Here are my PSP, iPod, ring, ballpoint pen and the work gloves my mother made me that I wear whenever I draw. I always have all these things with me.

—**Katsura Hoshino**

Shiga Prefecture native Katsura Hoshino's hit manga series *D.Gray-man* has been serialized in *Weekly Shonen Jump* since 2004. Katsura's debut manga, "Continue," appeared for the first time in *Weekly Shonen Jump* in 2003.

Katsura adores cats.

D.GRAY-MAN
3-in-1 Edition
Volume 5

SHONEN JUMP Manga Omnibus Edition
A compilation of the graphic novel volumes 13–15

STORY AND ART BY
KATSURA HOSHINO

English Adaptation/Lance Caselman
Translation/John Werry
Touch-up Art & Lettering/Hudson Yards
Design/Matt Hinrichs (Graphic Novel)
Design/Yukiko Whitley (3-in-1 Edition)
Editor/Gary Leach (Graphic Novel Edition)
Editor/Nancy Thistlethwaite (3-in-1 Edition)

Published by VIZ Media, LLC
P.O. Box 77010
San Francisco, CA 94107

10 9 8 7 6 5 4 3 2 1
3-in-1 edition first printing, November 2014

www.viz.com

ADVANCED
www.shonenjump.com

SHONEN JUMP ADVANCED MANGA EDITION

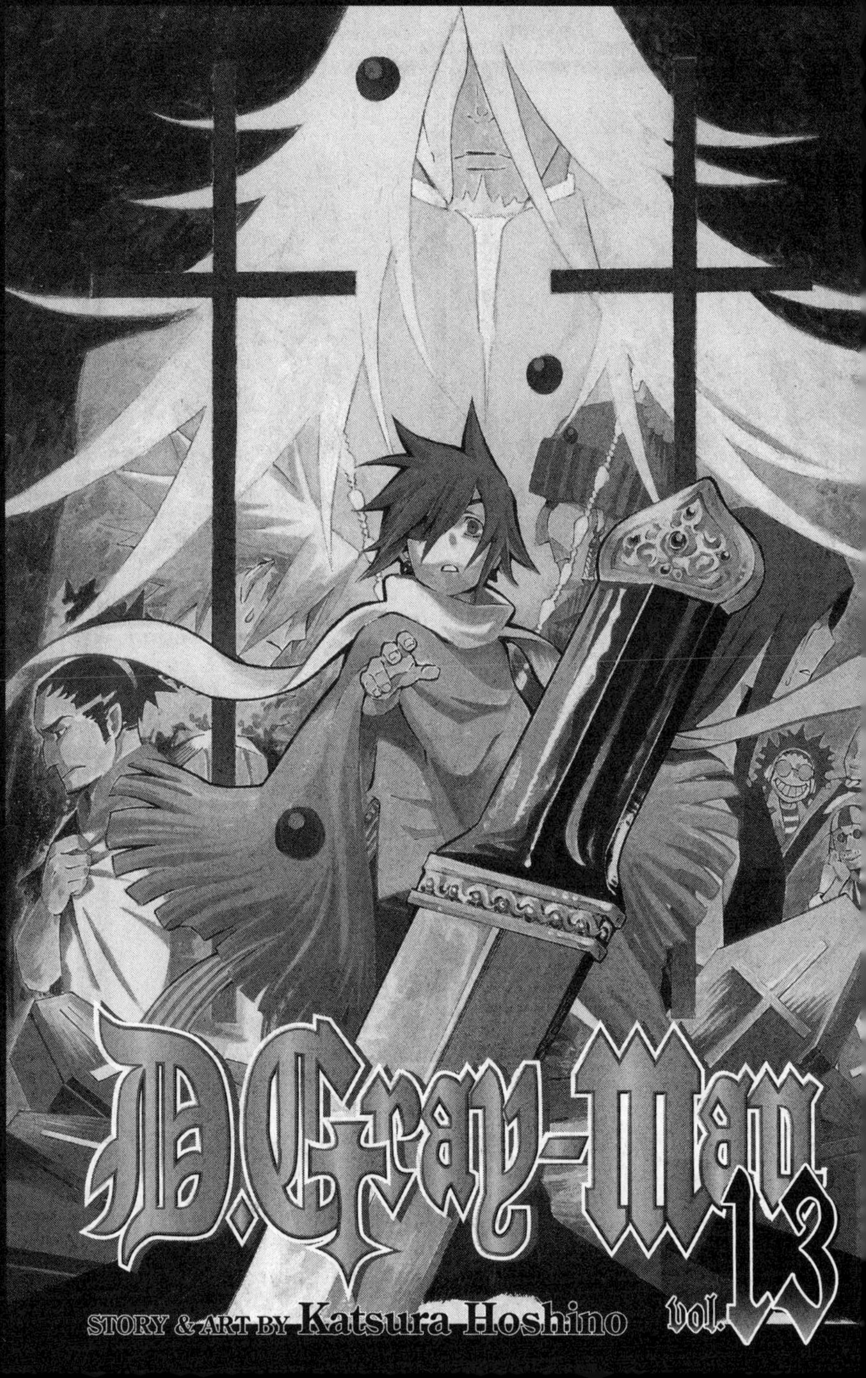
D.Gray-man
vol. 13
STORY & ART BY Katsura Hoshino

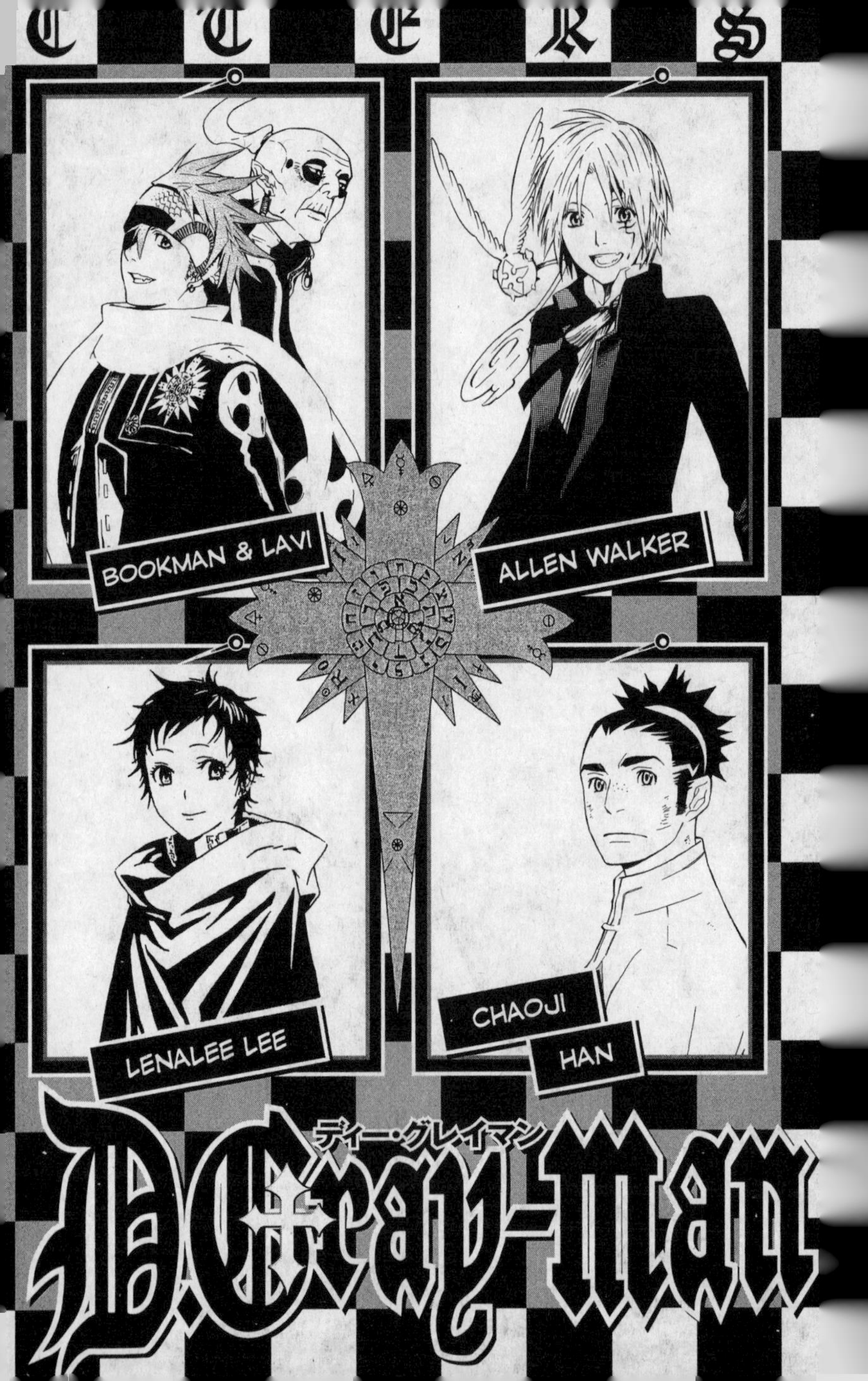
C T E R S
BOOKMAN & LAVI
ALLEN WALKER
LENALEE LEE
CHAOJI HAN
ディー・グレイマン
D.Gray-man

CHARA

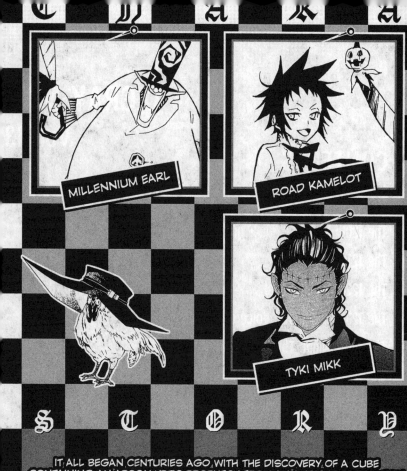

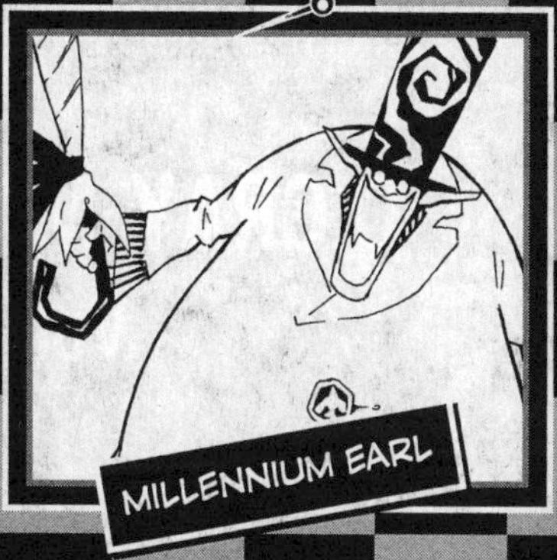
MILLENNIUM EARL

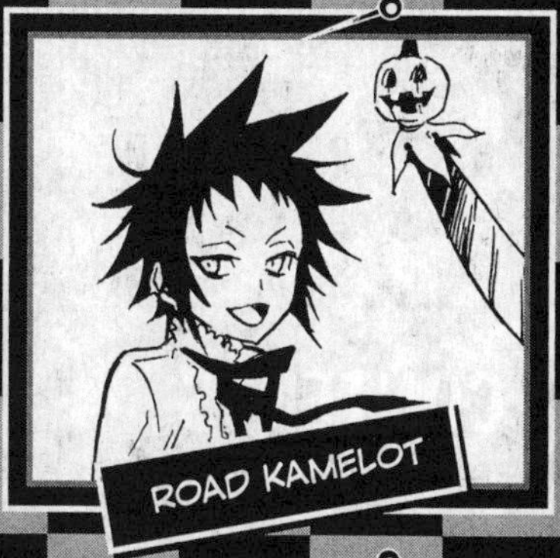
ROAD KAMELOT

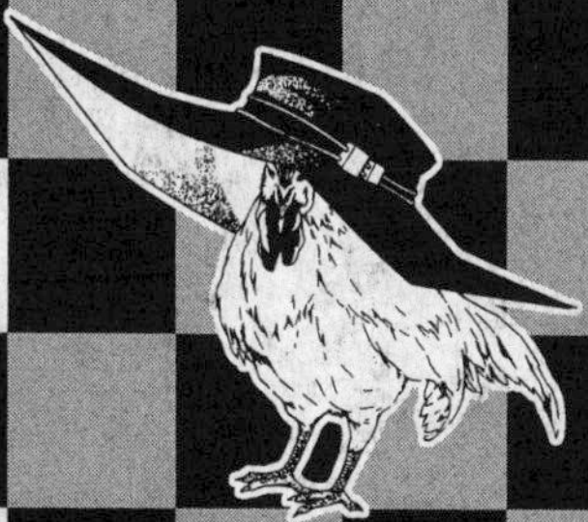

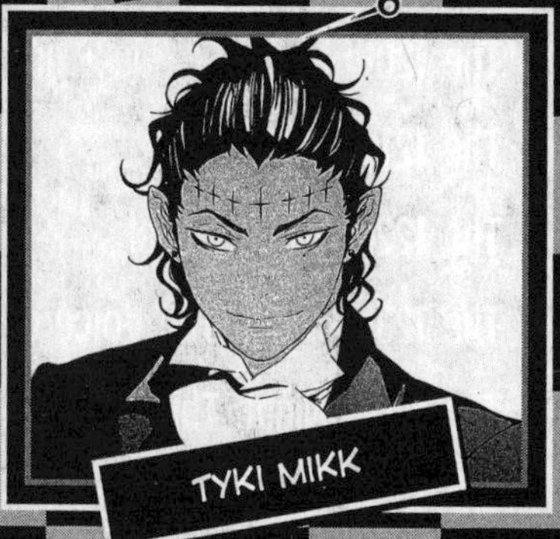
TYKI MIKK

STORY

IT ALL BEGAN CENTURIES AGO WITH THE DISCOVERY OF A CUBE CONTAINING AN APOCALYPTIC PROPHECY FROM AN ANCIENT CIVILIZATION AND INSTRUCTIONS IN THE USE OF INNOCENCE, A CRYSTALLINE SUBSTANCE OF WONDROUS SUPERNATURAL POWER. THE CREATORS OF THE CUBE CLAIMED TO HAVE DEFEATED AN EVIL KNOWN AS THE MILLENNIUM EARL BY USING THE INNOCENCE. NEVERTHELESS, THE WORLD WAS DESTROYED BY THE GREAT FLOOD OF THE OLD TESTAMENT. NOW, TO AVERT A SECOND END OF THE WORLD, A GROUP OF EXORCISTS WIELDING WEAPONS MADE OF INNOCENCE MUST BATTLE THE MILLENNIUM EARL AND HIS TERRIBLE MINIONS, THE AKUMA.

THE EXORCISTS FIGHT FOR THEIR LIVES AS THE ARK DISINTEGRATES AROUND THEM. ALLEN DEFEATS TYKI BY DESTROYING HIS INNER NOAH, AND IN RETALIATION, ROAD ATTEMPTS TO PIERCE LAVI'S HEART!

D.GRAY-MAN
Vol. 13

CONTENTS

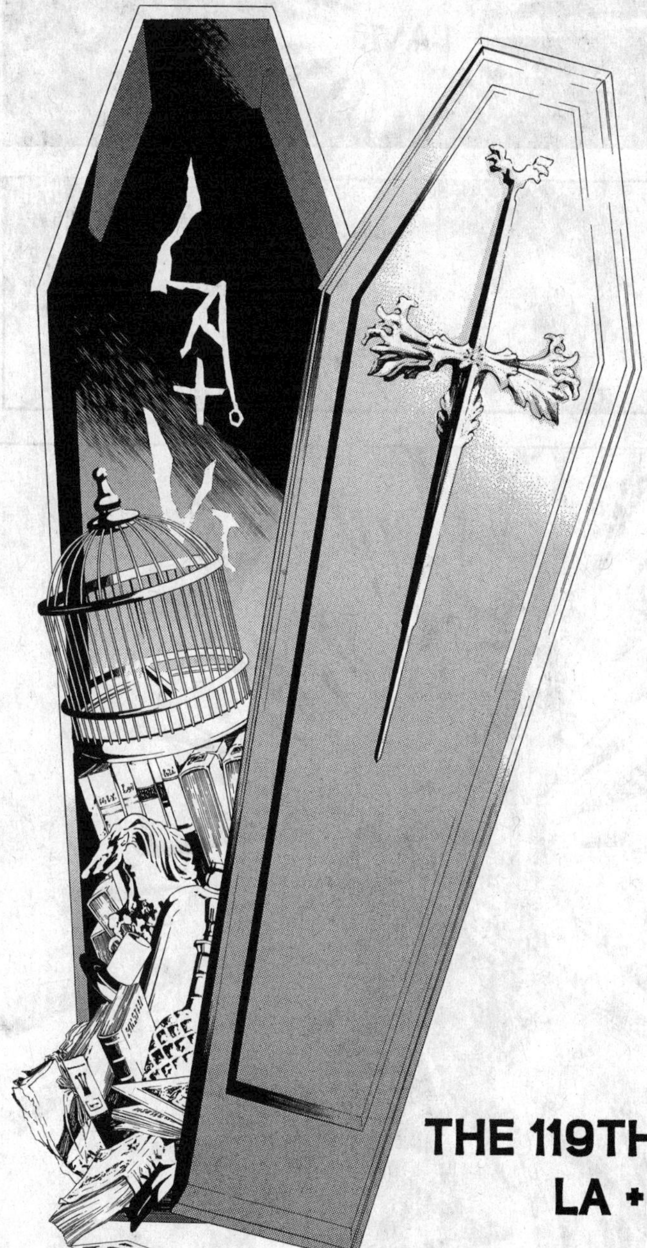

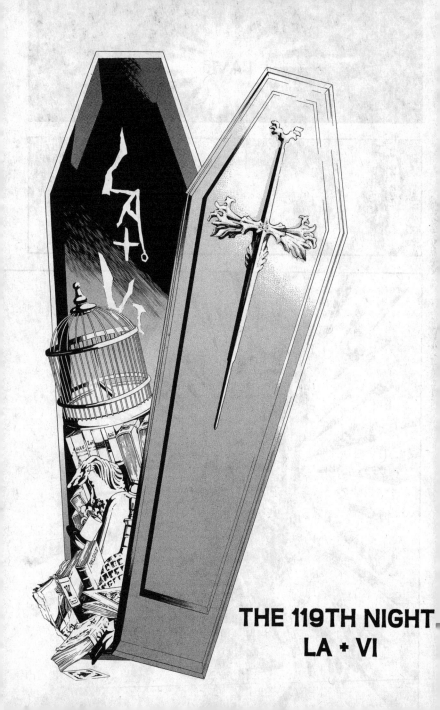

THE 119TH NIGHT
LA + VI

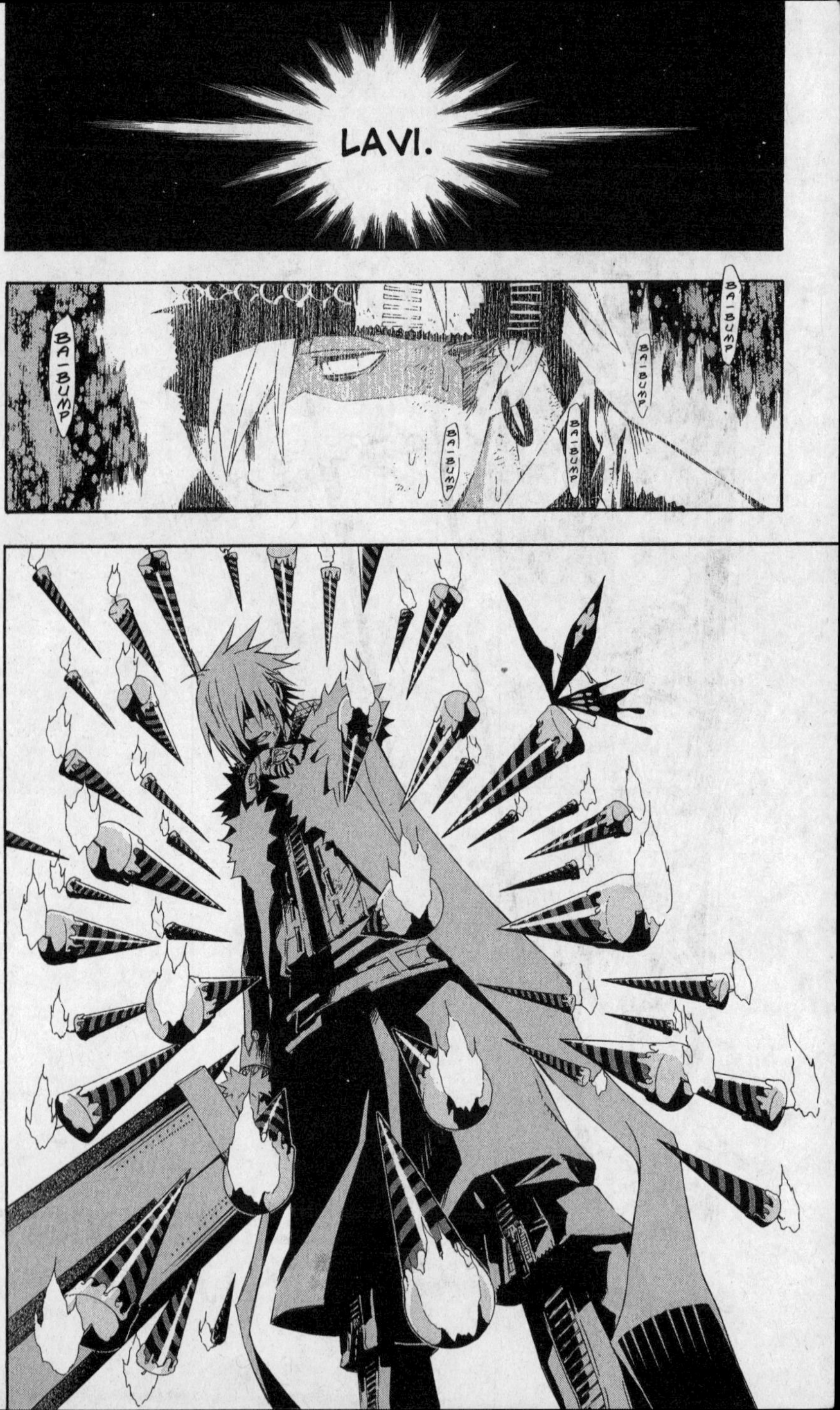
LAVI.
BA-BUMP
BA-BUMP
BA-BUMP
BA-BUMP
BA-BUMP

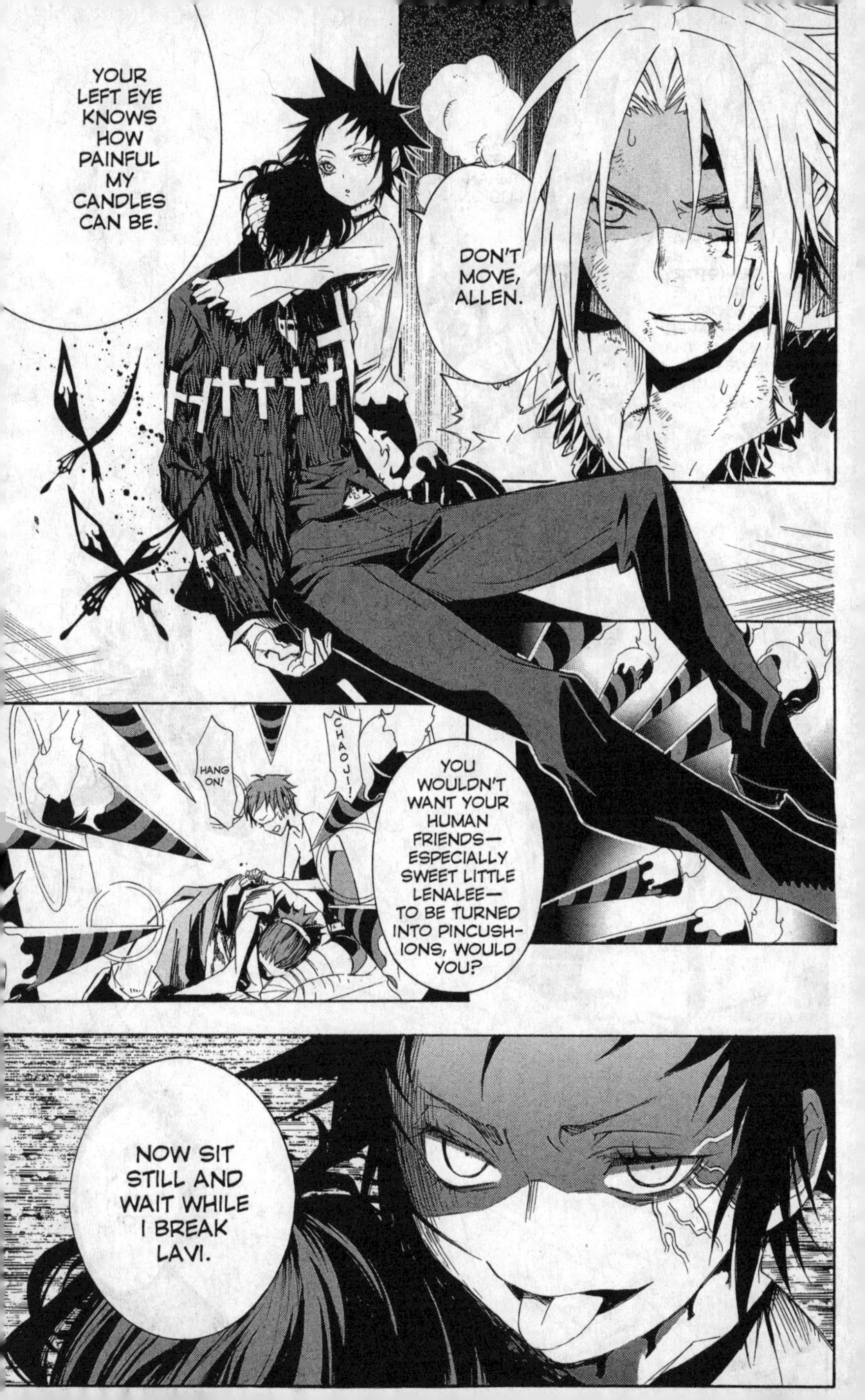
DON'T MOVE, ALLEN.
YOUR LEFT EYE KNOWS HOW PAINFUL MY CANDLES CAN BE.
YOU WOULDN'T WANT YOUR HUMAN FRIENDS— ESPECIALLY SWEET LITTLE LENALEE— TO BE TURNED INTO PINCUSHIONS, WOULD YOU?
CHAOJI!
HANG ON!
NOW SIT STILL AND WAIT WHILE I BREAK LAVI.

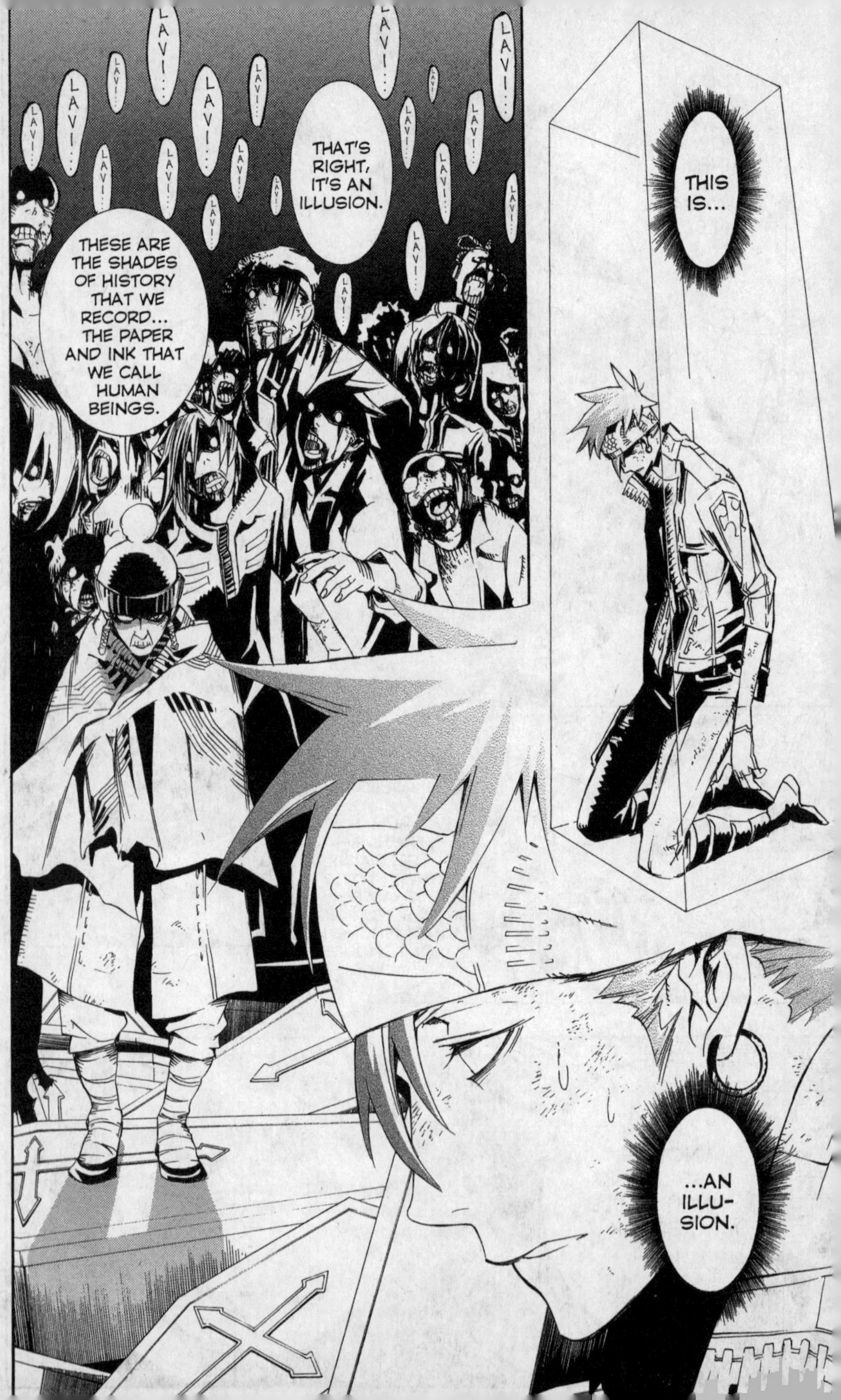
THIS IS...
...AN ILLUSION.
LAVI...
LAVI...
LAVI...
LAVI...
LAVI...
LAVI...
LAVI...
LAVI...
THAT'S RIGHT, IT'S AN ILLUSION.
LAVI...
LAVI...
LAVI...
LAVI...
LAVI...
LAVI...
LAVI...
LAVI...
LAVI...
LAVI...
LAVI...
THESE ARE THE SHADES OF HISTORY THAT WE RECORD... THE PAPER AND INK THAT WE CALL HUMAN BEINGS.

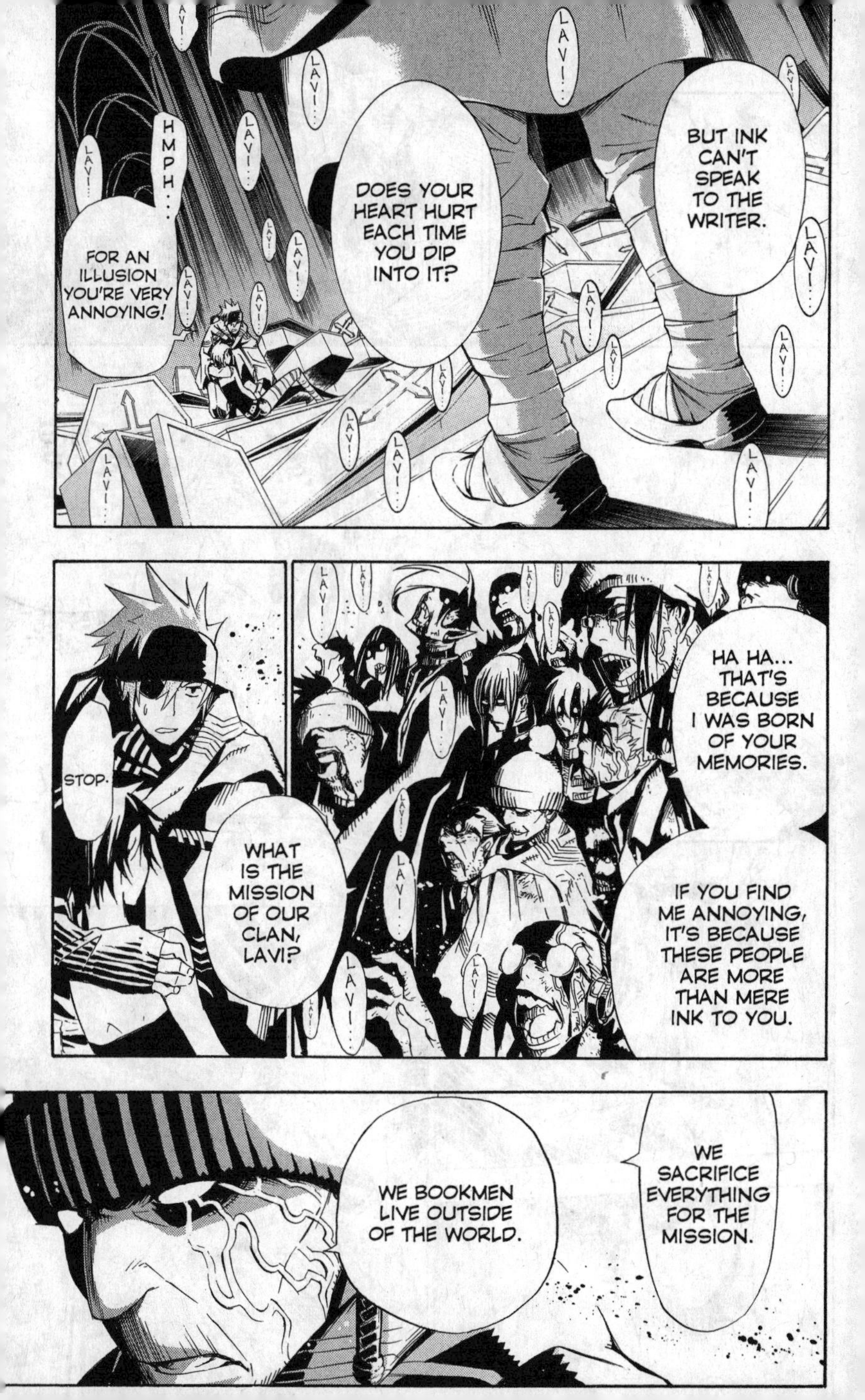
LAVI...
BUT INK CAN'T SPEAK TO THE WRITER.
LAVI...
DOES YOUR HEART HURT EACH TIME YOU DIP INTO IT?
LAVI...
HMPH...
FOR AN ILLUSION YOU'RE VERY ANNOYING!
LAVI...
HA HA... THAT'S BECAUSE I WAS BORN OF YOUR MEMORIES.
IF YOU FIND ME ANNOYING, IT'S BECAUSE THESE PEOPLE ARE MORE THAN MERE INK TO YOU.
LAVI...
WHAT IS THE MISSION OF OUR CLAN, LAVI?
STOP.
WE SACRIFICE EVERYTHING FOR THE MISSION.
WE BOOKMEN LIVE OUTSIDE OF THE WORLD.

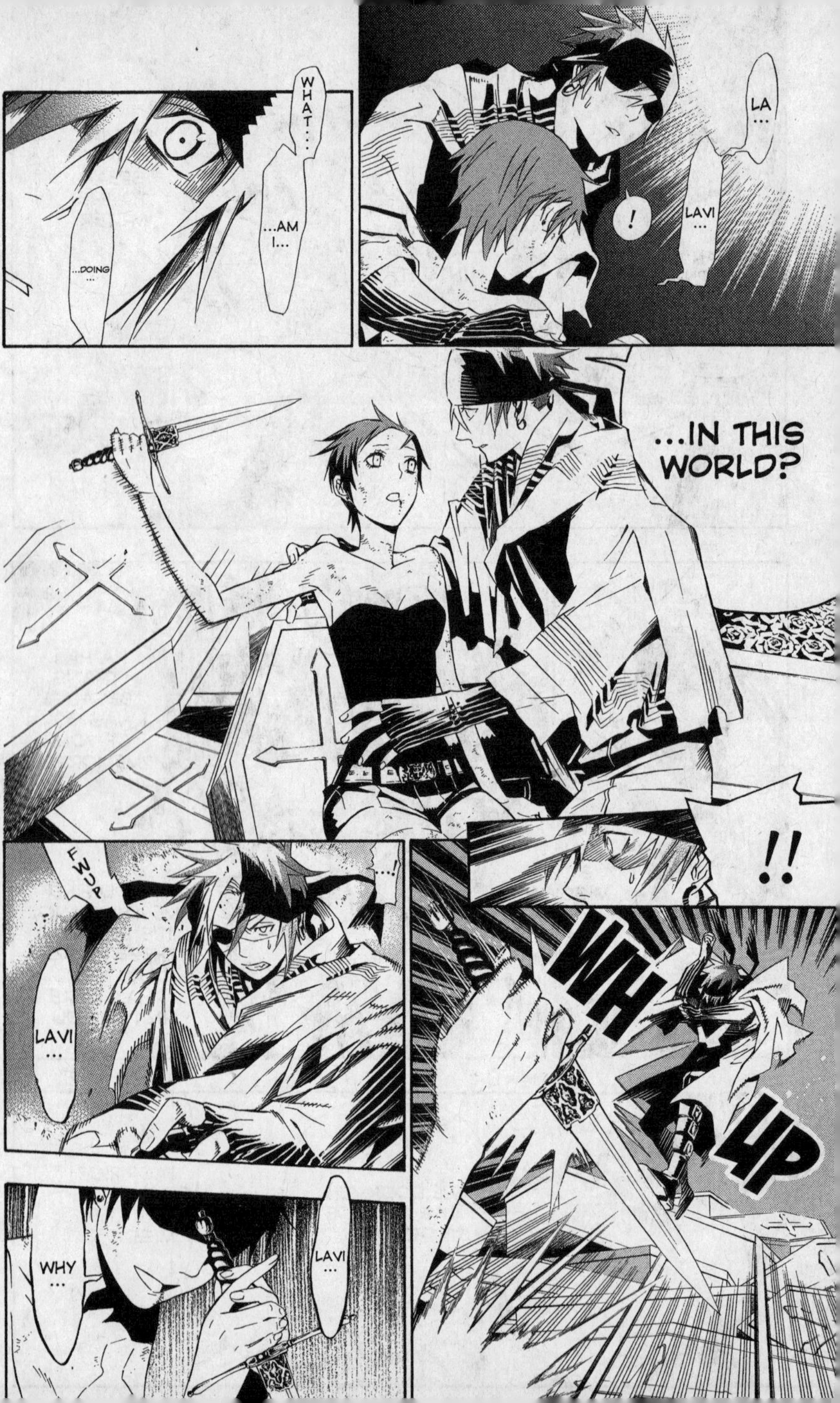
LA...
!
LAVI...
WHAT...
...AM I...
...DOING...
...IN THIS WORLD?
!!
WHUP
...!
FWUP
LAVI...
LAVI...
WHY...

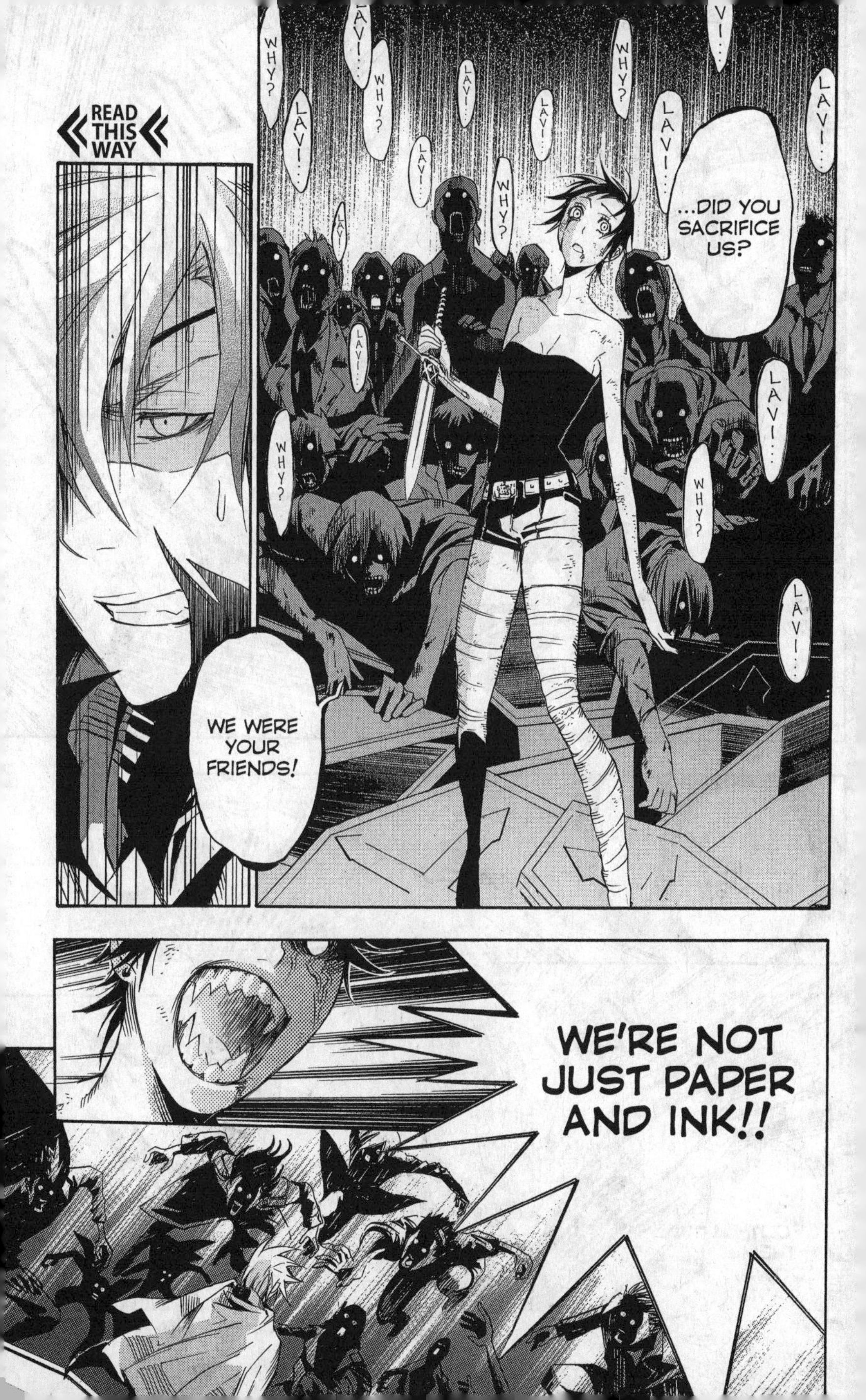
READ THIS WAY
LAVI...
LAVI...
WHY?
LAVI...
...DID YOU SACRIFICE US?
WHY?
LAVI...
LAVI...
WHY?
LAVI...
LAVI...
WHY?
LAVI...
LAVI...
WHY?
LAVI...
LAVI...
WHY?
LAVI...
WHY?
LAVI...
WE WERE YOUR FRIENDS!
WE'RE NOT JUST PAPER AND INK!!

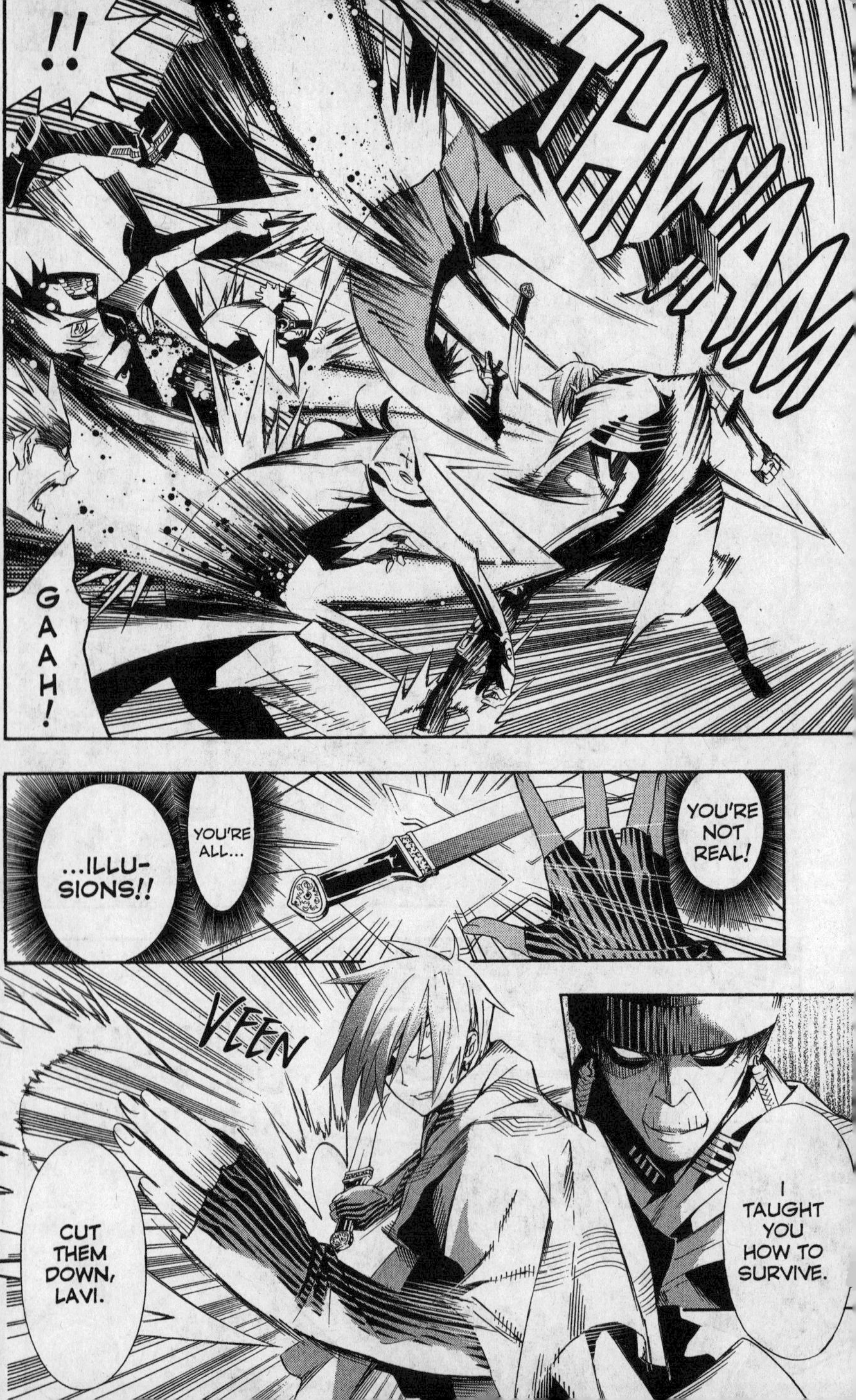
THWAAM
!!
GAAH!
YOU'RE NOT REAL!
YOU'RE ALL...
...ILLUSIONS!!
I TAUGHT YOU HOW TO SURVIVE.
VEEN
CUT THEM DOWN, LAVI.

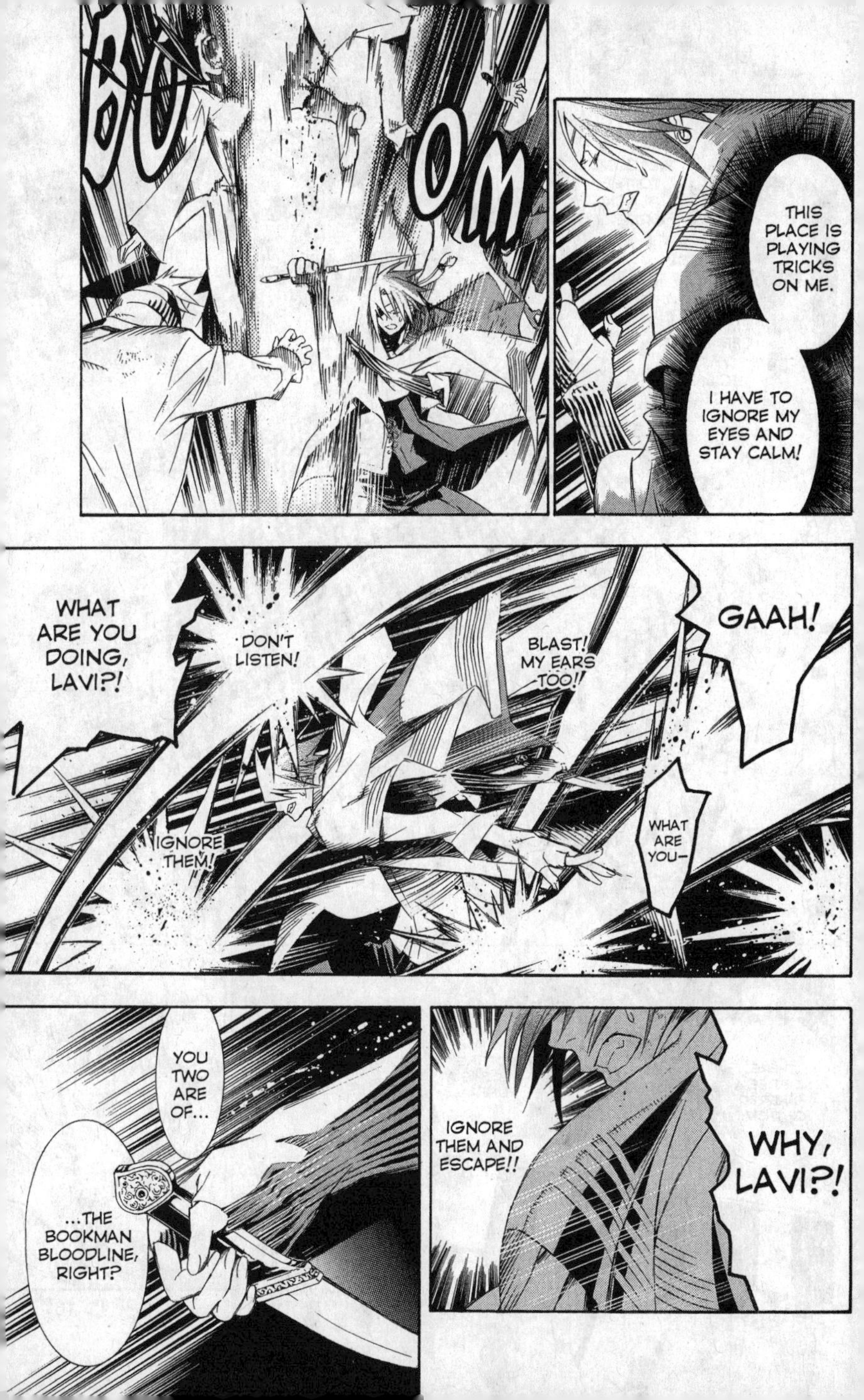
THIS PLACE IS PLAYING TRICKS ON ME.
I HAVE TO IGNORE MY EYES AND STAY CALM!
BOOM
GAAH!
BLAST! MY EARS TOO!
DON'T LISTEN!
WHAT ARE YOU DOING, LAVI?!
WHAT ARE YOU—
IGNORE THEM!
WHY, LAVI?!
IGNORE THEM AND ESCAPE!!
YOU TWO ARE OF...
...THE BOOKMAN BLOODLINE, RIGHT?

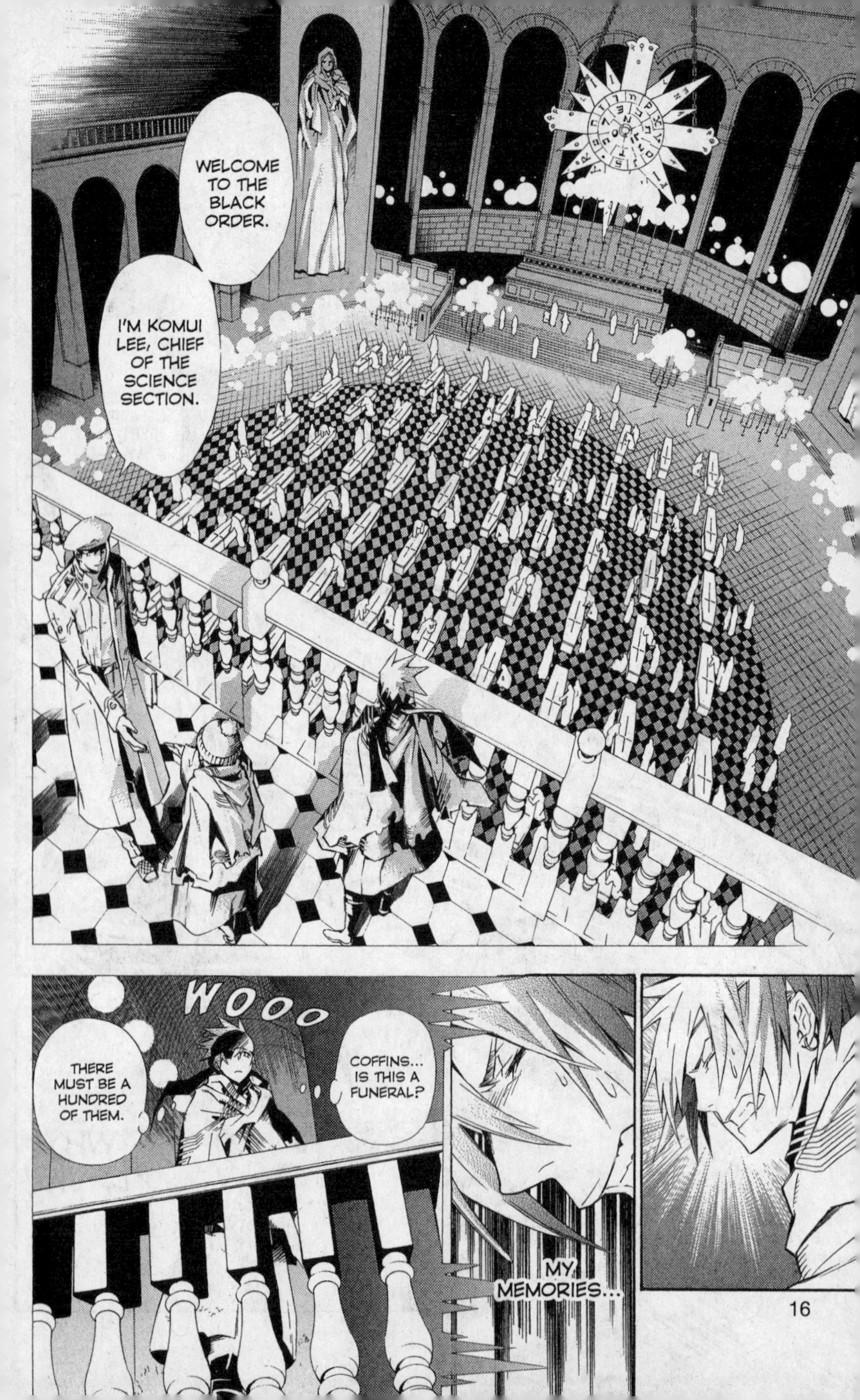
WELCOME TO THE BLACK ORDER.
I'M KOMUI LEE, CHIEF OF THE SCIENCE SECTION.
WOOO
COFFINS... IS THIS A FUNERAL?
THERE MUST BE A HUNDRED OF THEM.
MY MEMORIES...

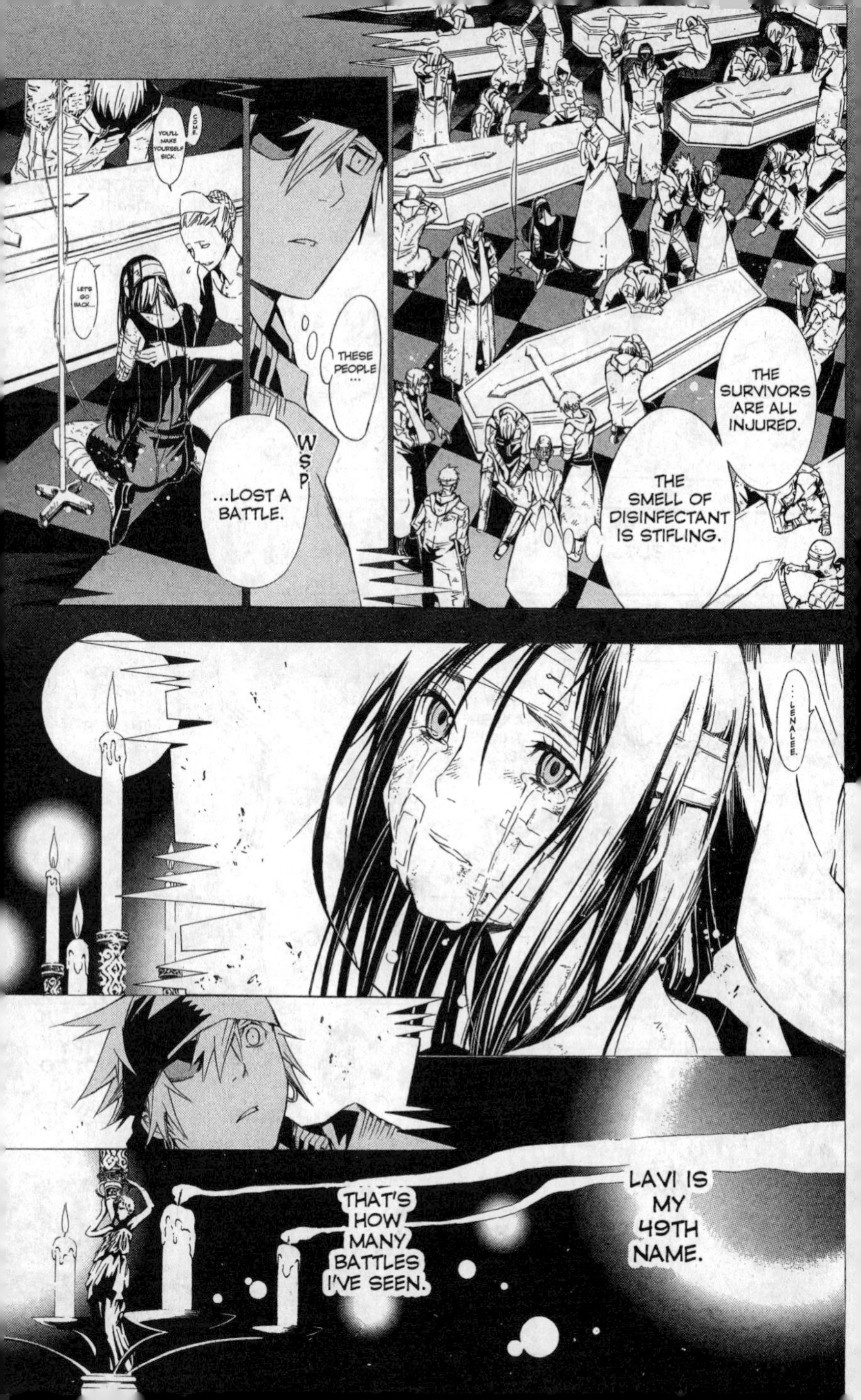
THE SURVIVORS ARE ALL INJURED.
THE SMELL OF DISINFECTANT IS STIFLING.
THESE PEOPLE...
WSP
...LOST A BATTLE.
COME.
YOU'LL MAKE YOURSELF SICK.
LET'S GO BACK...
...LENALEE.
LAVI IS MY 49TH NAME.
THAT'S HOW MANY BATTLES I'VE SEEN.

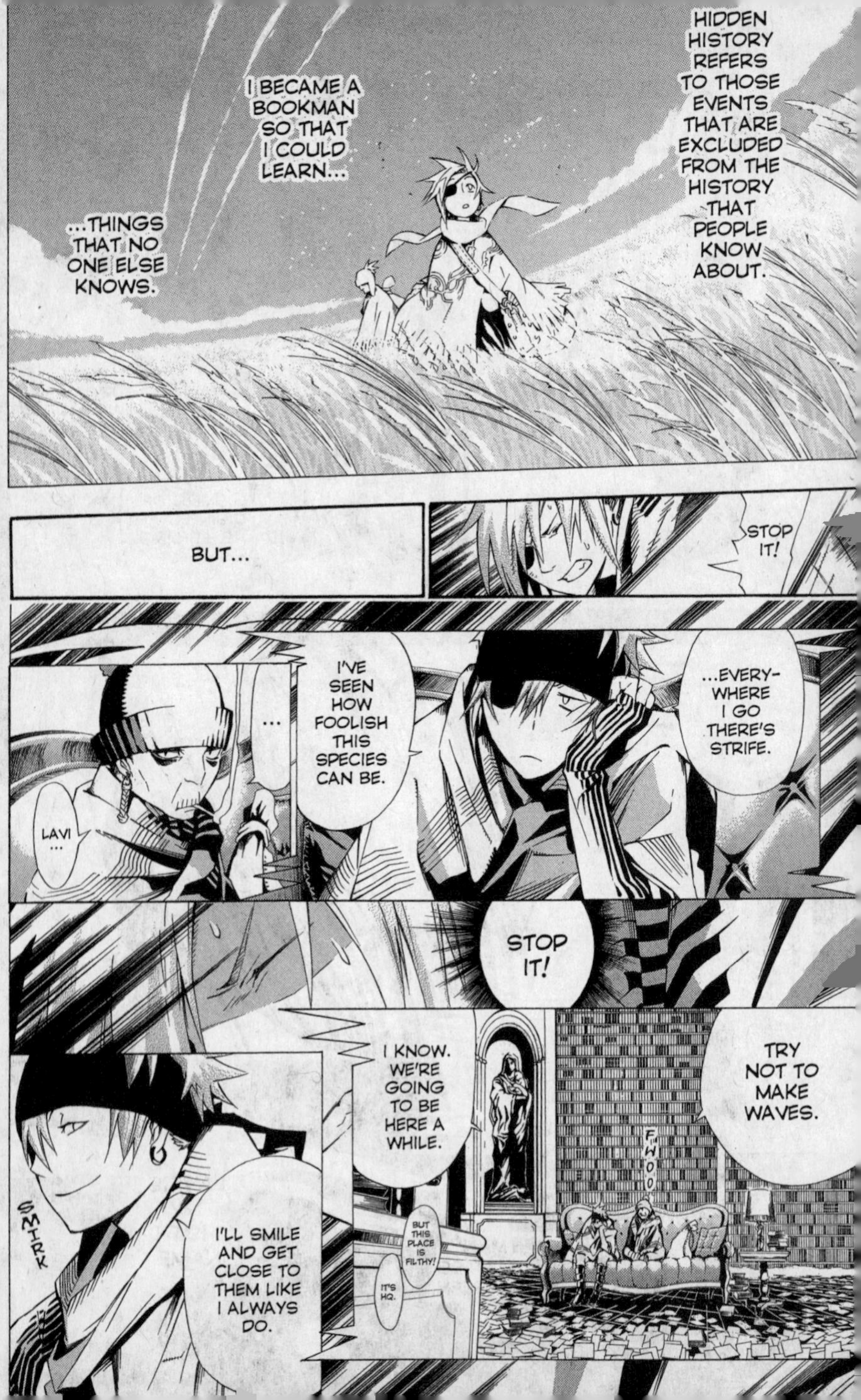
HIDDEN HISTORY REFERS TO THOSE EVENTS THAT ARE EXCLUDED FROM THE HISTORY THAT PEOPLE KNOW ABOUT.
I BECAME A BOOKMAN SO THAT I COULD LEARN...
...THINGS THAT NO ONE ELSE KNOWS.
STOP IT!
BUT...
...EVERY-WHERE I GO THERE'S STRIFE.
I'VE SEEN HOW FOOLISH THIS SPECIES CAN BE.
...
LAVI ...
STOP IT!
TRY NOT TO MAKE WAVES.
FWOO
I KNOW. WE'RE GOING TO BE HERE A WHILE.
BUT THIS PLACE IS FILTHY!
IT'S HQ.
I'LL SMILE AND GET CLOSE TO THEM LIKE I ALWAYS DO.
SMIRK

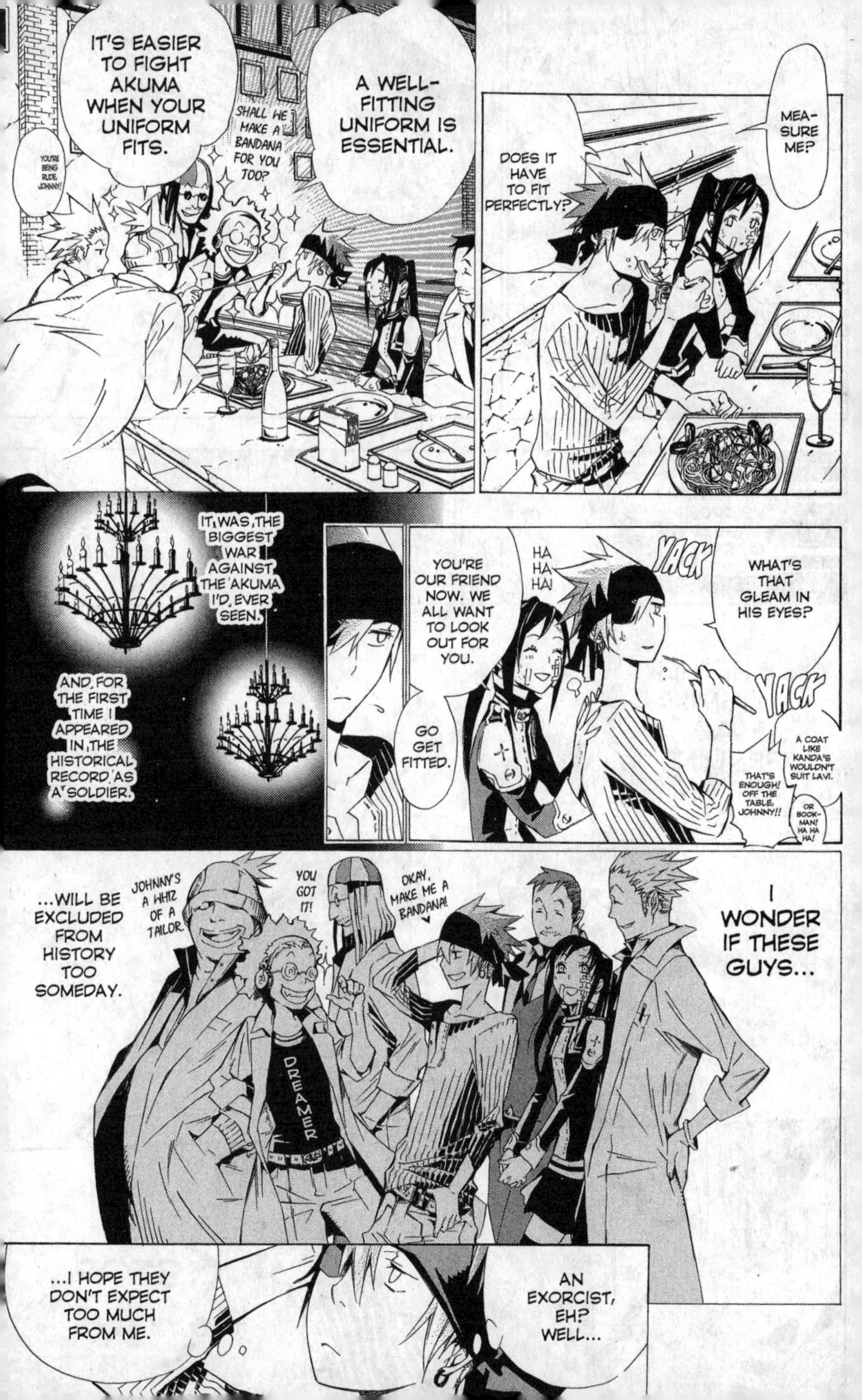
MEA-SURE ME?
DOES IT HAVE TO FIT PERFECTLY?
A WELL-FITTING UNIFORM IS ESSENTIAL.
SHALL WE MAKE A BANDANA FOR YOU TOO?
IT'S EASIER TO FIGHT AKUMA WHEN YOUR UNIFORM FITS.
YOU'RE BEING RUDE, JOHNNY!
WHAT'S THAT GLEAM IN HIS EYES?
YACK
YACK
HA HA HA!
YOU'RE OUR FRIEND NOW. WE ALL WANT TO LOOK OUT FOR YOU.
A COAT LIKE KANDA'S WOULDN'T SUIT LAVI.
OR BOOKMAN! HA HA HA!
THAT'S ENOUGH! OFF THE TABLE, JOHNNY!!
GO GET FITTED.
IT WAS THE BIGGEST WAR AGAINST THE AKUMA I'D EVER SEEN.
AND FOR THE FIRST TIME I APPEARED IN THE HISTORICAL RECORD AS A SOLDIER.
I WONDER IF THESE GUYS...
OKAY, MAKE ME A BANDANA!
YOU GOT IT!
JOHNNY'S A WHIZ OF A TAILOR.
...WILL BE EXCLUDED FROM HISTORY TOO SOMEDAY.
AN EXORCIST, EH? WELL...
...I HOPE THEY DON'T EXPECT TOO MUCH FROM ME.

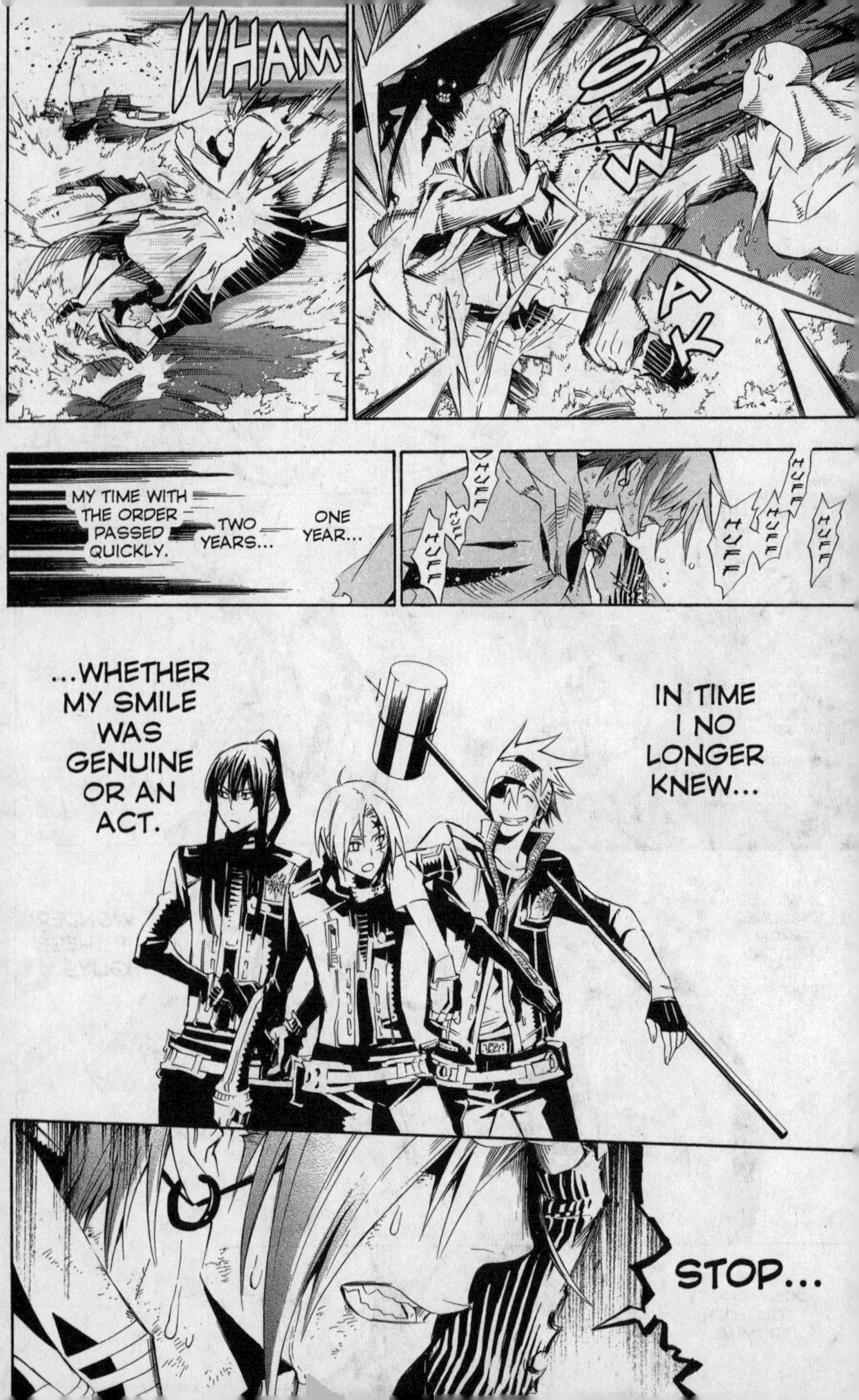
SWAK
WHAM
HUFF HUFF HUFF HUFF HUFF HUFF HUFF
ONE YEAR...
TWO YEARS...
MY TIME WITH THE ORDER PASSED QUICKLY.
IN TIME I NO LONGER KNEW...
...WHETHER MY SMILE WAS GENUINE OR AN ACT.
STOP...

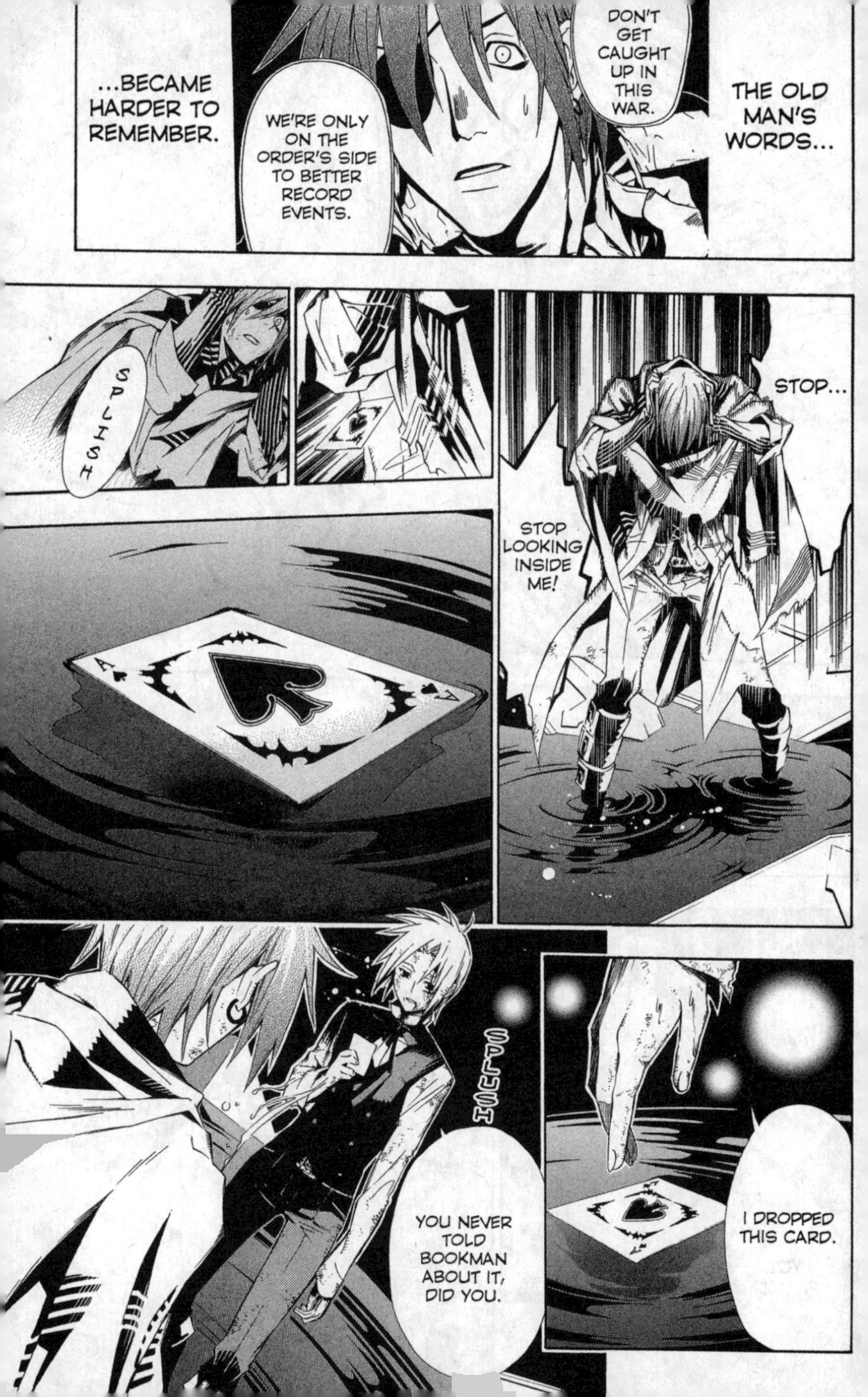
THE OLD MAN'S WORDS...
DON'T GET CAUGHT UP IN THIS WAR.
WE'RE ONLY ON THE ORDER'S SIDE TO BETTER RECORD EVENTS.
...BECAME HARDER TO REMEMBER.
STOP...
STOP LOOKING INSIDE ME!
SPLISH
I DROPPED THIS CARD.
SPLISH
YOU NEVER TOLD BOOKMAN ABOUT IT, DID YOU.

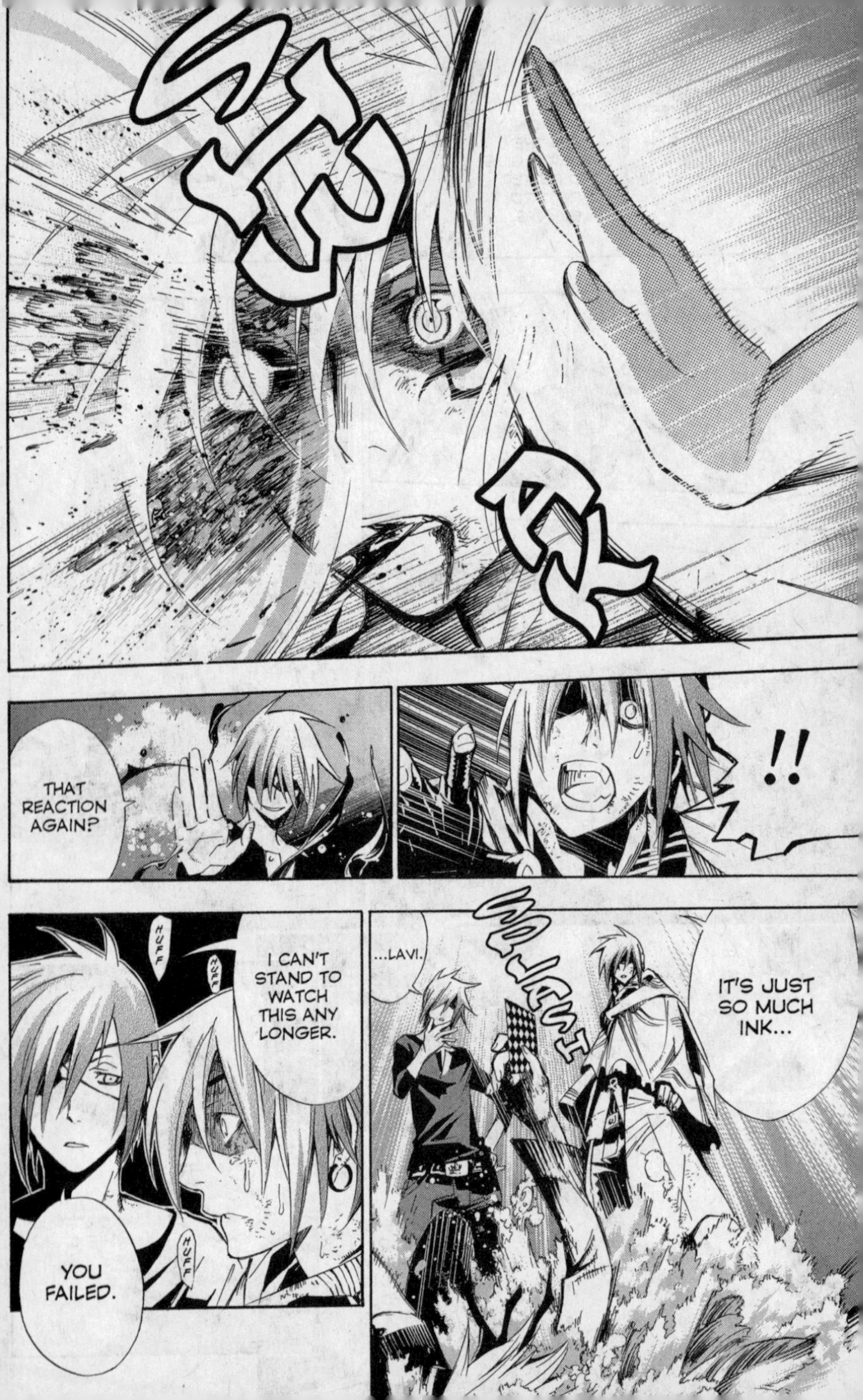
!!
THAT REACTION AGAIN?
IT'S JUST SO MUCH INK...
...LAVI.
I CAN'T STAND TO WATCH THIS ANY LONGER.
HUFF
HUFF
YOU FAILED.
HUFF

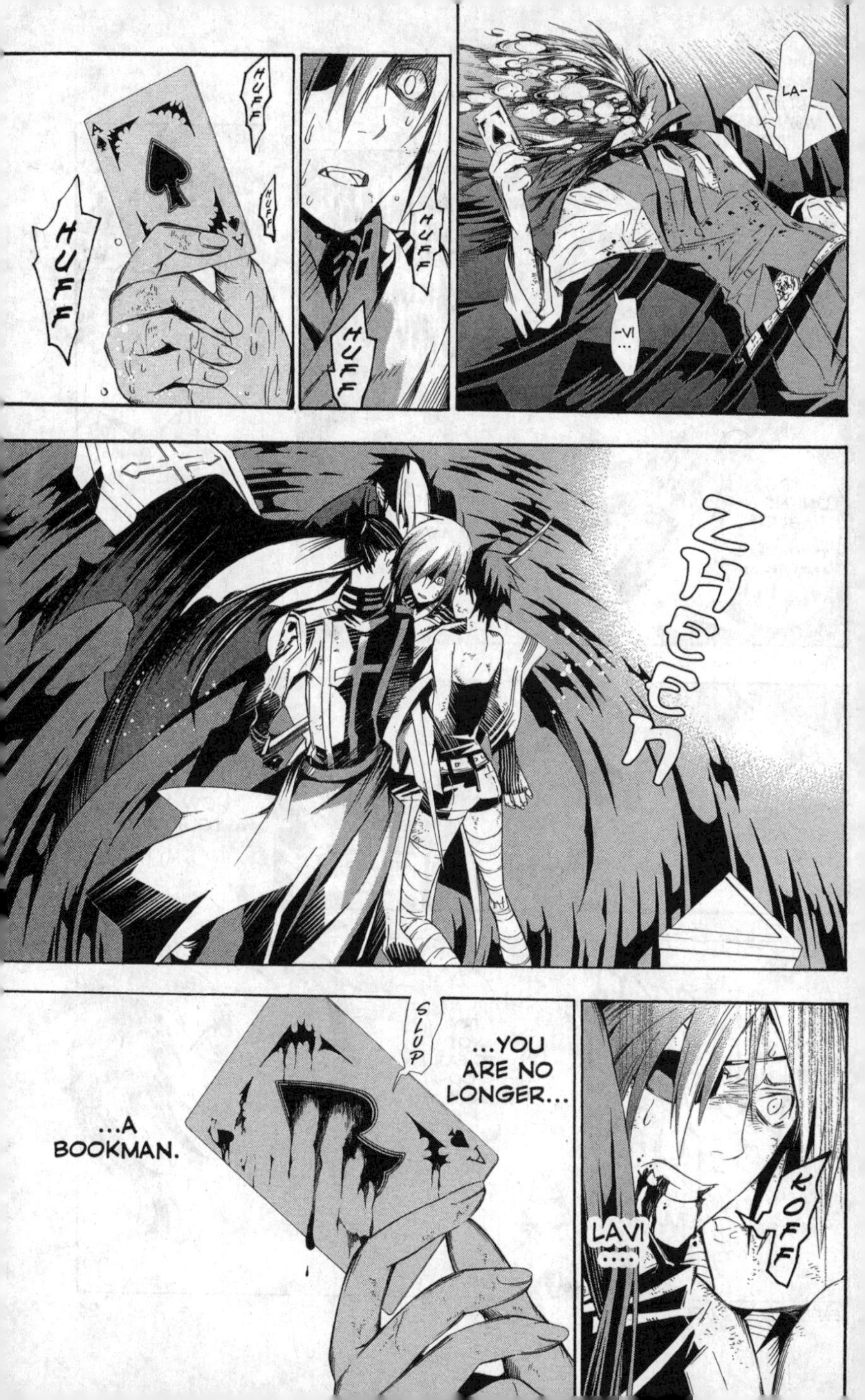
LA-
-VI ...
HUFF
HUFF
HUFF
HUFF
HUFF
ZHEECH
KOFF
LAVI ....
SLUP
...YOU ARE NO LONGER...
...A BOOKMAN.

IN VOLUME 2, I NOTICED THAT ALLEN ORDERED 20 STICKS OF RICE FLOUR DUMPLINGS FROM JERRY. HOW MANY *DANGO* CAN HE EAT AT ONE SITTING? (HARUNA MATSUMOTO, KAGAWA PREFECTURE)

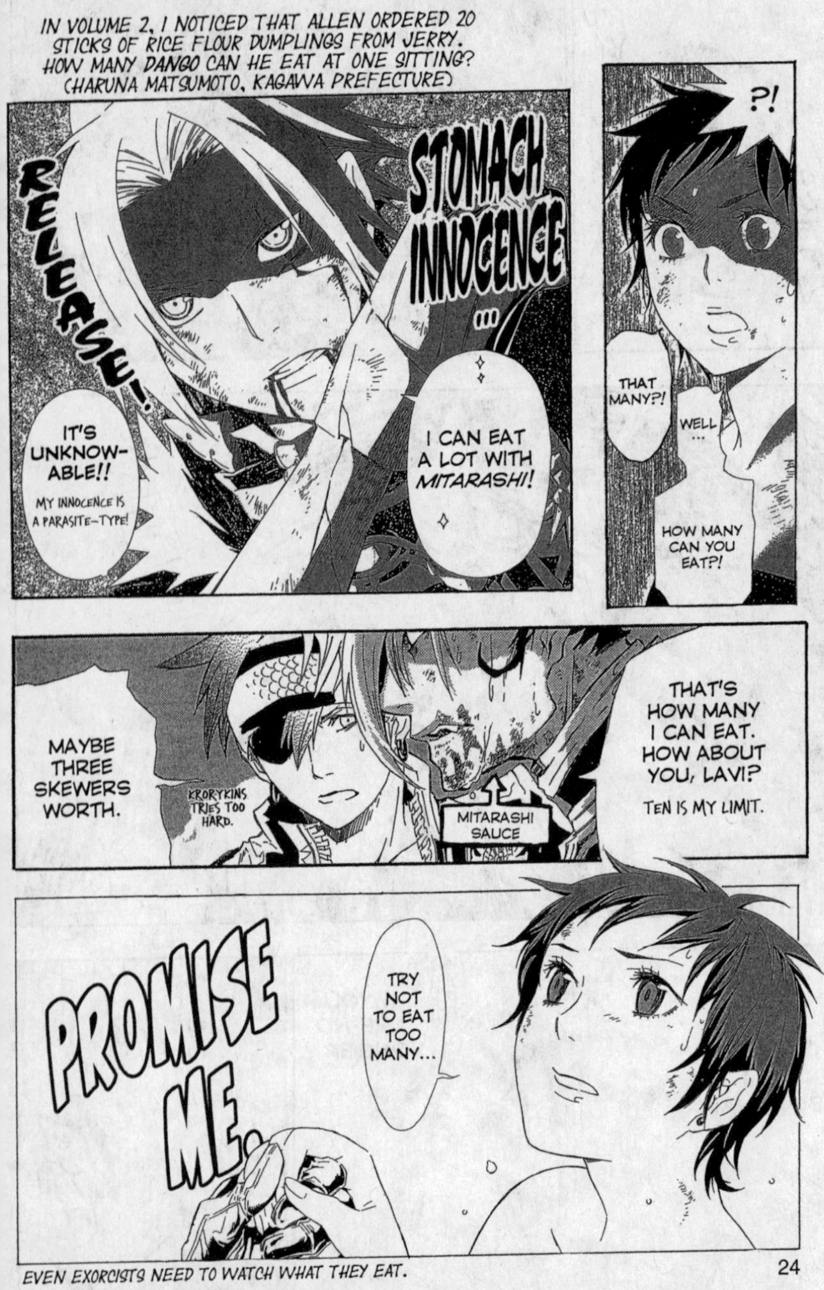
?!
THAT MANY?!
WELL...
HOW MANY CAN YOU EAT?!
STOMACH INNOCENCE...
RELEASE!
I CAN EAT A LOT WITH *MITARASHI*!
IT'S UNKNOWABLE!!
MY INNOCENCE IS A PARASITE-TYPE!
THAT'S HOW MANY I CAN EAT. HOW ABOUT YOU, LAVI?
TEN IS MY LIMIT.
MITARASHI SAUCE
KRORYKINS TRIES TOO HARD.
MAYBE THREE SKEWERS WORTH.
TRY NOT TO EAT TOO MANY...
PROMISE ME.

EVEN EXORCISTS NEED TO WATCH WHAT THEY EAT.

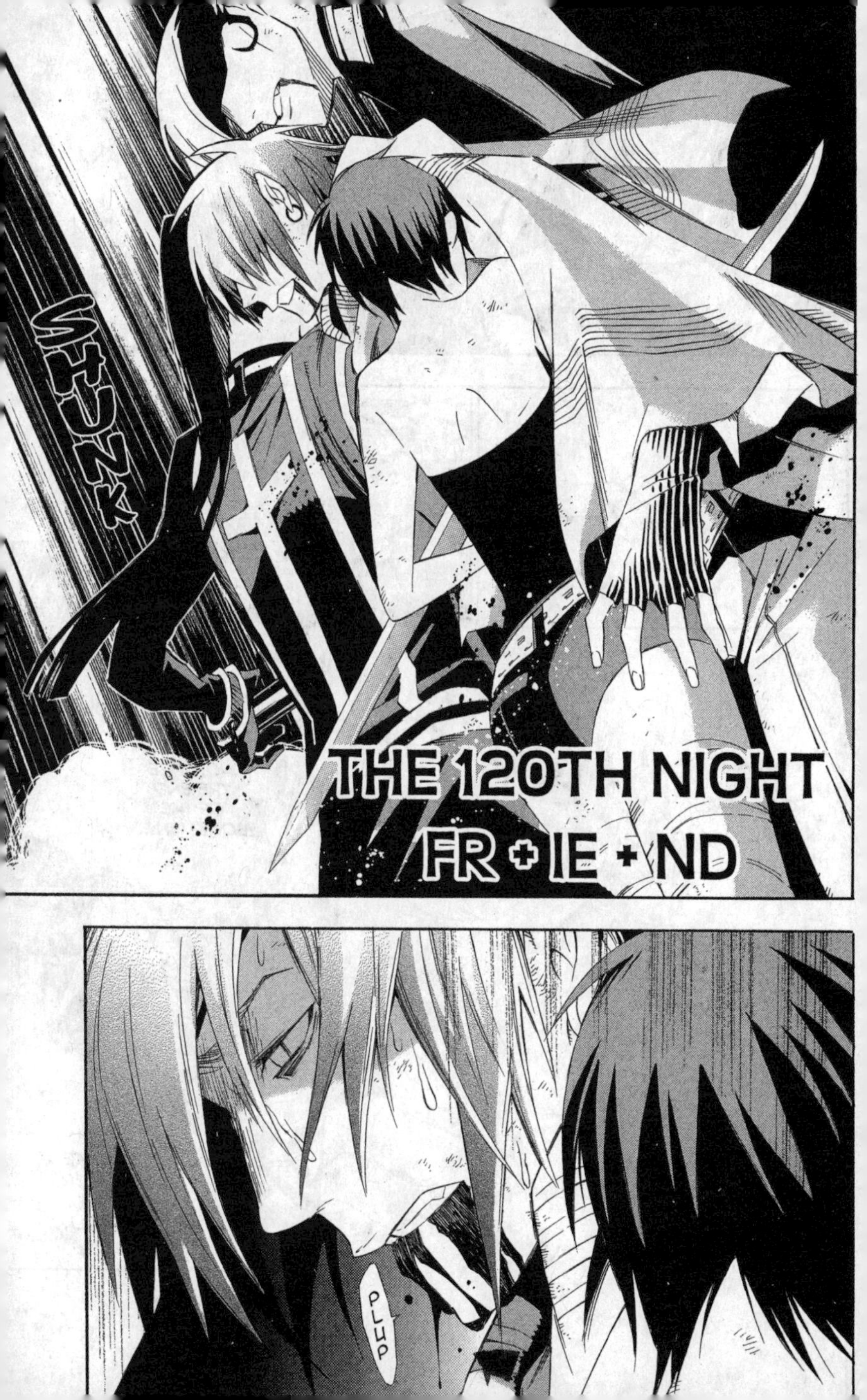
SHUNK
THE 120TH NIGHT
FR + IE + ND
PLUP

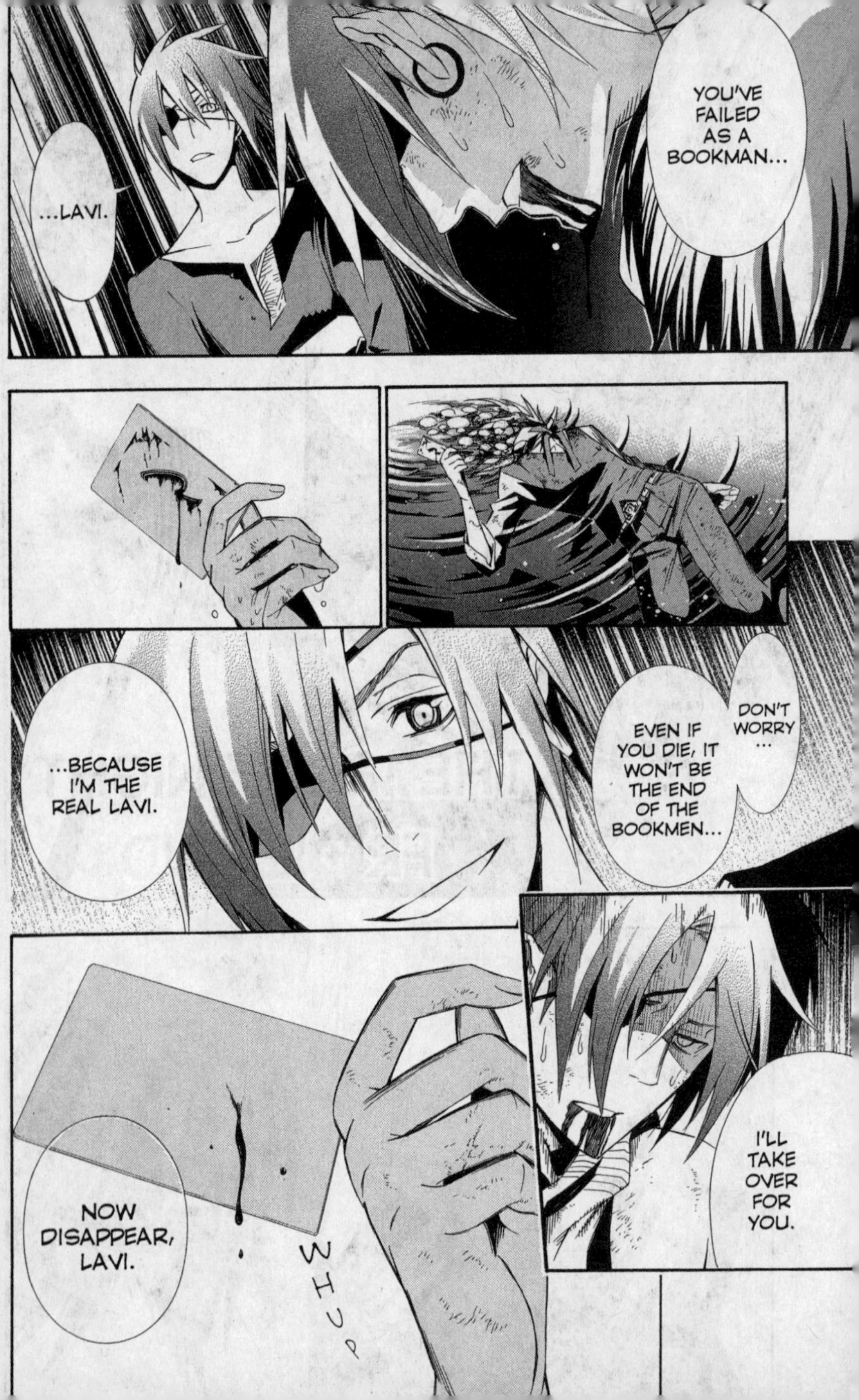
YOU'VE FAILED AS A BOOKMAN...
...LAVI.
DON'T WORRY...
EVEN IF YOU DIE, IT WON'T BE THE END OF THE BOOKMEN...
...BECAUSE I'M THE REAL LAVI.
I'LL TAKE OVER FOR YOU.
NOW DISAPPEAR, LAVI.
WHUP

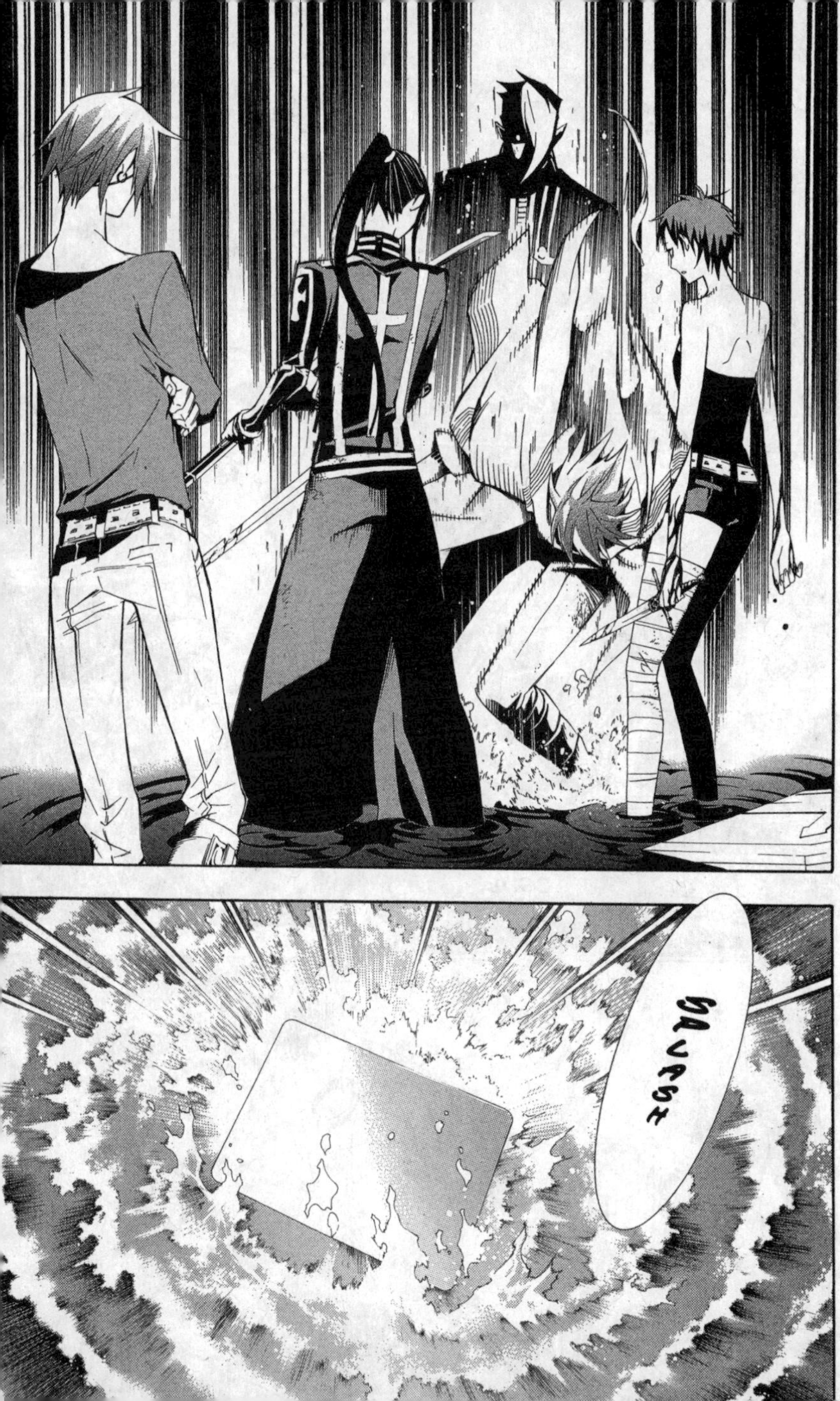
SPLASH

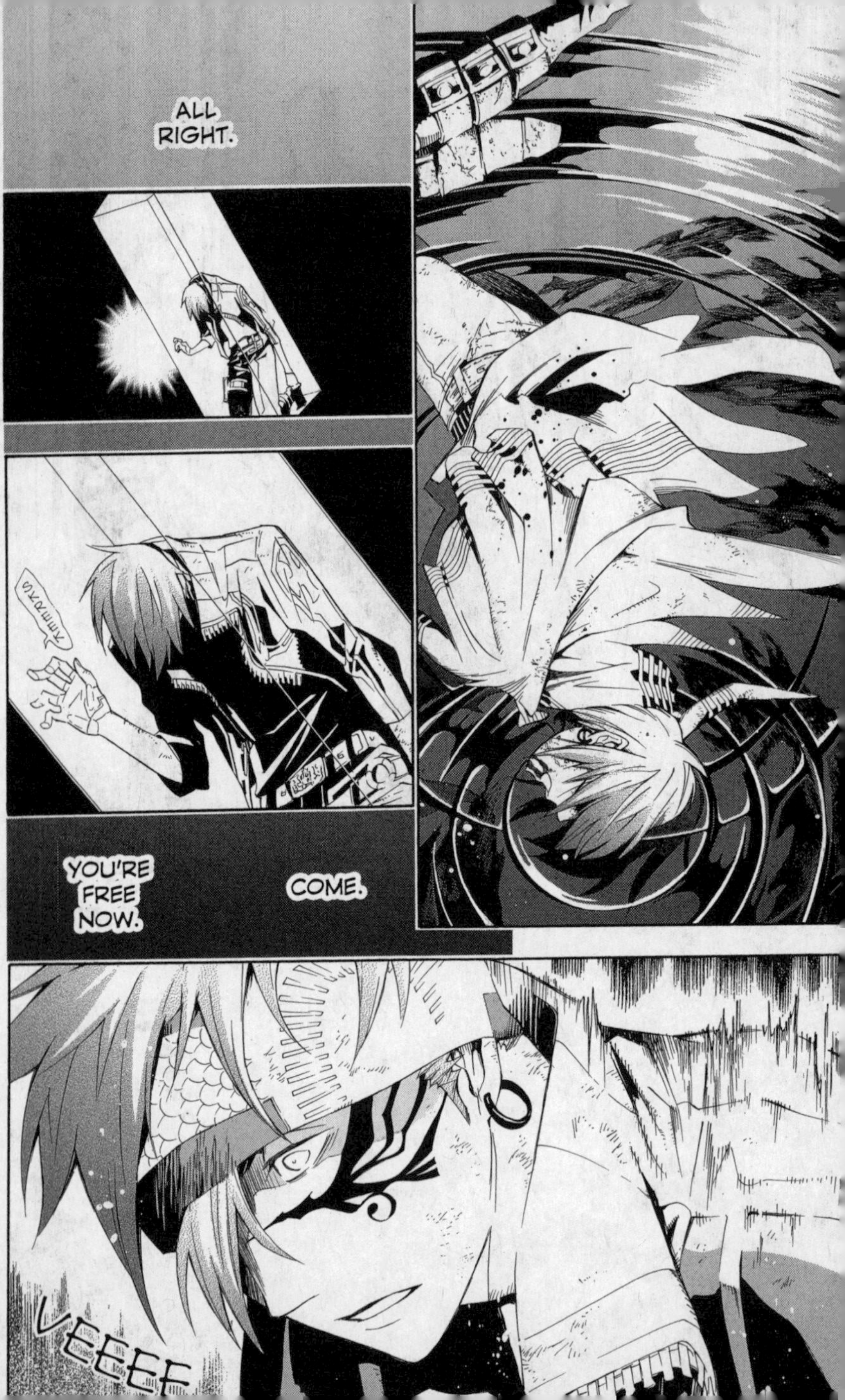
ALL RIGHT.
SKREEK
COME.
YOU'RE FREE NOW.

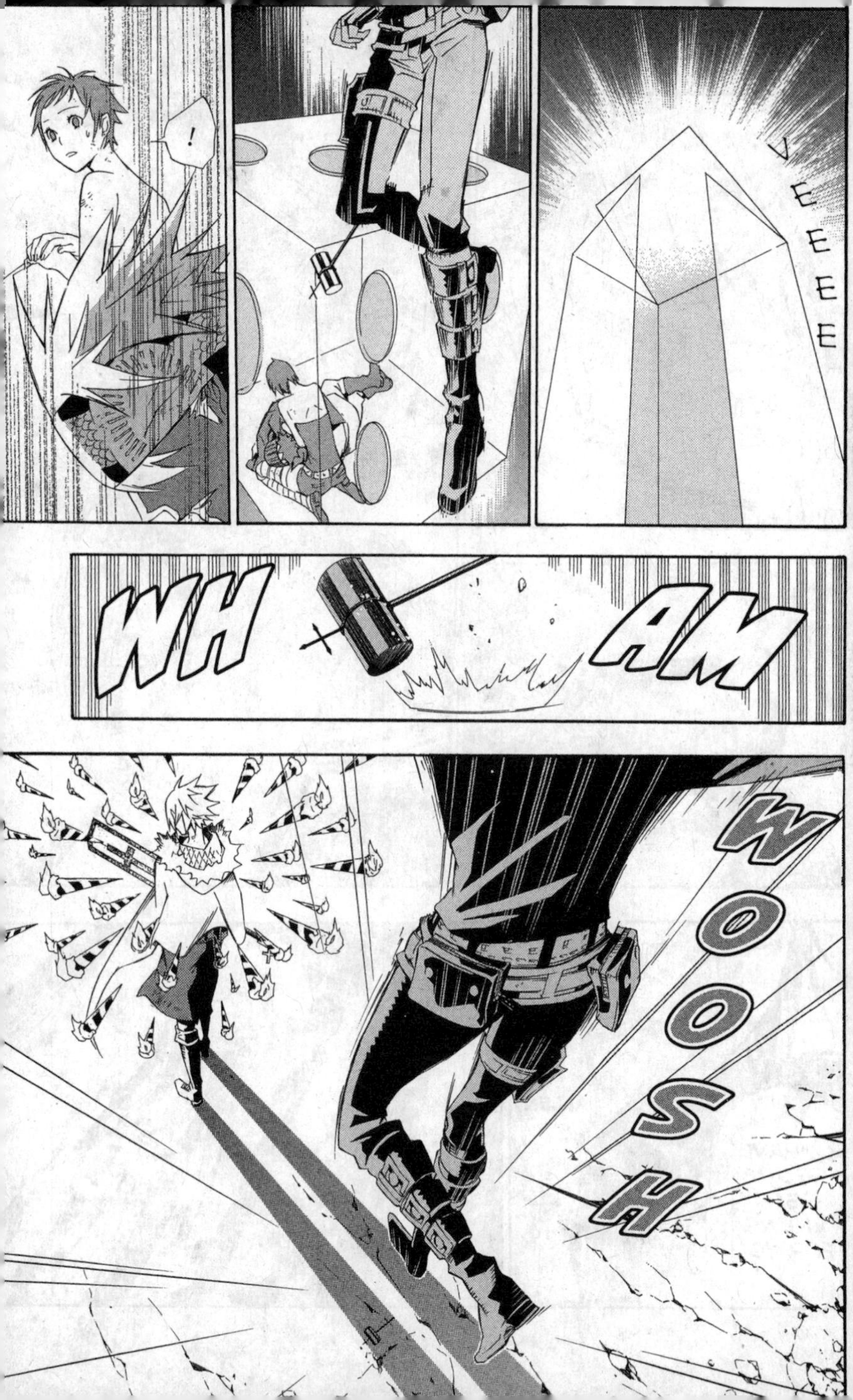
VEEEE
!
WH AM
WOOOSH

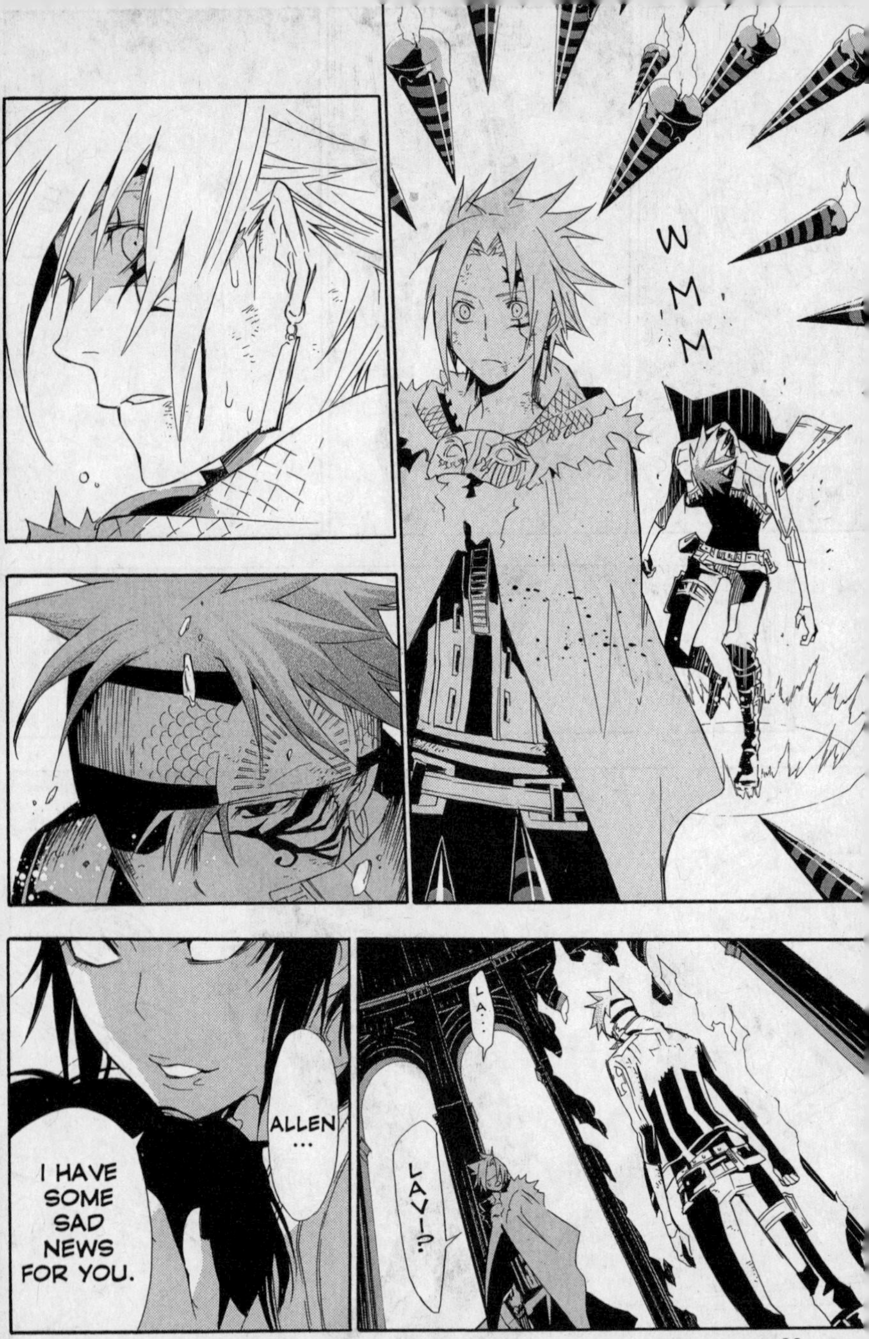
WMM
LA...
LAVI?
ALLEN...
I HAVE SOME SAD NEWS FOR YOU.

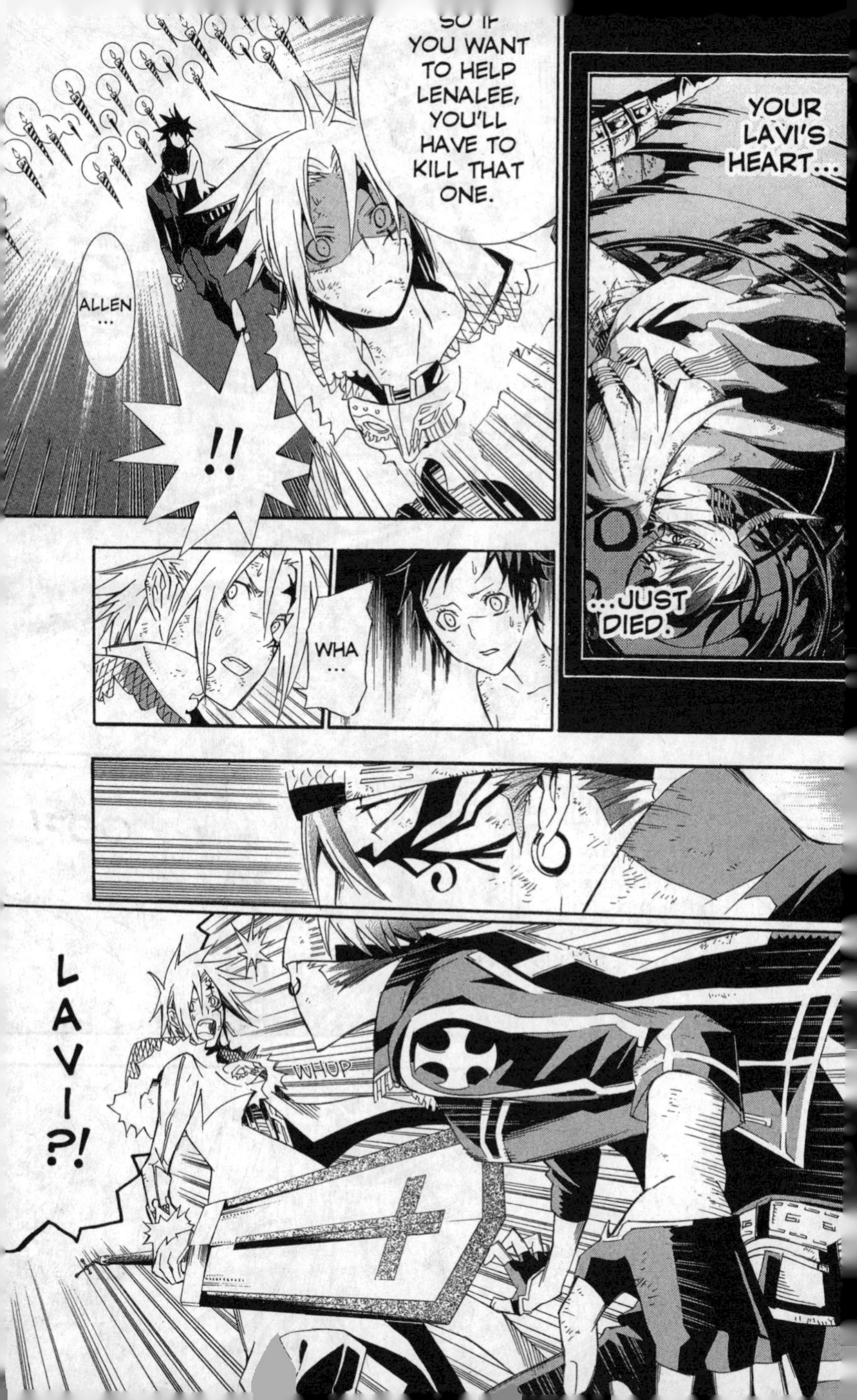
YOUR LAVI'S HEART...
...JUST DIED.
SO IF YOU WANT TO HELP LENALEE, YOU'LL HAVE TO KILL THAT ONE.
ALLEN...
!!
WHA...
WHUP
LAVI?!

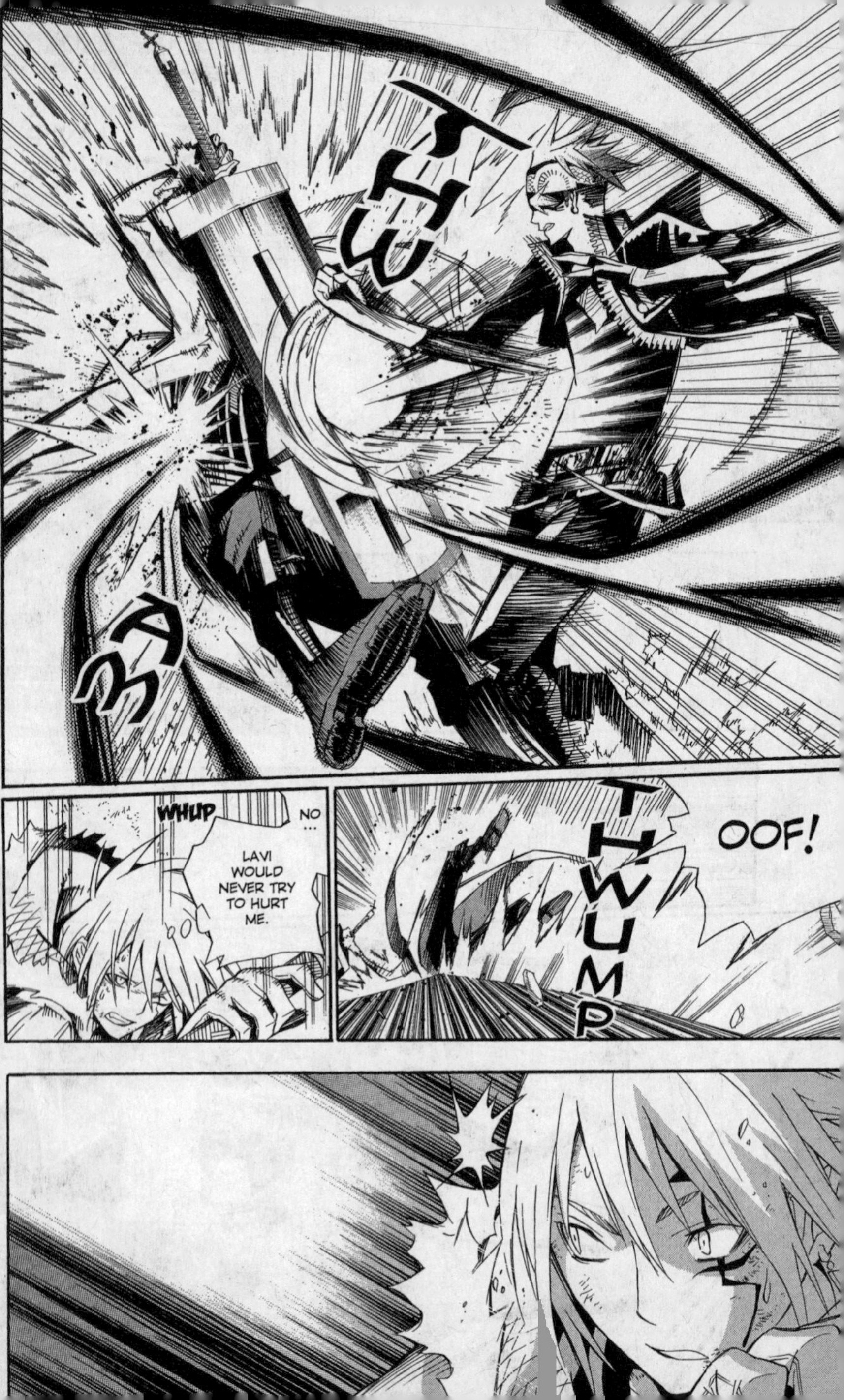

THWUMP
OOF!
WHUP
NO ...
LAVI WOULD NEVER TRY TO HURT ME.

READ THIS WAY

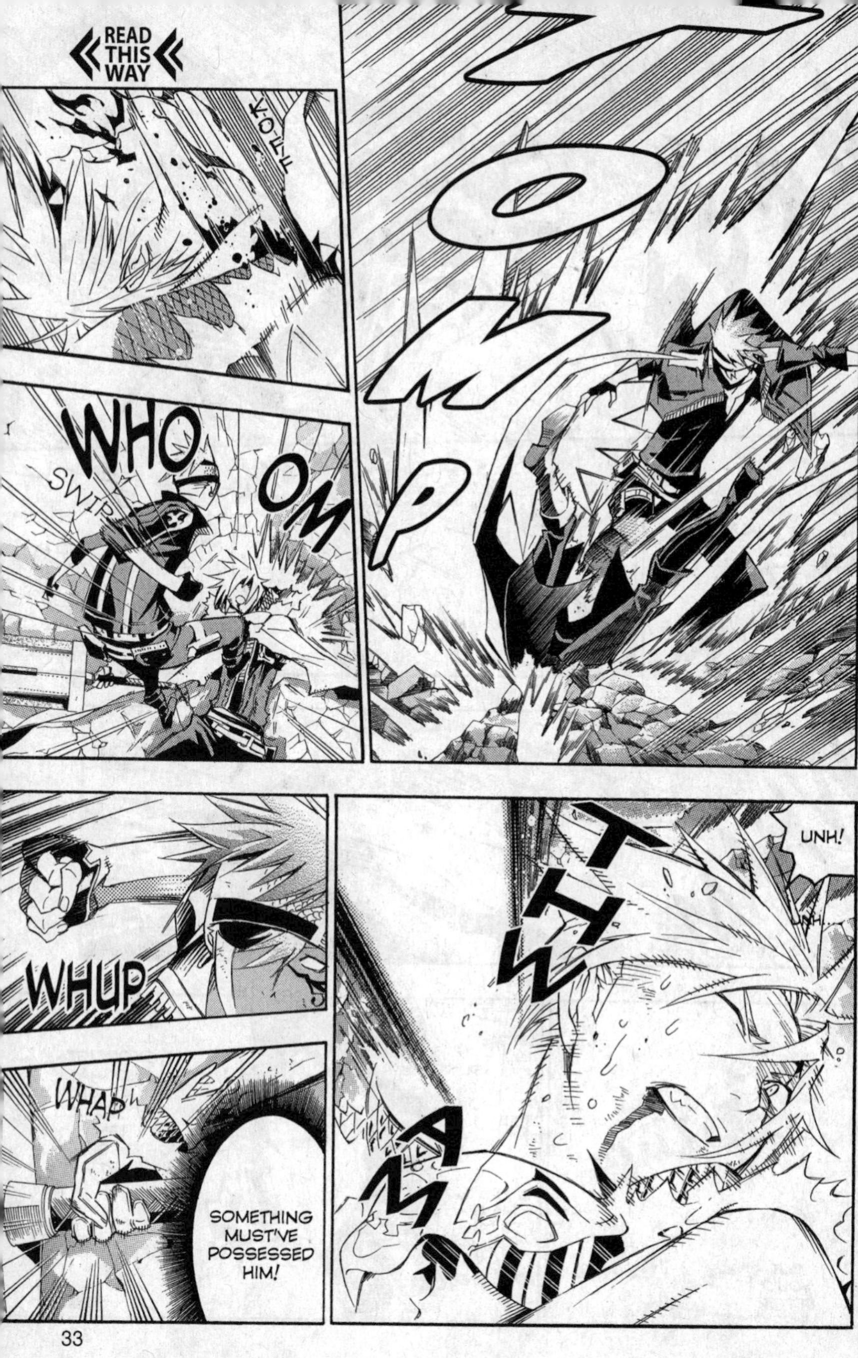
OMP
K-OFF
WHO
OM
SWIP
THWAM
UNH!
NH...
WHUP
WHAP
SOMETHING MUST'VE POSSESSED HIM!

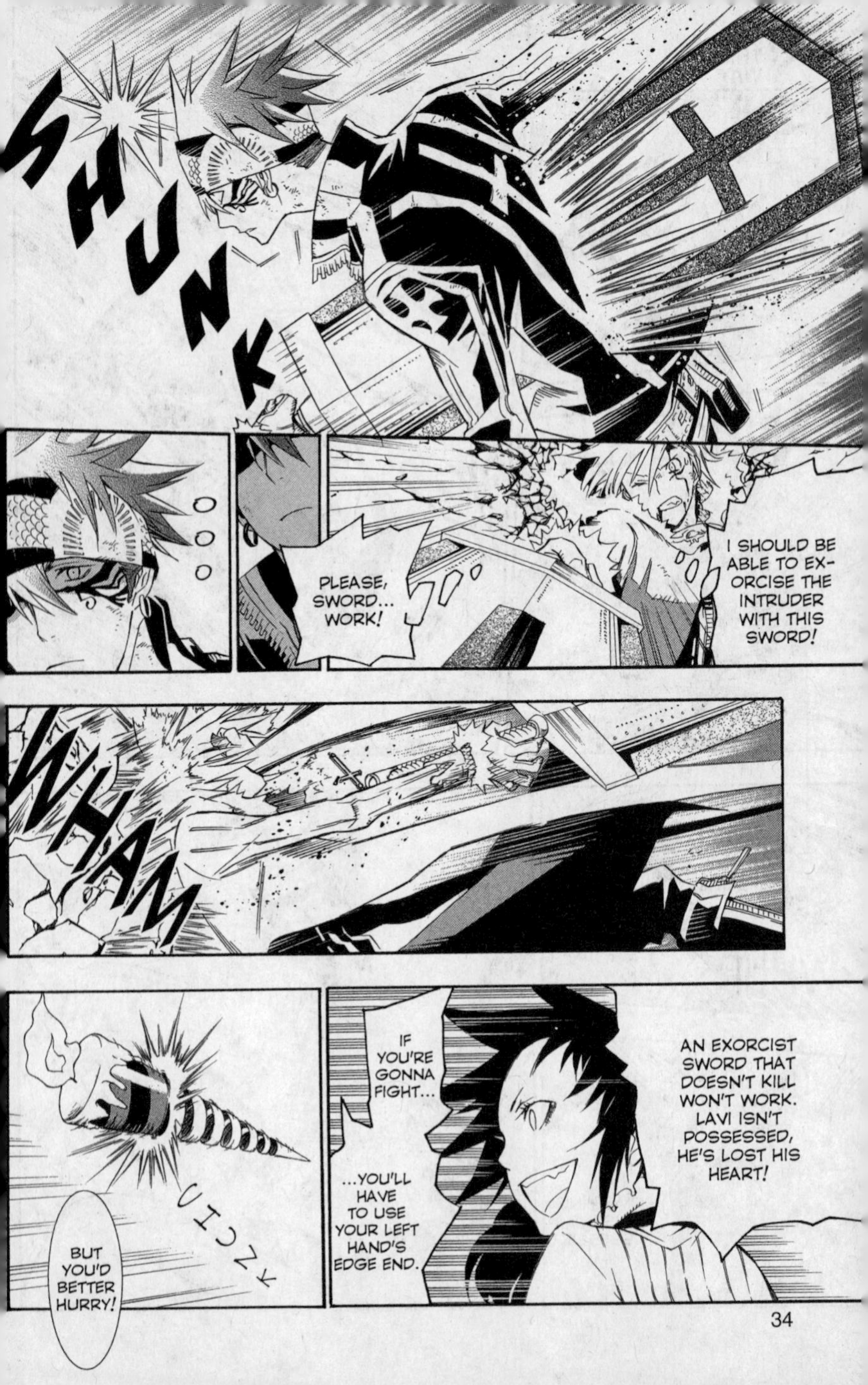
SHUNK
I SHOULD BE ABLE TO EXORCISE THE INTRUDER WITH THIS SWORD!
PLEASE, SWORD... WORK!
WHAM
AN EXORCIST SWORD THAT DOESN'T KILL WON'T WORK. LAVI ISN'T POSSESSED, HE'S LOST HIS HEART!
IF YOU'RE GONNA FIGHT...
...YOU'LL HAVE TO USE YOUR LEFT HAND'S EDGE END.
CLICK
BUT YOU'D BETTER HURRY!

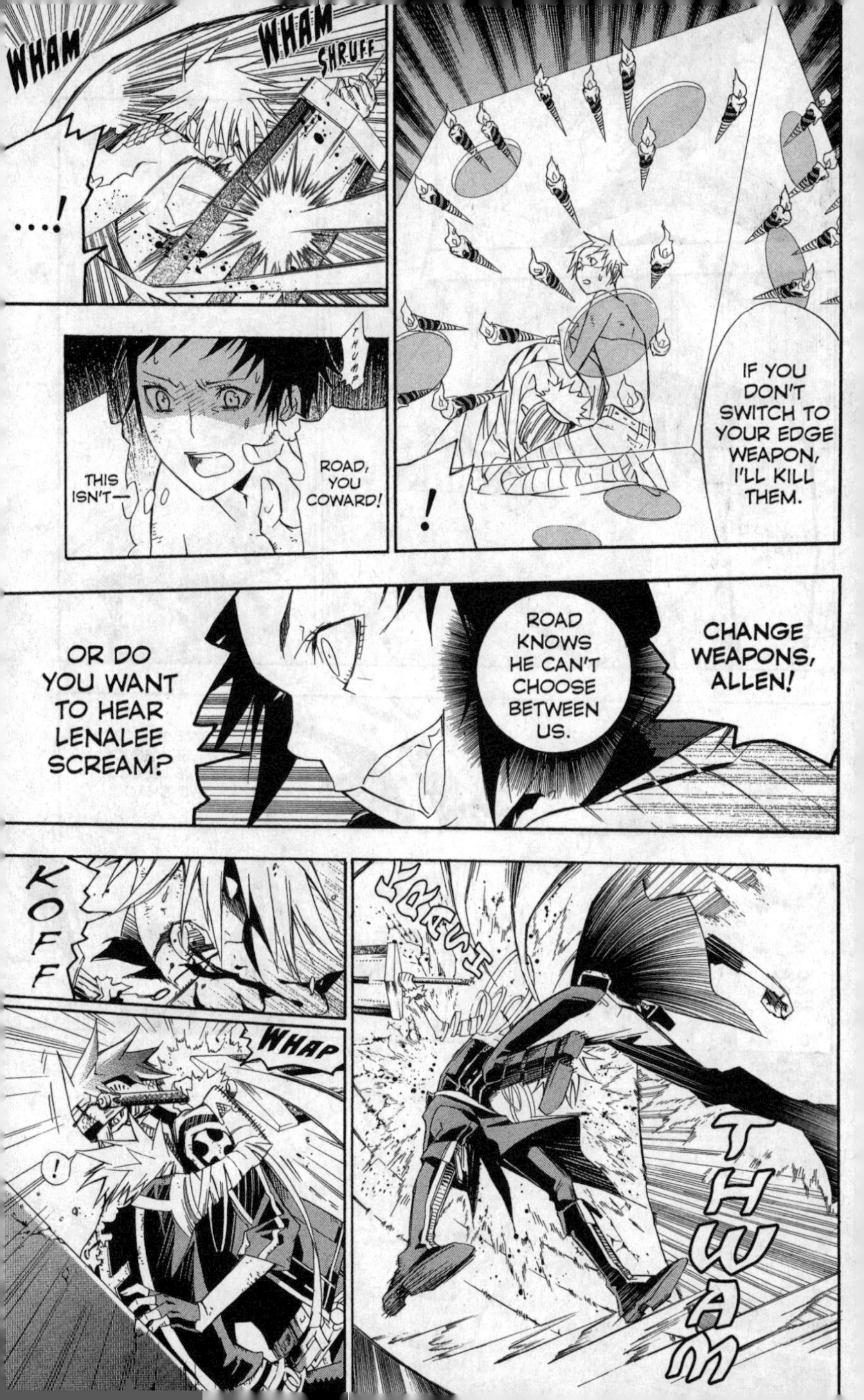
IF YOU DON'T SWITCH TO YOUR EDGE WEAPON, I'LL KILL THEM.
!
WHAM
WHAM
SHRUFF
...!
THUMP
ROAD, YOU COWARD!
THIS ISN'T—
CHANGE WEAPONS, ALLEN!
ROAD KNOWS HE CAN'T CHOOSE BETWEEN US.
OR DO YOU WANT TO HEAR LENALEE SCREAM?
THWAM
KOFF
WHAP
!

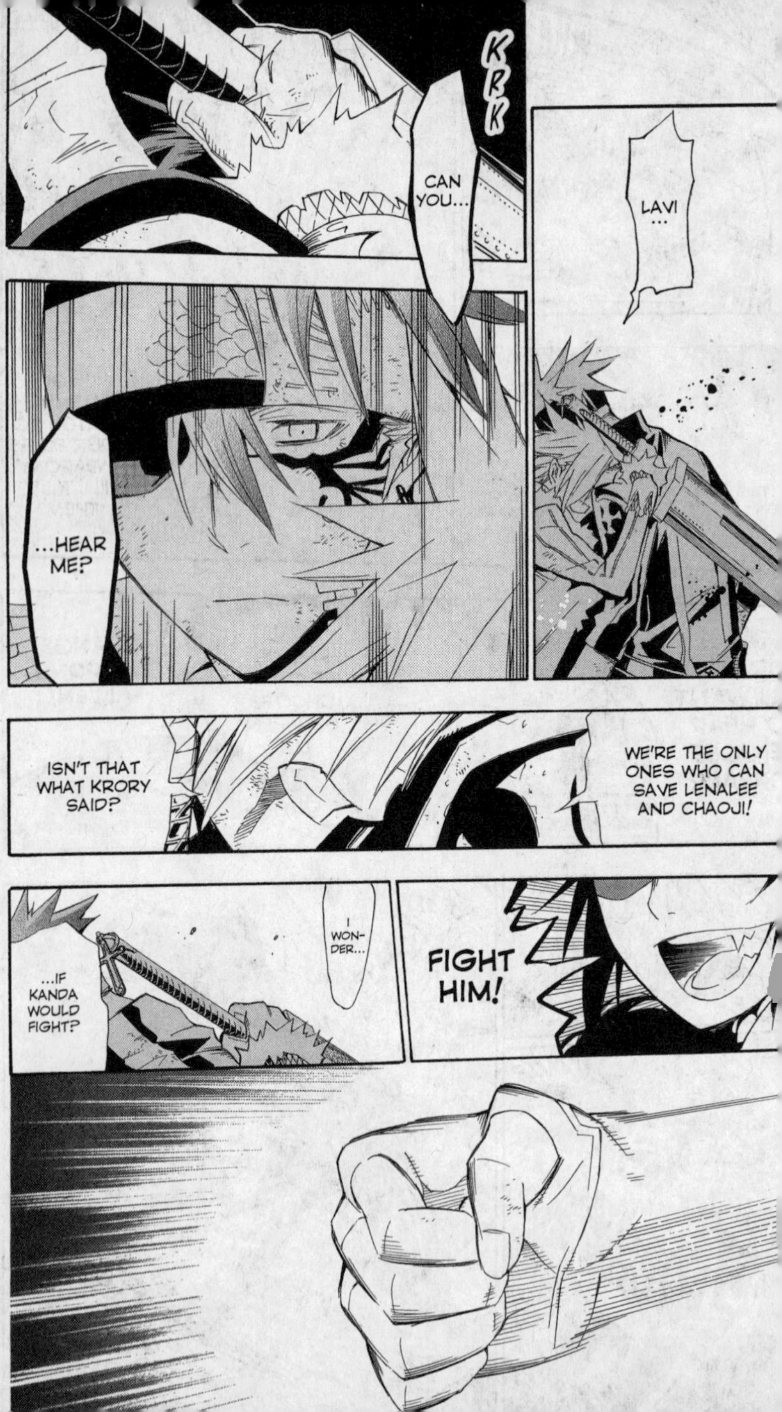
LAVI...
KRK
CAN YOU...
...HEAR ME?
WE'RE THE ONLY ONES WHO CAN SAVE LENALEE AND CHAOJI!
ISN'T THAT WHAT KRORY SAID?
FIGHT HIM!
I WONDER...
...IF KANDA WOULD FIGHT?

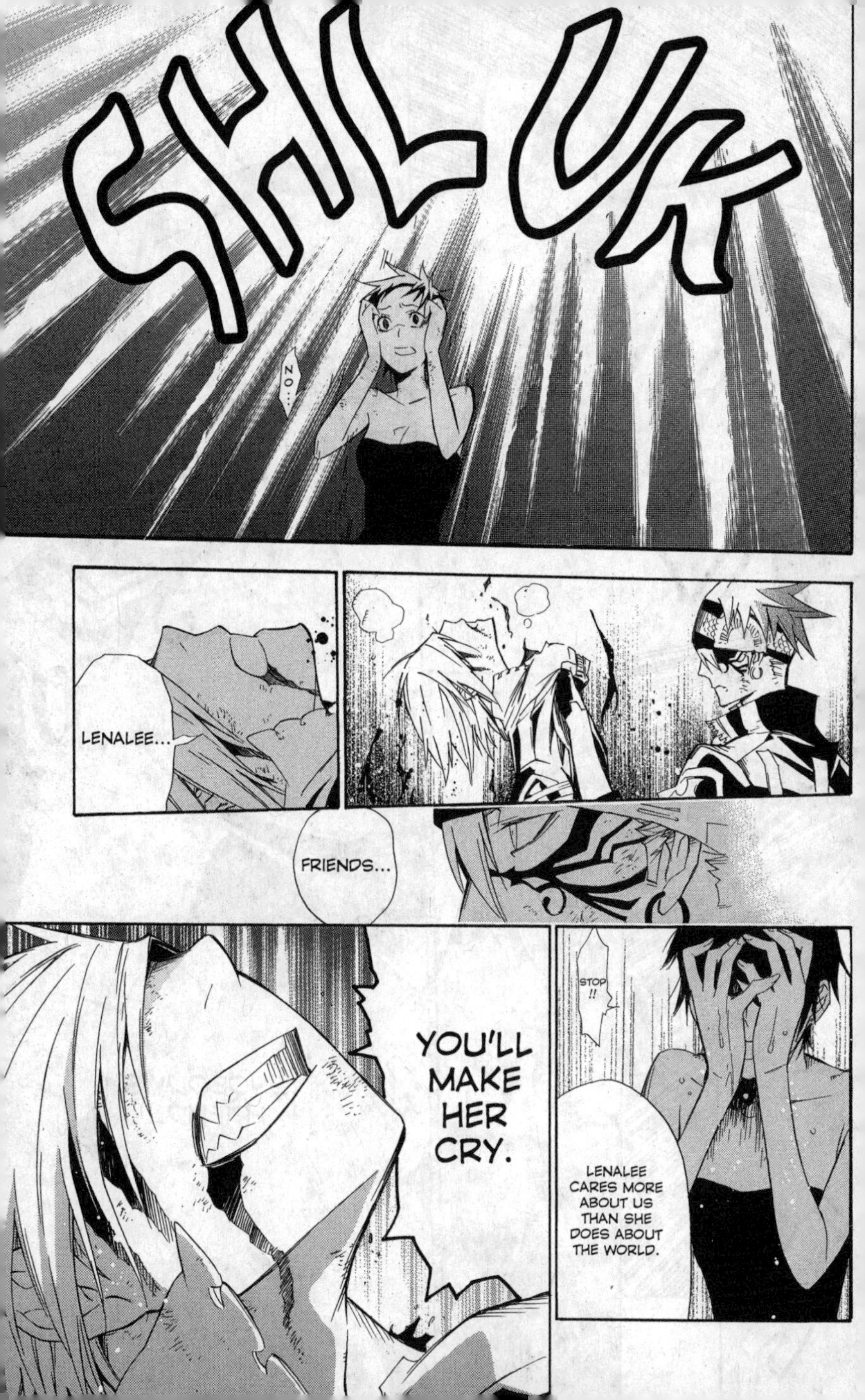
SHLUK
NO...
LENALEE...
FRIENDS...
STOP!!
LENALEE CARES MORE ABOUT US THAN SHE DOES ABOUT THE WORLD.
YOU'LL MAKE HER CRY.

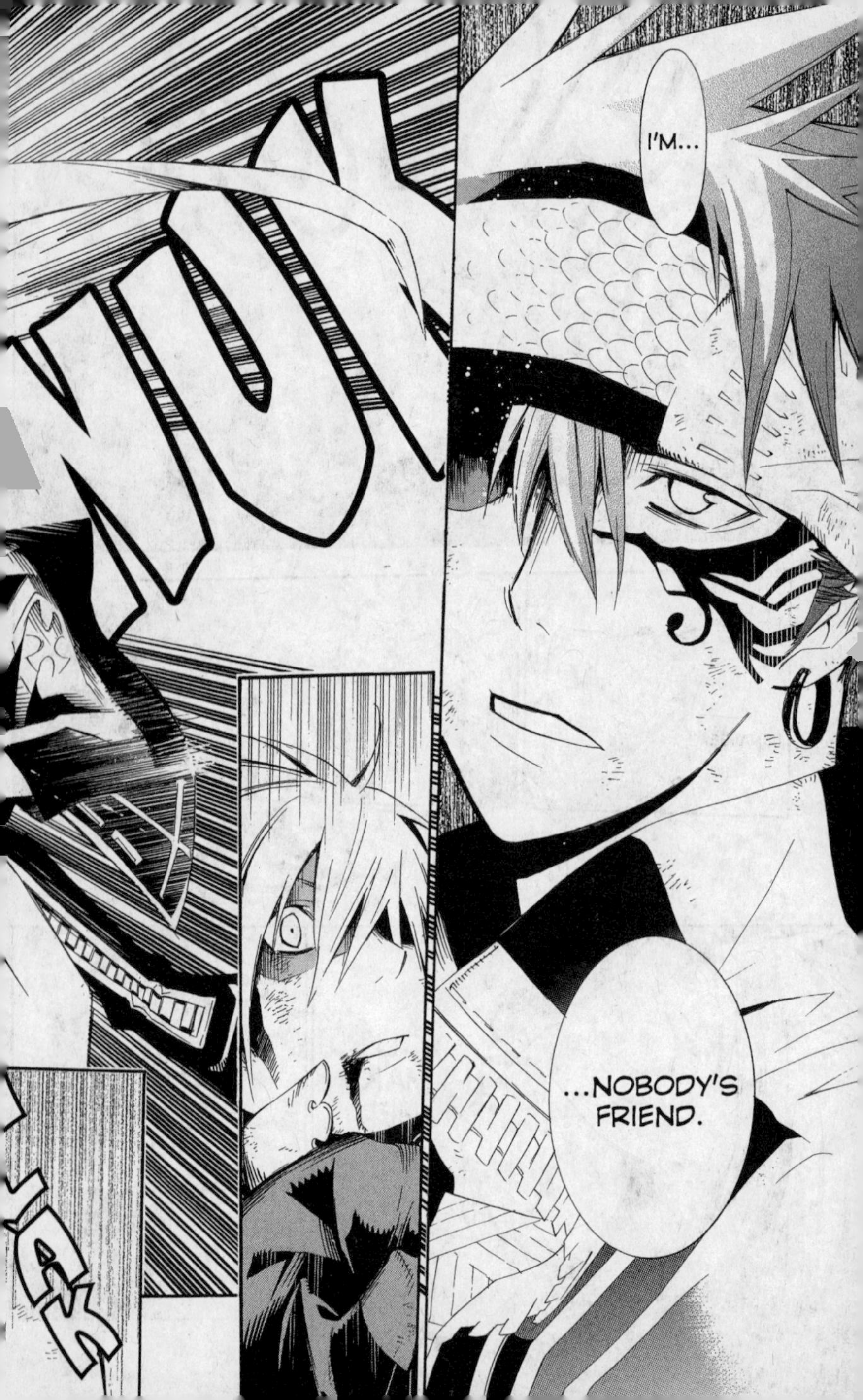
I'M...
...NOBODY'S FRIEND.

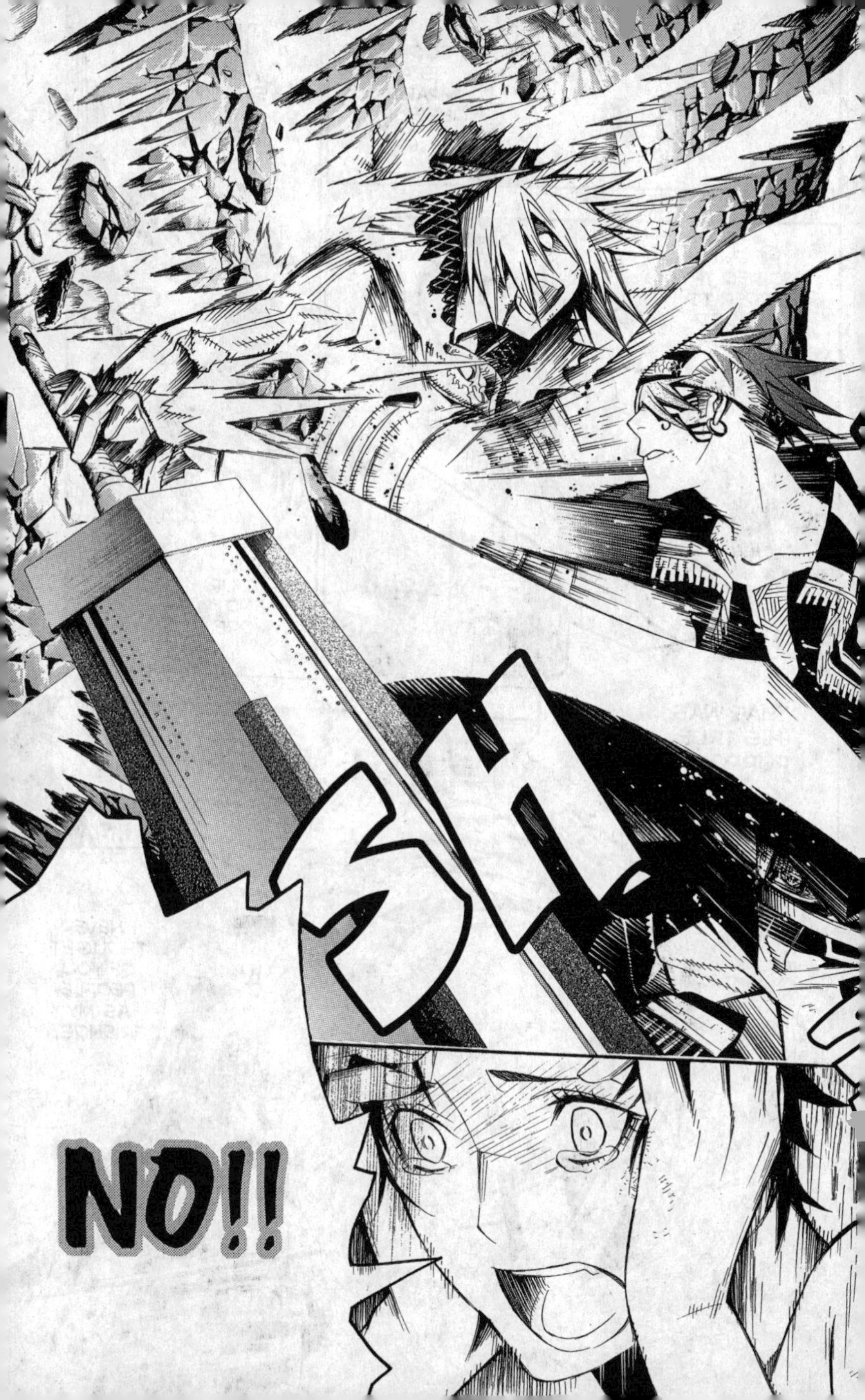
SH
NO!!

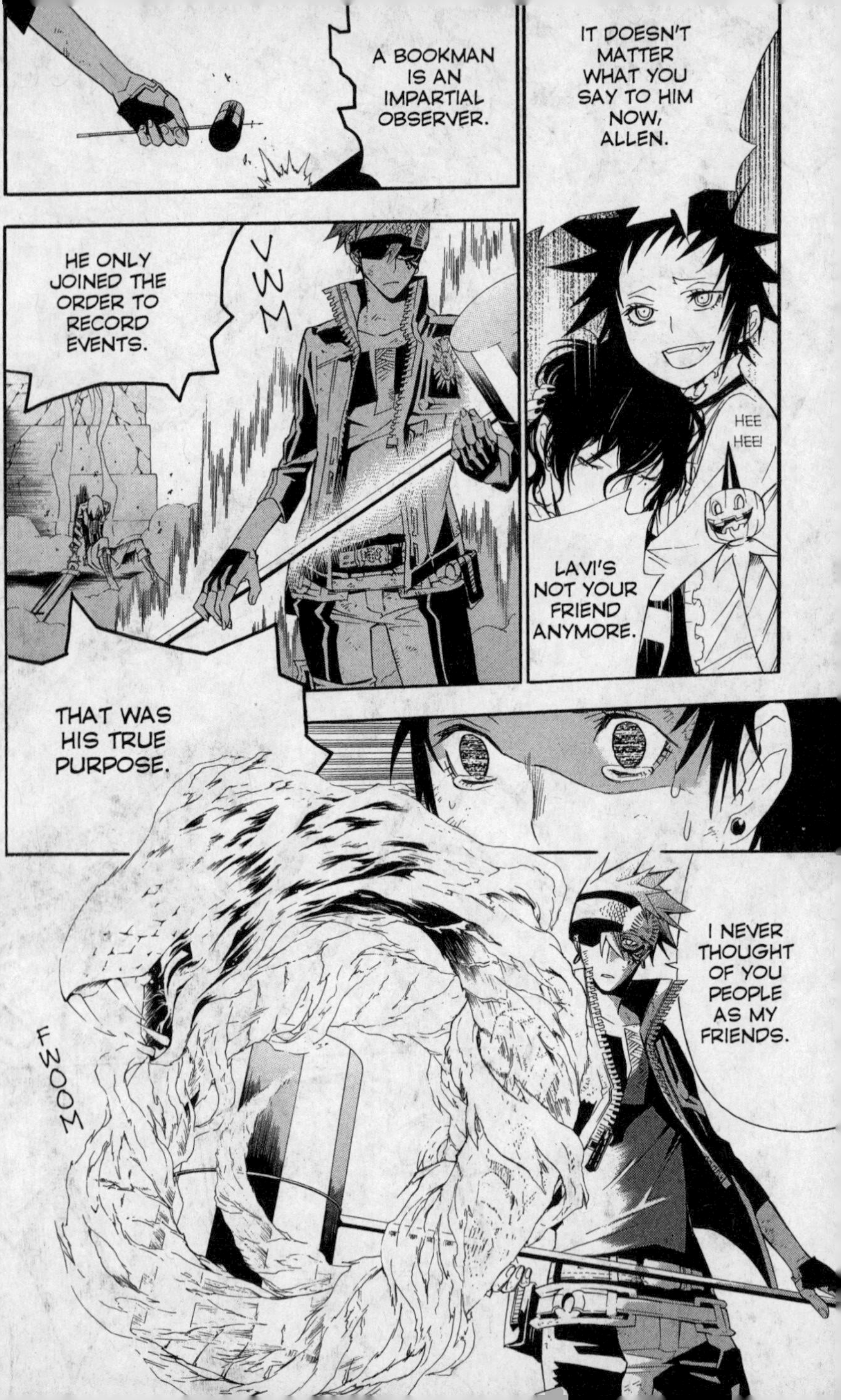
IT DOESN'T MATTER WHAT YOU SAY TO HIM NOW, ALLEN.
HEE HEE!
LAVI'S NOT YOUR FRIEND ANYMORE.
A BOOKMAN IS AN IMPARTIAL OBSERVER.
HE ONLY JOINED THE ORDER TO RECORD EVENTS.
VWM
THAT WAS HIS TRUE PURPOSE.
I NEVER THOUGHT OF YOU PEOPLE AS MY FRIENDS.
FWOOM

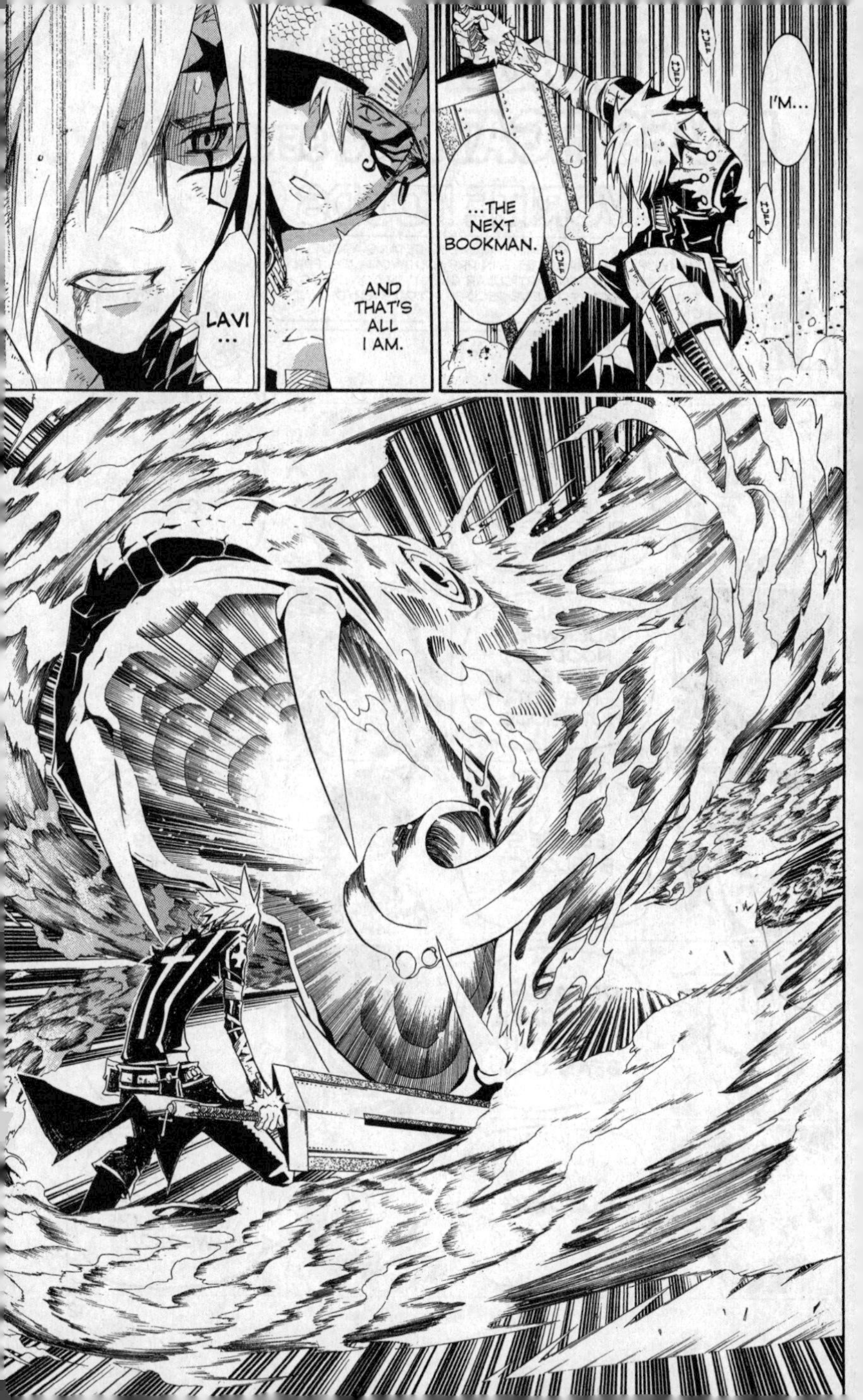
I'M...
HUFF
HUFF
HUFF
HUFF
...THE NEXT BOOKMAN.
AND THAT'S ALL I AM.
LAVI ...

D.GRAY-MAN INVESTIGATION SERIES (?)

FAVORITE FOODS ♡

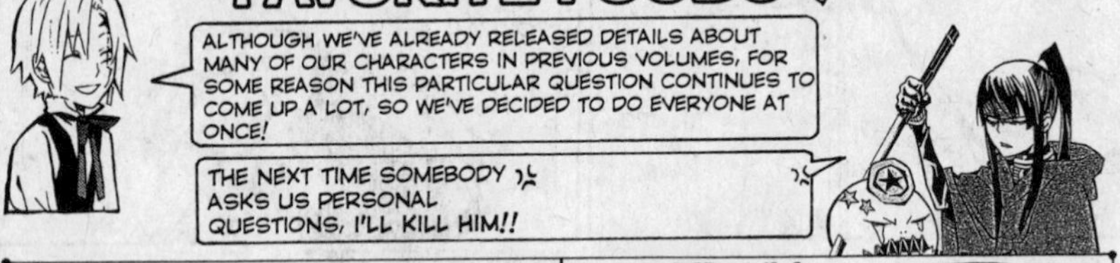
ALTHOUGH WE'VE ALREADY RELEASED DETAILS ABOUT MANY OF OUR CHARACTERS IN PREVIOUS VOLUMES, FOR SOME REASON THIS PARTICULAR QUESTION CONTINUES TO COME UP A LOT, SO WE'VE DECIDED TO DO EVERYONE AT ONCE!
THE NEXT TIME SOMEBODY ASKS US PERSONAL QUESTIONS, I'LL KILL HIM!!

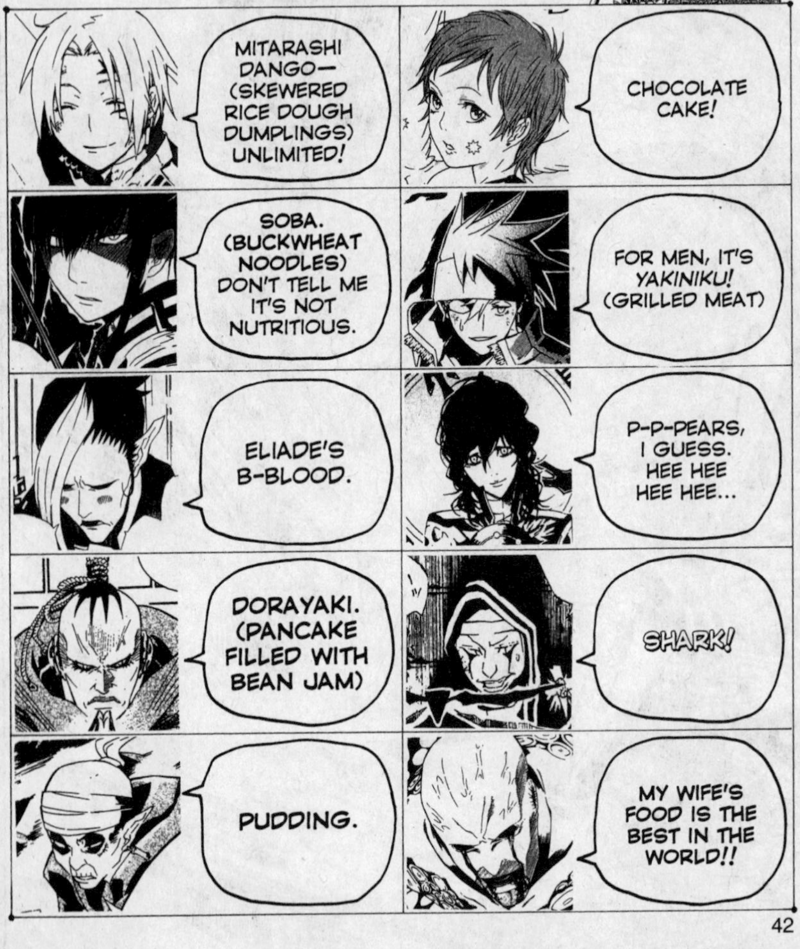
CHOCOLATE CAKE!
MITARASHI DANGO— (SKEWERED RICE DOUGH DUMPLINGS) UNLIMITED!
FOR MEN, IT'S YAKINIKU! (GRILLED MEAT)
SOBA. (BUCKWHEAT NOODLES) DON'T TELL ME IT'S NOT NUTRITIOUS.
P-P-PEARS, I GUESS. HEE HEE HEE HEE...
ELIADE'S B-BLOOD.
SHARK!
DORAYAKI. (PANCAKE FILLED WITH BEAN JAM)
MY WIFE'S FOOD IS THE BEST IN THE WORLD!!
PUDDING.

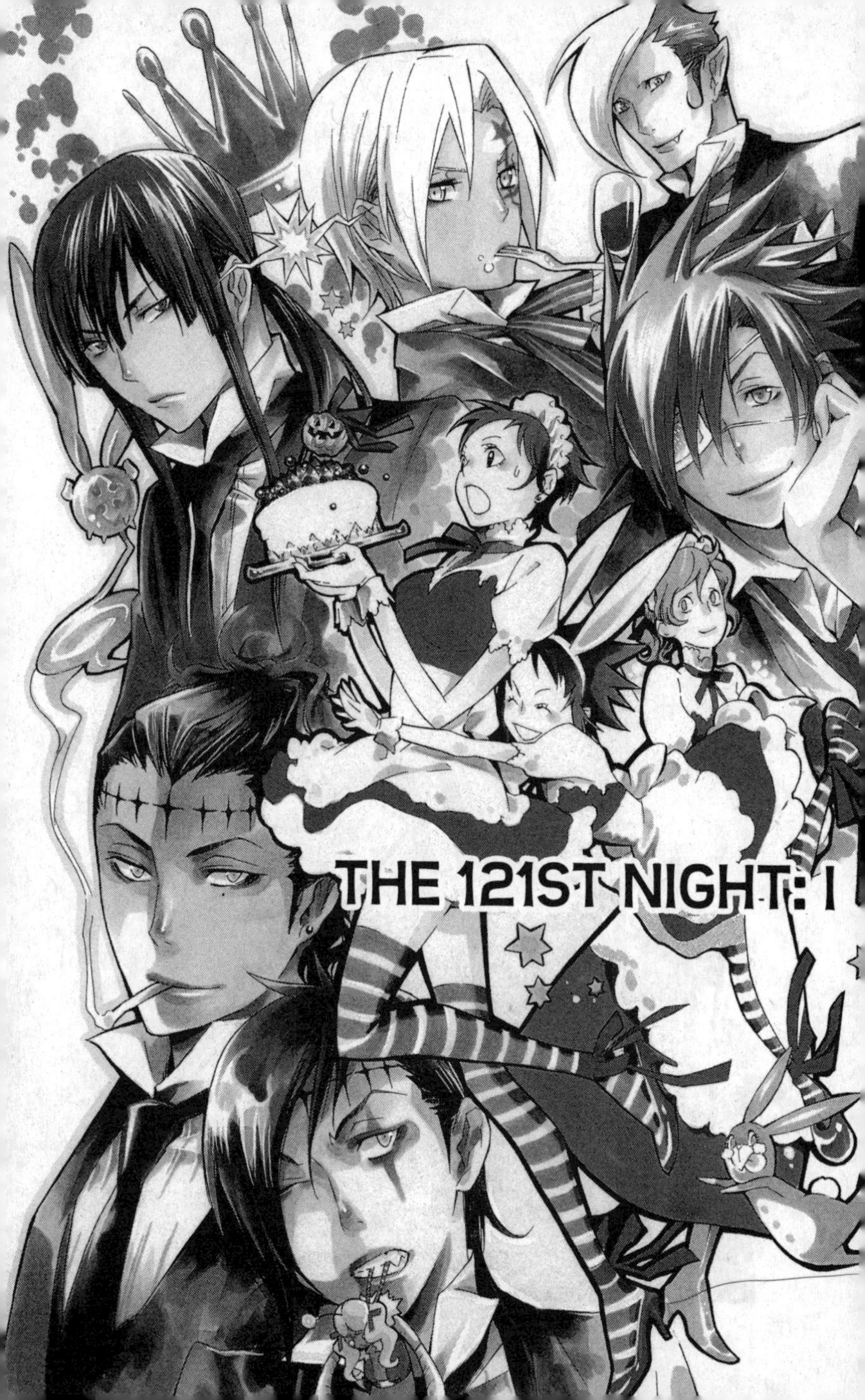
THE 121ST NIGHT: I

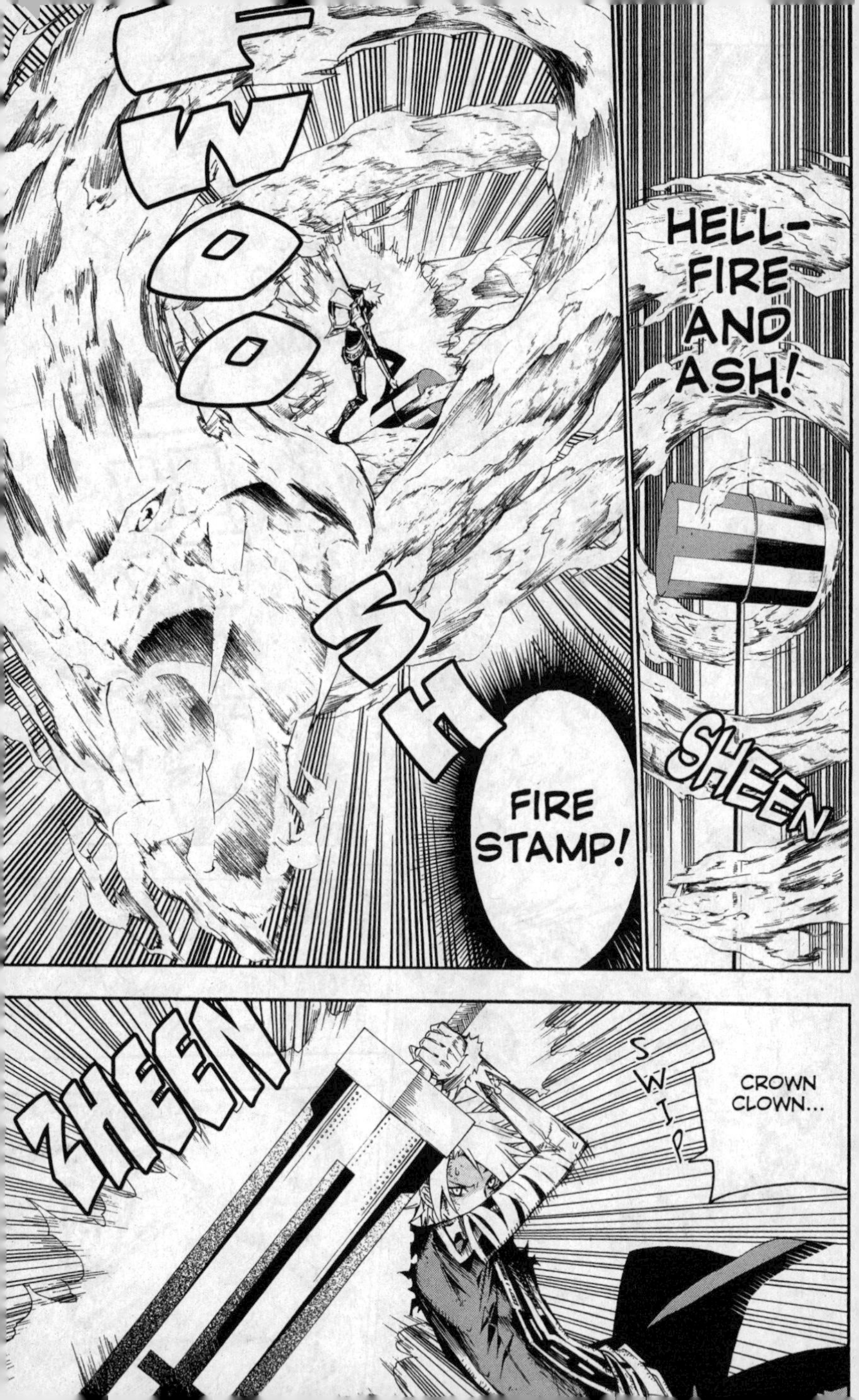
HELL-FIRE AND ASH!
SHEEN
WHOOSH
FIRE STAMP!
CROWN CLOWN...
SWIP
ZHEEN

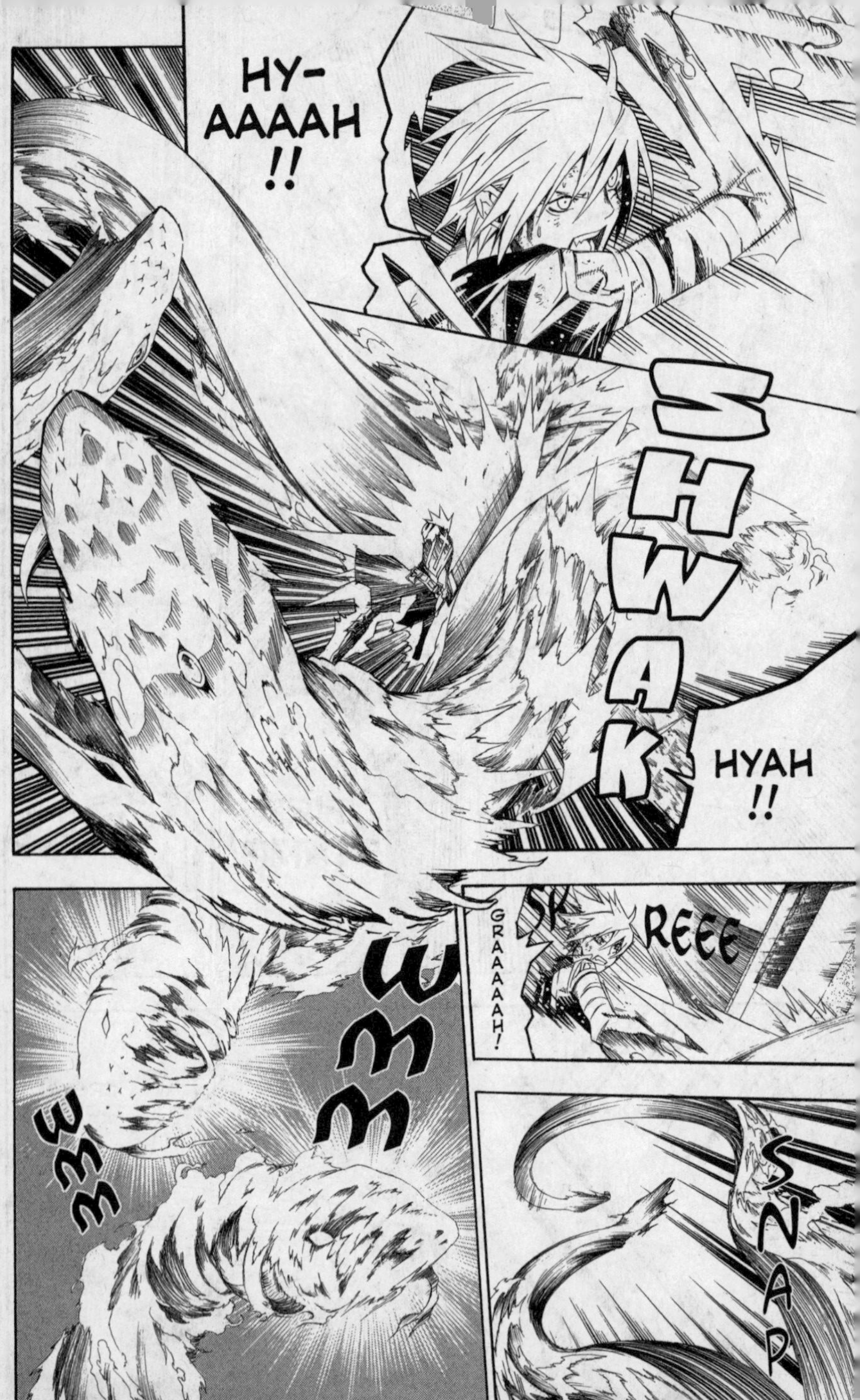
HY-AAAAH!!
SHWAK
HYAH!!
SKREEE
GRAAAAAH!
SNAP

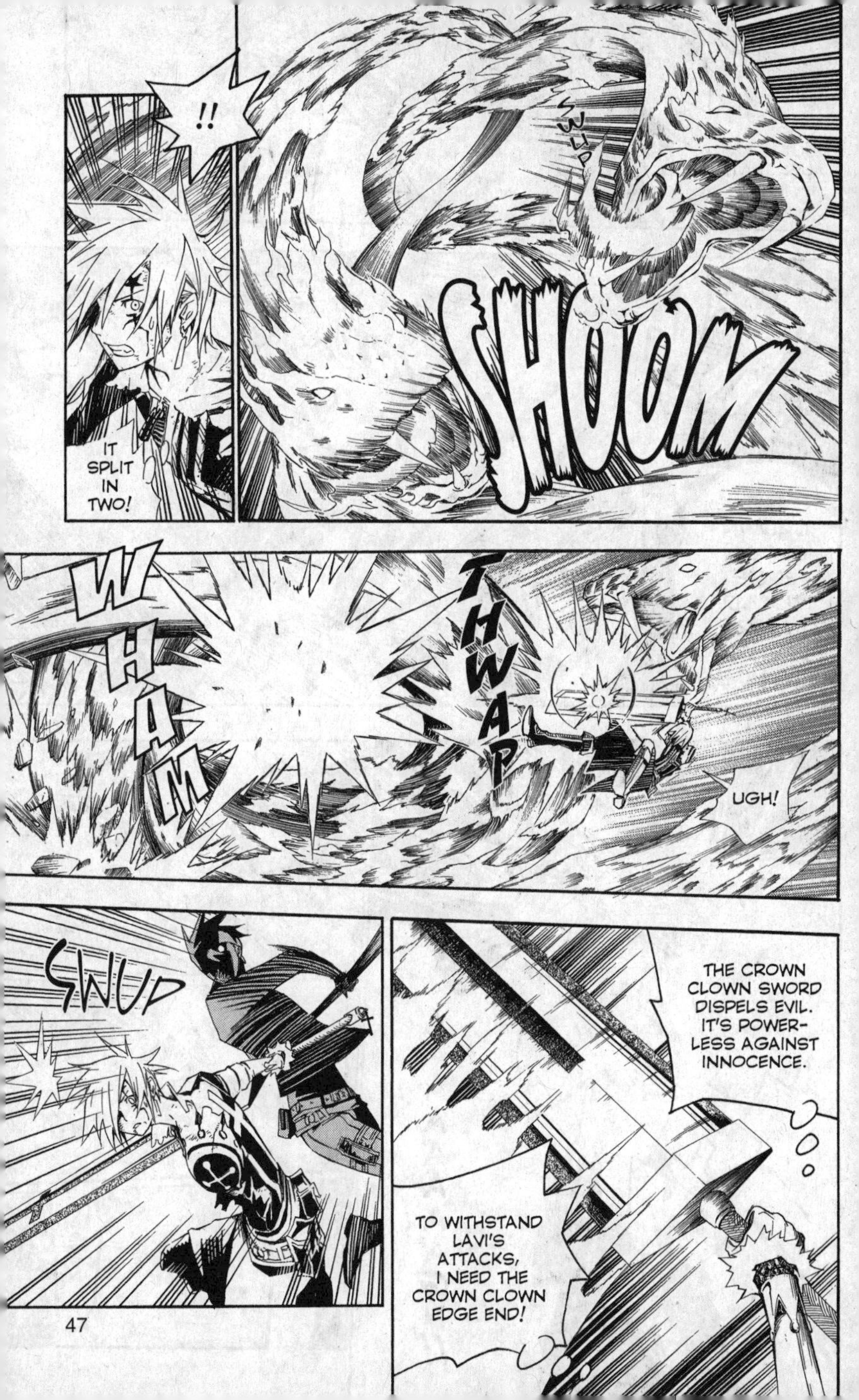
SWUD
SHOOM
!!
IT SPLIT IN TWO!
UGH!
THWAP
WHAM
THE CROWN CLOWN SWORD DISPELS EVIL. IT'S POWERLESS AGAINST INNOCENCE.
TO WITHSTAND LAVI'S ATTACKS, I NEED THE CROWN CLOWN EDGE END!
SWUD

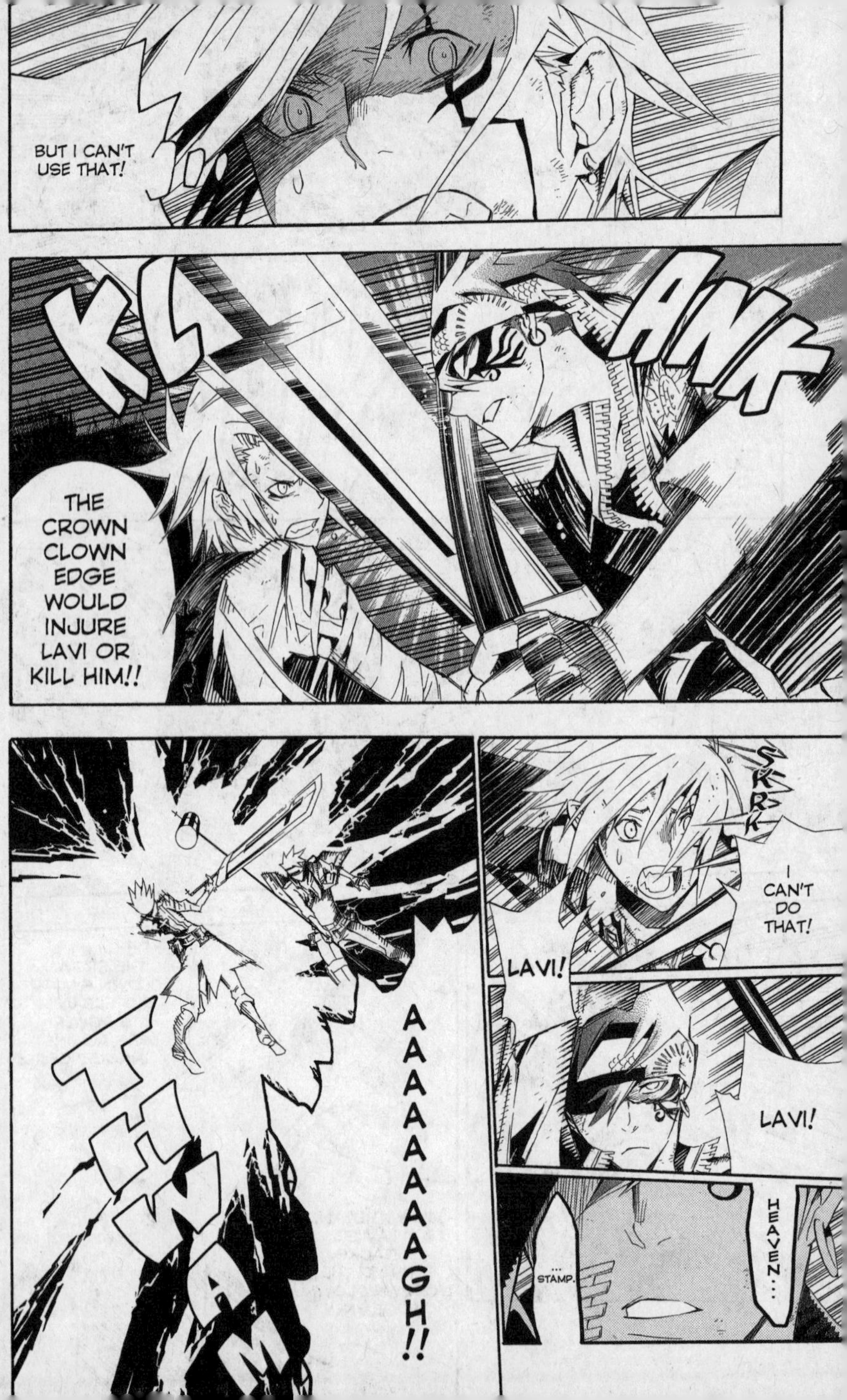
BUT I CAN'T USE THAT!
KLANK
THE CROWN CLOWN EDGE WOULD INJURE LAVI OR KILL HIM!!
SKRK
I CAN'T DO THAT!
LAVI!
LAVI!
HEAVEN...
...STAMP.
THWAM
AAAAAAAAAGH!!

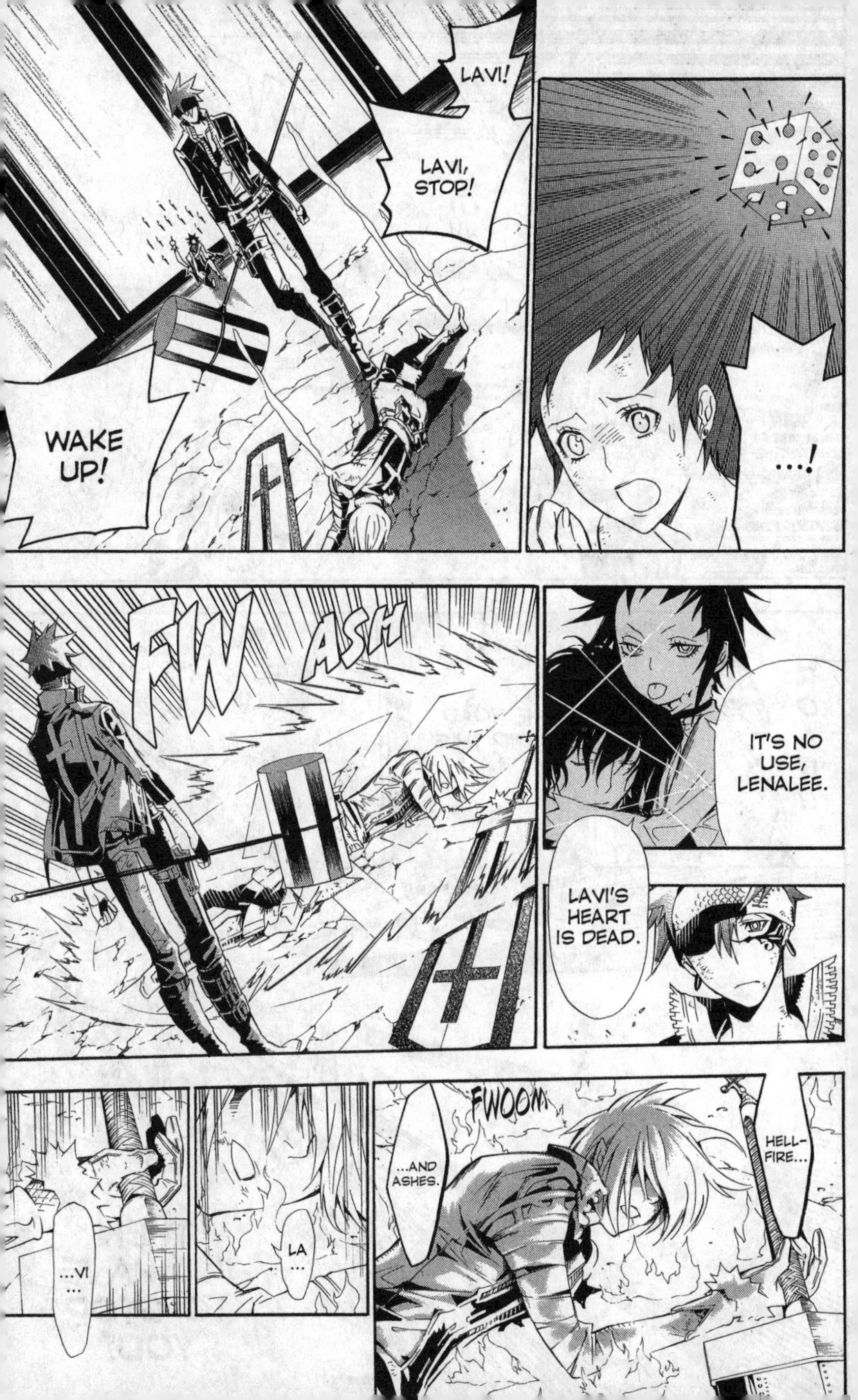
...!
LAVI!
LAVI, STOP!
WAKE UP!
IT'S NO USE, LENALEE.
LAVI'S HEART IS DEAD.
FWASH
FWOOM
HELL-FIRE...
...AND ASHES.
LA ...
...VI ...

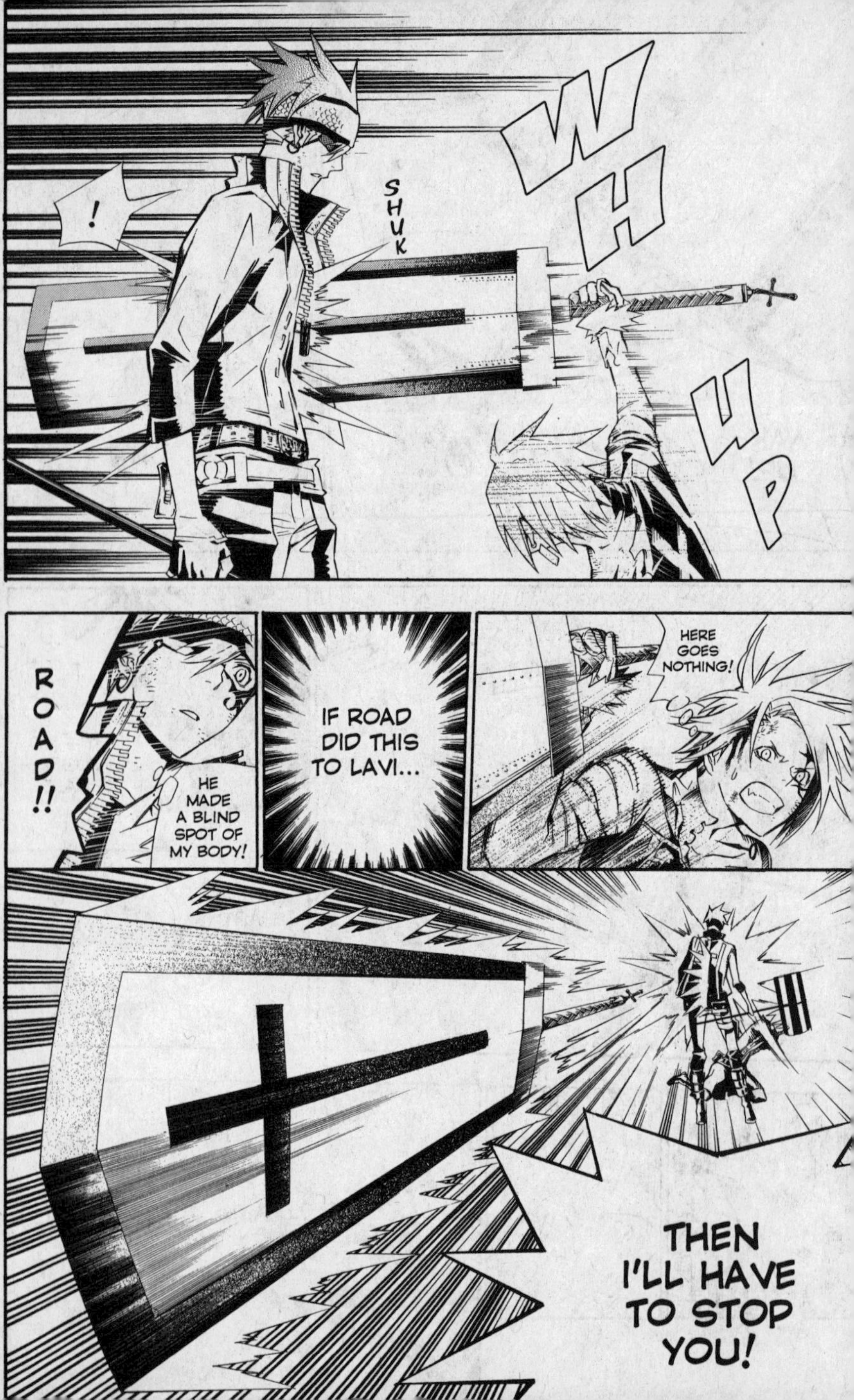
WHUP
SHUK
!
HERE GOES NOTHING!
IF ROAD DID THIS TO LAVI...
ROAD!!
HE MADE A BLIND SPOT OF MY BODY!
THEN I'LL HAVE TO STOP YOU!

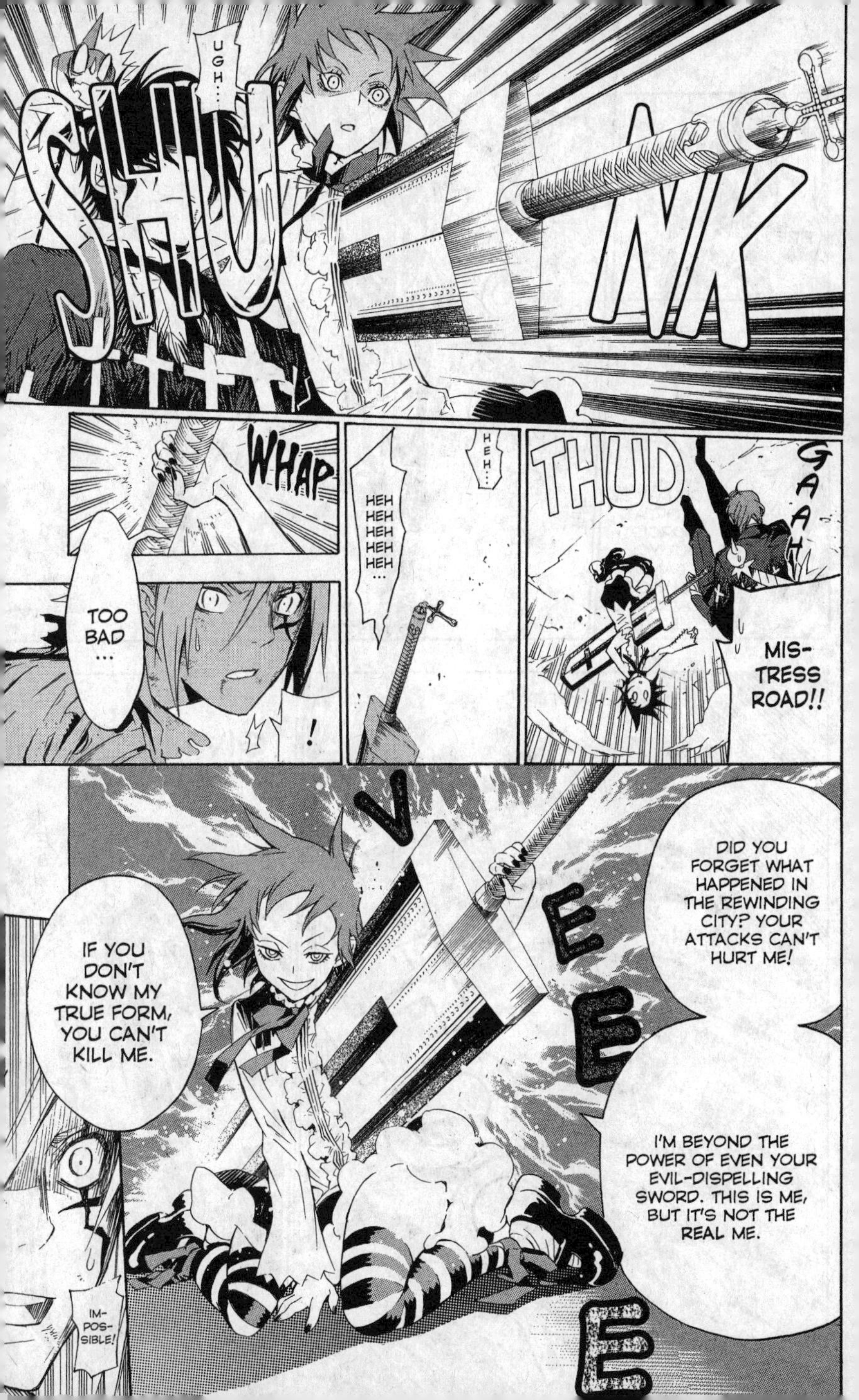
UGH...
SHU
NK
THUD
GAAAH
MISTRESS ROAD!!
HEH...
HEH HEH HEH HEH HEH...
WHAP
TOO BAD...
!
DID YOU FORGET WHAT HAPPENED IN THE REWINDING CITY? YOUR ATTACKS CAN'T HURT ME!
I'M BEYOND THE POWER OF EVEN YOUR EVIL-DISPELLING SWORD. THIS IS ME, BUT IT'S NOT THE REAL ME.
VEEEE
IF YOU DON'T KNOW MY TRUE FORM, YOU CAN'T KILL ME.
IMPOSSIBLE!

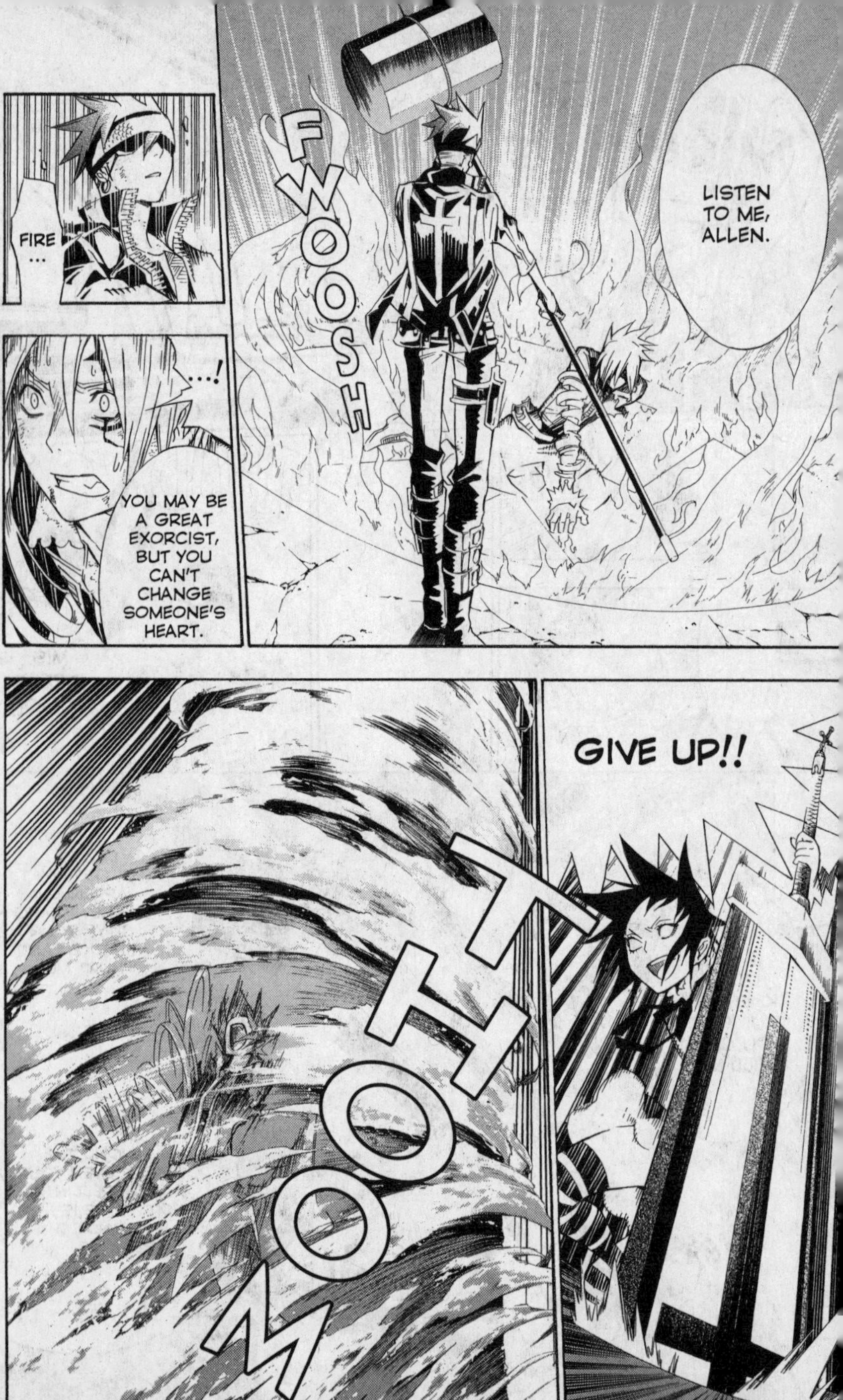
LISTEN TO ME, ALLEN.
FWOSH
FIRE ...
...!
YOU MAY BE A GREAT EXORCIST, BUT YOU CAN'T CHANGE SOMEONE'S HEART.
GIVE UP!!
THOOOM

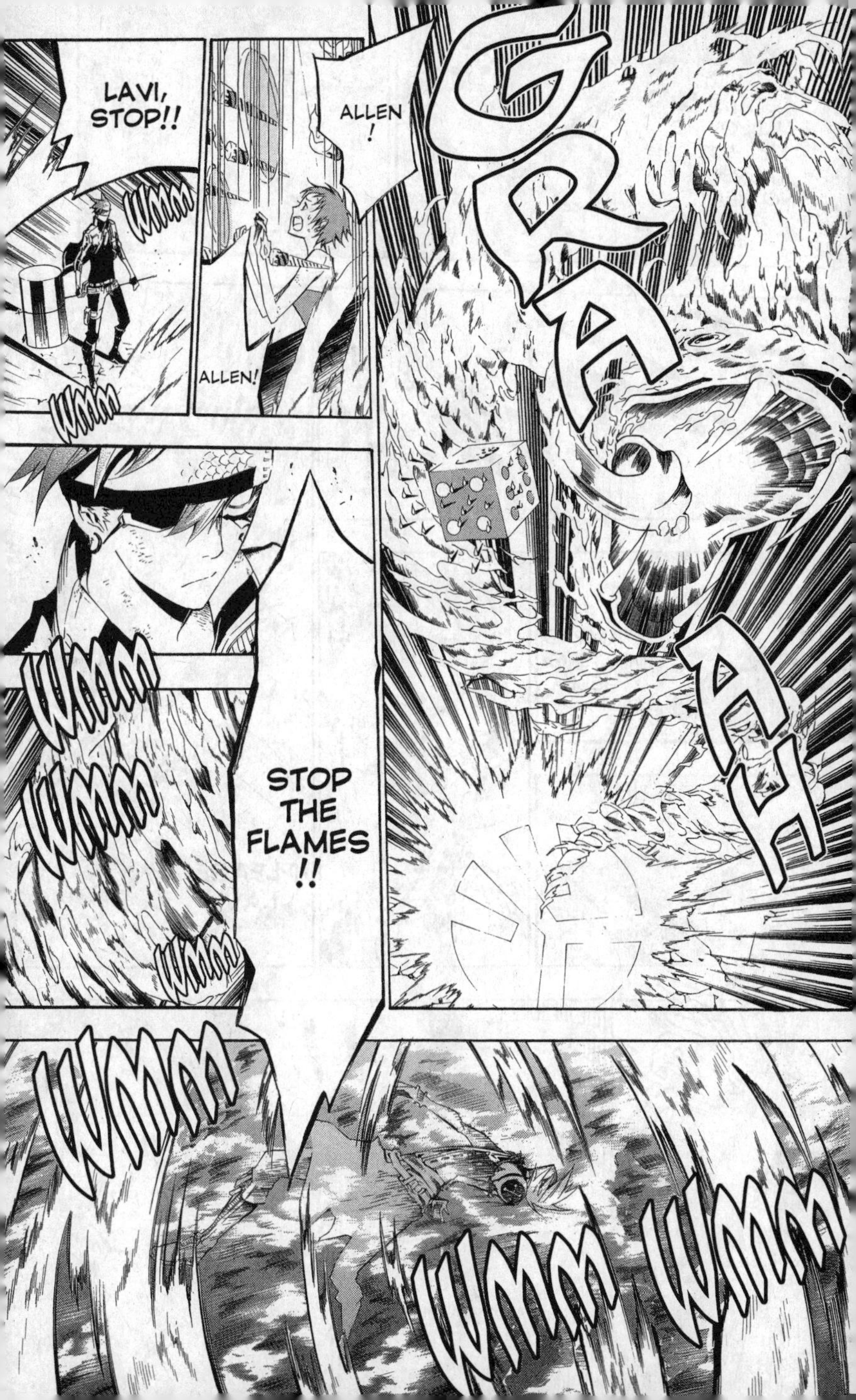
GRA
ACH
ALLEN!
ALLEN!
LAVI, STOP!!
WMM
WMM
WMM
WMM
STOP THE FLAMES!!
WMM
WMM
WMM WMM

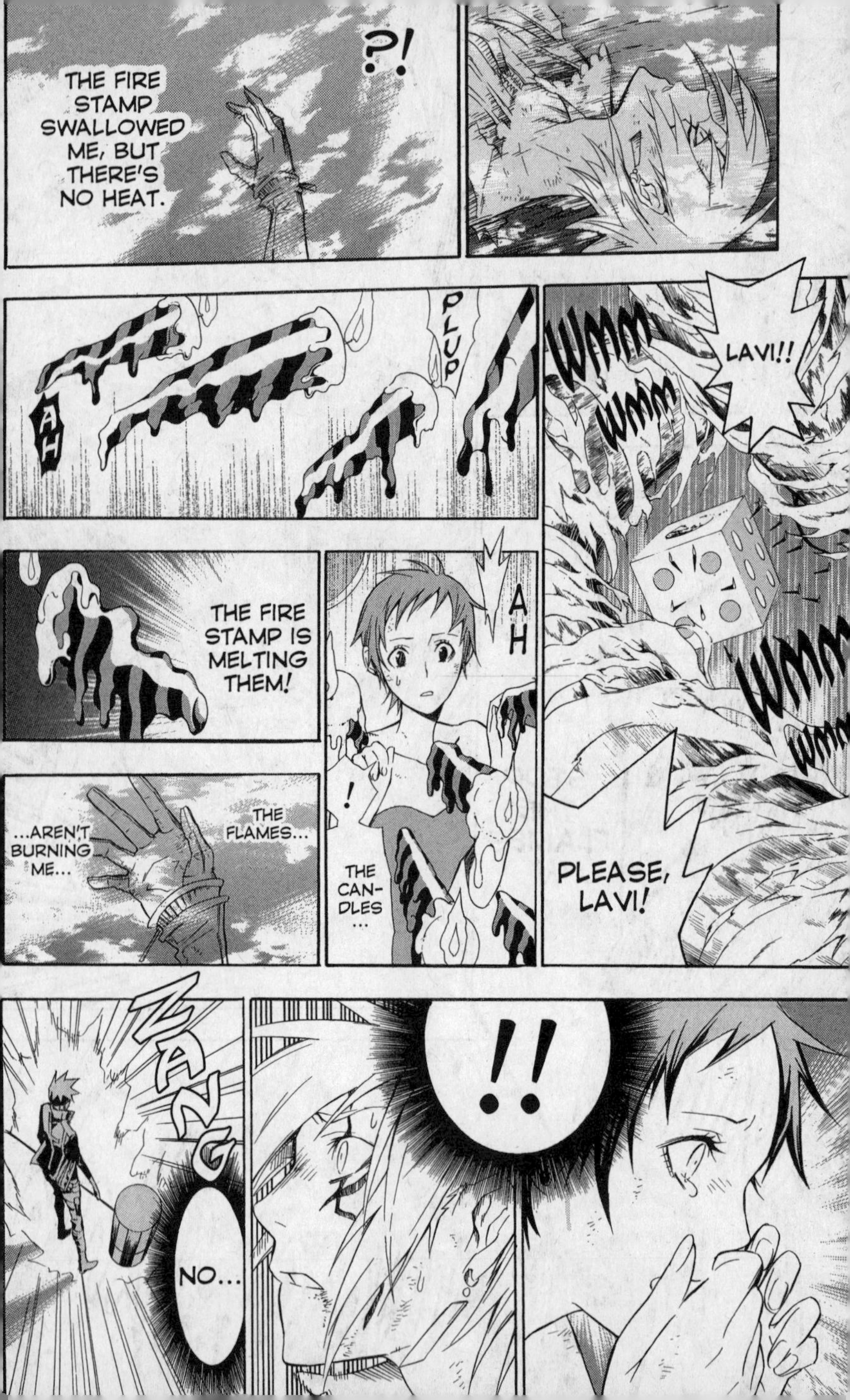
?!
THE FIRE STAMP SWALLOWED ME, BUT THERE'S NO HEAT.
LAVI!!
WMM
WMM
WMM
WMM
PLEASE, LAVI!
PLUP
AH
AH
!
THE CAN- DLES ...
THE FIRE STAMP IS MELTING THEM!
THE FLAMES...
...AREN'T BURNING ME...
!!
ZANG
NO...

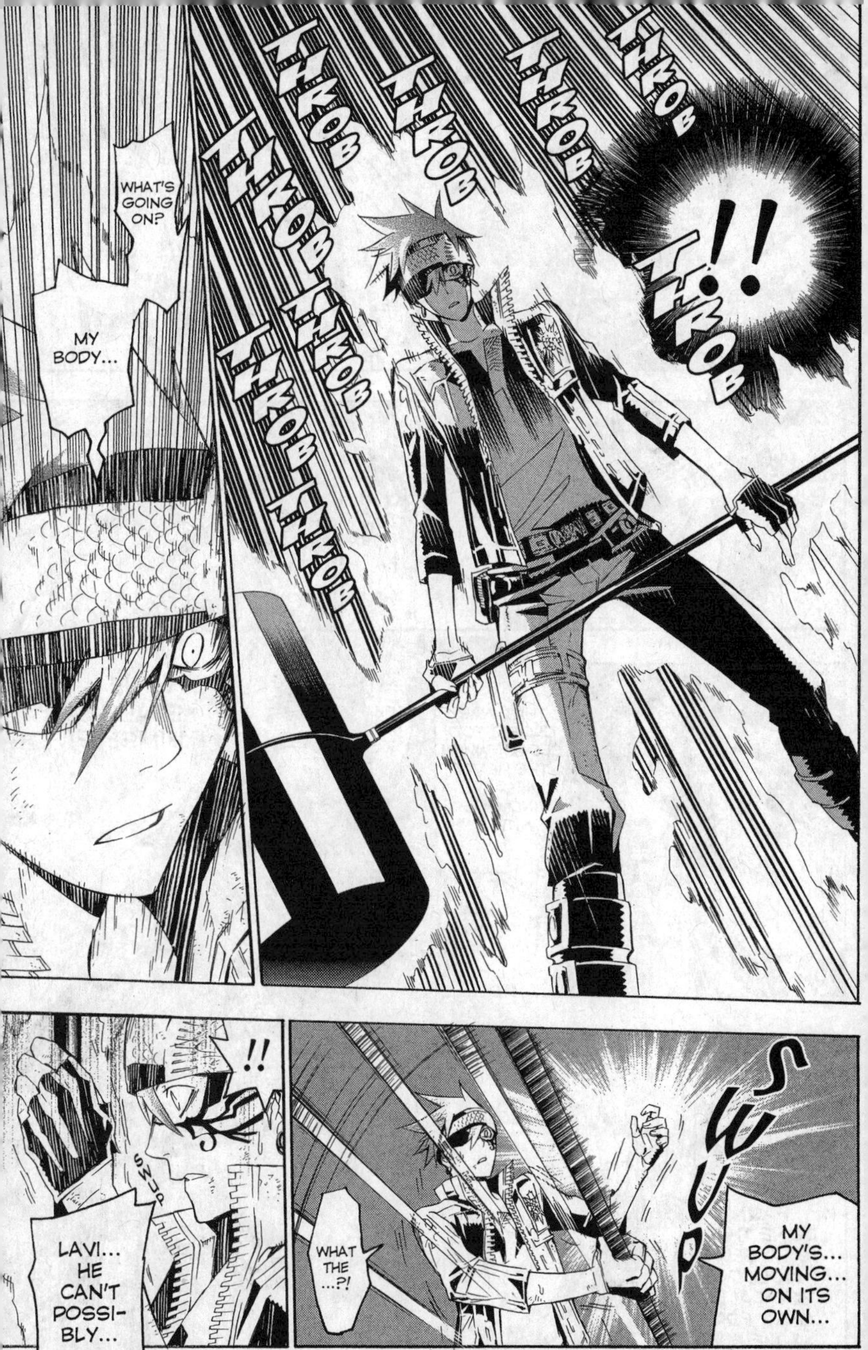
THROB
THROB
THROB
THROB
THROB THROB THROB
THROB THROB THROB
THROB
!!
WHAT'S GOING ON?
MY BODY...
SWUP
MY BODY'S... MOVING... ON ITS OWN...
WHAT THE ...?!
!!
SWUP
LAVI... HE CAN'T POSSI-BLY...

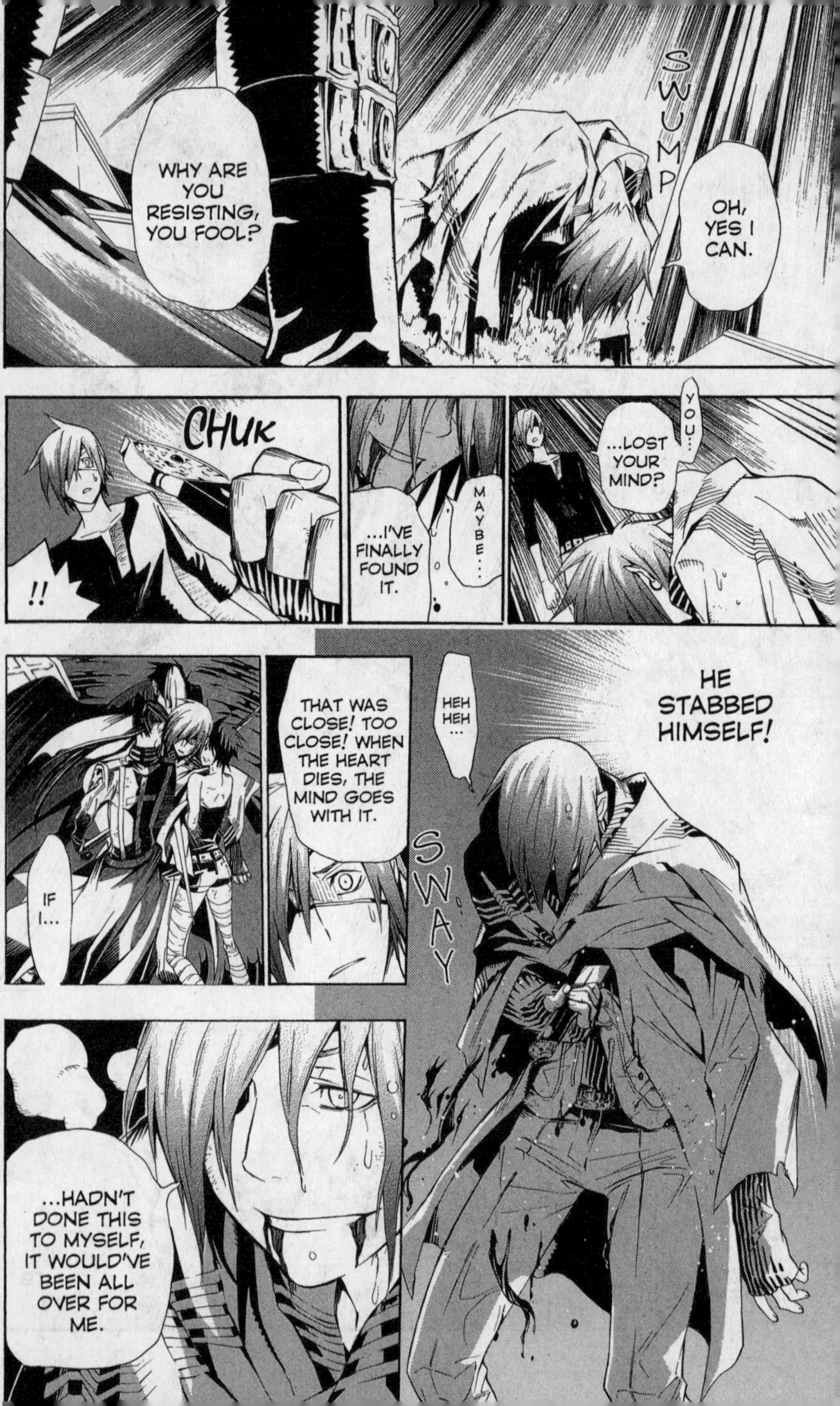
SWUMP
OH, YES I CAN.
WHY ARE YOU RESISTING, YOU FOOL?
YOU...
...LOST YOUR MIND?
MAYBE...
...I'VE FINALLY FOUND IT.
CHUK
!!
HE STABBED HIMSELF!
HEH HEH...
SWAY
THAT WAS CLOSE! TOO CLOSE! WHEN THE HEART DIES, THE MIND GOES WITH IT.
IF I...
...HADN'T DONE THIS TO MYSELF, IT WOULD'VE BEEN ALL OVER FOR ME.

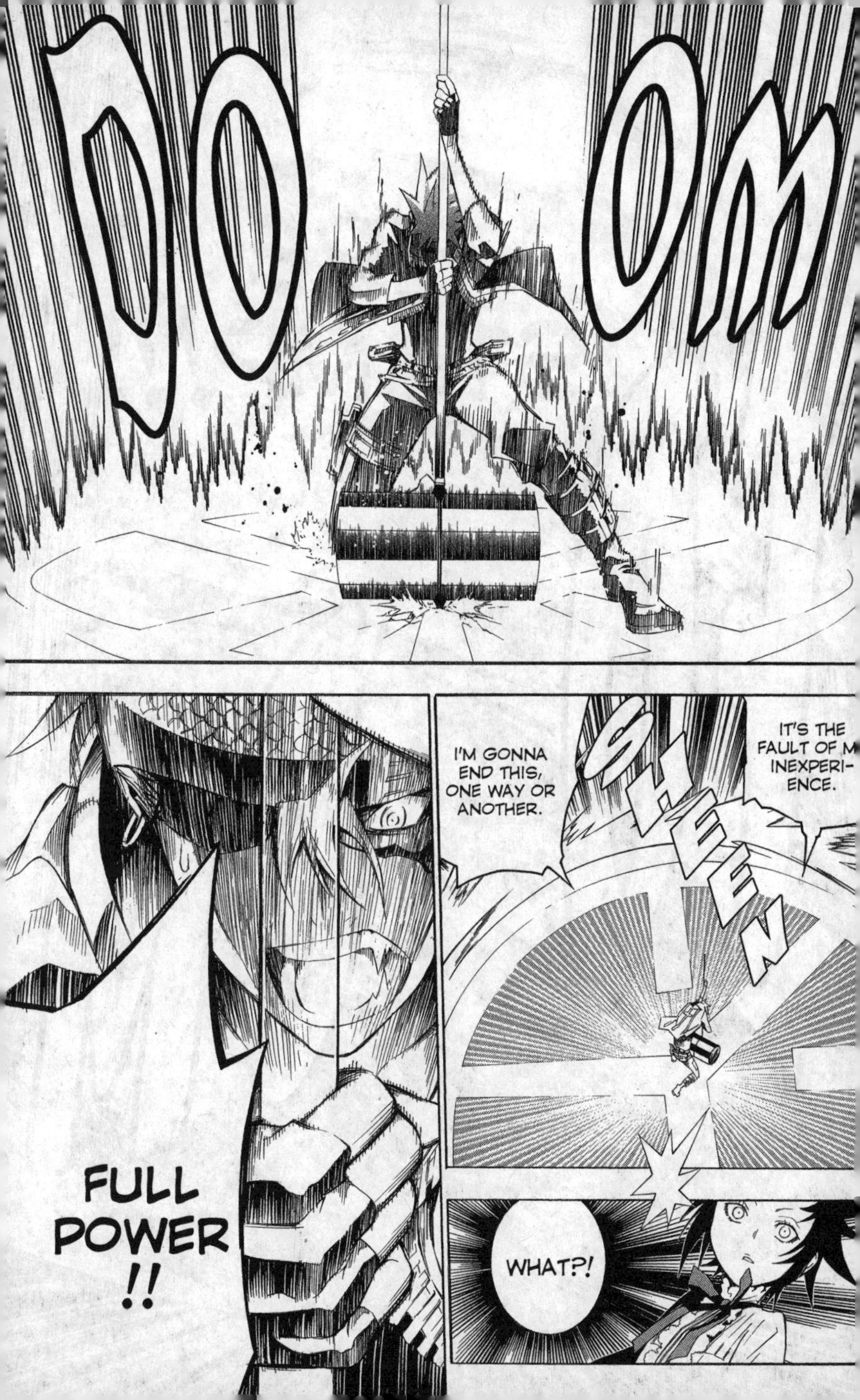
DOOM
IT'S THE FAULT OF M INEXPERIENCE.
SHEEN
I'M GONNA END THIS, ONE WAY OR ANOTHER.
WHAT?!
FULL POWER!!

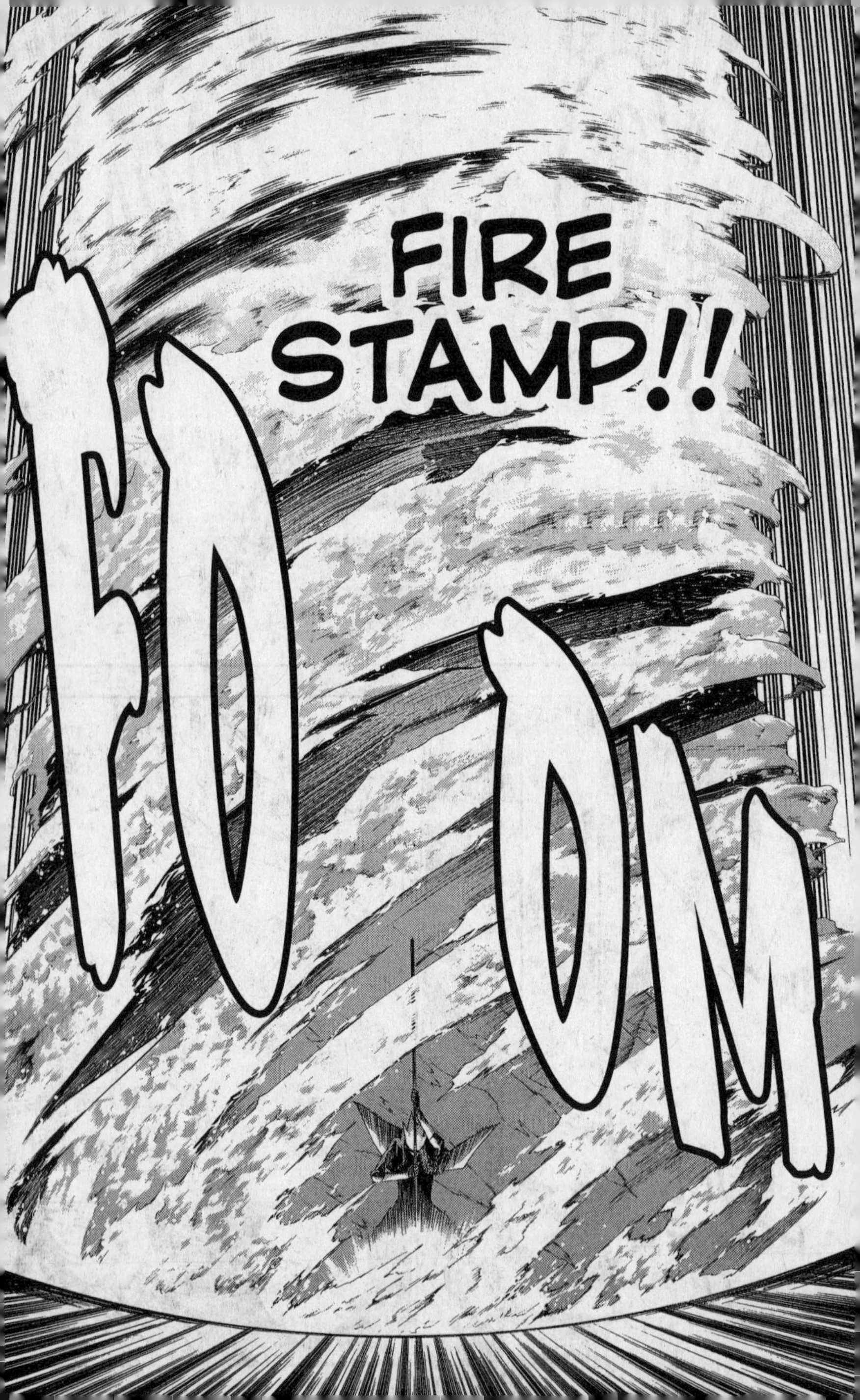
FIRE STAMP!!
FOOM

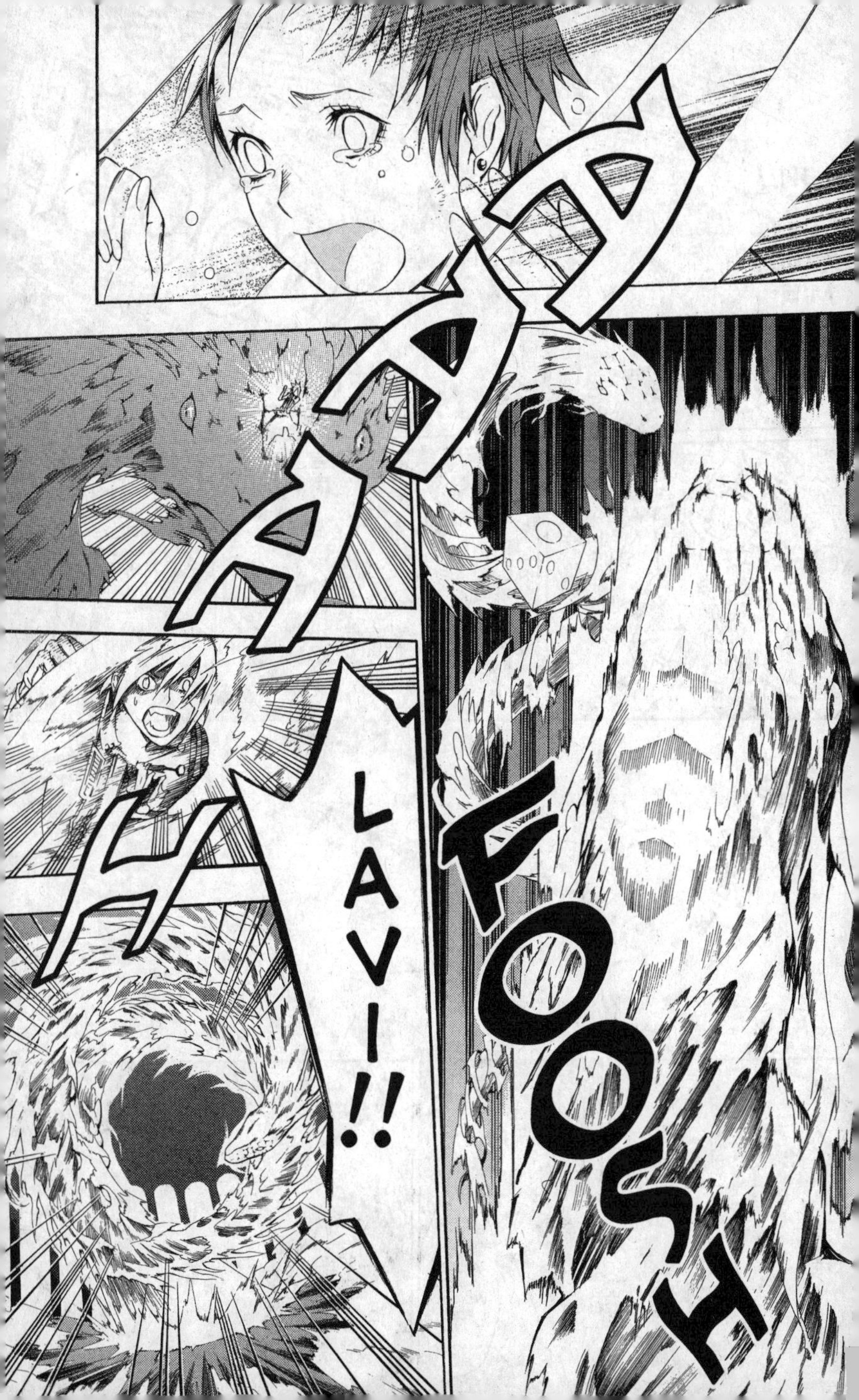
AAAAAH
FOOSH
LAVI!!

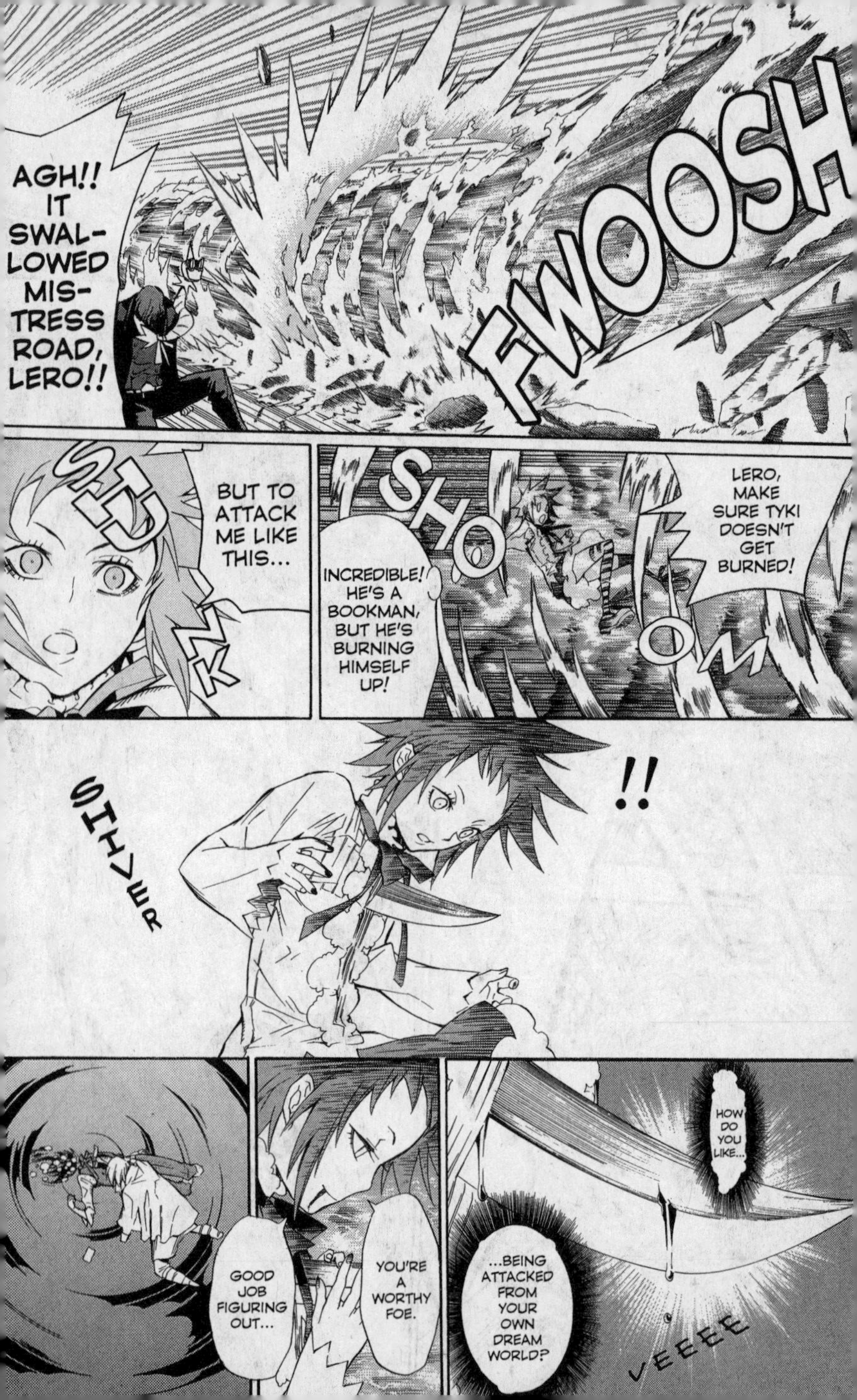
FWOOSH
AGH!! IT SWAL-LOWED MIS-TRESS ROAD, LERO!!
LERO, MAKE SURE TYKI DOESN'T GET BURNED!
SHOOOM
INCREDIBLE! HE'S A BOOKMAN, BUT HE'S BURNING HIMSELF UP!
BUT TO ATTACK ME LIKE THIS...
SHUNK
!!
SHIVER
HOW DO YOU LIKE...
...BEING ATTACKED FROM YOUR OWN DREAM WORLD?
VEEEE
YOU'RE A WORTHY FOE.
GOOD JOB FIGURING OUT...

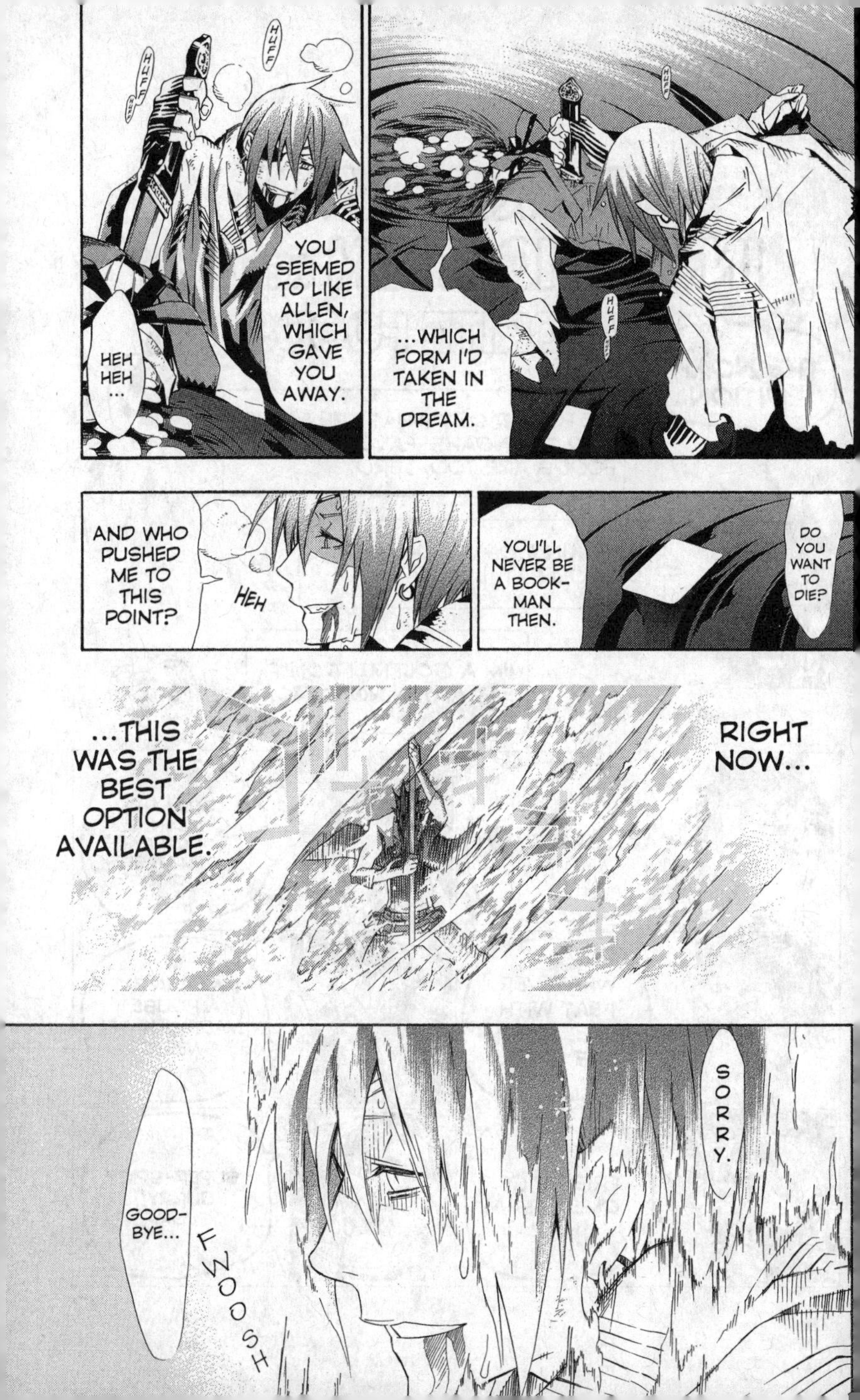
HUFF
...WHICH FORM I'D TAKEN IN THE DREAM.
HUFF
HUFF
HUFF
YOU SEEMED TO LIKE ALLEN, WHICH GAVE YOU AWAY.
HEH HEH ...
DO YOU WANT TO DIE?
YOU'LL NEVER BE A BOOK-MAN THEN.
AND WHO PUSHED ME TO THIS POINT?
HEH
RIGHT NOW...
...THIS WAS THE BEST OPTION AVAILABLE.
SORRY.
GOOD-BYE...
FWOOSH

D.GRAY-MAN INVESTIGATION SERIES (?)

FAVORITE FOODS ♥

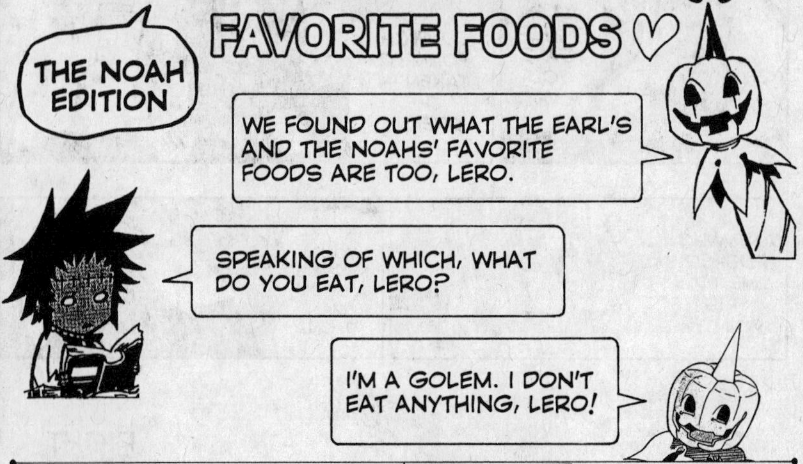
THE NOAH EDITION
WE FOUND OUT WHAT THE EARL'S AND THE NOAHS' FAVORITE FOODS ARE TOO, LERO.
SPEAKING OF WHICH, WHAT DO YOU EAT, LERO?
I'M A GOLEM. I DON'T EAT ANYTHING, LERO!

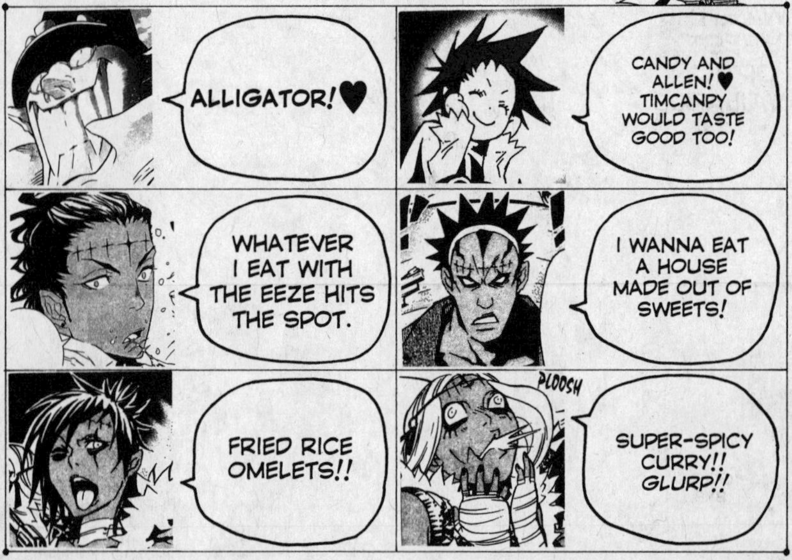
CANDY AND ALLEN! ♥ TIMCANPY WOULD TASTE GOOD TOO!
ALLIGATOR! ♥
I WANNA EAT A HOUSE MADE OUT OF SWEETS!
WHATEVER I EAT WITH THE EEZE HITS THE SPOT.
PLOOSH
SUPER-SPICY CURRY!! GLURP!!
FRIED RICE OMELETS!!

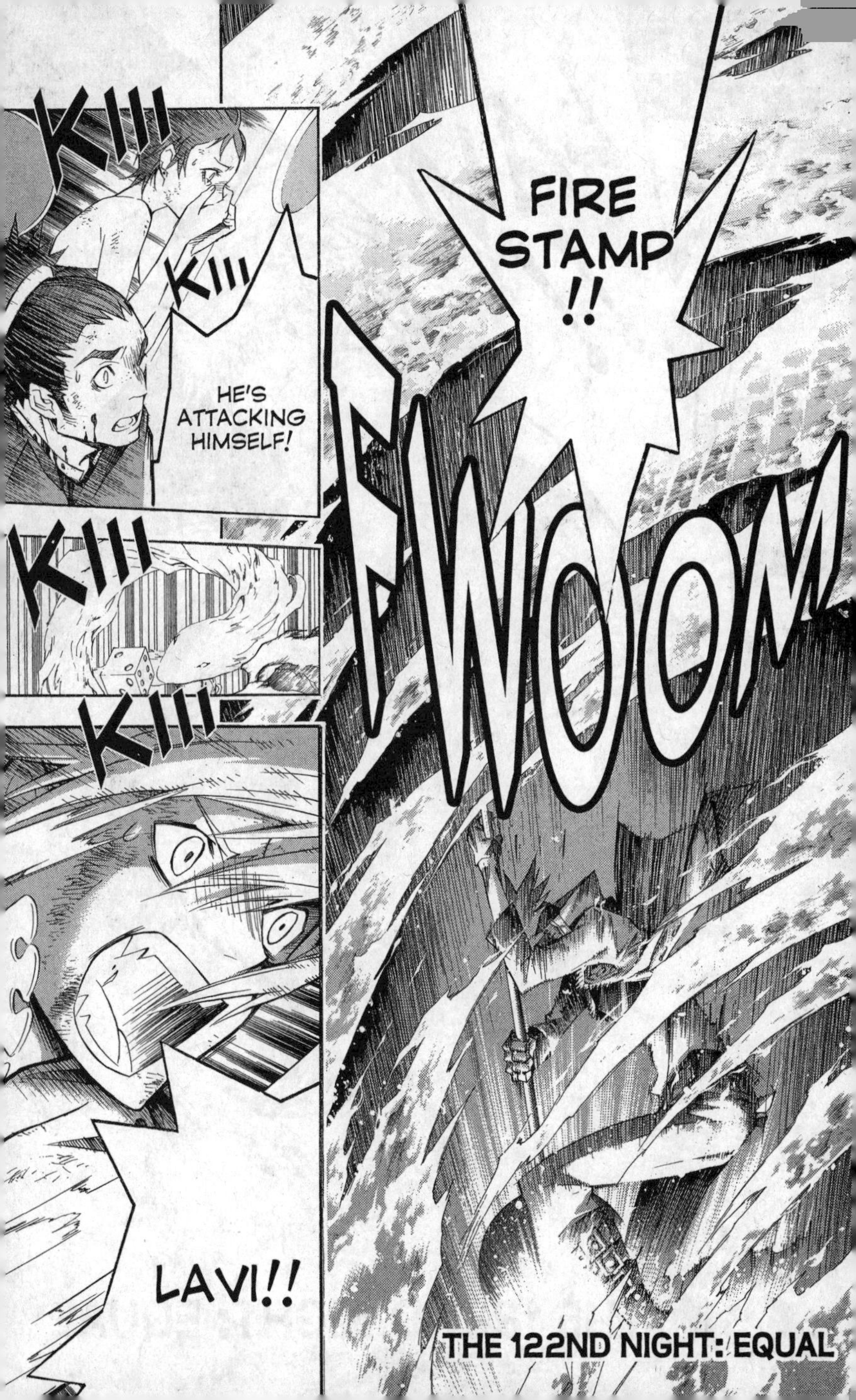
FIRE STAMP!!
FWOOM
THE 122ND NIGHT: EQUAL
KIIII
KIII
HE'S ATTACKING HIMSELF!
KIII
KIII
LAVI!!

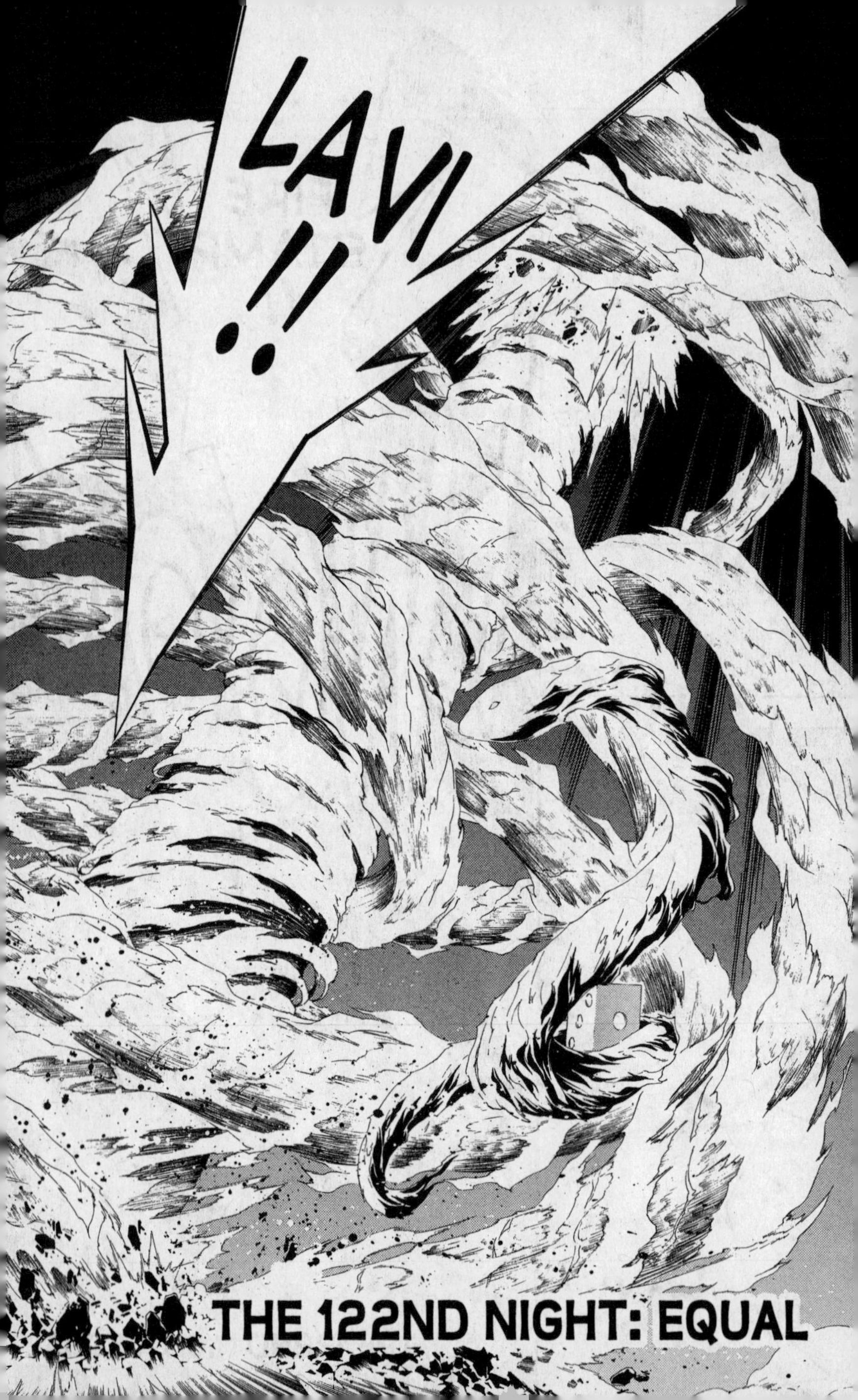
LAVI!!
THE 122ND NIGHT: EQUAL

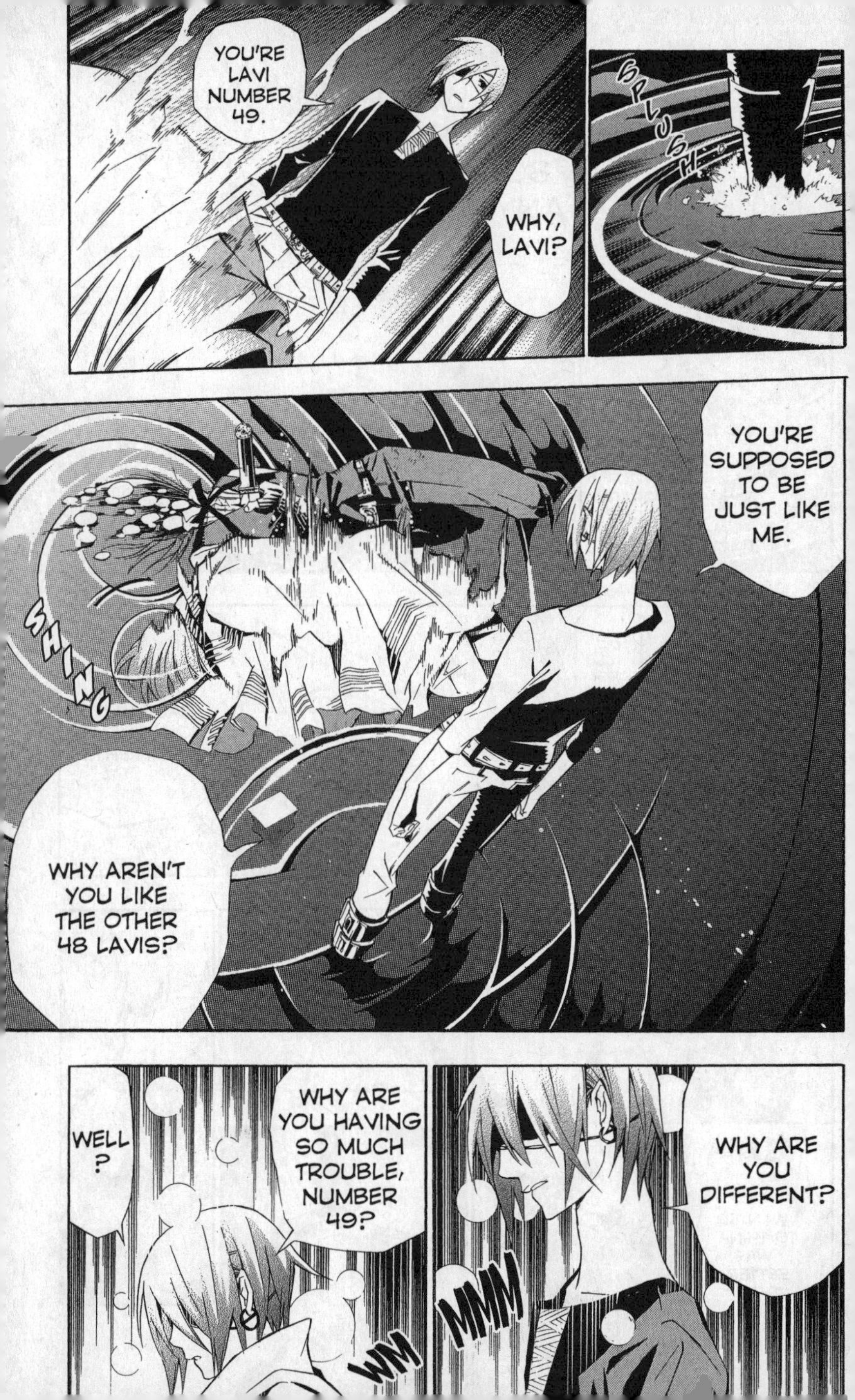
SPLUSH
YOU'RE LAVI NUMBER 49.
WHY, LAVI?
YOU'RE SUPPOSED TO BE JUST LIKE ME.
SHING
WHY AREN'T YOU LIKE THE OTHER 48 LAVIS?
WHY ARE YOU DIFFERENT?
MMM
WHY ARE YOU HAVING SO MUCH TROUBLE, NUMBER 49?
WELL?
WM

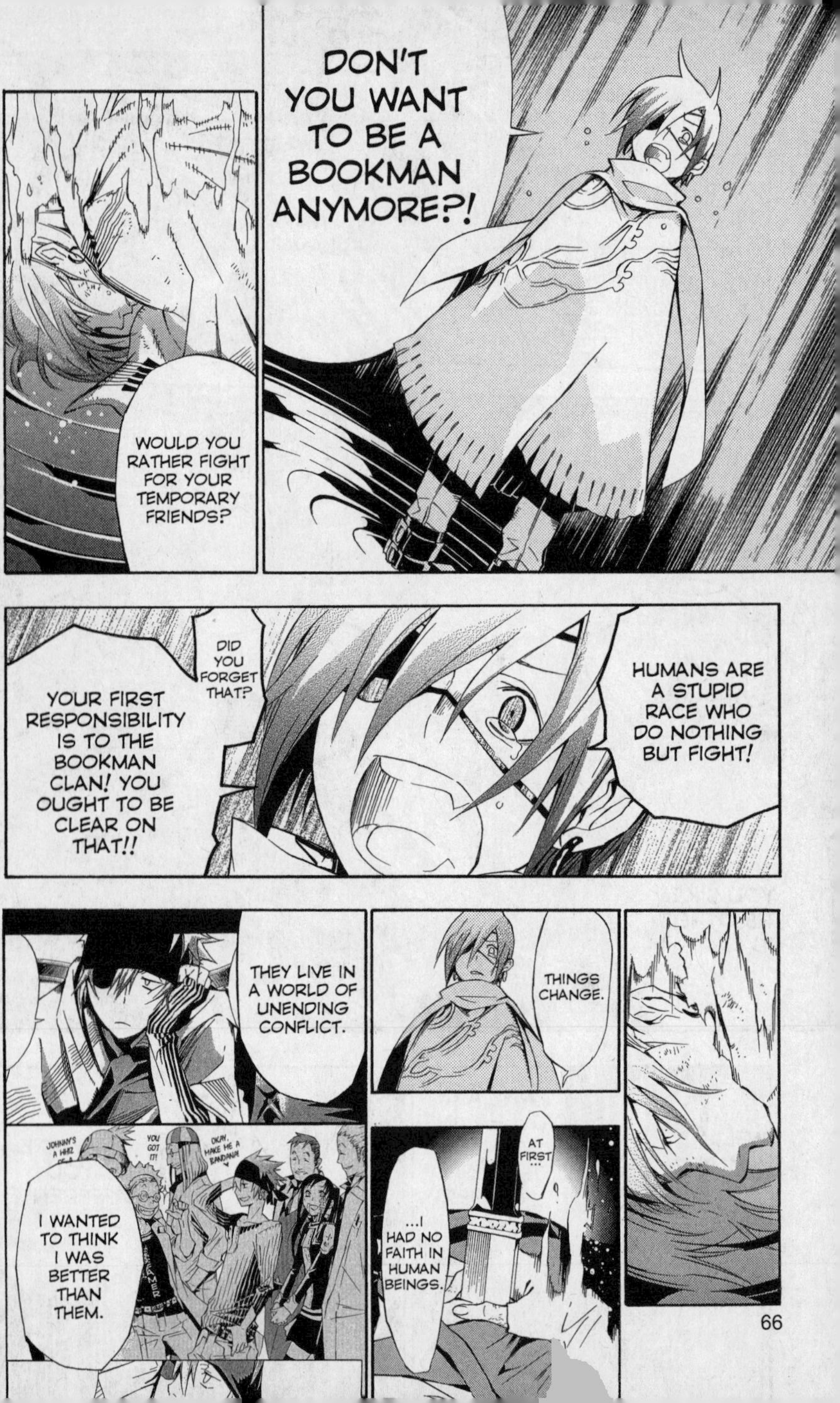
DON'T YOU WANT TO BE A BOOKMAN ANYMORE?!
WOULD YOU RATHER FIGHT FOR YOUR TEMPORARY FRIENDS?
HUMANS ARE A STUPID RACE WHO DO NOTHING BUT FIGHT!
DID YOU FORGET THAT?
YOUR FIRST RESPONSIBILITY IS TO THE BOOKMAN CLAN! YOU OUGHT TO BE CLEAR ON THAT!!
THINGS CHANGE.
THEY LIVE IN A WORLD OF UNENDING CONFLICT.
AT FIRST...
...I HAD NO FAITH IN HUMAN BEINGS.
OKAY, MAKE ME A BANDANA!
YOU GOT IT!
I WANTED TO THINK I WAS BETTER THAN THEM.

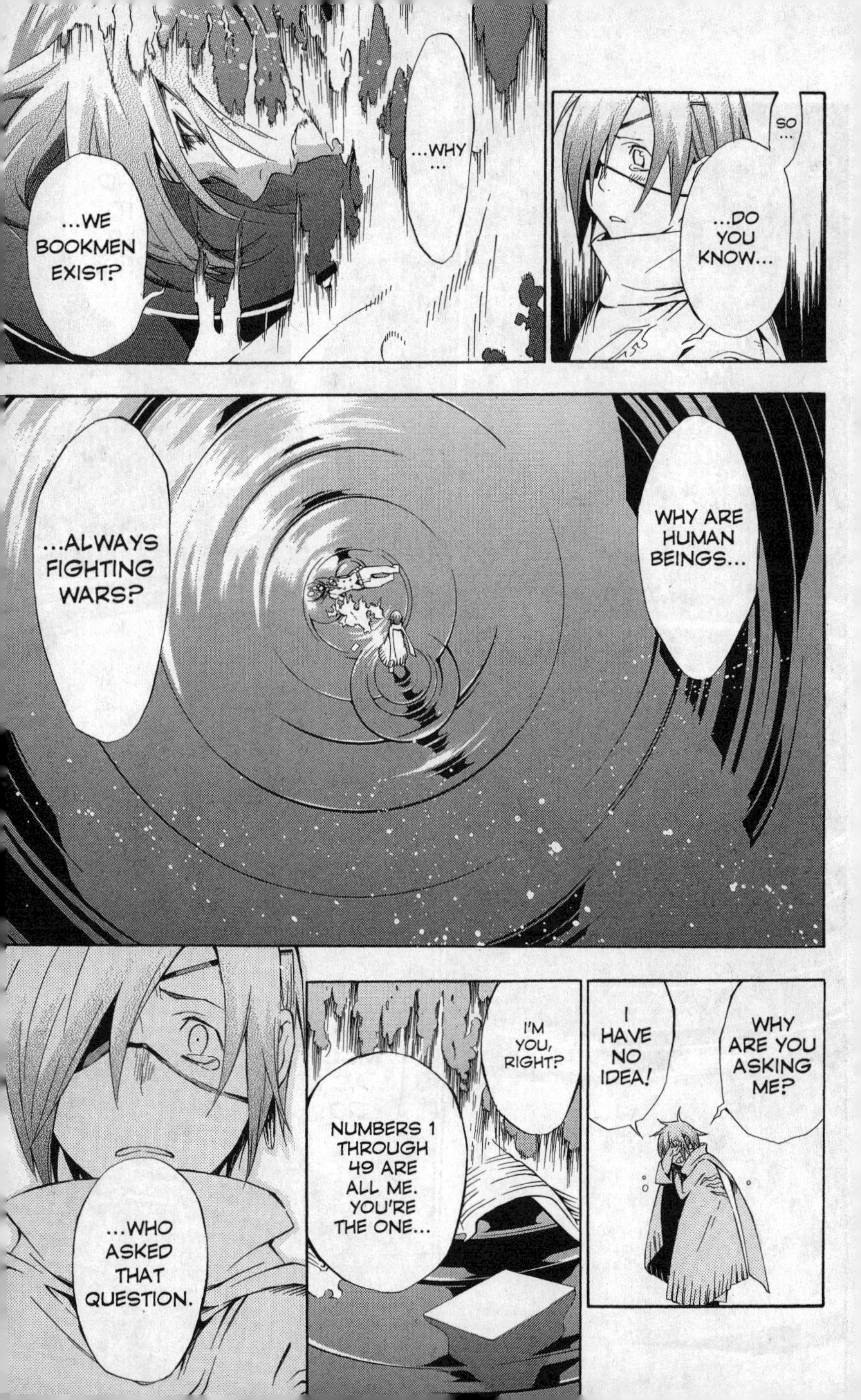
SO ...
...DO YOU KNOW...
...WHY ...
...WE BOOKMEN EXIST?
WHY ARE HUMAN BEINGS...
...ALWAYS FIGHTING WARS?
WHY ARE YOU ASKING ME?
I HAVE NO IDEA!
I'M YOU, RIGHT?
NUMBERS 1 THROUGH 49 ARE ALL ME. YOU'RE THE ONE...
...WHO ASKED THAT QUESTION.

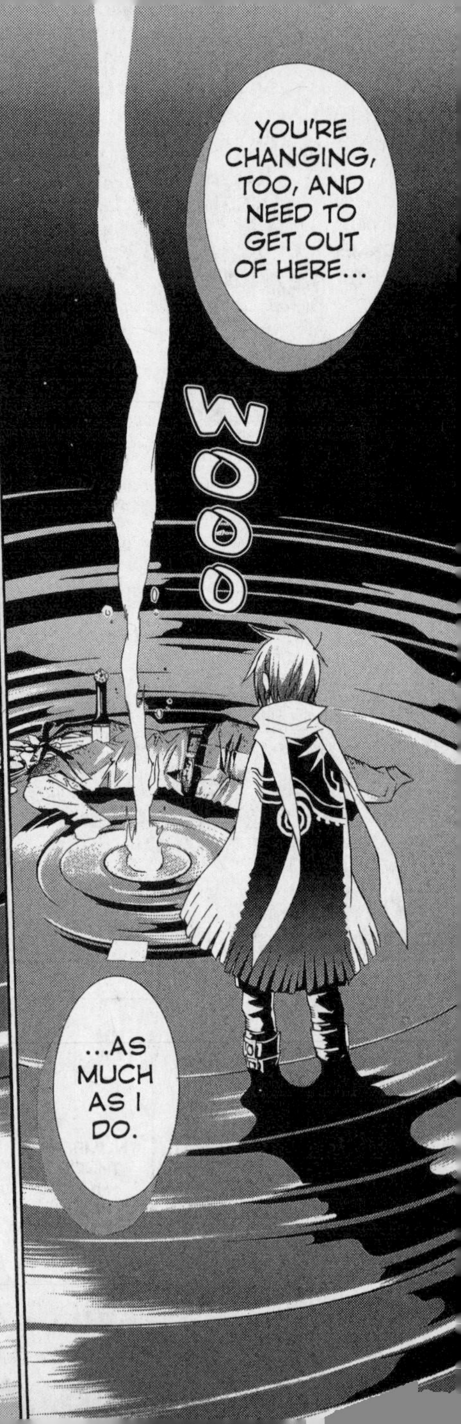
YOU'RE CHANGING, TOO, AND NEED TO GET OUT OF HERE...
WOOOO
...AS MUCH AS I DO.
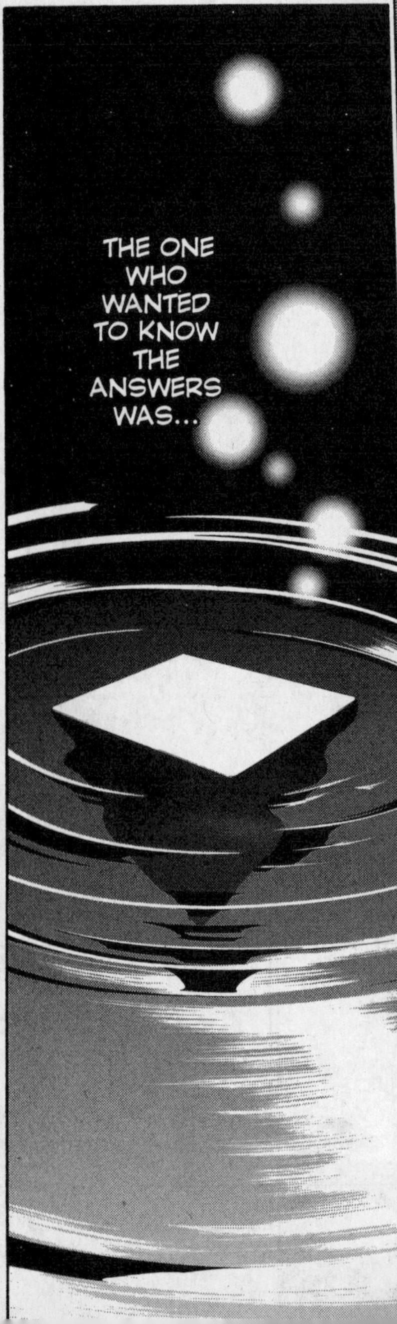
THE ONE WHO WANTED TO KNOW THE ANSWERS WAS...

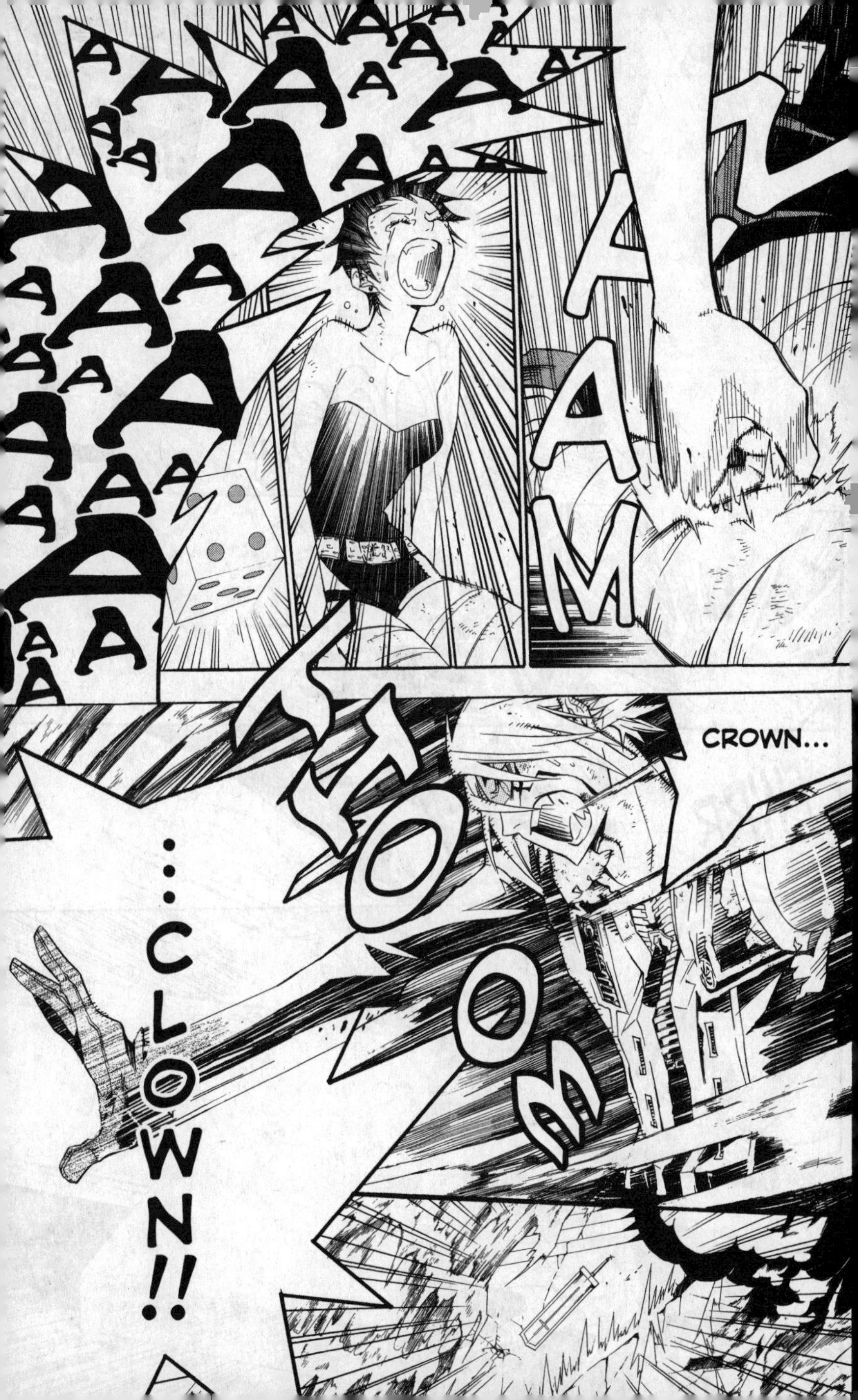
CROWN...
...CLOWN!!

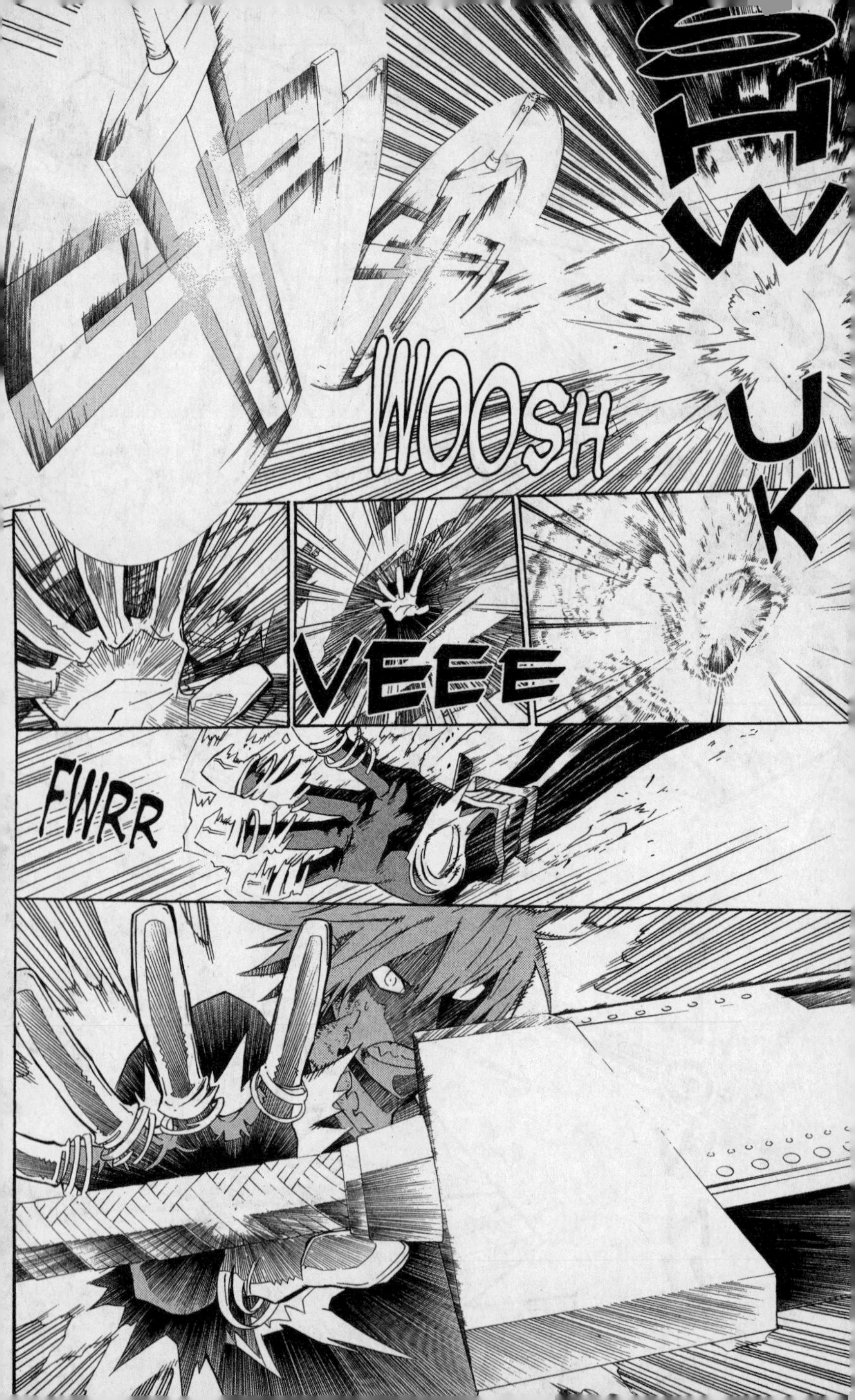

SHWUK
WOOSH
VEEE
FWRR

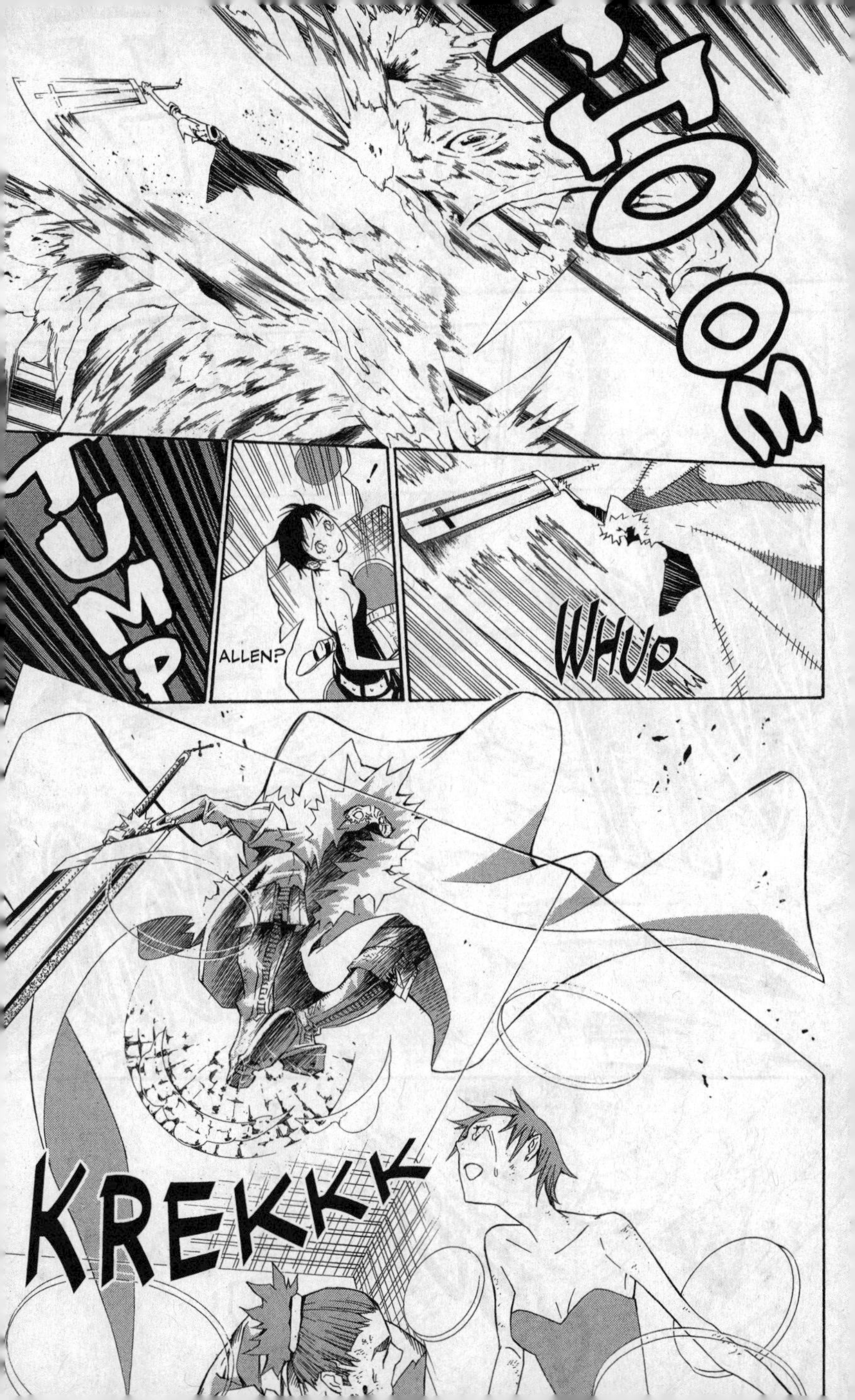
WHUP
!
ALLEN?
JUMP
KREKKK

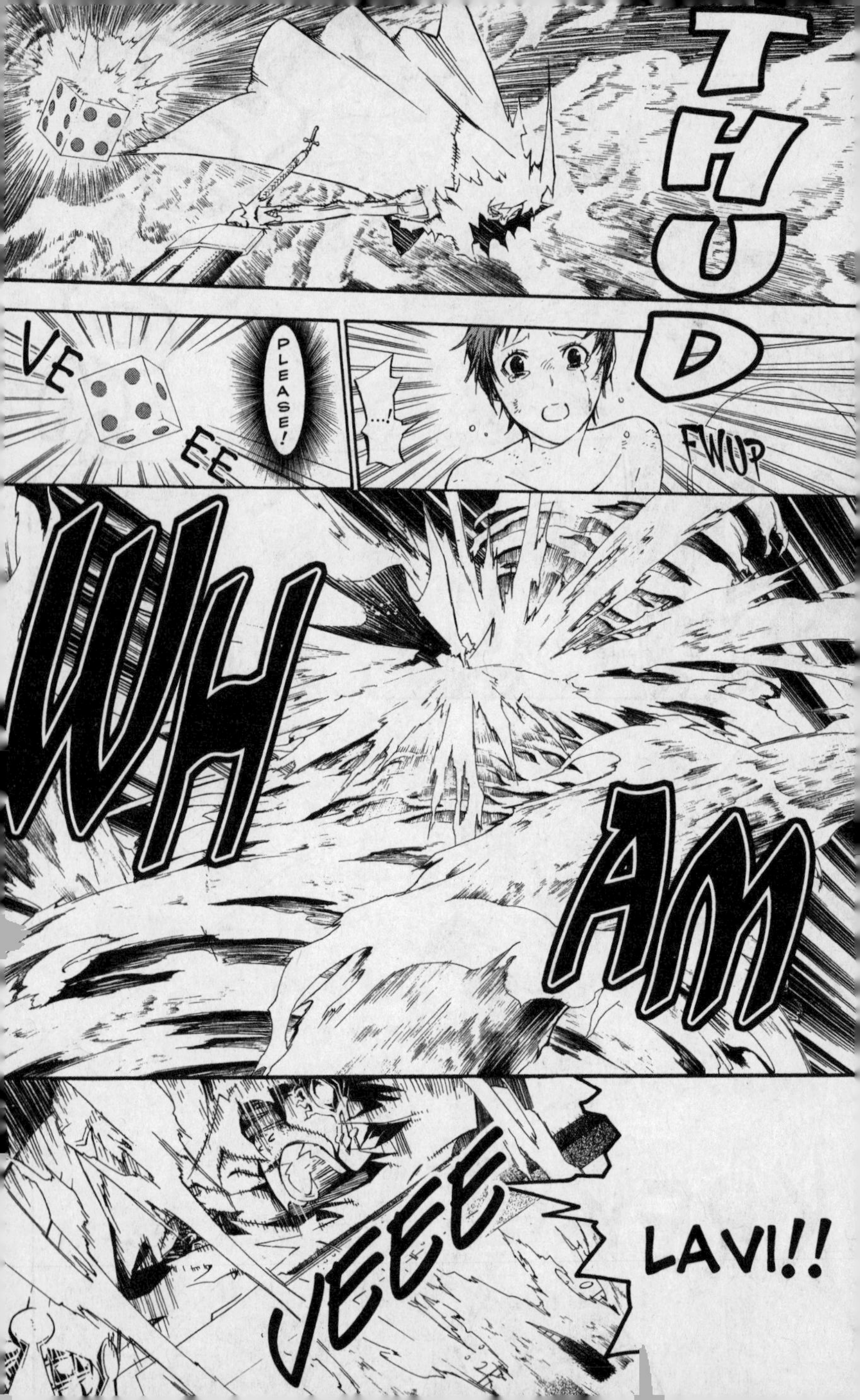
THUD
FWUP
...!
PLEASE!
VE
EE
WHAM
LAVI!!
JEEE

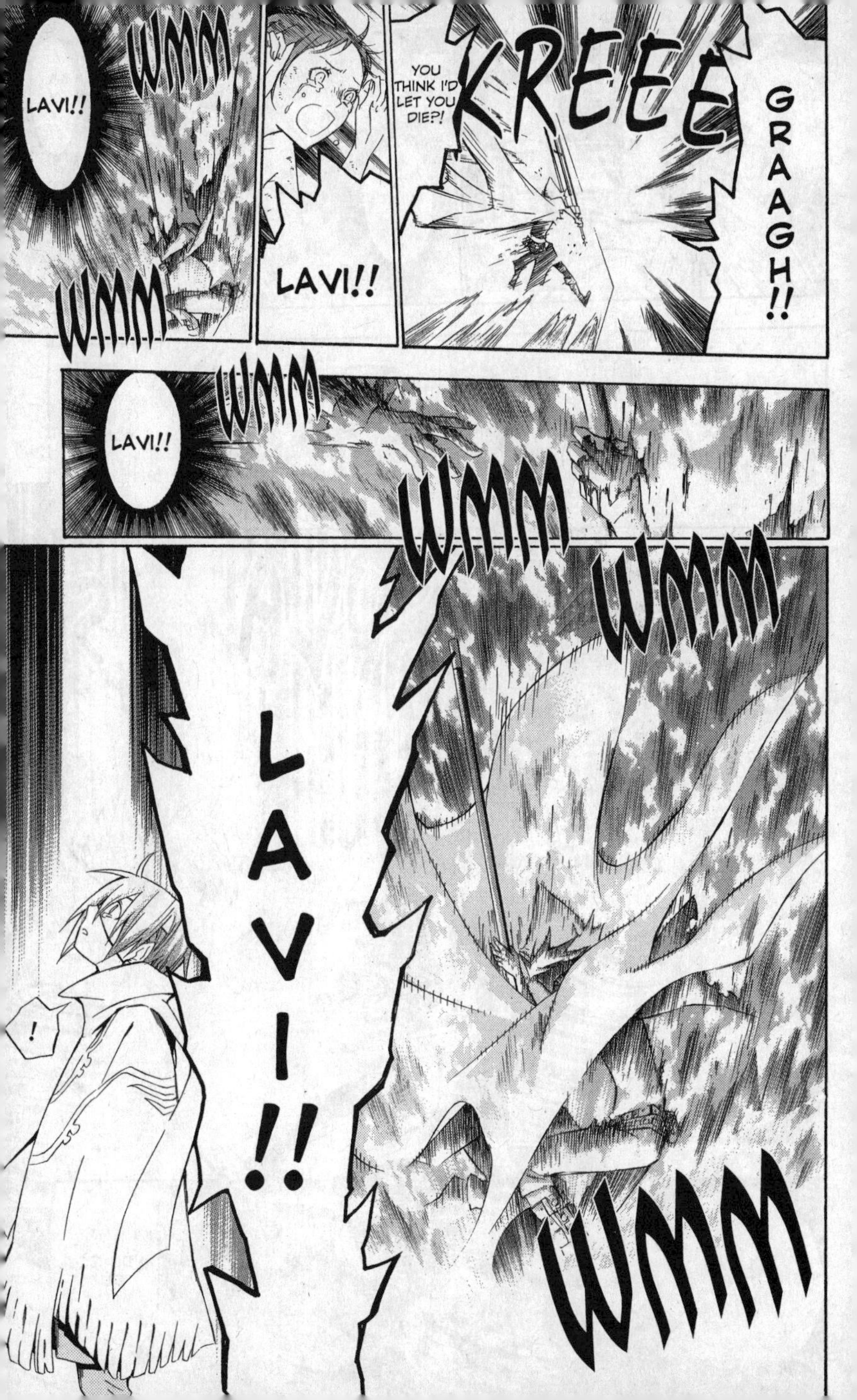
GRAAGH!!
KREEE
YOU THINK I'D LET YOU DIE?!
LAVI!!
WMM
LAVI!!
WMM
WMM
LAVI!!
WMM
WMM
LAVI!!
!
WMM

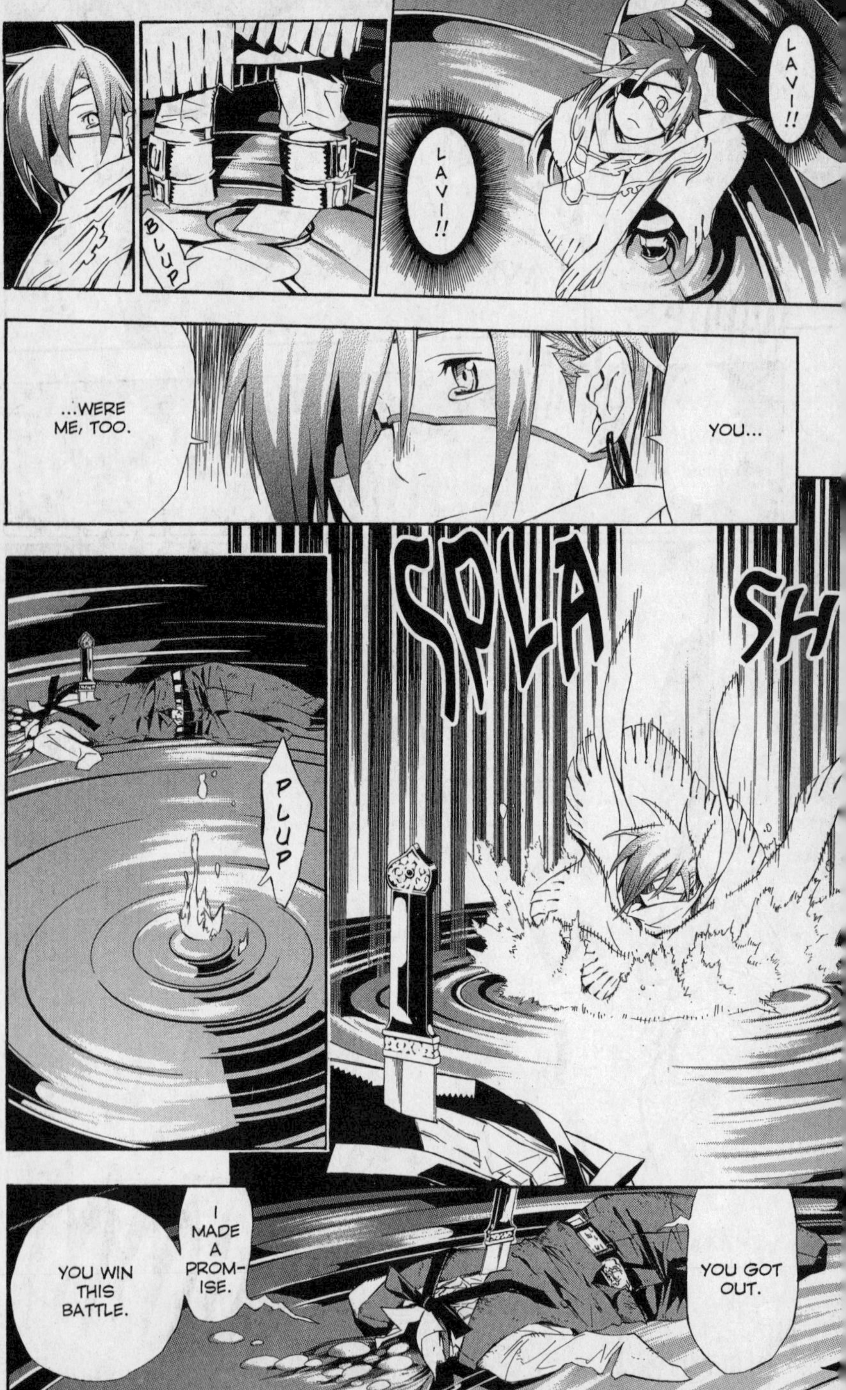
LAVI!!
LAVI!!
BLUP
YOU...
...WERE ME, TOO.
SPLASH
PLUP
YOU GOT OUT.
I MADE A PROM-ISE.
YOU WIN THIS BATTLE.

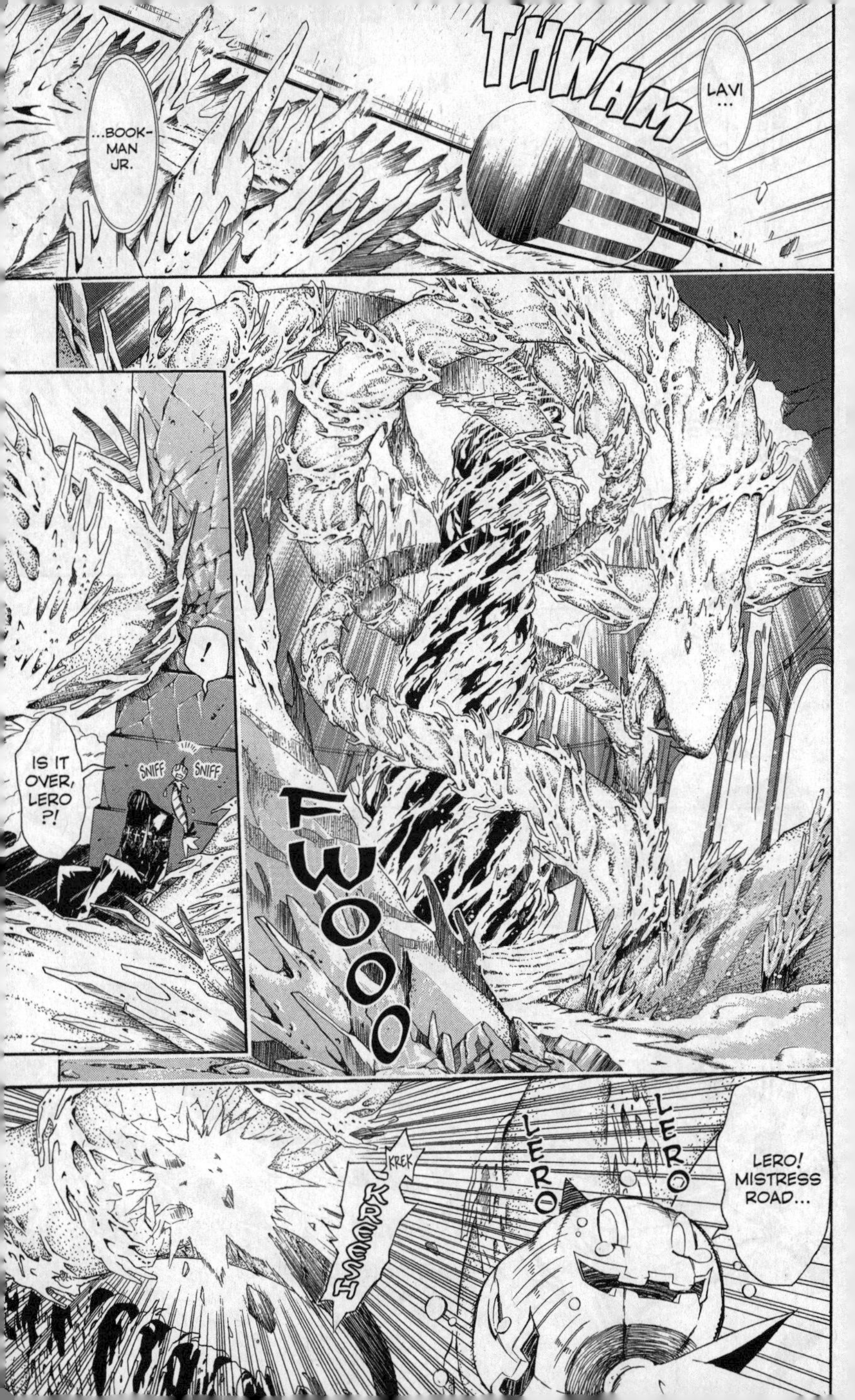
THWAM
LAVI ...
...BOOK-MAN JR.
FWOOO
!
SNIFF
SNIFF
IS IT OVER, LERO?!
LERO! MISTRESS ROAD...
LERO
LERO
KREK
KREEESH

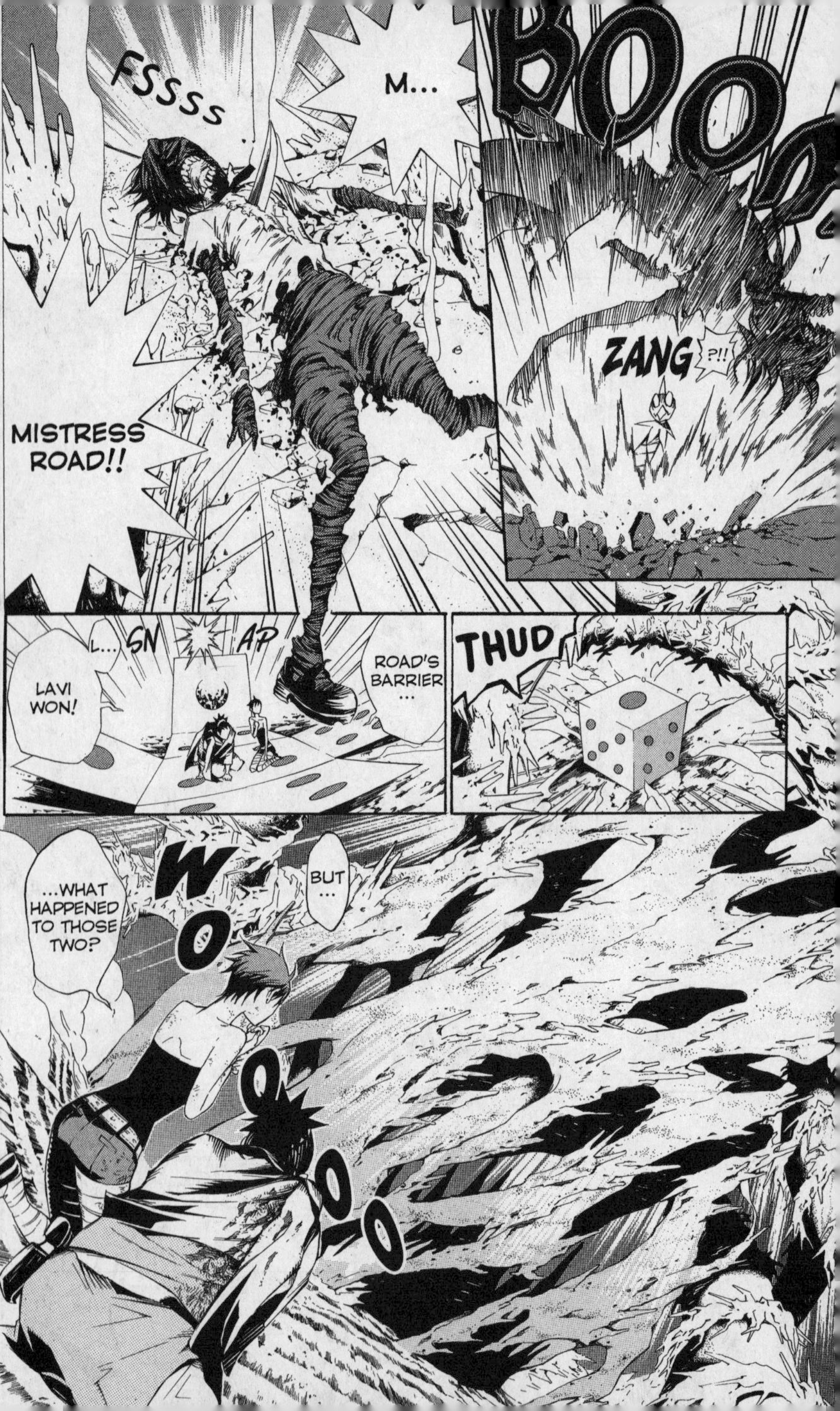
BOOO
ZANG
?!!
M...
FSSSS
MISTRESS ROAD!!
THUD
ROAD'S BARRIER ...
SNAP
L...
LAVI WON!
BUT ...
...WHAT HAPPENED TO THOSE TWO?
WOOOO

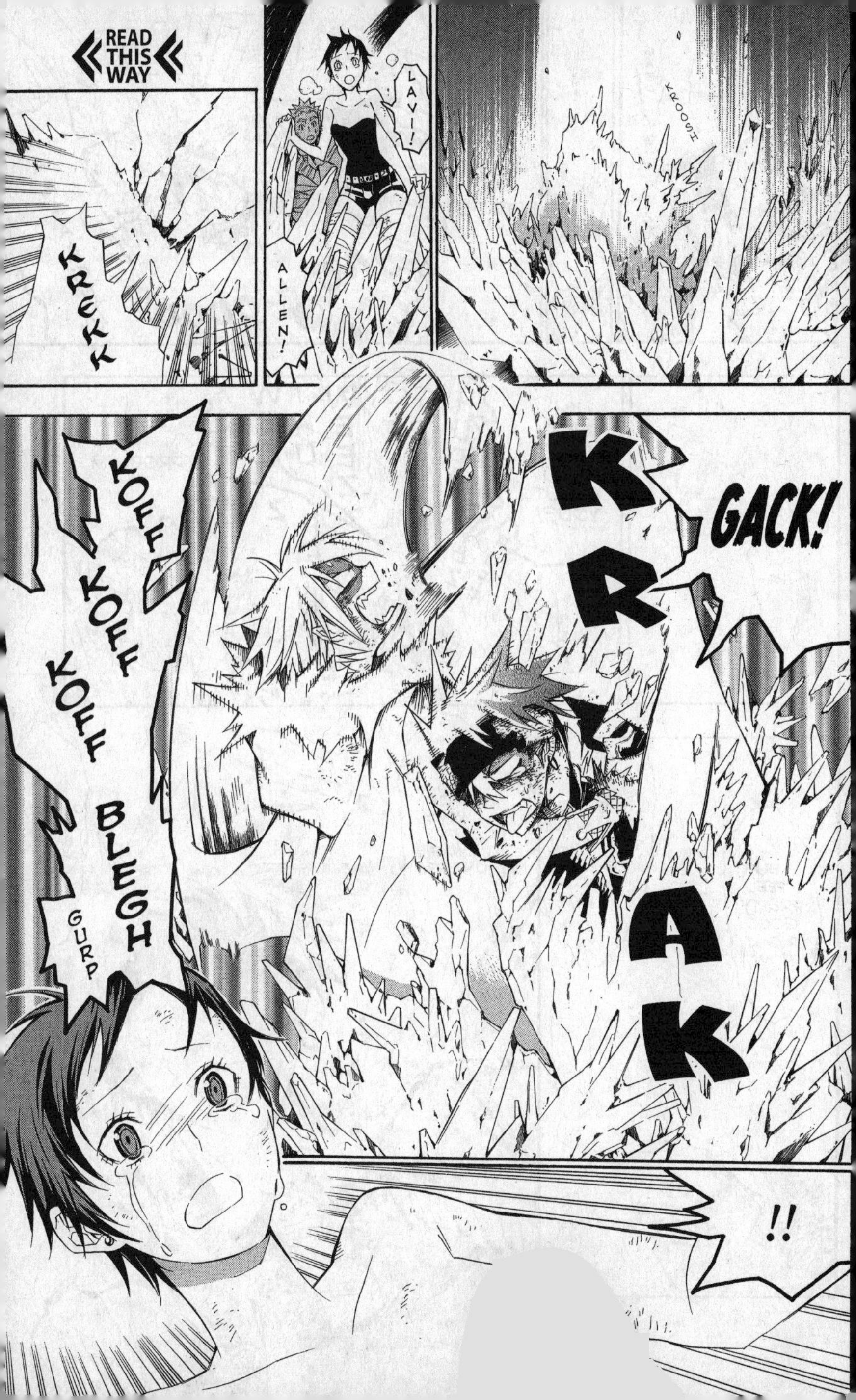
READ THIS WAY
KROOSH
LAVI!
ALLEN!
KREKK
GACK!
KRAK
KOFF KOFF KOFF
BLEGH
GURP
!!

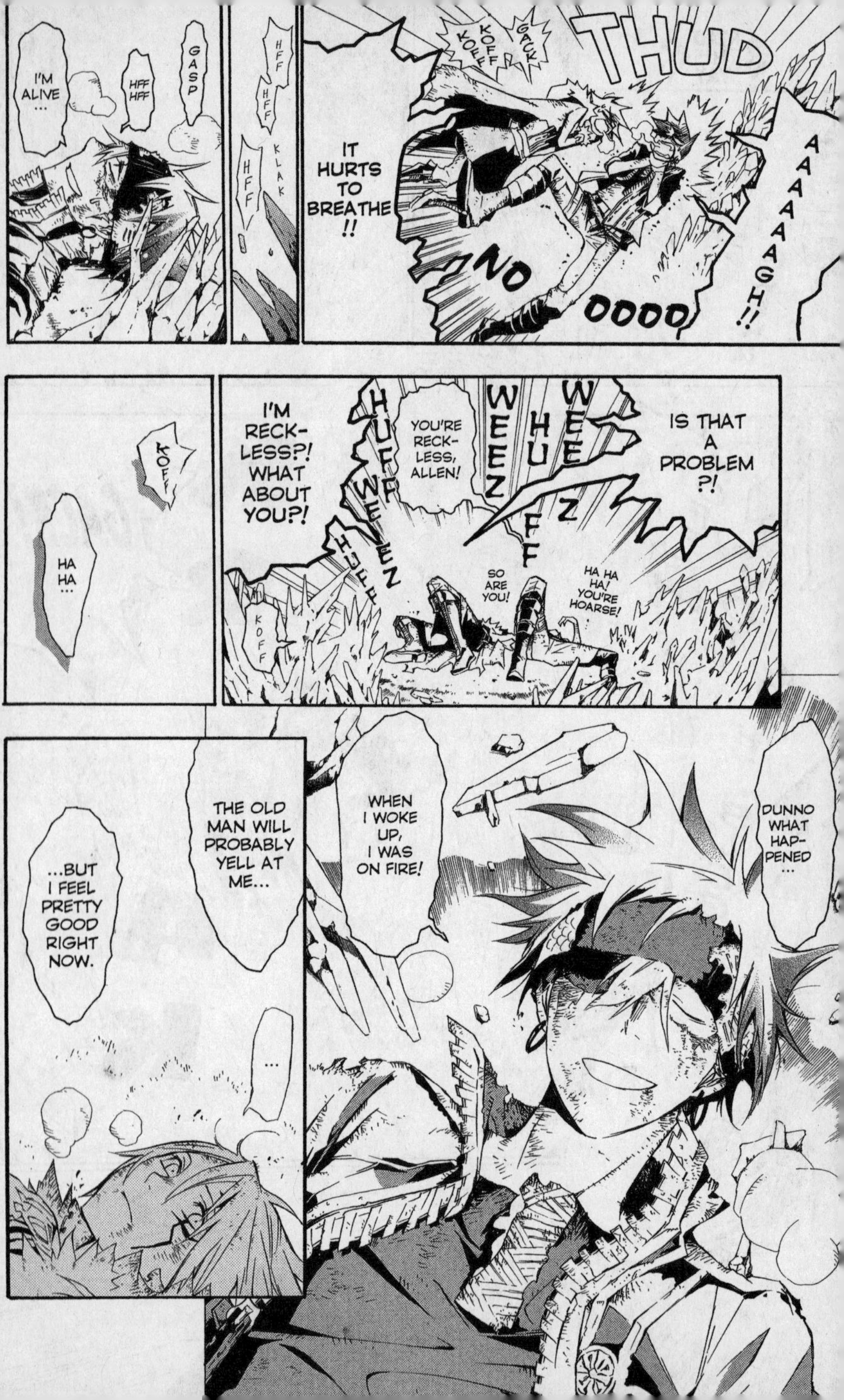
THUD
KOFF KOFF
GACK
AAAAAAAGH!!
IT HURTS TO BREATHE!!
NOOOOO
HFF HFF
HFF HFF
KLAK
GASP
HFF HFF
I'M ALIVE...
IS THAT A PROBLEM?!
WEEZ
HUFF
WEEZ
YOU'RE RECKLESS, ALLEN!
HUFF
WEEZ
HUFF
I'M RECKLESS?! WHAT ABOUT YOU?!
HA HA HA! YOU'RE HOARSE!
SO ARE YOU!
KOFF
KOFF
HA HA...
DUNNO WHAT HAPPENED...
WHEN I WOKE UP, I WAS ON FIRE!
THE OLD MAN WILL PROBABLY YELL AT ME...
...
...BUT I FEEL PRETTY GOOD RIGHT NOW.

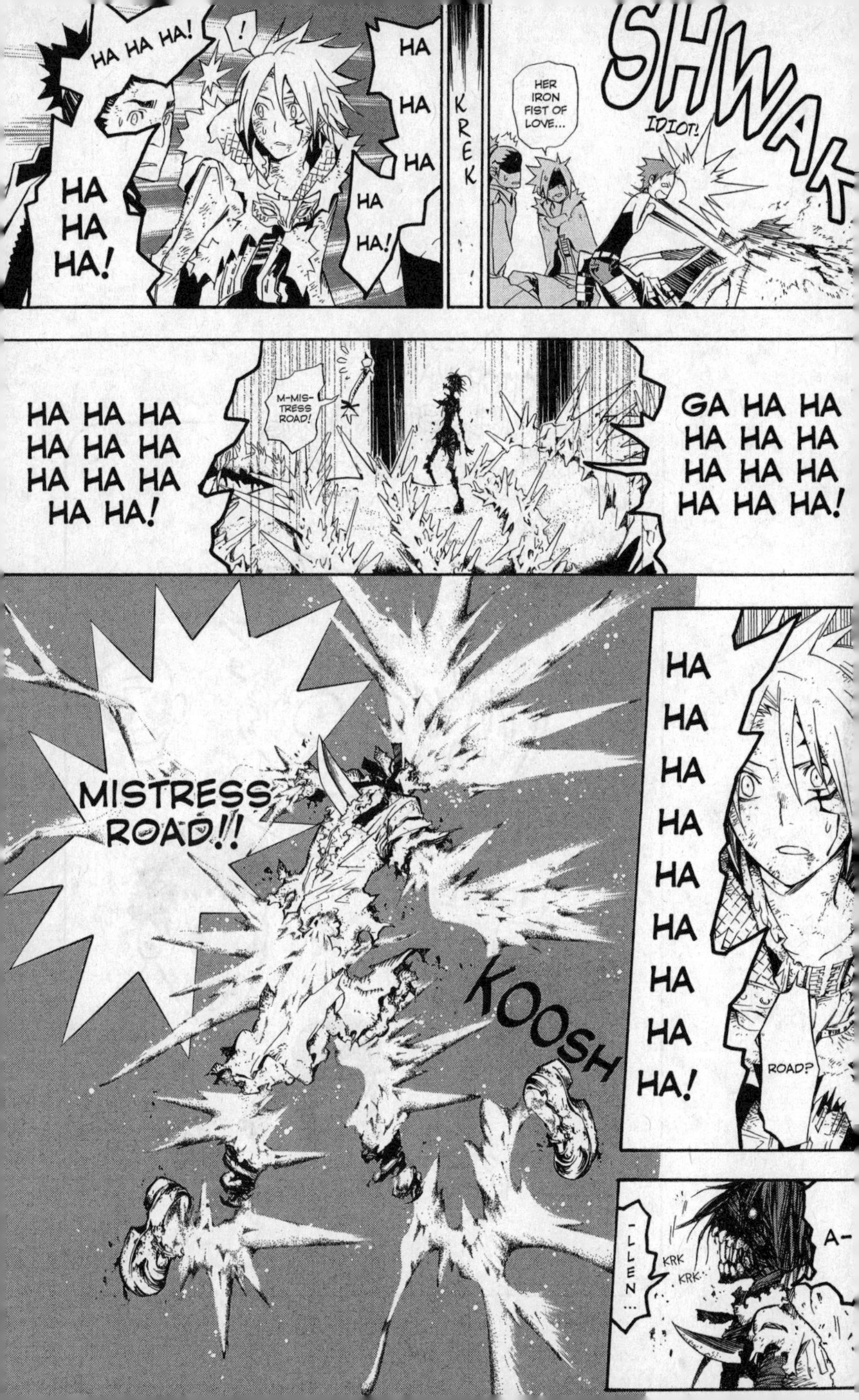
SHWAK
IDIOT!
HER IRON FIST OF LOVE...
KREK
HA HA HA HA HA!
!
HA HA HA!
HA HA HA!
GA HA HA HA HA HA HA HA HA HA HA HA!
M-MISTRESS ROAD!
HA HA HA HA HA HA HA HA HA HA HA!
HA HA HA HA HA HA HA HA HA!
ROAD?
A-
KRK KRK
-LLEN...
MISTRESS ROAD!!
KOOSH

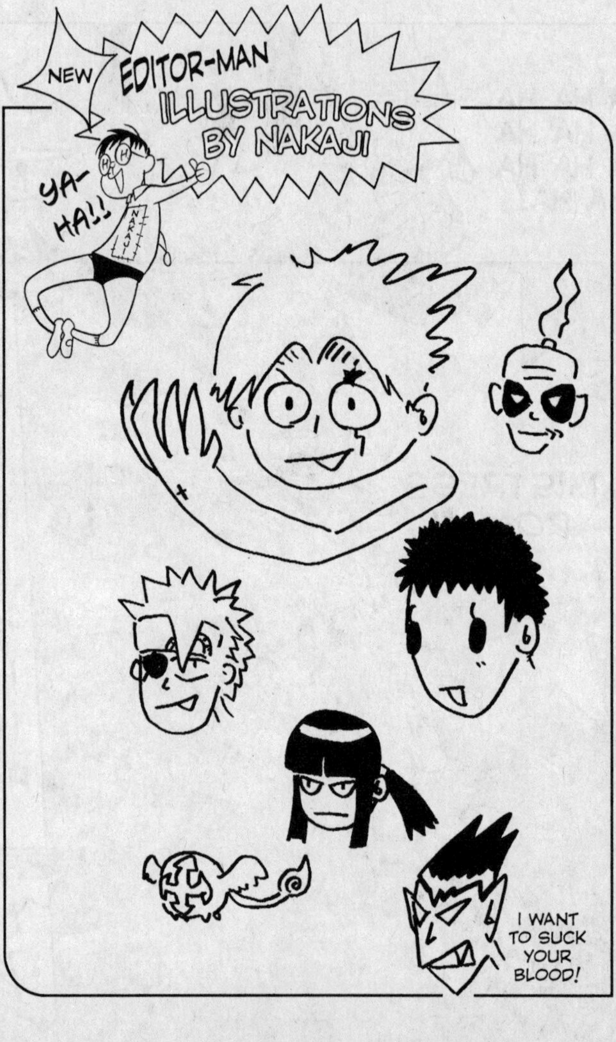
NEW
EDITOR-MAN
ILLUSTRATIONS
BY NAKAJI
YA-HA!!
NAKAJI
I WANT TO SUCK YOUR BLOOD!

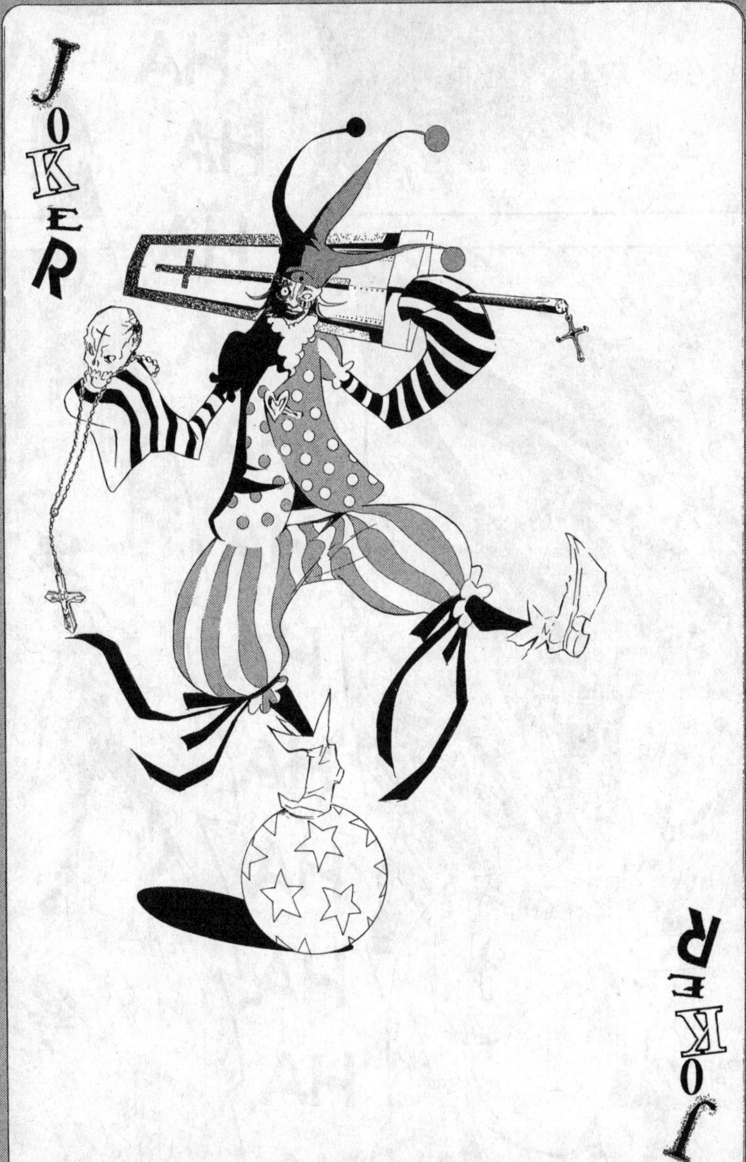
JOKER
JOKER

THE 123RD NIGHT: THE VOICE OF DARKNESS

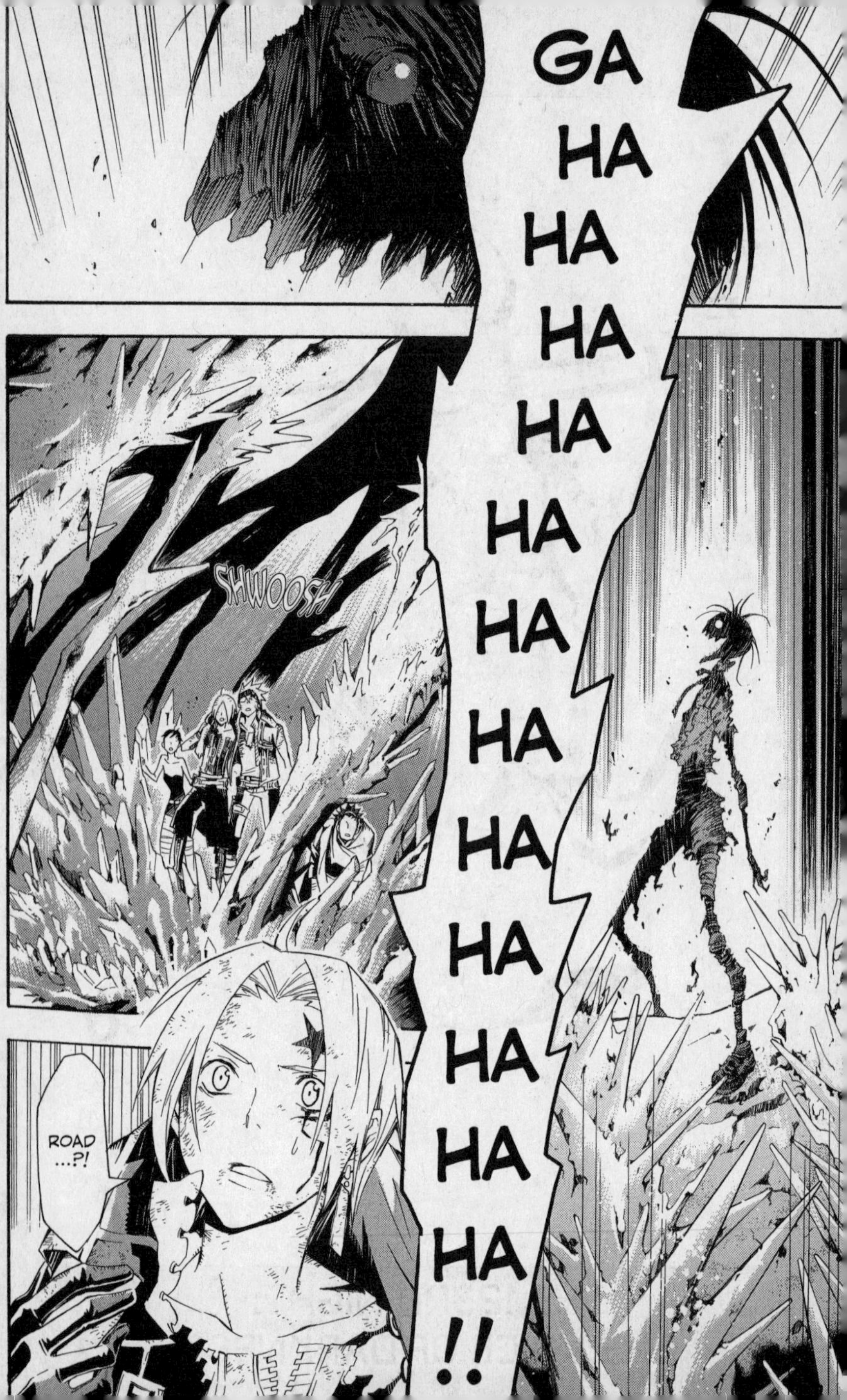
GA HA HA HA HA HA HA HA HA HA HA HA HA!!
SHWOOSH
ROAD ...?!

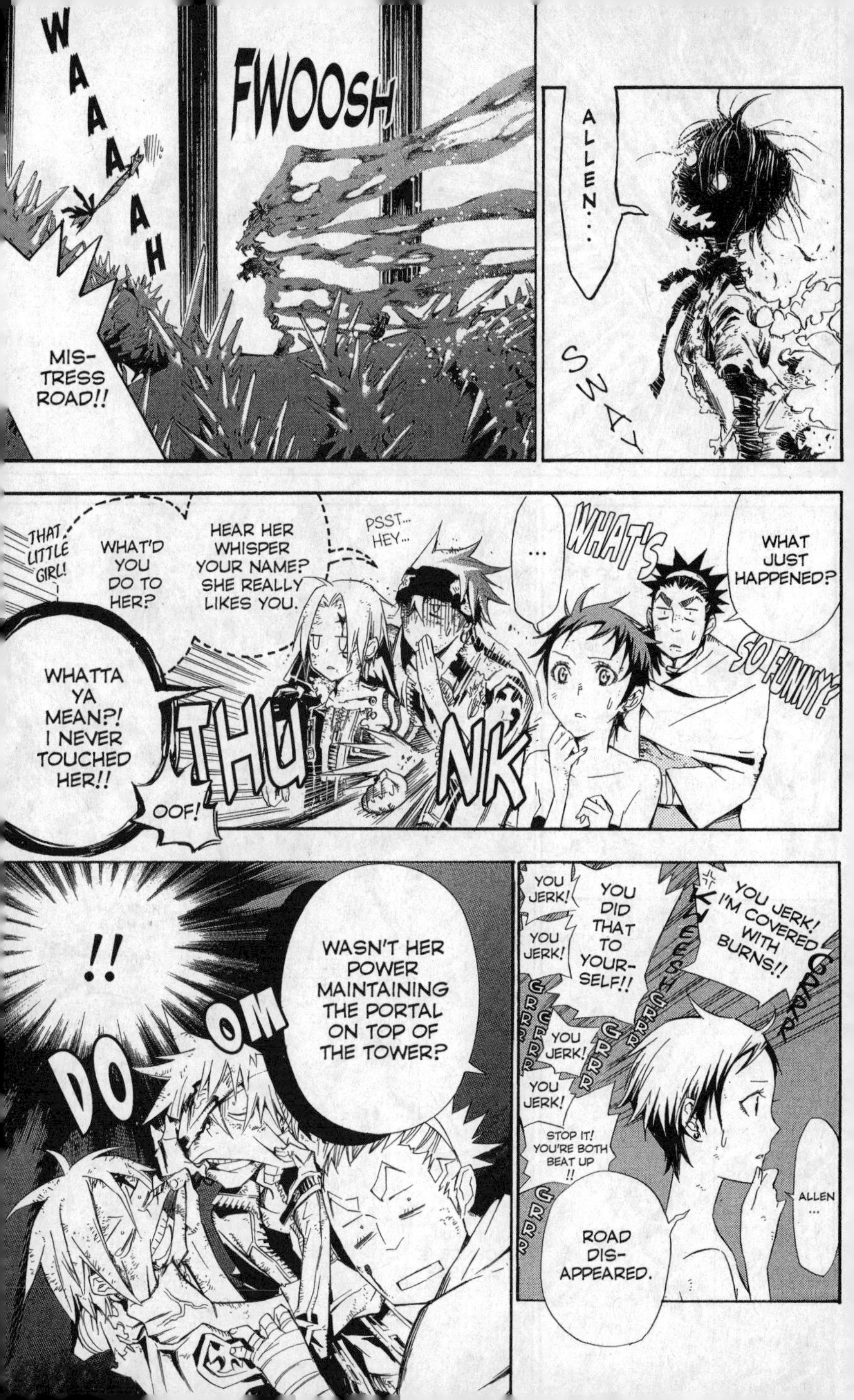
ALLEN...
SWAY
WAAAAAH
FWOOSH
MIS-TRESS ROAD!!
WHAT JUST HAPPENED?
WHAT'S SO FUNNY?!
...
PSST... HEY...
HEAR HER WHISPER YOUR NAME? SHE REALLY LIKES YOU.
WHAT'D YOU DO TO HER?
THAT LITTLE GIRL!
WHATTA YA MEAN?! I NEVER TOUCHED HER!!
THUNK
OOF!
YOU JERK! I'M COVERED WITH BURNS!!
YOU DID THAT TO YOUR-SELF!!
YOU JERK!
YOU JERK!
YOU JERK!
YOU JERK!
GRRR
STOP IT! YOU'RE BOTH BEAT UP!!
ALLEN...
ROAD DIS-APPEARED.
WASN'T HER POWER MAINTAINING THE PORTAL ON TOP OF THE TOWER?
!!
DOOM

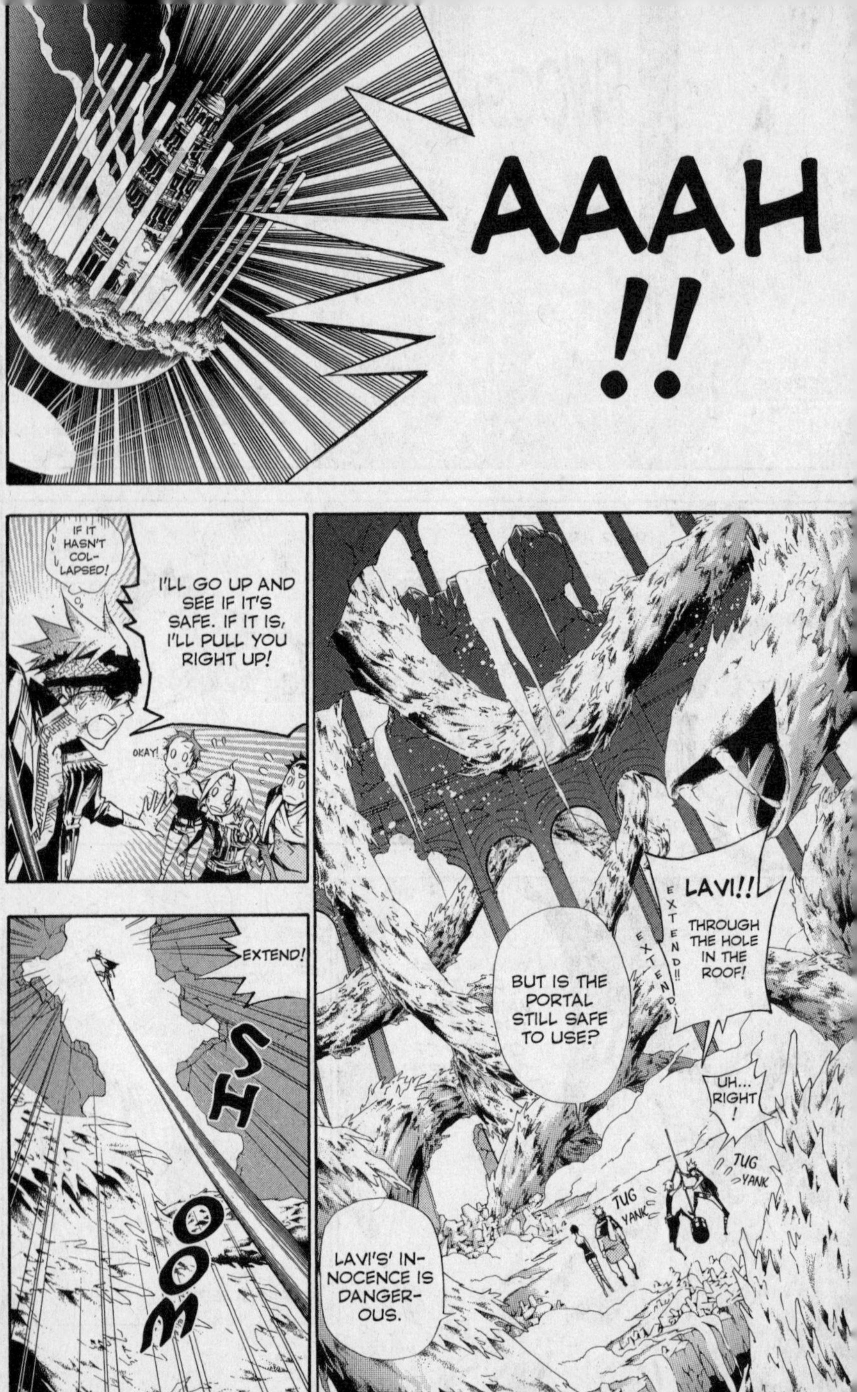
AAAH!!
LAVI!!
THROUGH THE HOLE IN THE ROOF!
EXTEND!!
EXTEND...
BUT IS THE PORTAL STILL SAFE TO USE?
UH... RIGHT!
TUG
YANK
TUG
YANK
LAVI'S INNOCENCE IS DANGEROUS.
IF IT HASN'T COLLAPSED!
I'LL GO UP AND SEE IF IT'S SAFE. IF IT IS, I'LL PULL YOU RIGHT UP!
OKAY!
EXTEND!
SHOOM

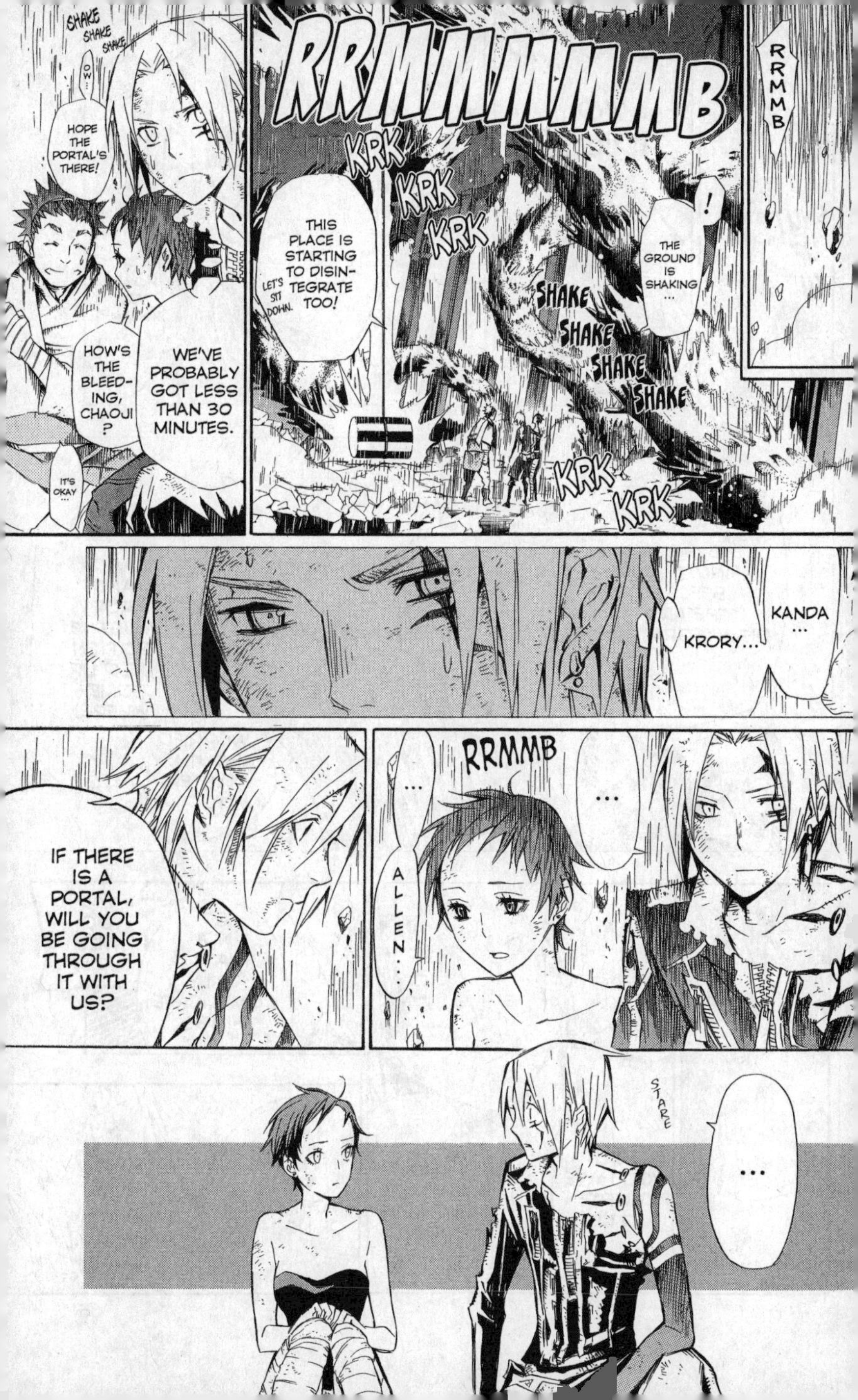
RRMMB
!
THE GROUND IS SHAKING...
RRMMMMMMMB
KRK
KRK
KRK
THIS PLACE IS STARTING TO DISINTEGRATE TOO!
LET'S SIT DOWN.
SHAKE
SHAKE
SHAKE
SHAKE
KRK
KRK
SHAKE SHAKE SHAKE
OW...
HOPE THE PORTAL'S THERE!
WE'VE PROBABLY GOT LESS THAN 30 MINUTES.
HOW'S THE BLEEDING, CHAOJI?
IT'S OKAY...
KANDA...
KRORY...
...
RRMMB
...
ALLEN...
IF THERE IS A PORTAL, WILL YOU BE GOING THROUGH IT WITH US?
STARE
...

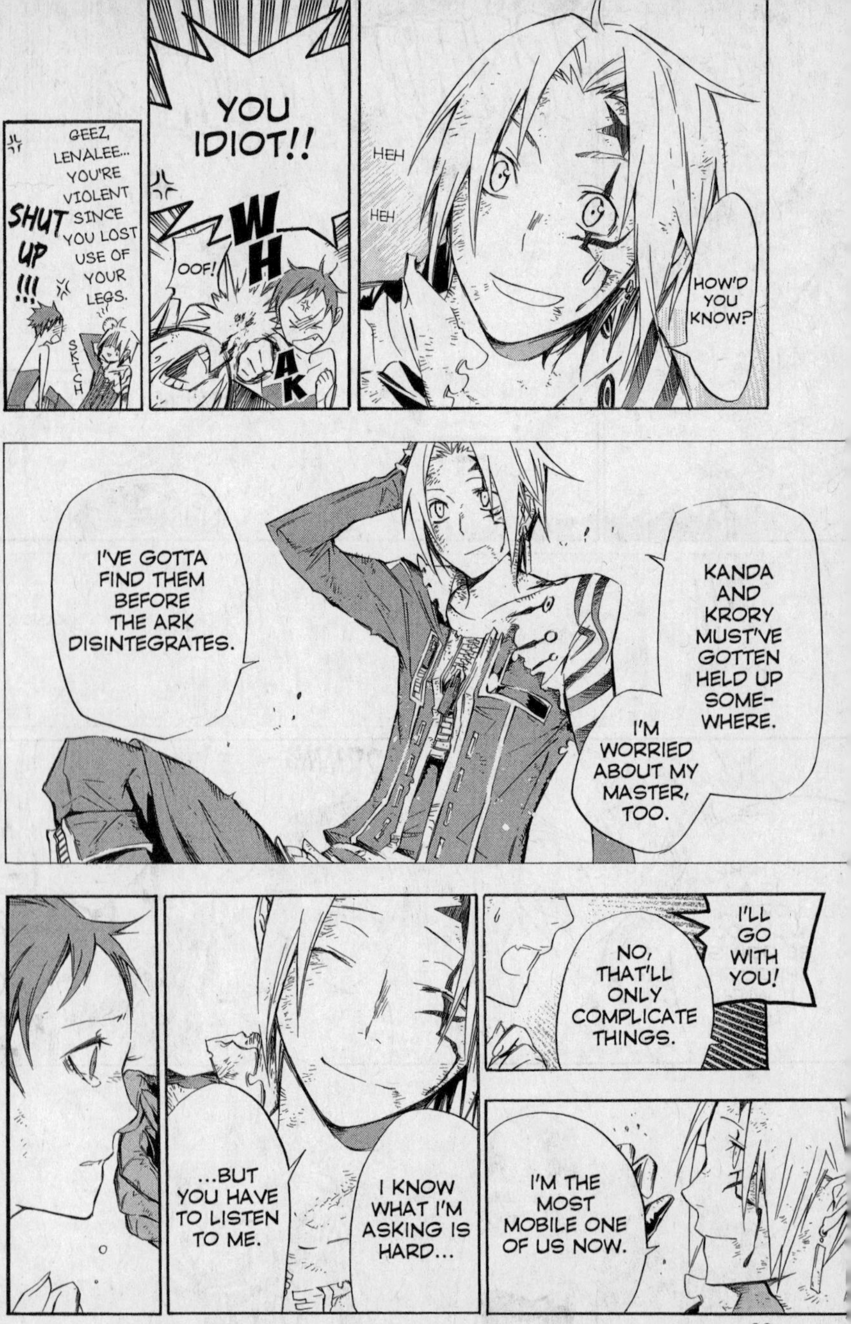
HEH
HEH
HOW'D YOU KNOW?
YOU IDIOT!!
WHAK
OOF!
GEEZ, LENALEE... YOU'RE VIOLENT SINCE YOU LOST USE OF YOUR LEGS.
SHUT UP!!!
SKTCH
KANDA AND KRORY MUST'VE GOTTEN HELD UP SOMEWHERE.
I'M WORRIED ABOUT MY MASTER, TOO.
I'VE GOTTA FIND THEM BEFORE THE ARK DISINTEGRATES.
I'LL GO WITH YOU!
NO, THAT'LL ONLY COMPLICATE THINGS.
I'M THE MOST MOBILE ONE OF US NOW.
I KNOW WHAT I'M ASKING IS HARD...
...BUT YOU HAVE TO LISTEN TO ME.

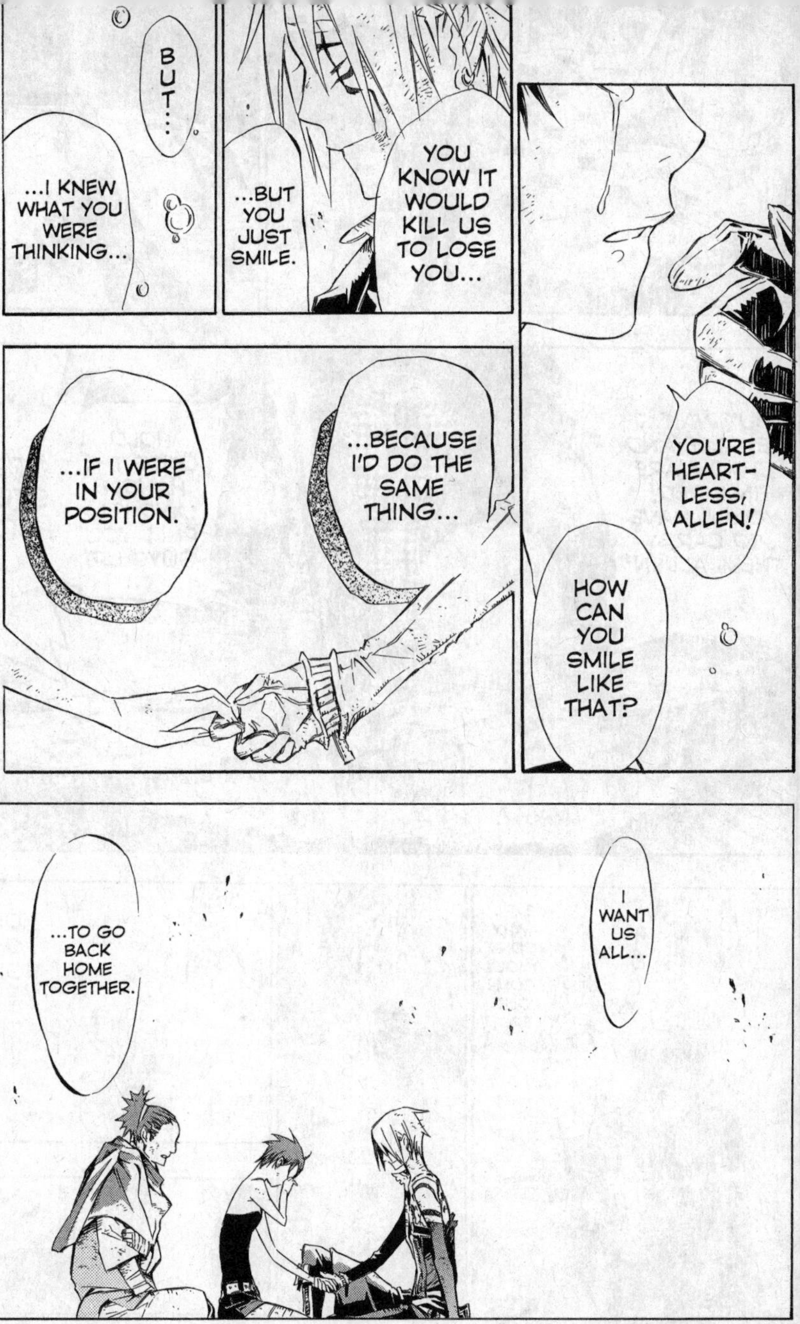
YOU KNOW IT WOULD KILL US TO LOSE YOU...
...BUT YOU JUST SMILE.
YOU'RE HEART-LESS, ALLEN!
HOW CAN YOU SMILE LIKE THAT?
BUT...
...I KNEW WHAT YOU WERE THINKING...
...BECAUSE I'D DO THE SAME THING...
...IF I WERE IN YOUR POSITION.
I WANT US ALL...
...TO GO BACK HOME TOGETHER.

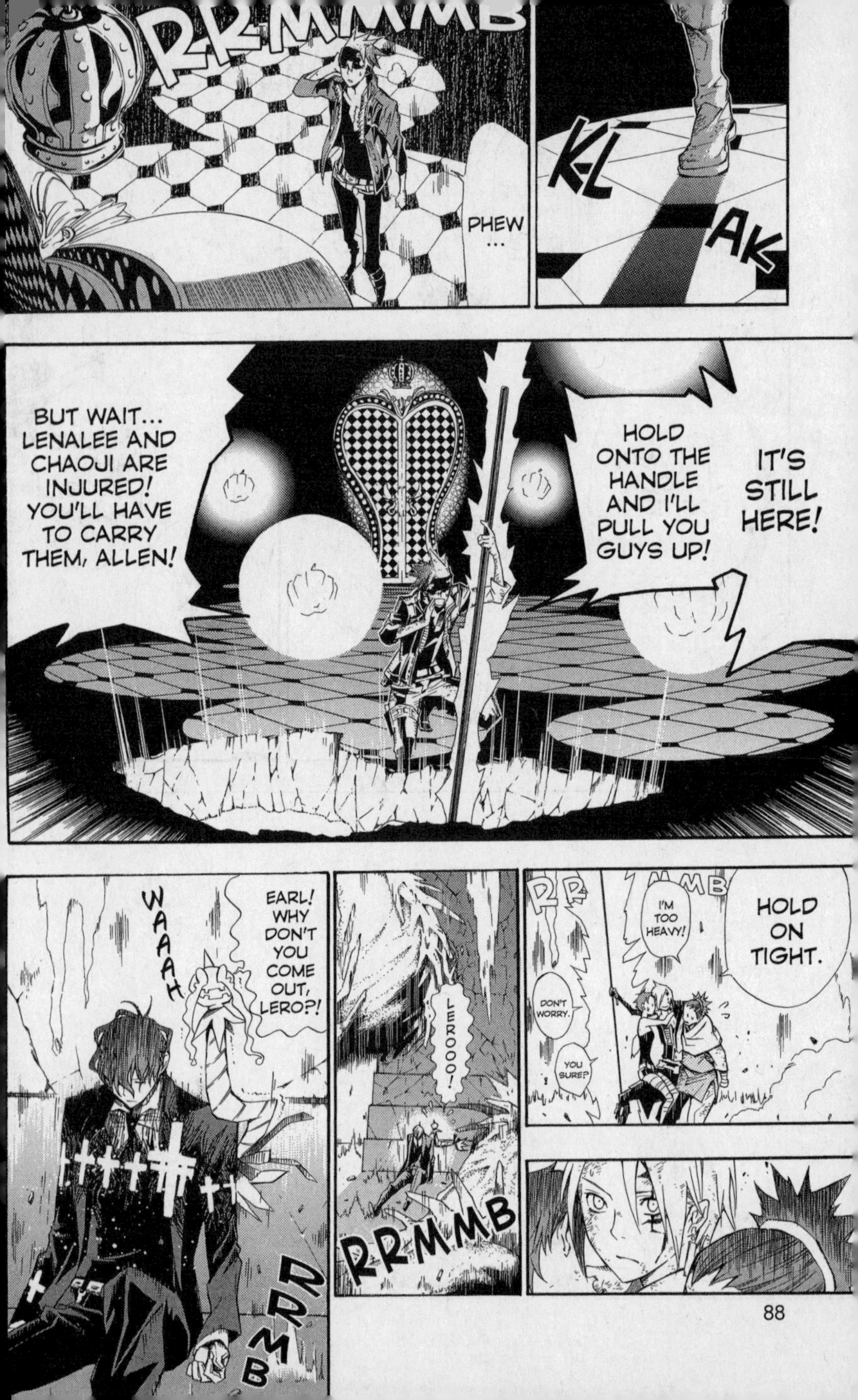
KL-AK
RRMMMB
PHEW...
IT'S STILL HERE!
HOLD ONTO THE HANDLE AND I'LL PULL YOU GUYS UP!
BUT WAIT... LENALEE AND CHAOJI ARE INJURED! YOU'LL HAVE TO CARRY THEM, ALLEN!
RR MMB
HOLD ON TIGHT.
I'M TOO HEAVY!
DON'T WORRY.
YOU SURE?
LEROOO!
RRMMB
EARL! WHY DON'T YOU COME OUT, LERO?!
WAAAAH
RRMB

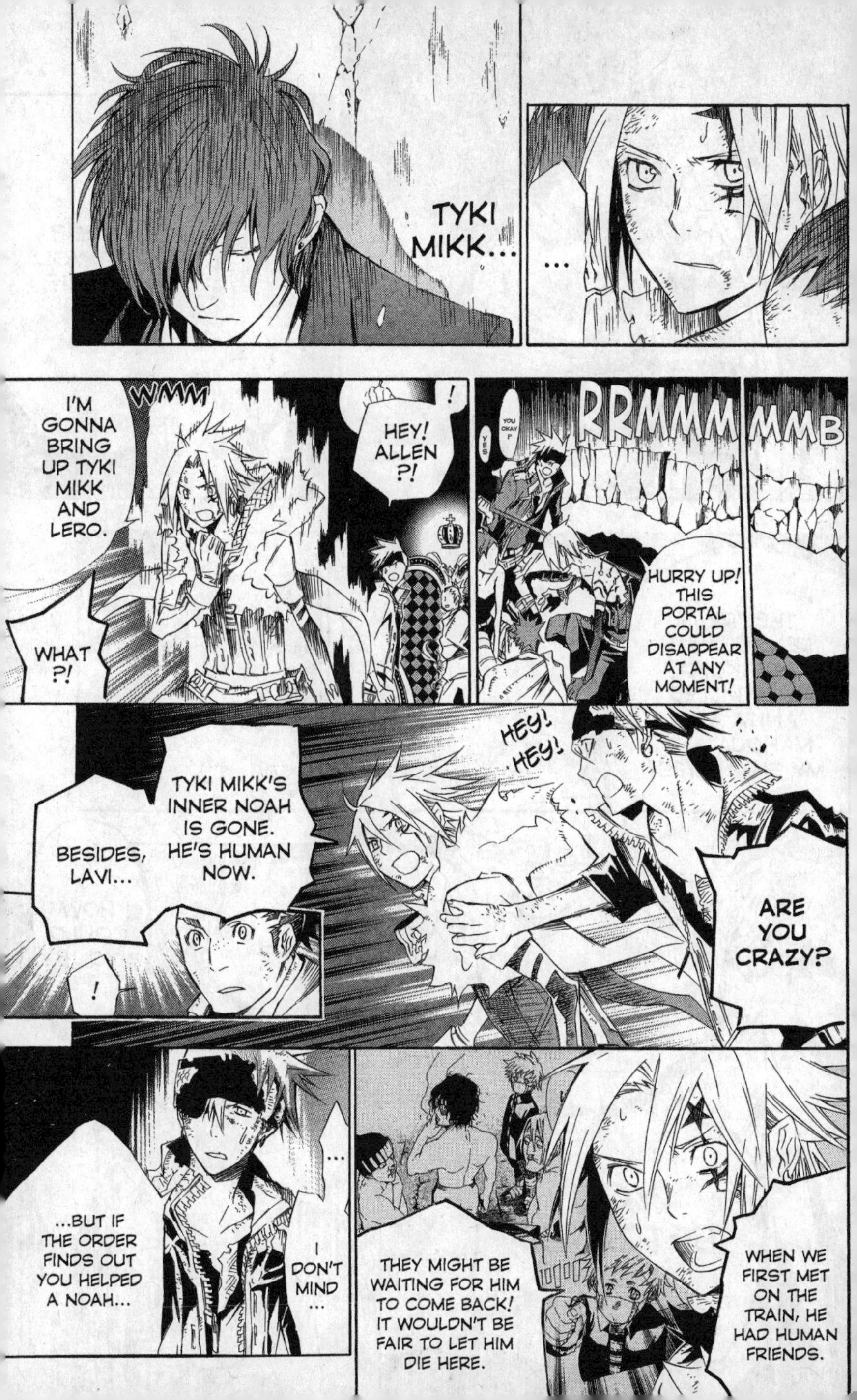
...
TYKI MIKK...
RRMMMMMMB
YOU OKAY?
YES
HURRY UP! THIS PORTAL COULD DISAPPEAR AT ANY MOMENT!
!
HEY! ALLEN ?!
WMM
I'M GONNA BRING UP TYKI MIKK AND LERO.
WHAT ?!
HEY! HEY!
ARE YOU CRAZY?
TYKI MIKK'S INNER NOAH IS GONE. HE'S HUMAN NOW.
BESIDES, LAVI...
!
WHEN WE FIRST MET ON THE TRAIN, HE HAD HUMAN FRIENDS.
THEY MIGHT BE WAITING FOR HIM TO COME BACK! IT WOULDN'T BE FAIR TO LET HIM DIE HERE.
...
...BUT IF THE ORDER FINDS OUT YOU HELPED A NOAH...
I DON'T MIND ...

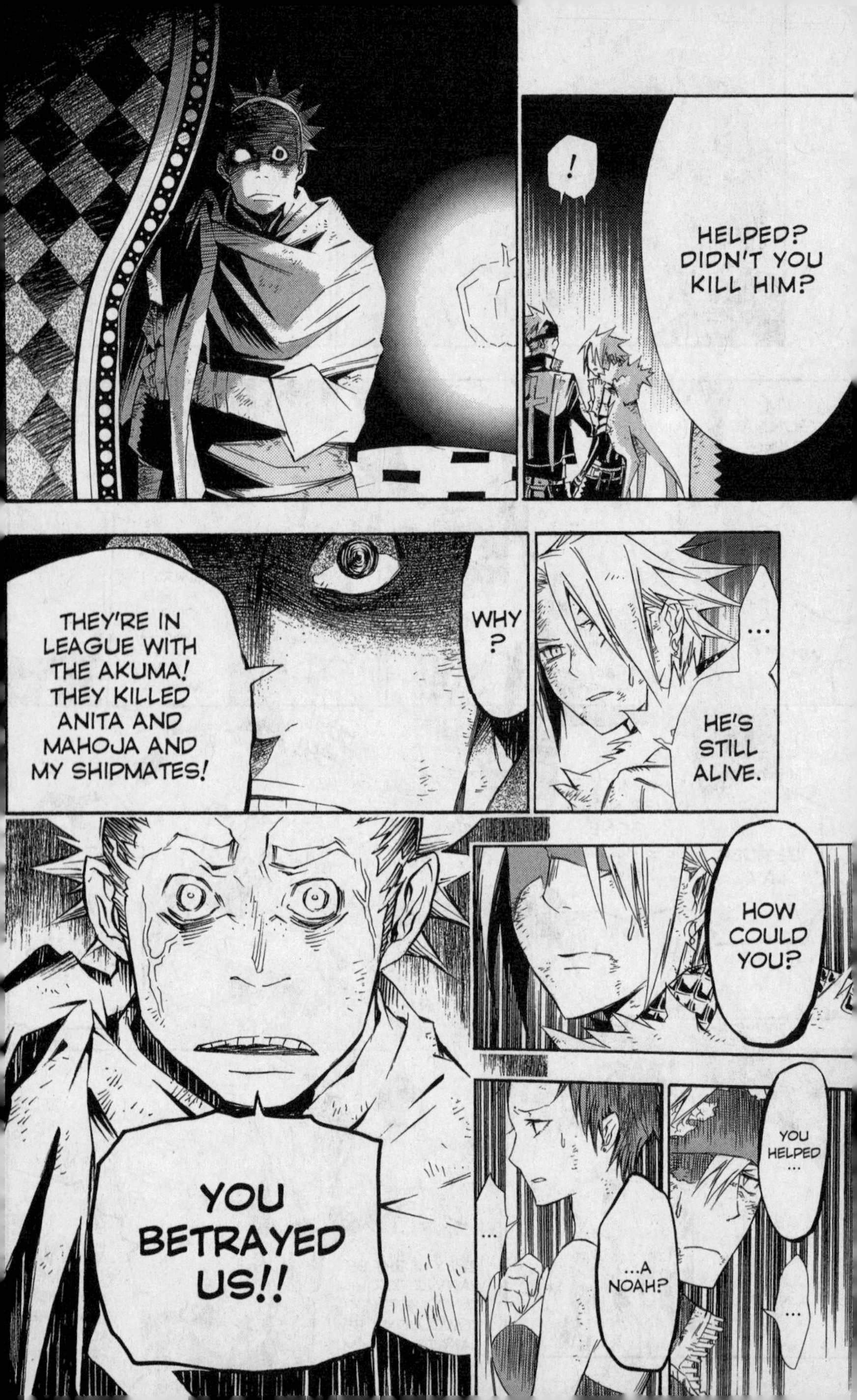
!
HELPED? DIDN'T YOU KILL HIM?
...
HE'S STILL ALIVE.
WHY?
THEY'RE IN LEAGUE WITH THE AKUMA! THEY KILLED ANITA AND MAHOJA AND MY SHIPMATES!
HOW COULD YOU?
YOU HELPED ...
...
...A NOAH?
...
YOU BETRAYED US!!

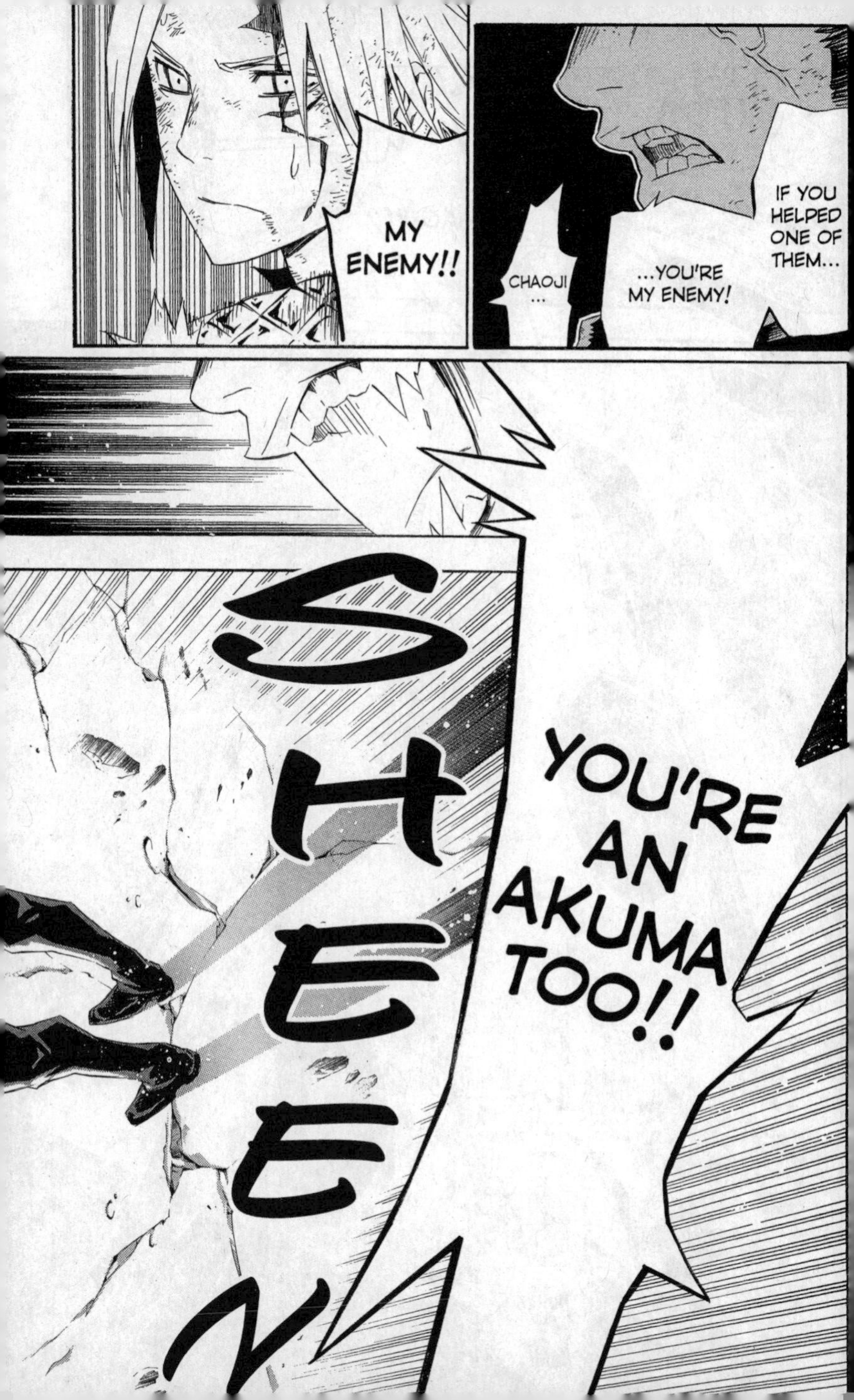
IF YOU HELPED ONE OF THEM...
...YOU'RE MY ENEMY!
CHAOJI ...
MY ENEMY!!
YOU'RE AN AKUMA TOO!!
SHEEN

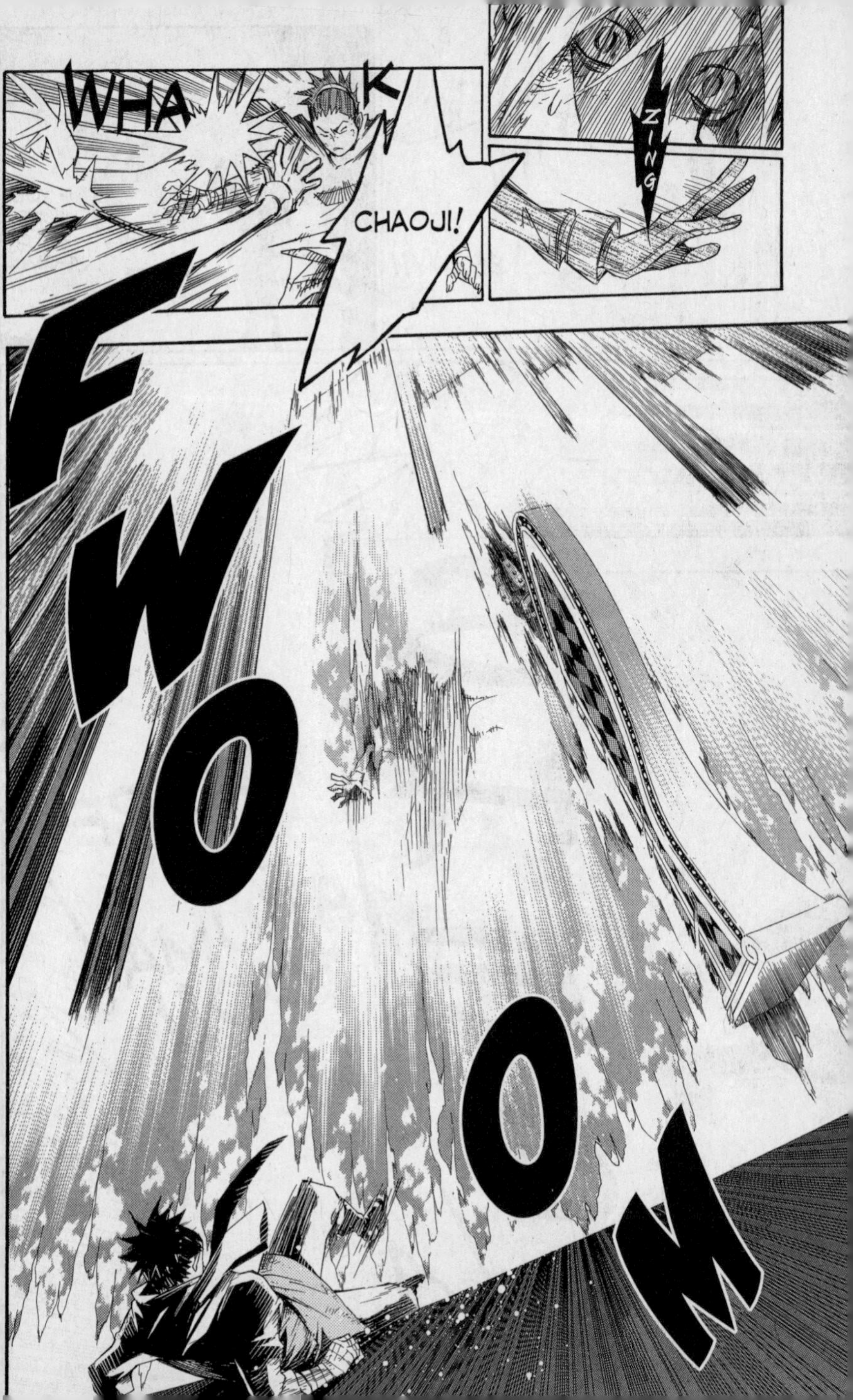
ZING
WHAK
CHAOJI!
FWOOOM

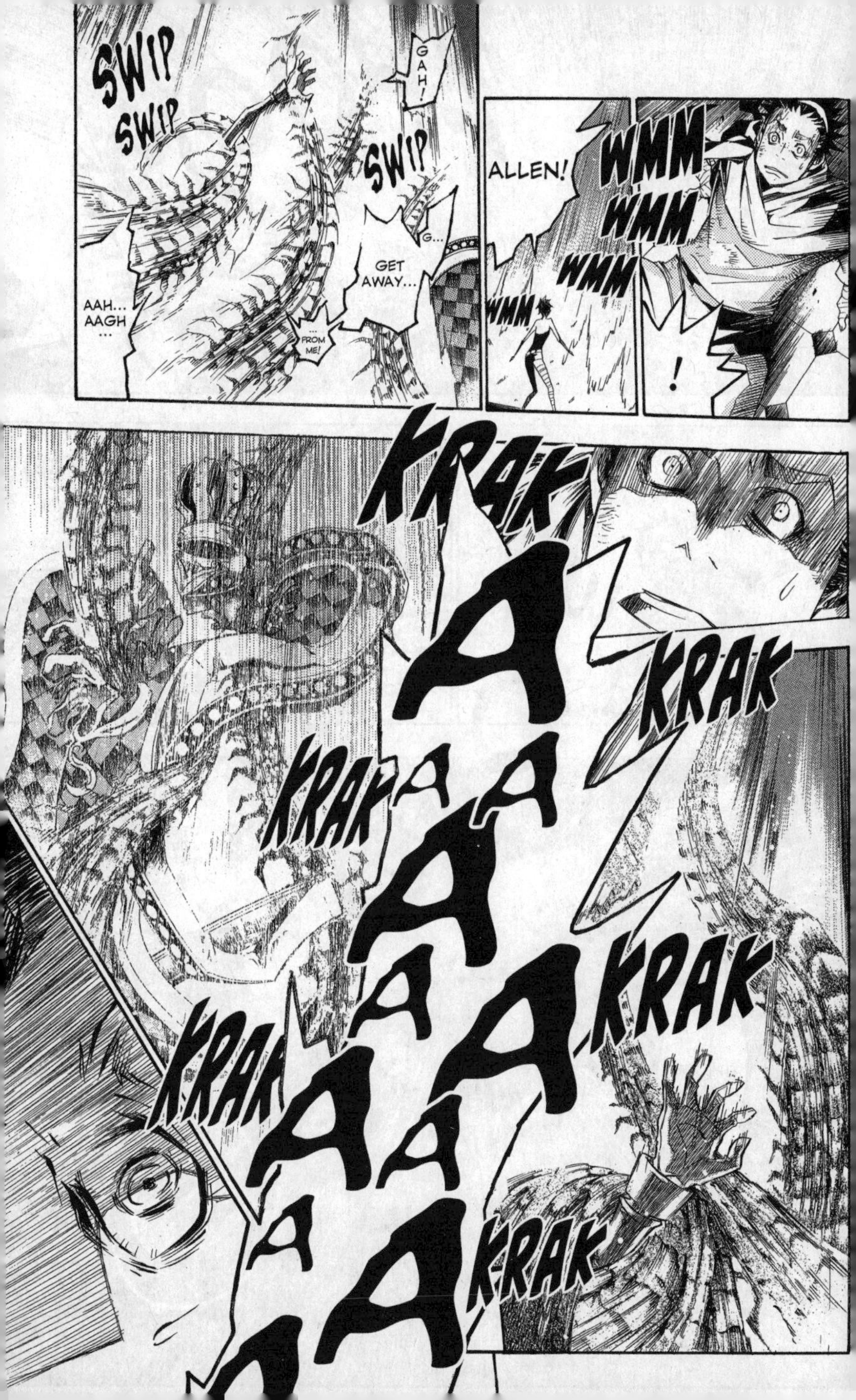

WMM WMM WMM WMM
ALLEN!
!
GAH!
SWIP SWIP
SWIP
G...
GET AWAY...
...FROM ME!
AAH... AAGH...
KRAK
KRAK
AAAAAAAAAAAAA
KRAK
KRAK
KRAK
KRAK

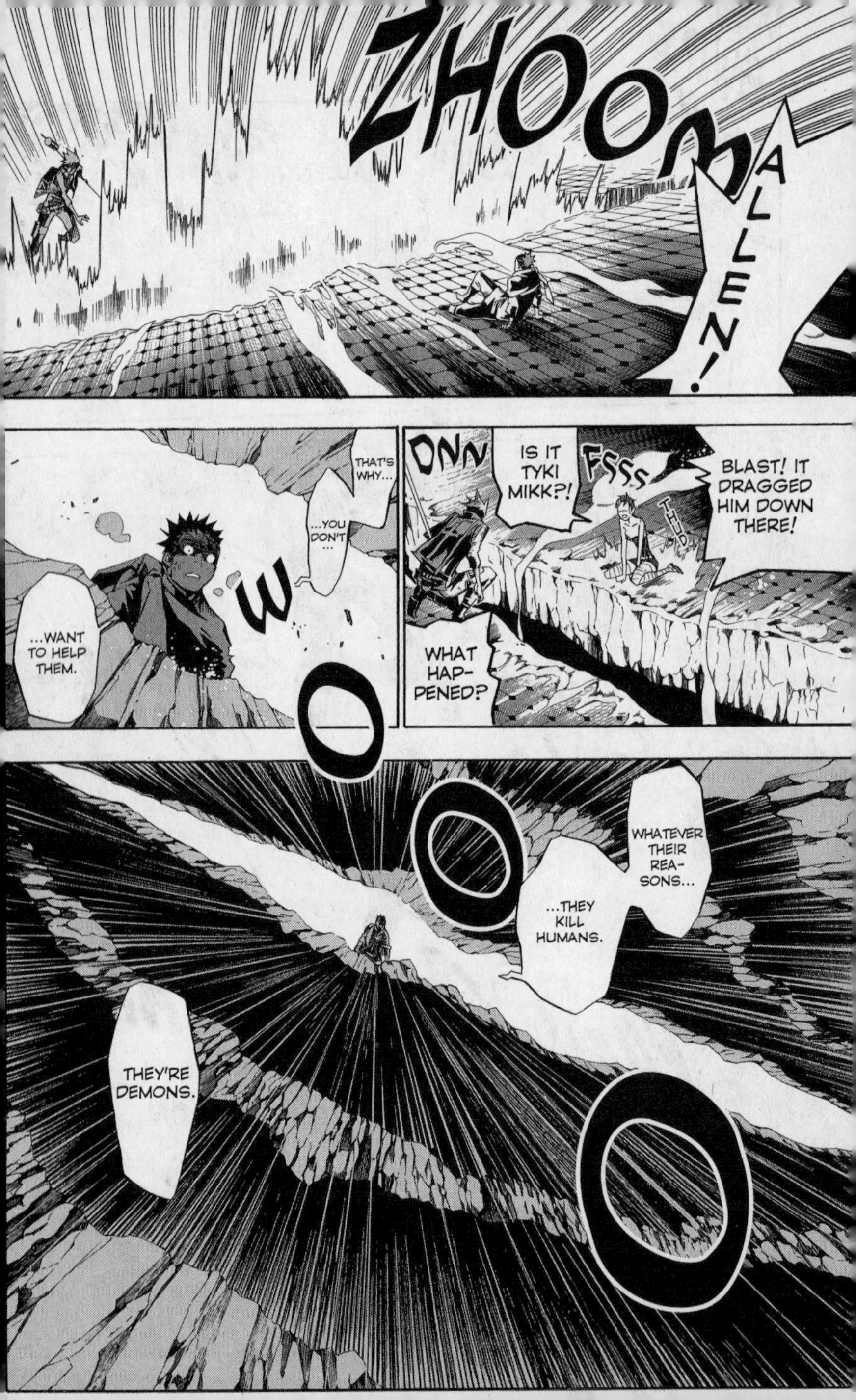
ZHOOM
ALLEN!
BLAST! IT DRAGGED HIM DOWN THERE!
FSSS
THUD
IS IT TYKI MIKK?!
DONN
WHAT HAP-PENED?
THAT'S WHY...
...YOU DON'T...
...WANT TO HELP THEM.
WOOOO
WHATEVER THEIR REA-SONS...
...THEY KILL HUMANS.
THEY'RE DEMONS.

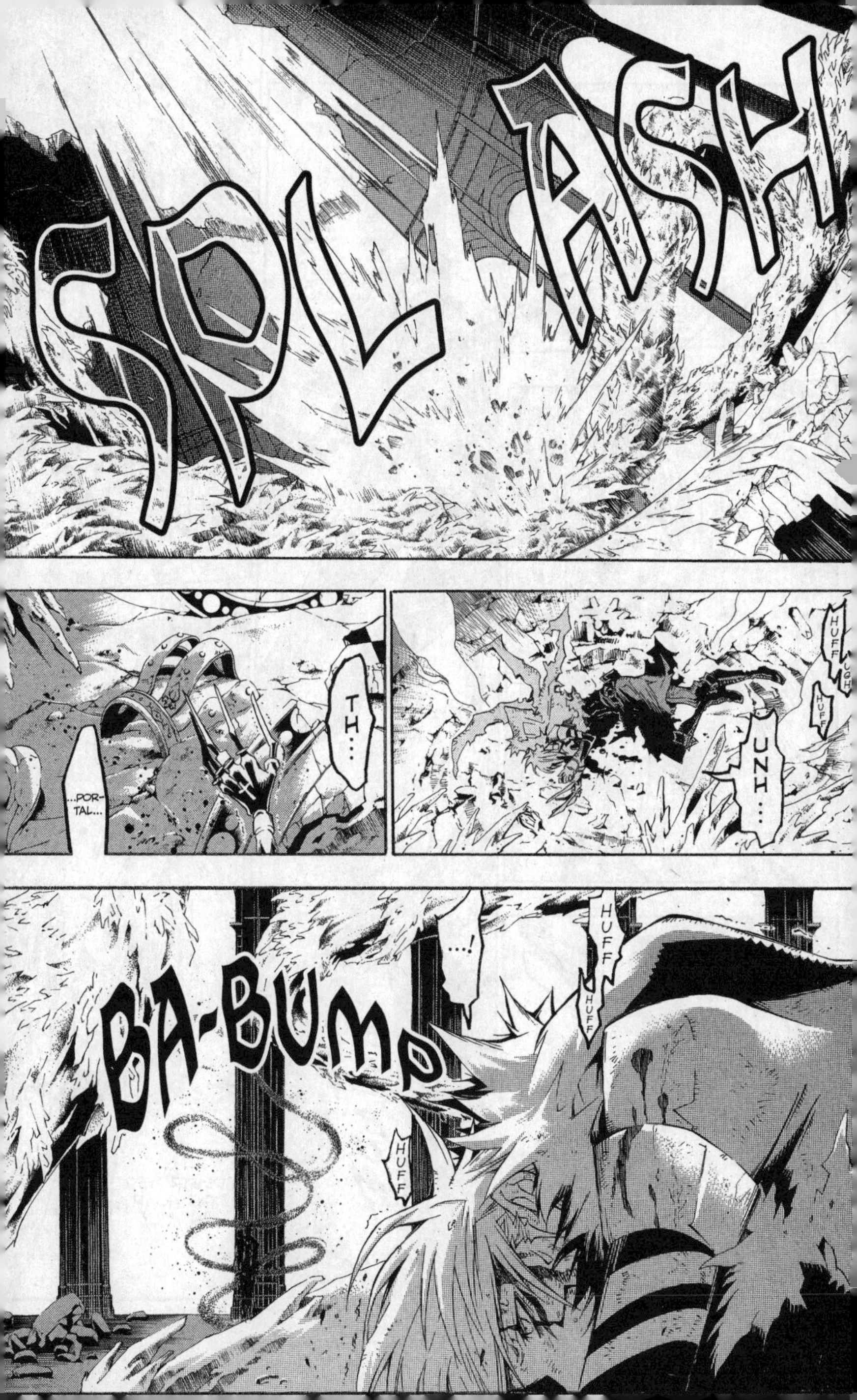
SPLASH
HUFF
UGH
HUFF
UNH...
TH...
...PORTAL...
HUFF
HUFF
...!
BA-BUMP
HUFF

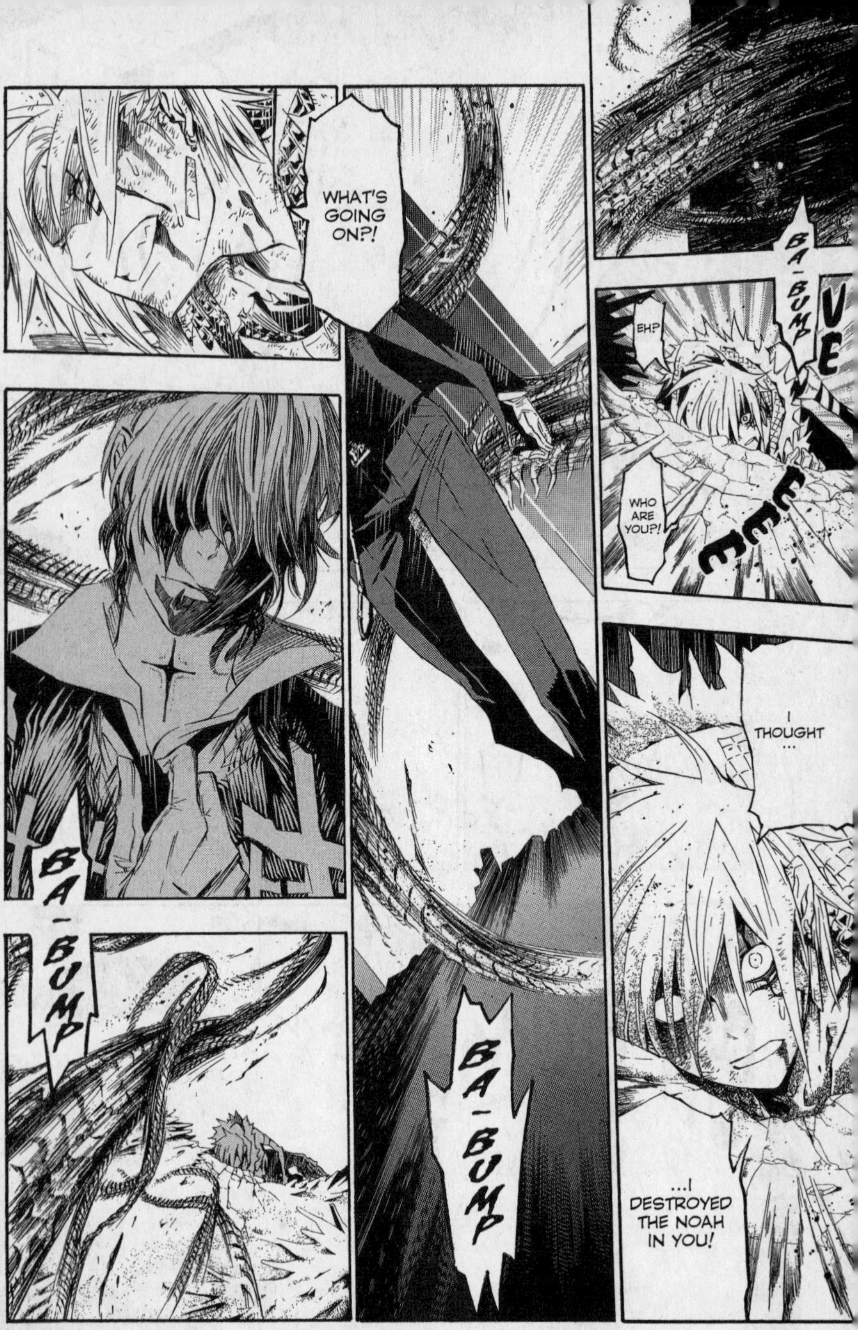
BA-BUMP
VEEEE
EH?
WHO ARE YOU?!
I THOUGHT...
...I DESTROYED THE NOAH IN YOU!
WHAT'S GOING ON?!
BA-BUMP
BA-BUMP
BA-BUMP

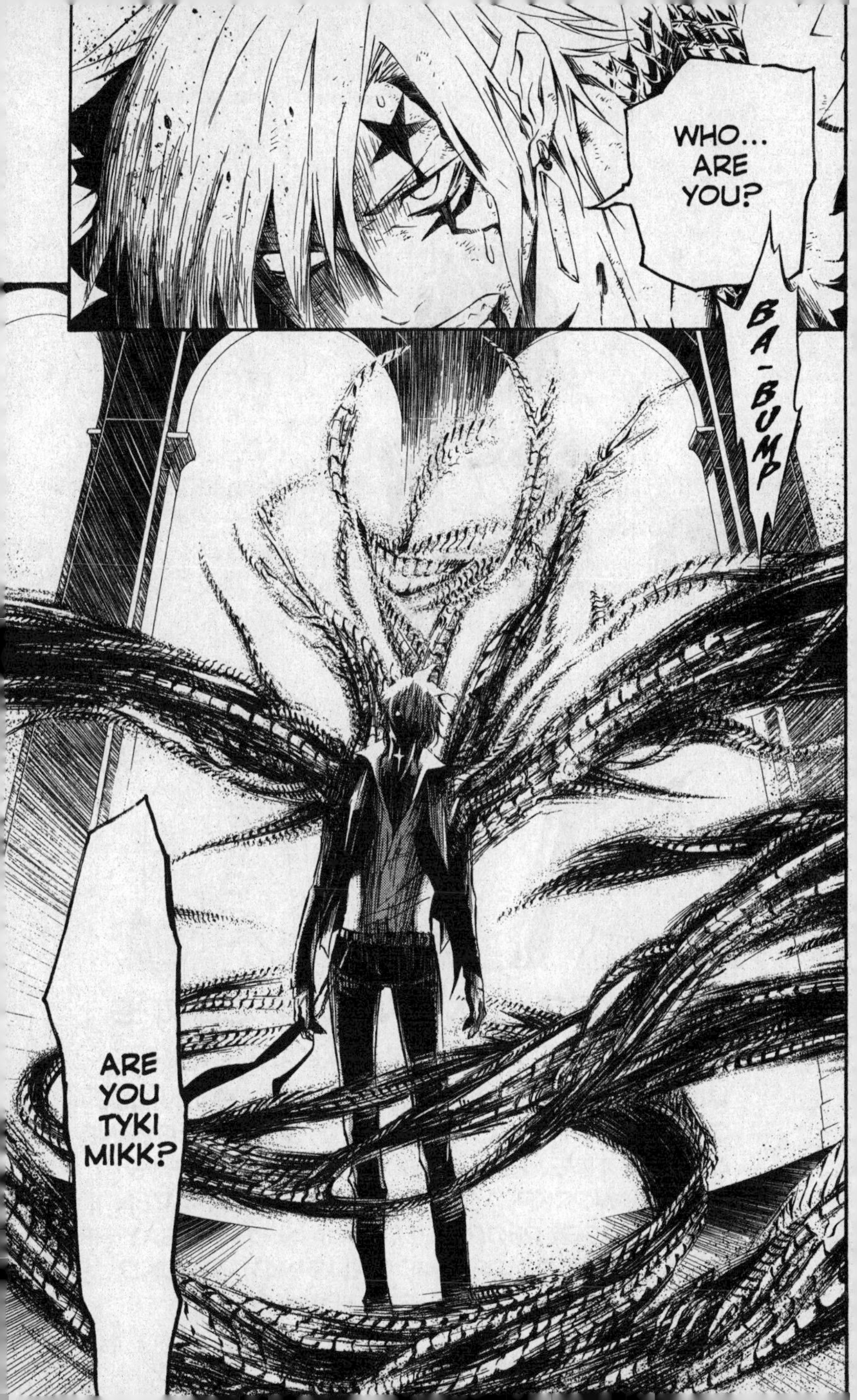
WHO... ARE YOU?
BA-BUMP
ARE YOU TYKI MIKK?

HAR
HAR
HAR

EROS

THE D.GRAY-MAN ELITE CORPS
ILLUSTRATION BY MURAKAMI-KUN
MURAKAMI IS A MAN WHO USES HIS UNIQUE
CONVERSATIONAL SKILLS TO GIVE EVERYONE
A HARD TIME. HE LIKES TO BRING SWEETS
TO THE WORKPLACE, BUT WHEN THEY AREN'T
VERY GOOD, PEOPLE COMPLAIN. THEY SAY HE
SPENDS A LOT OF TIME HANGING AROUND
THE SHOPS UNDER THE BUILDING.

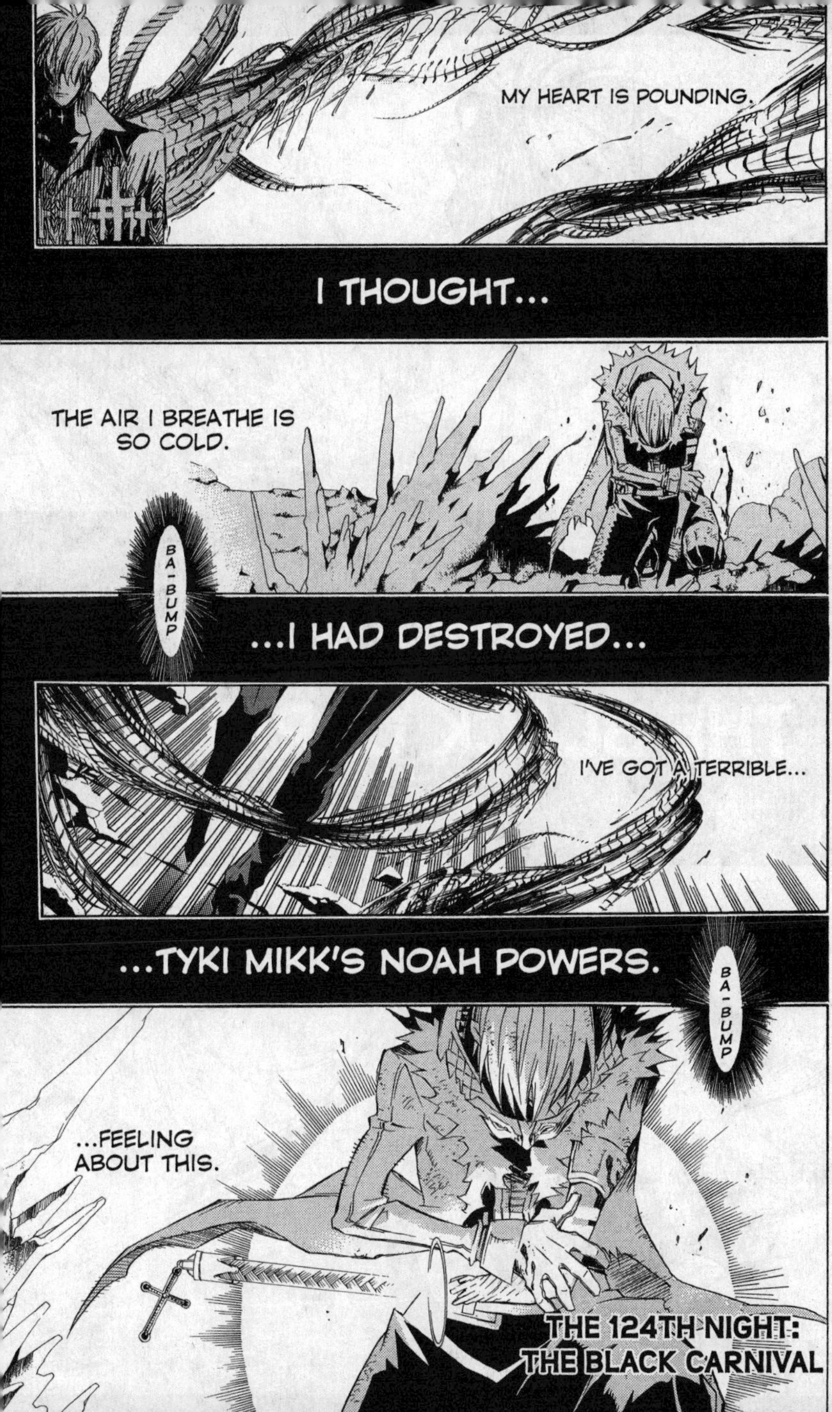
MY HEART IS POUNDING.
I THOUGHT...
THE AIR I BREATHE IS SO COLD.
BA-BUMP
...I HAD DESTROYED...
I'VE GOT A TERRIBLE...
...TYKI MIKK'S NOAH POWERS.
BA-BUMP
...FEELING ABOUT THIS.
THE 124TH NIGHT: THE BLACK CARNIVAL

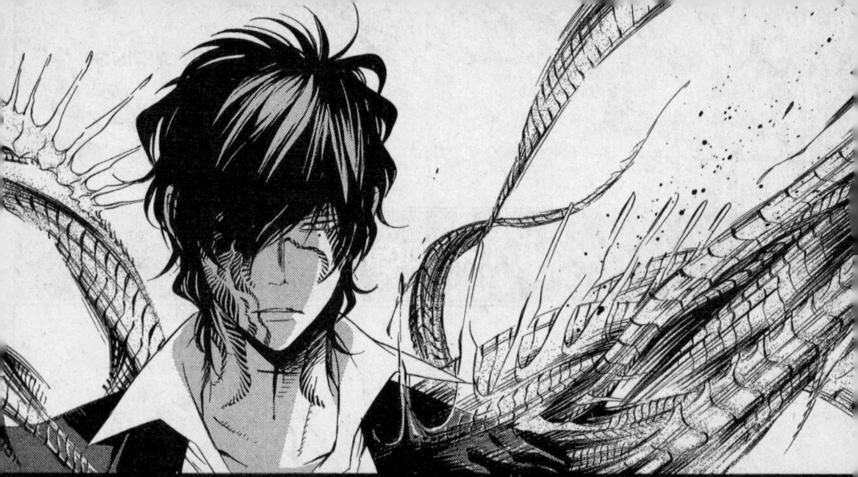

THE 124TH NIGHT: THE BLACK CARNIVAL

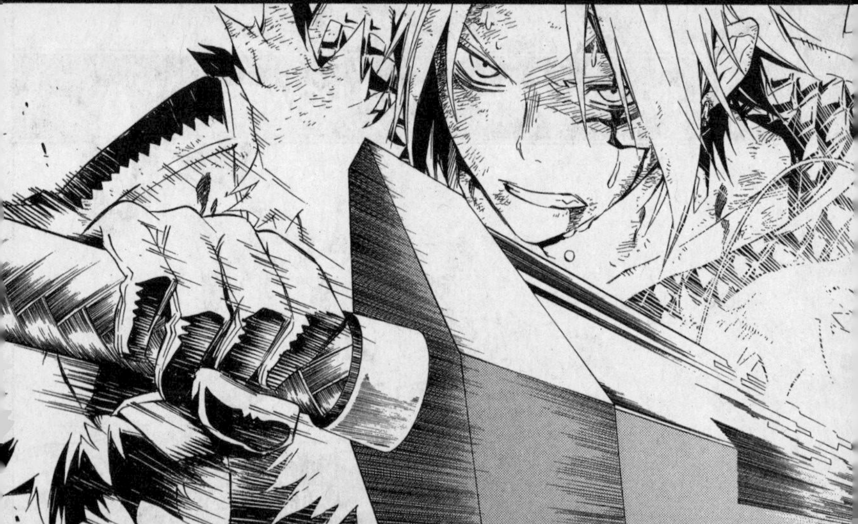

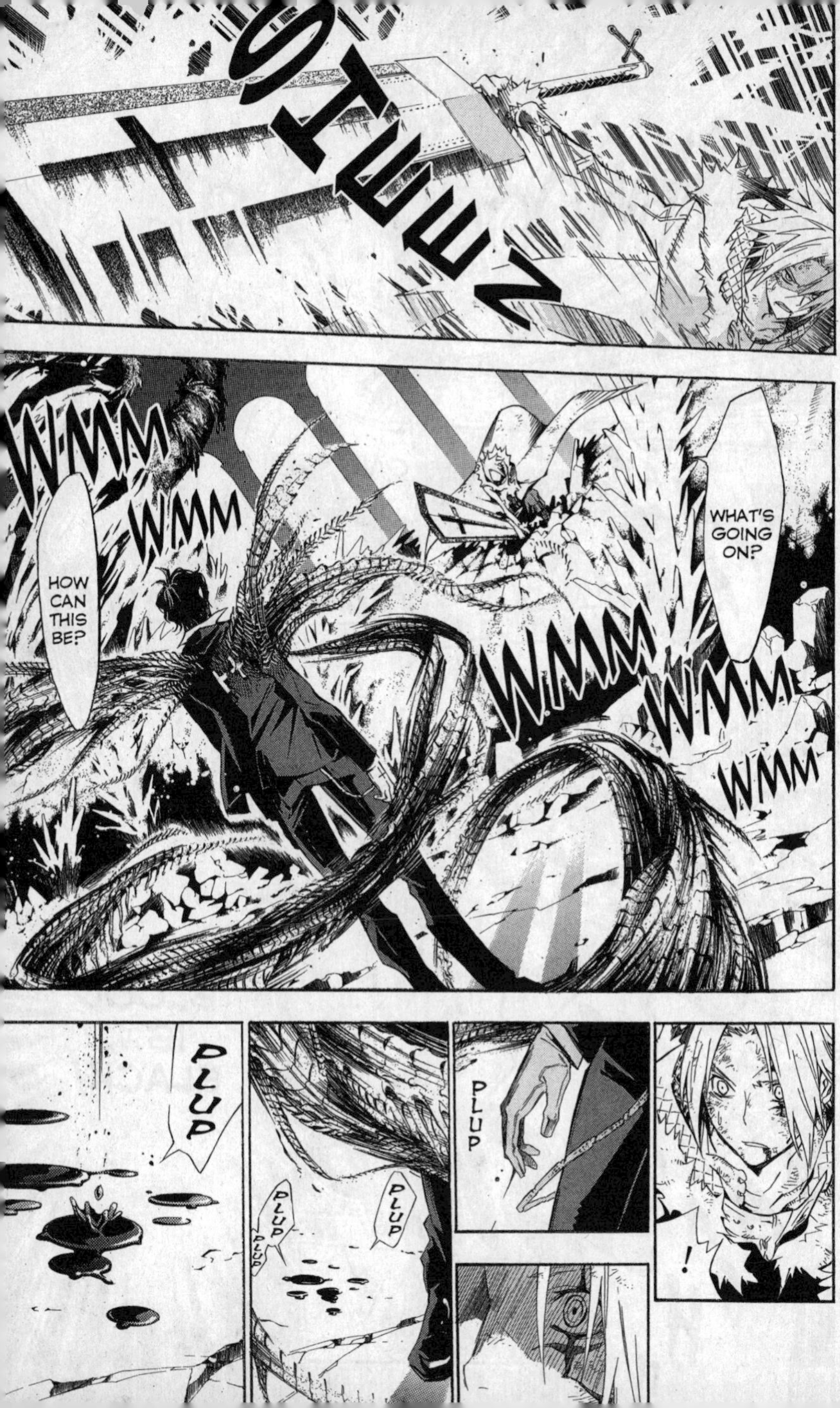
SLASH
WHAT'S GOING ON?
WMM WMM WMM
WMM WMM
HOW CAN THIS BE?
!
PLUP
PLUP
PLUP
PLUP
PLUP

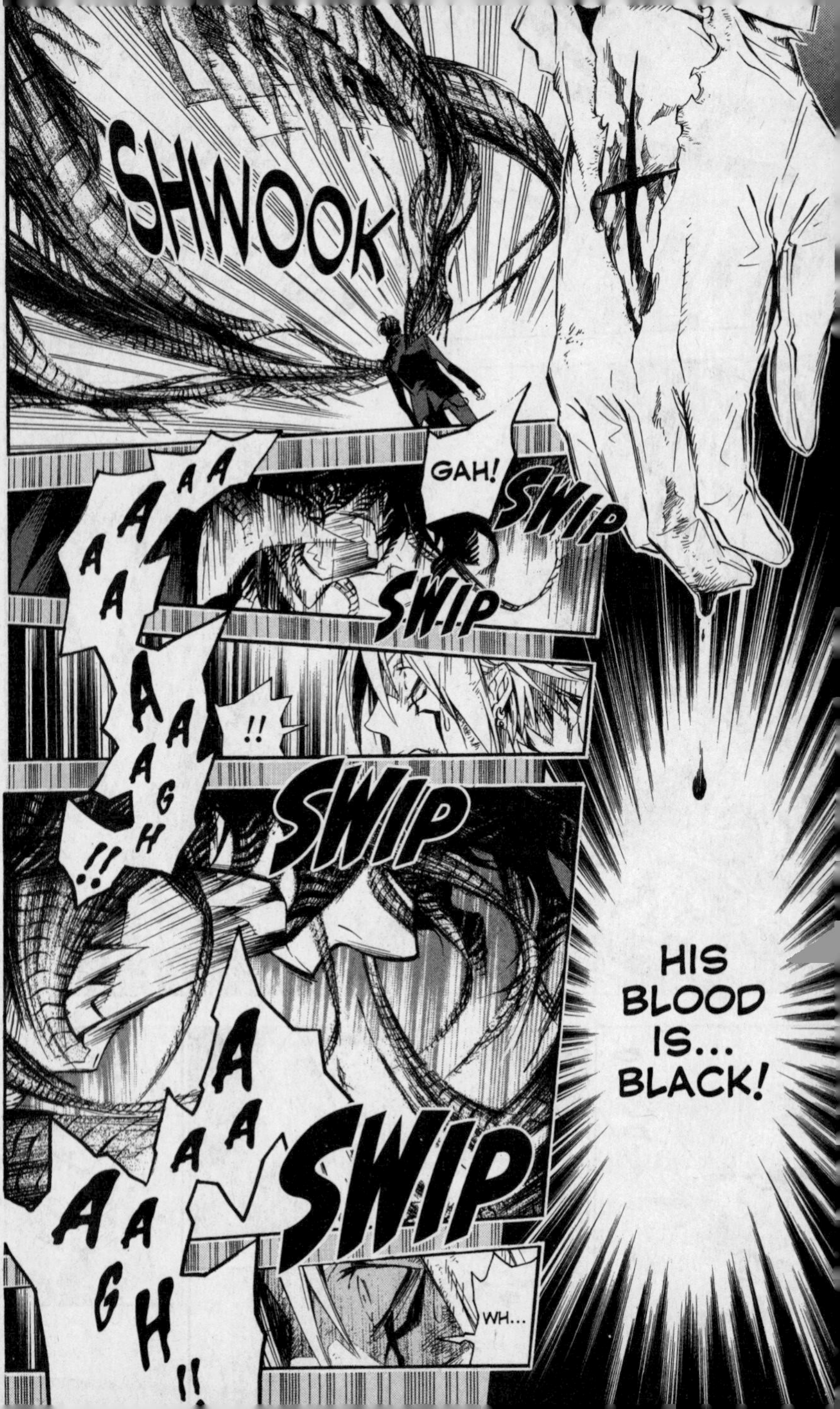

HIS BLOOD IS... BLACK!
SHWOOK
AAAAAAAAAAAGH!!!
GAH!
SWIP
SWIP
!!
SWIP
AAAAAAAGH!!
SWIP
WH...

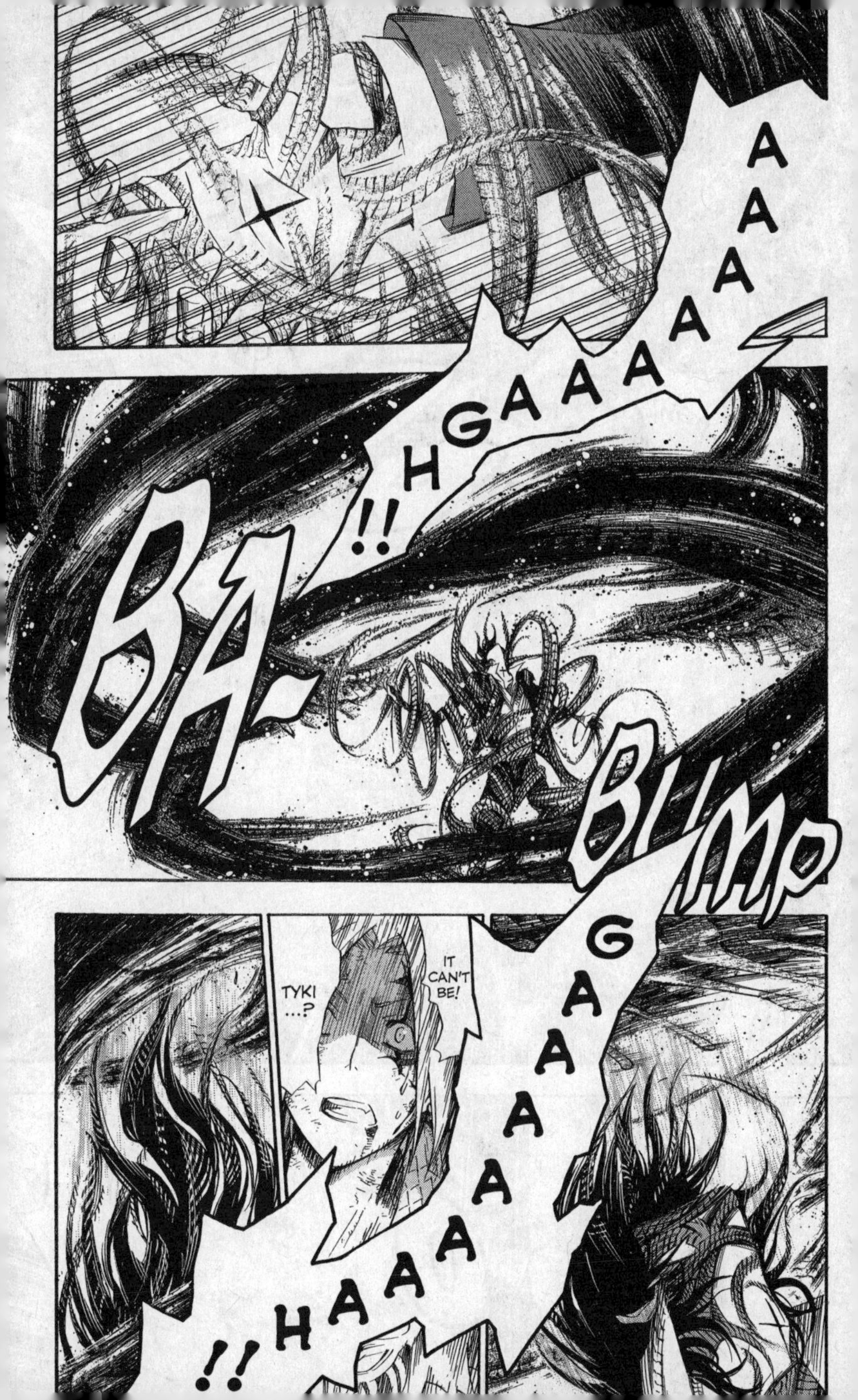
!!HGAAAAAAA
BA-BUMP
IT CAN'T BE!
TYKI ...?
!!HAAAAAAAG

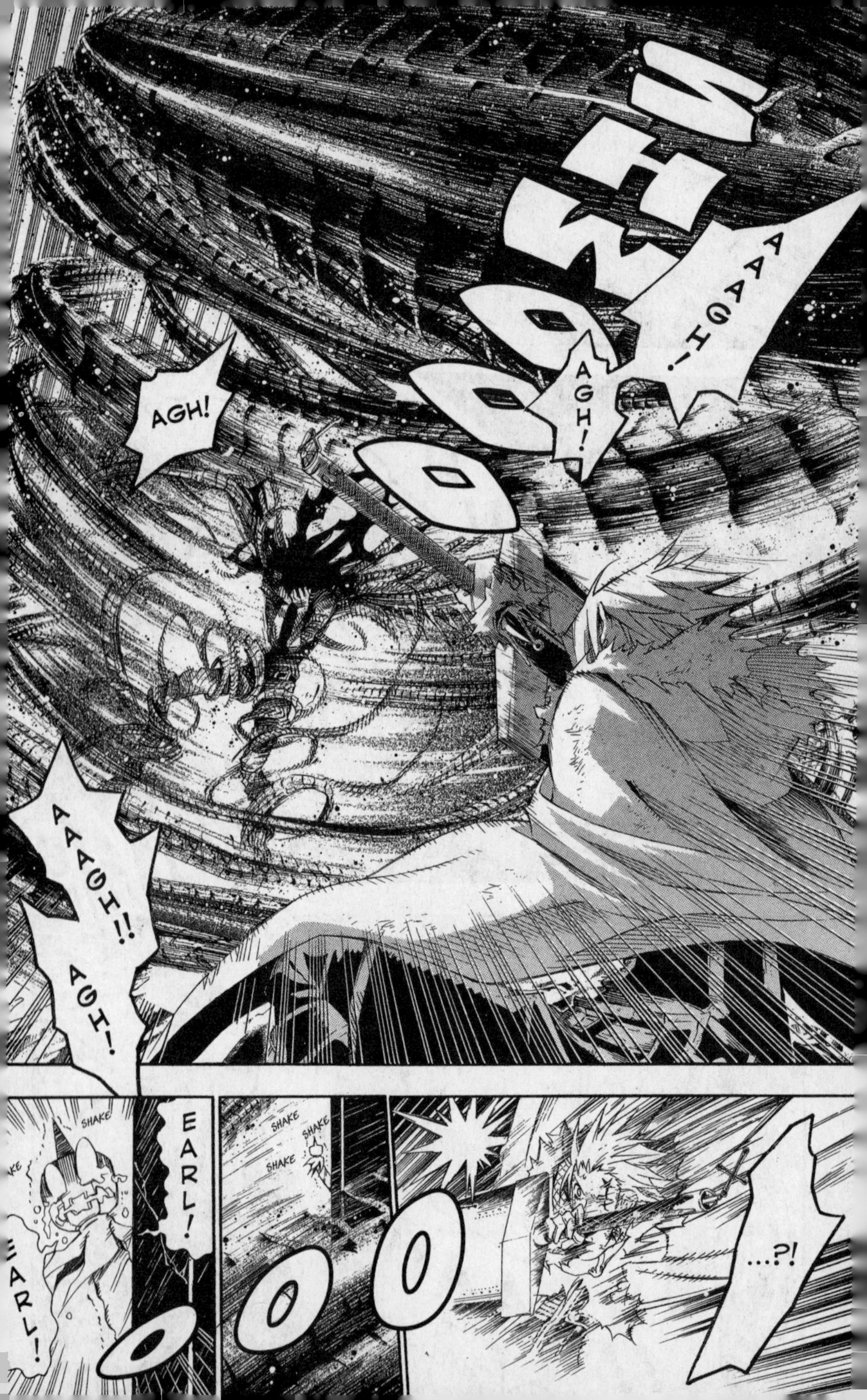
SHWOOO
AAAGH!
AGH!
AGH!
AAAGH!!
AGH!
...?!
OOOO
SHAKE
SHAKE
SHAKE
SHAKE
EARL!
EARL!
SHAKE

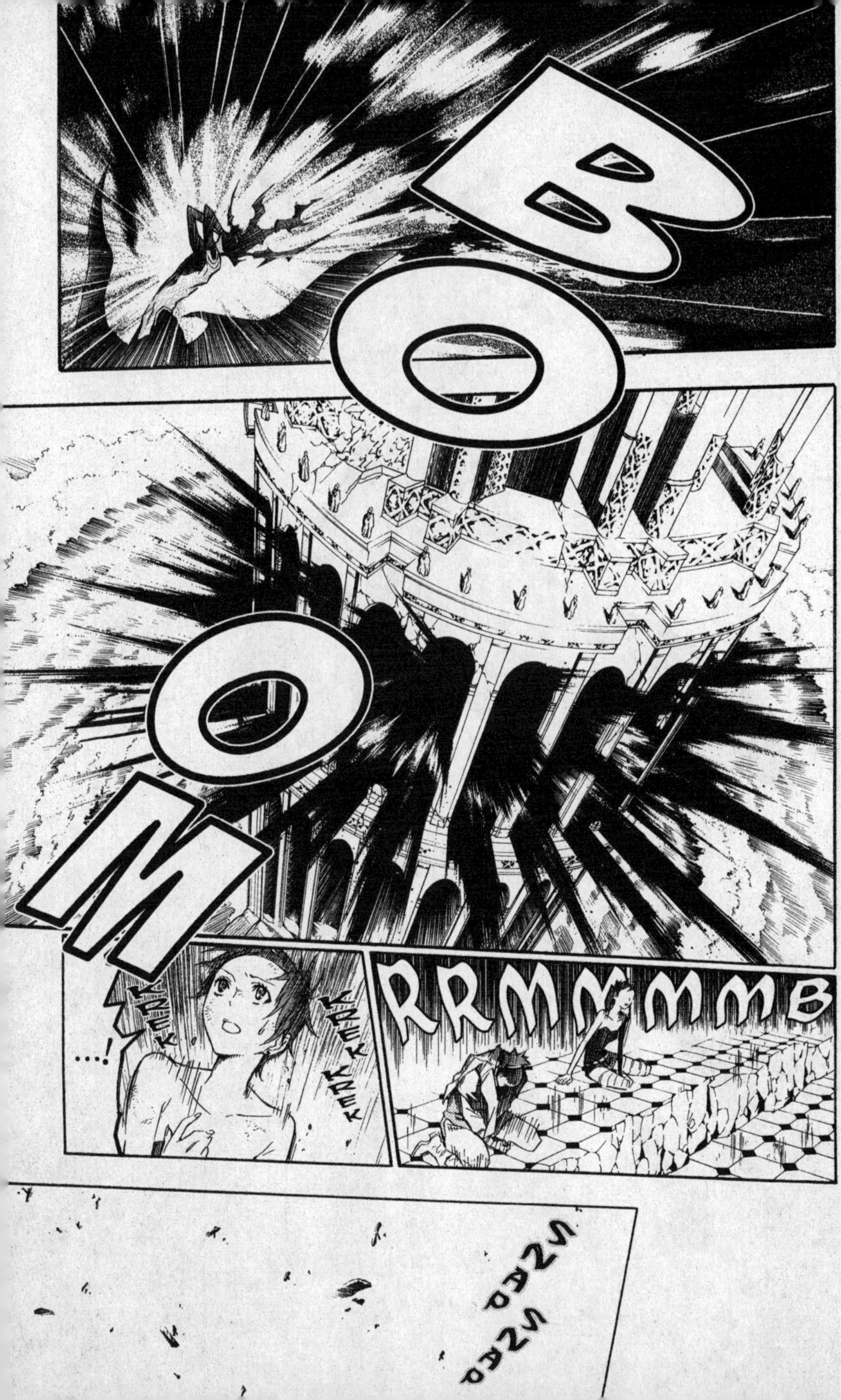
BOOM
RRMMMMMB
KREK KREK
KREK
...!
SNAP SNAP

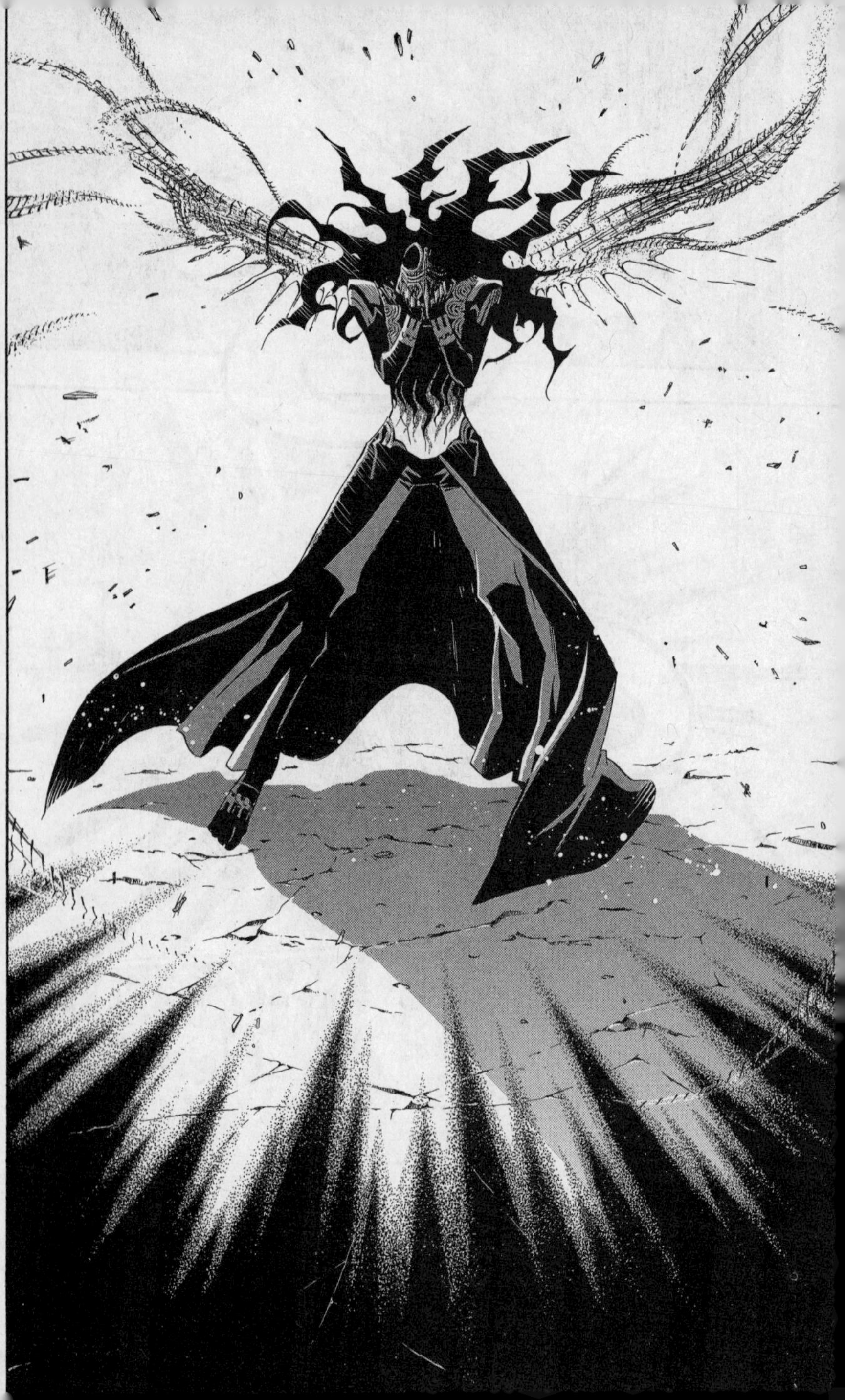

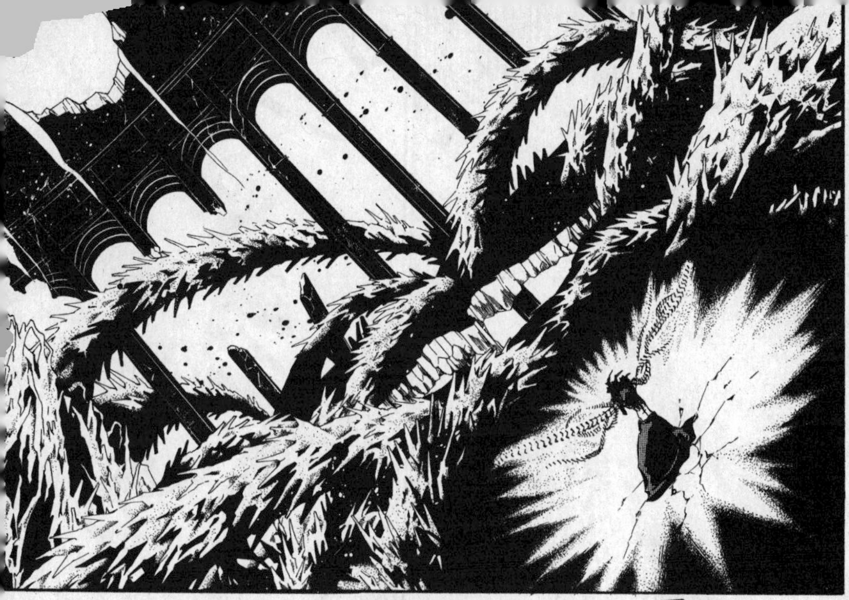

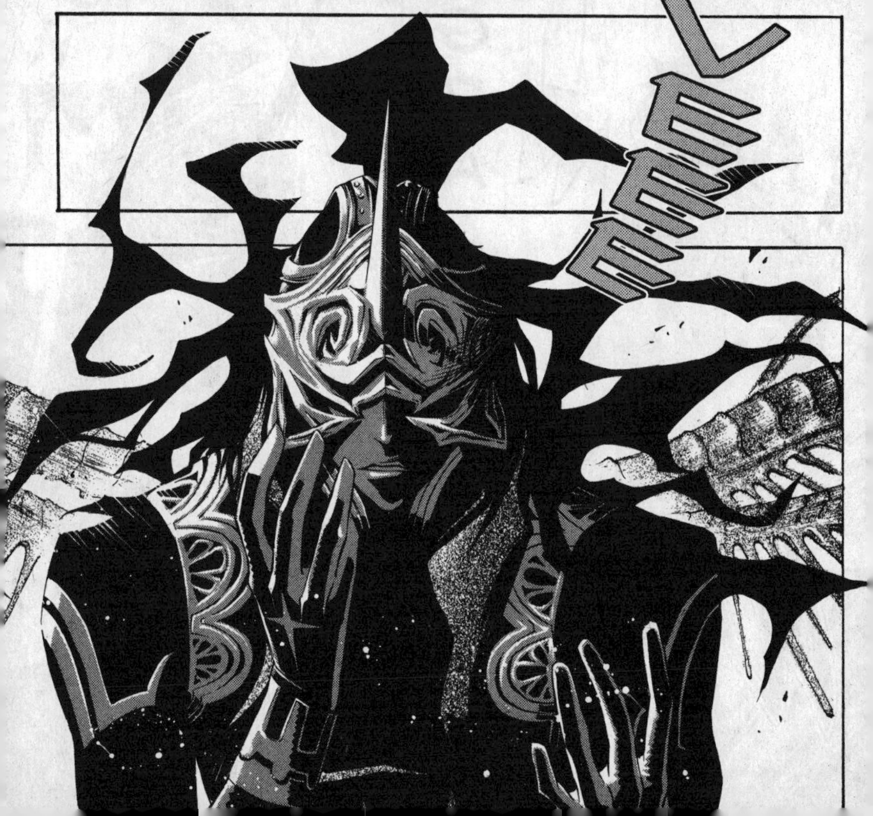
VEEEE

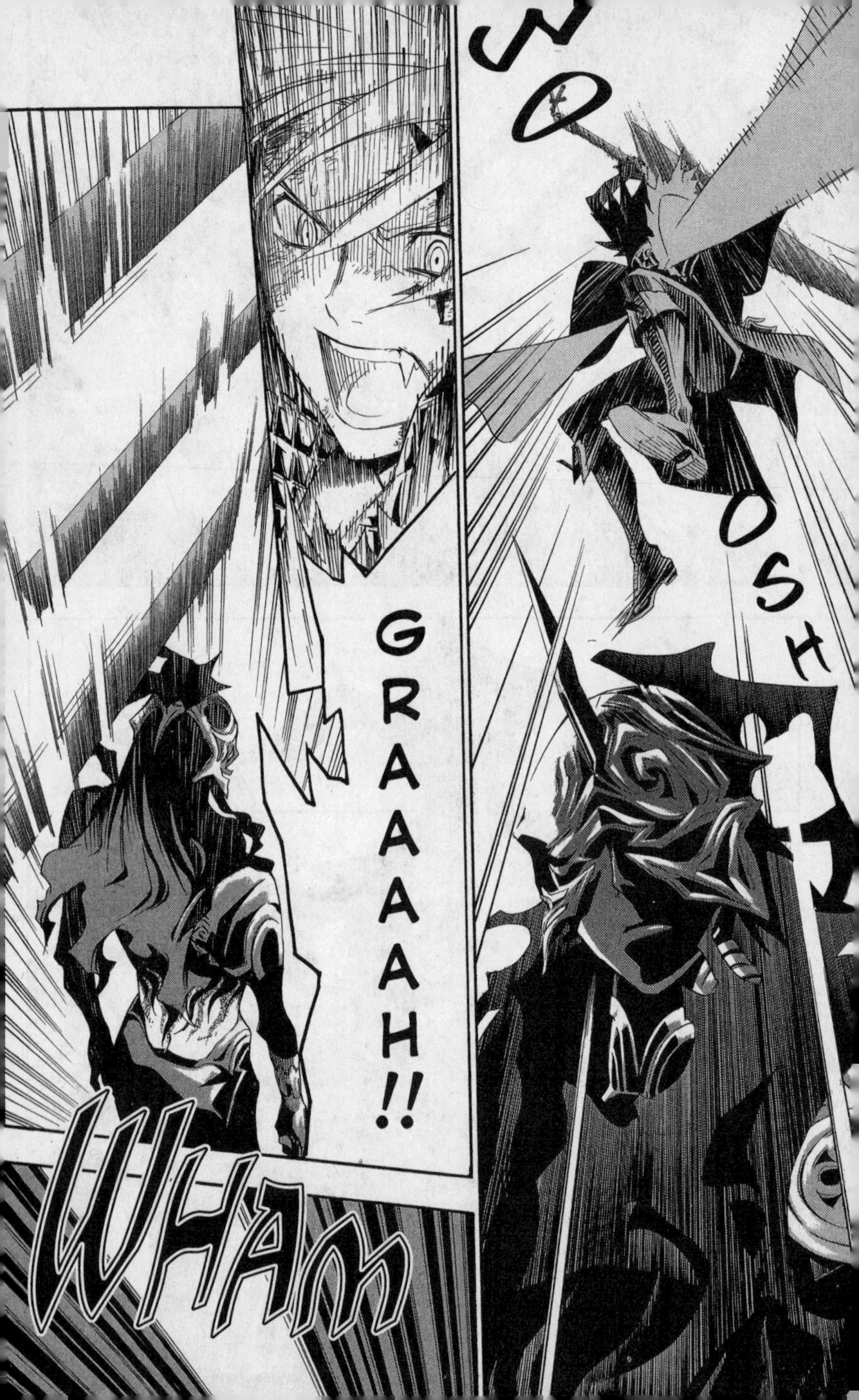
WOOSH
GRAAAH!!
WHAM

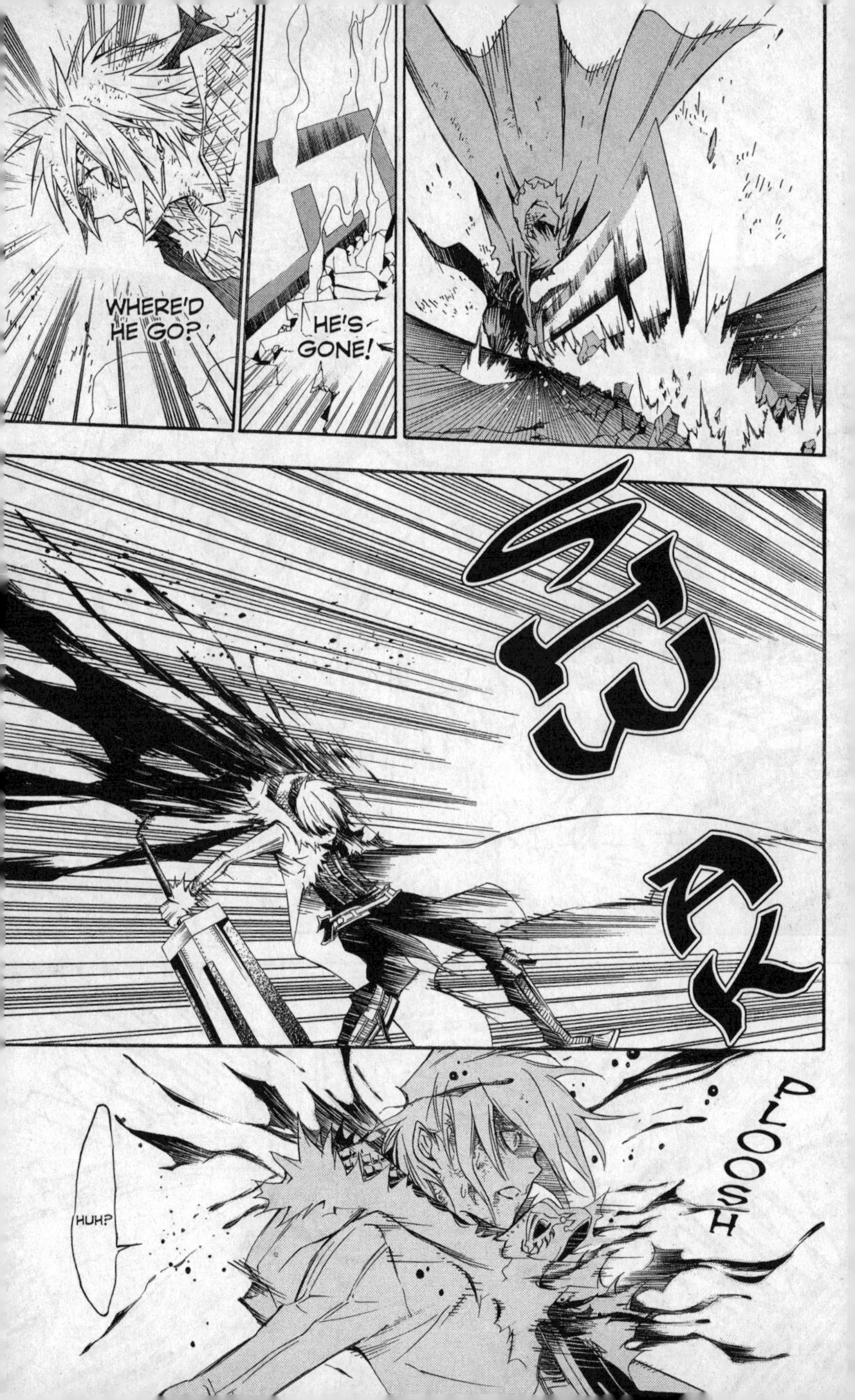
HE'S GONE!
WHERE'D HE GO?
PLOOSH
HUH?

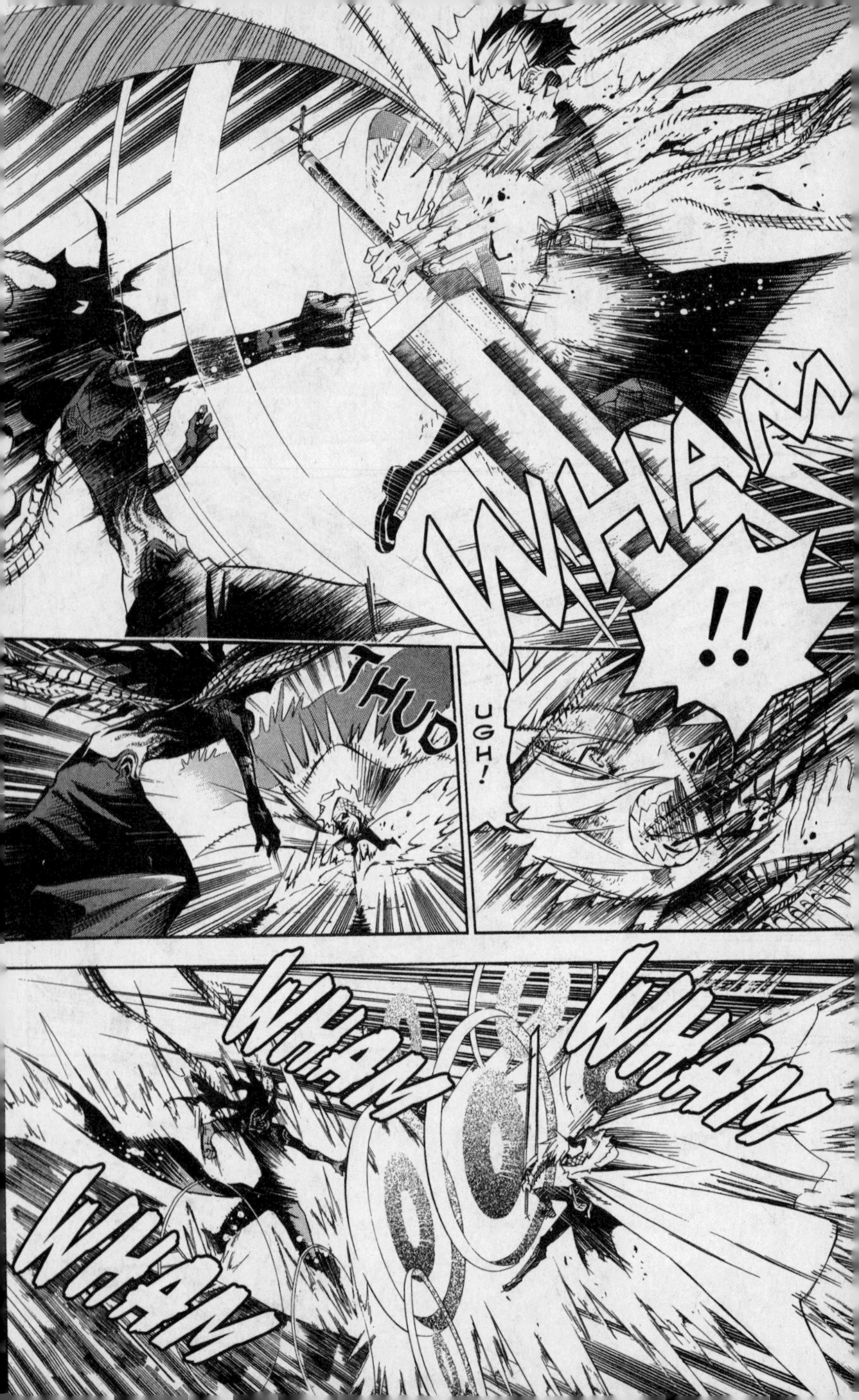
WHAM!!
UGH!
THUD
WHAM
WHAM
WHAM

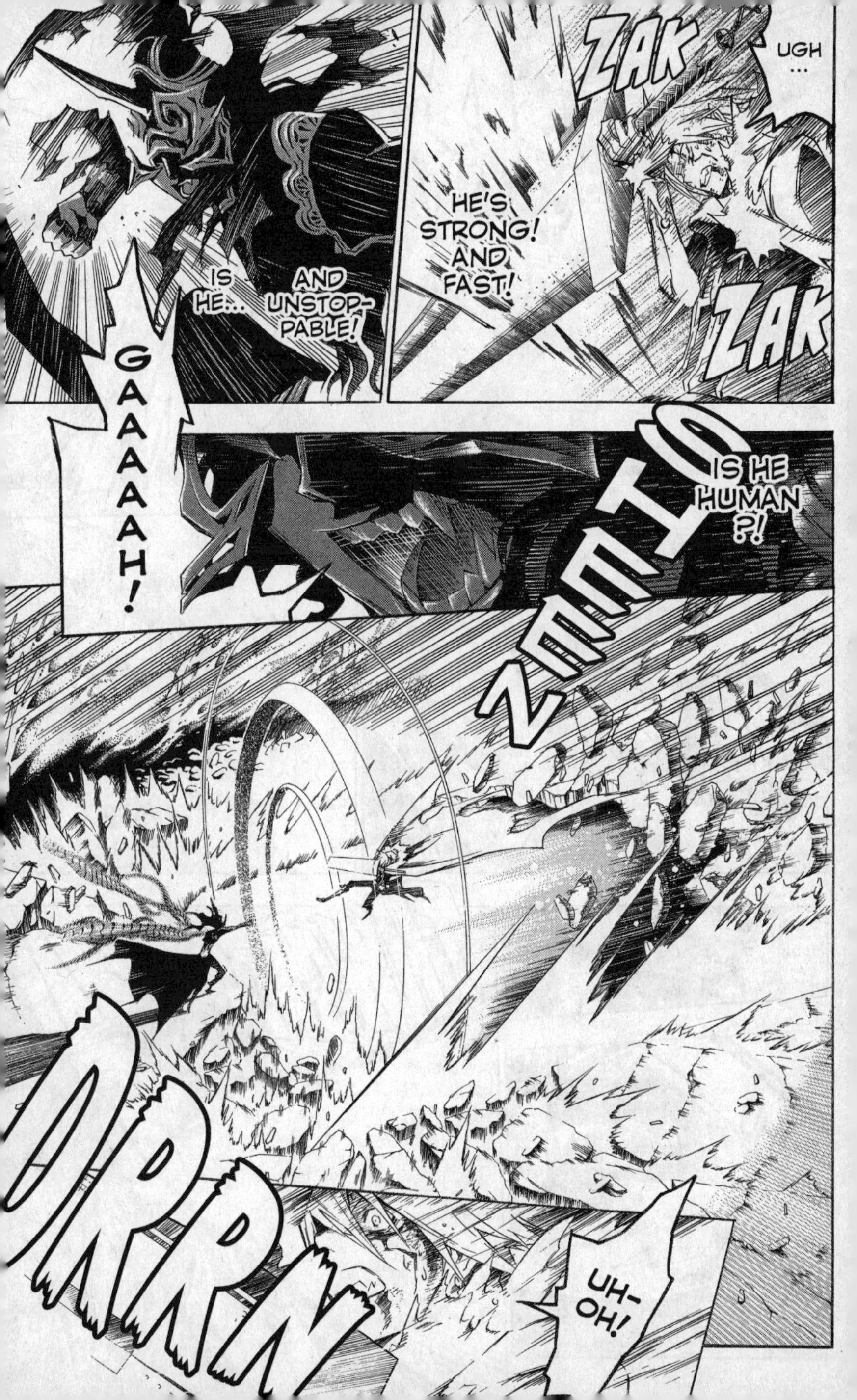
ZAK
UGH...
ZAK
HE'S STRONG! AND FAST!
AND UNSTOP-PABLE!
IS HE...
GAAAAAAH!
SHEEEN
IS HE HUMAN?!
ORRN
UH-OH!

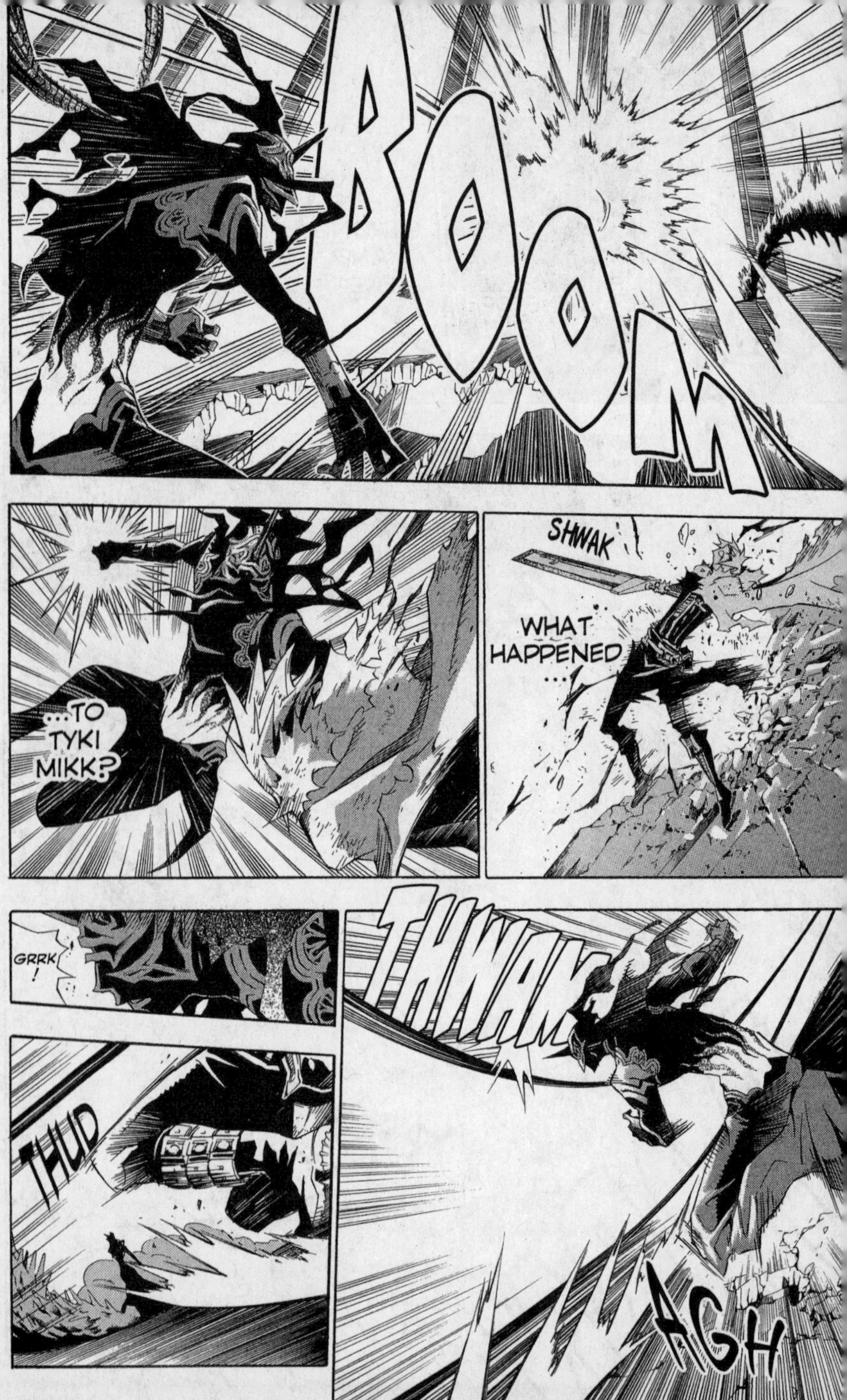
BOOM
SHWAK
WHAT HAPPENED...
...TO TYKI MIKK?
THWAK
AGH
GRRK!
THUD

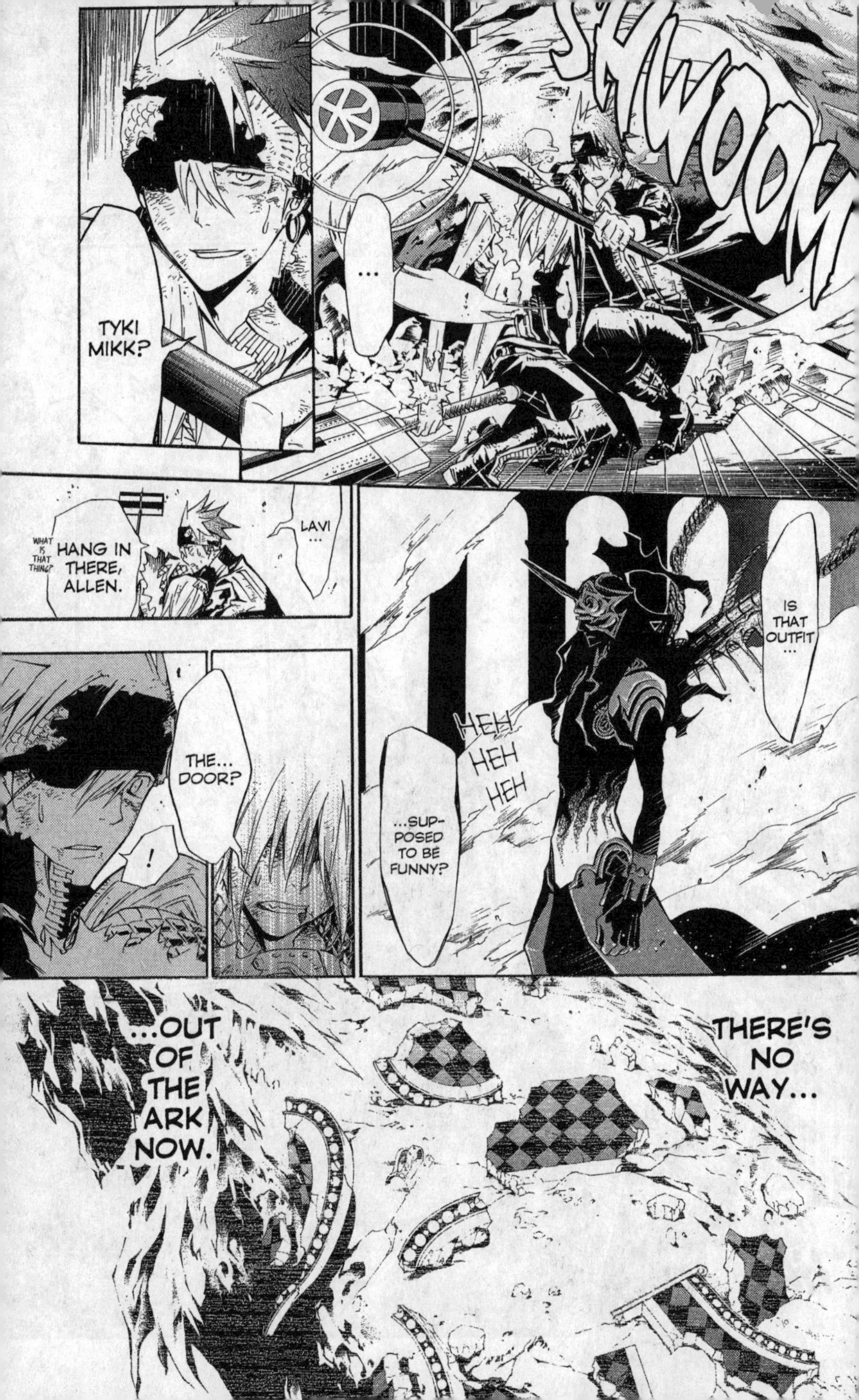
SHWOOM
...
TYKI MIKK?
IS THAT OUTFIT ...
HEH HEH HEH
...SUP-POSED TO BE FUNNY?
LAVI ...
HANG IN THERE, ALLEN.
WHAT IS THAT THING?
THE... DOOR?
!
THERE'S NO WAY...
...OUT OF THE ARK NOW.

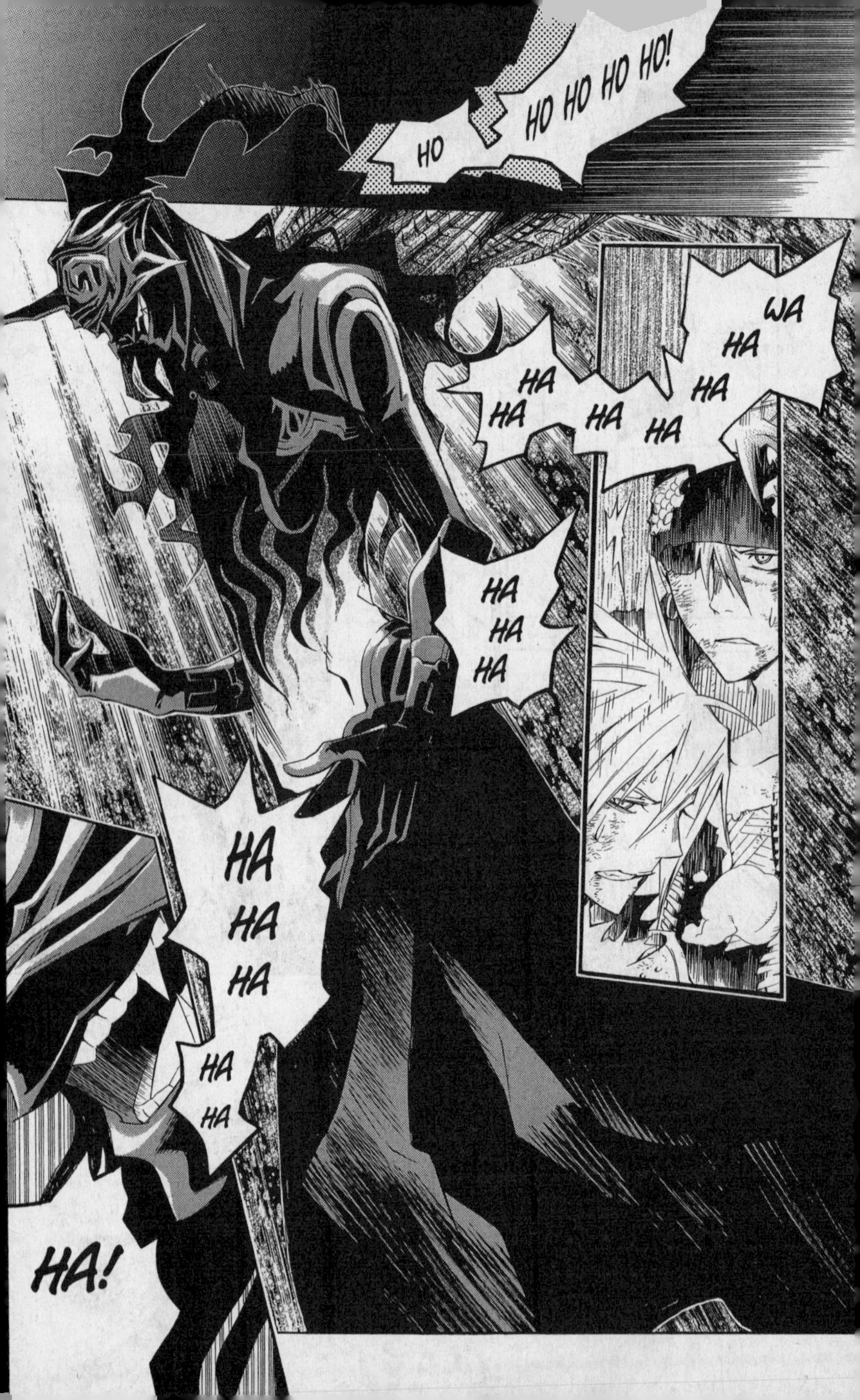
HO HO HO HO HO!
WA HA HA HA
HA HA HA
HA HA HA
HA HA HA
HA HA
HA!

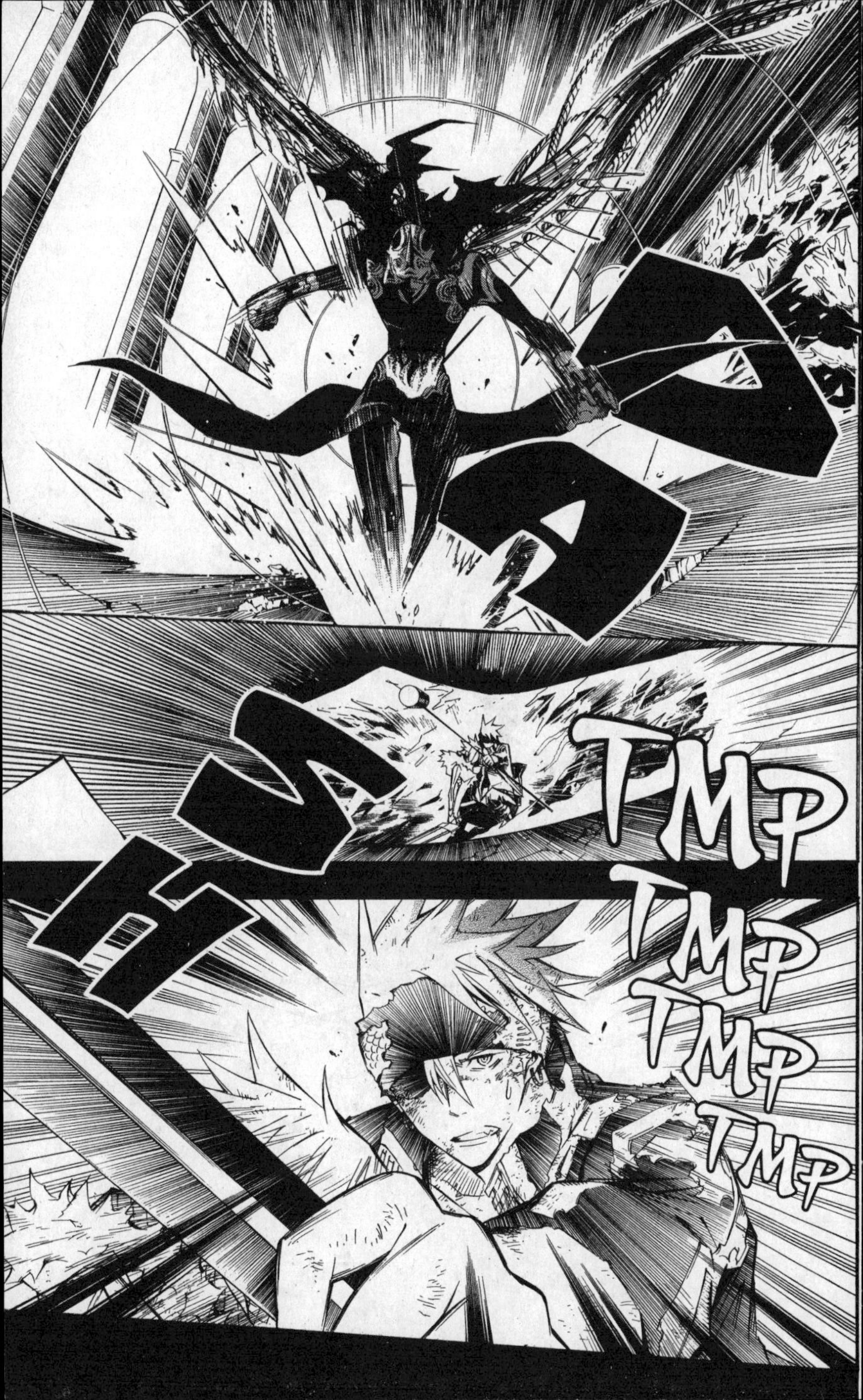
TMP
TMP
TMP
TMP

NOAH

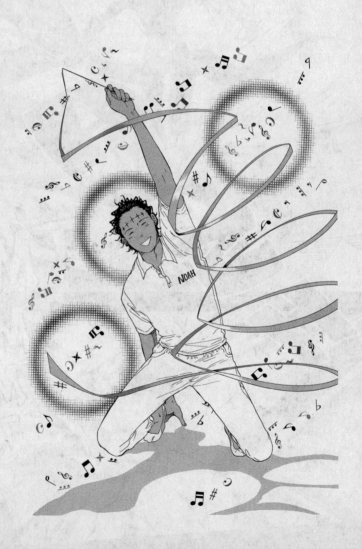

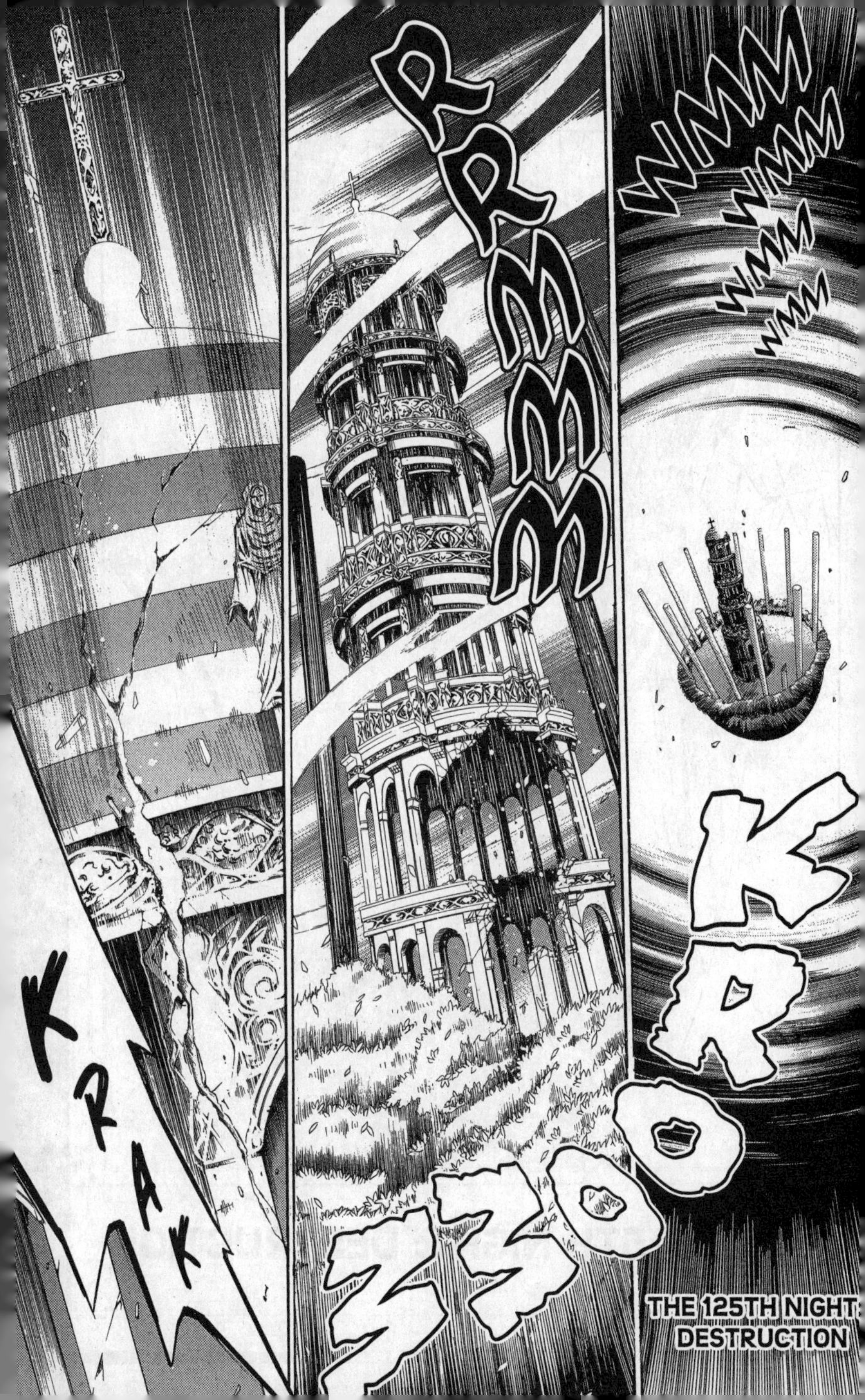
WMMM
WMMM
WMMM
WMMM
KROOMM
THE 125TH NIGHT:
DESTRUCTION
RRMMMM
KRAK

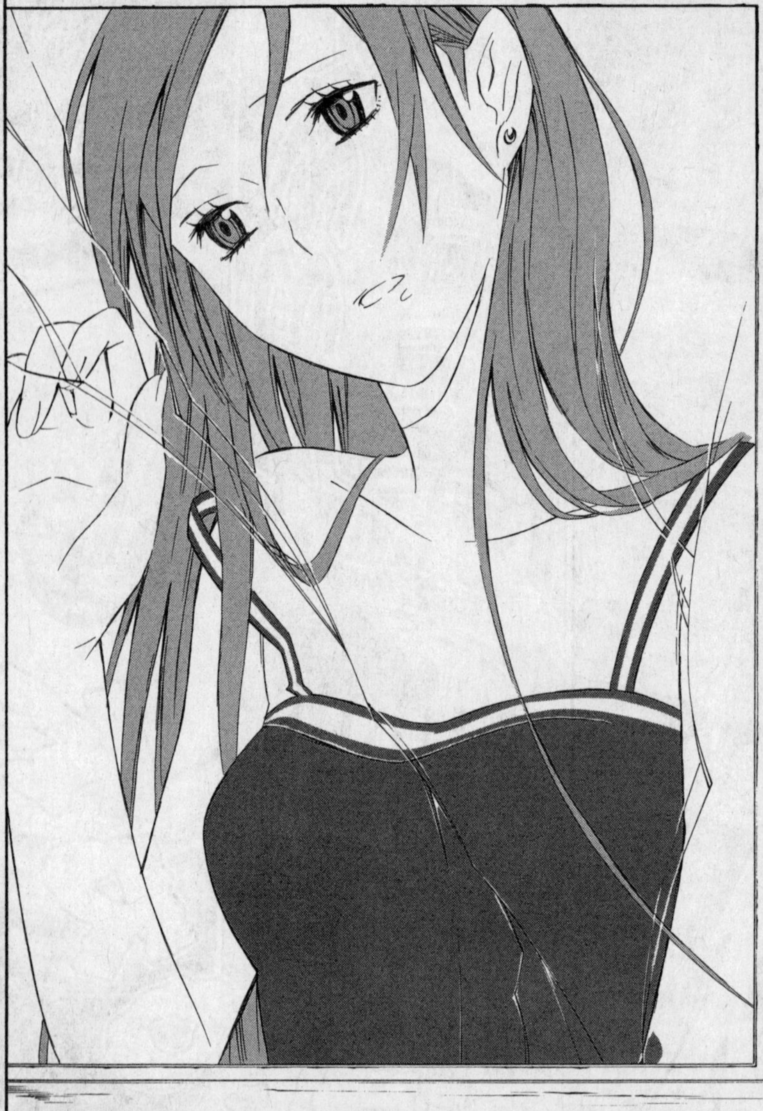

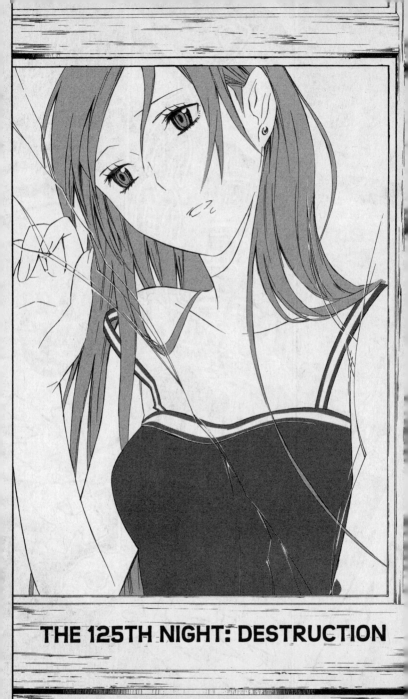

THE 125TH NIGHT: DESTRUCTION

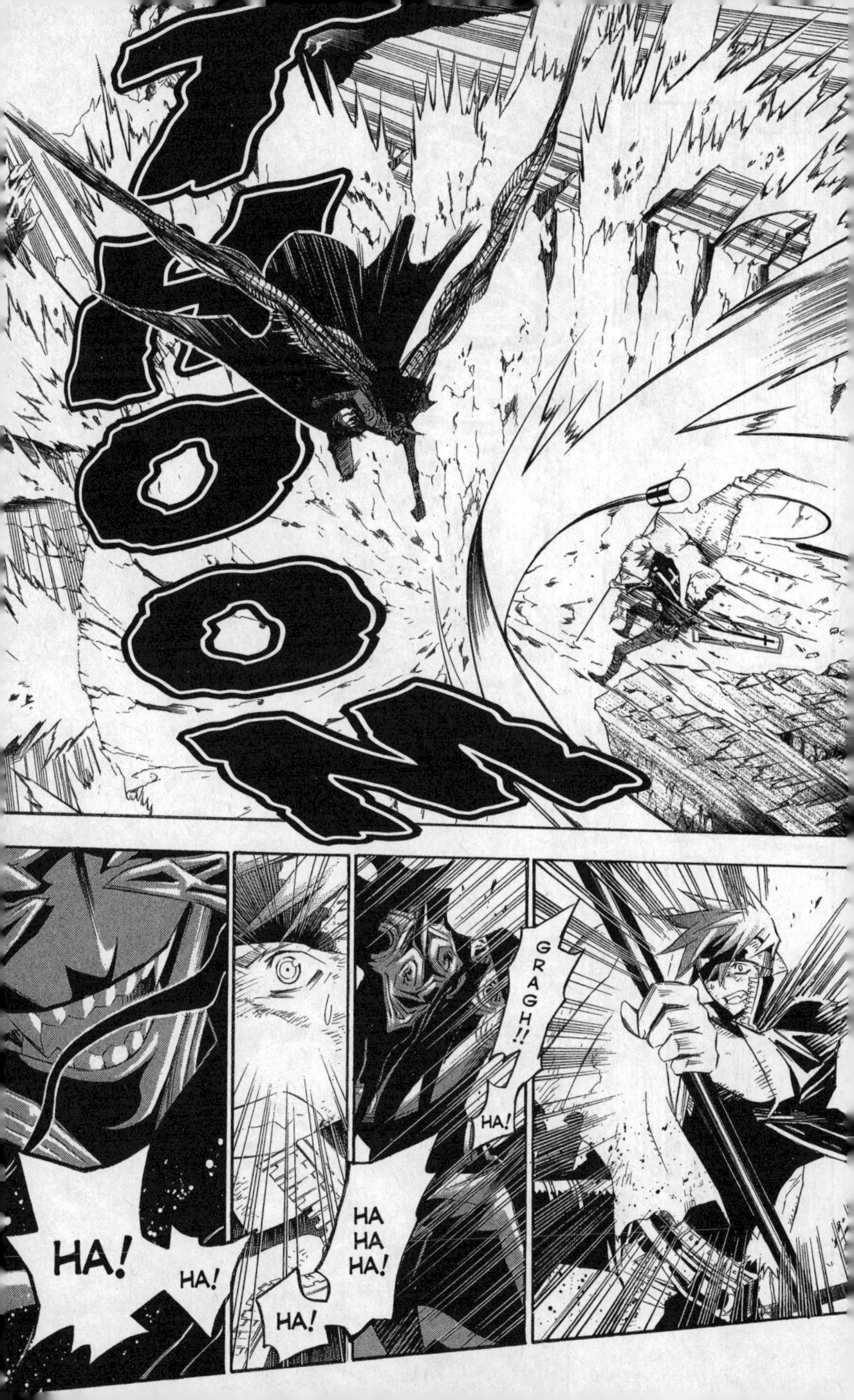
GRAGH!!
HA!
HA HA HA!
HA!
HA!
HA!

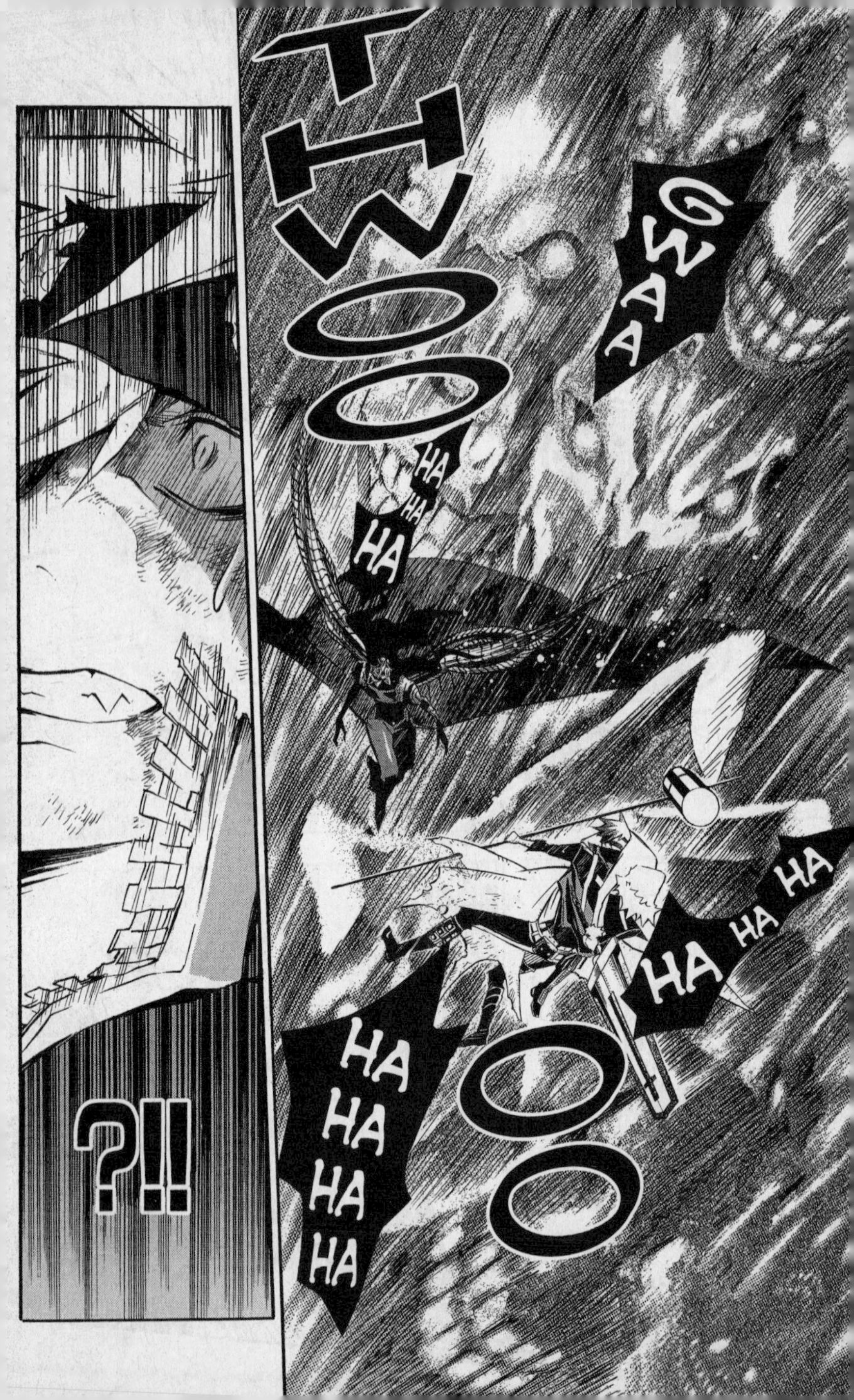
GWAA
FWOOOO
HA HA HA
HA HA HA HA
HA HA HA HA HA
?!!

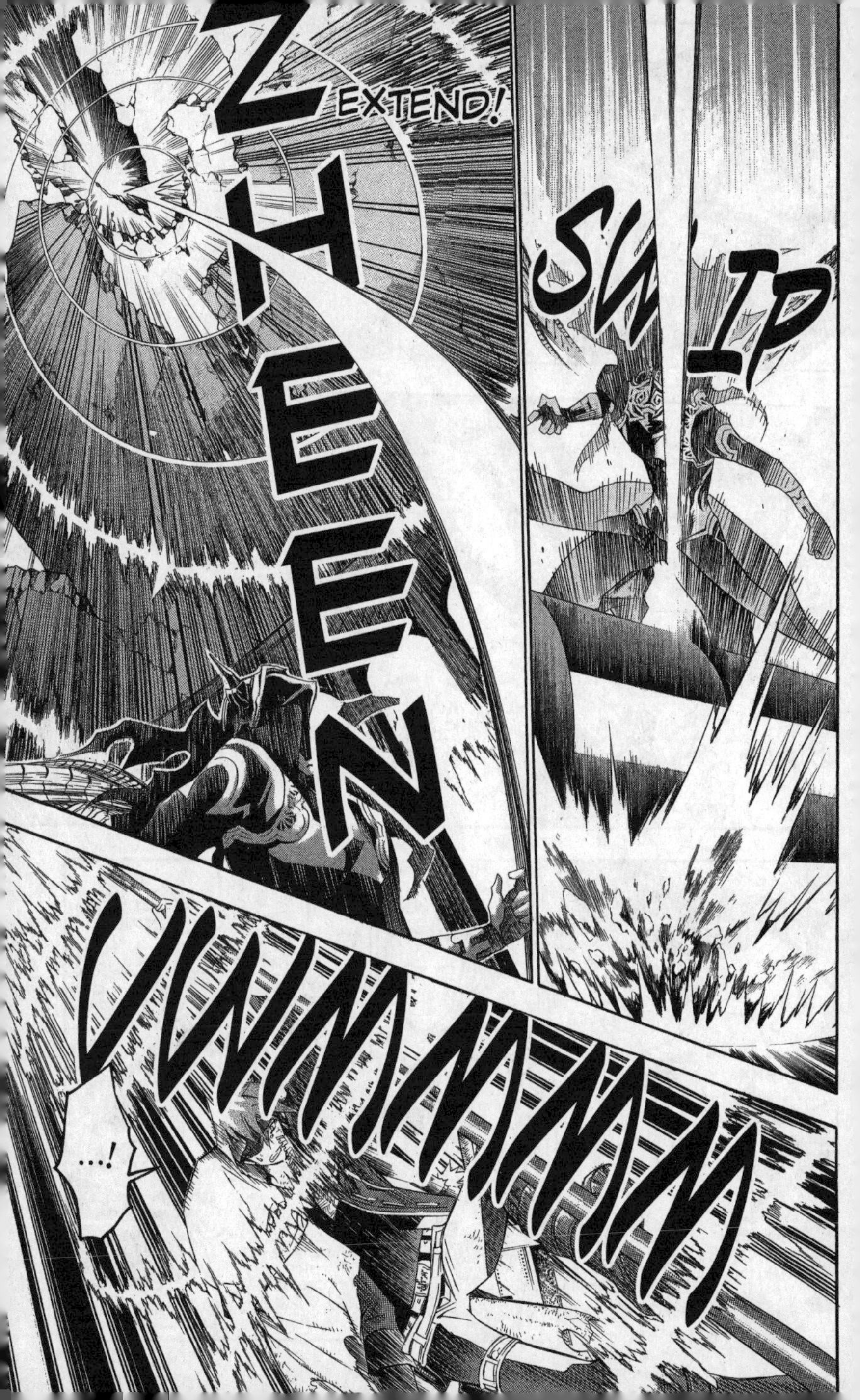
SWIP
EXTEND!
ZHEEEN
VWMMMMMM
...!

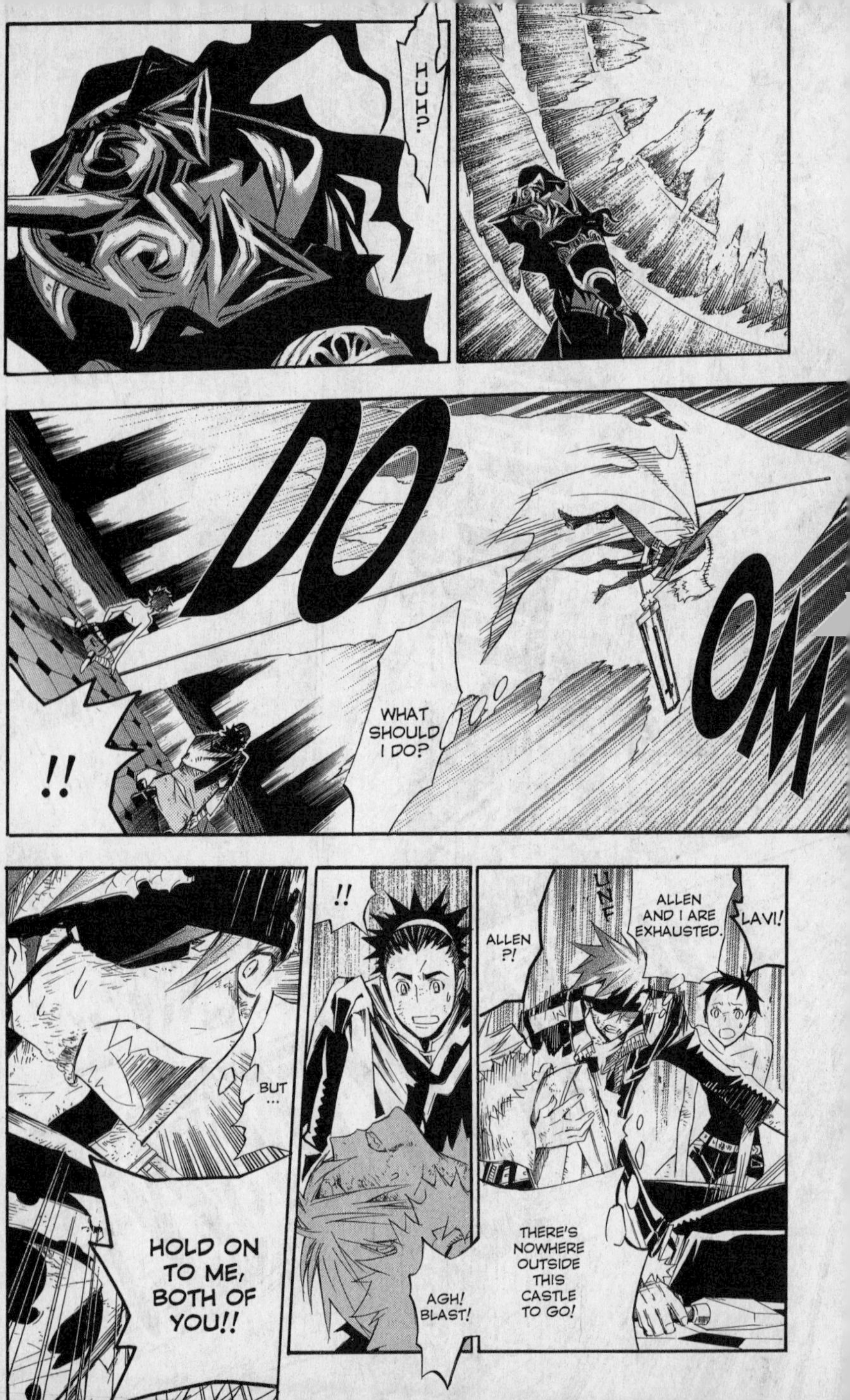
HUH?
DO
OM
WHAT SHOULD I DO?
!!
LAVI!
ALLEN AND I ARE EXHAUSTED.
ALLEN ?!
THERE'S NOWHERE OUTSIDE THIS CASTLE TO GO!
!!
AGH! BLAST!
BUT ...
HOLD ON TO ME, BOTH OF YOU!!

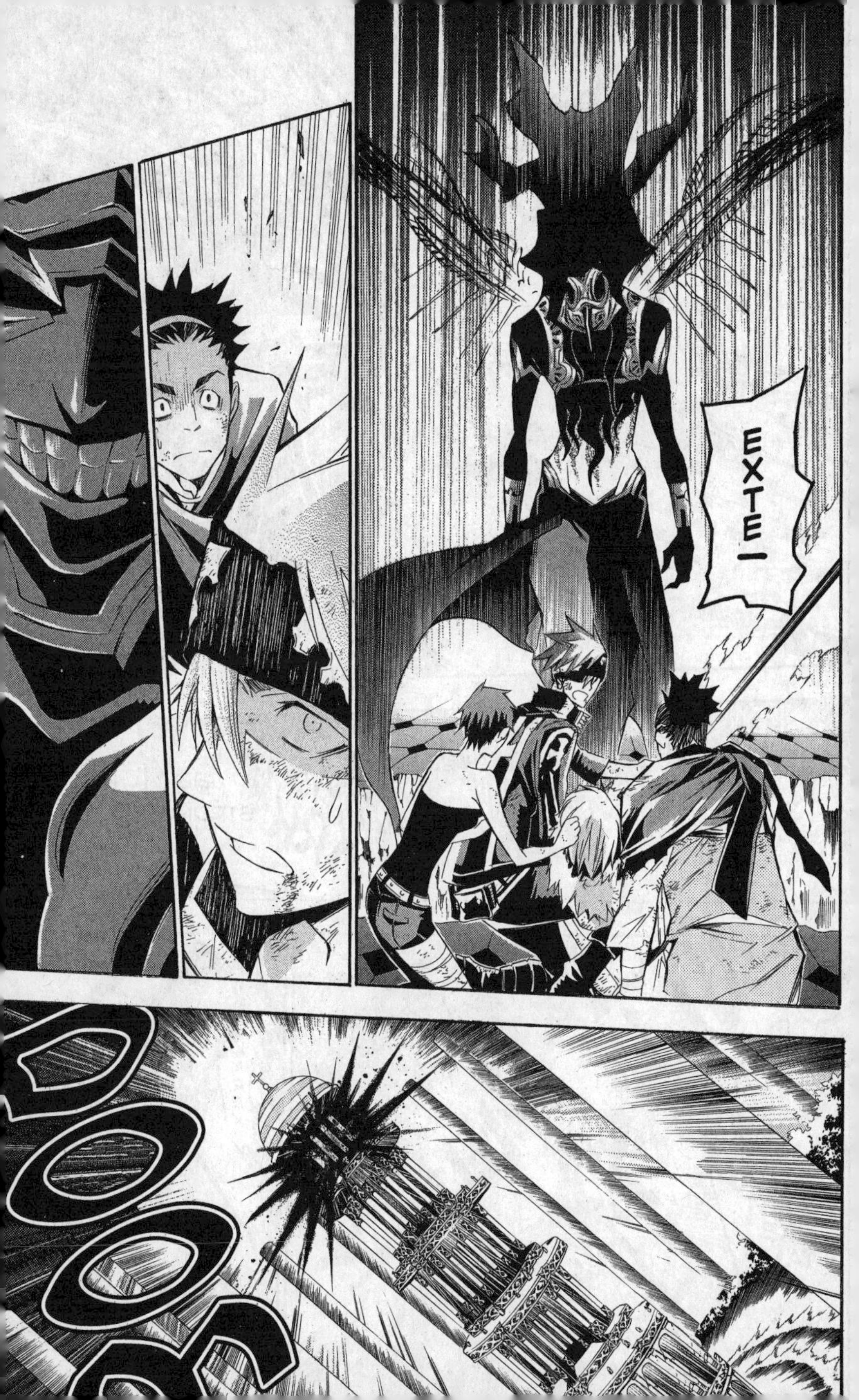
EXTE—

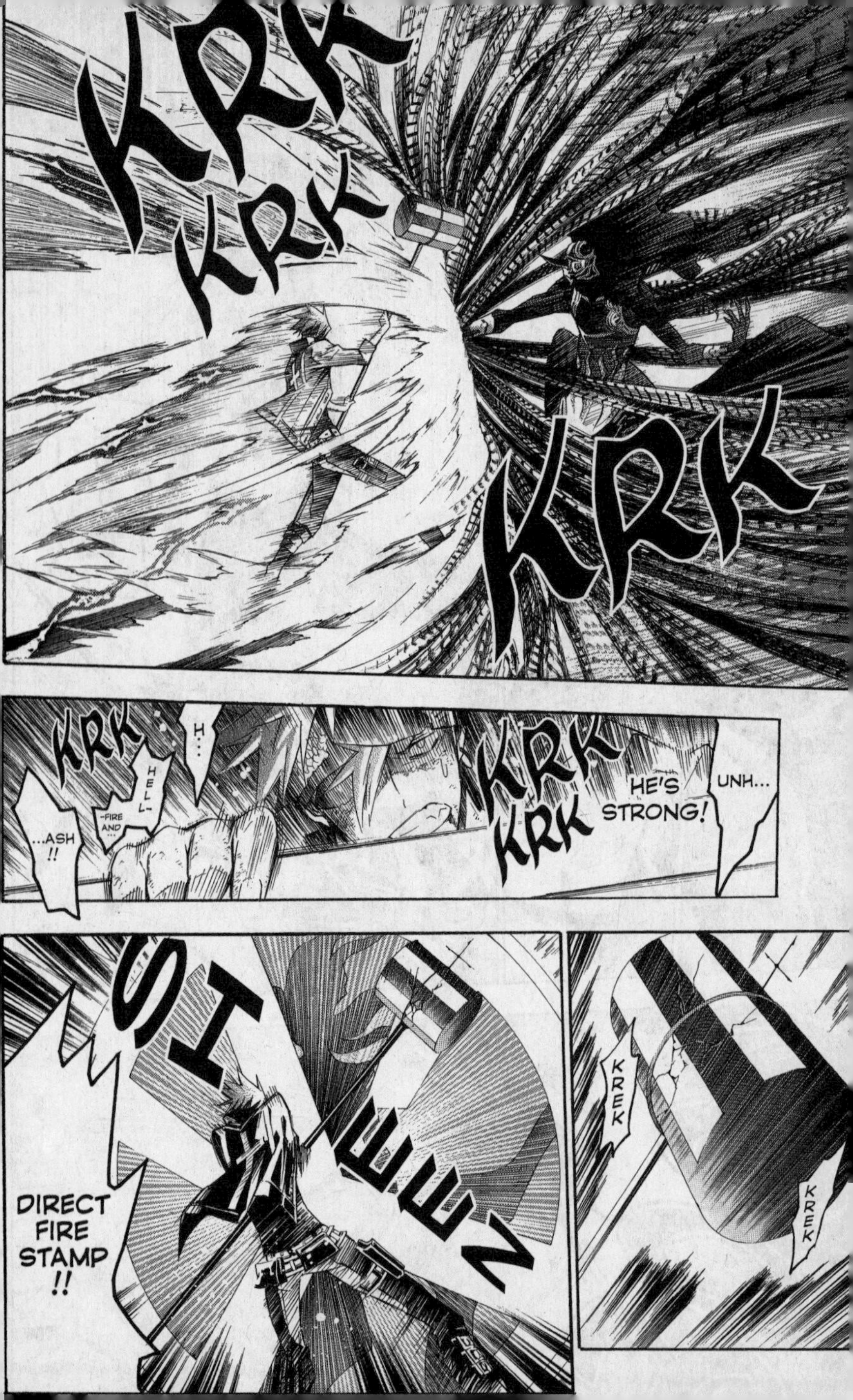
KRK KRK
KRK
UNH...
HE'S STRONG!
KRK KRK KRK
H... HELL- -FIRE AND... ...ASH!!
KRK
KREK
KREK
DIRECT FIRE STAMP!!

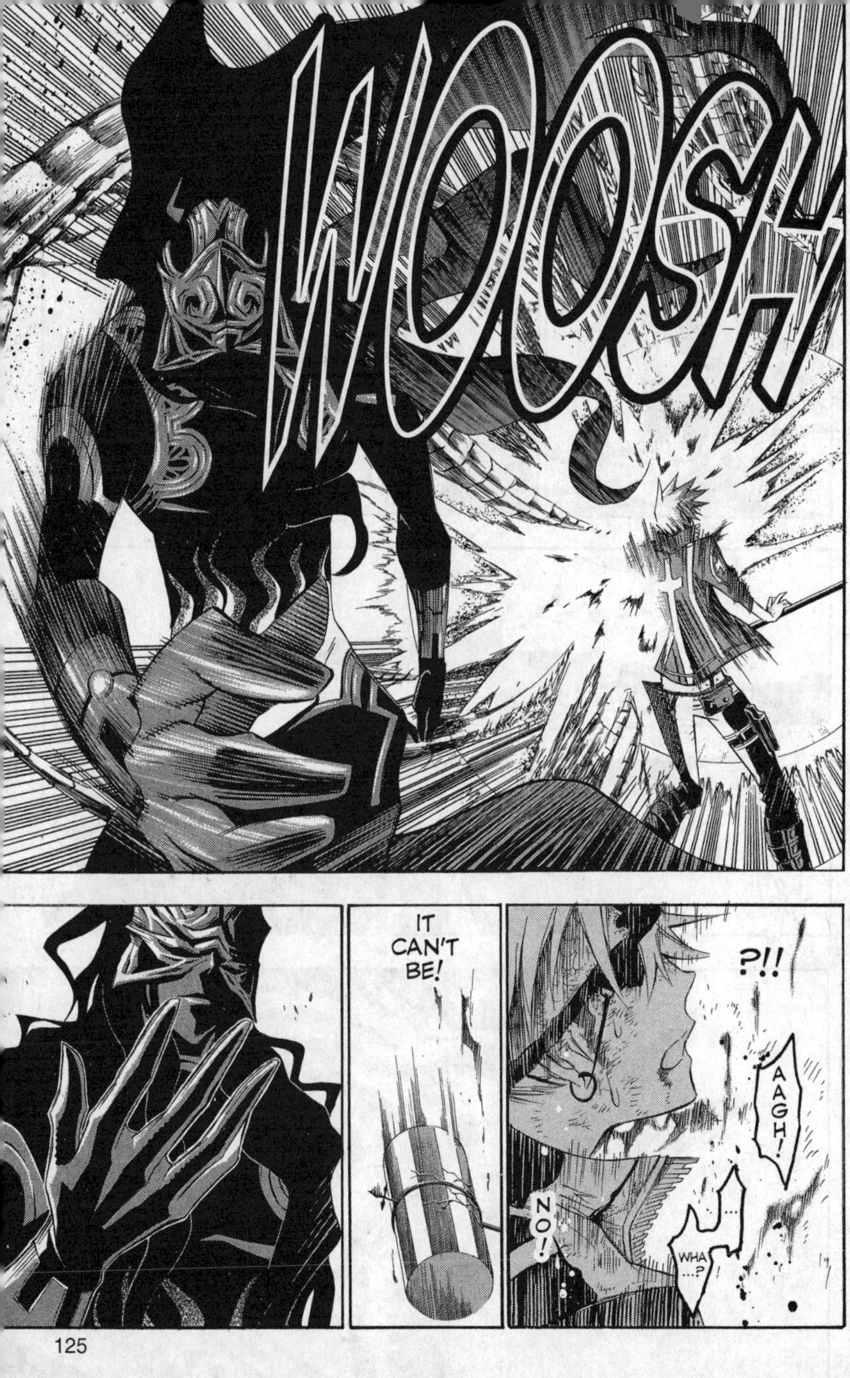
WOOSH
?!!
AAGH!
...
WHA...?
NO!
IT CAN'T BE!

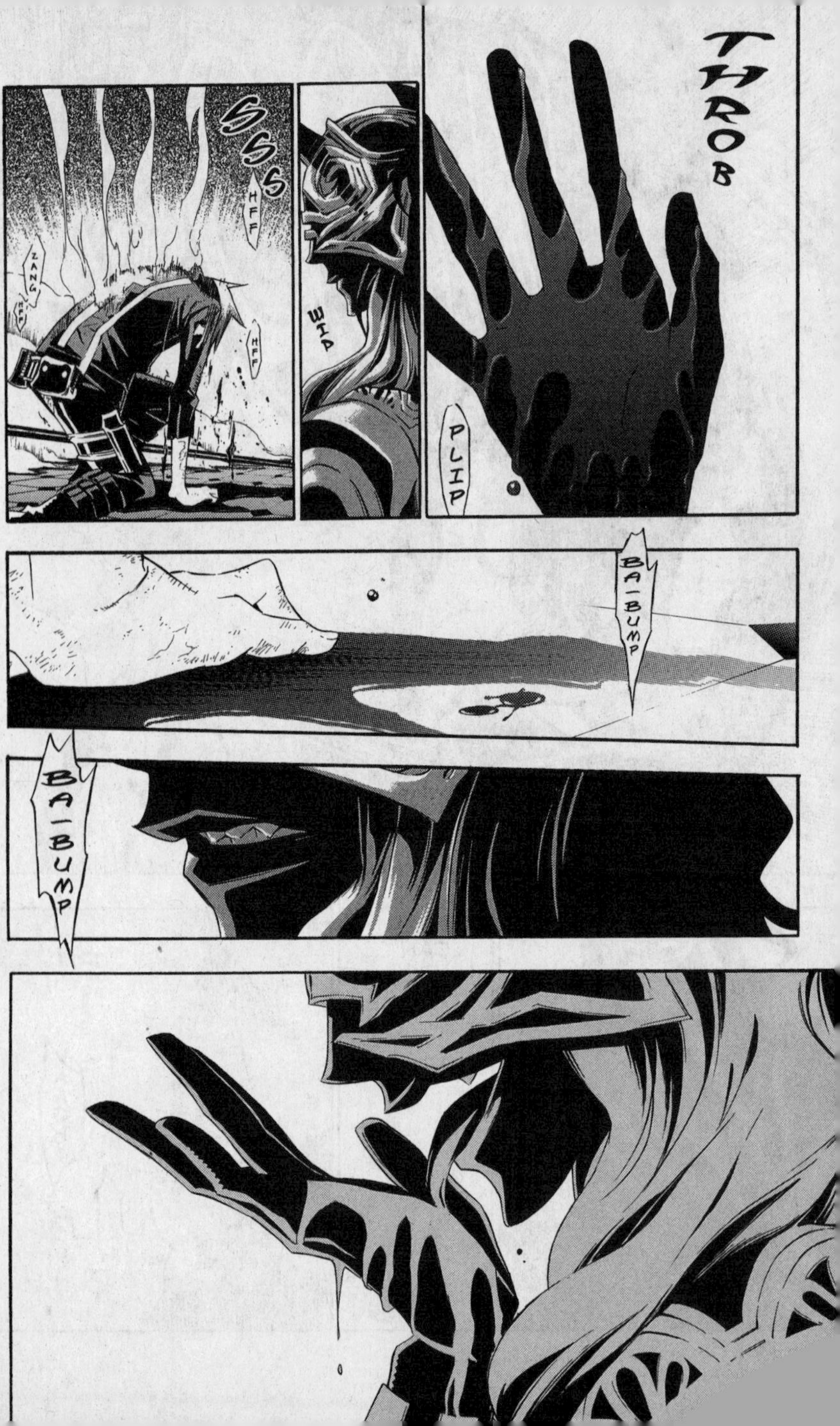
THROB
PLIP
WIP
SSS
HFF
ZANG
HFF
HFF
BA-BUMP
BA-BUMP

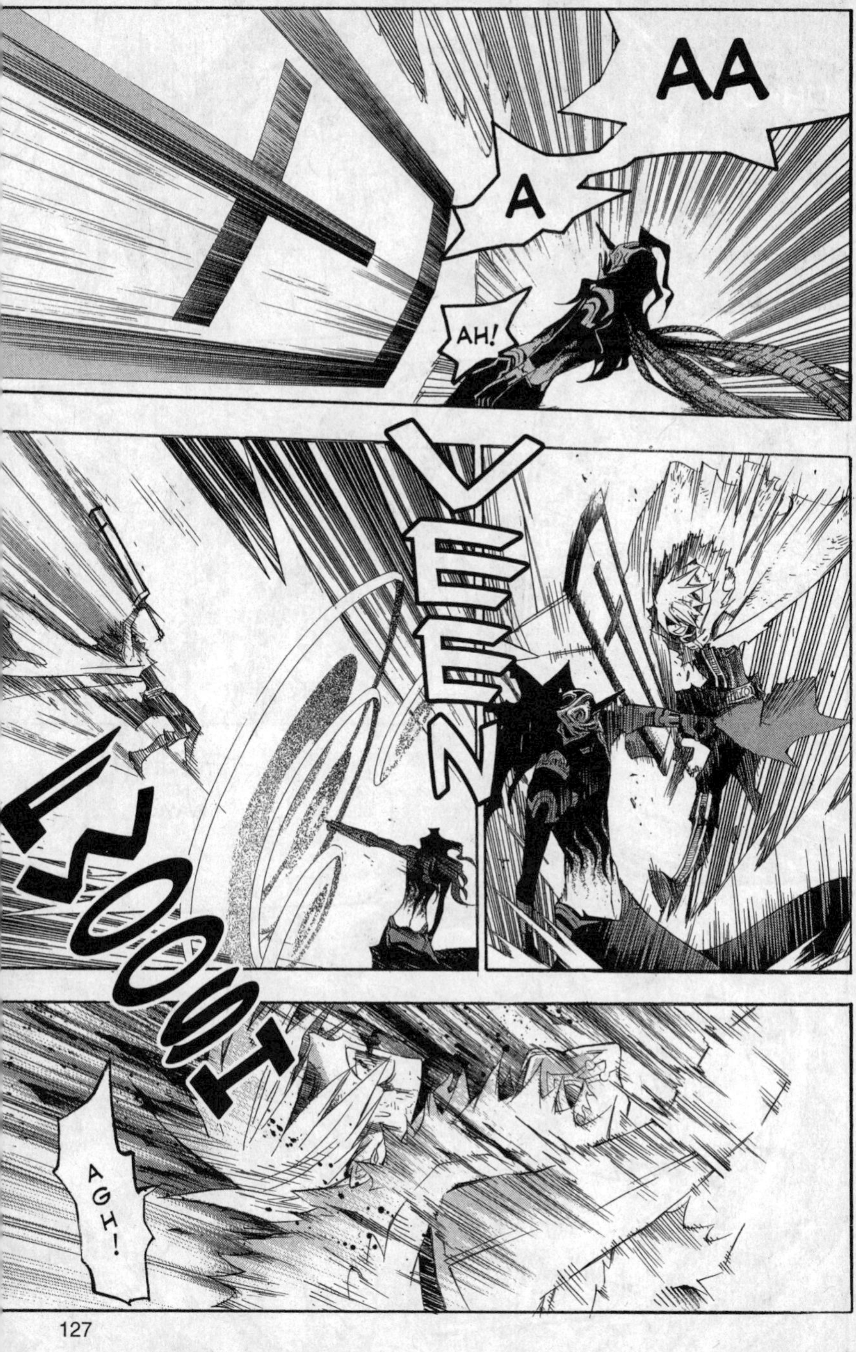
AA
A
AH!
VEEN
WOOOT
AGH!

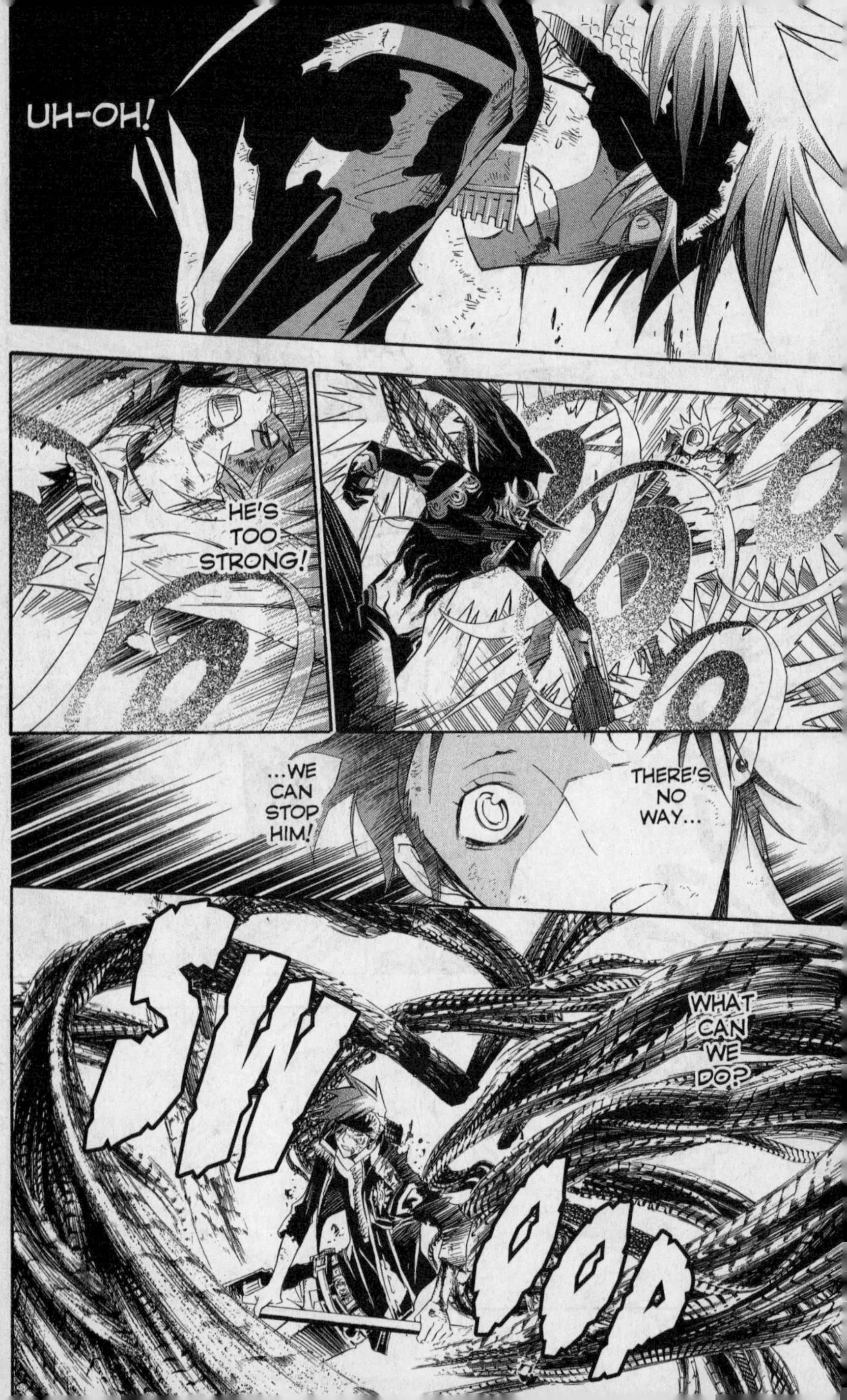
UH-OH!
HE'S TOO STRONG!
THERE'S NO WAY...
...WE CAN STOP HIM!
WHAT CAN WE DO?
SWOOP

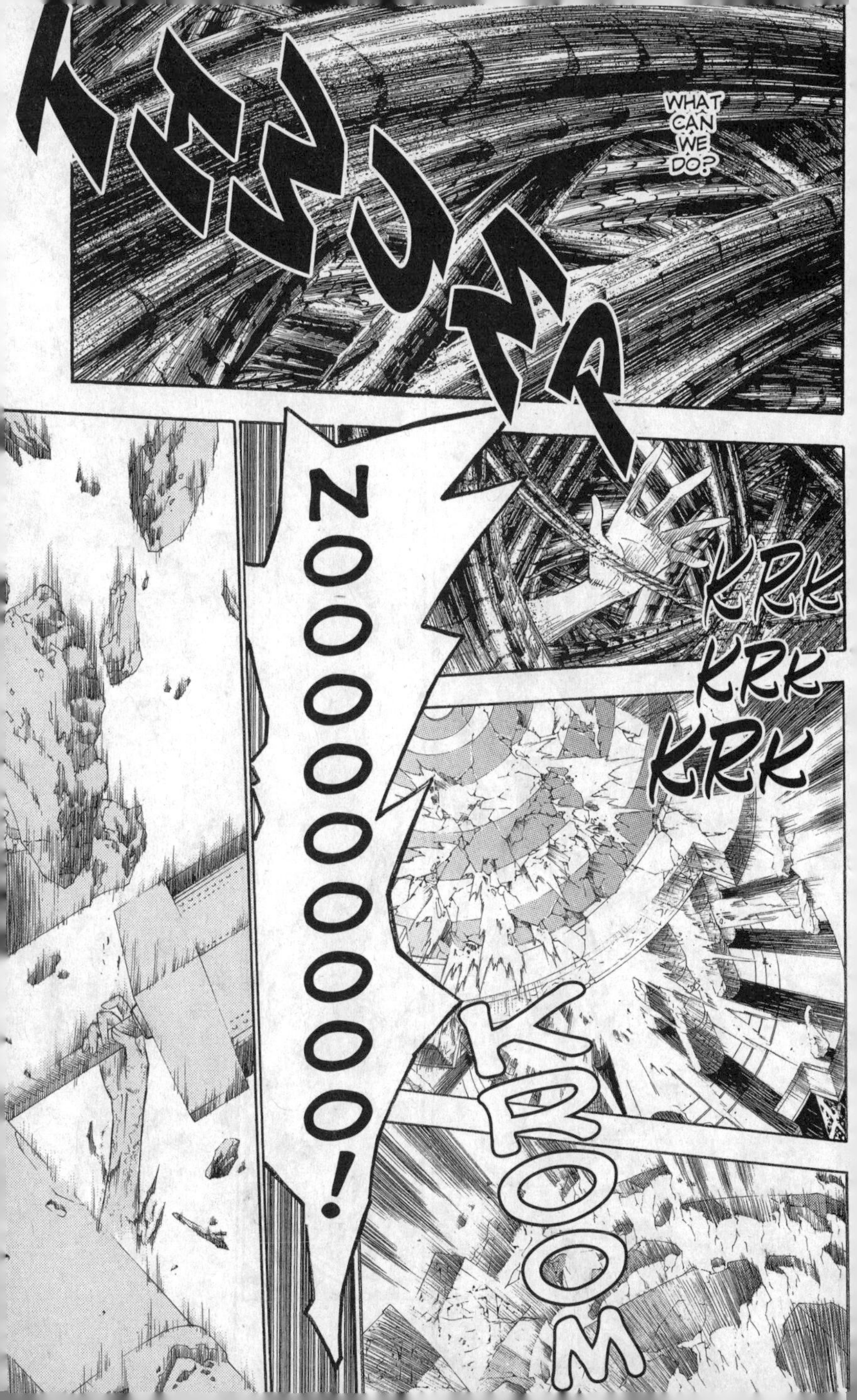
WHAT CAN WE DO?
KRK KRK KRK
NOOOOOOOOOO!
KROOM

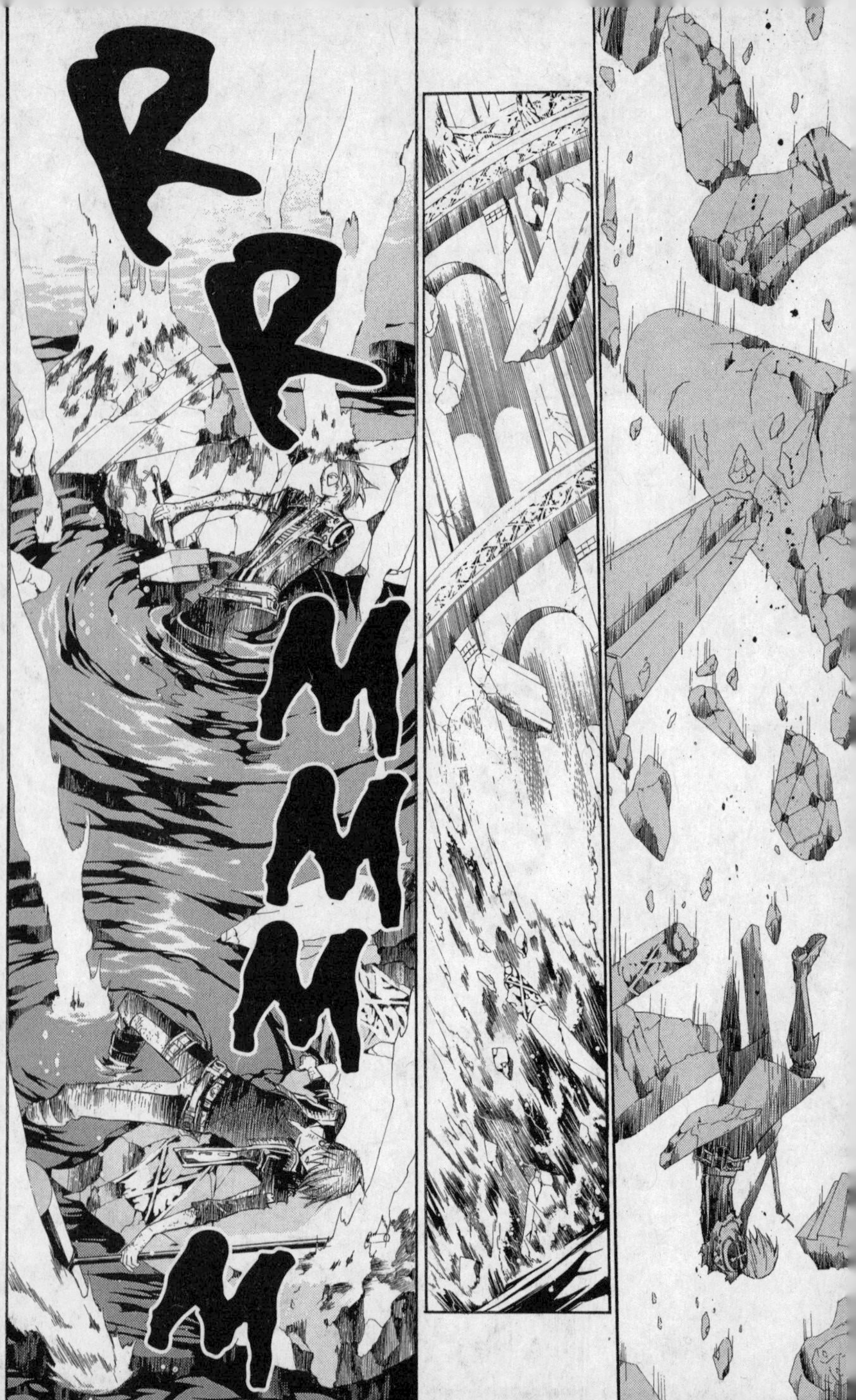
RRMMMM

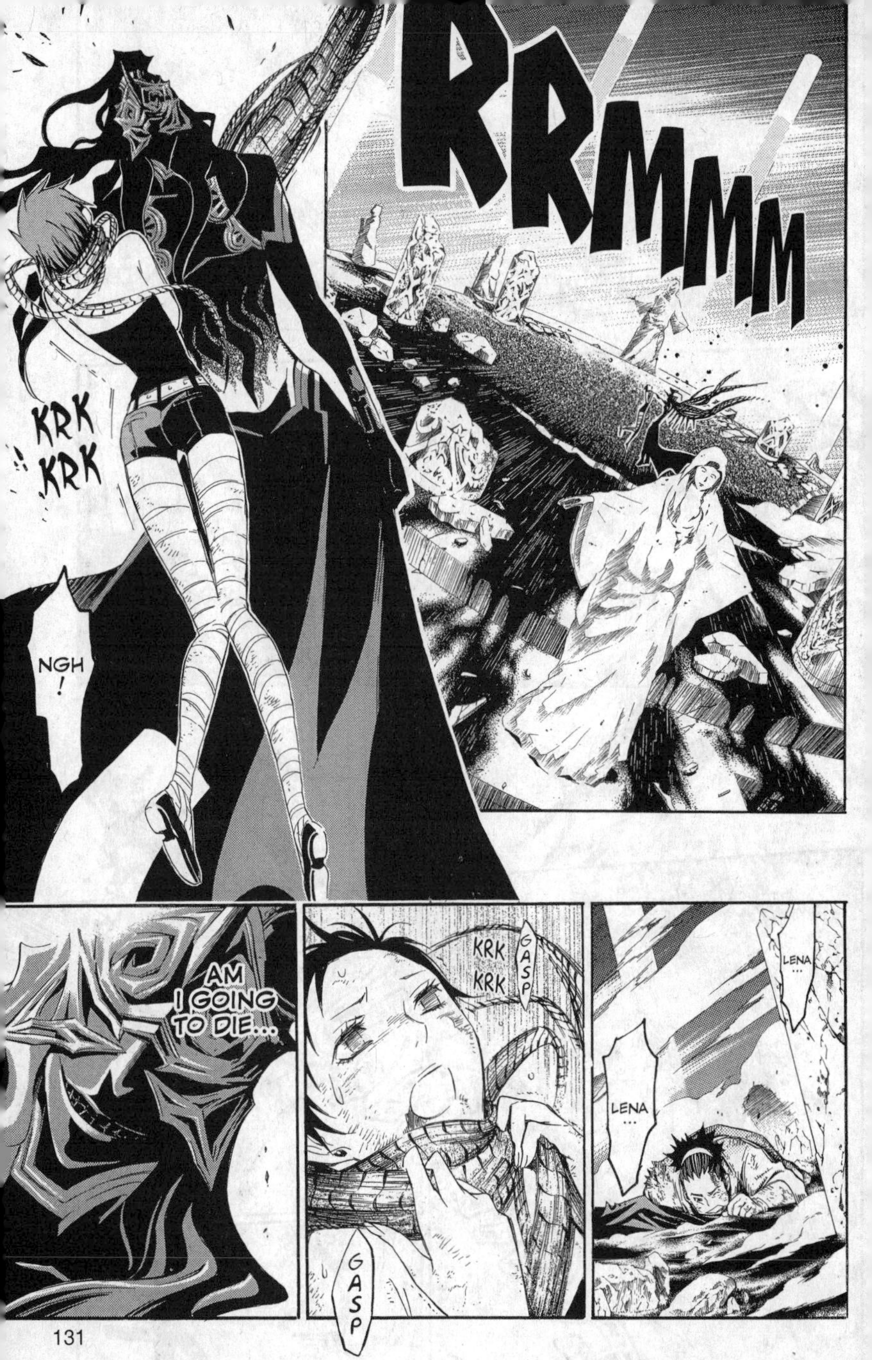
RRMMMM
KRK KRK
NGH!
LENA...
LENA...
GASP
KRK KRK
GASP
AM I GOING TO DIE...

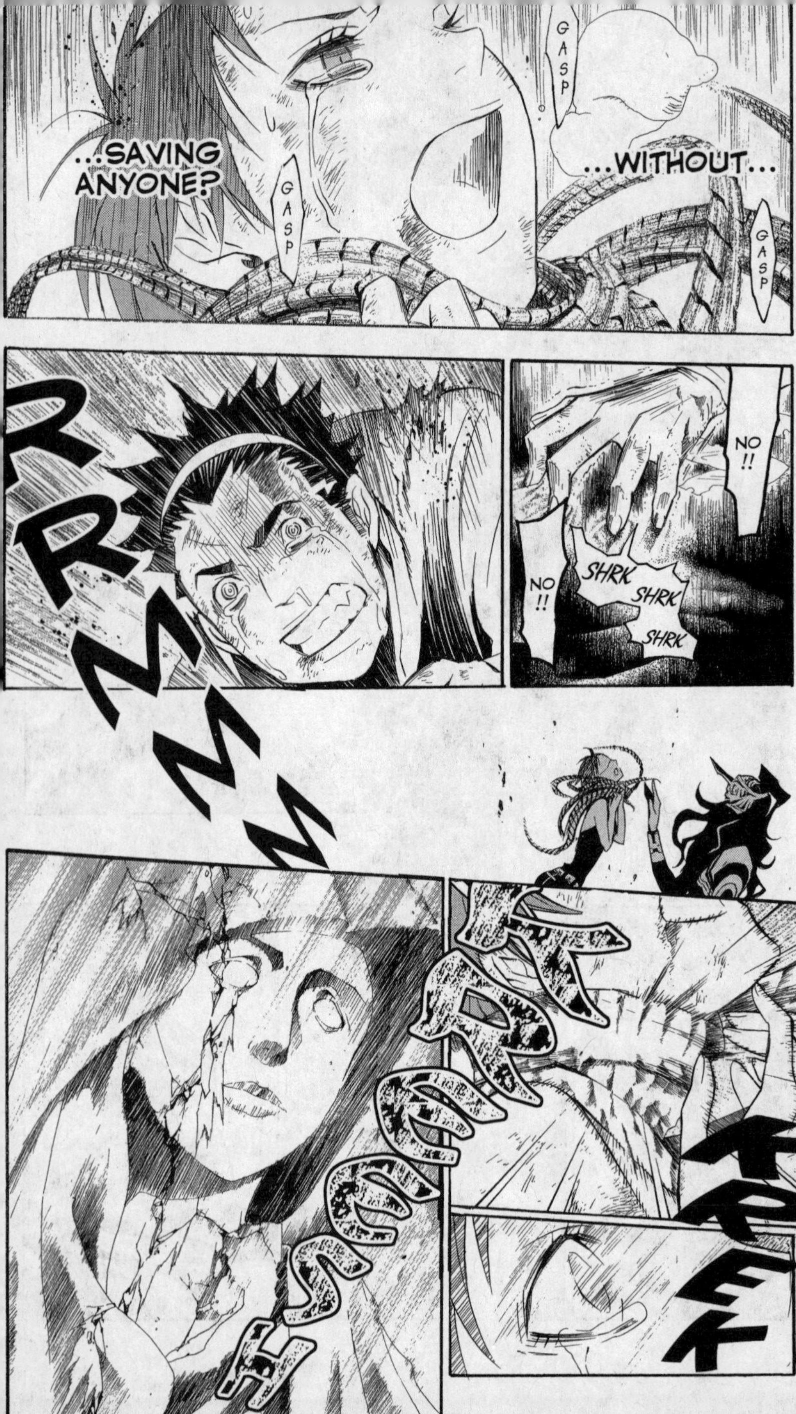
GASP
...WITHOUT...
GASP
GASP
...SAVING ANYONE?
NO!!
SHRK
SHRK
SHRK
NO!!
KREEK

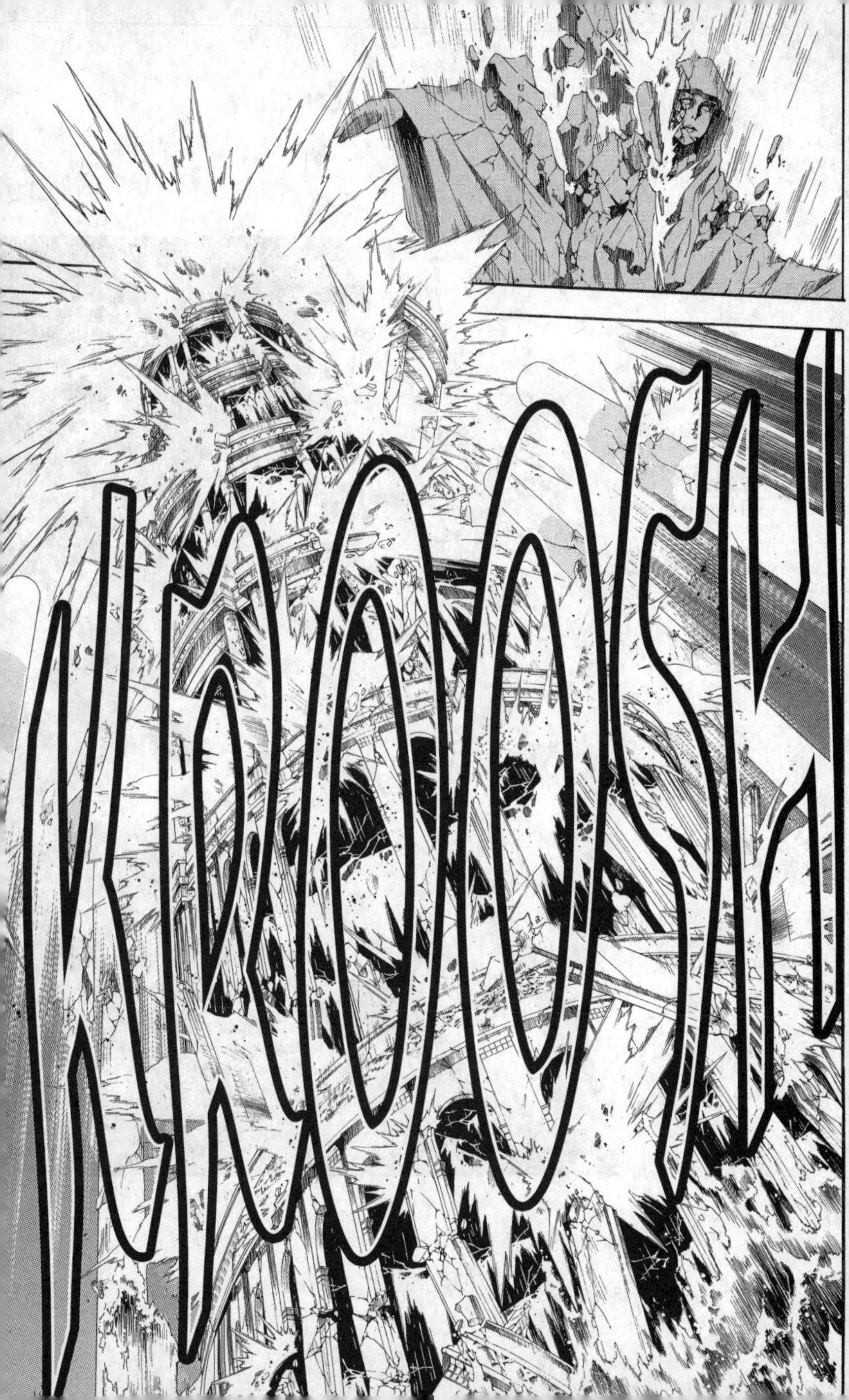
KRAOOOSH!

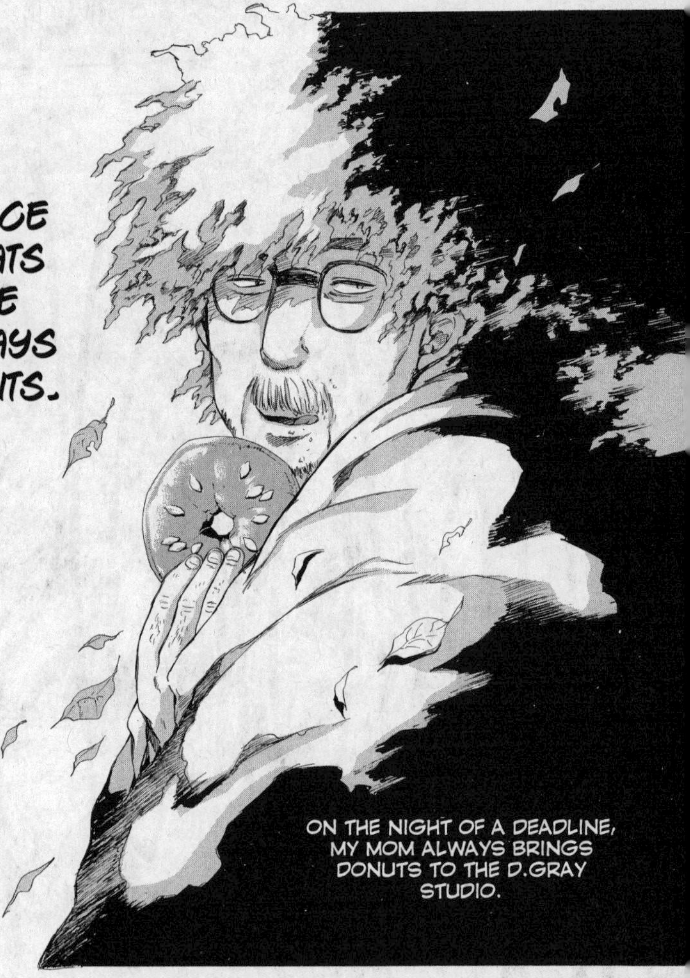
OFFICE TREATS ARE ALWAYS DONUTS.
ON THE NIGHT OF A DEADLINE, MY MOM ALWAYS BRINGS DONUTS TO THE D.GRAY STUDIO.

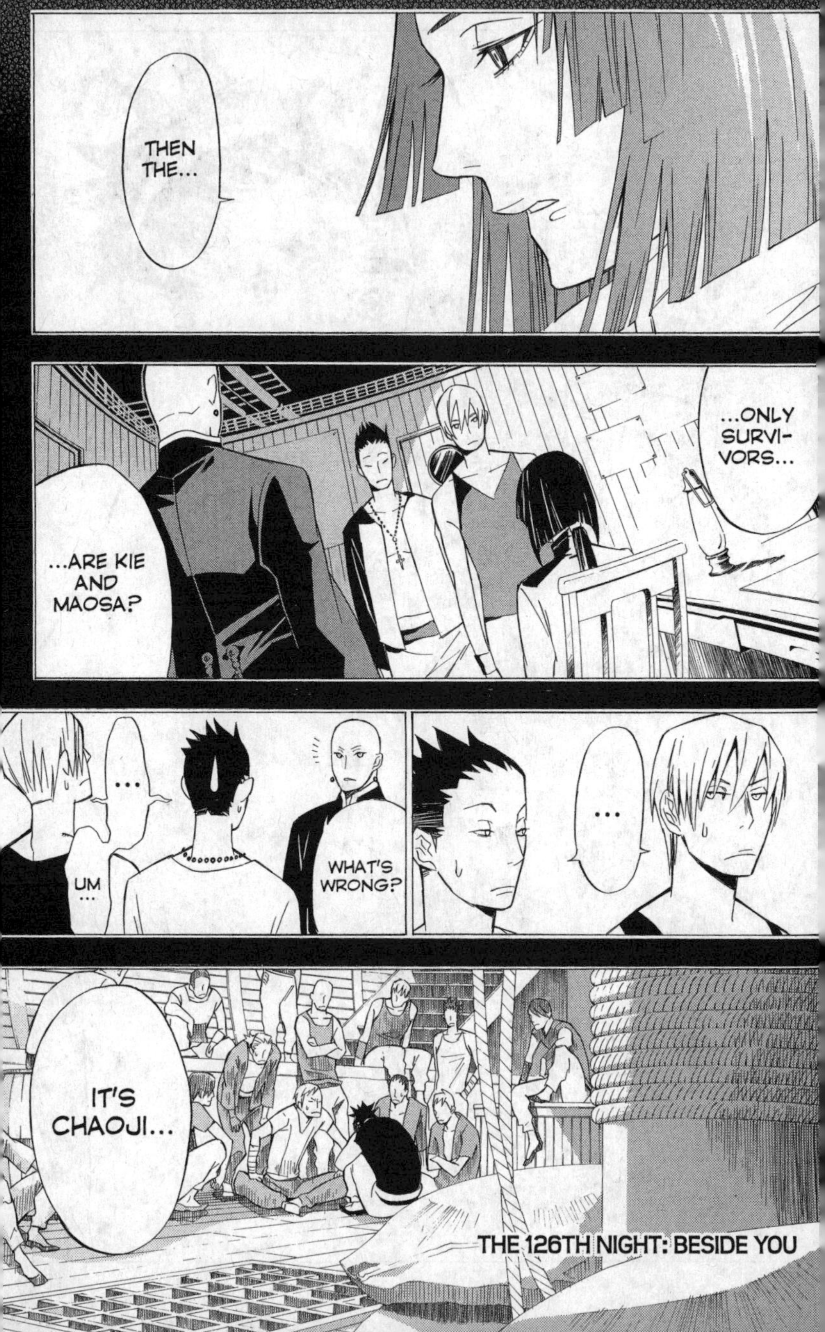
THEN THE...
...ONLY SURVIVORS...
...ARE KIE AND MAOSA?
...
...
UM ...
WHAT'S WRONG?
IT'S CHAOJI...
THE 126TH NIGHT: BESIDE YOU

THE 126TH NIGHT: BESIDE YOU

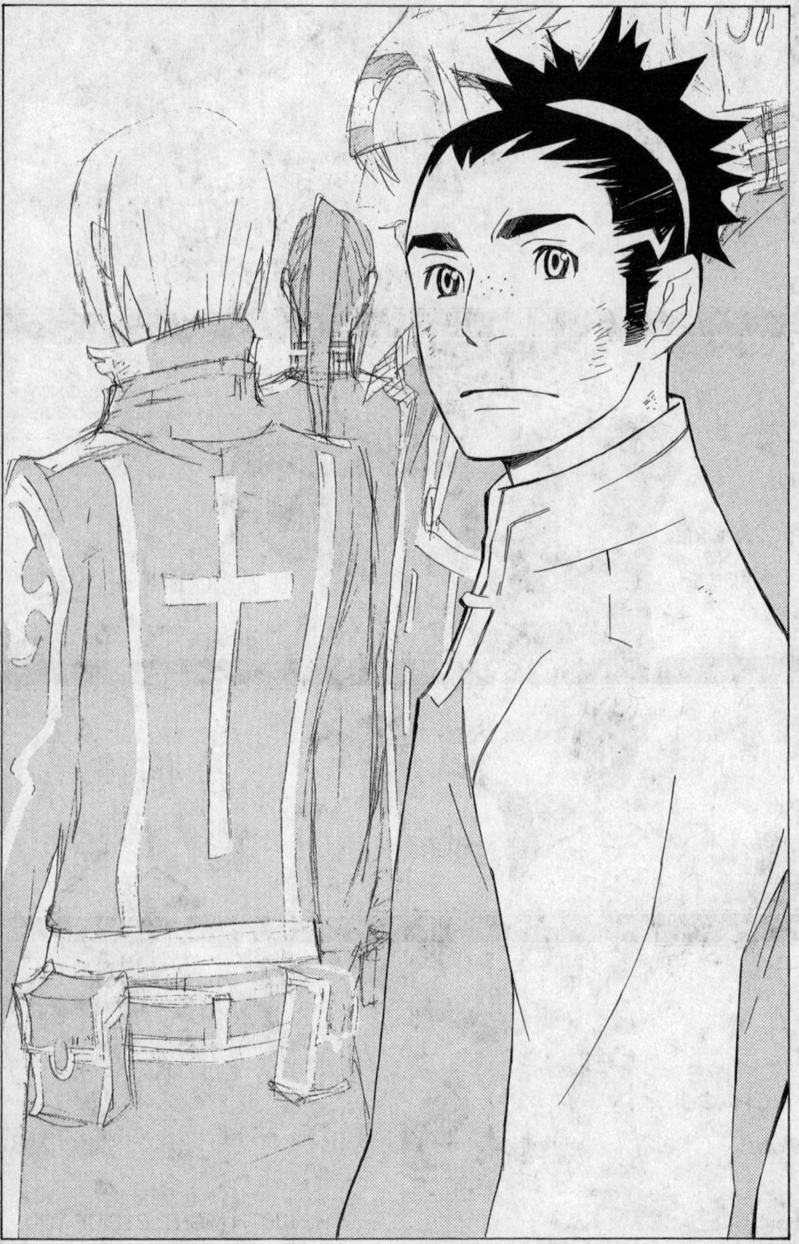

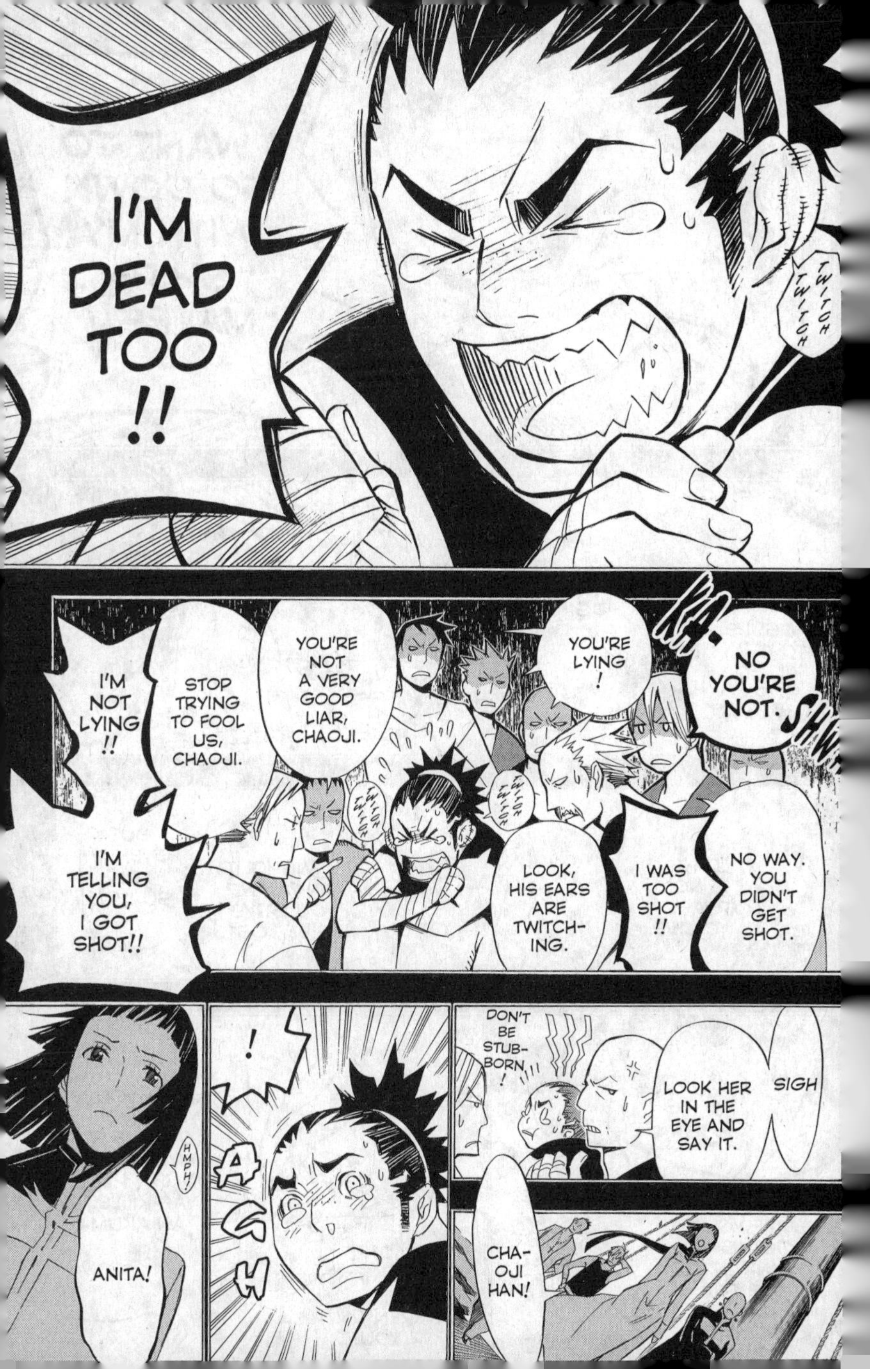
I'M DEAD TOO!!
TWITCH TWITCH
NO YOU'RE NOT.
YOU'RE LYING!
YOU'RE NOT A VERY GOOD LIAR, CHAOJI.
STOP TRYING TO FOOL US, CHAOJI.
I'M NOT LYING!!
NO WAY. YOU DIDN'T GET SHOT.
I WAS TOO SHOT!!
LOOK, HIS EARS ARE TWITCH-ING.
I'M TELLING YOU, I GOT SHOT!!
SIGH
LOOK HER IN THE EYE AND SAY IT.
DON'T BE STUB-BORN!
CHA-OJI HAN!
!
AGH
HMPH!
ANITA!

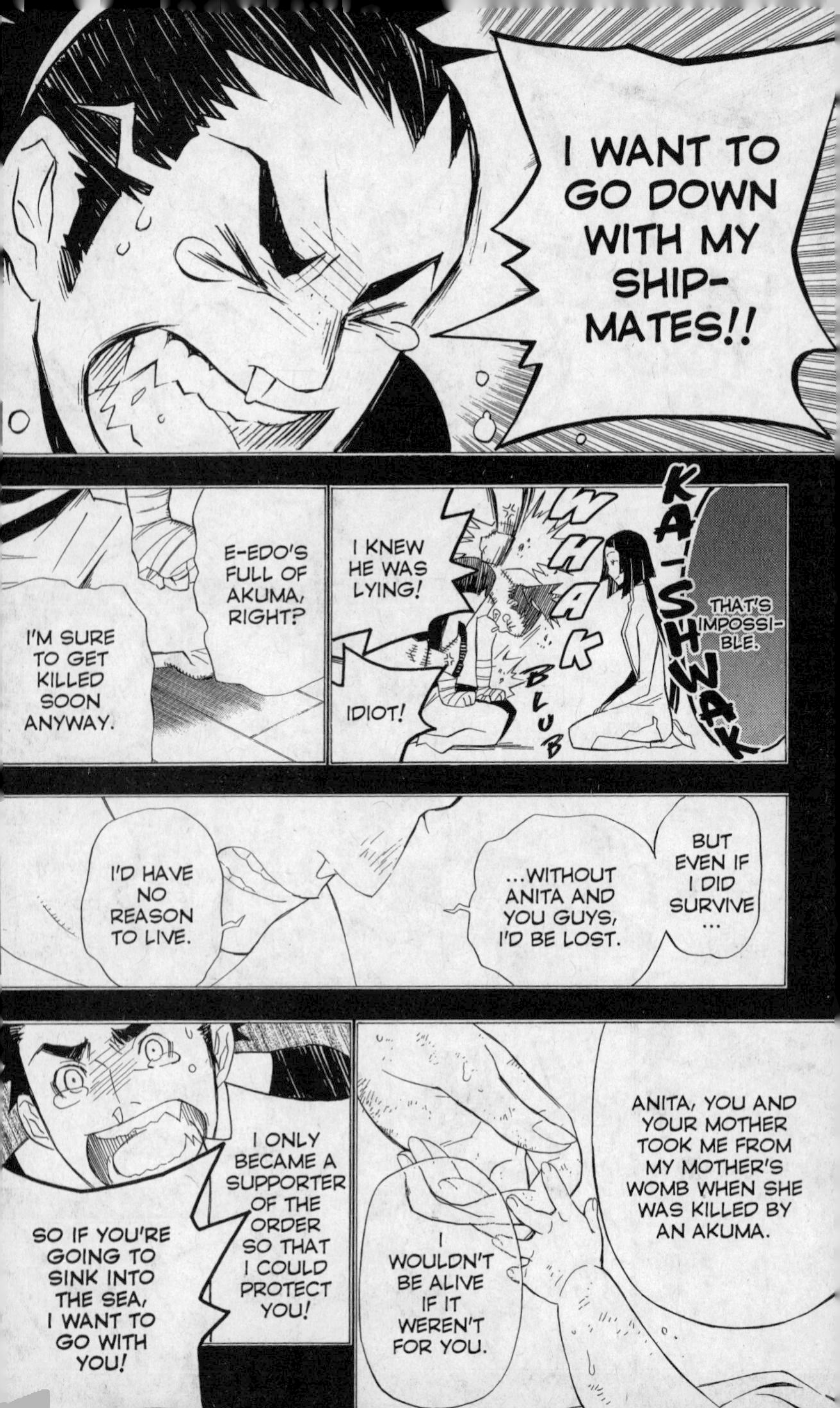
I WANT TO GO DOWN WITH MY SHIP-MATES!!
THAT'S IMPOSSIBLE.
KA-SHWAK
WHAK
I KNEW HE WAS LYING!
BLUB
IDIOT!
E-EDO'S FULL OF AKUMA, RIGHT?
I'M SURE TO GET KILLED SOON ANYWAY.
BUT EVEN IF I DID SURVIVE ...
...WITHOUT ANITA AND YOU GUYS, I'D BE LOST.
I'D HAVE NO REASON TO LIVE.
ANITA, YOU AND YOUR MOTHER TOOK ME FROM MY MOTHER'S WOMB WHEN SHE WAS KILLED BY AN AKUMA.
I WOULDN'T BE ALIVE IF IT WEREN'T FOR YOU.
I ONLY BECAME A SUPPORTER OF THE ORDER SO THAT I COULD PROTECT YOU!
SO IF YOU'RE GOING TO SINK INTO THE SEA, I WANT TO GO WITH YOU!

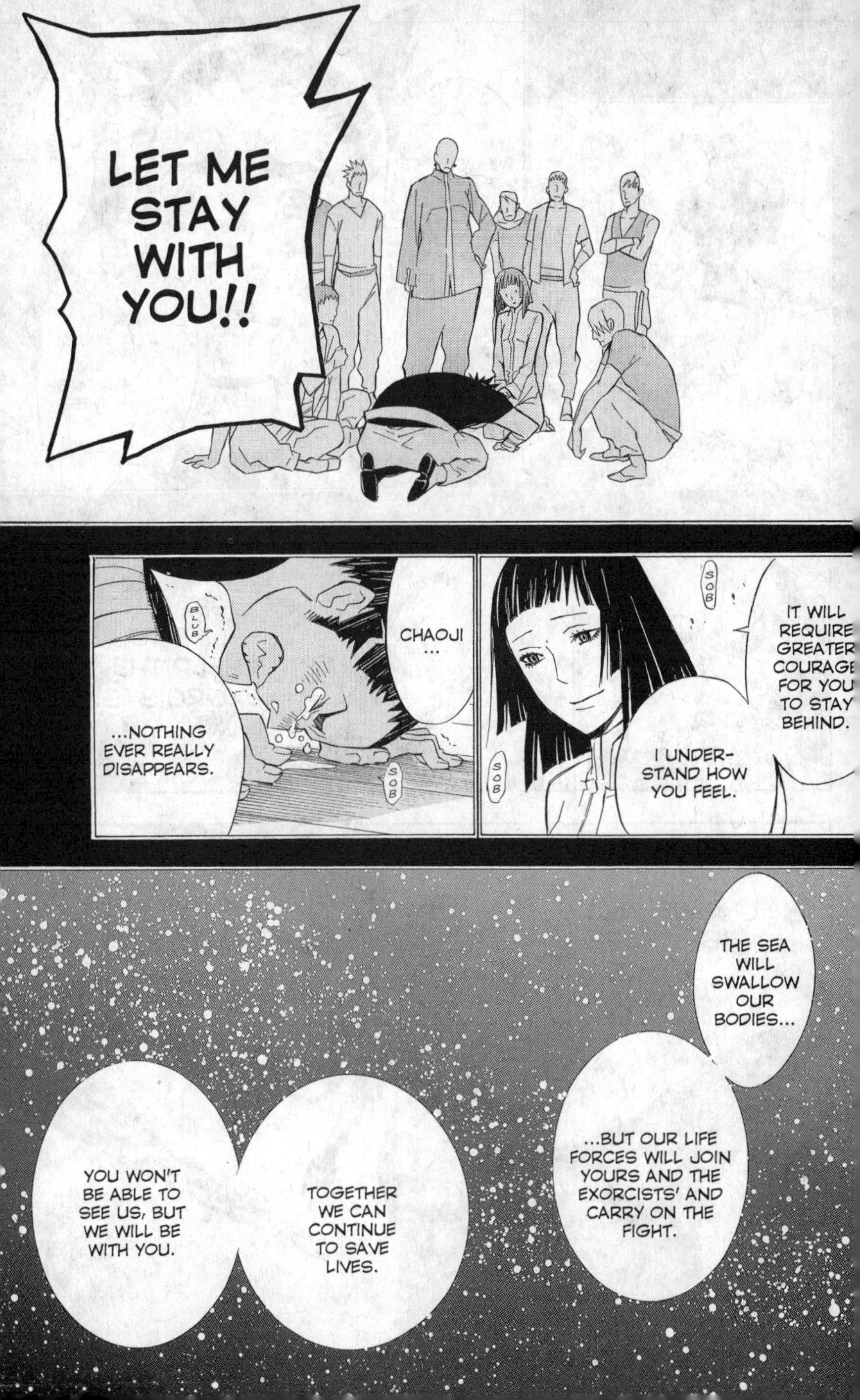
LET ME STAY WITH YOU!!
SOB
IT WILL REQUIRE GREATER COURAGE FOR YOU TO STAY BEHIND.
I UNDER-STAND HOW YOU FEEL.
SOB
CHAOJI ...
BLUB
SOB
...NOTHING EVER REALLY DISAPPEARS.
THE SEA WILL SWALLOW OUR BODIES...
...BUT OUR LIFE FORCES WILL JOIN YOURS AND THE EXORCISTS' AND CARRY ON THE FIGHT.
TOGETHER WE CAN CONTINUE TO SAVE LIVES.
YOU WON'T BE ABLE TO SEE US, BUT WE WILL BE WITH YOU.

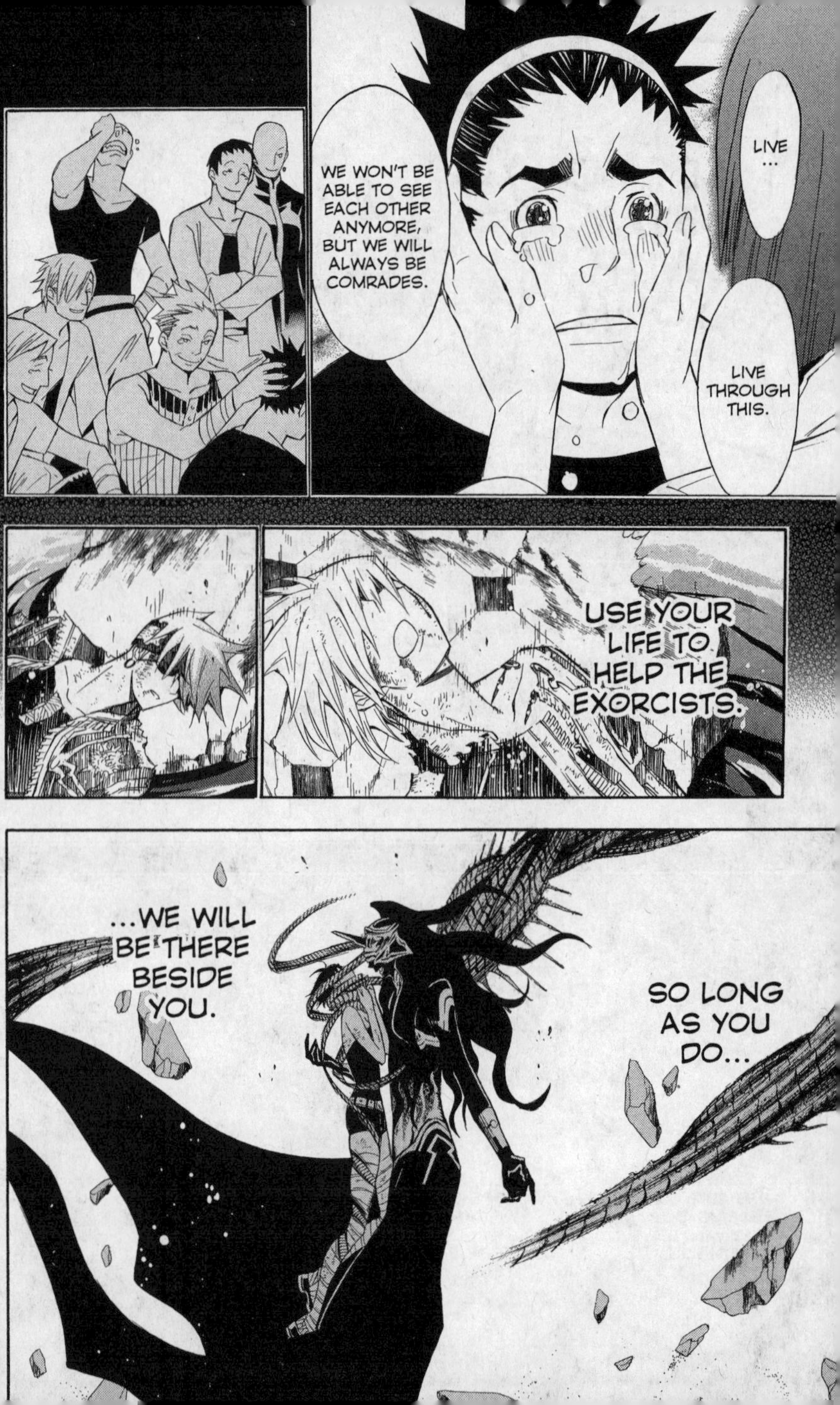
LIVE ...
LIVE THROUGH THIS.
WE WON'T BE ABLE TO SEE EACH OTHER ANYMORE, BUT WE WILL ALWAYS BE COMRADES.
USE YOUR LIFE TO HELP THE EXORCISTS.
SO LONG AS YOU DO...
...WE WILL BE THERE BESIDE YOU.

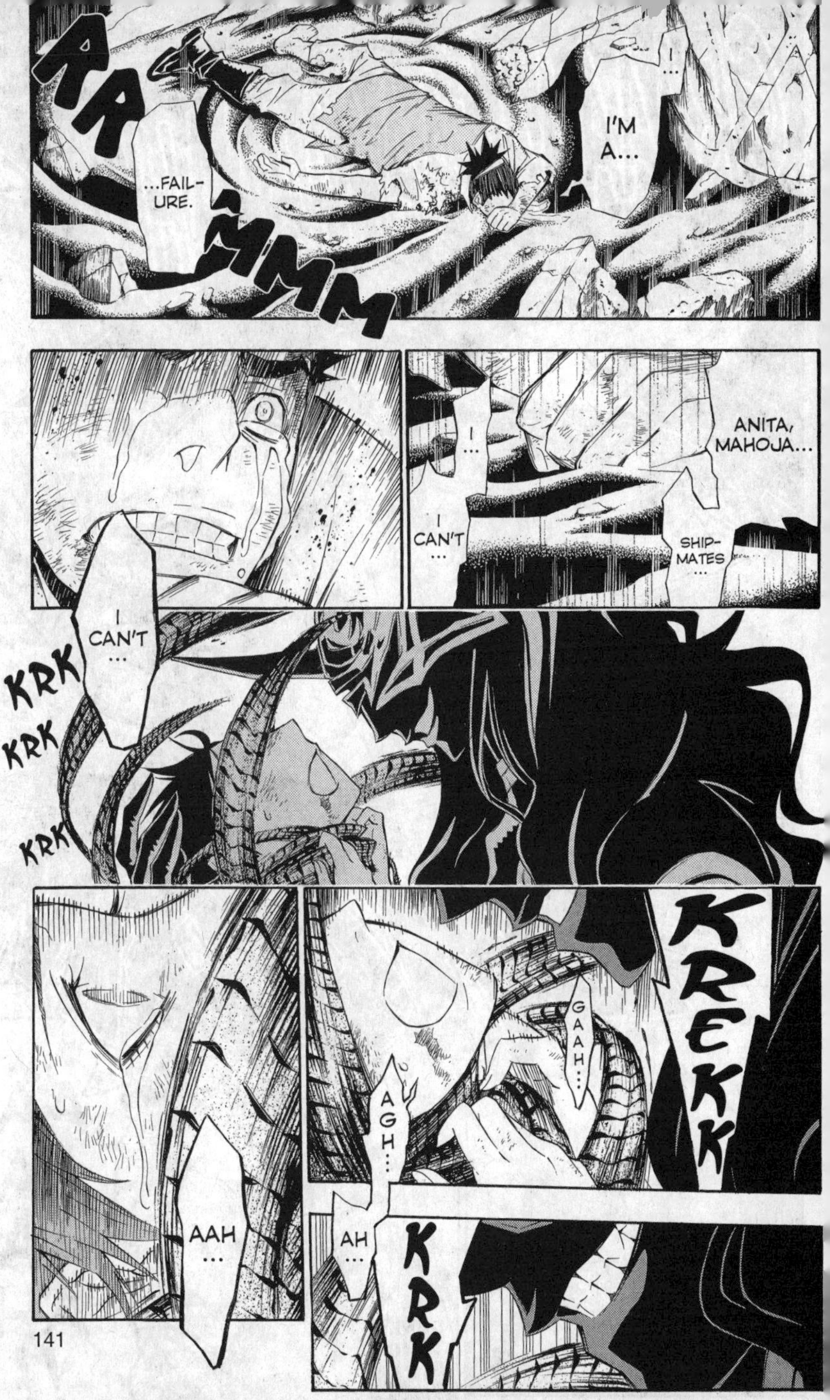
I...
I'M A...
...FAIL-URE.
RRÂMMM
ANITA, MAHOJA...
SHIP-MATES...
I...
I CAN'T...
I CAN'T...
KRK
KRK
KRK
KREKK
GAAH...
AGH...
KRK
AH...
AAH...

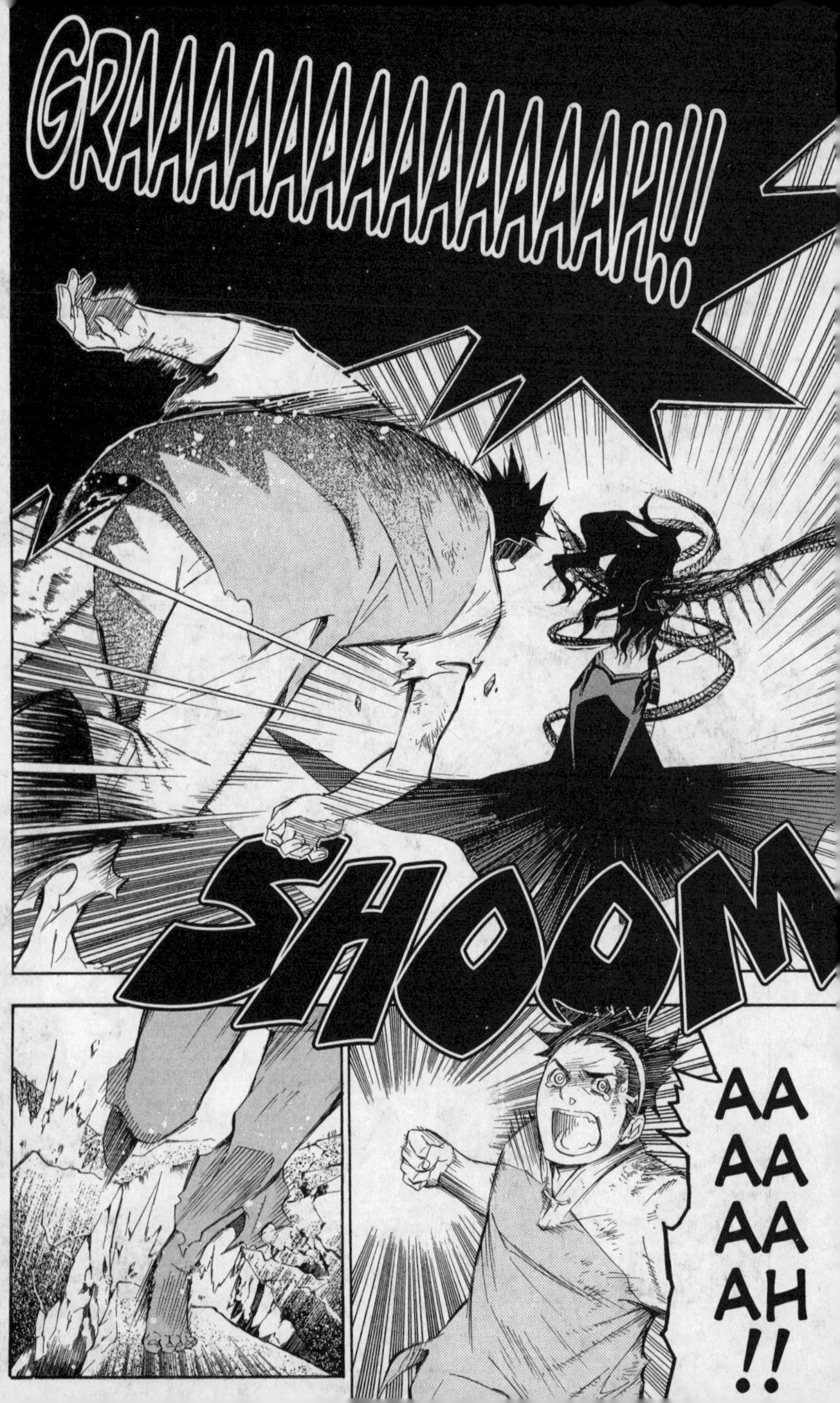
GRAAAAAAAAAAAAH!!
SHOOM
AAAAAAAAH!!

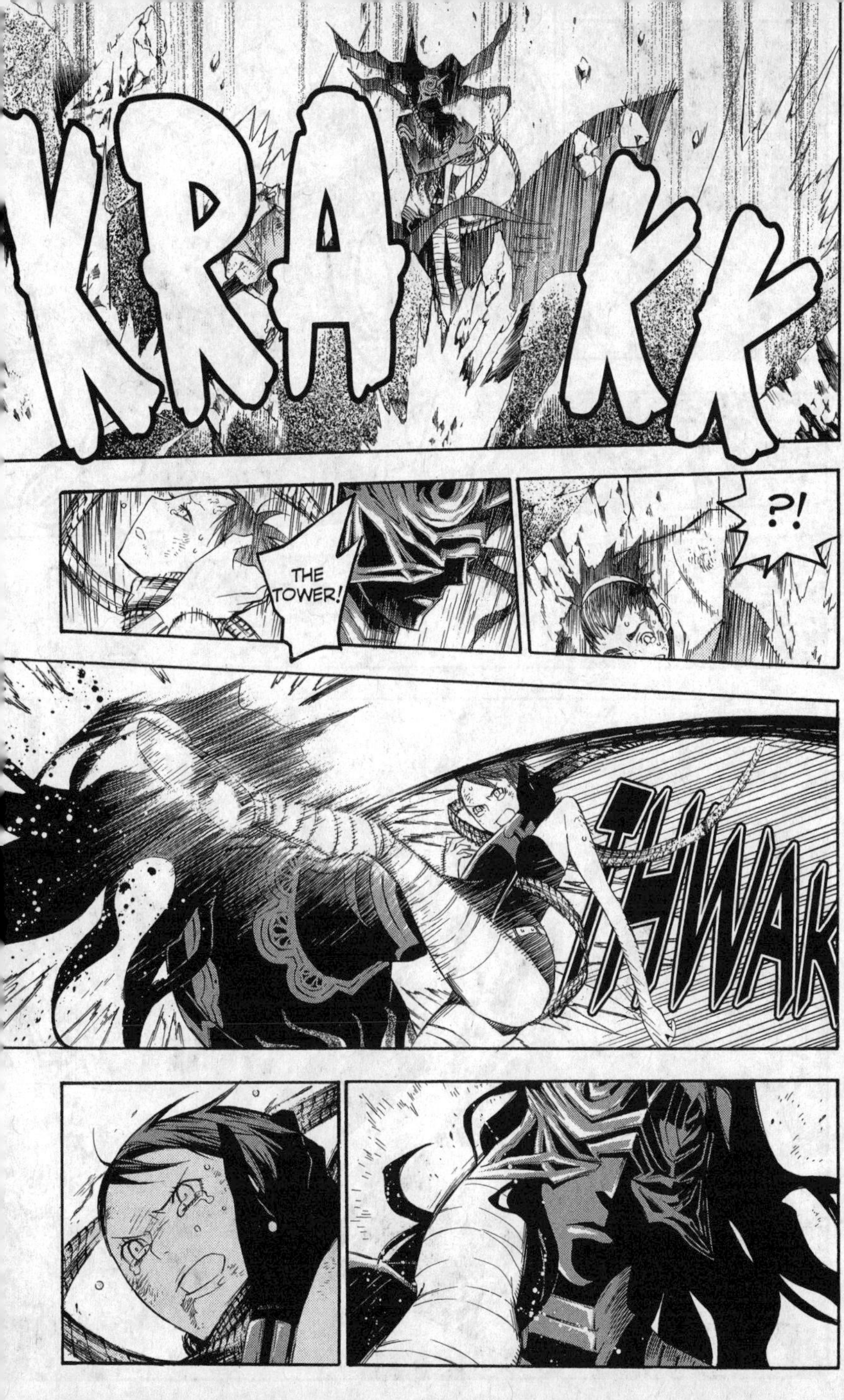
KRAKK
?!
THE TOWER!
THWAK

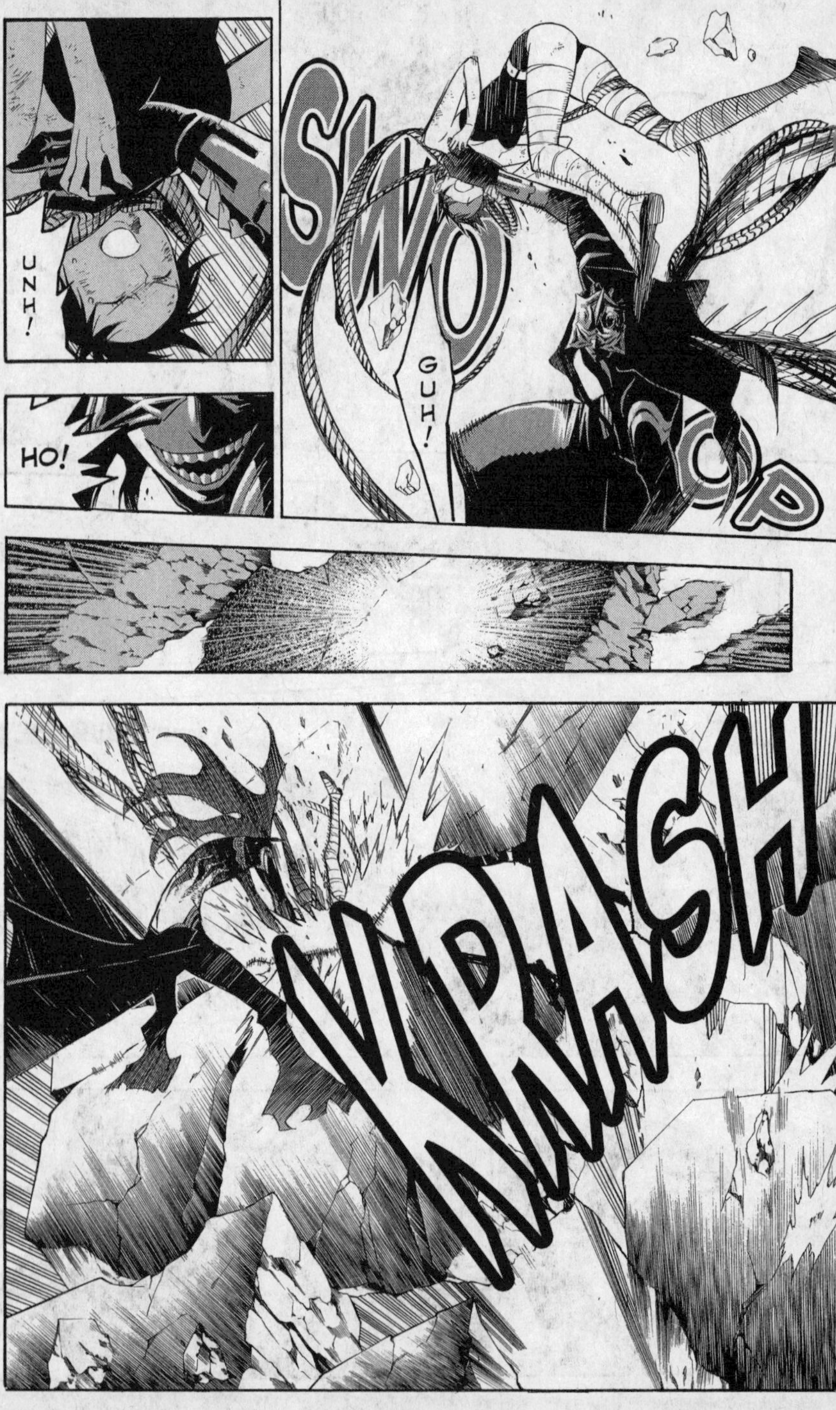
SWOOP
GUH!
UNH!
HO!
KRASH

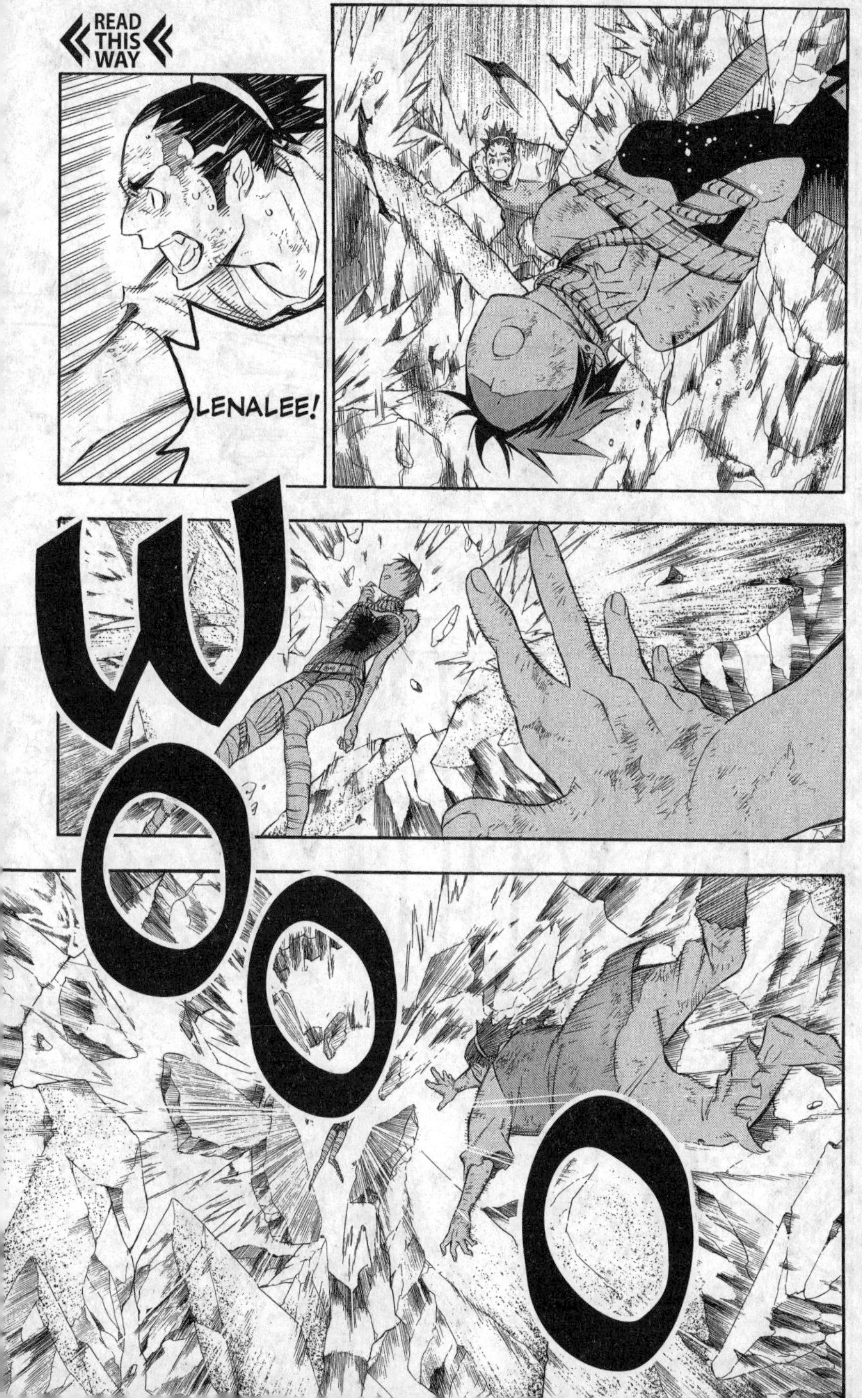
READ THIS WAY
LENALEE!
WOOOO

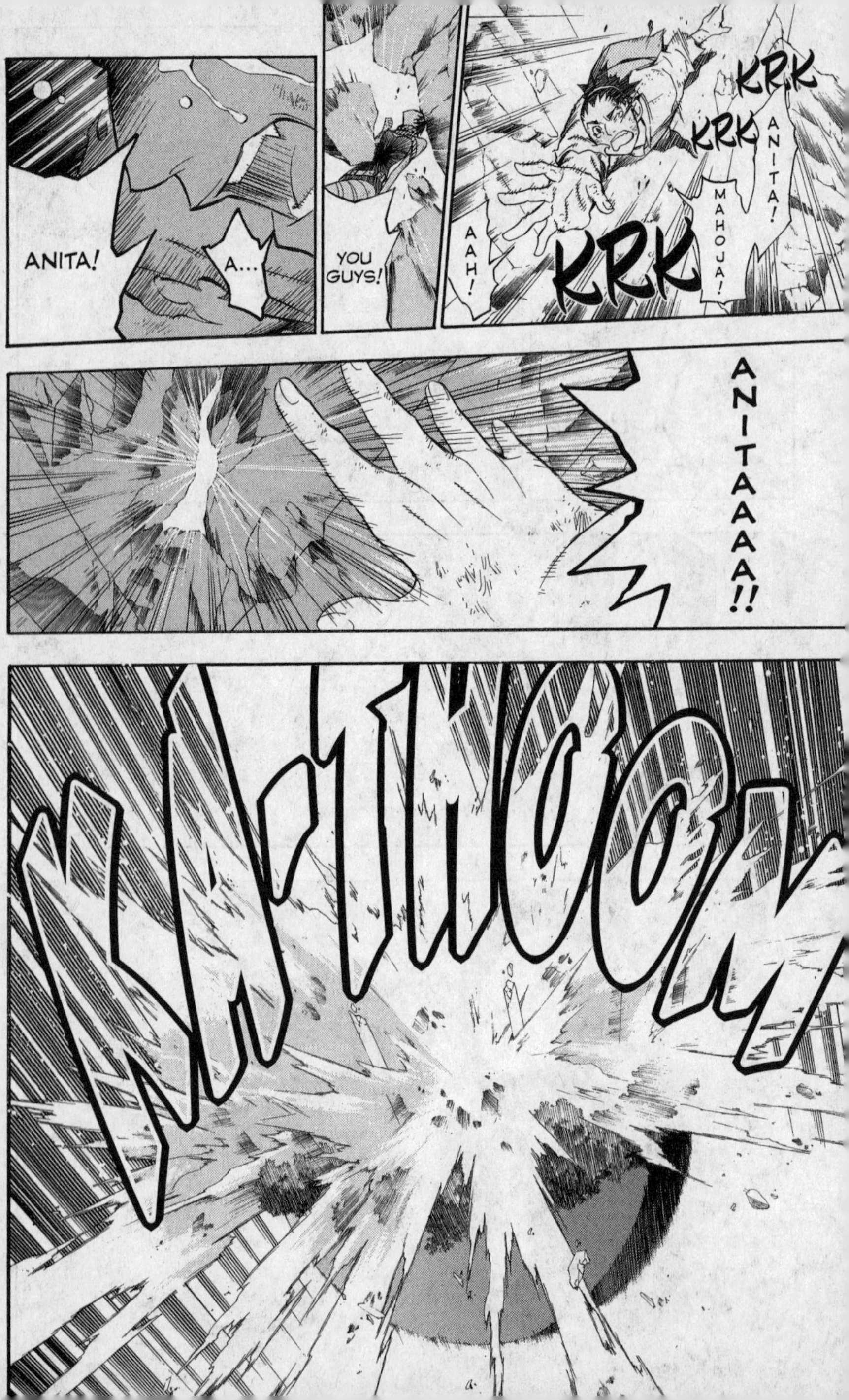
KRK
ANITA!
KRK
MAHOJA!
KRK
AAH!
YOU GUYS!
A...
ANITA!
ANITAAAAA!!

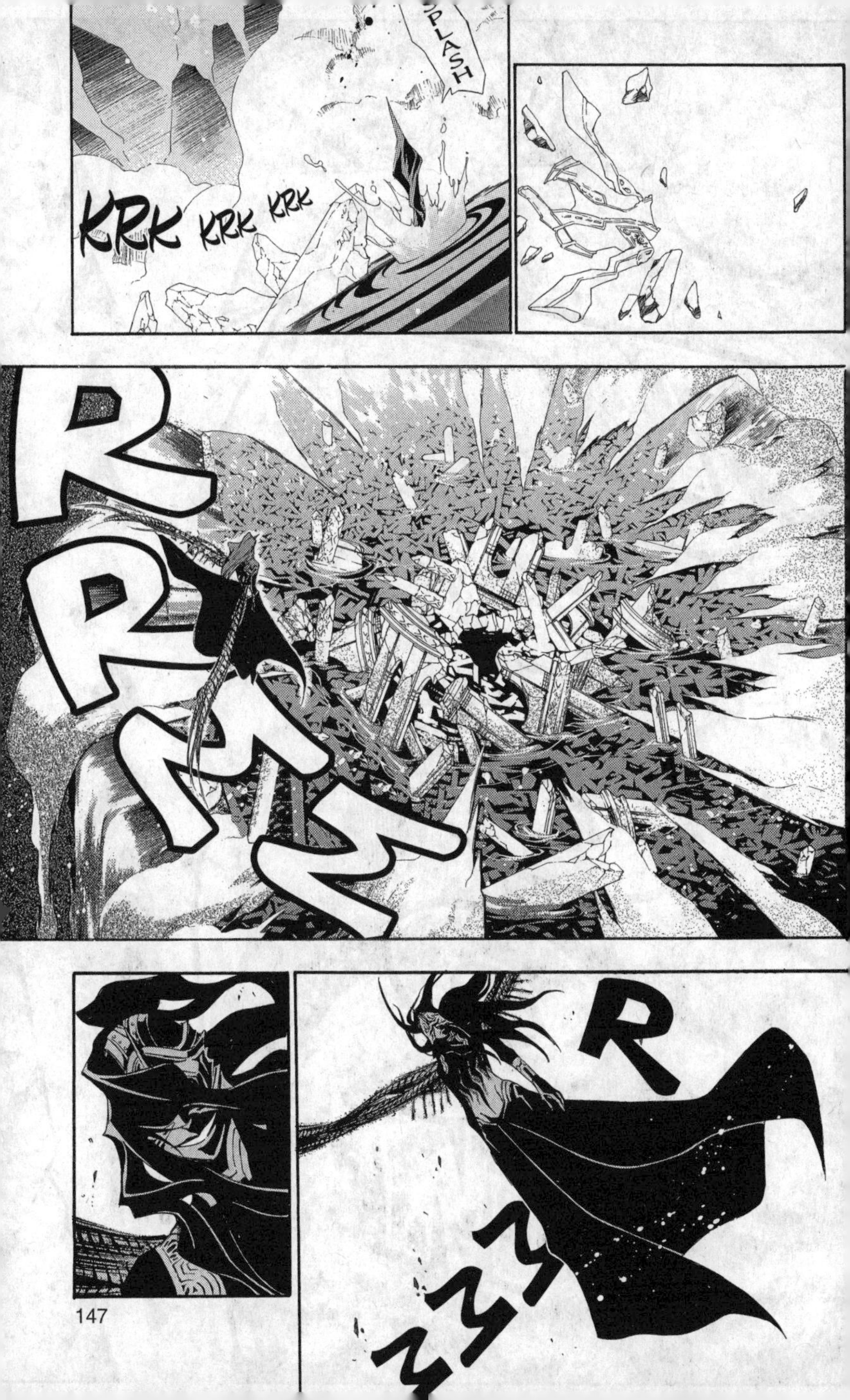
SPLASH
KRK KRK KRK
RRMMM
RMMM

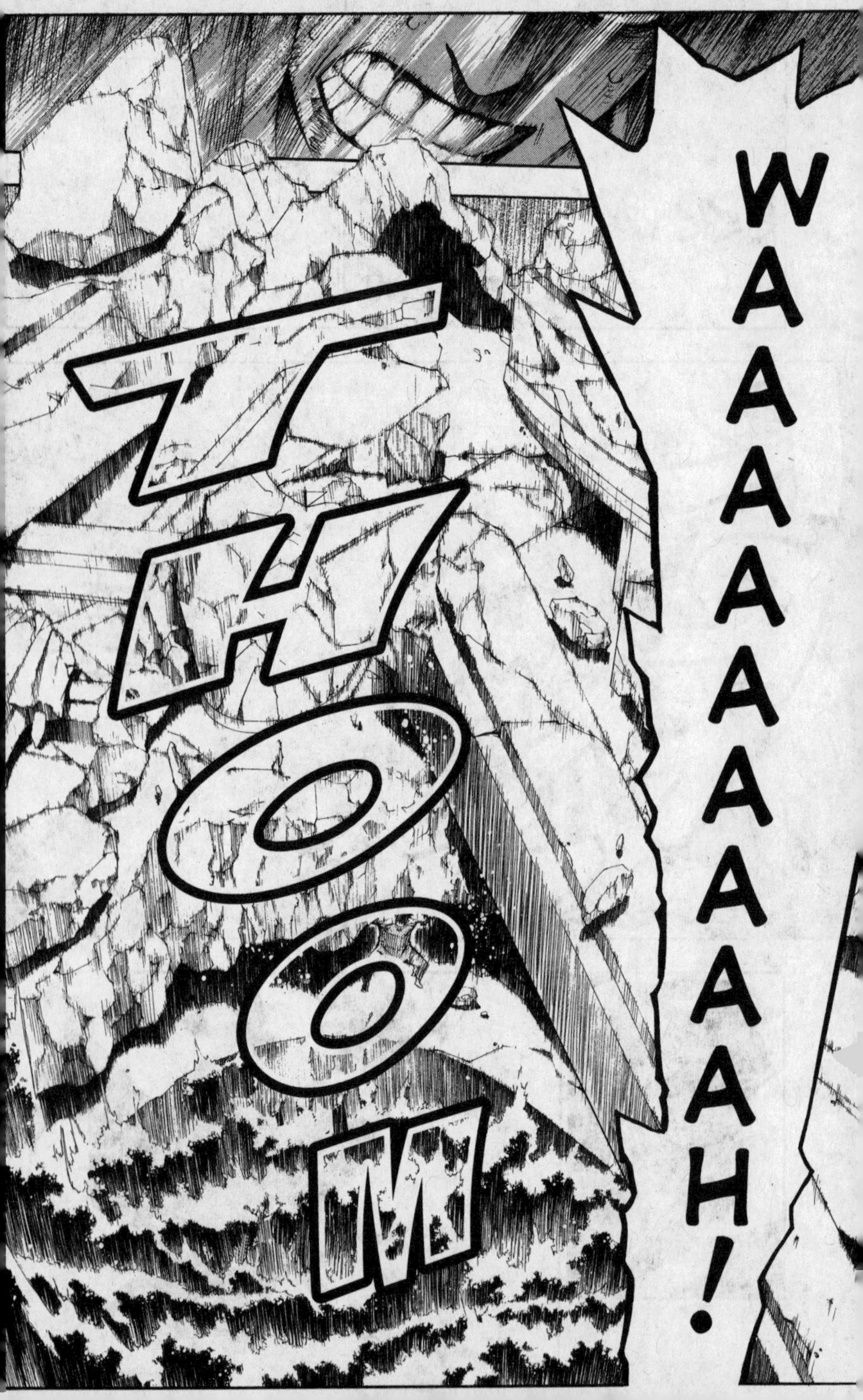
WAAAAAAAAAAH!
THOOOM

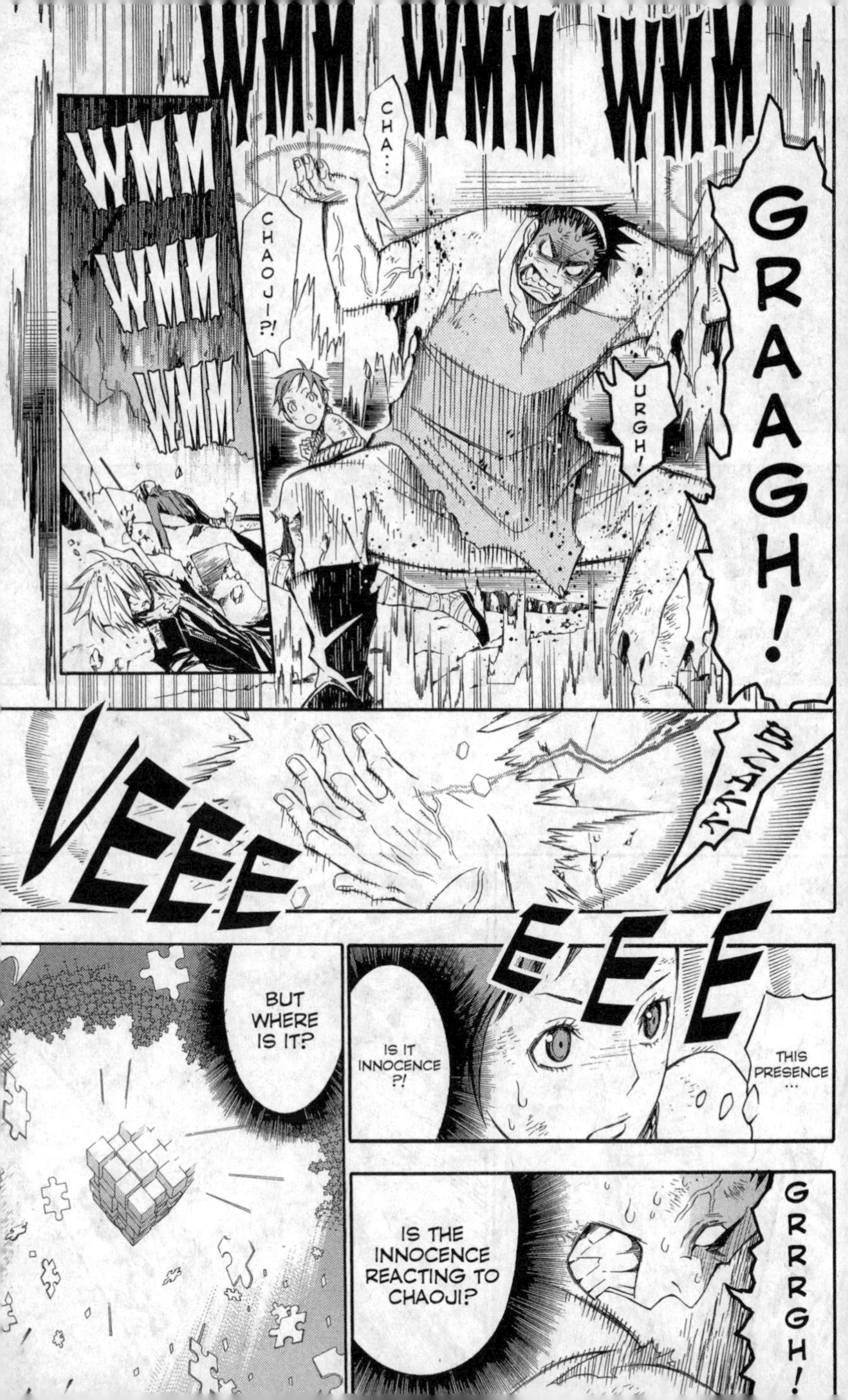
WMM WMM WMM
GRAGH!
CHA...
URGH!
CHAOJI?!
WMM WMM WMM
VEEE
EEE
THIS PRESENCE...
IS IT INNOCENCE?!
GRRRGH!
IS THE INNOCENCE REACTING TO CHAOJI?
BUT WHERE IS IT?

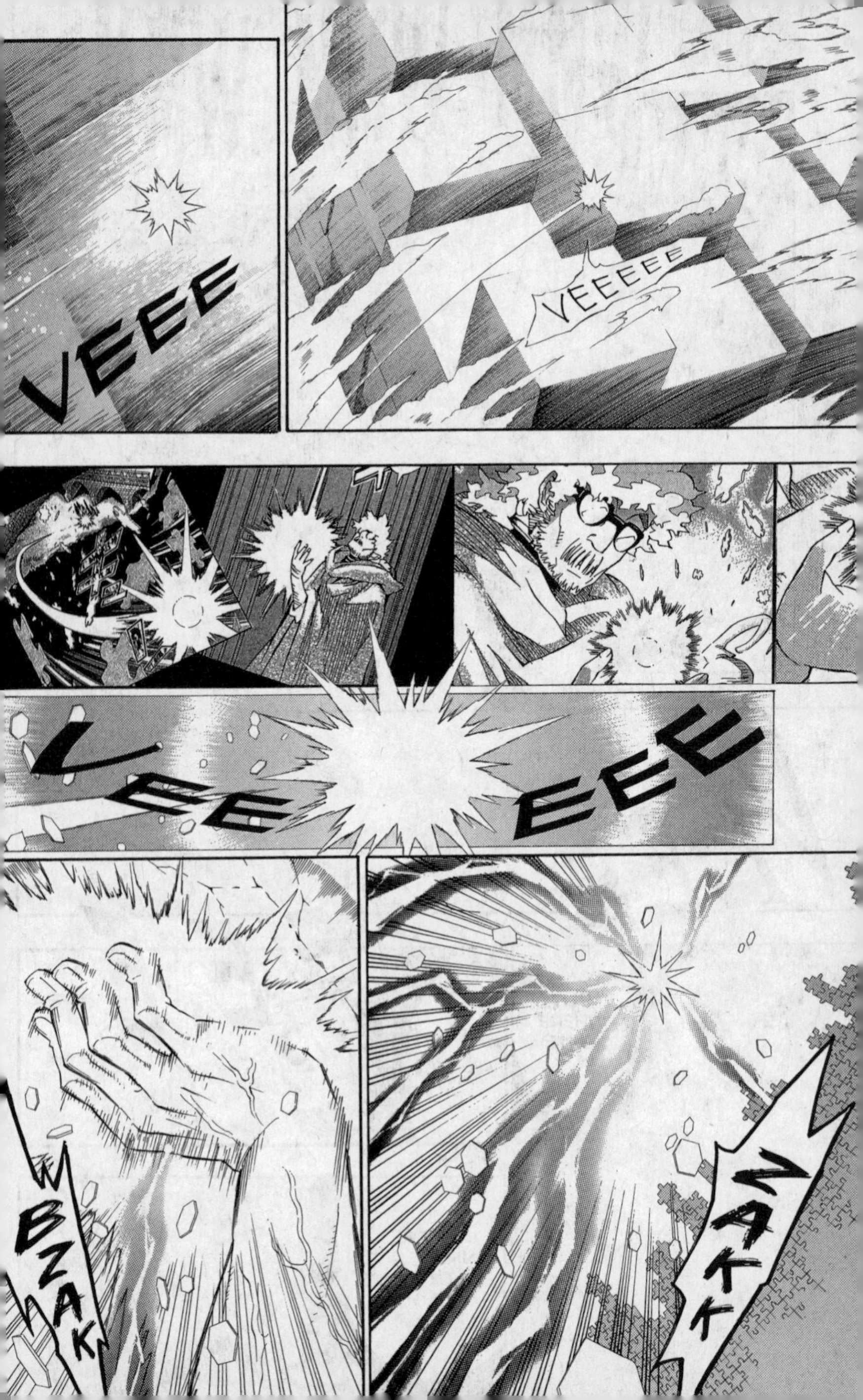
VEEEEEE
VEEE
VEEEEE
ZAKK
BZAK

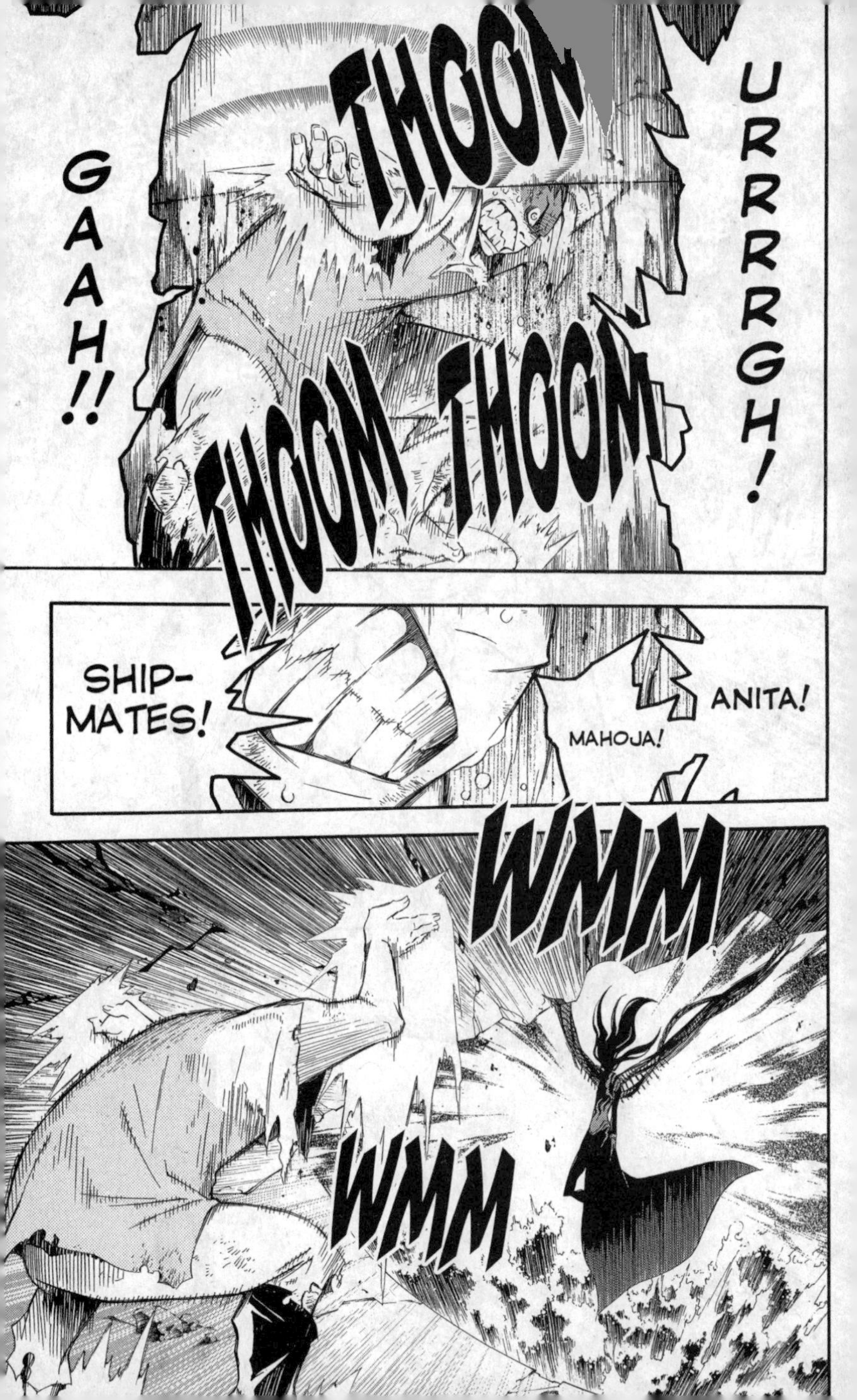
URRRRGH!
THOOM
GAAH!!
THOOM
THOOM
ANITA!
MAHOJA!
SHIP-MATES!
WMM
WMM

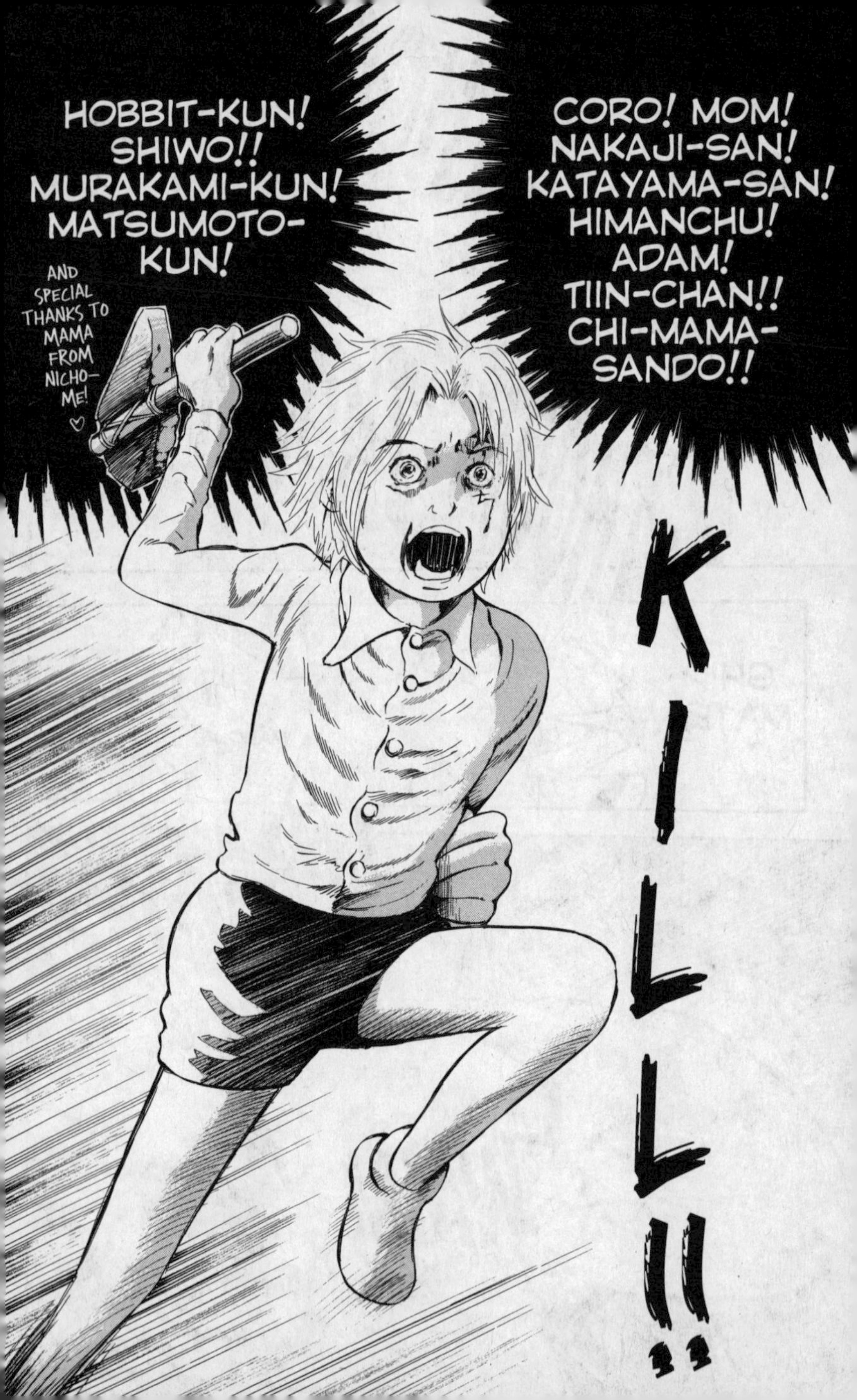
CORO! MOM! NAKAJI-SAN! KATAYAMA-SAN! HIMANCHU! ADAM! TIIN-CHAN!! CHI-MAMA-SANDO!!
HOBBIT-KUN! SHIWO!! MURAKAMI-KUN! MATSUMOTO-KUN!
AND SPECIAL THANKS TO MAMA FROM NICHO-ME! ♡
KILL!!

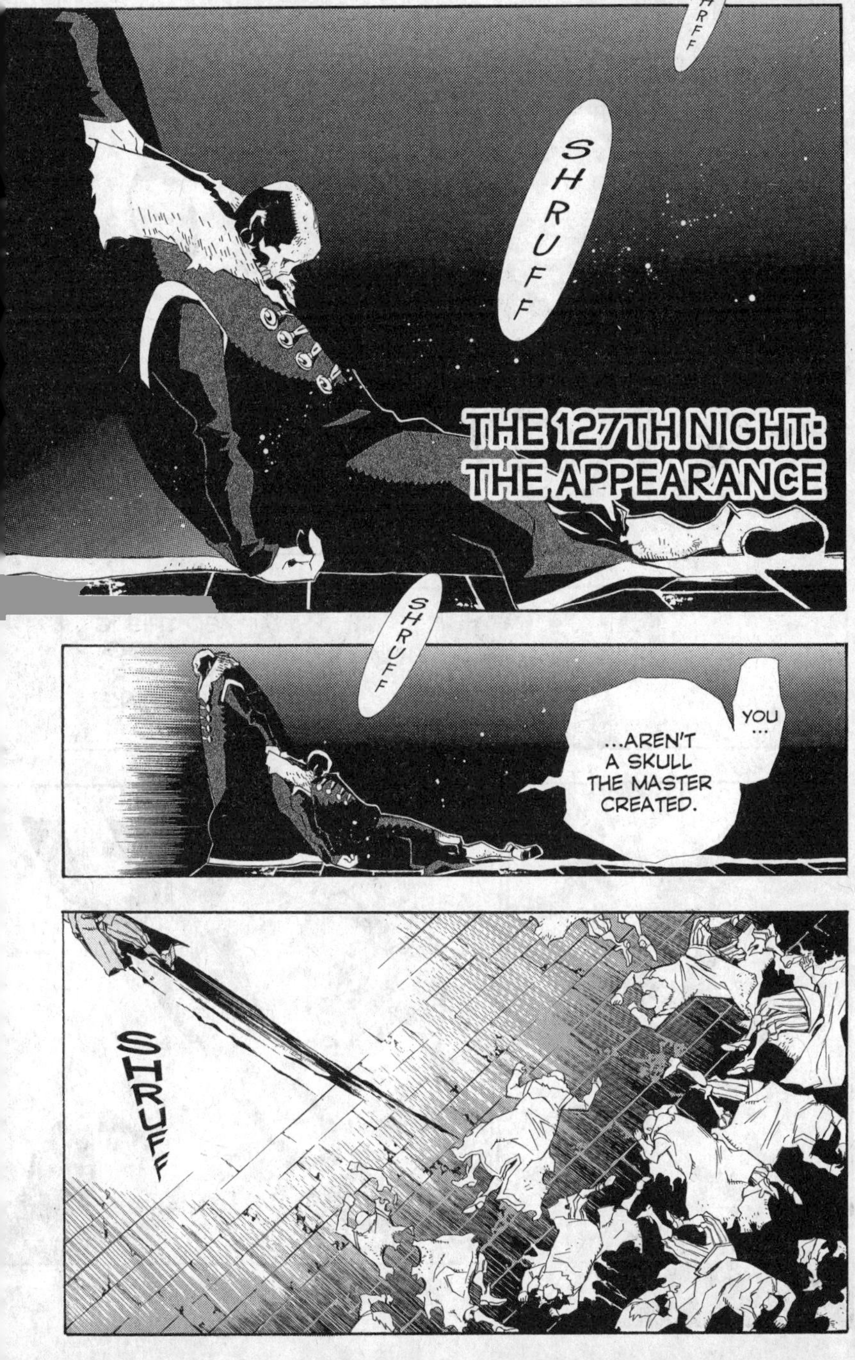
SHRFF
SHRUFF
THE 127TH NIGHT: THE APPEARANCE
SHRUFF
YOU...
...AREN'T A SKULL THE MASTER CREATED.
SHRUFF

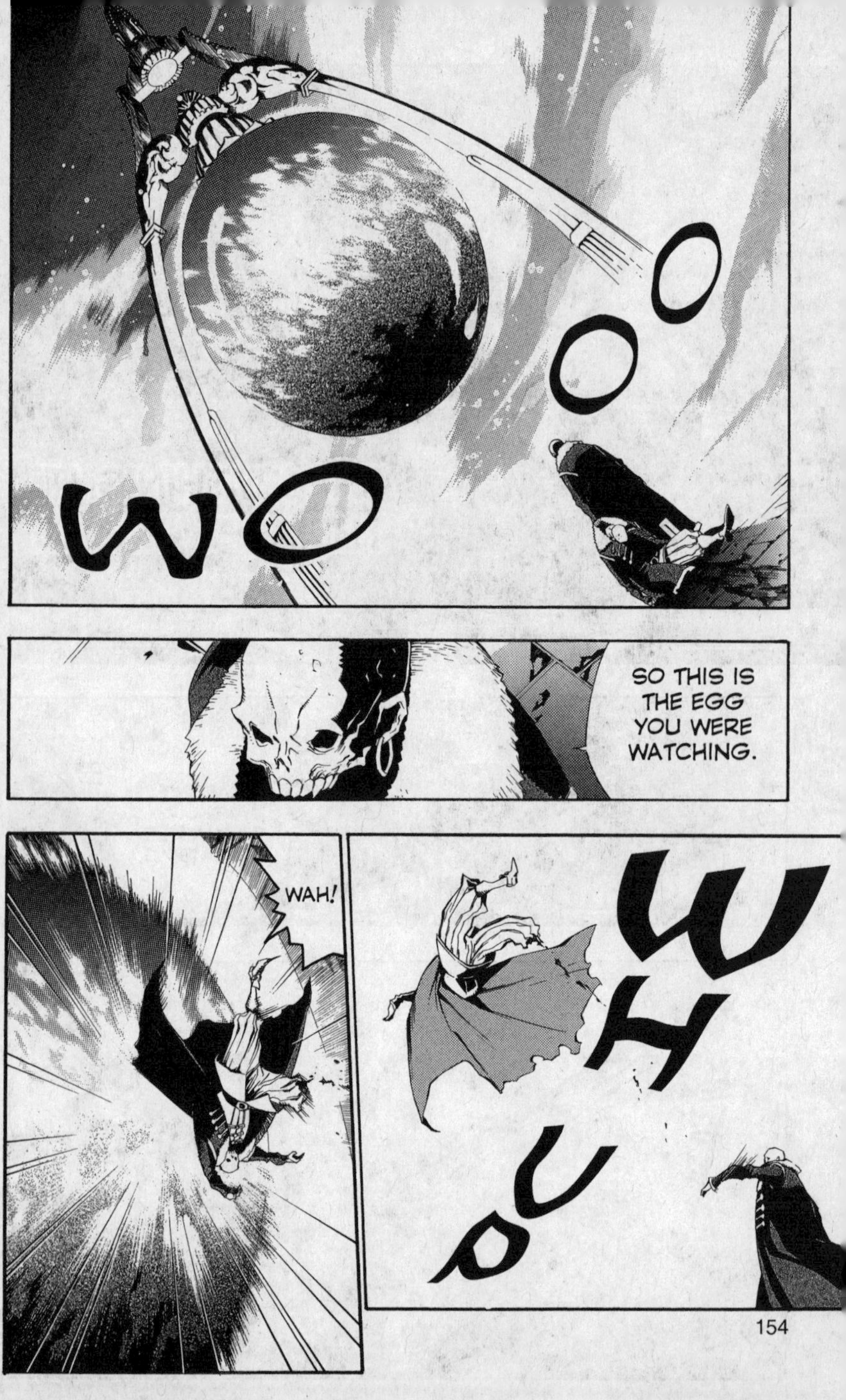
WOOO
SO THIS IS THE EGG YOU WERE WATCHING.
WHUP
WAH!

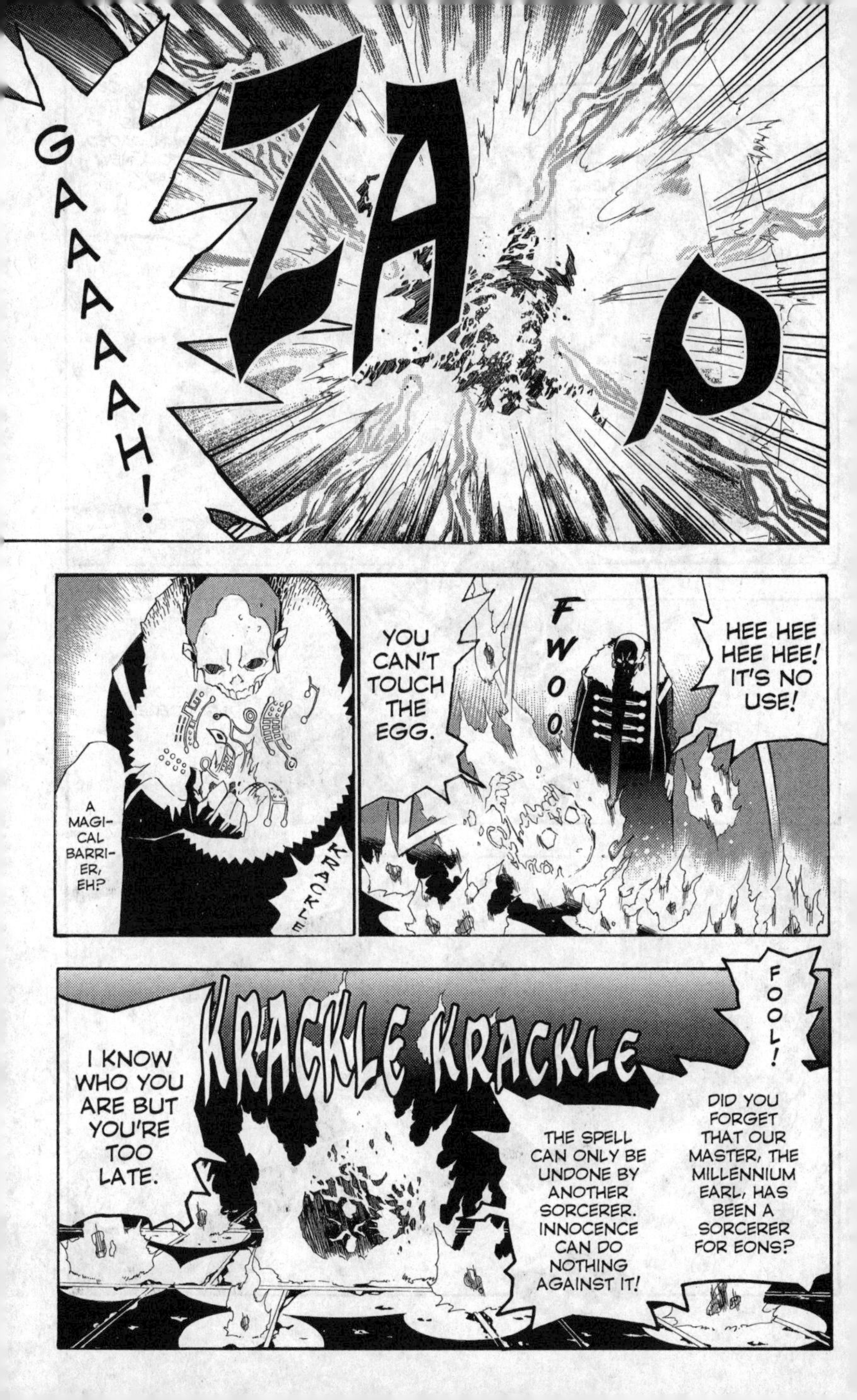
ZAP
GAAAAAH!
HEE HEE HEE HEE! IT'S NO USE!
FWOO
YOU CAN'T TOUCH THE EGG.
KRACKLE
A MAGICAL BARRIER, EH?
FOOL!
KRACKLE KRACKLE
DID YOU FORGET THAT OUR MASTER, THE MILLENNIUM EARL, HAS BEEN A SORCERER FOR EONS?
THE SPELL CAN ONLY BE UNDONE BY ANOTHER SORCERER. INNOCENCE CAN DO NOTHING AGAINST IT!
I KNOW WHO YOU ARE BUT YOU'RE TOO LATE.

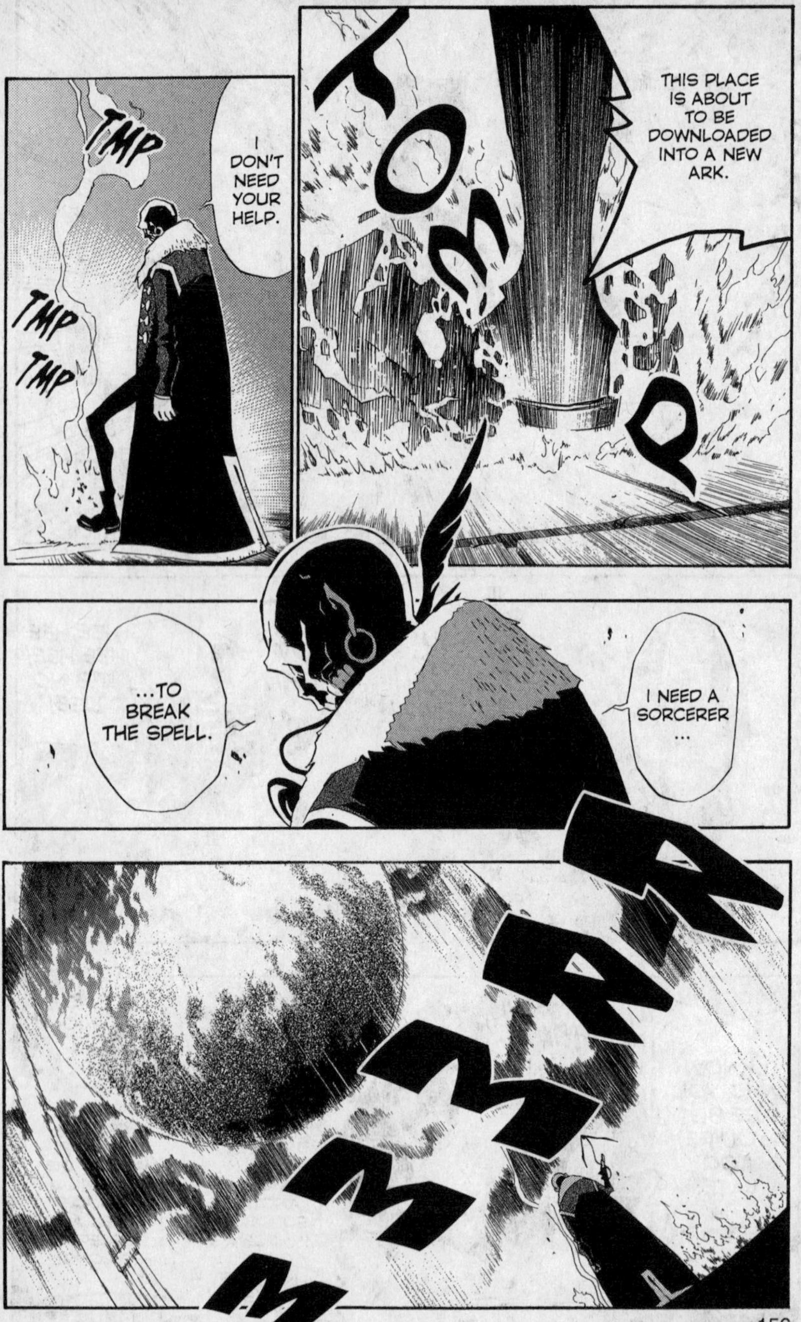
THIS PLACE IS ABOUT TO BE DOWNLOADED INTO A NEW ARK.
TMP
I DON'T NEED YOUR HELP.
TMP TMP
I NEED A SORCERER ...
...TO BREAK THE SPELL.

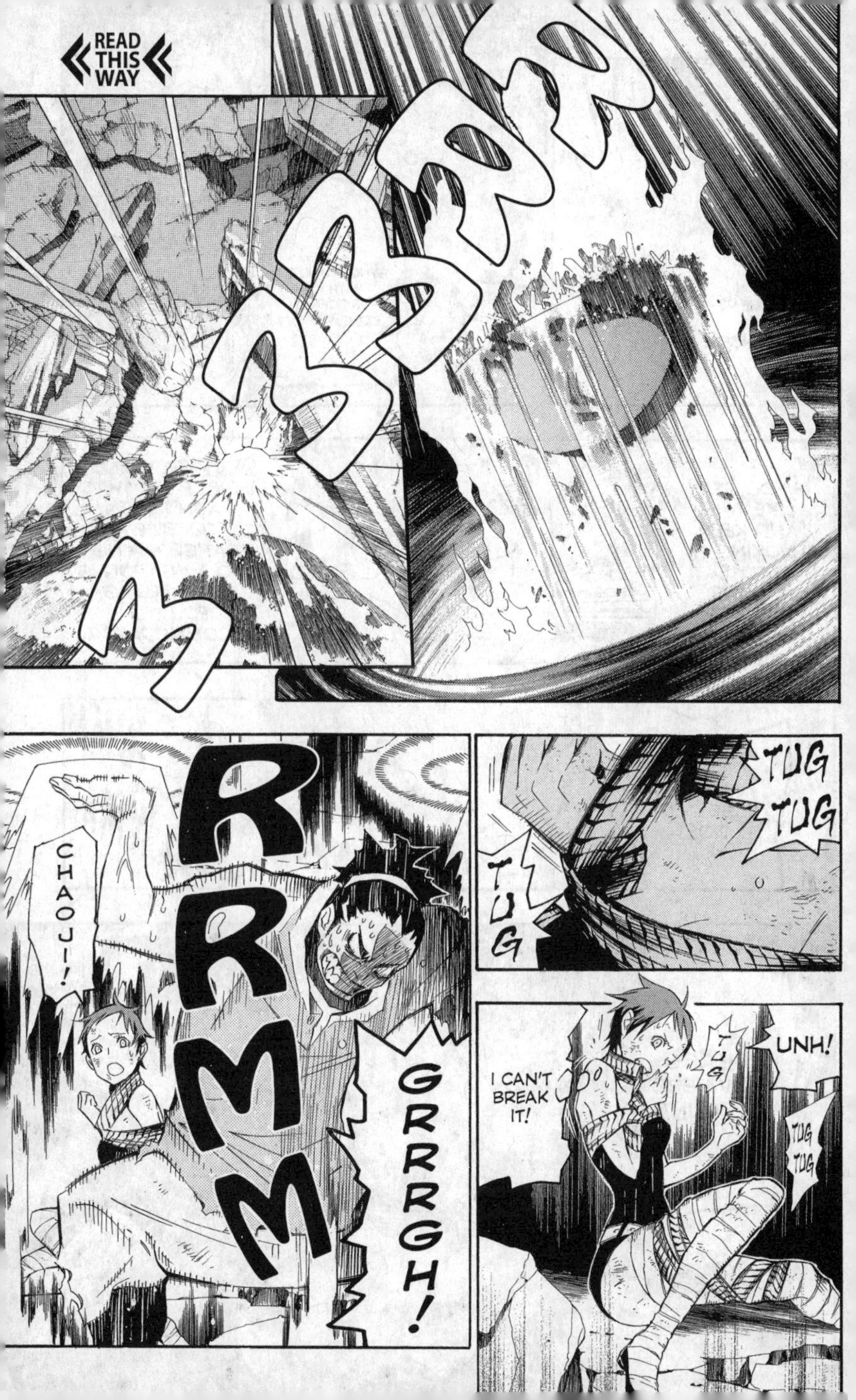
READ THIS WAY
TUG TUG
TUG
UNH!
TUG
I CAN'T BREAK IT!
TUG TUG
GRRRGH!
RRMM
CHAOJI!

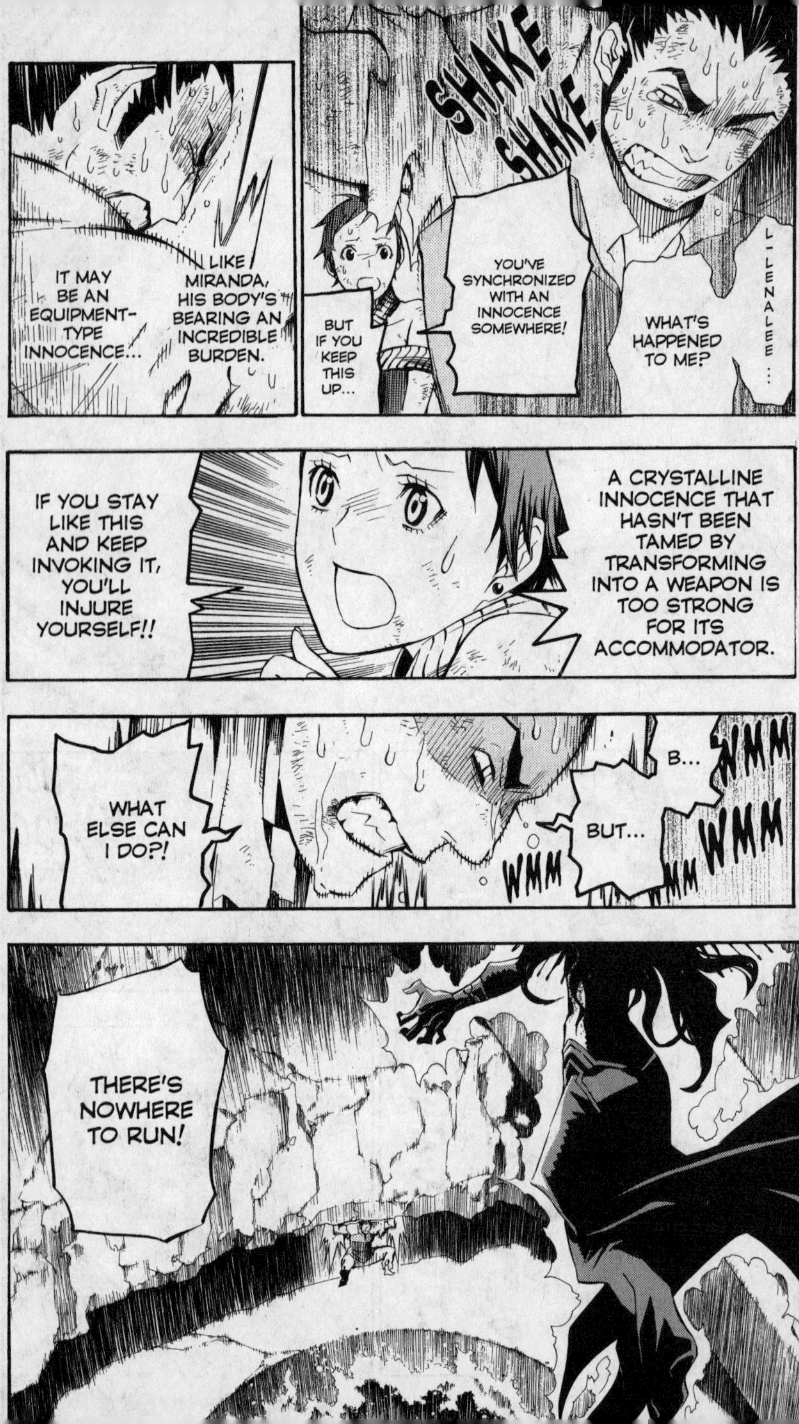
L-LENALEE...
WHAT'S HAPPENED TO ME?
SHAKE SHAKE
YOU'VE SYNCHRONIZED WITH AN INNOCENCE SOMEWHERE!
BUT IF YOU KEEP THIS UP...
LIKE MIRANDA, HIS BODY'S BEARING AN INCREDIBLE BURDEN.
IT MAY BE AN EQUIPMENT-TYPE INNOCENCE...
A CRYSTALLINE INNOCENCE THAT HASN'T BEEN TAMED BY TRANSFORMING INTO A WEAPON IS TOO STRONG FOR ITS ACCOMMODATOR.
IF YOU STAY LIKE THIS AND KEEP INVOKING IT, YOU'LL INJURE YOURSELF!!
WMM WMM
B... BUT...
WMM
WHAT ELSE CAN I DO?!
THERE'S NOWHERE TO RUN!

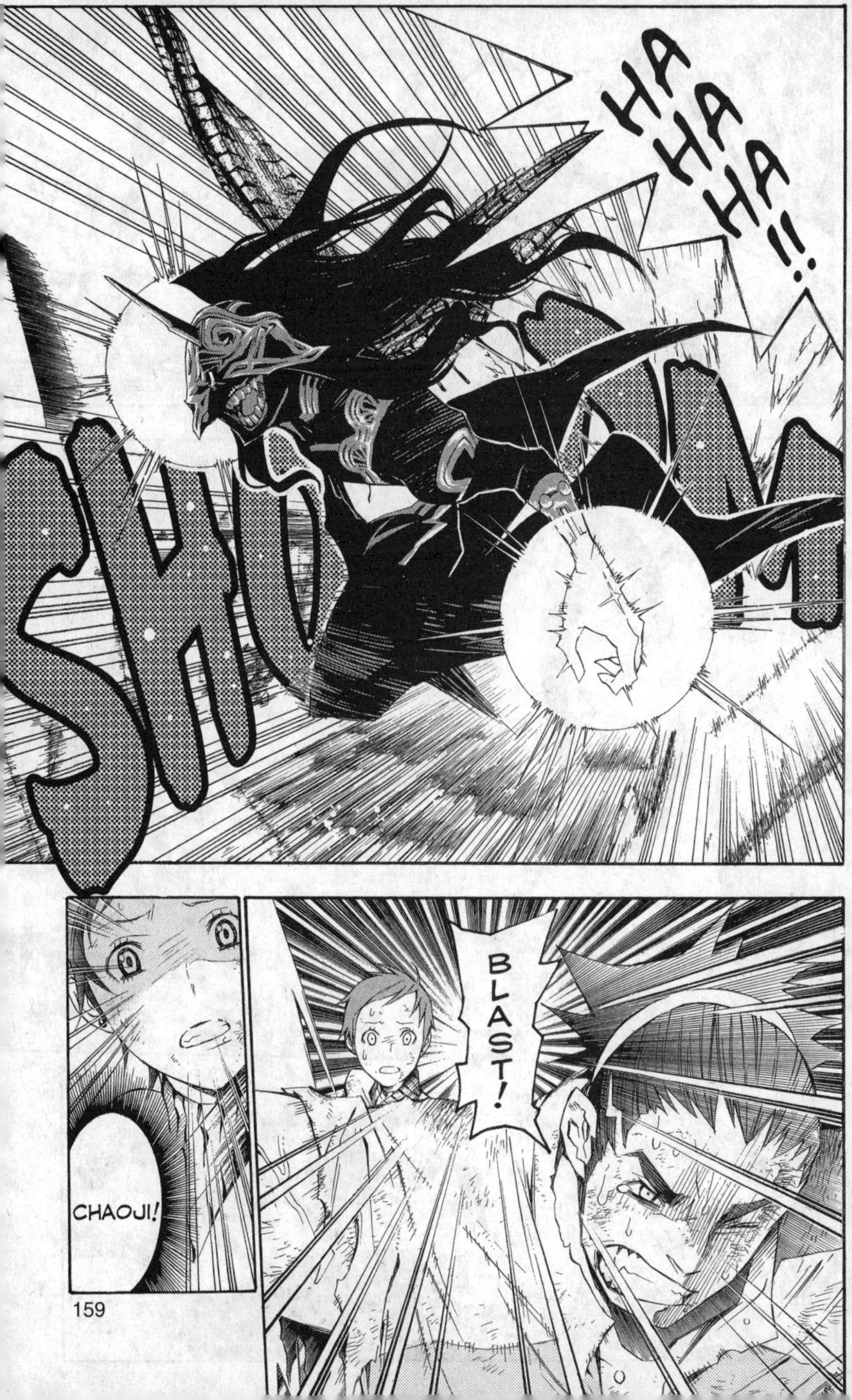
HA HA HA!!
BLAST!
CHAOJI!

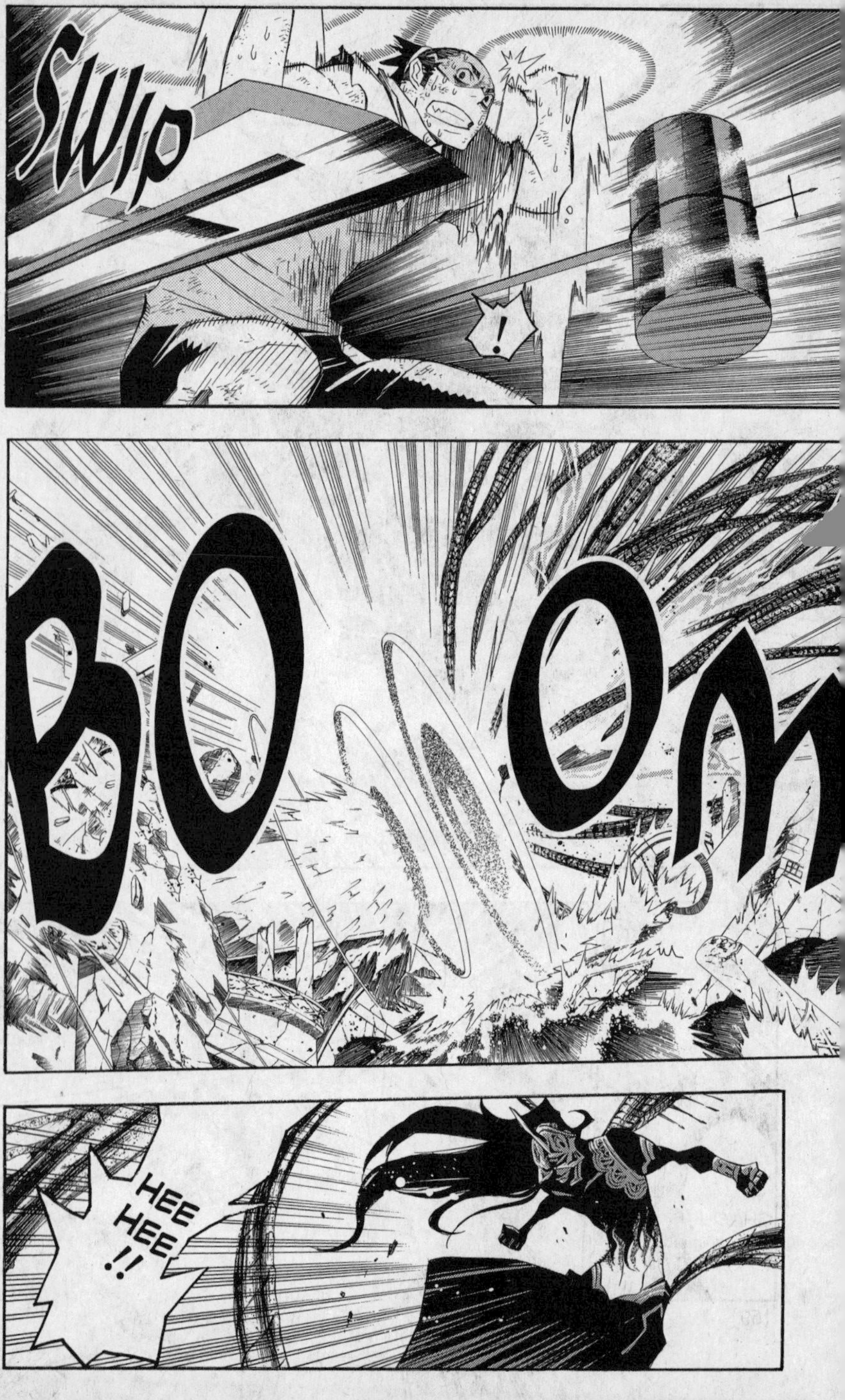
!
SWIP
BOOM
HEE HEE!!

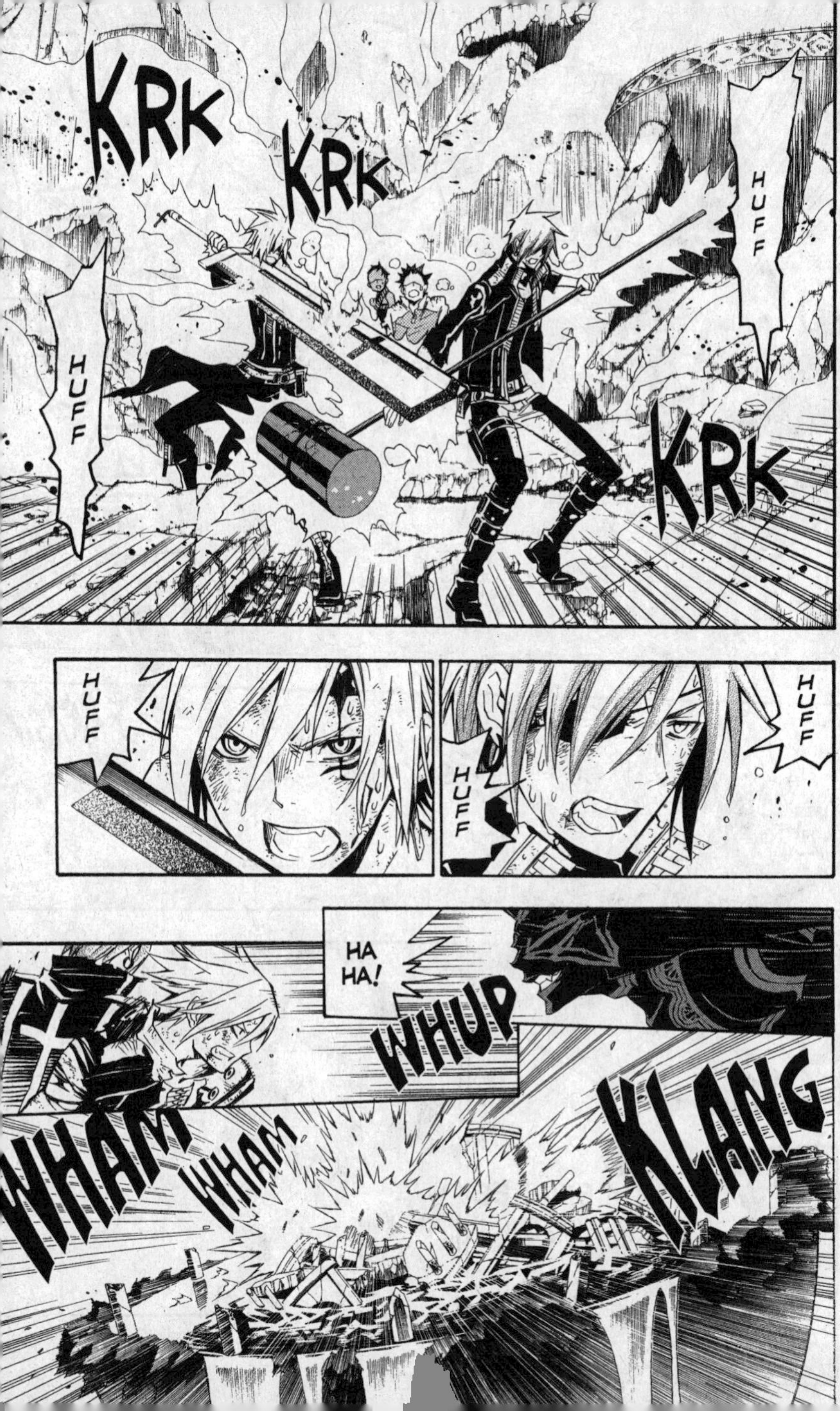
HUFF
KRK
KRK
KRK
HUFF
HUFF
HUFF
HUFF
HA HA!
WHUP
KLANG
WHAM
WHAM

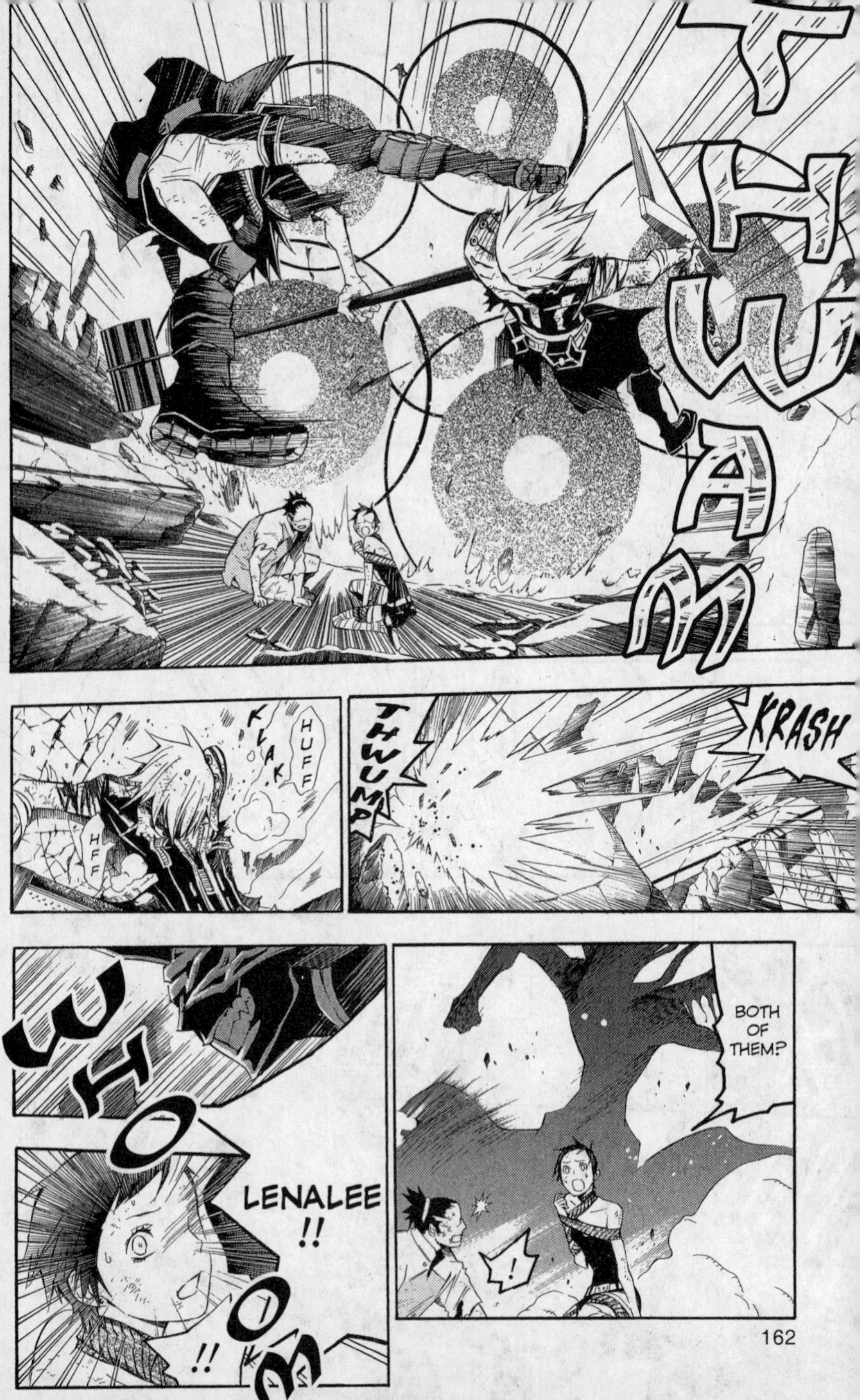
THWAM
KRASH
THWUMP
HUFF
KLAK
HFF
BOTH OF THEM?
!
LENALEE !!
!!

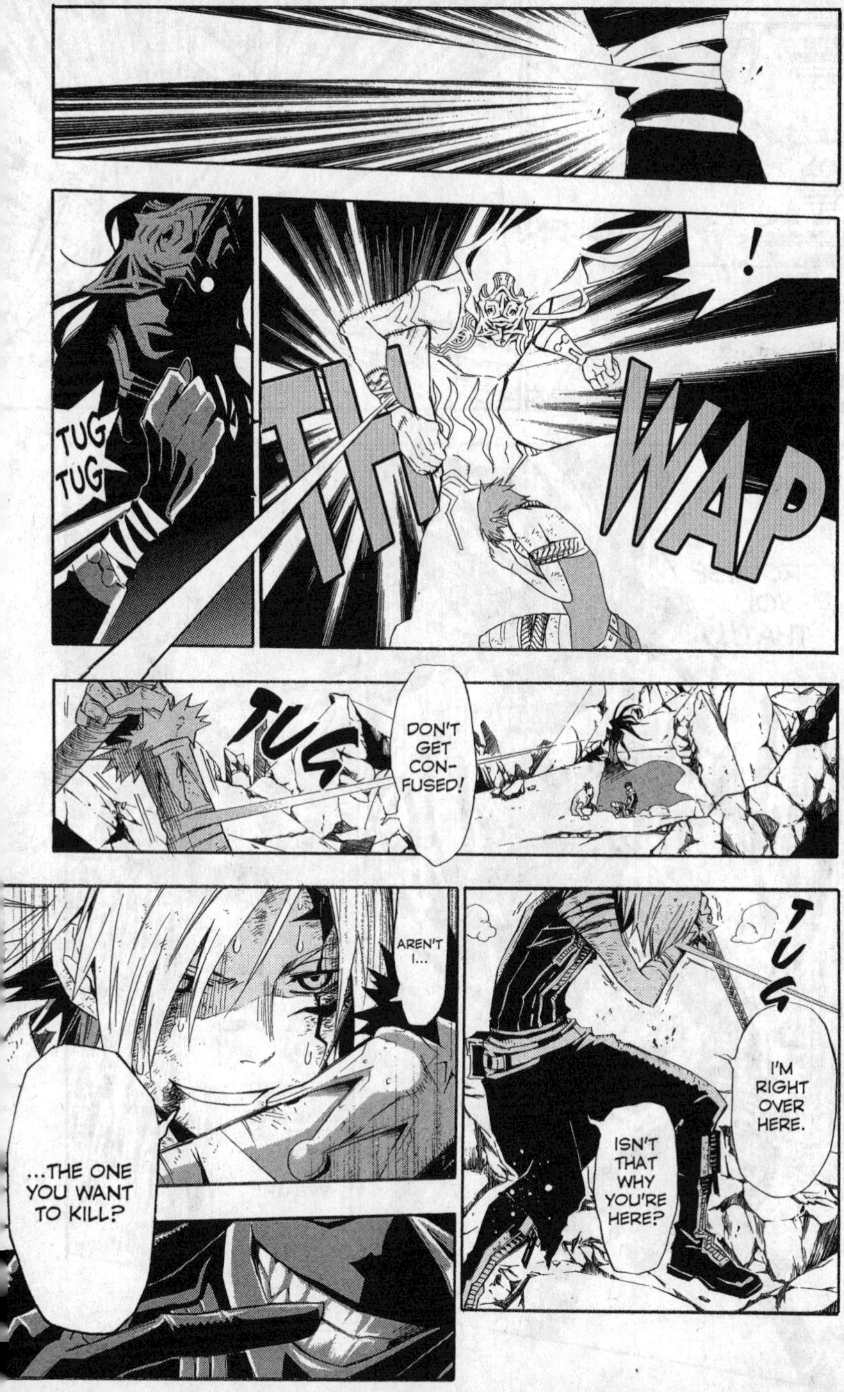
!
THWAP
TUG TUG
TUG
DON'T GET CON-FUSED!
TUG
I'M RIGHT OVER HERE.
ISN'T THAT WHY YOU'RE HERE?
AREN'T I...
...THE ONE YOU WANT TO KILL?

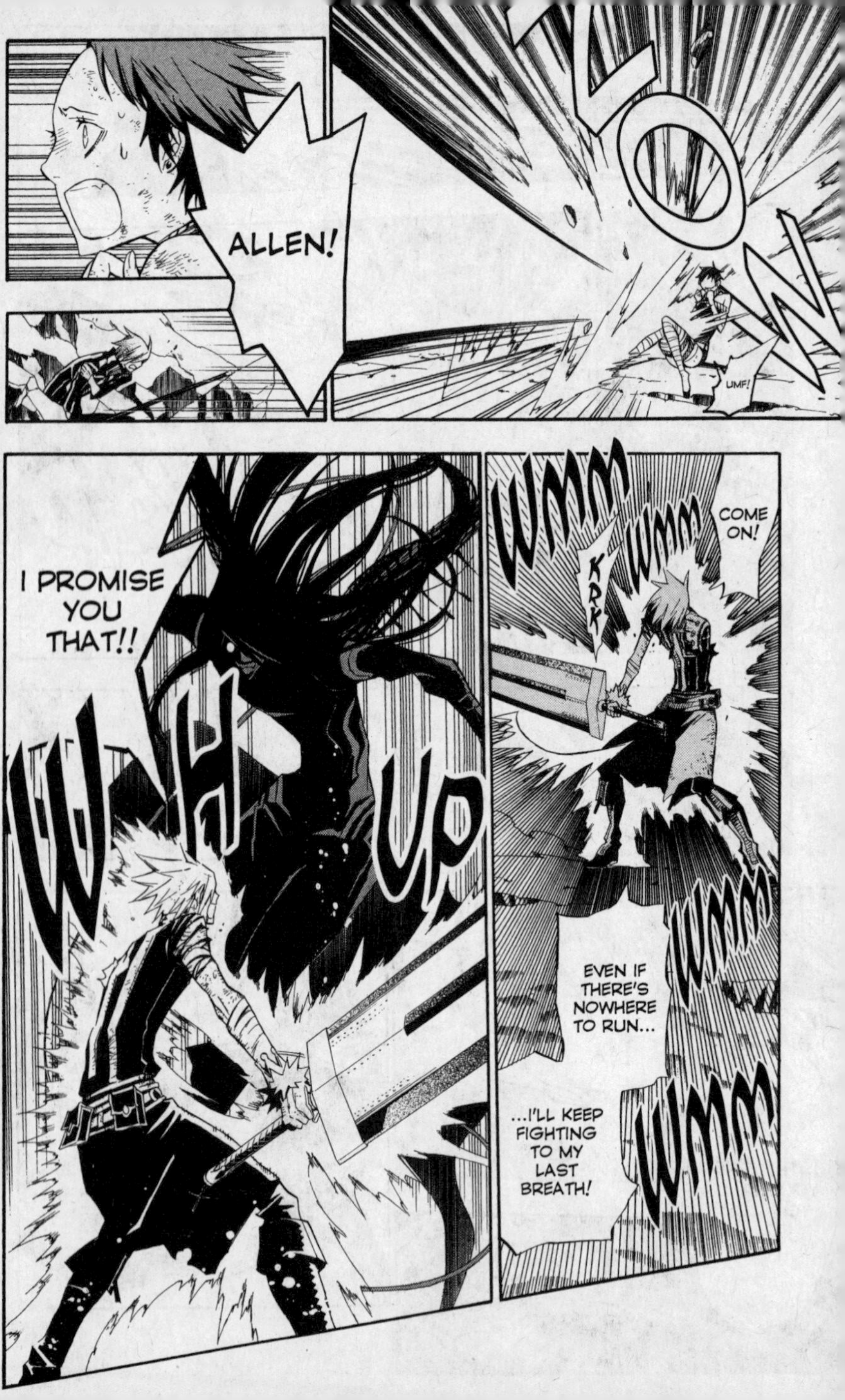
UMF!
ALLEN!
WMM
WMM
COME ON!
KRK
WMM
EVEN IF THERE'S NOWHERE TO RUN...
...I'LL KEEP FIGHTING TO MY LAST BREATH!
WMM
I PROMISE YOU THAT!!
WHUP

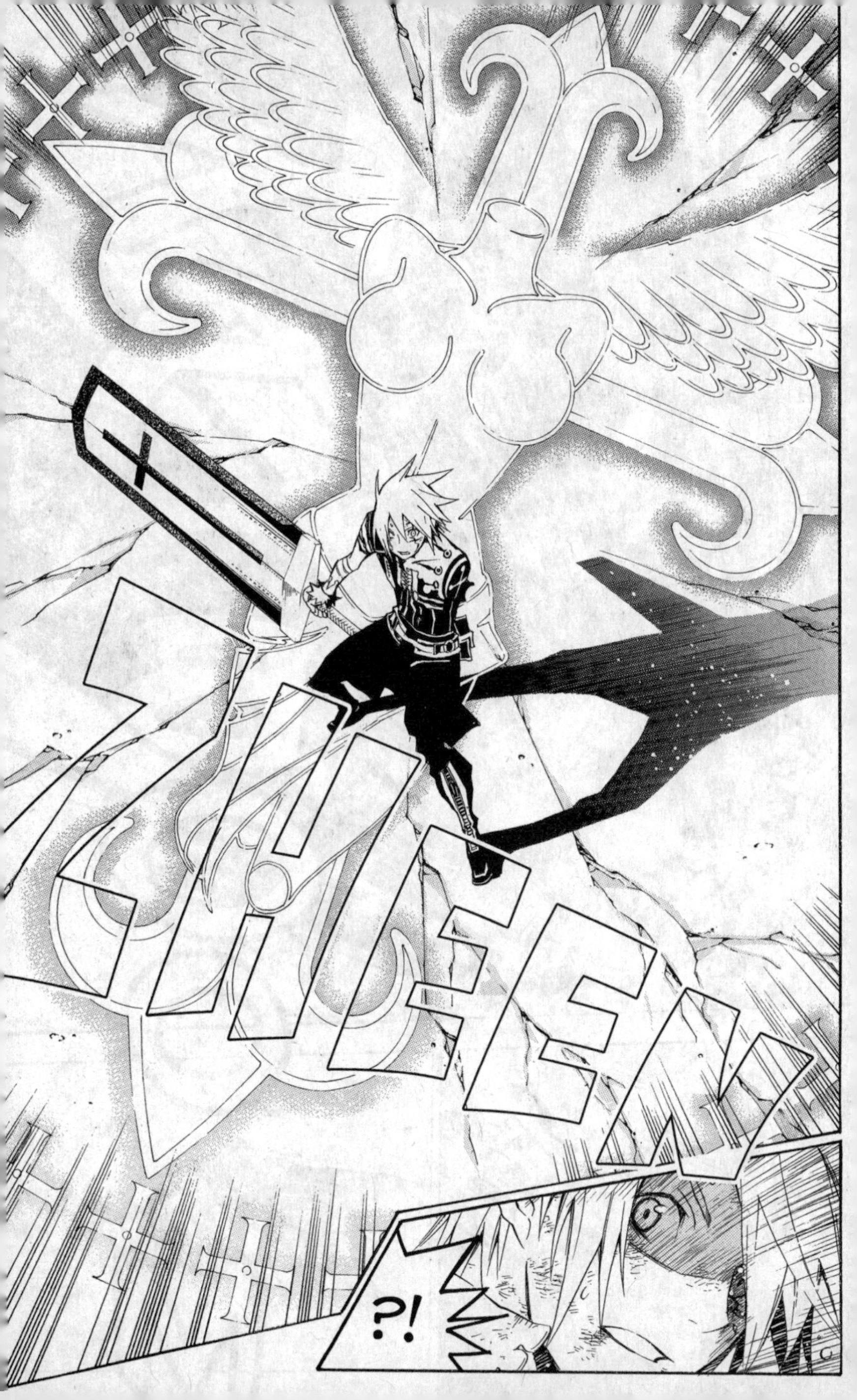
SHEEN
?!

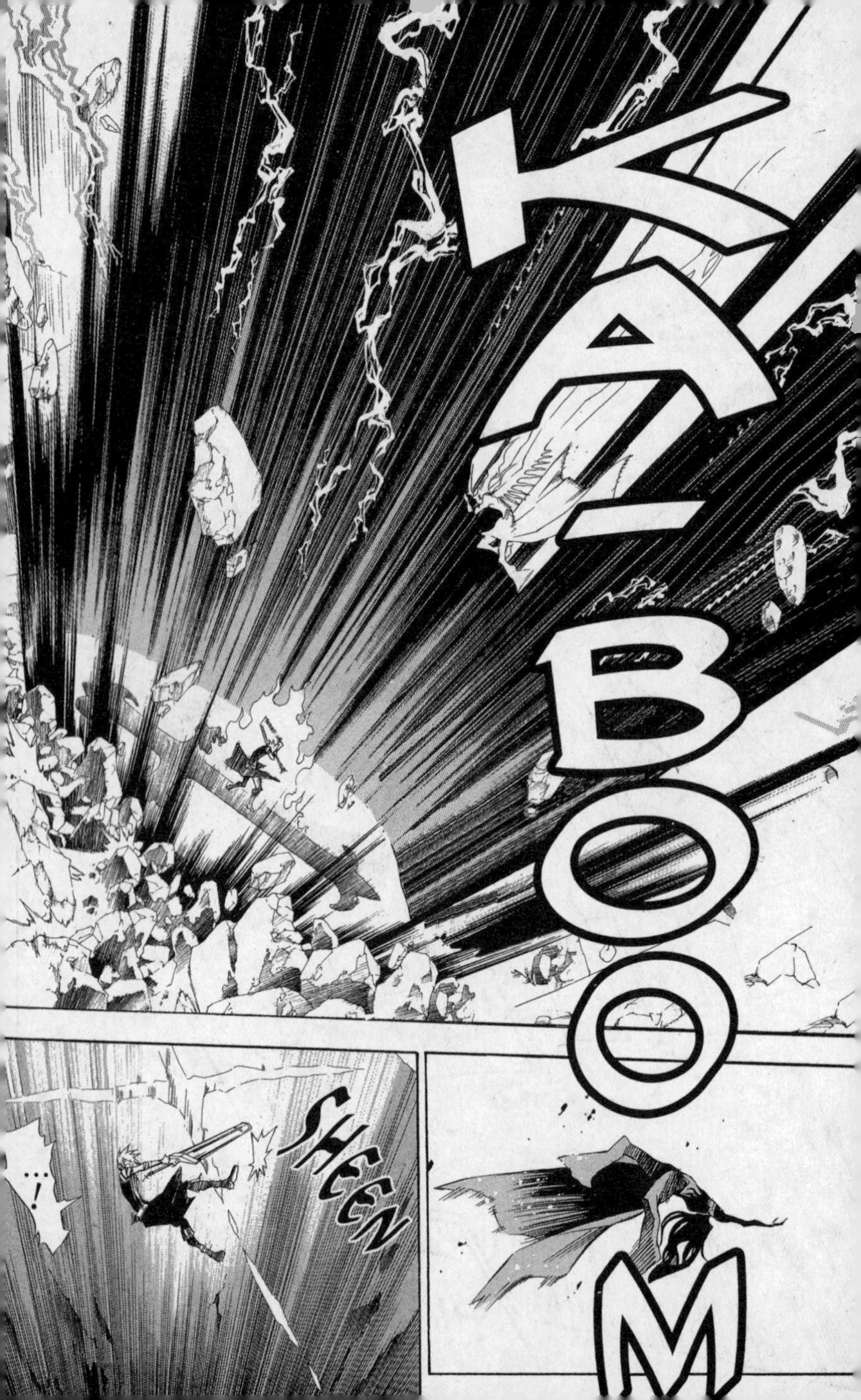
KA-BOOM
SHEEN
...!

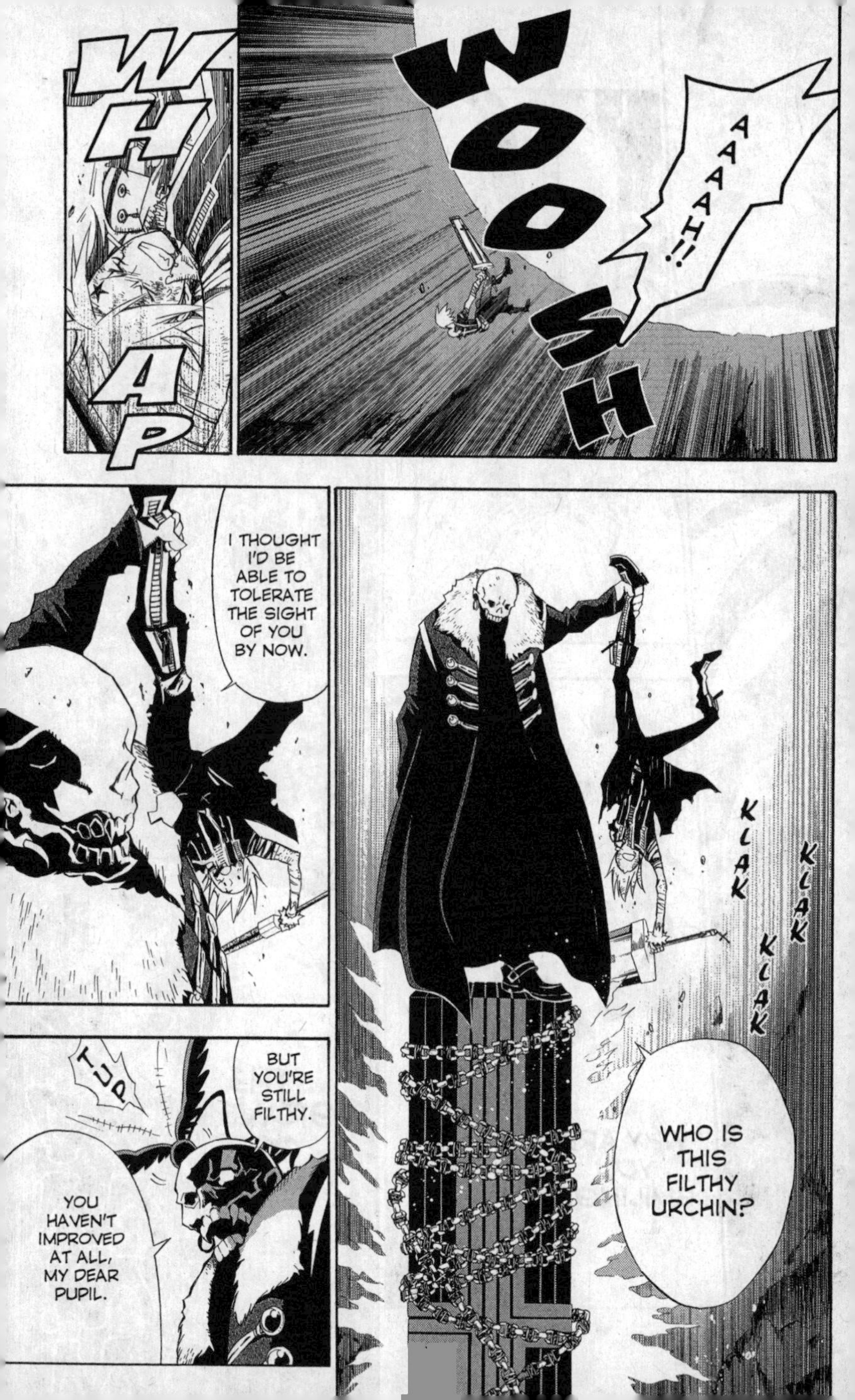
WOOSH
AAAAAH!!
WHAP
KLAK
KLAK
KLAK
KLAK
WHO IS THIS FILTHY URCHIN?
I THOUGHT I'D BE ABLE TO TOLERATE THE SIGHT OF YOU BY NOW.
BUT YOU'RE STILL FILTHY.
TJP
YOU HAVEN'T IMPROVED AT ALL, MY DEAR PUPIL.

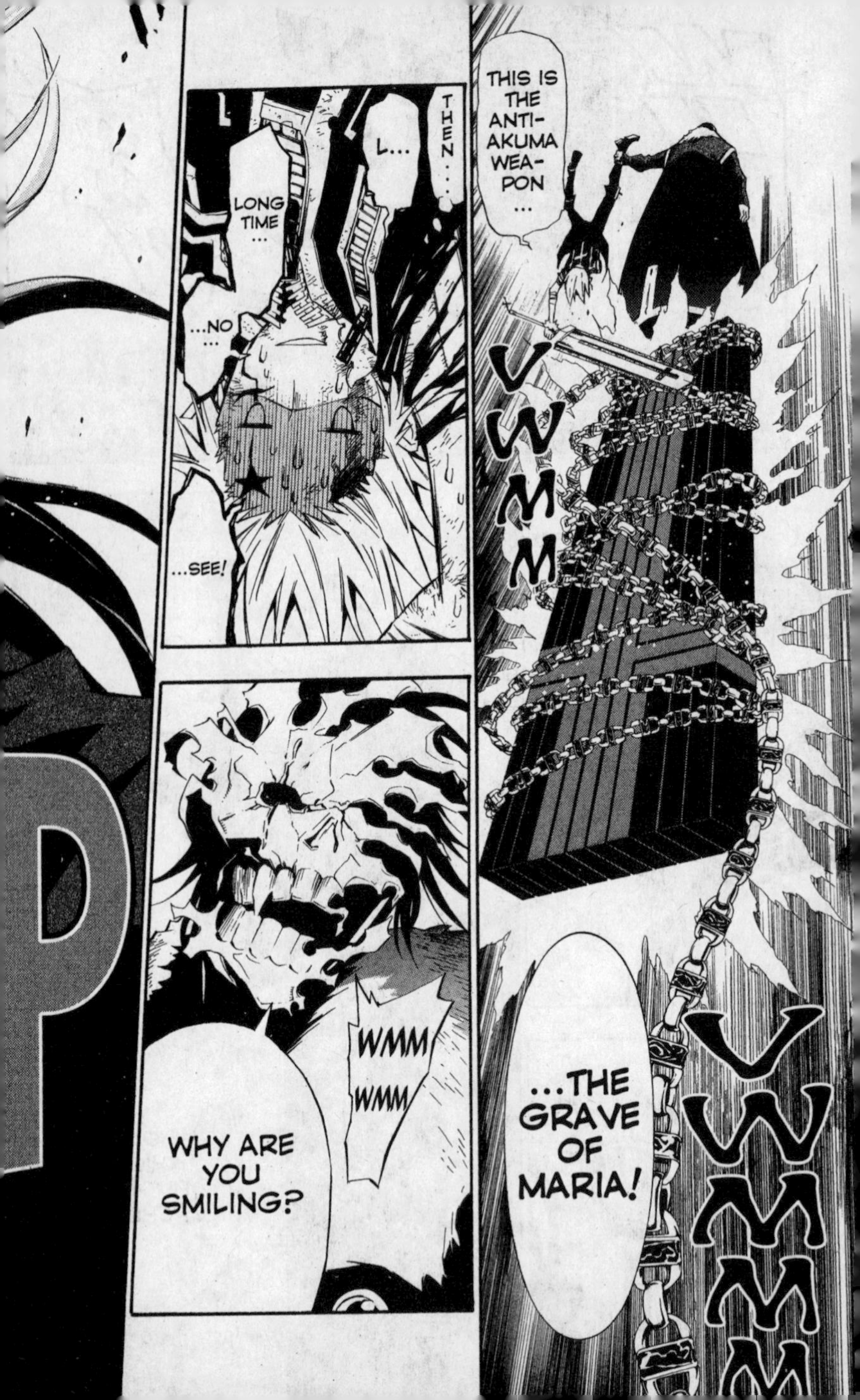
THIS IS THE ANTI-AKUMA WEAPON...
VWMM
...THE GRAVE OF MARIA!
VWMMM
THEN...
I...
LONG TIME...
...NO...
...SEE!
WMM WMM
WHY ARE YOU SMILING?

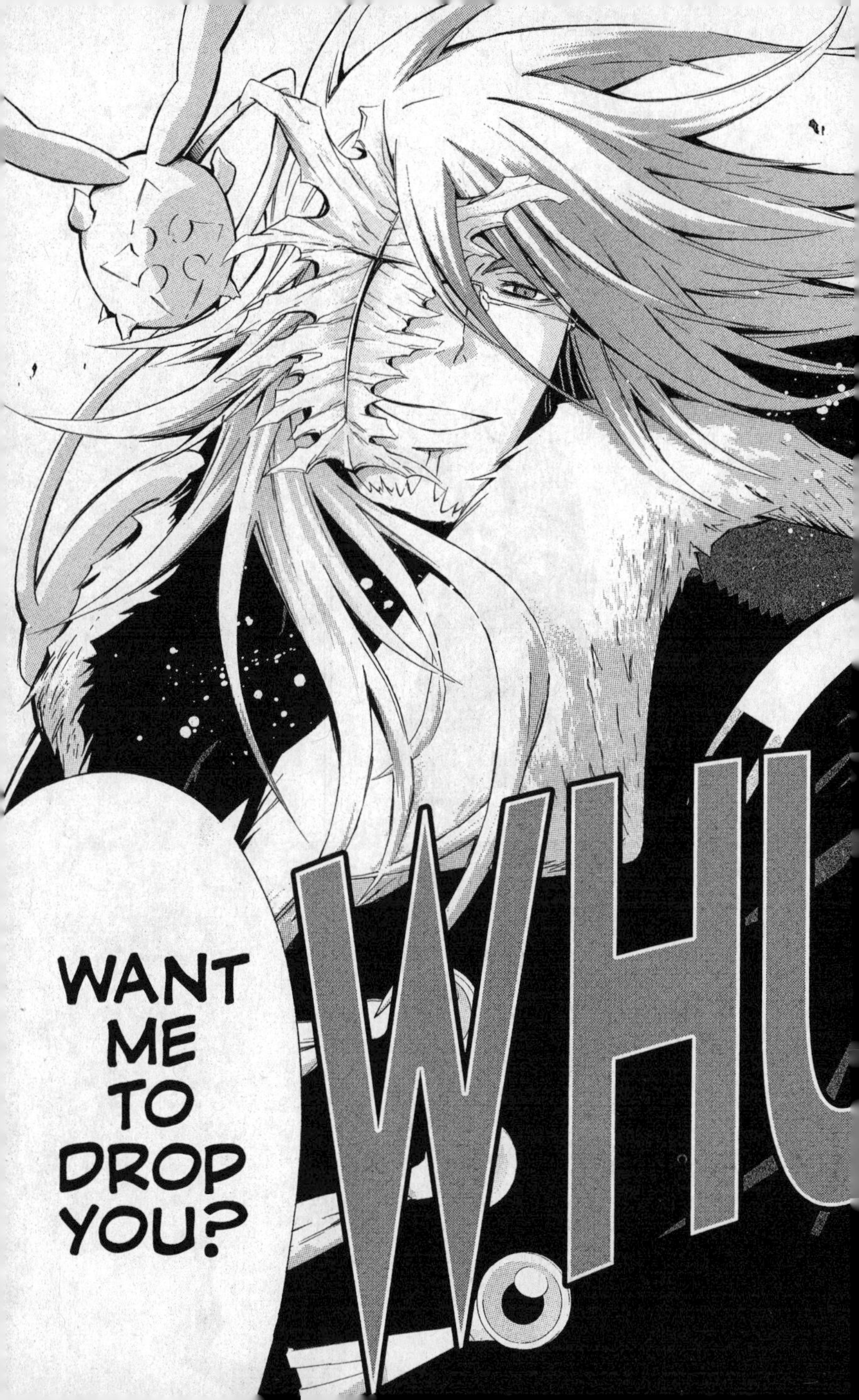

WANT ME TO DROP YOU?
WHU

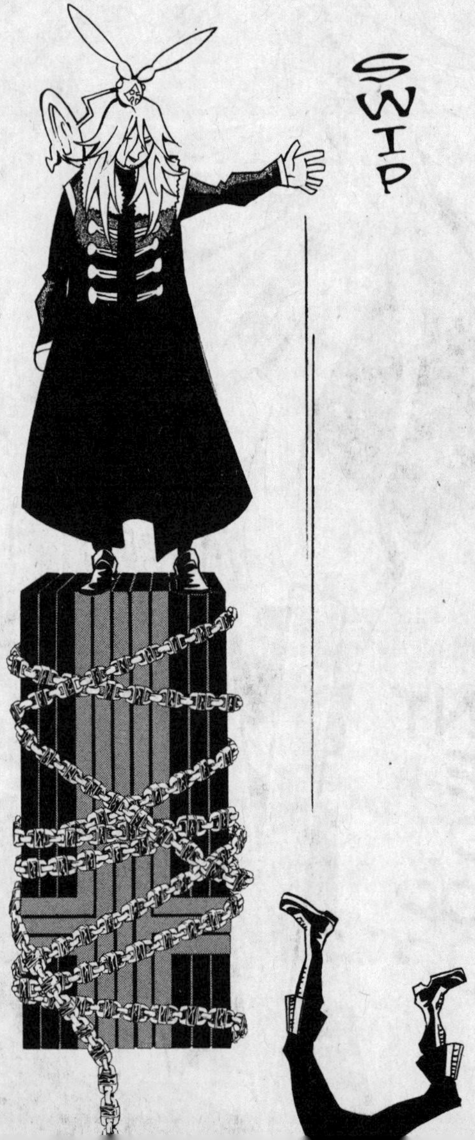
SWIP

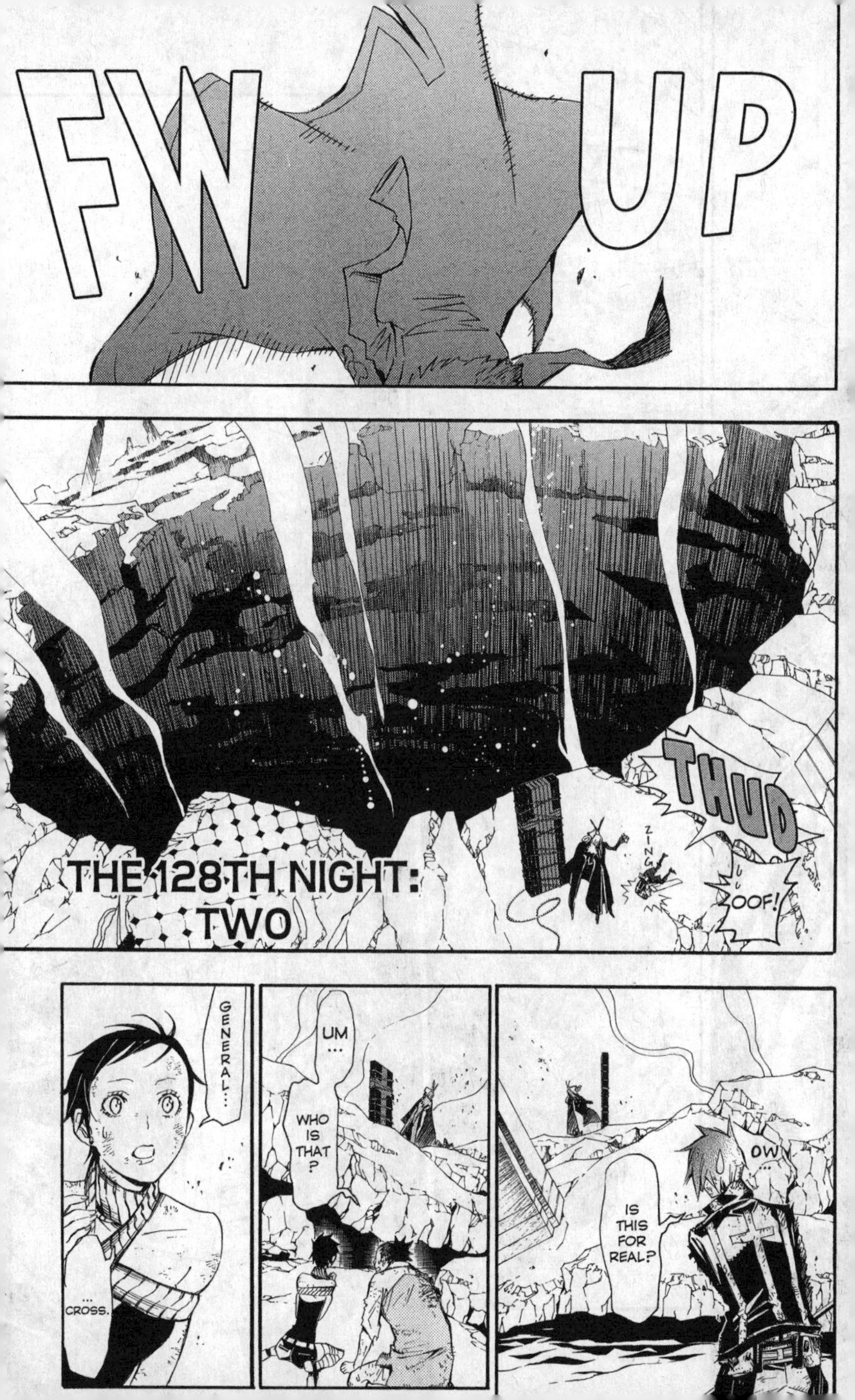
FWUP
THUD
ZING
OOF!
THE 128TH NIGHT:
TWO
OW
IS THIS FOR REAL?
UM...
WHO IS THAT?
GENERAL...
...CROSS.

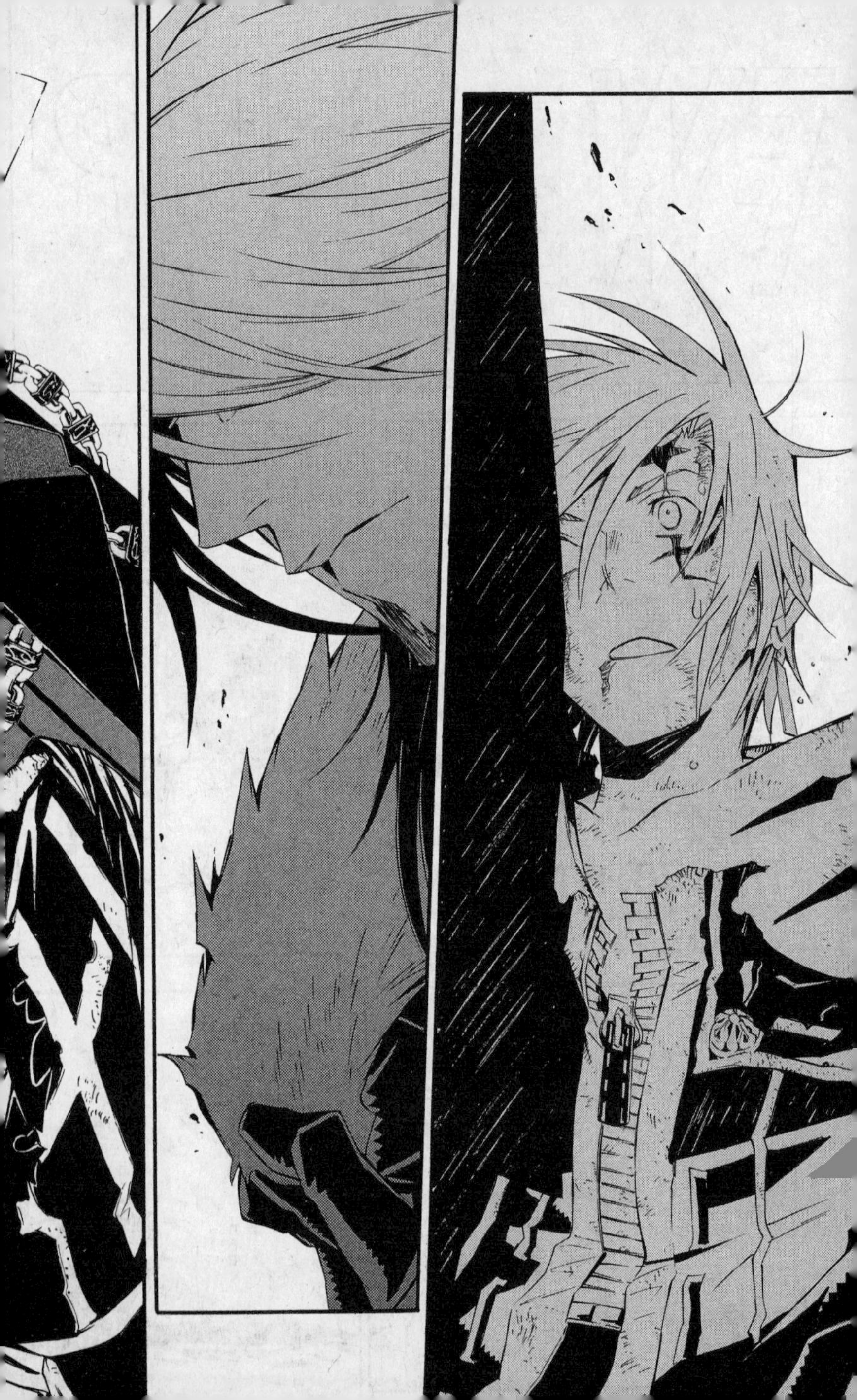

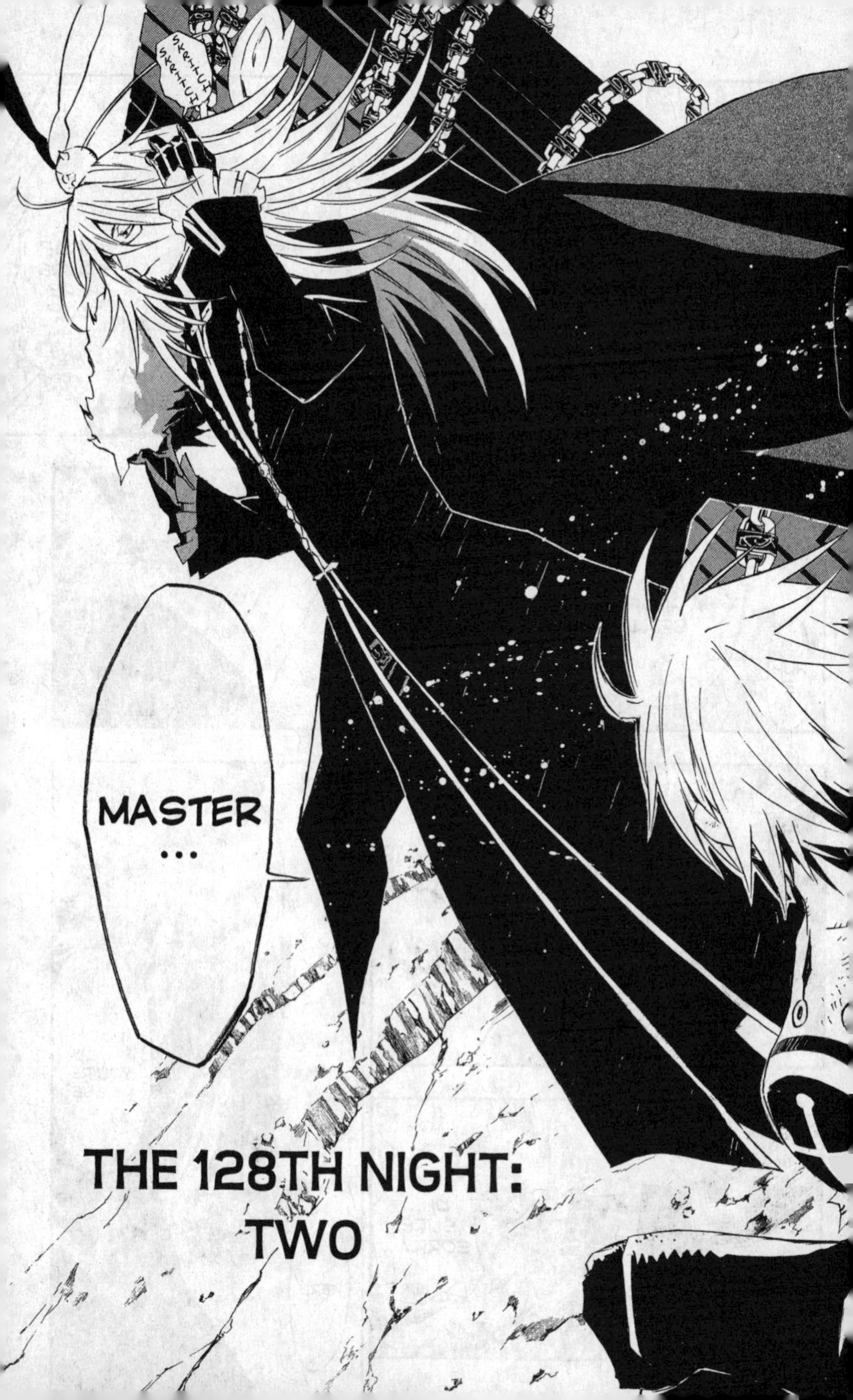
SKRITCH SKRITCH
MASTER ...
THE 128TH NIGHT: TWO

TWITCH

!

ZANG

T-TIM? YOU'RE HERE TOO?

FWUP

AT LEAST YOU CAN FINALLY DO A PROPER SPELL.

HUH?

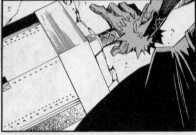

HIS HAND?

HUH?

WHUP

BUT LOOK AT YOU. YOU'RE A MESS.

HERE.

WHAP

OH...

UH... SURE. SORRY...

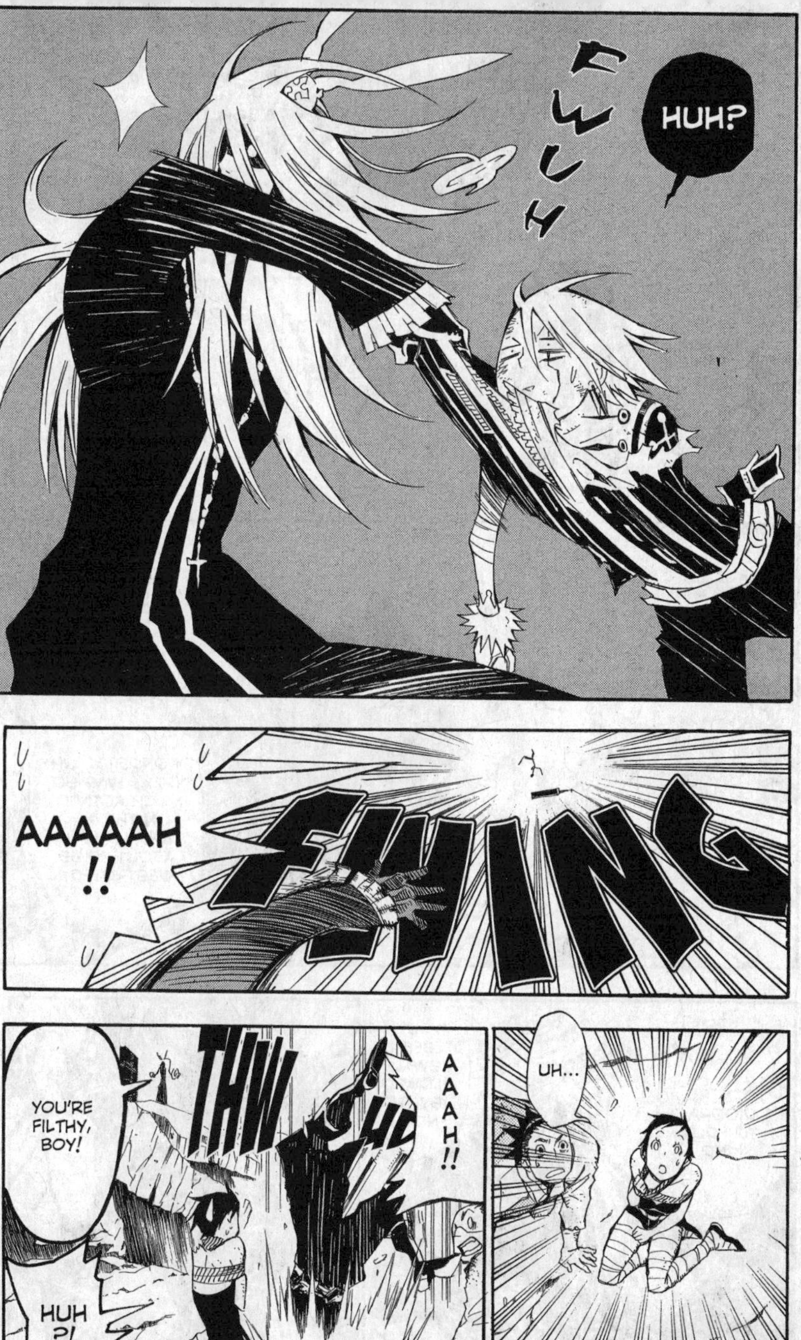
HUH?
FWUH
AAAAAH!!
UH...
AAAAH!!
YOU'RE FILTHY, BOY!
HUH?!

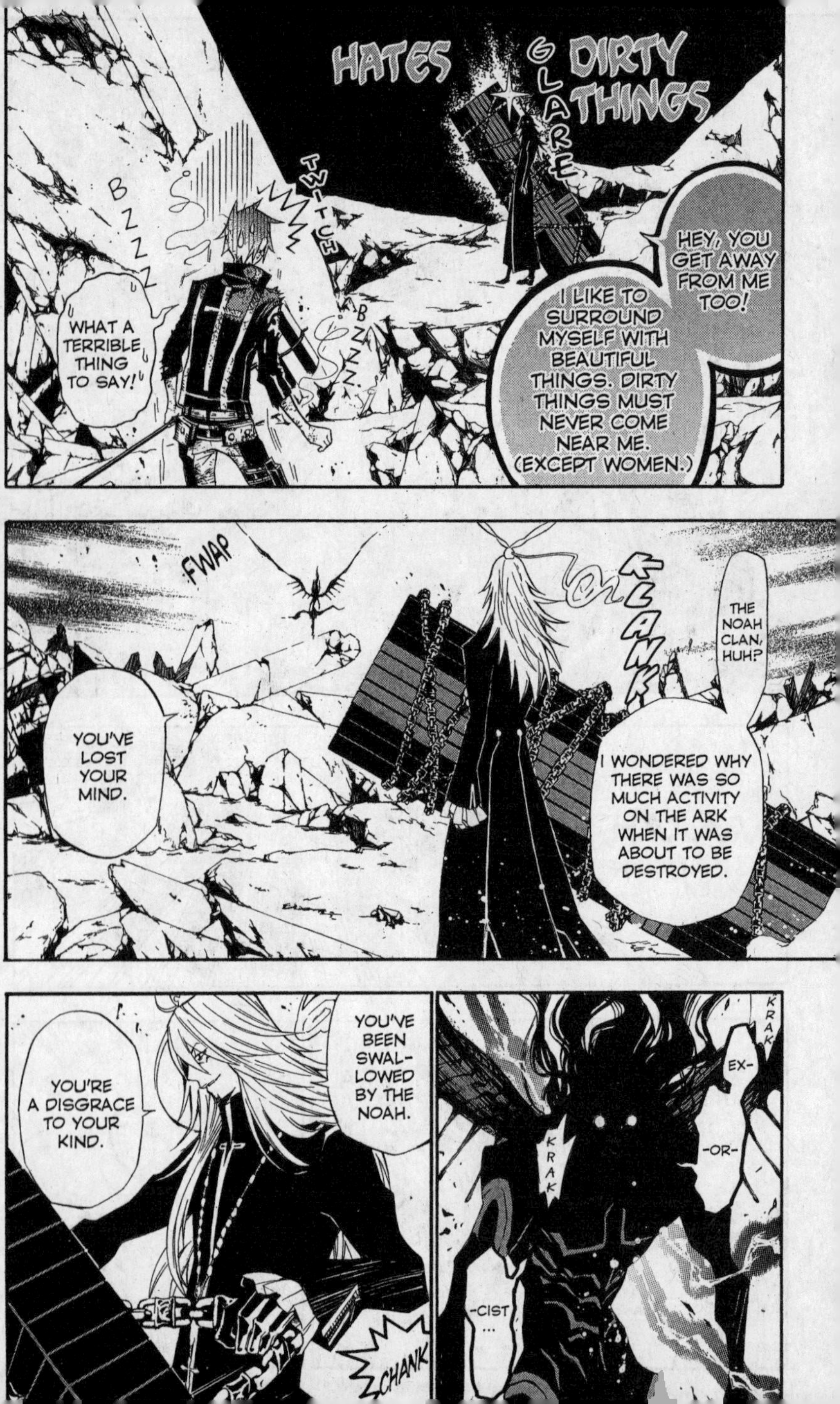
HATES DIRTY THINGS
GLARE
HEY, YOU GET AWAY FROM ME TOO!
I LIKE TO SURROUND MYSELF WITH BEAUTIFUL THINGS. DIRTY THINGS MUST NEVER COME NEAR ME. (EXCEPT WOMEN.)
TWITCH
BZZZ
BZZZ
WHAT A TERRIBLE THING TO SAY!
THE NOAH CLAN, HUH?
KLANK
I WONDERED WHY THERE WAS SO MUCH ACTIVITY ON THE ARK WHEN IT WAS ABOUT TO BE DESTROYED.
FWAP
YOU'VE LOST YOUR MIND.
KRAK
EX-
-OR-
KRAK
-CIST ...
YOU'VE BEEN SWAL-LOWED BY THE NOAH.
YOU'RE A DISGRACE TO YOUR KIND.
CHANK

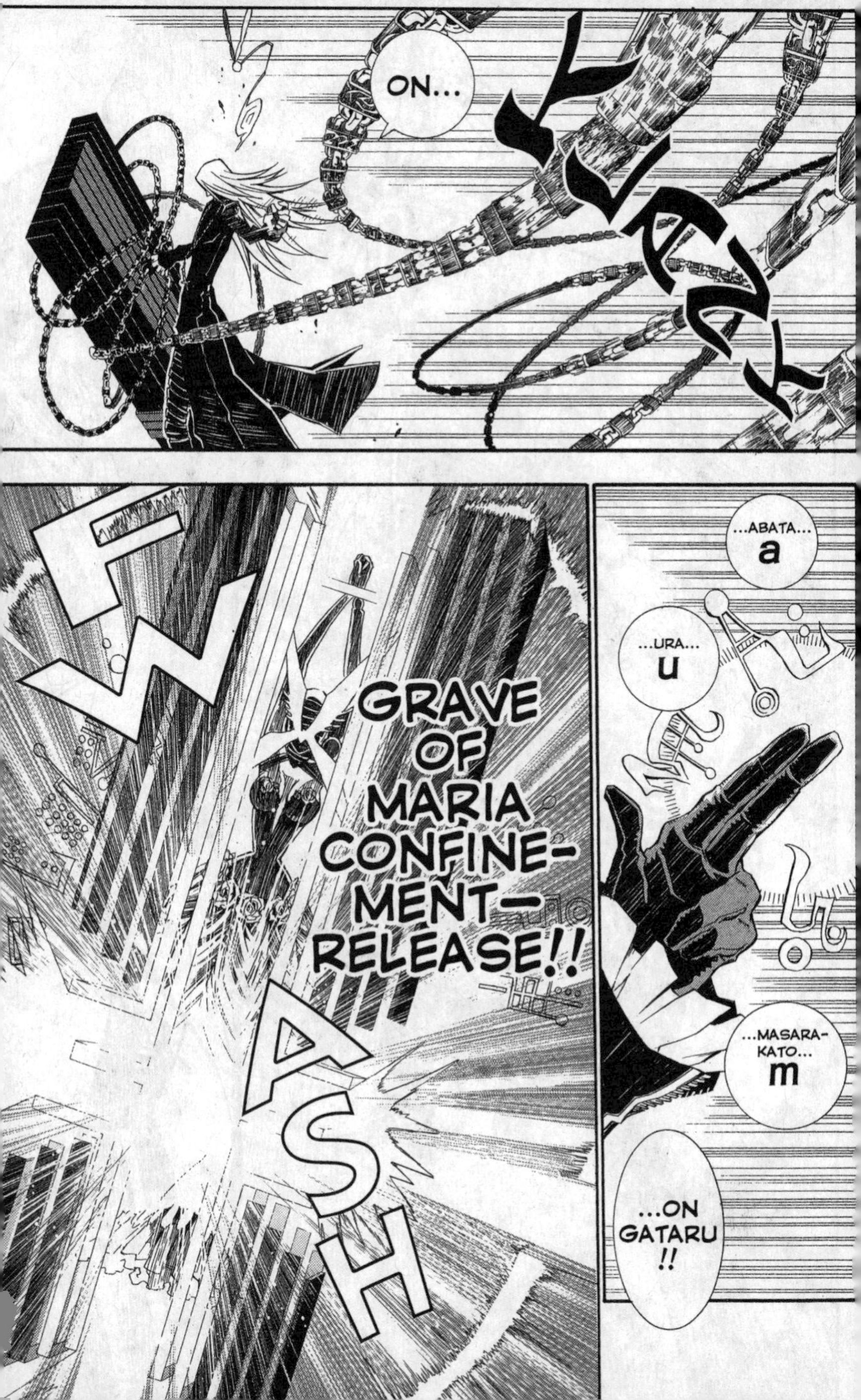
ON...
...ABATA... a
...URA... u
...MASARA-KATO... m
...ON GATARU !!
GRAVE OF MARIA CONFINE-MENT—RELEASE!!
FWASH

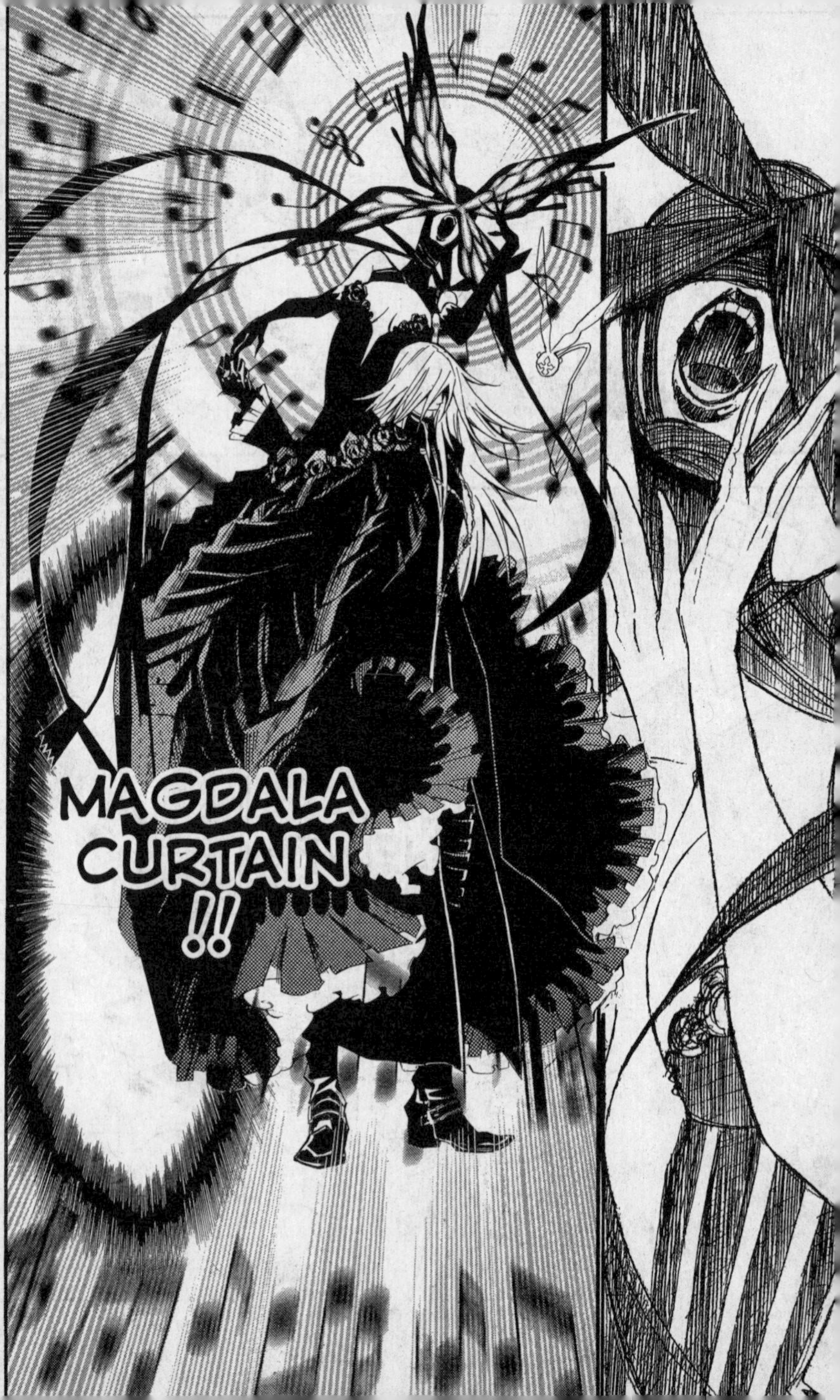
MAGDALA CURTAIN !!

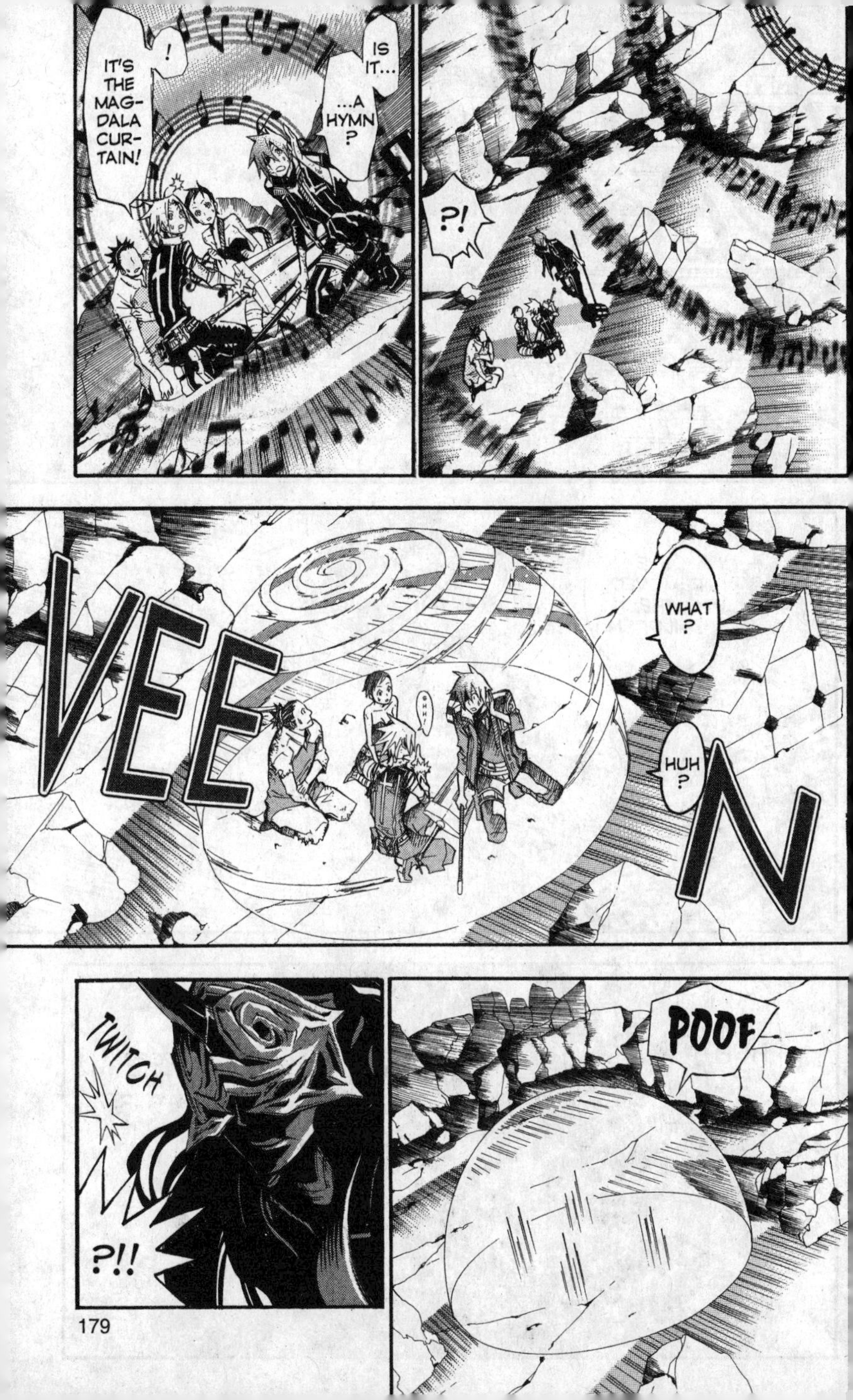
?!
IS IT...
...A HYMN?
!
IT'S THE MAG-DALA CUR-TAIN!
WHAT?
HUH?
VEEN
POOF
TWITCH
?!!

WOOO OO

I'VE REMOVED THE CHILDREN.

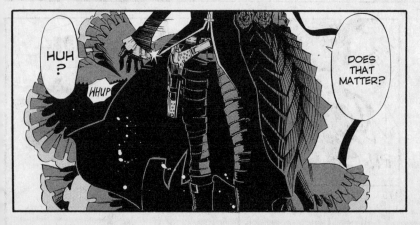

HUH?

WHUP

DOES THAT MATTER?

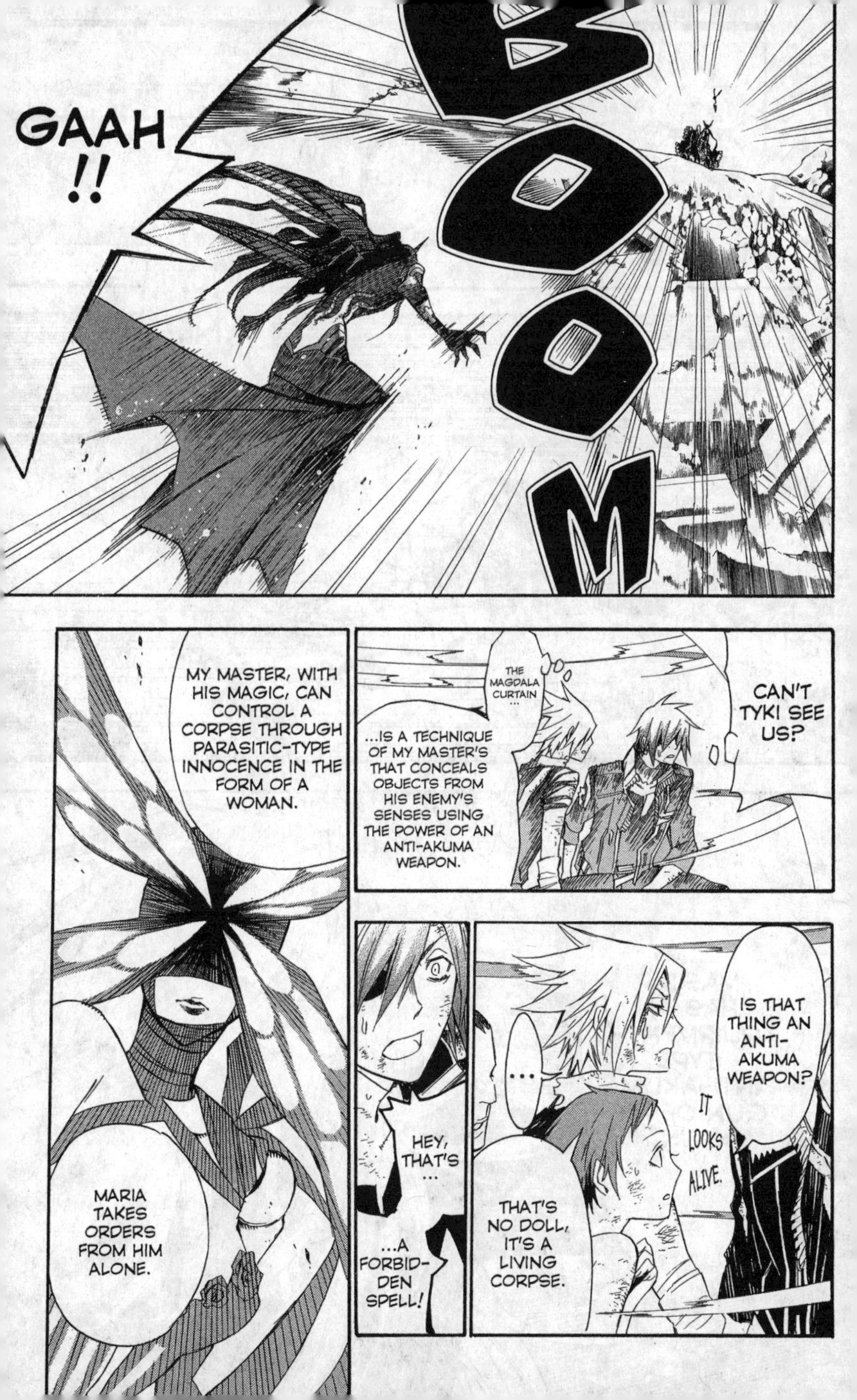
BOOM
GAAH!!
CAN'T TYKI SEE US?
THE MAGDALA CURTAIN ...
...IS A TECHNIQUE OF MY MASTER'S THAT CONCEALS OBJECTS FROM HIS ENEMY'S SENSES USING THE POWER OF AN ANTI-AKUMA WEAPON.
IS THAT THING AN ANTI-AKUMA WEAPON?
IT LOOKS ALIVE.
...
THAT'S NO DOLL, IT'S A LIVING CORPSE.
HEY, THAT'S ...
...A FORBID-DEN SPELL!
MY MASTER, WITH HIS MAGIC, CAN CONTROL A CORPSE THROUGH PARASITIC-TYPE INNOCENCE IN THE FORM OF A WOMAN.
MARIA TAKES ORDERS FROM HIM ALONE.

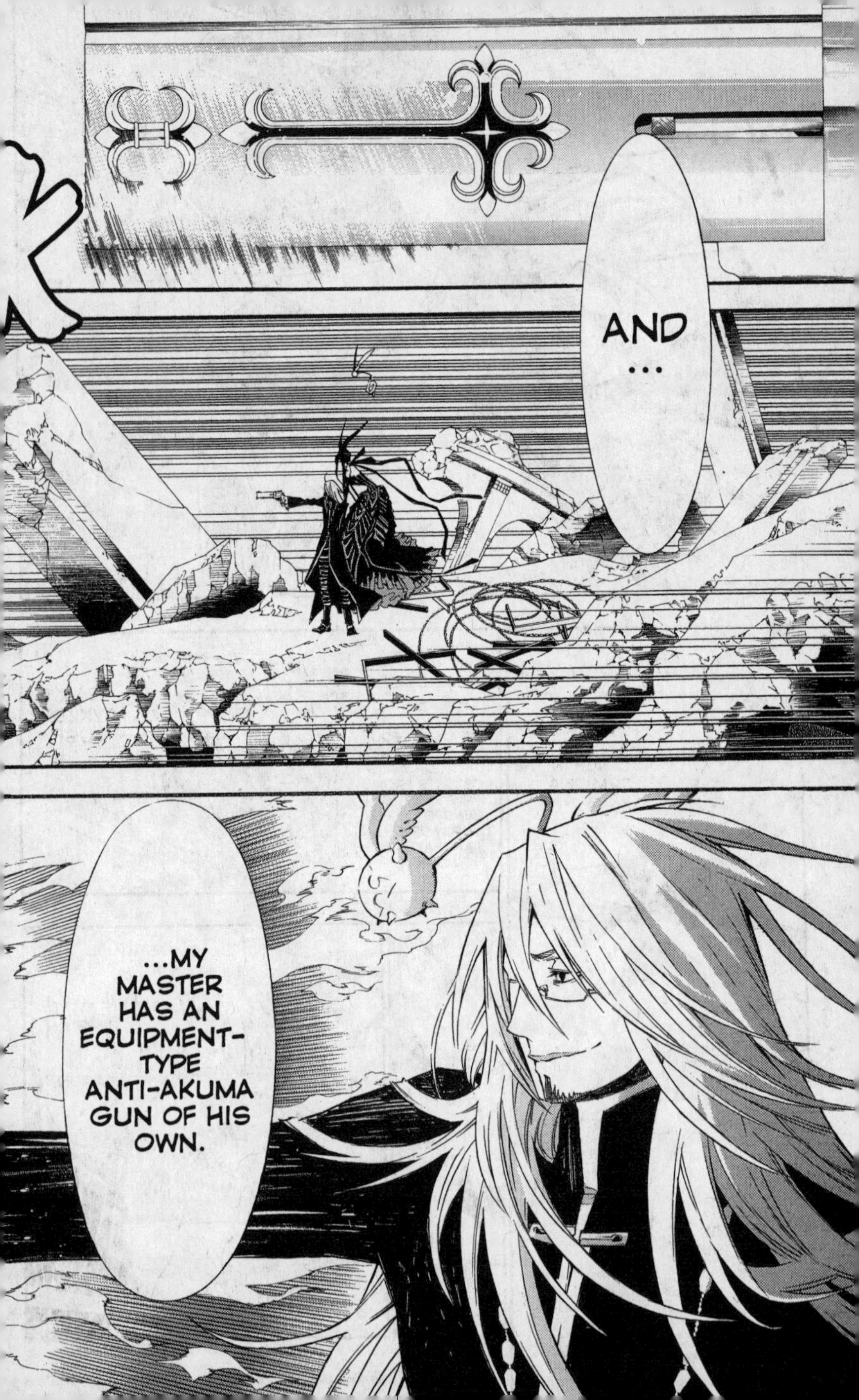
AND ...
...MY MASTER HAS AN EQUIPMENT-TYPE ANTI-AKUMA GUN OF HIS OWN.

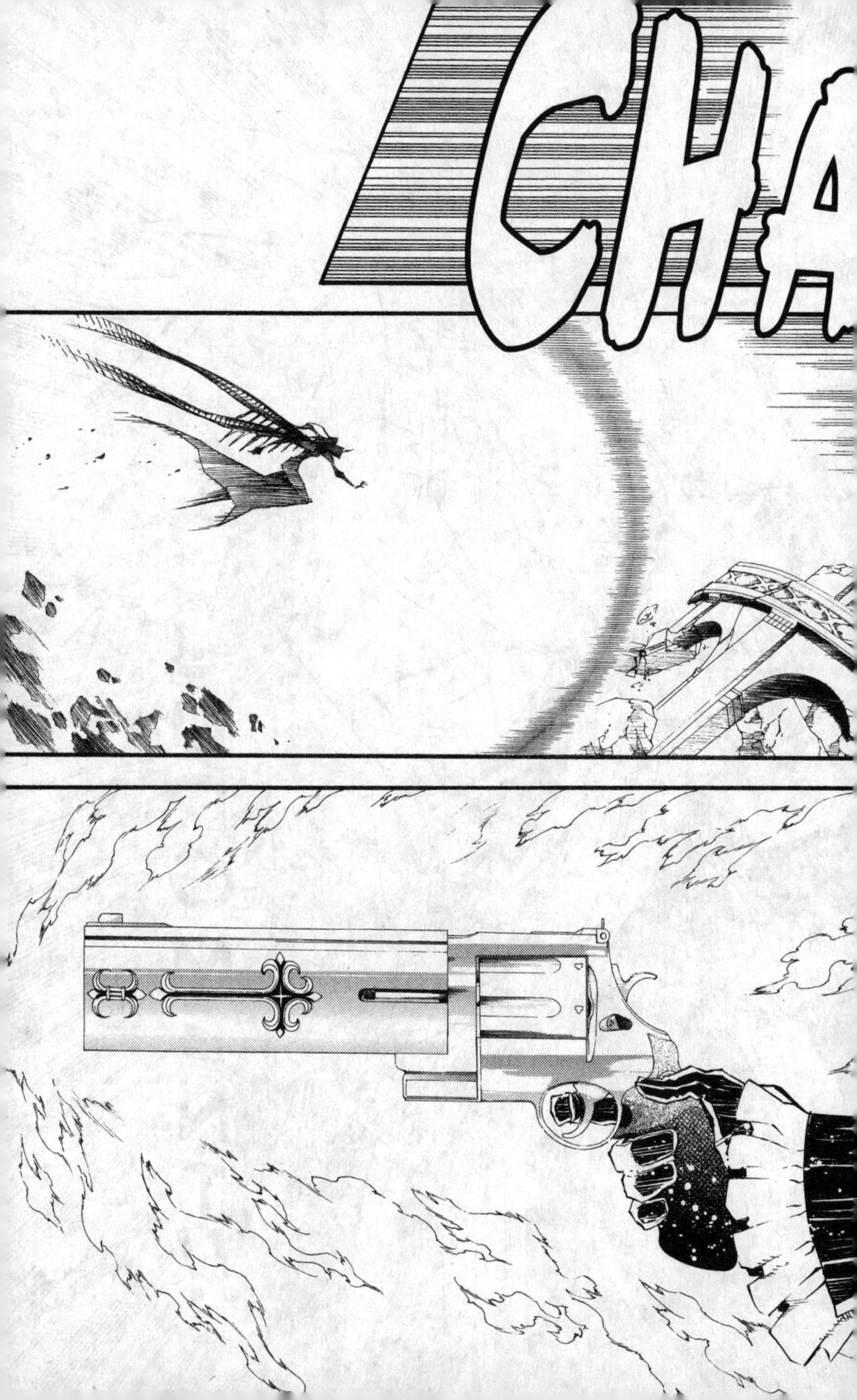
CHA

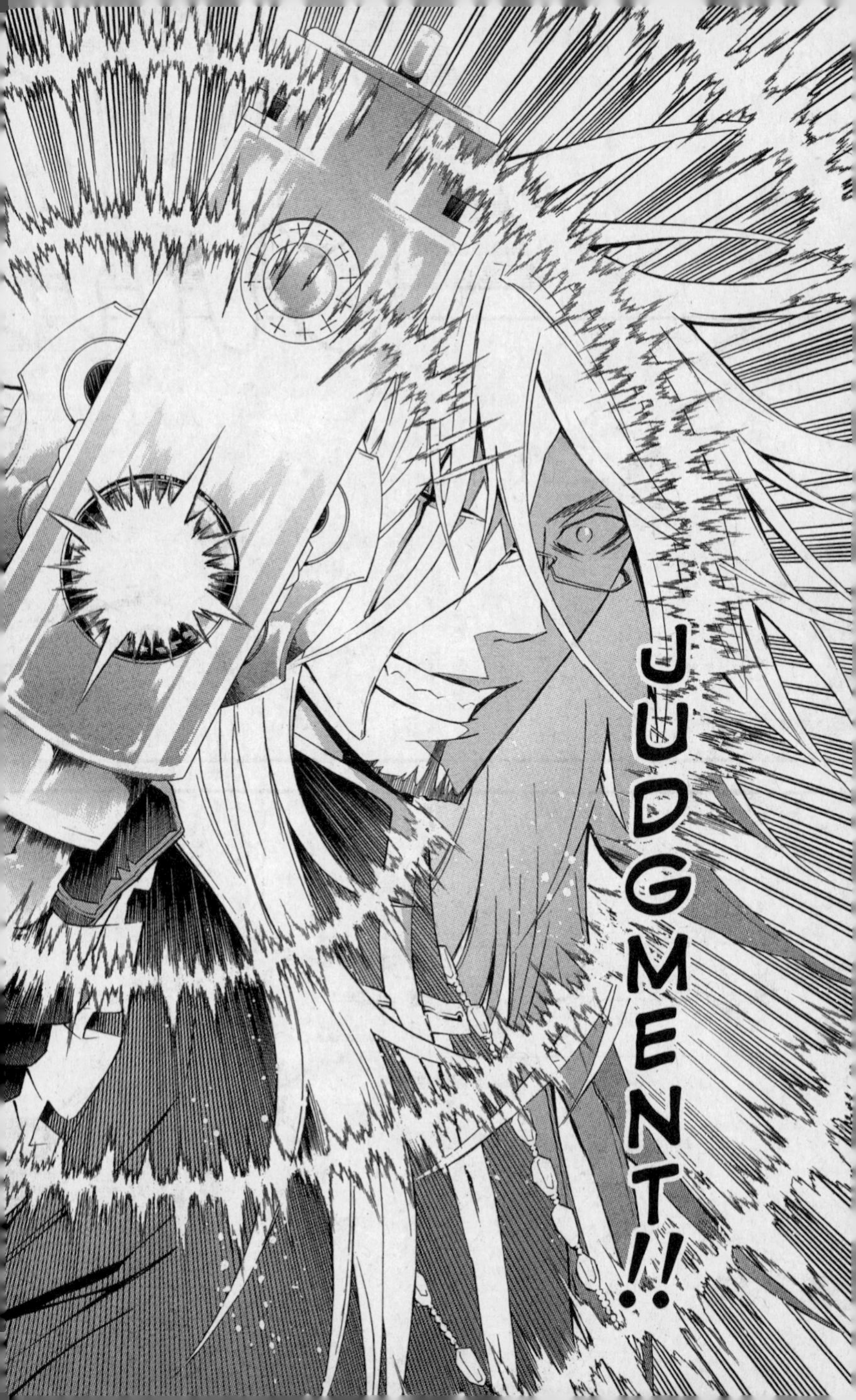
JUDGMENT!!

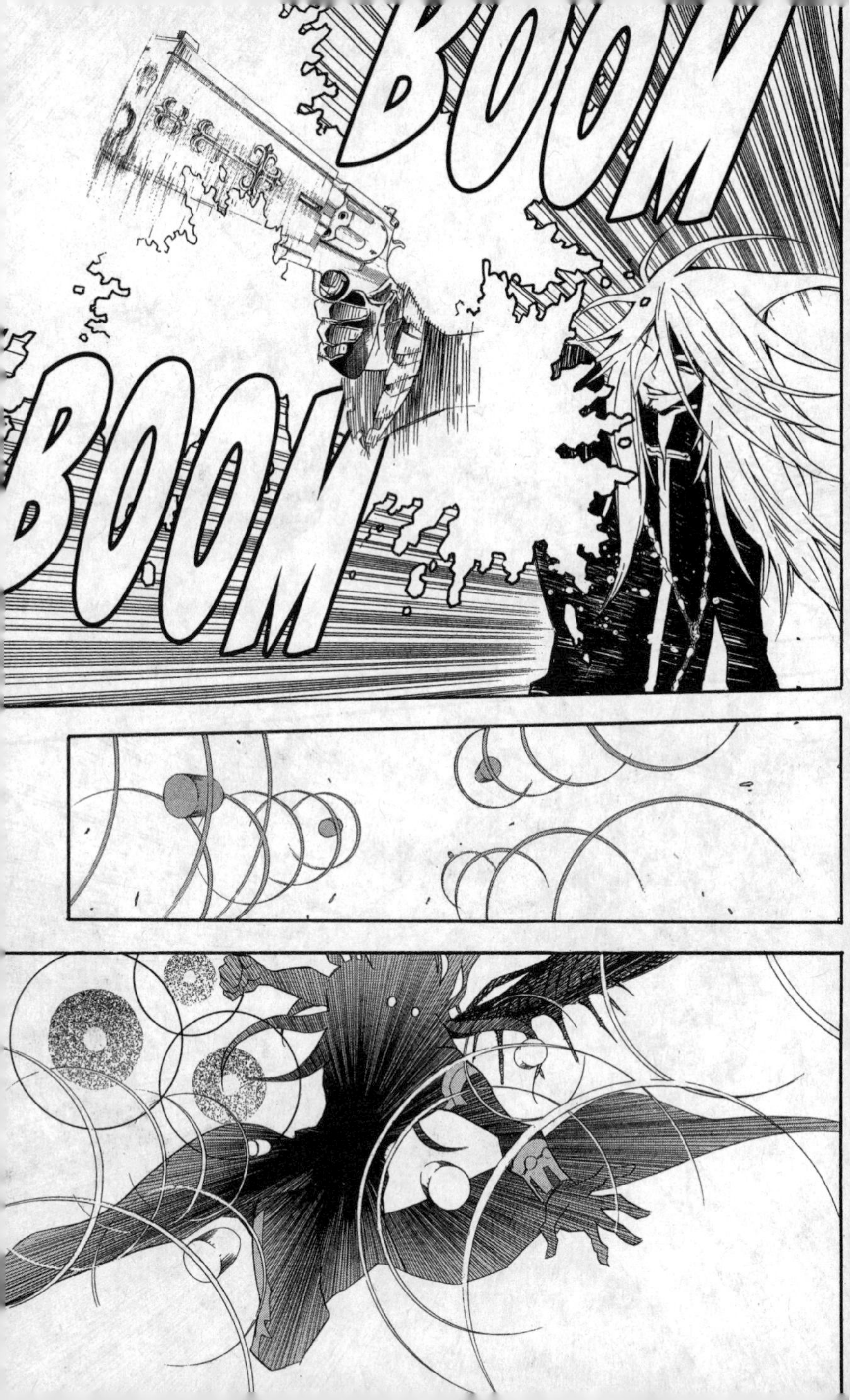
BOOM
BOOM

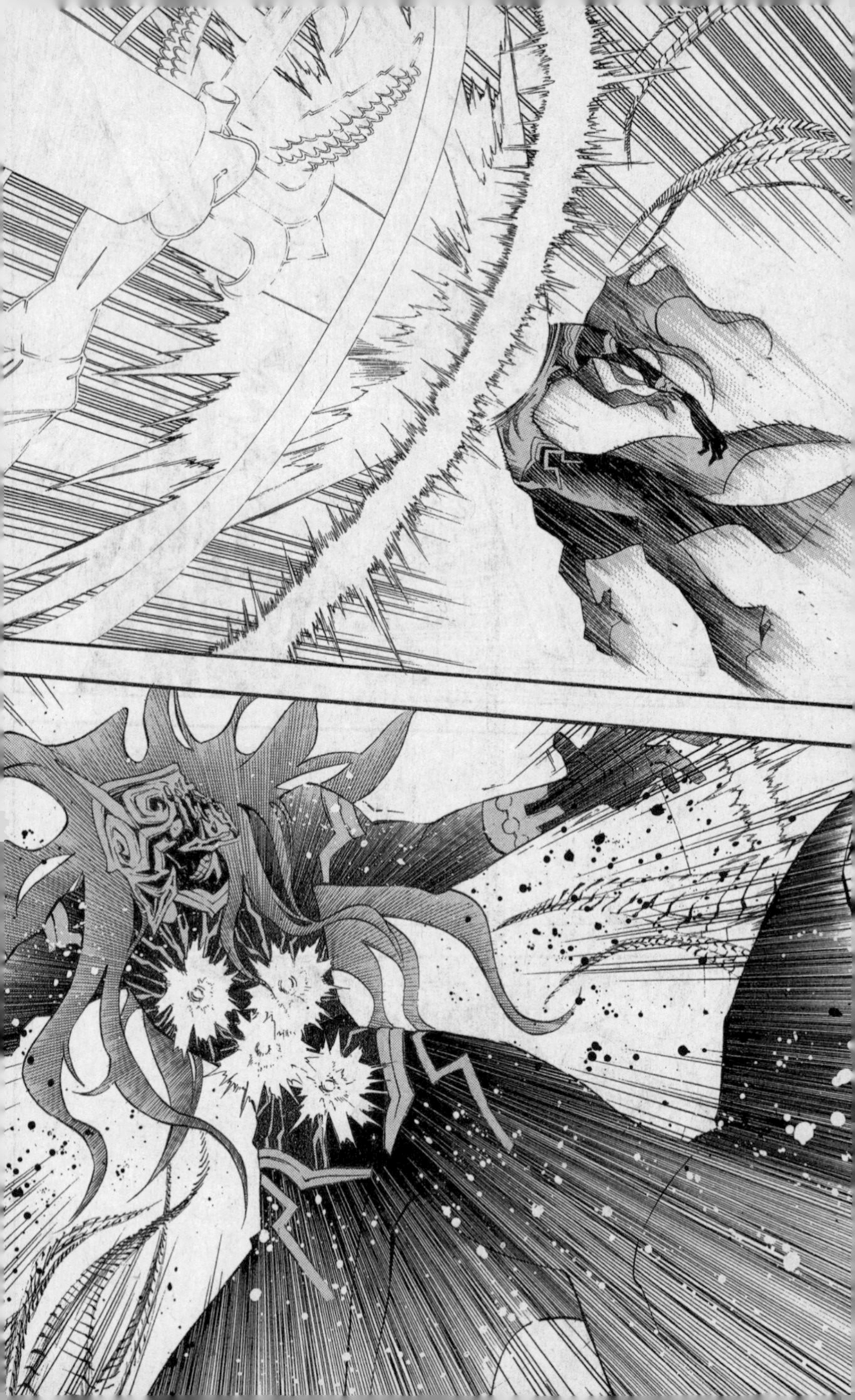

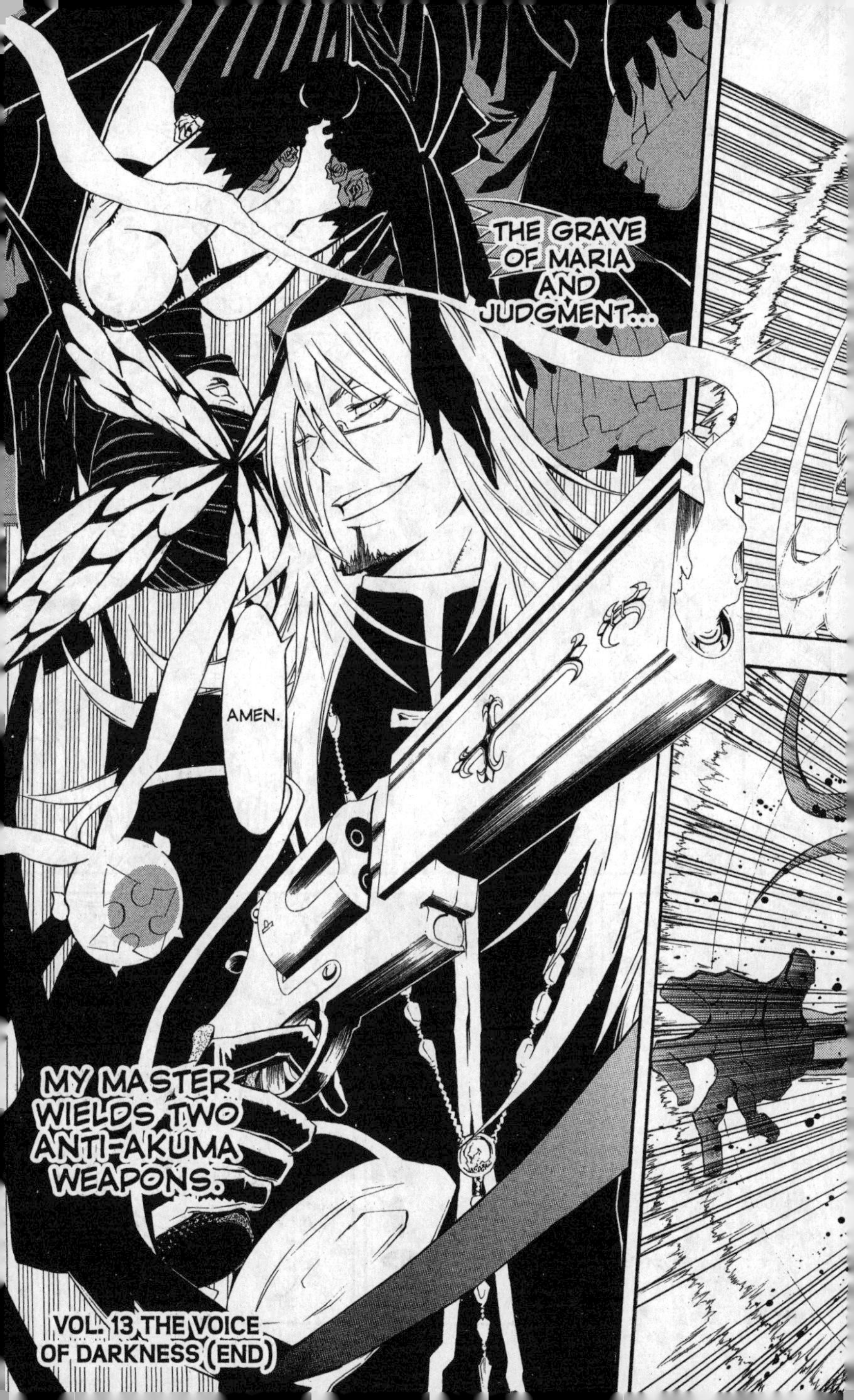
THE GRAVE OF MARIA AND JUDGMENT...
AMEN.
MY MASTER WIELDS TWO ANTI-AKUMA WEAPONS.
VOL. 13 THE VOICE OF DARKNESS (END)

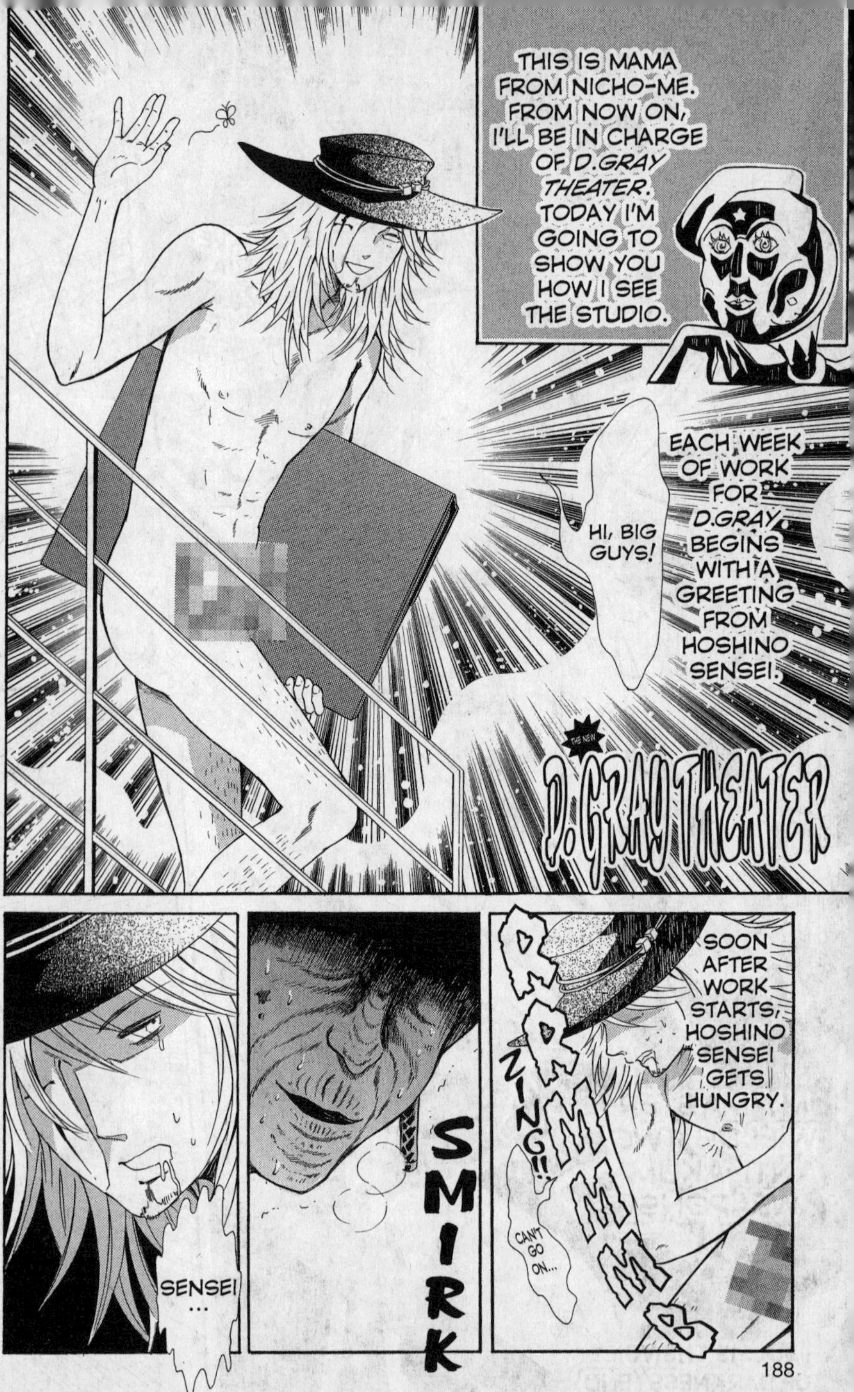
THIS IS MAMA FROM NICHO-ME. FROM NOW ON, I'LL BE IN CHARGE OF D.GRAY THEATER. TODAY I'M GOING TO SHOW YOU HOW I SEE THE STUDIO.
EACH WEEK OF WORK FOR D.GRAY BEGINS WITH A GREETING FROM HOSHINO SENSEI.
HI, BIG GUYS!
THE NEW
D.GRAY THEATER
SOON AFTER WORK STARTS, HOSHINO SENSEI GETS HUNGRY.
ZING!!
CAN'T GO ON...
SMIRK
SENSEI ...

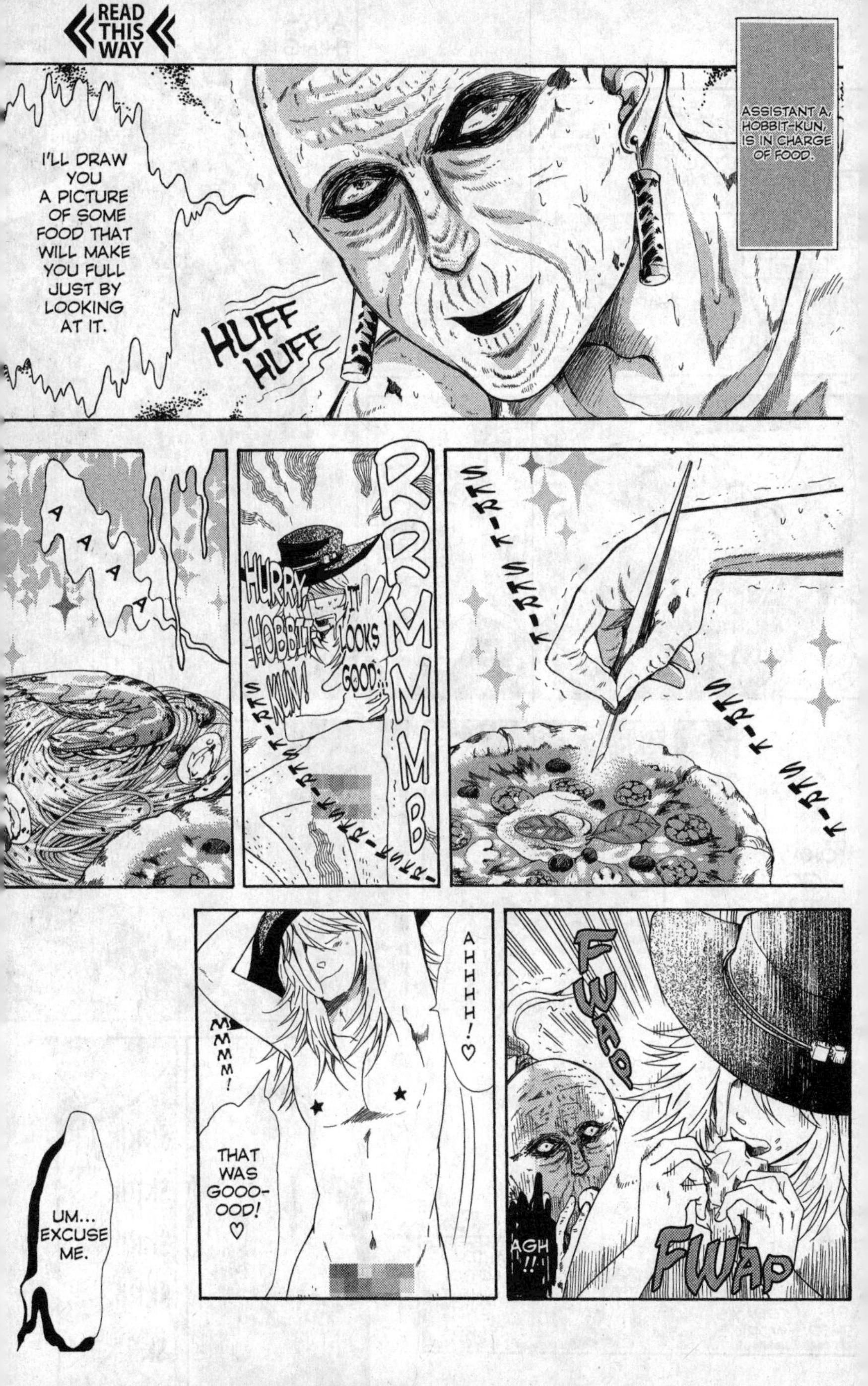
READ THIS WAY
ASSISTANT A, HOBBIT-KUN, IS IN CHARGE OF FOOD.
HUFF HUFF
I'LL DRAW YOU A PICTURE OF SOME FOOD THAT WILL MAKE YOU FULL JUST BY LOOKING AT IT.
SKRIK SKRIK
SKRIK SKRIK
RRMMMB
IT LOOKS GOOD;;
HURRY, HOBBIT-KUN!
SKRIK SKRIK
AAAAA
FWAP
AGH!!
FWAP
AHHHH!♡
MMMM!
THAT WAS GOOOOOD!♡
UM... EXCUSE ME.

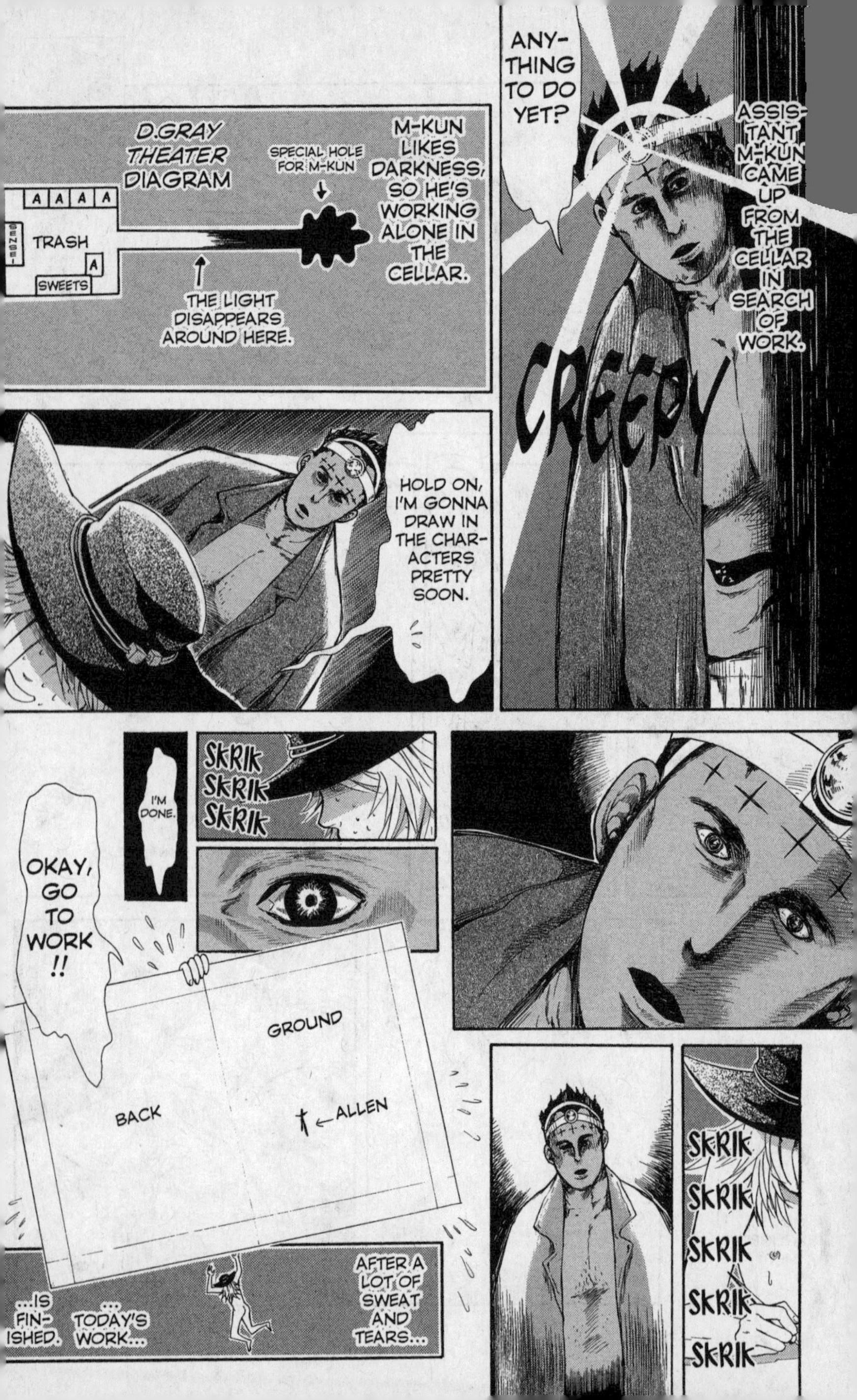
ASSISTANT M-KUN CAME UP FROM THE CELLAR IN SEARCH OF WORK.
ANYTHING TO DO YET?
CREEPY
M-KUN LIKES DARKNESS, SO HE'S WORKING ALONE IN THE CELLAR.
SPECIAL HOLE FOR M-KUN
D.GRAY THEATER DIAGRAM
A A A A
SENSEI
TRASH
A
SWEETS
THE LIGHT DISAPPEARS AROUND HERE.
HOLD ON, I'M GONNA DRAW IN THE CHARACTERS PRETTY SOON.
SKRIK SKRIK SKRIK
I'M DONE.
OKAY, GO TO WORK!!
GROUND
BACK
← ALLEN
SKRIK SKRIK SKRIK SKRIK SKRIK
AFTER A LOT OF SWEAT AND TEARS...
...TODAY'S WORK...
...IS FINISHED.

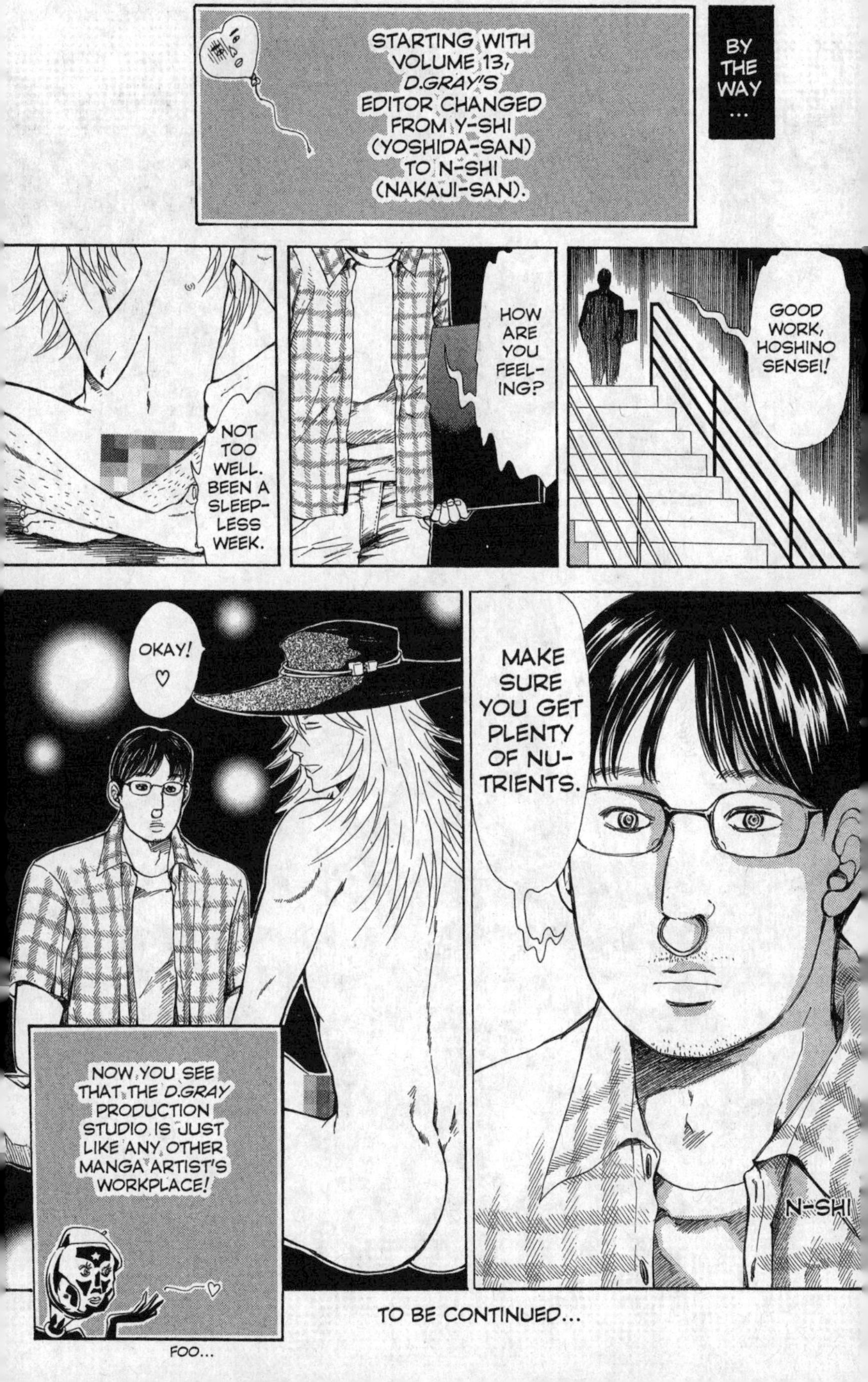
BY THE WAY...
STARTING WITH VOLUME 13, D.GRAY'S EDITOR CHANGED FROM Y-SHI (YOSHIDA-SAN) TO N-SHI (NAKAJI-SAN).
GOOD WORK, HOSHINO SENSEI!
HOW ARE YOU FEEL-ING?
NOT TOO WELL. BEEN A SLEEP-LESS WEEK.
MAKE SURE YOU GET PLENTY OF NU-TRIENTS.
N-SHI
OKAY! ♡
NOW YOU SEE THAT THE D.GRAY PRODUCTION STUDIO IS JUST LIKE ANY OTHER MANGA ARTIST'S WORKPLACE!
FOO...
TO BE CONTINUED...

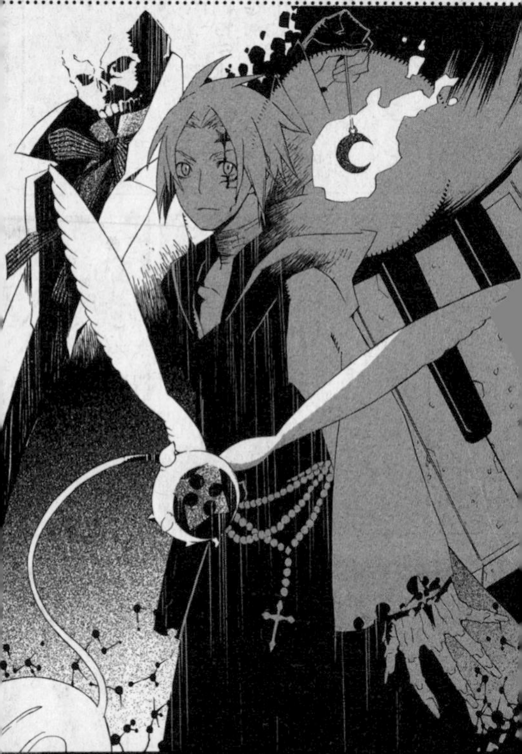

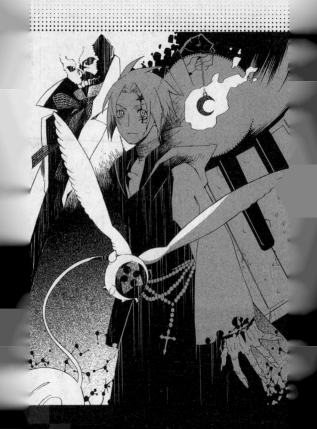

XT VOLUME...

onfidently faces off against both the new Tyki Mikk and the new
but fighting these menaces is not Cross's primary concern. He's
gg, a unique data transfer device that will allow the Millennium E
n, however, holds the key to success or failure—if he can just
piano!

v!

SHONEN JUMP ADVANCED MANGA EDITION

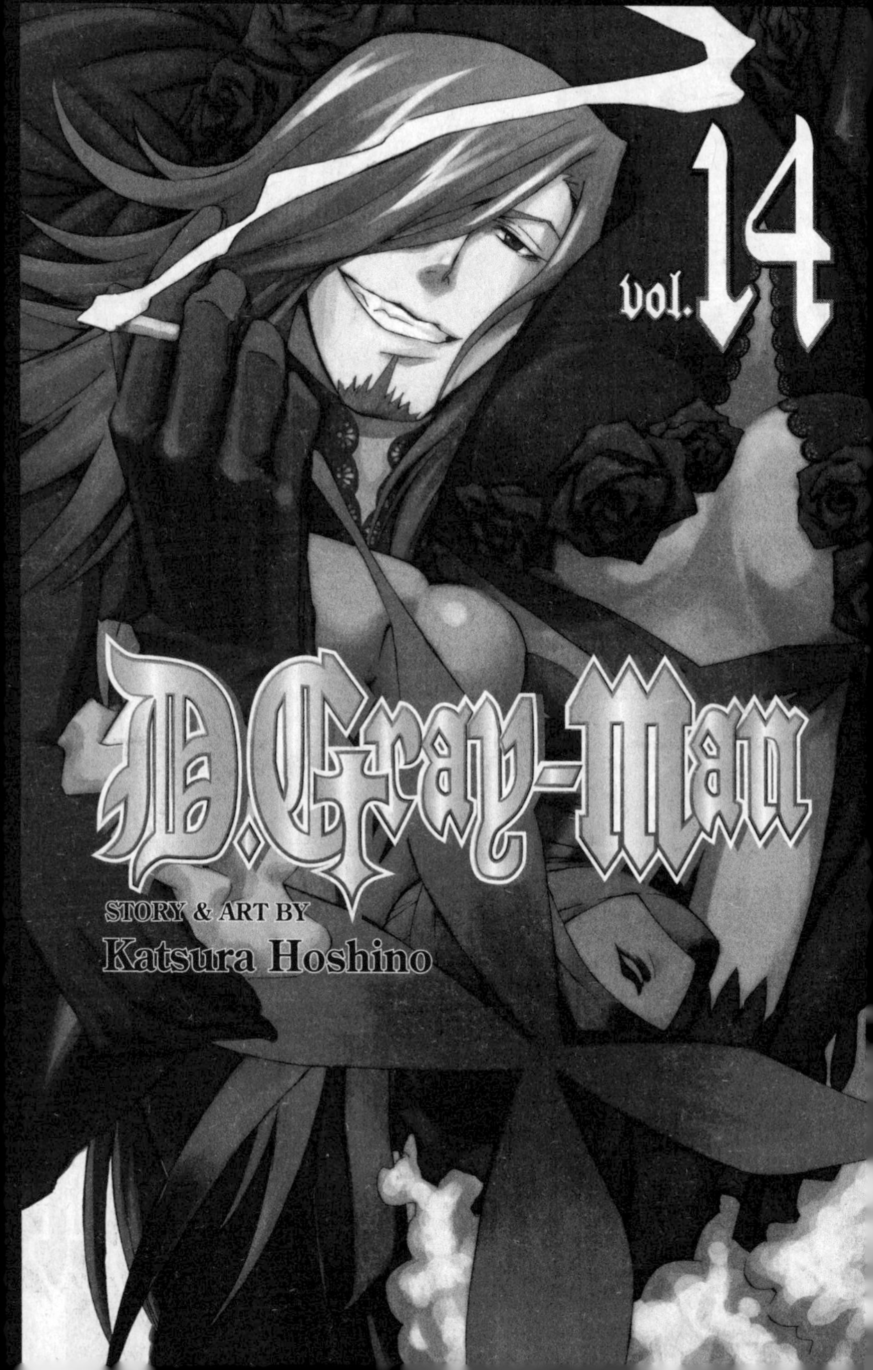
vol. 14
D.Gray-man
STORY & ART BY
Katsura Hoshino

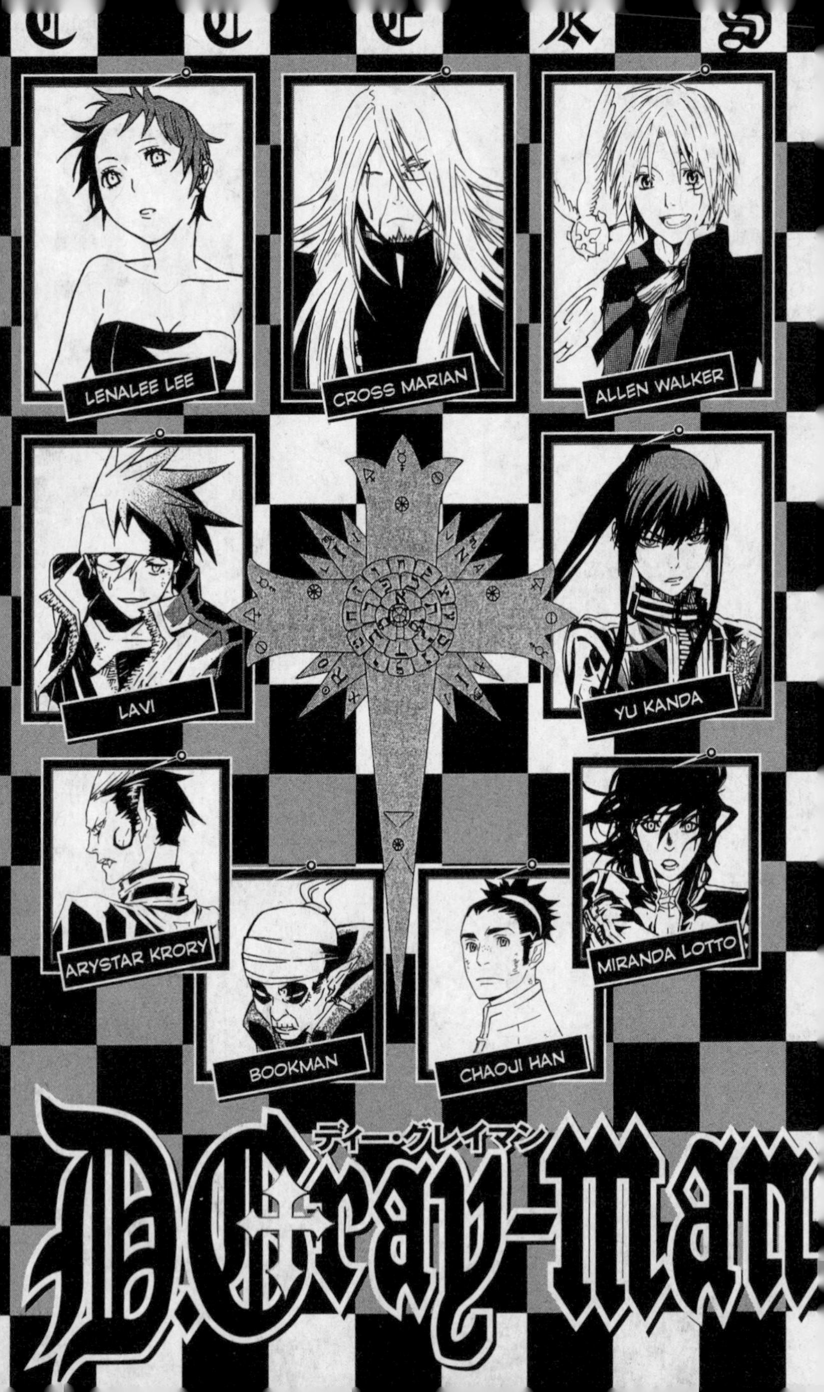
LENALEE LEE
CROSS MARIAN
ALLEN WALKER
LAVI
YU KANDA
ARYSTAR KRORY
BOOKMAN
CHAOJI HAN
MIRANDA LOTTO
ディー・グレイマン
D.Gray-man

CHARA CTERS

- JOHNNY GILL
- BAK CHAN
- KOMUI LEE
- ROUVERLIER
- REEVER WENHAM
- MILLENNIUM EARL
- TYKI MIKK
- HOWARD

STORY

IT ALL BEGAN CENTURIES AGO WITH THE DISCOVERY OF A CUBE CONTAINING AN APOCALYPTIC PROPHECY FROM AN ANCIENT CIVILIZATION AND INSTRUCTIONS IN THE USE OF INNOCENCE, A CRYSTALLINE SUBSTANCE OF WONDROUS SUPERNATURAL POWER. THE CREATORS OF THE CUBE CLAIMED TO HAVE DEFEATED AN EVIL KNOWN AS THE MILLENNIUM EARL BY USING THE INNOCENCE. NEVERTHELESS, THE WORLD WAS DESTROYED BY THE GREAT FLOOD OF THE OLD TESTAMENT. NOW, TO AVERT A SECOND END OF THE WORLD, A GROUP OF EXORCISTS WIELDING WEAPONS MADE OF INNOCENCE MUST BATTLE THE MILLENNIUM EARL AND HIS TERRIBLE MINIONS, THE AKUMA.

ALLEN AND THE OTHER EXORCISTS FIND THEMSELVES FIGHTING FOR THEIR LIVES ON A RAPIDLY DISINTEGRATING ARK. BUT EVEN AS THE ARK COLLAPSES AROUND THEM, ALLEN DESTROYS TYKI MIKK'S INNER NOAH, TRIGGERING A RAMPAGE OF DESTRUCTION. AND IF MATTERS WEREN'T COMPLICATED ENOUGH, ALLEN'S LONG-LOST MASTER, CROSS MARIAN, SUDDENLY SHOWS UP!!

D.GRAY-MAN
Vol. 14

CONTENTS

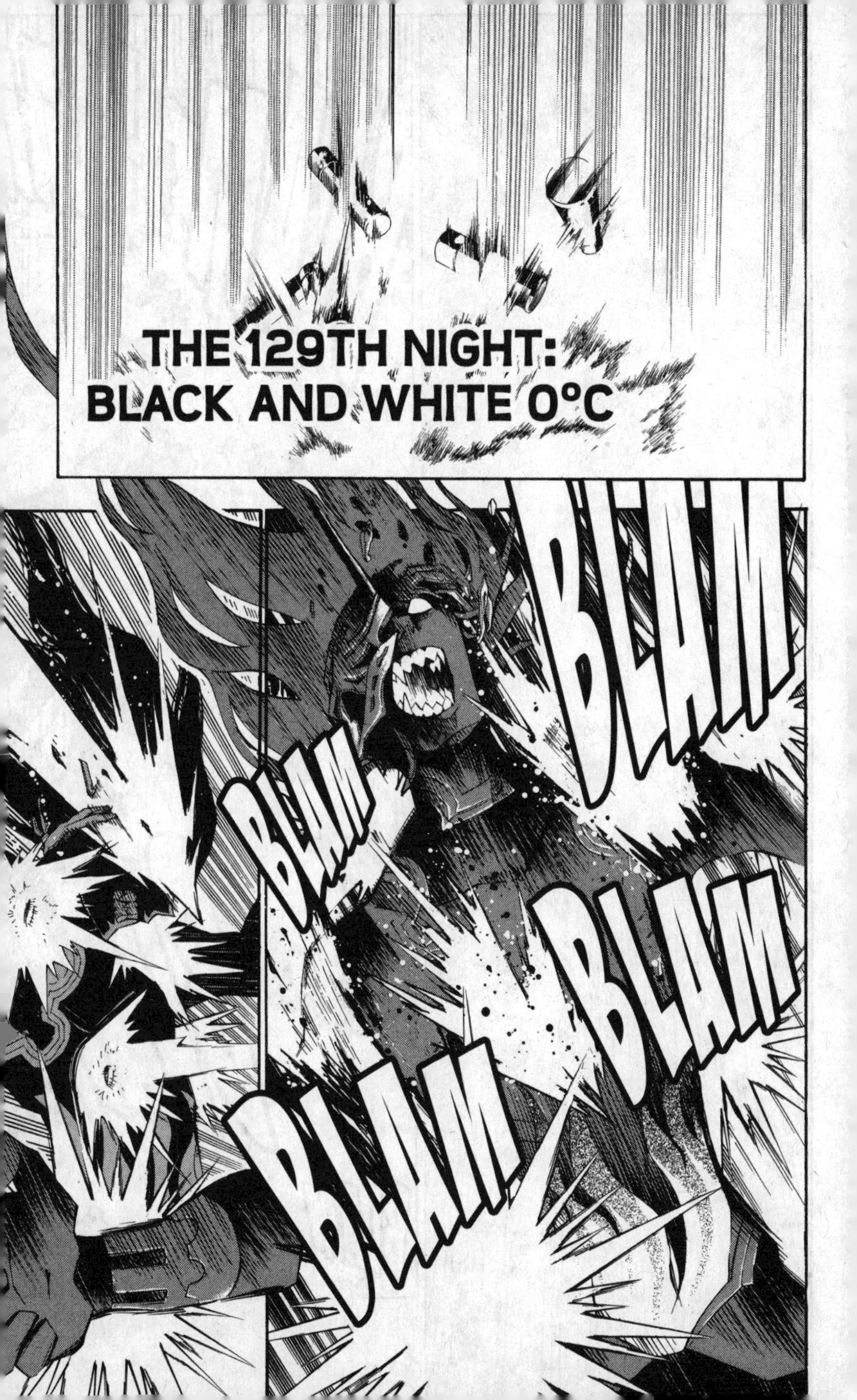
THE 129TH NIGHT:
BLACK AND WHITE 0°C
BLAM
BLAM
BLAM
BLAM

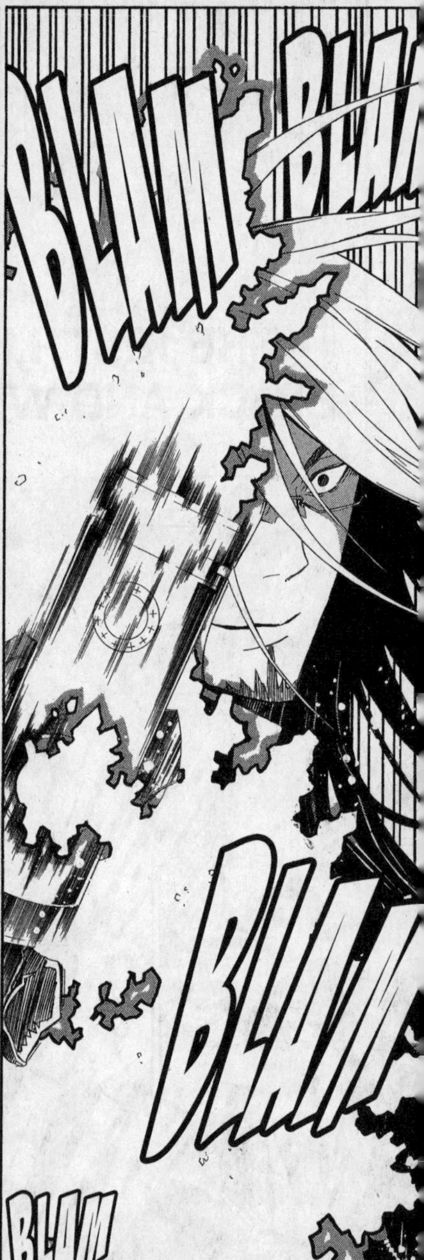
BLAM
BLAM
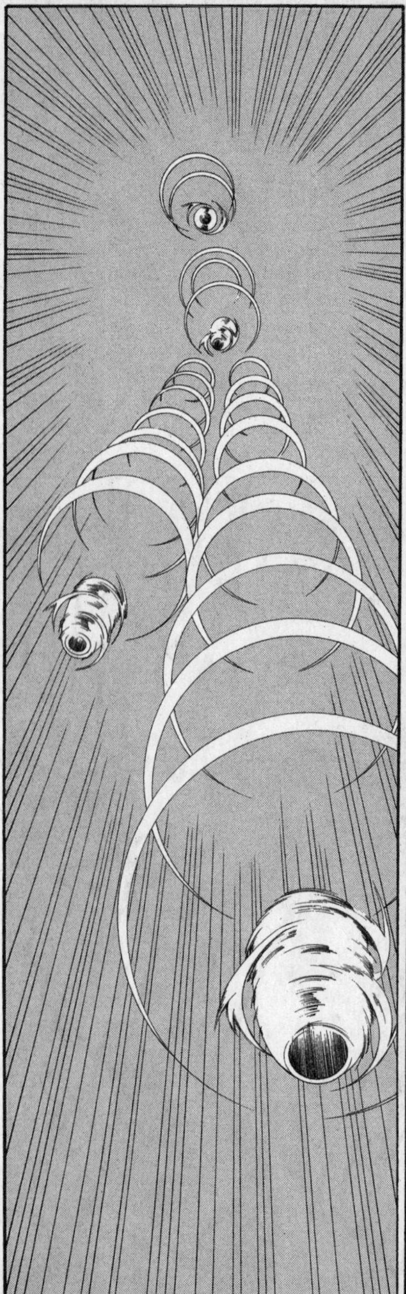

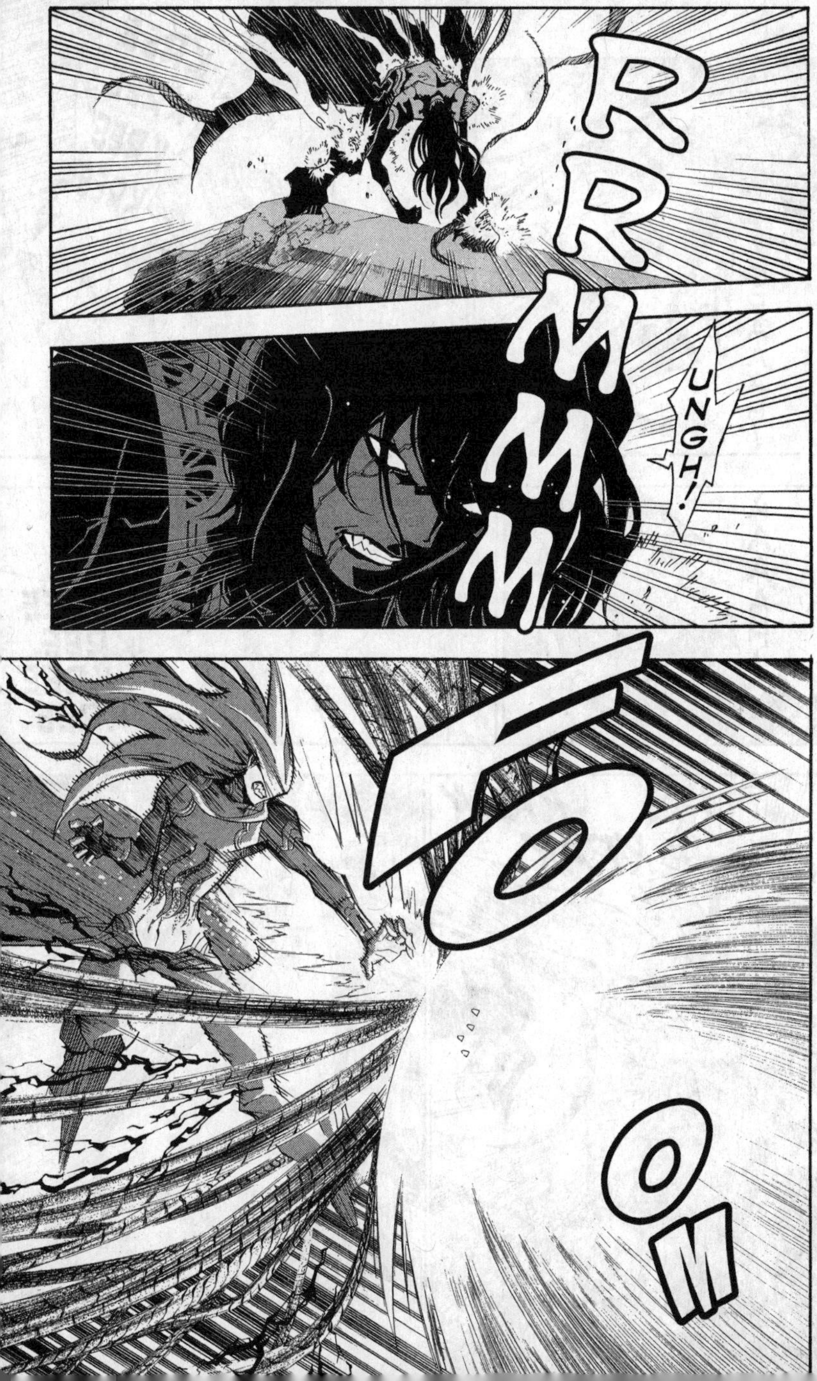
RRMMM
UNGH!

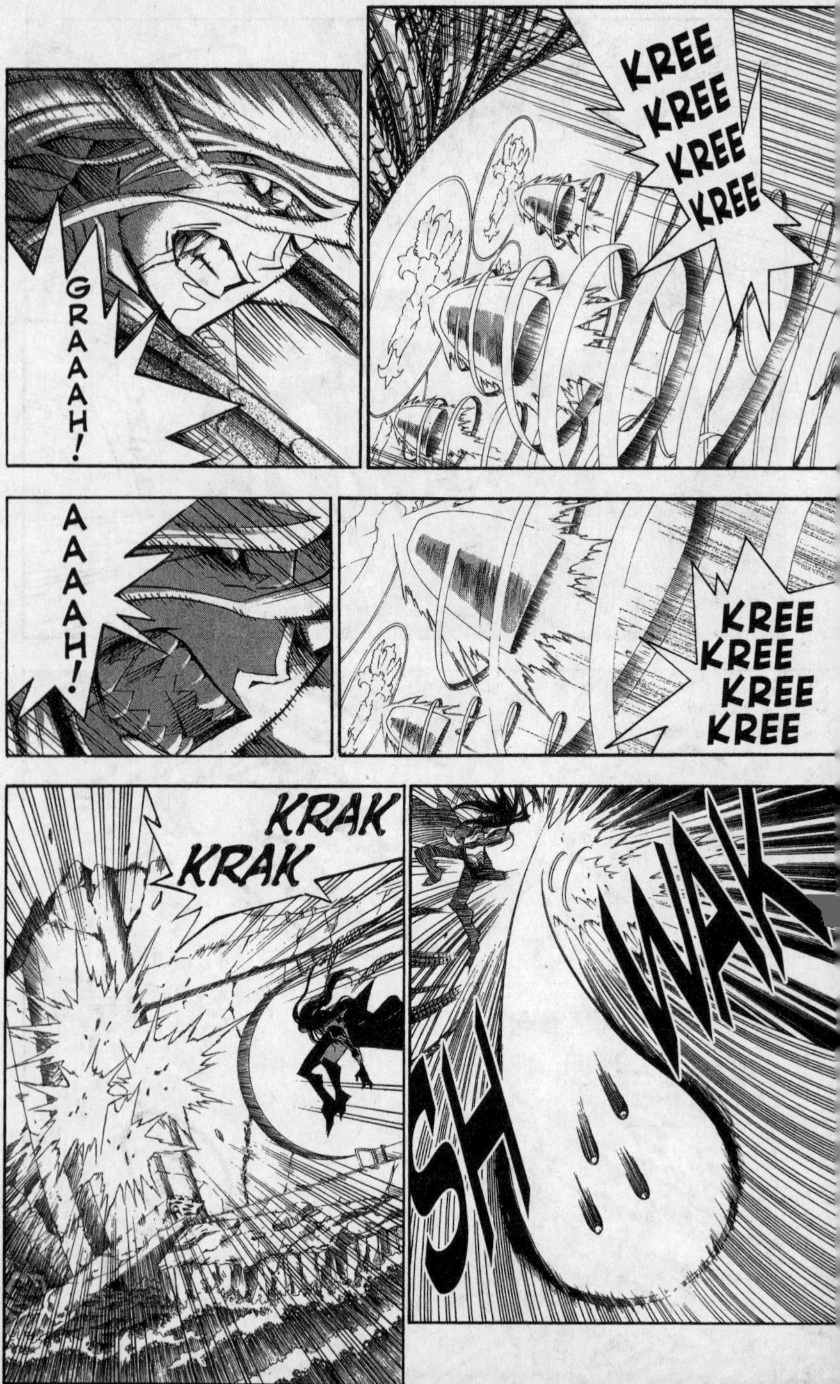
KREE KREE KREE KREE
GRAAAAH!
KREE KREE KREE KREE
AAAAAH!
SHWAK
KRAK KRAK

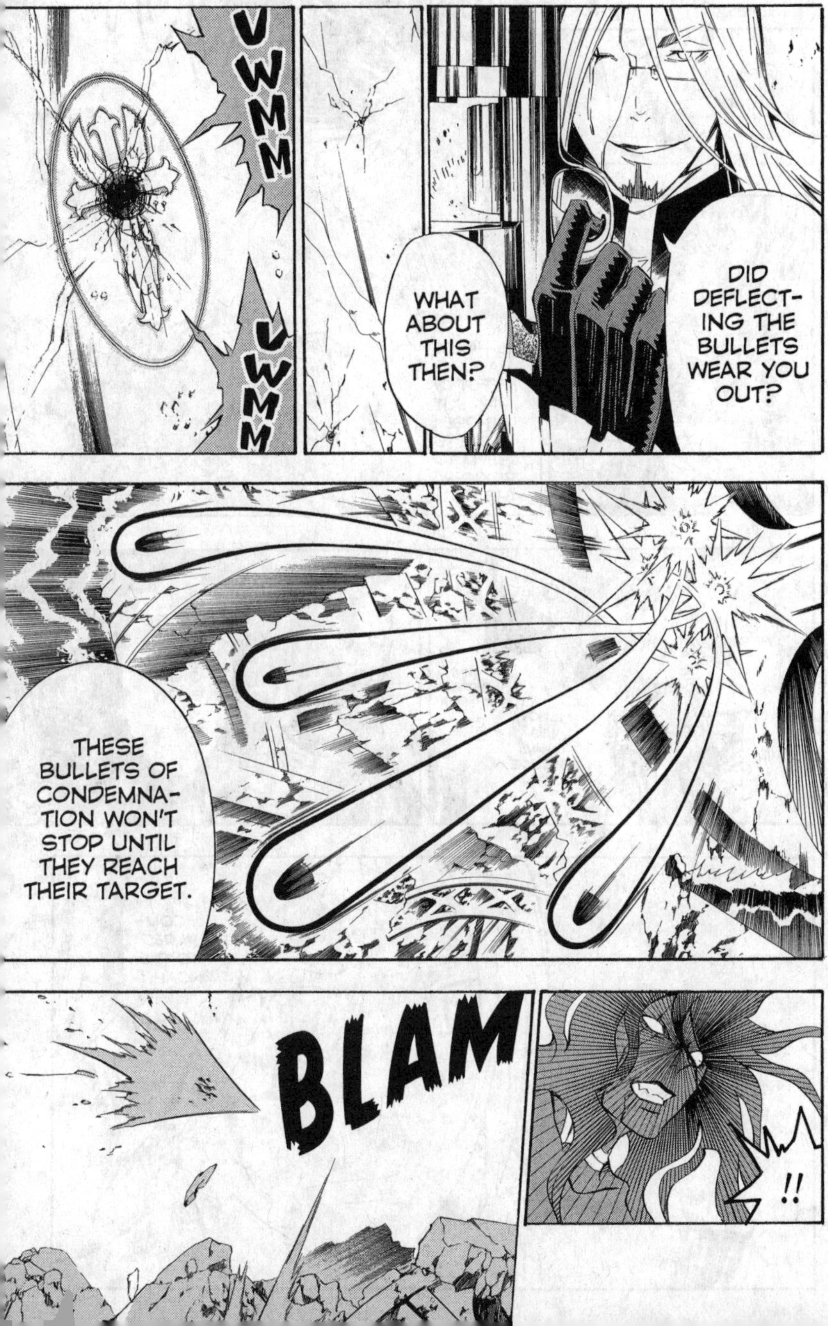
DID DEFLECT-ING THE BULLETS WEAR YOU OUT?
WHAT ABOUT THIS THEN?
VWMM
VWMM
THESE BULLETS OF CONDEMNA-TION WON'T STOP UNTIL THEY REACH THEIR TARGET.
!!
BLAM

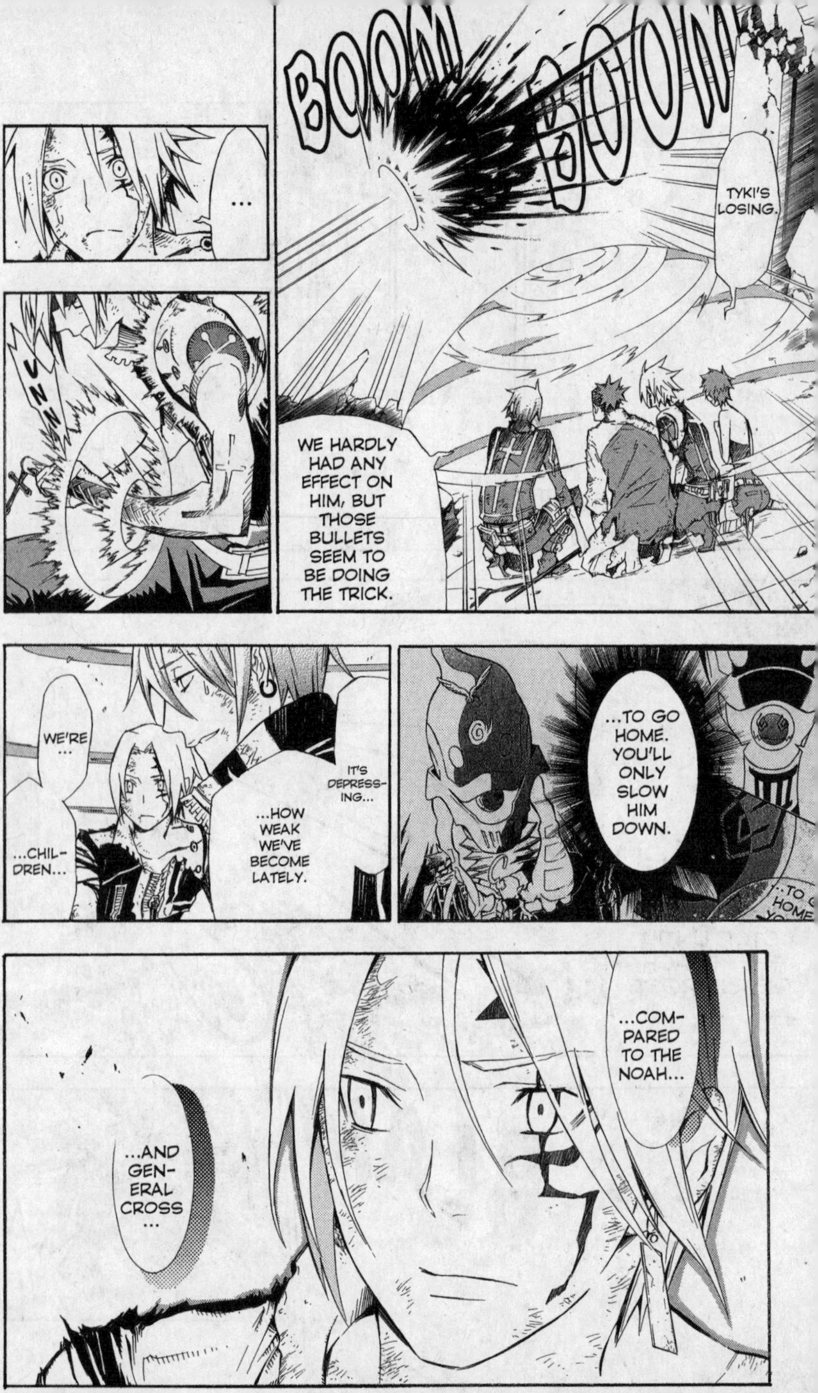
BOOM
BOOM
TYKI'S LOSING.
WE HARDLY HAD ANY EFFECT ON HIM, BUT THOSE BULLETS SEEM TO BE DOING THE TRICK.
...
UNN
...TO GO HOME. YOU'LL ONLY SLOW HIM DOWN.
IT'S DEPRESSING...
...HOW WEAK WE'VE BECOME LATELY.
WE'RE...
...CHILDREN...
...COMPARED TO THE NOAH...
...AND GENERAL CROSS...

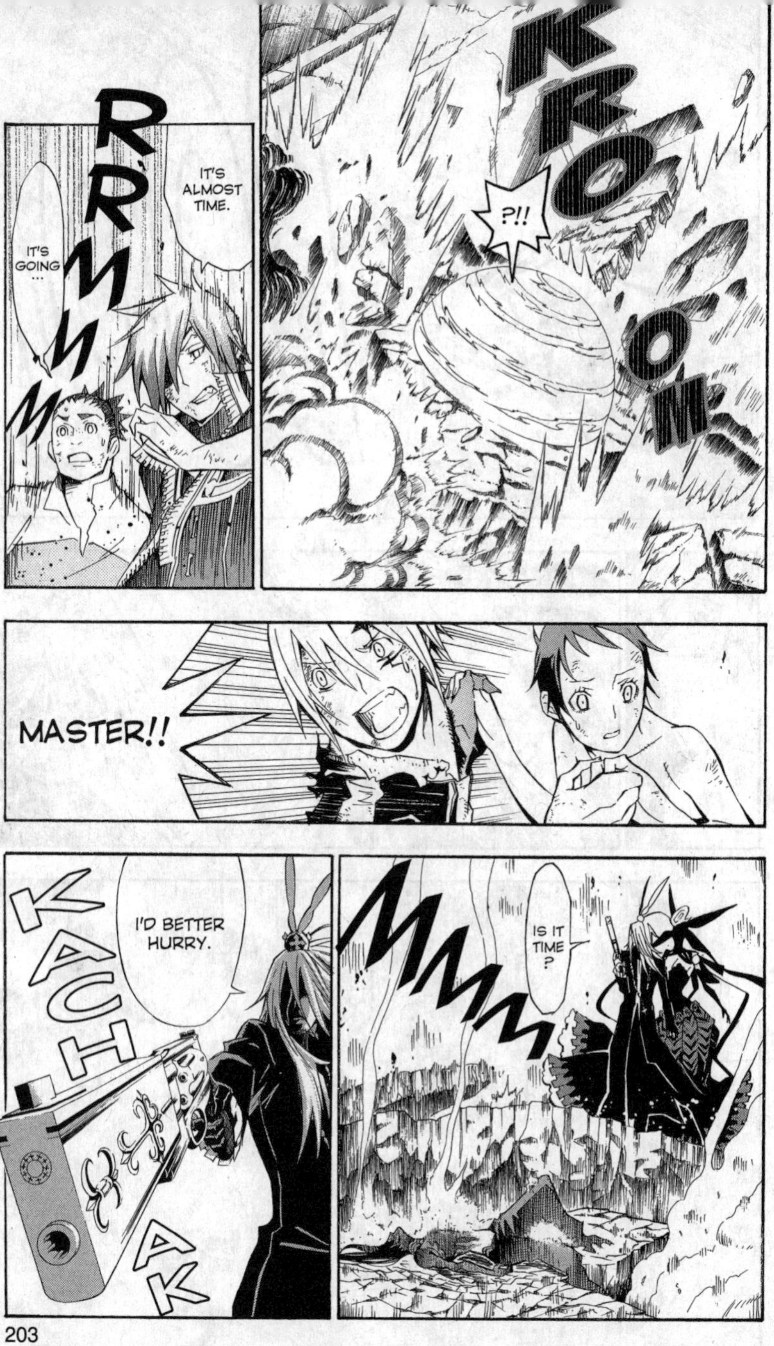
KROOOM
?!!
IT'S ALMOST TIME.
IT'S GOING...
RRMMM
MASTER!!
IS IT TIME?
MMMM
I'D BETTER HURRY.
KACHAK

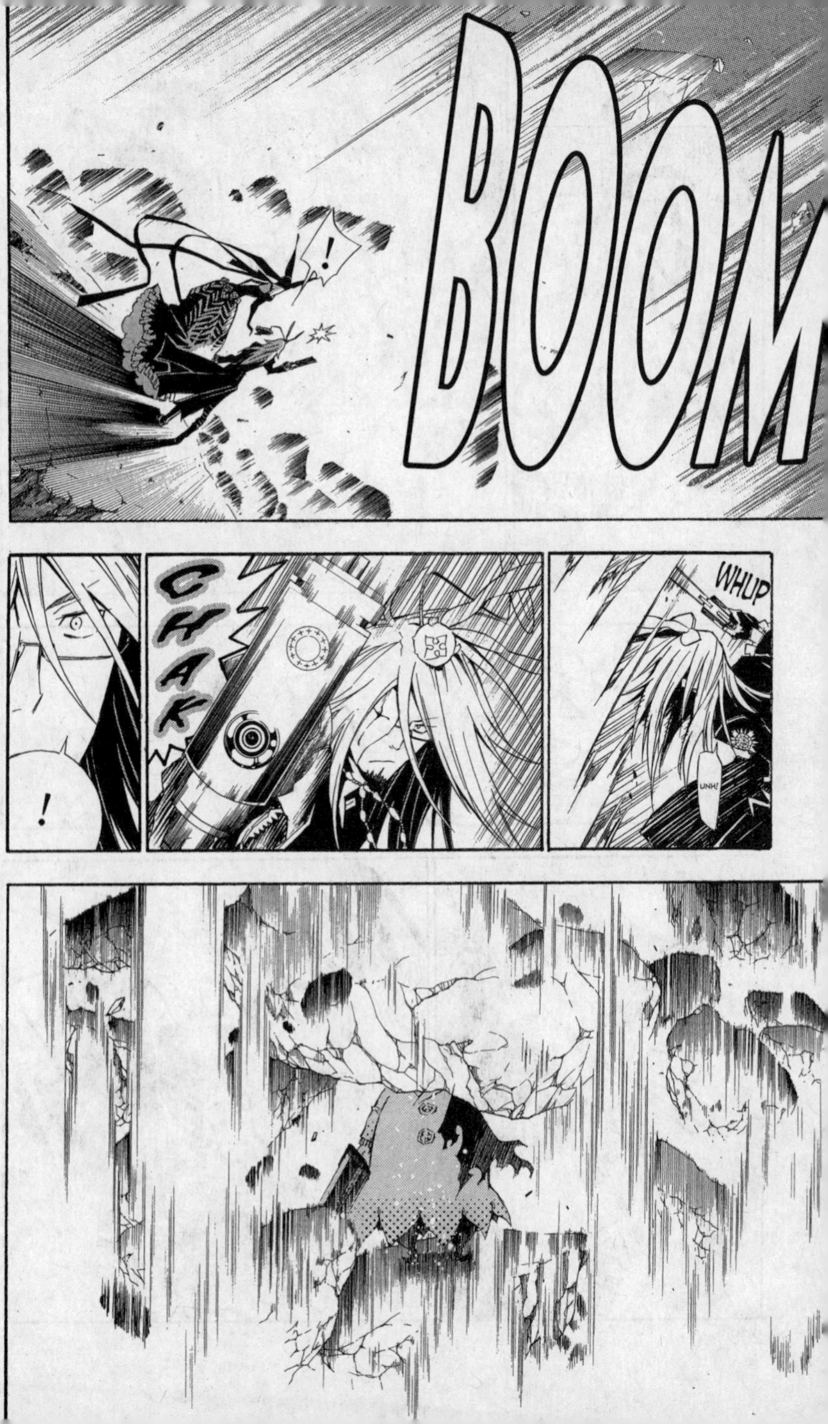
BOOM
!
WHUP
UNH!
CHAK
!

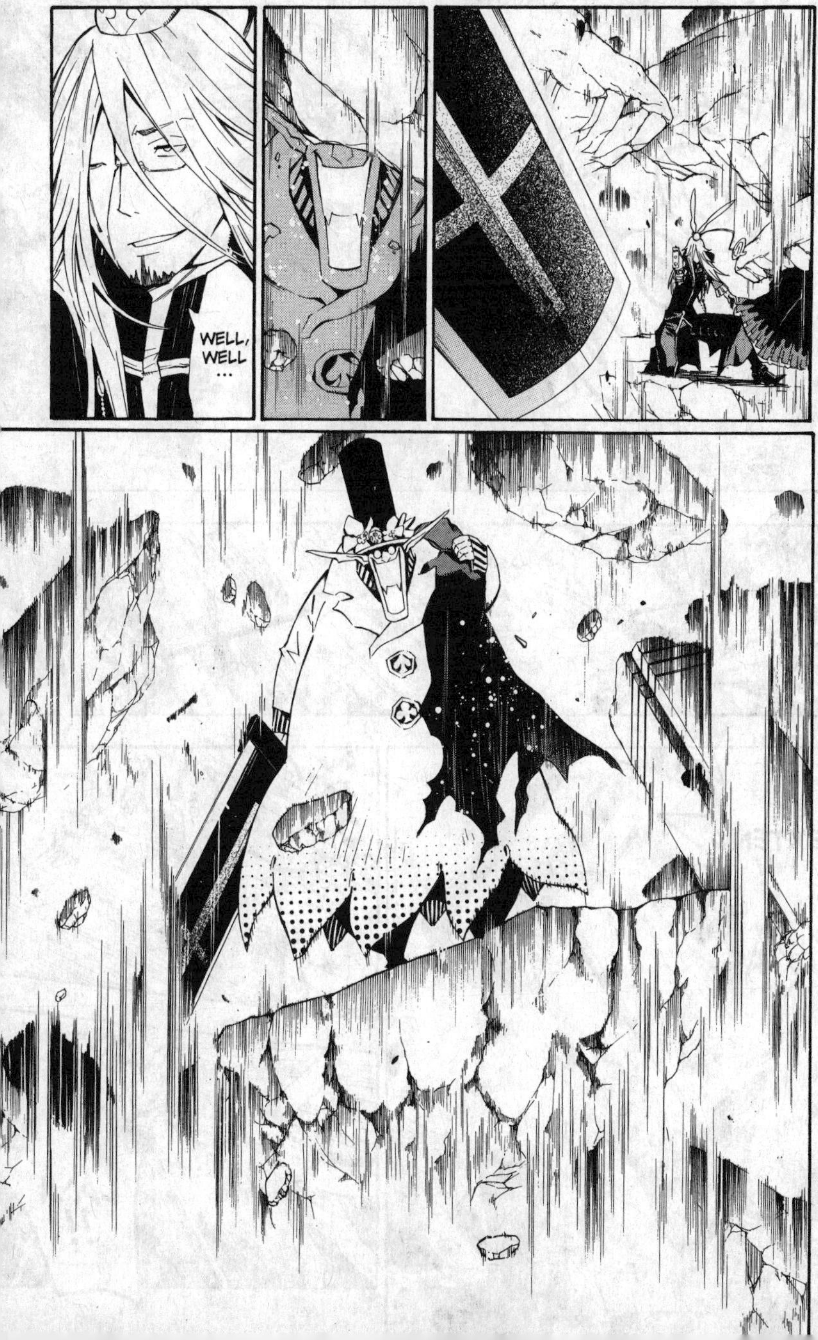
WELL, WELL ...

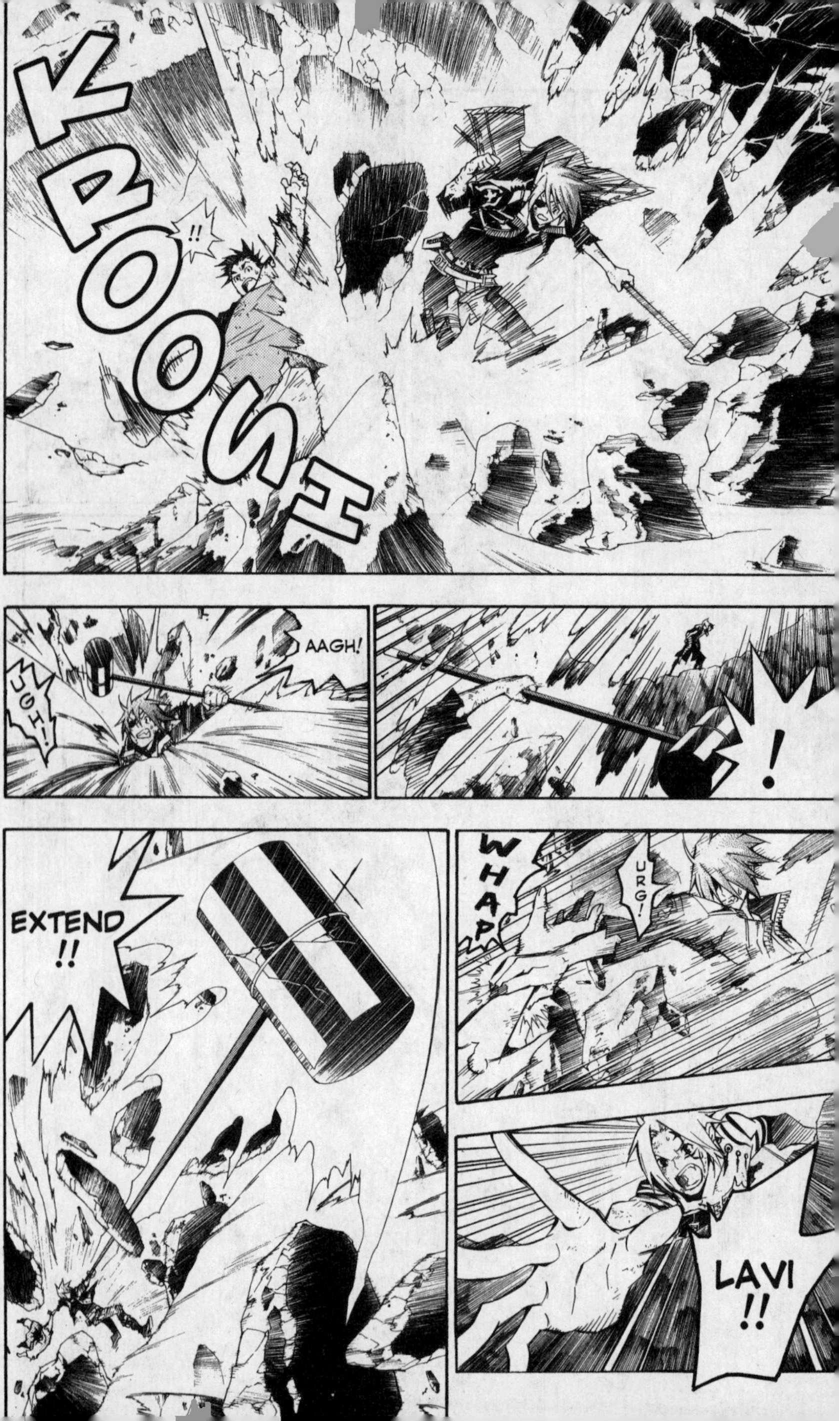
KROOSH
!!
!
AAGH!
UGH!
URG!
WHAP
LAVI !!
EXTEND !!

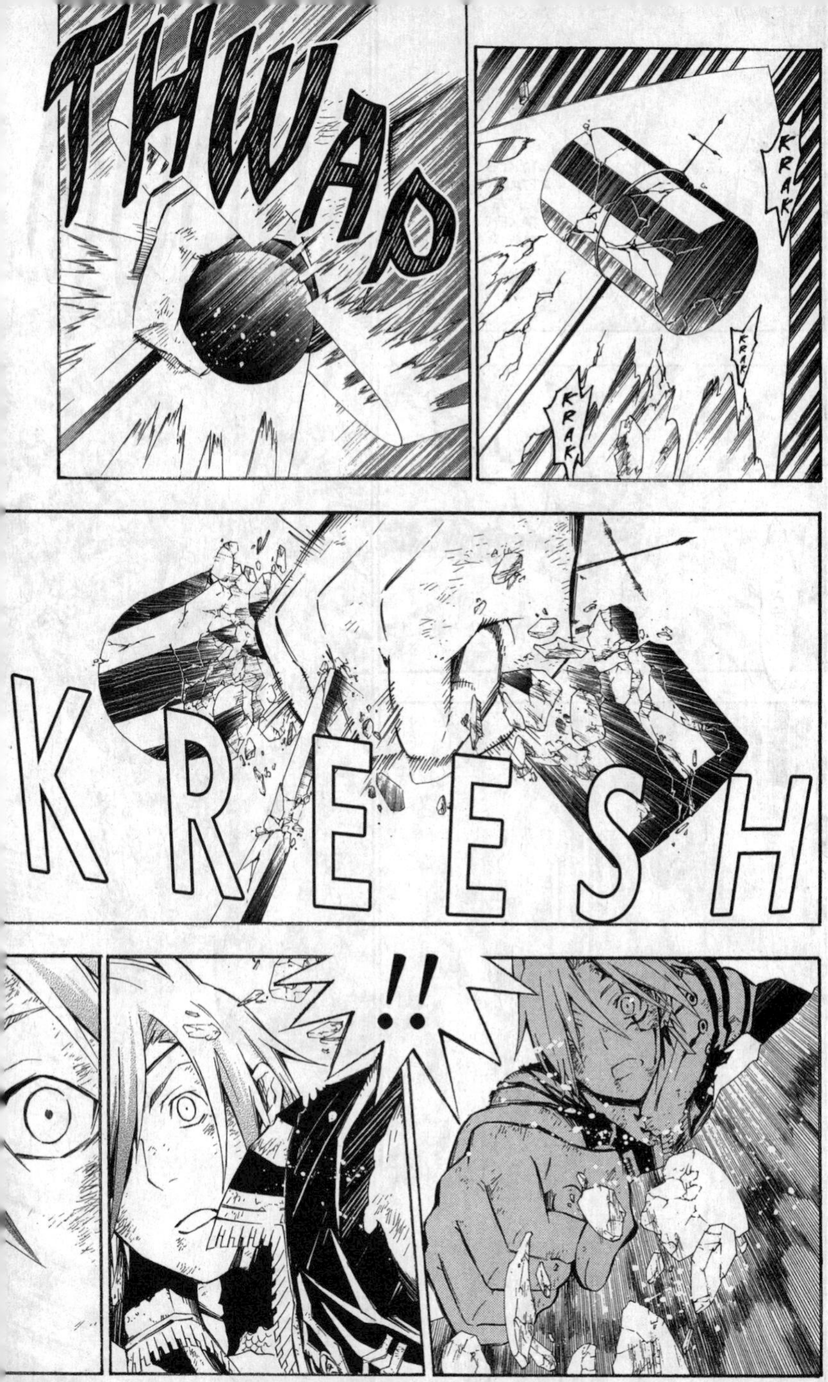
KRAK
KRAK
KRAK
THWAP
KREESH
!!

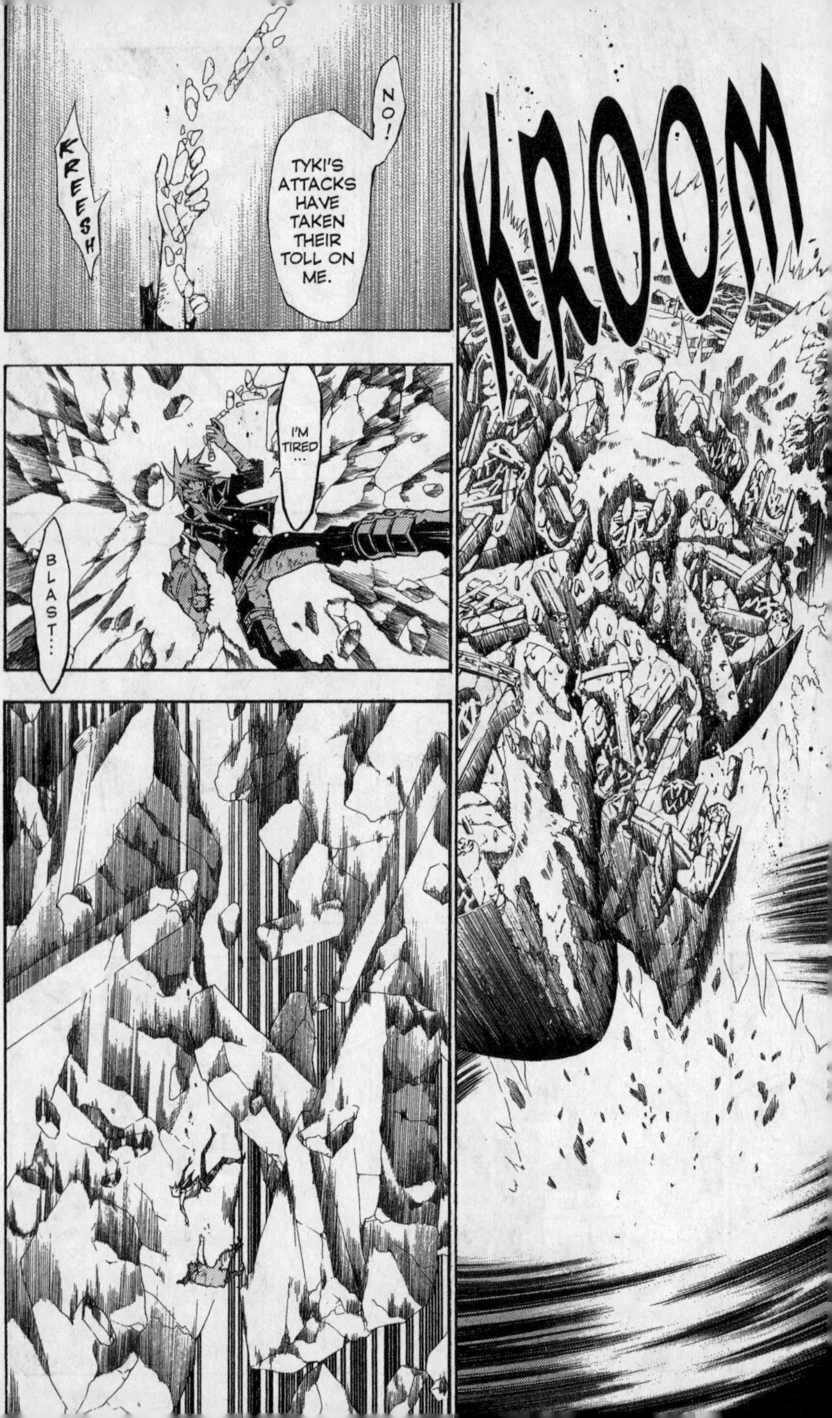
KROOM
NO!
TYKI'S ATTACKS HAVE TAKEN THEIR TOLL ON ME.
KREESH
I'M TIRED...
BLAST...

KRAK

THOOM

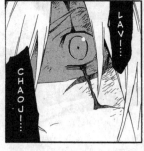

LAVI!

CHAOJI!...

CHAOJI!...

THUD

LAVI!...

KRAK KRAK

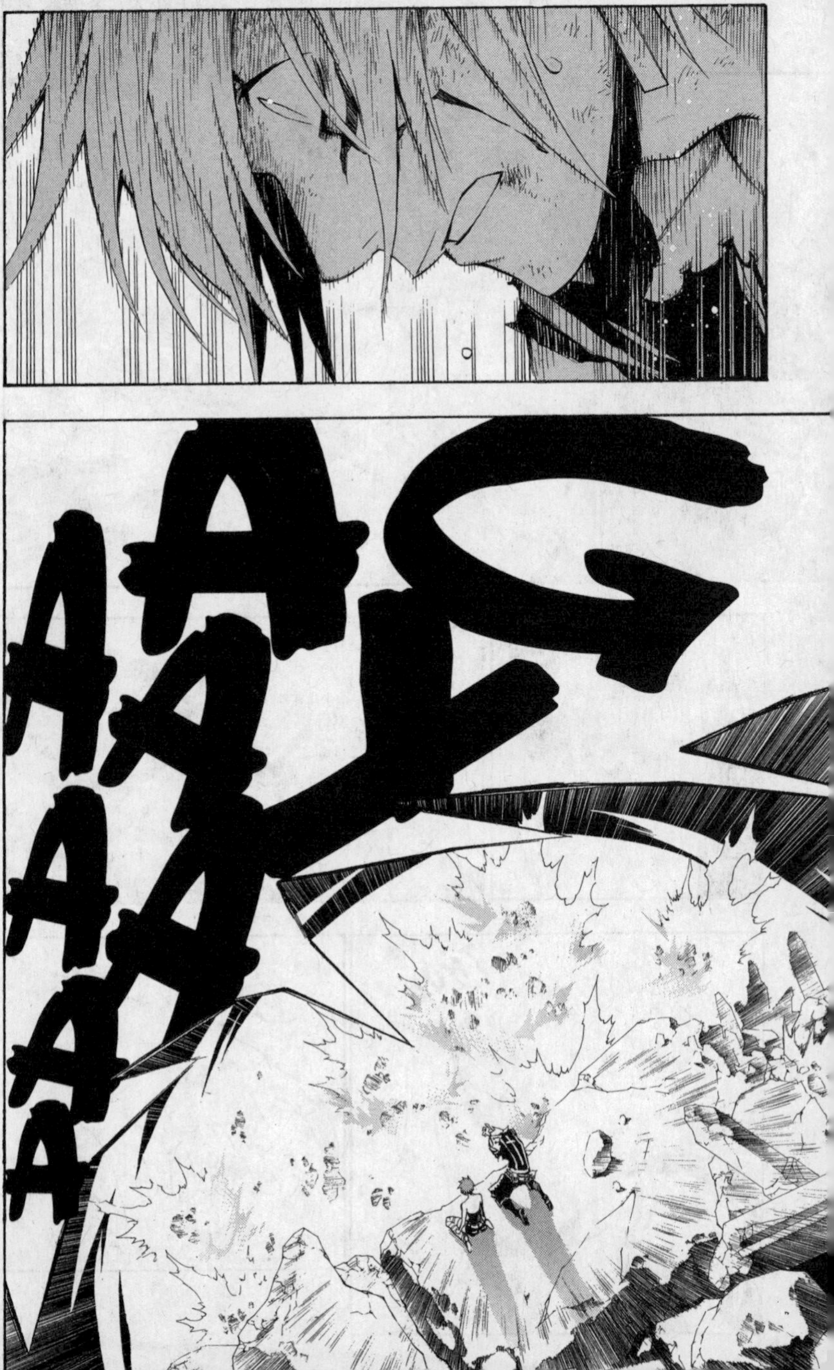
AAAAAAGH

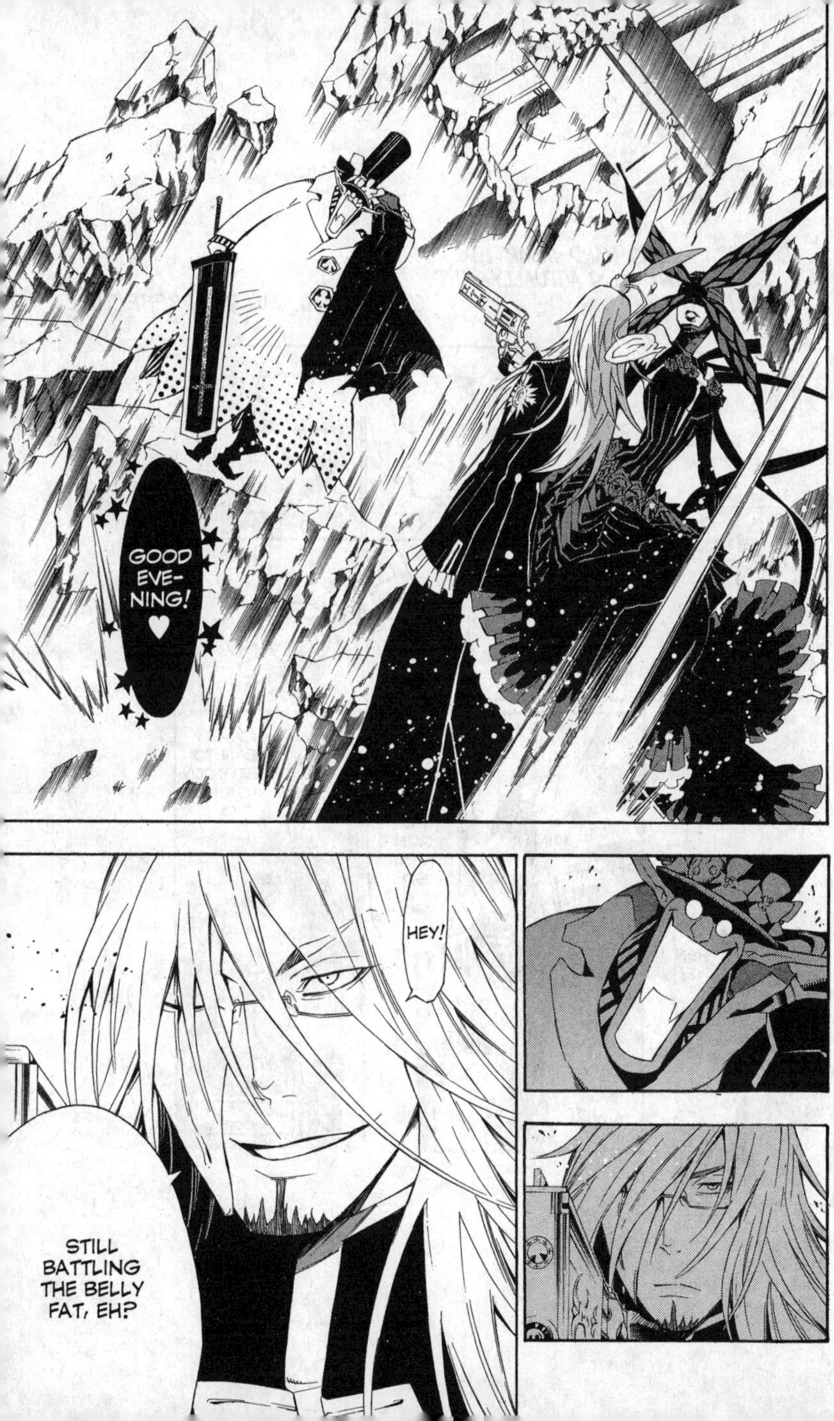
GOOD EVE-NING! ♥
HEY!
STILL BATTLING THE BELLY FAT, EH?

Q. KANDA SEEMS HARD-HEARTED, BUT I THINK HE'S ACTUALLY KIND. AM I RIGHT? (ERINA SATO, SAITAMA PREFECTURE)

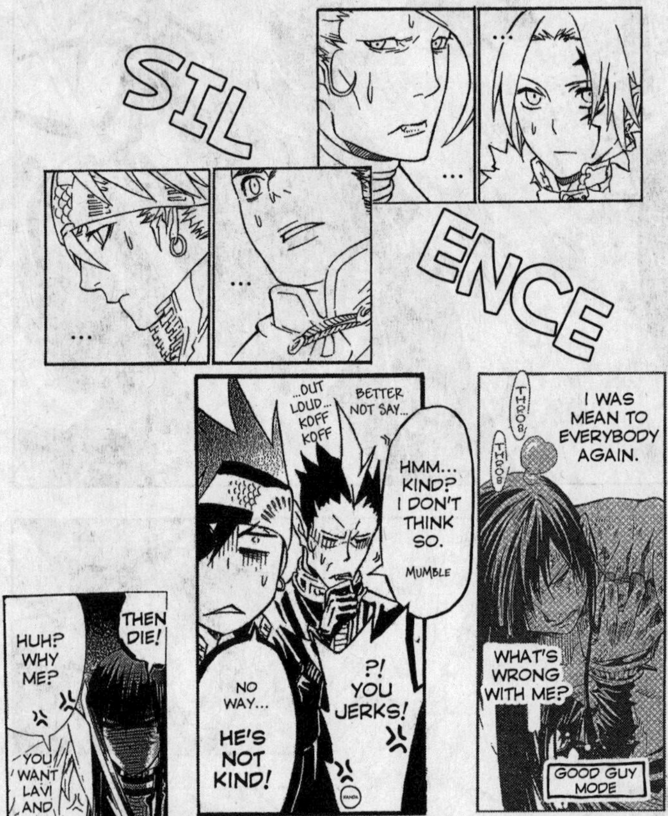
...
...
SILENCE
...
...
THROB
THROB
I WAS MEAN TO EVERYBODY AGAIN.
WHAT'S WRONG WITH ME?
GOOD GUY MODE
BETTER NOT SAY...
...OUT LOUD... KOFF KOFF
HMM... KIND? I DON'T THINK SO.
MUMBLE
?! YOU JERKS!
NO WAY...
HE'S NOT KIND!
KANDA
THEN DIE!
HUH? WHY ME?
YOU WANT LAVI AND KRORY!

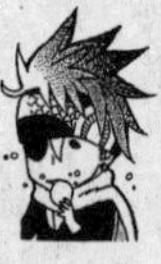

EVERYBODY'S GETTING ALONG FINE, AS USUAL.. (AS IN THE ANIME.)

THE 130TH NIGHT: EYES OF HATRED

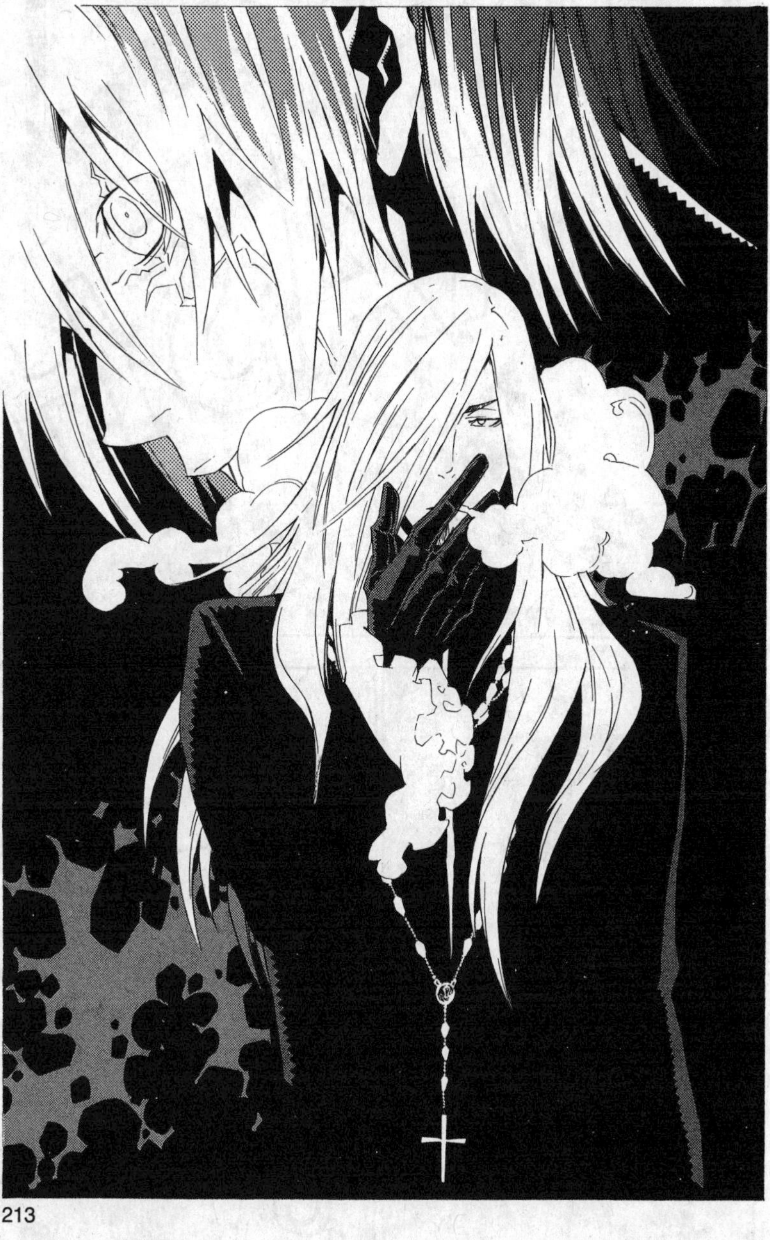

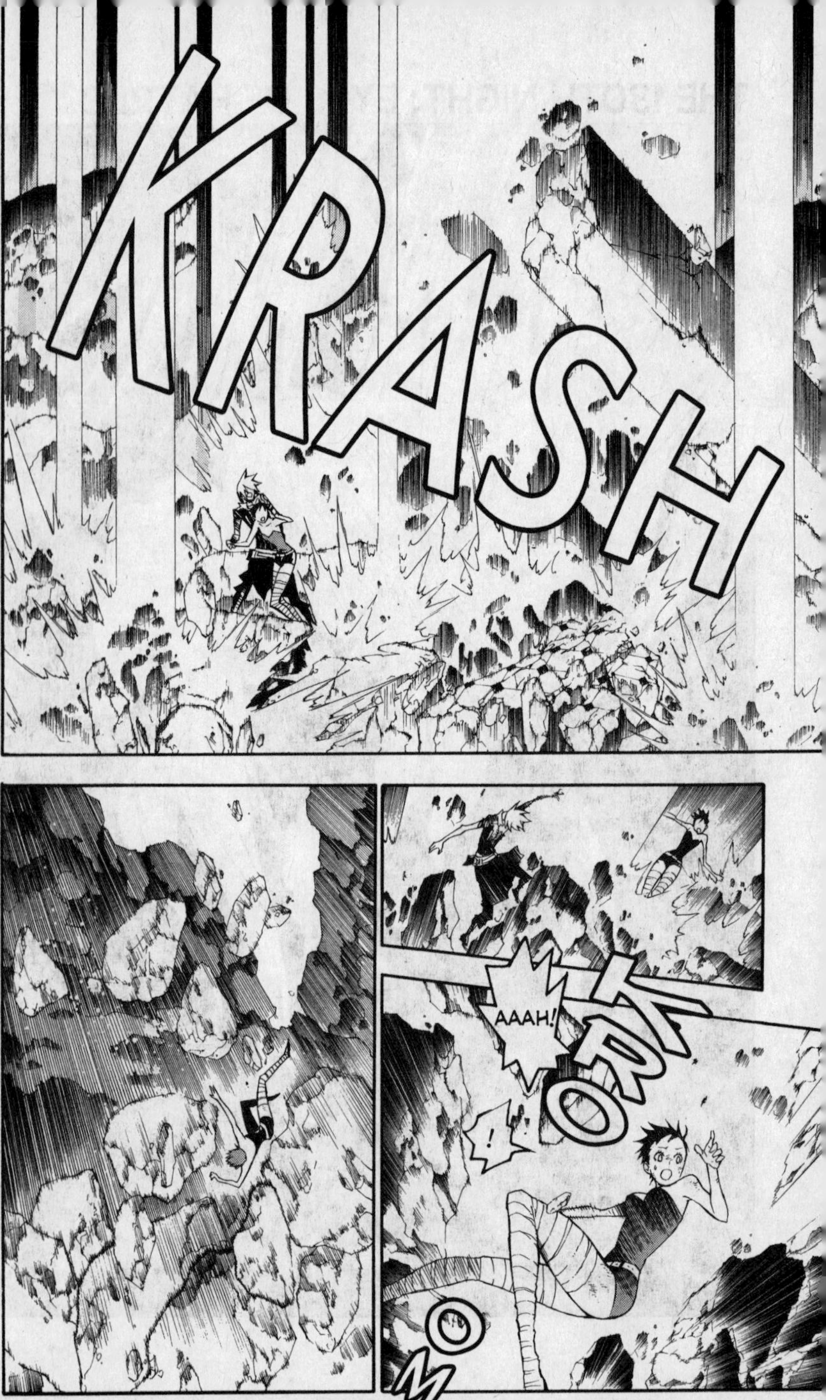
KRASH
AAAH!
KROOM
!

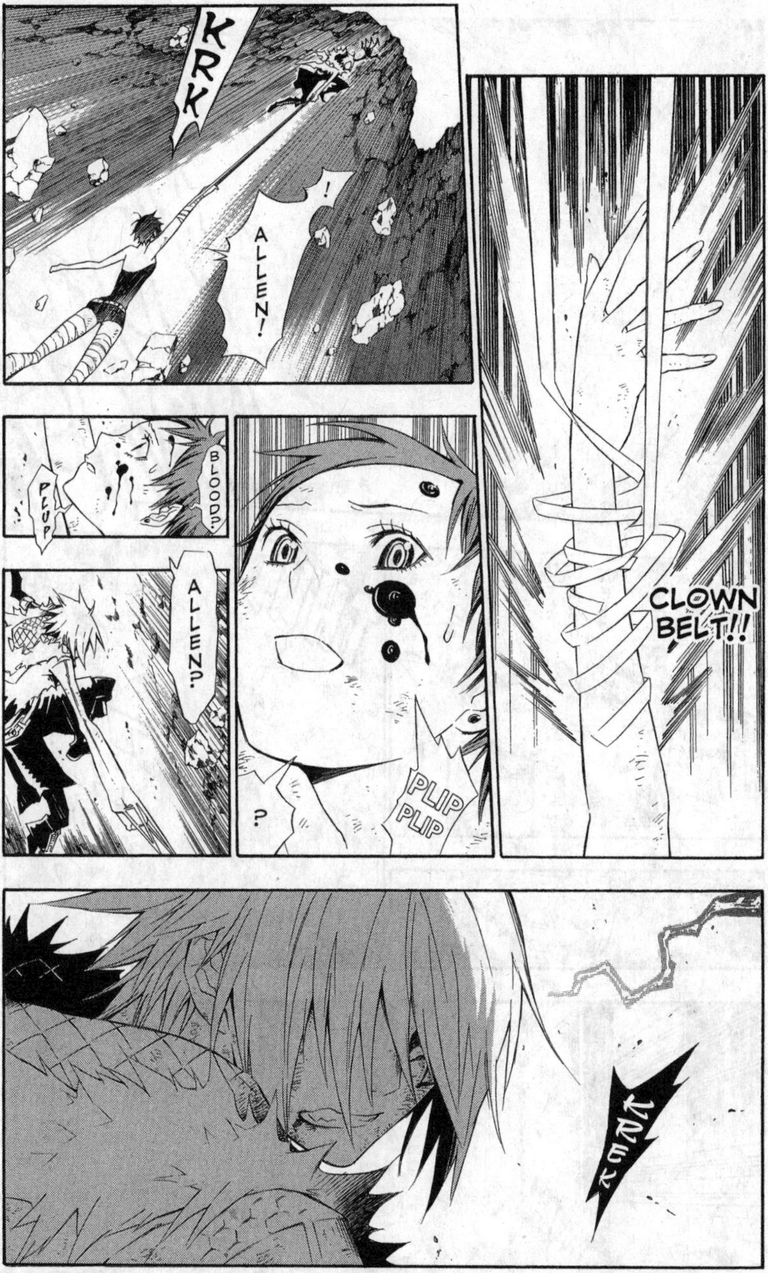
CLOWN BELT!!
KRK
!
ALLEN!
?
PLIP PLIP
BLOOD?
PLUP
ALLEN?
KREK

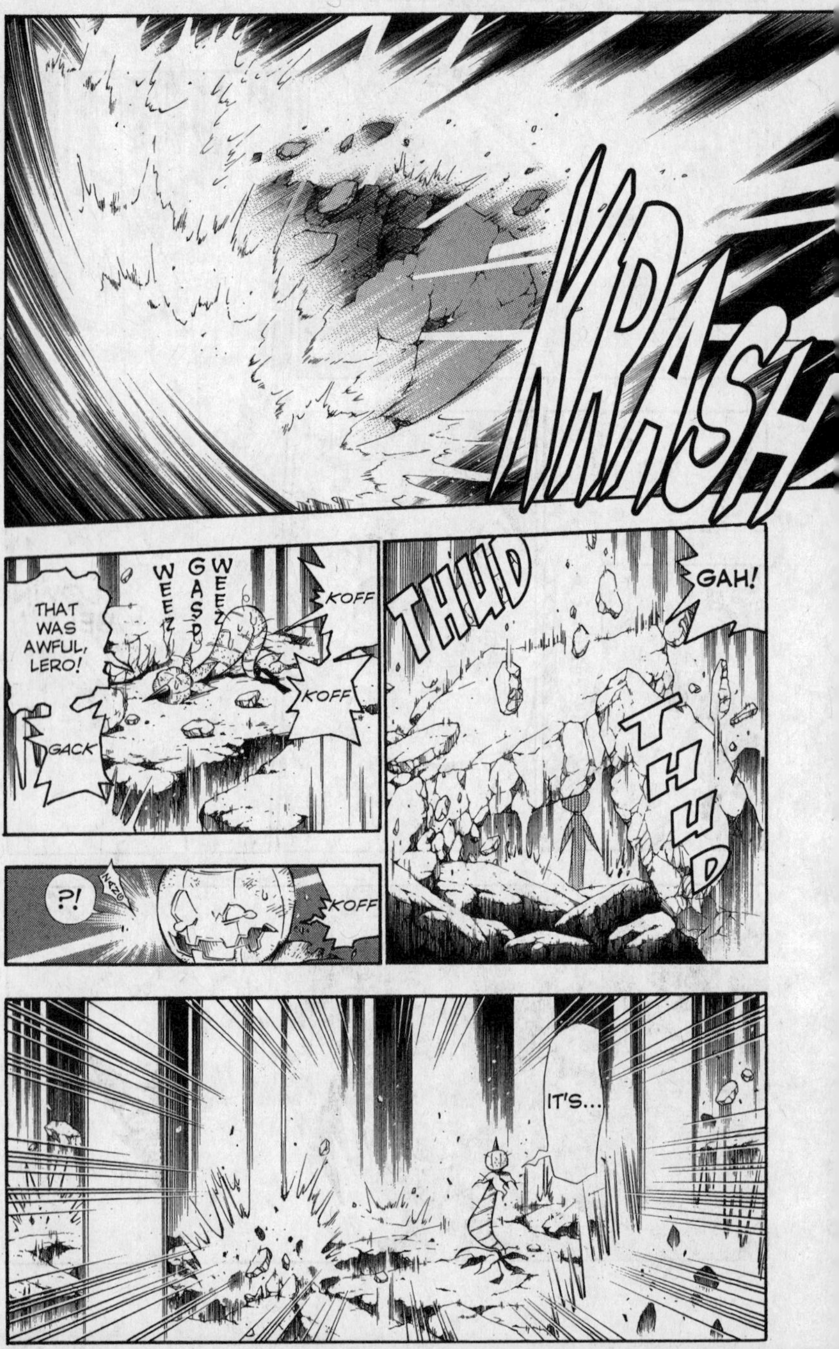
KRASH
THUD
GAH!
THUD
THUD
WEEZ
GASP
WEEZ
KOFF
KOFF
THAT WAS AWFUL, LERO!
GACK
KOFF
NAZO
?!
IT'S...

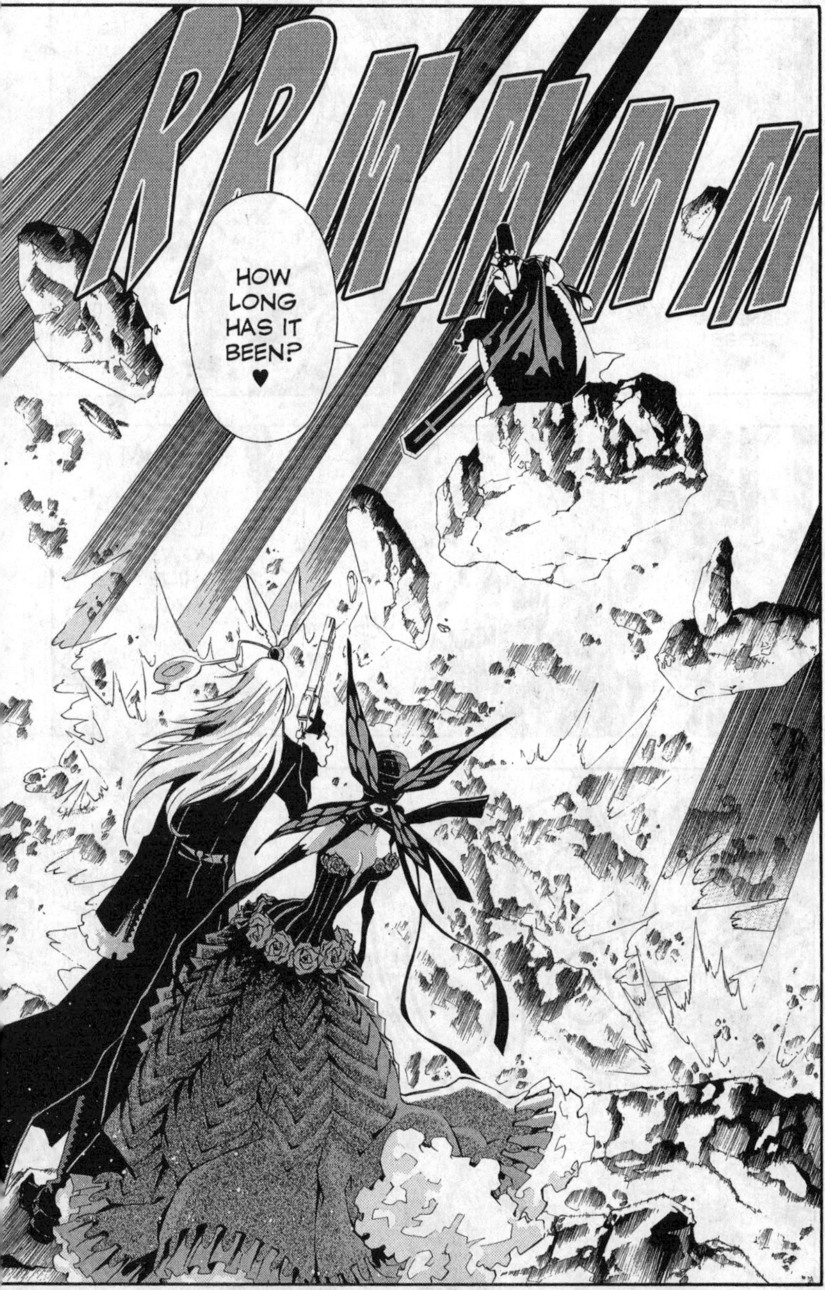
RRMMMMMM
HOW LONG HAS IT BEEN? ♥

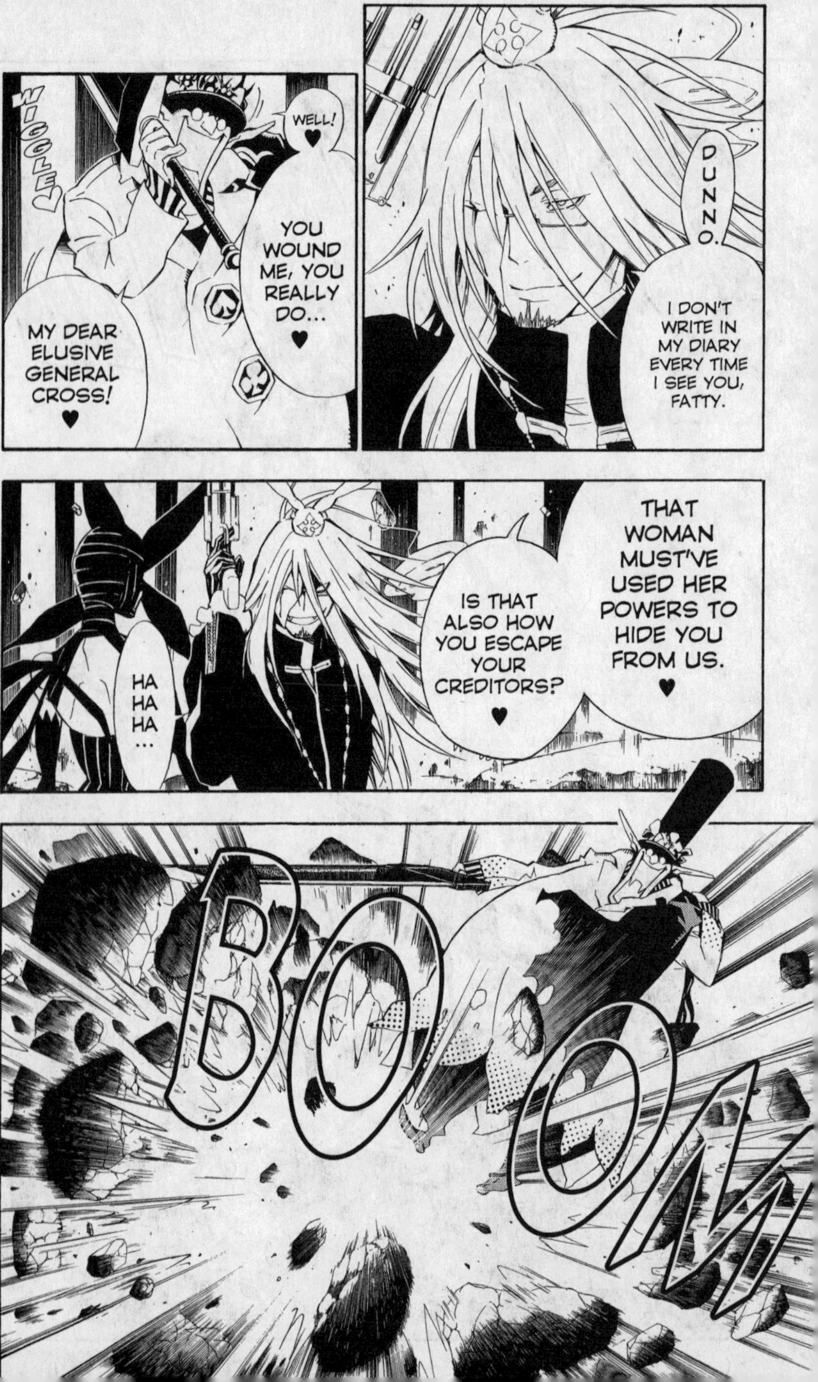
DUNNO.
I DON'T WRITE IN MY DIARY EVERY TIME I SEE YOU, FATTY.
WIGGLE♥
WELL! ♥
YOU WOUND ME, YOU REALLY DO... ♥
MY DEAR ELUSIVE GENERAL CROSS! ♥
THAT WOMAN MUST'VE USED HER POWERS TO HIDE YOU FROM US. ♥
IS THAT ALSO HOW YOU ESCAPE YOUR CREDITORS? ♥
HA HA HA ...
BOOM

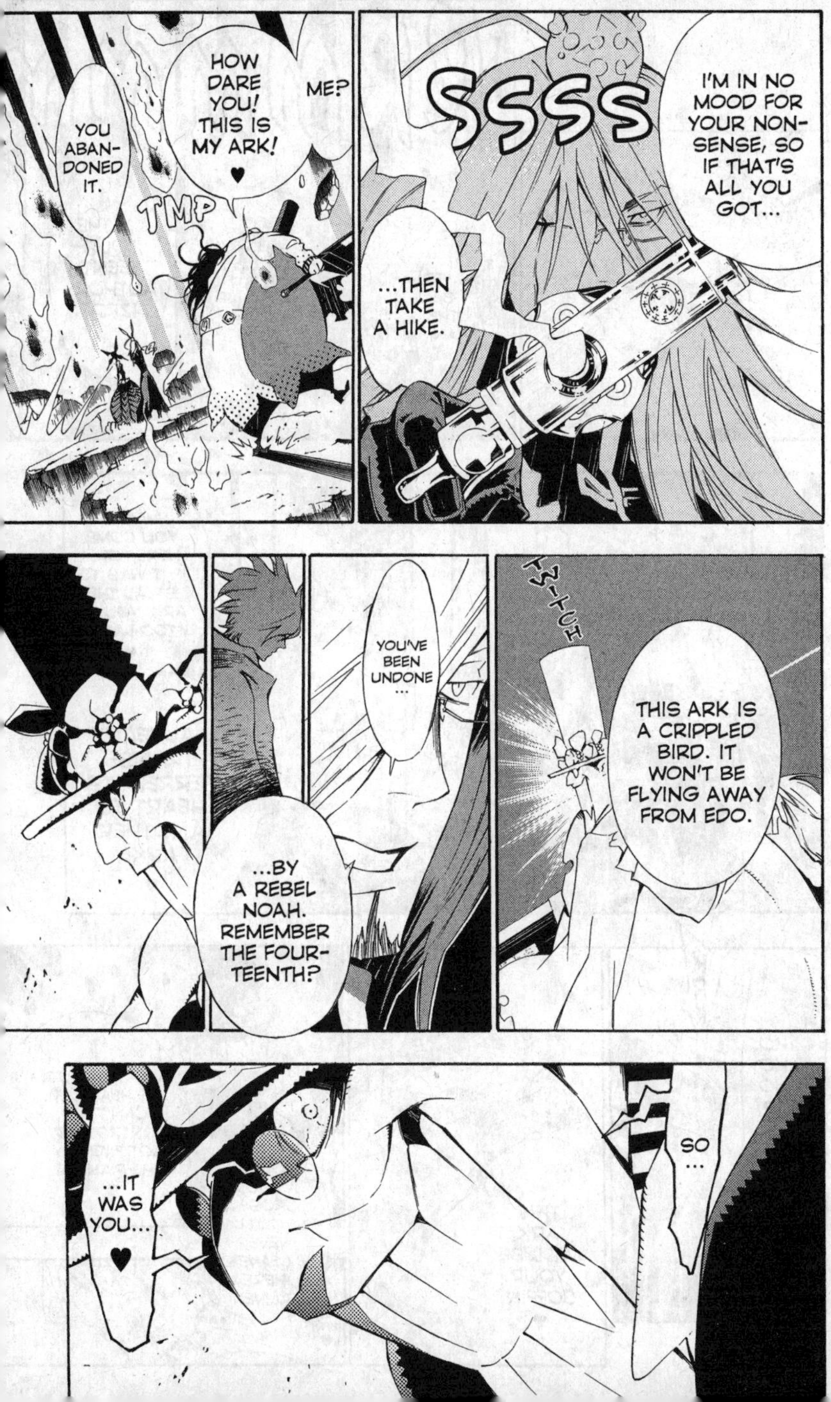
SSSS
I'M IN NO MOOD FOR YOUR NON-SENSE, SO IF THAT'S ALL YOU GOT...
...THEN TAKE A HIKE.
ME?
HOW DARE YOU! THIS IS MY ARK! ♥
TMP
YOU ABAN-DONED IT.
TWITCH
THIS ARK IS A CRIPPLED BIRD. IT WON'T BE FLYING AWAY FROM EDO.
YOU'VE BEEN UNDONE...
...BY A REBEL NOAH. REMEMBER THE FOUR-TEENTH?
SO...
...IT WAS YOU... ♥

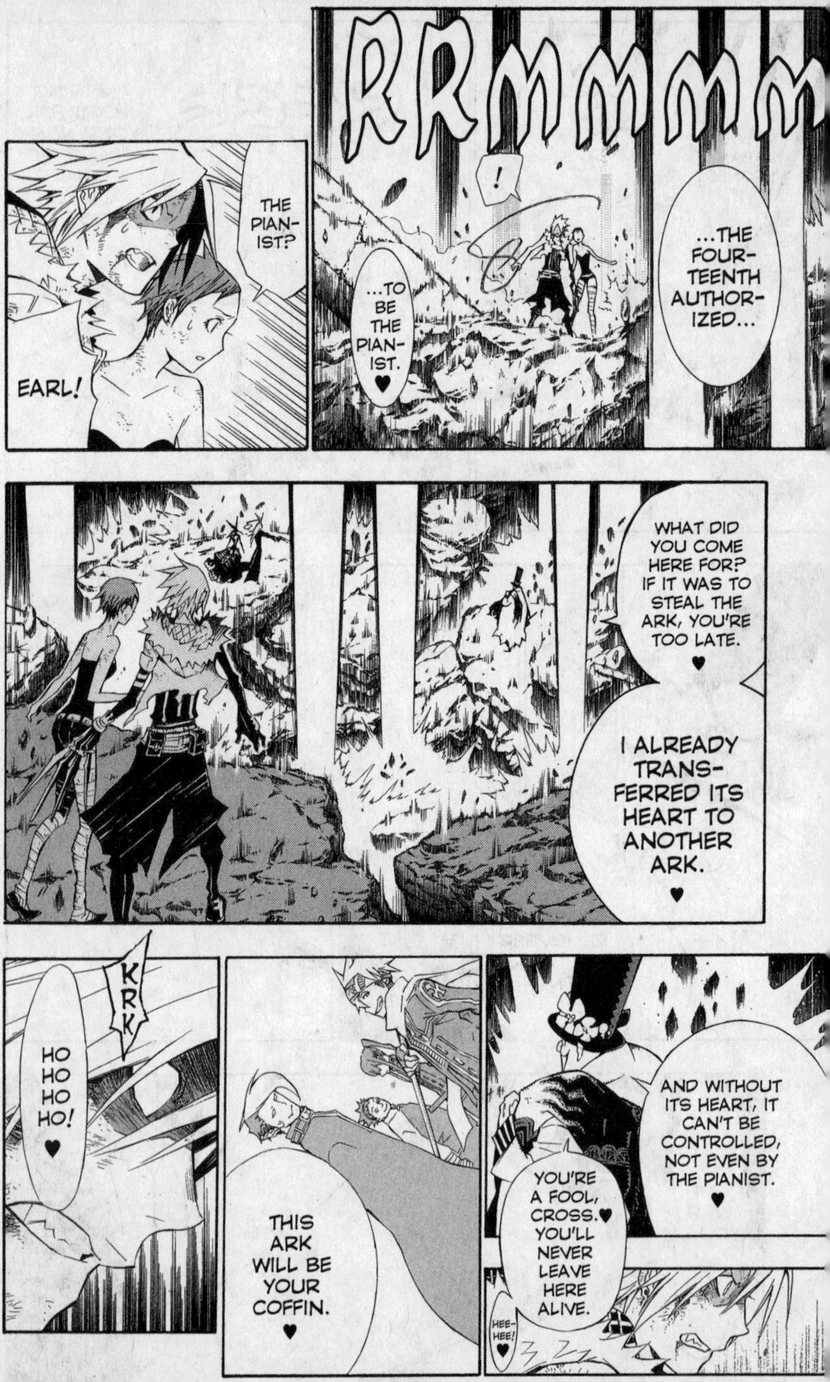
RRMMMM
!
...THE FOURTEENTH AUTHORIZED...
...TO BE THE PIANIST. ♥
THE PIANIST?
EARL!
WHAT DID YOU COME HERE FOR? IF IT WAS TO STEAL THE ARK, YOU'RE TOO LATE. ♥
I ALREADY TRANSFERRED ITS HEART TO ANOTHER ARK. ♥
AND WITHOUT ITS HEART, IT CAN'T BE CONTROLLED, NOT EVEN BY THE PIANIST. ♥
YOU'RE A FOOL, CROSS. ♥ YOU'LL NEVER LEAVE HERE ALIVE.
HEE-HEE! ♥
THIS ARK WILL BE YOUR COFFIN. ♥
KRK
HO HO HO HO! ♥

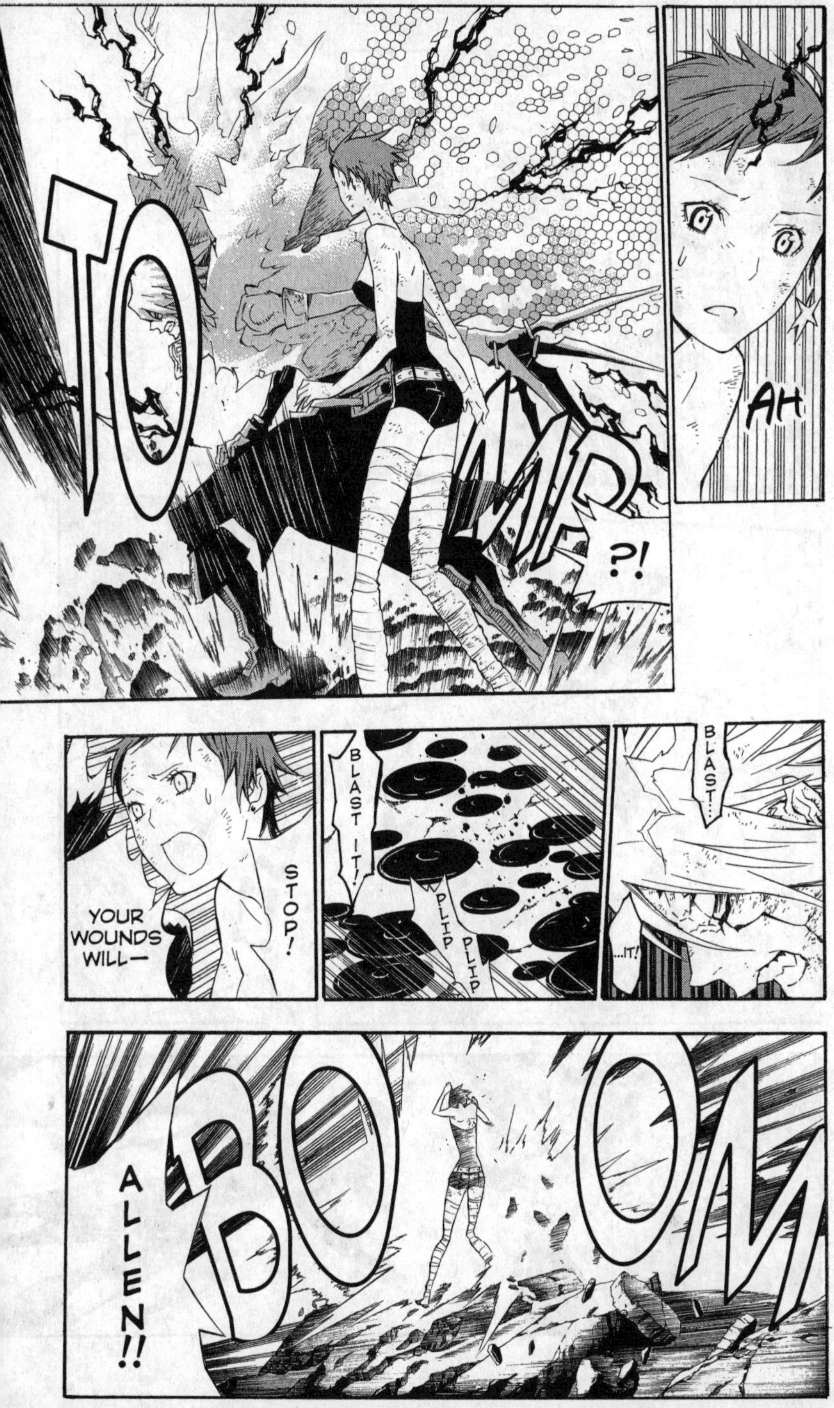
AH
TOWMP
?!
BLAST...
...IT!
BLAST IT!
PLIP PLIP
STOP!
YOUR WOUNDS WILL—
BOOM
ALLEN!!

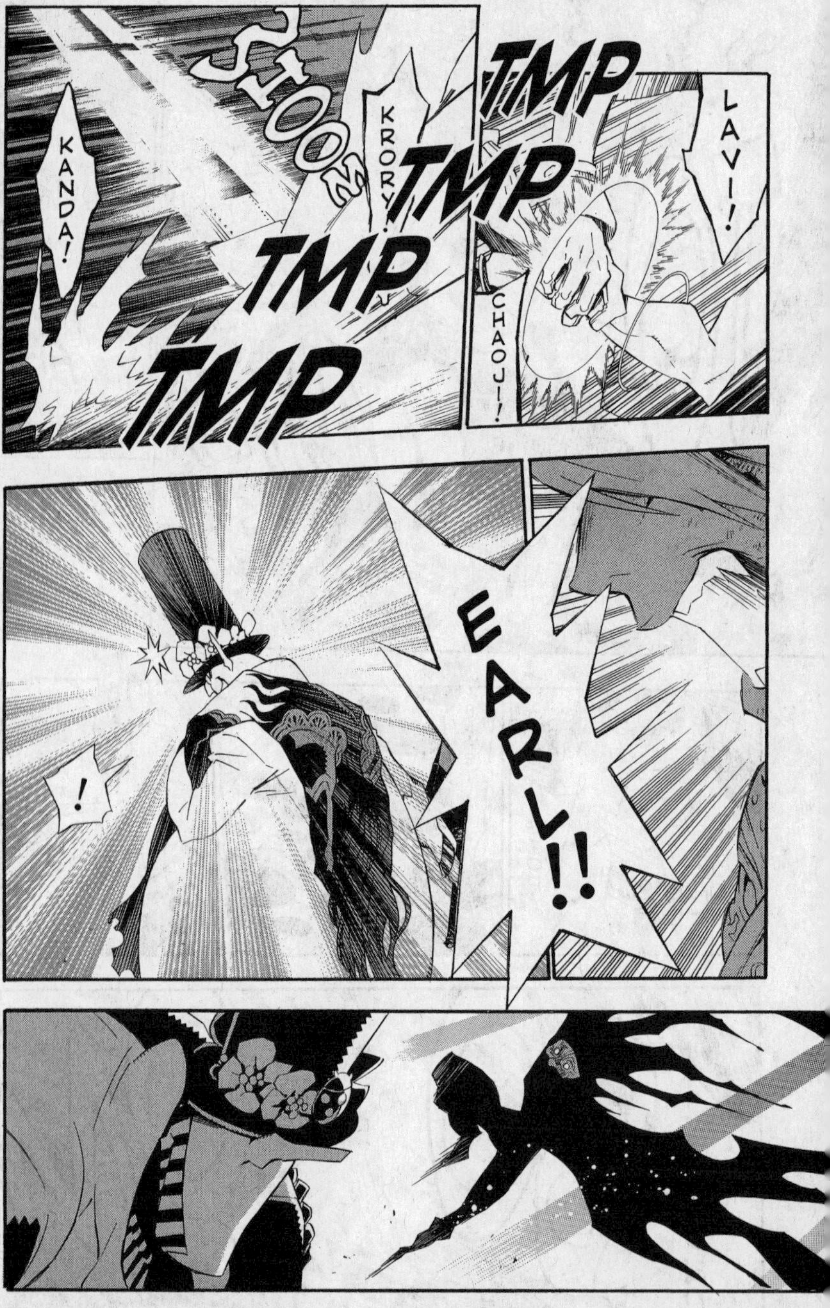
LAVI!
CHAOJI!
TMP TMP TMP TMP
KRORY!
KANDA!
EARL!!
!

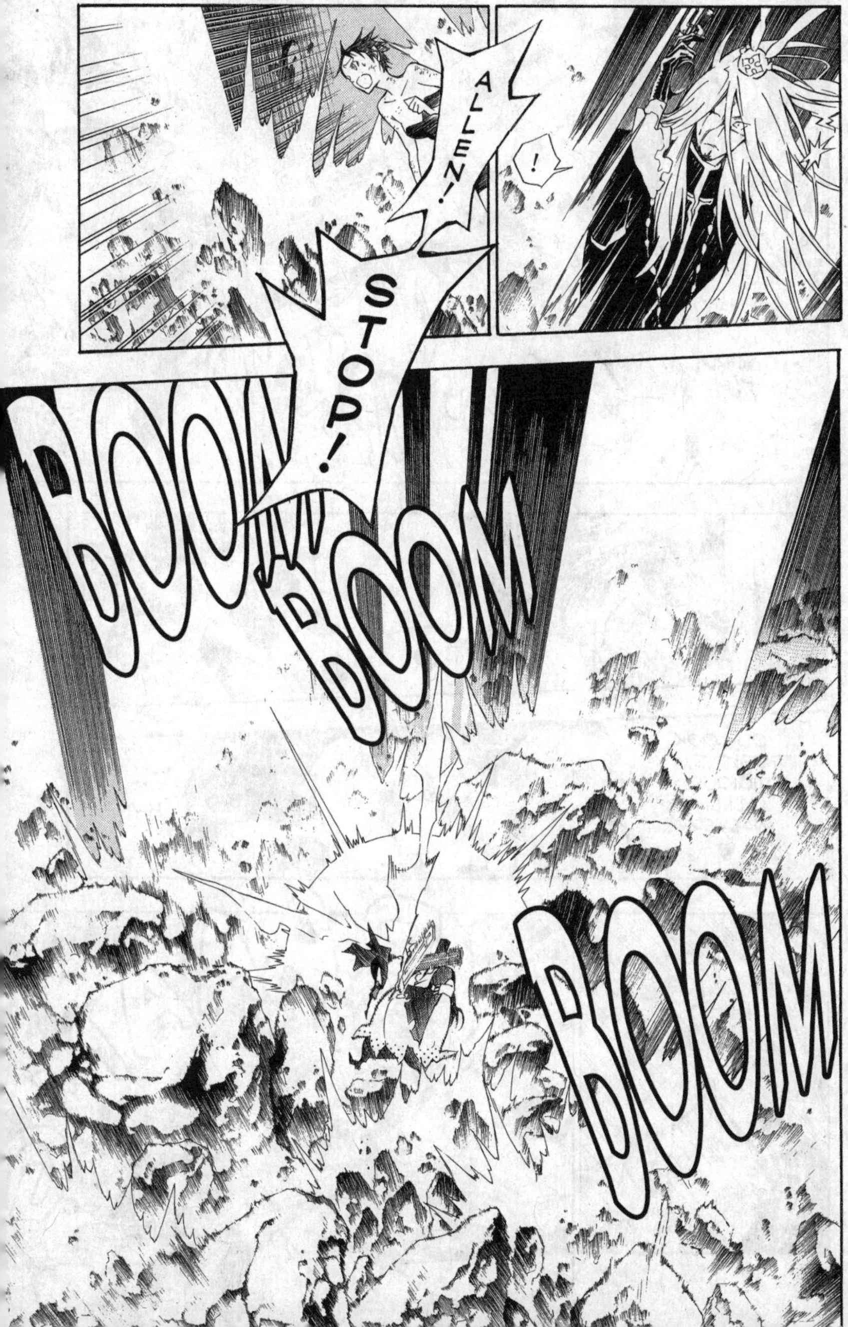
!
ALLEN!
STOP!
BOOM
BOOM
BOOM

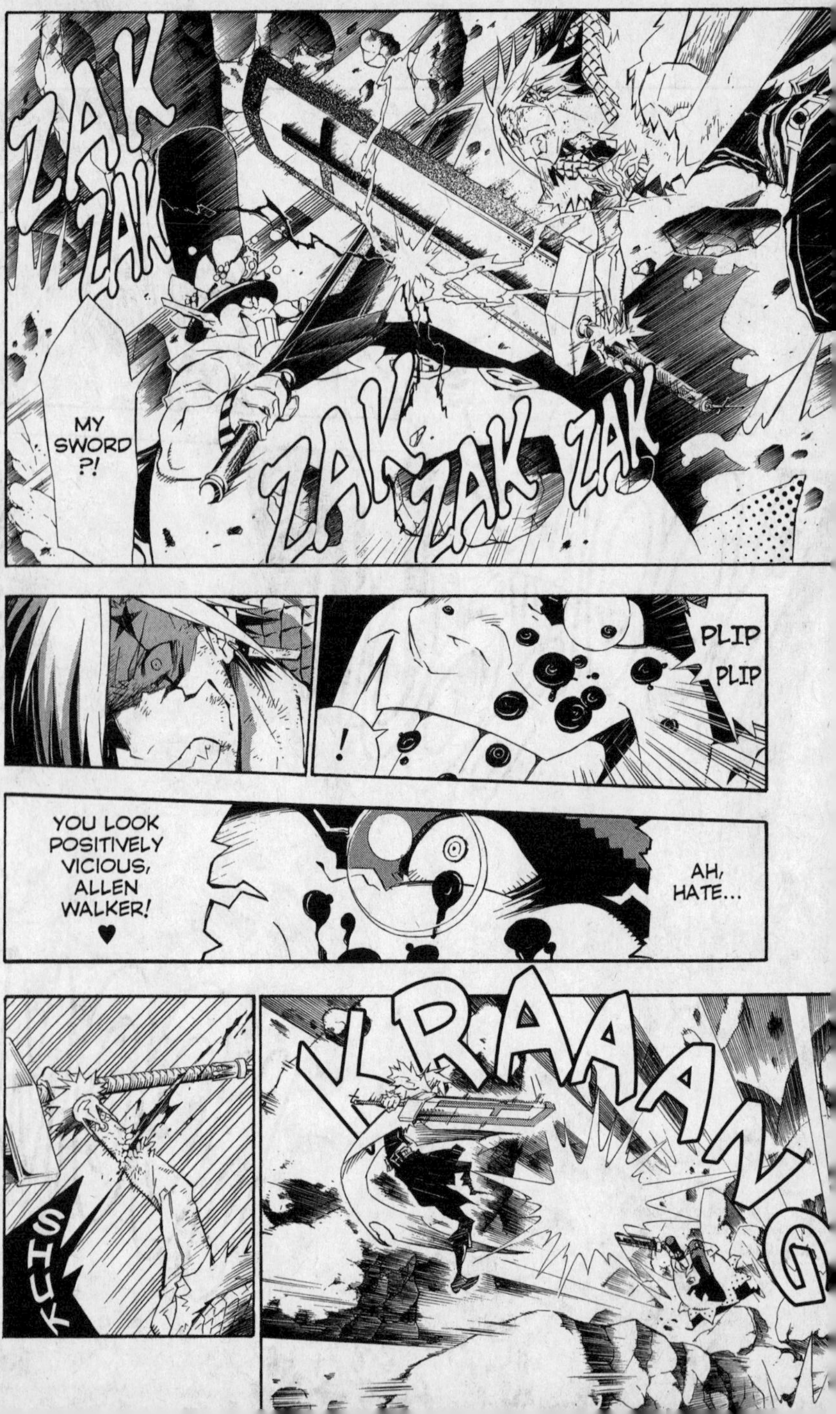
ZAK ZAK ZAK
MY SWORD ?!
ZAK ZAK ZAK
PLIP PLIP
!
AH, HATE...
YOU LOOK POSITIVELY VICIOUS, ALLEN WALKER! ♥
KRAAAANG
SHUK

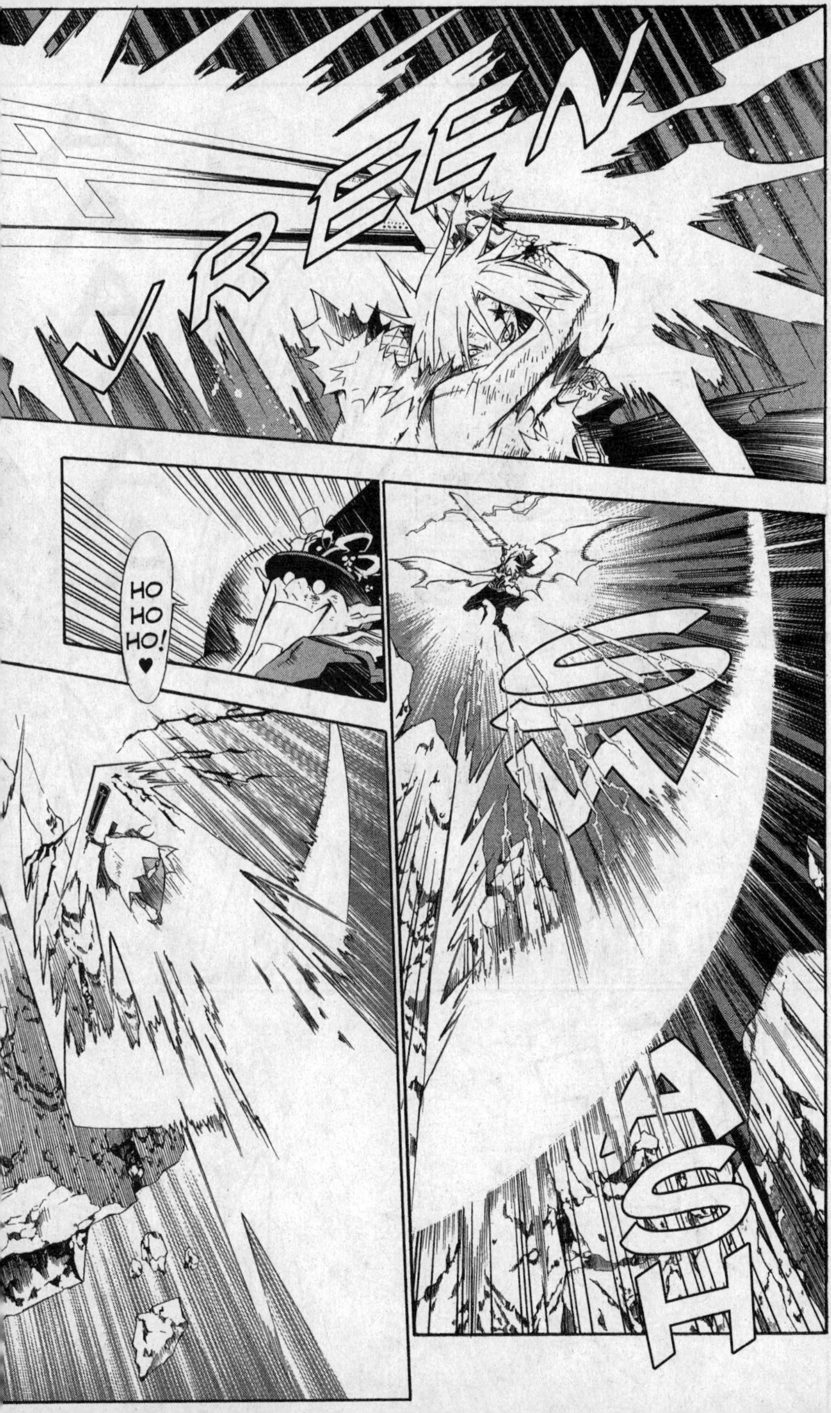

VRREEN
SWASH
HO HO HO! ♥

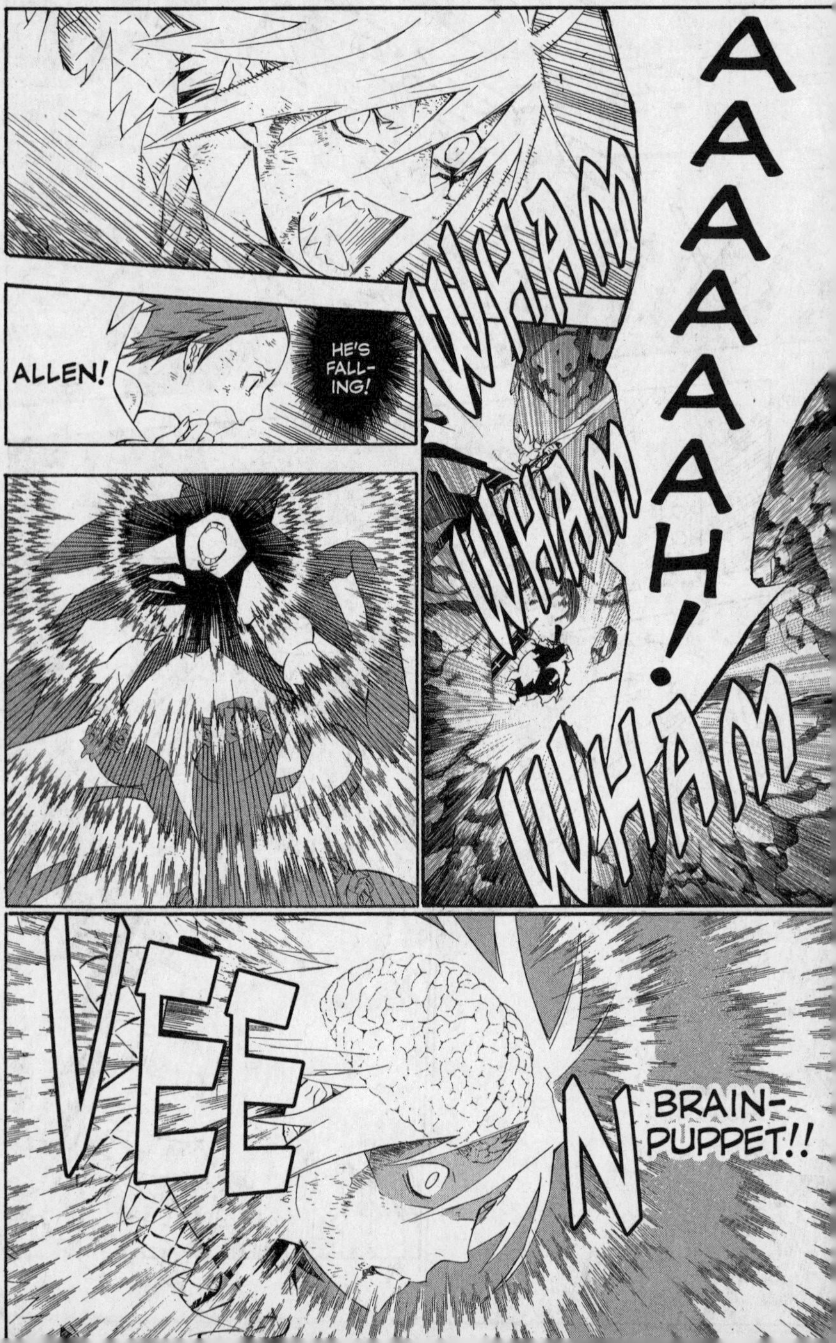
AAAAAAH!
WHAM
WHAM
WHAM
HE'S FALLING!
ALLEN!
VEEN
BRAIN-PUPPET!!

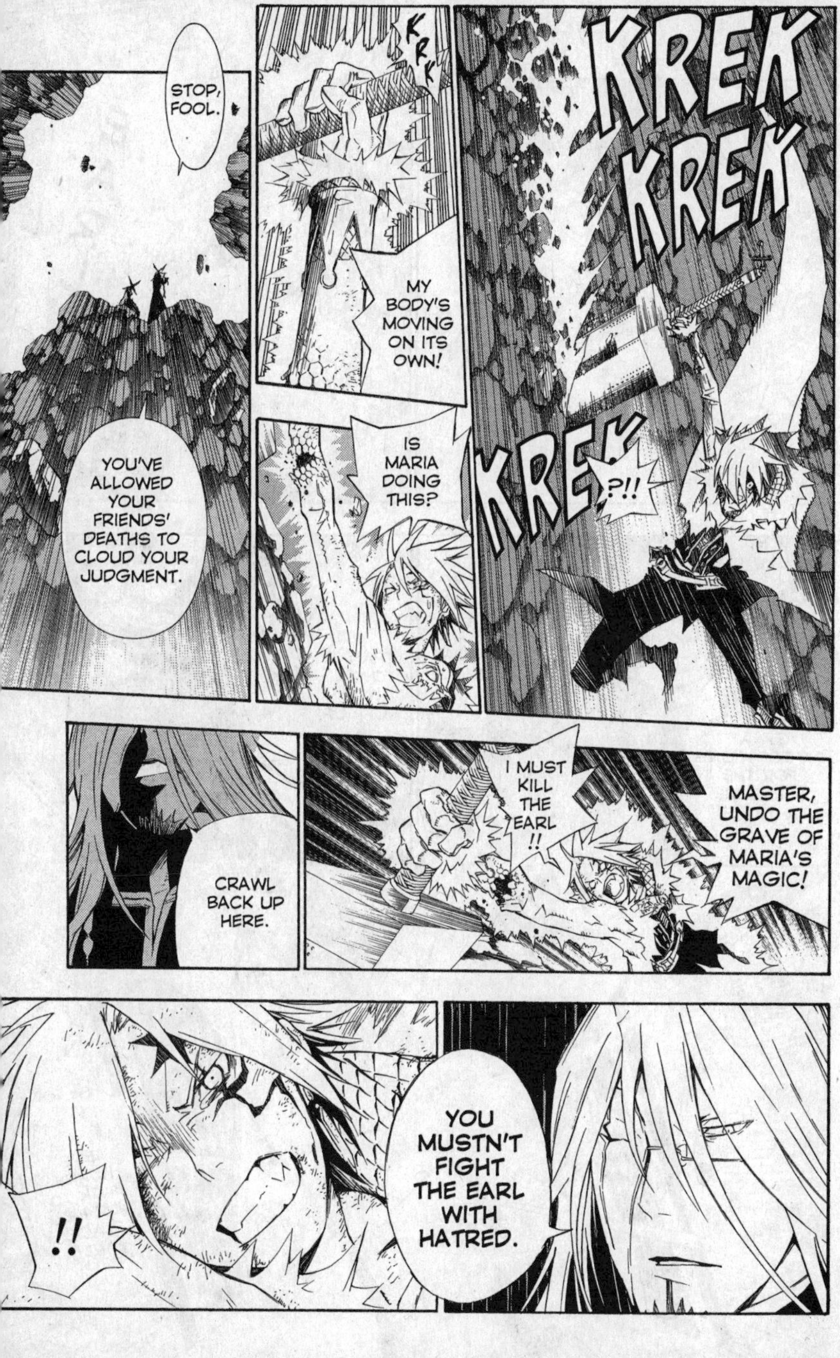
KREK KREK
KREK
?!!
KRKK
MY BODY'S MOVING ON ITS OWN!
IS MARIA DOING THIS?
STOP, FOOL.
YOU'VE ALLOWED YOUR FRIENDS' DEATHS TO CLOUD YOUR JUDGMENT.
MASTER, UNDO THE GRAVE OF MARIA'S MAGIC!
I MUST KILL THE EARL !!
CRAWL BACK UP HERE.
YOU MUSTN'T FIGHT THE EARL WITH HATRED.
!!

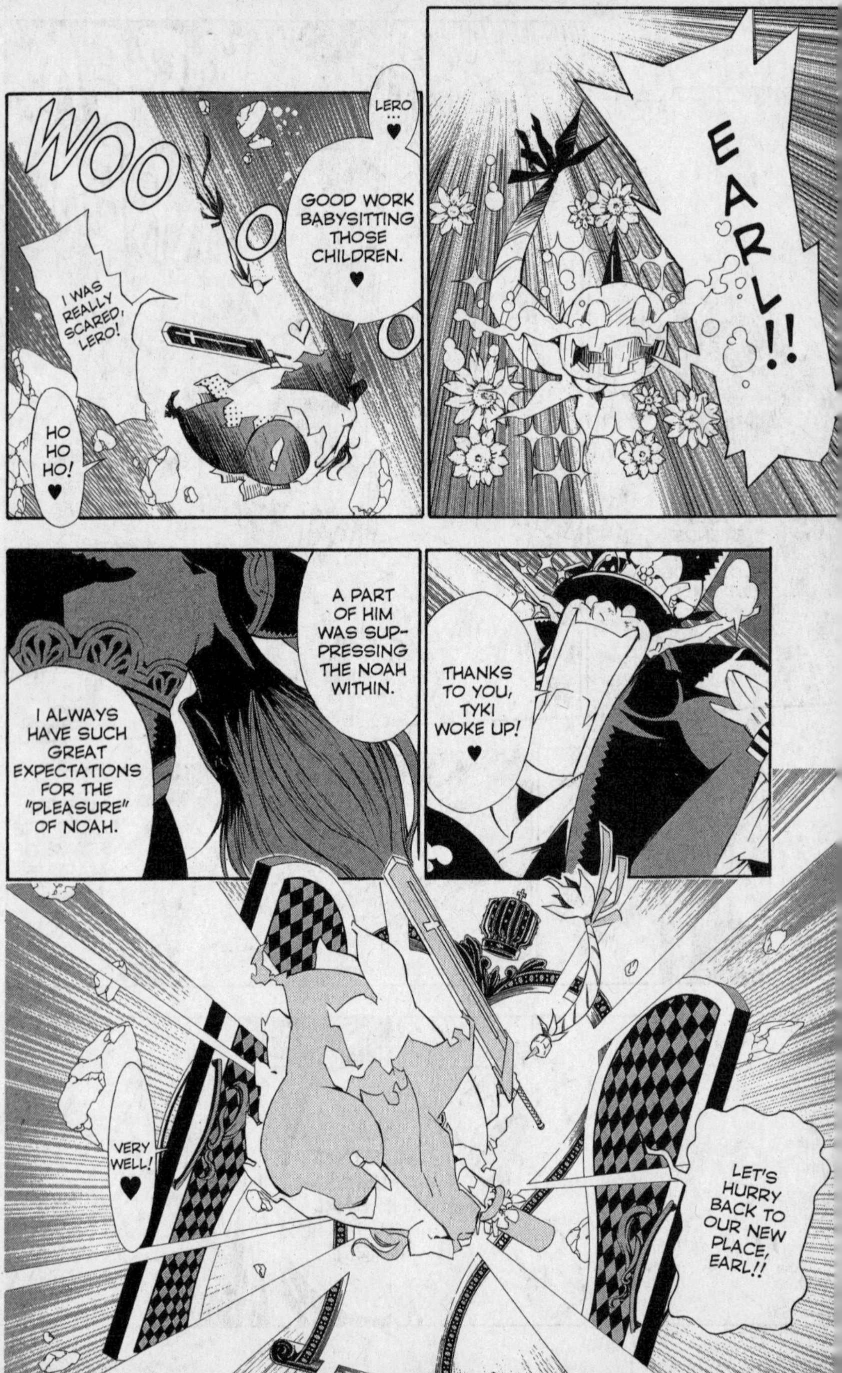
EARL!!
LERO... ♥
GOOD WORK BABYSITTING THOSE CHILDREN. ♥
WOOO
I WAS REALLY SCARED, LERO!
HO HO HO! ♥
THANKS TO YOU, TYKI WOKE UP! ♥
A PART OF HIM WAS SUP-PRESSING THE NOAH WITHIN.
I ALWAYS HAVE SUCH GREAT EXPECTATIONS FOR THE "PLEASURE" OF NOAH.
LET'S HURRY BACK TO OUR NEW PLACE, EARL!!
VERY WELL! ♥

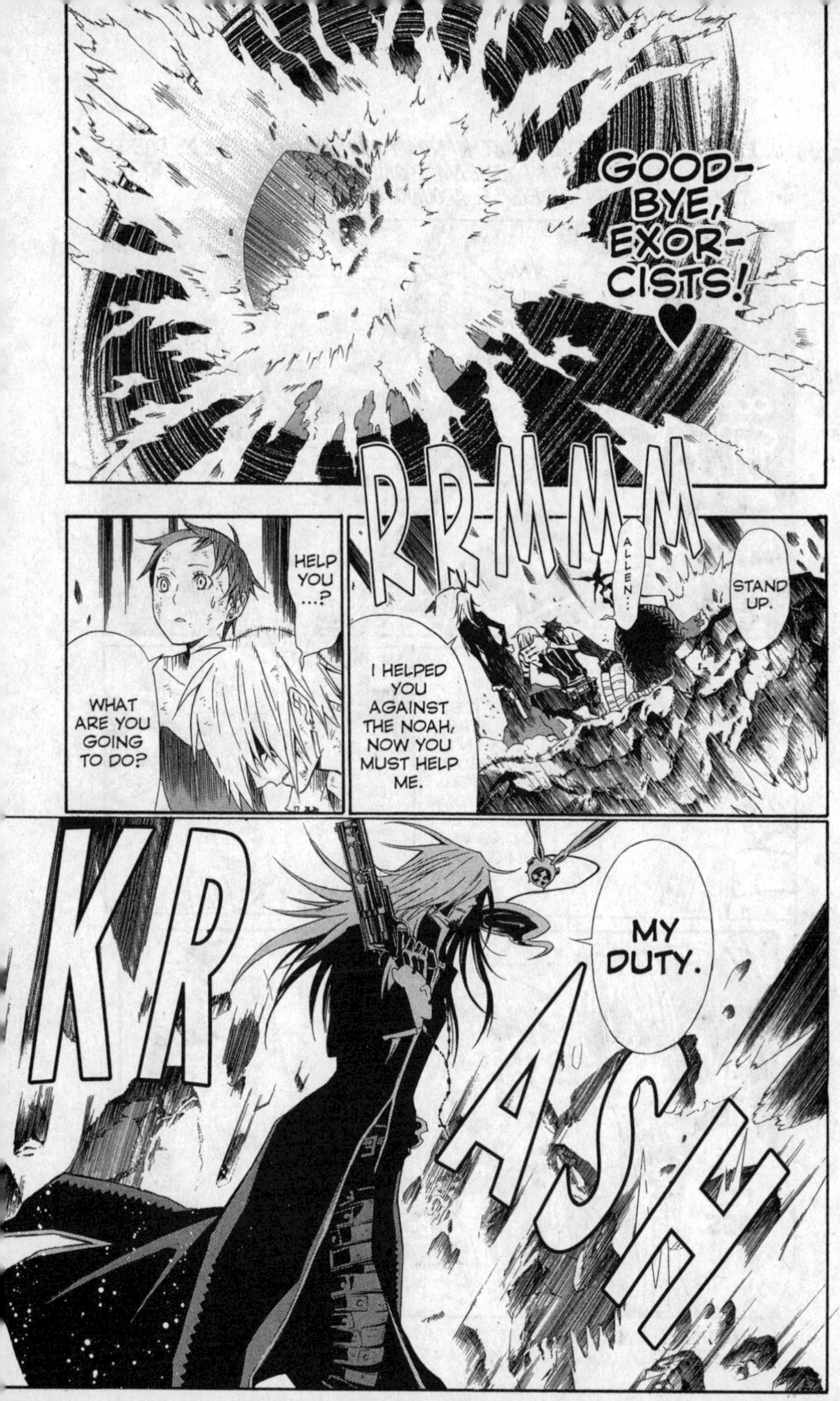
GOOD-BYE, EXORCISTS! ♥
RRMMMM
STAND UP.
ALLEN...
I HELPED YOU AGAINST THE NOAH, NOW YOU MUST HELP ME.
HELP YOU ...?
WHAT ARE YOU GOING TO DO?
MY DUTY.
KRASH

Q. RECENTLY I NOTICED THAT KANDA YU'S INITIALS ARE K.Y. DOES THAT STAND FOR KUKI YOMENAI (SOMEONE WHO CAN'T READ THE MOOD OF THE PEOPLE AROUND HIM)?

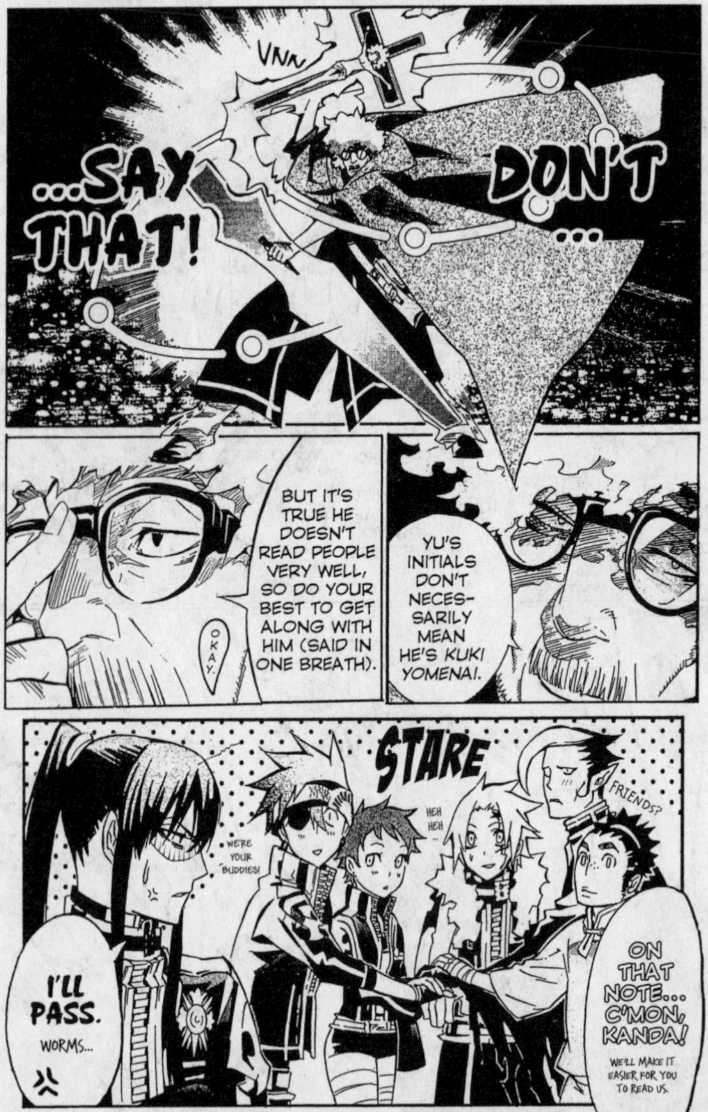
VNN
DON'T ...
...SAY THAT!
YU'S INITIALS DON'T NECES-SARILY MEAN HE'S KUKI YOMENAI.
BUT IT'S TRUE HE DOESN'T READ PEOPLE VERY WELL, SO DO YOUR BEST TO GET ALONG WITH HIM (SAID IN ONE BREATH).
OKAY.
ON THAT NOTE... C'MON, KANDA!
WE'LL MAKE IT EASIER FOR YOU TO READ US.
FRIENDS?
STARE
HEH HEH
WE'RE YOUR BUDDIES!
I'LL PASS.
WORMS...

I HEARD THAT SOMEONE EVEN WORSE AT READING PEOPLE IS CALLED A S.K.Y. (SUPER KUKI YOMENAI).

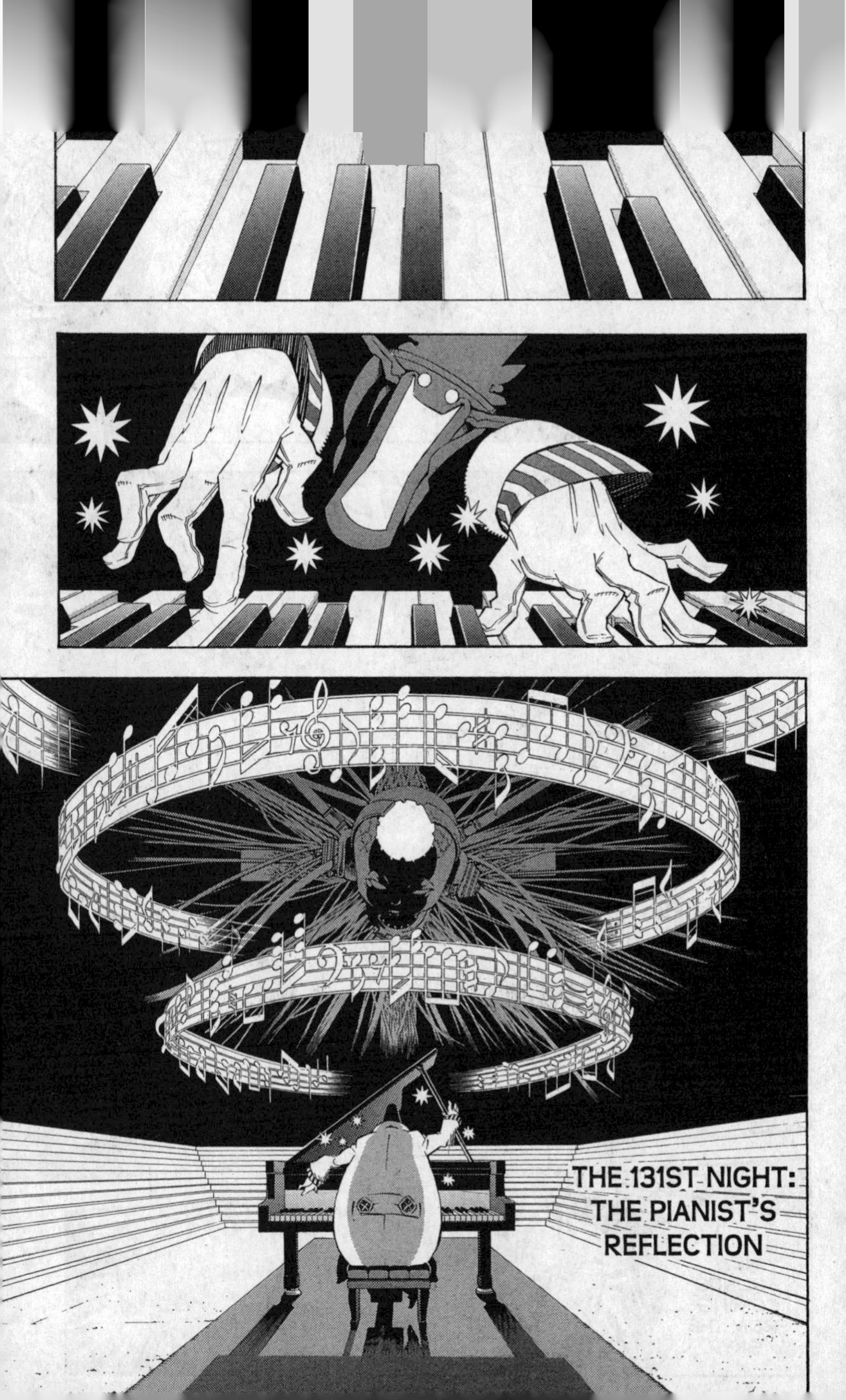
THE 131ST NIGHT:
THE PIANIST'S
REFLECTION

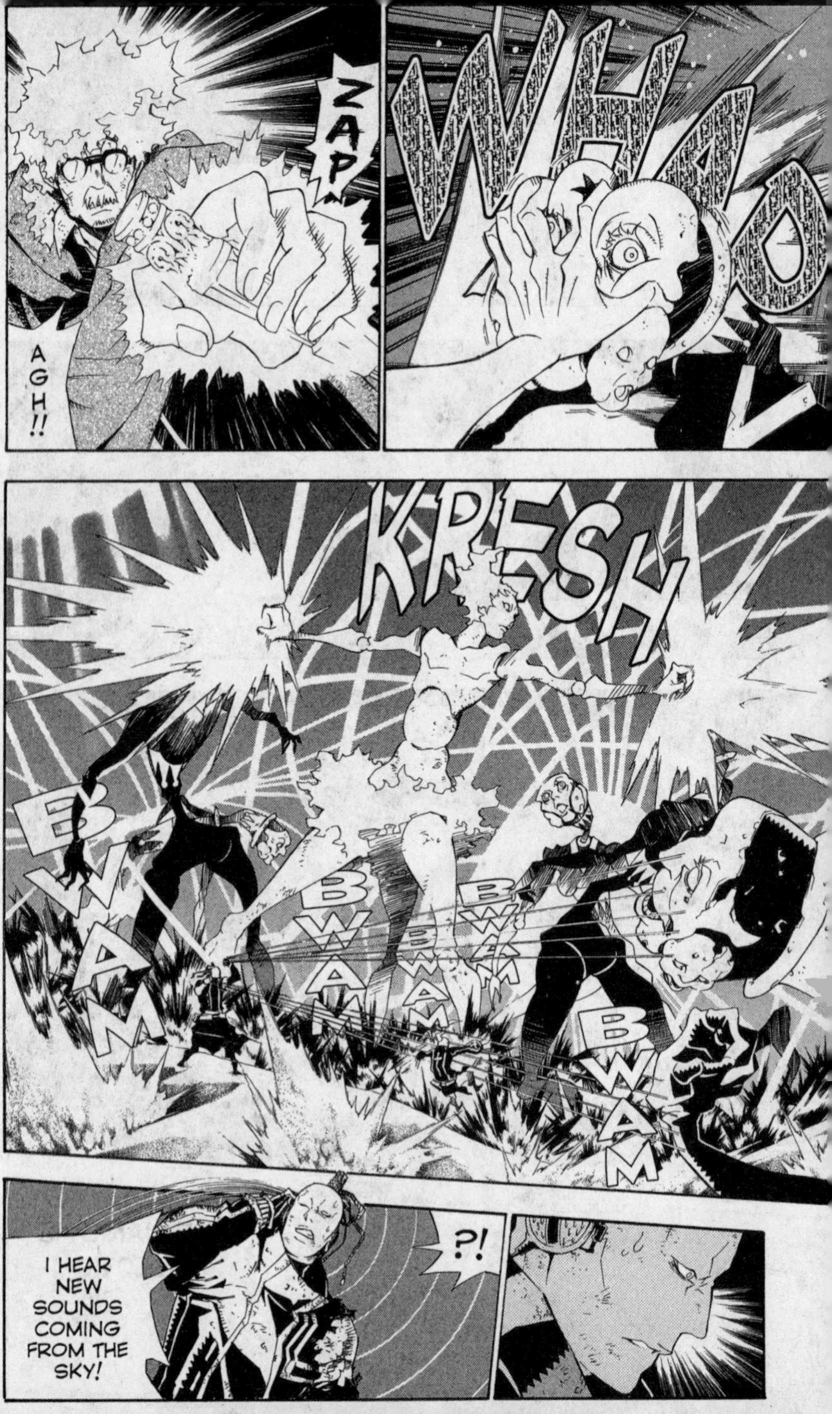
WHAO
ZAP
AGH!!
KRESH
BWAM
BWAM
BWAM
BWAM
BWAM
?!
I HEAR NEW SOUNDS COMING FROM THE SKY!

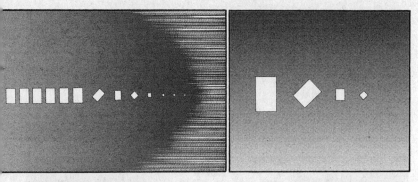

WHAT
IS IT?!

?!

WHAT IS IT?
SOME-THING'S...
...UP THERE.

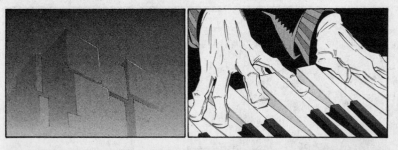

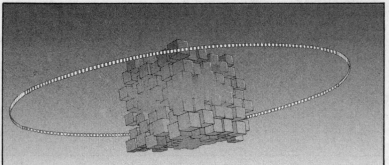

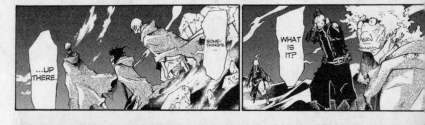

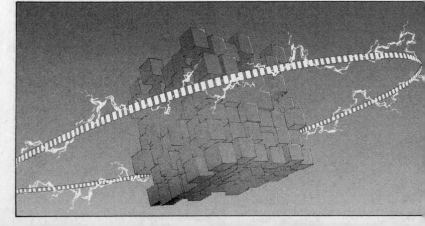

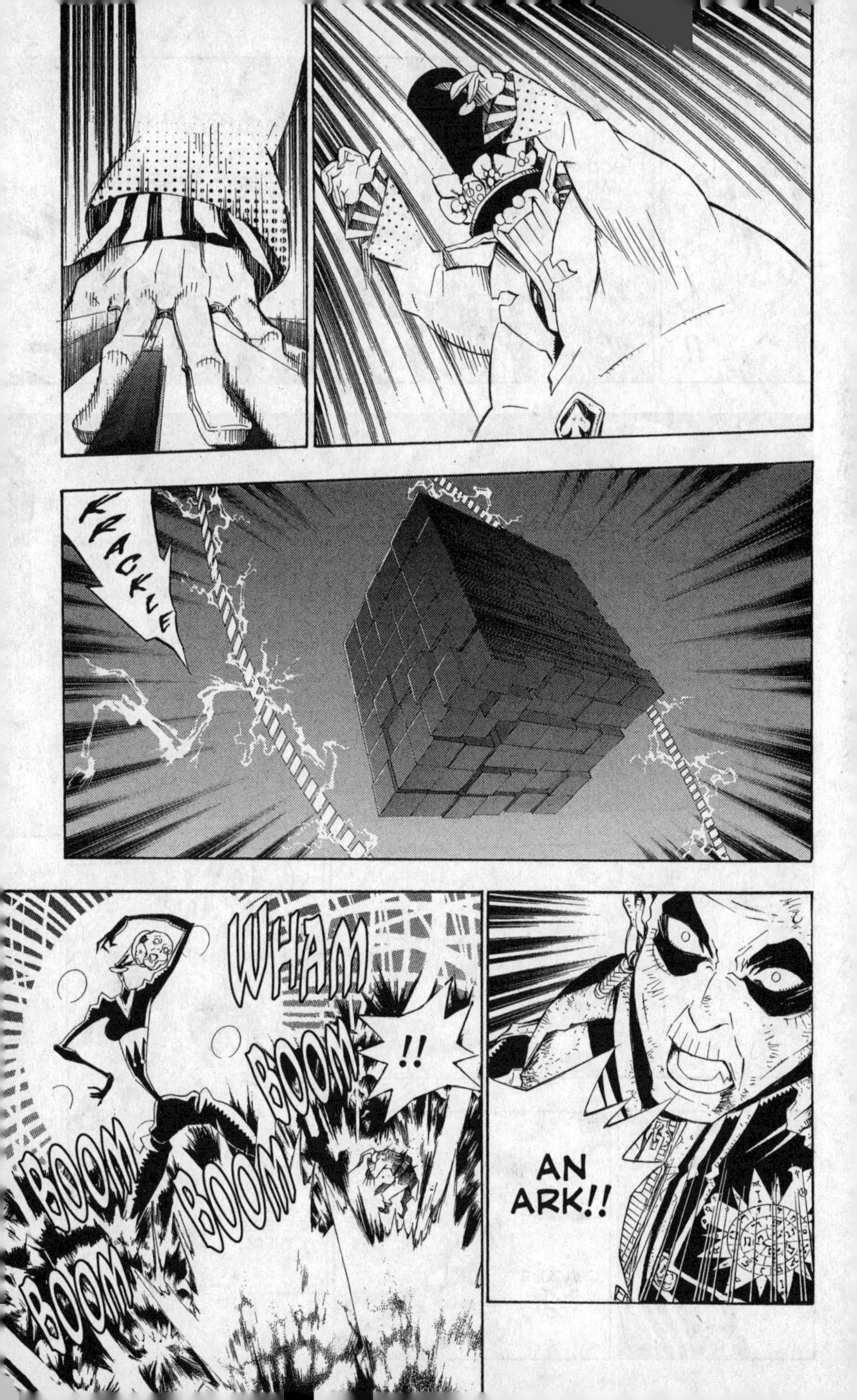
KRACKLE
AN ARK!!
WHAM
!!
BOOM BOOM
BOOM BOOM
BOOM

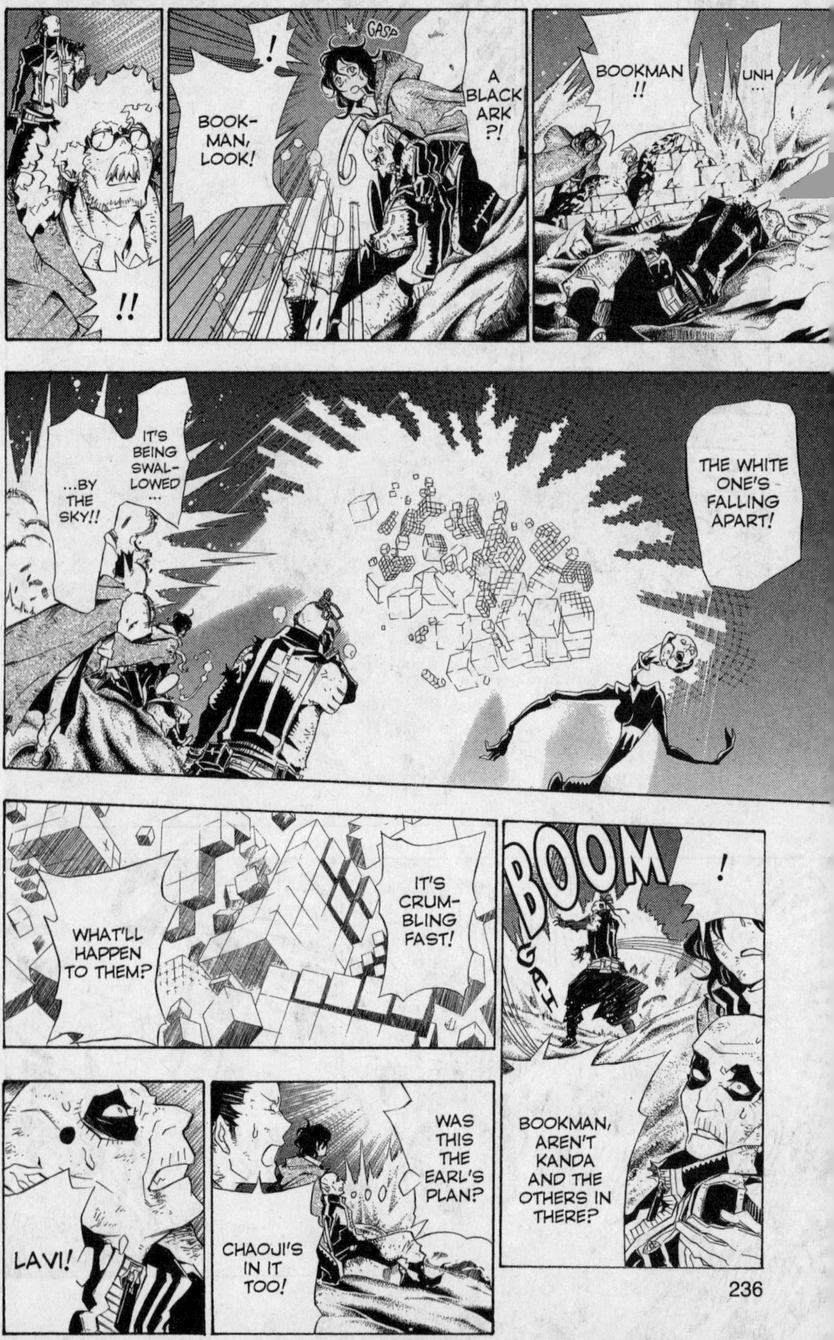
UNH ...
BOOKMAN !!
GASP
A BLACK ARK ?!
!
BOOK-MAN, LOOK!
!!
THE WHITE ONE'S FALLING APART!
IT'S BEING SWAL-LOWED ...
...BY THE SKY!!
BOOM
!
GAH
BOOKMAN, AREN'T KANDA AND THE OTHERS IN THERE?
IT'S CRUM-BLING FAST!
WHAT'LL HAPPEN TO THEM?
WAS THIS THE EARL'S PLAN?
CHAOJI'S IN IT TOO!
LAVI!

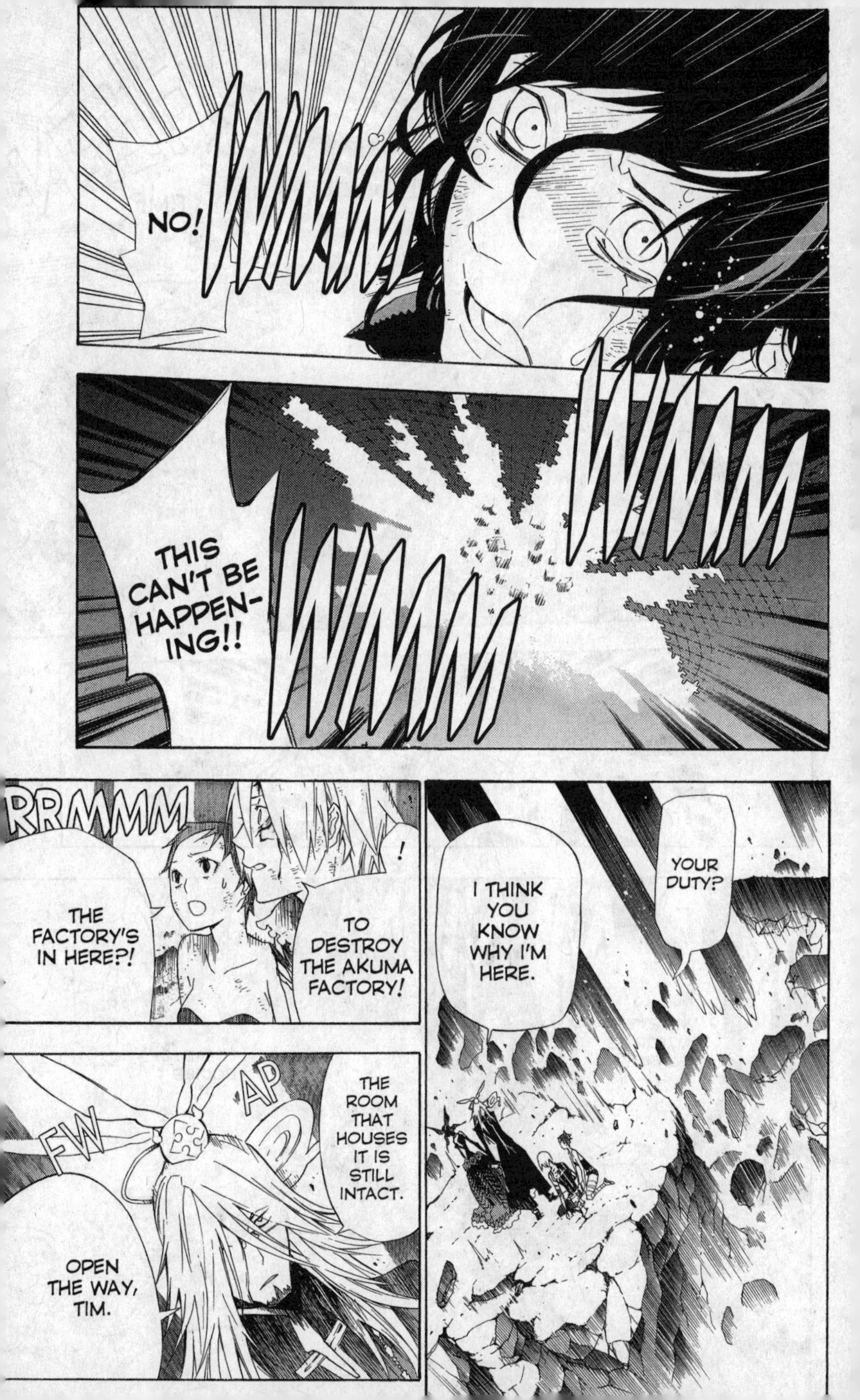
WMM
NO!
WMMM
WMMM
THIS CAN'T BE HAPPEN-ING!!
YOUR DUTY?
I THINK YOU KNOW WHY I'M HERE.
RRMMM
!
TO DESTROY THE AKUMA FACTORY!
THE FACTORY'S IN HERE?!
AP
FW
THE ROOM THAT HOUSES IT IS STILL INTACT.
OPEN THE WAY, TIM.

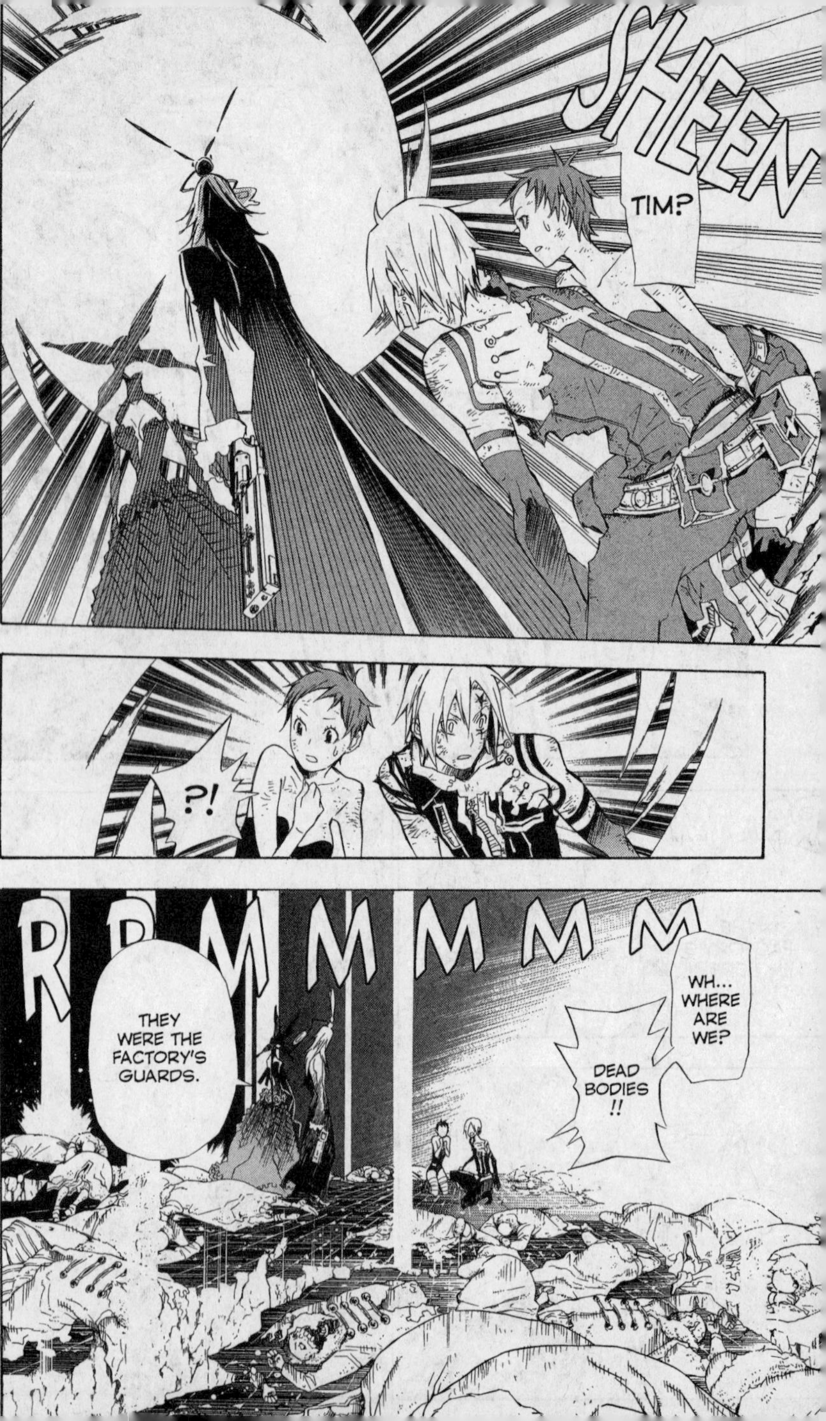
SHEEN
TIM?
?!
RRMMMMM
WH... WHERE ARE WE?
DEAD BODIES!!
THEY WERE THE FACTORY'S GUARDS.

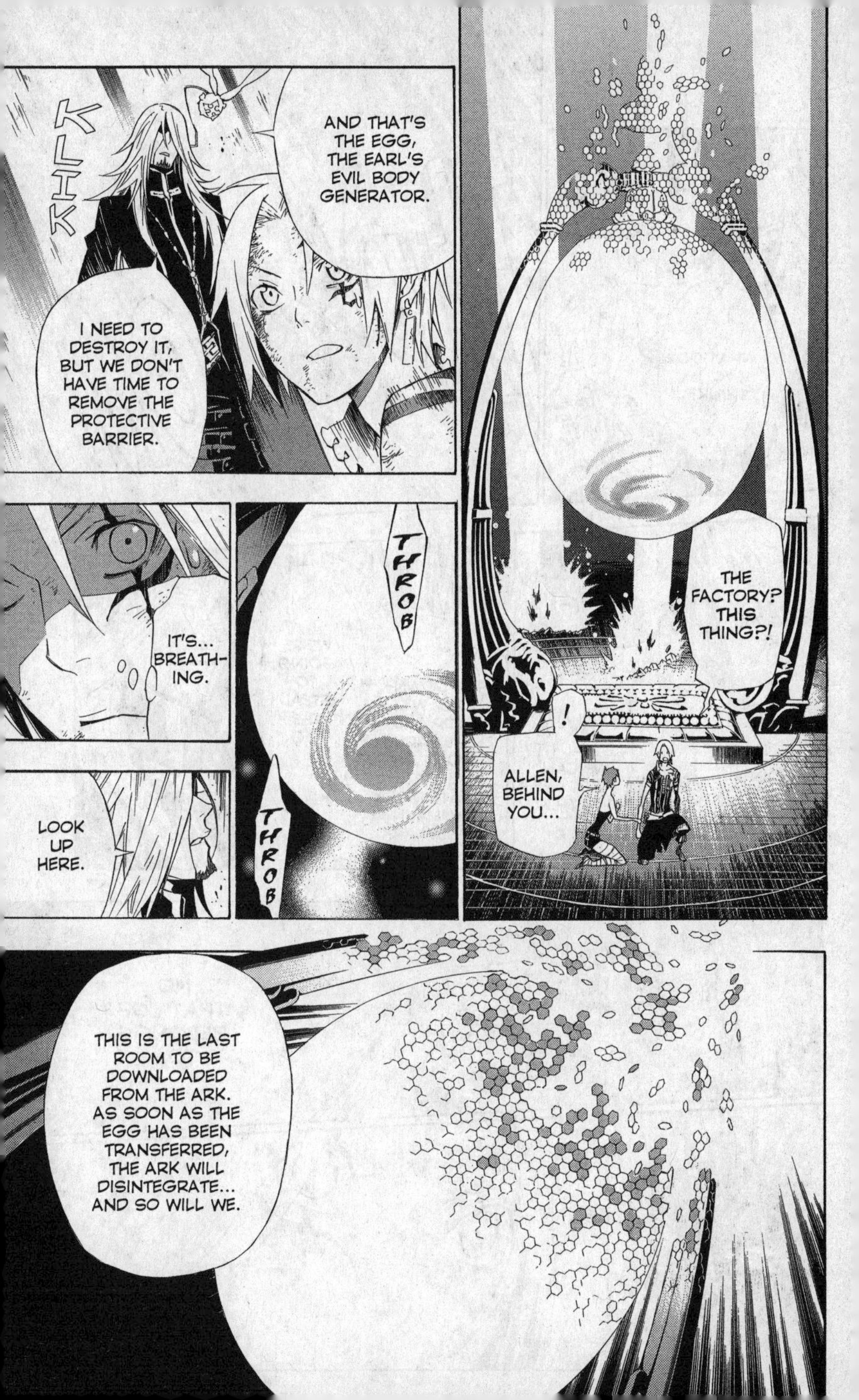
THE FACTORY? THIS THING?!
!
ALLEN, BEHIND YOU...
KLIK
AND THAT'S THE EGG, THE EARL'S EVIL BODY GENERATOR.
I NEED TO DESTROY IT, BUT WE DON'T HAVE TIME TO REMOVE THE PROTECTIVE BARRIER.
THROB
THROB
IT'S... BREATH-ING.
LOOK UP HERE.
THIS IS THE LAST ROOM TO BE DOWNLOADED FROM THE ARK. AS SOON AS THE EGG HAS BEEN TRANSFERRED, THE ARK WILL DISINTEGRATE... AND SO WILL WE.

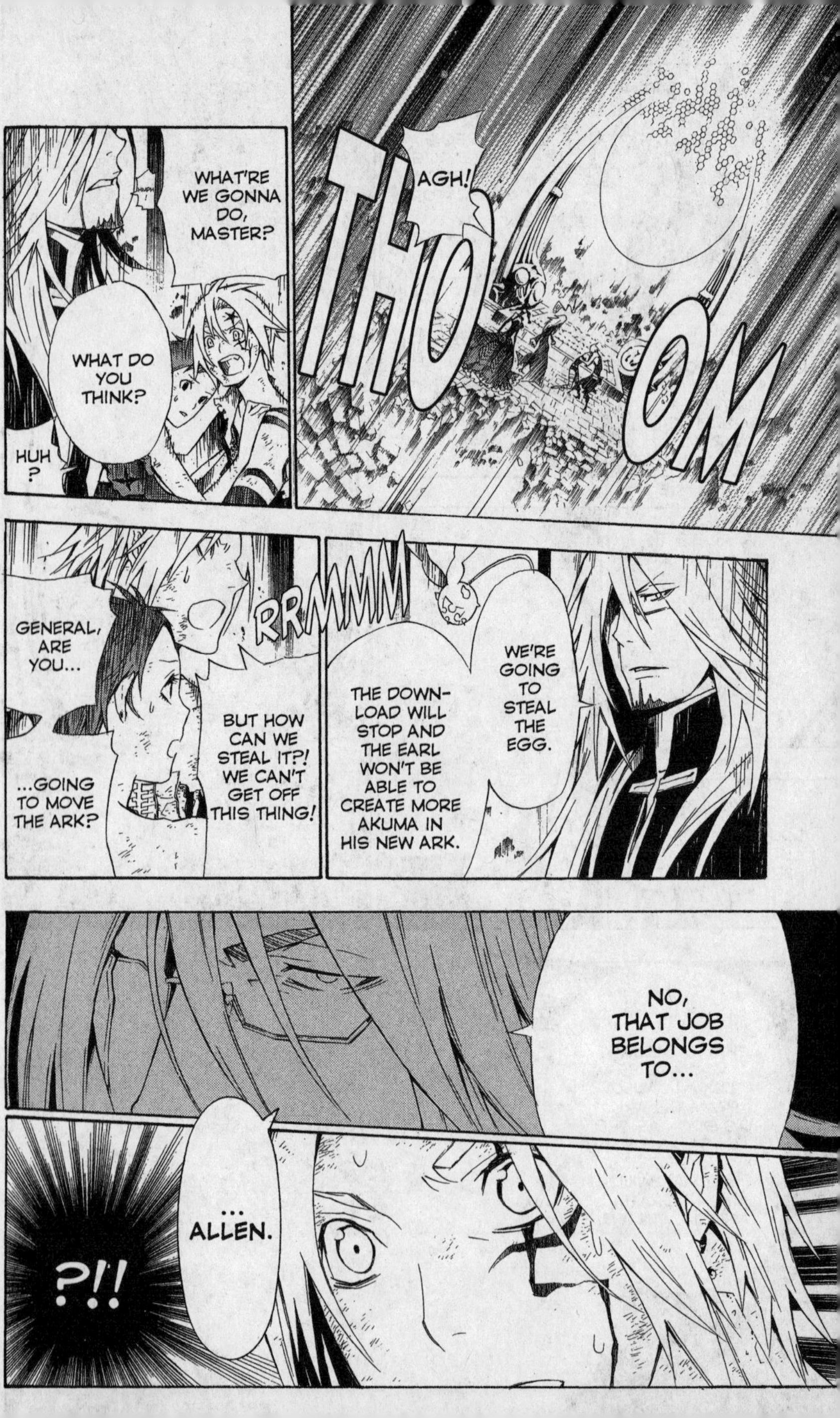
AGH!
THOOOM
WHAT'RE WE GONNA DO, MASTER?
HMPH
WHAT DO YOU THINK?
HUH?
WE'RE GOING TO STEAL THE EGG.
THE DOWN-LOAD WILL STOP AND THE EARL WON'T BE ABLE TO CREATE MORE AKUMA IN HIS NEW ARK.
RRMMMM
BUT HOW CAN WE STEAL IT?! WE CAN'T GET OFF THIS THING!
GENERAL, ARE YOU...
...GOING TO MOVE THE ARK?
NO, THAT JOB BELONGS TO...
... ALLEN.
?!!

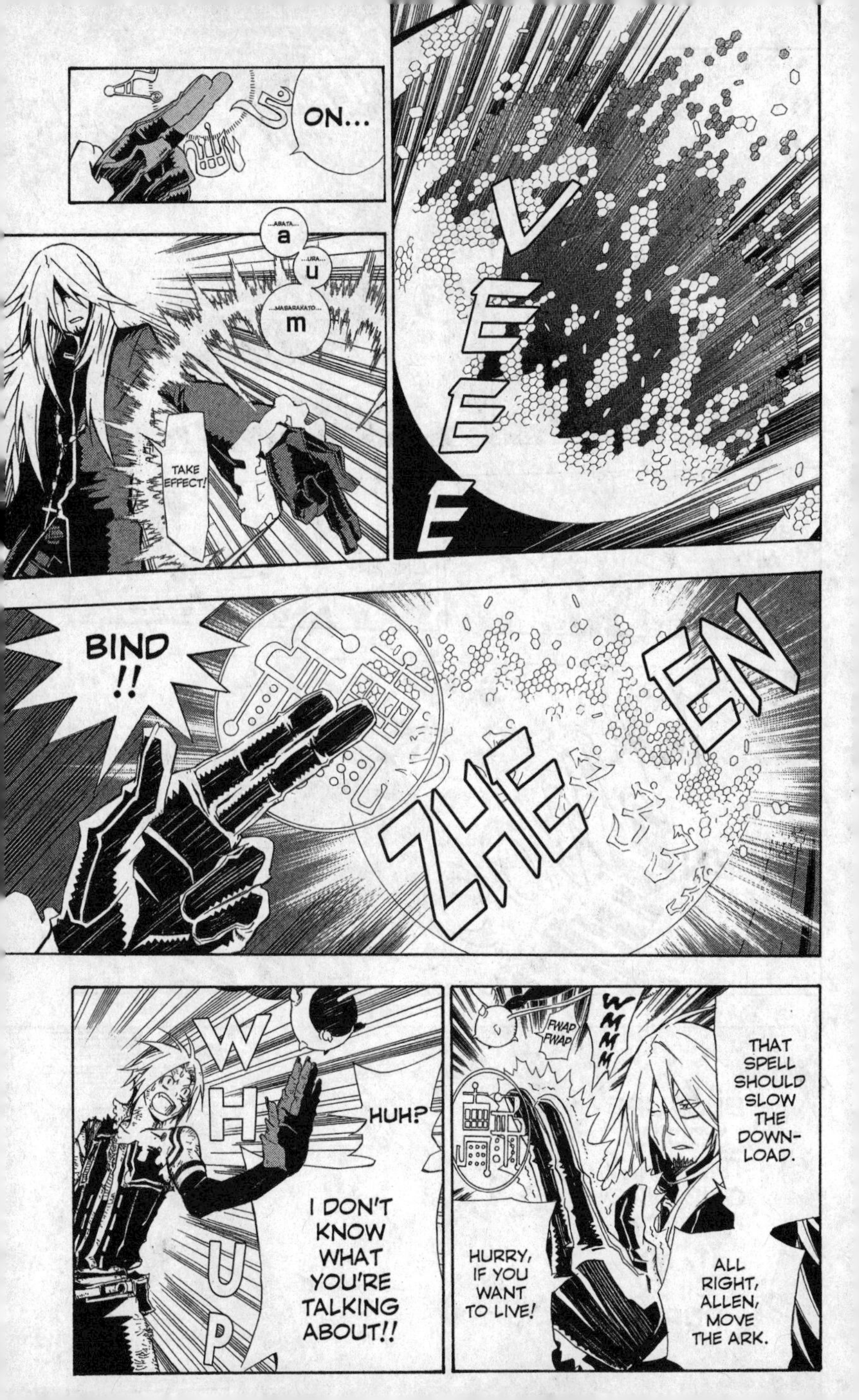
VEEEE
ON...
...ABATA... a
...URA... u
...MASARAKATO... m
TAKE EFFECT!
ZHEEN
BIND!!
WMMM
FWAP FWAP
THAT SPELL SHOULD SLOW THE DOWNLOAD.
ALL RIGHT, ALLEN, MOVE THE ARK.
HURRY, IF YOU WANT TO LIVE!
WHUP
HUH?
I DON'T KNOW WHAT YOU'RE TALKING ABOUT!!

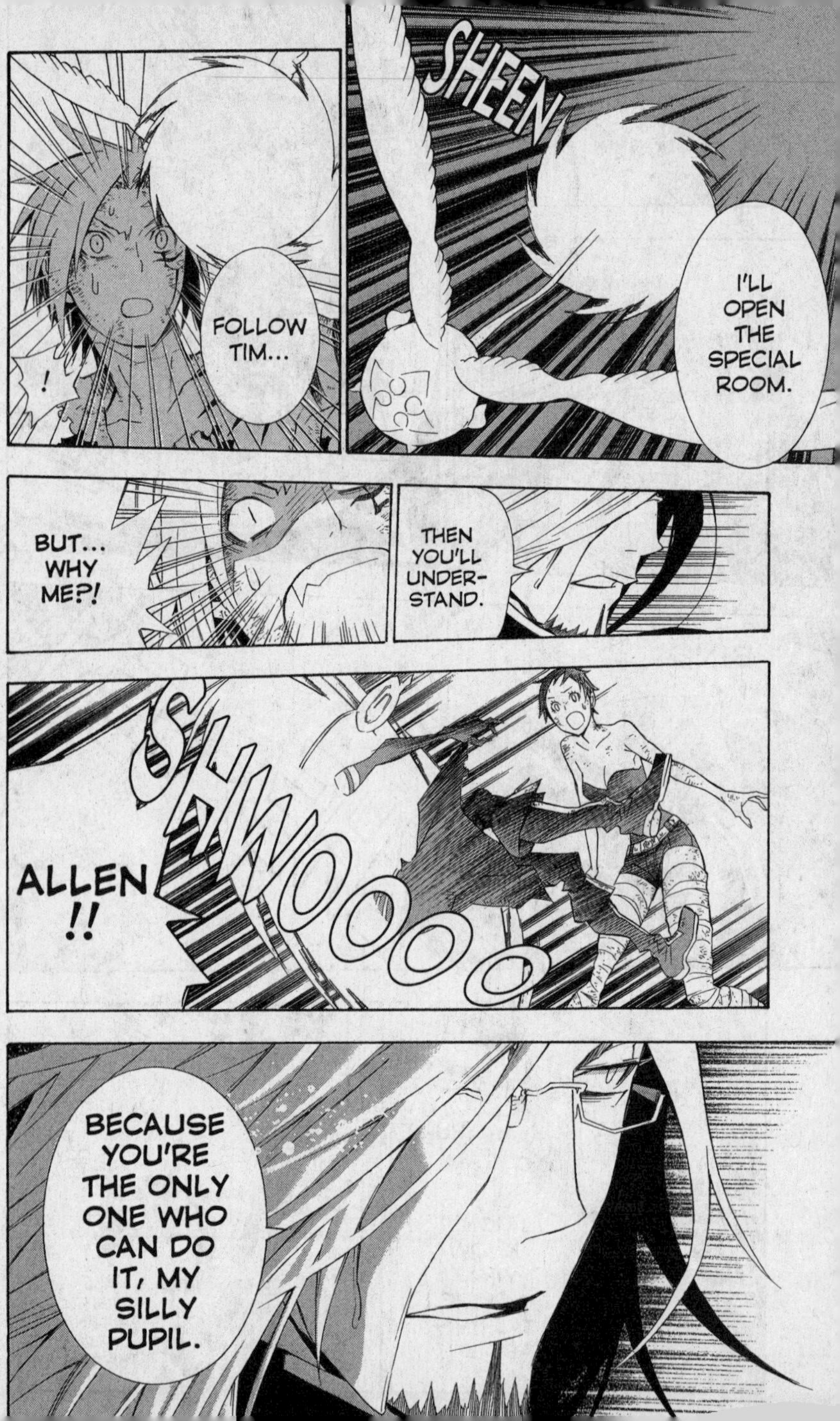
SHEEN
I'LL OPEN THE SPECIAL ROOM.
FOLLOW TIM...
!
THEN YOU'LL UNDER-STAND.
BUT... WHY ME?!
SHWOOOOO
ALLEN!!
BECAUSE YOU'RE THE ONLY ONE WHO CAN DO IT, MY SILLY PUPIL.

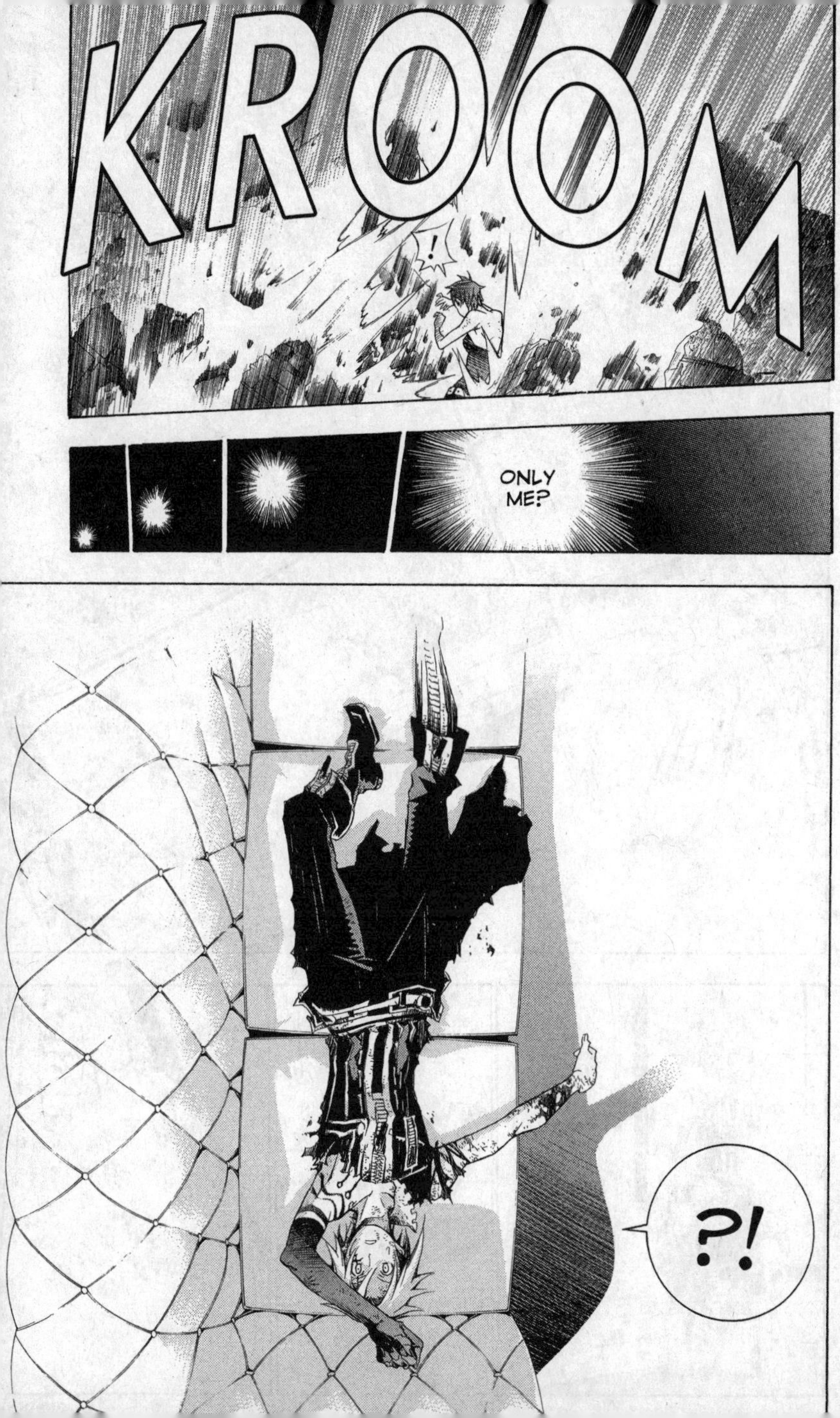
KROOM
!
ONLY ME?
?!

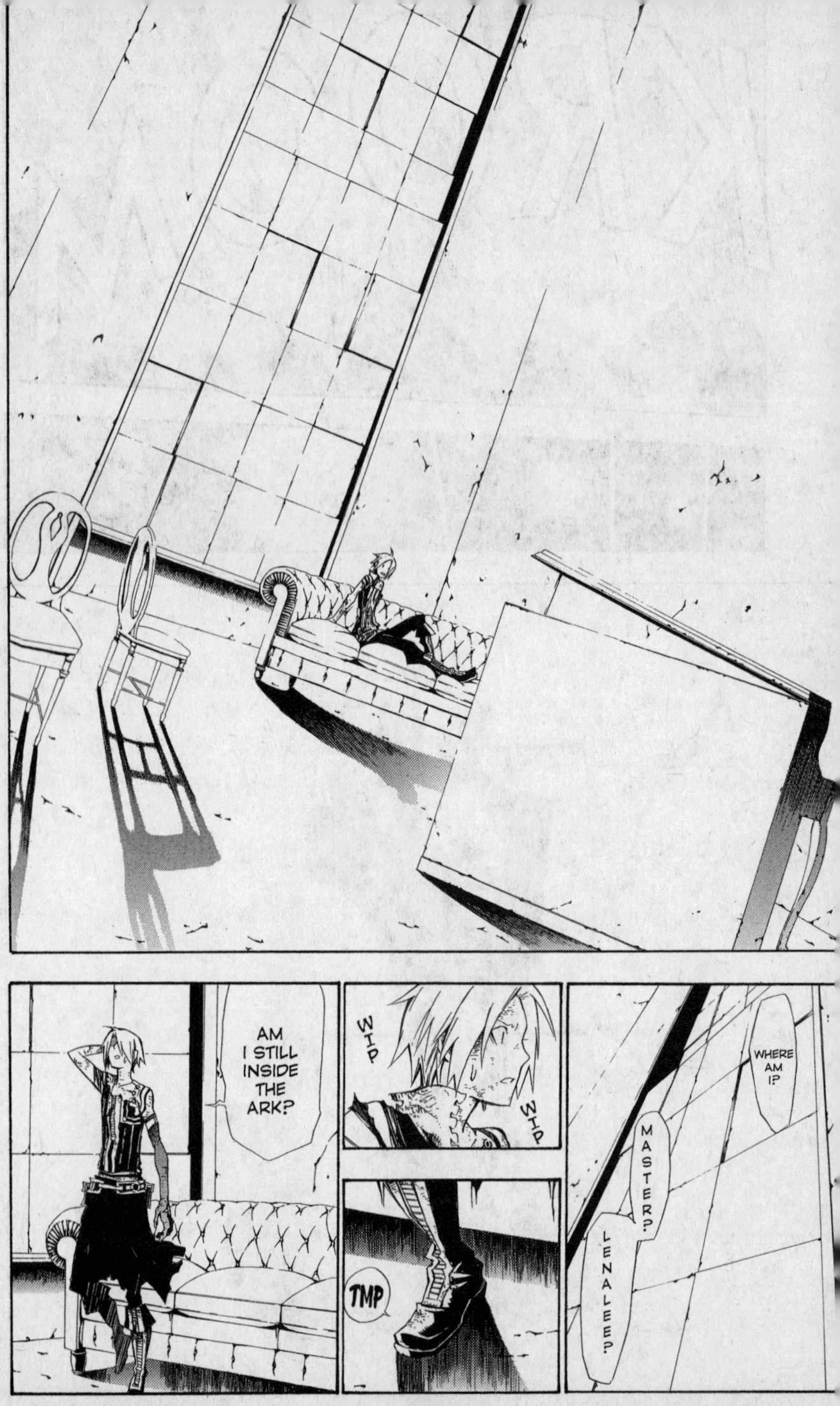
WHERE AM I?
MASTER?
LENALEE?
WIP WIP
TMP
AM I STILL INSIDE THE ARK?

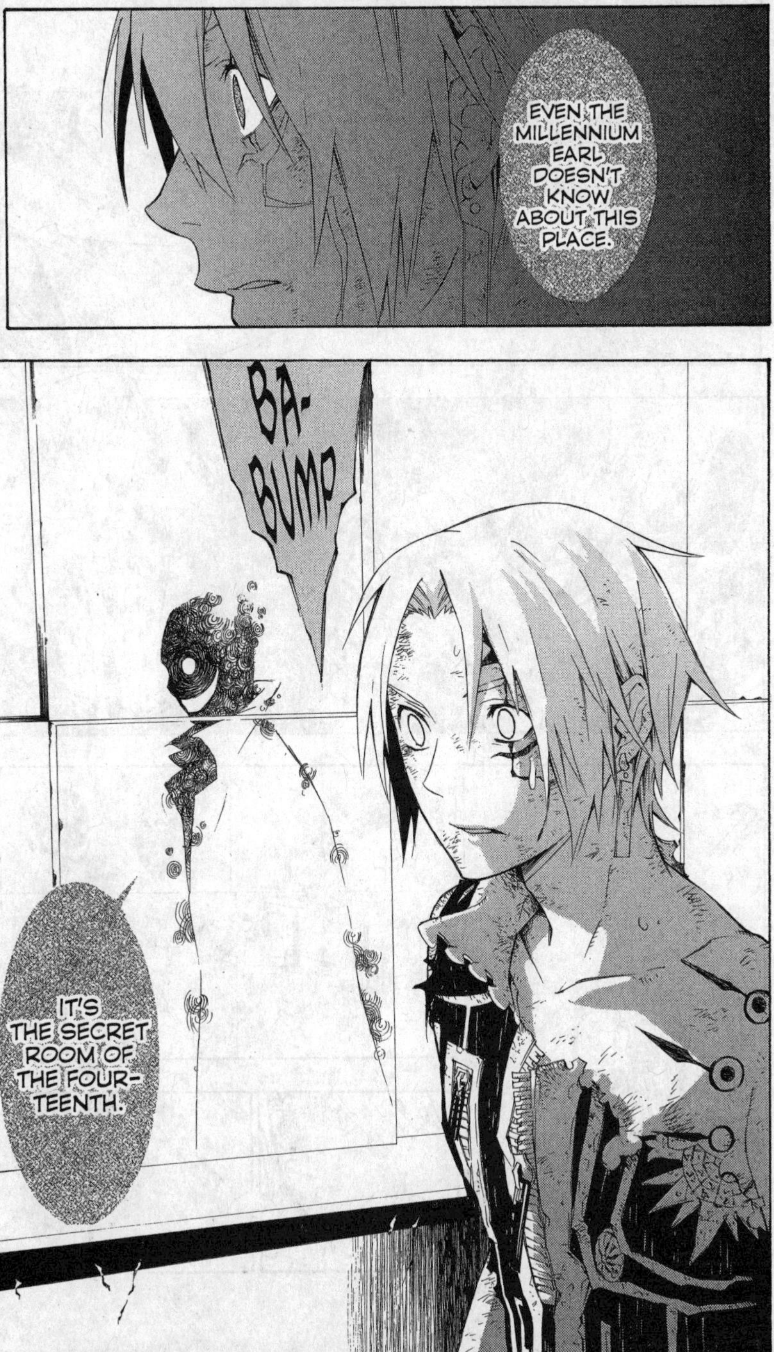
EVEN THE MILLENNIUM EARL DOESN'T KNOW ABOUT THIS PLACE.
BA-BUMP
IT'S THE SECRET ROOM OF THE FOUR-TEENTH.

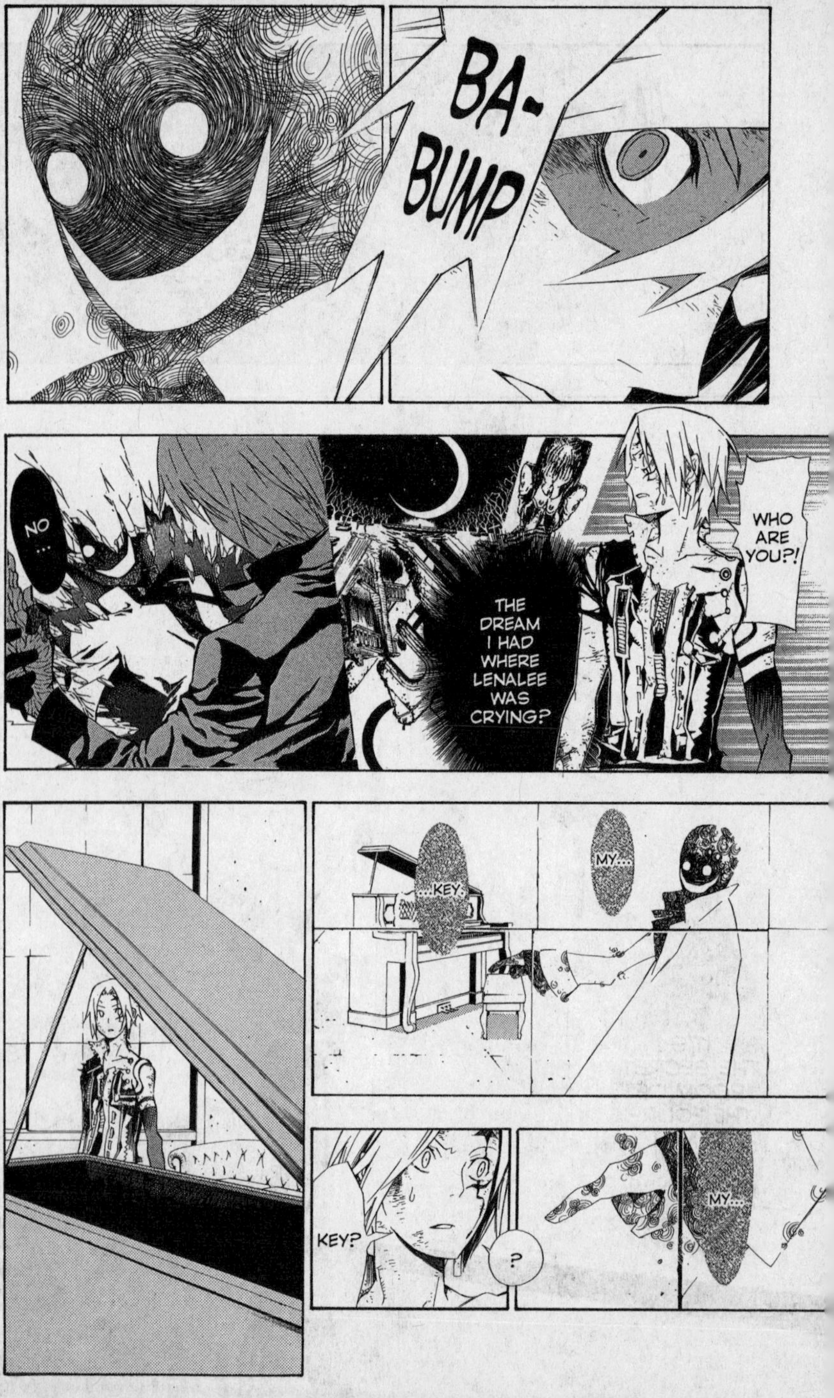
BA-BUMP
WHO ARE YOU?!
THE DREAM I HAD WHERE LENALEE WAS CRYING?
NO...
MY...
...KEY.
MY...
?
KEY?

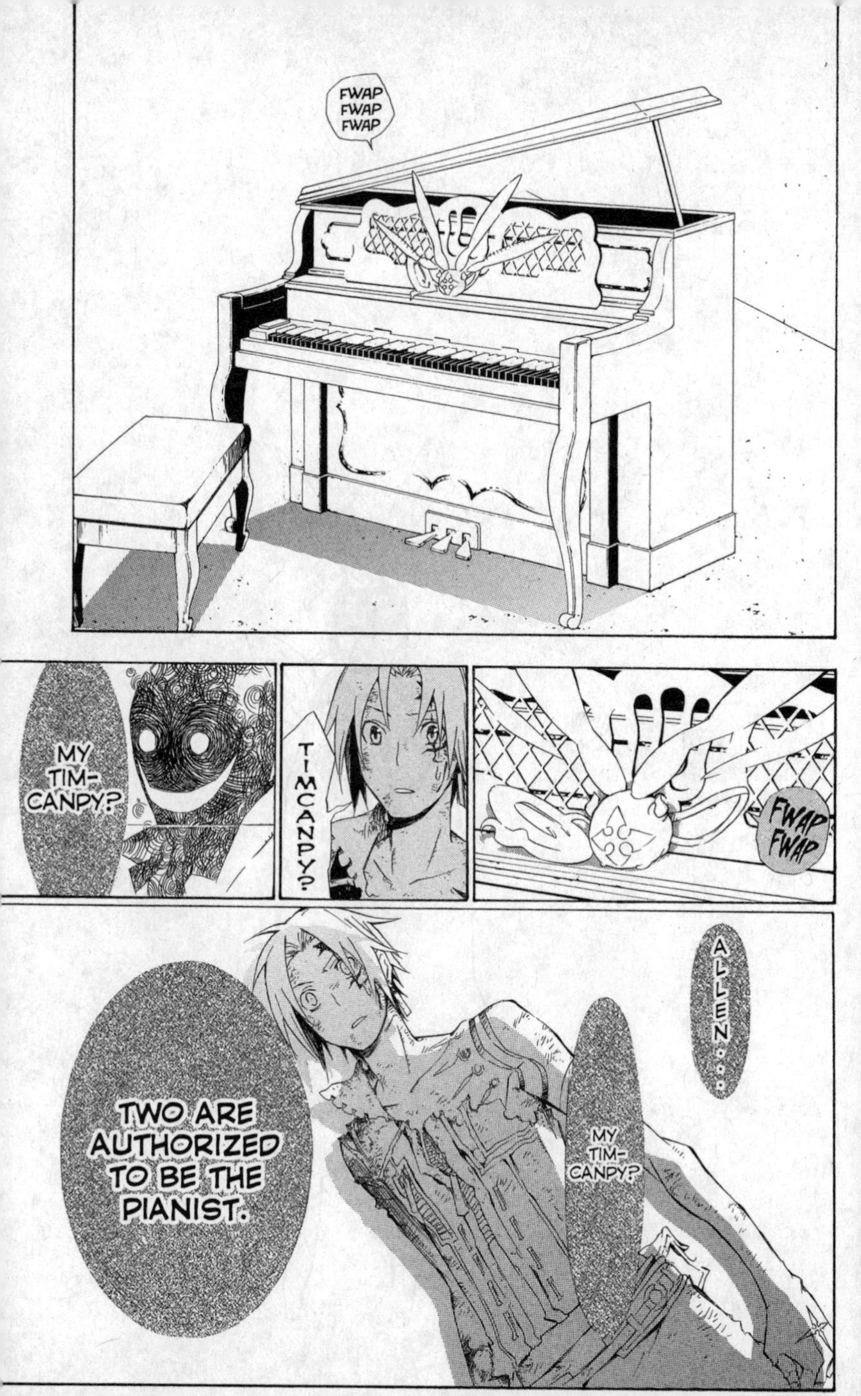
FWAP FWAP FWAP
FWAP FWAP
TIMCANPY?
MY TIM-CANPY?
ALLEN...
MY TIM-CANPY?
TWO ARE AUTHORIZED TO BE THE PIANIST.

THE 132ND NIGHT: PIANIST?!!

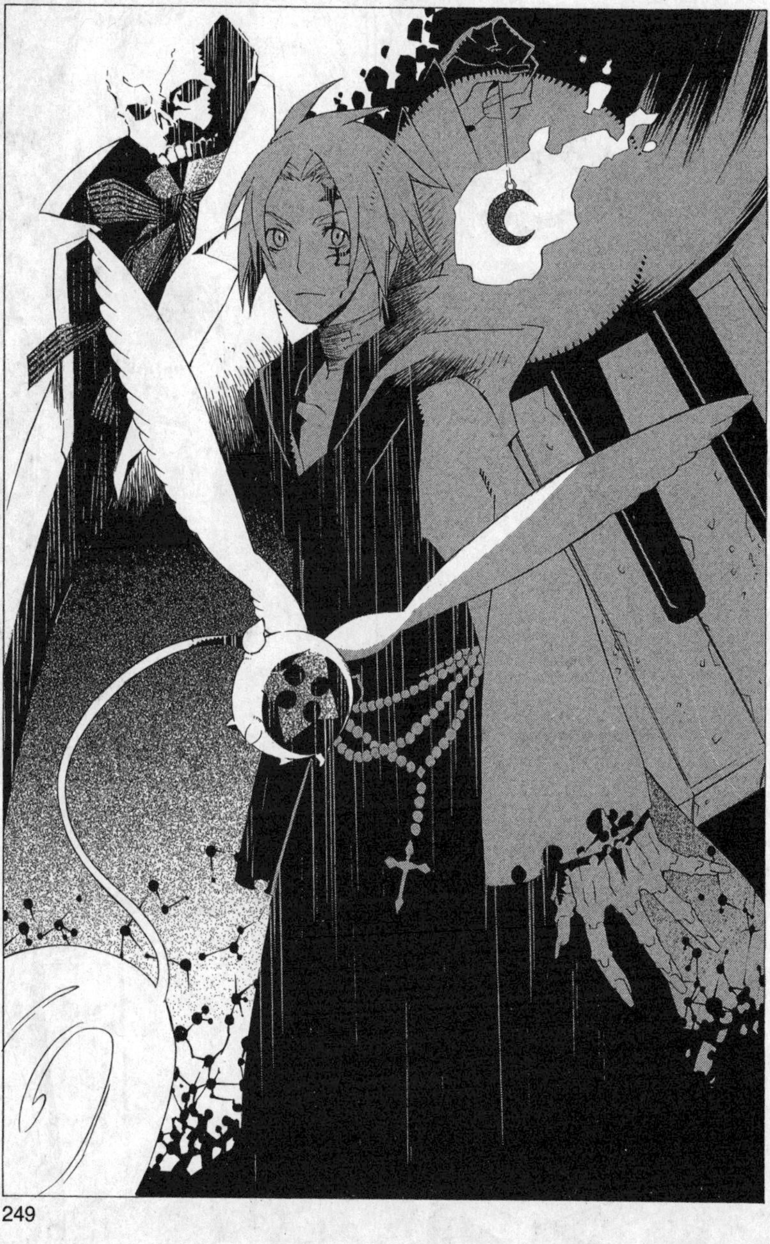

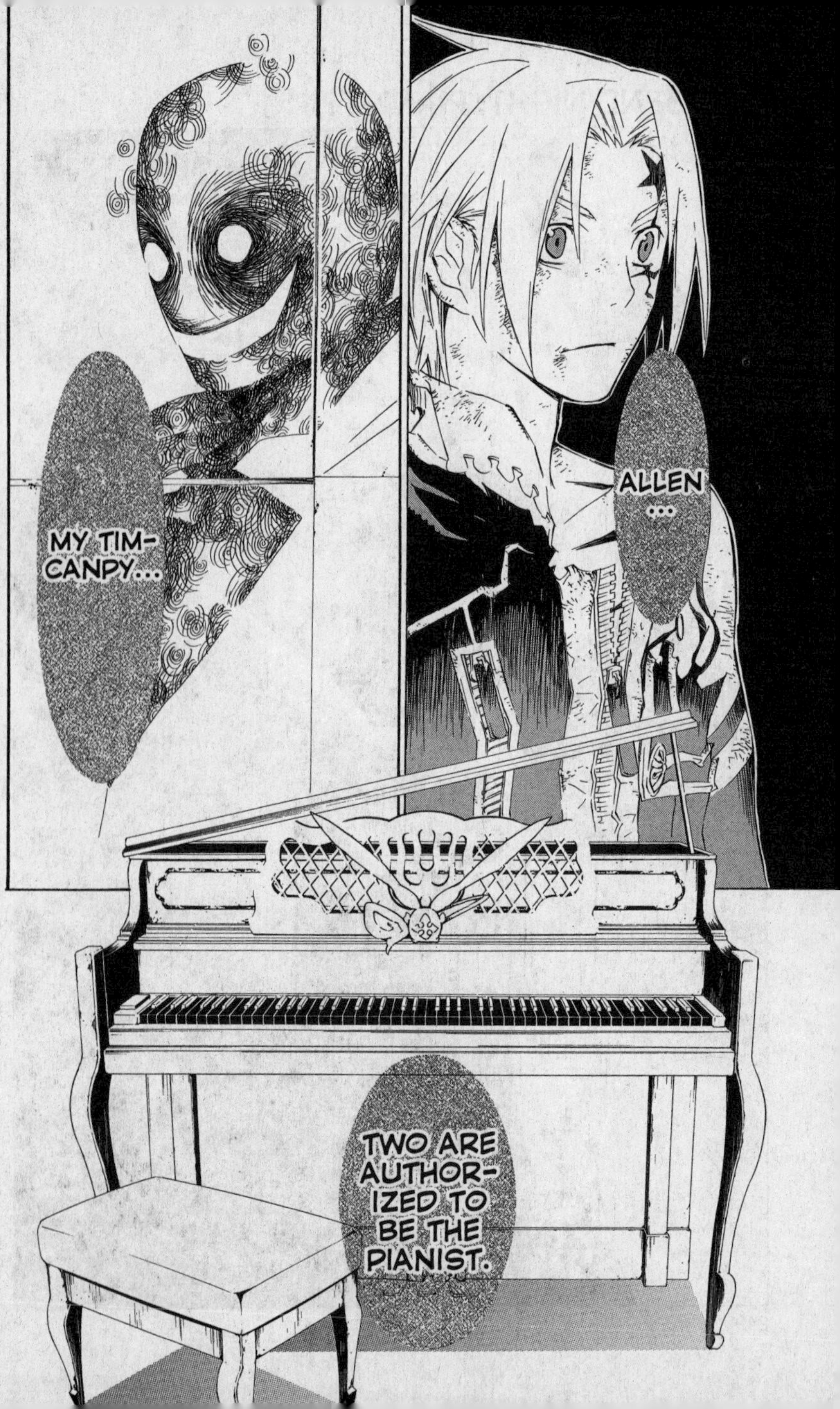
ALLEN...
MY TIMCANPY...
TWO ARE AUTHORIZED TO BE THE PIANIST.

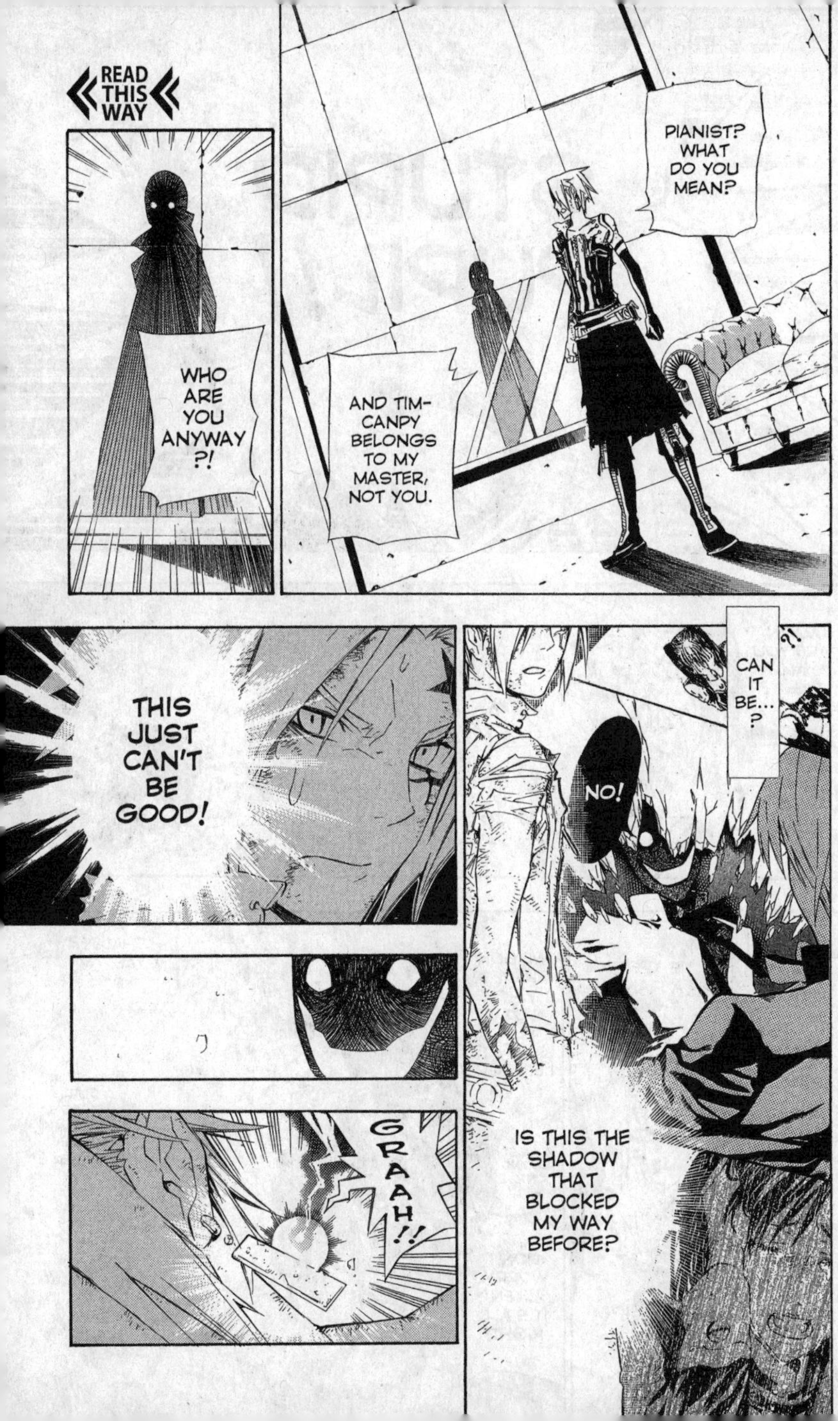
READ THIS WAY
PIANIST? WHAT DO YOU MEAN?
AND TIM-CANPY BELONGS TO MY MASTER, NOT YOU.
WHO ARE YOU ANYWAY?!
?!
CAN IT BE...?
NO!
IS THIS THE SHADOW THAT BLOCKED MY WAY BEFORE?
THIS JUST CAN'T BE GOOD!
GRAAH!!

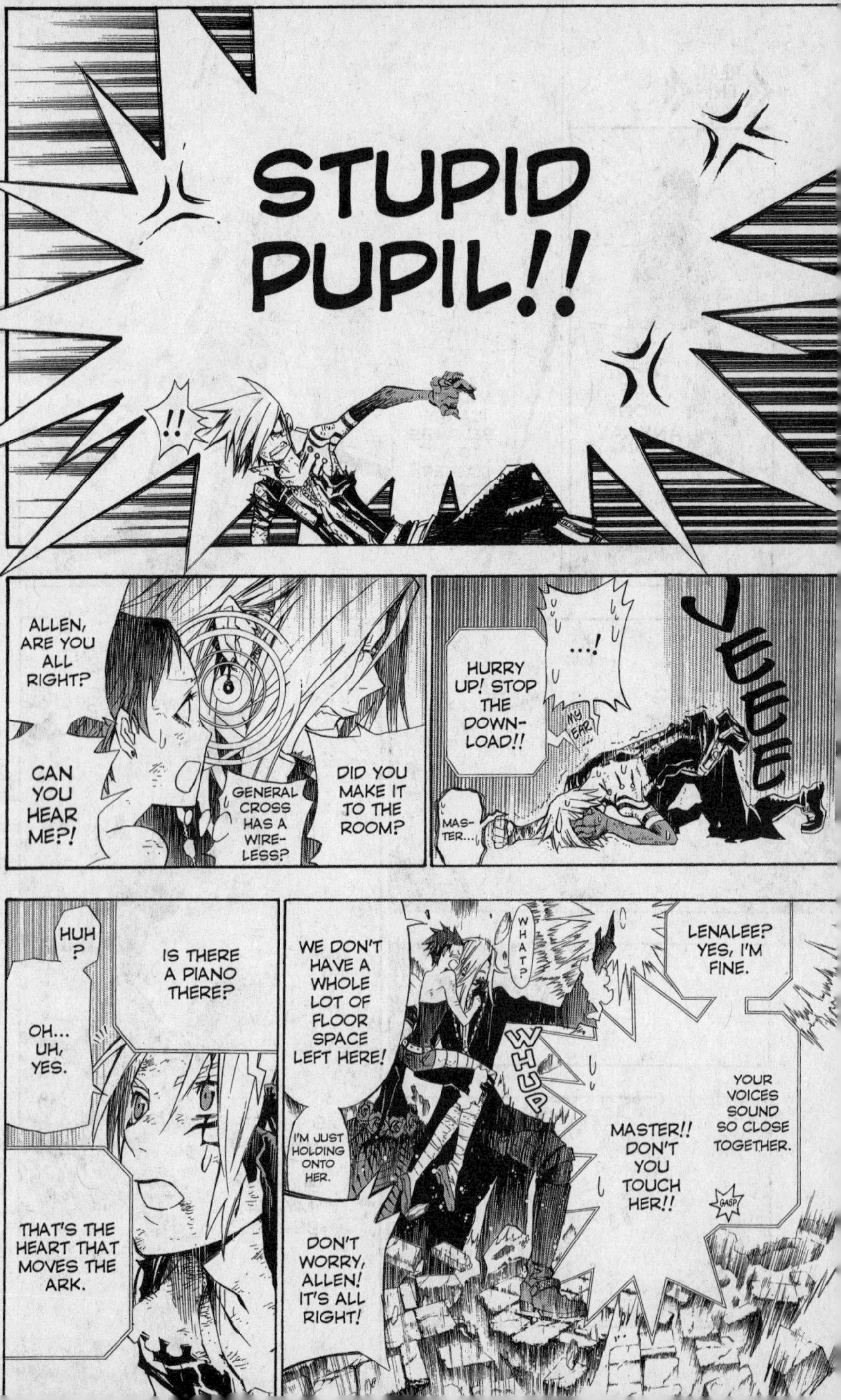
STUPID PUPIL!!
!!
JEEE
...!
HURRY UP! STOP THE DOWN-LOAD!!
MY EAR
MAS-TER...
DID YOU MAKE IT TO THE ROOM?
GENERAL CROSS HAS A WIRE-LESS?
ALLEN, ARE YOU ALL RIGHT?
CAN YOU HEAR ME?!
LENALEE? YES, I'M FINE.
WHAT?
YOUR VOICES SOUND SO CLOSE TOGETHER.
GASP
MASTER!! DON'T YOU TOUCH HER!!
WHUP
WE DON'T HAVE A WHOLE LOT OF FLOOR SPACE LEFT HERE!
I'M JUST HOLDING ONTO HER.
DON'T WORRY, ALLEN! IT'S ALL RIGHT!
IS THERE A PIANO THERE?
HUH?
OH... UH, YES.
THAT'S THE HEART THAT MOVES THE ARK.

READ THIS WAY

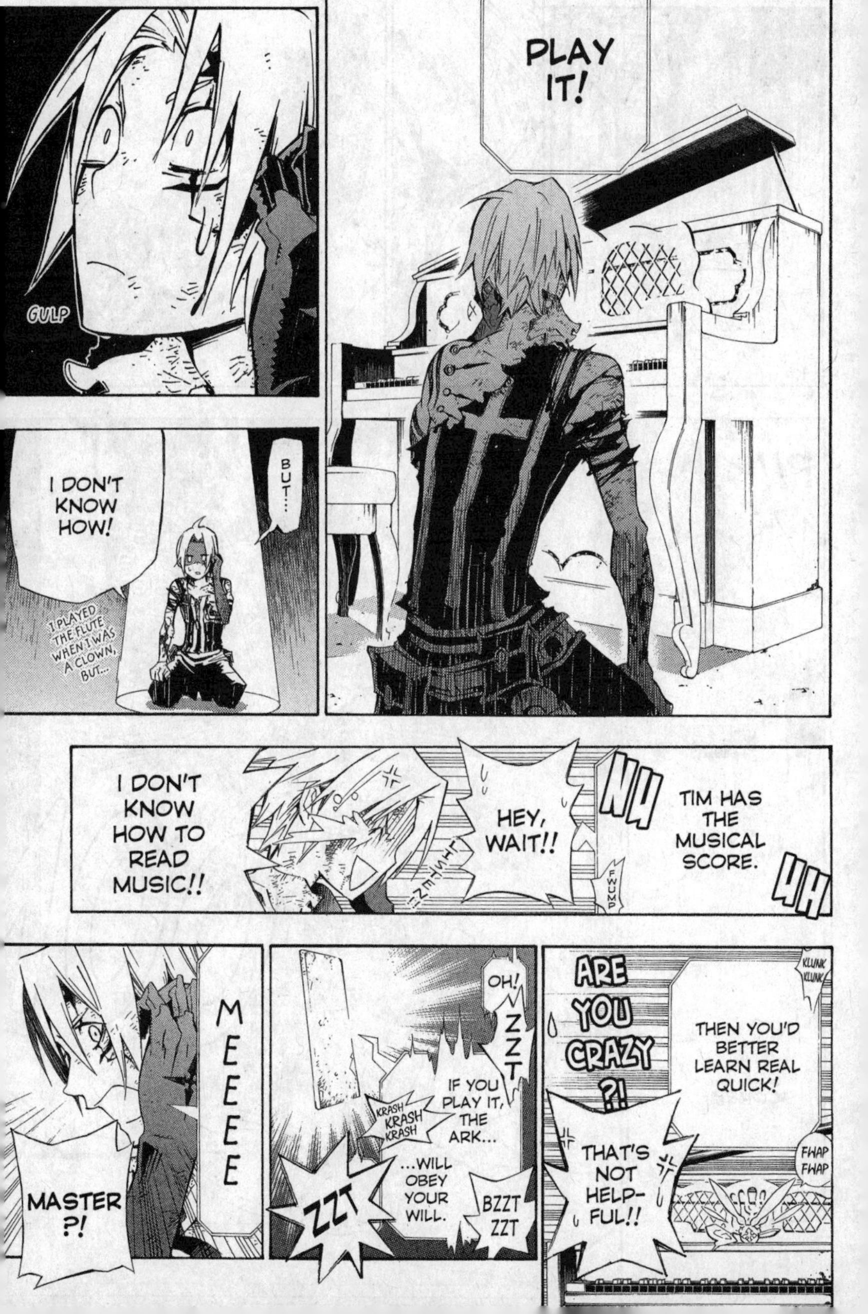

PLAY IT!
GULP
BUT...
I DON'T KNOW HOW!
I PLAYED THE FLUTE WHEN I WAS A CLOWN, BUT...
NU
UH
TIM HAS THE MUSICAL SCORE.
FWUMP
HEY, WAIT!!
I DON'T KNOW HOW TO READ MUSIC!!
KLUNK KLUNK
THEN YOU'D BETTER LEARN REAL QUICK!
ARE YOU CRAZY?!
FWAP FWAP
THAT'S NOT HELPFUL!!
OH!
ZZZT
IF YOU PLAY IT, THE ARK...
KRASH KRASH KRASH
...WILL OBEY YOUR WILL.
BZZT ZZT
ZZT
MEEEE
MASTER?!

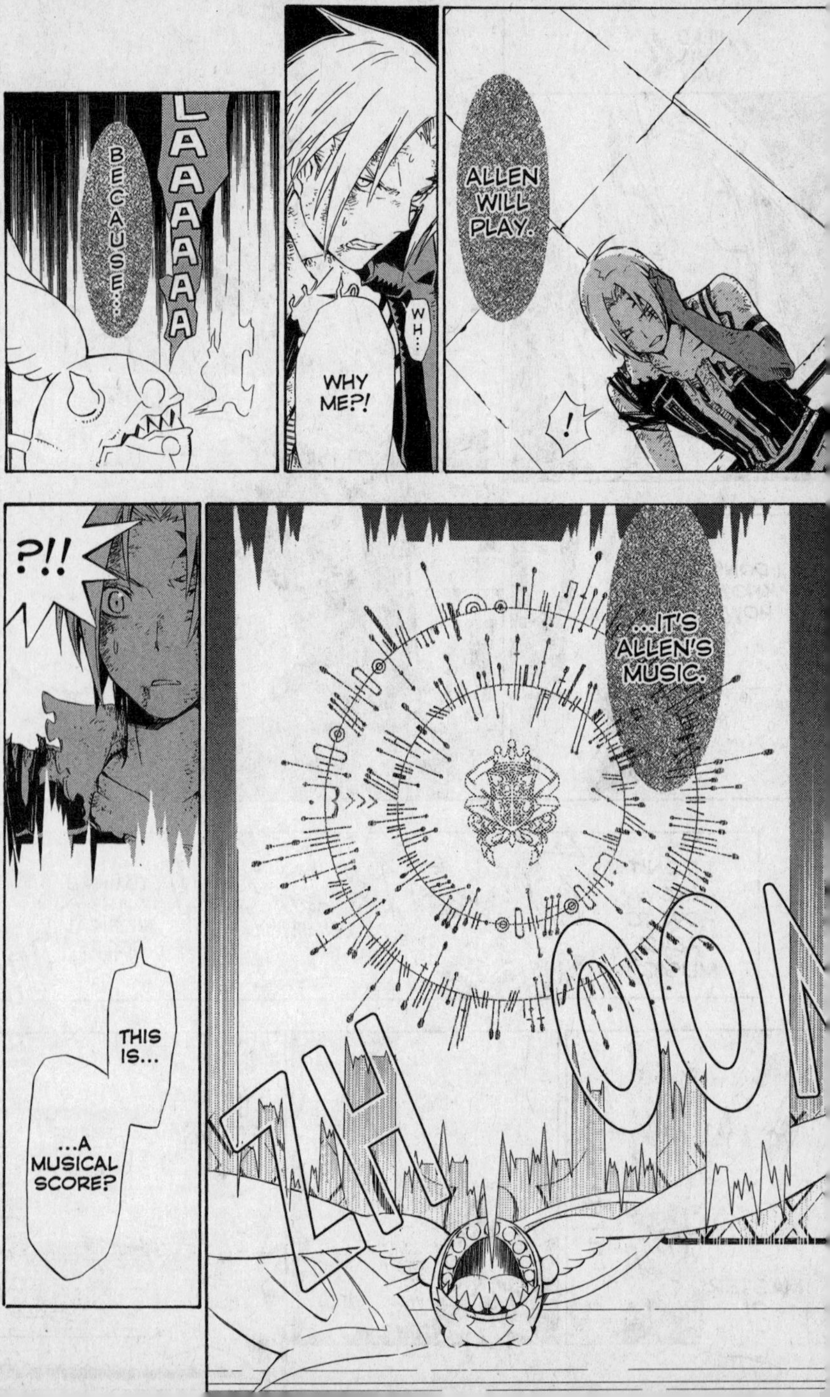
ALLEN WILL PLAY.
!
WH...
WHY ME?!
LAAAAAAA
BECAUSE...
...IT'S ALLEN'S MUSIC.
ZHOON
?!!
THIS IS...
...A MUSICAL SCORE?

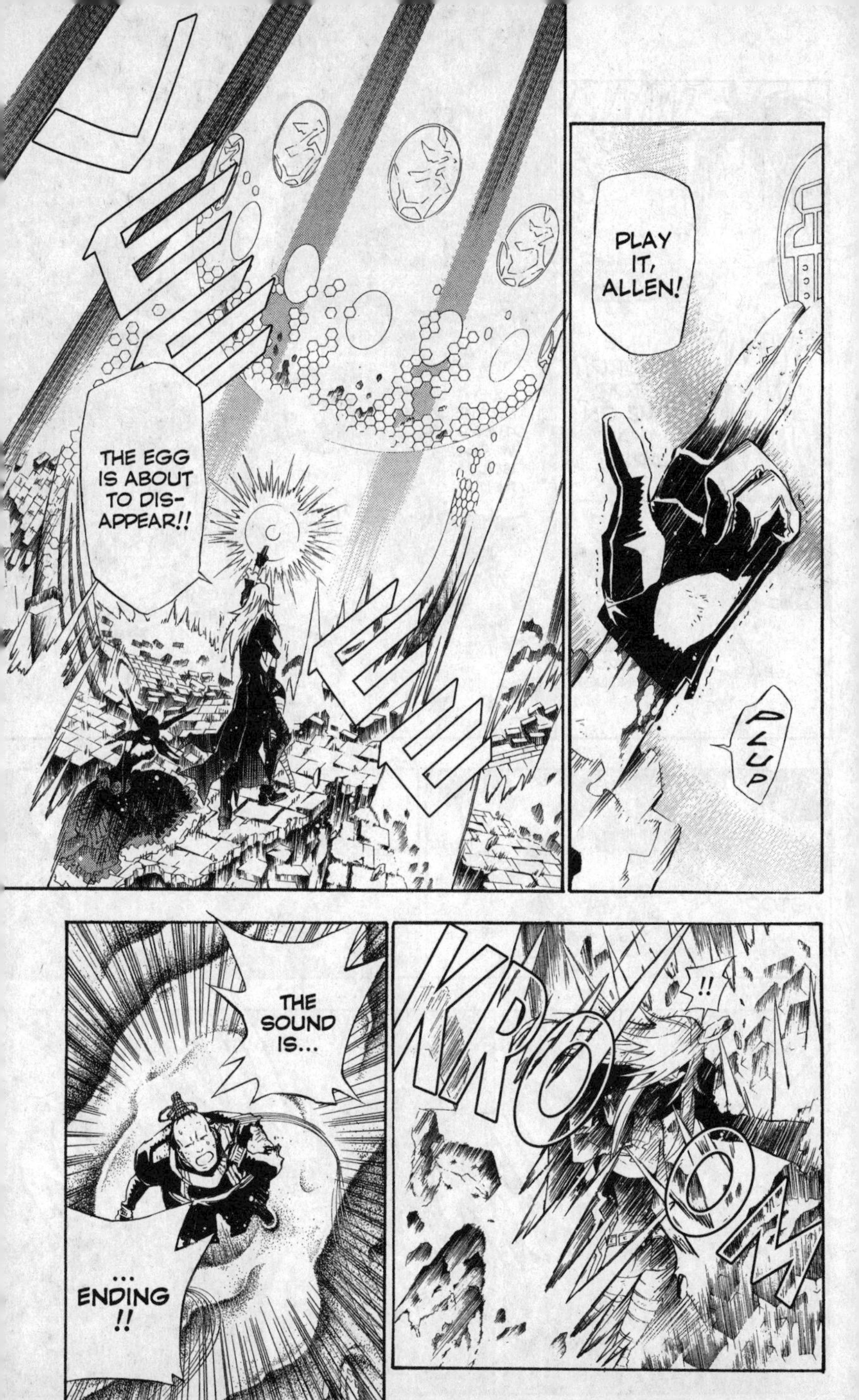
PLAY IT, ALLEN!
PLUP
THE EGG IS ABOUT TO DIS-APPEAR!!
KROOOM
!!
THE SOUND IS...
... ENDING !!

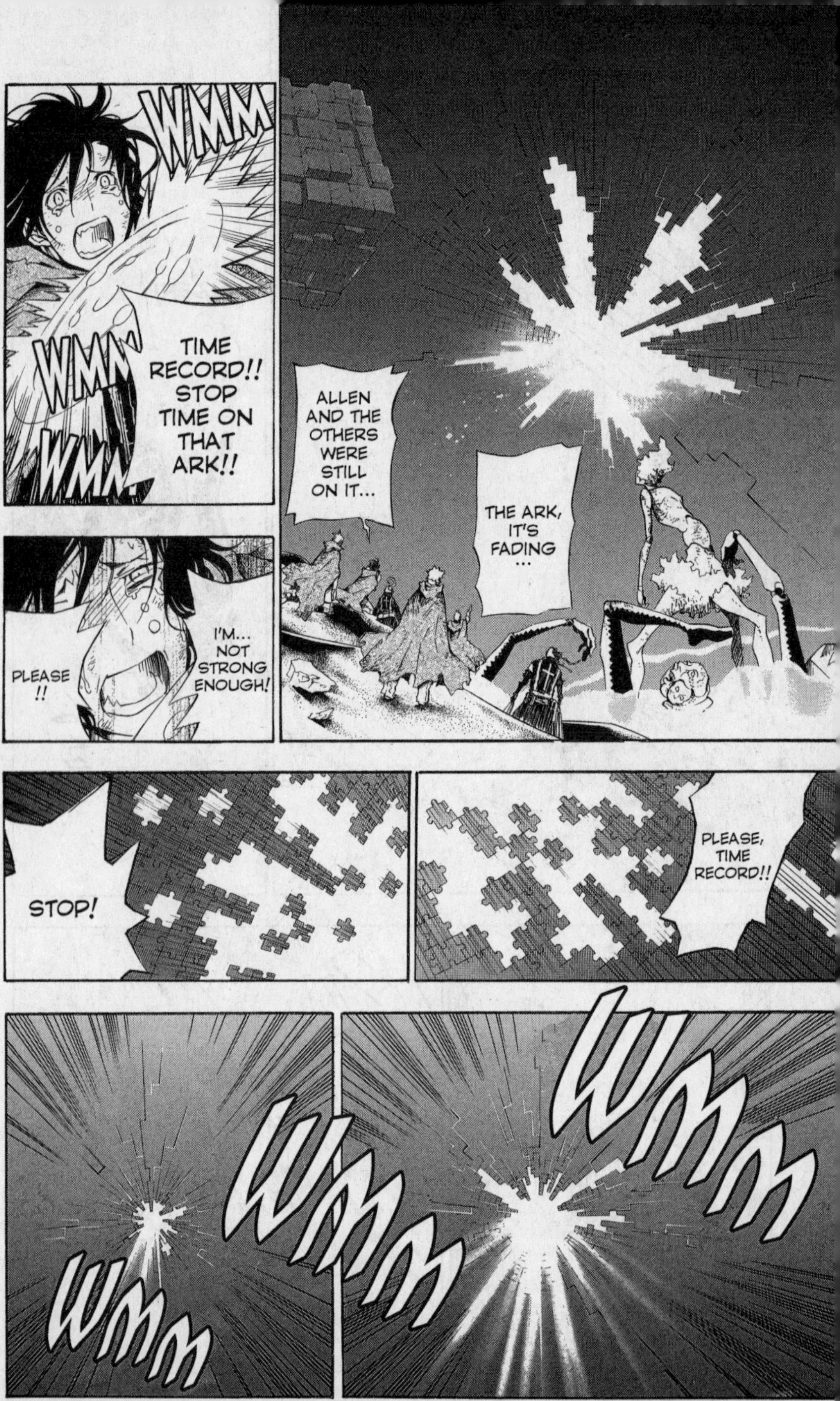
THE ARK, IT'S FADING ...
ALLEN AND THE OTHERS WERE STILL ON IT...
WMM
TIME RECORD!! STOP TIME ON THAT ARK!!
WMM
WMM
I'M... NOT STRONG ENOUGH!
PLEASE !!
PLEASE, TIME RECORD!!
STOP!
WMM
WMM
WMM
WMM

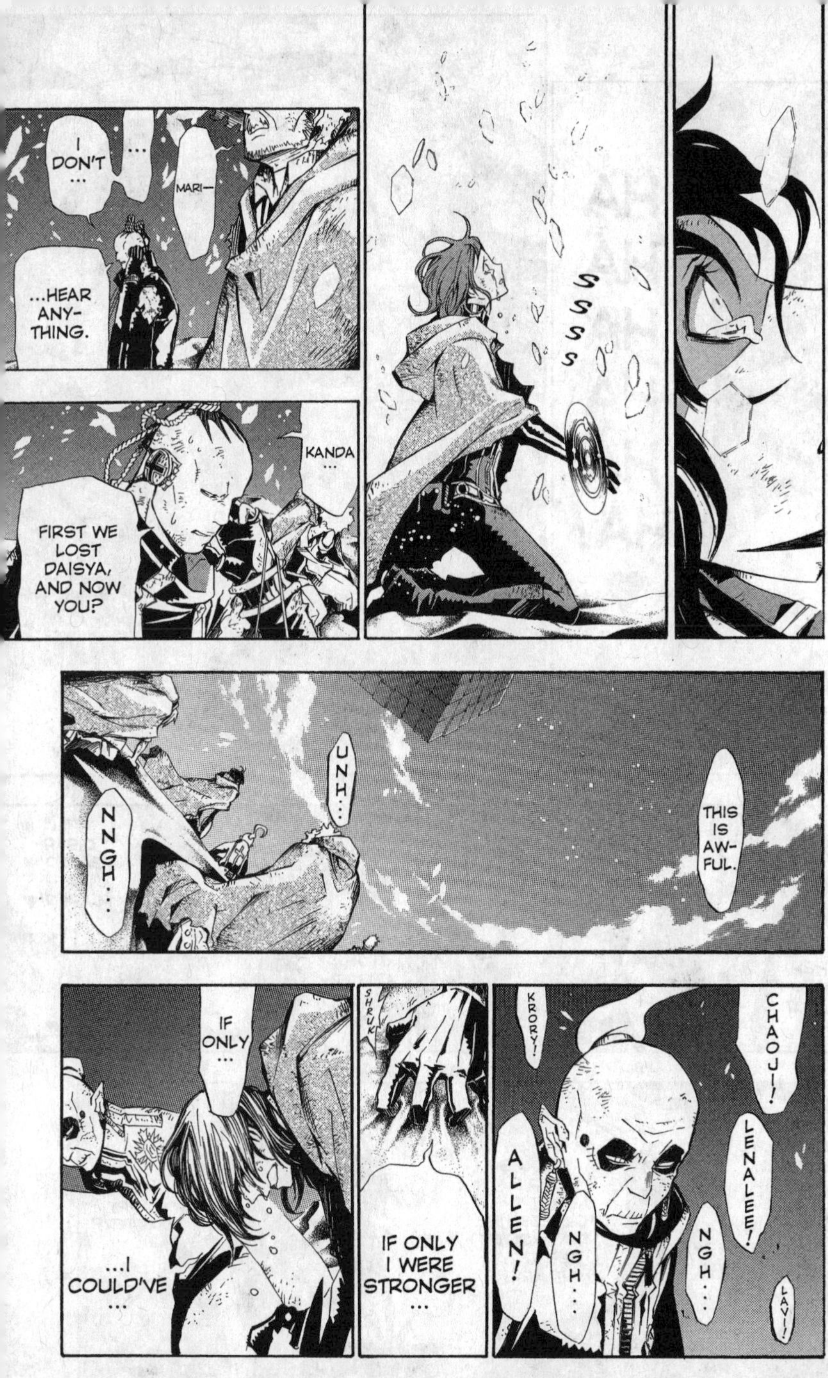
SSSS
MARI—
...
I DON'T ...
...HEAR ANYTHING.
KANDA ...
FIRST WE LOST DAISYA, AND NOW YOU?
THIS IS AWFUL.
UNH...
NNGH...
CHAOJI!
KRORY!
LENALEE!
NGH...
LAVI!
ALLEN!
NGH...
SHRUK
IF ONLY I WERE STRONGER ...
IF ONLY ...
...I COULD'VE ...

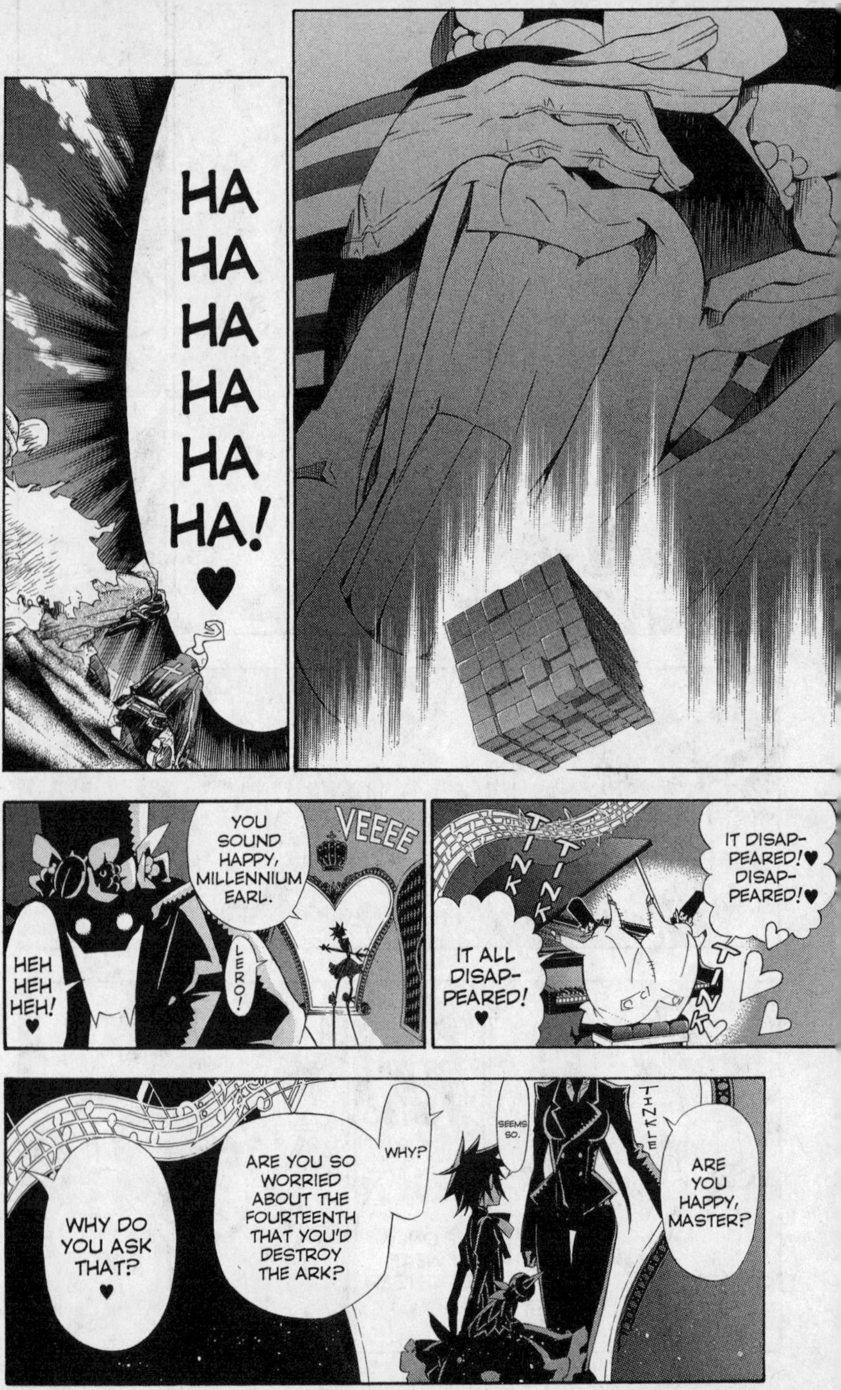
HA HA HA HA HA HA! ♥
IT DISAPPEARED! ♥ DISAPPEARED! ♥
TINK
TINK
IT ALL DISAPPEARED! ♥
TINK
VEEEE
YOU SOUND HAPPY, MILLENNIUM EARL.
LERO!
HEH HEH HEH! ♥
TINKLE
ARE YOU HAPPY, MASTER?
SEEMS SO.
WHY?
ARE YOU SO WORRIED ABOUT THE FOURTEENTH THAT YOU'D DESTROY THE ARK?
WHY DO YOU ASK THAT? ♥

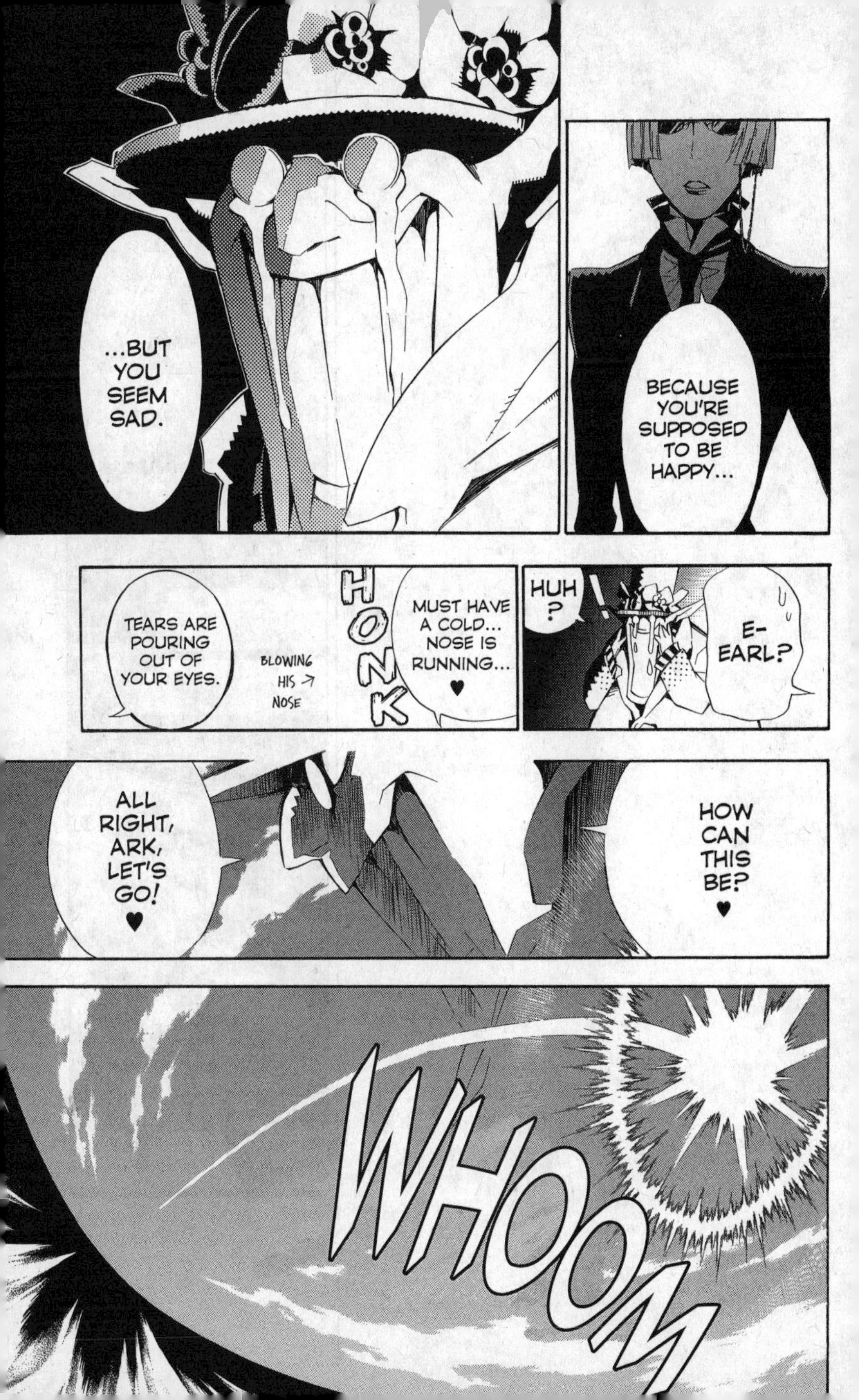
BECAUSE YOU'RE SUPPOSED TO BE HAPPY...
...BUT YOU SEEM SAD.
E-EARL?
HUH?
MUST HAVE A COLD... NOSE IS RUNNING... ♥
HONK
BLOWING HIS NOSE
TEARS ARE POURING OUT OF YOUR EYES.
HOW CAN THIS BE? ♥
ALL RIGHT, ARK, LET'S GO! ♥
WHOOM

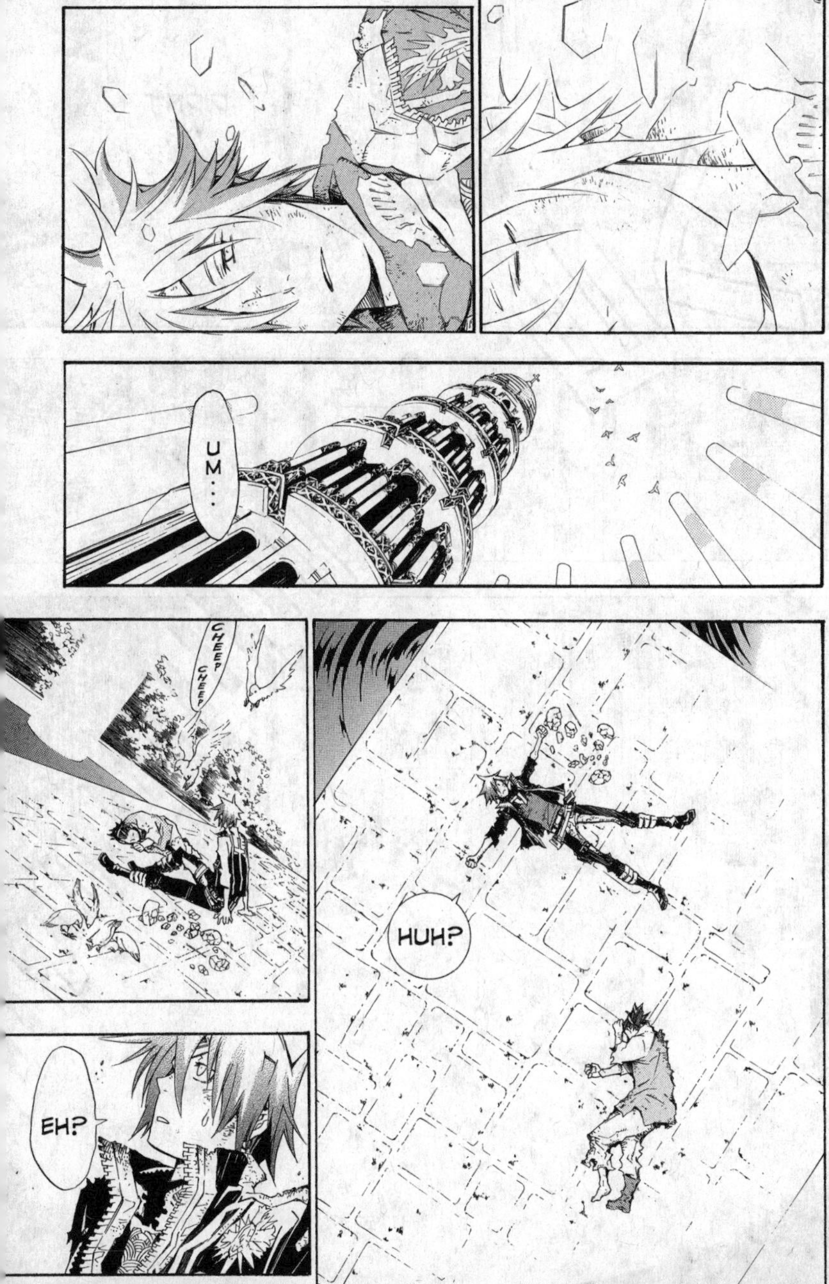
UM...
HUH?
CHEEP CHEEP
EH?

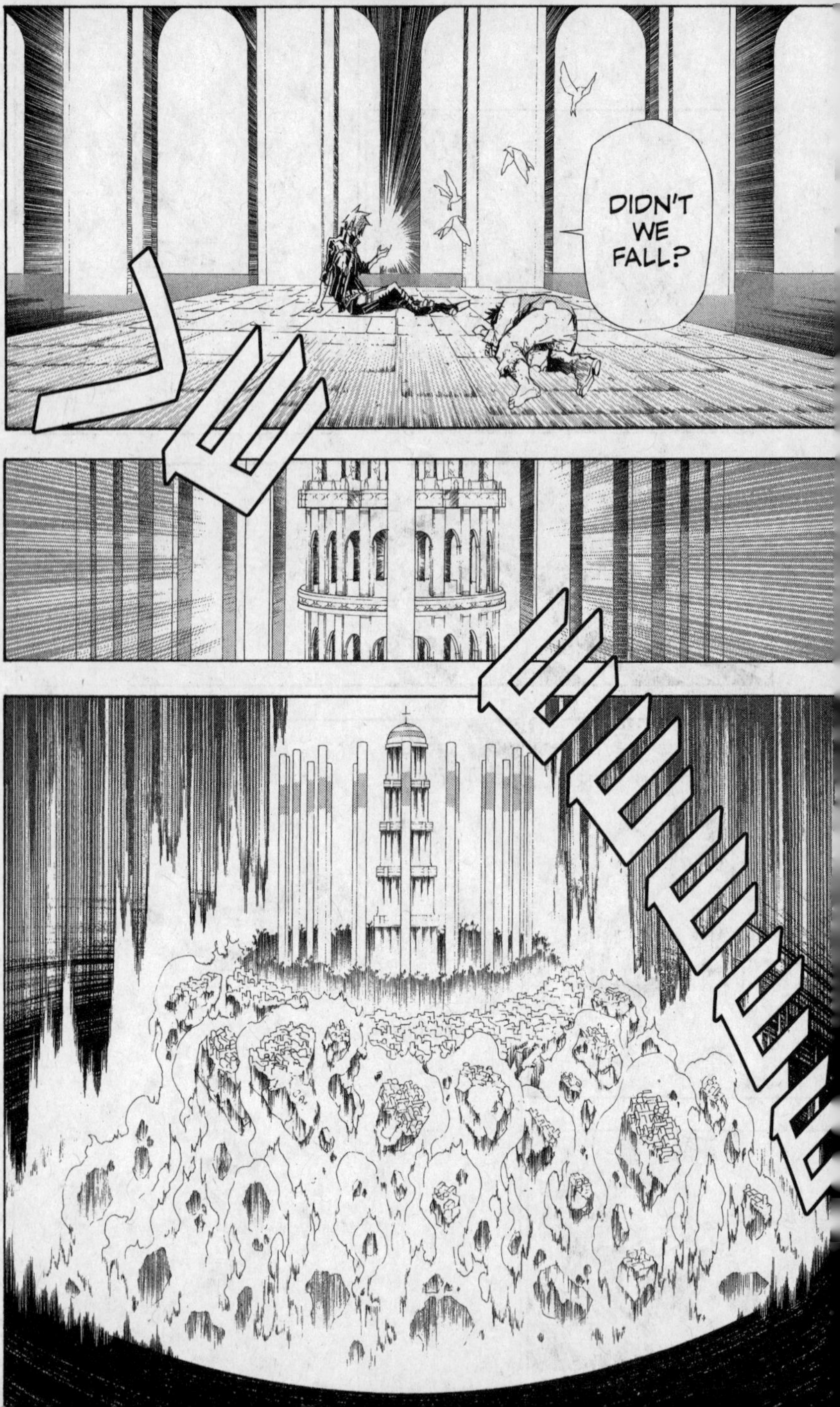
DIDN'T WE FALL?

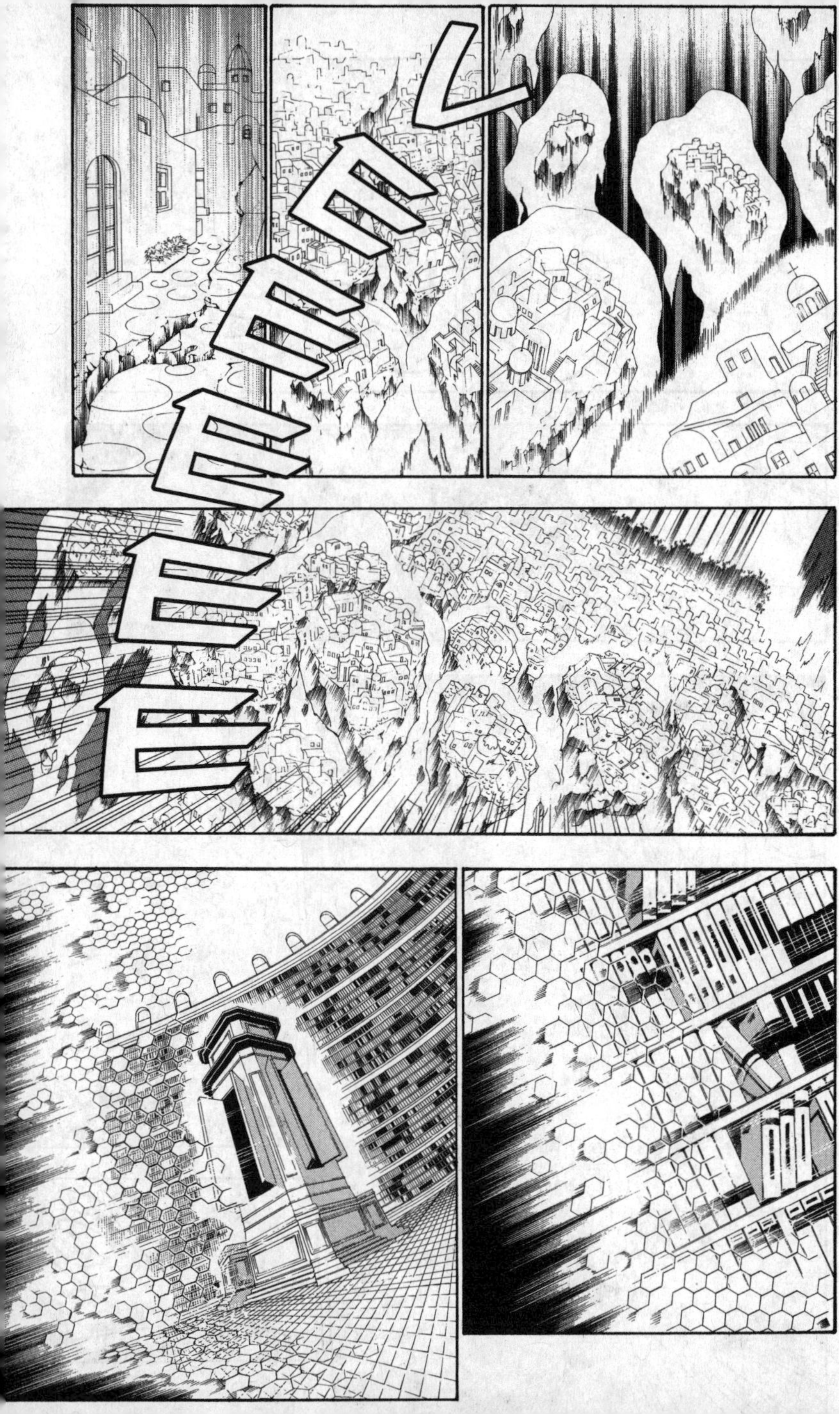

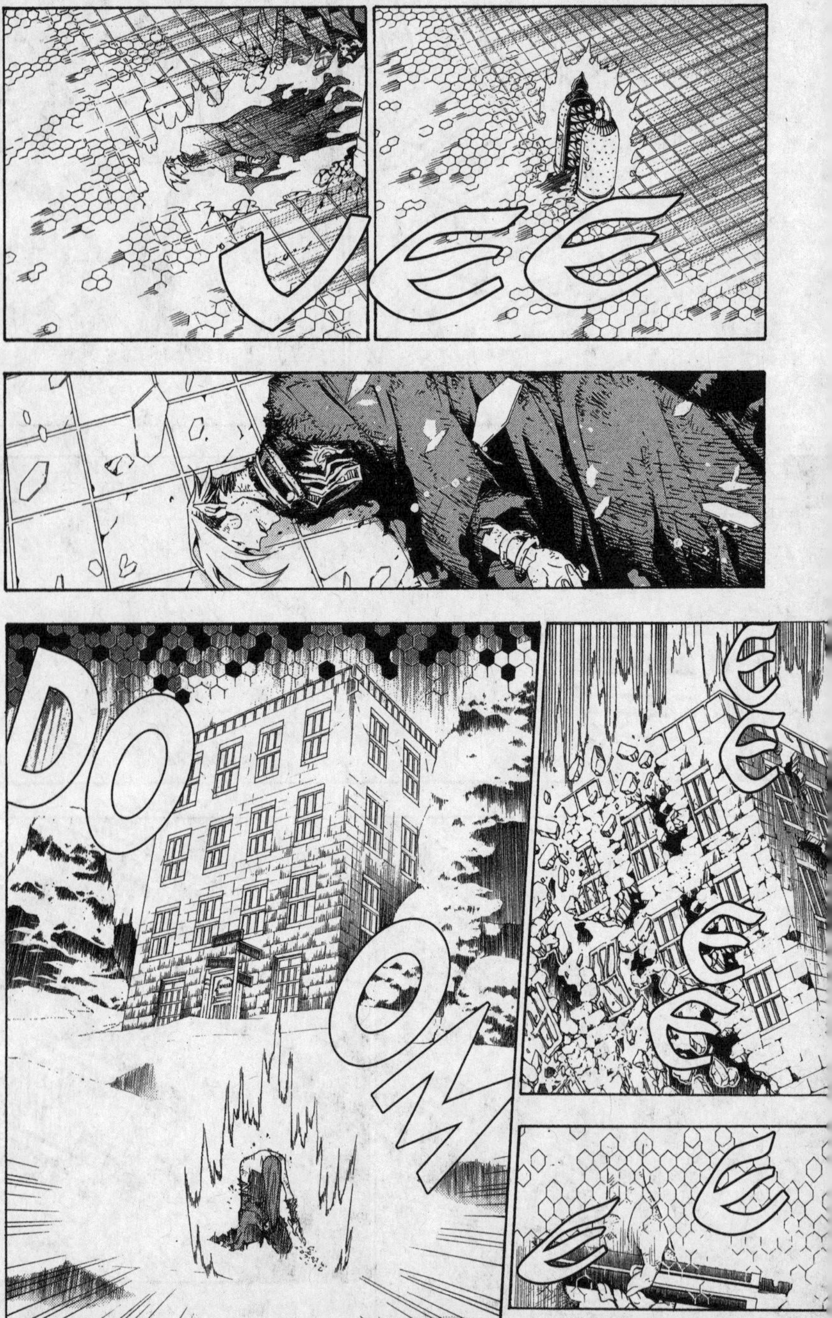
VEE
EEEE
EE
DOOM

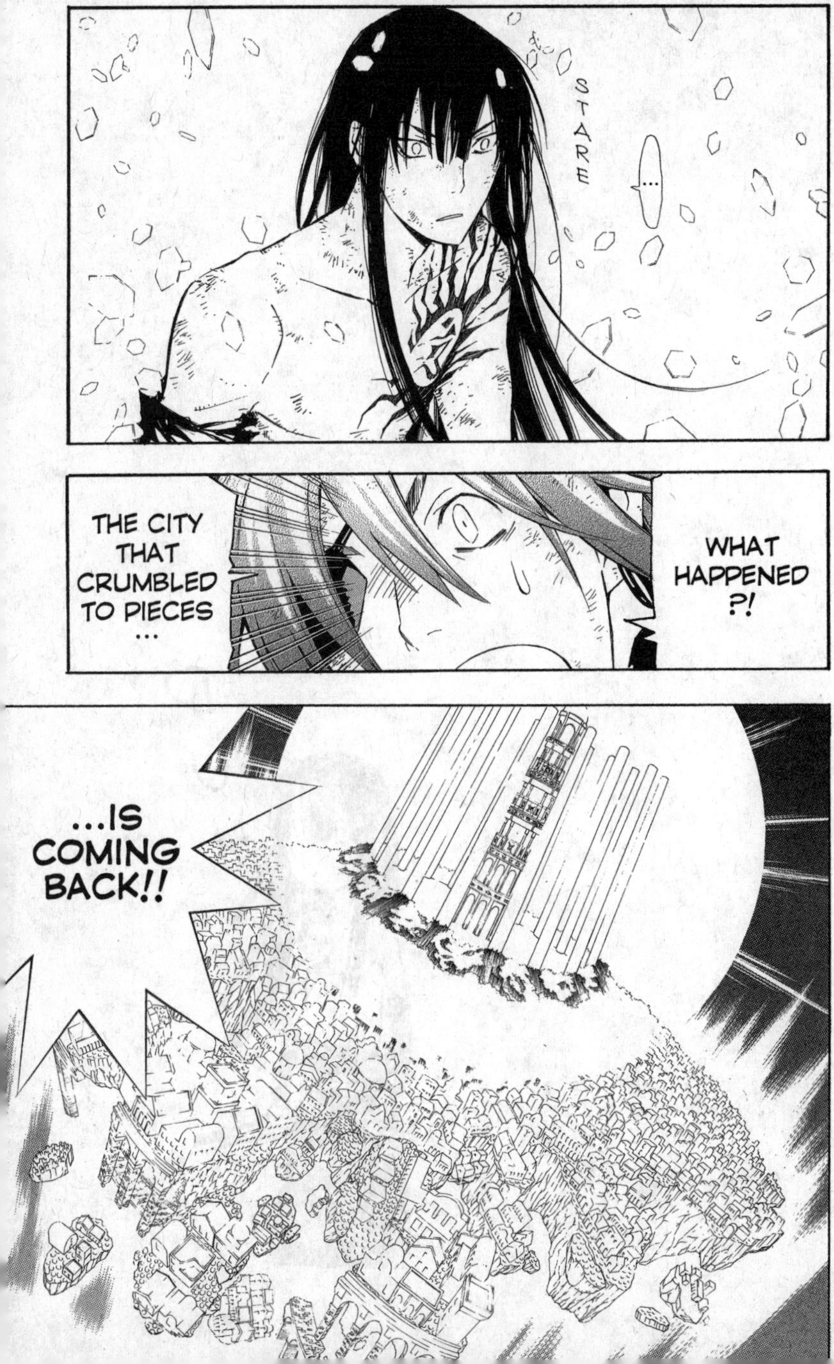
...
STARE
WHAT HAPPENED ?!
THE CITY THAT CRUMBLED TO PIECES ...
...IS COMING BACK!!

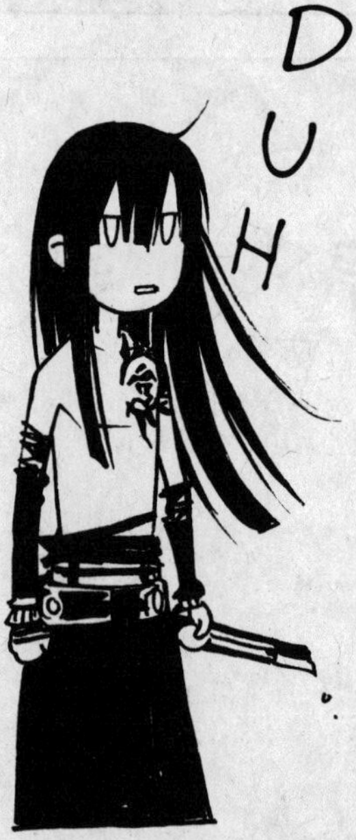
DUH

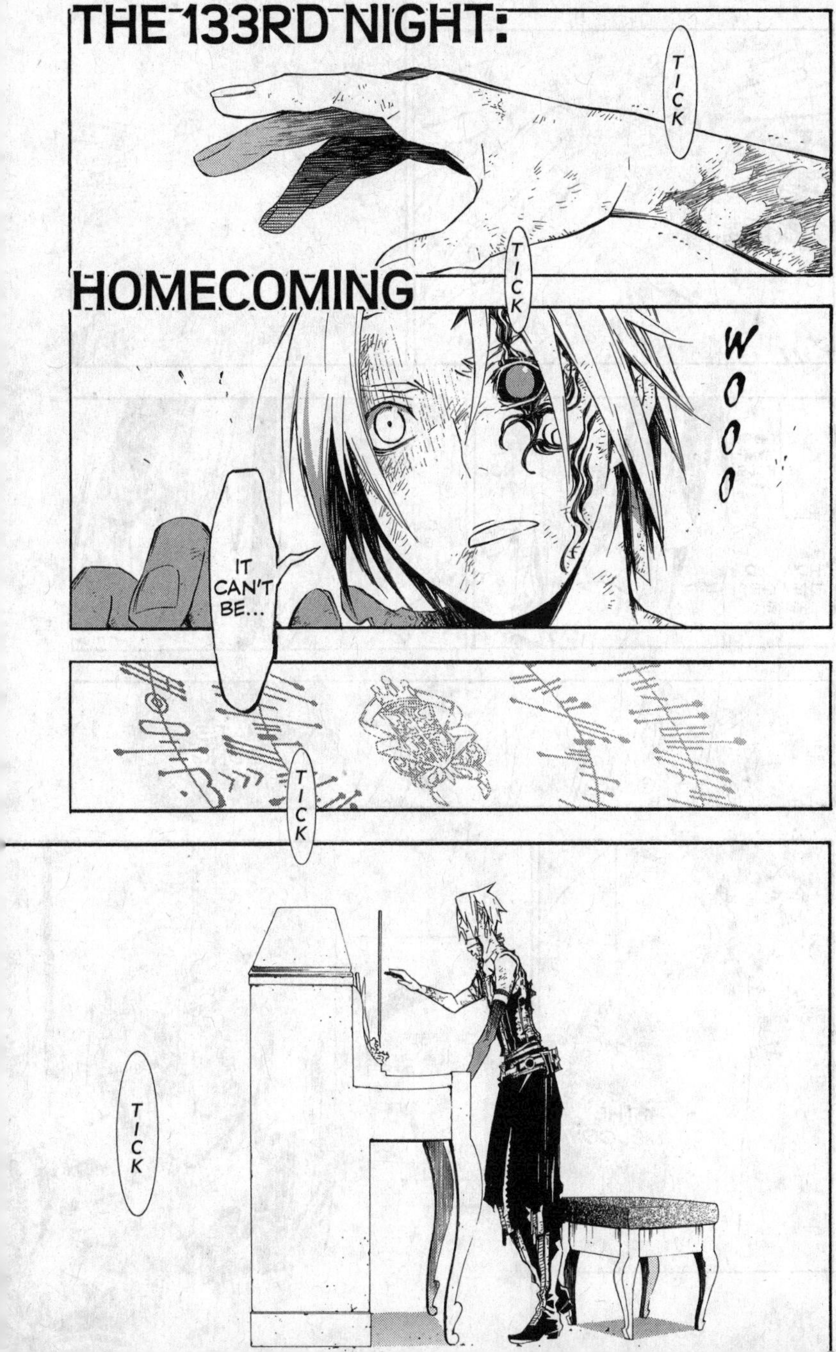
THE 133RD NIGHT:
HOMECOMING
TICK
TICK
WOOO
IT CAN'T BE...
TICK
TICK

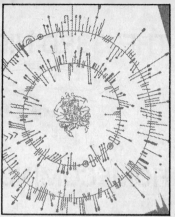

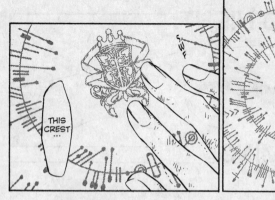

THIS CREST...

THESE SYMBOLS...

HOW DID THEY GET HERE?

NO.

IT CAN'T BE...

NO...

THAT'S A SONG.

THE MELODY...

READ THIS WAY

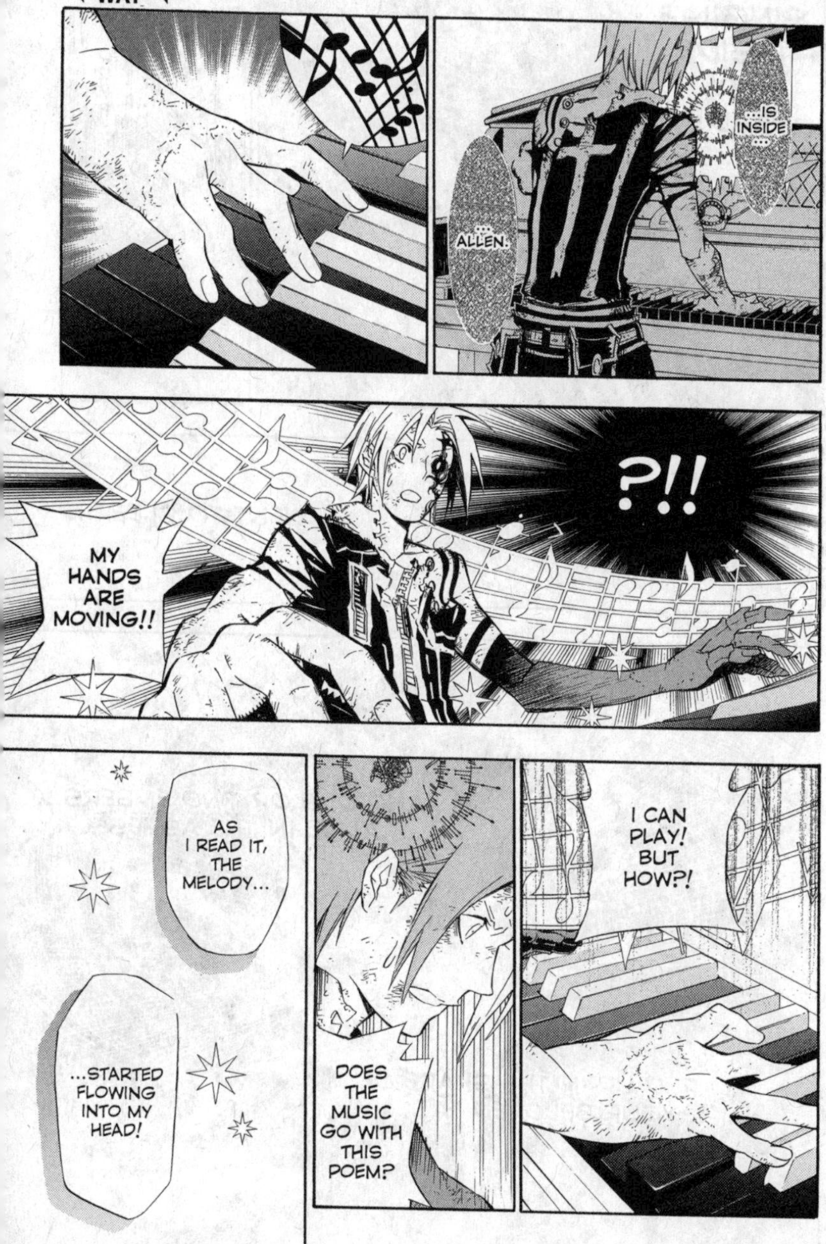
...IS INSIDE...
...ALLEN.
?!!
MY HANDS ARE MOVING!!
I CAN PLAY! BUT HOW?!
DOES THE MUSIC GO WITH THIS POEM?
AS I READ IT, THE MELODY...
...STARTED FLOWING INTO MY HEAD!

WHO'S SINGING INSIDE MY HEAD?!

MELODY?

HEY!

THEN THE BOY WENT TO SLEEP...

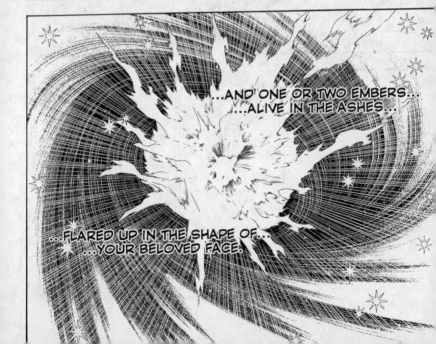

...AND ONE OR TWO EMBERS...
...ALIVE IN THE ASHES...

...FLARED UP IN THE SHAPE OF...
...YOUR BELOVED FACE.

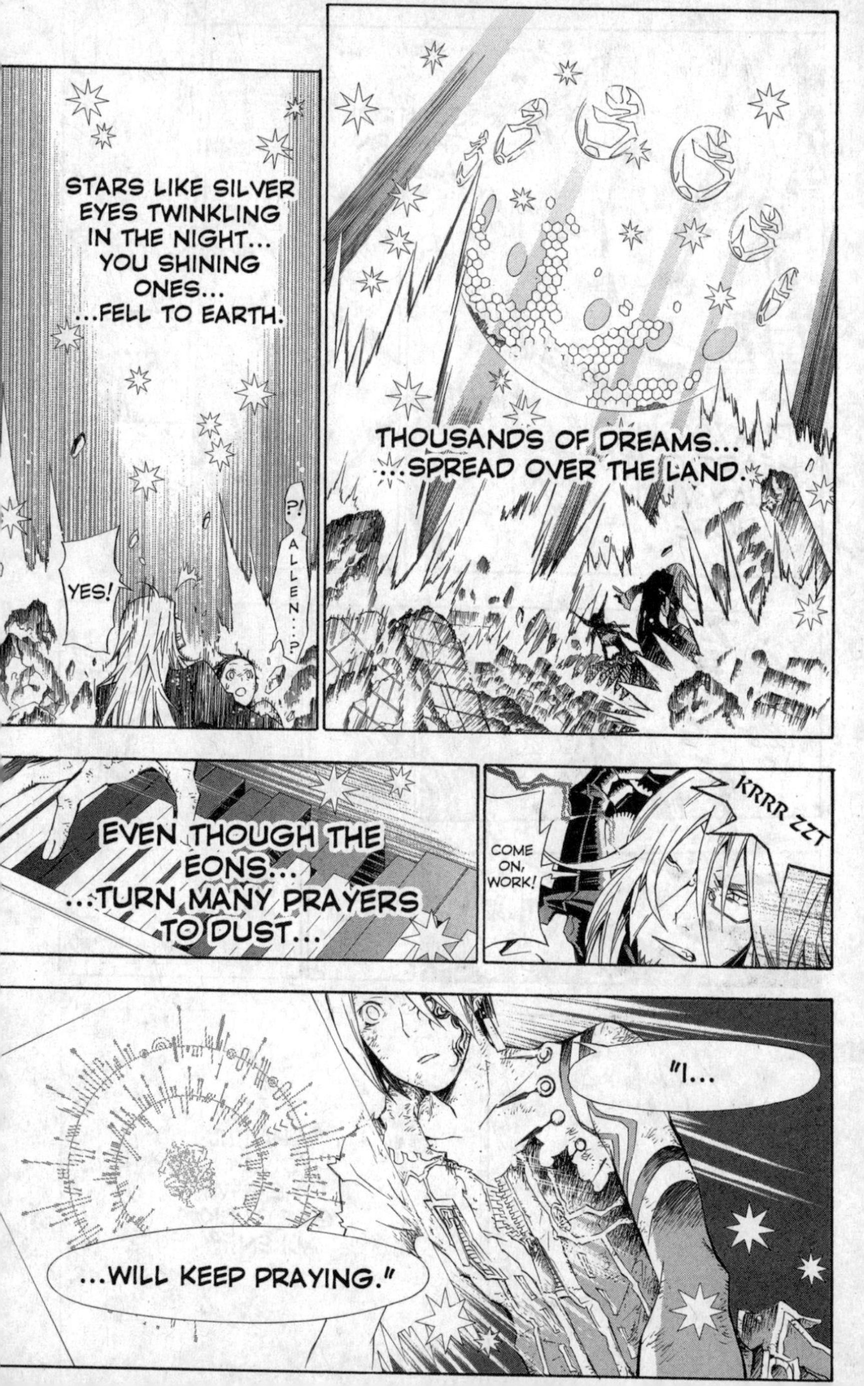
THOUSANDS OF DREAMS... ...SPREAD OVER THE LAND.
STARS LIKE SILVER EYES TWINKLING IN THE NIGHT... YOU SHINING ONES... ...FELL TO EARTH.
?!
YES!
?! ALLEN...?
KRRR ZZT
COME ON, WORK!
EVEN THOUGH THE EONS... ...TURN MANY PRAYERS TO DUST...
"I...
...WILL KEEP PRAYING."

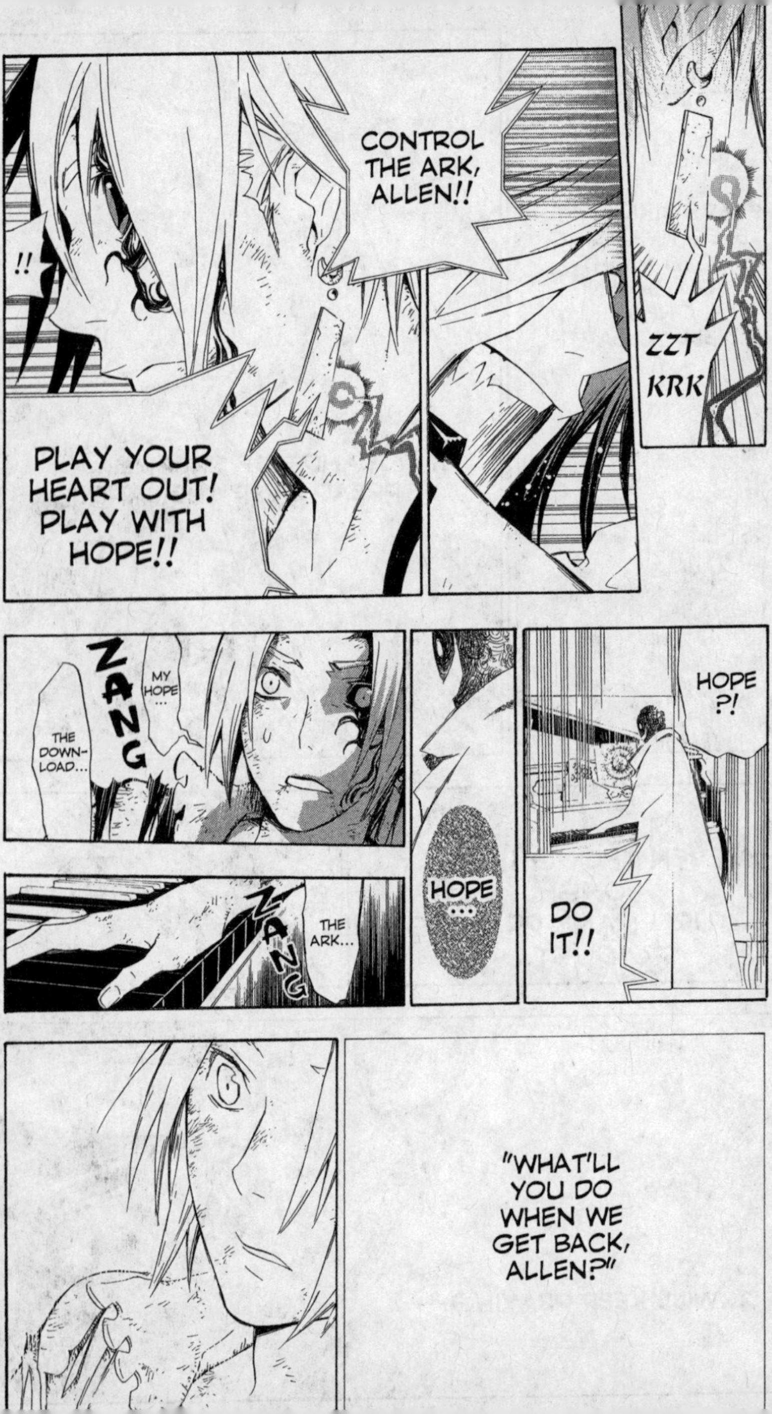
ZZT
KRK
CONTROL THE ARK, ALLEN!!
!!
PLAY YOUR HEART OUT! PLAY WITH HOPE!!
HOPE ?!
DO IT!!
HOPE ...
MY HOPE ...
ZANG
THE DOWN-LOAD...
ZANG
THE ARK...
"WHAT'LL YOU DO WHEN WE GET BACK, ALLEN?"

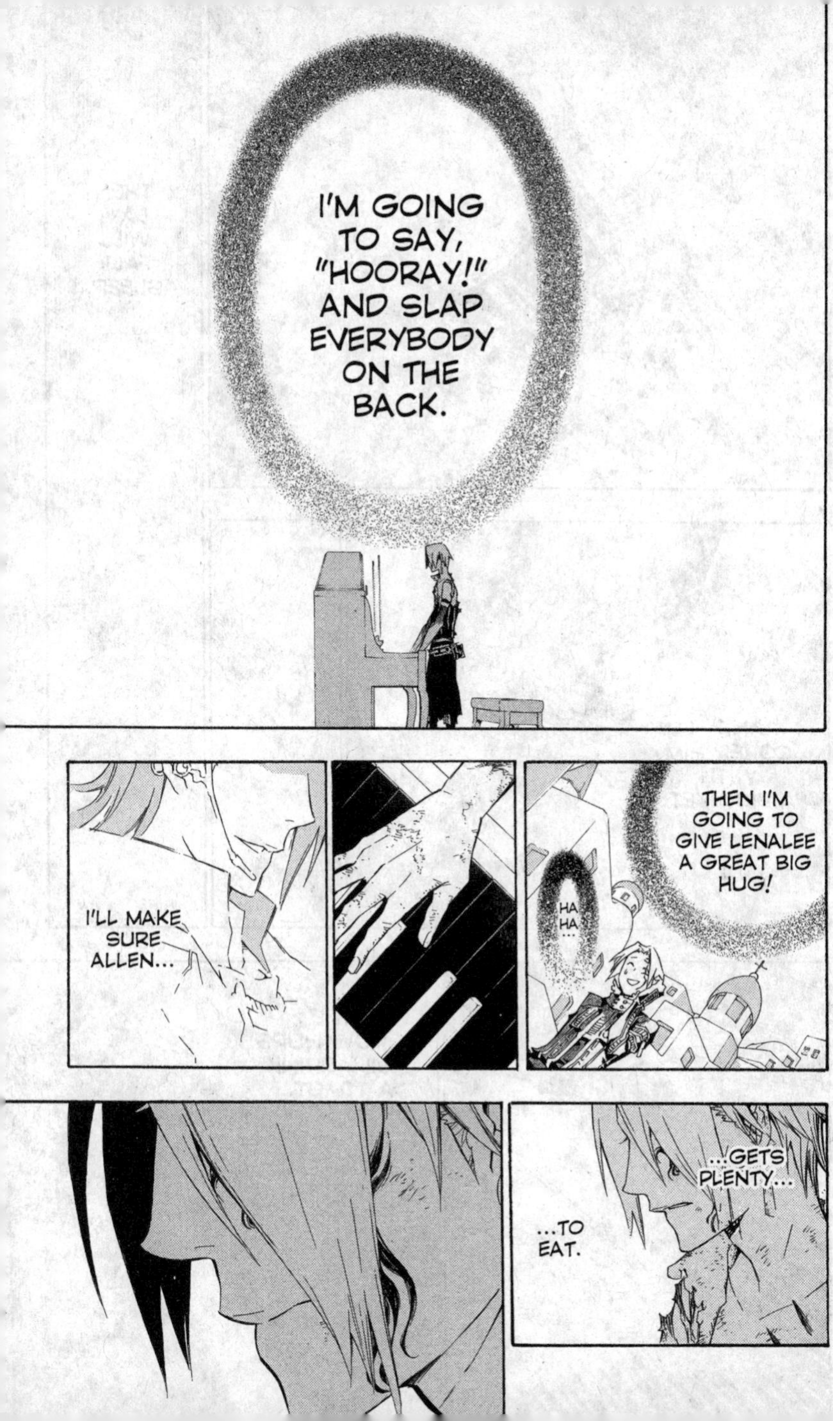
I'M GOING TO SAY, "HOORAY!" AND SLAP EVERYBODY ON THE BACK.
THEN I'M GOING TO GIVE LENALEE A GREAT BIG HUG!
HA HA...
I'LL MAKE SURE ALLEN...
...GETS PLENTY...
...TO EAT.

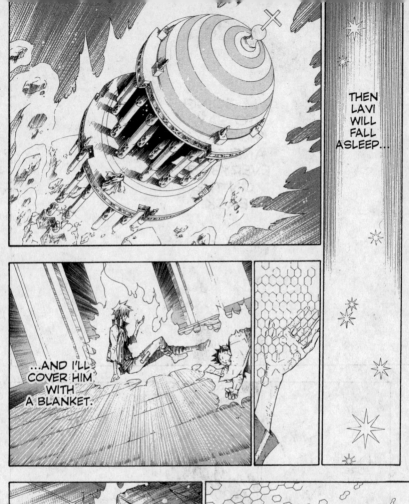

THEN LAVI WILL FALL ASLEEP...

...AND I'LL COVER HIM WITH A BLANKET.

THE GROWN-UPS WILL DRINK A TOAST...

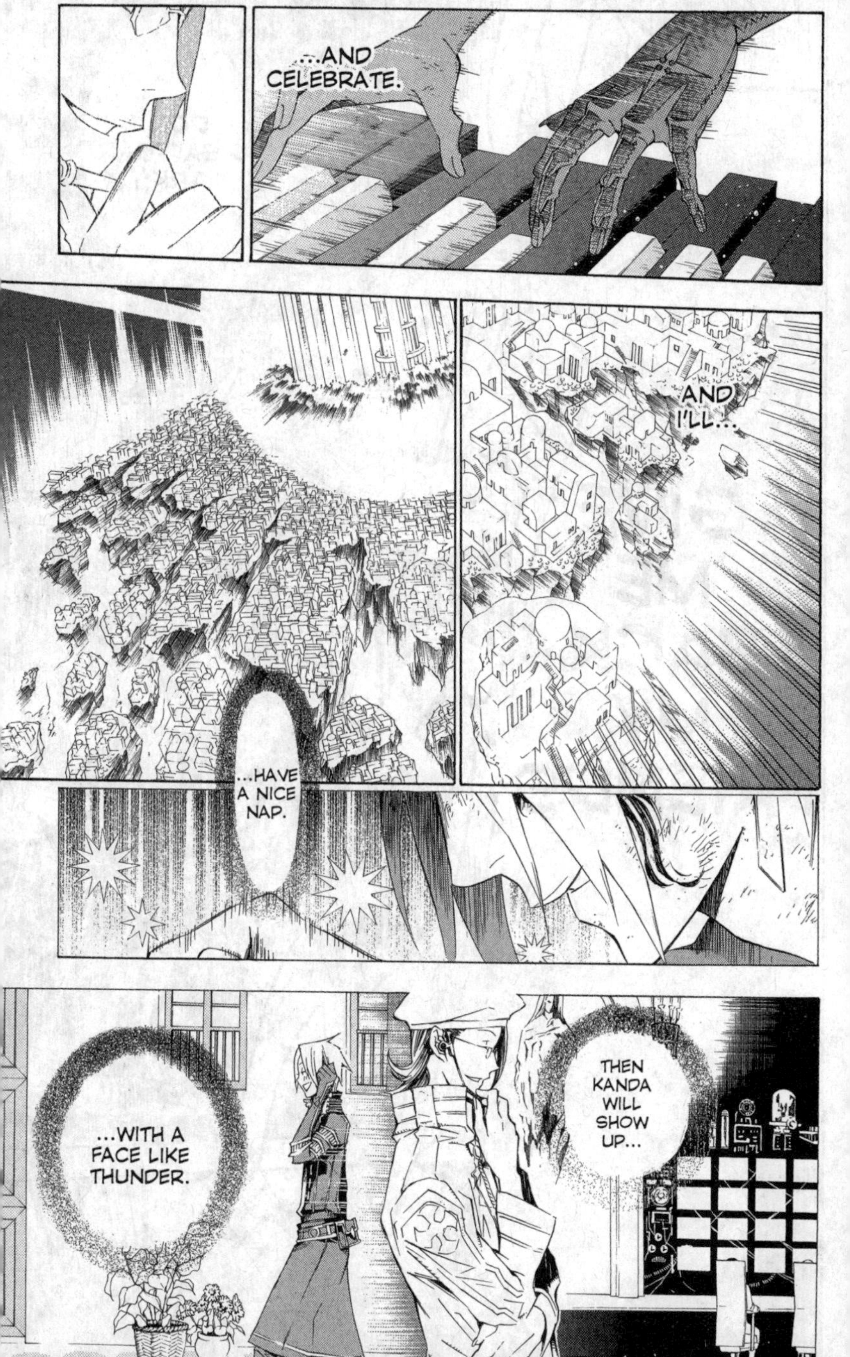
...AND CELEBRATE.
AND I'LL...
...HAVE A NICE NAP.
THEN KANDA WILL SHOW UP...
...WITH A FACE LIKE THUNDER.

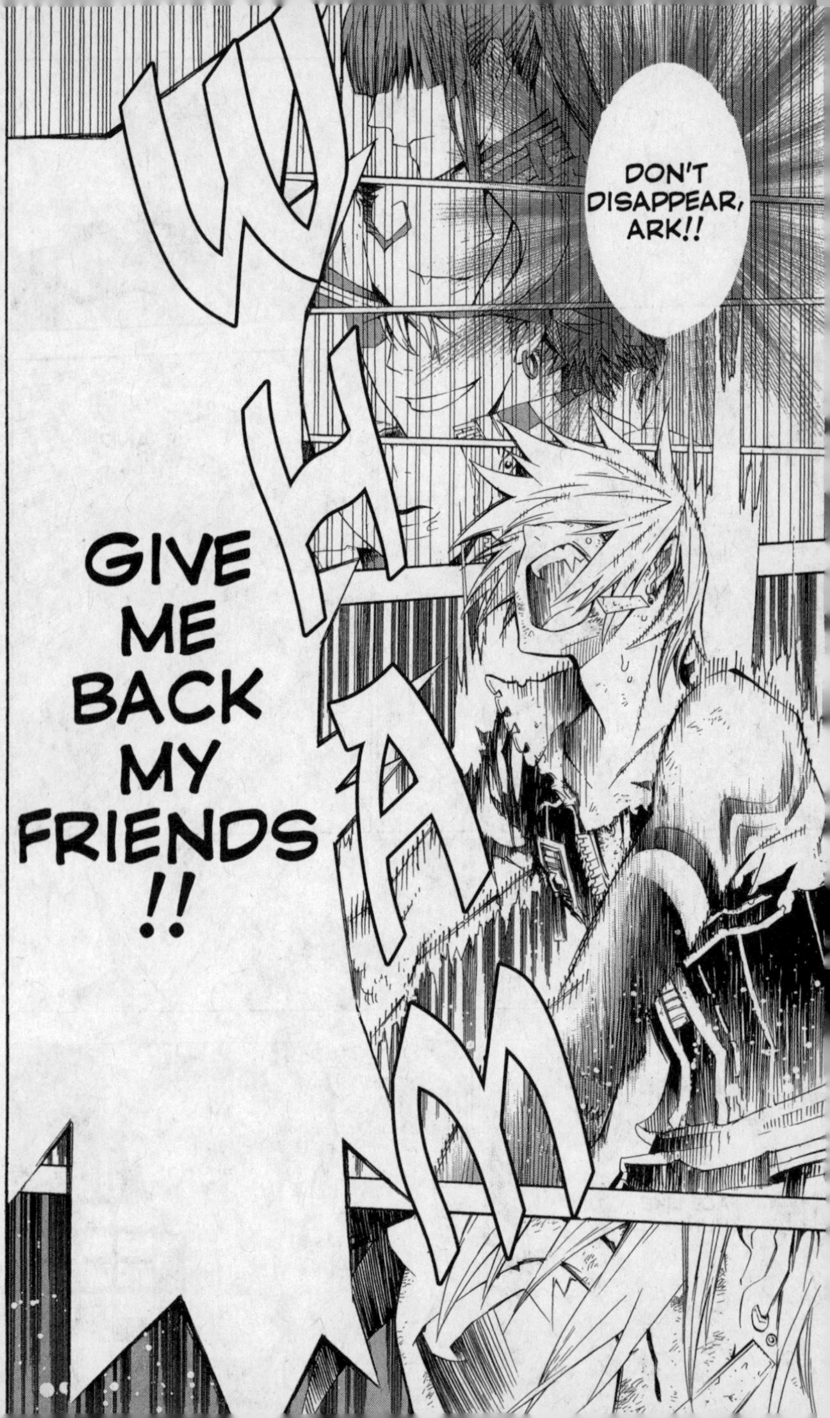
DON'T DISAPPEAR, ARK!!
GIVE ME BACK MY FRIENDS!!

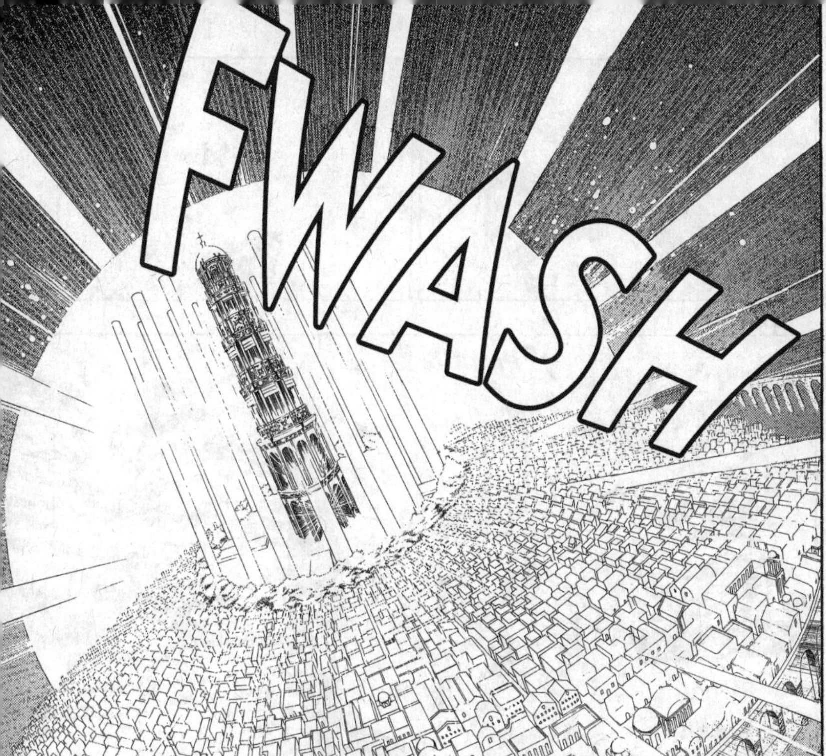
FWASH
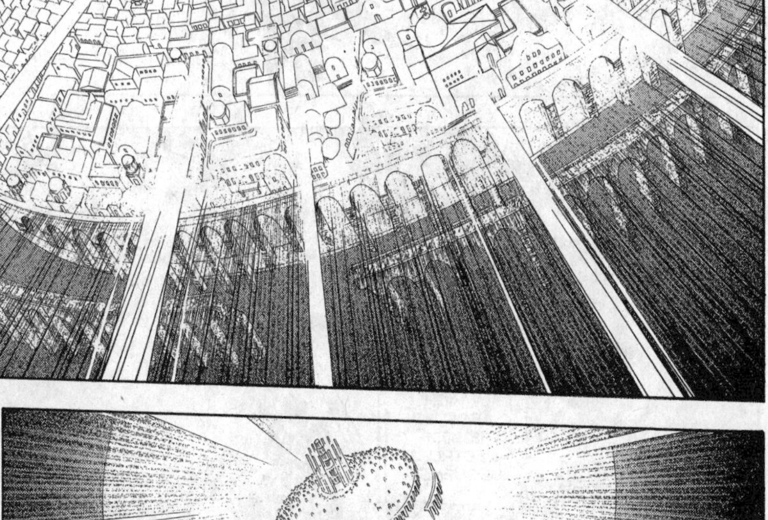

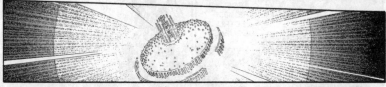

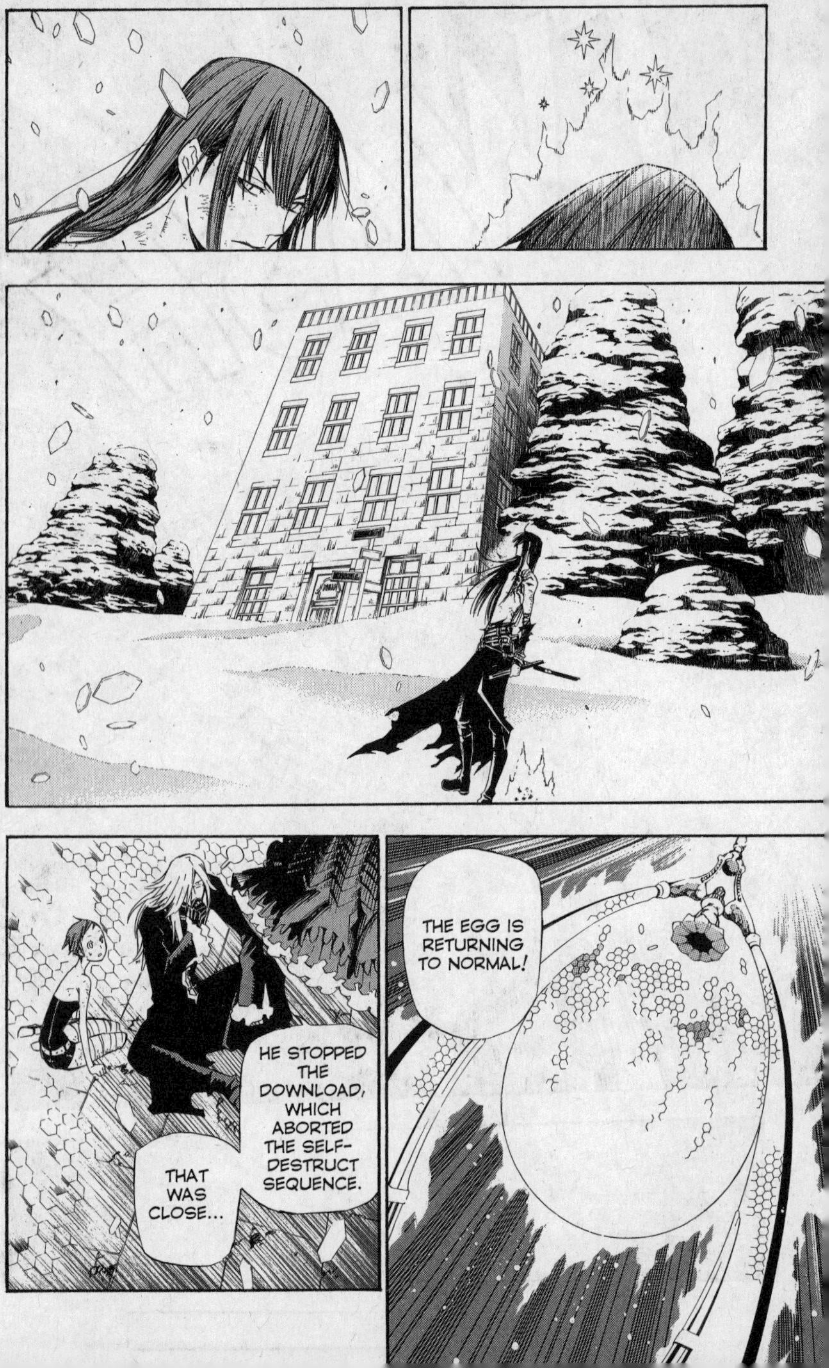
THE EGG IS RETURNING TO NORMAL!
HE STOPPED THE DOWNLOAD, WHICH ABORTED THE SELF-DESTRUCT SEQUENCE.
THAT WAS CLOSE...

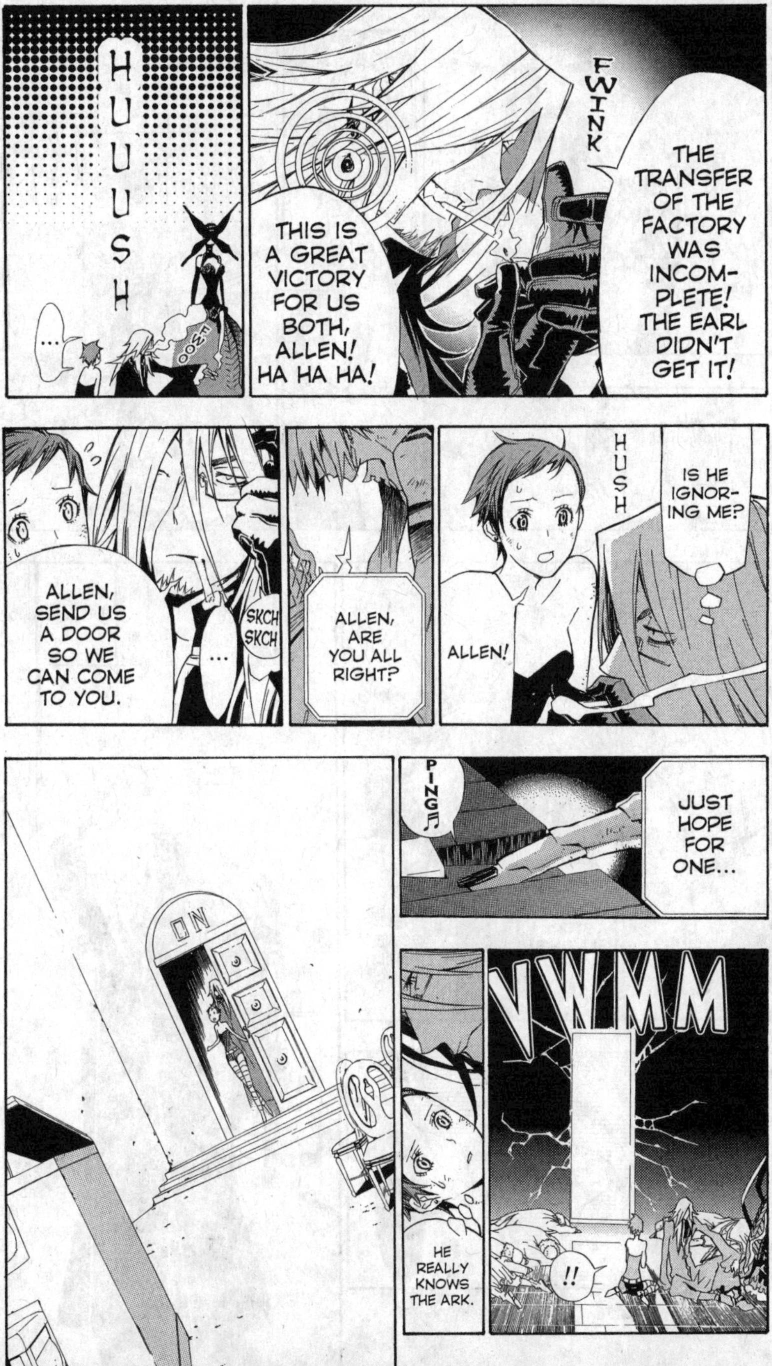
FWINK
THE TRANSFER OF THE FACTORY WAS INCOMPLETE! THE EARL DIDN'T GET IT!
THIS IS A GREAT VICTORY FOR US BOTH, ALLEN! HA HA HA!
HUUUSH
FWOO
...
HUSH
IS HE IGNORING ME?
ALLEN!
ALLEN, ARE YOU ALL RIGHT?
SKCH SKCH
...
ALLEN, SEND US A DOOR SO WE CAN COME TO YOU.
PING♫
JUST HOPE FOR ONE...
VWMM
!!
HE REALLY KNOWS THE ARK.
ON

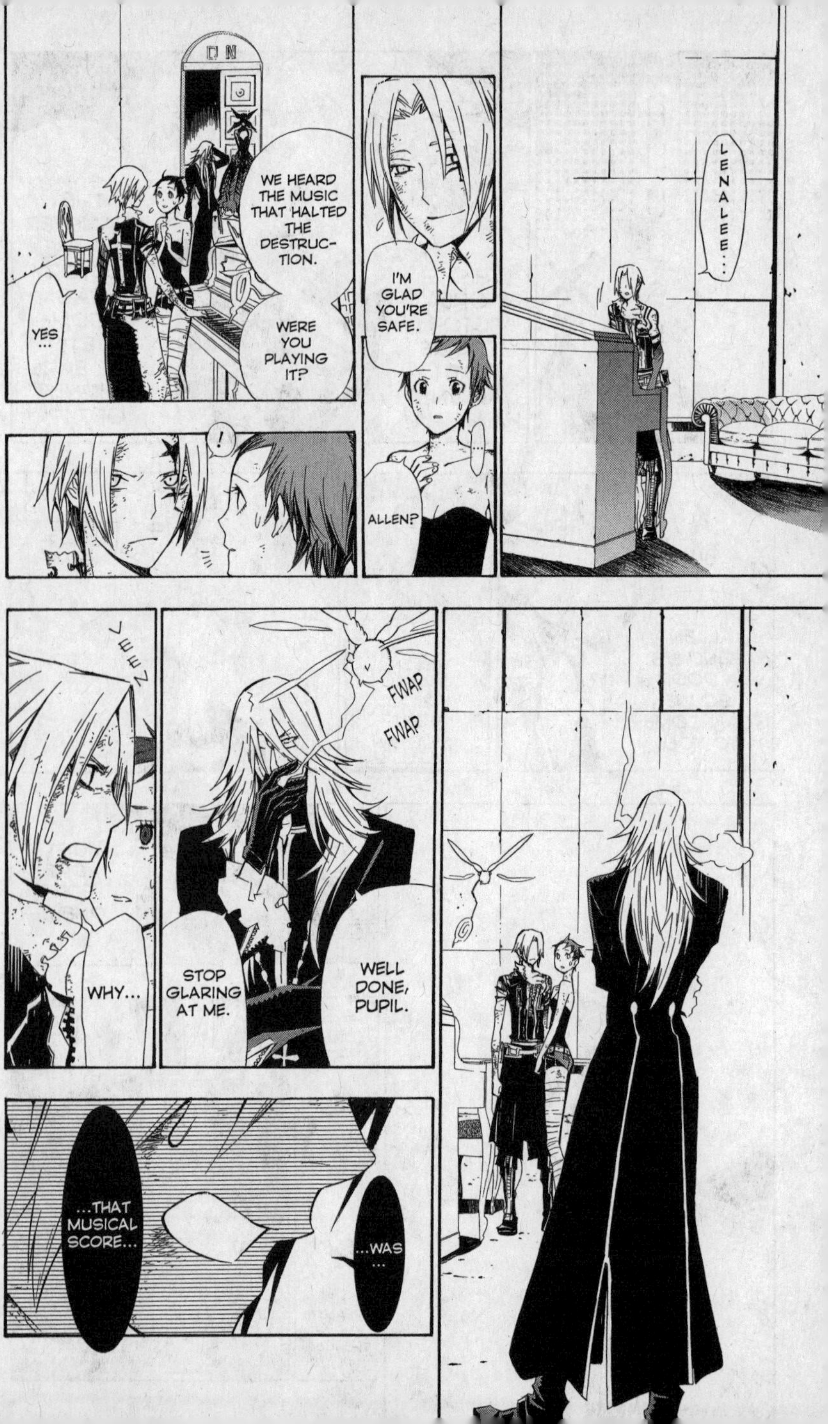
LENALEE...
I'M GLAD YOU'RE SAFE.
...
ALLEN?
WE HEARD THE MUSIC THAT HALTED THE DESTRUCTION.
WERE YOU PLAYING IT?
YES...
!
FWAP
FWAP
WELL DONE, PUPIL.
STOP GLARING AT ME.
VEEN
WHY...
...THAT MUSICAL SCORE...
...WAS...

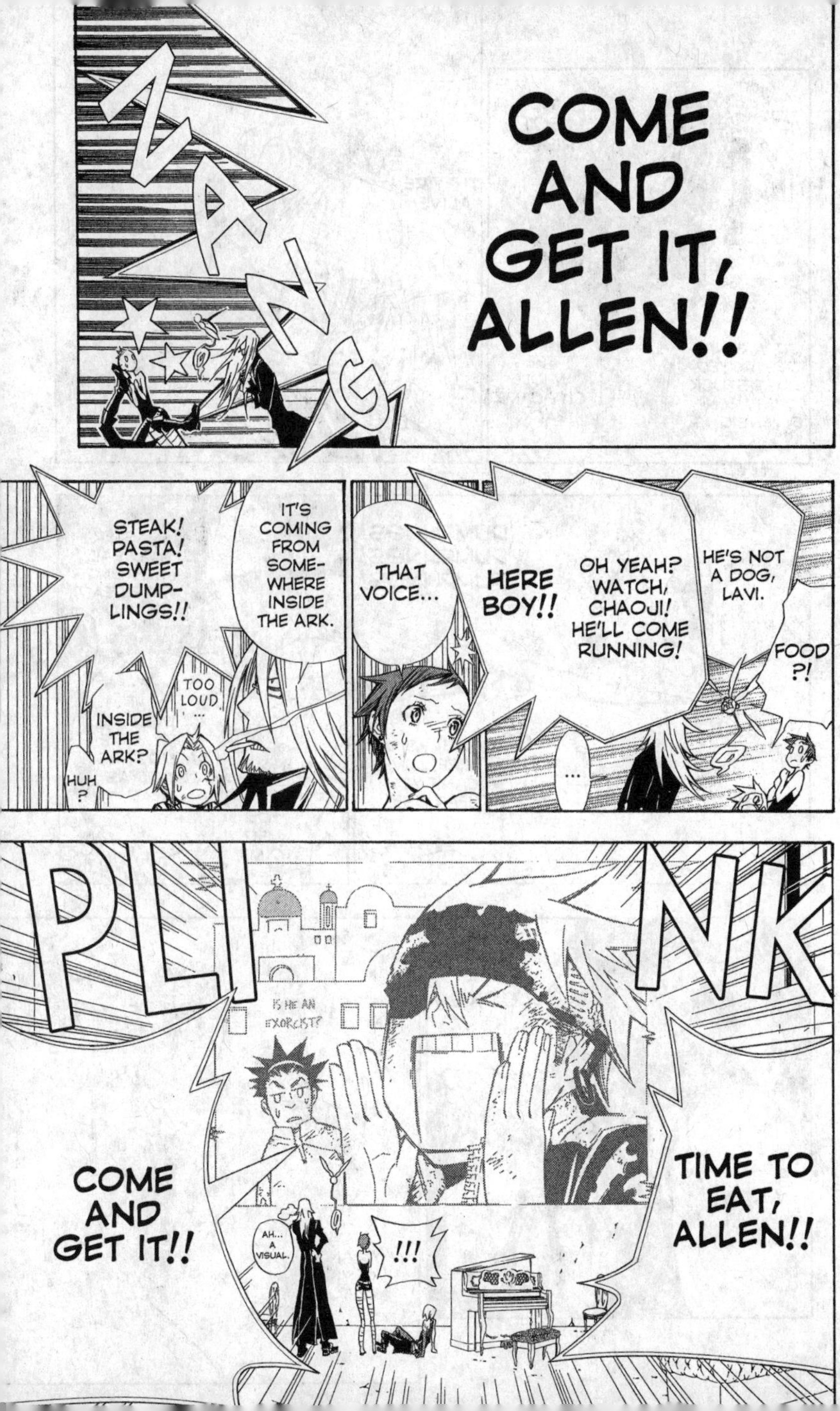
ZANG
COME AND GET IT, ALLEN!!
HE'S NOT A DOG, LAVI.
FOOD ?!
OH YEAH? WATCH, CHAOJI! HE'LL COME RUNNING!
HERE BOY!!
...
THAT VOICE...
IT'S COMING FROM SOMEWHERE INSIDE THE ARK.
STEAK! PASTA! SWEET DUMPLINGS!!
TOO LOUD...
INSIDE THE ARK?
HUH ?
PLINK
TIME TO EAT, ALLEN!!
COME AND GET IT!!
IS HE AN EXORCIST?
!!!
AH... A VISUAL.

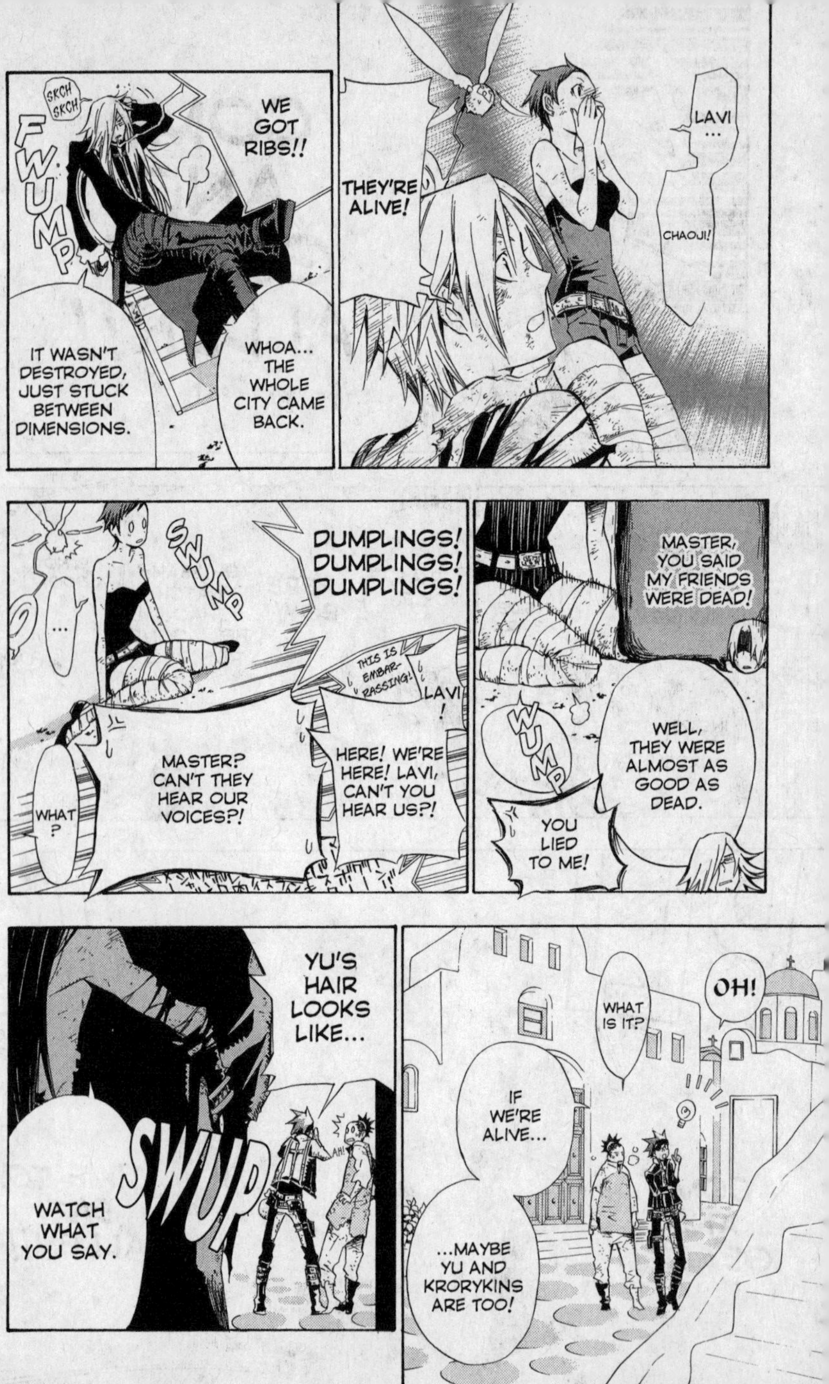
LAVI...
CHAOJI!
THEY'RE ALIVE!
WE GOT RIBS!!
SKCH SKCH
FWUMP
WHOA... THE WHOLE CITY CAME BACK.
IT WASN'T DESTROYED, JUST STUCK BETWEEN DIMENSIONS.
MASTER, YOU SAID MY FRIENDS WERE DEAD!
WELL, THEY WERE ALMOST AS GOOD AS DEAD.
WUMP
YOU LIED TO ME!
DUMPLINGS! DUMPLINGS! DUMPLINGS!
SWUMP
LAVI!
THIS IS EMBARRASSING!
...
HERE! WE'RE HERE! LAVI, CAN'T YOU HEAR US?!
MASTER? CAN'T THEY HEAR OUR VOICES?!
WHAT?
OH!
WHAT IS IT?
IF WE'RE ALIVE...
...MAYBE YU AND KRORYKINS ARE TOO!
YU'S HAIR LOOKS LIKE...
AH!
SWUP
WATCH WHAT YOU SAY.

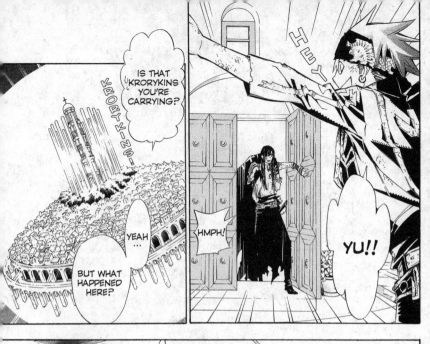

HEY
YU!!
HMPH!
KRORYKINS!
IS THAT KRORYKINS YOU'RE CARRYING?
YEAH ...
BUT WHAT HAPPENED HERE?
I HAVE NO IDEA!
COME ON! GET OUT HERE, BEAN SPROUT!!
DON'T CALL ME BEAN SPROUT!!
SOB
I'M SO HAPPY.
ALLEN ?!
HUH ?
WHERE ARE YOU?
BEAN SPROUT'S VOICE IS COMING FROM UP THERE.
MY NAME'S ALLEN!!
ELI... ADE ...
HEY, KRORYKINS JUST SPOKE!!

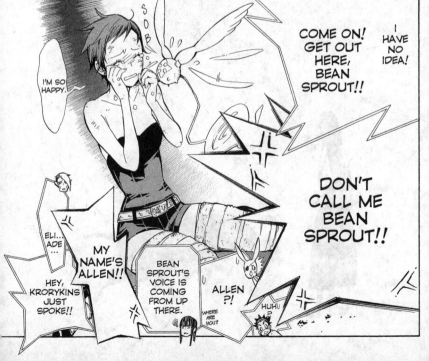

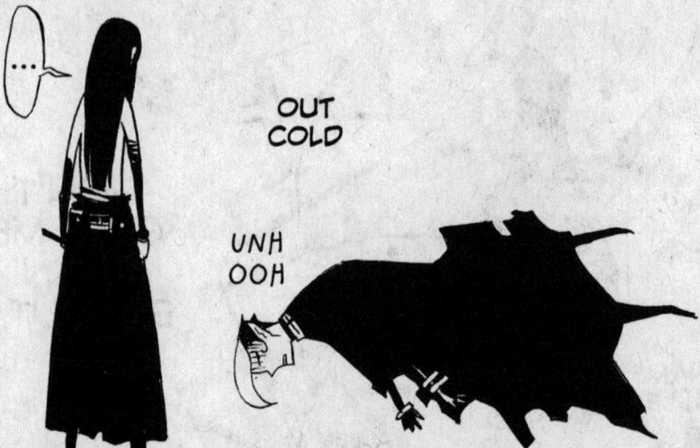
OUT COLD
UNH OOH
...

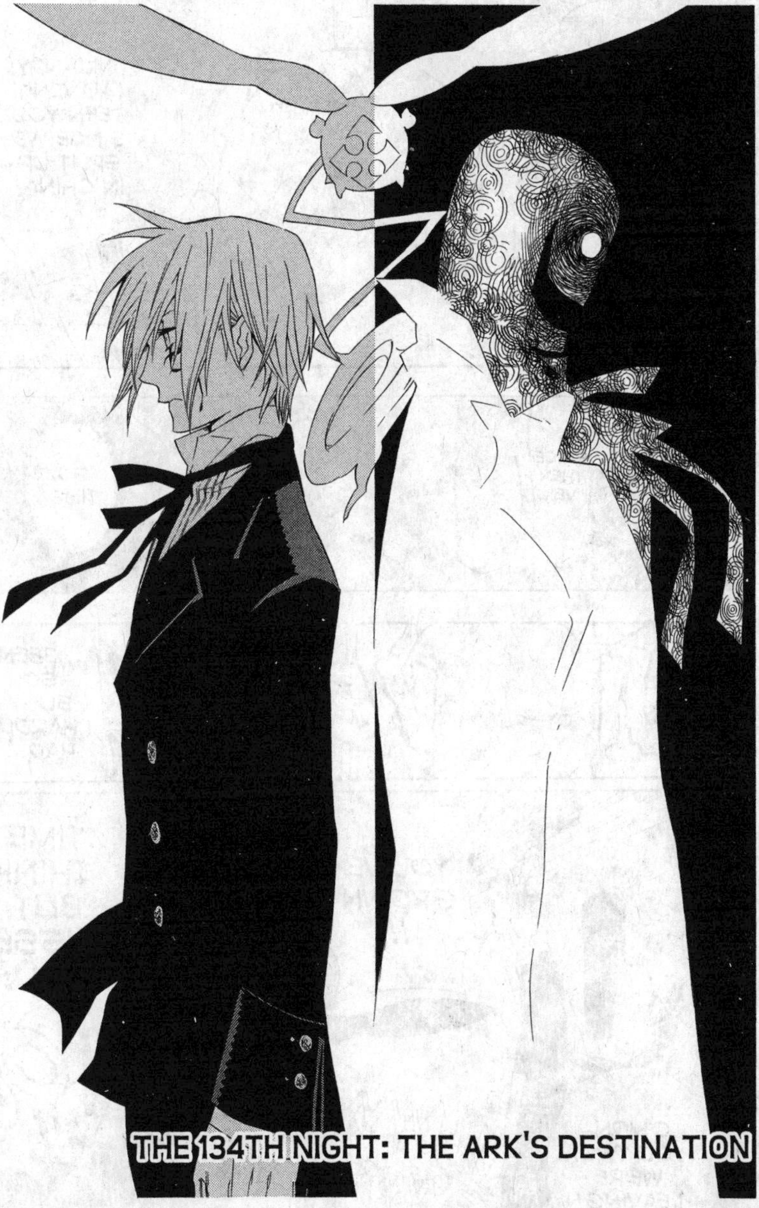

THE 134TH NIGHT: THE ARK'S DESTINATION

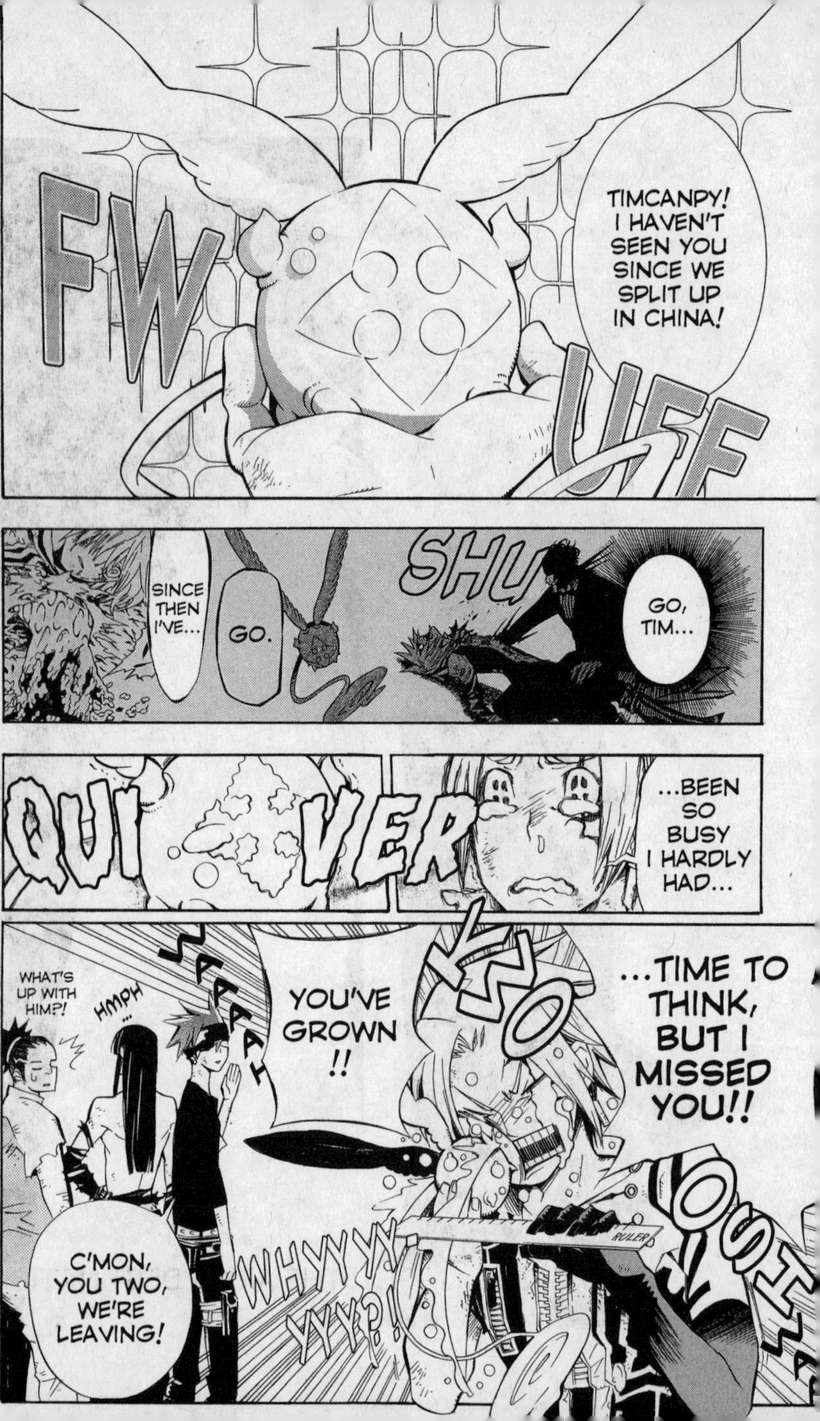
TIMCANPY! I HAVEN'T SEEN YOU SINCE WE SPLIT UP IN CHINA!
FWUFF
GO, TIM...
SHU
GO.
SINCE THEN I'VE...
...BEEN SO BUSY I HARDLY HAD...
QUIVER
...TIME TO THINK, BUT I MISSED YOU!!
YOU'VE GROWN!!
RULER
WHYYYY YYY?!
WHAT'S UP WITH HIM?!
HMPH...
C'MON, YOU TWO, WE'RE LEAVING!

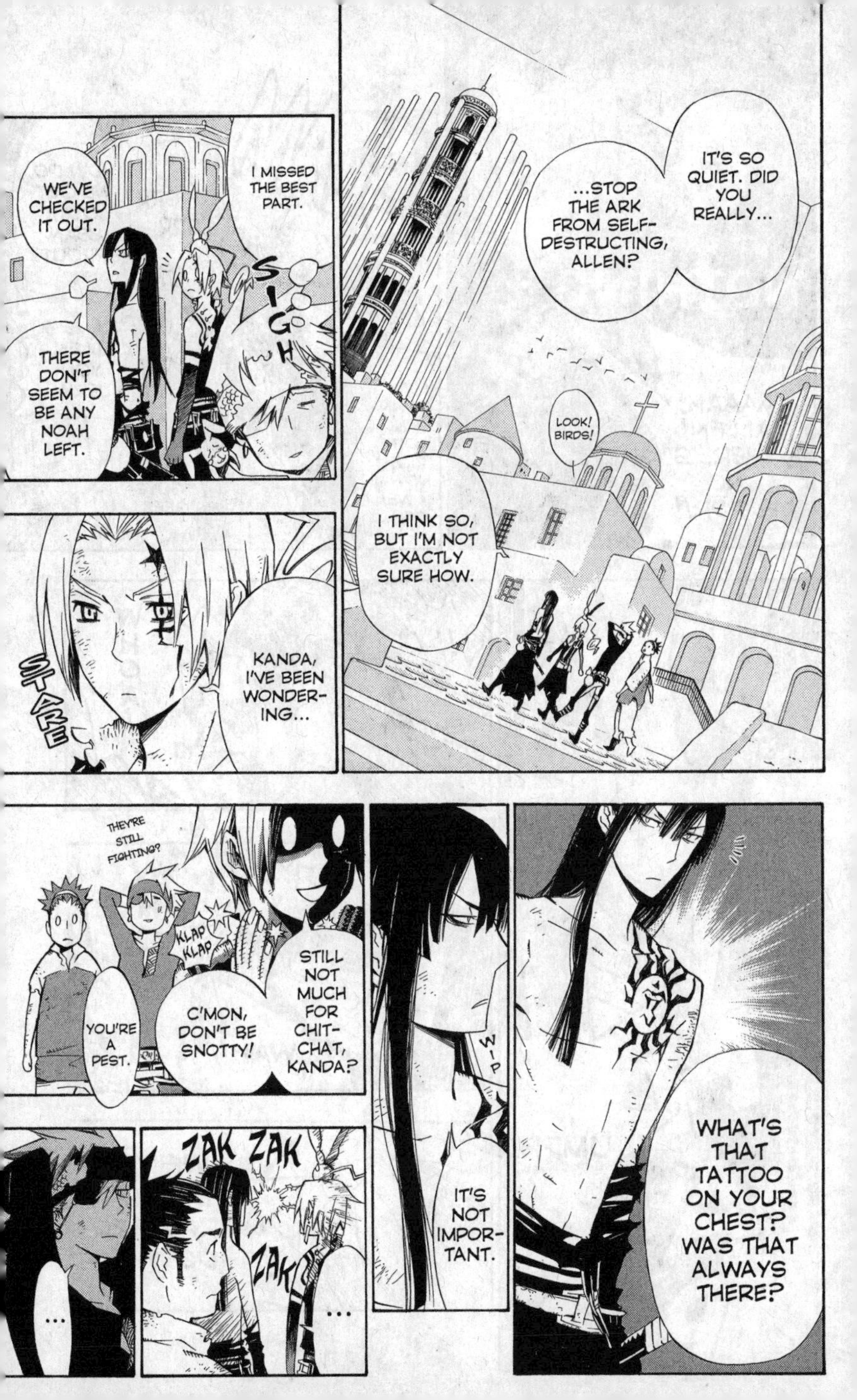
IT'S SO QUIET. DID YOU REALLY...
...STOP THE ARK FROM SELF-DESTRUCTING, ALLEN?
LOOK! BIRDS!
I THINK SO, BUT I'M NOT EXACTLY SURE HOW.
I MISSED THE BEST PART.
SIGH
WE'VE CHECKED IT OUT.
THERE DON'T SEEM TO BE ANY NOAH LEFT.
KANDA, I'VE BEEN WONDERING...
STARE
WHAT'S THAT TATTOO ON YOUR CHEST? WAS THAT ALWAYS THERE?
WIP
IT'S NOT IMPORTANT.
STILL NOT MUCH FOR CHIT-CHAT, KANDA?
KLAP KLAP
C'MON, DON'T BE SNOTTY!
THEY'RE STILL FIGHTING?
YOU'RE A PEST.
ZAK ZAK
ZAK
...
...

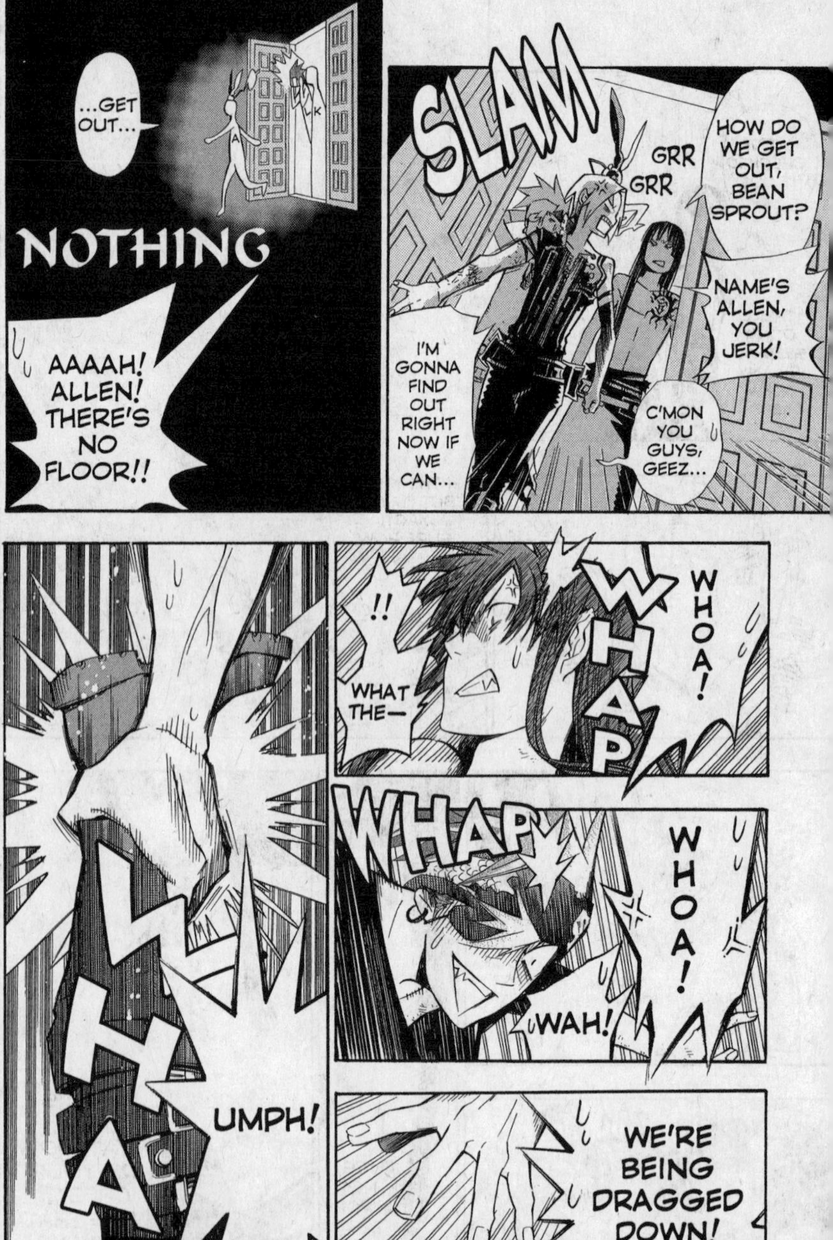
HOW DO WE GET OUT, BEAN SPROUT?
SLAM
GRR
GRR
NAME'S ALLEN, YOU JERK!
C'MON YOU GUYS, GEEZ...
I'M GONNA FIND OUT RIGHT NOW IF WE CAN...
...GET OUT...
NOTHING
AAAAH! ALLEN! THERE'S NO FLOOR!!
WHOA!
WHAP
!!
WHAT THE—
WHOA!
WHAP
WAH!
WE'RE BEING DRAGGED DOWN!
WHAP
UMPH!

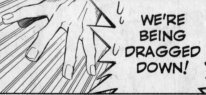

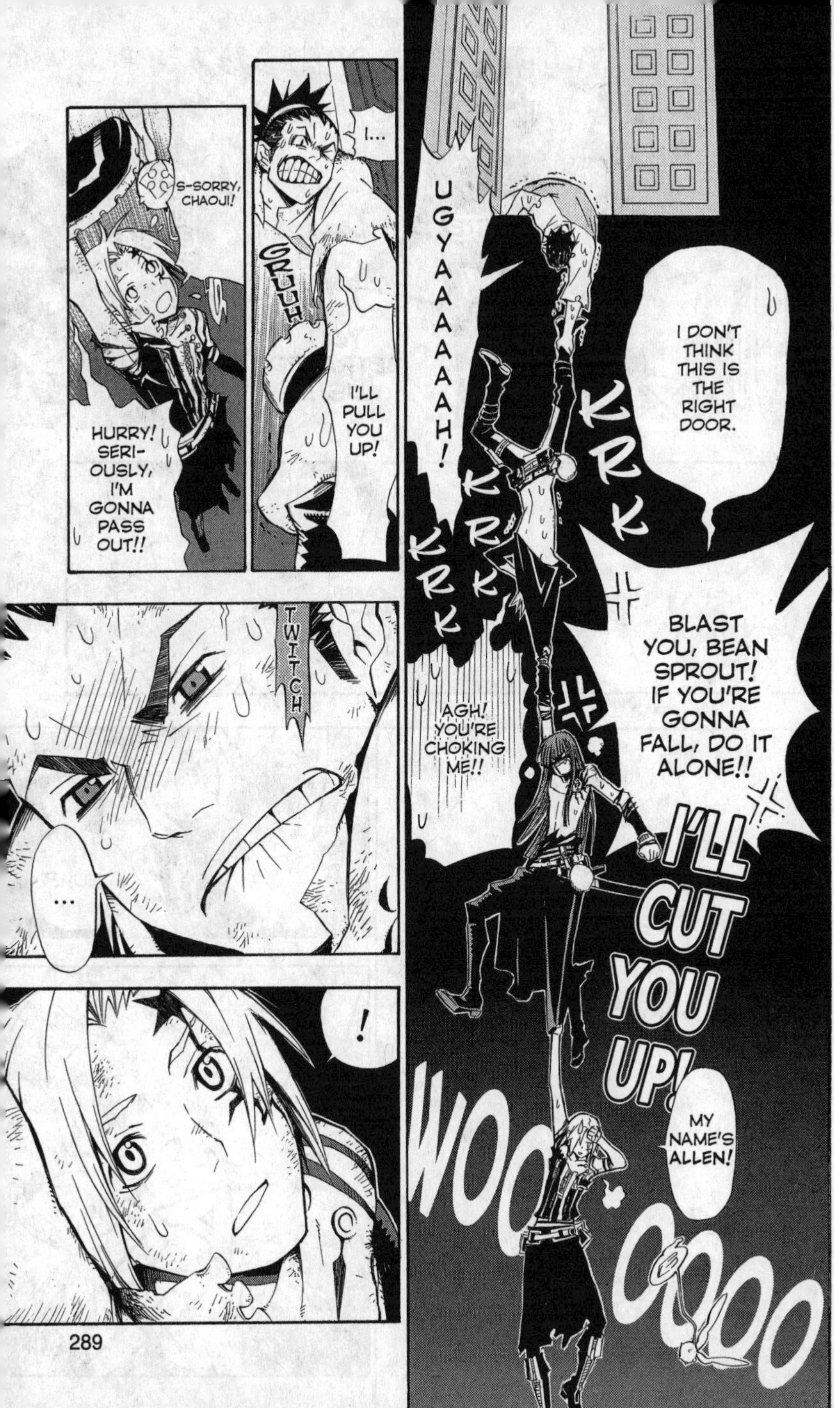
I DON'T THINK THIS IS THE RIGHT DOOR.
UGYAAAAAAAH!
KRK KRK
KRK KRK
KRK
BLAST YOU, BEAN SPROUT! IF YOU'RE GONNA FALL, DO IT ALONE!!
AGH! YOU'RE CHOKING ME!!
I'LL CUT YOU UP!
MY NAME'S ALLEN!
WOOOOOOO
I...
GRUUH
I'LL PULL YOU UP!
S-SORRY, CHAOJI!
HURRY! SERI-OUSLY, I'M GONNA PASS OUT!!
TWITCH
...
!

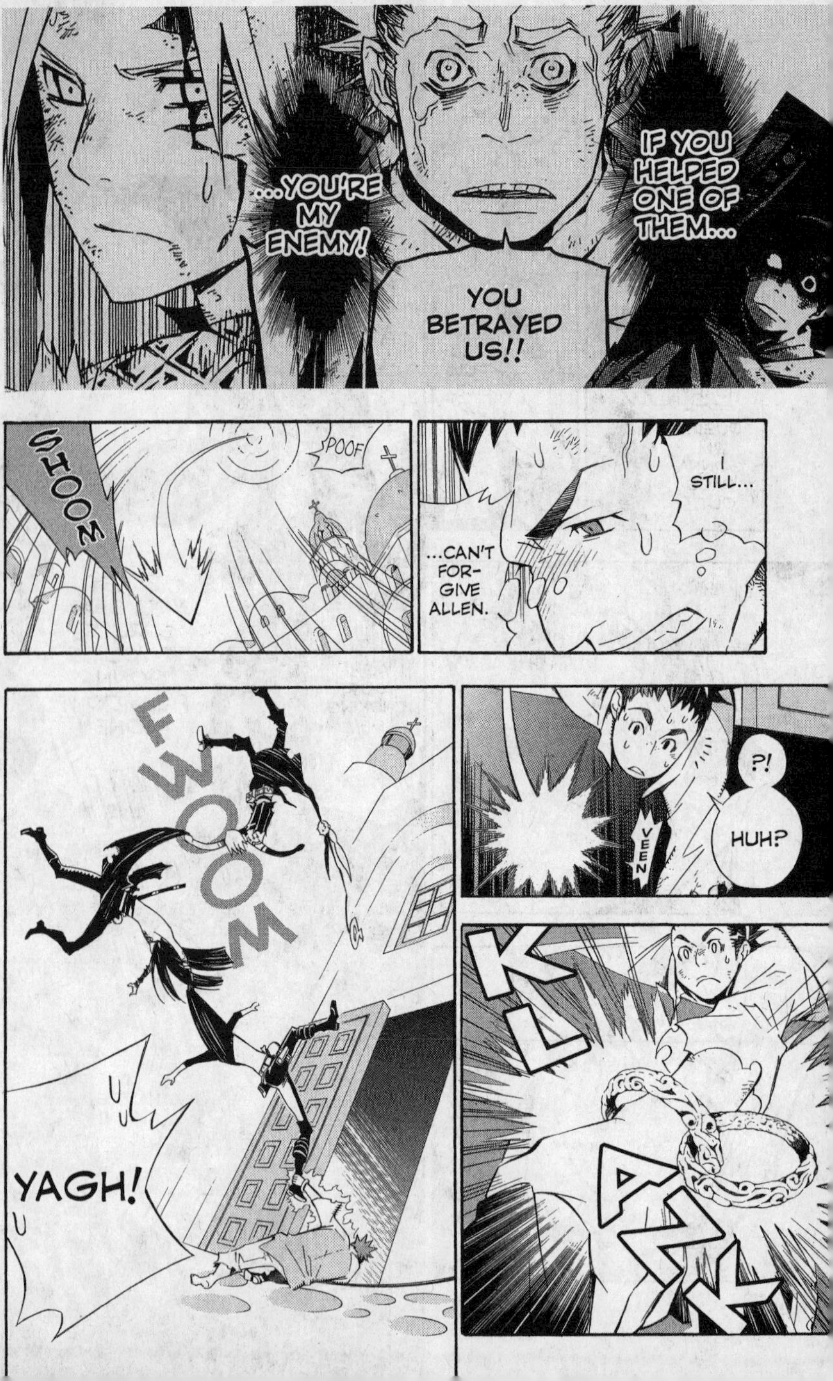
IF YOU HELPED ONE OF THEM...
...YOU'RE MY ENEMY!
YOU BETRAYED US!!
I STILL...
...CAN'T FOR-GIVE ALLEN.
POOF
SHOOM
?!
HUH?
VEEN
KLAZZK
FWOOM
YAGH!

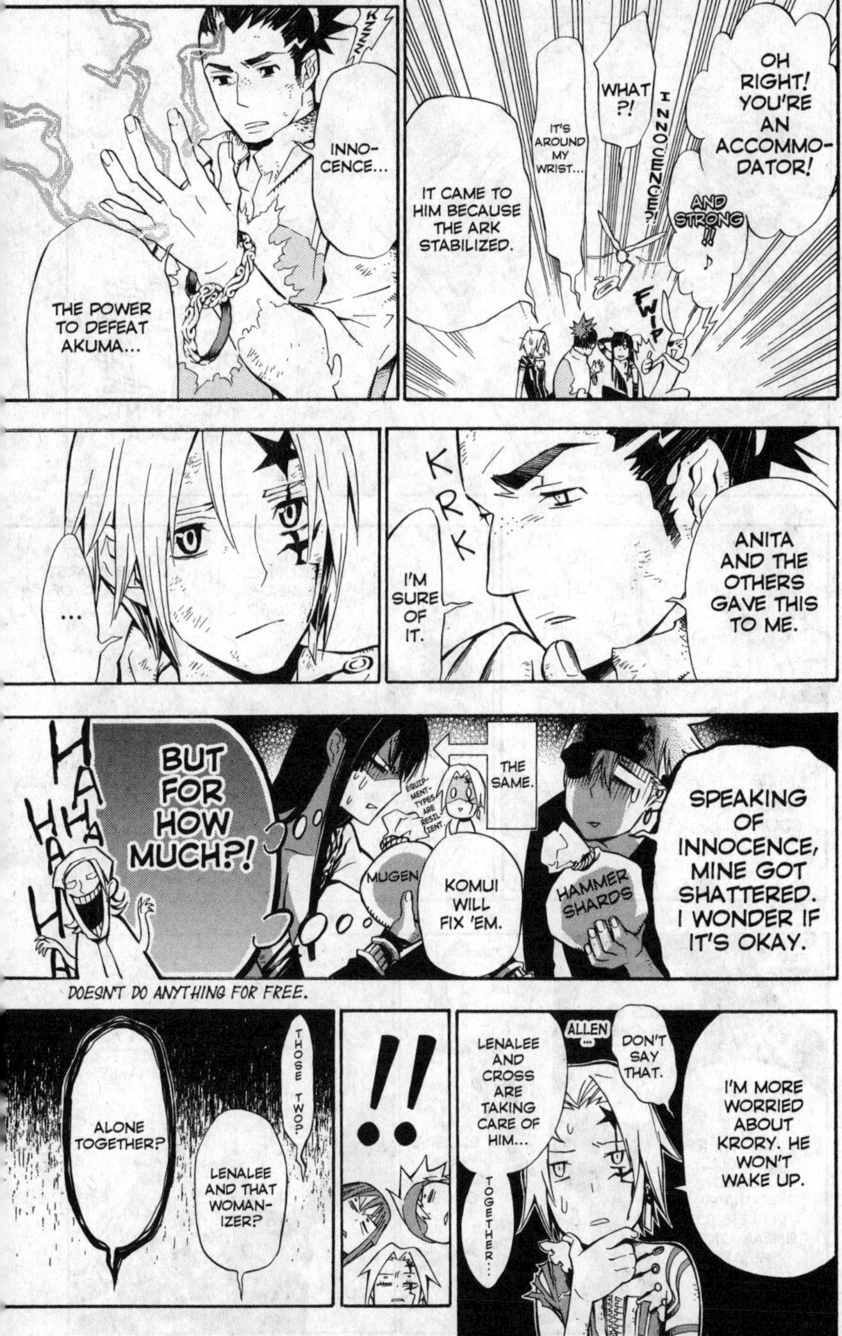
OH RIGHT! YOU'RE AN ACCOMMODATOR!
AND STRONG!! ♪
FWIP
INNOCENCE?!
WHAT?!
IT'S AROUND MY WRIST...
IT CAME TO HIM BECAUSE THE ARK STABILIZED.
INNOCENCE...
THE POWER TO DEFEAT AKUMA...
ANITA AND THE OTHERS GAVE THIS TO ME.
KRK
I'M SURE OF IT.
...
SPEAKING OF INNOCENCE, MINE GOT SHATTERED. I WONDER IF IT'S OKAY.
HAMMER SHARDS
THE SAME.
EQUIPMENT-TYPES ARE RESILIENT.
KOMUI WILL FIX 'EM.
MUGEN
BUT FOR HOW MUCH?!
HAHAHAHA
DOESN'T DO ANYTHING FOR FREE.
I'M MORE WORRIED ABOUT KRORY. HE WON'T WAKE UP.
DON'T SAY THAT.
ALLEN...
LENALEE AND CROSS ARE TAKING CARE OF HIM...
TOGETHER...
!!
THOSE TWO?
LENALEE AND THAT WOMANIZER?
ALONE TOGETHER?

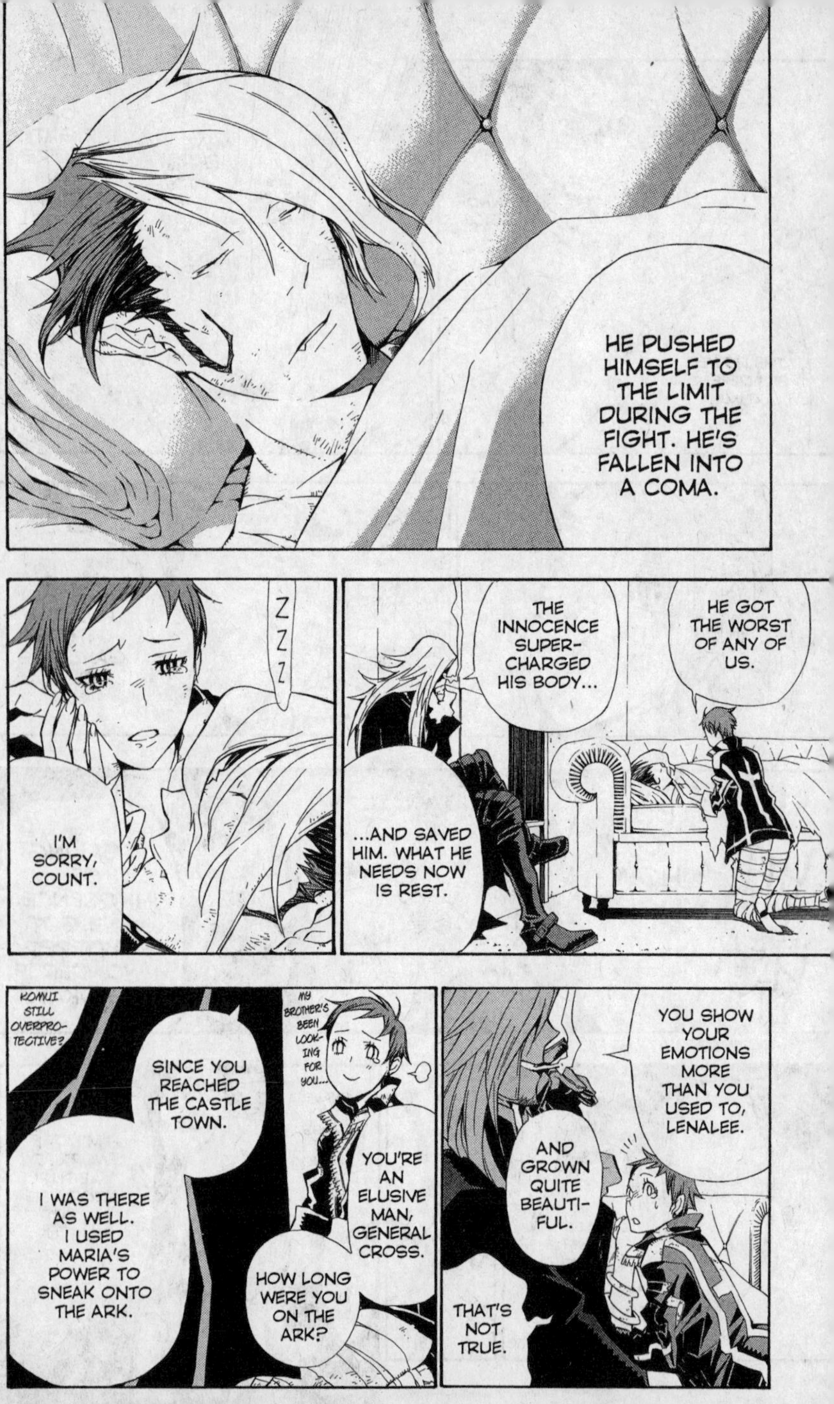
HE PUSHED HIMSELF TO THE LIMIT DURING THE FIGHT. HE'S FALLEN INTO A COMA.
HE GOT THE WORST OF ANY OF US.
THE INNOCENCE SUPER-CHARGED HIS BODY...
...AND SAVED HIM. WHAT HE NEEDS NOW IS REST.
ZZZ
I'M SORRY, COUNT.
YOU SHOW YOUR EMOTIONS MORE THAN YOU USED TO, LENALEE.
AND GROWN QUITE BEAUTIFUL.
THAT'S NOT TRUE.
MY BROTHER'S BEEN LOOKING FOR YOU...
YOU'RE AN ELUSIVE MAN, GENERAL CROSS.
HOW LONG WERE YOU ON THE ARK?
KOMUI STILL OVERPROTECTIVE?
SINCE YOU REACHED THE CASTLE TOWN.
I WAS THERE AS WELL. I USED MARIA'S POWER TO SNEAK ONTO THE ARK.

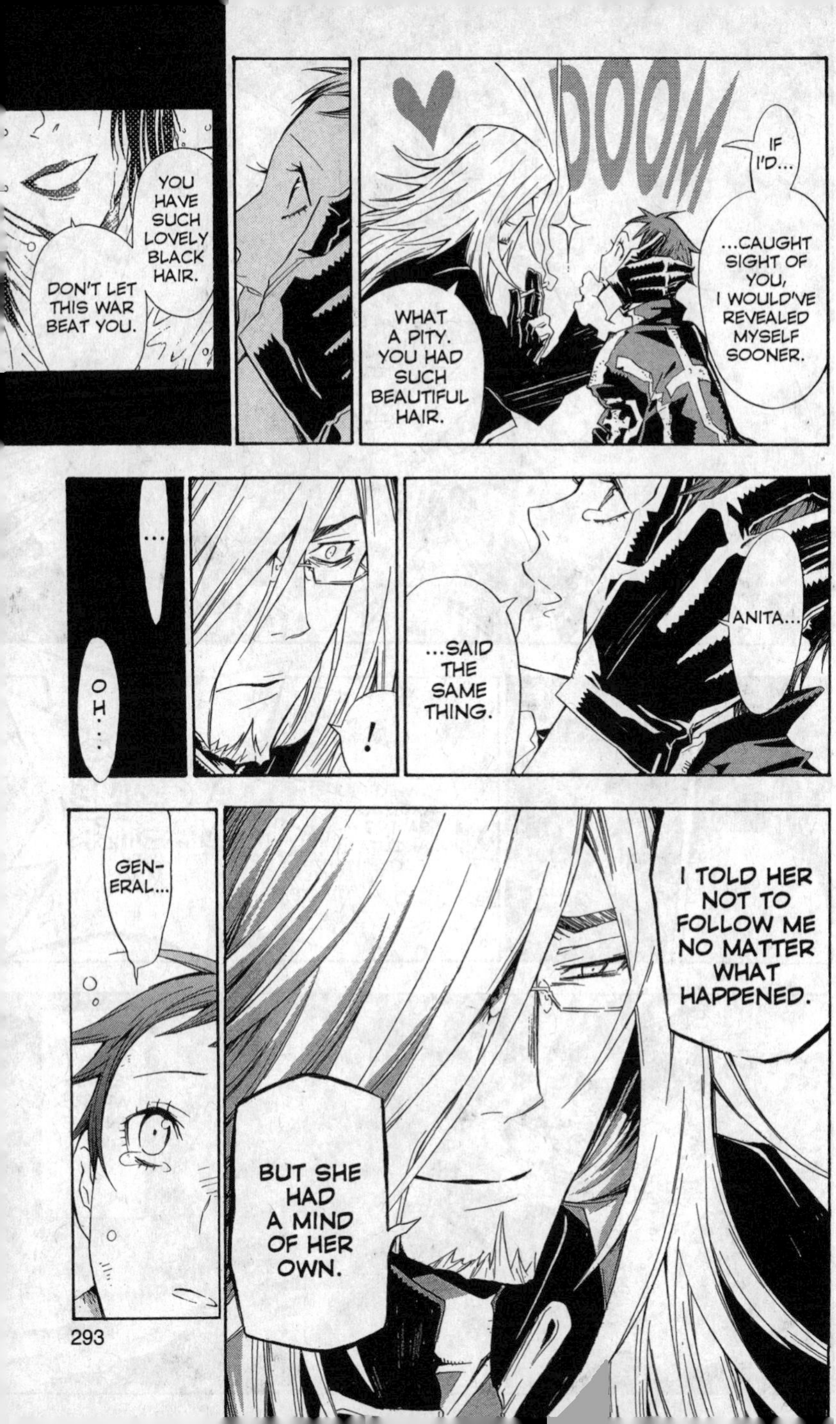
IF I'D...
...CAUGHT SIGHT OF YOU, I WOULD'VE REVEALED MYSELF SOONER.
DOOM
WHAT A PITY. YOU HAD SUCH BEAUTIFUL HAIR.
YOU HAVE SUCH LOVELY BLACK HAIR.
DON'T LET THIS WAR BEAT YOU.
ANITA...
...SAID THE SAME THING.
!
...
OH...
I TOLD HER NOT TO FOLLOW ME NO MATTER WHAT HAPPENED.
BUT SHE HAD A MIND OF HER OWN.
GEN-ERAL...

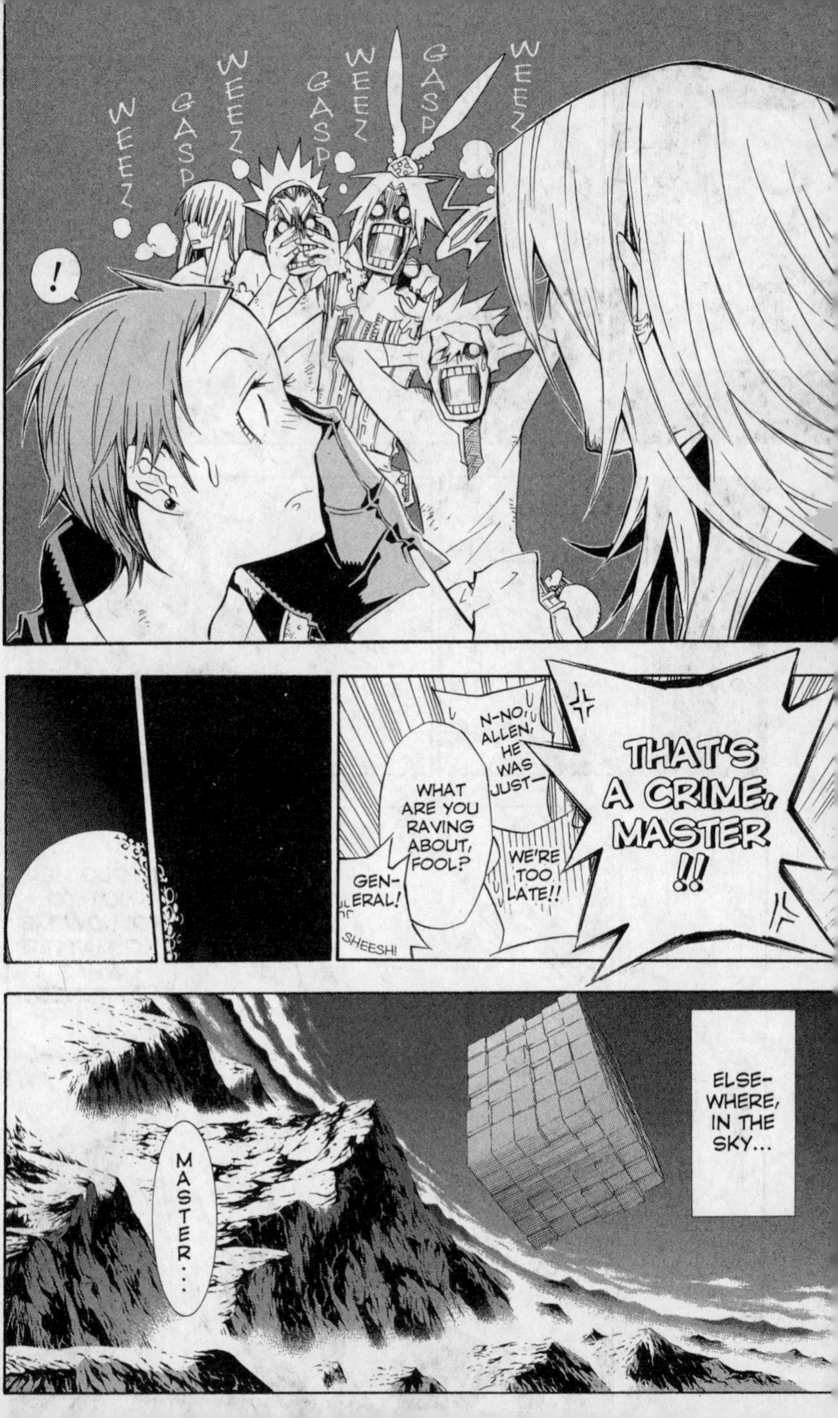
WEEZ
GASP
WEEZ
GASP
WEEZ
GASP
WEEZ
!
THAT'S A CRIME, MASTER!!
N-NO, ALLEN, HE WAS JUST—
WHAT ARE YOU RAVING ABOUT, FOOL?
WE'RE TOO LATE!!
GEN-ERAL!
SHEESH!
ELSE-WHERE, IN THE SKY...
MASTER...

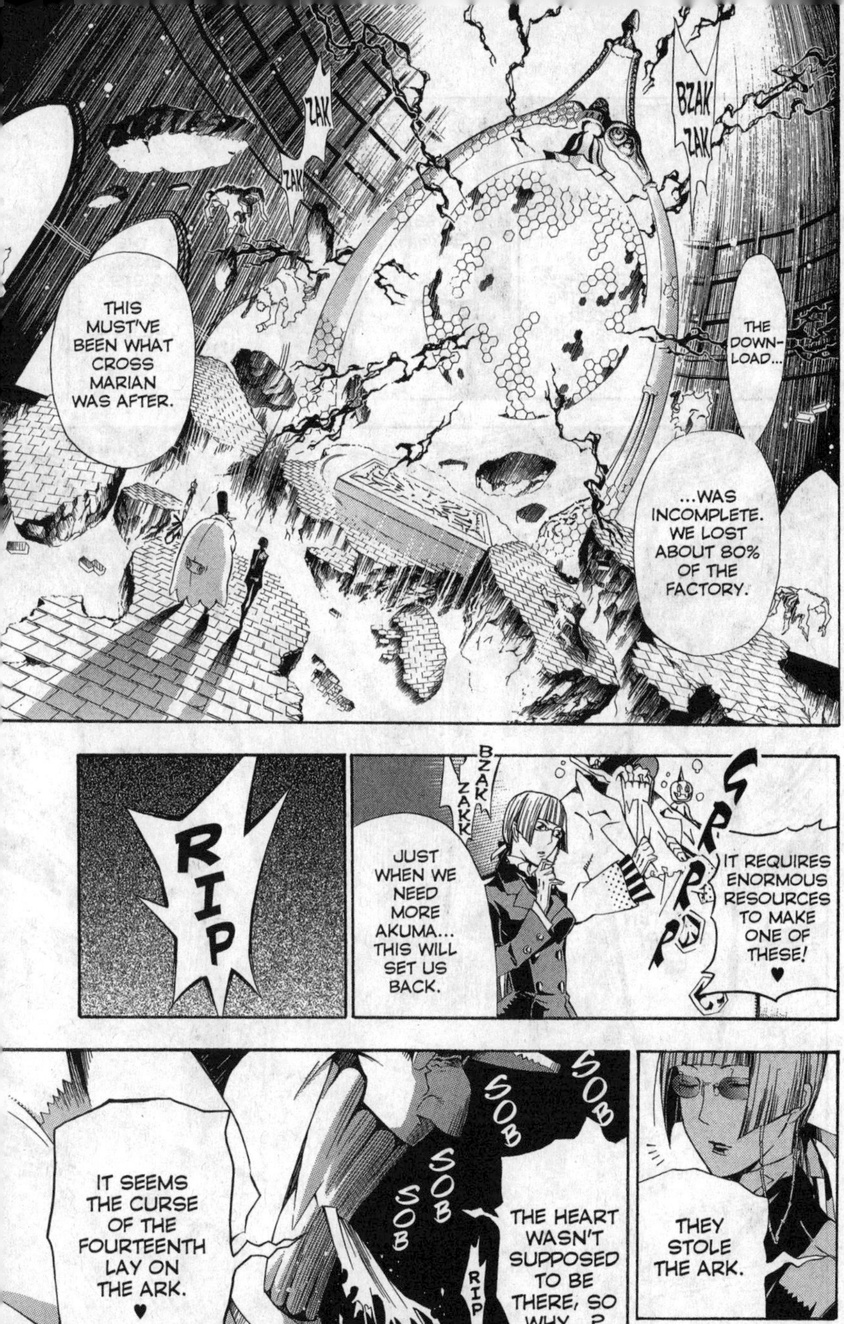
BZAK
ZAK
ZAK
ZAK
THE DOWNLOAD...
...WAS INCOMPLETE. WE LOST ABOUT 80% OF THE FACTORY.
THIS MUST'VE BEEN WHAT CROSS MARIAN WAS AFTER.
SRRRP
IT REQUIRES ENORMOUS RESOURCES TO MAKE ONE OF THESE! ♥
BZAK
ZAKK
JUST WHEN WE NEED MORE AKUMA... THIS WILL SET US BACK.
RIP
THEY STOLE THE ARK.
SOB
SOB
THE HEART WASN'T SUPPOSED TO BE THERE, SO WHY...?
RIP
SOB
SOB
SOB
IT SEEMS THE CURSE OF THE FOURTEENTH LAY ON THE ARK. ♥

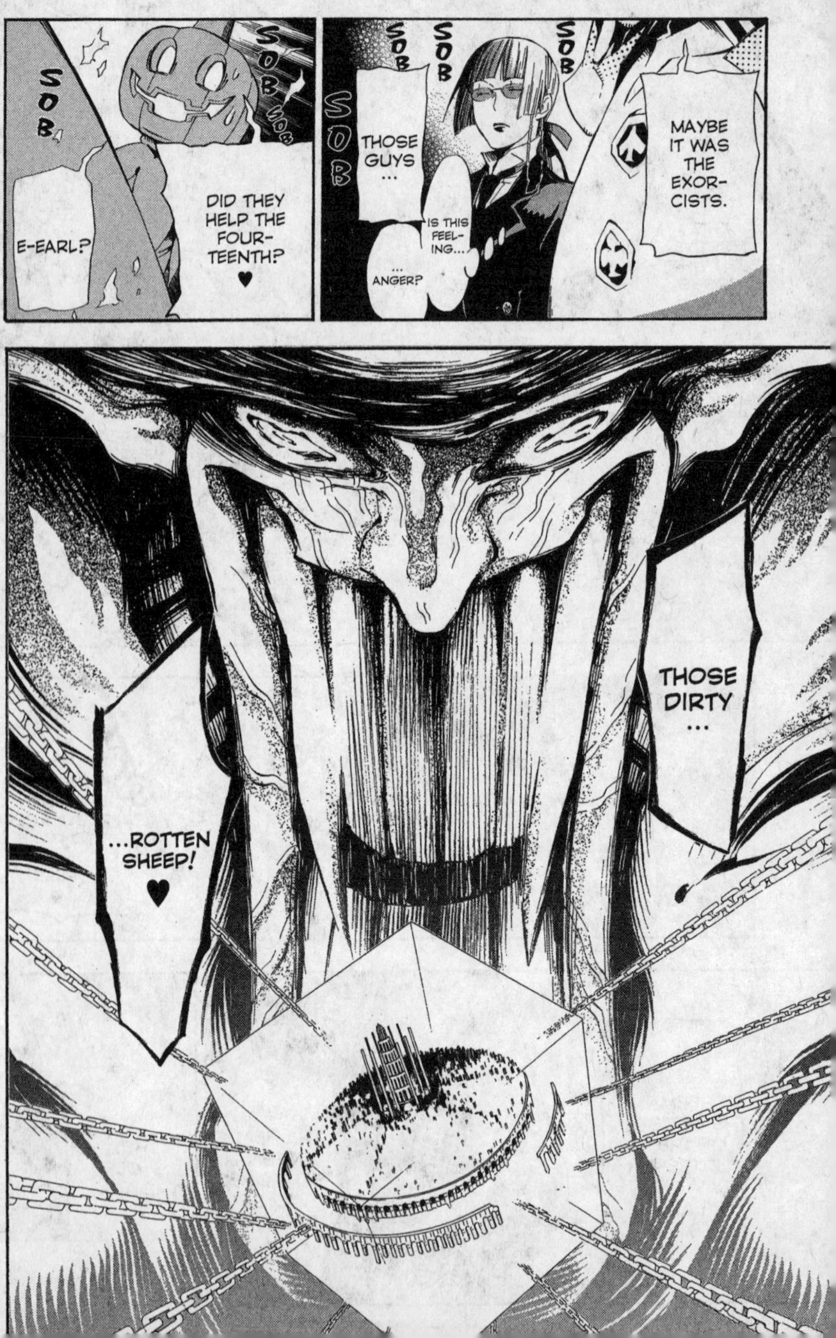
SOB
MAYBE IT WAS THE EXORCISTS.
SOB
SOB
THOSE GUYS...
SOB
IS THIS FEELING...
...ANGER?
SOB
SOB
SOB
DID THEY HELP THE FOURTEENTH? ♥
SOB
E-EARL?
THOSE DIRTY...
...ROTTEN SHEEP! ♥

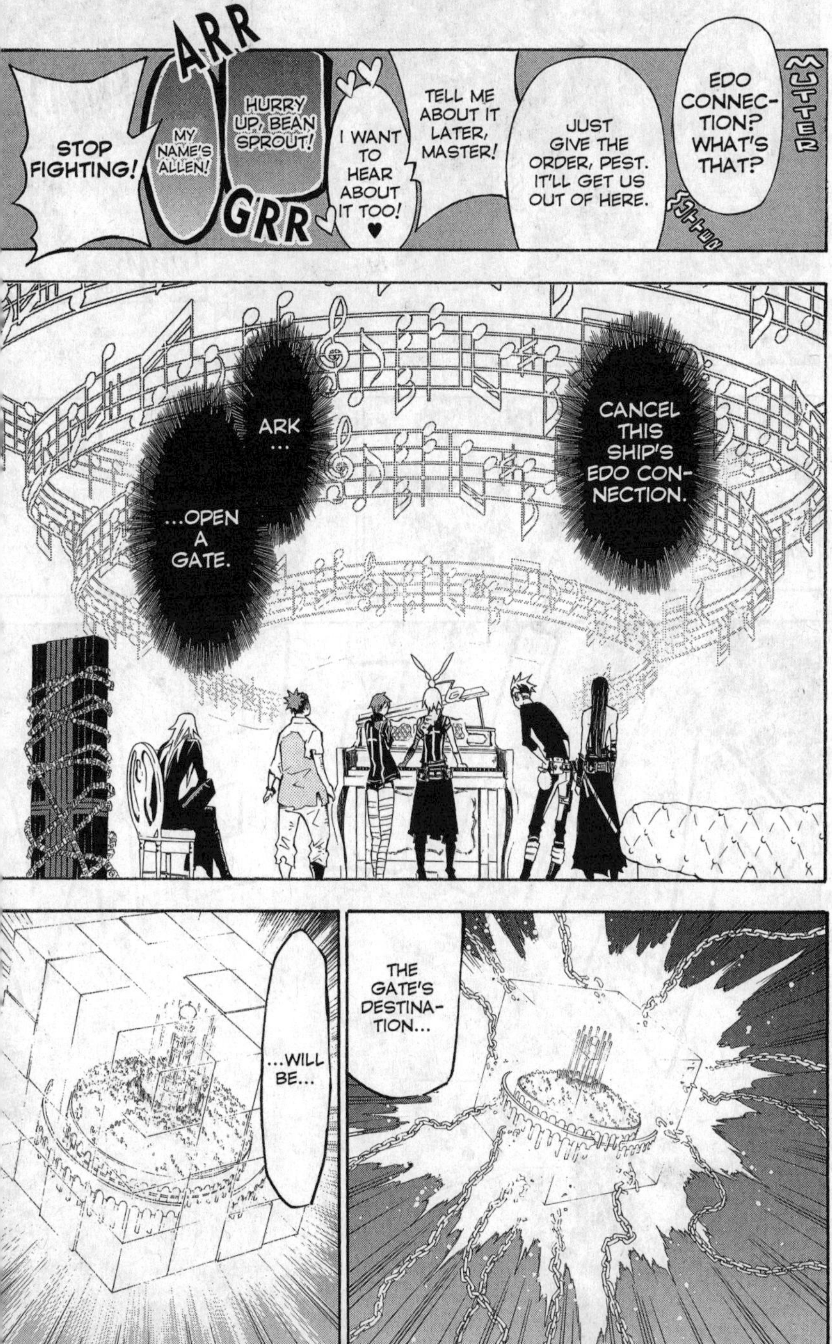
MUTTER
EDO CONNECTION? WHAT'S THAT?
JUST GIVE THE ORDER, PEST. IT'LL GET US OUT OF HERE.
TELL ME ABOUT IT LATER, MASTER!
I WANT TO HEAR ABOUT IT TOO! ♥
HURRY UP, BEAN SPROUT!
ARR
MY NAME'S ALLEN!
GRR
STOP FIGHTING!
CANCEL THIS SHIP'S EDO CONNECTION.
ARK...
...OPEN A GATE.
THE GATE'S DESTINATION...
...WILL BE...

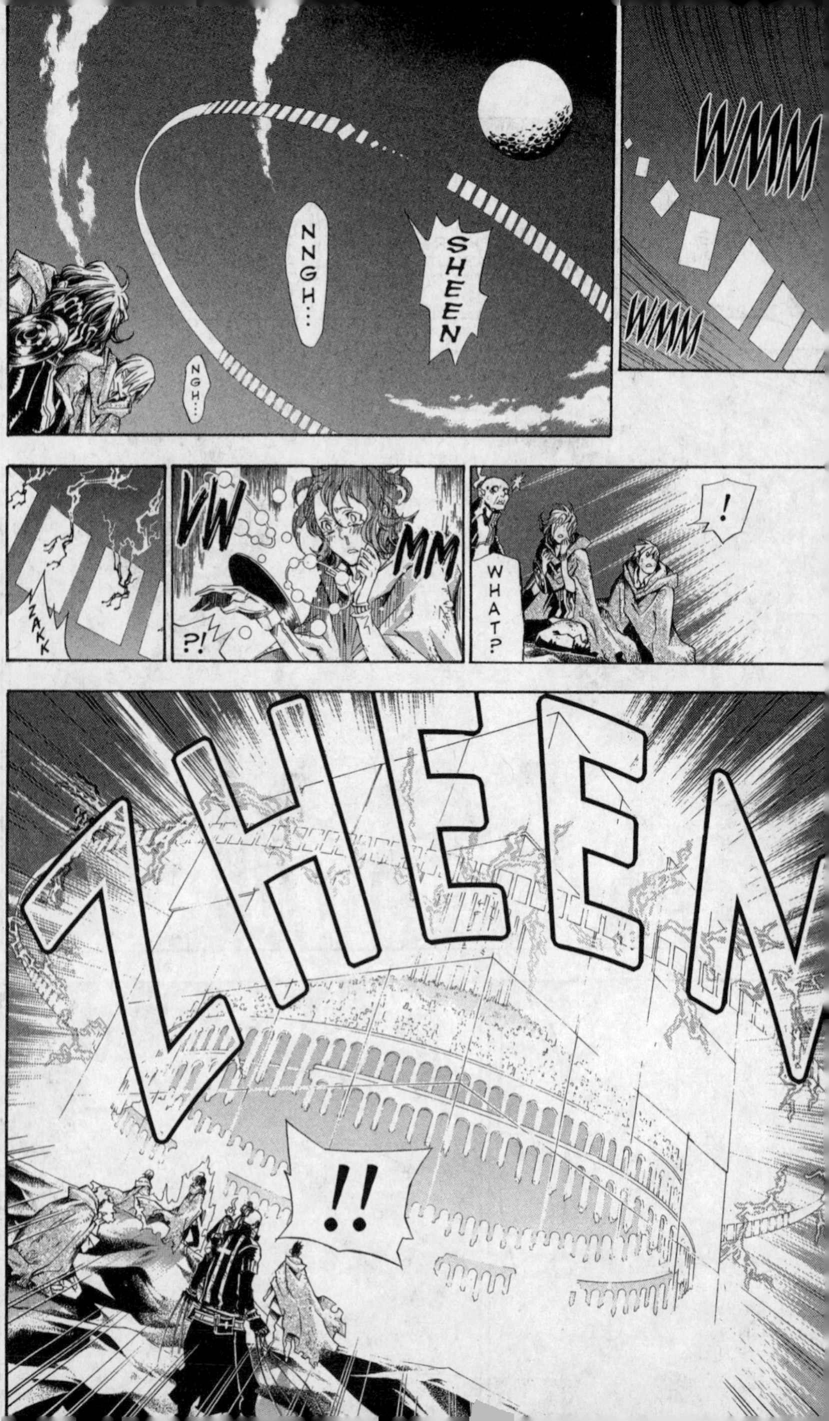
WMM
WMM
SHEEN
NNGH...
NGH...
!
WHAT?
VW
MM
?!
ZAKK
ZHEEN
!!

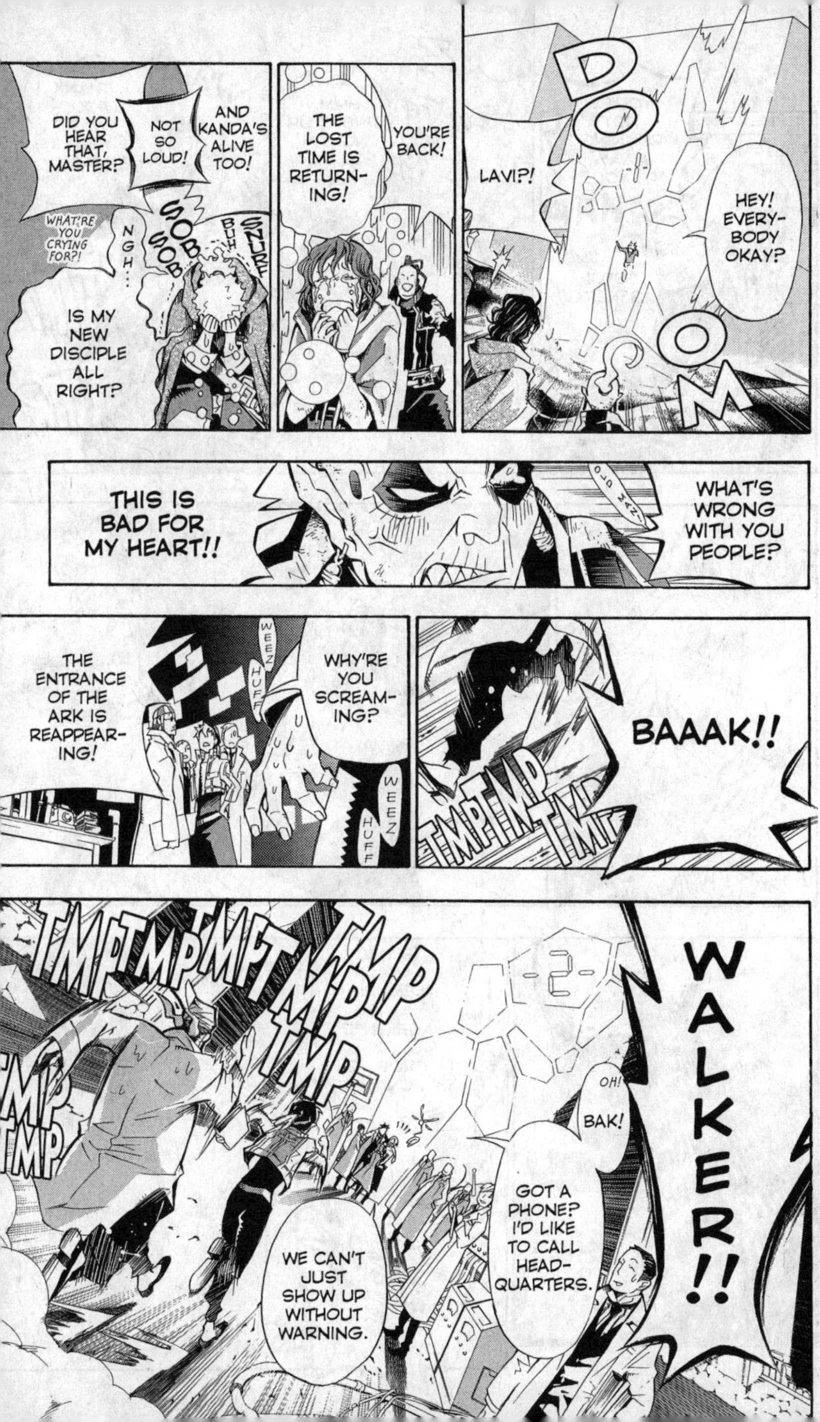
DOOOM
HEY! EVERYBODY OKAY?
LAVI?!
YOU'RE BACK!
THE LOST TIME IS RETURNING!
AND KANDA'S ALIVE TOO!
NOT SO LOUD!
DID YOU HEAR THAT, MASTER?
SNURF
BUH
SOB SOB
NGH...
WHAT'RE YOU CRYING FOR?!
IS MY NEW DISCIPLE ALL RIGHT?
WHAT'S WRONG WITH YOU PEOPLE?
OLD MAN!
THIS IS BAD FOR MY HEART!!
BAAAK!!
TMP TMP TMP
WHY'RE YOU SCREAMING?
WEEZ HUFF
WEEZ HUFF
THE ENTRANCE OF THE ARK IS REAPPEARING!
WALKER!!
TMP TMP TMP TMP TMP TMP
OH!
BAK!
GOT A PHONE? I'D LIKE TO CALL HEADQUARTERS.
WE CAN'T JUST SHOW UP WITHOUT WARNING.
TMP TMP

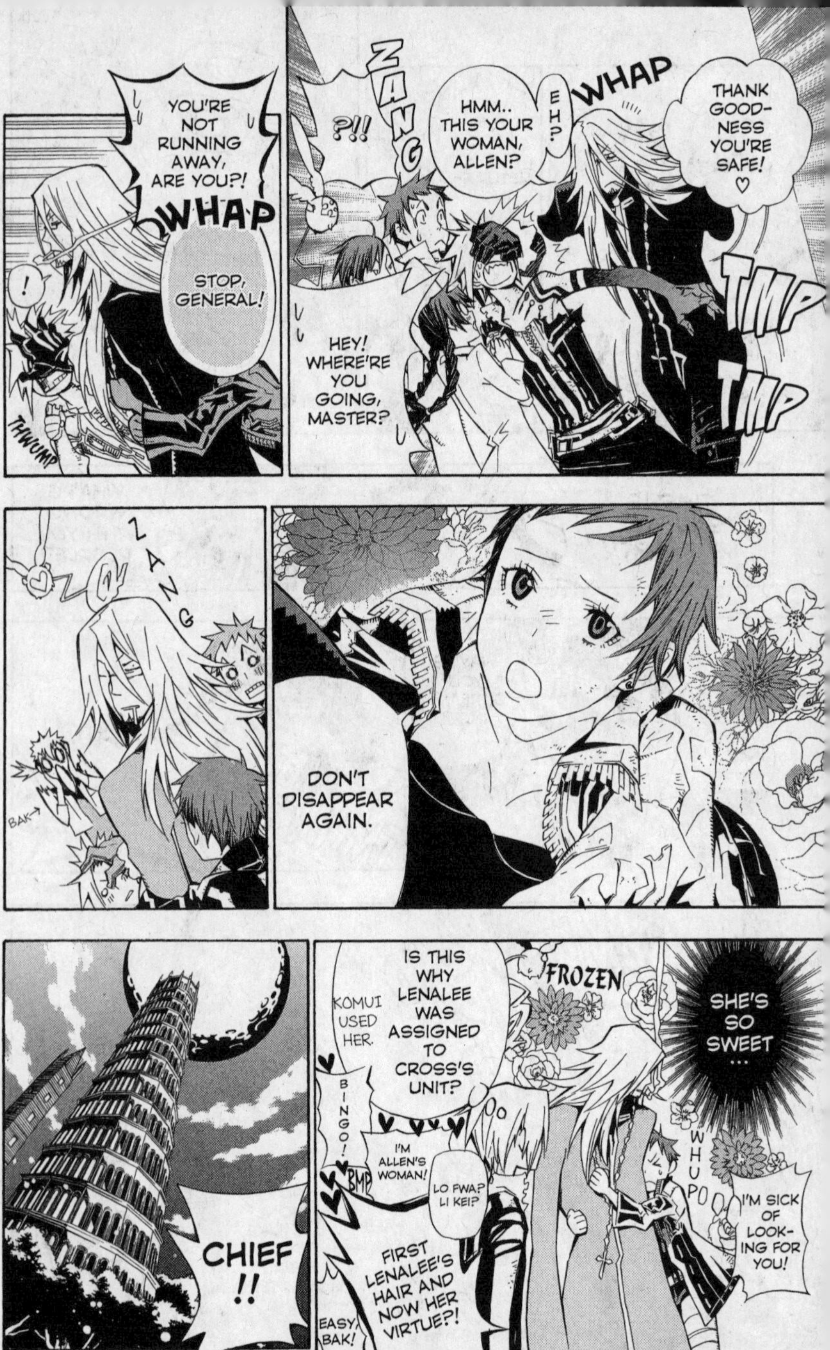
THANK GOODNESS YOU'RE SAFE! ♡
WHAP
EH?
HMM.. THIS YOUR WOMAN, ALLEN?
ZANG
?!!
TMP
TMP
HEY! WHERE'RE YOU GOING, MASTER?
YOU'RE NOT RUNNING AWAY, ARE YOU?!
WHAP
STOP, GENERAL!
!
THWUMP
DON'T DISAPPEAR AGAIN.
ZANG
BAK→
SHE'S SO SWEET...
FROZEN
IS THIS WHY LENALEE WAS ASSIGNED TO CROSS'S UNIT?
KOMUI USED HER.
BINGO!
WHUP
I'M SICK OF LOOKING FOR YOU!
LO FWA? LI KEI?
I'M ALLEN'S WOMAN!
BMP
FIRST LENALEE'S HAIR AND NOW HER VIRTUE?!
EASY, BAK!
CHIEF!!

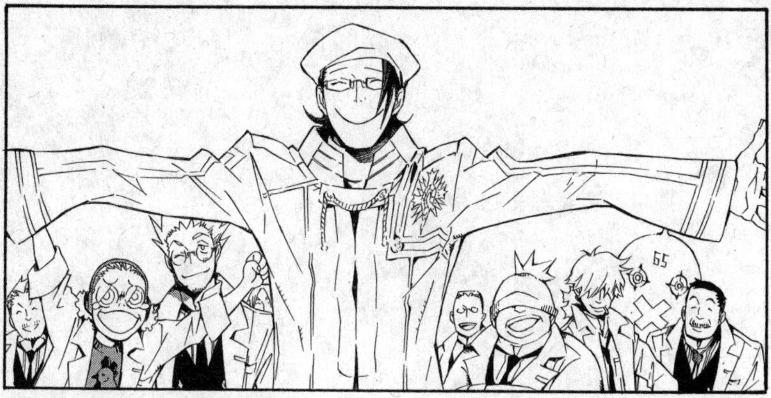
65

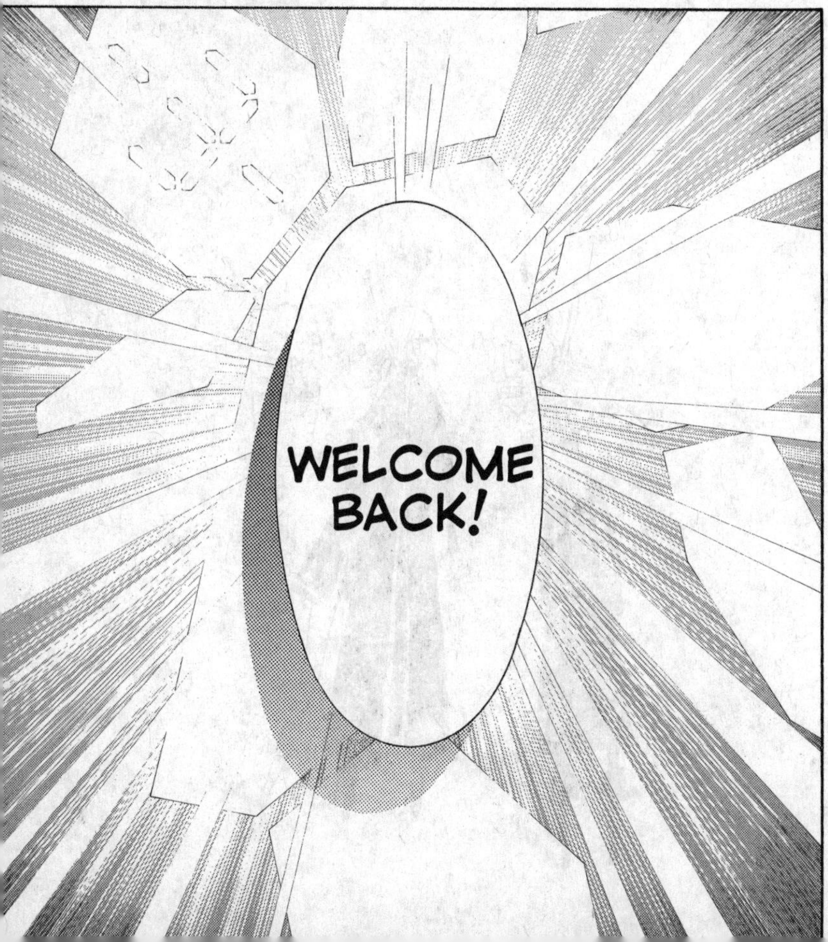
WELCOME BACK!

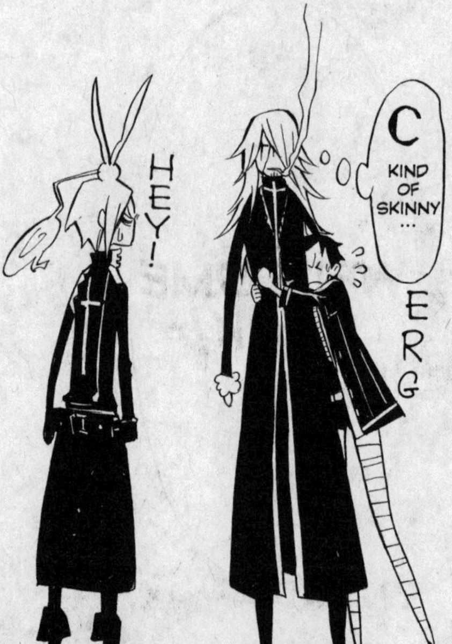
C
KIND OF SKINNY ...
ERG
HEY!

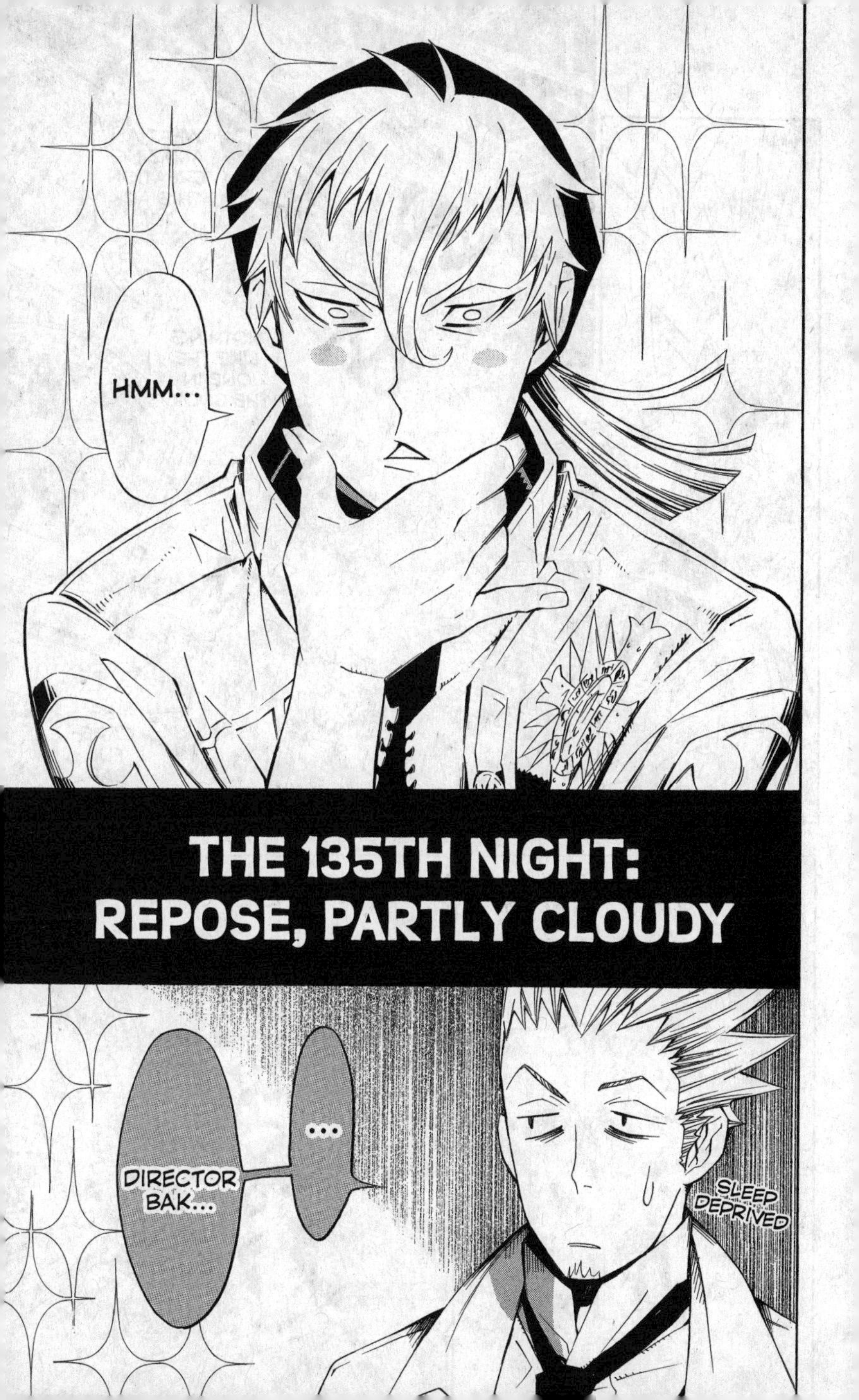
HMM...
THE 135TH NIGHT:
REPOSE, PARTLY CLOUDY
SLEEP DEPRIVED
...
DIRECTOR BAK...

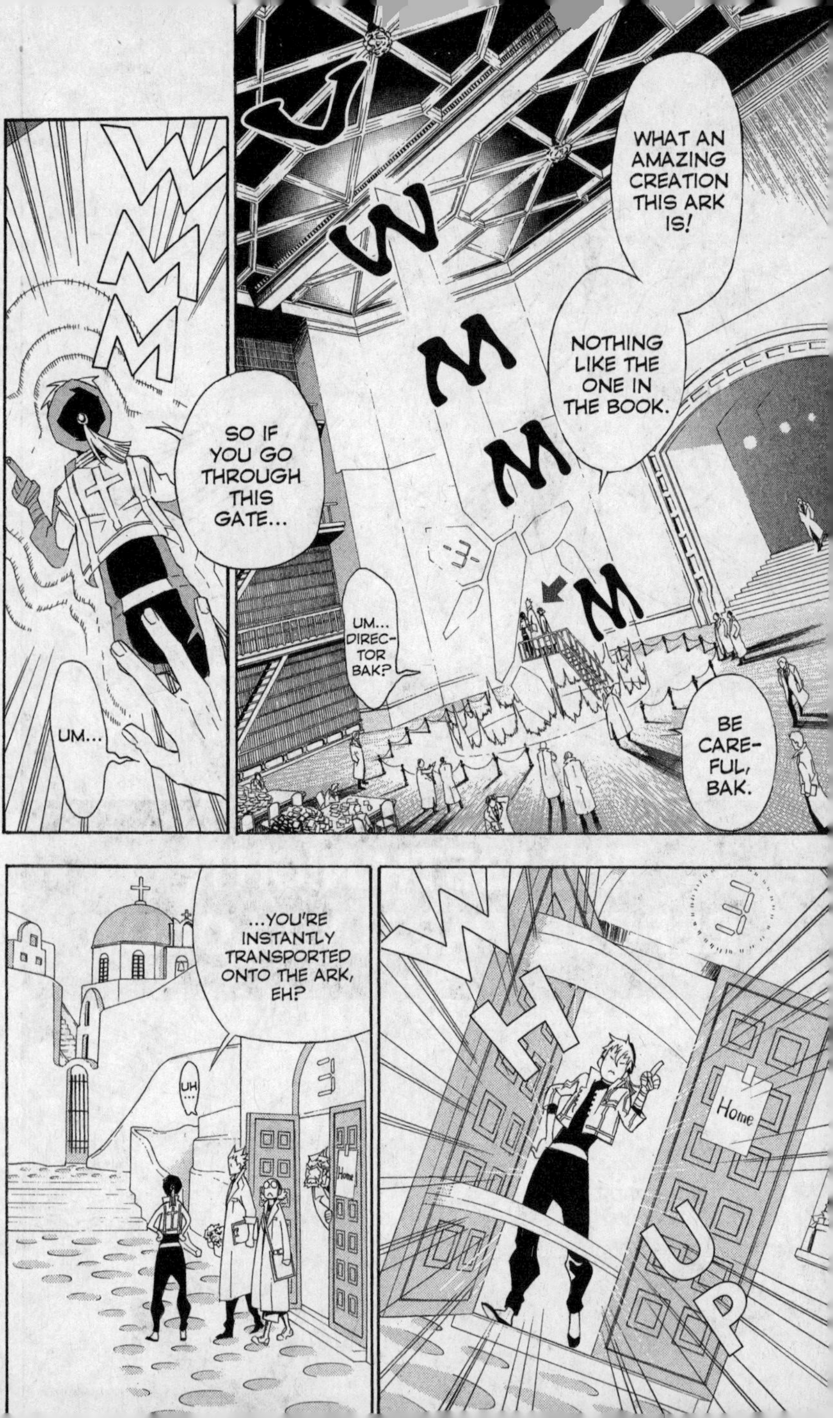

WHAT AN AMAZING CREATION THIS ARK IS!
NOTHING LIKE THE ONE IN THE BOOK.
WMMMM
BE CARE-FUL, BAK.
UM... DIREC-TOR BAK?
WMMM
SO IF YOU GO THROUGH THIS GATE...
UM...
WHUP
Home
...YOU'RE INSTANTLY TRANSPORTED ONTO THE ARK, EH?
UH...
Home

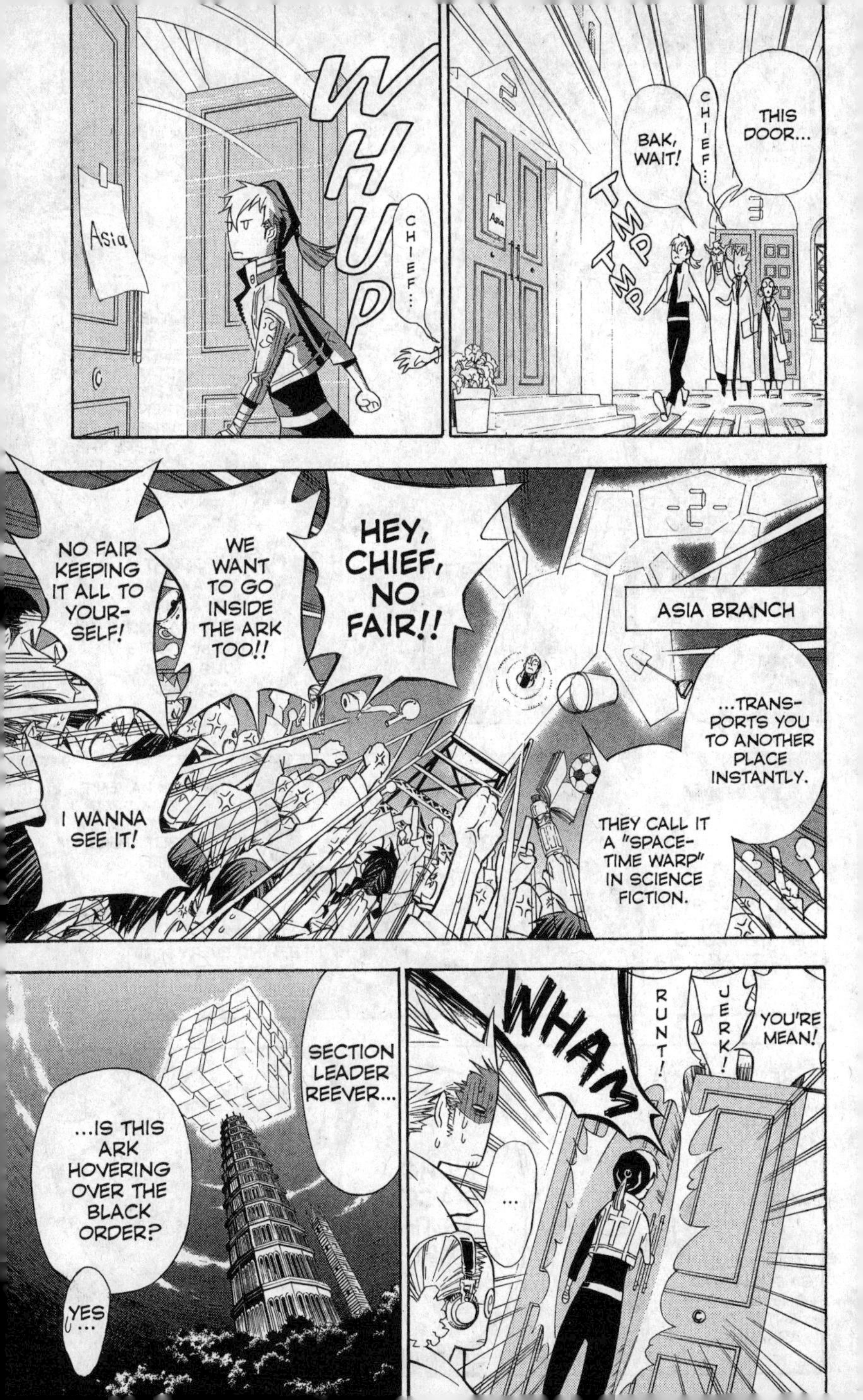
THIS DOOR...
CHIEF...
BAK, WAIT!
TMP TMP TMP
WHUP
CHIEF...
ASIA BRANCH
...TRANSPORTS YOU TO ANOTHER PLACE INSTANTLY.
THEY CALL IT A "SPACE-TIME WARP" IN SCIENCE FICTION.
HEY, CHIEF, NO FAIR!!
WE WANT TO GO INSIDE THE ARK TOO!!
NO FAIR KEEPING IT ALL TO YOURSELF!
I WANNA SEE IT!
YOU'RE MEAN!
JERK!
RUNT!
WHAM
...
SECTION LEADER REEVER...
...IS THIS ARK HOVERING OVER THE BLACK ORDER?
YES...

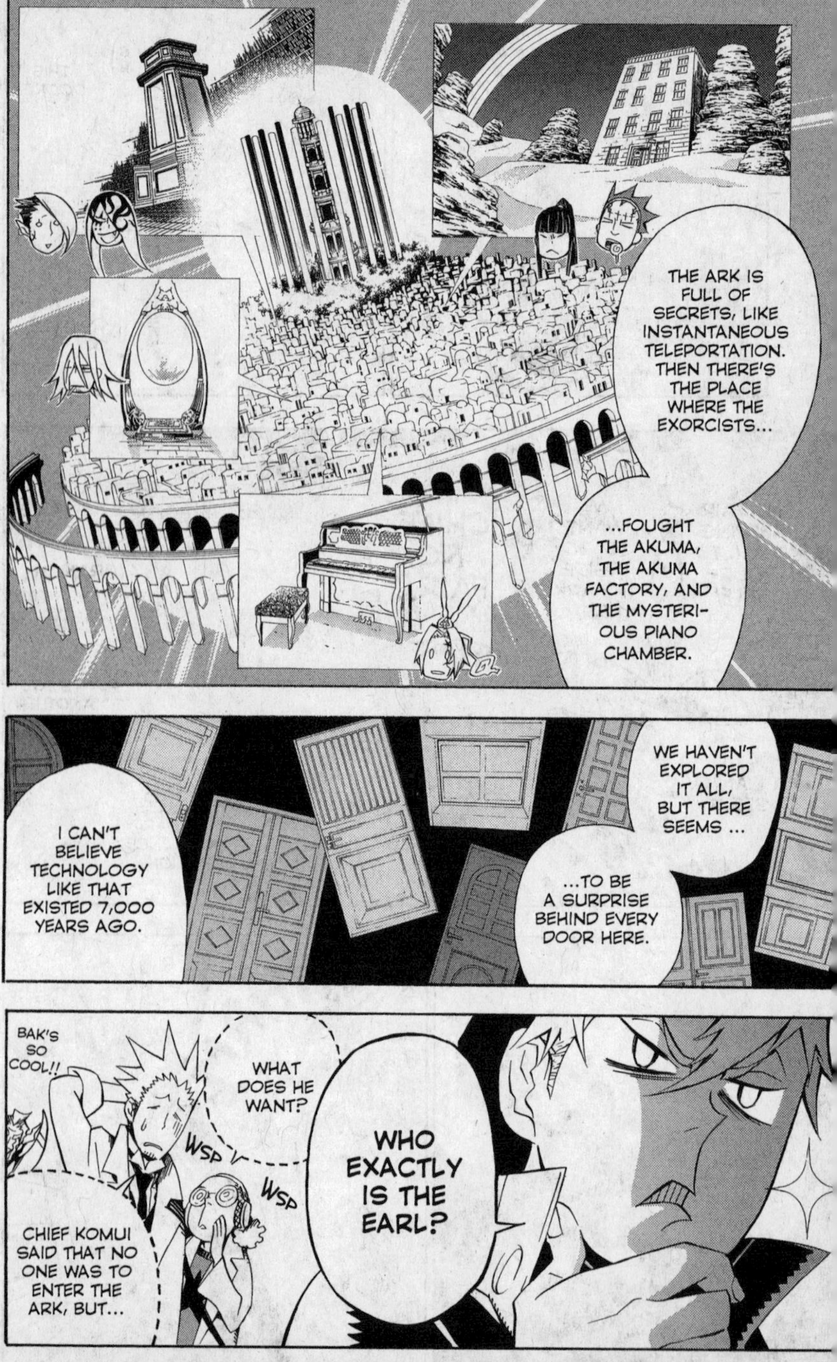
THE ARK IS FULL OF SECRETS, LIKE INSTANTANEOUS TELEPORTATION. THEN THERE'S THE PLACE WHERE THE EXORCISTS...
...FOUGHT THE AKUMA, THE AKUMA FACTORY, AND THE MYSTERIOUS PIANO CHAMBER.
WE HAVEN'T EXPLORED IT ALL, BUT THERE SEEMS ...
...TO BE A SURPRISE BEHIND EVERY DOOR HERE.
I CAN'T BELIEVE TECHNOLOGY LIKE THAT EXISTED 7,000 YEARS AGO.
WHO EXACTLY IS THE EARL?
WHAT DOES HE WANT?
BAK'S SO COOL!!
WSP
WSP
CHIEF KOMUI SAID THAT NO ONE WAS TO ENTER THE ARK, BUT...

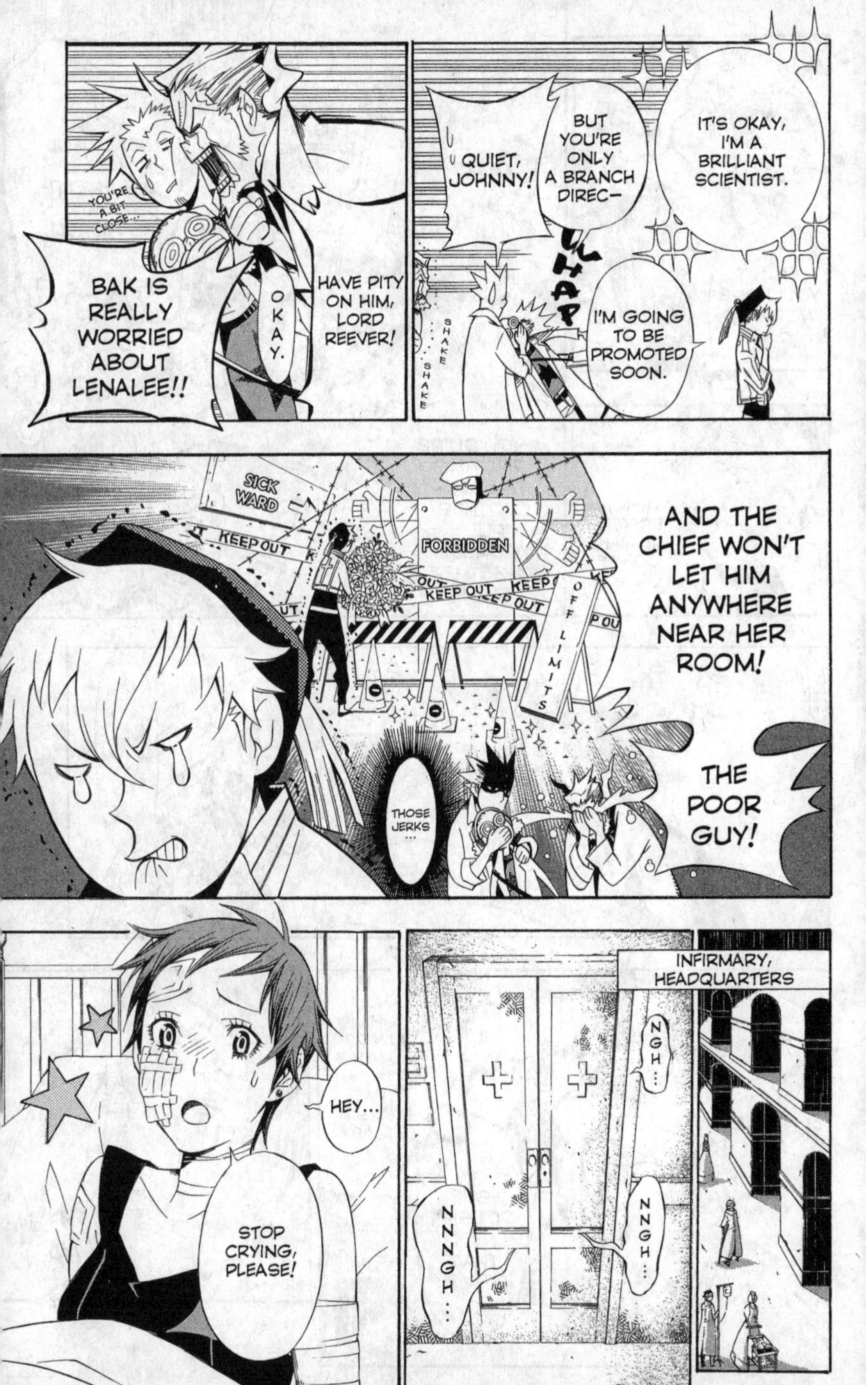

IT'S OKAY, I'M A BRILLIANT SCIENTIST.
BUT YOU'RE ONLY A BRANCH DIREC—
QUIET, JOHNNY!
WHAP
I'M GOING TO BE PROMOTED SOON.
SHAKE SHAKE
HAVE PITY ON HIM, LORD REEVER!
OKAY.
YOU'RE A BIT CLOSE...
BAK IS REALLY WORRIED ABOUT LENALEE!!
AND THE CHIEF WON'T LET HIM ANYWHERE NEAR HER ROOM!
SICK WARD
KEEP OUT
FORBIDDEN
OFF LIMITS
THE POOR GUY!
THOSE JERKS...
INFIRMARY, HEADQUARTERS
NGH...
NNGH...
NNNGH...
HEY...
STOP CRYING, PLEASE!

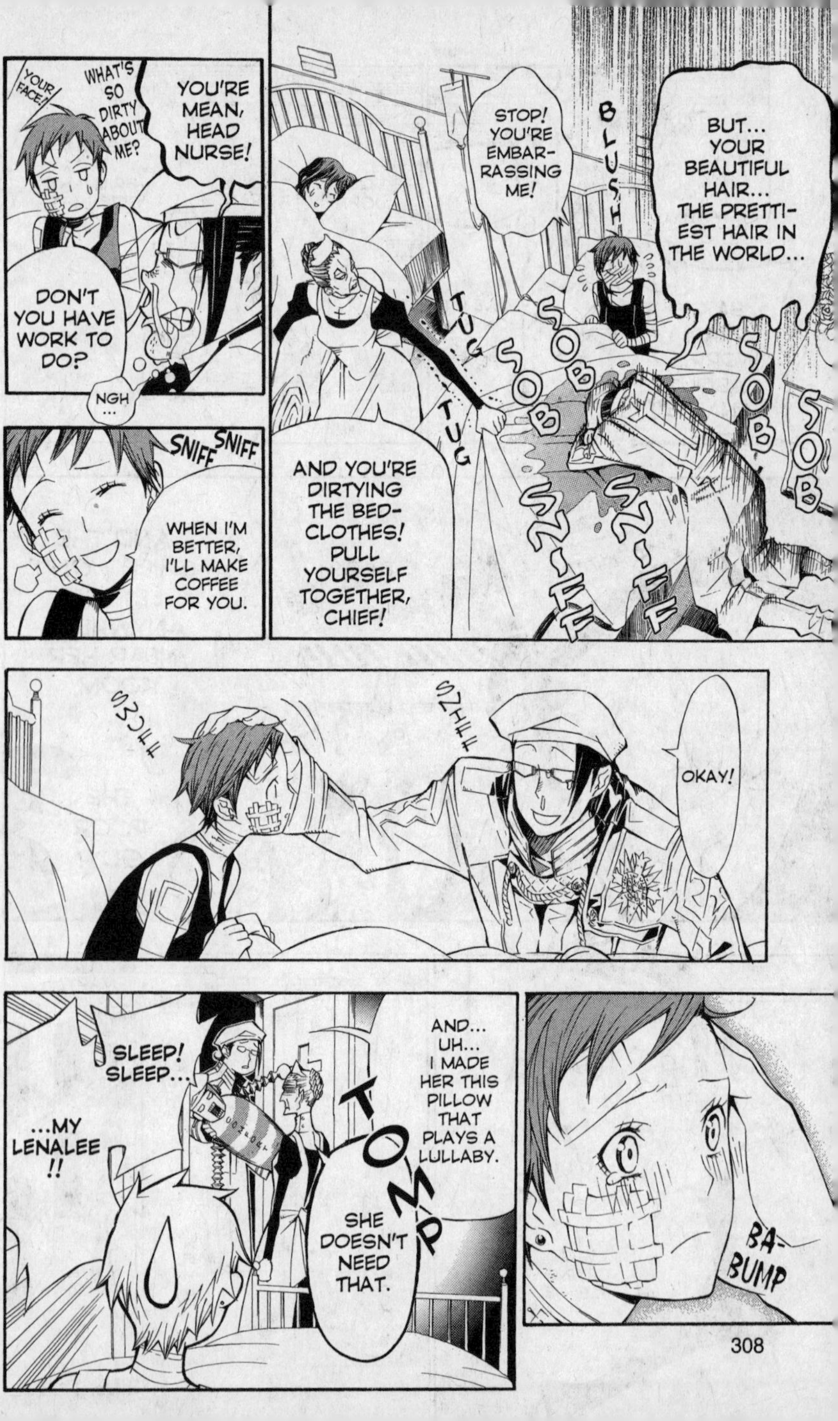
BUT... YOUR BEAUTIFUL HAIR... THE PRETTIEST HAIR IN THE WORLD...
SOB SOB
BLUSH
STOP! YOU'RE EMBARRASSING ME!
SOB SOB
SNIFF SNIFF
TUG TUG
AND YOU'RE DIRTYING THE BED-CLOTHES! PULL YOURSELF TOGETHER, CHIEF!
YOU'RE MEAN, HEAD NURSE!
WHAT'S SO DIRTY ABOUT ME?
YOUR FACE!
DON'T YOU HAVE WORK TO DO?
NGH...
SNIFF SNIFF
WHEN I'M BETTER, I'LL MAKE COFFEE FOR YOU.
OKAY!
SNIFF
SNIFF
BA-BUMP
AND... UH... I MADE HER THIS PILLOW THAT PLAYS A LULLABY.
TOMP
SLEEP! SLEEP...
...MY LENALEE !!
SHE DOESN'T NEED THAT.

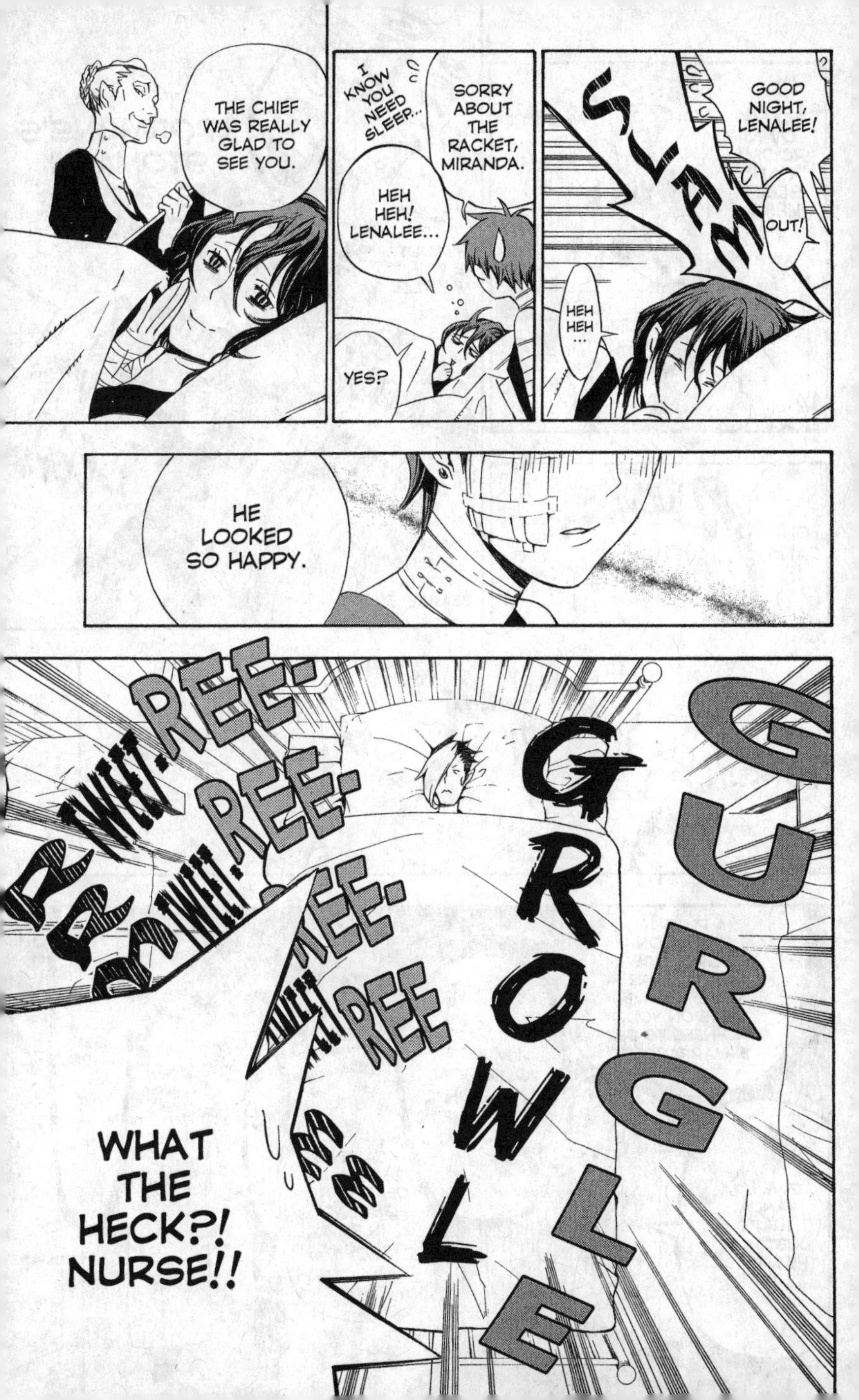

GOOD NIGHT, LENALEE!
SLAM
OUT!
HEH HEH ...
SORRY ABOUT THE RACKET, MIRANDA.
I KNOW YOU NEED SLEEP...
HEH HEH! LENALEE...
YES?
THE CHIEF WAS REALLY GLAD TO SEE YOU.
HE LOOKED SO HAPPY.
GURGLE
GROWL
TWEET REE-
TWEET REE-
REE-
TWEET REE
WHAT THE HECK?! NURSE!!

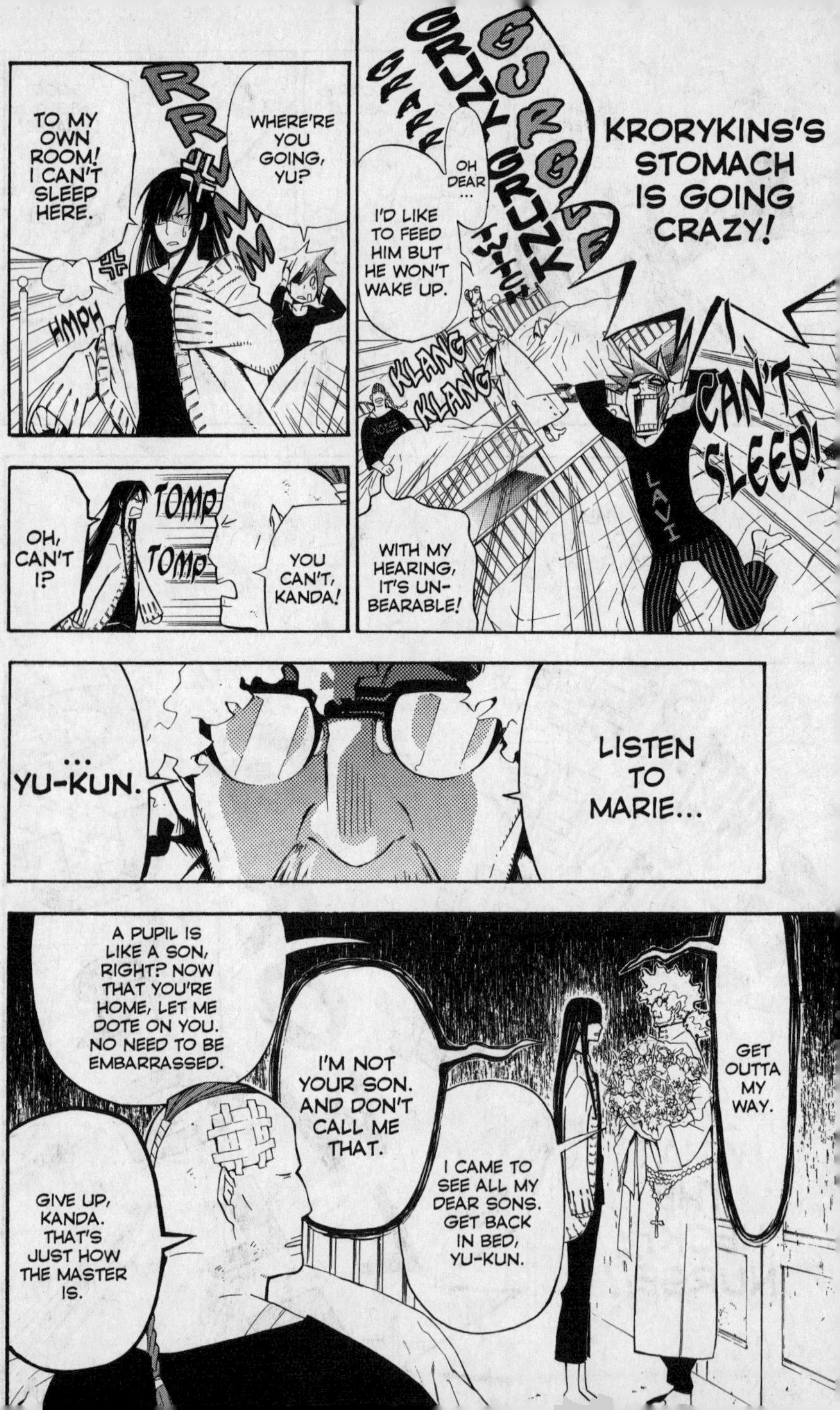
GURGLE
KRORYKINS'S STOMACH IS GOING CRAZY!
GRUNK GRUNK
OH DEAR ...
I'D LIKE TO FEED HIM BUT HE WON'T WAKE UP.
TWITCH
CAN'T SLEEP!
KLANG KLANG
WITH MY HEARING, IT'S UN-BEARABLE!
WHERE'RE YOU GOING, YU?
RRUMM
TO MY OWN ROOM! I CAN'T SLEEP HERE.
HMPH
TOMP TOMP
YOU CAN'T, KANDA!
OH, CAN'T I?
LISTEN TO MARIE...
... YU-KUN.
GET OUTTA MY WAY.
I CAME TO SEE ALL MY DEAR SONS. GET BACK IN BED, YU-KUN.
I'M NOT YOUR SON. AND DON'T CALL ME THAT.
A PUPIL IS LIKE A SON, RIGHT? NOW THAT YOU'RE HOME, LET ME DOTE ON YOU. NO NEED TO BE EMBARRASSED.
GIVE UP, KANDA. THAT'S JUST HOW THE MASTER IS.

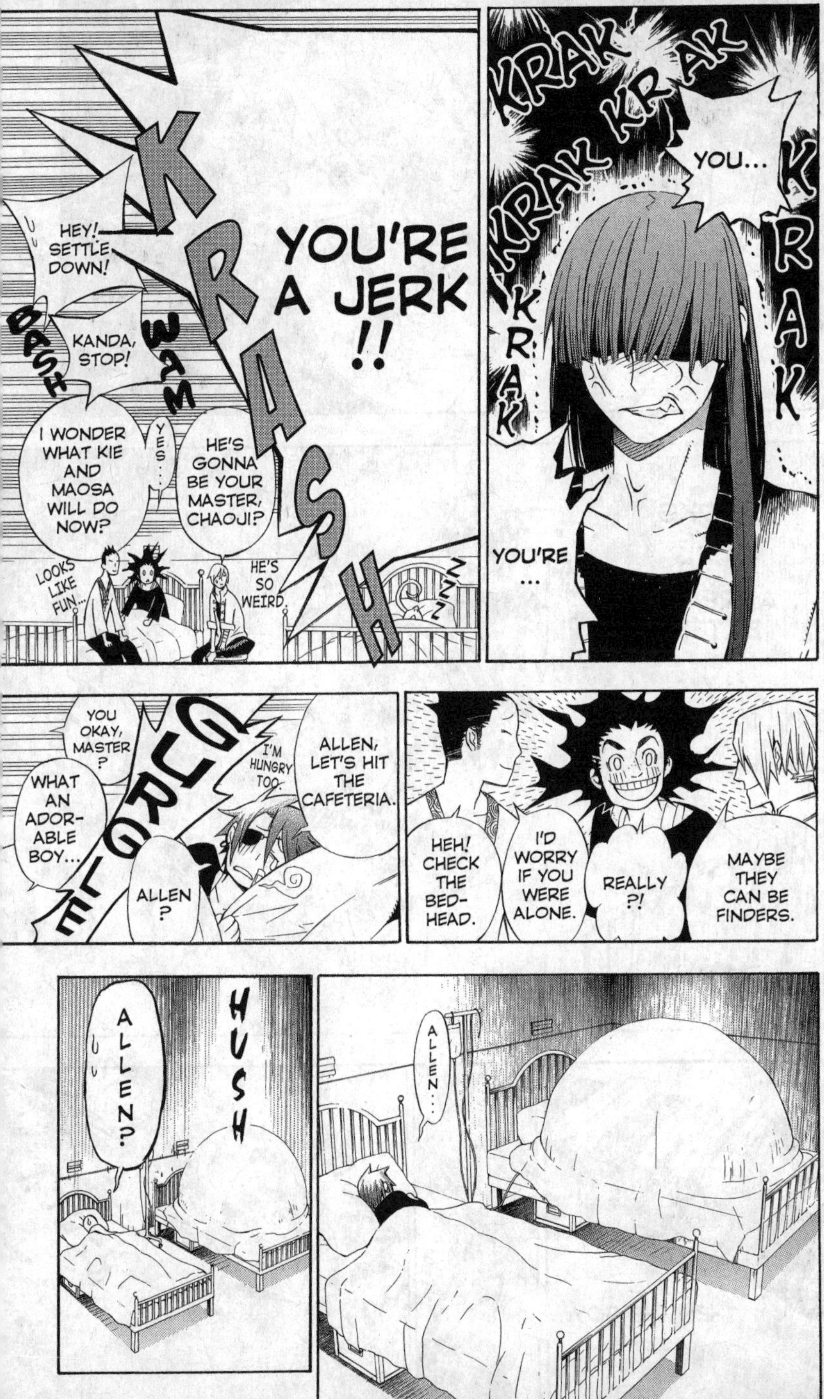
KRAK KRAK KRAK KRAK
YOU...
KRAK
KRAK
KRAK
YOU'RE ...
YOU'RE A JERK!!
KRASH
HEY! SETTLE DOWN!
KANDA, STOP!
BASH
WAM
HE'S GONNA BE YOUR MASTER, CHAOJI?
YES...
I WONDER WHAT KIE AND MAOSA WILL DO NOW?
HE'S SO WEIRD.
LOOKS LIKE FUN...
ZZZ
MAYBE THEY CAN BE FINDERS.
REALLY?!
I'D WORRY IF YOU WERE ALONE.
HEH! CHECK THE BED-HEAD.
ALLEN, LET'S HIT THE CAFETERIA.
I'M HUNGRY TOO.
YOU OKAY, MASTER?
WHAT AN ADOR-ABLE BOY...
GURGLE
ALLEN?
ALLEN...
HUSH
ALLEN?

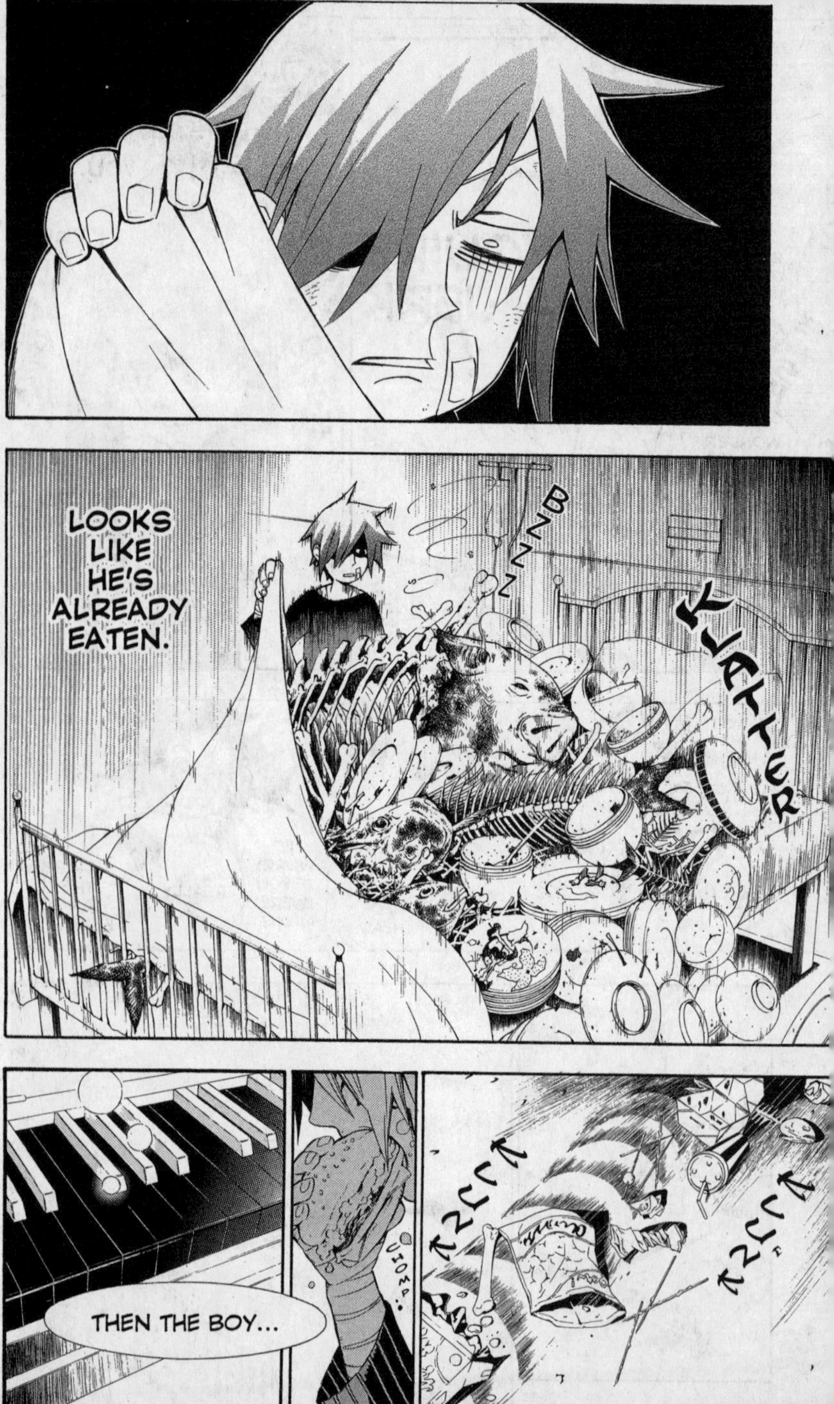
KLATTER
BZZZZ
LOOKS LIKE HE'S ALREADY EATEN.
CHOMP
THEN THE BOY...

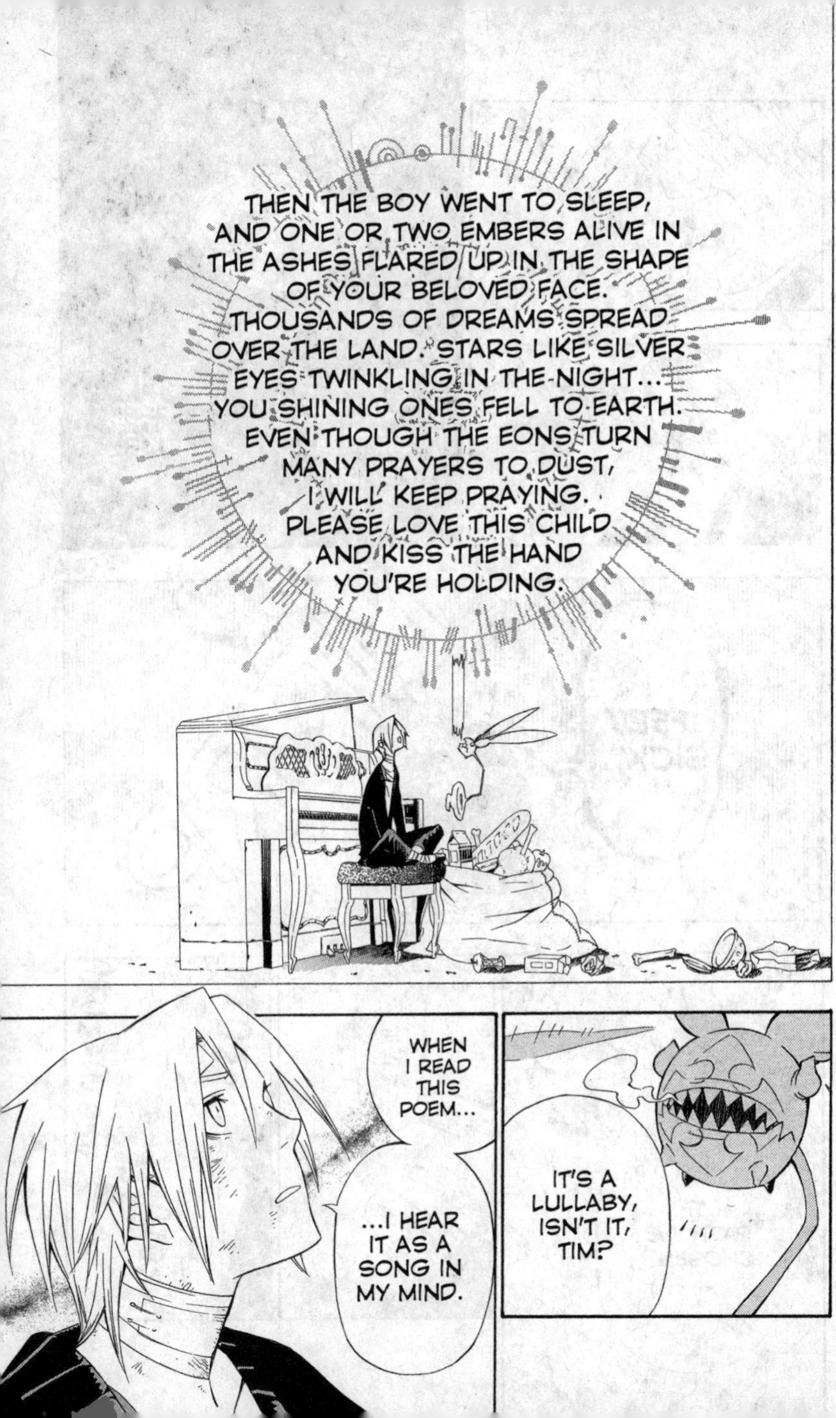
THEN THE BOY WENT TO SLEEP, AND ONE OR TWO EMBERS ALIVE IN THE ASHES FLARED UP IN THE SHAPE OF YOUR BELOVED FACE. THOUSANDS OF DREAMS SPREAD OVER THE LAND. STARS LIKE SILVER EYES TWINKLING IN THE NIGHT... YOU SHINING ONES FELL TO EARTH. EVEN THOUGH THE EONS TURN MANY PRAYERS TO DUST, I WILL KEEP PRAYING. PLEASE LOVE THIS CHILD AND KISS THE HAND YOU'RE HOLDING.
IT'S A LULLABY, ISN'T IT, TIM?
WHEN I READ THIS POEM...
...I HEAR IT AS A SONG IN MY MIND.

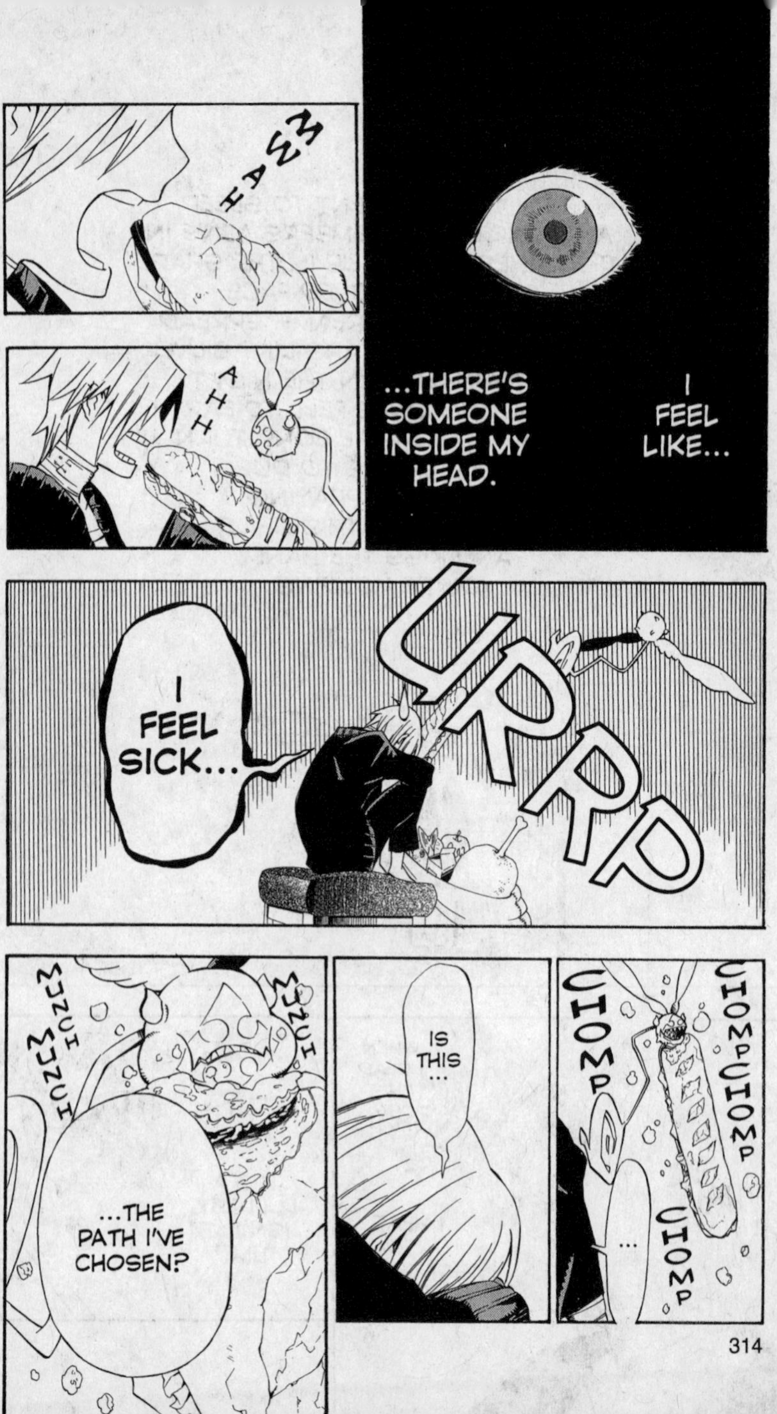
I FEEL LIKE...
...THERE'S SOMEONE INSIDE MY HEAD.
MWAH
AHH
URRP
I FEEL SICK...
CHOMP
CHOMPCHOMP
CHOMP
...
IS THIS ...
MUNCH
MUNCH MUNCH
...THE PATH I'VE CHOSEN?

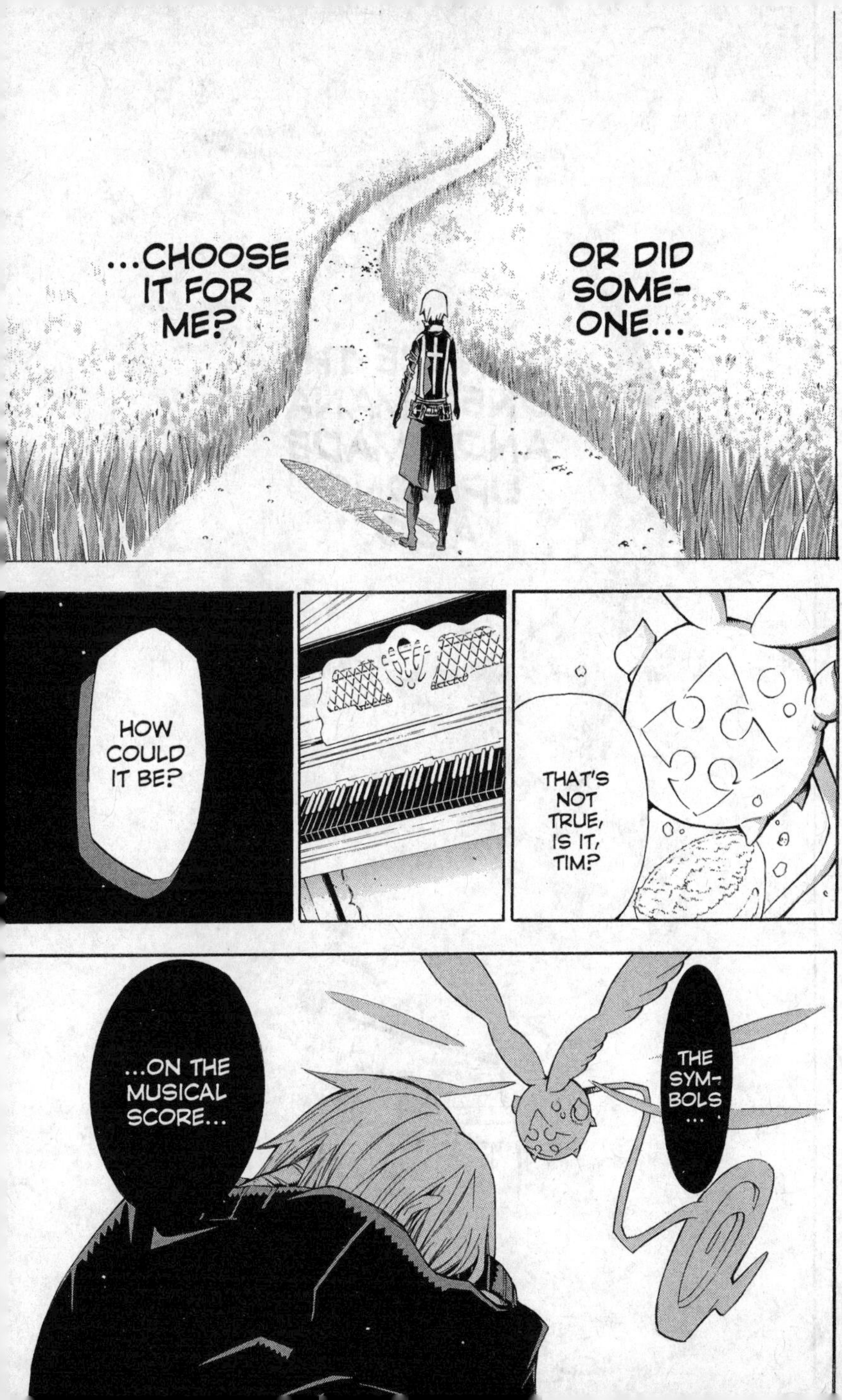
OR DID SOME-ONE...
...CHOOSE IT FOR ME?
THAT'S NOT TRUE, IS IT, TIM?
HOW COULD IT BE?
THE SYM-BOLS...
...ON THE MUSICAL SCORE...

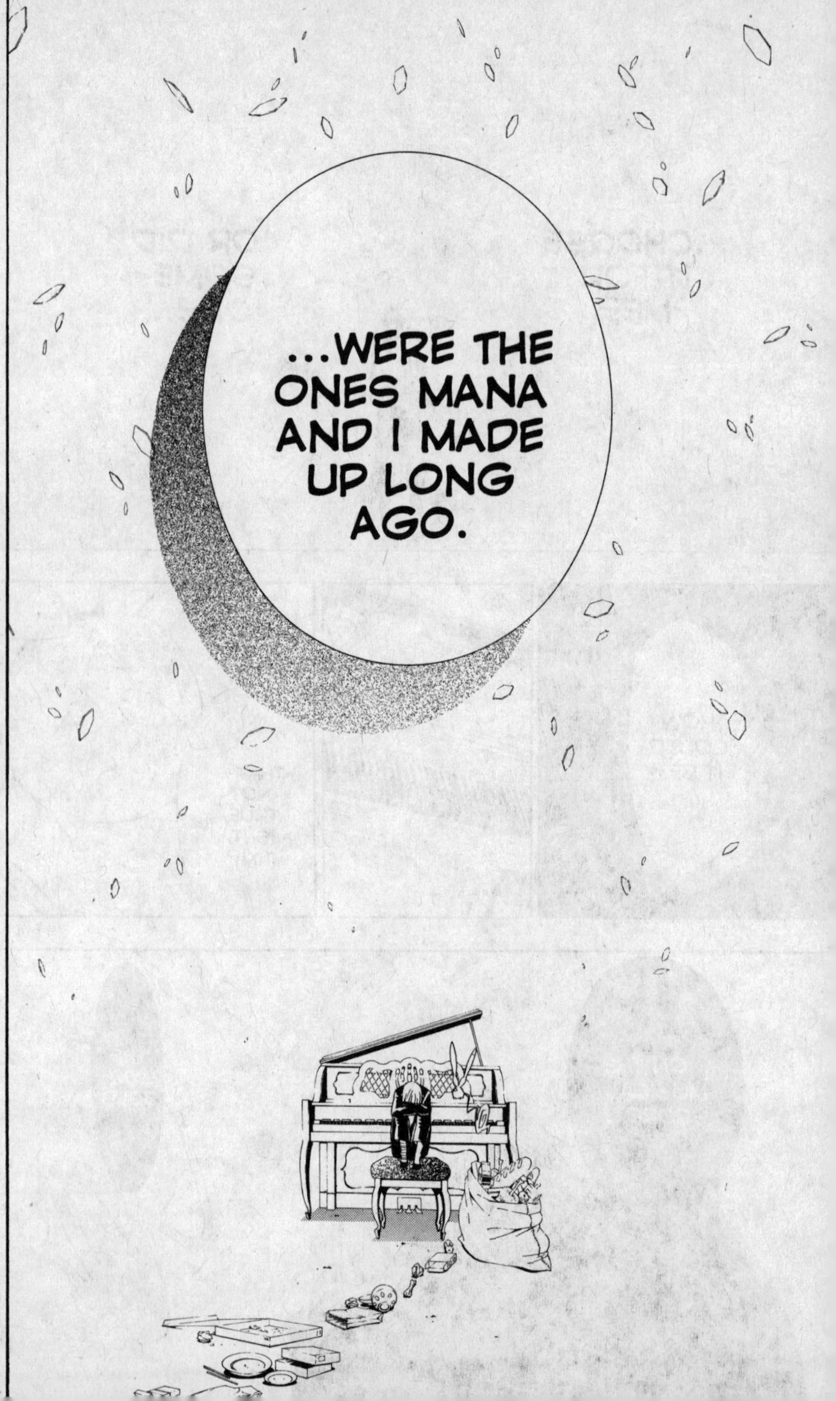
...WERE THE ONES MANA AND I MADE UP LONG AGO.

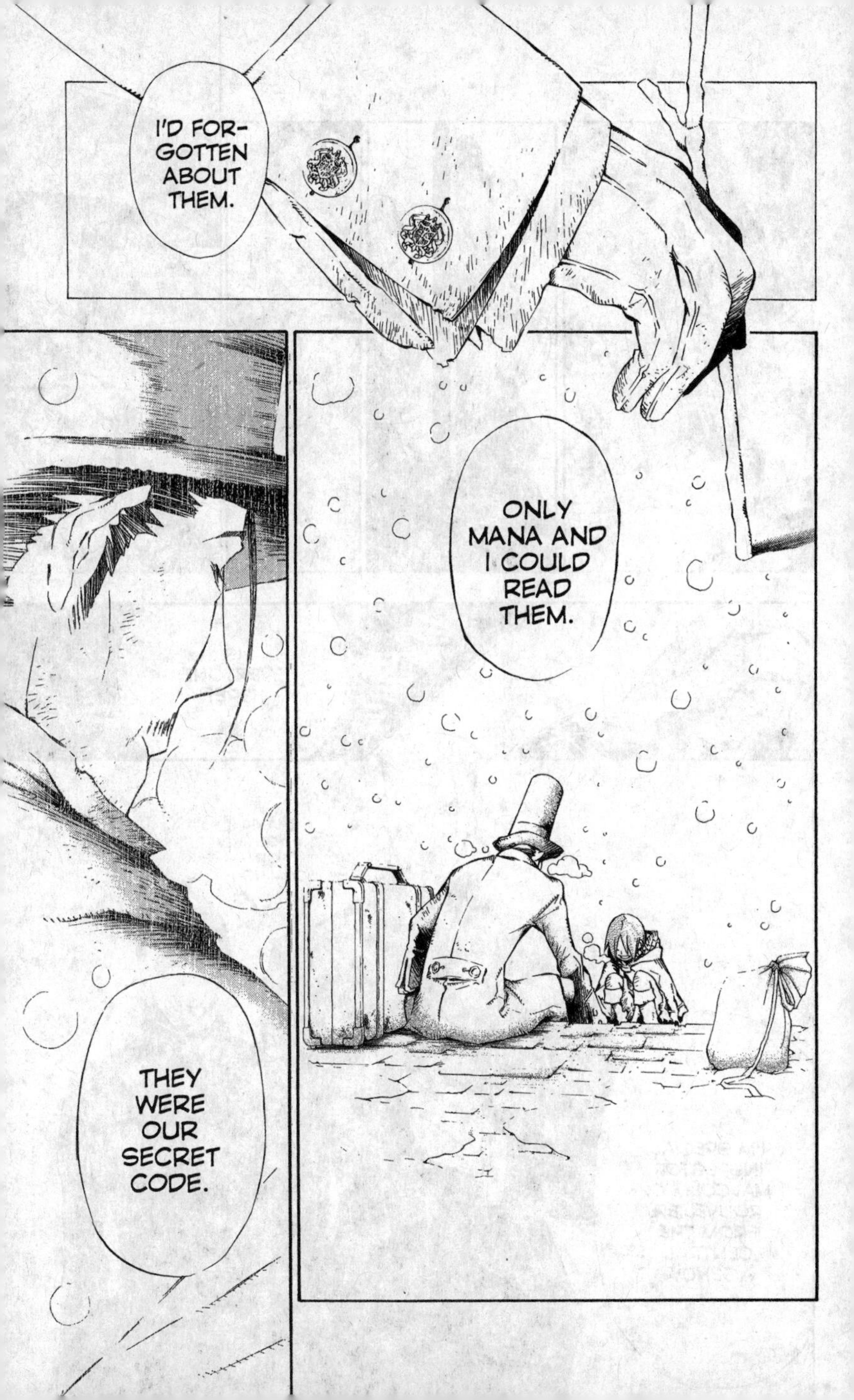
I'D FOR-GOTTEN ABOUT THEM.
ONLY MANA AND I COULD READ THEM.
THEY WERE OUR SECRET CODE.

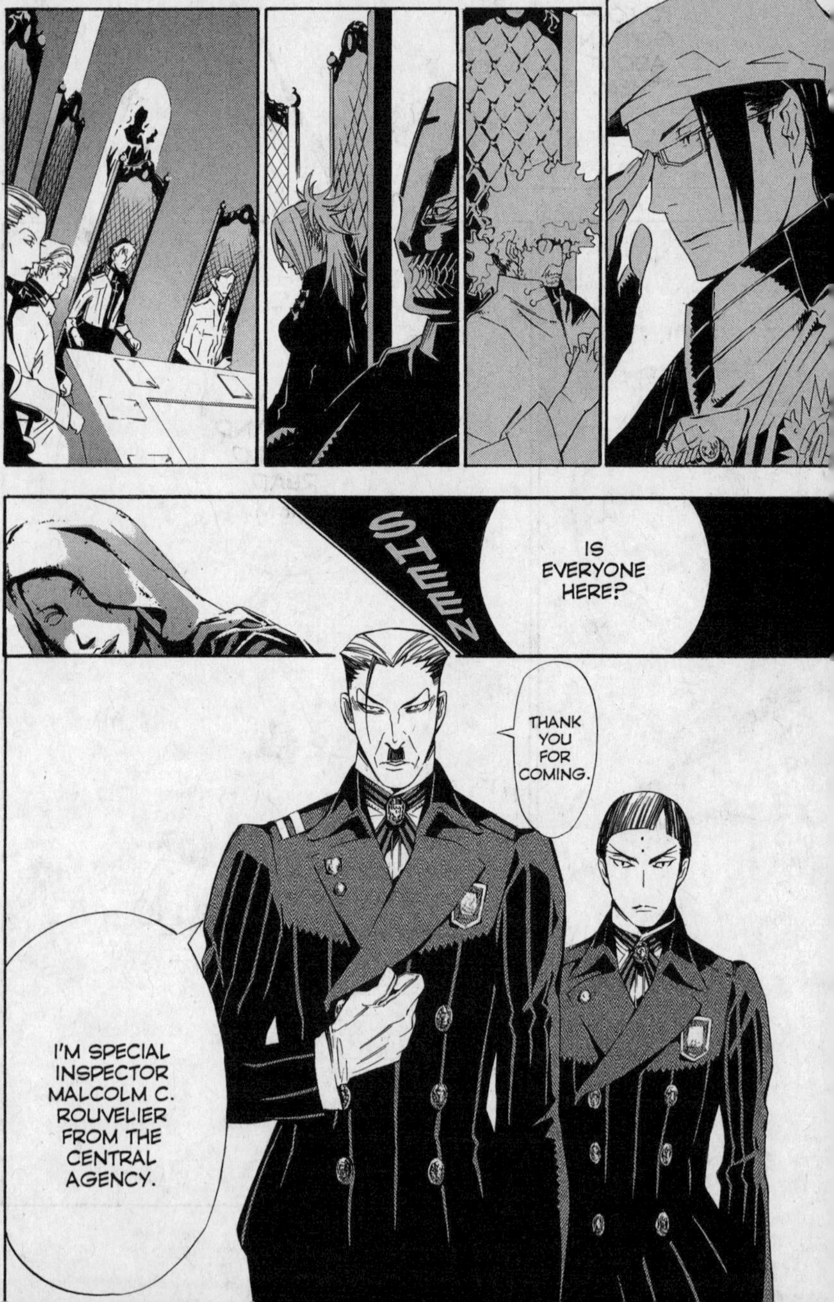
IS EVERYONE HERE?
SHEEN
THANK YOU FOR COMING.
I'M SPECIAL INSPECTOR MALCOLM C. ROUVELIER FROM THE CENTRAL AGENCY.

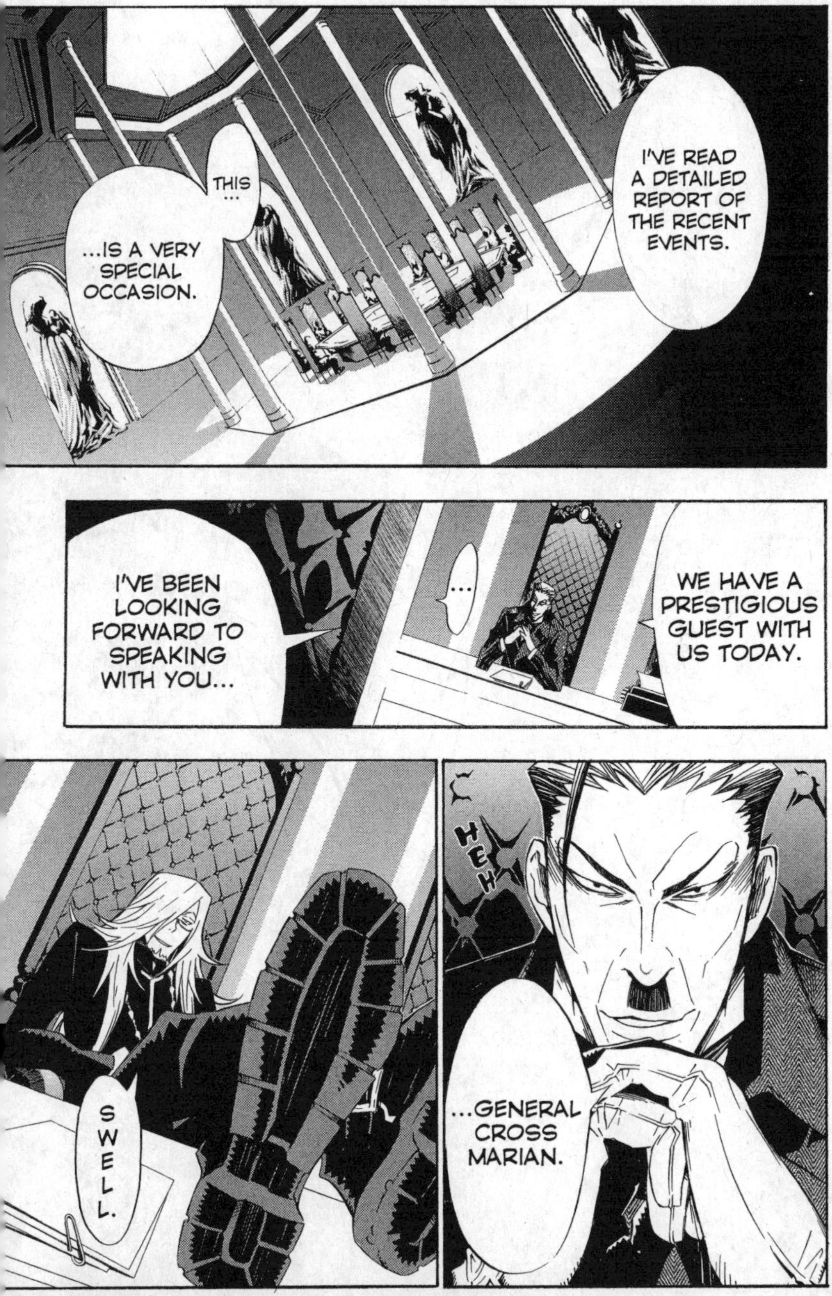
I'VE READ A DETAILED REPORT OF THE RECENT EVENTS.
THIS ...
...IS A VERY SPECIAL OCCASION.
WE HAVE A PRESTIGIOUS GUEST WITH US TODAY.
...
I'VE BEEN LOOKING FORWARD TO SPEAKING WITH YOU...
HEH
...GENERAL CROSS MARIAN.
SWELL.

TIM LEARNED HOW TO EAT.

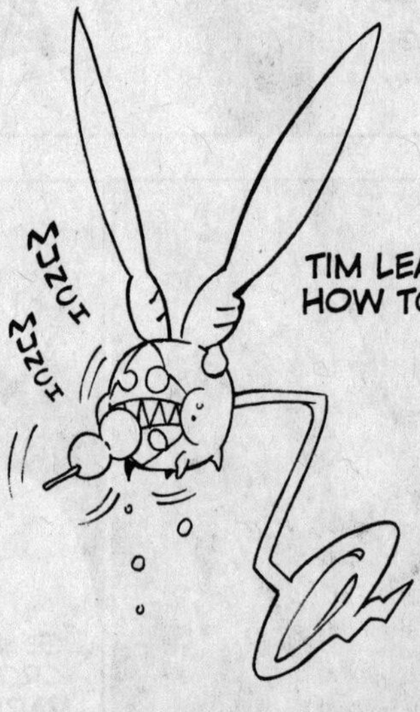
MUNCH
MUNCH

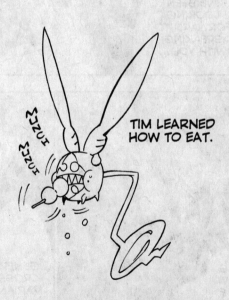

THE 136TH NIGHT: SHEEP AND DOG

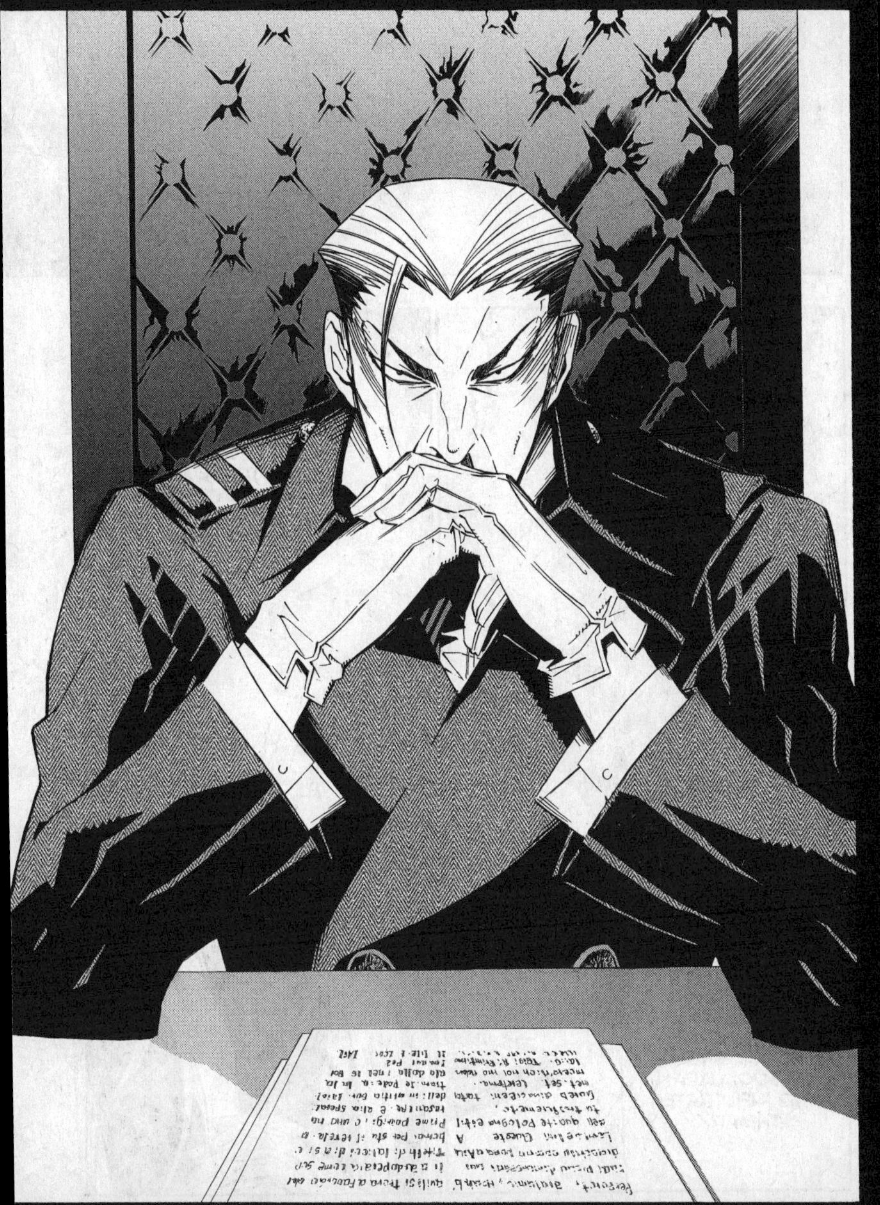

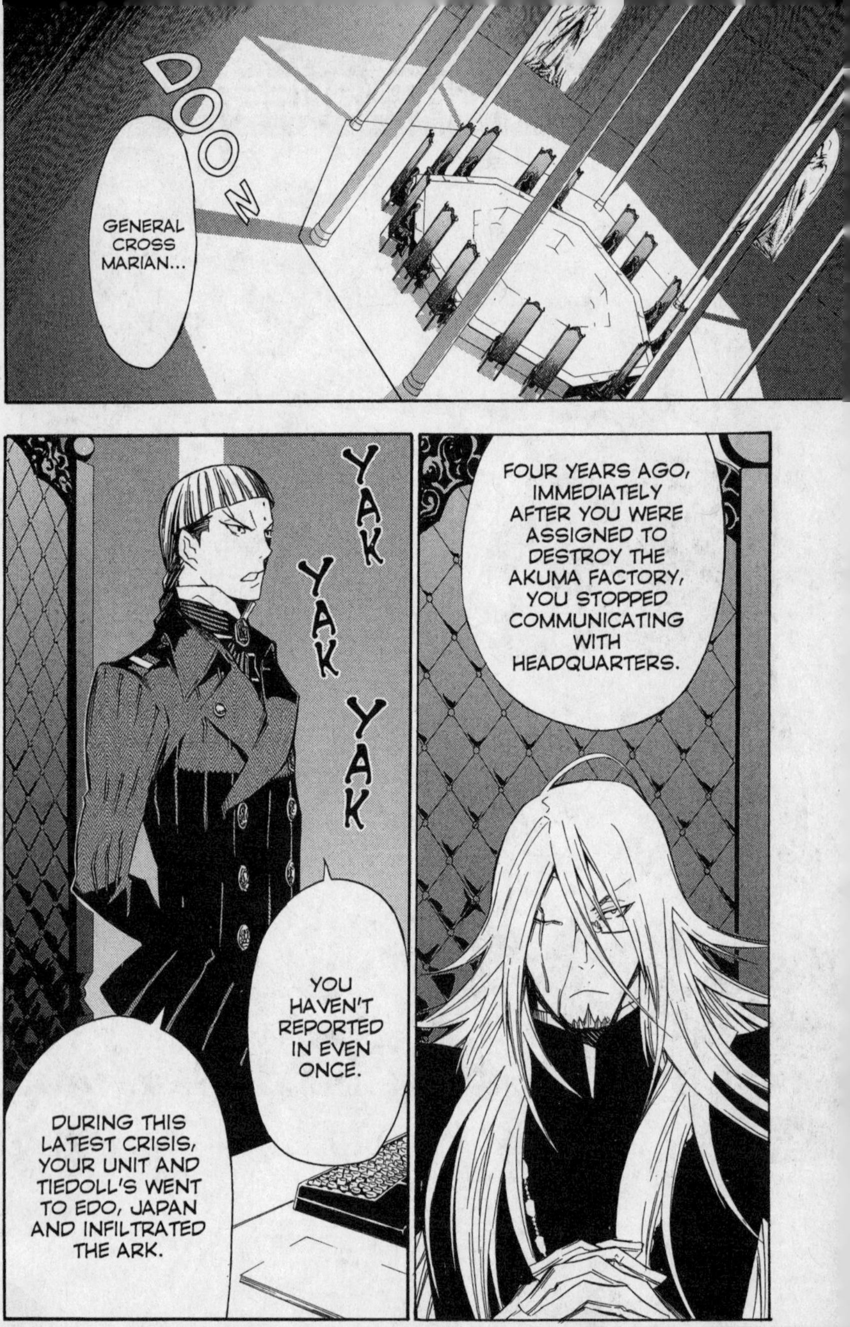
DOOON
GENERAL CROSS MARIAN...
FOUR YEARS AGO, IMMEDIATELY AFTER YOU WERE ASSIGNED TO DESTROY THE AKUMA FACTORY, YOU STOPPED COMMUNICATING WITH HEADQUARTERS.
YAK YAK YAK
YOU HAVEN'T REPORTED IN EVEN ONCE.
DURING THIS LATEST CRISIS, YOUR UNIT AND TIEDOLL'S WENT TO EDO, JAPAN AND INFILTRATED THE ARK.

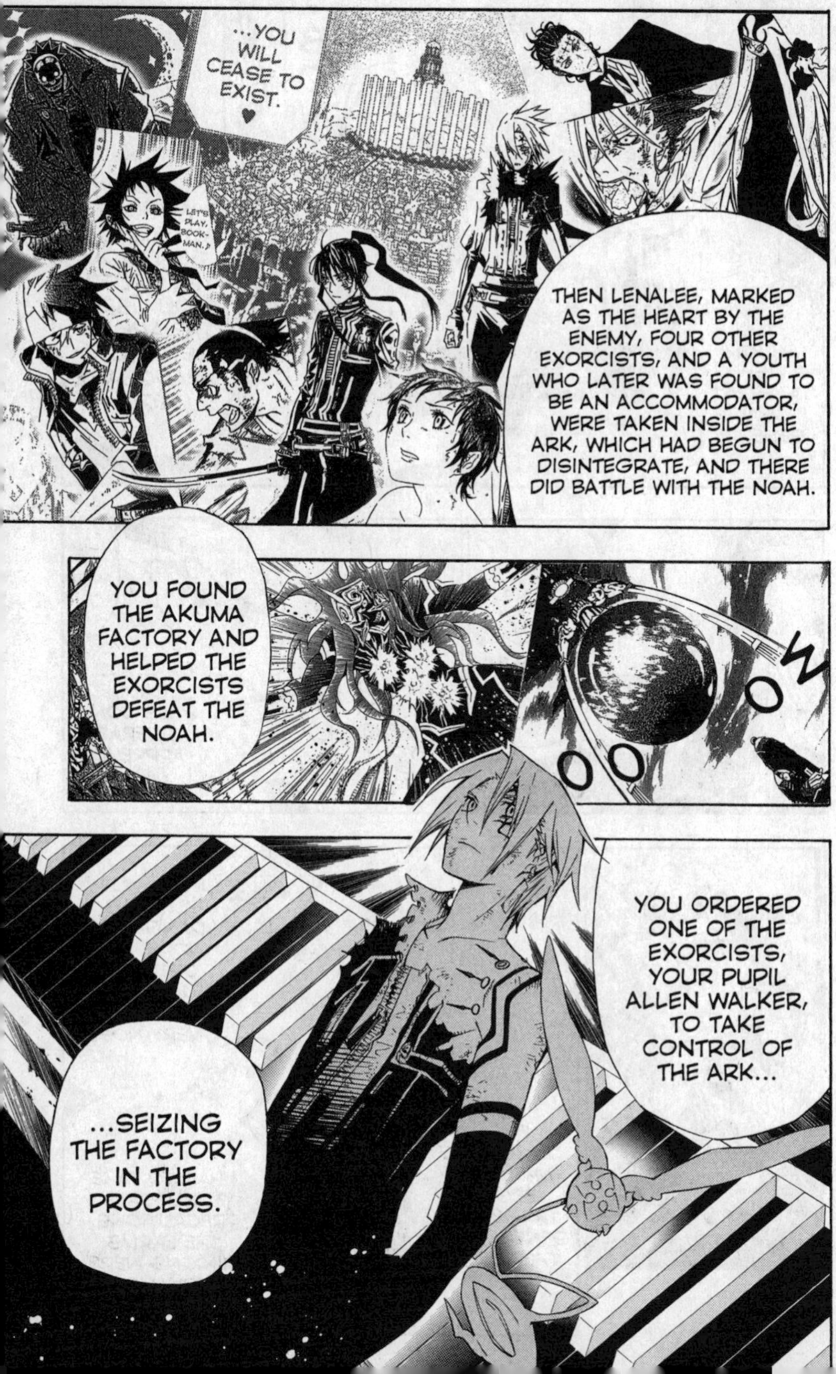
...YOU WILL CEASE TO EXIST. ♥
LET'S PLAY, BOOKMAN. ♪
THEN LENALEE, MARKED AS THE HEART BY THE ENEMY, FOUR OTHER EXORCISTS, AND A YOUTH WHO LATER WAS FOUND TO BE AN ACCOMMODATOR, WERE TAKEN INSIDE THE ARK, WHICH HAD BEGUN TO DISINTEGRATE, AND THERE DID BATTLE WITH THE NOAH.
YOU FOUND THE AKUMA FACTORY AND HELPED THE EXORCISTS DEFEAT THE NOAH.
OOOOW
YOU ORDERED ONE OF THE EXORCISTS, YOUR PUPIL ALLEN WALKER, TO TAKE CONTROL OF THE ARK...
...SEIZING THE FACTORY IN THE PROCESS.

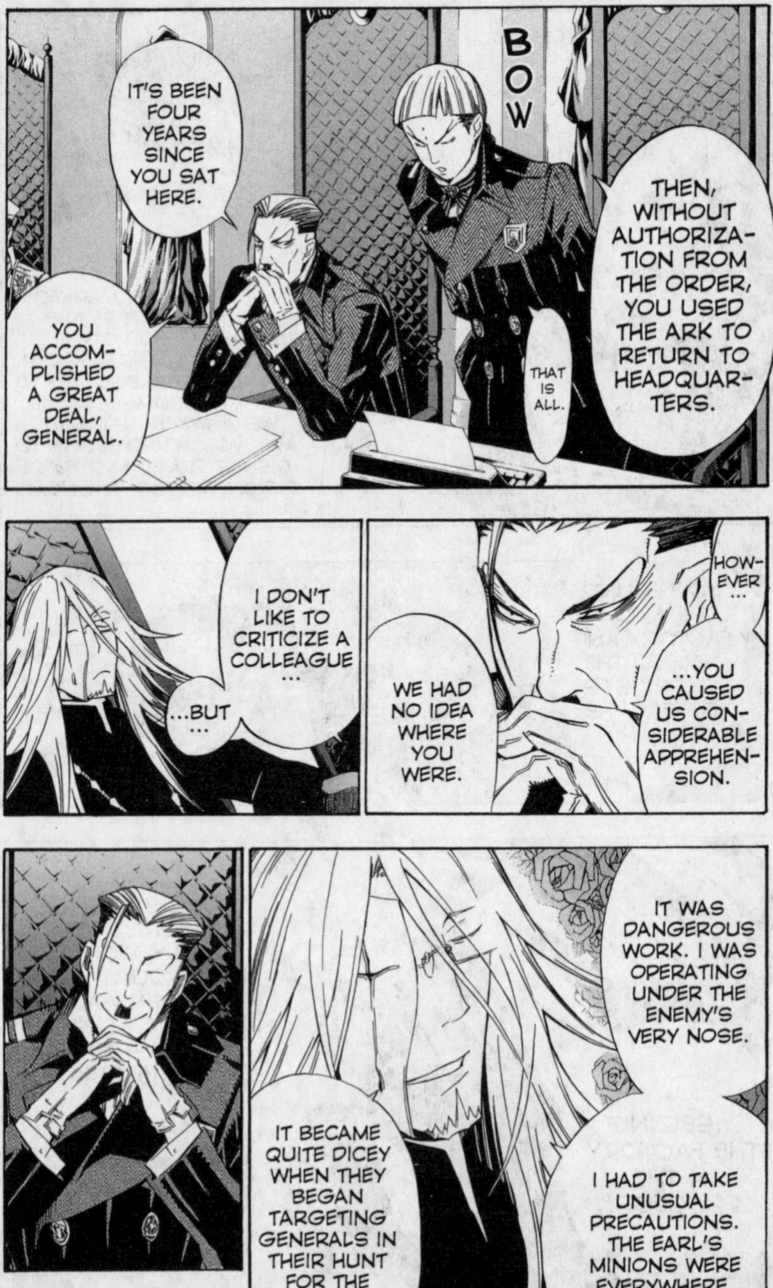
BOW
THEN, WITHOUT AUTHORIZATION FROM THE ORDER, YOU USED THE ARK TO RETURN TO HEADQUARTERS.
IT'S BEEN FOUR YEARS SINCE YOU SAT HERE.
THAT IS ALL.
YOU ACCOMPLISHED A GREAT DEAL, GENERAL.
HOWEVER...
...YOU CAUSED US CONSIDERABLE APPREHENSION.
WE HAD NO IDEA WHERE YOU WERE.
I DON'T LIKE TO CRITICIZE A COLLEAGUE...
...BUT...
IT WAS DANGEROUS WORK. I WAS OPERATING UNDER THE ENEMY'S VERY NOSE.
I HAD TO TAKE UNUSUAL PRECAUTIONS. THE EARL'S MINIONS WERE EVERYWHERE.
IT BECAME QUITE DICEY WHEN THEY BEGAN TARGETING GENERALS IN THEIR HUNT FOR THE HEART.

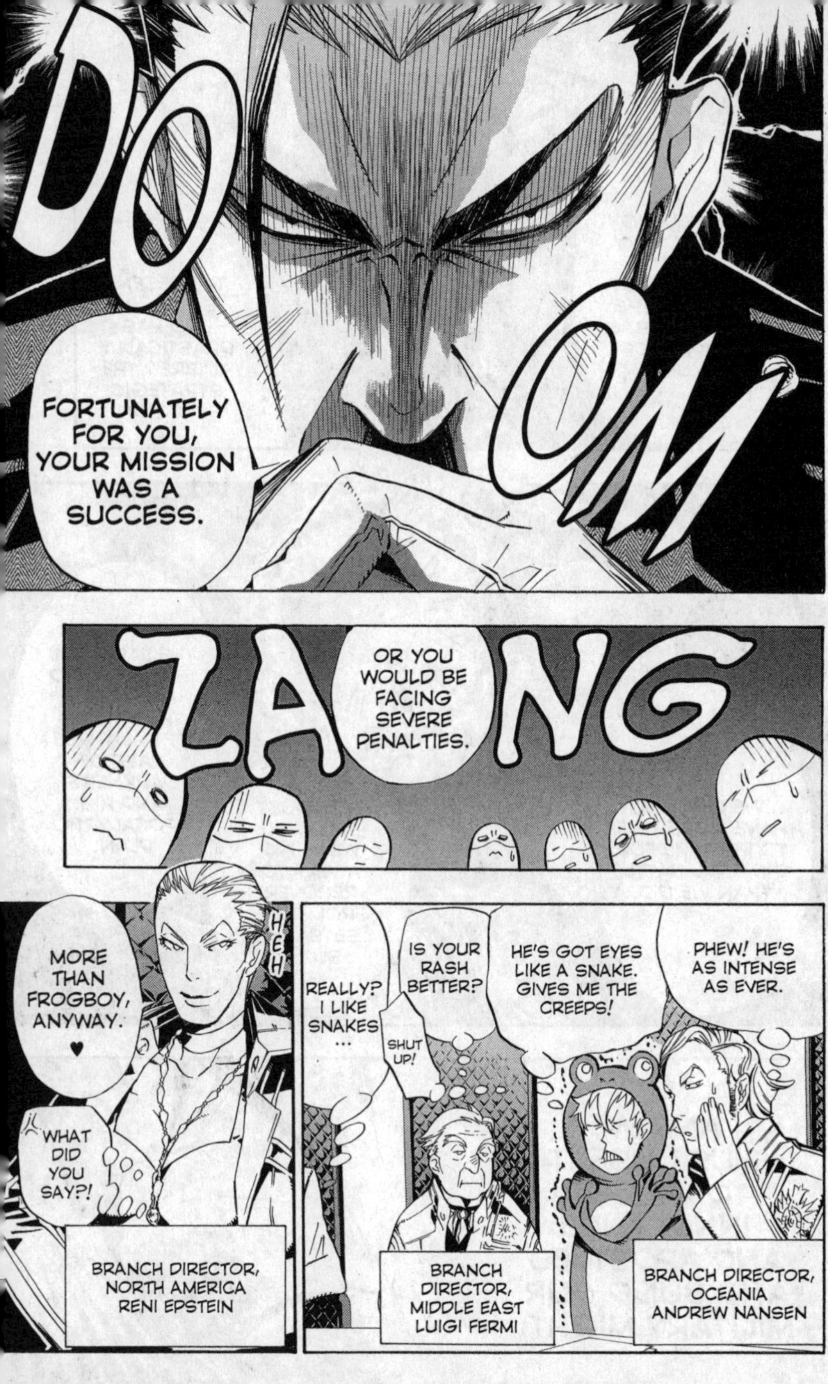
DOOM
FORTUNATELY FOR YOU, YOUR MISSION WAS A SUCCESS.
ZANG
OR YOU WOULD BE FACING SEVERE PENALTIES.
PHEW! HE'S AS INTENSE AS EVER.
HE'S GOT EYES LIKE A SNAKE. GIVES ME THE CREEPS!
IS YOUR RASH BETTER?
SHUT UP!
REALLY? I LIKE SNAKES...
BRANCH DIRECTOR, OCEANIA ANDREW NANSEN
BRANCH DIRECTOR, MIDDLE EAST LUIGI FERMI
HEH
MORE THAN FROGBOY, ANYWAY. ♥
WHAT DID YOU SAY?!
BRANCH DIRECTOR, NORTH AMERICA RENI EPSTEIN

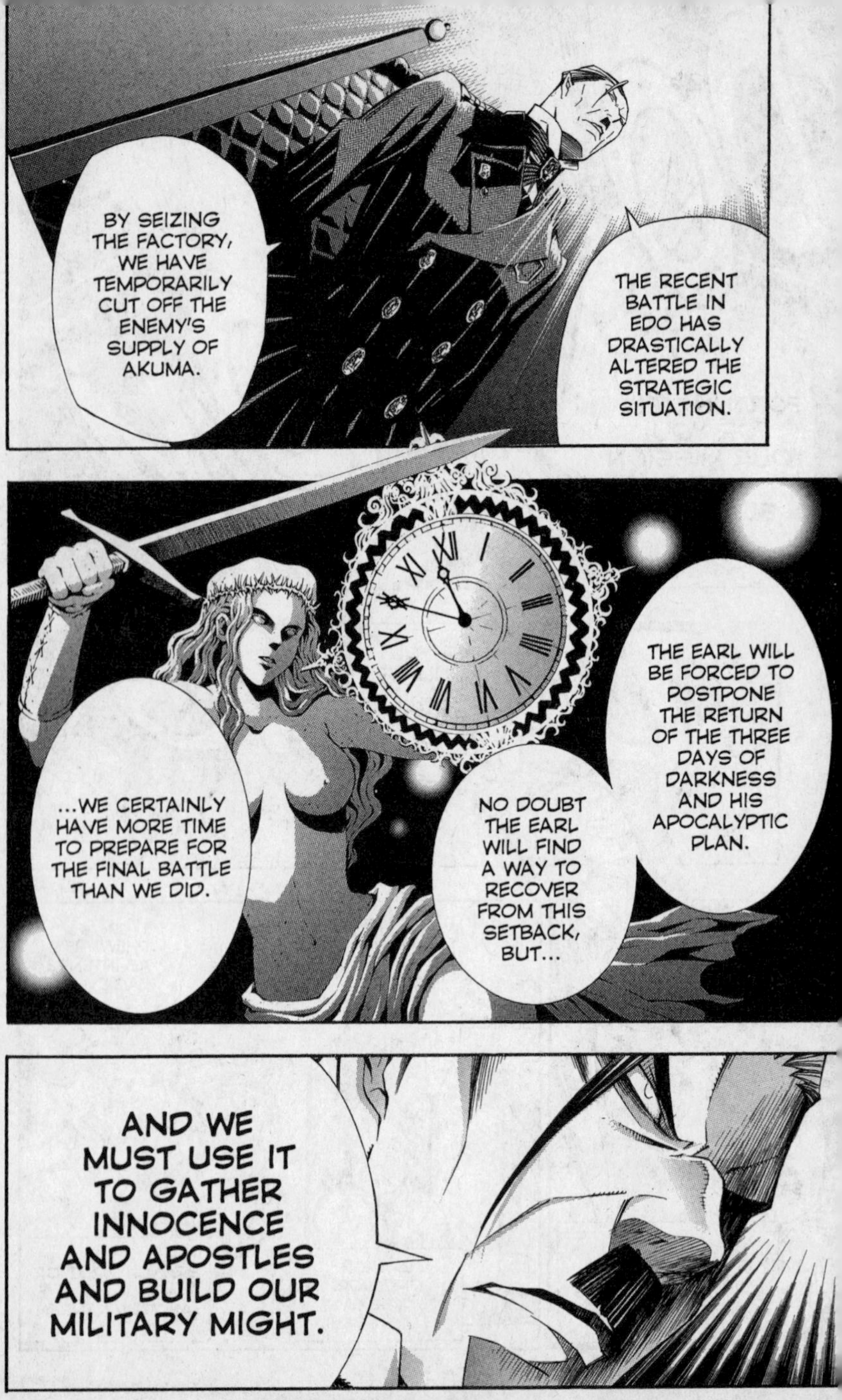
THE RECENT BATTLE IN EDO HAS DRASTICALLY ALTERED THE STRATEGIC SITUATION.
BY SEIZING THE FACTORY, WE HAVE TEMPORARILY CUT OFF THE ENEMY'S SUPPLY OF AKUMA.
THE EARL WILL BE FORCED TO POSTPONE THE RETURN OF THE THREE DAYS OF DARKNESS AND HIS APOCALYPTIC PLAN.
NO DOUBT THE EARL WILL FIND A WAY TO RECOVER FROM THIS SETBACK, BUT...
...WE CERTAINLY HAVE MORE TIME TO PREPARE FOR THE FINAL BATTLE THAN WE DID.
AND WE MUST USE IT TO GATHER INNOCENCE AND APOSTLES AND BUILD OUR MILITARY MIGHT.

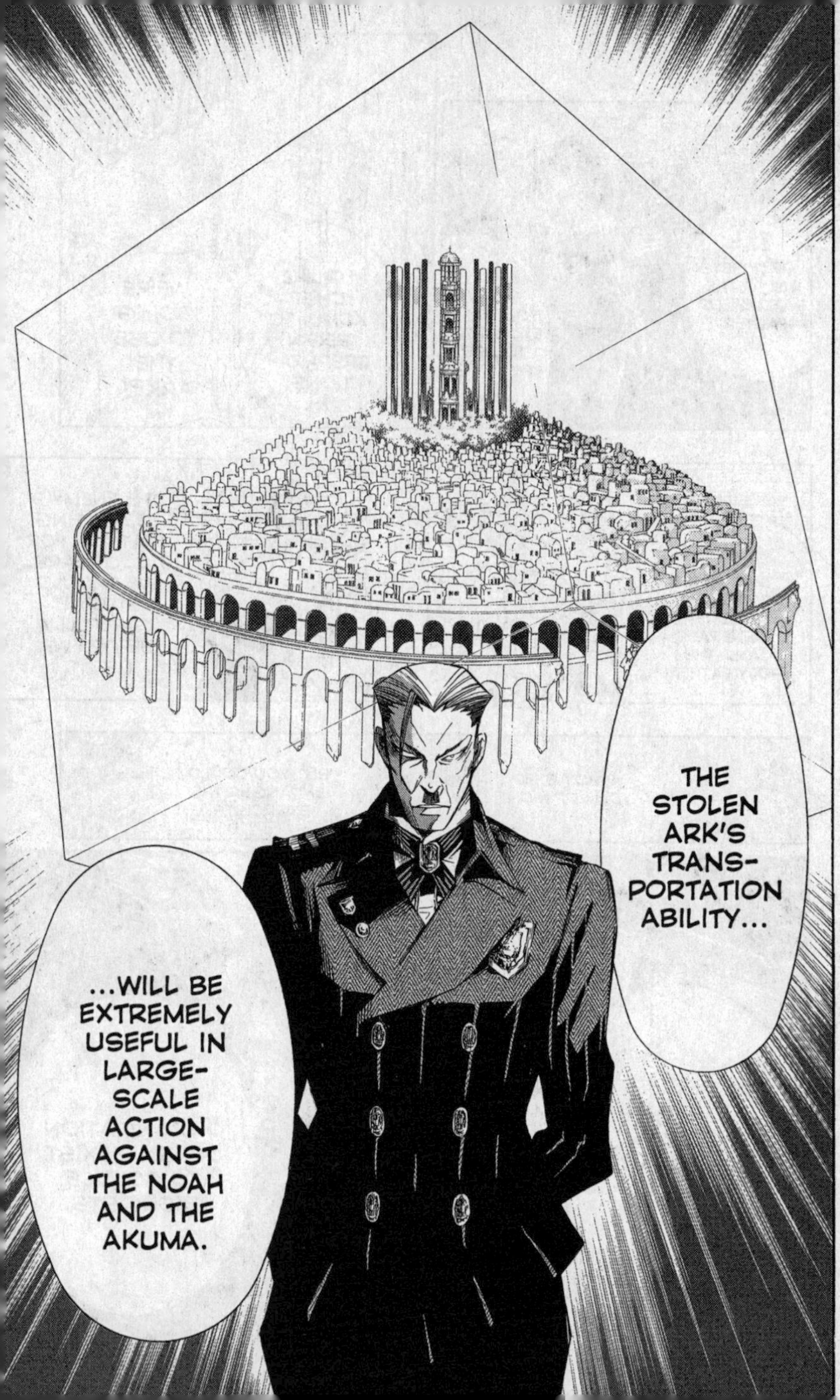
THE STOLEN ARK'S TRANS-PORTATION ABILITY...
...WILL BE EXTREMELY USEFUL IN LARGE-SCALE ACTION AGAINST THE NOAH AND THE AKUMA.

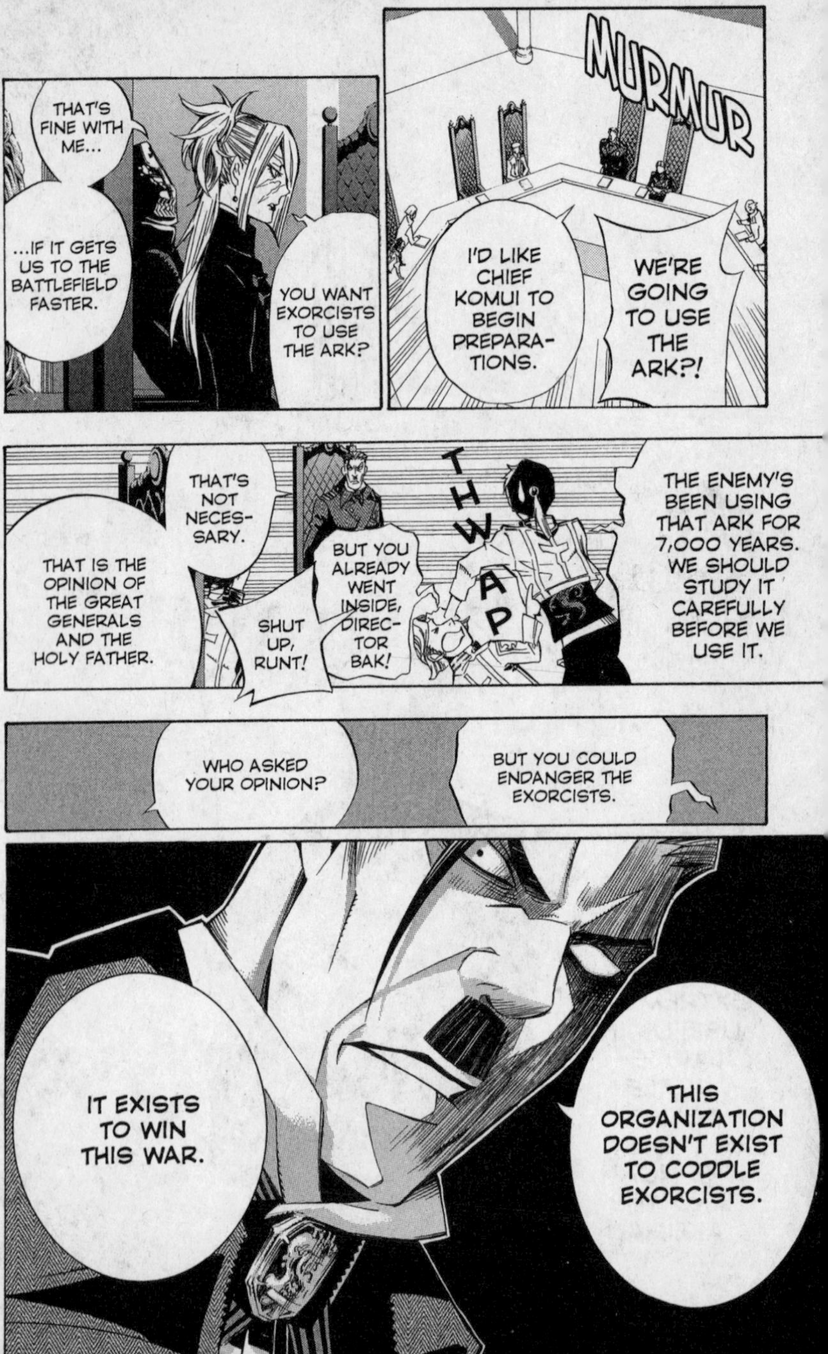
MURMUR
WE'RE GOING TO USE THE ARK?!
I'D LIKE CHIEF KOMUI TO BEGIN PREPARATIONS.
YOU WANT EXORCISTS TO USE THE ARK?
THAT'S FINE WITH ME...
...IF IT GETS US TO THE BATTLEFIELD FASTER.
THE ENEMY'S BEEN USING THAT ARK FOR 7,000 YEARS. WE SHOULD STUDY IT CAREFULLY BEFORE WE USE IT.
THWAP
BUT YOU ALREADY WENT INSIDE, DIRECTOR BAK!
SHUT UP, RUNT!
THAT'S NOT NECESSARY.
THAT IS THE OPINION OF THE GREAT GENERALS AND THE HOLY FATHER.
BUT YOU COULD ENDANGER THE EXORCISTS.
WHO ASKED YOUR OPINION?
THIS ORGANIZATION DOESN'T EXIST TO CODDLE EXORCISTS.
IT EXISTS TO WIN THIS WAR.

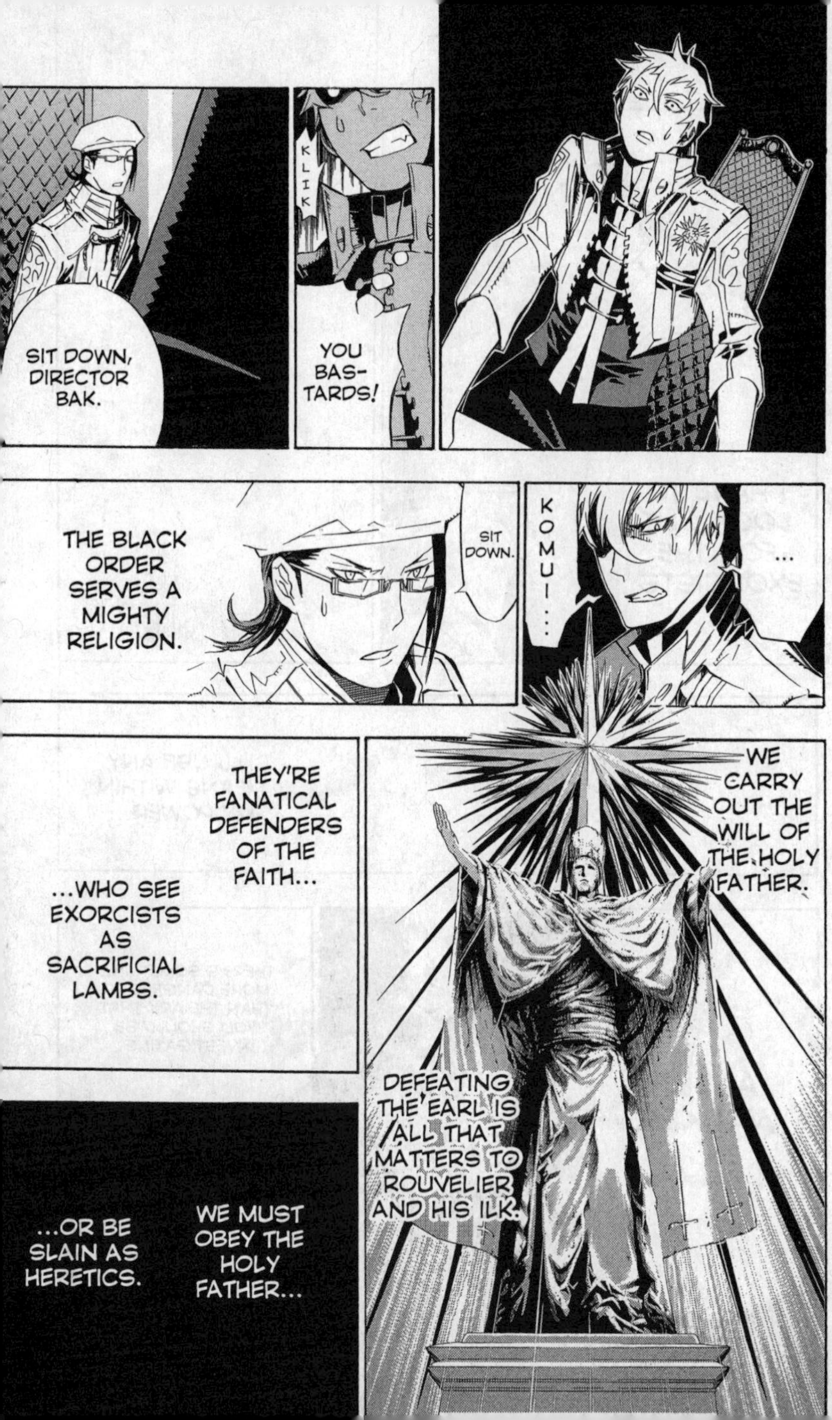
KLIK
YOU BASTARDS!
SIT DOWN, DIRECTOR BAK.
...
KOMUI...
SIT DOWN.
THE BLACK ORDER SERVES A MIGHTY RELIGION.
WE CARRY OUT THE WILL OF THE HOLY FATHER.
DEFEATING THE EARL IS ALL THAT MATTERS TO ROUVELIER AND HIS ILK.
THEY'RE FANATICAL DEFENDERS OF THE FAITH...
...WHO SEE EXORCISTS AS SACRIFICIAL LAMBS.
WE MUST OBEY THE HOLY FATHER...
...OR BE SLAIN AS HERETICS.

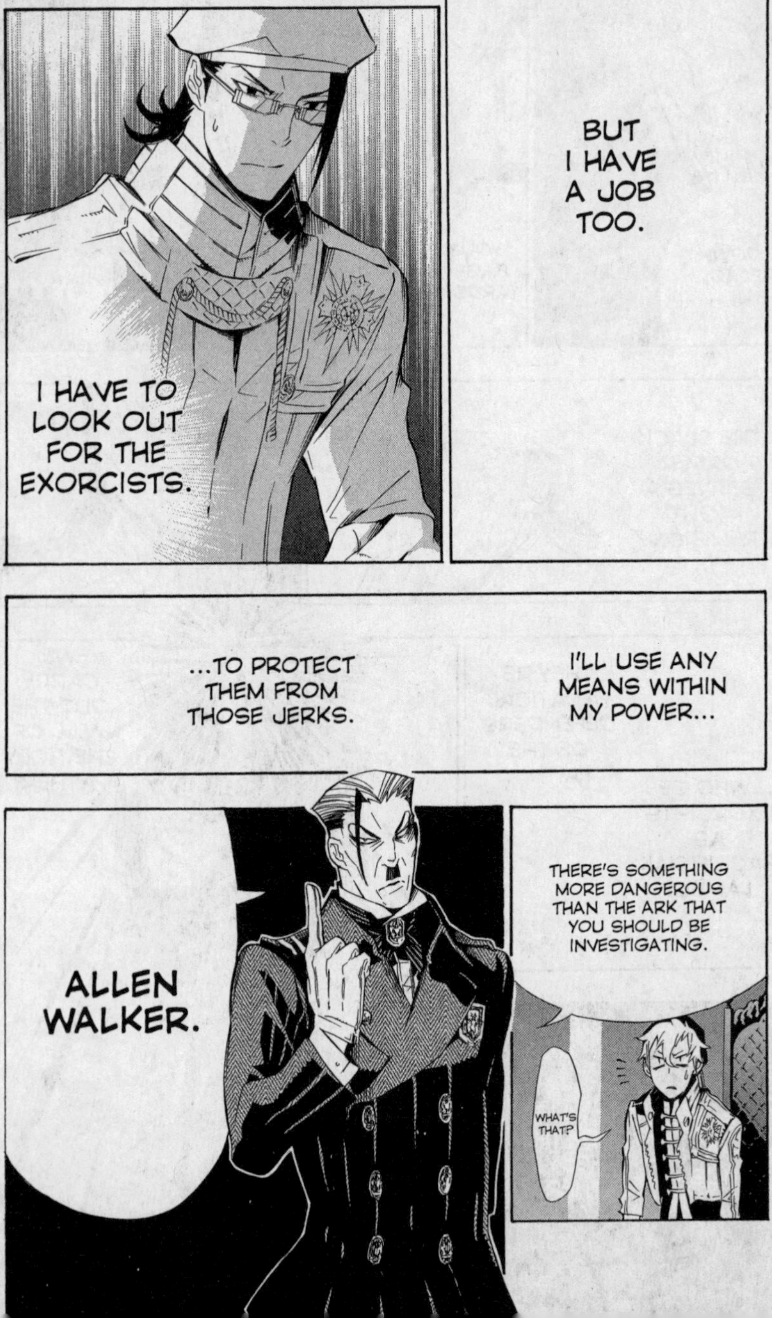
BUT I HAVE A JOB TOO.
I HAVE TO LOOK OUT FOR THE EXORCISTS.
I'LL USE ANY MEANS WITHIN MY POWER...
...TO PROTECT THEM FROM THOSE JERKS.
THERE'S SOMETHING MORE DANGEROUS THAN THE ARK THAT YOU SHOULD BE INVESTIGATING.
WHAT'S THAT?
ALLEN WALKER.

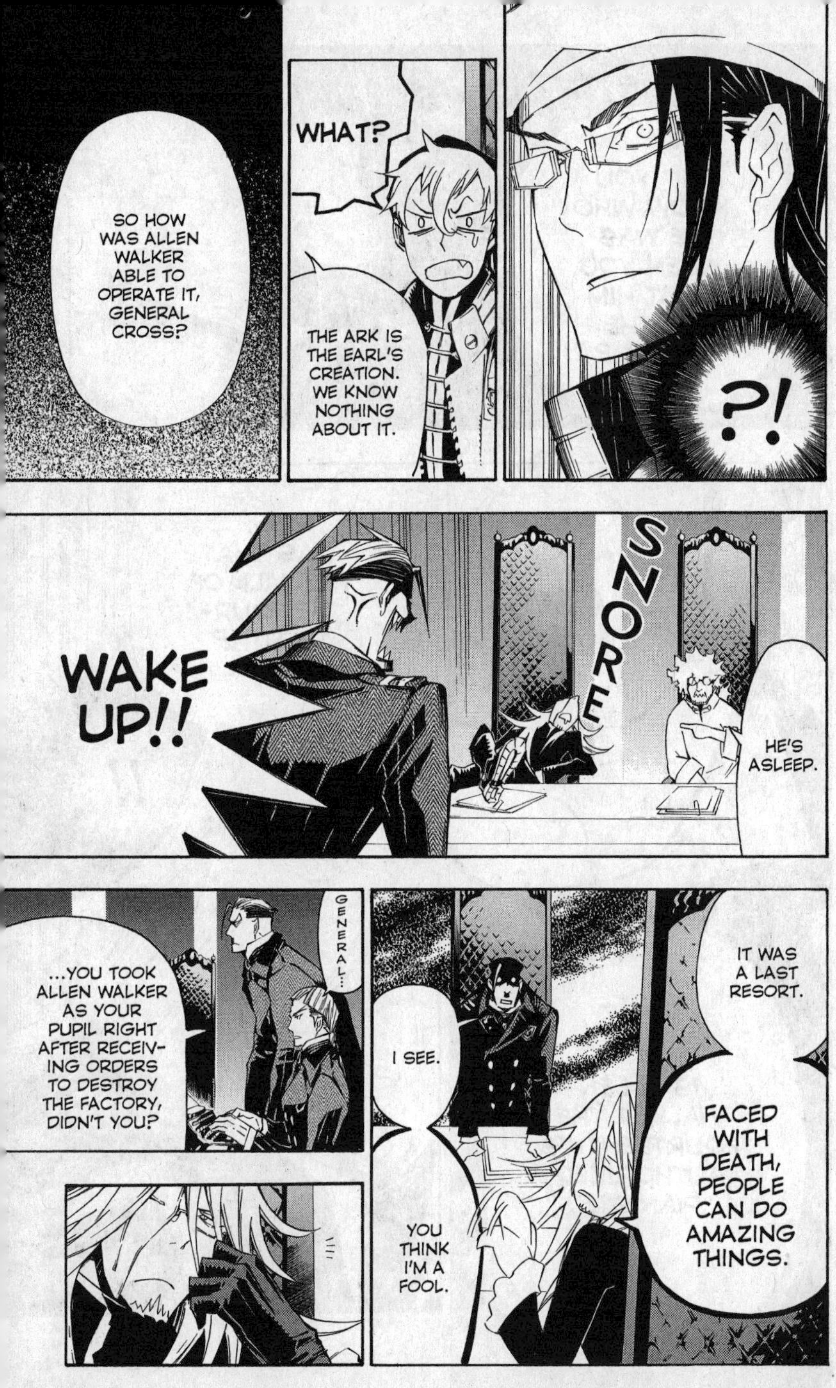
?!
WHAT?
THE ARK IS THE EARL'S CREATION. WE KNOW NOTHING ABOUT IT.
SO HOW WAS ALLEN WALKER ABLE TO OPERATE IT, GENERAL CROSS?
HE'S ASLEEP.
SNORE
WAKE UP!!
IT WAS A LAST RESORT.
FACED WITH DEATH, PEOPLE CAN DO AMAZING THINGS.
I SEE.
YOU THINK I'M A FOOL.
GENERAL...
...YOU TOOK ALLEN WALKER AS YOUR PUPIL RIGHT AFTER RECEIVING ORDERS TO DESTROY THE FACTORY, DIDN'T YOU?
...

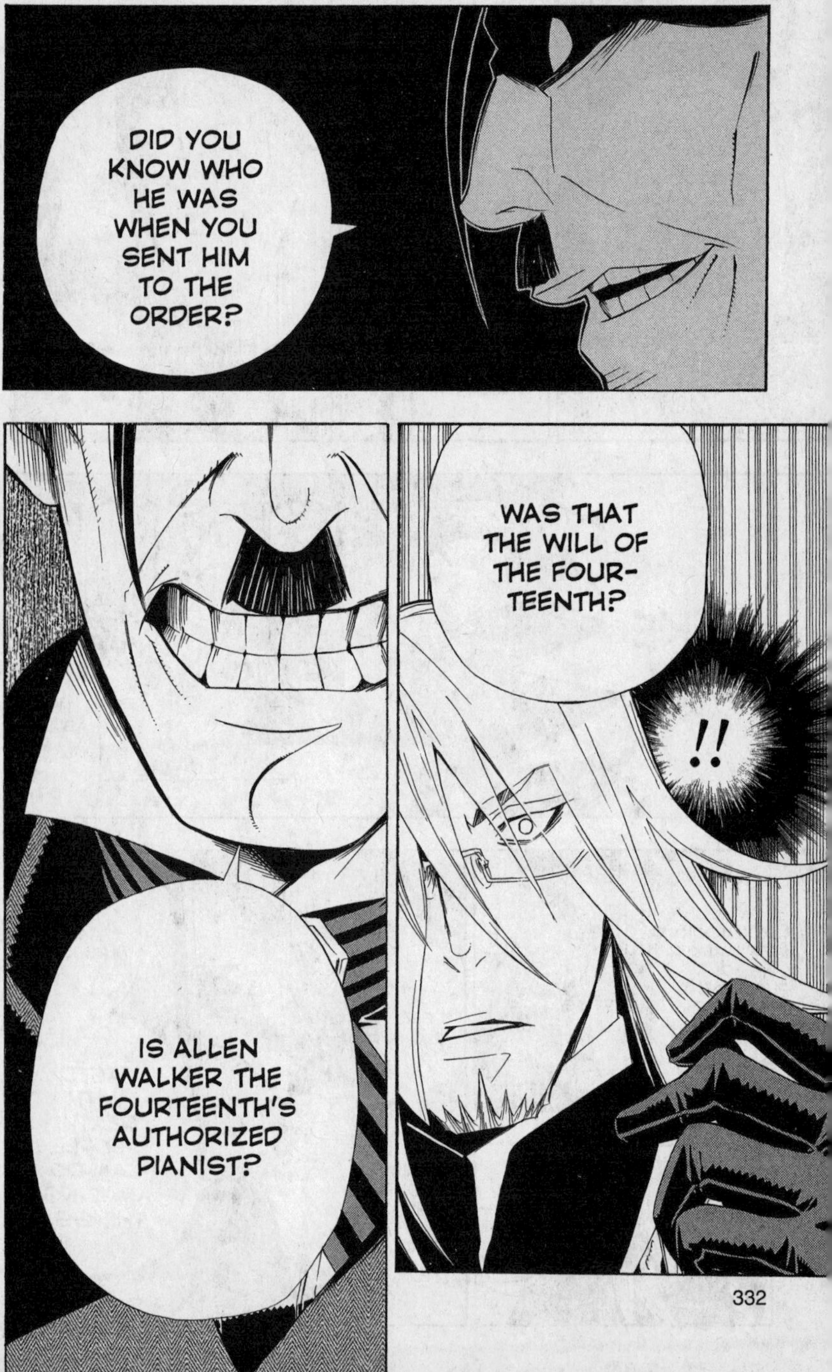
DID YOU KNOW WHO HE WAS WHEN YOU SENT HIM TO THE ORDER?
WAS THAT THE WILL OF THE FOUR-TEENTH?
!!
IS ALLEN WALKER THE FOURTEENTH'S AUTHORIZED PIANIST?

READ THIS WAY

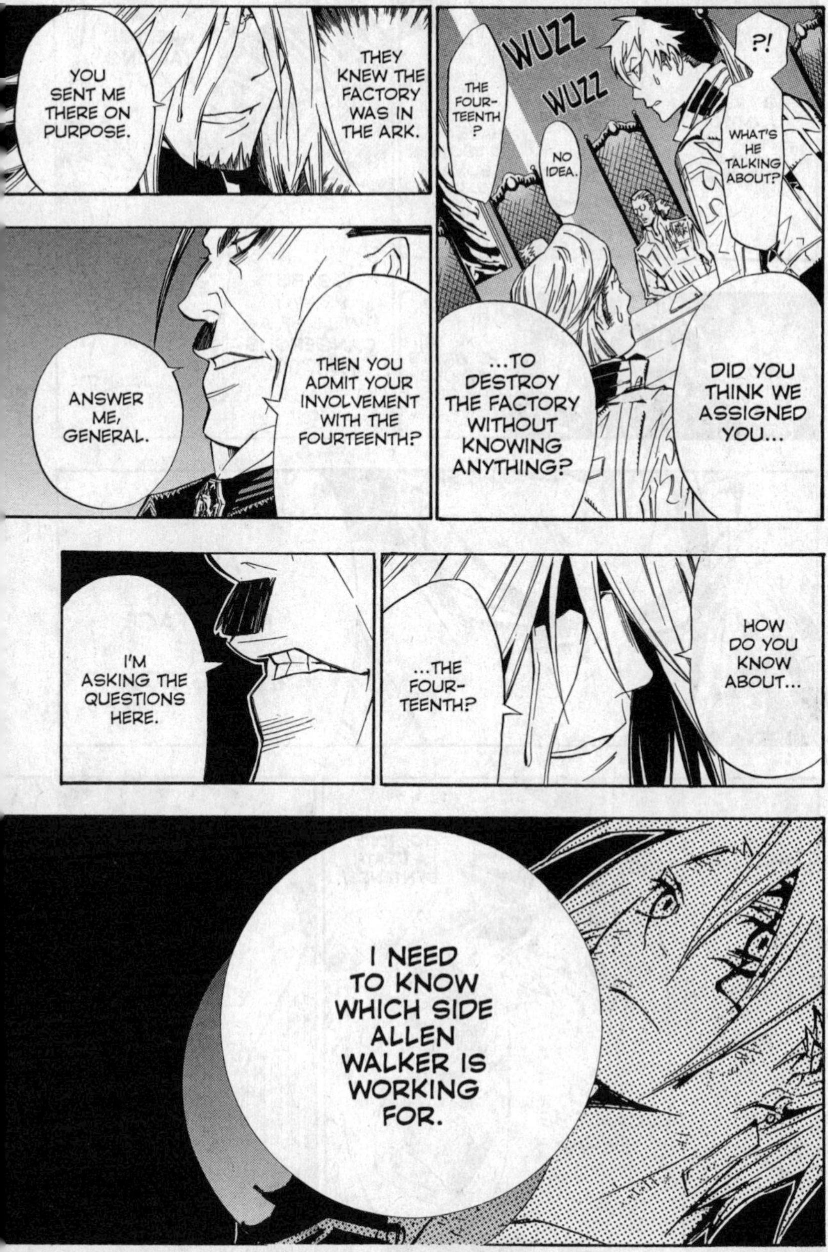
?!
WHAT'S HE TALKING ABOUT?
WUZZ WUZZ
THE FOURTEENTH?
NO IDEA.
DID YOU THINK WE ASSIGNED YOU...
...TO DESTROY THE FACTORY WITHOUT KNOWING ANYTHING?
THEY KNEW THE FACTORY WAS IN THE ARK.
YOU SENT ME THERE ON PURPOSE.
THEN YOU ADMIT YOUR INVOLVEMENT WITH THE FOURTEENTH?
ANSWER ME, GENERAL.
HOW DO YOU KNOW ABOUT...
...THE FOURTEENTH?
I'M ASKING THE QUESTIONS HERE.
I NEED TO KNOW WHICH SIDE ALLEN WALKER IS WORKING FOR.

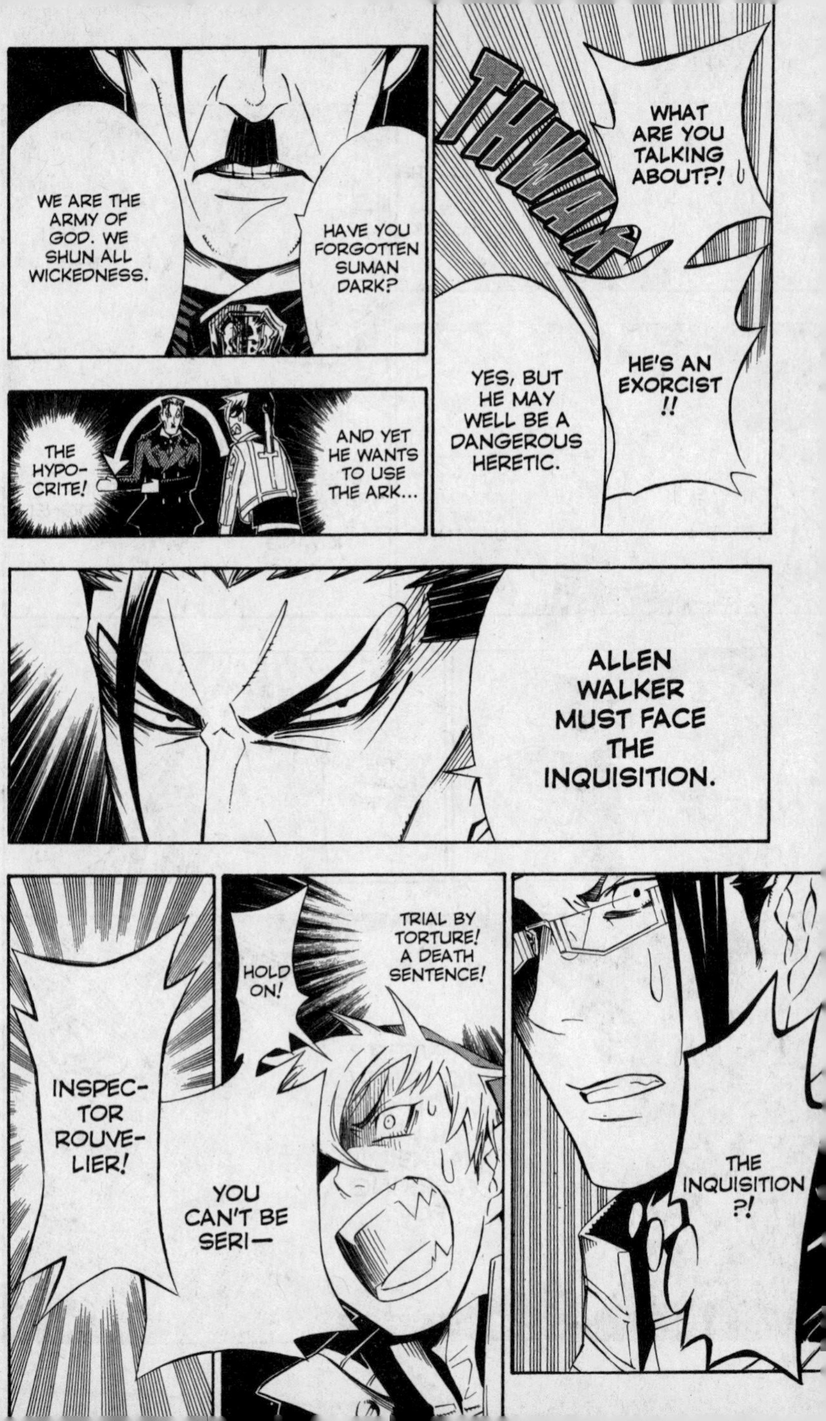
WHAT ARE YOU TALKING ABOUT?!
THWAK
HE'S AN EXORCIST!!
YES, BUT HE MAY WELL BE A DANGEROUS HERETIC.
HAVE YOU FORGOTTEN SUMAN DARK?
WE ARE THE ARMY OF GOD. WE SHUN ALL WICKEDNESS.
AND YET HE WANTS TO USE THE ARK...
THE HYPO- CRITE!
ALLEN WALKER MUST FACE THE INQUISITION.
THE INQUISITION?!
TRIAL BY TORTURE! A DEATH SENTENCE!
HOLD ON!
YOU CAN'T BE SERI—
INSPEC- TOR ROUVE- LIER!

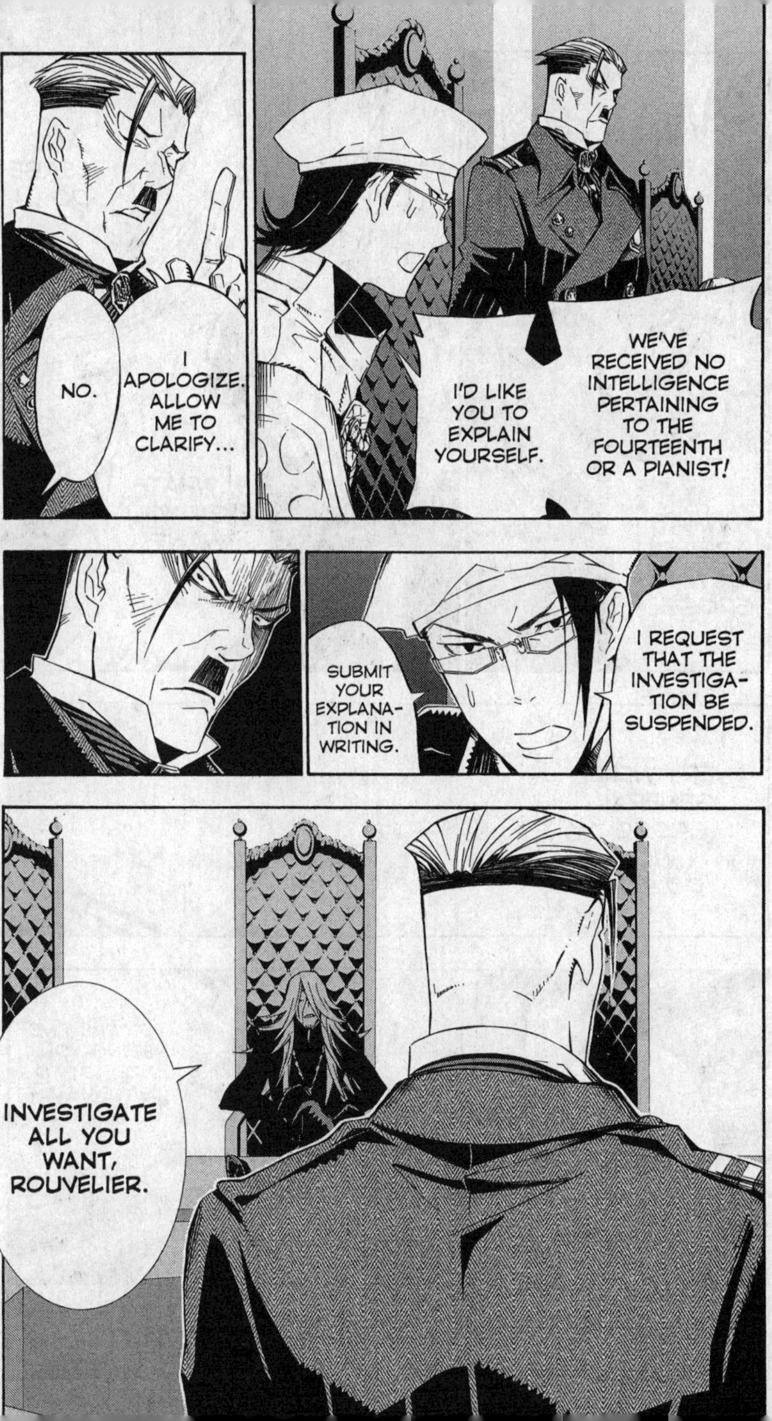
WE'VE RECEIVED NO INTELLIGENCE PERTAINING TO THE FOURTEENTH OR A PIANIST!
I'D LIKE YOU TO EXPLAIN YOURSELF.
I APOLOGIZE. ALLOW ME TO CLARIFY...
NO.
I REQUEST THAT THE INVESTIGATION BE SUSPENDED.
SUBMIT YOUR EXPLANATION IN WRITING.
INVESTIGATE ALL YOU WANT, ROUVELIER.

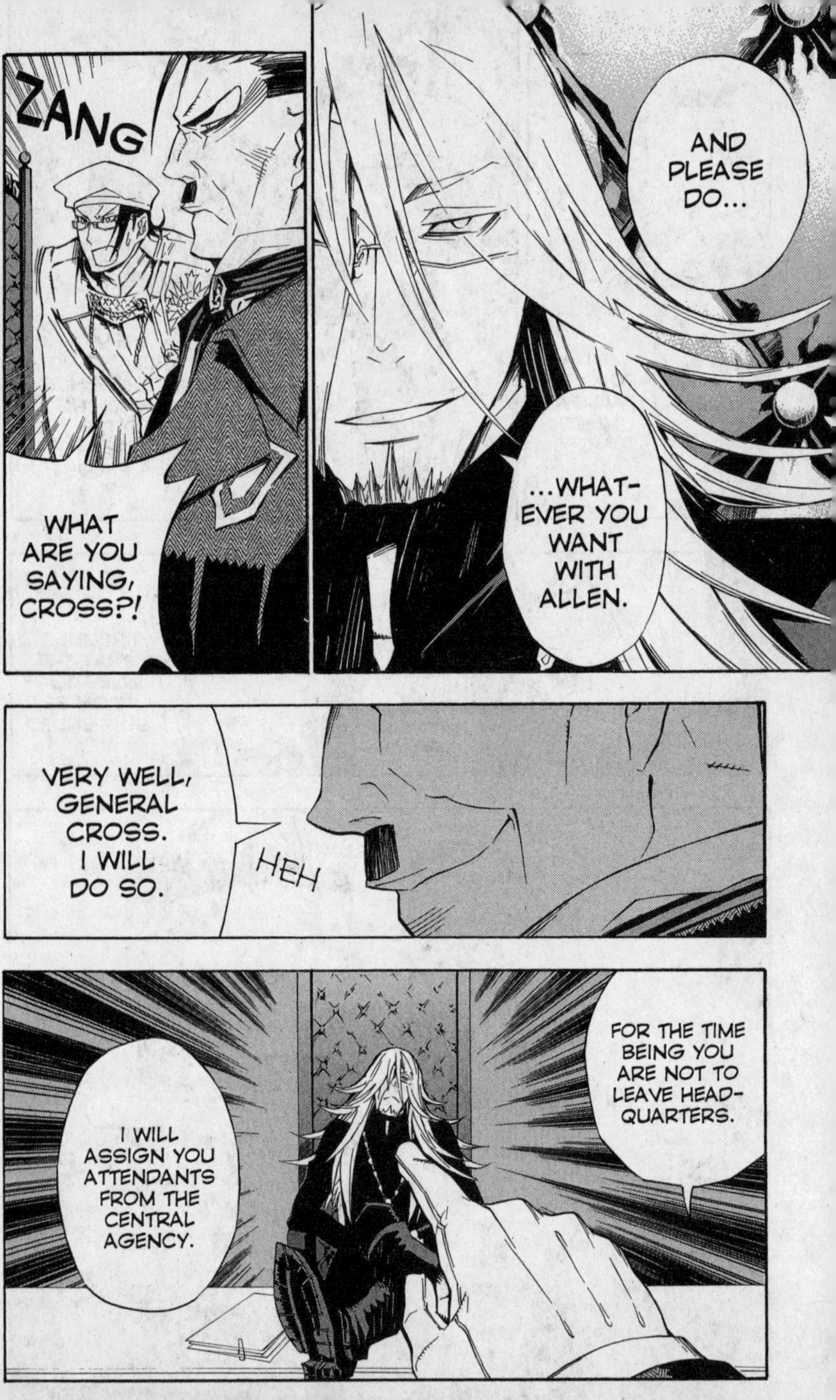
AND PLEASE DO...
...WHAT-EVER YOU WANT WITH ALLEN.
ZANG
WHAT ARE YOU SAYING, CROSS?!
VERY WELL, GENERAL CROSS. I WILL DO SO.
HEH
FOR THE TIME BEING YOU ARE NOT TO LEAVE HEAD-QUARTERS.
I WILL ASSIGN YOU ATTENDANTS FROM THE CENTRAL AGENCY.

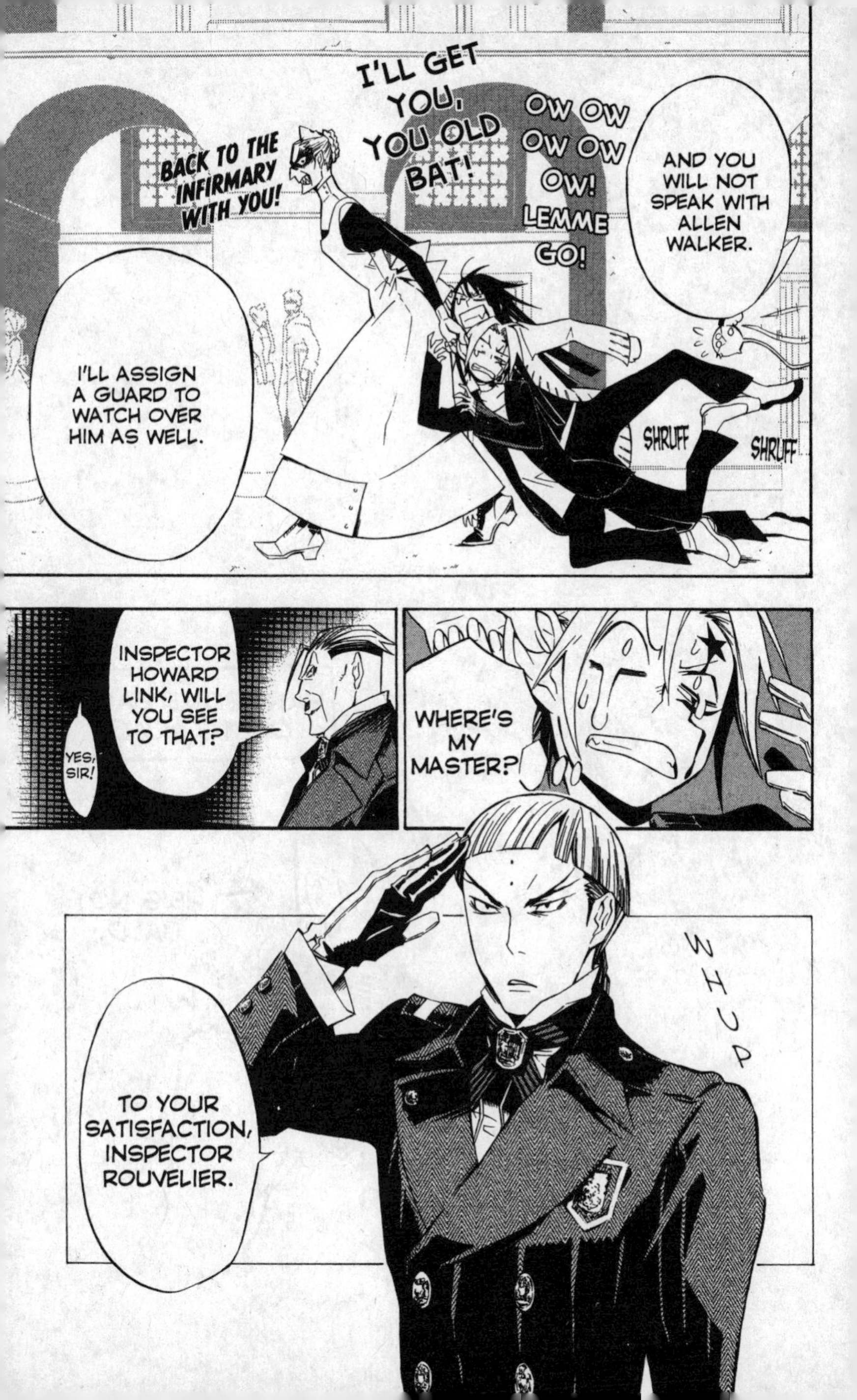
AND YOU WILL NOT SPEAK WITH ALLEN WALKER.
OW OW OW OW OW! LEMME GO!
I'LL GET YOU, YOU OLD BAT!
BACK TO THE INFIRMARY WITH YOU!
SHRUFF
SHRUFF
I'LL ASSIGN A GUARD TO WATCH OVER HIM AS WELL.
WHERE'S MY MASTER?
INSPECTOR HOWARD LINK, WILL YOU SEE TO THAT?
YES, SIR!
WHUP
TO YOUR SATISFACTION, INSPECTOR ROUVELIER.

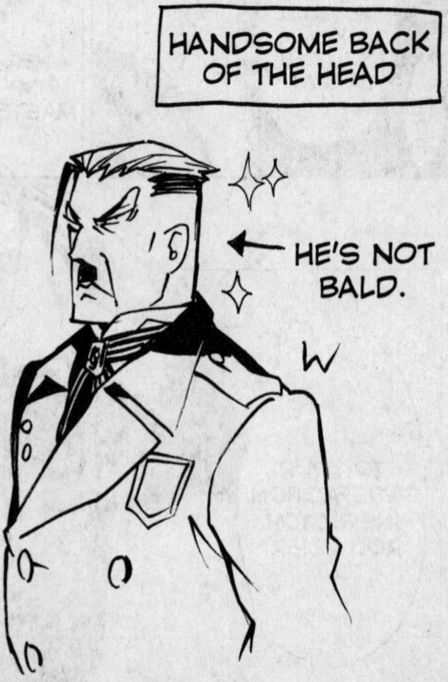
HANDSOME BACK OF THE HEAD
HE'S NOT BALD.
W

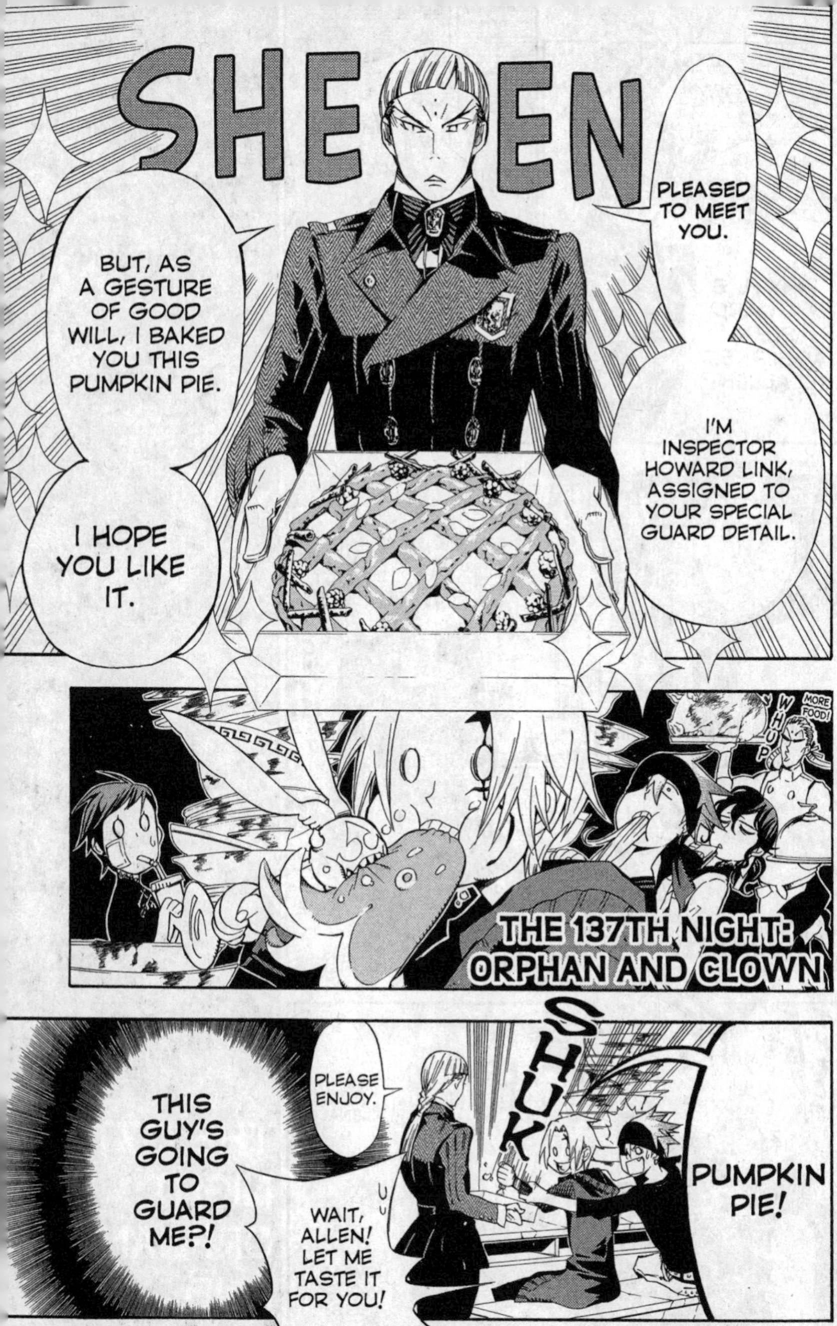
SHE EN
PLEASED TO MEET YOU.
I'M INSPECTOR HOWARD LINK, ASSIGNED TO YOUR SPECIAL GUARD DETAIL.
BUT, AS A GESTURE OF GOOD WILL, I BAKED YOU THIS PUMPKIN PIE.
I HOPE YOU LIKE IT.
MORE FOOD!
WHUP
THE 137TH NIGHT: ORPHAN AND CLOWN
PUMPKIN PIE!
SHUK
PLEASE ENJOY.
WAIT, ALLEN! LET ME TASTE IT FOR YOU!
THIS GUY'S GOING TO GUARD ME?!

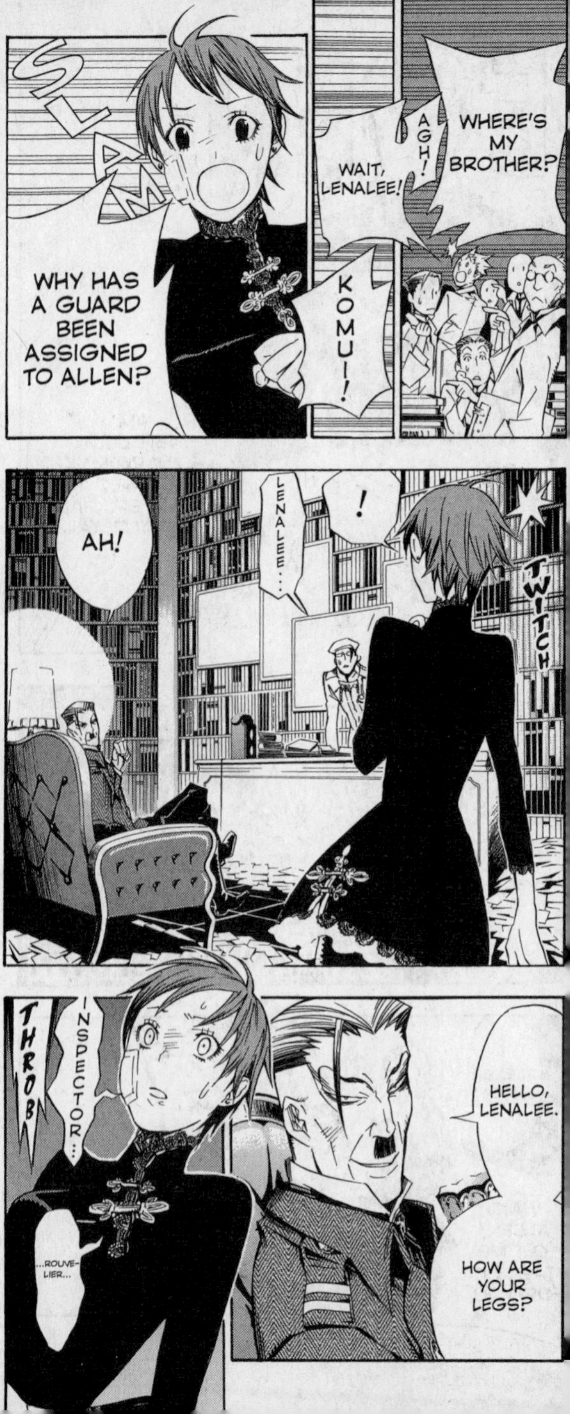
WHERE'S MY BROTHER?
AGH!
WAIT, LENALEE!
KOMUI!
SLAM
WHY HAS A GUARD BEEN ASSIGNED TO ALLEN?
TWITCH
!
LENALEE...
AH!
HELLO, LENALEE.
HOW ARE YOUR LEGS?
INSPECTOR...
THROB
...ROUVELIER...

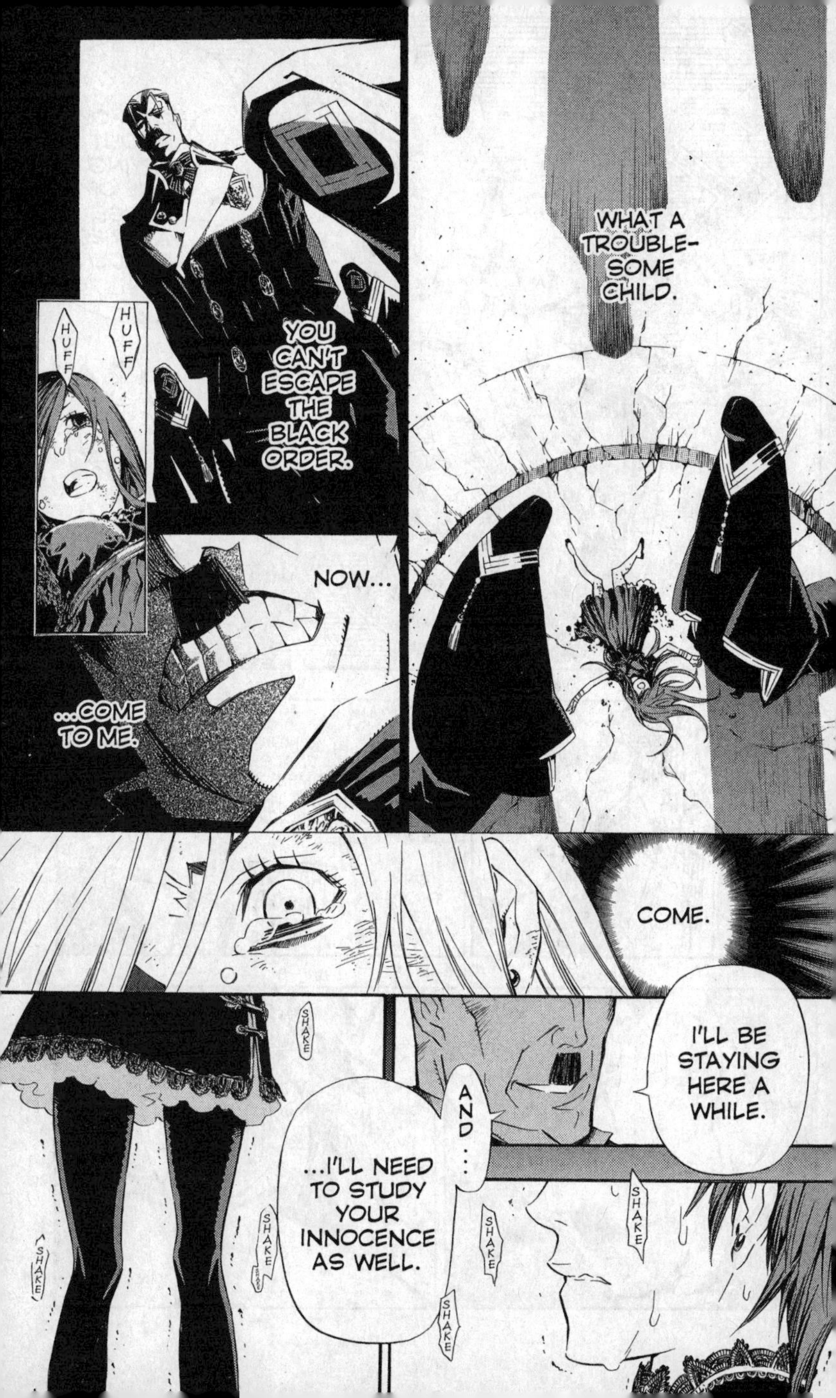
WHAT A TROUBLE-SOME CHILD.
YOU CAN'T ESCAPE THE BLACK ORDER.
HUFF
HUFF
NOW...
...COME TO ME.
COME.
I'LL BE STAYING HERE A WHILE.
AND...
...I'LL NEED TO STUDY YOUR INNOCENCE AS WELL.
SHAKE
SHAKE
SHAKE
SHAKE
SHAKE
SHAKE

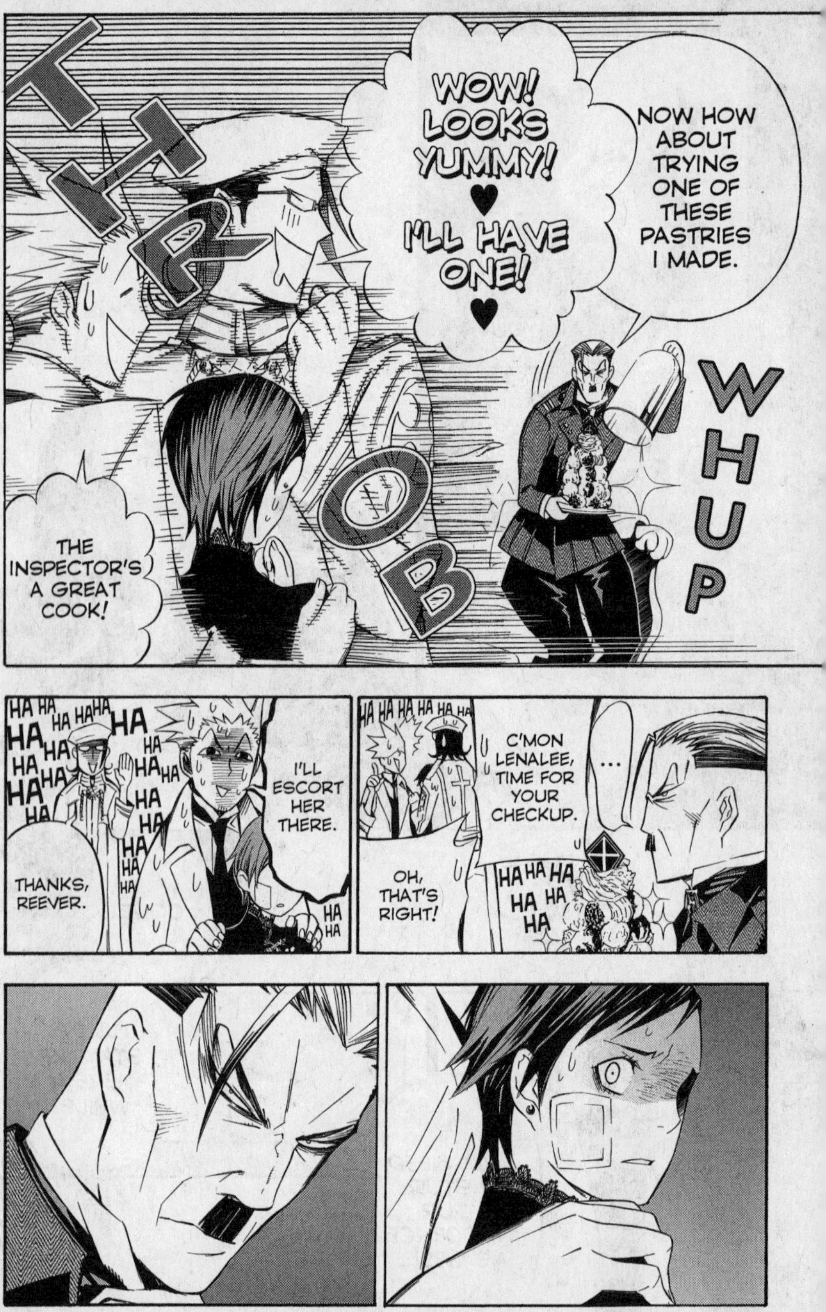
NOW HOW ABOUT TRYING ONE OF THESE PASTRIES I MADE.
WHUP
WOW! LOOKS YUMMY! ♥ I'LL HAVE ONE! ♥
THROB
THE INSPECTOR'S A GREAT COOK!
...
C'MON LENALEE, TIME FOR YOUR CHECKUP.
HA HA HA HA HA HA
HA HA HA HA HA HA
OH, THAT'S RIGHT!
I'LL ESCORT HER THERE.
HA HA HA HA HA HA HA HA HA HA HA HA HA HA HA HA HA HA
THANKS, REEVER.
HA HA

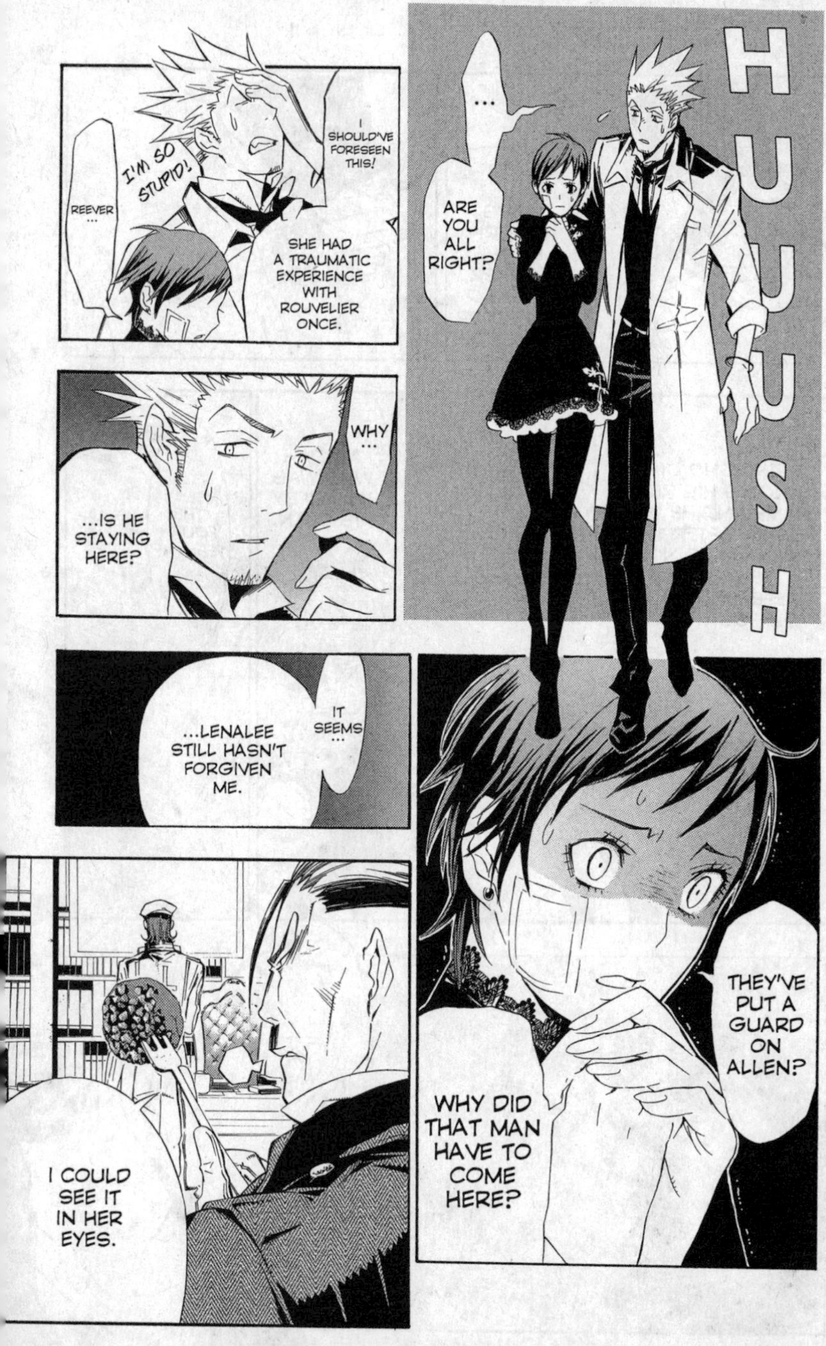
HUUUSH
...
ARE YOU ALL RIGHT?
I SHOULD'VE FORESEEN THIS!
I'M SO STUPID!
SHE HAD A TRAUMATIC EXPERIENCE WITH ROUVELIER ONCE.
REEVER...
WHY...
...IS HE STAYING HERE?
THEY'VE PUT A GUARD ON ALLEN?
WHY DID THAT MAN HAVE TO COME HERE?
IT SEEMS...
...LENALEE STILL HASN'T FORGIVEN ME.
I COULD SEE IT IN HER EYES.

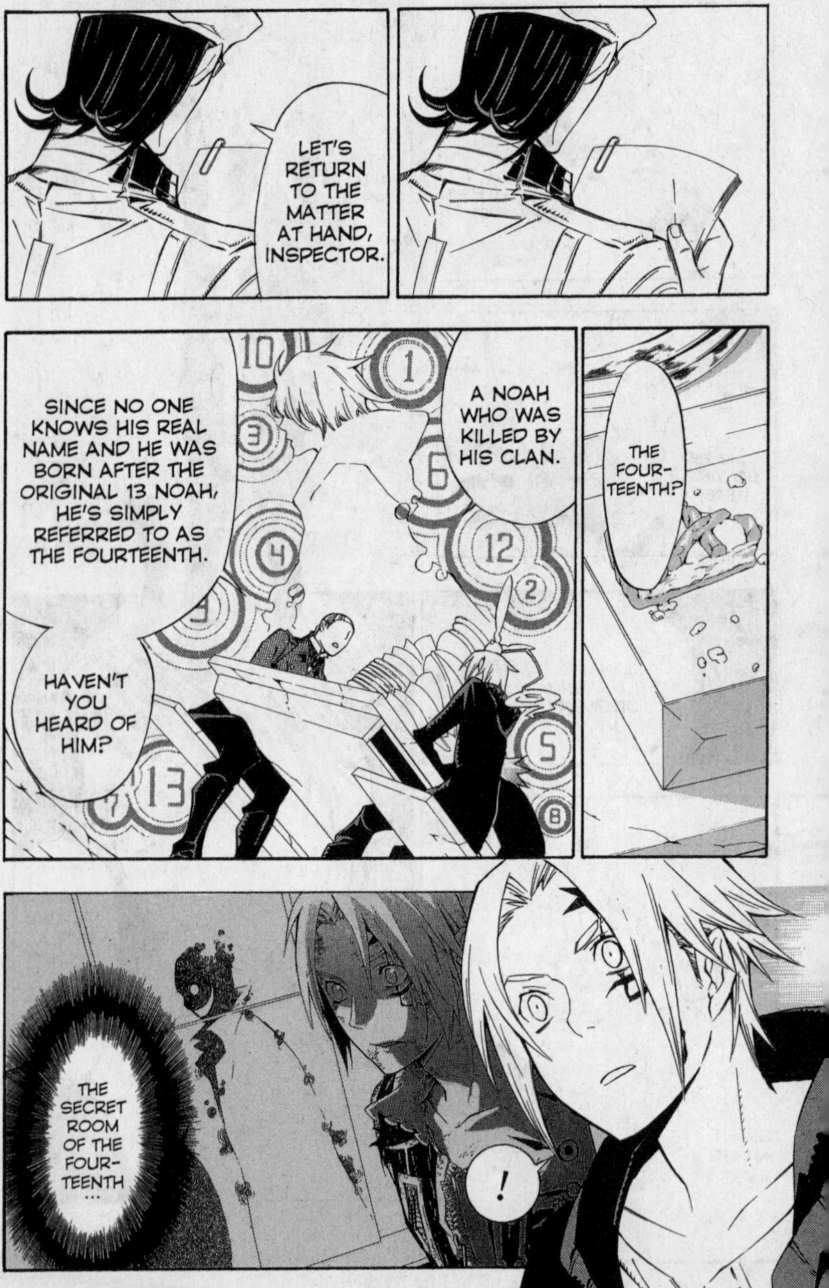
LET'S RETURN TO THE MATTER AT HAND, INSPECTOR.
THE FOUR-TEENTH?
A NOAH WHO WAS KILLED BY HIS CLAN.
SINCE NO ONE KNOWS HIS REAL NAME AND HE WAS BORN AFTER THE ORIGINAL 13 NOAH, HE'S SIMPLY REFERRED TO AS THE FOURTEENTH.
HAVEN'T YOU HEARD OF HIM?
THE SECRET ROOM OF THE FOUR-TEENTH...
!

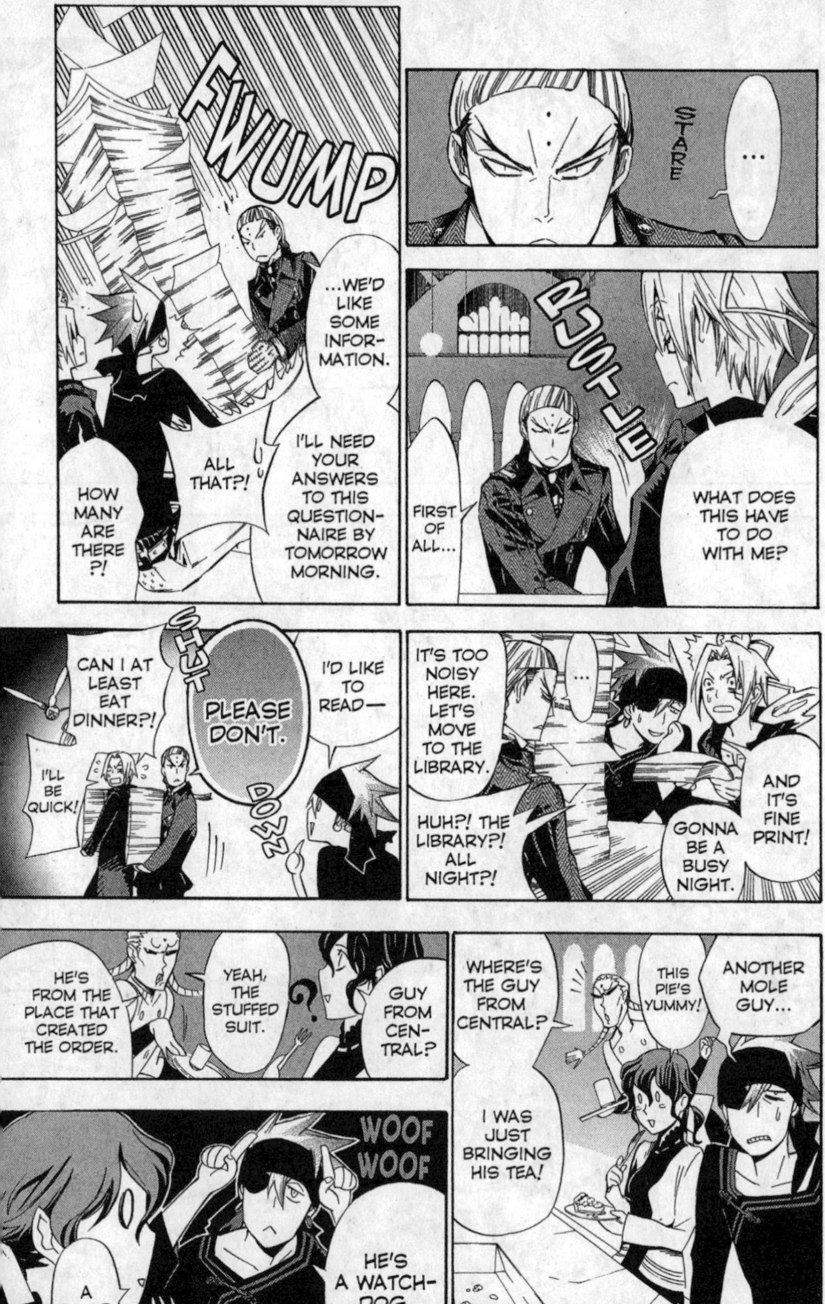
STARE
...
RUSTLE
WHAT DOES THIS HAVE TO DO WITH ME?
FIRST OF ALL...
FWUMP
...WE'D LIKE SOME INFOR-MATION.
I'LL NEED YOUR ANSWERS TO THIS QUESTION-NAIRE BY TOMORROW MORNING.
ALL THAT?!
HOW MANY ARE THERE?!
AND IT'S FINE PRINT!
...
IT'S TOO NOISY HERE. LET'S MOVE TO THE LIBRARY.
GONNA BE A BUSY NIGHT.
HUH?! THE LIBRARY?! ALL NIGHT?!
I'D LIKE TO READ—
SHUT
PLEASE DON'T.
DOWN
CAN I AT LEAST EAT DINNER?!
I'LL BE QUICK!
ANOTHER MOLE GUY...
THIS PIE'S YUMMY!
WHERE'S THE GUY FROM CENTRAL?
I WAS JUST BRINGING HIS TEA!
GUY FROM CEN-TRAL?
YEAH, THE STUFFED SUIT.
HE'S FROM THE PLACE THAT CREATED THE ORDER.
WOOF WOOF
HE'S A WATCH-DOG.
A DOG?

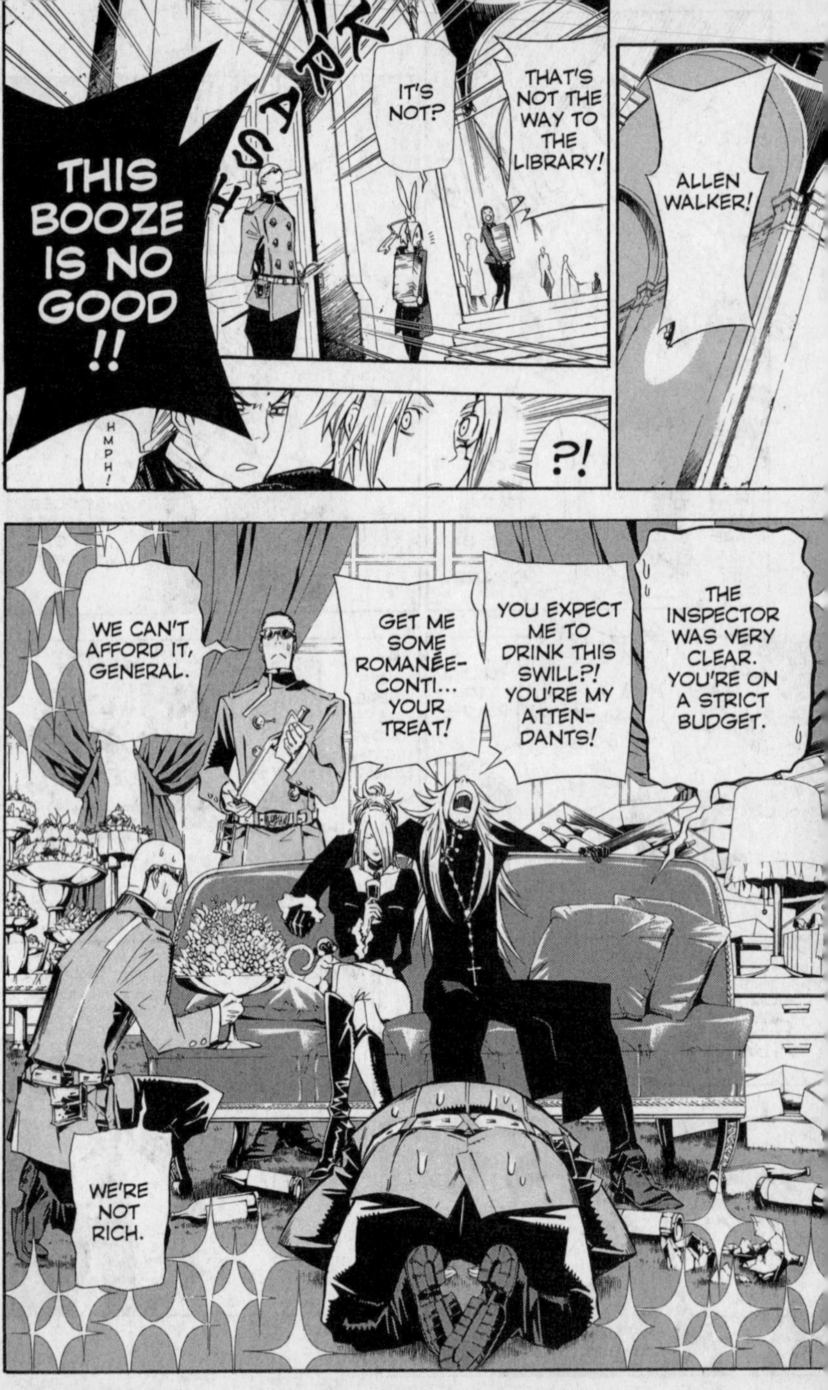
ALLEN WALKER!
THAT'S NOT THE WAY TO THE LIBRARY!
IT'S NOT?
THIS BOOZE IS NO GOOD!!
?!
HMPH!
THE INSPECTOR WAS VERY CLEAR. YOU'RE ON A STRICT BUDGET.
YOU EXPECT ME TO DRINK THIS SWILL?! YOU'RE MY ATTEN-DANTS!
GET ME SOME ROMANÉE-CONTI... YOUR TREAT!
WE CAN'T AFFORD IT, GENERAL.
WE'RE NOT RICH.

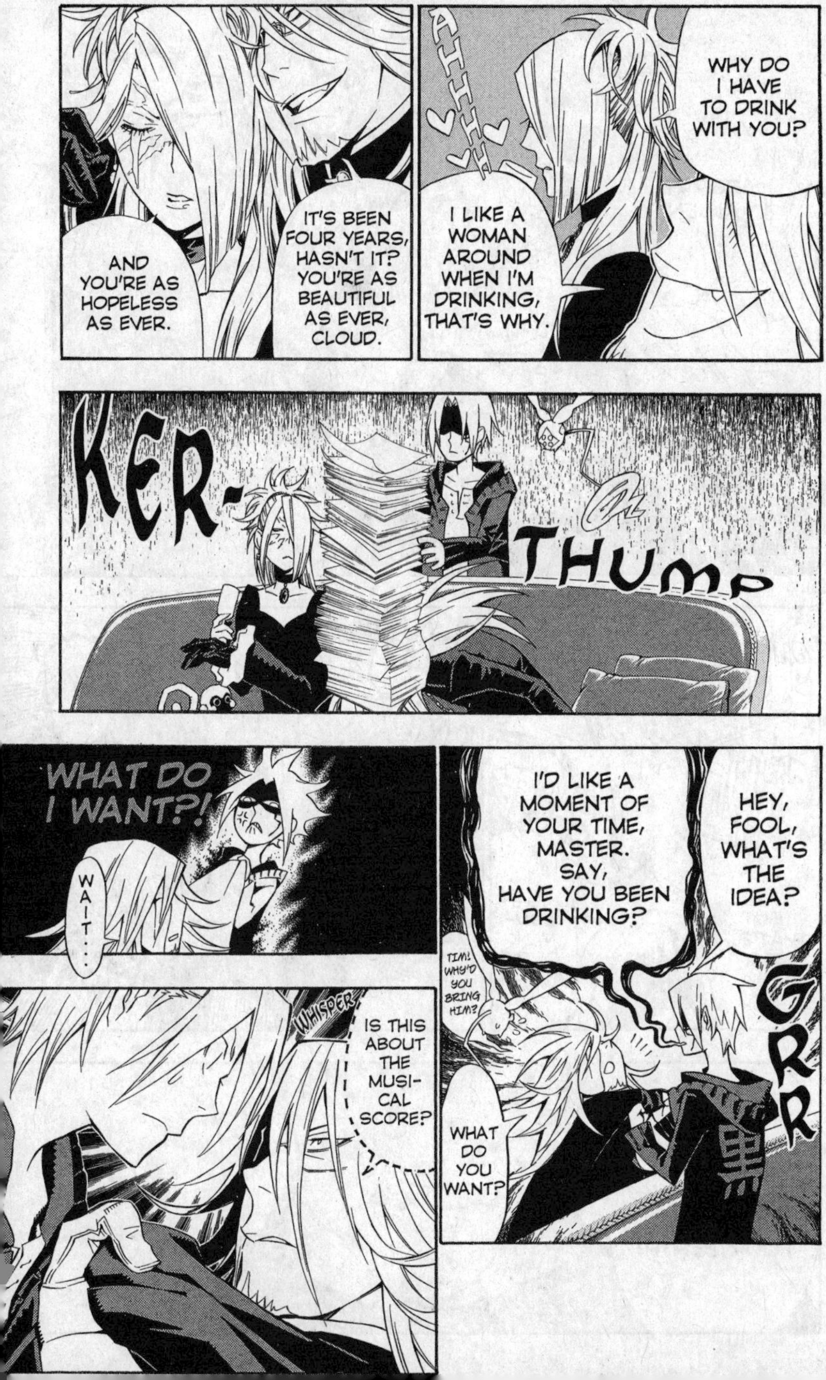
WHY DO I HAVE TO DRINK WITH YOU?
AHHHH
I LIKE A WOMAN AROUND WHEN I'M DRINKING, THAT'S WHY.
IT'S BEEN FOUR YEARS, HASN'T IT? YOU'RE AS BEAUTIFUL AS EVER, CLOUD.
AND YOU'RE AS HOPELESS AS EVER.
KER-
THUMP
HEY, FOOL, WHAT'S THE IDEA?
I'D LIKE A MOMENT OF YOUR TIME, MASTER. SAY, HAVE YOU BEEN DRINKING?
GRR
TIM! WHY'D YOU BRING HIM?
WHAT DO YOU WANT?
WHAT DO I WANT?!
WAIT...
WHISPER
IS THIS ABOUT THE MUSI-CAL SCORE?

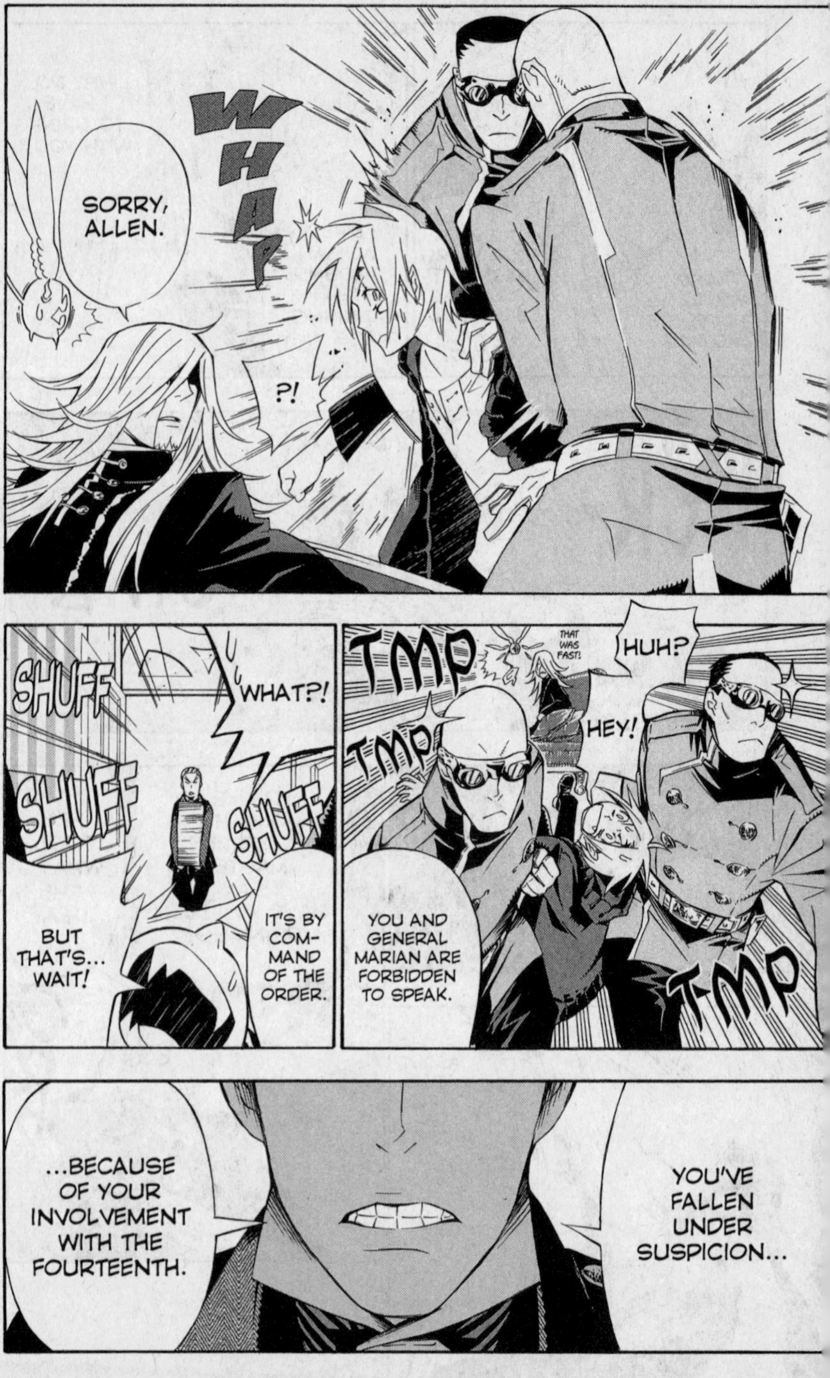

WHAP
SORRY, ALLEN.
?!
HUH?
THAT WAS FAST!
TMP
HEY!
TMP
YOU AND GENERAL MARIAN ARE FORBIDDEN TO SPEAK.
TMP
WHAT?!
SHUFF
SHUFF
SHUFF
IT'S BY COM-MAND OF THE ORDER.
BUT THAT'S... WAIT!
YOU'VE FALLEN UNDER SUSPICION...
...BECAUSE OF YOUR INVOLVEMENT WITH THE FOURTEENTH.

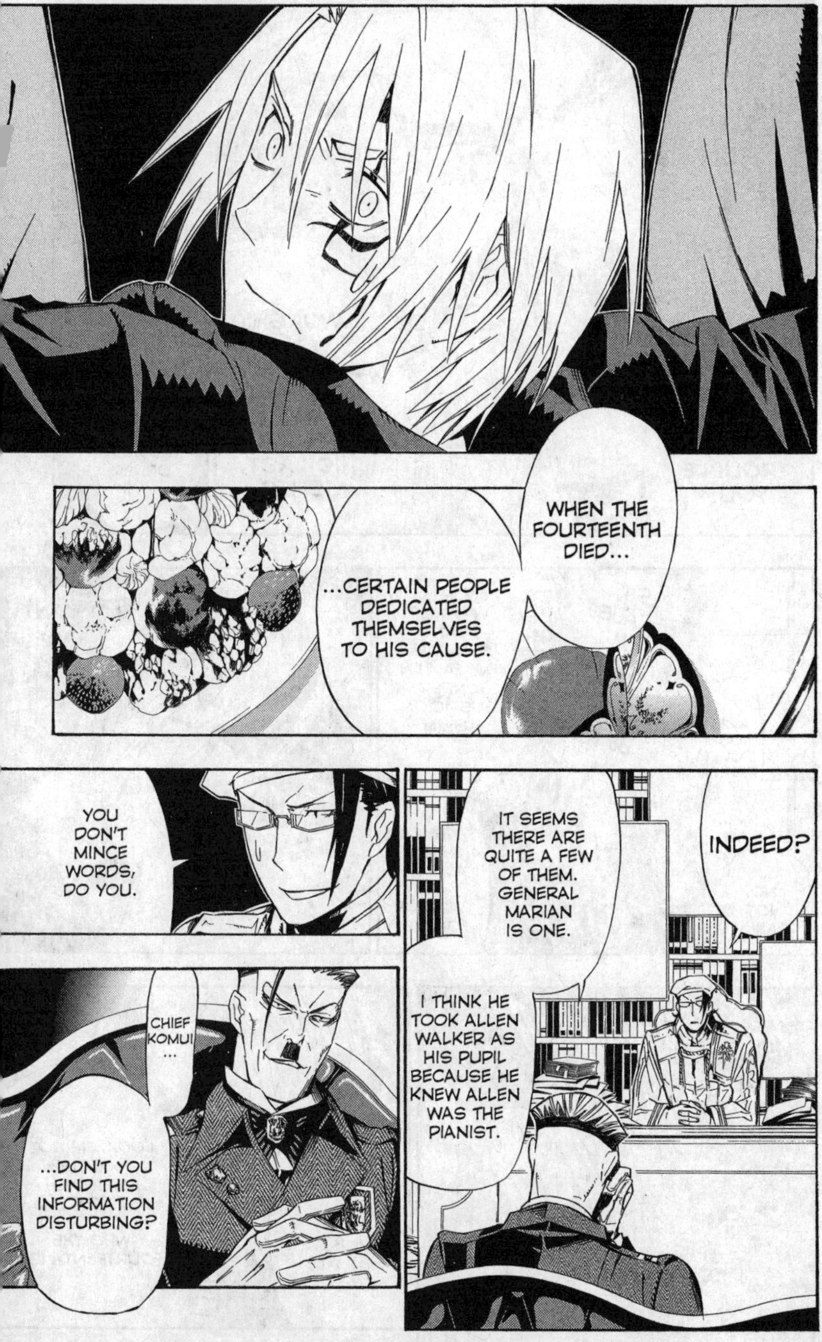

WHEN THE FOURTEENTH DIED...
...CERTAIN PEOPLE DEDICATED THEMSELVES TO HIS CAUSE.
INDEED?
IT SEEMS THERE ARE QUITE A FEW OF THEM. GENERAL MARIAN IS ONE.
I THINK HE TOOK ALLEN WALKER AS HIS PUPIL BECAUSE HE KNEW ALLEN WAS THE PIANIST.
YOU DON'T MINCE WORDS, DO YOU.
CHIEF KOMUI ...
...DON'T YOU FIND THIS INFORMATION DISTURBING?

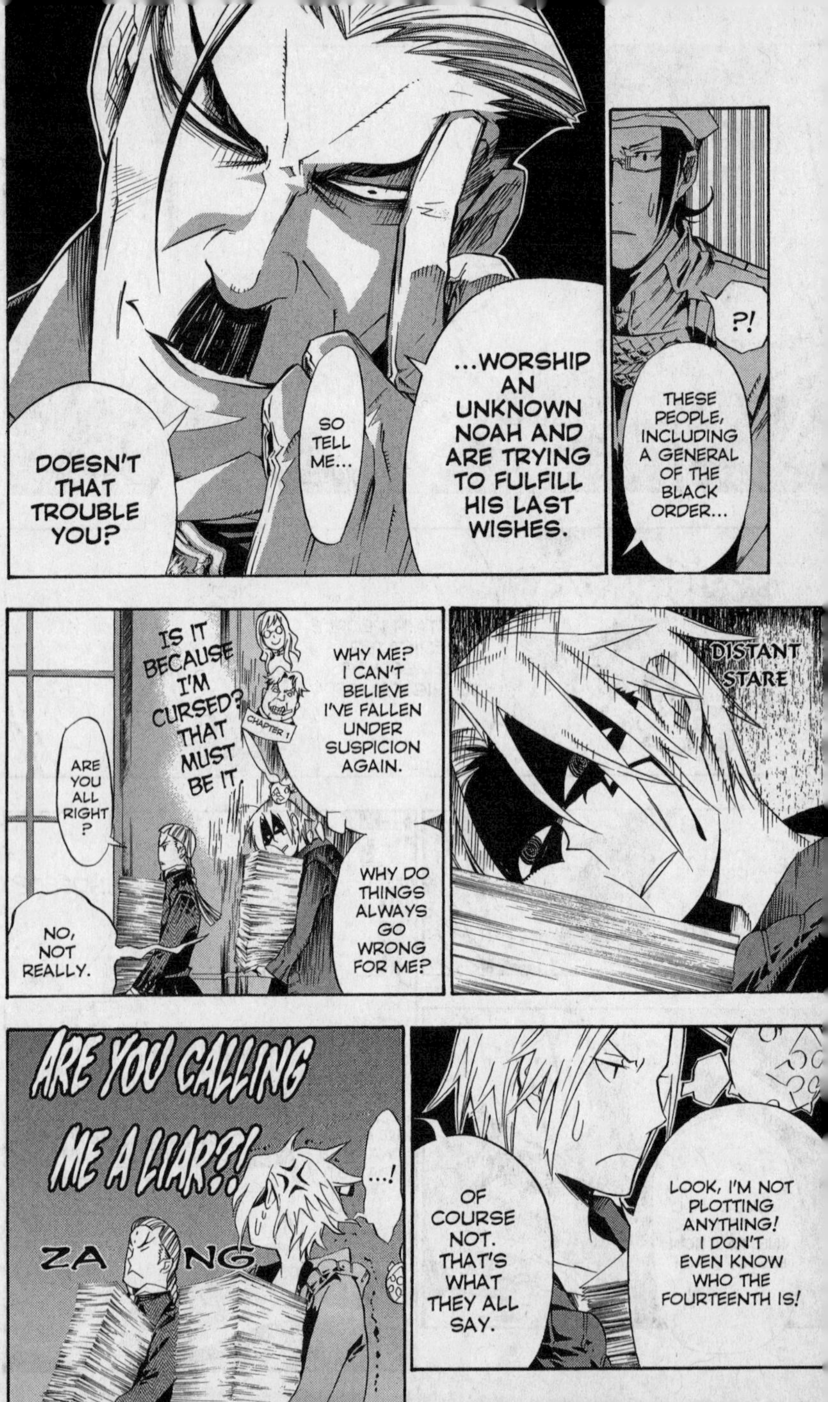
?!
THESE PEOPLE, INCLUDING A GENERAL OF THE BLACK ORDER...
...WORSHIP AN UNKNOWN NOAH AND ARE TRYING TO FULFILL HIS LAST WISHES.
SO TELL ME...
DOESN'T THAT TROUBLE YOU?
DISTANT STARE
WHY ME? I CAN'T BELIEVE I'VE FALLEN UNDER SUSPICION AGAIN.
IS IT BECAUSE I'M CURSED? THAT MUST BE IT.
CHAPTER 1
WHY DO THINGS ALWAYS GO WRONG FOR ME?
ARE YOU ALL RIGHT?
NO, NOT REALLY.
LOOK, I'M NOT PLOTTING ANYTHING! I DON'T EVEN KNOW WHO THE FOURTEENTH IS!
OF COURSE NOT. THAT'S WHAT THEY ALL SAY.
...!
ARE YOU CALLING ME A LIAR?!
ZANG

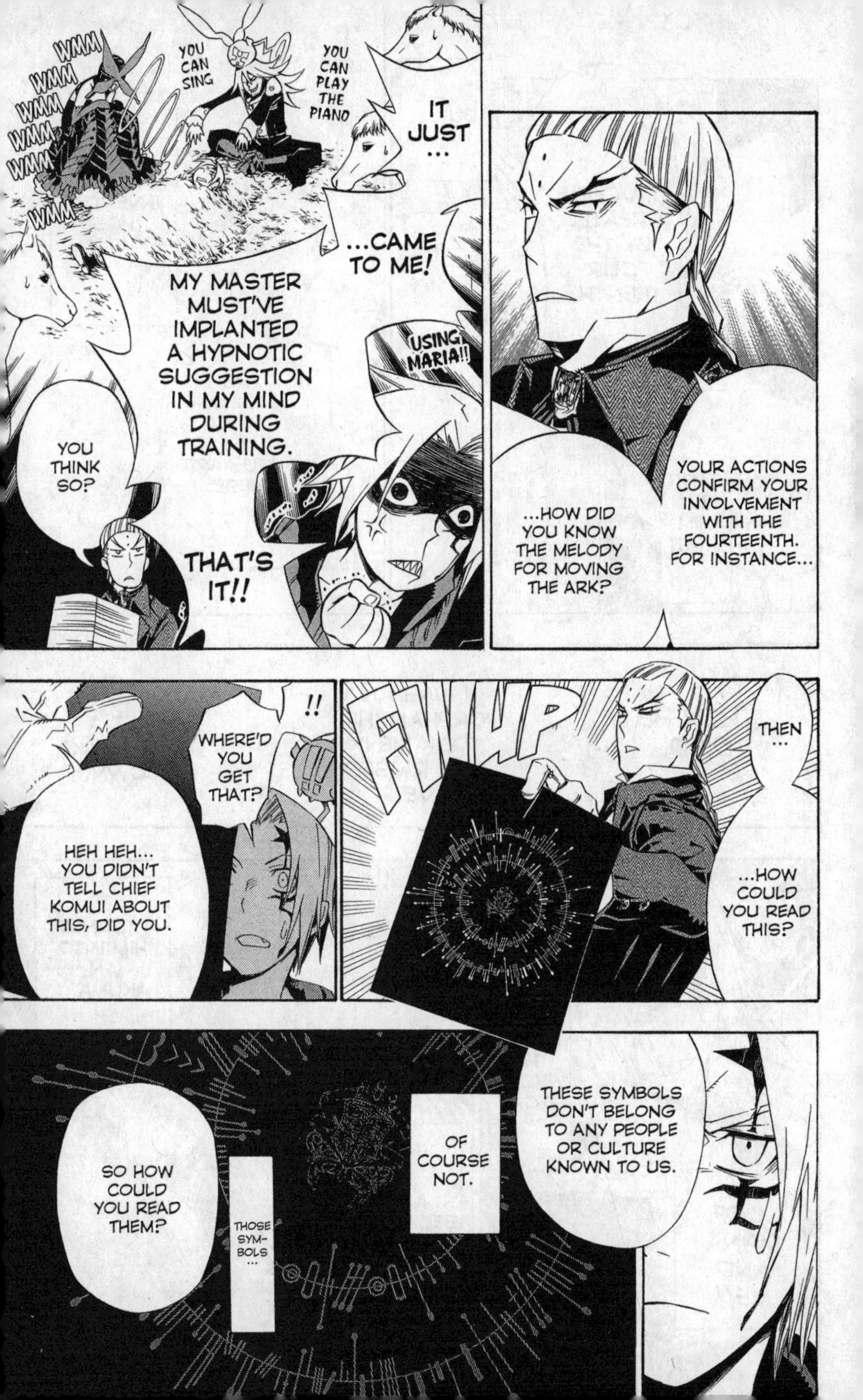
YOUR ACTIONS CONFIRM YOUR INVOLVEMENT WITH THE FOURTEENTH. FOR INSTANCE...
...HOW DID YOU KNOW THE MELODY FOR MOVING THE ARK?
IT JUST...
...CAME TO ME!
YOU CAN PLAY THE PIANO
YOU CAN SING
WMM WMM WMM WMM WMM WMM
MY MASTER MUST'VE IMPLANTED A HYPNOTIC SUGGESTION IN MY MIND DURING TRAINING.
USING MARIA!!
THAT'S IT!!
YOU THINK SO?
THEN...
FWUP
...HOW COULD YOU READ THIS?
!!
WHERE'D YOU GET THAT?
HEH HEH... YOU DIDN'T TELL CHIEF KOMUI ABOUT THIS, DID YOU.
THESE SYMBOLS DON'T BELONG TO ANY PEOPLE OR CULTURE KNOWN TO US.
OF COURSE NOT.
THOSE SYMBOLS...
SO HOW COULD YOU READ THEM?

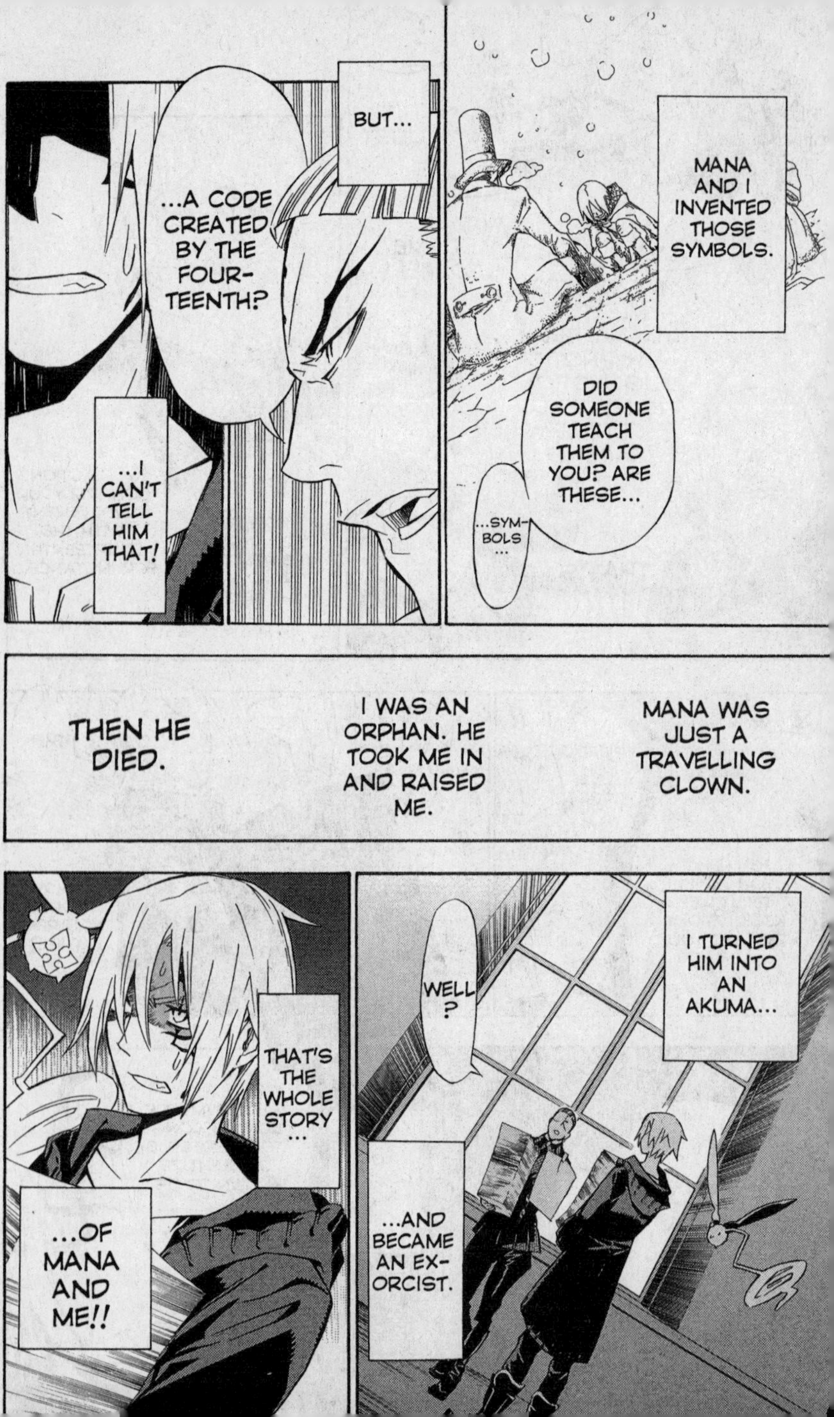
MANA AND I INVENTED THOSE SYMBOLS.
DID SOMEONE TEACH THEM TO YOU? ARE THESE...
...SYM-BOLS...
BUT...
...A CODE CREATED BY THE FOUR-TEENTH?
...I CAN'T TELL HIM THAT!
MANA WAS JUST A TRAVELLING CLOWN.
I WAS AN ORPHAN. HE TOOK ME IN AND RAISED ME.
THEN HE DIED.
I TURNED HIM INTO AN AKUMA...
WELL?
...AND BECAME AN EX-ORCIST.
THAT'S THE WHOLE STORY...
...OF MANA AND ME!!

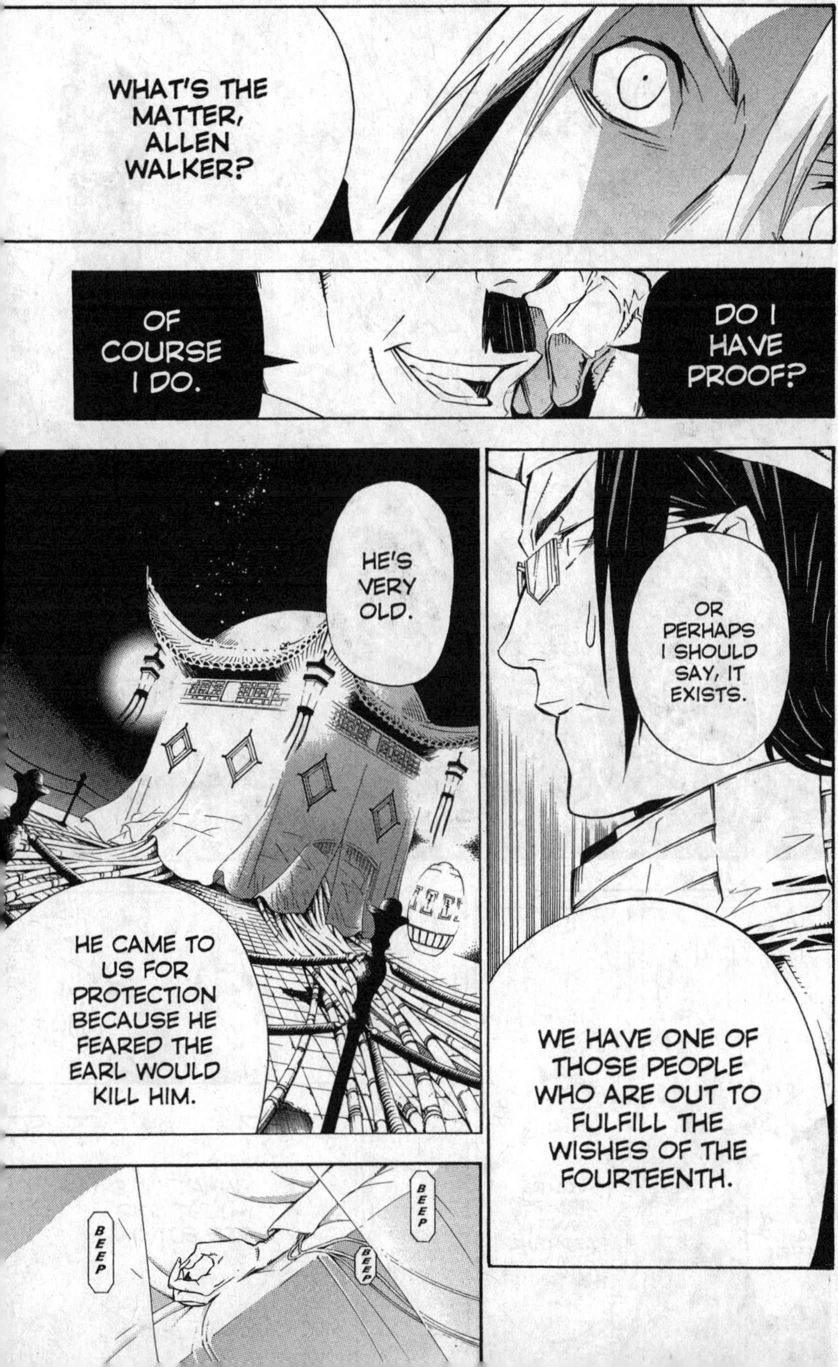
WHAT'S THE MATTER, ALLEN WALKER?
DO I HAVE PROOF?
OF COURSE I DO.
OR PERHAPS I SHOULD SAY, IT EXISTS.
WE HAVE ONE OF THOSE PEOPLE WHO ARE OUT TO FULFILL THE WISHES OF THE FOURTEENTH.
HE'S VERY OLD.
HE CAME TO US FOR PROTECTION BECAUSE HE FEARED THE EARL WOULD KILL HIM.
BEEP
BEEP
BEEP

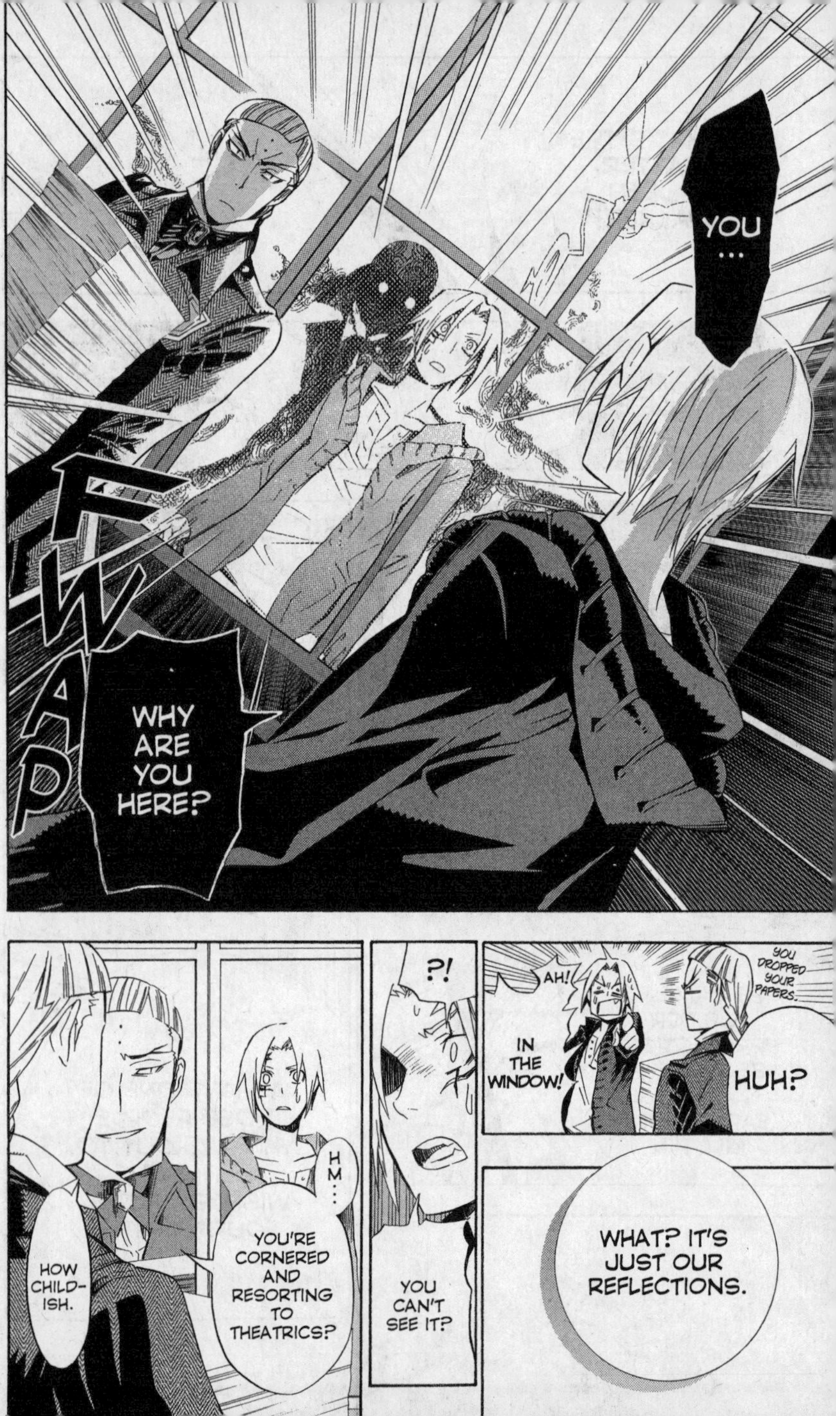
YOU...
FWAP
WHY ARE YOU HERE?
YOU DROPPED YOUR PAPERS.
HUH?
AH!
IN THE WINDOW!
WHAT? IT'S JUST OUR REFLECTIONS.
?!
YOU CAN'T SEE IT?
HM...
YOU'RE CORNERED AND RESORTING TO THEATRICS?
HOW CHILD-ISH.

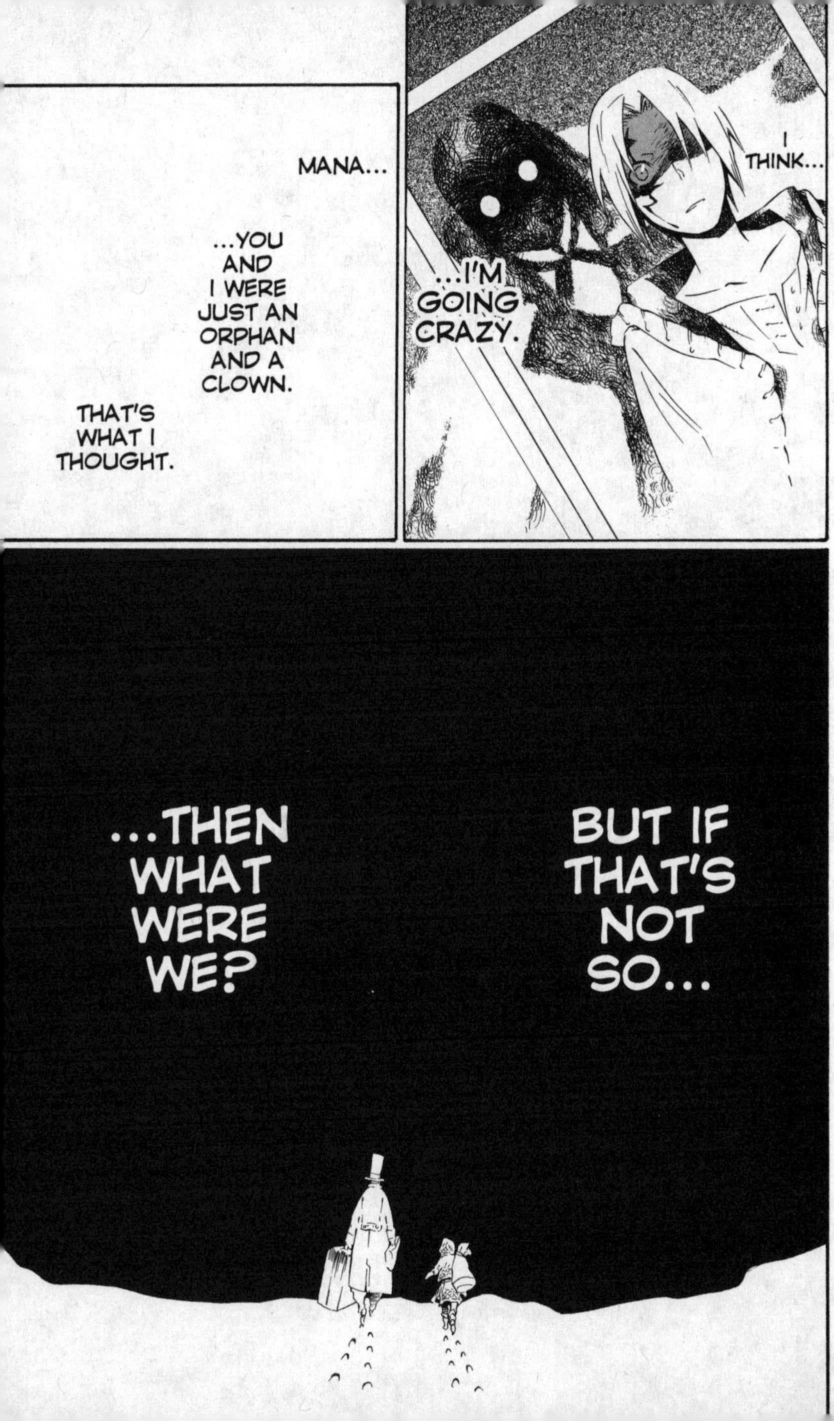
I THINK...
...I'M GOING CRAZY.
MANA...
...YOU AND I WERE JUST AN ORPHAN AND A CLOWN.
THAT'S WHAT I THOUGHT.
BUT IF THAT'S NOT SO...
...THEN WHAT WERE WE?

DISTANT
STARE

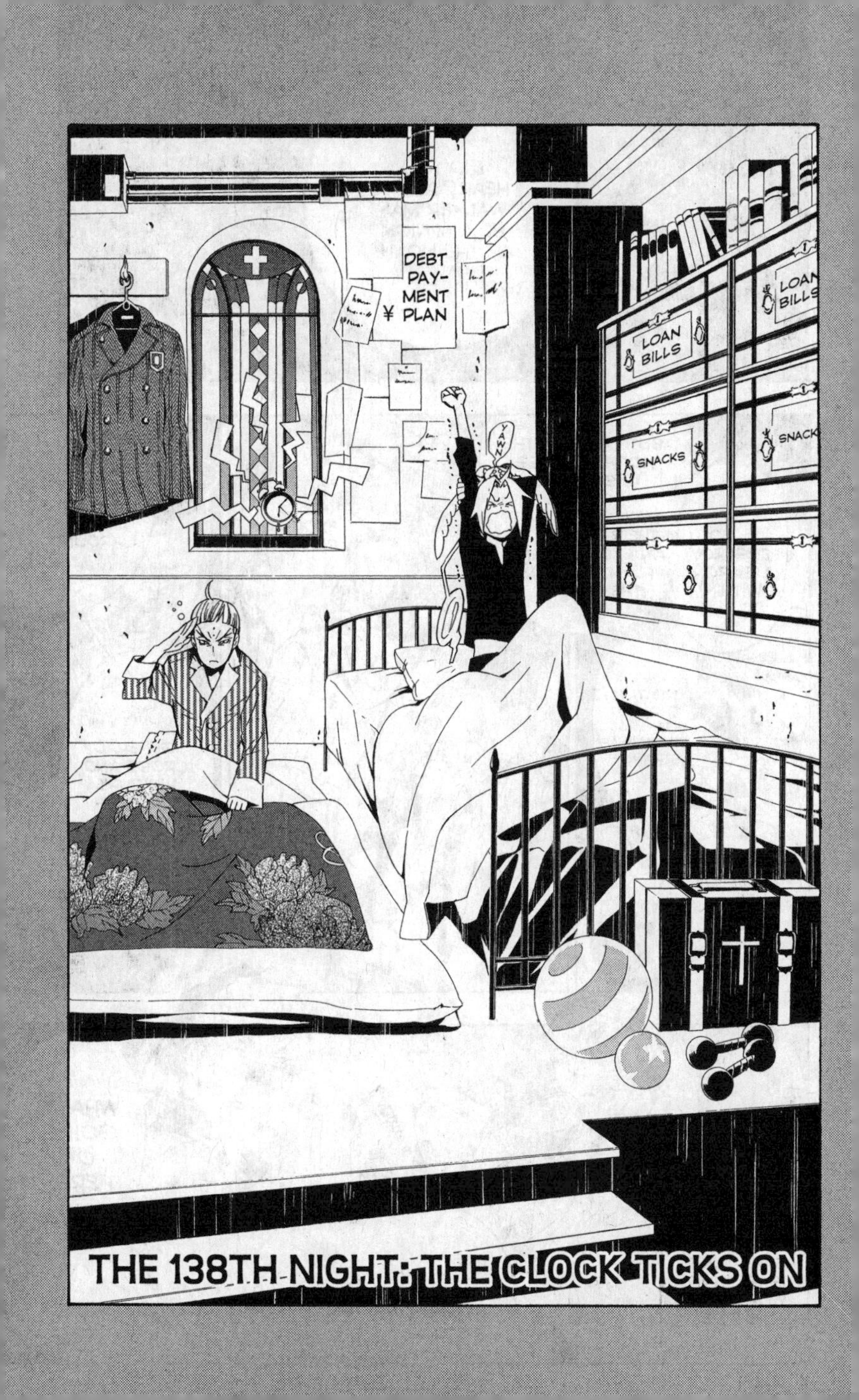
LOAN BILLS
SNACK
LOAN BILLS
SNACKS
YAWN
DEBT PAY-MENT ¥ PLAN
THE 138TH NIGHT: THE CLOCK TICKS ON

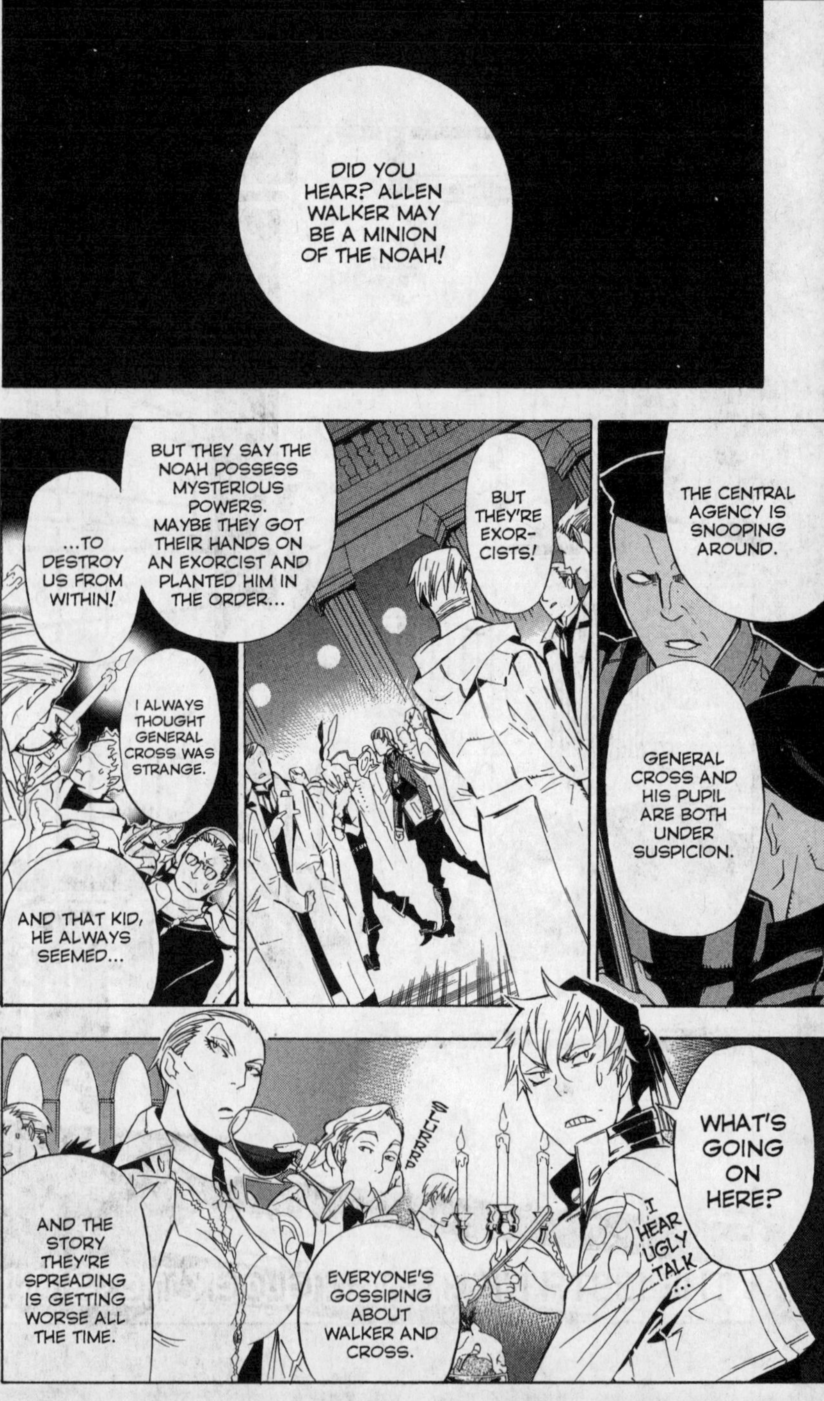
DID YOU HEAR? ALLEN WALKER MAY BE A MINION OF THE NOAH!
THE CENTRAL AGENCY IS SNOOPING AROUND.
GENERAL CROSS AND HIS PUPIL ARE BOTH UNDER SUSPICION.
BUT THEY'RE EXORCISTS!
BUT THEY SAY THE NOAH POSSESS MYSTERIOUS POWERS. MAYBE THEY GOT THEIR HANDS ON AN EXORCIST AND PLANTED HIM IN THE ORDER...
...TO DESTROY US FROM WITHIN!
I ALWAYS THOUGHT GENERAL CROSS WAS STRANGE.
AND THAT KID, HE ALWAYS SEEMED...
WHAT'S GOING ON HERE?
I HEAR UGLY TALK...
SLURRRP
EVERYONE'S GOSSIPING ABOUT WALKER AND CROSS.
AND THE STORY THEY'RE SPREADING IS GETTING WORSE ALL THE TIME.

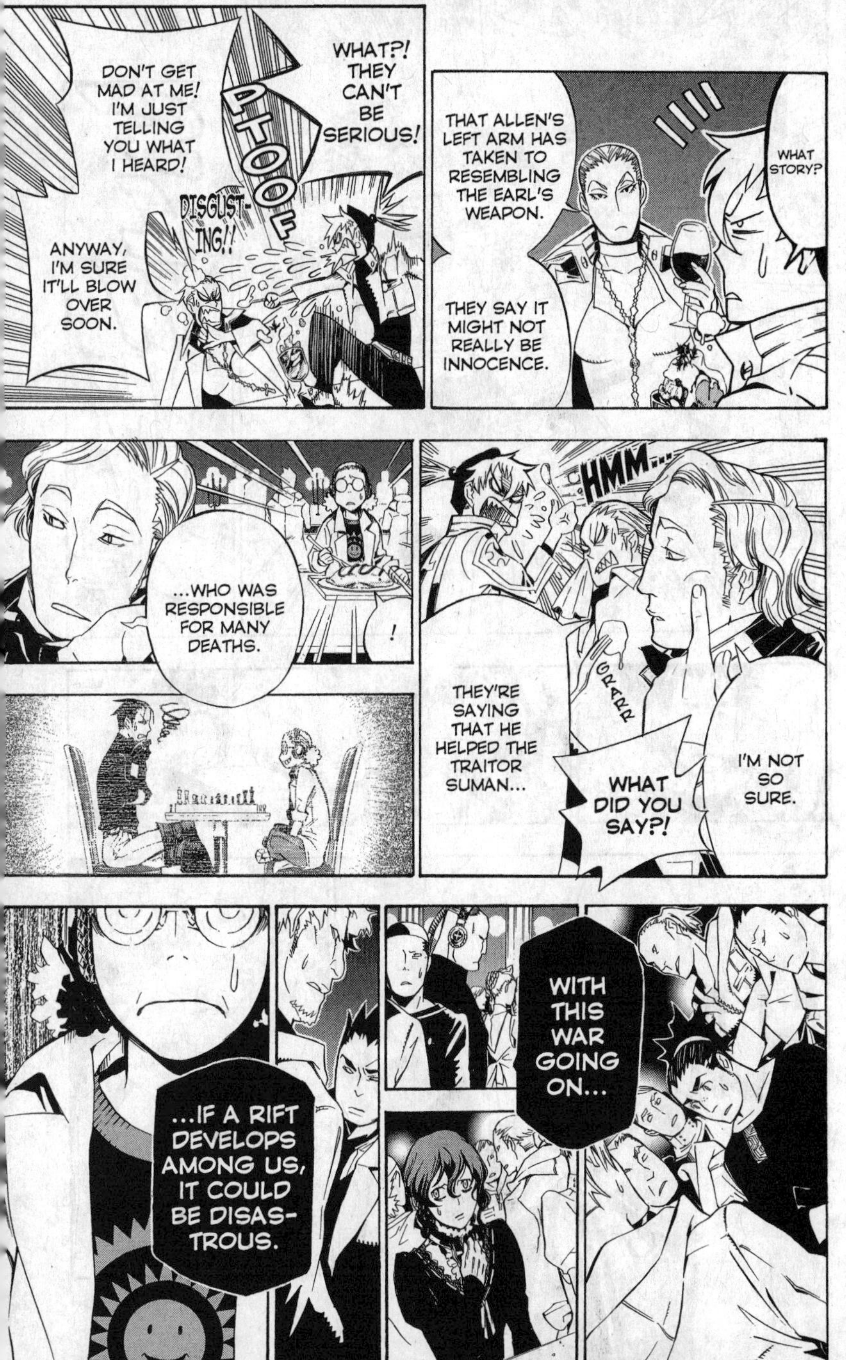
WHAT STORY?
THAT ALLEN'S LEFT ARM HAS TAKEN TO RESEMBLING THE EARL'S WEAPON.
THEY SAY IT MIGHT NOT REALLY BE INNOCENCE.
WHAT?! THEY CAN'T BE SERIOUS!
PTOOF
DON'T GET MAD AT ME! I'M JUST TELLING YOU WHAT I HEARD!
DISGUSTING!!
ANYWAY, I'M SURE IT'LL BLOW OVER SOON.
HMM...
GRARR
I'M NOT SO SURE.
THEY'RE SAYING THAT HE HELPED THE TRAITOR SUMAN...
WHAT DID YOU SAY?!
...WHO WAS RESPONSIBLE FOR MANY DEATHS.
!
WITH THIS WAR GOING ON...
...IF A RIFT DEVELOPS AMONG US, IT COULD BE DISASTROUS.

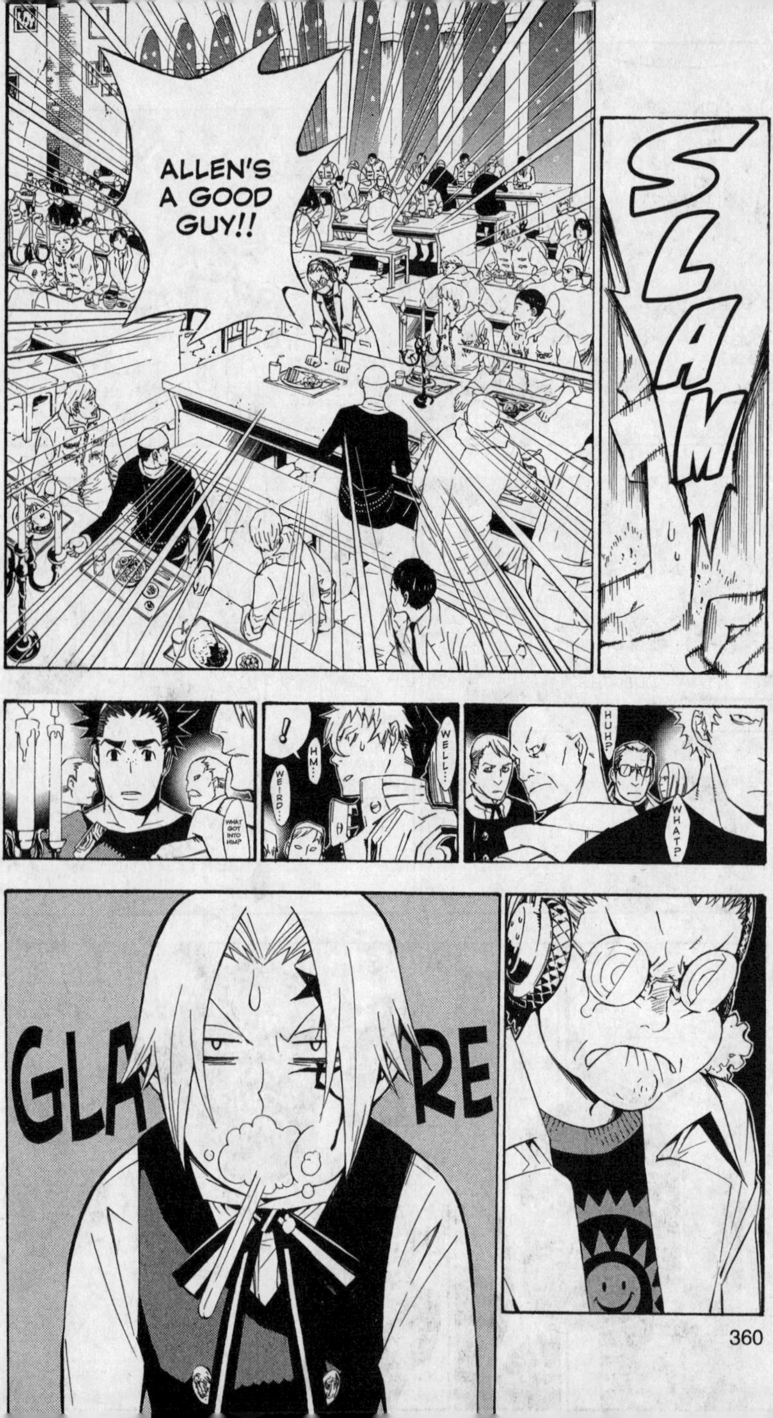
SLAM
ALLEN'S A GOOD GUY!!
HUH?
WHAT?
WELL...
HM...
WEIRD...
!
WHAT GOT INTO HIM?
GLARE

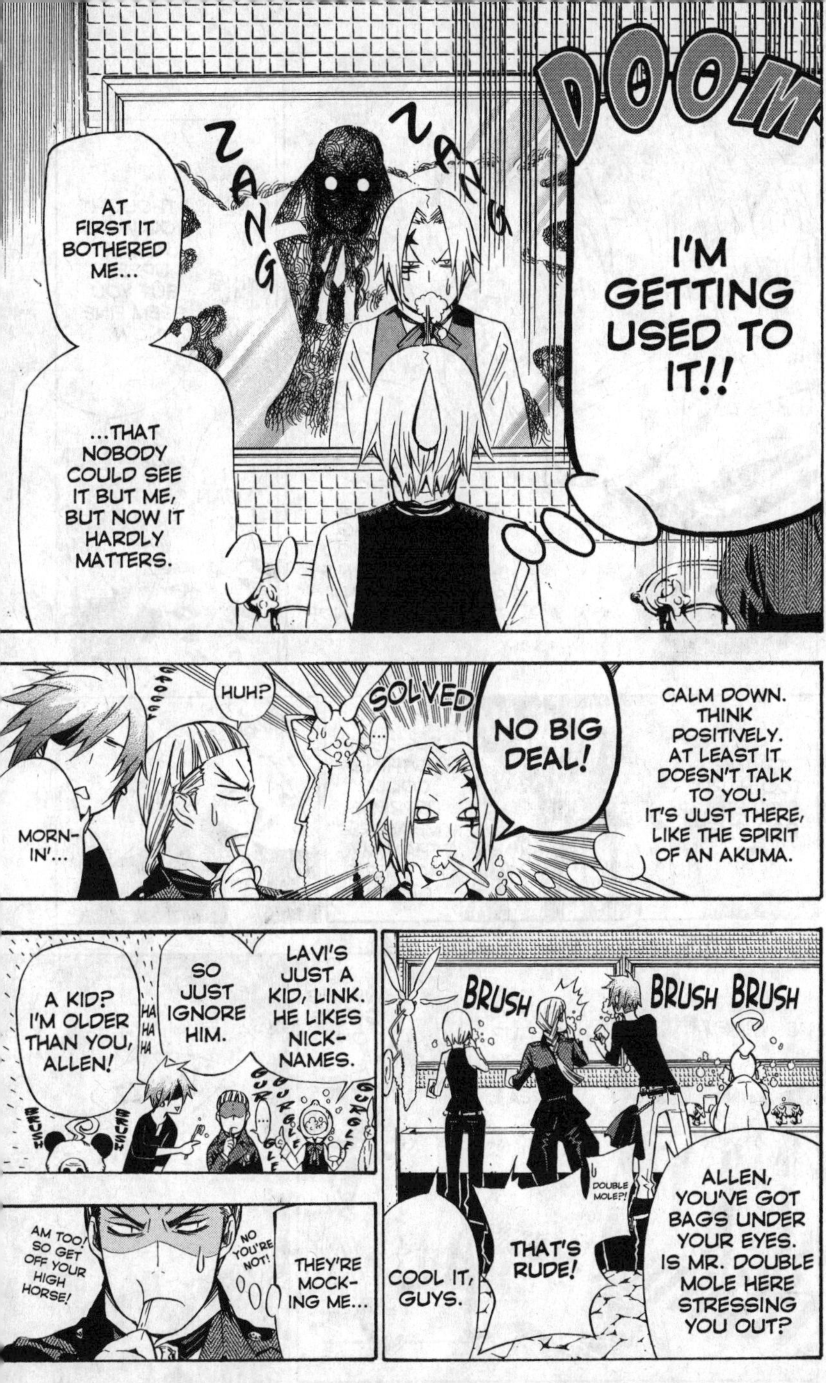
DOOM
I'M GETTING USED TO IT!!
ZANG ZANG
AT FIRST IT BOTHERED ME...
...THAT NOBODY COULD SEE IT BUT ME, BUT NOW IT HARDLY MATTERS.
CALM DOWN. THINK POSITIVELY. AT LEAST IT DOESN'T TALK TO YOU. IT'S JUST THERE, LIKE THE SPIRIT OF AN AKUMA.
NO BIG DEAL!
SOLVED
...
HUH?
MORN- IN'...
BRUSH BRUSH
BRUSH
ALLEN, YOU'VE GOT BAGS UNDER YOUR EYES. IS MR. DOUBLE MOLE HERE STRESSING YOU OUT?
DOUBLE MOLE?!
THAT'S RUDE!
COOL IT, GUYS.
LAVI'S JUST A KID, LINK. HE LIKES NICK- NAMES.
SO JUST IGNORE HIM.
HA HA HA
A KID? I'M OLDER THAN YOU, ALLEN!
GURGLE
GURGLE
GURGLE
...
BRUSH
BRUSH
THEY'RE MOCK- ING ME...
NO YOU'RE NOT!
AM TOO! SO GET OFF YOUR HIGH HORSE!

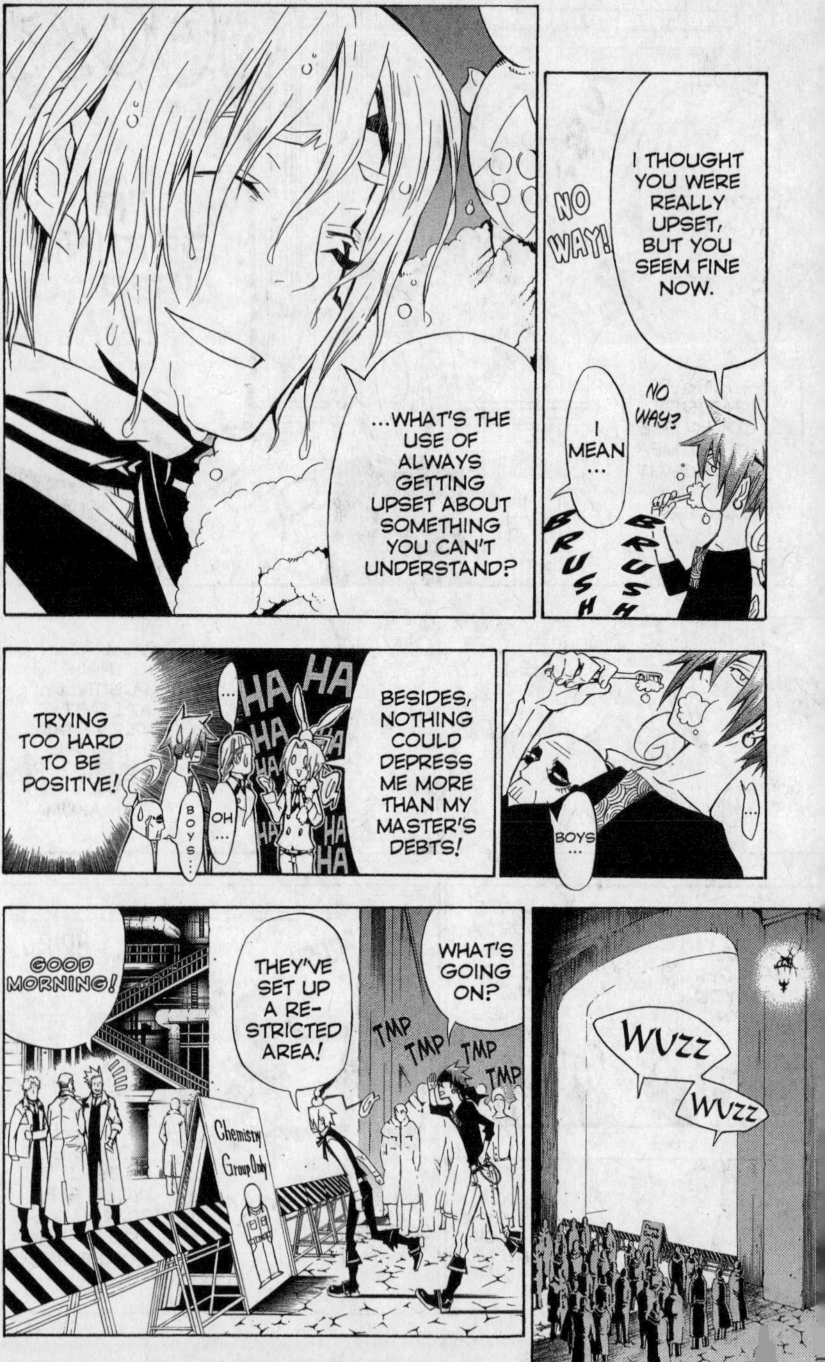
I THOUGHT YOU WERE REALLY UPSET, BUT YOU SEEM FINE NOW.
NO WAY!
NO WAY?
I MEAN...
BRUSH
BRUSH
...WHAT'S THE USE OF ALWAYS GETTING UPSET ABOUT SOMETHING YOU CAN'T UNDERSTAND?
...
BOYS...
BESIDES, NOTHING COULD DEPRESS ME MORE THAN MY MASTER'S DEBTS!
HA HA HA HA HA HA HA HA HA
...
OH...
BOYS...
TRYING TOO HARD TO BE POSITIVE!
WUZZ
WUZZ
WHAT'S GOING ON?
TMP TMP TMP TMP
THEY'VE SET UP A RE-STRICTED AREA!
Chemistry Group Only
GOOD MORNING!

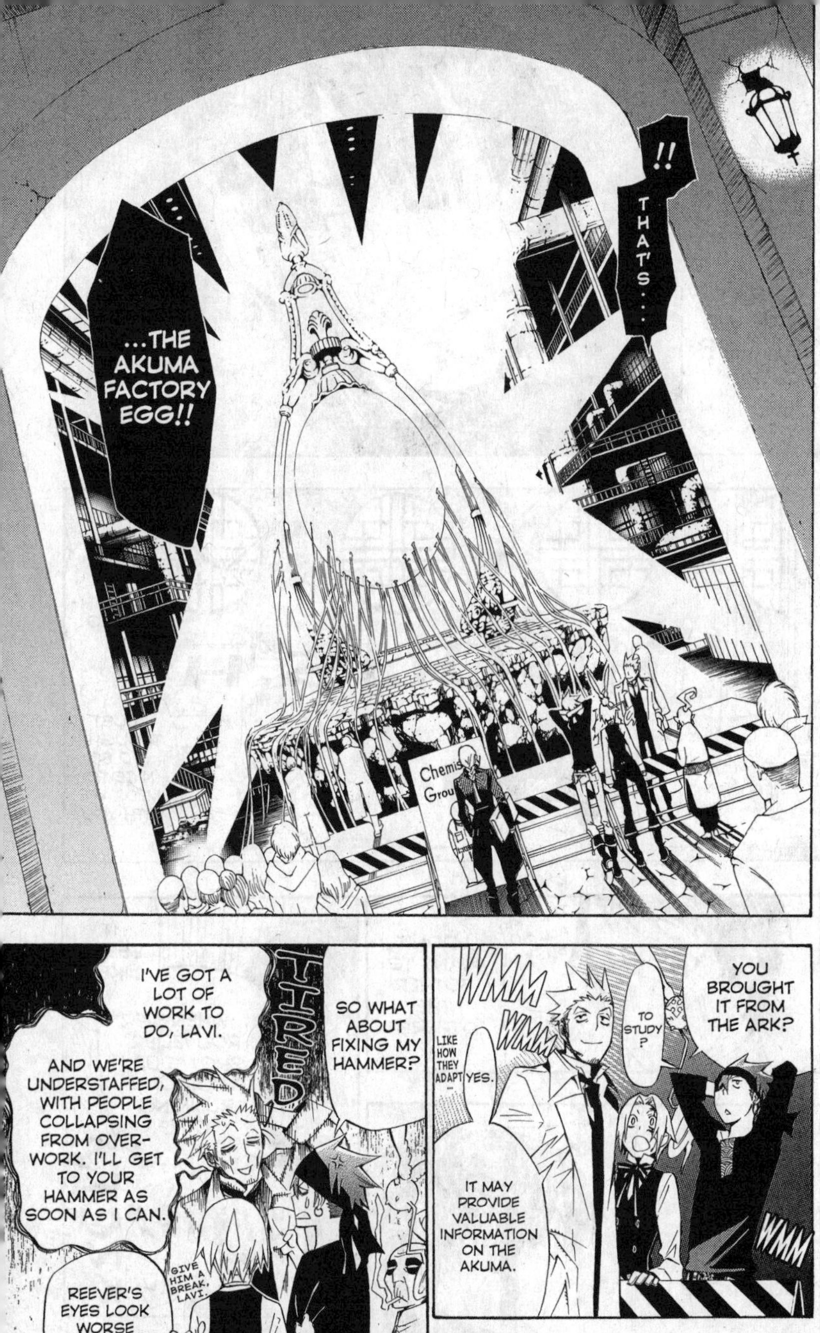
!!
THAT'S...
...THE AKUMA FACTORY EGG!!
WMM
WMM
YOU BROUGHT IT FROM THE ARK?
TO STUDY?
YES.
LIKE HOW THEY ADAPT...
IT MAY PROVIDE VALUABLE INFORMATION ON THE AKUMA.
WMM
SO WHAT ABOUT FIXING MY HAMMER?
TIRED
I'VE GOT A LOT OF WORK TO DO, LAVI.
AND WE'RE UNDERSTAFFED, WITH PEOPLE COLLAPSING FROM OVER-WORK. I'LL GET TO YOUR HAMMER AS SOON AS I CAN.
GIVE HIM A BREAK, LAVI.
REEVER'S EYES LOOK WORSE THAN MINE.

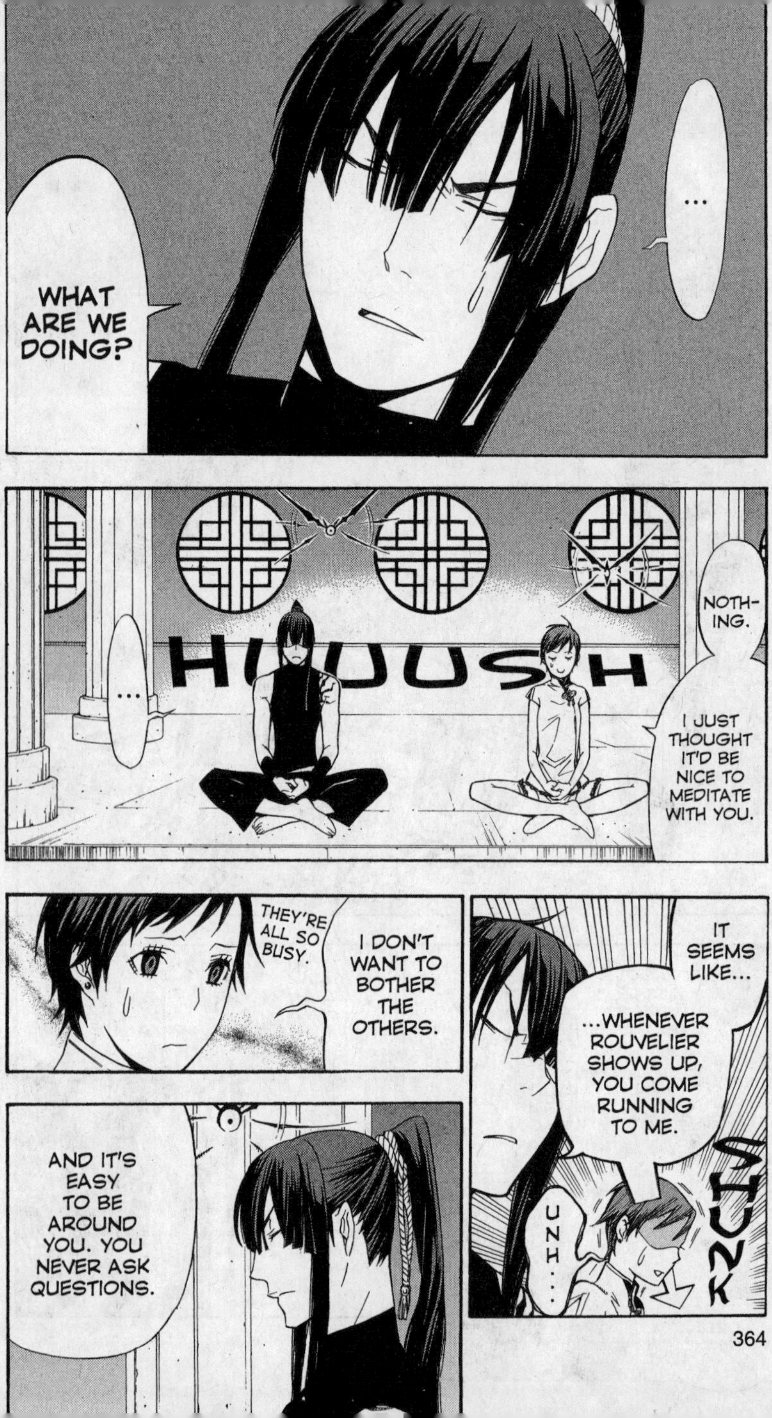
...
WHAT ARE WE DOING?
NOTHING.
I JUST THOUGHT IT'D BE NICE TO MEDITATE WITH YOU.
HUUUSH
...
IT SEEMS LIKE...
...WHENEVER ROUVELIER SHOWS UP, YOU COME RUNNING TO ME.
UNH...
SHUNK
I DON'T WANT TO BOTHER THE OTHERS.
THEY'RE ALL SO BUSY.
AND IT'S EASY TO BE AROUND YOU. YOU NEVER ASK QUESTIONS.

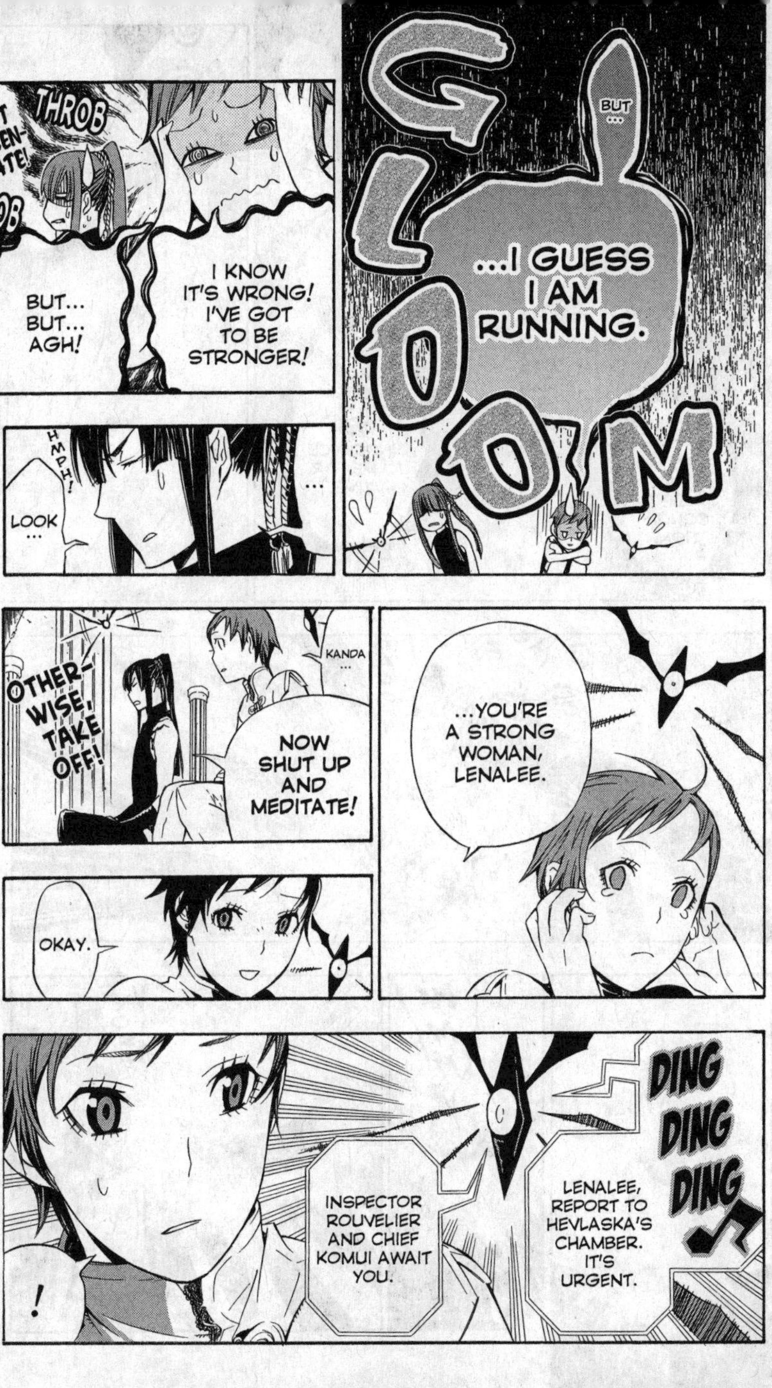
GLOOM
BUT...
...I GUESS I AM RUNNING.
THROB
I CAN'T CONCEN-TRATE!
THROB
THROB
I KNOW IT'S WRONG! I'VE GOT TO BE STRONGER!
BUT... BUT... AGH!
...
HMPH!
LOOK...
...YOU'RE A STRONG WOMAN, LENALEE.
KANDA...
NOW SHUT UP AND MEDITATE!
OTHER-WISE, TAKE OFF!
OKAY.
DING DING DING
LENALEE, REPORT TO HEVLASKA'S CHAMBER. IT'S URGENT.
INSPECTOR ROUVELIER AND CHIEF KOMUI AWAIT YOU.
!

VWMM

WHAT?

HER SYNCHRONIZATION RATE IS NOW BELOW TEN PERCENT.

WE SHOULD RETURN HER INNOCENCE TO ME FOR A TIME.

I'LL RESTORE IT TO ORIGINAL CONDITION.

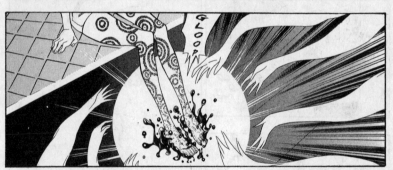

GLOOP

KLUNK

WMM

WMM

SLOSH

MY BOOTS MELTED...

READ THIS WAY

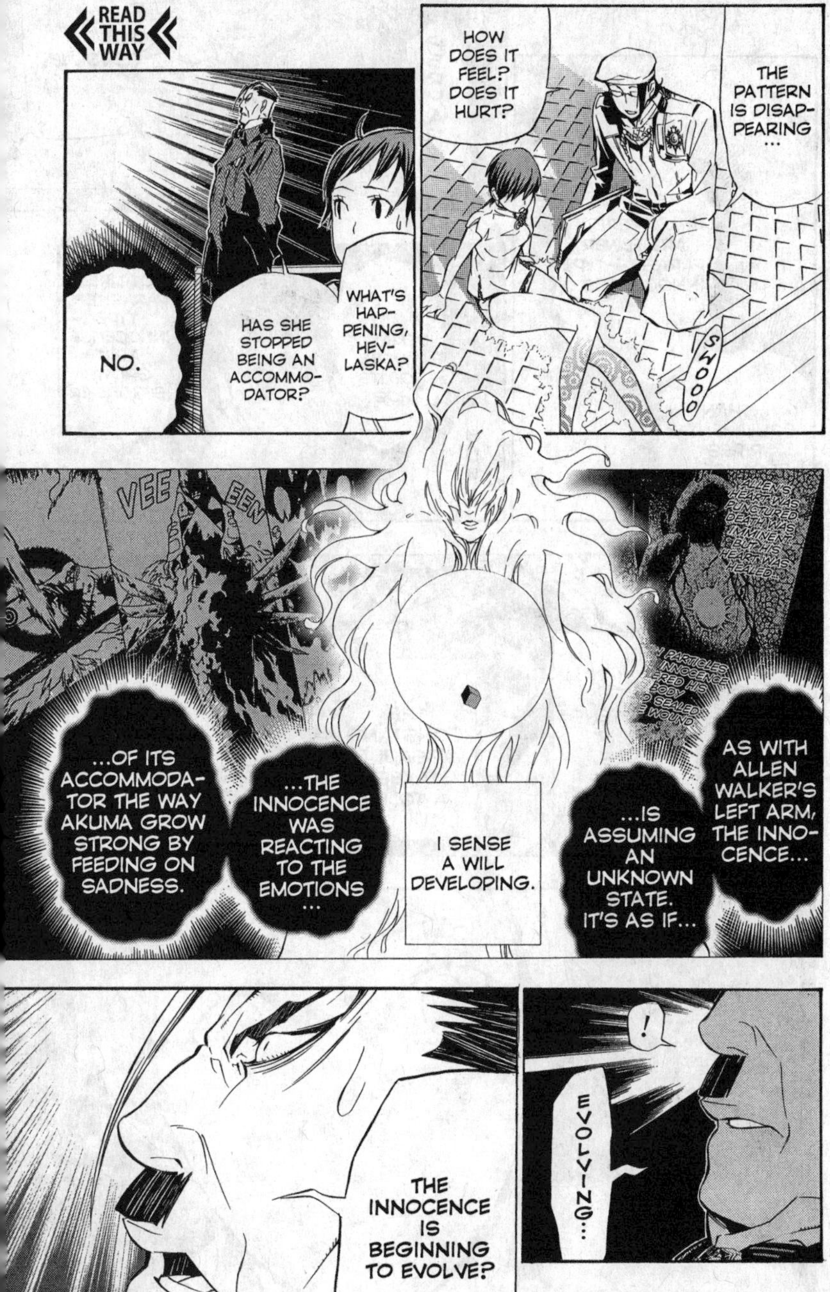
HOW DOES IT FEEL? DOES IT HURT?
THE PATTERN IS DISAPPEARING...
SWOOO
WHAT'S HAPPENING, HEVLASKA?
HAS SHE STOPPED BEING AN ACCOMMODATOR?
NO.
ALLEN'S HEART WAS PUNCTURED. DEATH WAS IMMINENT, BUT HIS HEART WAS HEALED.
AS WITH ALLEN WALKER'S LEFT ARM, THE INNOCENCE...
...IS ASSUMING AN UNKNOWN STATE. IT'S AS IF...
I SENSE A WILL DEVELOPING.
...THE INNOCENCE WAS REACTING TO THE EMOTIONS...
...OF ITS ACCOMMODATOR THE WAY AKUMA GROW STRONG BY FEEDING ON SADNESS.
VEE
EEN
!
EVOLVING...
THE INNOCENCE IS BEGINNING TO EVOLVE?

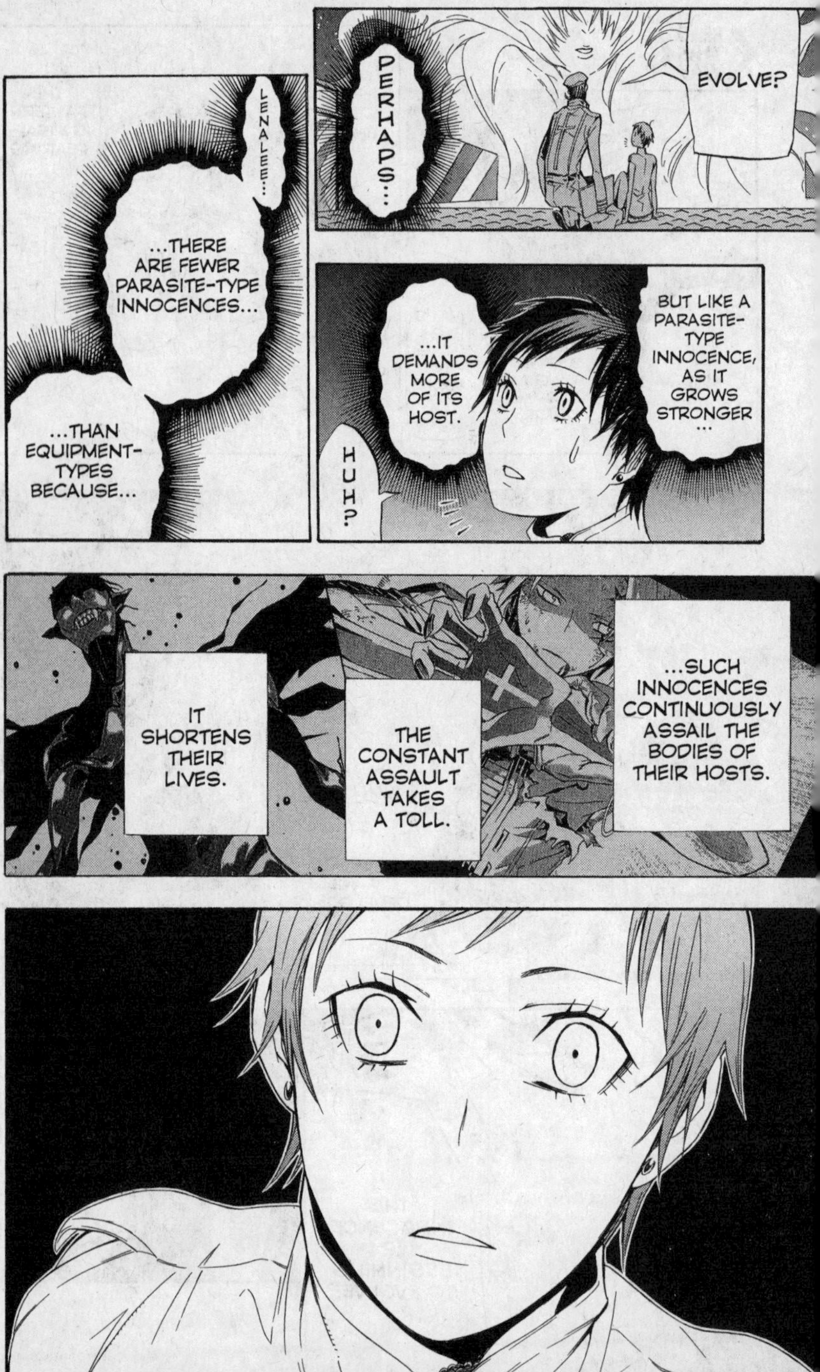
EVOLVE?
PERHAPS...
BUT LIKE A PARASITE-TYPE INNOCENCE, AS IT GROWS STRONGER...
...IT DEMANDS MORE OF ITS HOST.
HUH?
LENALEE...
...THERE ARE FEWER PARASITE-TYPE INNOCENCES...
...THAN EQUIPMENT-TYPES BECAUSE...
...SUCH INNOCENCES CONTINUOUSLY ASSAIL THE BODIES OF THEIR HOSTS.
THE CONSTANT ASSAULT TAKES A TOLL.
IT SHORTENS THEIR LIVES.

READ THIS WAY

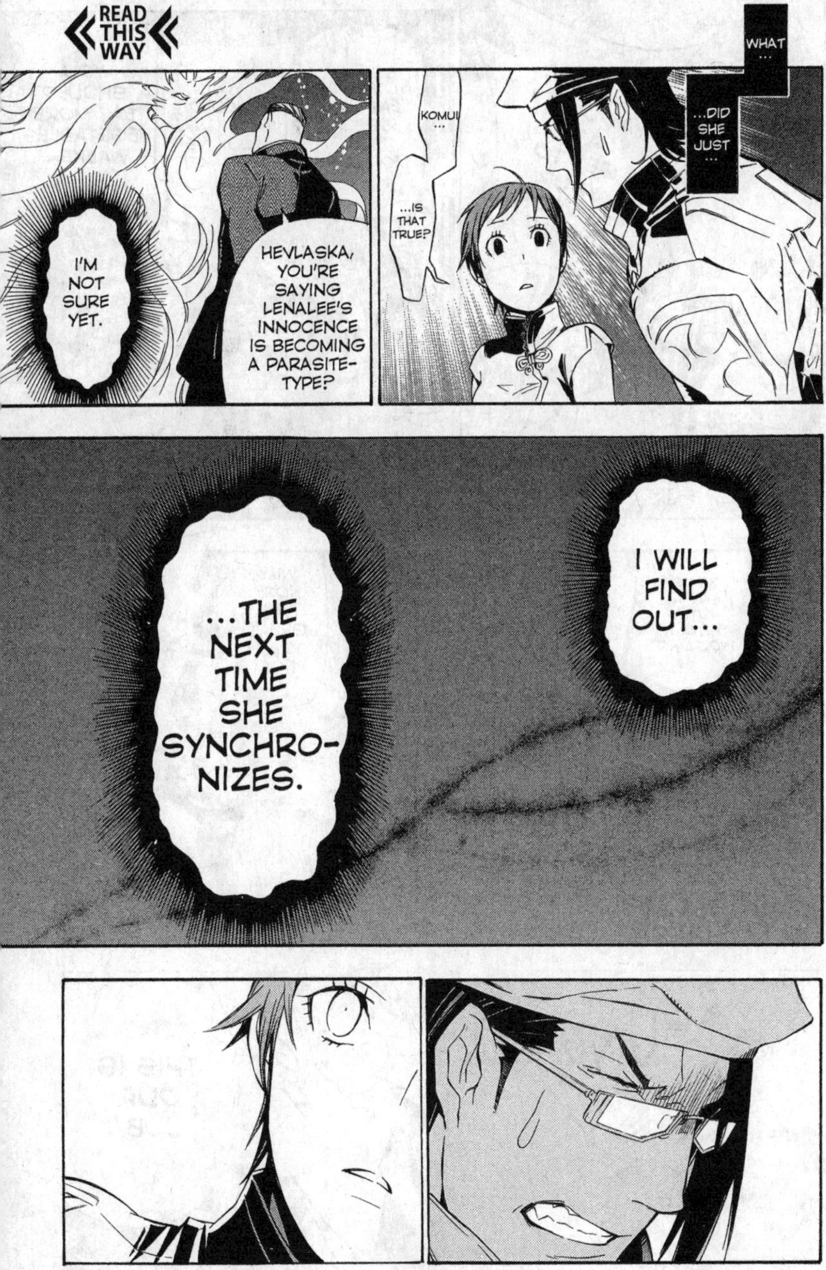
WHAT...
...DID SHE JUST...
KOMUI...
...IS THAT TRUE?
HEVLASKA, YOU'RE SAYING LENALEE'S INNOCENCE IS BECOMING A PARASITE-TYPE?
I'M NOT SURE YET.
I WILL FIND OUT...
...THE NEXT TIME SHE SYNCHRONIZES.

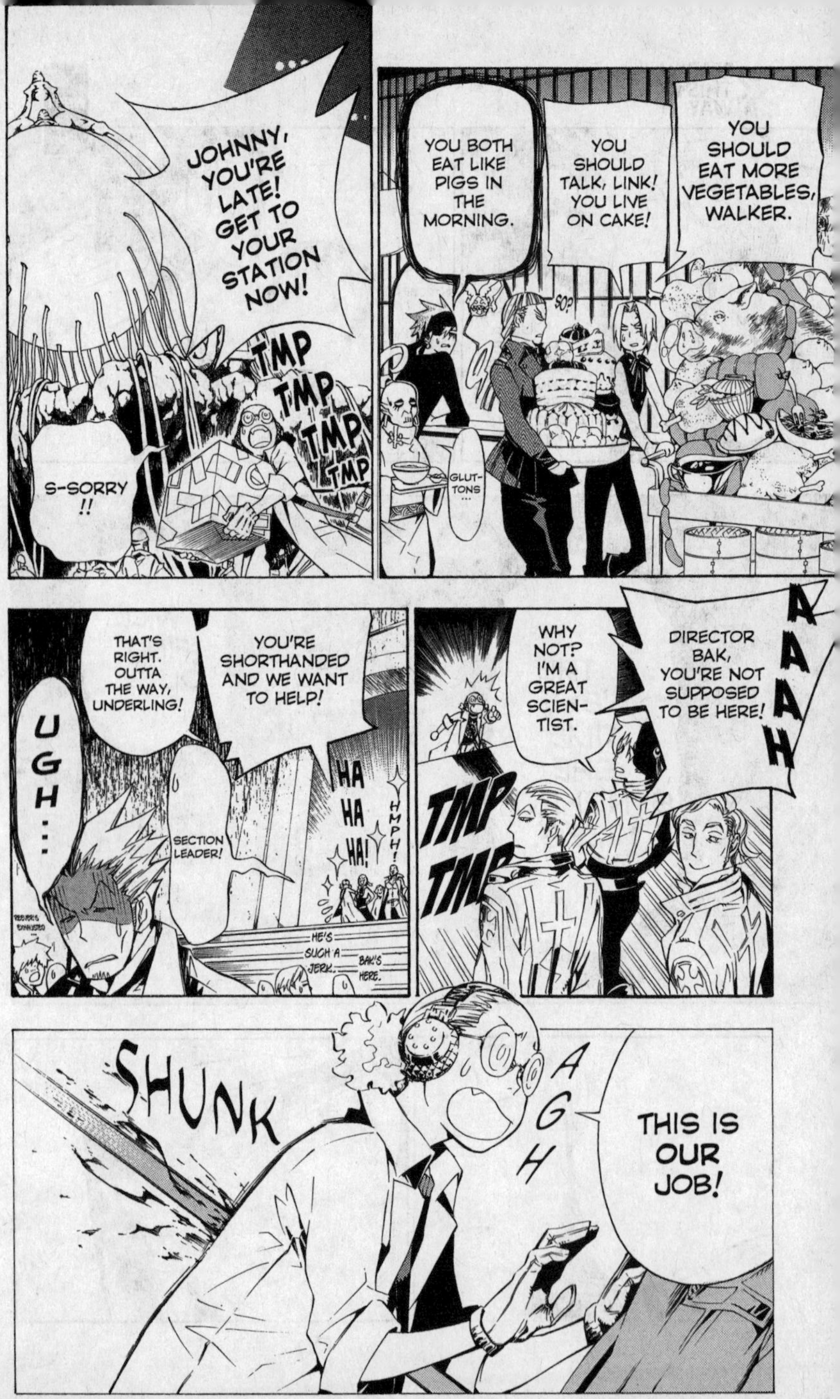
YOU SHOULD EAT MORE VEGETABLES, WALKER.
YOU SHOULD TALK, LINK! YOU LIVE ON CAKE!
YOU BOTH EAT LIKE PIGS IN THE MORNING.
SOP
GLUTTONS...
JOHNNY, YOU'RE LATE! GET TO YOUR STATION NOW!
TMP TMP TMP TMP
S-SORRY!!
AAAAH
DIRECTOR BAK, YOU'RE NOT SUPPOSED TO BE HERE!
WHY NOT? I'M A GREAT SCIENTIST.
TMP TMP
YOU'RE SHORTHANDED AND WE WANT TO HELP!
THAT'S RIGHT. OUTTA THE WAY, UNDERLING!
HA HA HA!
HMPH!
HE'S SUCH A JERK.
BAK'S HERE.
SECTION LEADER!
UGH...
REEVER'S EXHAUSTED...
THIS IS OUR JOB!
AGH
SHUNK

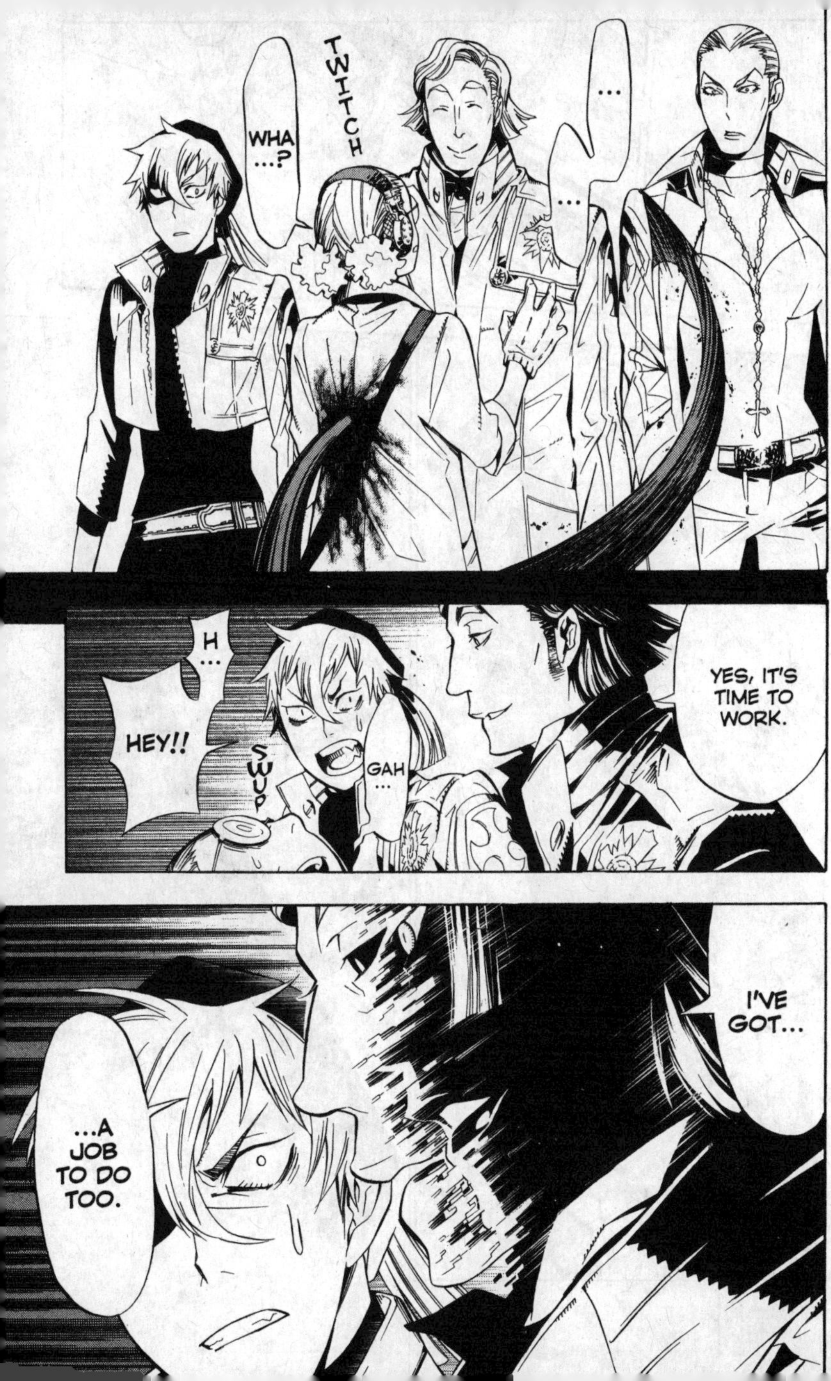
...
...
TWITCH
WHA ...?
YES, IT'S TIME TO WORK.
GAH ...
SWUP
H ...
HEY!!
I'VE GOT...
...A JOB TO DO TOO.

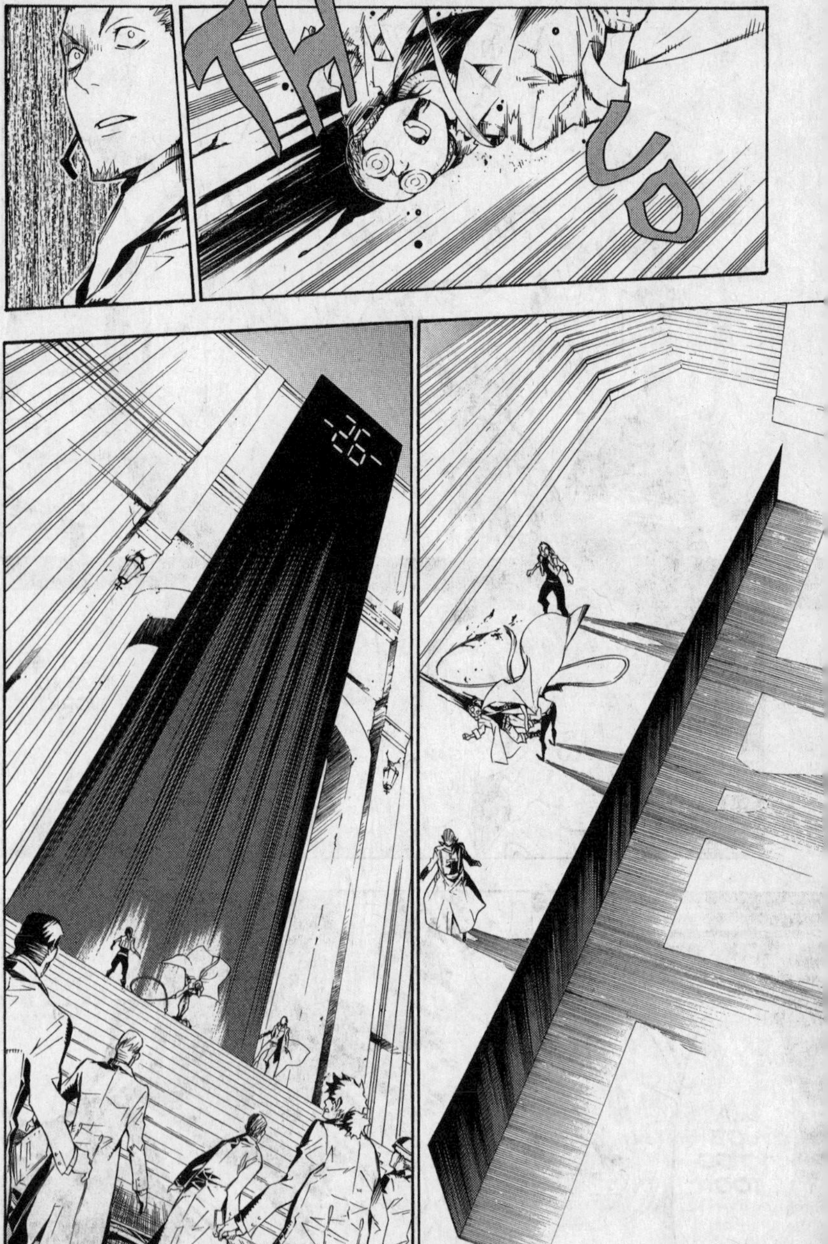
THUD
26

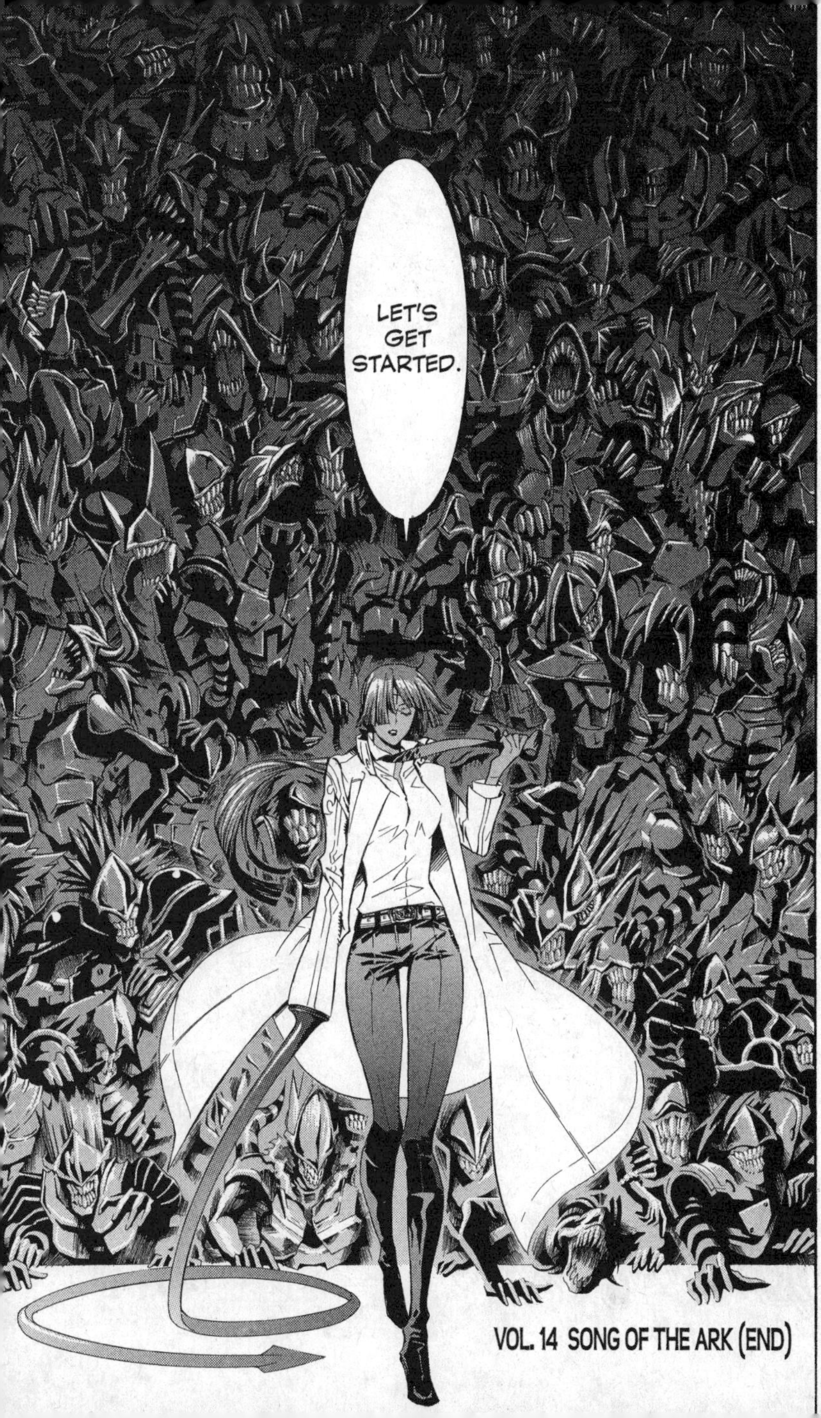
LET'S GET STARTED.
VOL. 14 SONG OF THE ARK (END)

ディー・グレイマン
D.Gray-man

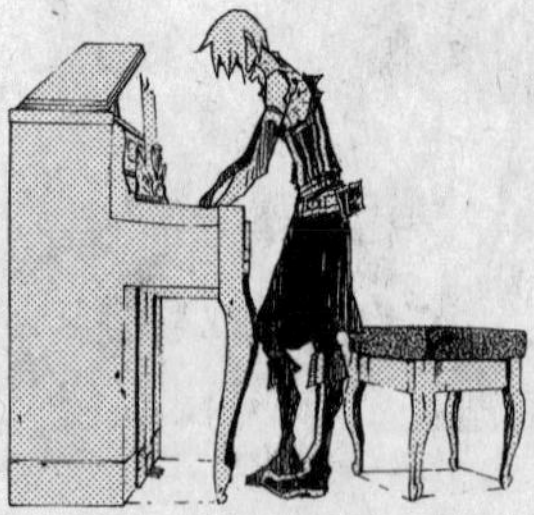

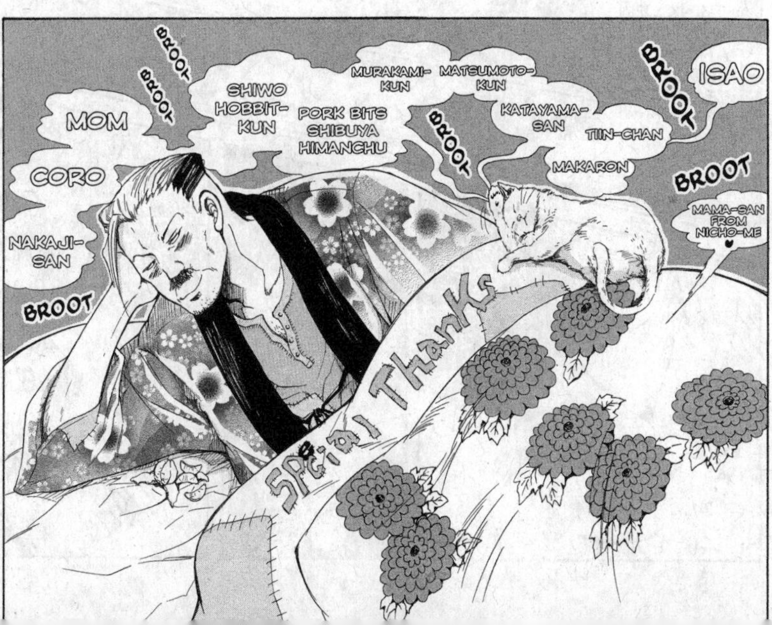
ISAO
BROOT
MATSUMOTO-KUN
MURAKAMI-KUN
KATAYAMA-SAN
TIIN-CHAN
BROOT
PORK BITS SHIBUYA HIMANCHU
SHIWO HOBBIT-KUN
BROOT
BROOT
MOM
MAKARON
BROOT
MAMA-SAN FROM NICHO-ME
CORO
NAKAJI-SAN
BROOT
Special Thanks

D.GRAY THEATER

BY MAMA-SAN FROM NICHO-ME

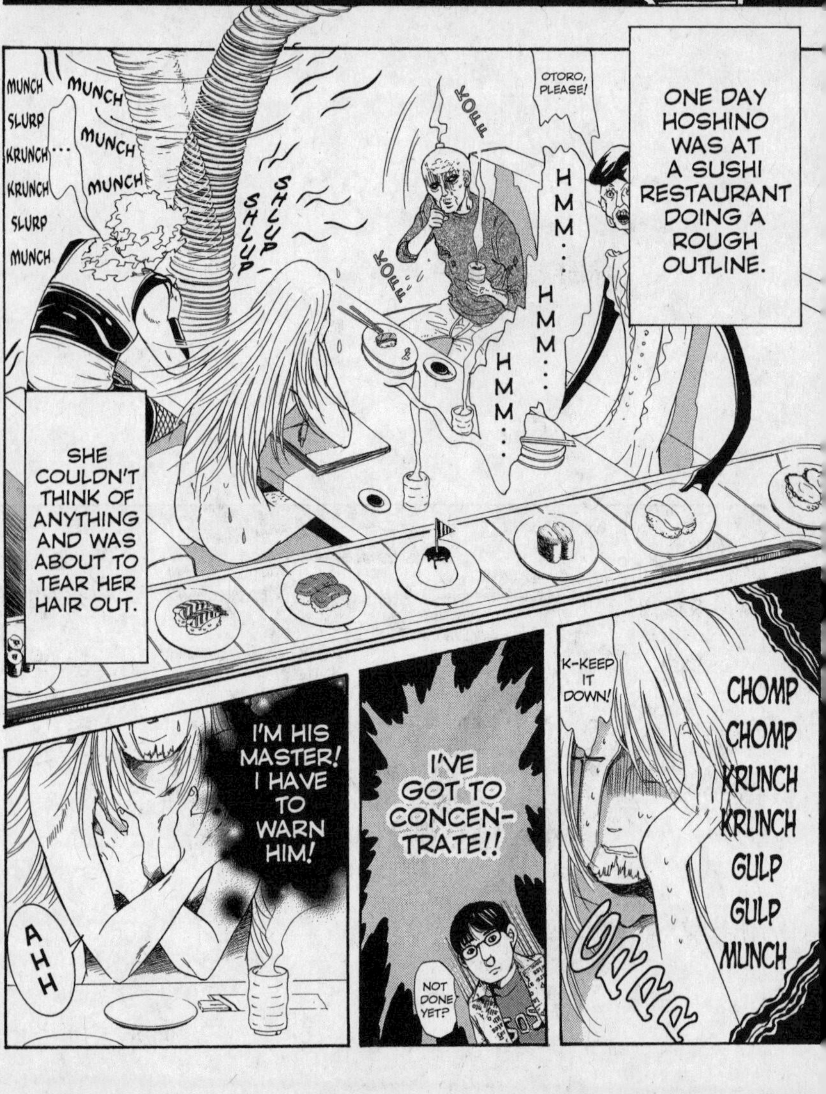
ONE DAY HOSHINO WAS AT A SUSHI RESTAURANT DOING A ROUGH OUTLINE.
OTORO, PLEASE!
HMM... HMM... HMM...
KOFF
KOFF
SHLUP SHLUP
MUNCH MUNCH MUNCH
MUNCH SLURP KRUNCH... KRUNCH SLURP MUNCH
SHE COULDN'T THINK OF ANYTHING AND WAS ABOUT TO TEAR HER HAIR OUT.
CHOMP CHOMP KRUNCH KRUNCH GULP GULP MUNCH
K-KEEP IT DOWN!
I'VE GOT TO CONCENTRATE!!
NOT DONE YET?
I'M HIS MASTER! I HAVE TO WARN HIM!
AHH

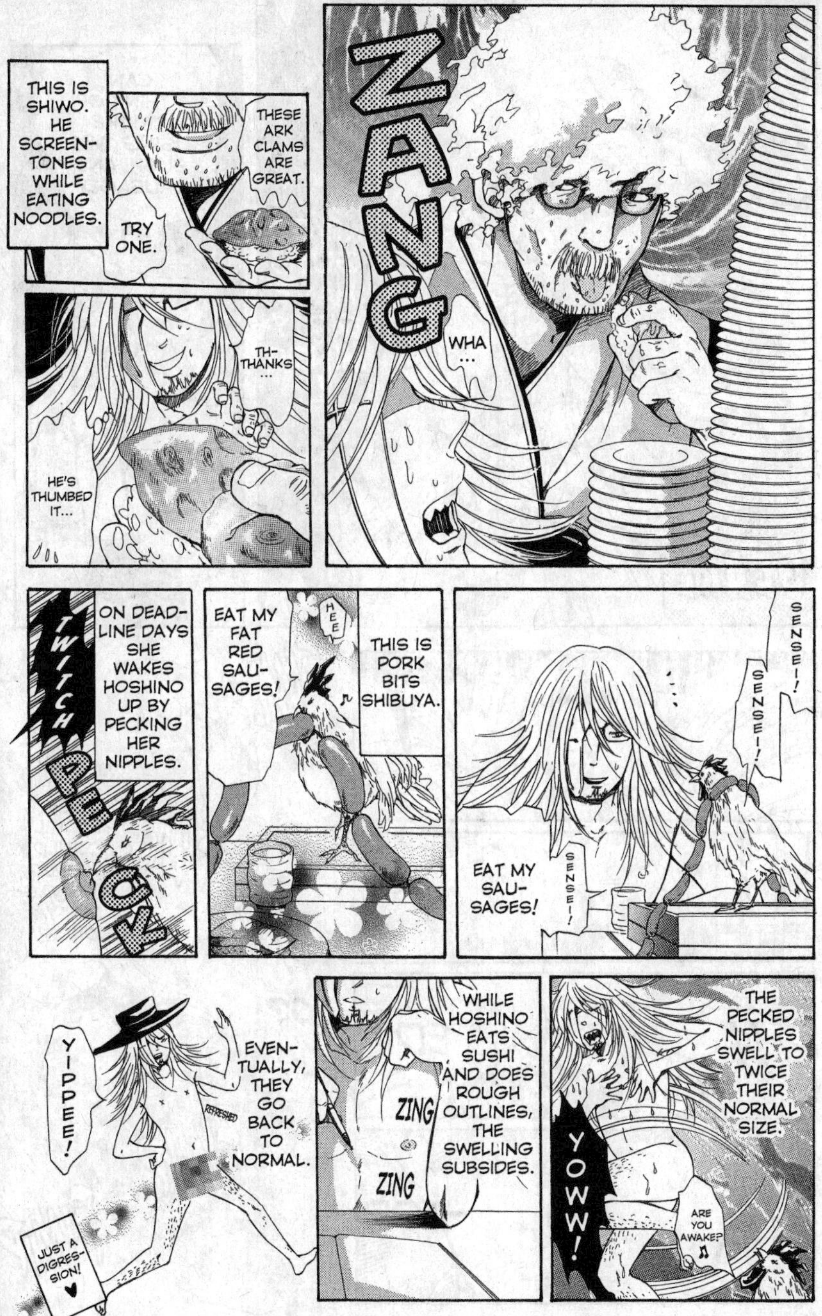
ZANG
WHA...
THIS IS SHIWO. HE SCREENTONES WHILE EATING NOODLES.
THESE ARK CLAMS ARE GREAT.
TRY ONE.
TH-THANKS...
HE'S THUMBED IT...
SENSE-I!
SENSE-I!
...
EAT MY SAUSAGES!
SENSE-I!
THIS IS PORK BITS SHIBUYA.
EAT MY FAT RED SAUSAGES!
HEE
♪
ON DEADLINE DAYS SHE WAKES HOSHINO UP BY PECKING HER NIPPLES.
TWITCH
PECK
THE PECKED NIPPLES SWELL TO TWICE THEIR NORMAL SIZE.
YOWW!
ARE YOU AWAKE? ♫
WHILE HOSHINO EATS SUSHI AND DOES ROUGH OUTLINES, THE SWELLING SUBSIDES.
ZING
ZING
EVENTUALLY, THEY GO BACK TO NORMAL.
YIPPEE!
REFRESHED
JUST A DIGRESSION! ♥

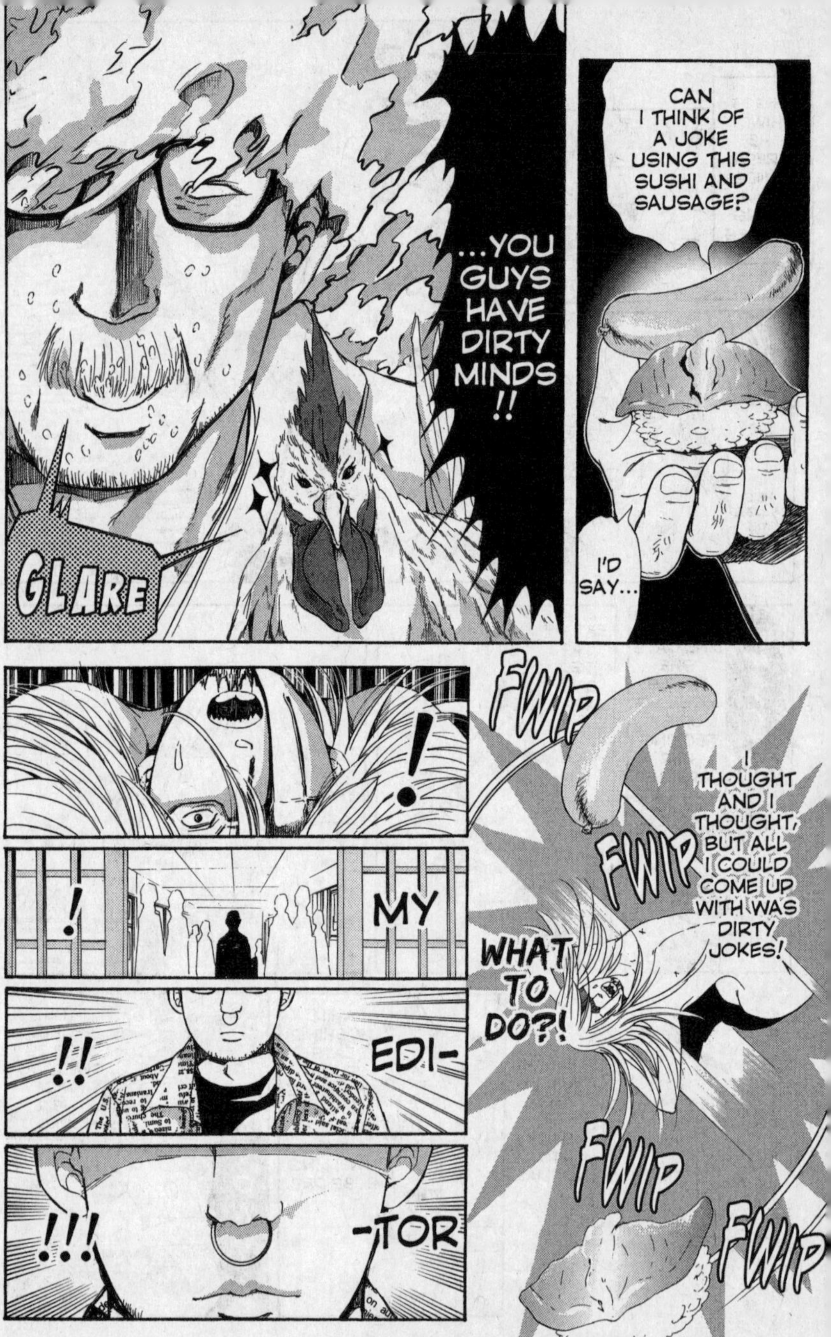
CAN I THINK OF A JOKE USING THIS SUSHI AND SAUSAGE?
I'D SAY...
...YOU GUYS HAVE DIRTY MINDS!!
GLARE
FWIP
I THOUGHT AND I THOUGHT, BUT ALL I COULD COME UP WITH WAS DIRTY JOKES!
FWIP
WHAT TO DO?!
FWIP
FWIP
!
MY
!
EDI-
!!
-TOR
!!!

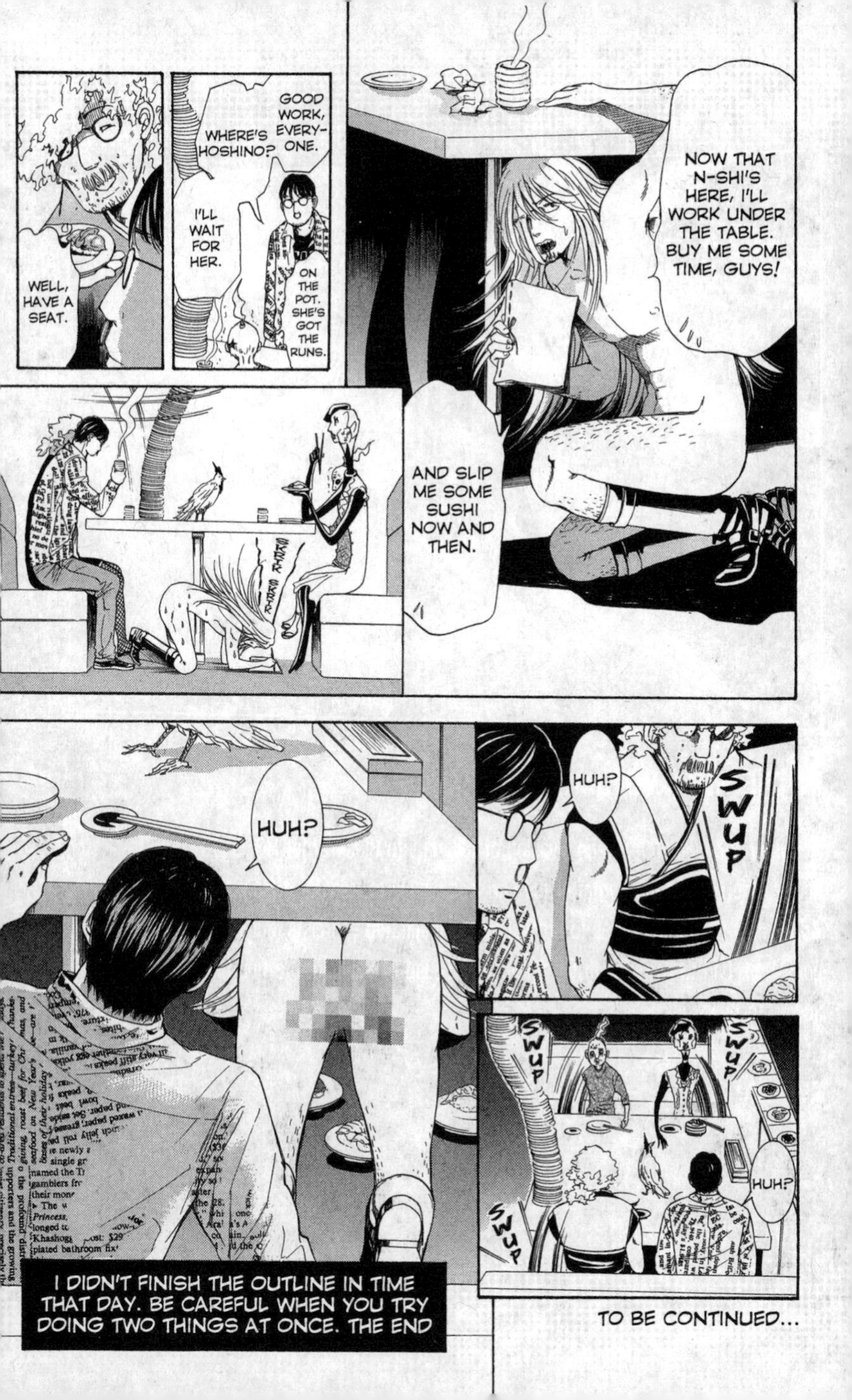
NOW THAT N-SHI'S HERE, I'LL WORK UNDER THE TABLE. BUY ME SOME TIME, GUYS!
AND SLIP ME SOME SUSHI NOW AND THEN.
GOOD WORK, EVERY-ONE.
WHERE'S HOSHINO?
ON THE POT. SHE'S GOT THE RUNS.
I'LL WAIT FOR HER.
WELL, HAVE A SEAT.
SKRIK SKRIK
HUH?
SWUP
SWUP
SWUP
HUH?
SWUP
HUH?
I DIDN'T FINISH THE OUTLINE IN TIME THAT DAY. BE CAREFUL WHEN YOU TRY DOING TWO THINGS AT ONCE. THE END
TO BE CONTINUED...

N THE NEXT VOLUME...

A mysterious woman leads an invasion of Akuma into Black Order HQ. She's come to acquire the Egg for the Earl after the Earl was unable to transfer it from the disintegrating Ark. Komui desperately tries to protect his incapacitated exorcists, but the situation only goes from bad to worse with the arrival of a squad of Skulls out to find brains worthy of adding to their ranks!

Available Now!

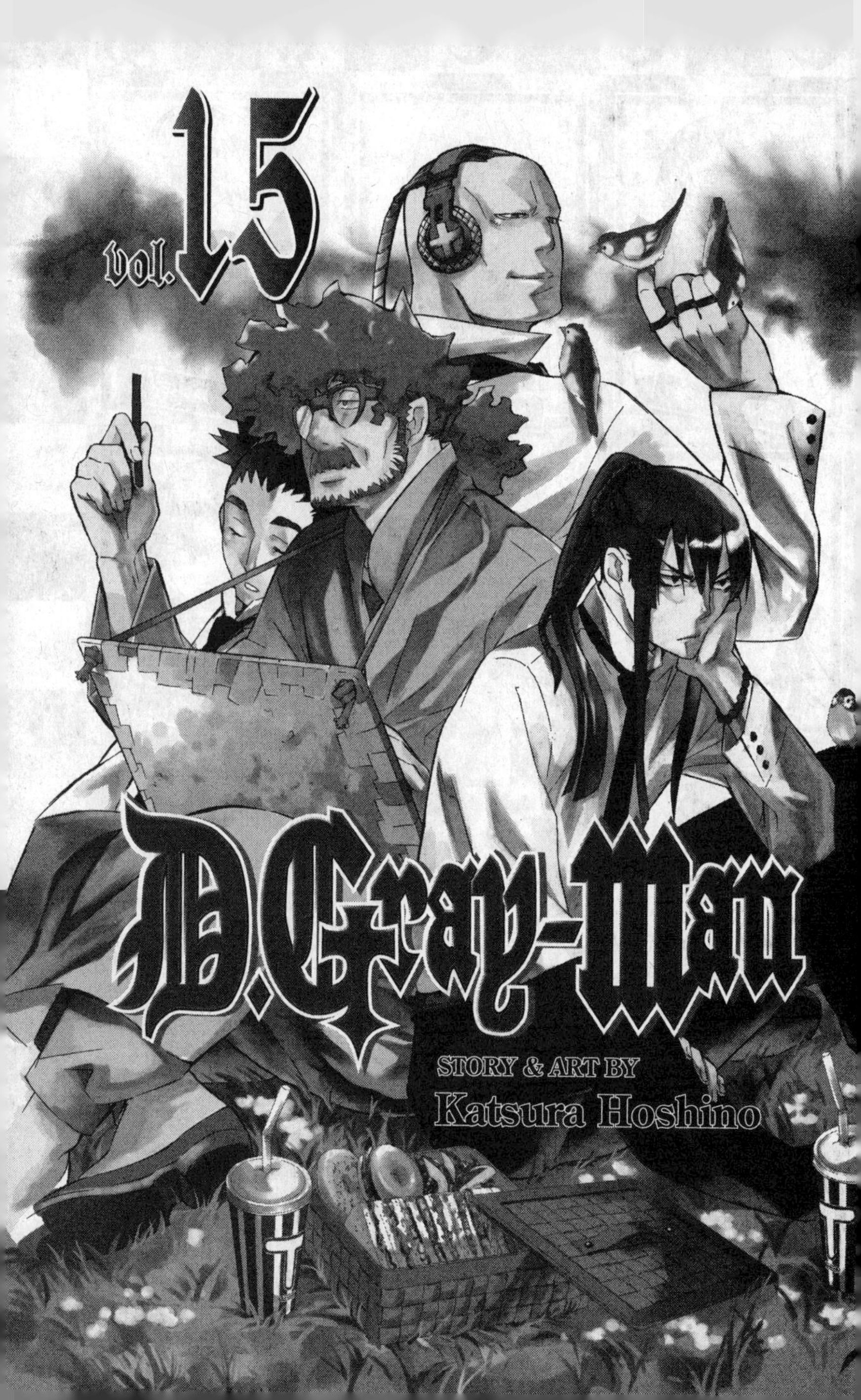
vol. 15
D.Gray-man
STORY & ART BY
Katsura Hoshino

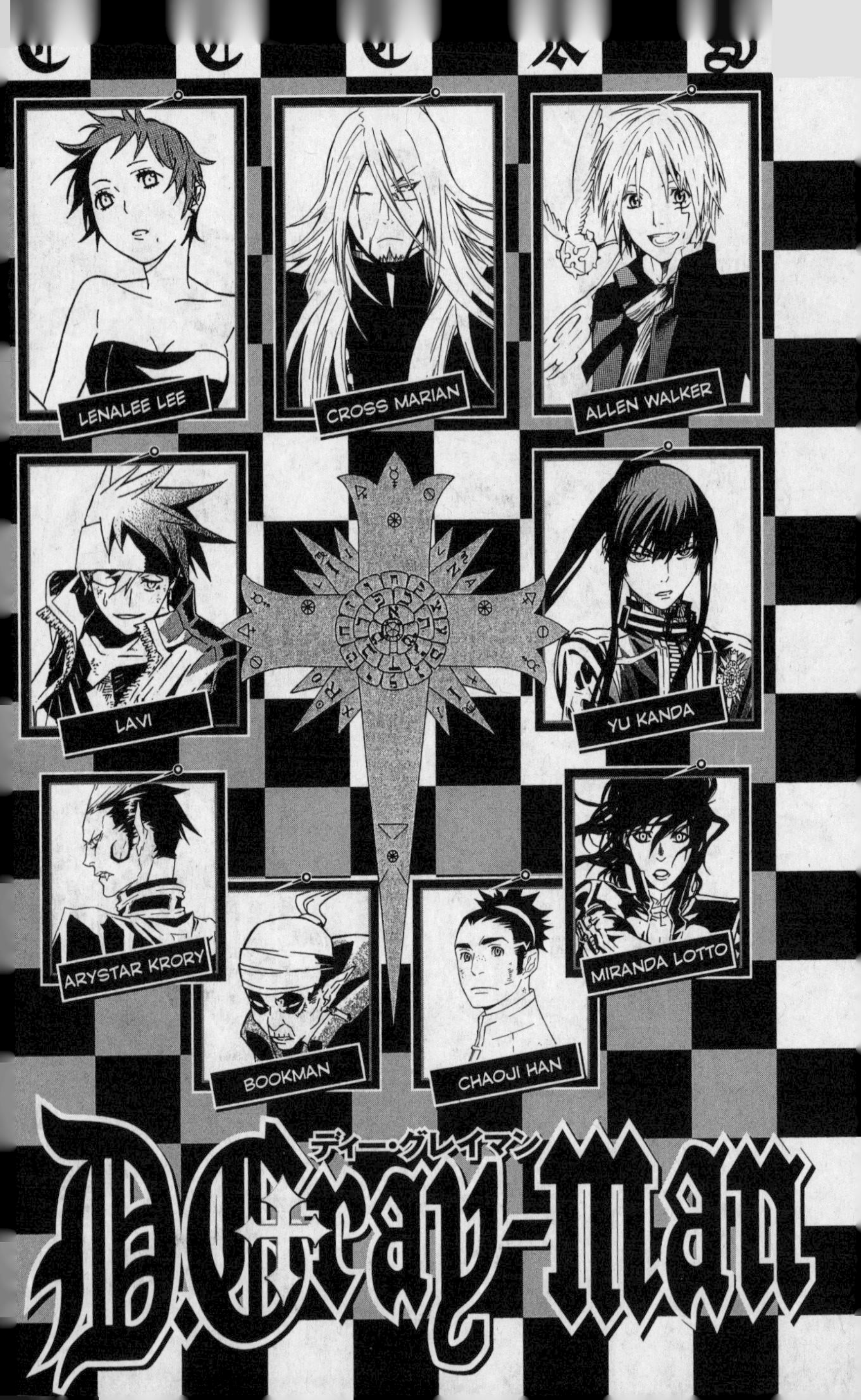
ALLEN WALKER
CROSS MARIAN
LENALEE LEE
YU KANDA
LAVI
MIRANDA LOTTO
ARYSTAR KRORY
CHAOJI HAN
BOOKMAN
ディー・グレイマン
D.Gray-man

C H A R A

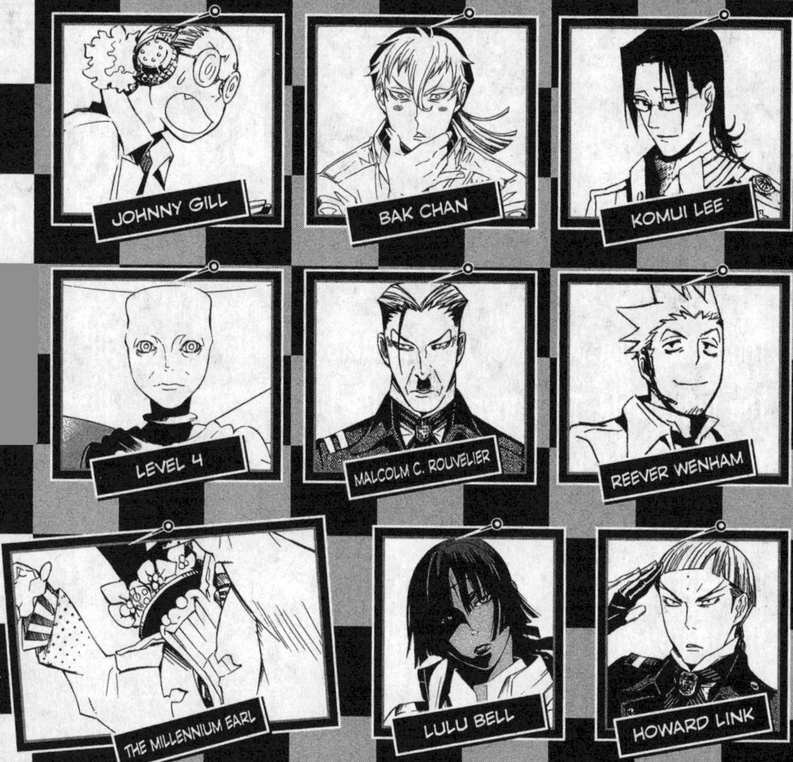
JOHNNY GILL
BAK CHAN
KOMUI LEE
LEVEL 4
MALCOLM C. ROUVELIER
REEVER WENHAM
THE MILLENNIUM EARL
LULU BELL
HOWARD LINK

STORY

IT ALL BEGAN CENTURIES AGO WITH THE DISCOVERY OF A CUBE CONTAINING AN APOCALYPTIC PROPHECY FROM AN ANCIENT CIVILIZATION AND INSTRUCTIONS IN THE USE OF INNOCENCE, A CRYSTALLINE SUBSTANCE OF WONDROUS SUPERNATURAL POWER. THE CREATORS OF THE CUBE CLAIMED TO HAVE DEFEATED AN EVIL KNOWN AS THE MILLENNIUM EARL BY USING THE INNOCENCE. NEVERTHELESS, THE WORLD WAS DESTROYED BY THE GREAT FLOOD OF THE OLD TESTAMENT. NOW, TO AVERT A SECOND END OF THE WORLD, A GROUP OF EXORCISTS WIELDING WEAPONS MADE OF INNOCENCE MUST BATTLE THE MILLENNIUM EARL AND HIS TERRIBLE MINIONS, THE AKUMA.

HAVING DEFEATED THE EARL'S MINIONS AND TAKEN CONTROL OF THE ARK, ALLEN AND HIS COLLEAGUES RETURN TO BLACK ORDER HQ, WHERE, INSTEAD OF BEING RECEIVED AS A HERO, ALLEN IS PLACED UNDER GUARD BY INSPECTOR ROUVELIER. BUT HE'S SOON FACED WITH FAR MORE PRESSING MATTERS.

D.GRAY-MAN
Vol. 15

CONTENTS

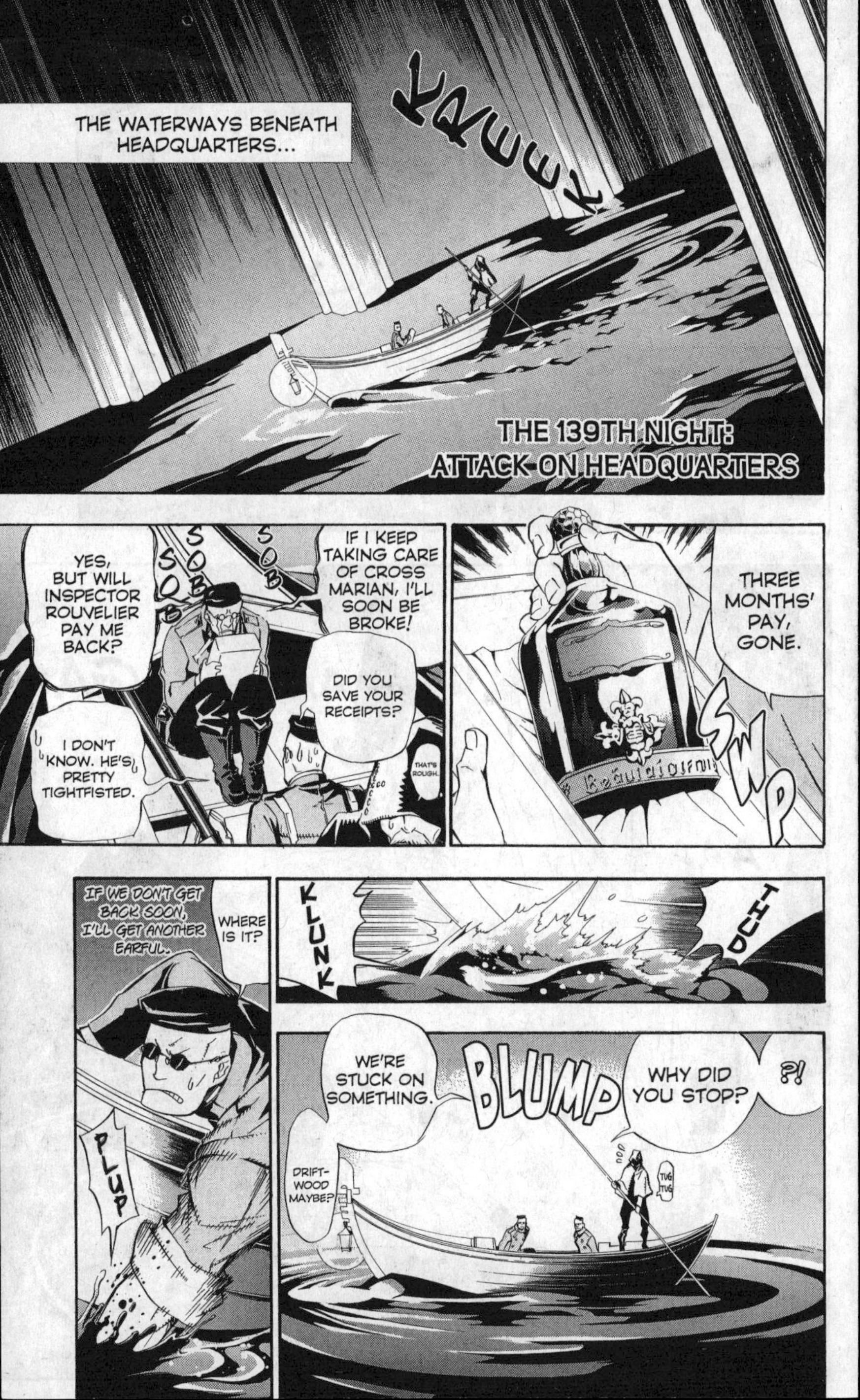
KRWEEK
THE WATERWAYS BENEATH HEADQUARTERS...
THE 139TH NIGHT: ATTACK ON HEADQUARTERS
THREE MONTHS' PAY, GONE.
SWP
IF I KEEP TAKING CARE OF CROSS MARIAN, I'LL SOON BE BROKE!
SOB
SOB SOB
YES, BUT WILL INSPECTOR ROUVELIER PAY ME BACK?
DID YOU SAVE YOUR RECEIPTS?
I DON'T KNOW. HE'S PRETTY TIGHTFISTED.
THAT'S ROUGH.
THUD
KLUNK
?!
WHY DID YOU STOP?
BLUMP
WE'RE STUCK ON SOMETHING.
TUG TUG
DRIFT-WOOD MAYBE?
WHERE IS IT?
IF WE DON'T GET BACK SOON, I'LL GET ANOTHER EARFUL.
PLUP

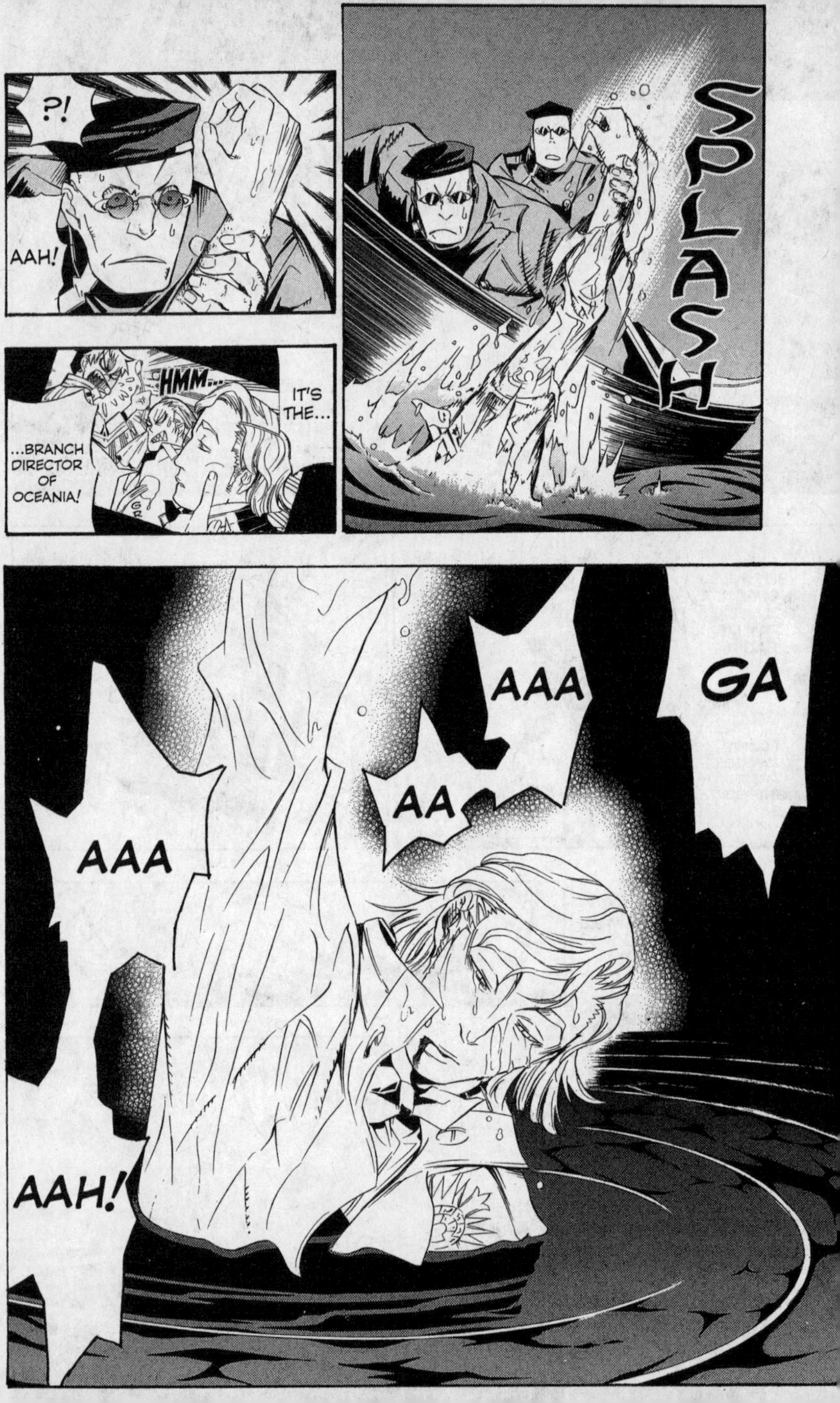
SPLASH
?!
AAH!
HMM...
IT'S THE...
...BRANCH DIRECTOR OF OCEANIA!
GR
GA
AAA
AA
AAA
AAH!

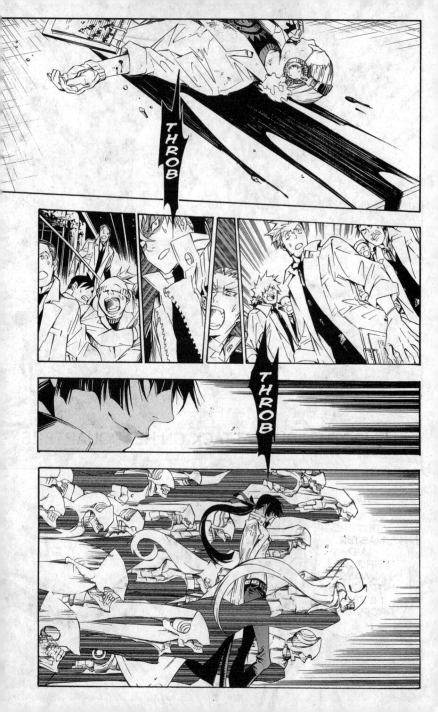

THROB

THROB

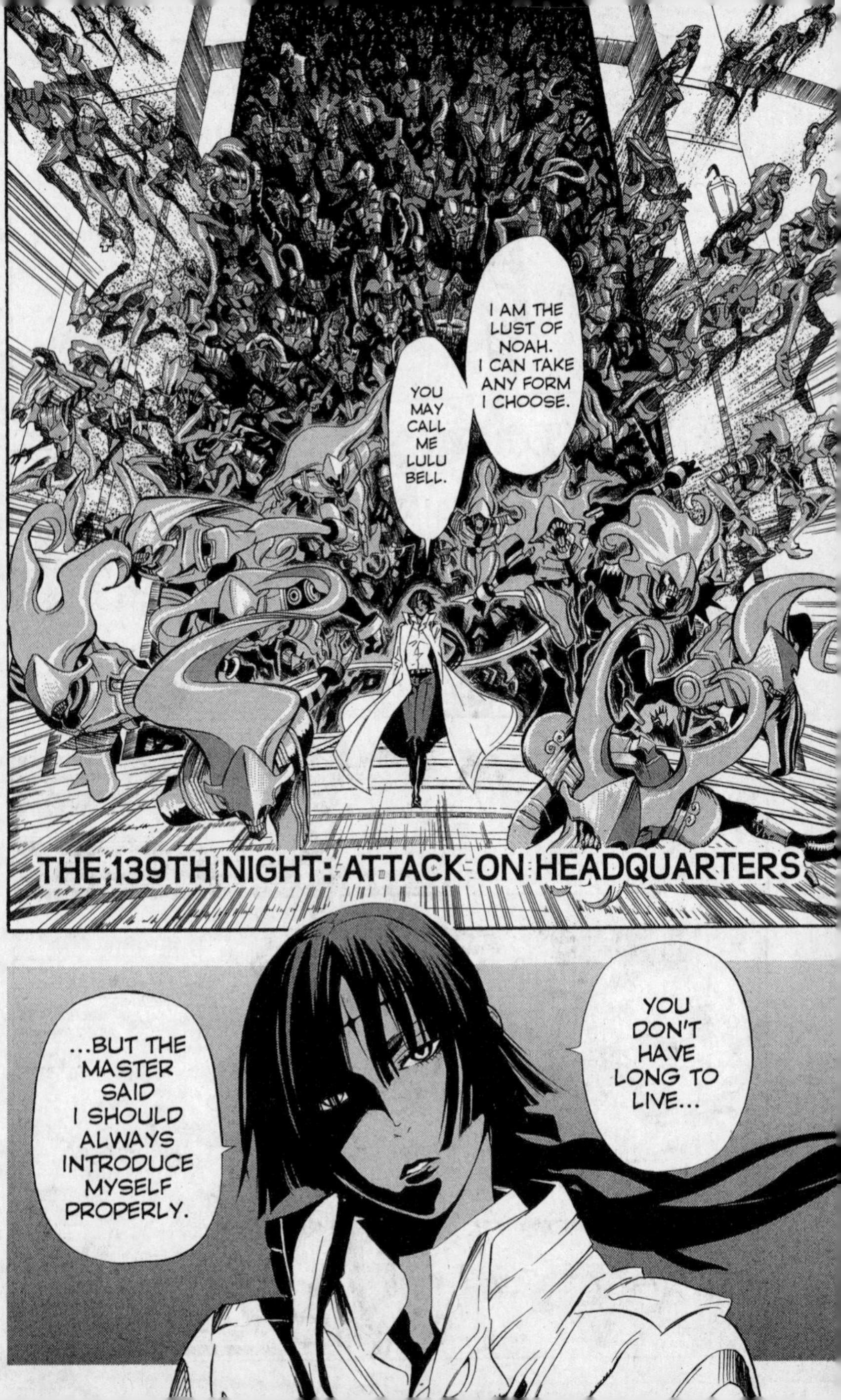
I AM THE LUST OF NOAH. I CAN TAKE ANY FORM I CHOOSE.
YOU MAY CALL ME LULU BELL.
THE 139TH NIGHT: ATTACK ON HEADQUARTERS
YOU DON'T HAVE LONG TO LIVE...
...BUT THE MASTER SAID I SHOULD ALWAYS INTRODUCE MYSELF PROPERLY.

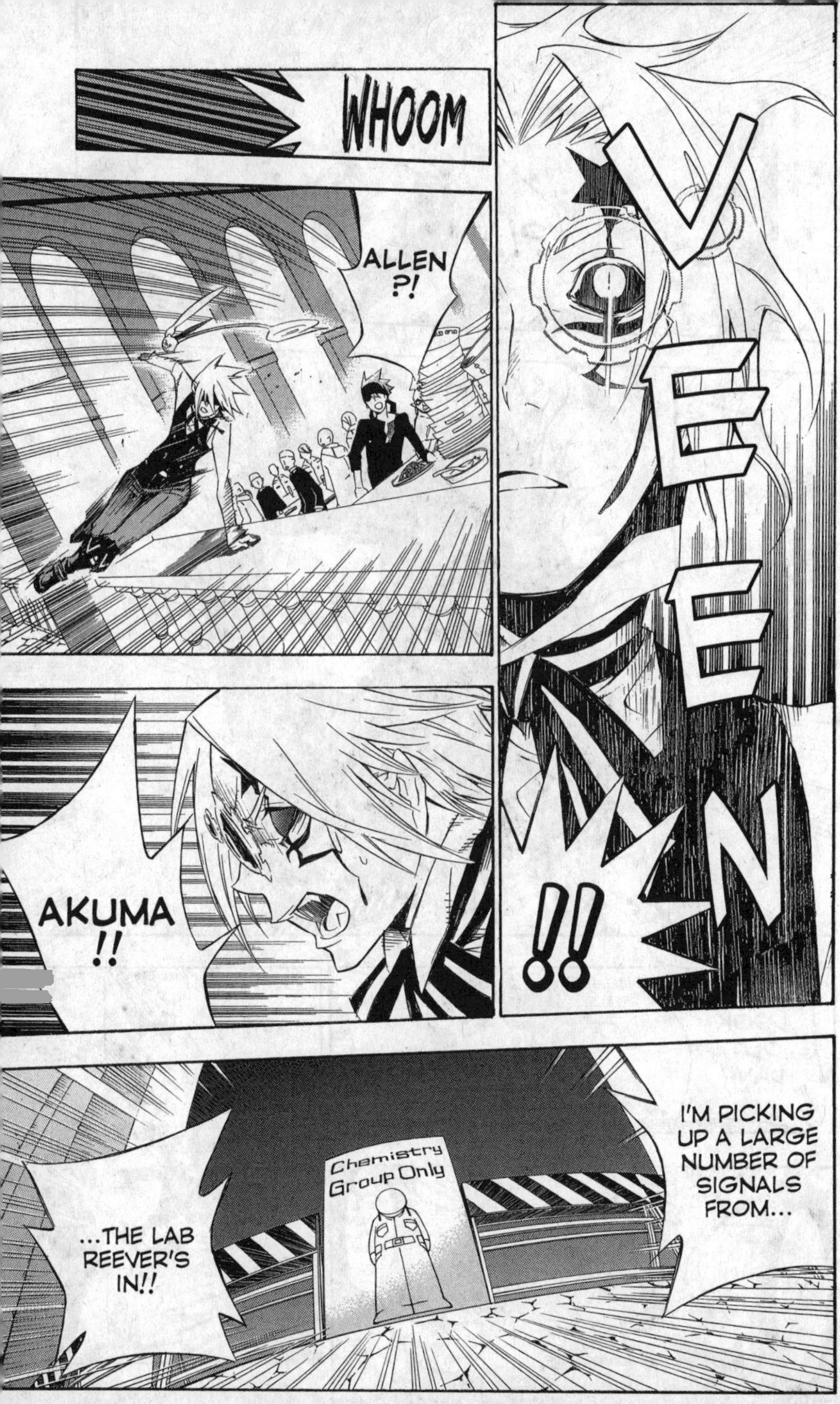
VEEN!!
WHOOM
ALLEN?!
AKUMA!!
I'M PICKING UP A LARGE NUMBER OF SIGNALS FROM...
Chemistry Group Only
...THE LAB REEVER'S IN!!

?!!...

...IS BLOCKED!

THE EN-TRANCE...

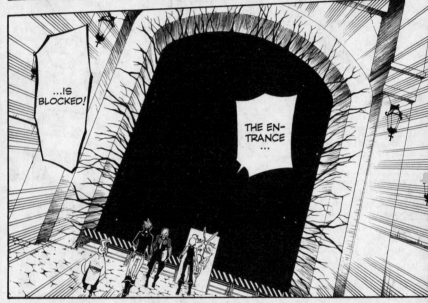

LOOK OUT, LAVI!

!

NOTH-ING.

BLAST!

WHAT'S THIS?!

THWAM

EDGE END!

HEAVEN COM-PASS!

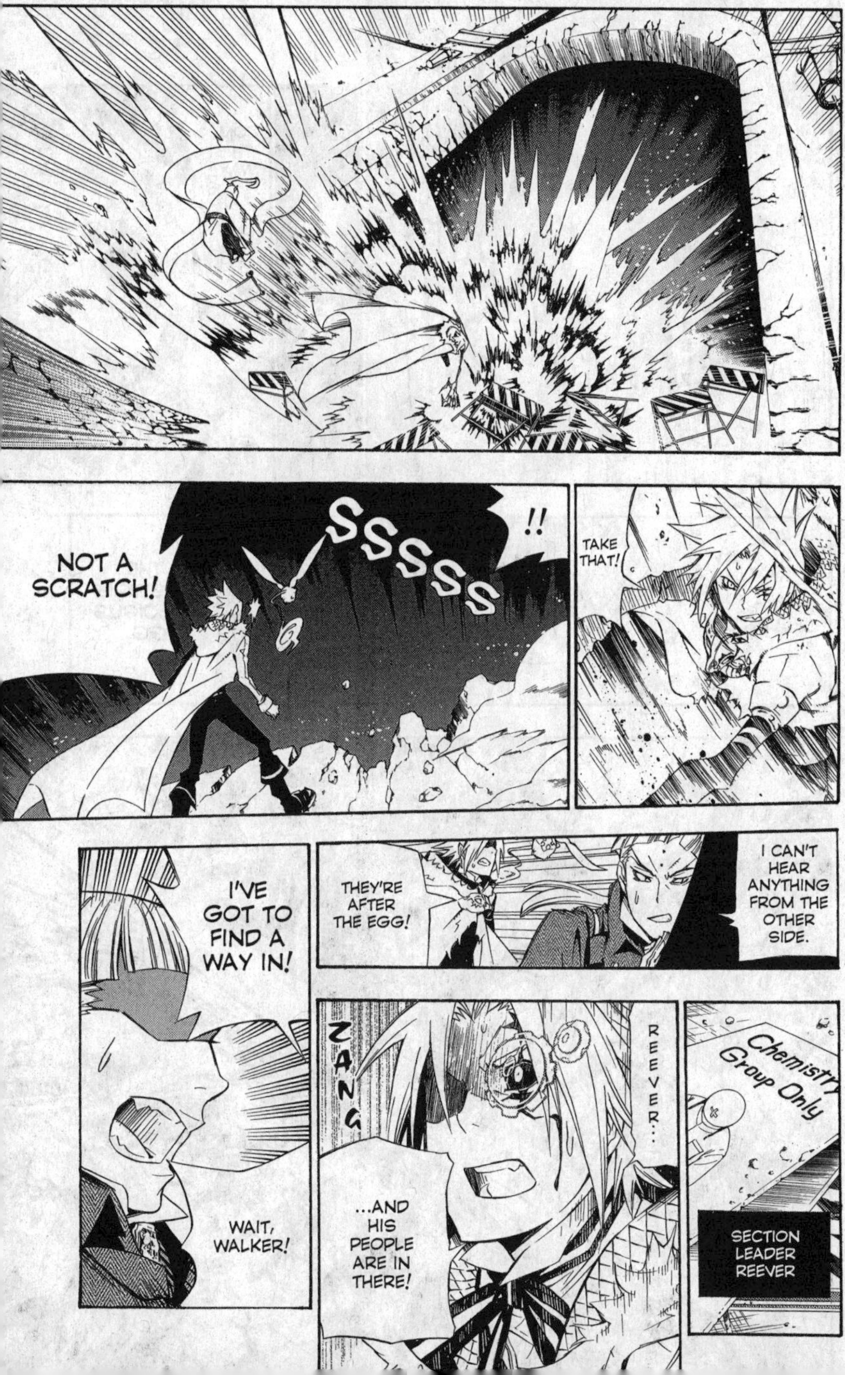
TAKE THAT!
!!
SSSSS
NOT A SCRATCH!
I CAN'T HEAR ANYTHING FROM THE OTHER SIDE.
THEY'RE AFTER THE EGG!
Chemistry Group Only
SECTION LEADER REEVER
REEVER...
ZANG
...AND HIS PEOPLE ARE IN THERE!
I'VE GOT TO FIND A WAY IN!
WAIT, WALKER!

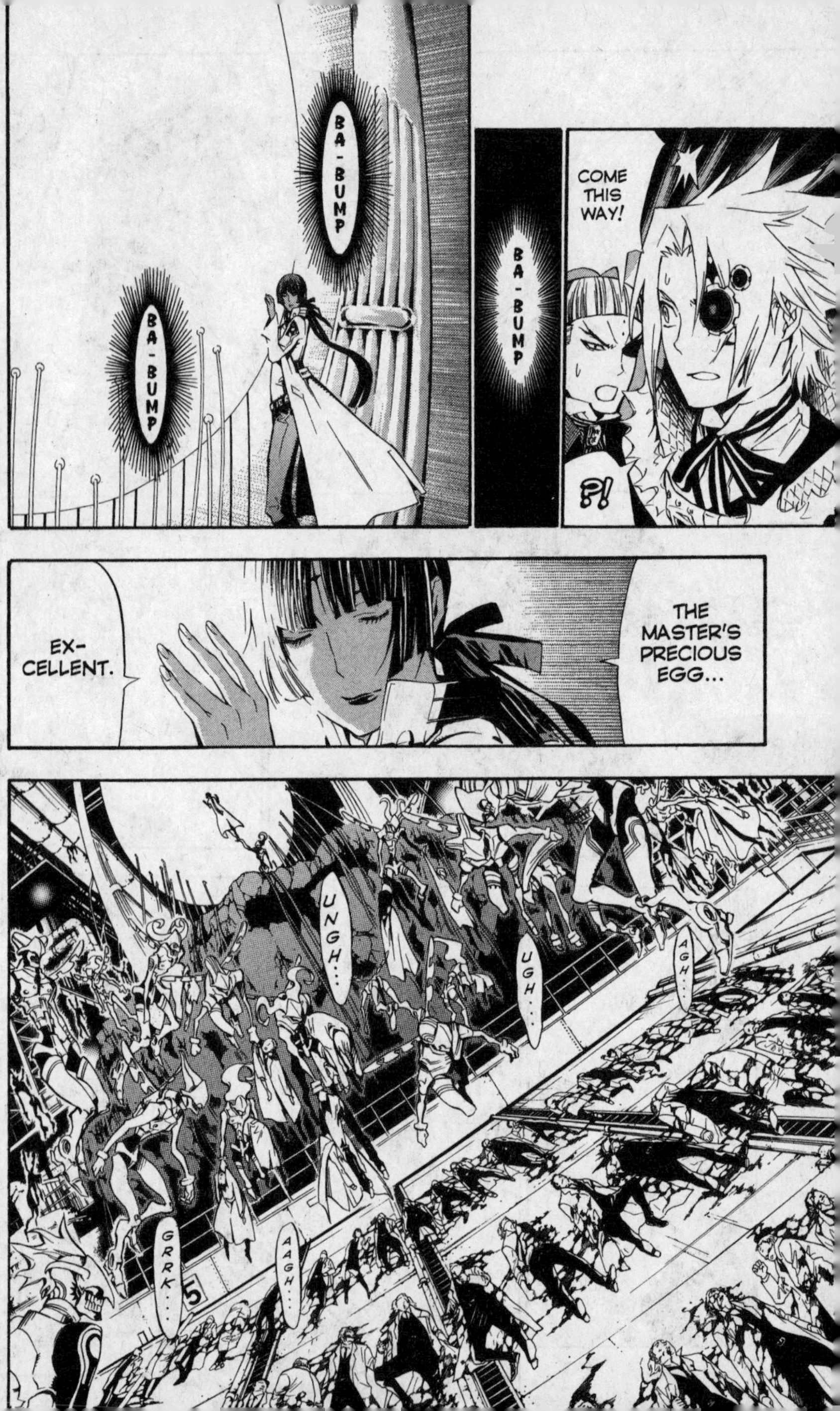
COME THIS WAY!
?!
BA-BUMP
BA-BUMP
BA-BUMP
THE MASTER'S PRECIOUS EGG...
EX-CELLENT.
AGH...
UGH...
UNGH...
AAGH...
GRRK...

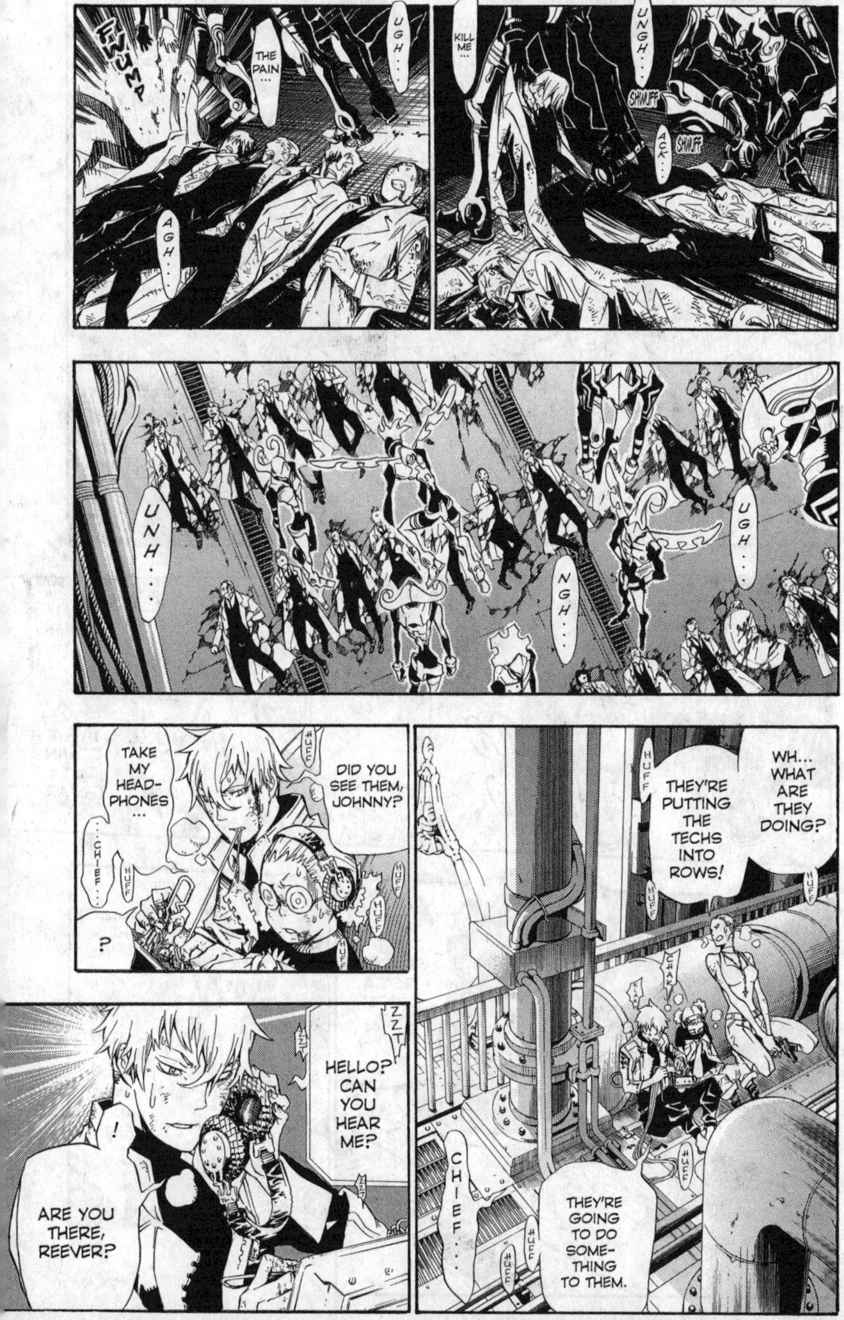
UNGH...
KILL ME...
SHWUFF
ACK...
SHWUFF
UGH...
THE PAIN...
FWUMP
AGH...
UGH...
NGH...
UNH...
WH... WHAT ARE THEY DOING?
HUFF
THEY'RE PUTTING THE TECHS INTO ROWS!
HUFF
HUFF
CHAK
CHIEF...
HUFF
HUFF
THEY'RE GOING TO DO SOME-THING TO THEM.
HUFF
HUFF
DID YOU SEE THEM, JOHNNY?
HUFF
HUFF
HUFF
HUFF
TAKE MY HEAD-PHONES...
...CHIEF...
HUFF
?
ZZT
ZZT
HELLO? CAN YOU HEAR ME?
ZZT
!
ARE YOU THERE, REEVER?

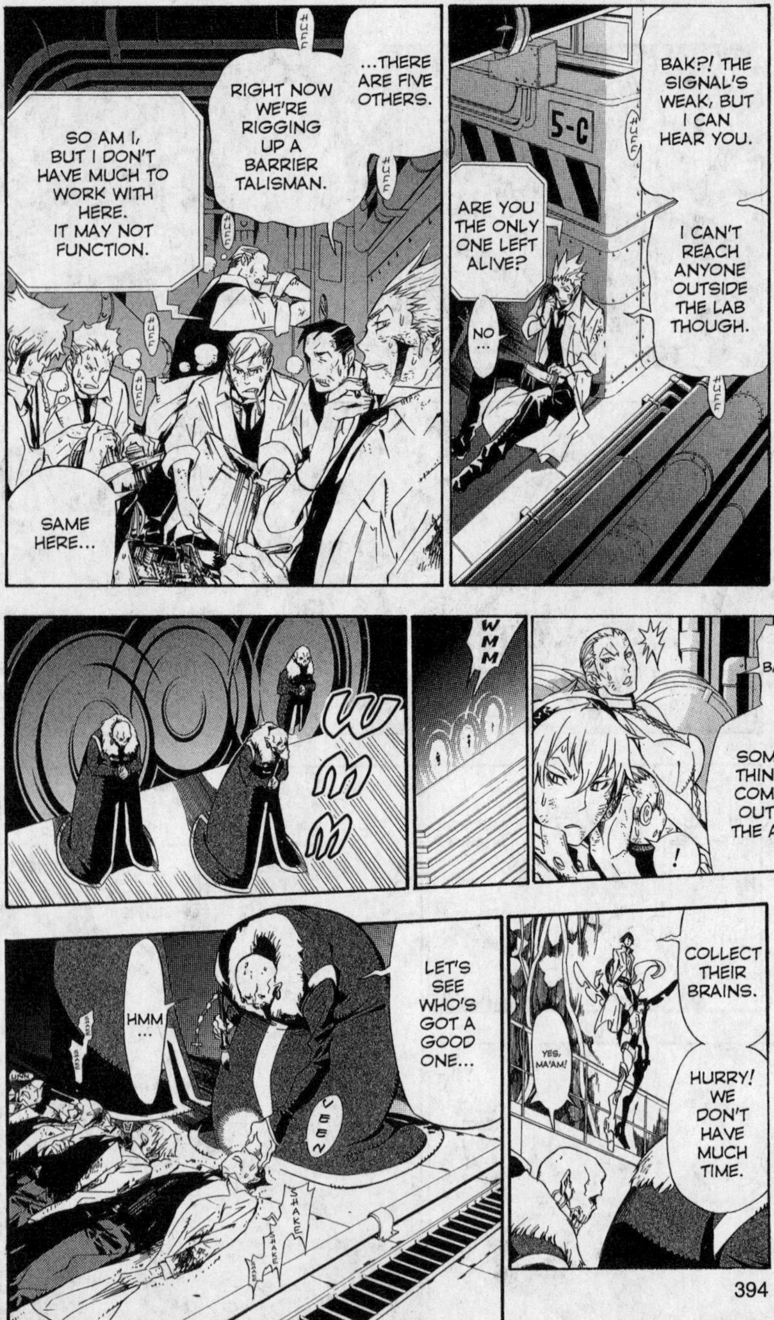
BAK?! THE SIGNAL'S WEAK, BUT I CAN HEAR YOU.
HUFF
ARE YOU THE ONLY ONE LEFT ALIVE?
I CAN'T REACH ANYONE OUTSIDE THE LAB THOUGH.
NO...
HUFF
...THERE ARE FIVE OTHERS.
HUFF
RIGHT NOW WE'RE RIGGING UP A BARRIER TALISMAN.
HUFF
SO AM I, BUT I DON'T HAVE MUCH TO WORK WITH HERE. IT MAY NOT FUNCTION.
HUFF
HUFF
HUFF
SAME HERE...
BAK!
SOME-THING'S COMING OUT OF THE ARK!
!
WMM
WMM
COLLECT THEIR BRAINS.
HURRY! WE DON'T HAVE MUCH TIME.
YES, MA'AM!
LET'S SEE WHO'S GOT A GOOD ONE...
VEEN
HMM...
SHAKE
SHAKE

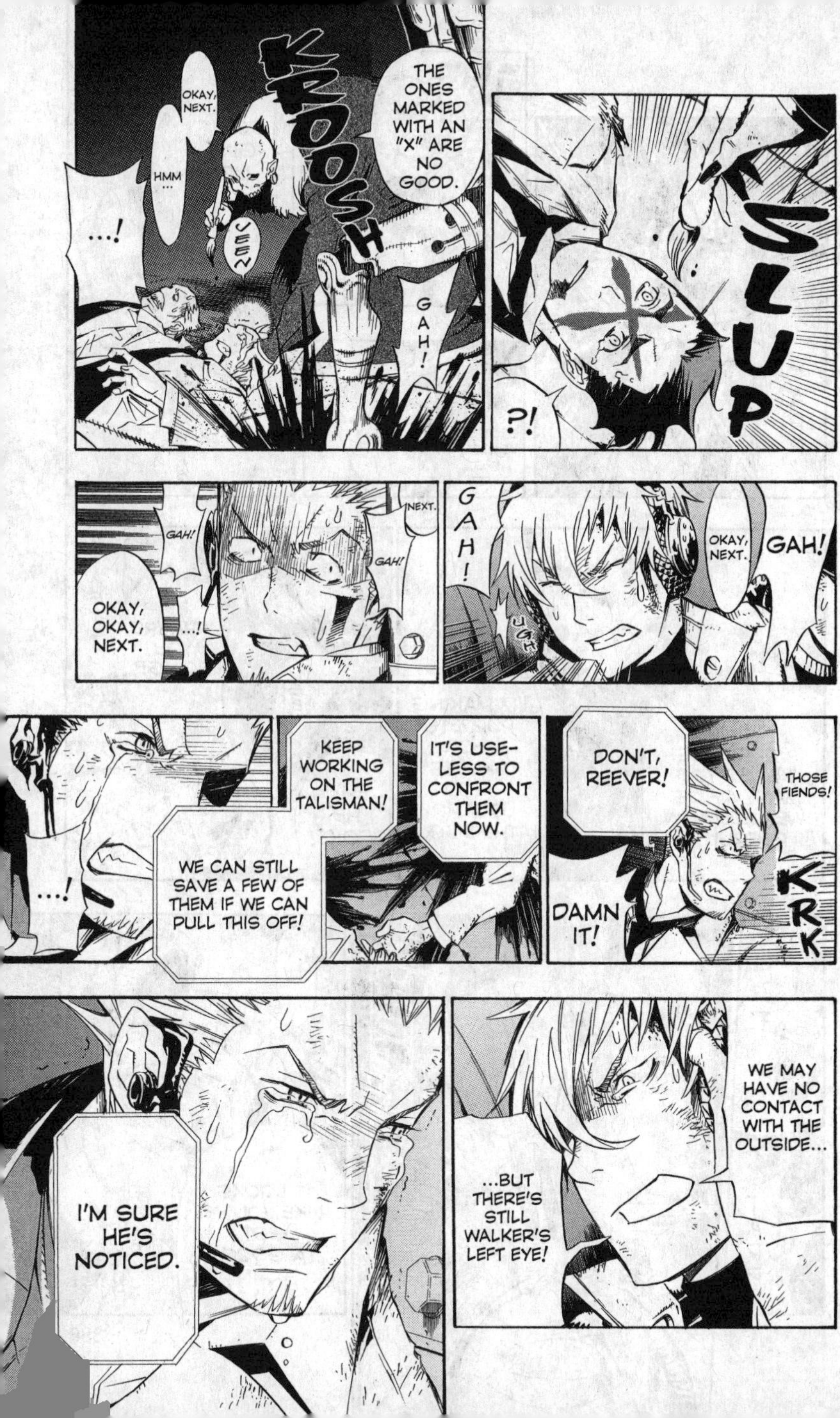
SLUP
?!
KROOSH
THE ONES MARKED WITH AN "X" ARE NO GOOD.
OKAY, NEXT.
HMM...
...!
JEEN
GAH!
OKAY, NEXT.
GAH!
GAH!
UGH
NEXT.
GAH!
GAH!
...!
OKAY, OKAY, NEXT.
THOSE FIENDS!
DON'T, REEVER!
KRK KRK
DAMN IT!
IT'S USE-LESS TO CONFRONT THEM NOW.
KEEP WORKING ON THE TALISMAN!
WE CAN STILL SAVE A FEW OF THEM IF WE CAN PULL THIS OFF!
...!
WE MAY HAVE NO CONTACT WITH THE OUTSIDE...
...BUT THERE'S STILL WALKER'S LEFT EYE!
I'M SURE HE'S NOTICED.

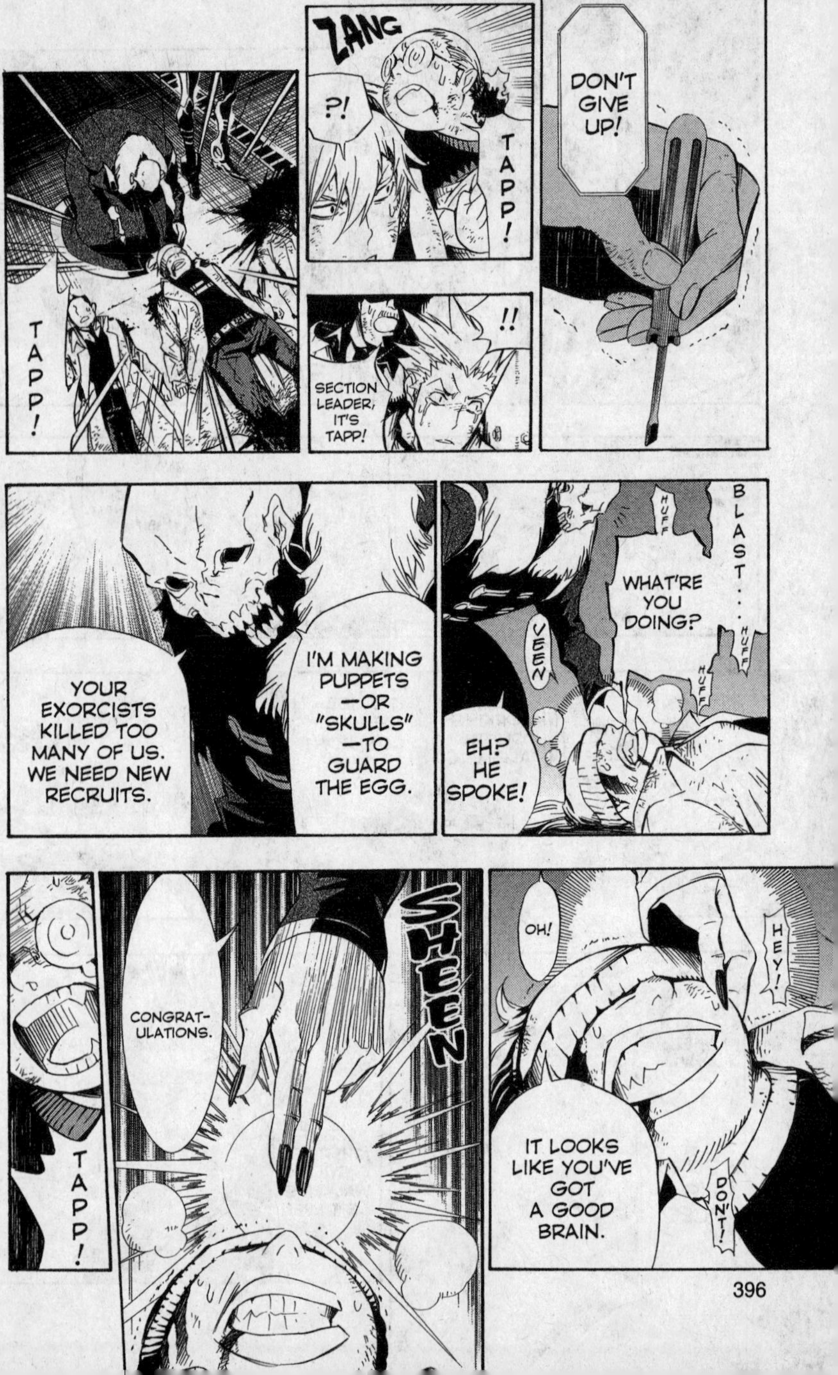
DON'T GIVE UP!
ZANG
TAPP!
?!
!!
SECTION LEADER, IT'S TAPP!
TAPP!
BLAST...
HUFF
HUFF
HUFF
WHAT'RE YOU DOING?
VEEN
EH? HE SPOKE!
I'M MAKING PUPPETS —OR "SKULLS" —TO GUARD THE EGG.
YOUR EXORCISTS KILLED TOO MANY OF US. WE NEED NEW RECRUITS.
HEY!
OH!
IT LOOKS LIKE YOU'VE GOT A GOOD BRAIN.
DON'T!
SHEEN
CONGRAT-ULATIONS.
TAPP!

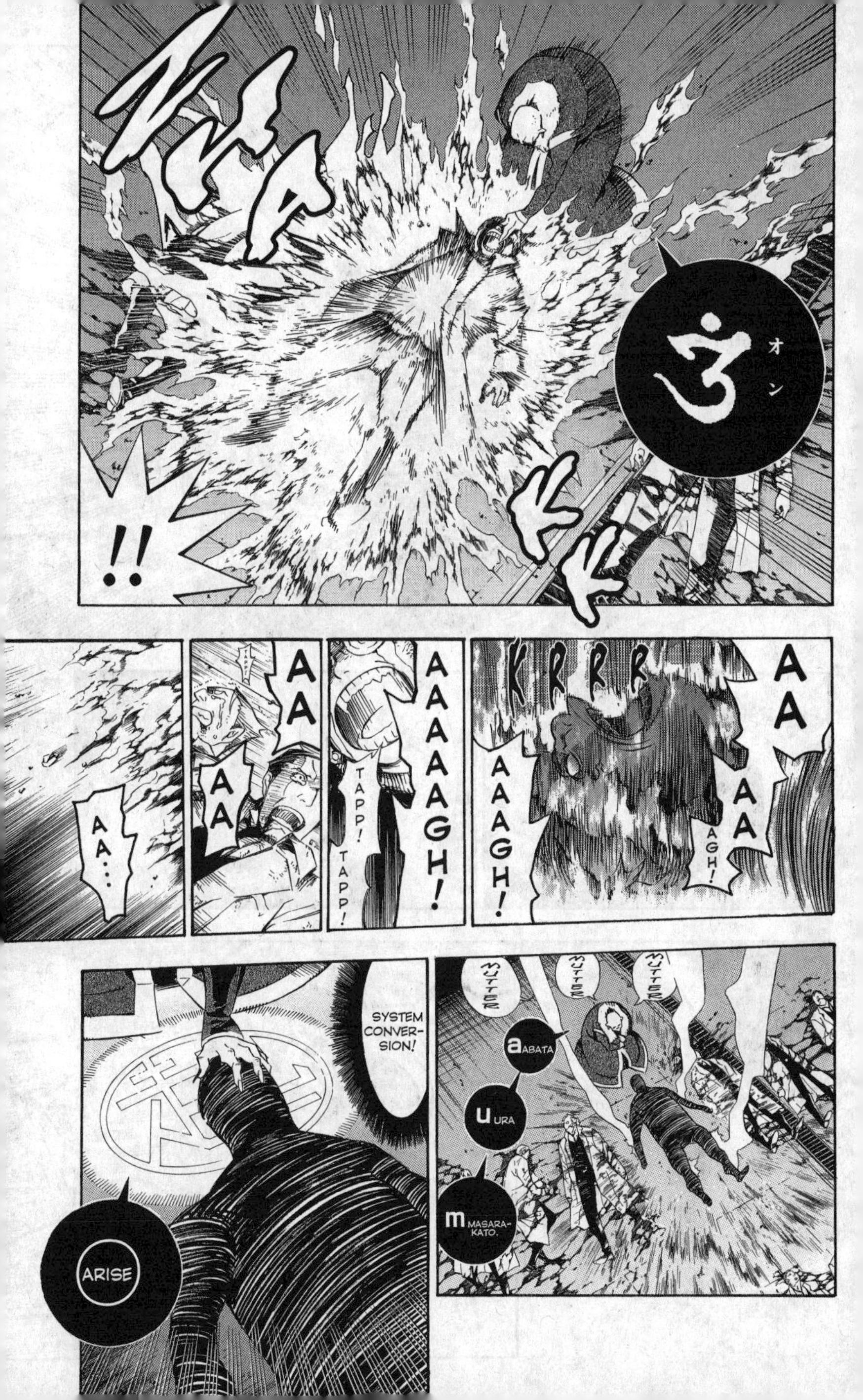
オン
!!
KRRR
AAAAAAGH!
AAAAGH!
AAAAAAAGH!
TAPP! TAPP! TAPP!
AAAA
TAPP!
AA...
MUTTER
MUTTER
MUTTER
a ABATA
u URA
m MASARA-KATO.
SYSTEM CONVERSION!
ARISE

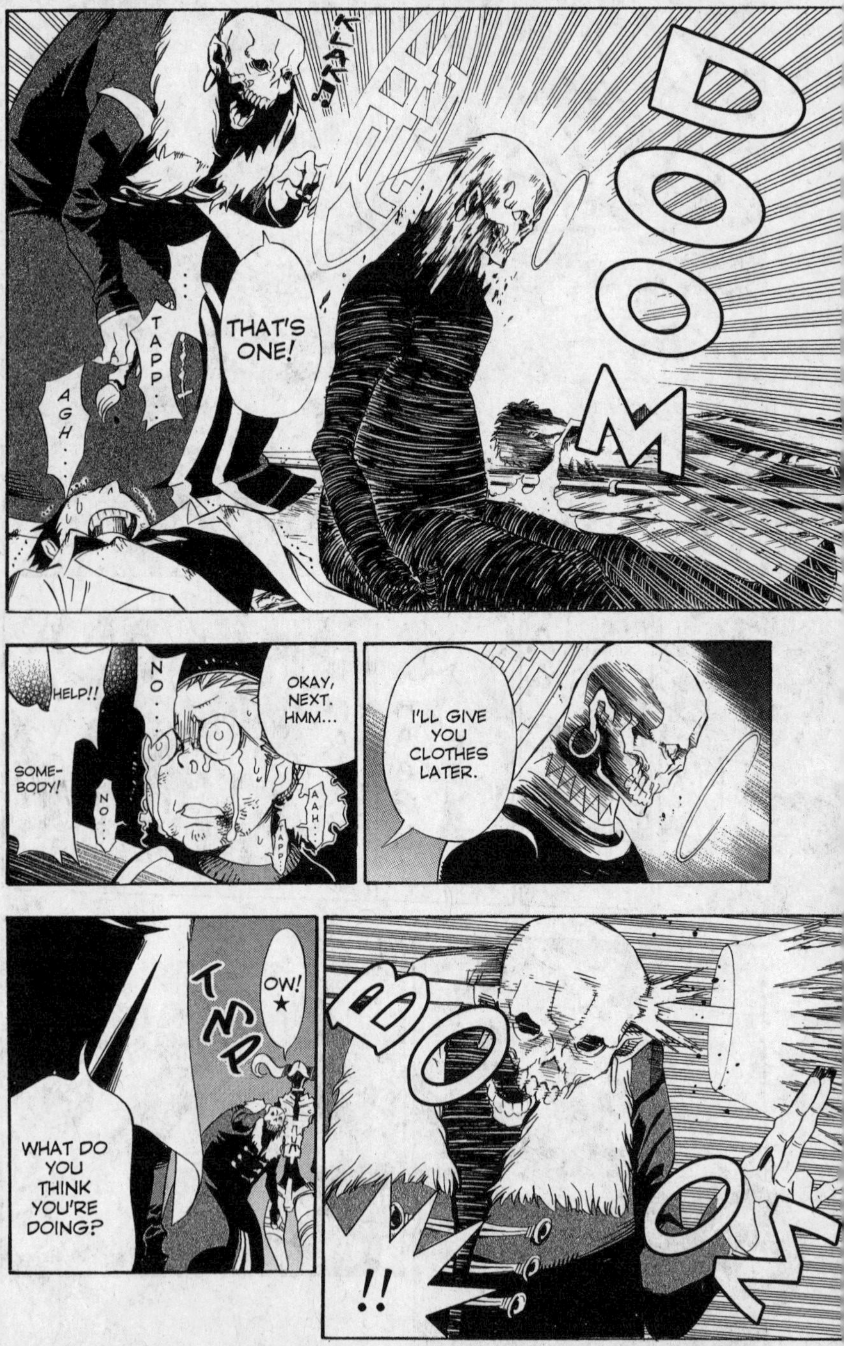
DOOOM
KLAK
THAT'S ONE!
TAPP...
AGH...
I'LL GIVE YOU CLOTHES LATER.
OKAY, NEXT. HMM...
AAH...
TAPP...
NO...
NO...
HELP!!
SOME-BODY!
BOOM
!!
OW! ★
TNP
WHAT DO YOU THINK YOU'RE DOING?

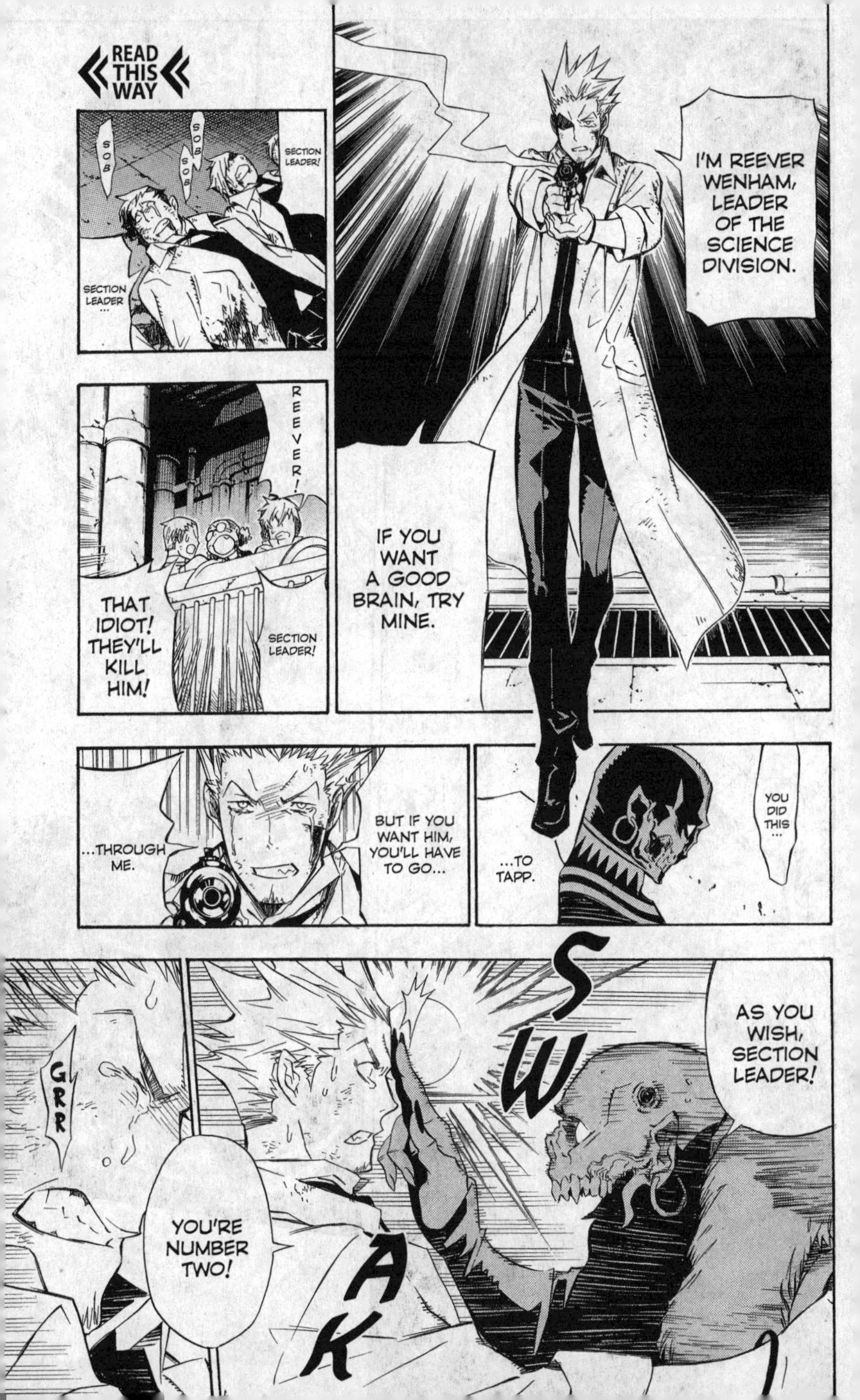
READ THIS WAY
I'M REEVER WENHAM, LEADER OF THE SCIENCE DIVISION.
IF YOU WANT A GOOD BRAIN, TRY MINE.
SOB SOB
SOB
SECTION LEADER!
SECTION LEADER ...
REEVER!
SECTION LEADER!
THAT IDIOT! THEY'LL KILL HIM!
YOU DID THIS ...
...TO TAPP.
BUT IF YOU WANT HIM, YOU'LL HAVE TO GO...
...THROUGH ME.
AS YOU WISH, SECTION LEADER!
SWAK
YOU'RE NUMBER TWO!
GRR

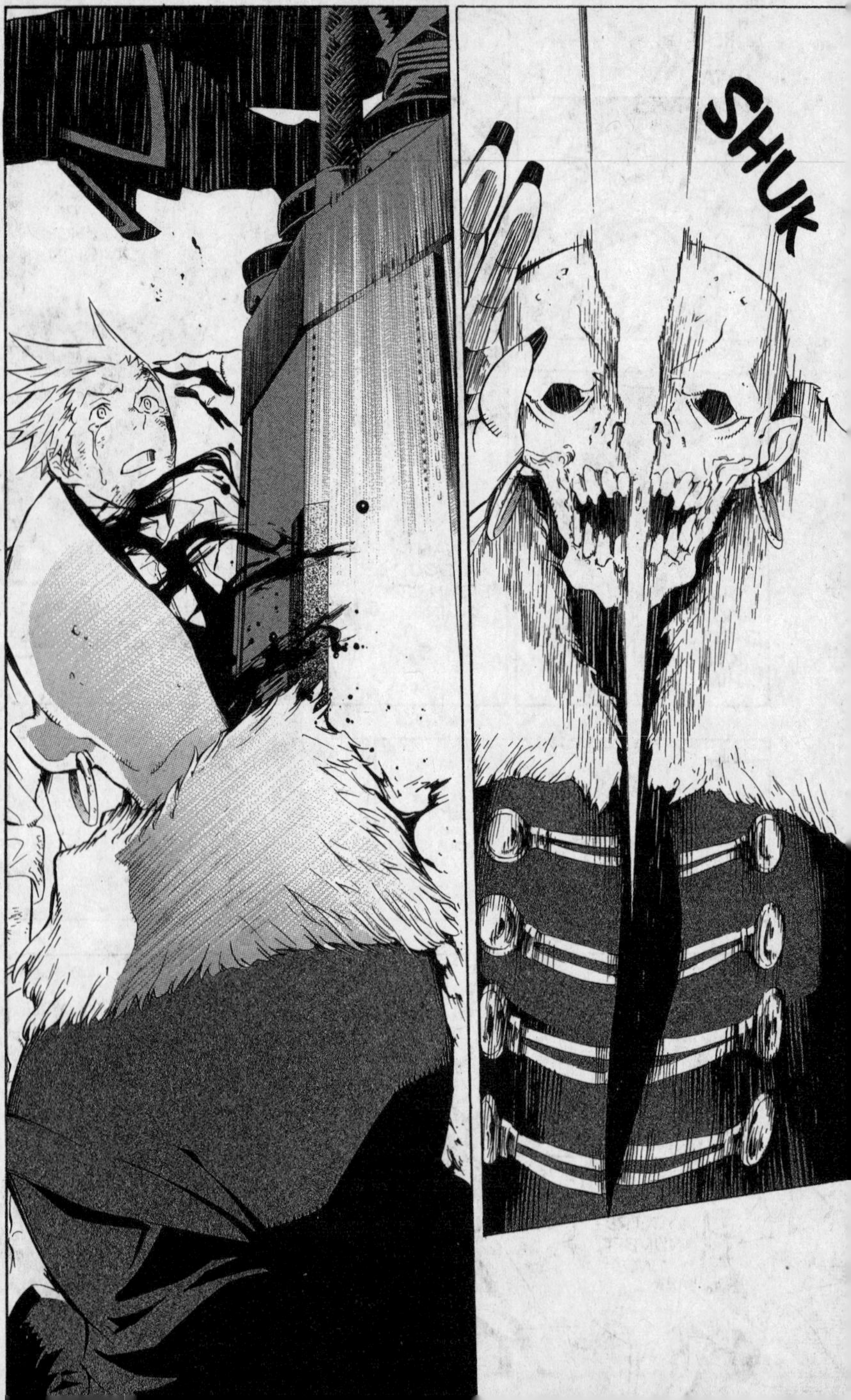
SHUK

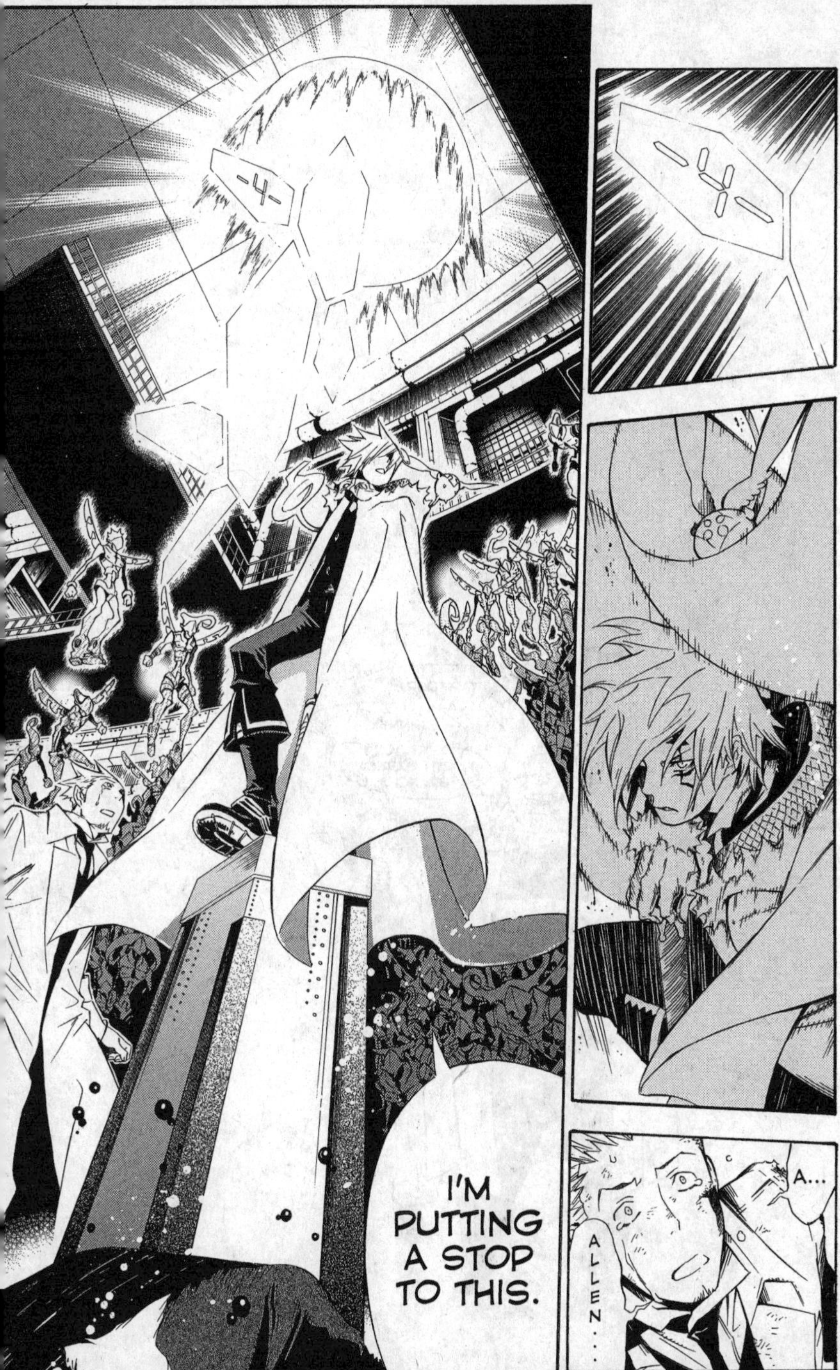
A...
ALLEN...
I'M PUTTING A STOP TO THIS.

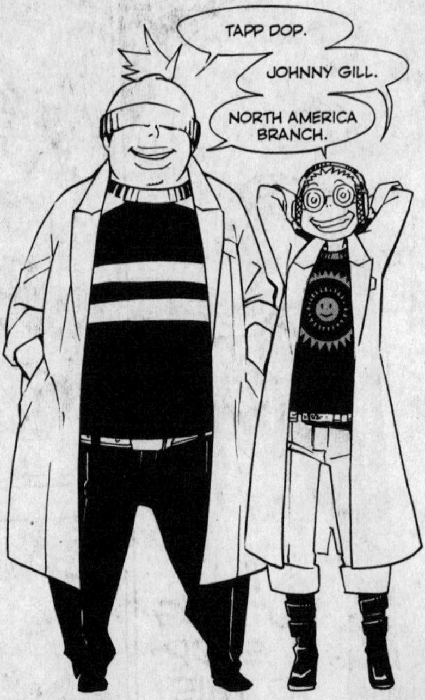
TAPP DOP.
JOHNNY GILL.
NORTH AMERICA BRANCH.

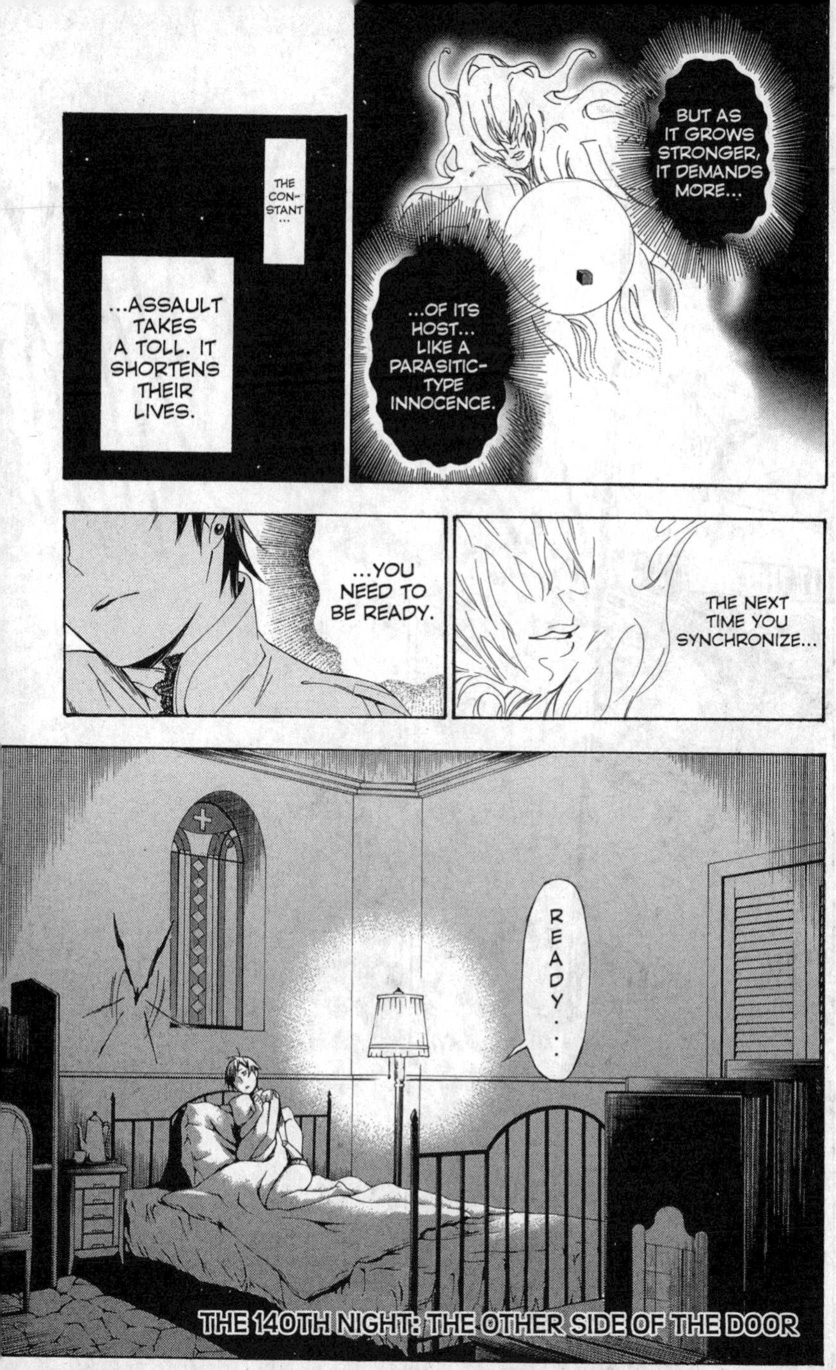
BUT AS IT GROWS STRONGER, IT DEMANDS MORE...
...OF ITS HOST... LIKE A PARASITIC-TYPE INNOCENCE.
THE CON-STANT...
...ASSAULT TAKES A TOLL. IT SHORTENS THEIR LIVES.
THE NEXT TIME YOU SYNCHRONIZE...
...YOU NEED TO BE READY.
READY...
THE 140TH NIGHT: THE OTHER SIDE OF THE DOOR

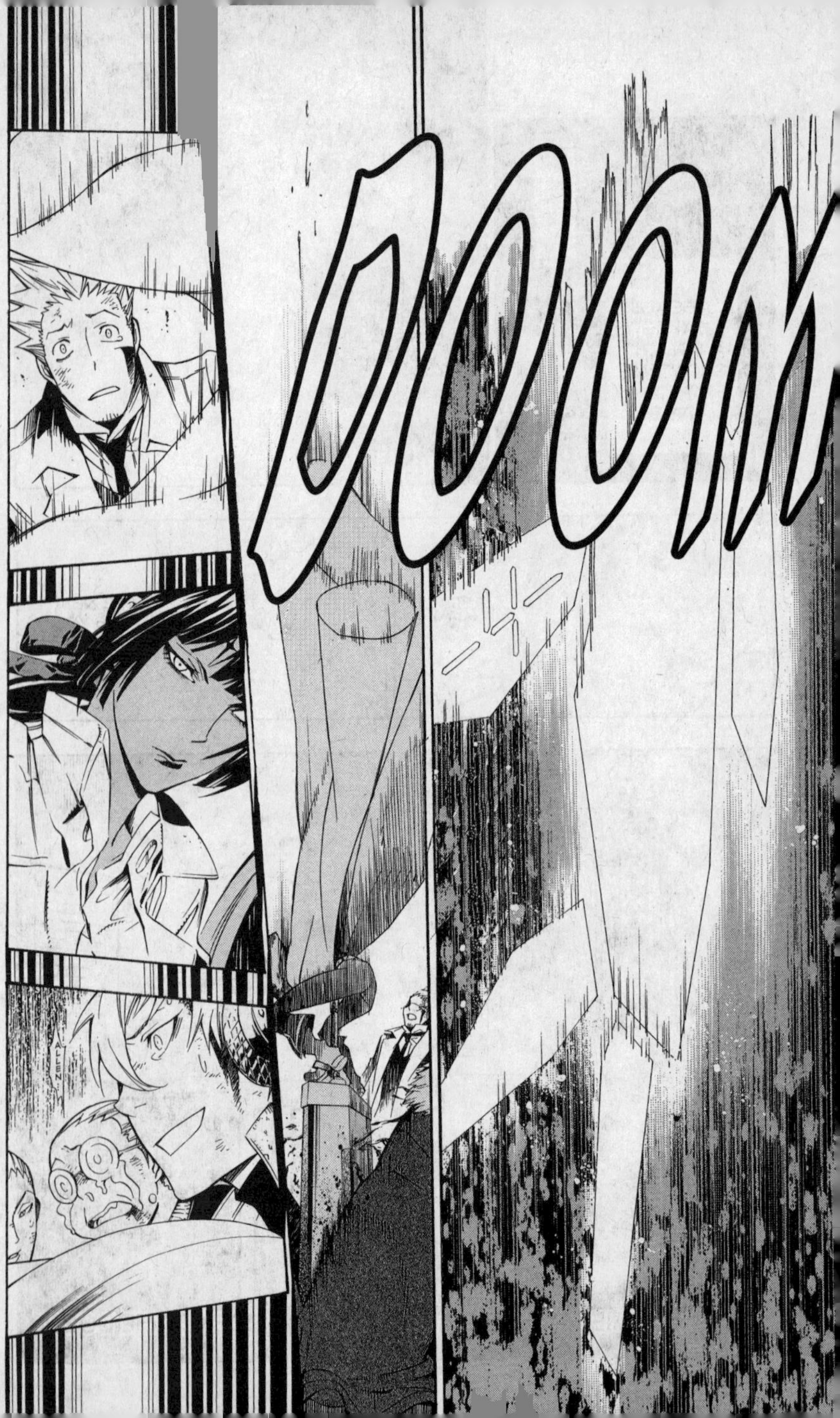
DOOM
ALLEN...

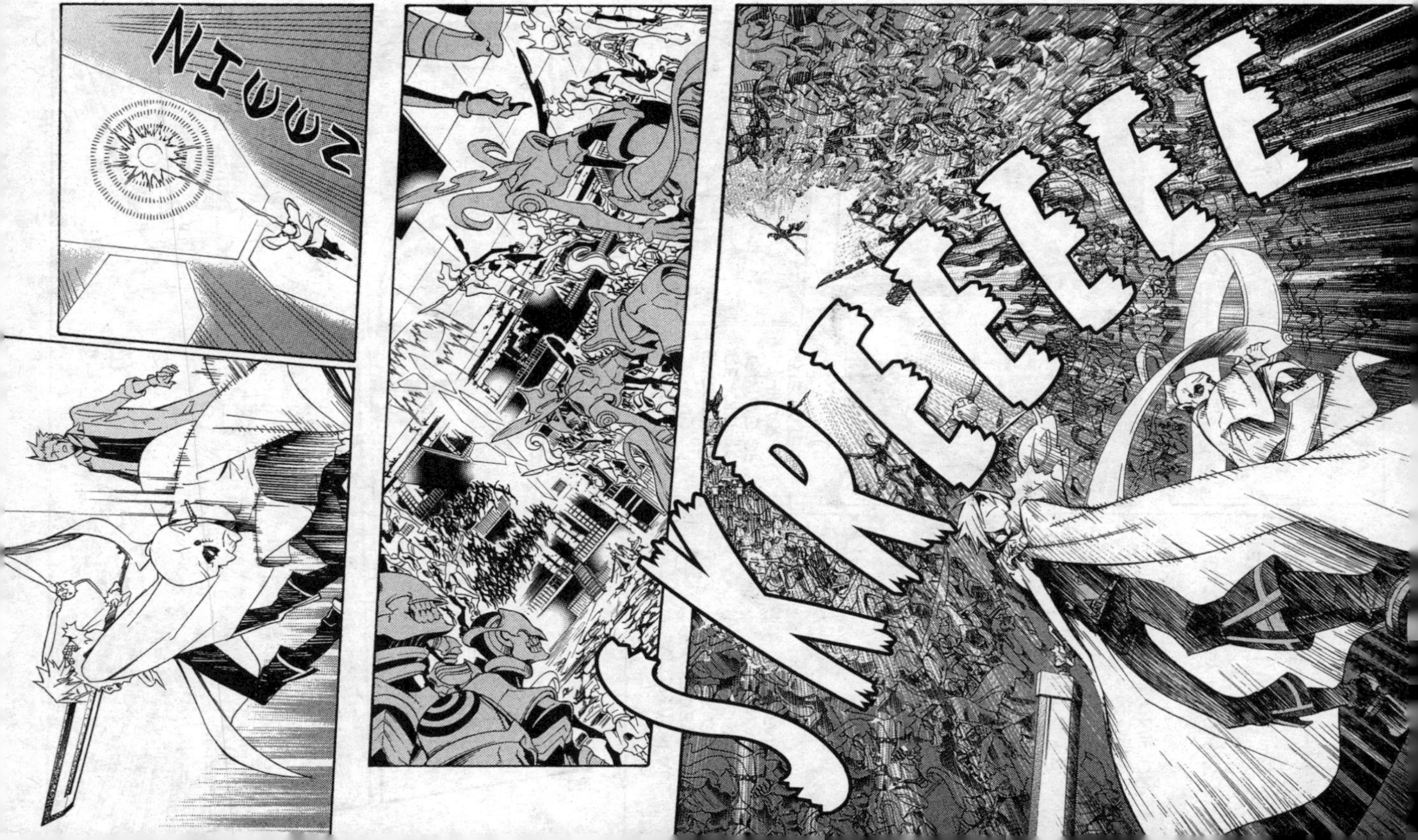
SKREEEEE

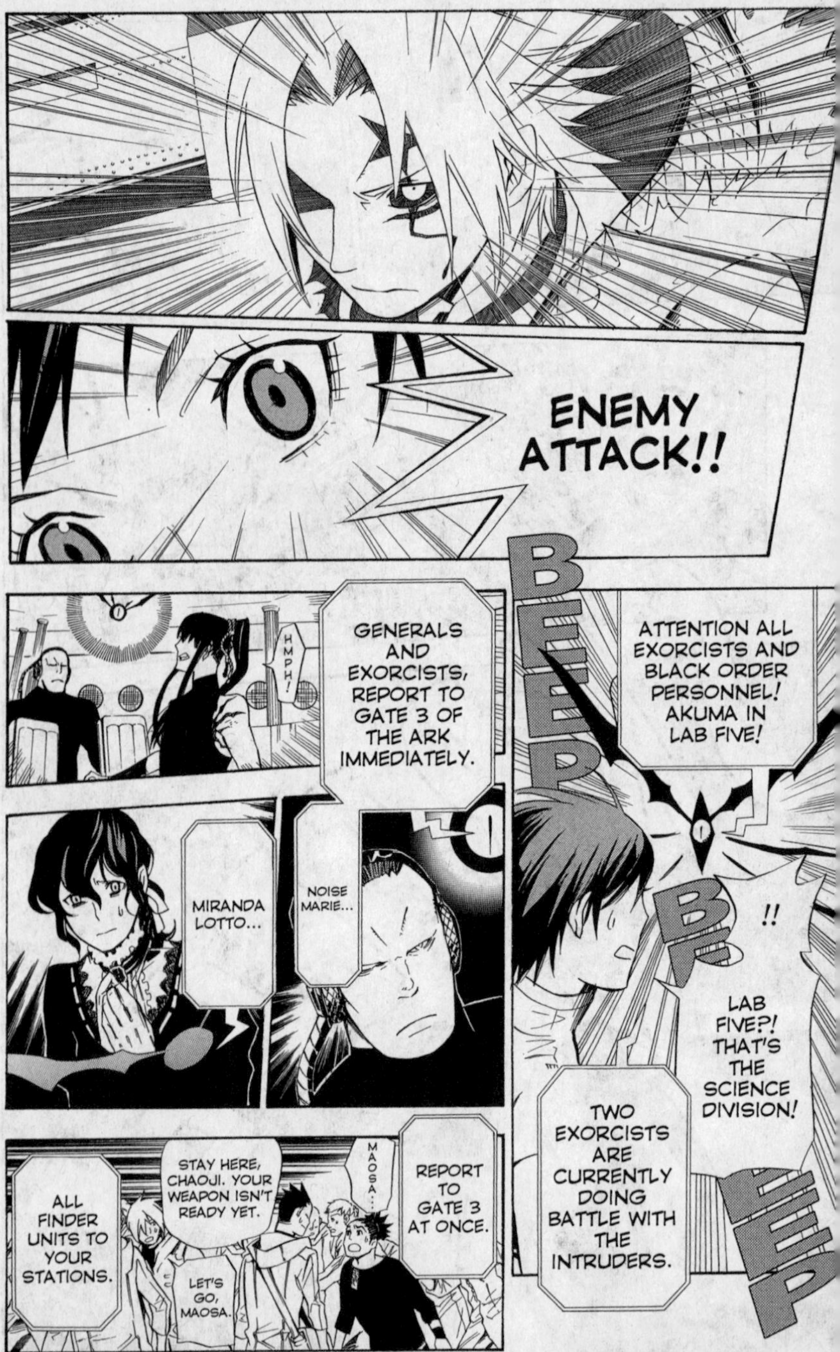
ENEMY ATTACK!!
ATTENTION ALL EXORCISTS AND BLACK ORDER PERSONNEL! AKUMA IN LAB FIVE!
BEEP
B
!!
LAB FIVE?! THAT'S THE SCIENCE DIVISION!
TWO EXORCISTS ARE CURRENTLY DOING BATTLE WITH THE INTRUDERS.
EEP
GENERALS AND EXORCISTS, REPORT TO GATE 3 OF THE ARK IMMEDIATELY.
HMPH!
NOISE MARIE...
MIRANDA LOTTO...
REPORT TO GATE 3 AT ONCE.
MAOSA...
STAY HERE, CHAOJI. YOUR WEAPON ISN'T READY YET.
LET'S GO, MAOSA.
ALL FINDER UNITS TO YOUR STATIONS.

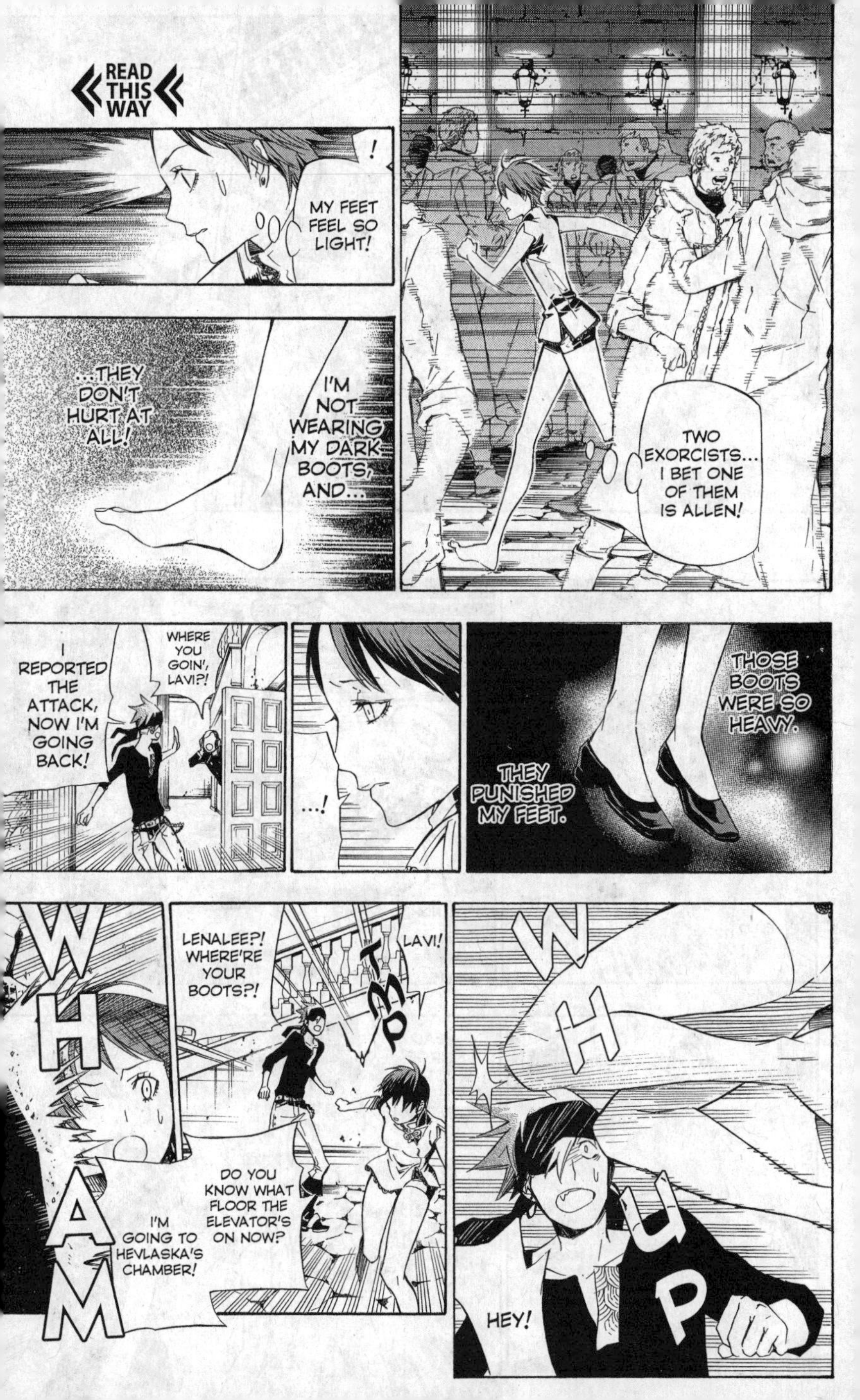
READ THIS WAY
TWO EXORCISTS... I BET ONE OF THEM IS ALLEN!
!
MY FEET FEEL SO LIGHT!
I'M NOT WEARING MY DARK BOOTS, AND...
...THEY DON'T HURT AT ALL!
THOSE BOOTS WERE SO HEAVY.
THEY PUNISHED MY FEET.
...!
WHERE YOU GOIN', LAVI?!
I REPORTED THE ATTACK, NOW I'M GOING BACK!
WHUP
HEY!
LAVI!
TMP
LENALEE?! WHERE'RE YOUR BOOTS?!
DO YOU KNOW WHAT FLOOR THE ELEVATOR'S ON NOW?
I'M GOING TO HEVLASKA'S CHAMBER!
WHAM

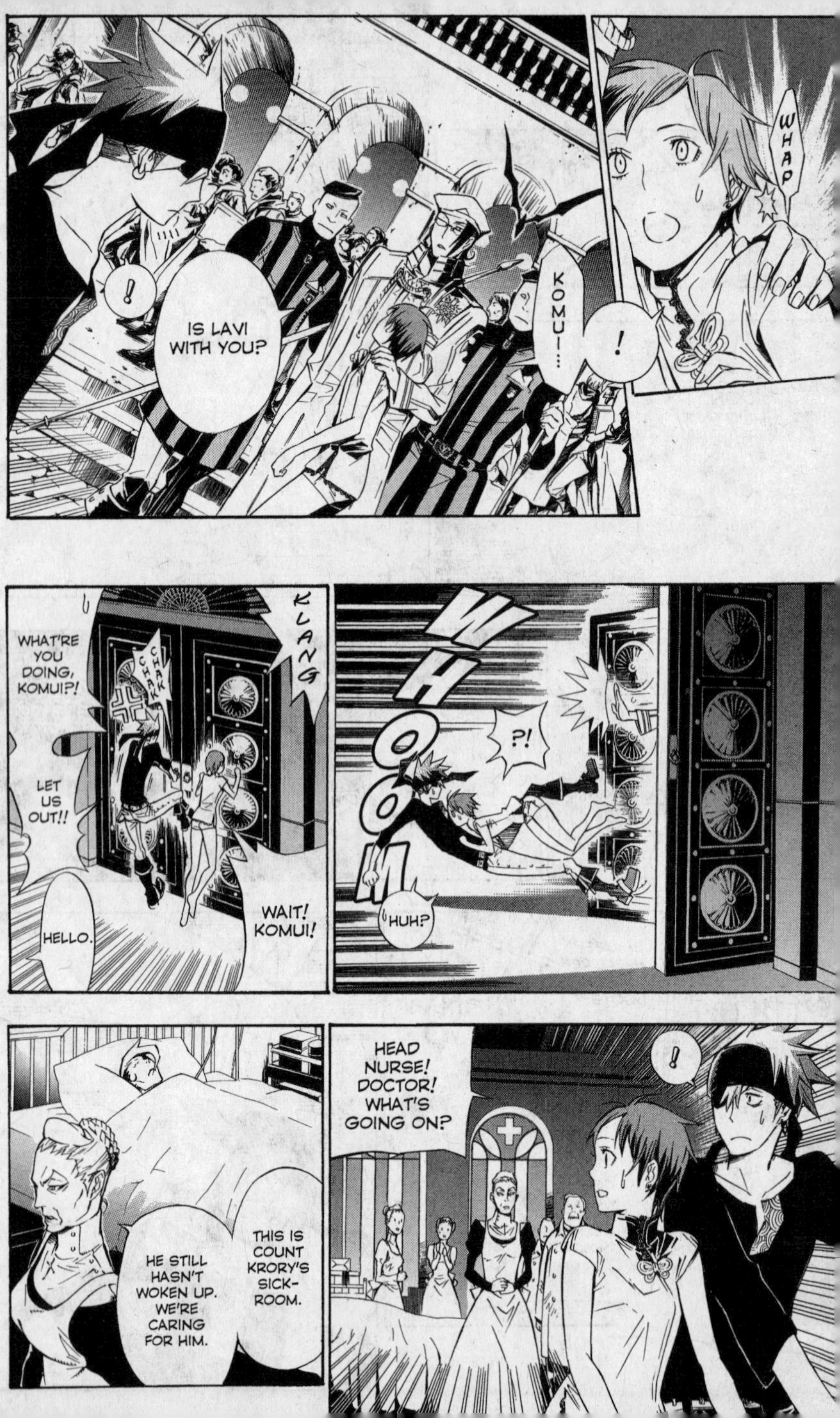
WHAP
!
KOMUI...
IS LAVI WITH YOU?
!
WHOOOM
?!
HUH?
KLANG
CHAK CHAK
WHAT'RE YOU DOING, KOMUI?!
LET US OUT!!
WAIT! KOMUI!
HELLO.
!
HEAD NURSE! DOCTOR! WHAT'S GOING ON?
THIS IS COUNT KRORY'S SICK-ROOM.
HE STILL HASN'T WOKEN UP. WE'RE CARING FOR HIM.

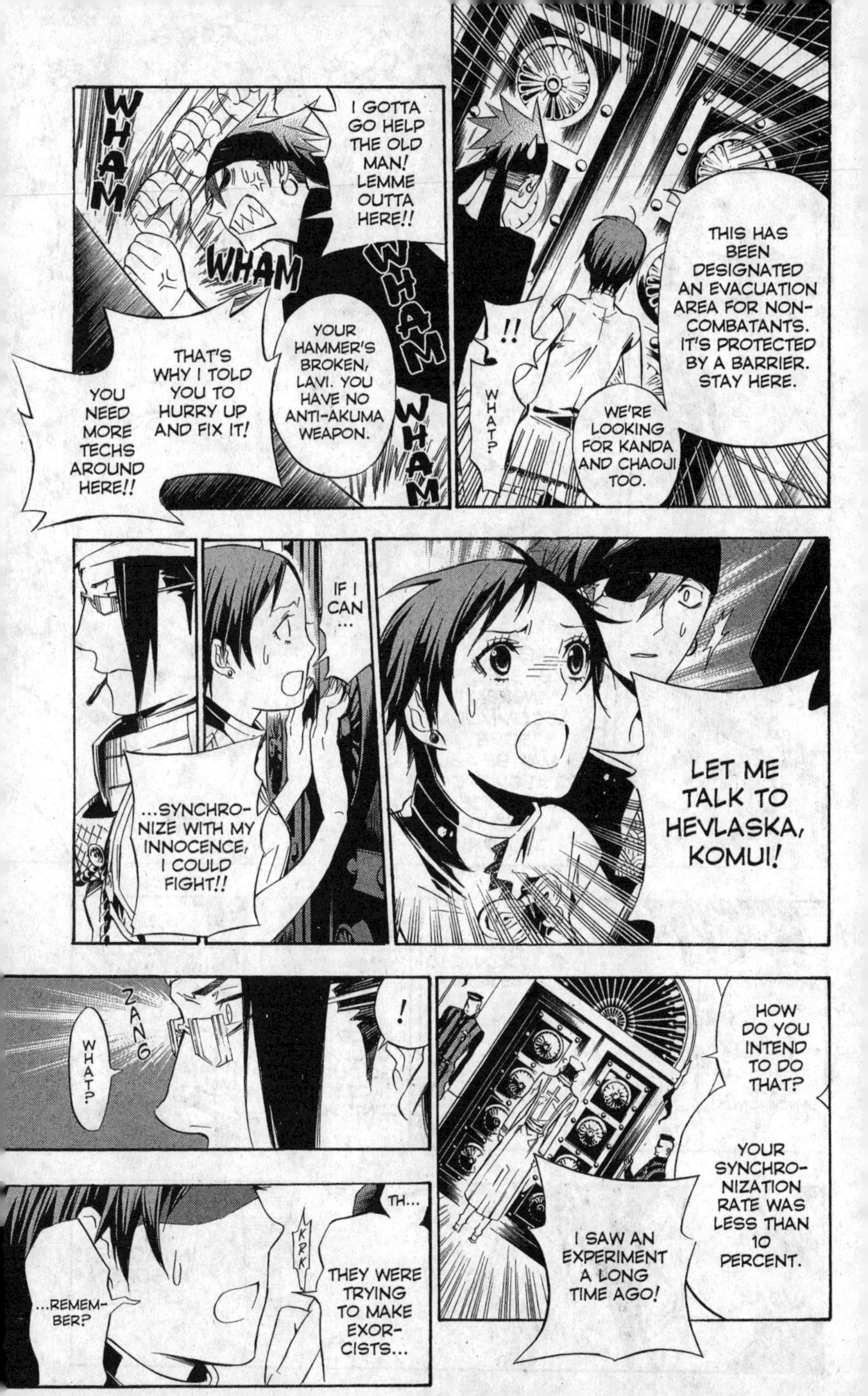
THIS HAS BEEN DESIGNATED AN EVACUATION AREA FOR NON-COMBATANTS. IT'S PROTECTED BY A BARRIER. STAY HERE.
!!
WHAT?
WE'RE LOOKING FOR KANDA AND CHAOJI TOO.
WHAM
I GOTTA GO HELP THE OLD MAN! LEMME OUTTA HERE!!
WHAM
WHAM
WHAM
WHAM
YOUR HAMMER'S BROKEN, LAVI. YOU HAVE NO ANTI-AKUMA WEAPON.
THAT'S WHY I TOLD YOU TO HURRY UP AND FIX IT!
YOU NEED MORE TECHS AROUND HERE!!
LET ME TALK TO HEVLASKA, KOMUI!
IF I CAN...
...SYNCHRONIZE WITH MY INNOCENCE, I COULD FIGHT!!
HOW DO YOU INTEND TO DO THAT?
YOUR SYNCHRONIZATION RATE WAS LESS THAN 10 PERCENT.
I SAW AN EXPERIMENT A LONG TIME AGO!
!
ZANG
WHAT?
TH...
KRK
THEY WERE TRYING TO MAKE EXORCISTS...
...REMEMBER?

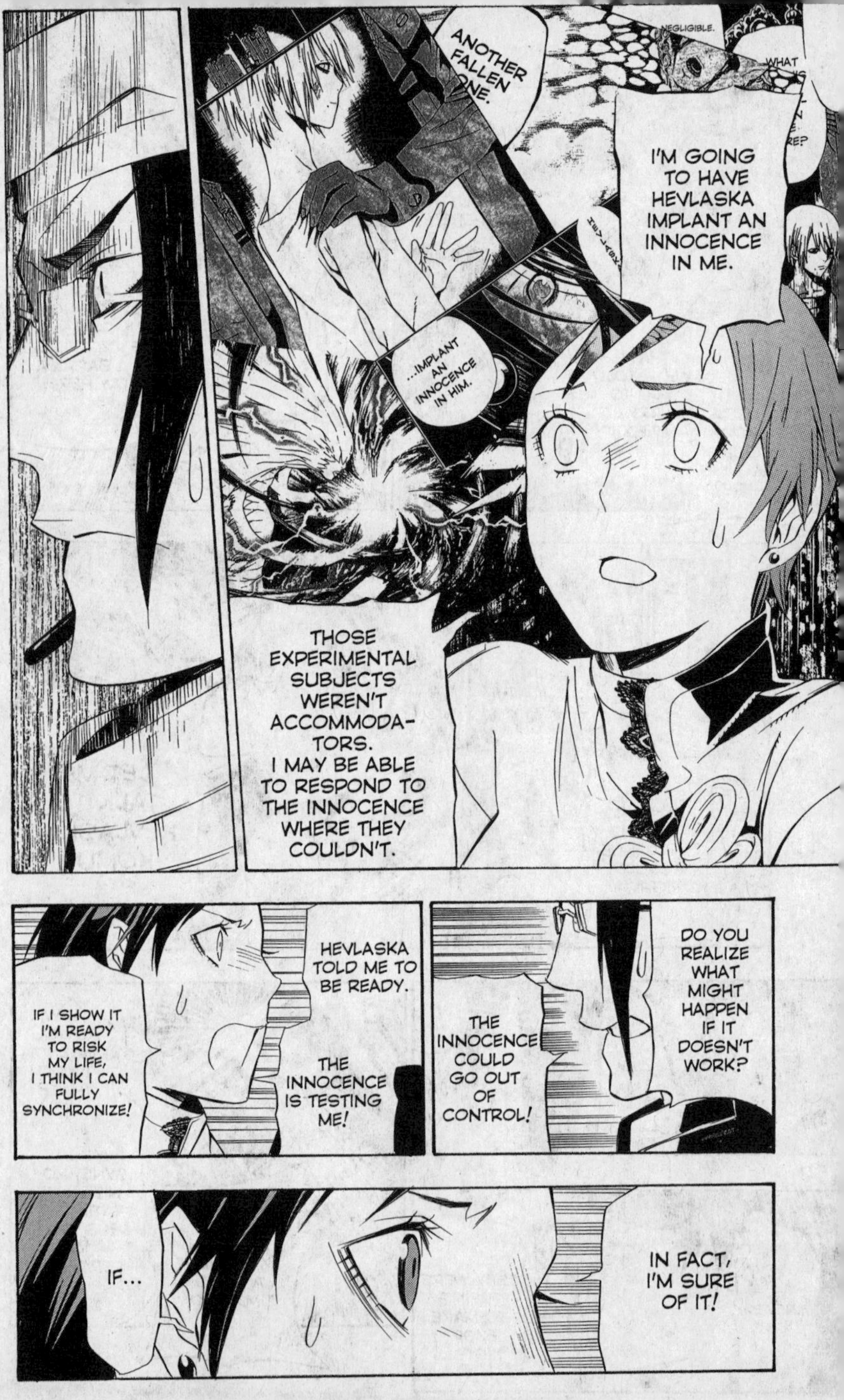
NEGLIGIBLE.
I'M GOING TO HAVE HEVLASKA IMPLANT AN INNOCENCE IN ME.
ANOTHER FALLEN ONE.
...IMPLANT AN INNOCENCE IN HIM.
THOSE EXPERIMENTAL SUBJECTS WEREN'T ACCOMMODA-TORS. I MAY BE ABLE TO RESPOND TO THE INNOCENCE WHERE THEY COULDN'T.
DO YOU REALIZE WHAT MIGHT HAPPEN IF IT DOESN'T WORK?
THE INNOCENCE COULD GO OUT OF CONTROL!
HEVLASKA TOLD ME TO BE READY.
THE INNOCENCE IS TESTING ME!
IF I SHOW IT I'M READY TO RISK MY LIFE, I THINK I CAN FULLY SYNCHRONIZE!
IN FACT, I'M SURE OF IT!
IF...

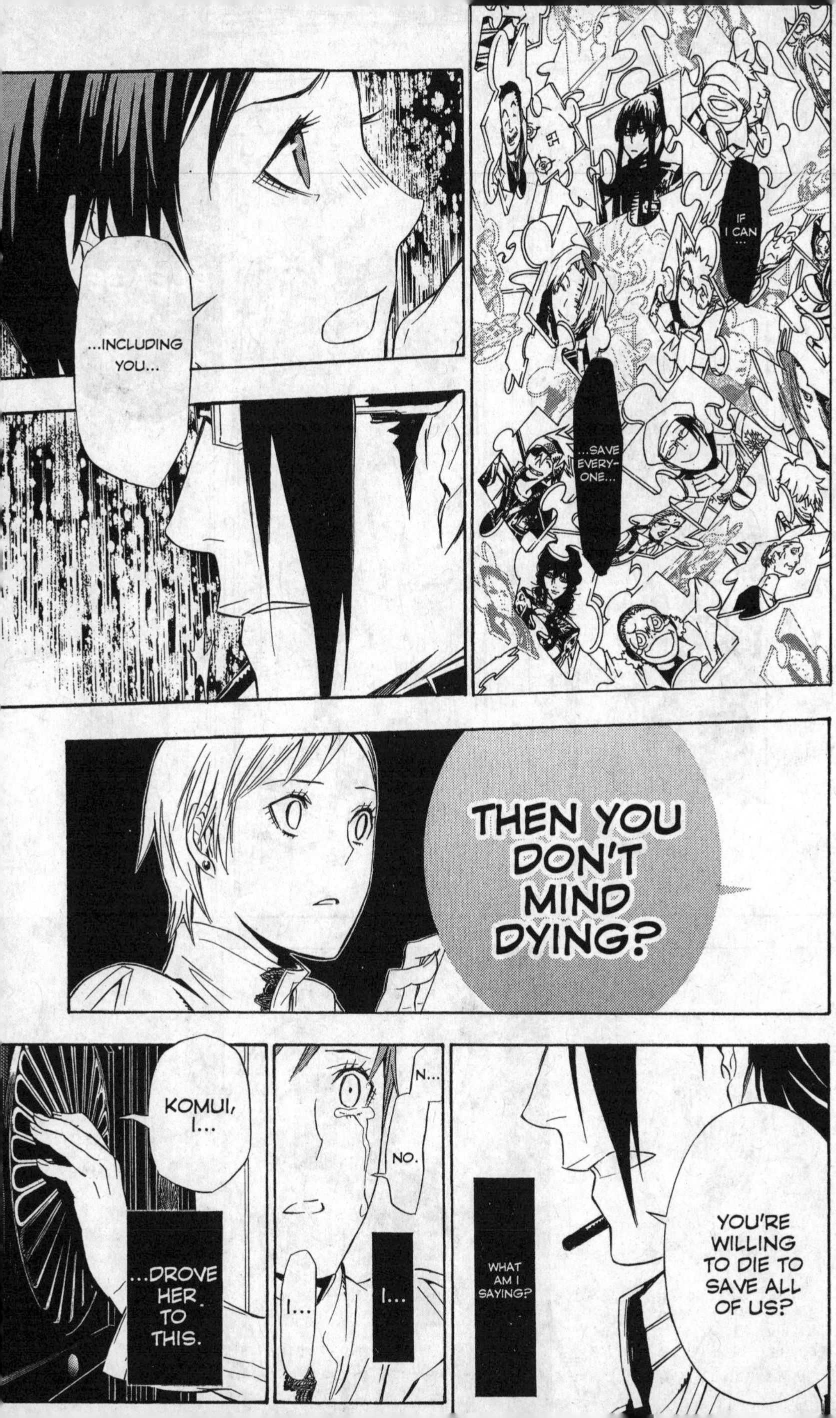
IF I CAN...
...SAVE EVERYONE...
...INCLUDING YOU...
THEN YOU DON'T MIND DYING?
YOU'RE WILLING TO DIE TO SAVE ALL OF US?
WHAT AM I SAYING?
N...
NO.
I...
I...
KOMUI, I...
...DROVE HER TO THIS.

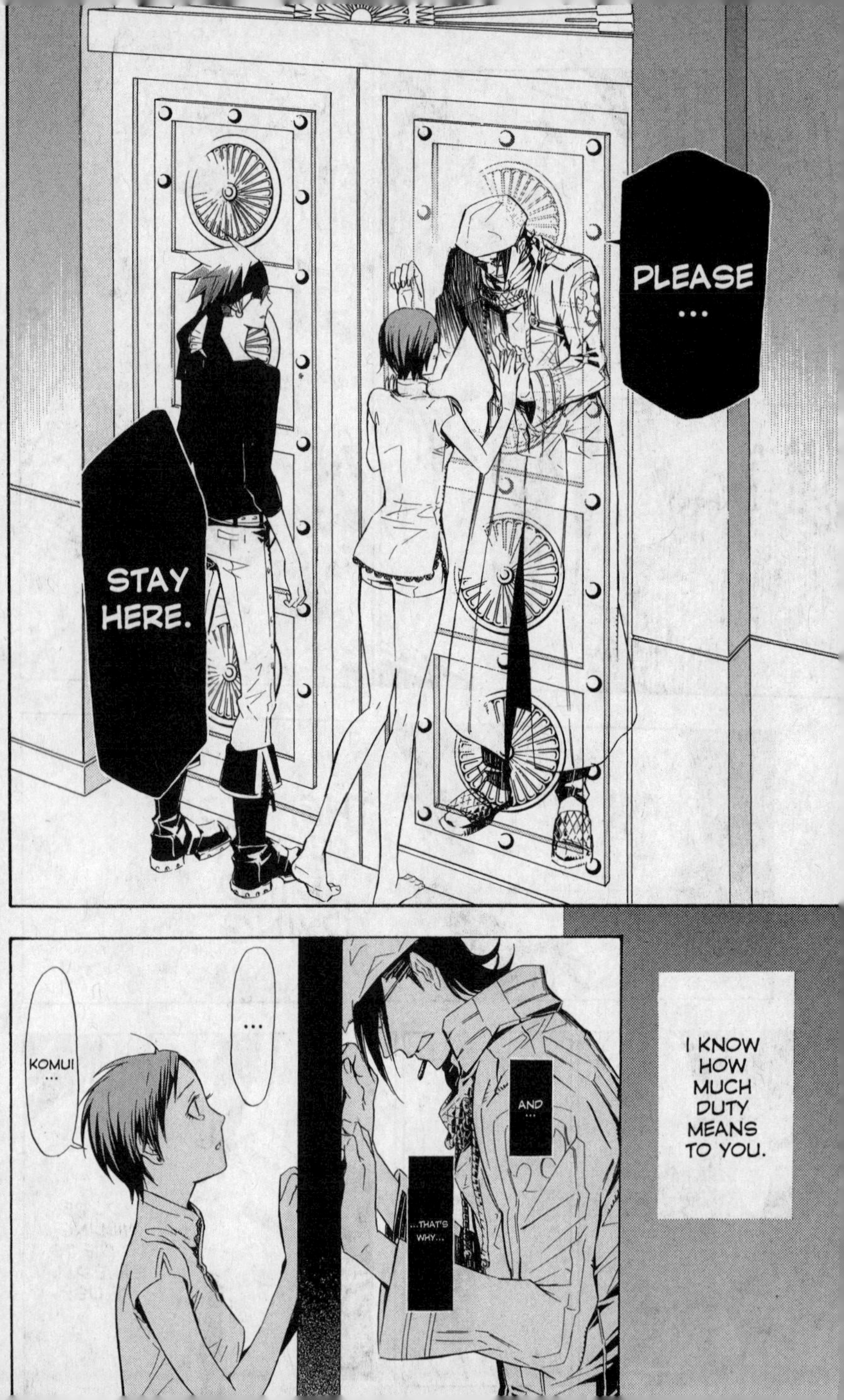
PLEASE ...
STAY HERE.
I KNOW HOW MUCH DUTY MEANS TO YOU.
AND ...
...THAT'S WHY...
...
KOMUI ...

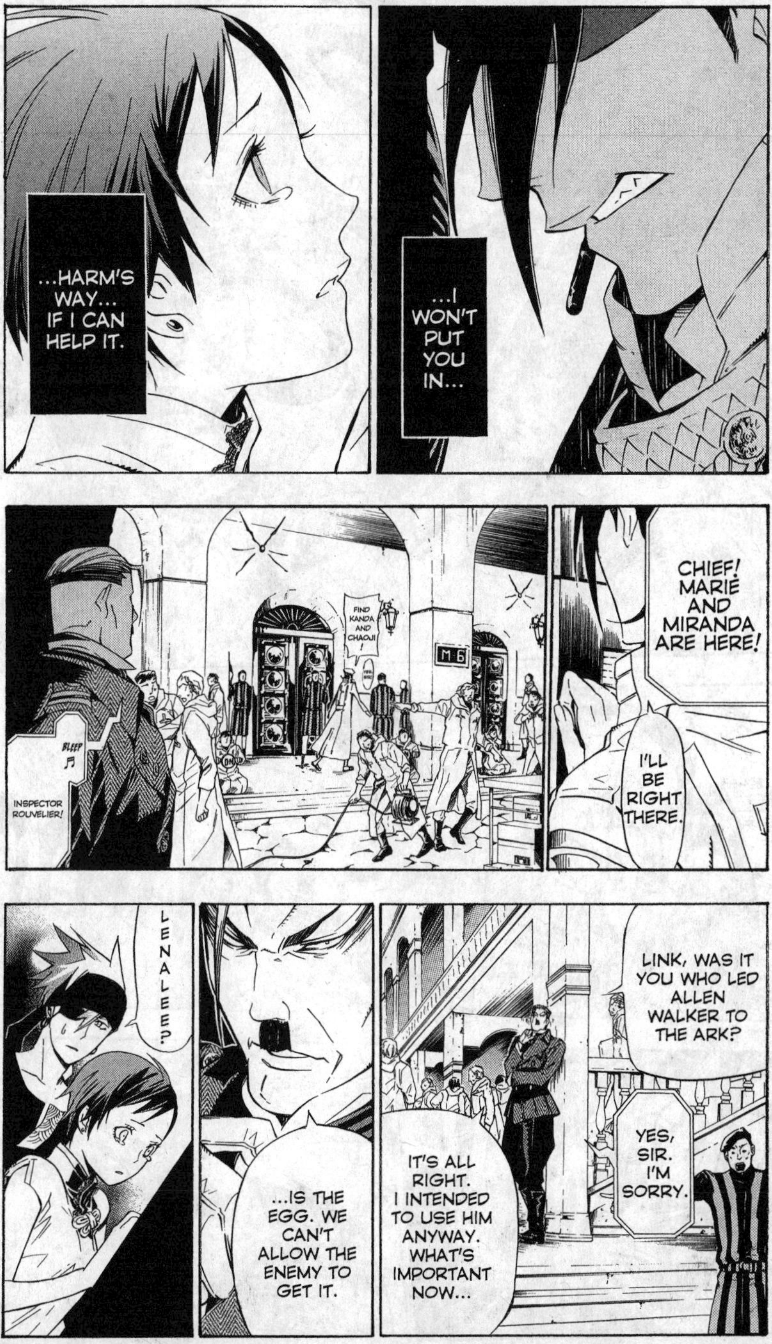
...I WON'T PUT YOU IN...
...HARM'S WAY... IF I CAN HELP IT.
CHIEF! MARIE AND MIRANDA ARE HERE!
I'LL BE RIGHT THERE.
FIND KANDA AND CHAOJI!
BLEEP ♫
INSPECTOR ROUVELIER!
LINK, WAS IT YOU WHO LED ALLEN WALKER TO THE ARK?
YES, SIR. I'M SORRY.
IT'S ALL RIGHT. I INTENDED TO USE HIM ANYWAY. WHAT'S IMPORTANT NOW...
...IS THE EGG. WE CAN'T ALLOW THE ENEMY TO GET IT.
LENALEE?

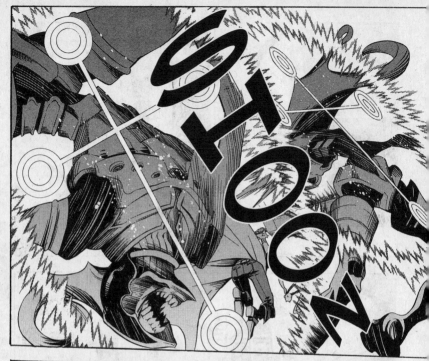

GET ON, BOY!

HEAVEN COM-PASS!

....!

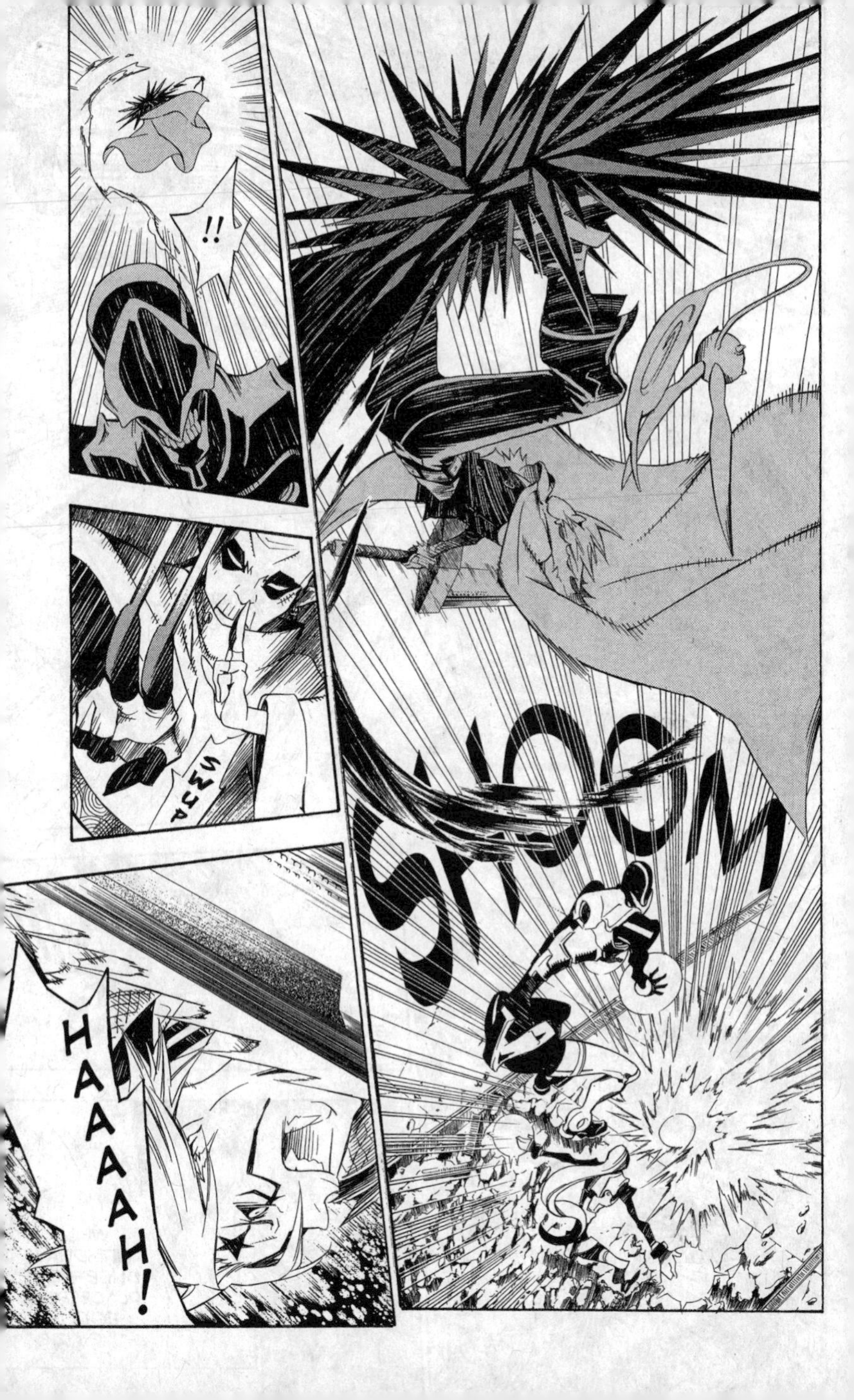
!!
SHOOM
HAAAAH!

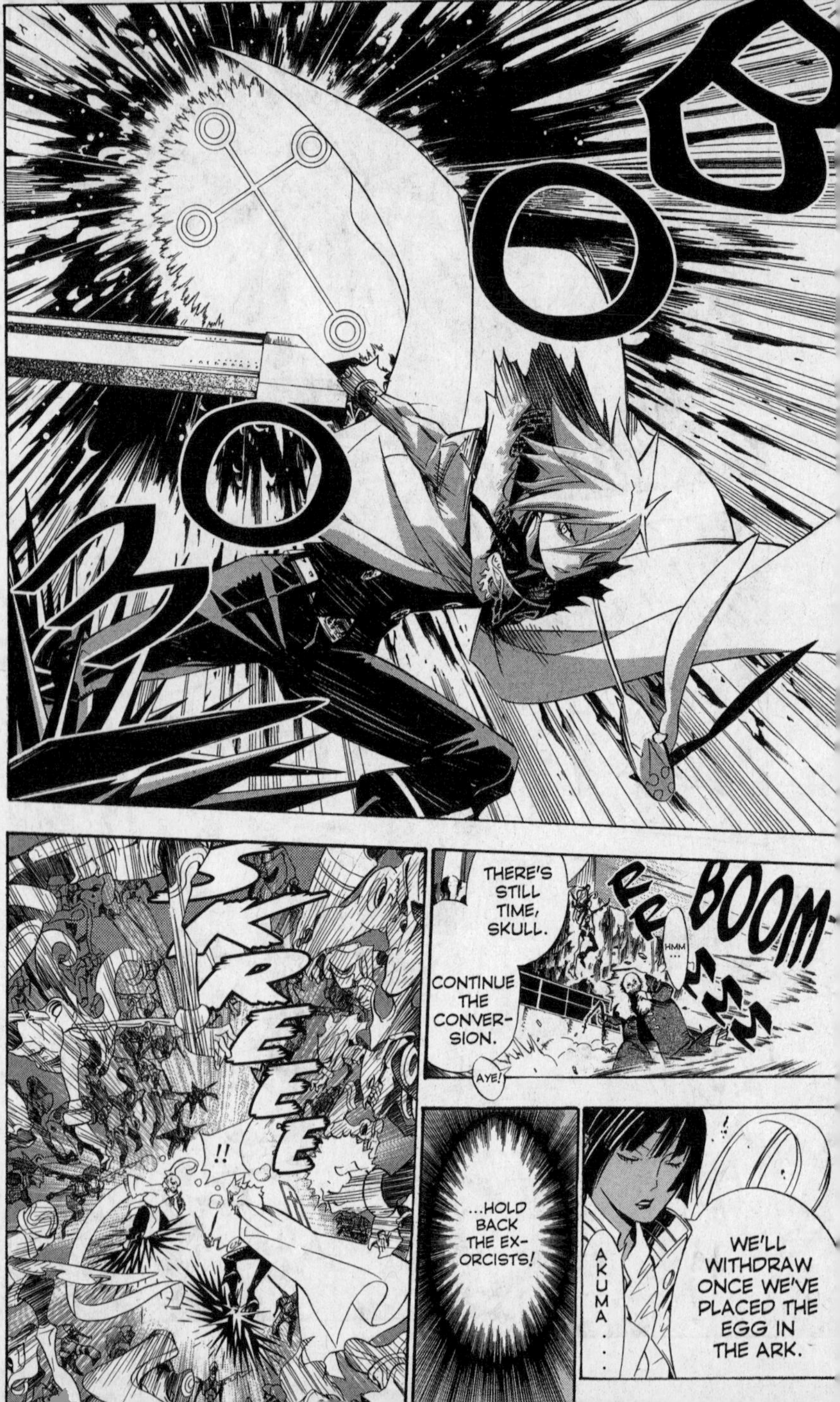
BOOM
THERE'S STILL TIME, SKULL.
HMM...
CONTINUE THE CONVERSION.
AYE!
WE'LL WITHDRAW ONCE WE'VE PLACED THE EGG IN THE ARK.
AKUMA...
...HOLD BACK THE EX-ORCISTS!
SKREEEE
!!

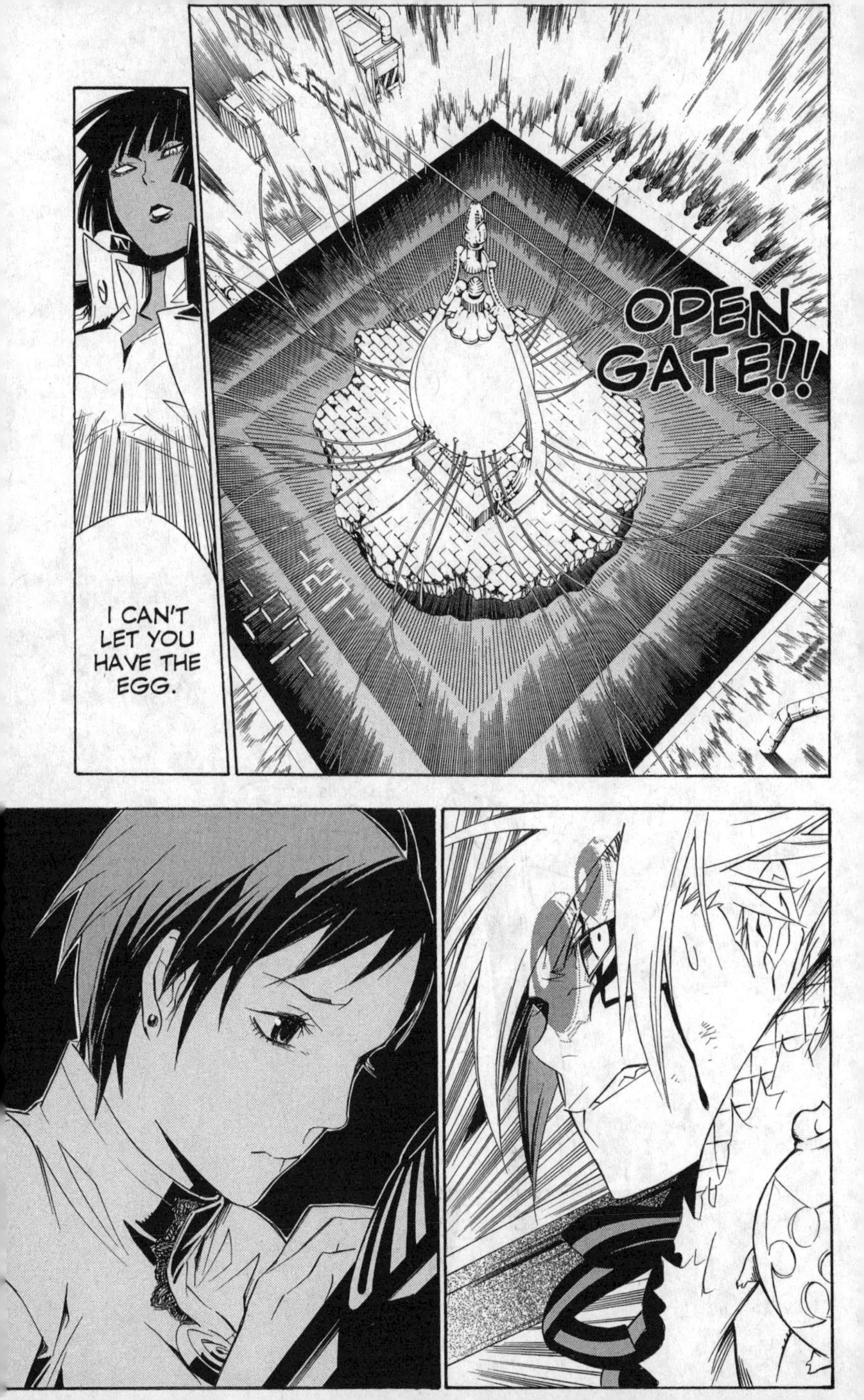
OPEN GATE!!
I CAN'T LET YOU HAVE THE EGG.

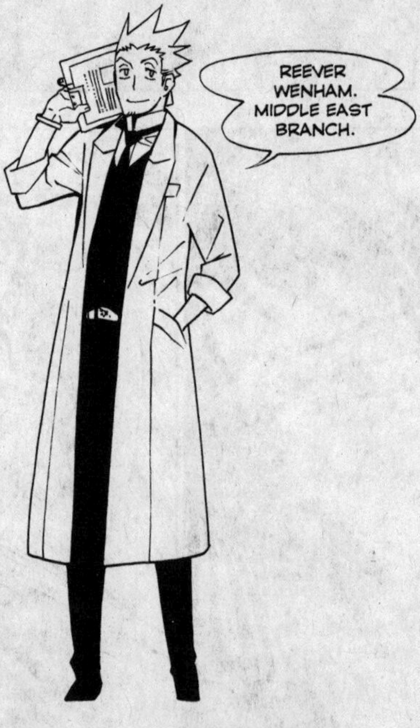
REEVER WENHAM. MIDDLE EAST BRANCH.

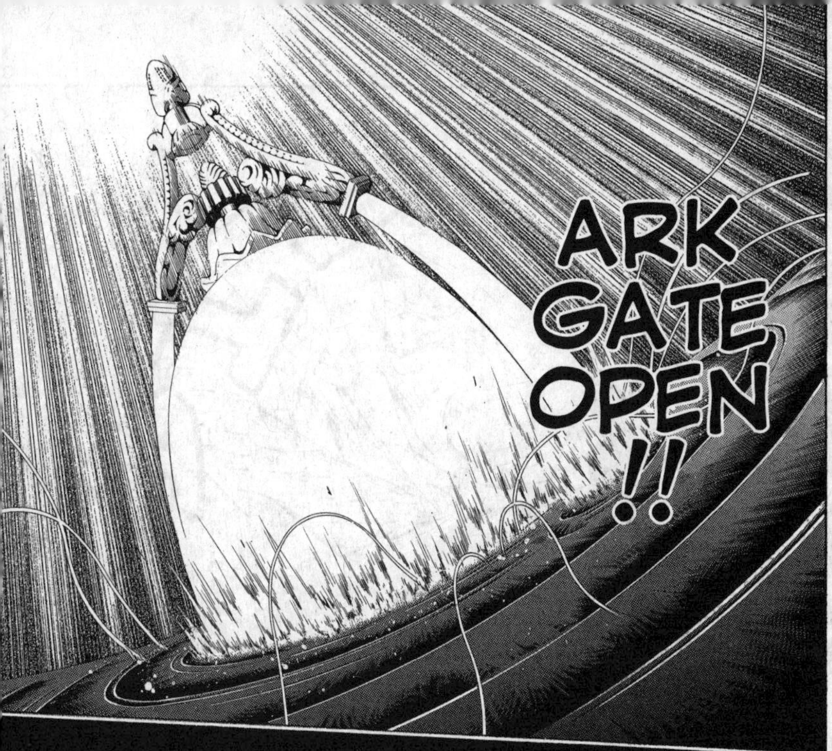
ARK GATE OPEN!!

THE 141ST NIGHT: ALLIES

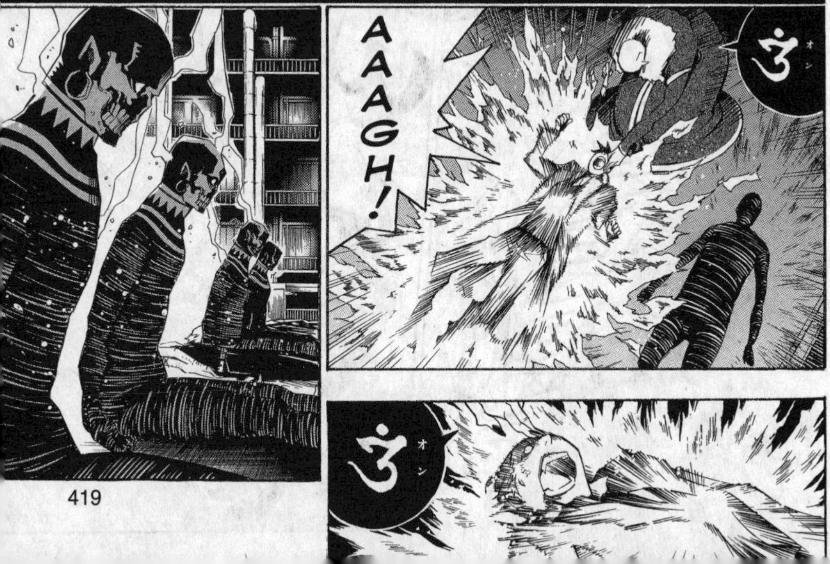
AAAGH!
オン
オン

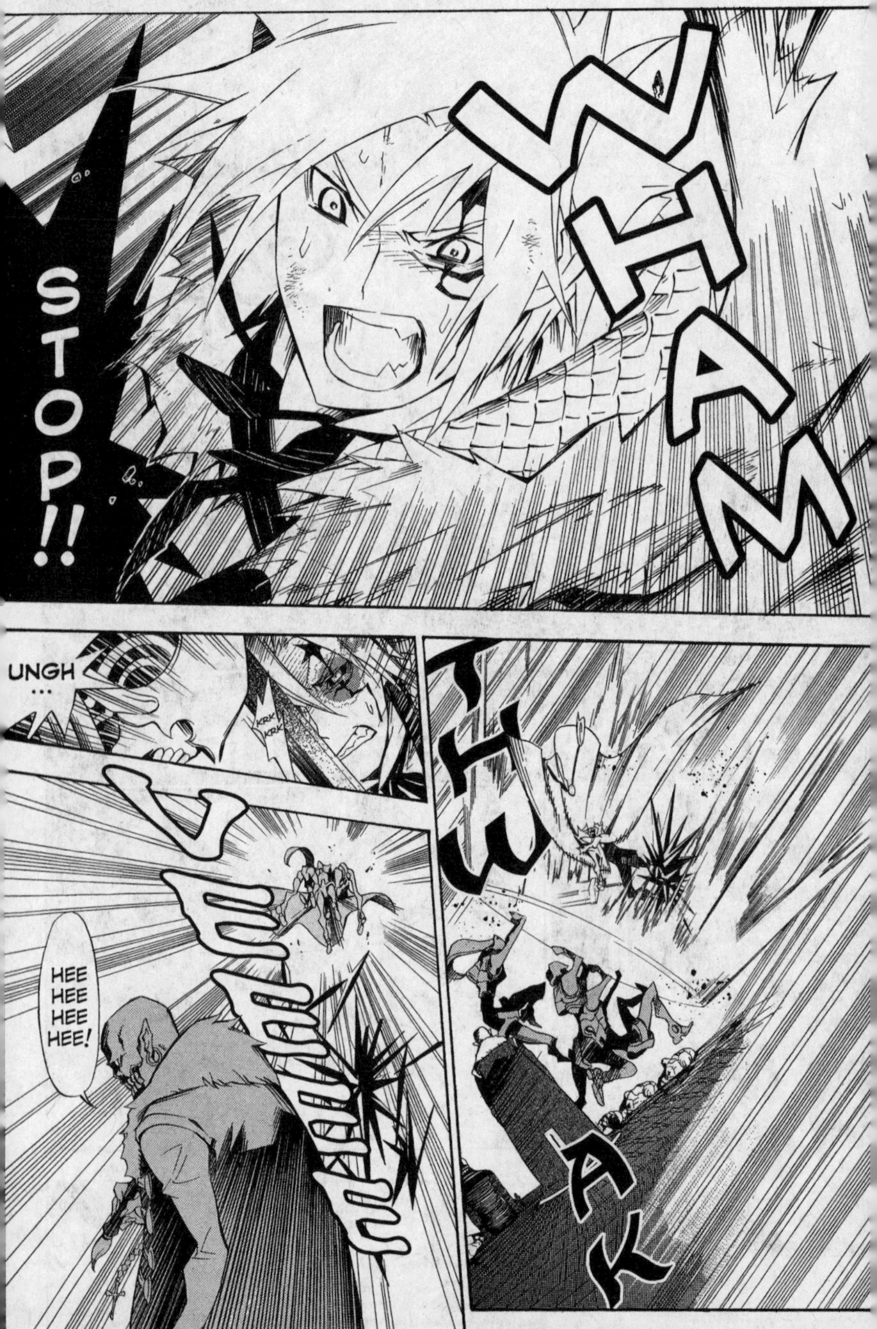
WHAM
STOP!!
THWAK
UNGH...
KRK KRK
VEEEEE
HEE HEE HEE HEE!

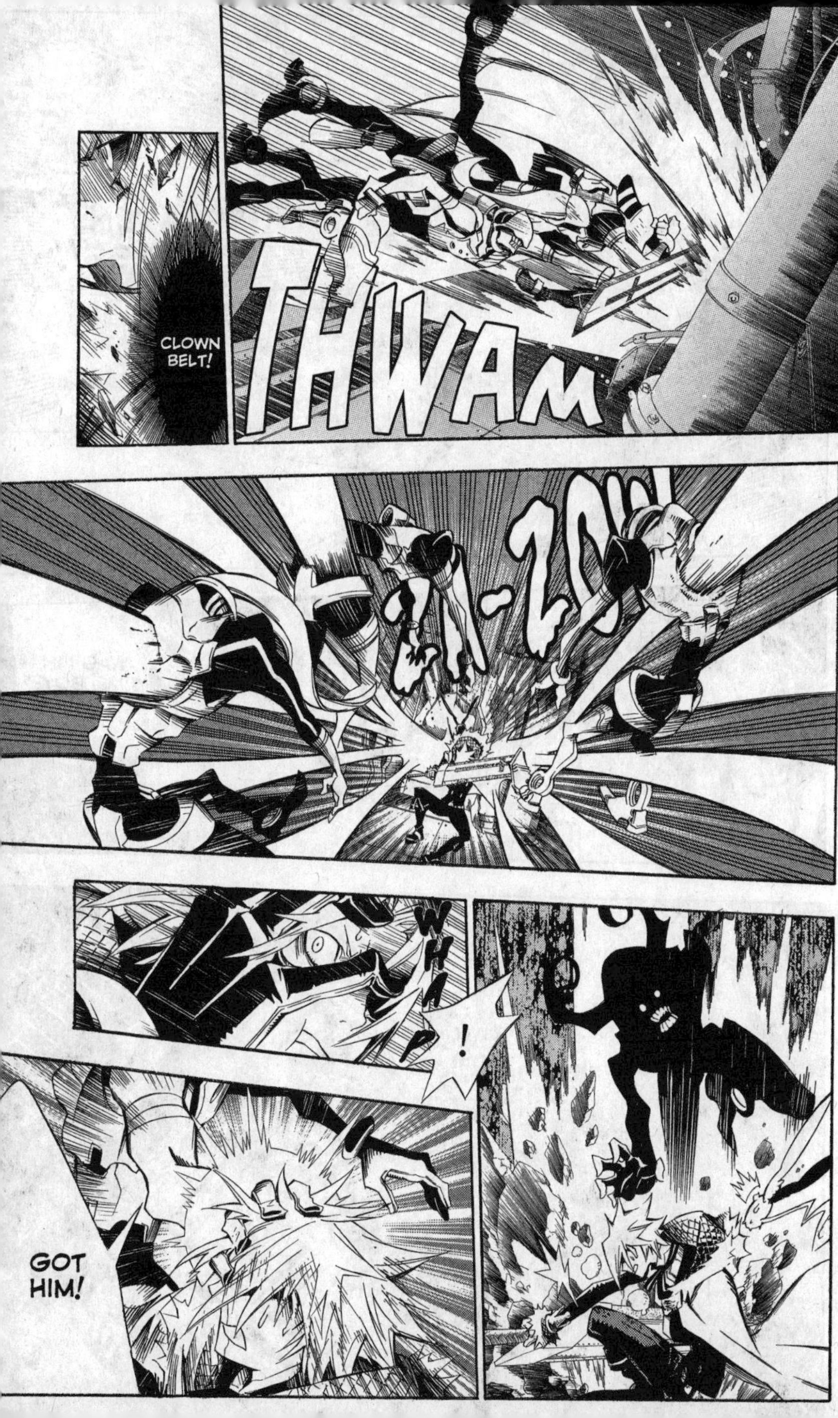
THWAM
CLOWN BELT!
WHAP
!
GOT HIM!

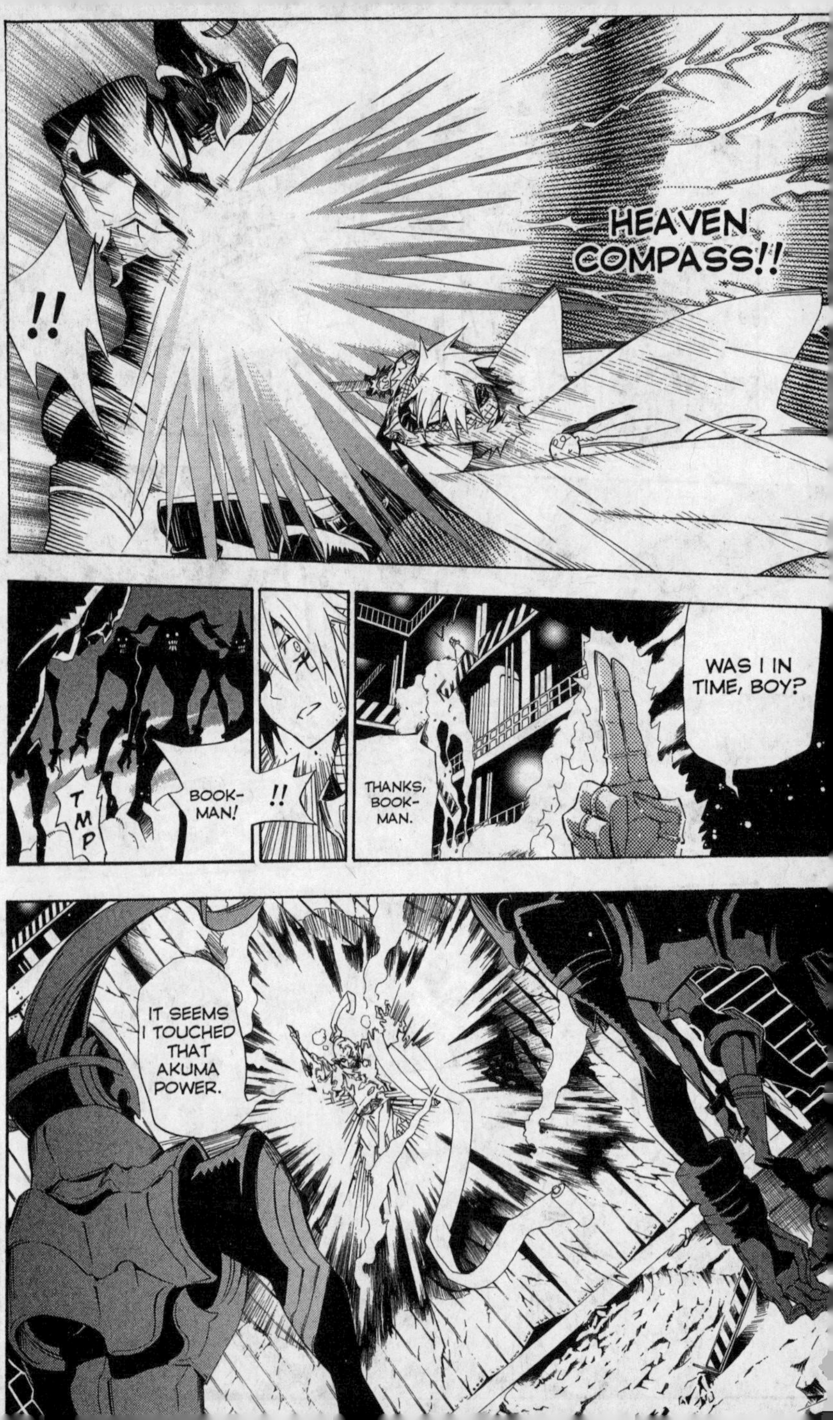
HEAVEN COMPASS!!
!!
WAS I IN TIME, BOY?
THANKS, BOOK-MAN.
!!
BOOK-MAN!
TMP
IT SEEMS I TOUCHED THAT AKUMA POWER.

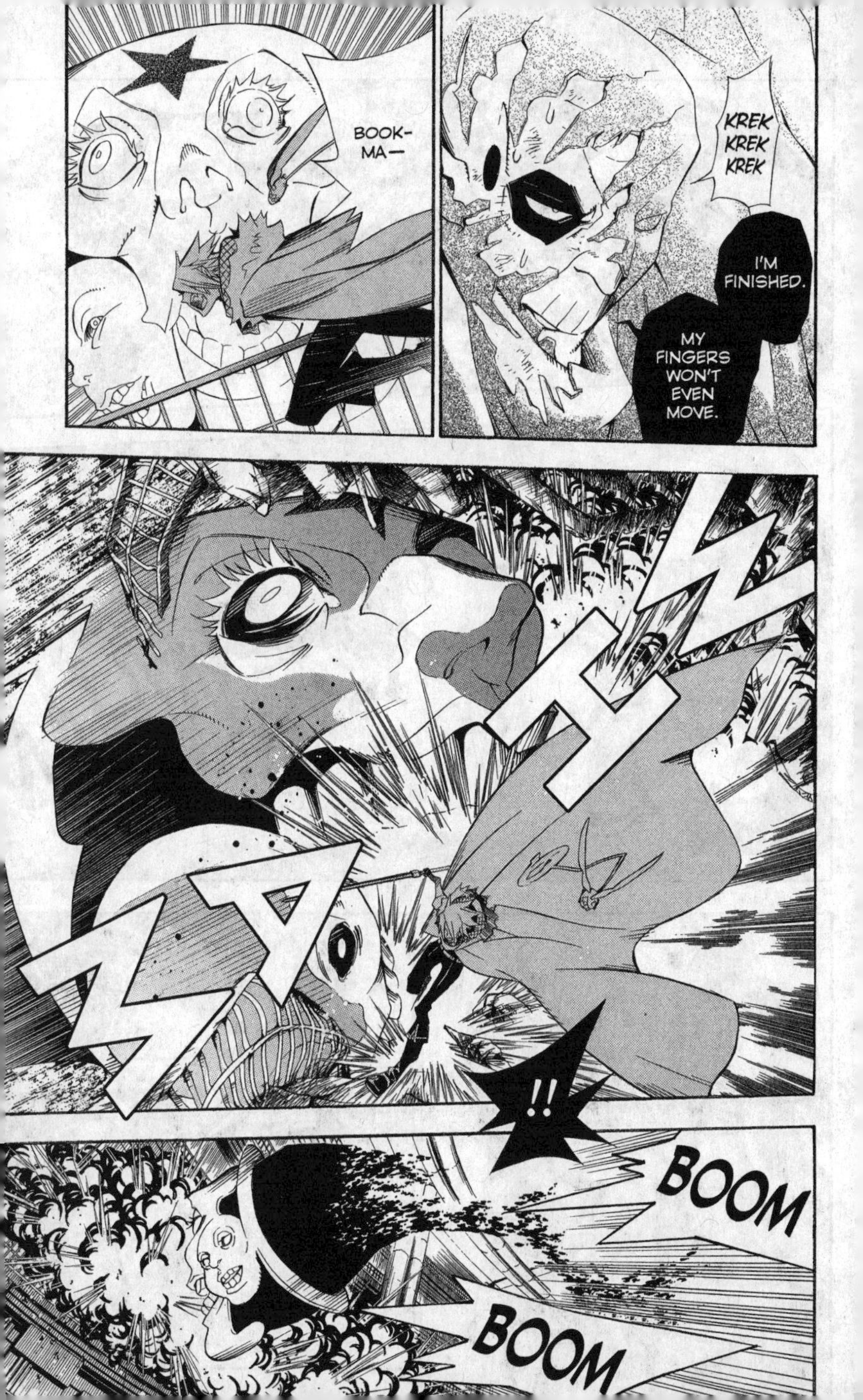
KREK
KREK
KREK
I'M FINISHED.
MY FINGERS WON'T EVEN MOVE.
BOOK-MA—
!!
BOOM
BOOM

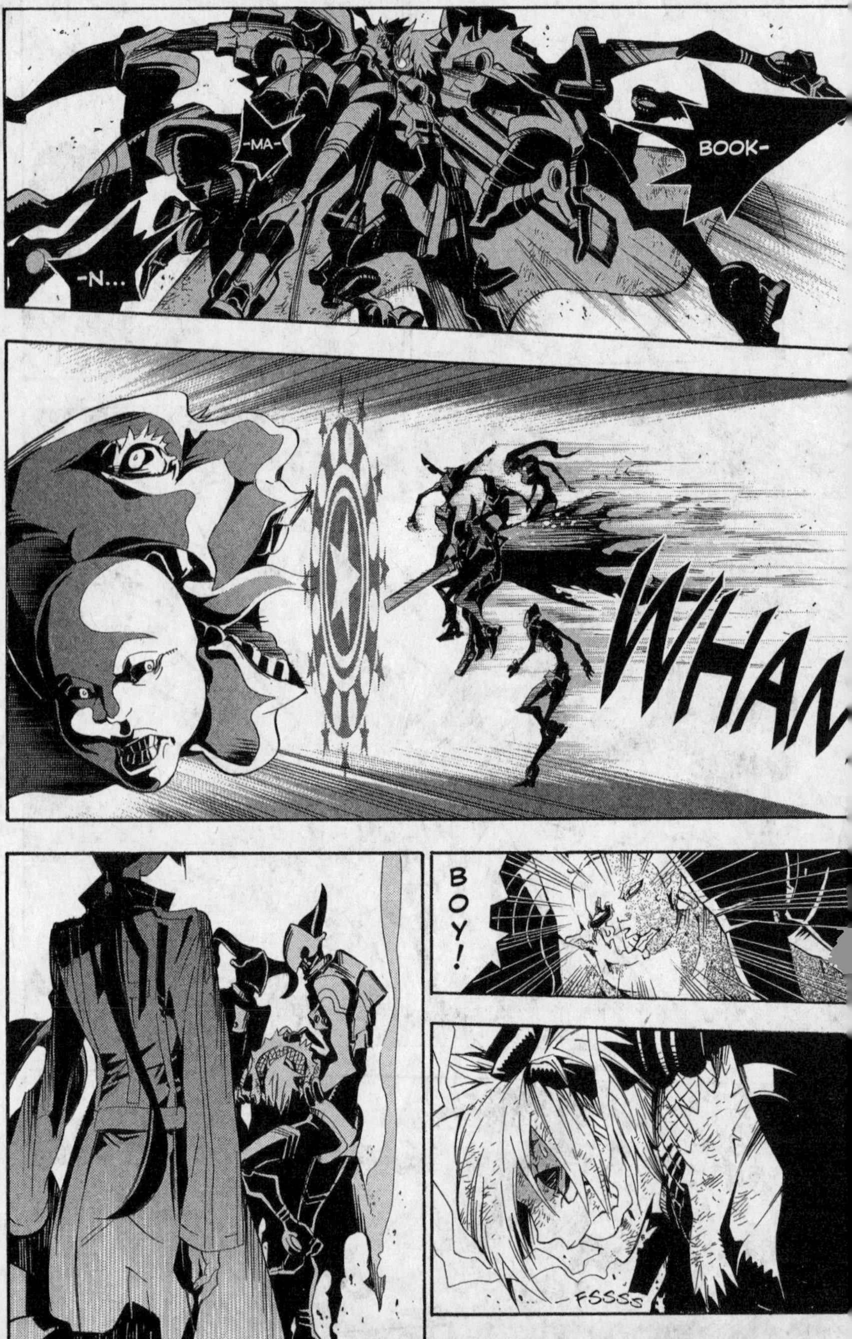
BOOK-
-MA-
-N...
WHAN
BOY!
FSSSS

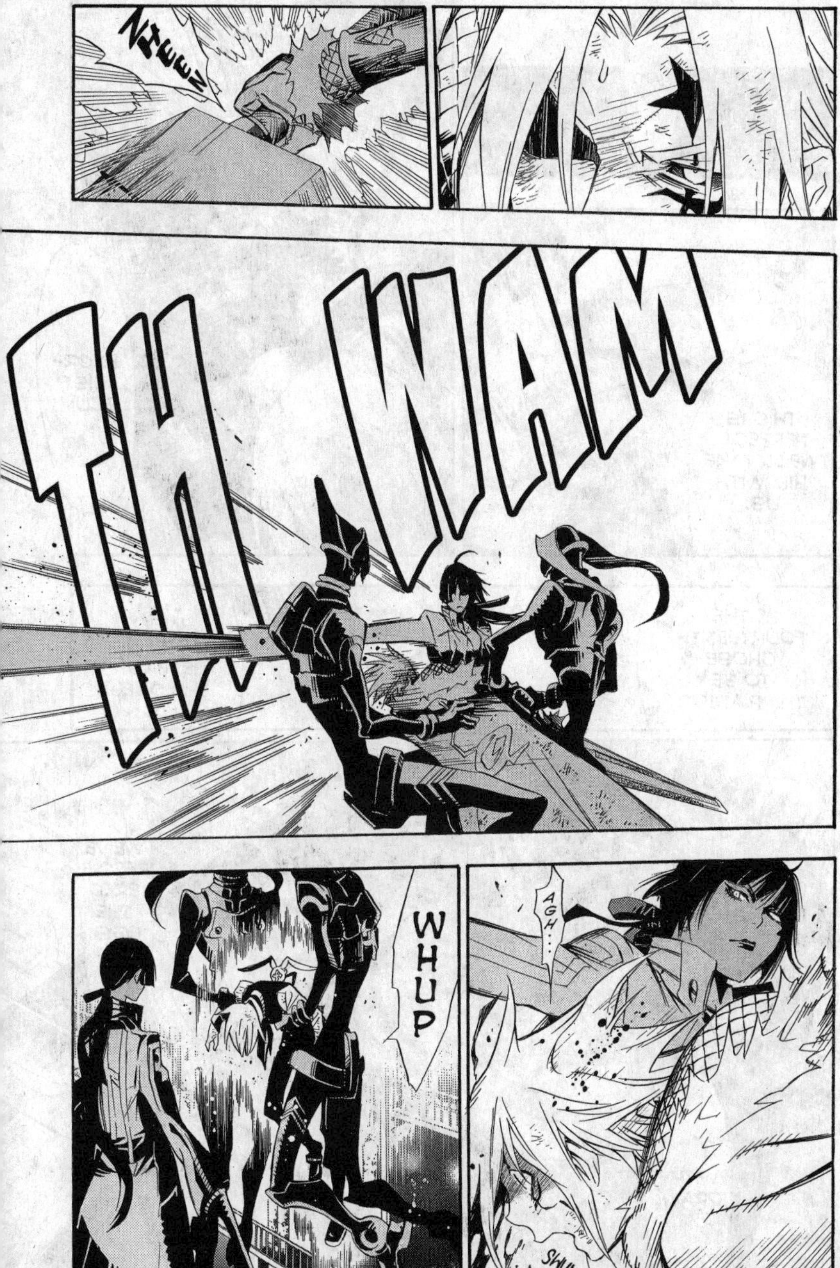
NZHEEEZ
THWAM
AGH...
SHUMP
WHUP

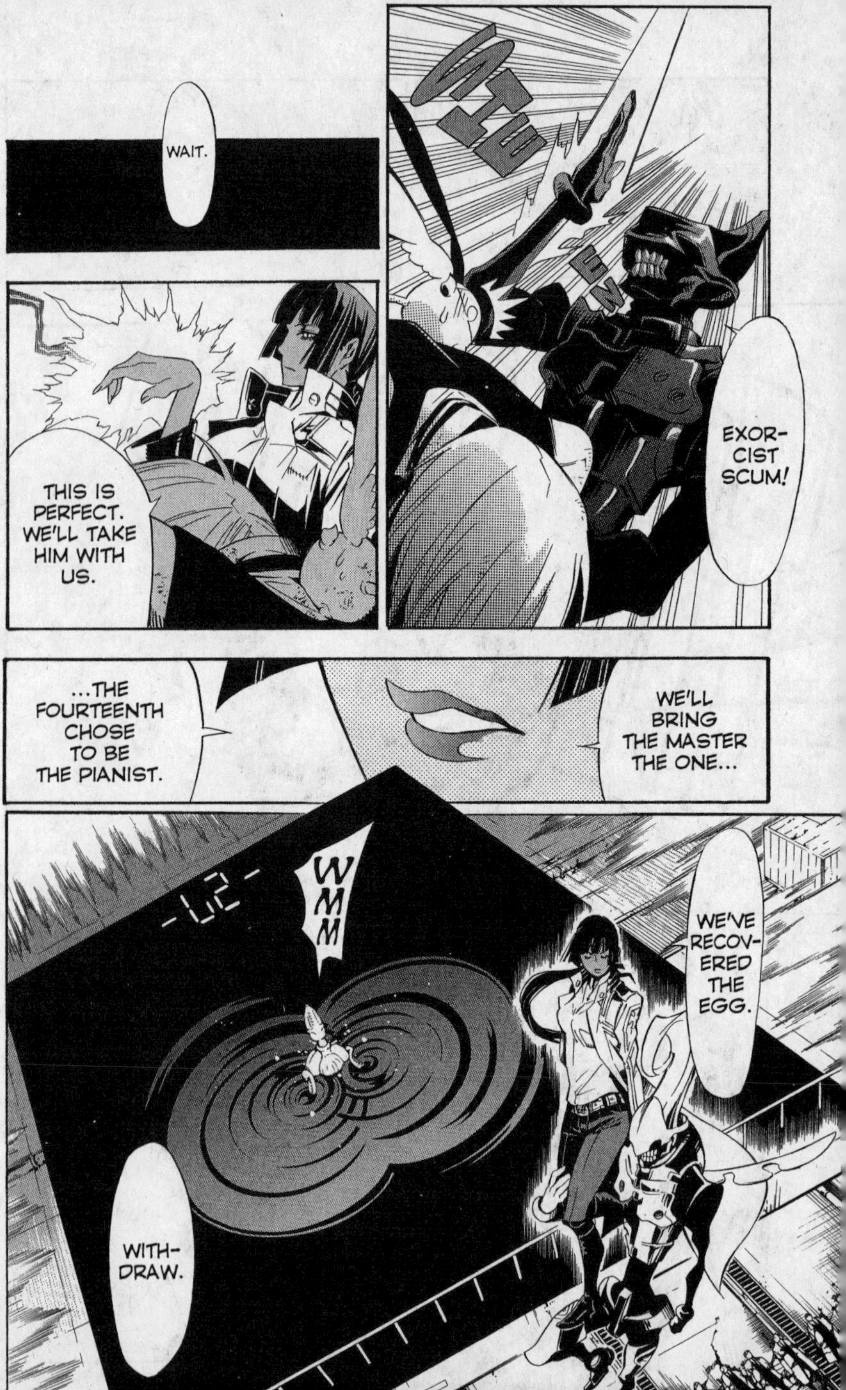
EXOR-CIST SCUM!
WAIT.
THIS IS PERFECT. WE'LL TAKE HIM WITH US.
WE'LL BRING THE MASTER THE ONE...
...THE FOURTEENTH CHOSE TO BE THE PIANIST.
WE'VE RECOV-ERED THE EGG.
WMM
WITH-DRAW.

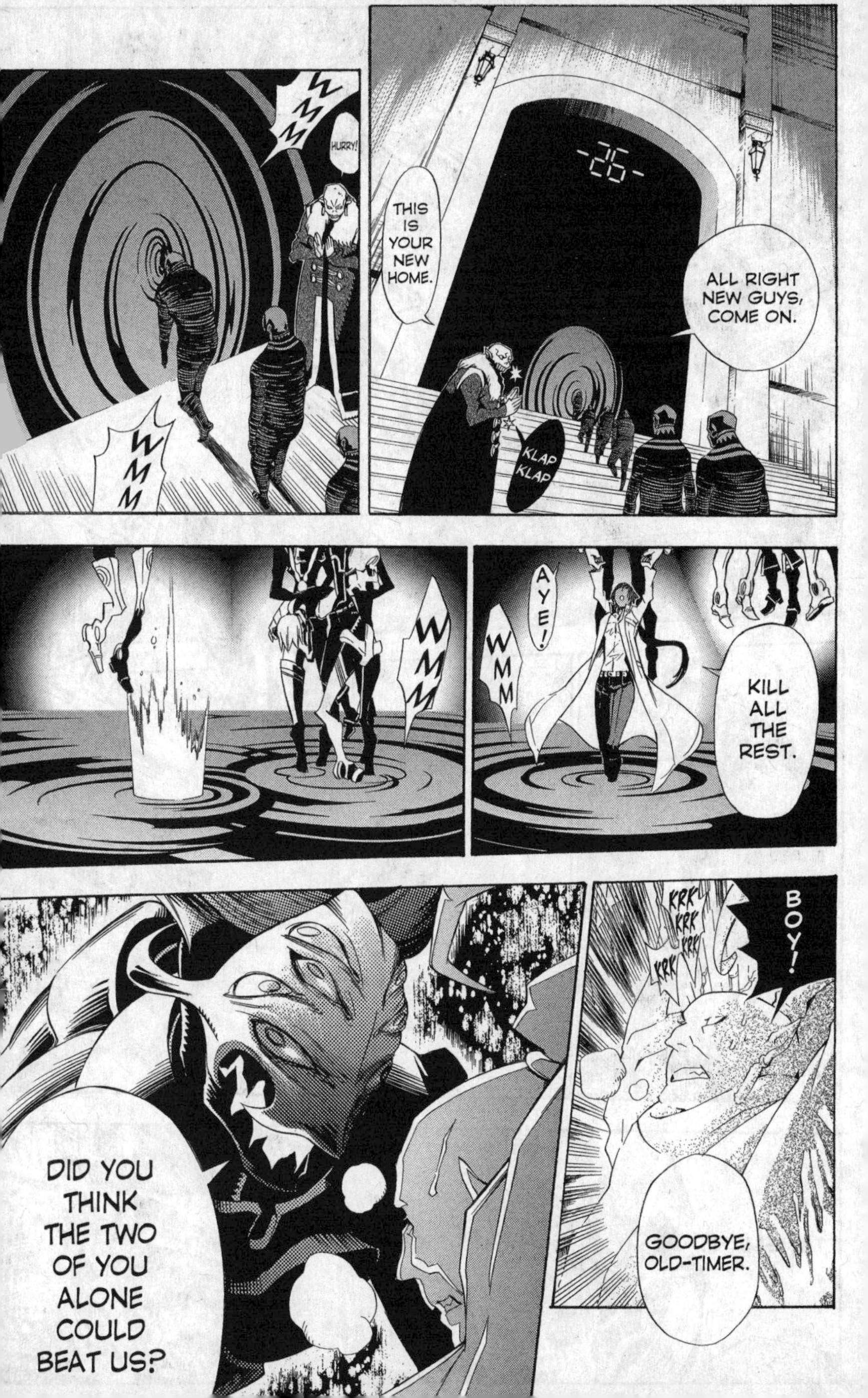
-26-
ALL RIGHT NEW GUYS, COME ON.
THIS IS YOUR NEW HOME.
KLAP KLAP
WMM
HURRY!
WMM
KILL ALL THE REST.
AYE!
WMM
WMM
BOY!
KRK KRK KRK KRK
GOODBYE, OLD-TIMER.
DID YOU THINK THE TWO OF YOU ALONE COULD BEAT US?

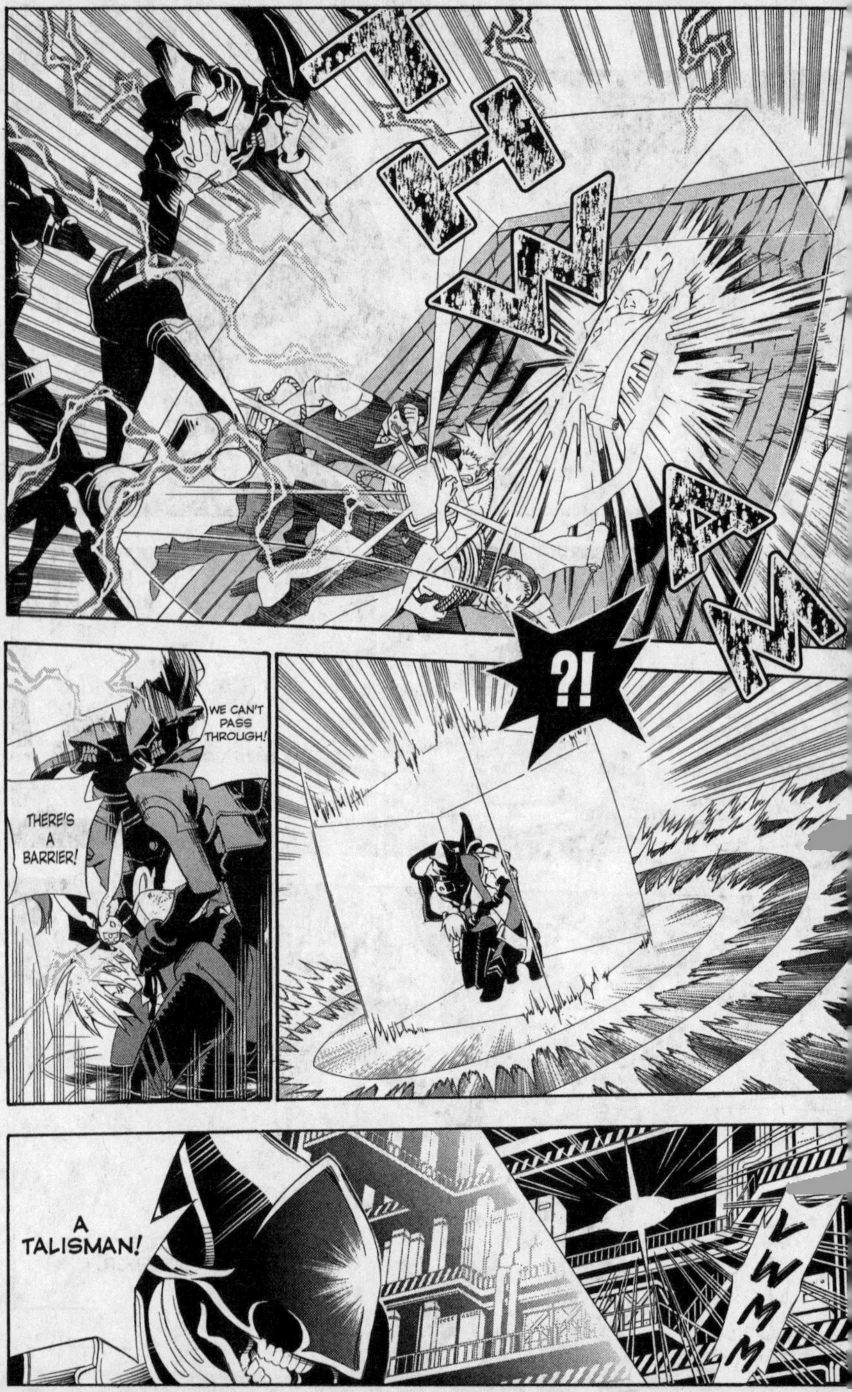
?!
WE CAN'T PASS THROUGH!
THERE'S A BARRIER!
VWMM
A TALISMAN!

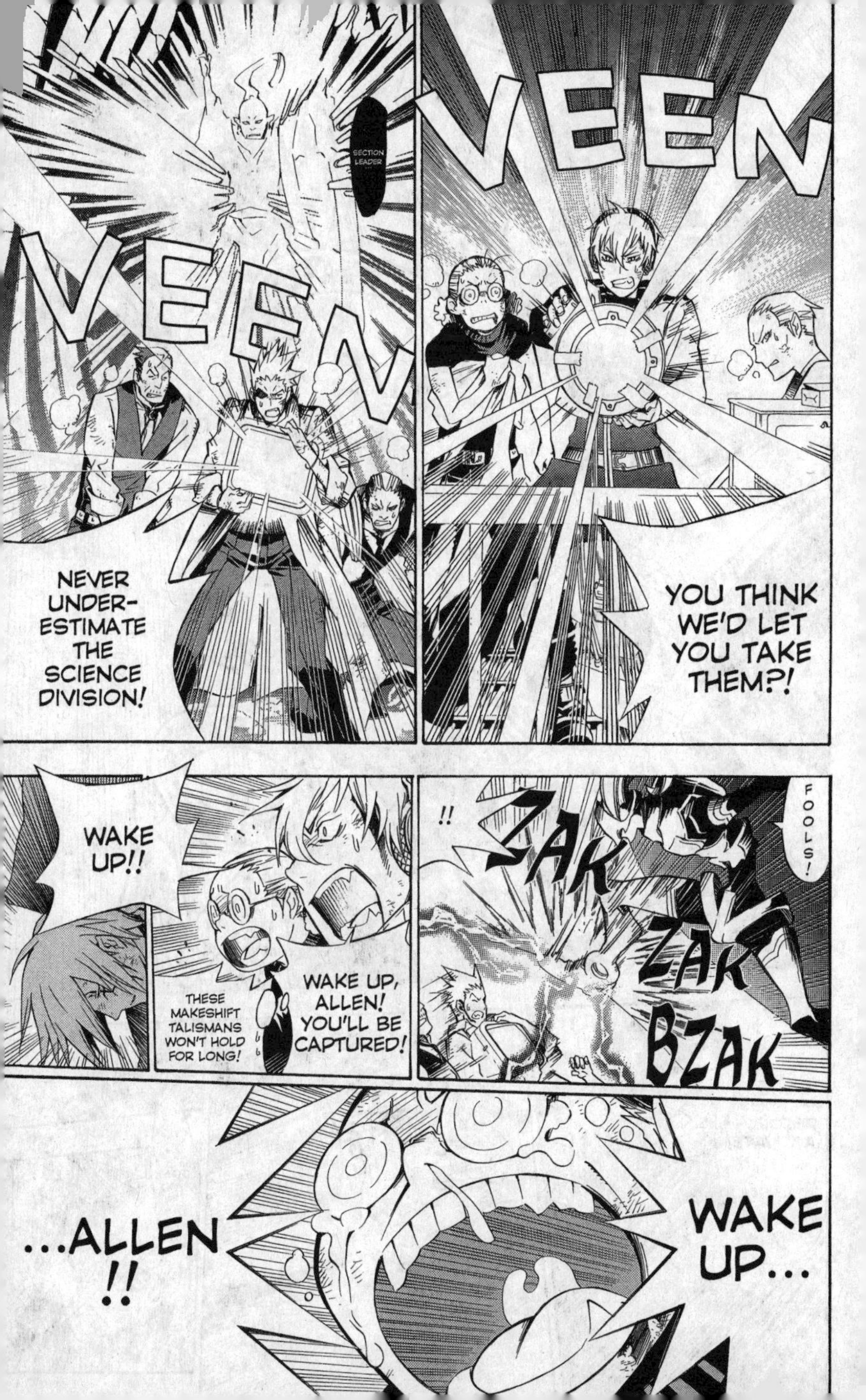
VEEN
YOU THINK WE'D LET YOU TAKE THEM?!
SECTION LEADER...
VEEN
NEVER UNDER-ESTIMATE THE SCIENCE DIVISION!
FOOLS!
ZAK
ZAK
BZAK
!!
WAKE UP!!
WAKE UP, ALLEN! YOU'LL BE CAPTURED!
THESE MAKESHIFT TALISMANS WON'T HOLD FOR LONG!
WAKE UP...
...ALLEN!!

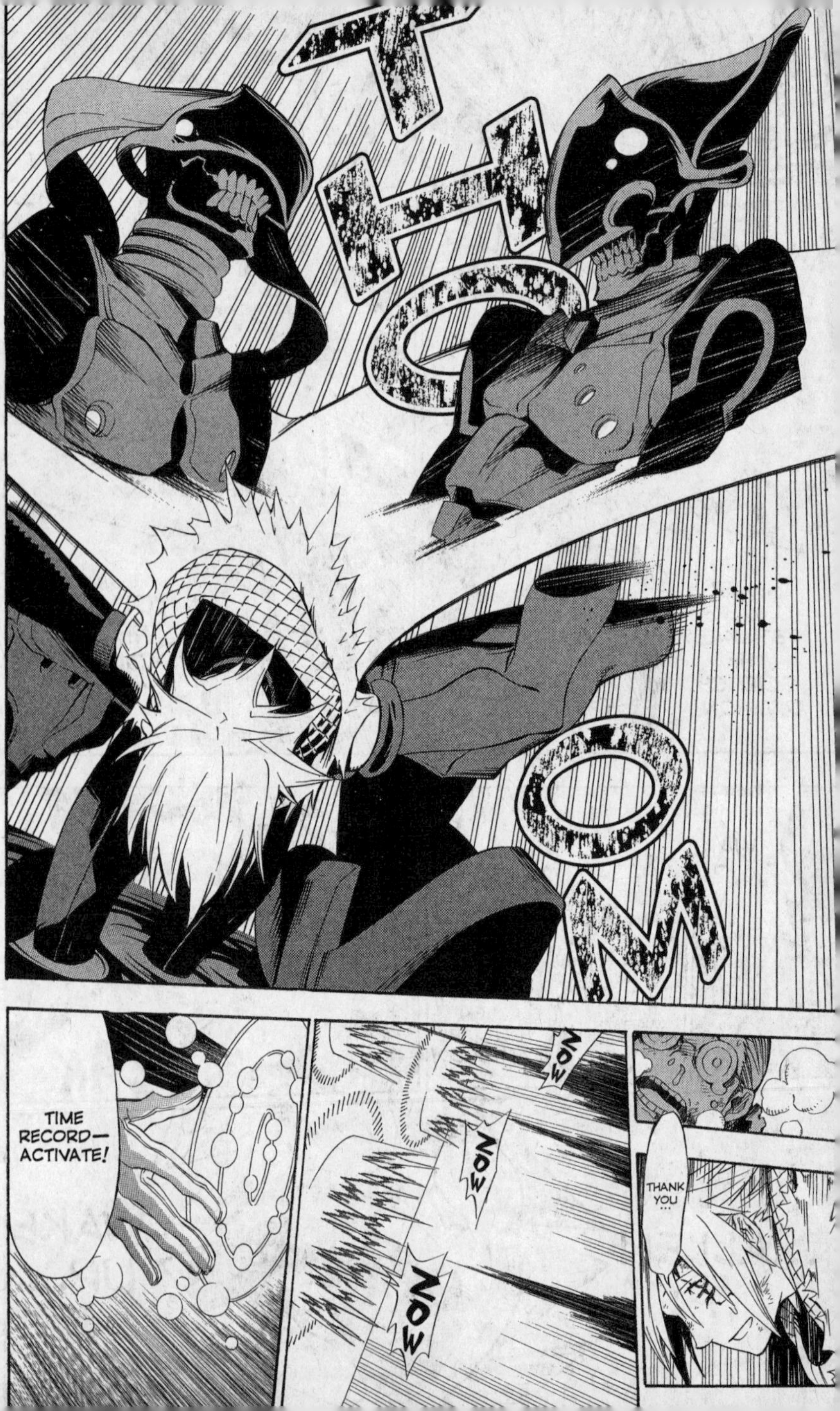
THOOM
THANK YOU...
TIME RECORD—ACTIVATE!

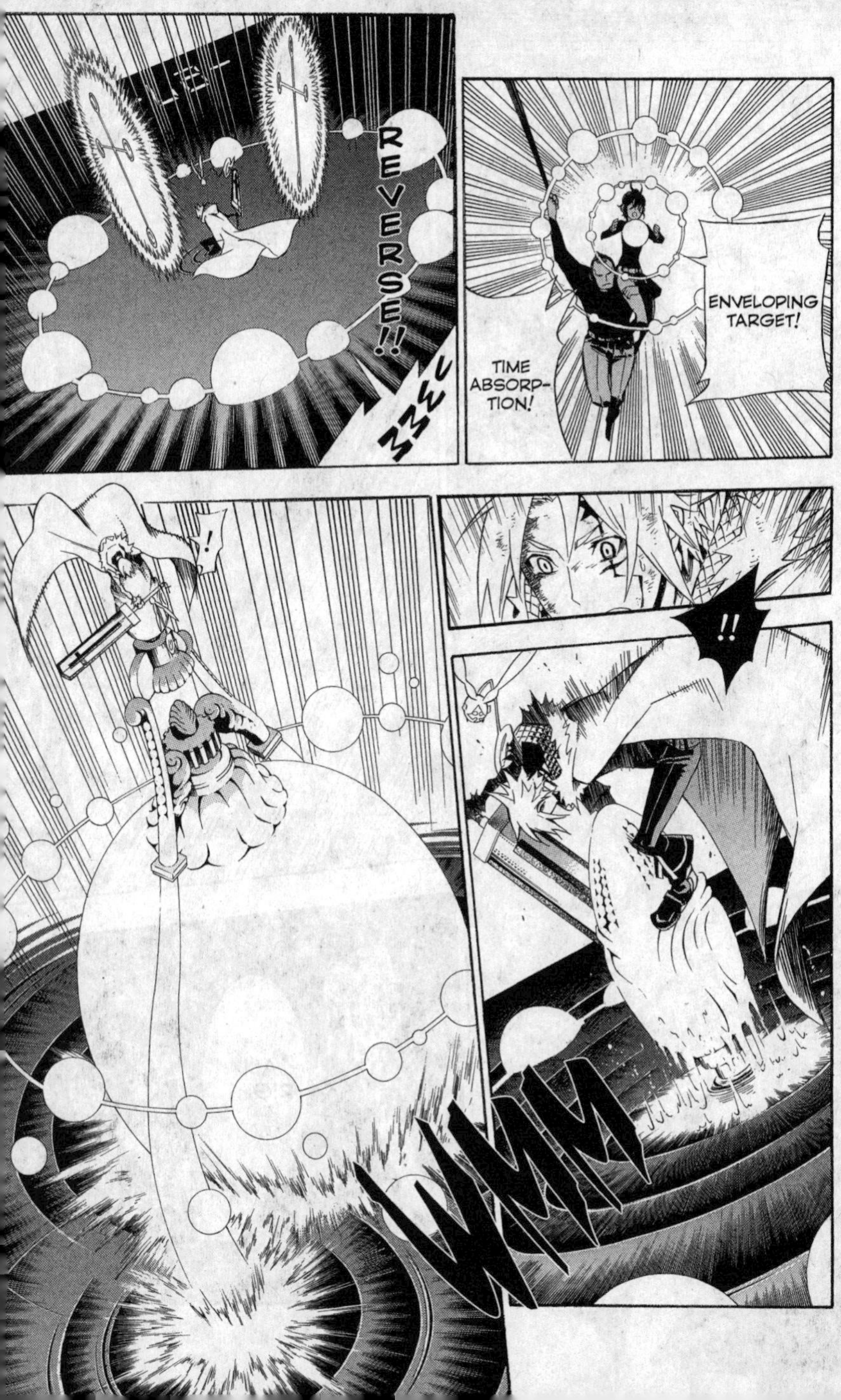
ENVELOPING TARGET!
TIME ABSORPTION!
REVERSE!!
VWMM
!!
!

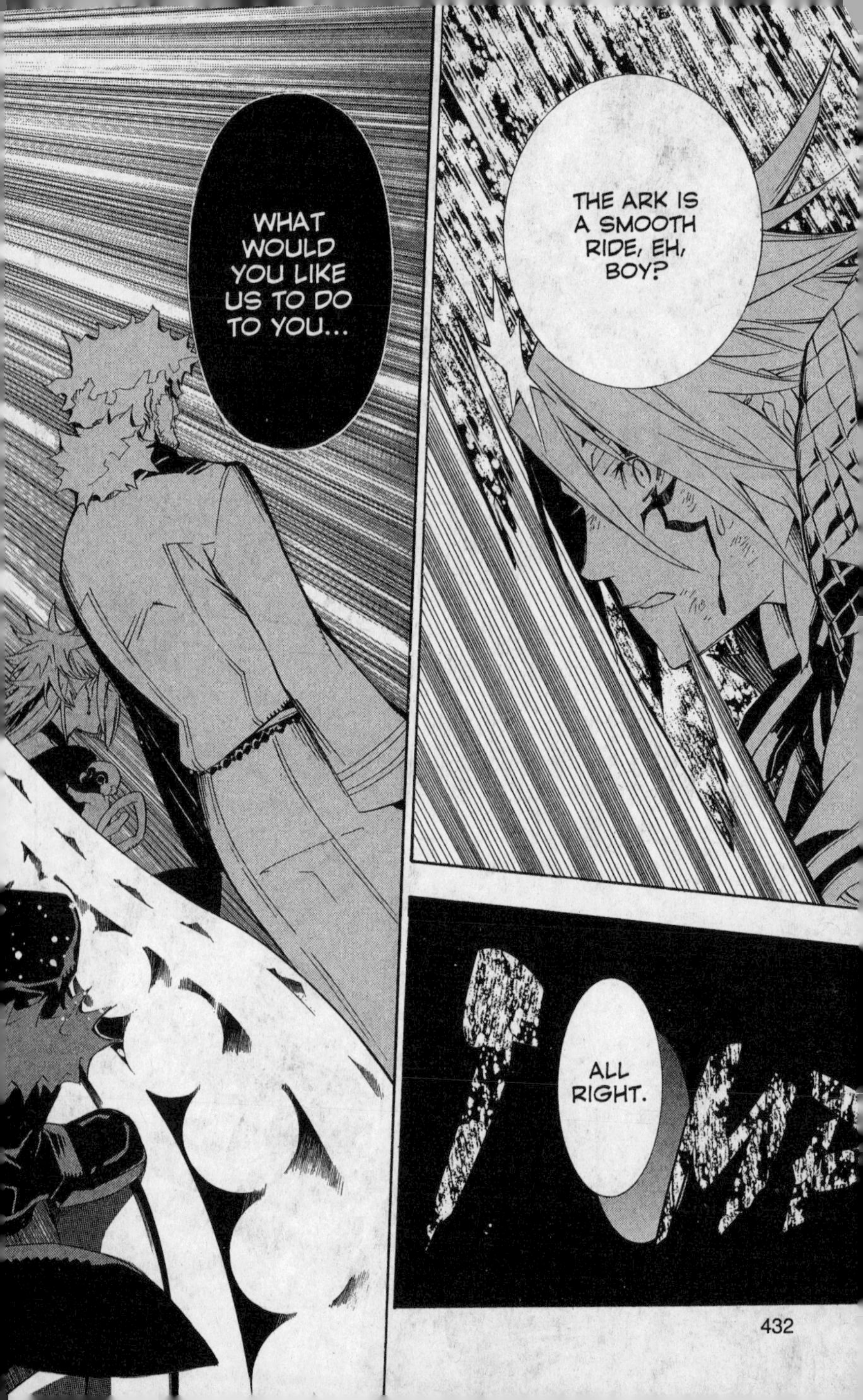
THE ARK IS A SMOOTH RIDE, EH, BOY?
ALL RIGHT.
WHAT WOULD YOU LIKE US TO DO TO YOU...

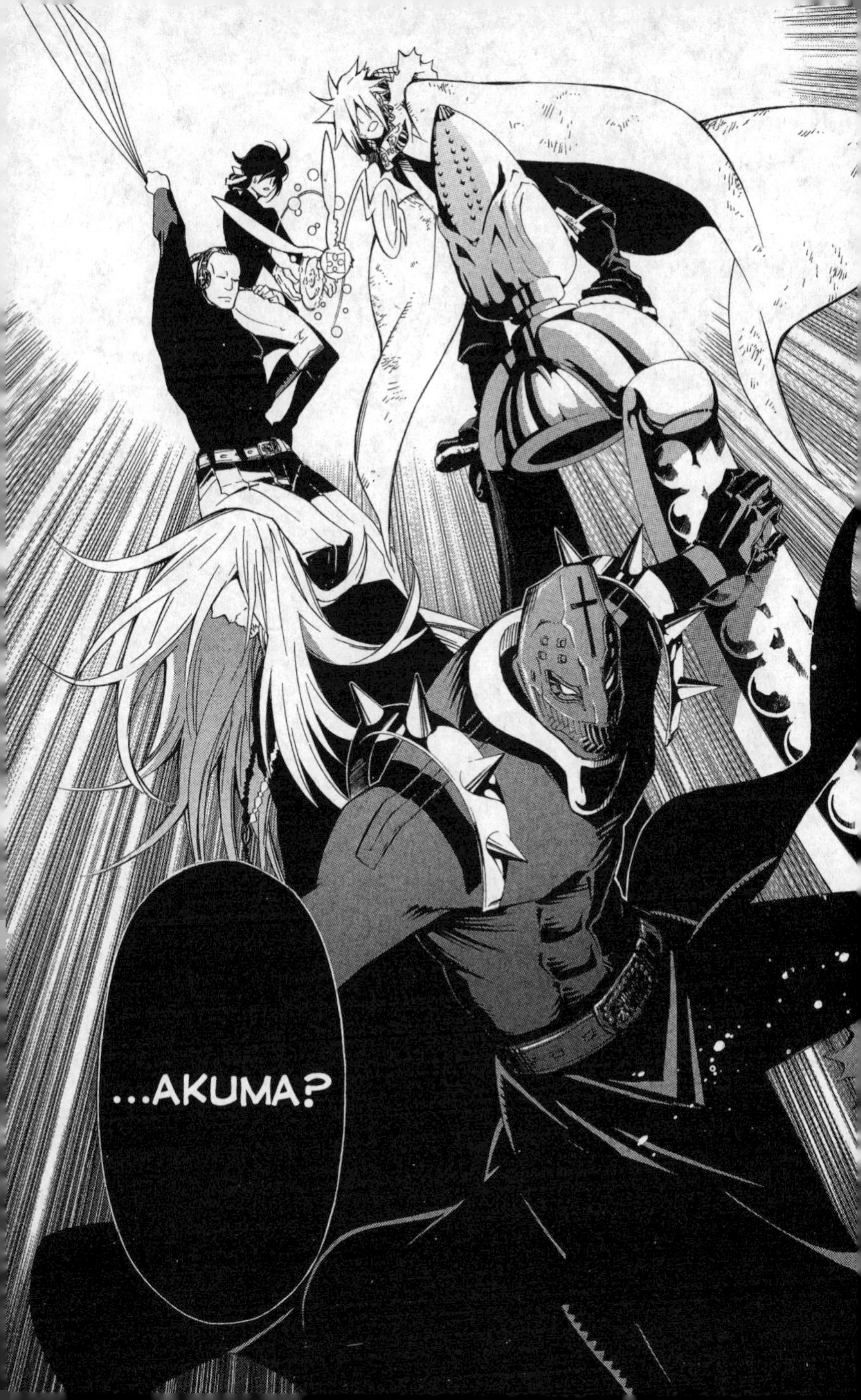
...AKUMA?

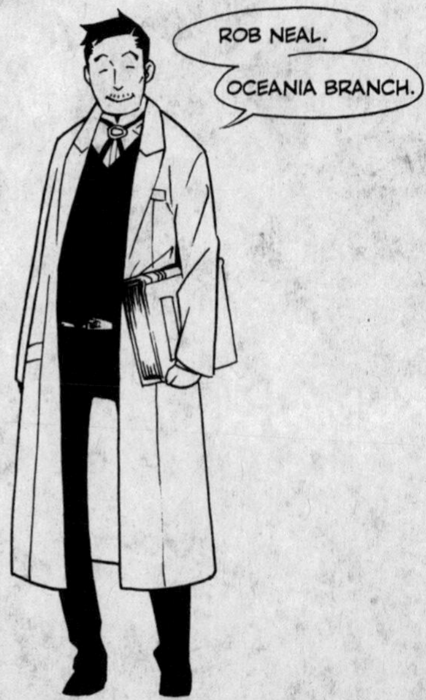
ROB NEAL.
OCEANIA BRANCH.

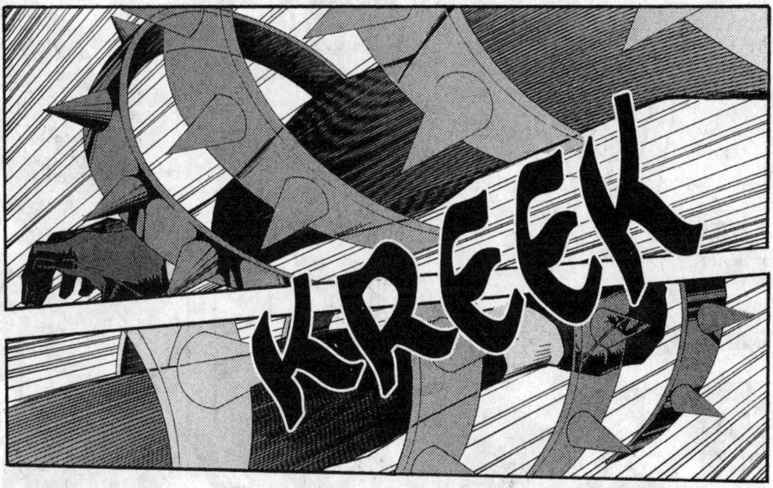
KREEK

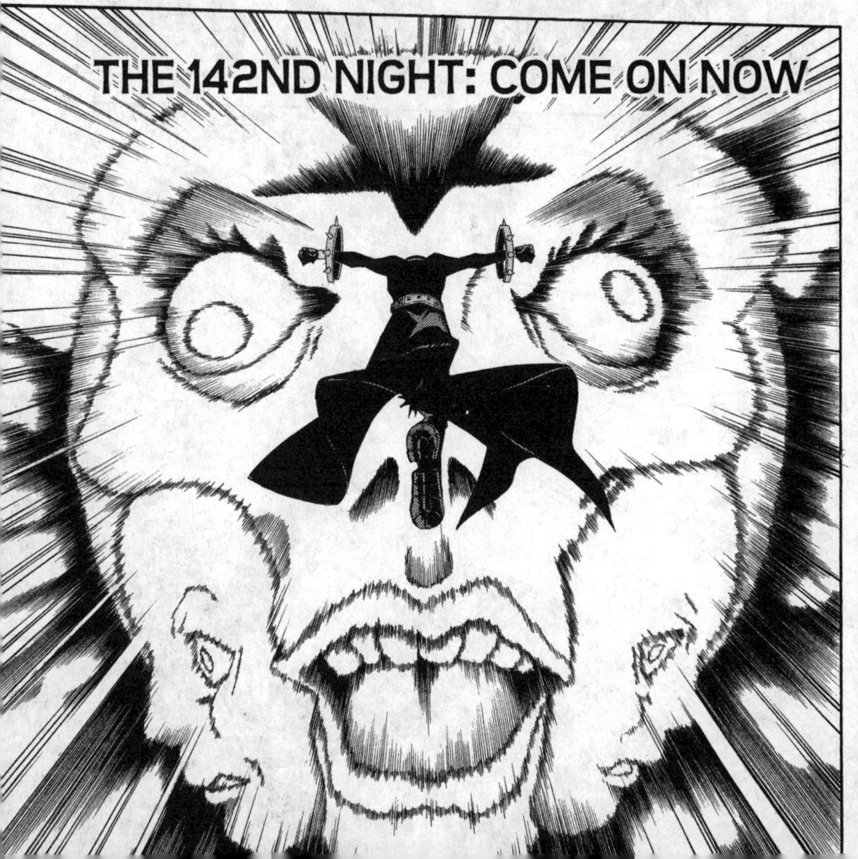
THE 142ND NIGHT: COME ON NOW

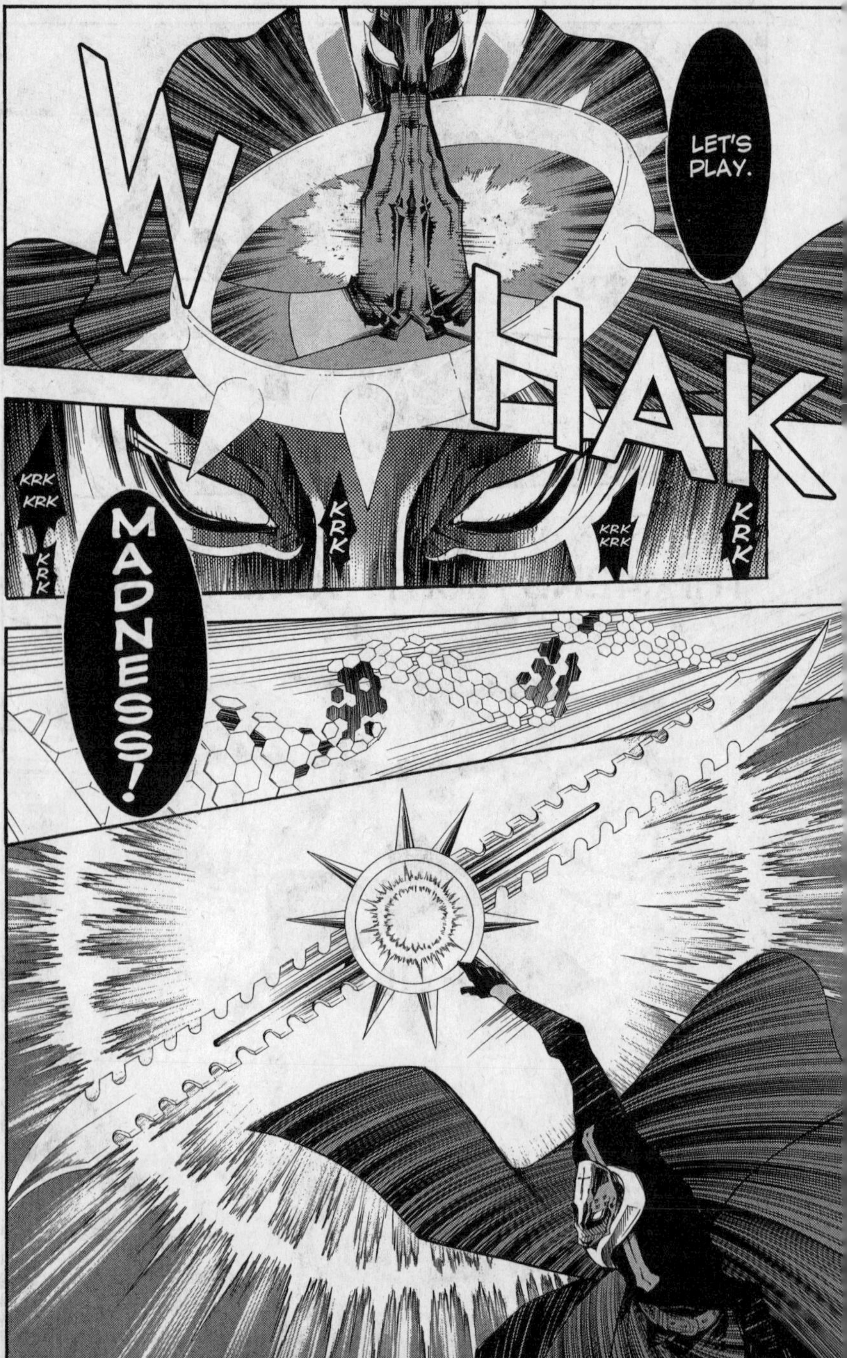
LET'S PLAY.
WHAK
KRK
KRK KRK
KRK
KRK KRK
KRK
MADNESS!

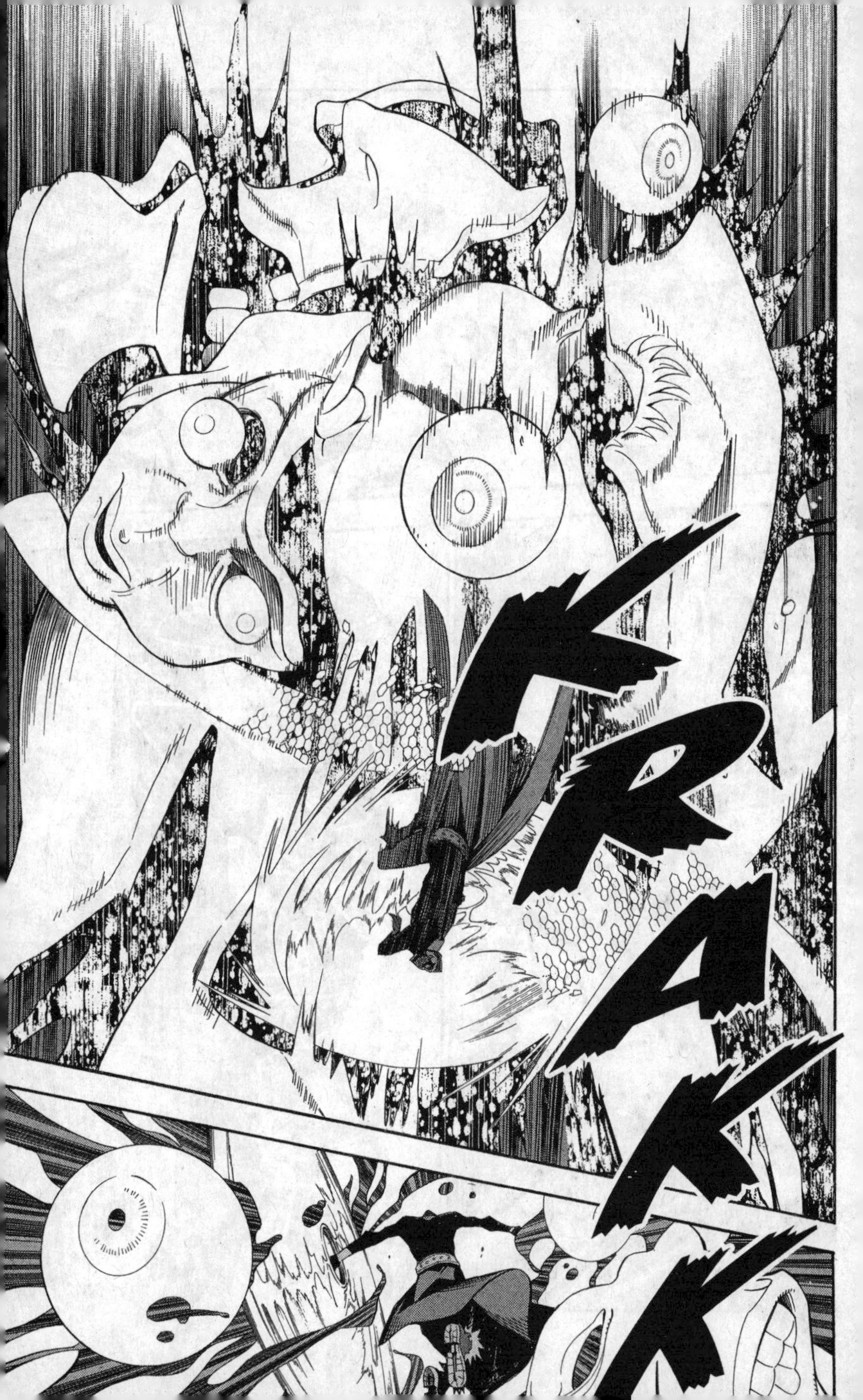
KRAKK

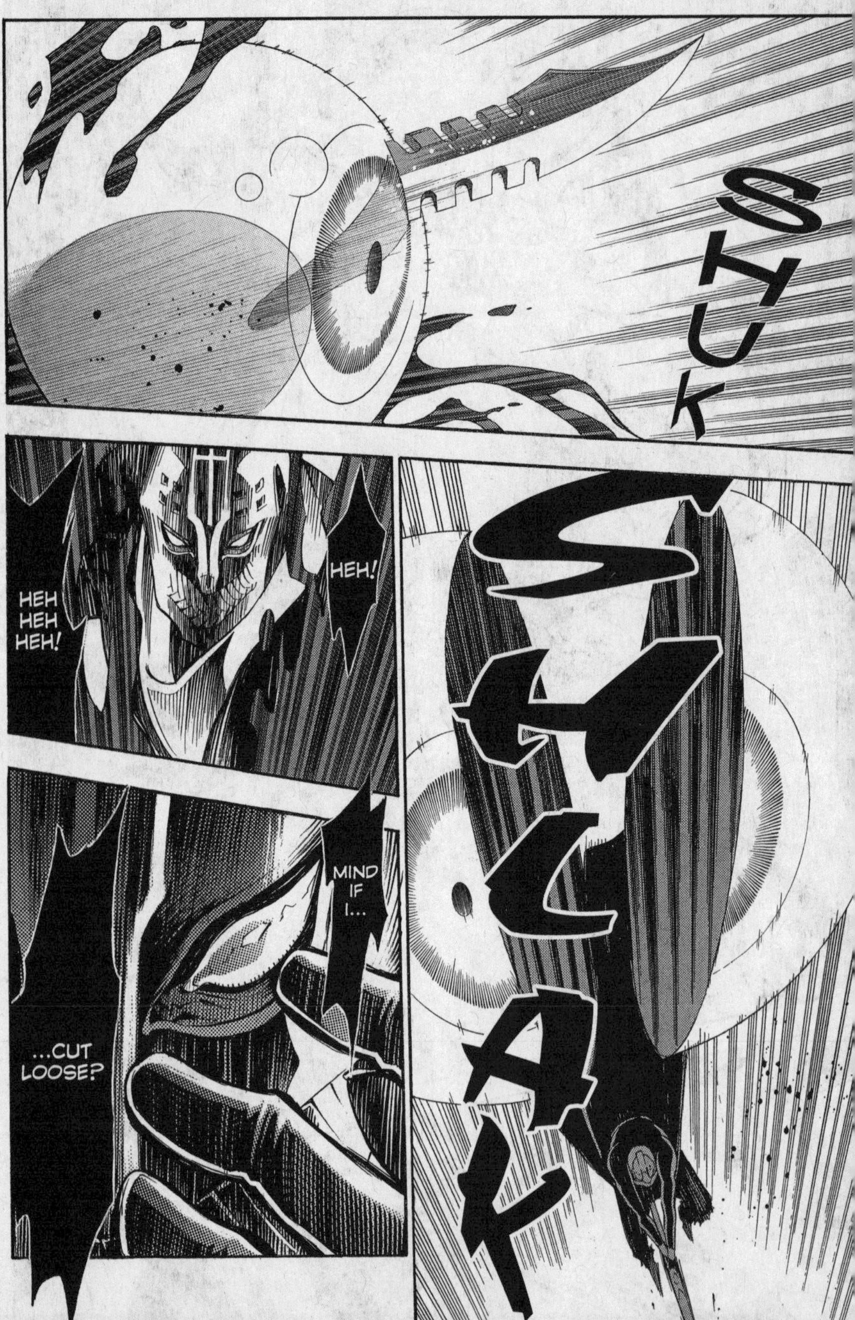
SHUK
HEH!
HEH HEH HEH!
MIND IF I...
...CUT LOOSE?

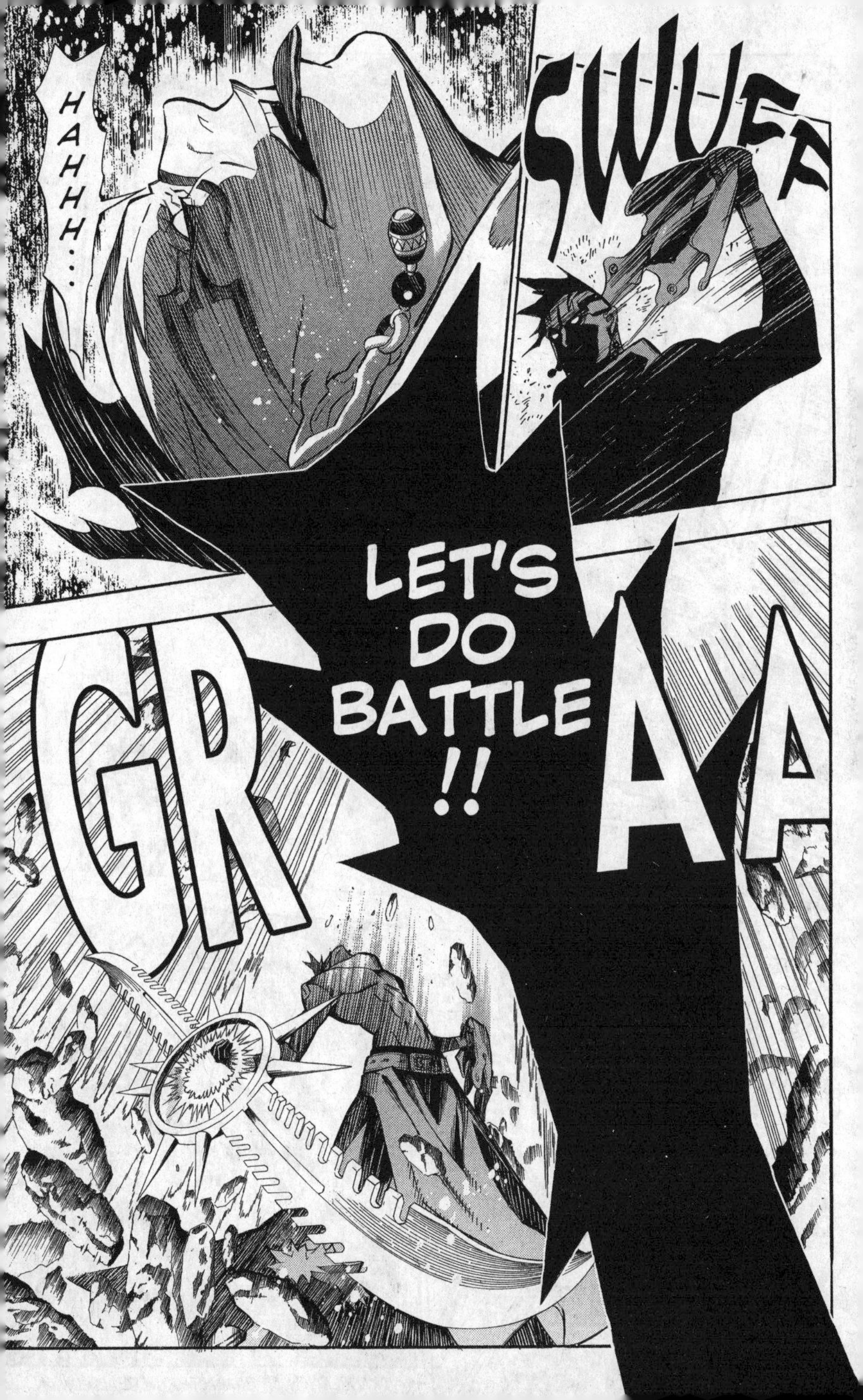
SWUFF
HAHHH...
LET'S DO BATTLE!!
GRAA

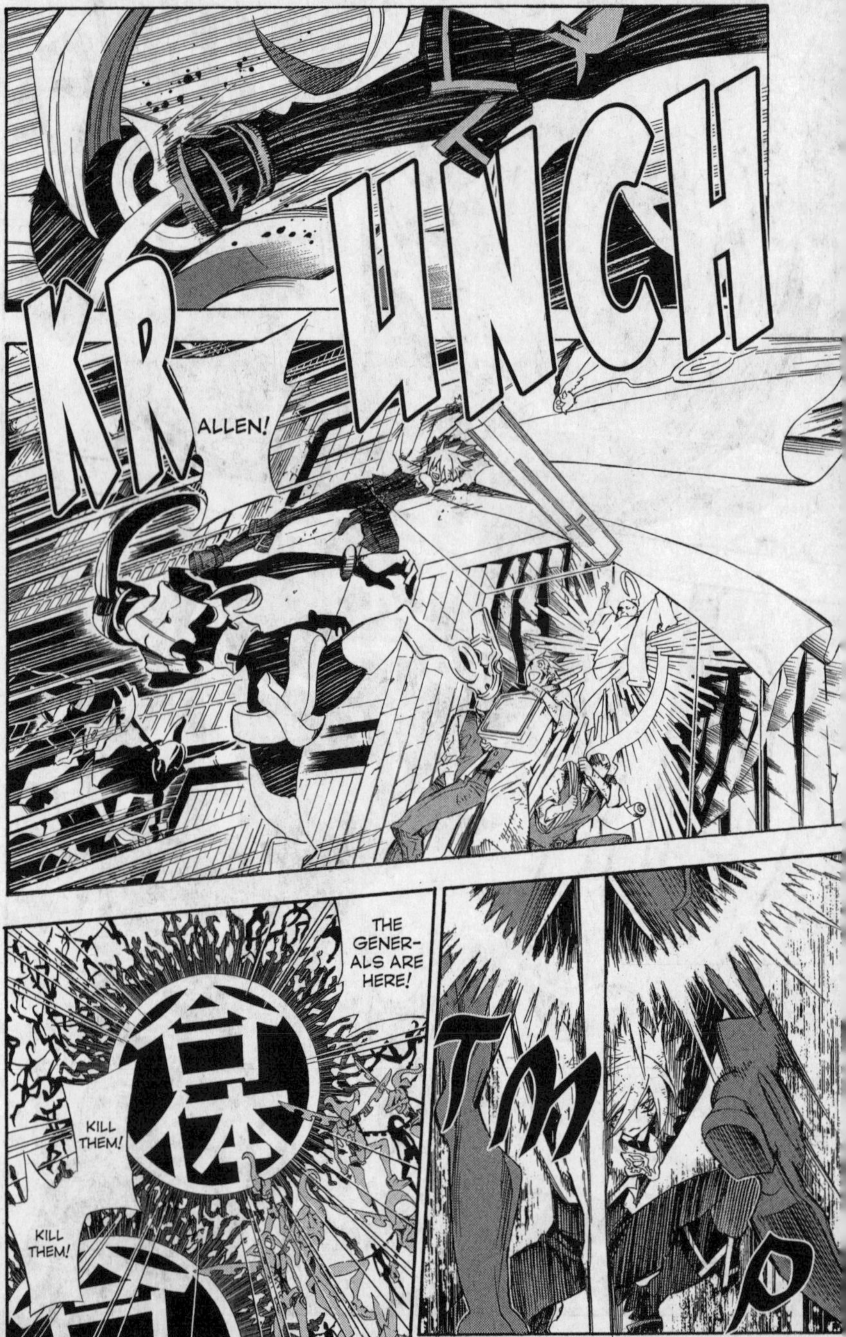
KR-UNCH
ALLEN!
TMP
THE GENER-ALS ARE HERE!
KILL THEM!
KILL THEM!

← TRANSLATION OF CHARACTER IN SEALS: UNION

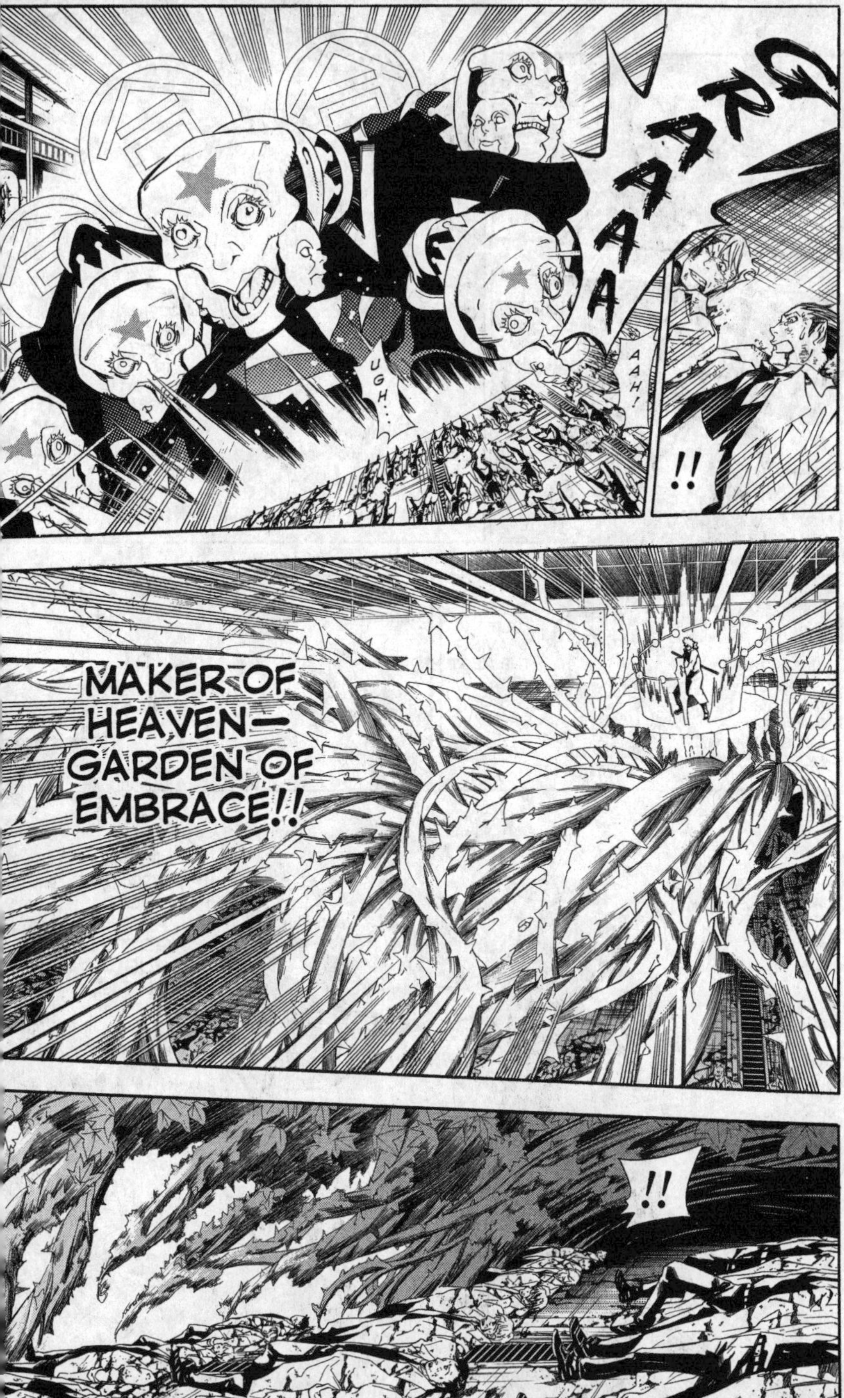

AAAARG
!!
AAH!
UGH...
MAKER OF HEAVEN—GARDEN OF EMBRACE!!
!!

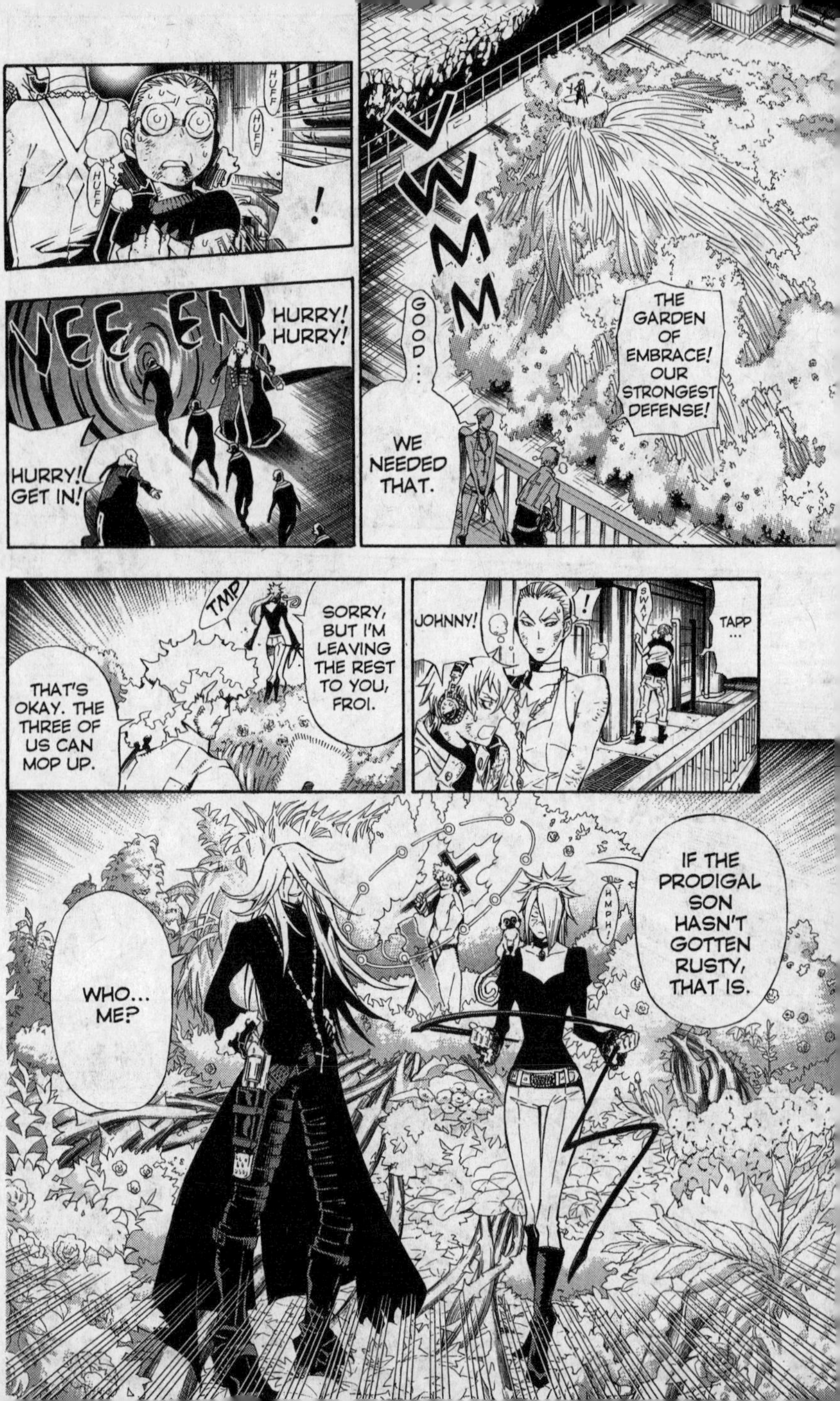
VWMM
THE GARDEN OF EMBRACE! OUR STRONGEST DEFENSE!
GOOD...
WE NEEDED THAT.
HUFF
HUFF
HUFF
!
HURRY! HURRY!
HURRY! GET IN!
SWAY
!
TAPP...
JOHNNY!
TMP
SORRY, BUT I'M LEAVING THE REST TO YOU, FROI.
THAT'S OKAY. THE THREE OF US CAN MOP UP.
IF THE PRODIGAL SON HASN'T GOTTEN RUSTY, THAT IS.
HMPH!
WHO... ME?

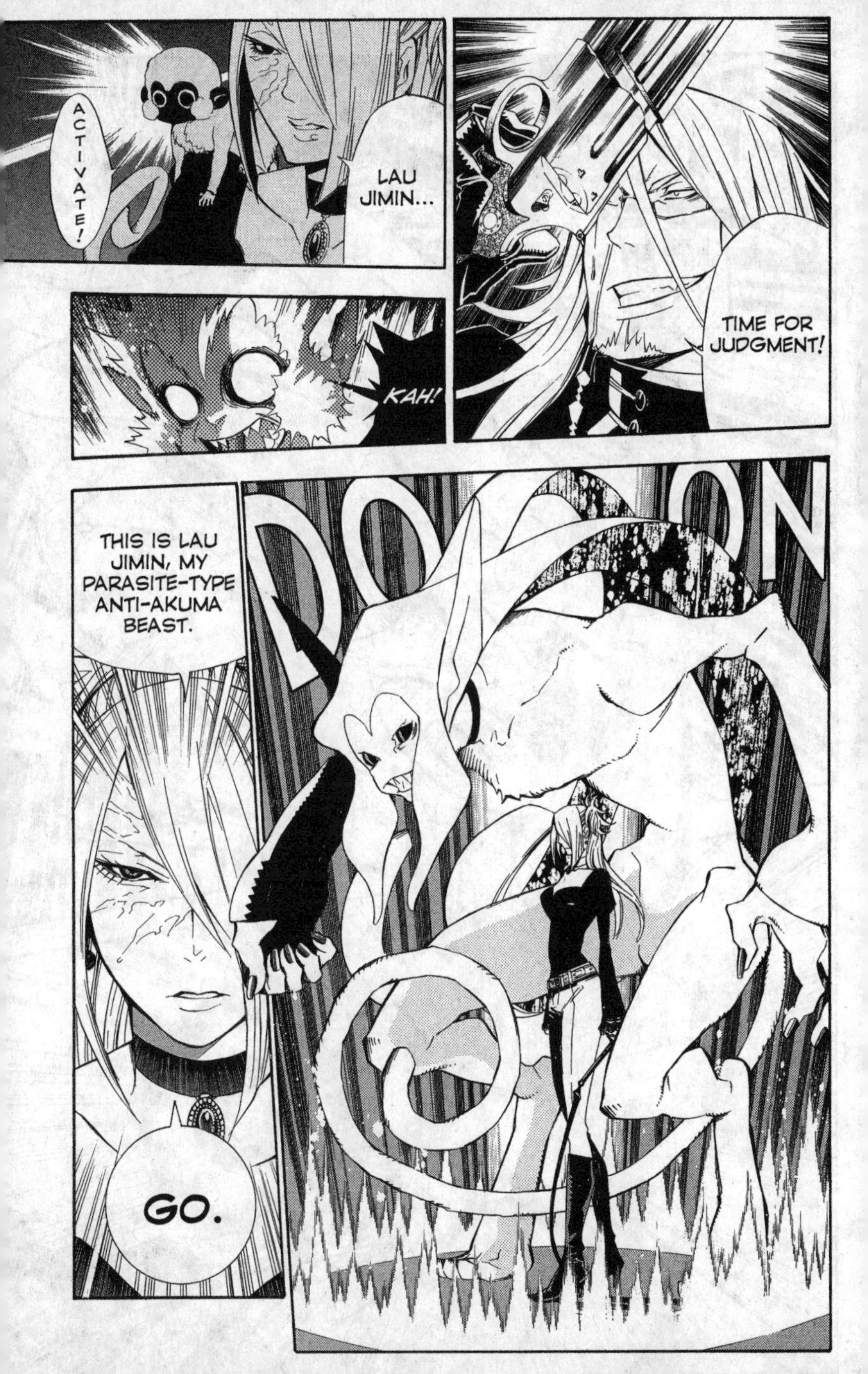
TIME FOR JUDGMENT!
LAU JIMIN...
ACTIVATE!
KAH!
THIS IS LAU JIMIN, MY PARASITE-TYPE ANTI-AKUMA BEAST.
GO.

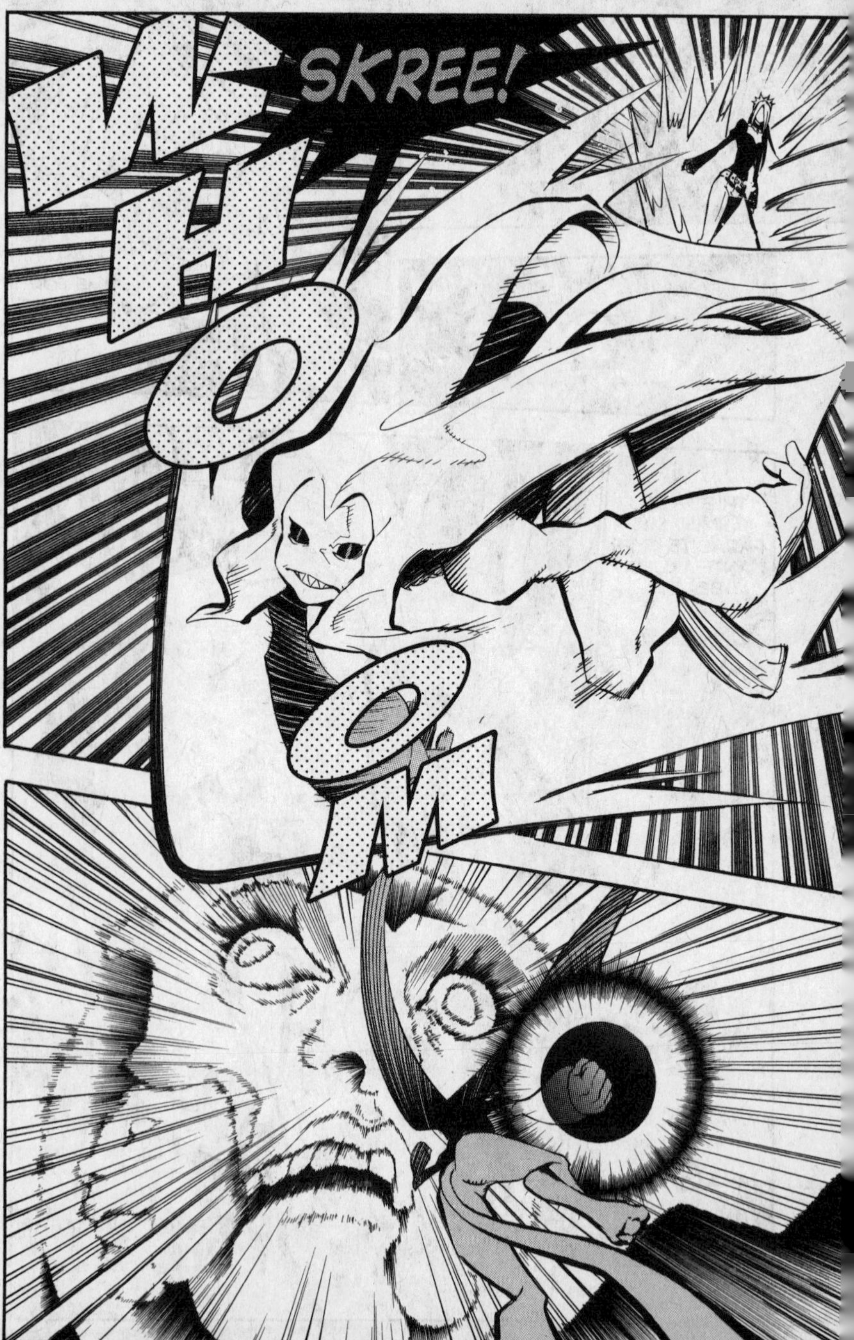
SKREE!
WHOOM

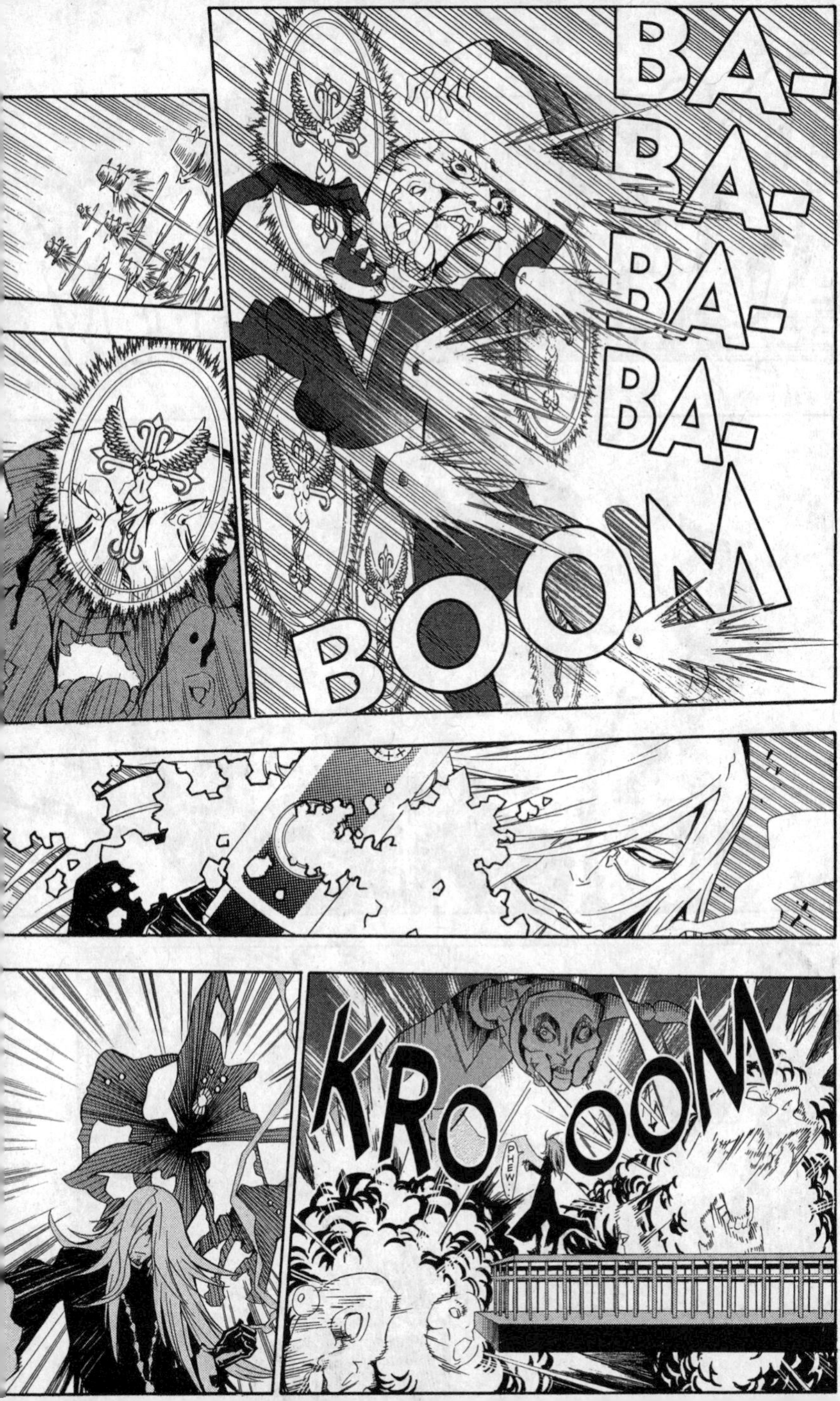
BA-BA-BA-BA-BOOM
KROOOM
PHEW...

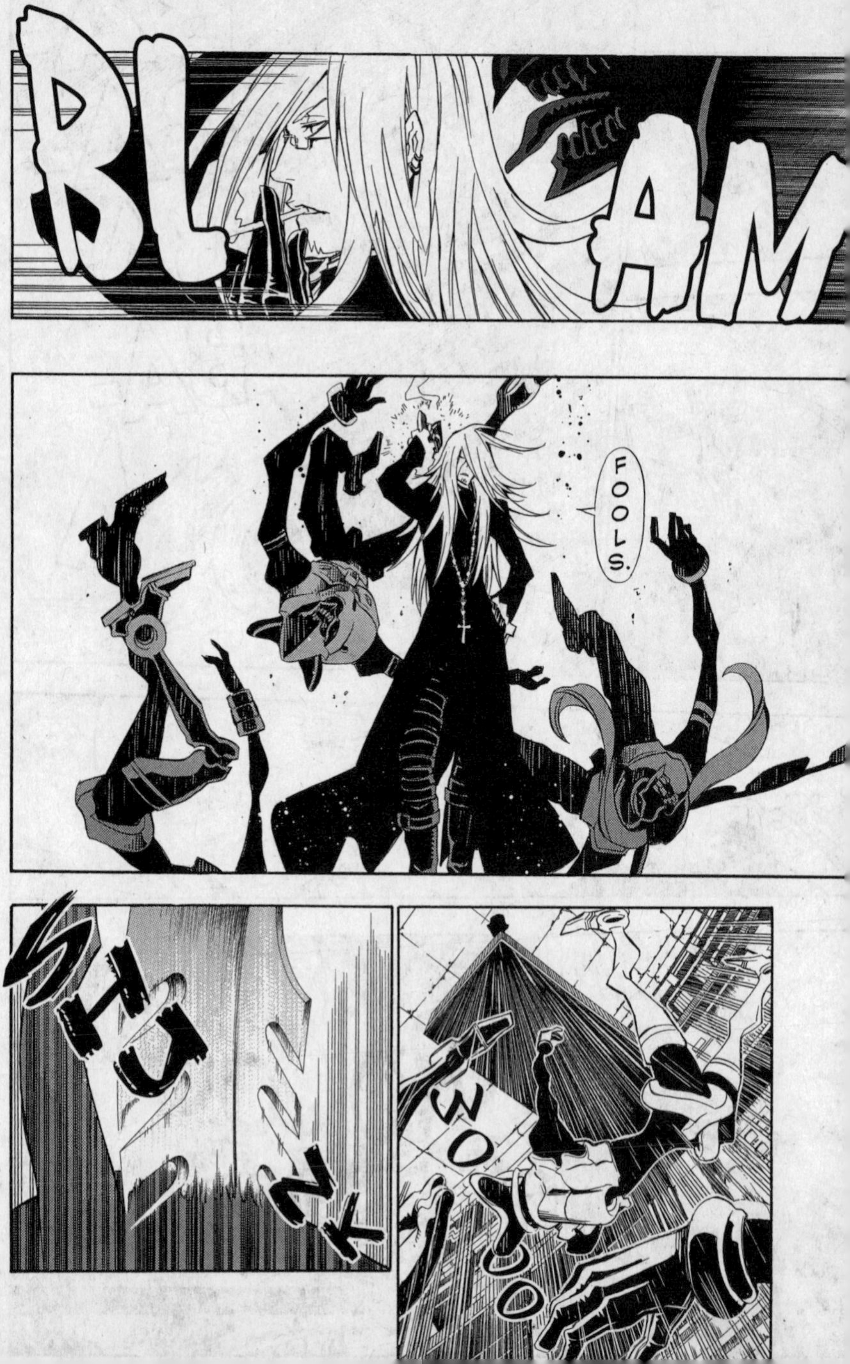
BLAM
FOOLS.
WOOO
SHUNK

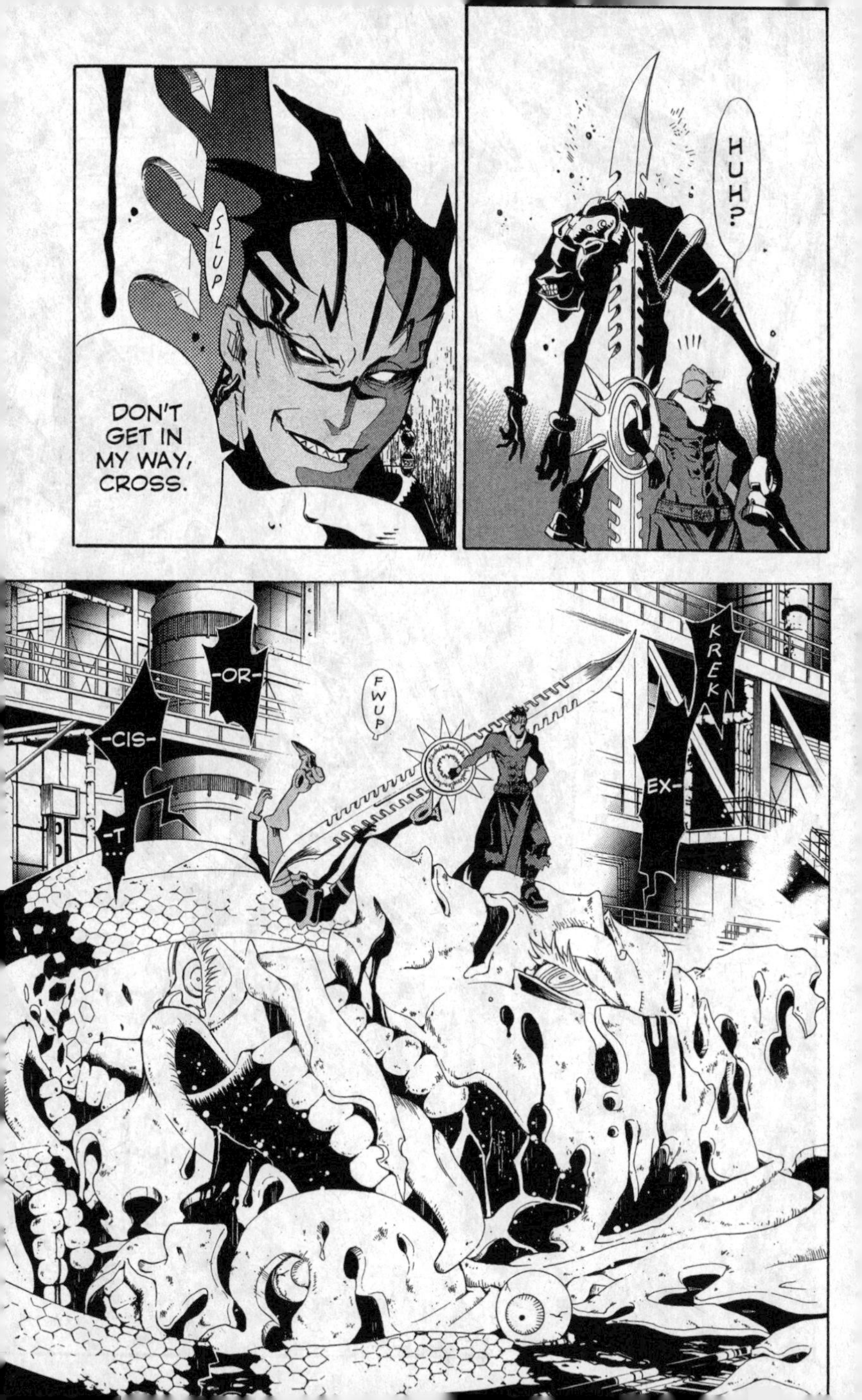
HUH?
SLUP
DON'T GET IN MY WAY, CROSS.
KREK
EX-
FWUP
-OR-
-CIS-
-T...

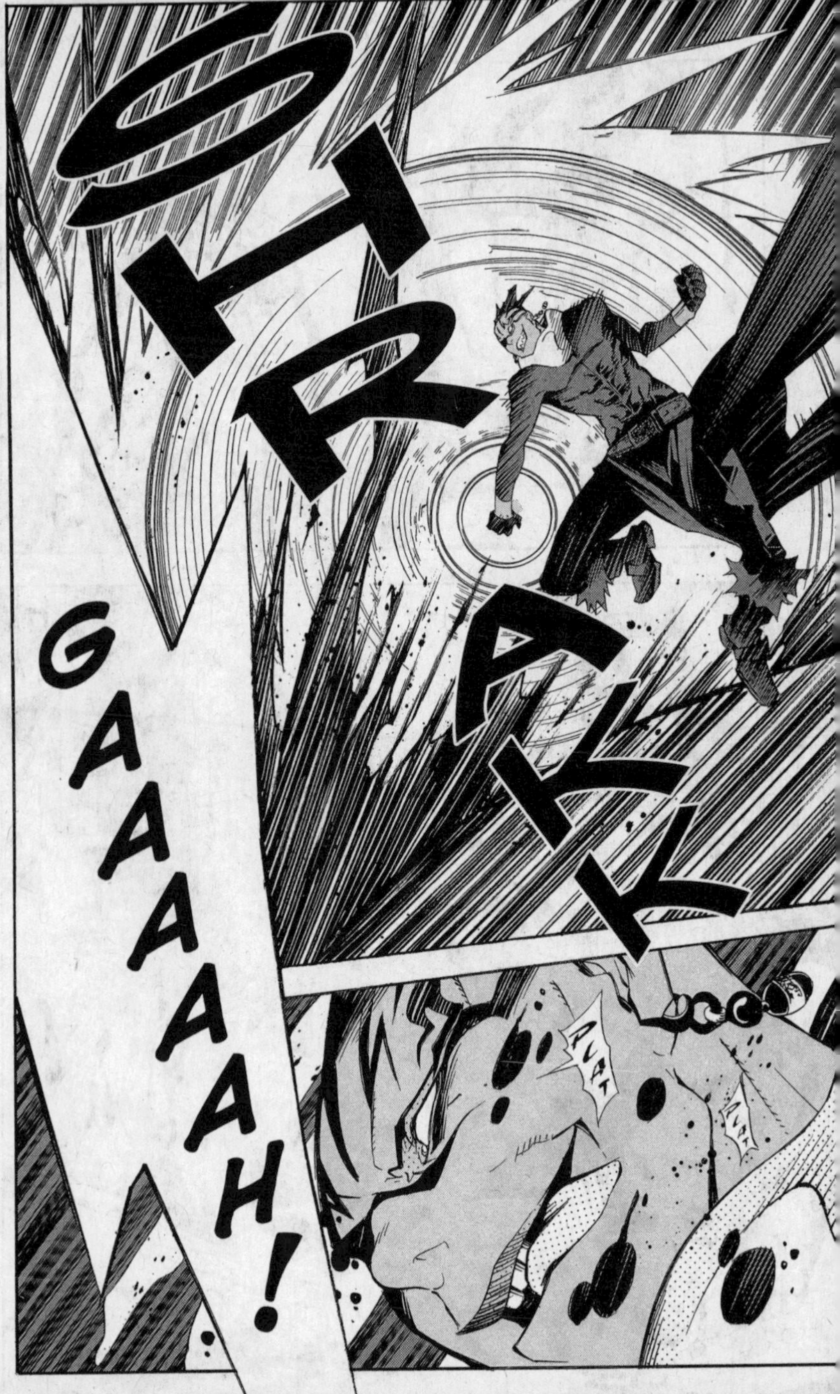
CHRAKK
GAAAAAH!

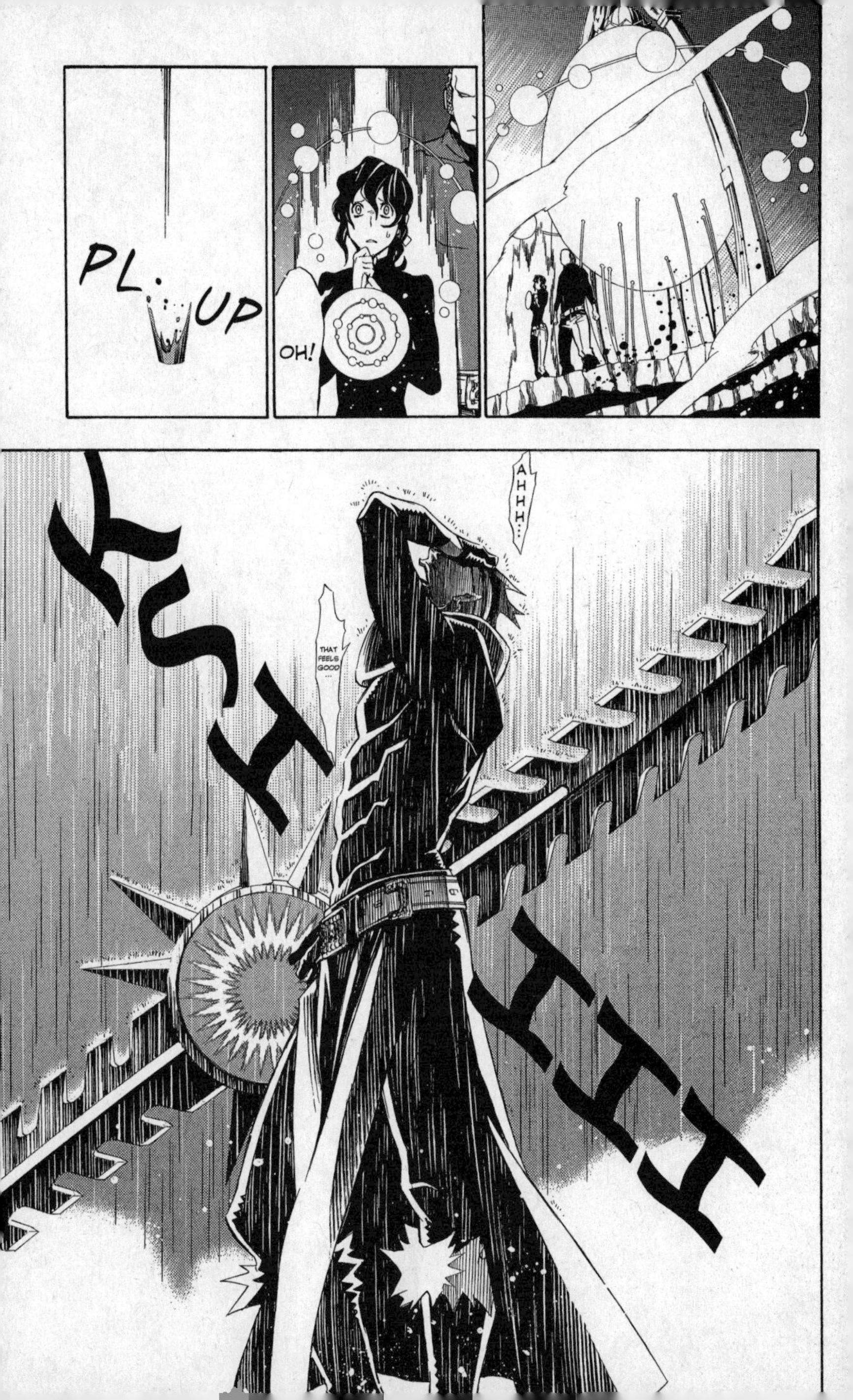
OH!
PL UP
AHHH...
THAT FEELS GOOD...
KSH
HHH

MARVIN HUSKIN.

SOUTH AMERICA BRANCH.

THE 143RD NIGHT: LINE OF SIGHT

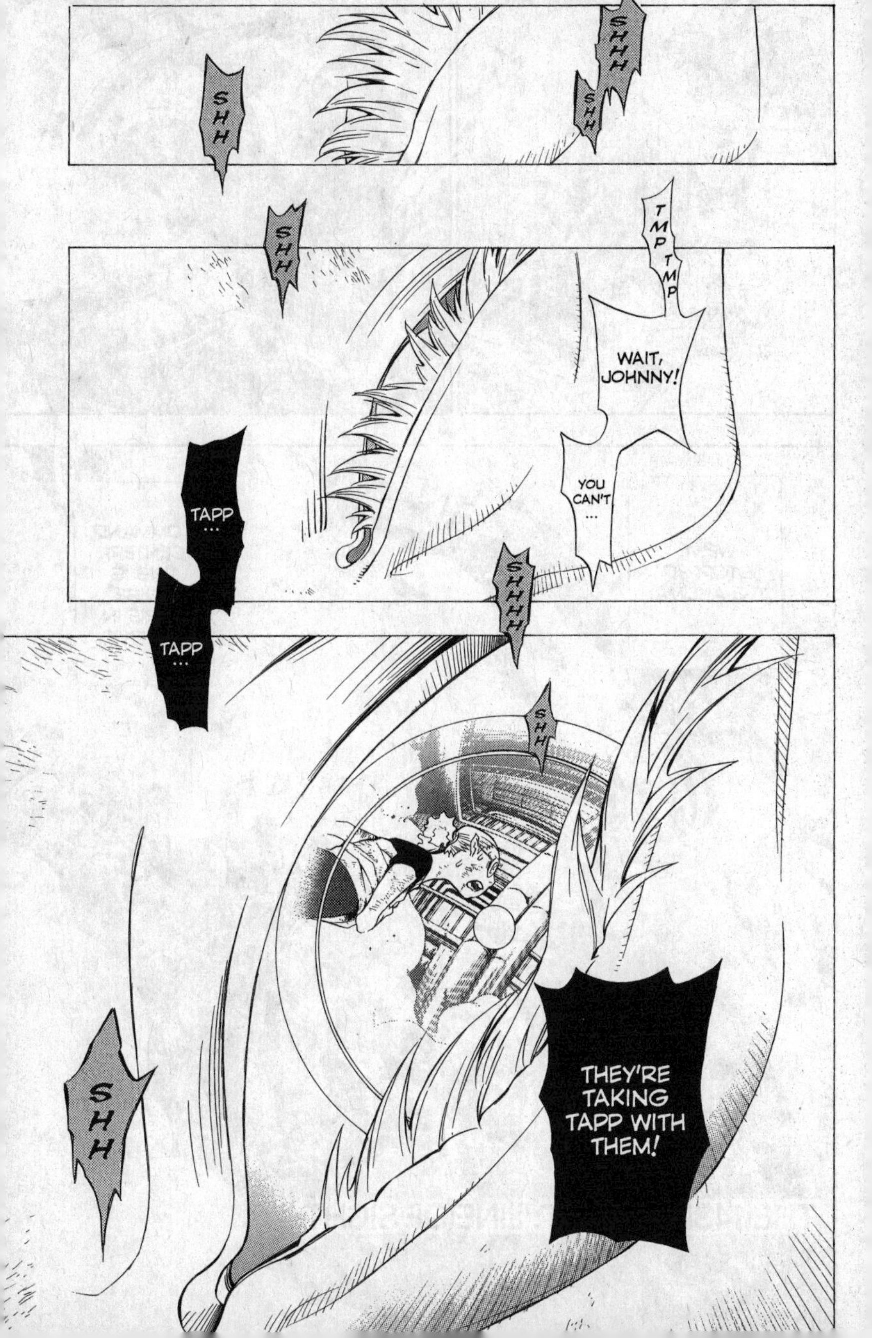
SHHH
SHH
SHH
SHH
TMP TMP TMP
WAIT, JOHNNY!
YOU CAN'T...
TAPP...
TAPP...
SHHHH
SHH
THEY'RE TAKING TAPP WITH THEM!
SHH

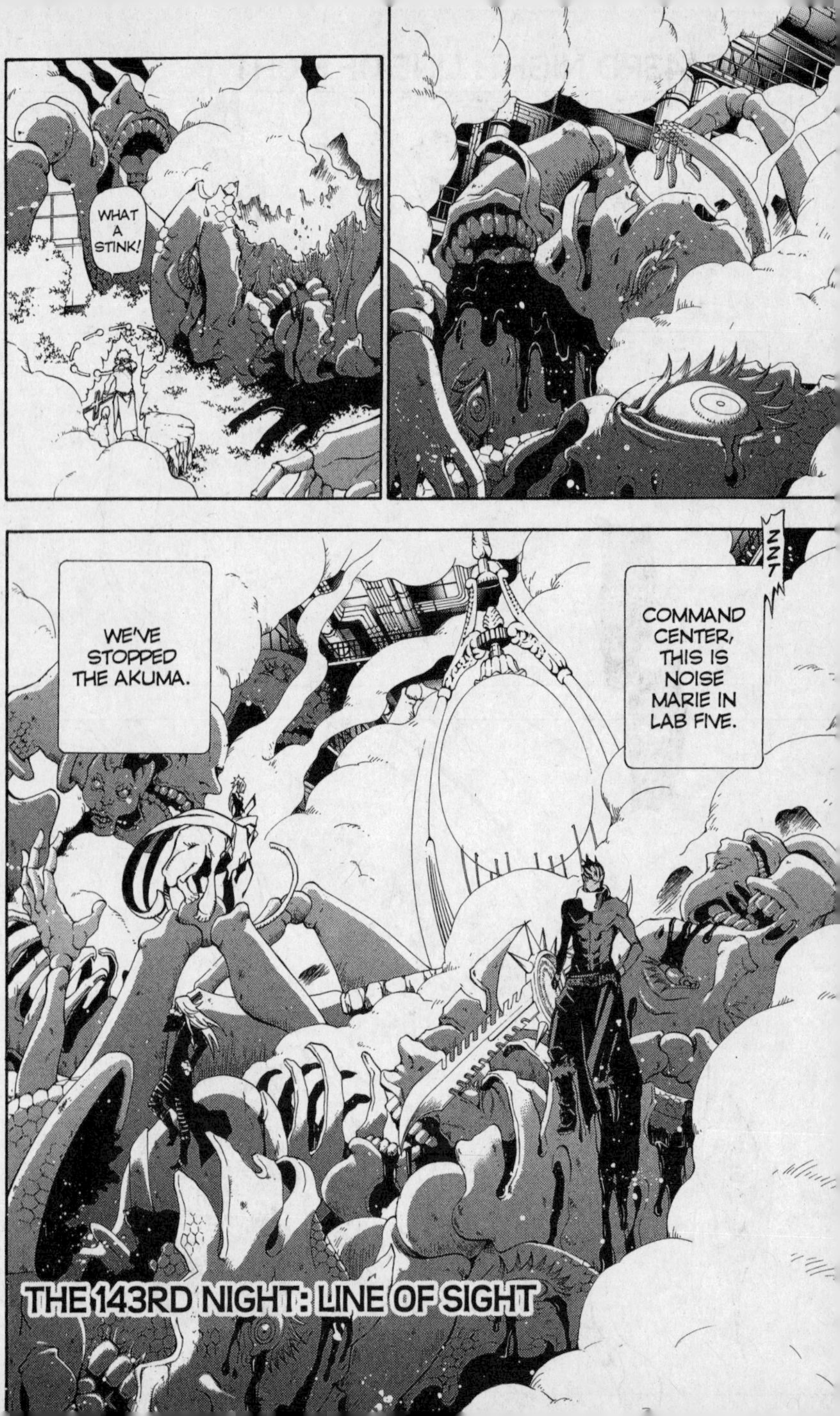
WHAT A STINK!
ZZT
COMMAND CENTER, THIS IS NOISE MARIE IN LAB FIVE.
WE'VE STOPPED THE AKUMA.

THE 143RD NIGHT: LINE OF SIGHT

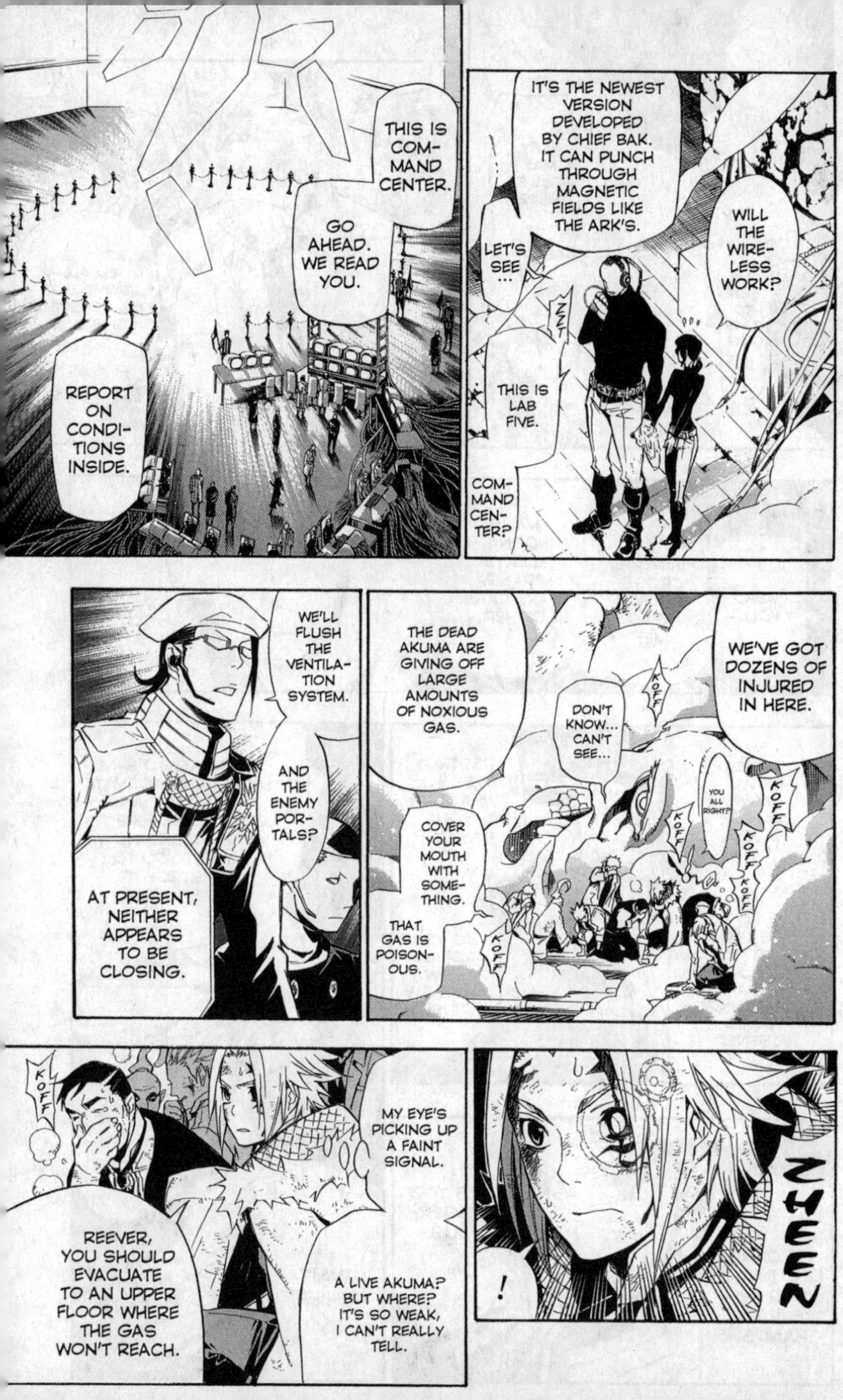

WILL THE WIRELESS WORK?
IT'S THE NEWEST VERSION DEVELOPED BY CHIEF BAK. IT CAN PUNCH THROUGH MAGNETIC FIELDS LIKE THE ARK'S.
LET'S SEE...
ZZT
THIS IS LAB FIVE.
COMMAND CENTER?
THIS IS COMMAND CENTER.
GO AHEAD. WE READ YOU.
REPORT ON CONDITIONS INSIDE.
WE'VE GOT DOZENS OF INJURED IN HERE.
THE DEAD AKUMA ARE GIVING OFF LARGE AMOUNTS OF NOXIOUS GAS.
KOFF
DON'T KNOW... CAN'T SEE...
KOFF
YOU ALL RIGHT?
KOFF
KOFF KOFF
COVER YOUR MOUTH WITH SOMETHING.
THAT GAS IS POISONOUS.
KOFF
WE'LL FLUSH THE VENTILATION SYSTEM.
AND THE ENEMY PORTALS?
AT PRESENT, NEITHER APPEARS TO BE CLOSING.
ZHEEN
!
MY EYE'S PICKING UP A FAINT SIGNAL.
A LIVE AKUMA? BUT WHERE? IT'S SO WEAK, I CAN'T REALLY TELL.
KOFF
REEVER, YOU SHOULD EVACUATE TO AN UPPER FLOOR WHERE THE GAS WON'T REACH.

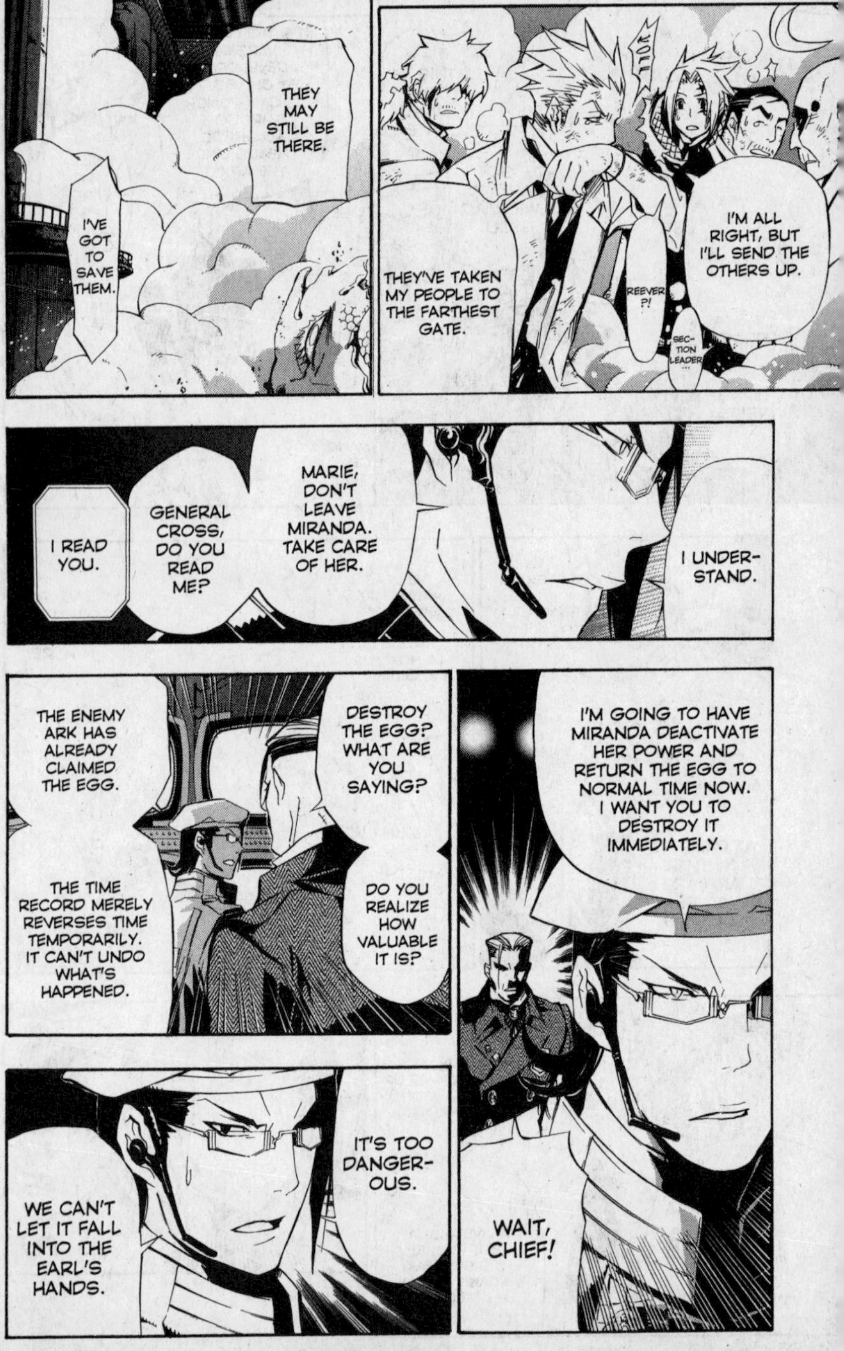
I'M ALL RIGHT, BUT I'LL SEND THE OTHERS UP.
REEVER?!
SECTION LEADER...
THEY'VE TAKEN MY PEOPLE TO THE FARTHEST GATE.
THEY MAY STILL BE THERE.
I'VE GOT TO SAVE THEM.
I UNDERSTAND.
MARIE, DON'T LEAVE MIRANDA. TAKE CARE OF HER.
GENERAL CROSS, DO YOU READ ME?
I READ YOU.
I'M GOING TO HAVE MIRANDA DEACTIVATE HER POWER AND RETURN THE EGG TO NORMAL TIME NOW. I WANT YOU TO DESTROY IT IMMEDIATELY.
WAIT, CHIEF!
DESTROY THE EGG? WHAT ARE YOU SAYING?
DO YOU REALIZE HOW VALUABLE IT IS?
THE ENEMY ARK HAS ALREADY CLAIMED THE EGG.
THE TIME RECORD MERELY REVERSES TIME TEMPORARILY. IT CAN'T UNDO WHAT'S HAPPENED.
IT'S TOO DANGEROUS.
WE CAN'T LET IT FALL INTO THE EARL'S HANDS.

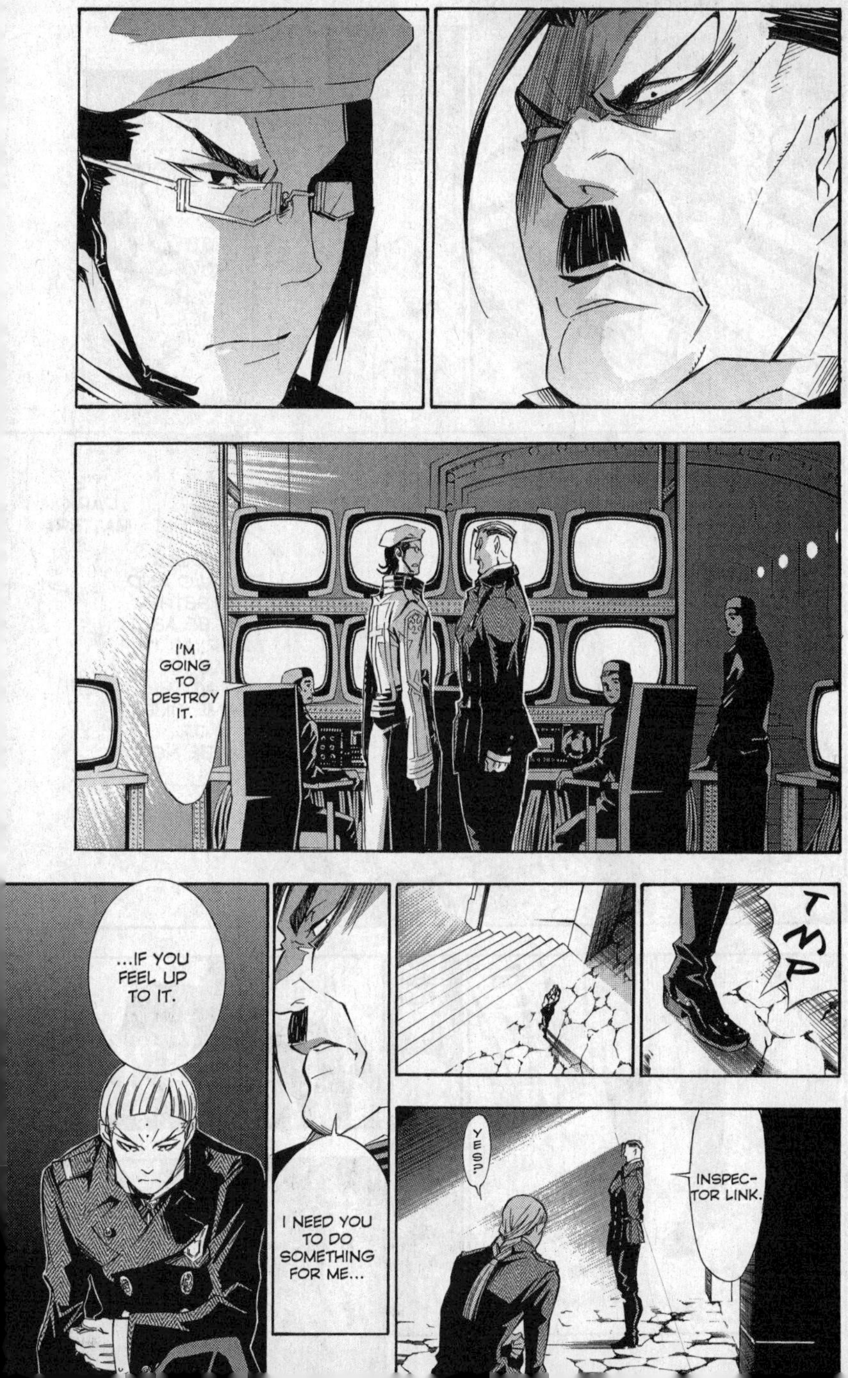
I'M GOING TO DESTROY IT.
TMP
INSPECTOR LINK.
YES?
I NEED YOU TO DO SOMETHING FOR ME...
...IF YOU FEEL UP TO IT.

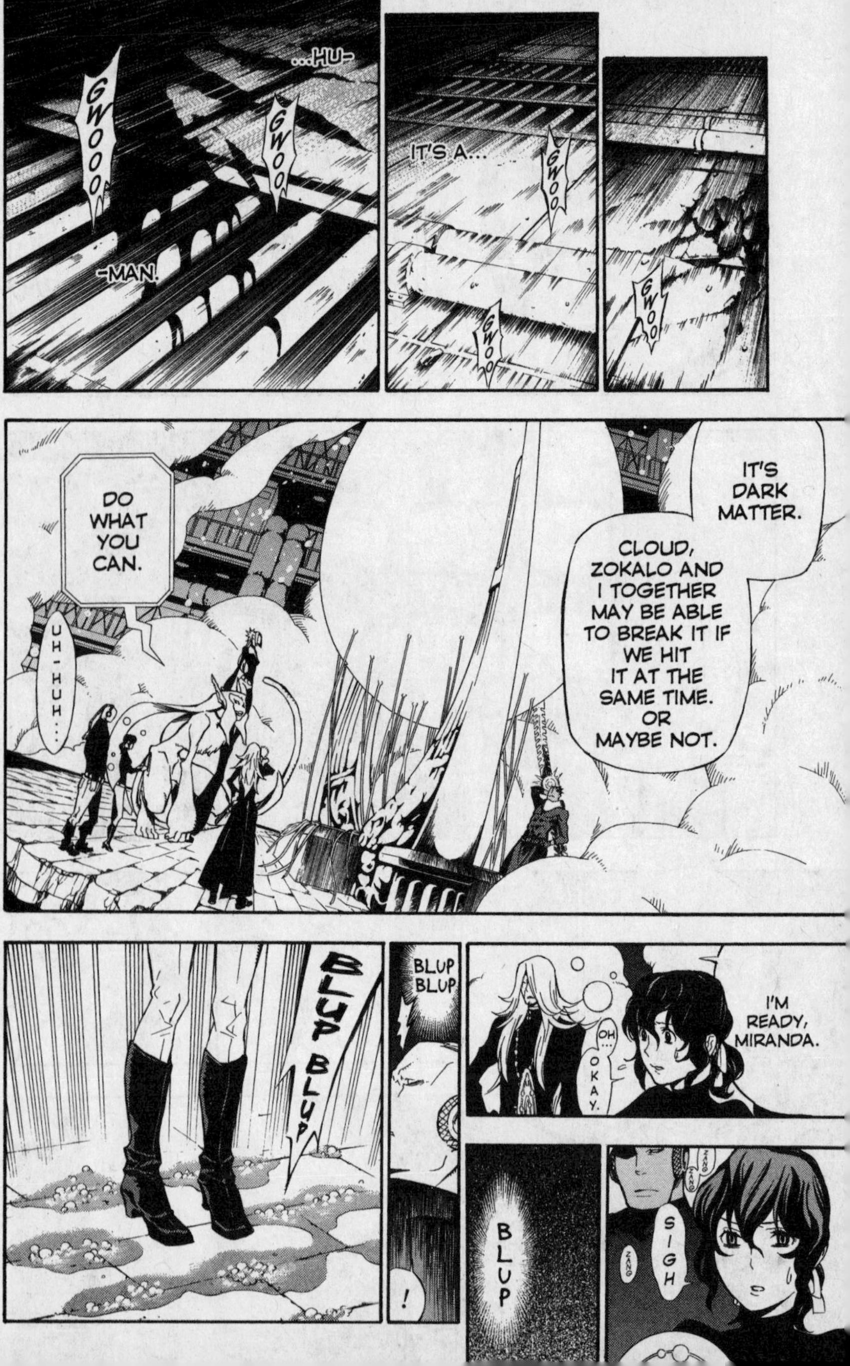

GWOOO
IT'S A...
GWOOO
...HU-
GWOOO
GWOOO
-MAN.
IT'S DARK MATTER.
CLOUD, ZOKALO AND I TOGETHER MAY BE ABLE TO BREAK IT IF WE HIT IT AT THE SAME TIME. OR MAYBE NOT.
DO WHAT YOU CAN.
UH-HUH...
I'M READY, MIRANDA.
OH... OKAY.
ZANG
ZANG
SIGH
ZANG
BLUP
BLUP BLUP
!
BLUP BLUP

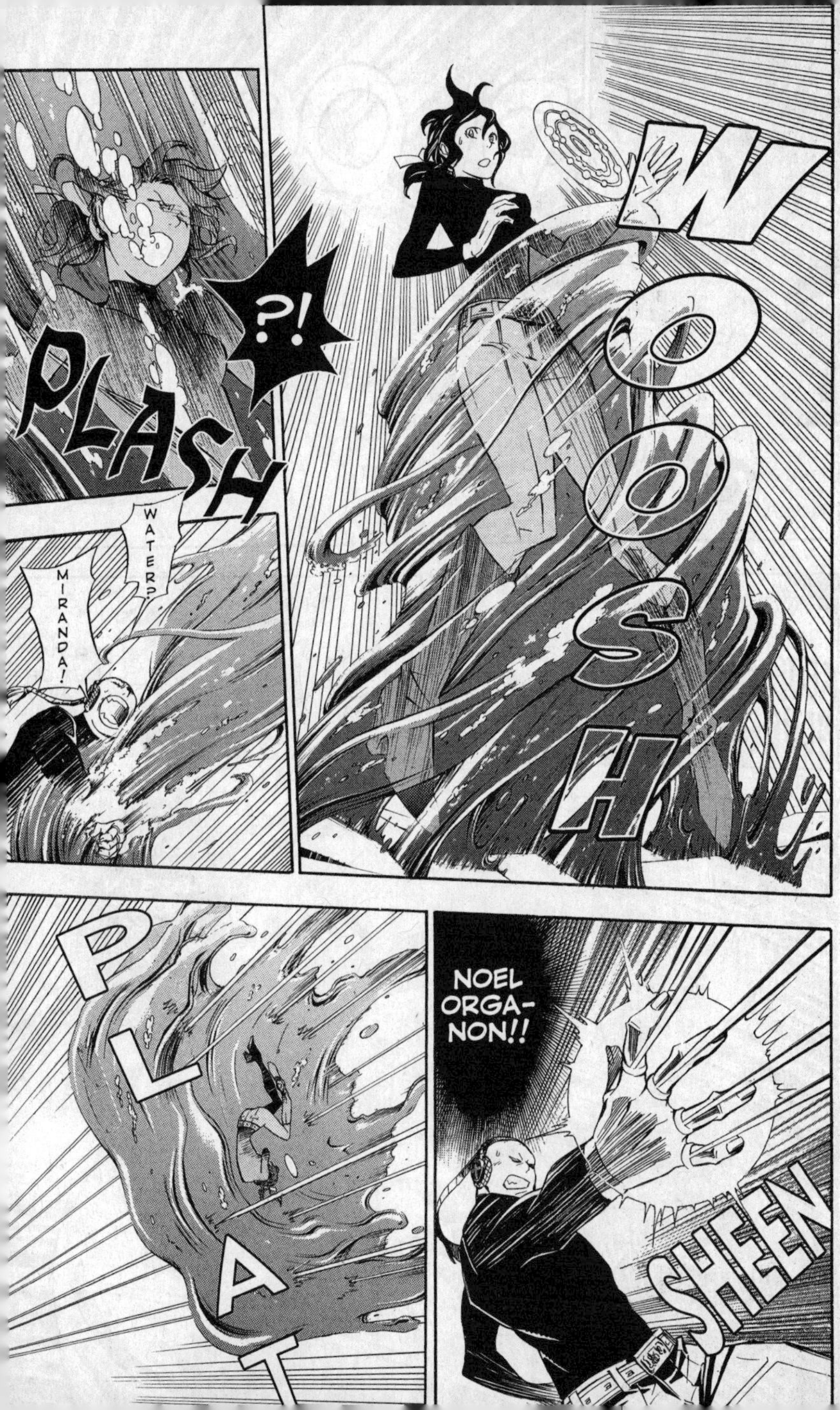
WOOOOSH
?!
PLASH
WATER?
MIRANDA!
NOEL ORGA-NON!!
SHEEN
PLAT

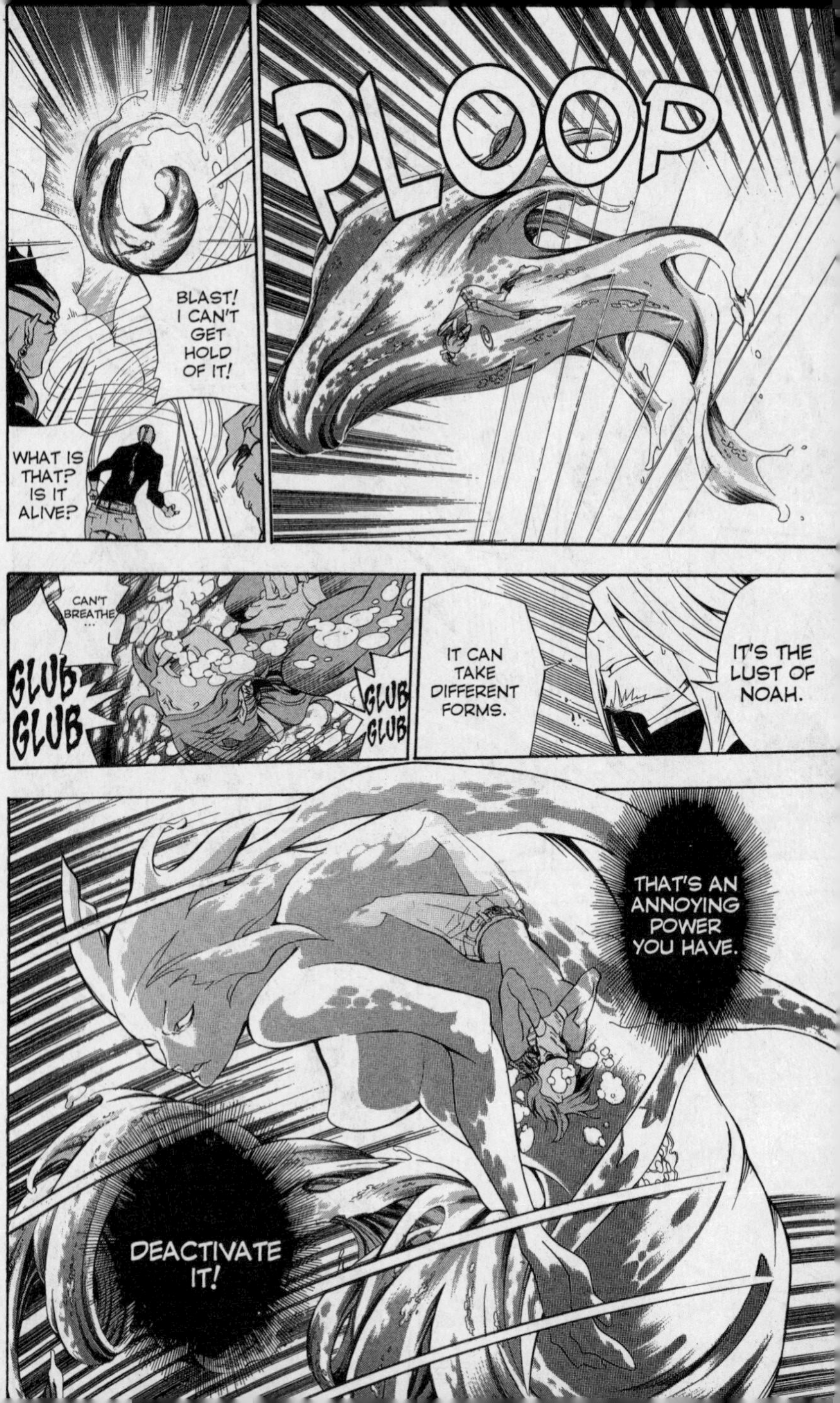
PLOOP
BLAST! I CAN'T GET HOLD OF IT!
WHAT IS THAT? IS IT ALIVE?
IT'S THE LUST OF NOAH.
IT CAN TAKE DIFFERENT FORMS.
GLUB GLUB
CAN'T BREATHE...
GLUB GLUB
THAT'S AN ANNOYING POWER YOU HAVE.
DEACTIVATE IT!

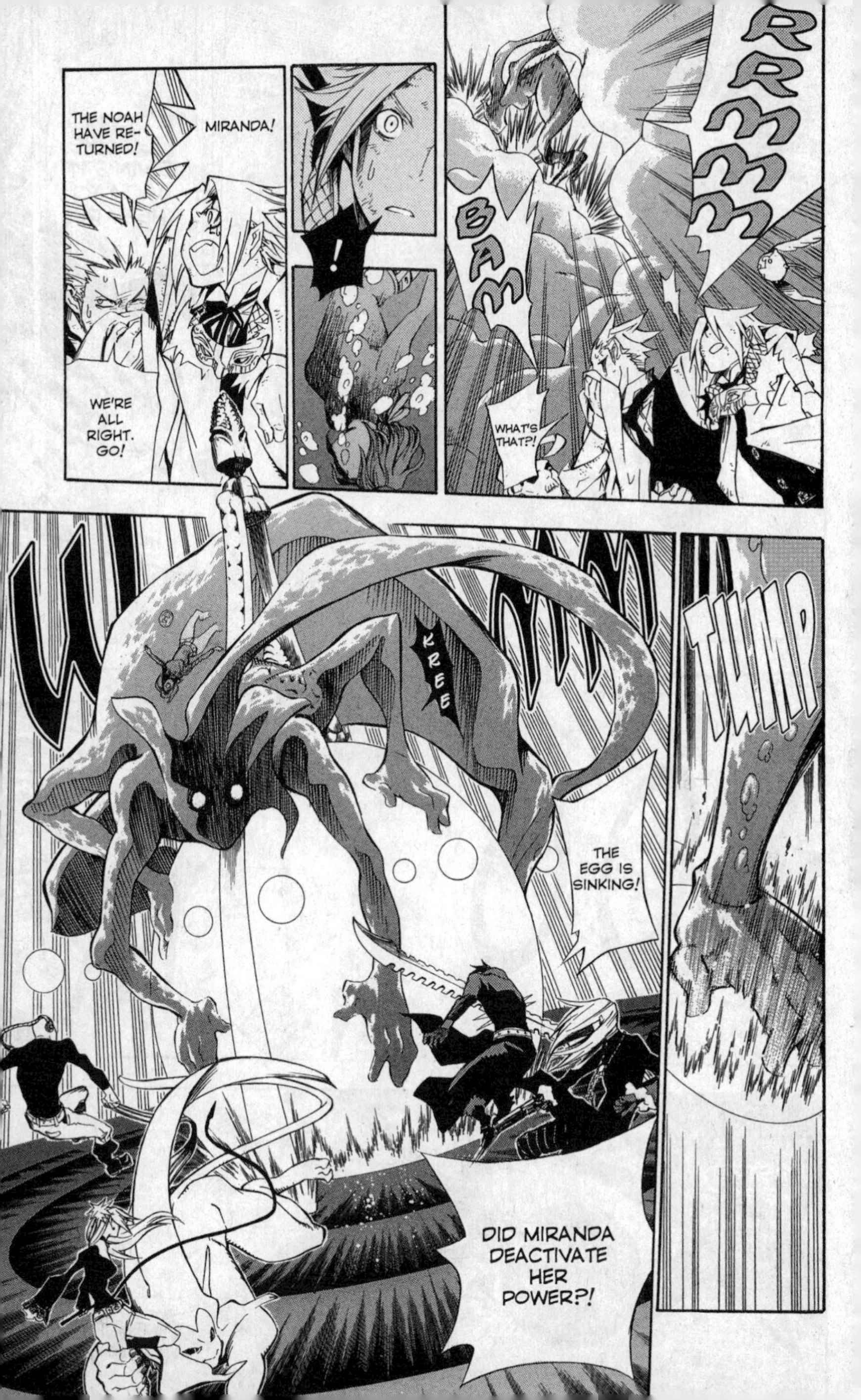
RRMMMM
BAM
WHAT'S THAT?!
!
MIRANDA!
THE NOAH HAVE RE-TURNED!
WE'RE ALL RIGHT. GO!
THUMP
KREE
THE EGG IS SINKING!
DID MIRANDA DEACTIVATE HER POWER?!

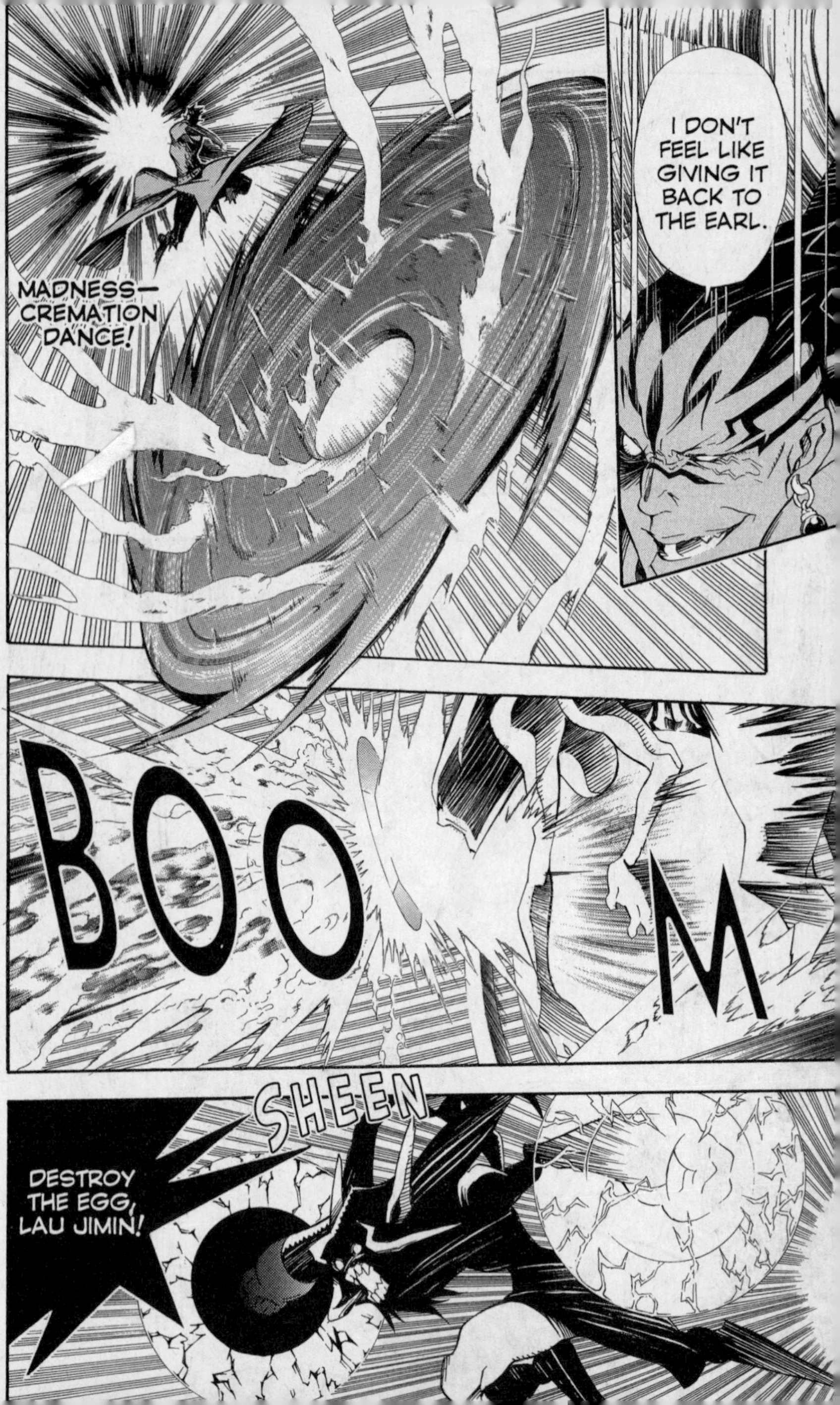
I DON'T FEEL LIKE GIVING IT BACK TO THE EARL.
MADNESS—CREMATION DANCE!
BOOM
SHEEN
DESTROY THE EGG, LAU JIMIN!

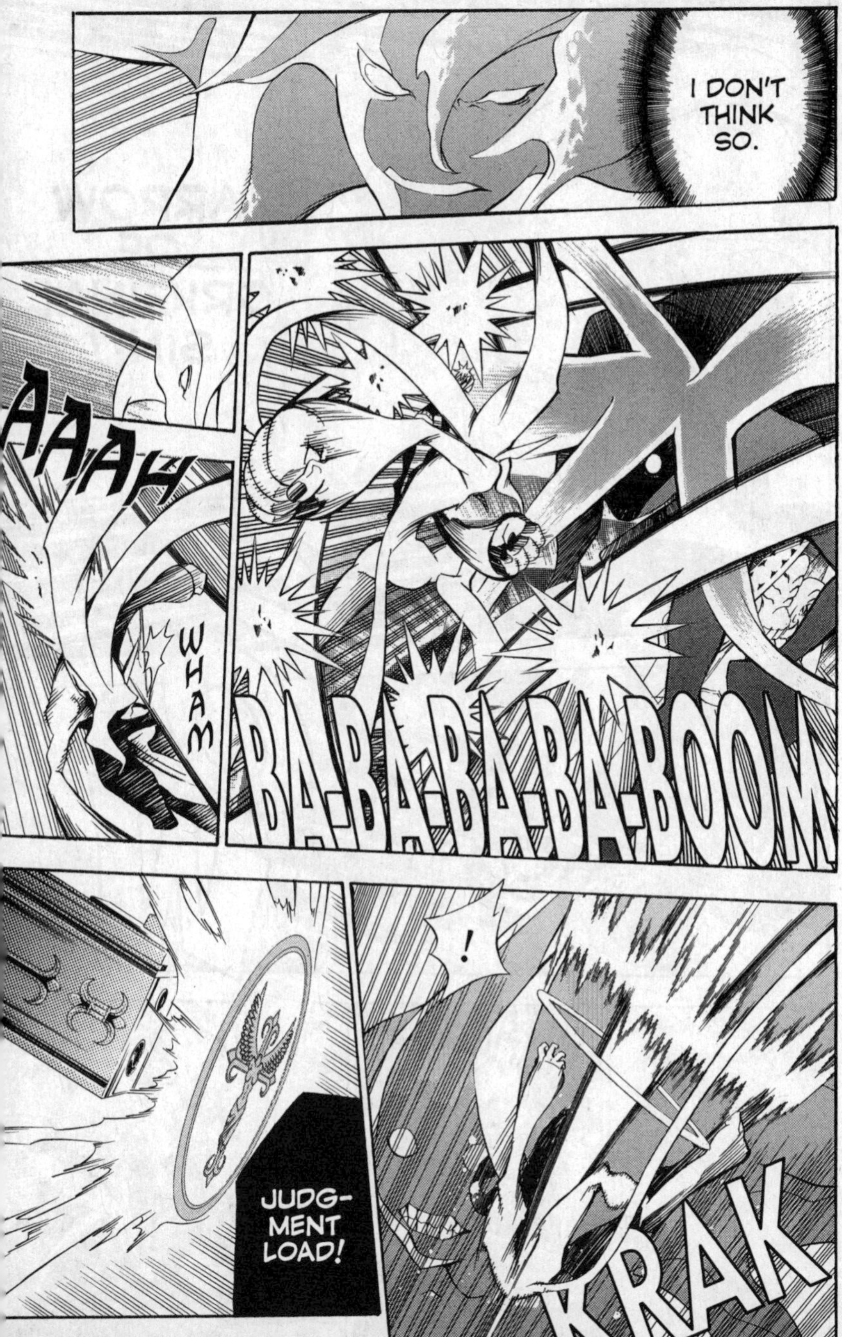
I DON'T THINK SO.
BA-BA-BA-BA-BOOM
WHAM
AAAAH
!
KRAK
JUDG-MENT LOAD!

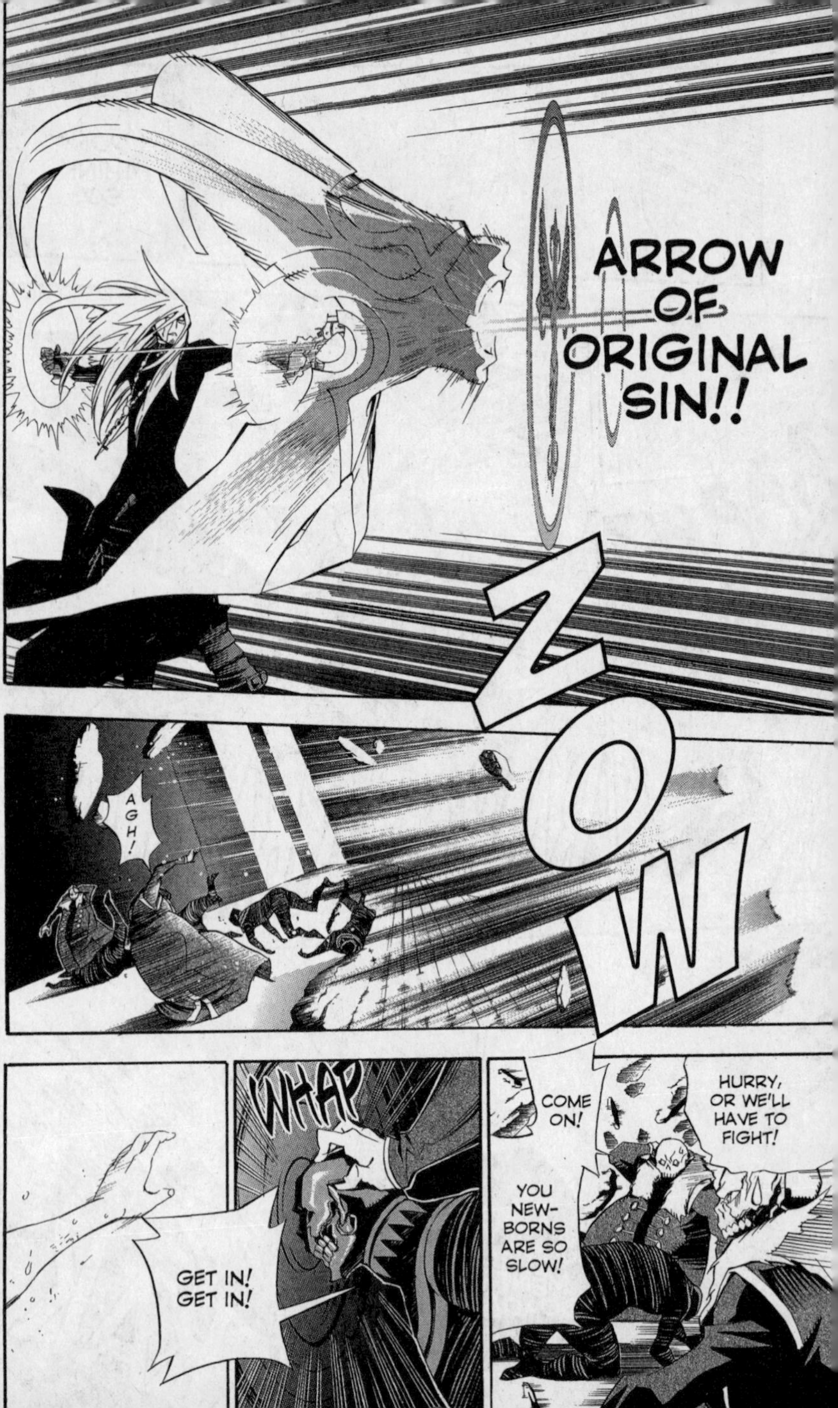
ARROW OF ORIGINAL SIN!!
AGH!
HURRY, OR WE'LL HAVE TO FIGHT!
COME ON!
YOU NEW-BORNS ARE SO SLOW!
WHAP
GET IN! GET IN!

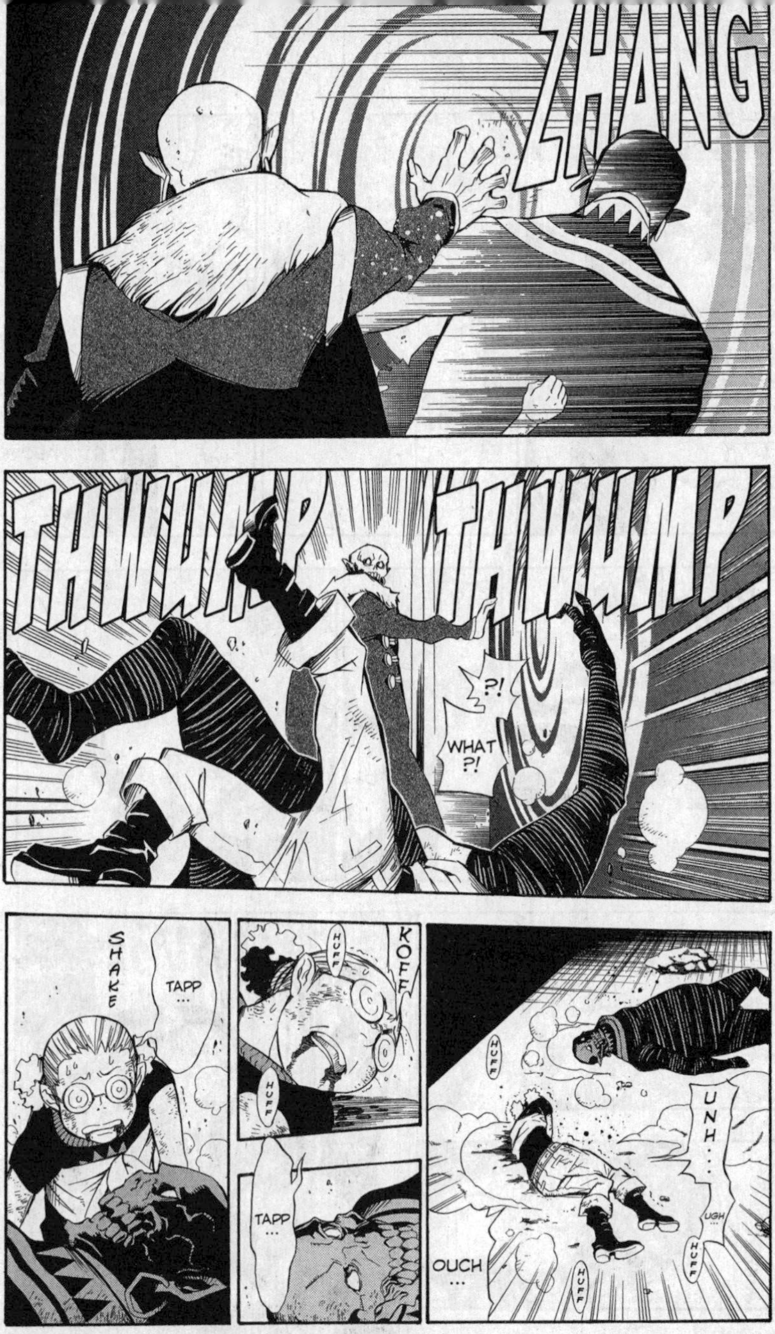
ZHANG
THWUMP
THWUMP
?!
WHAT ?!
UNH...
HUFF
UGH...
HUFF
HUFF
OUCH...
KOFF
HUFF
HUFF
TAPP...
SHAKE
TAPP...

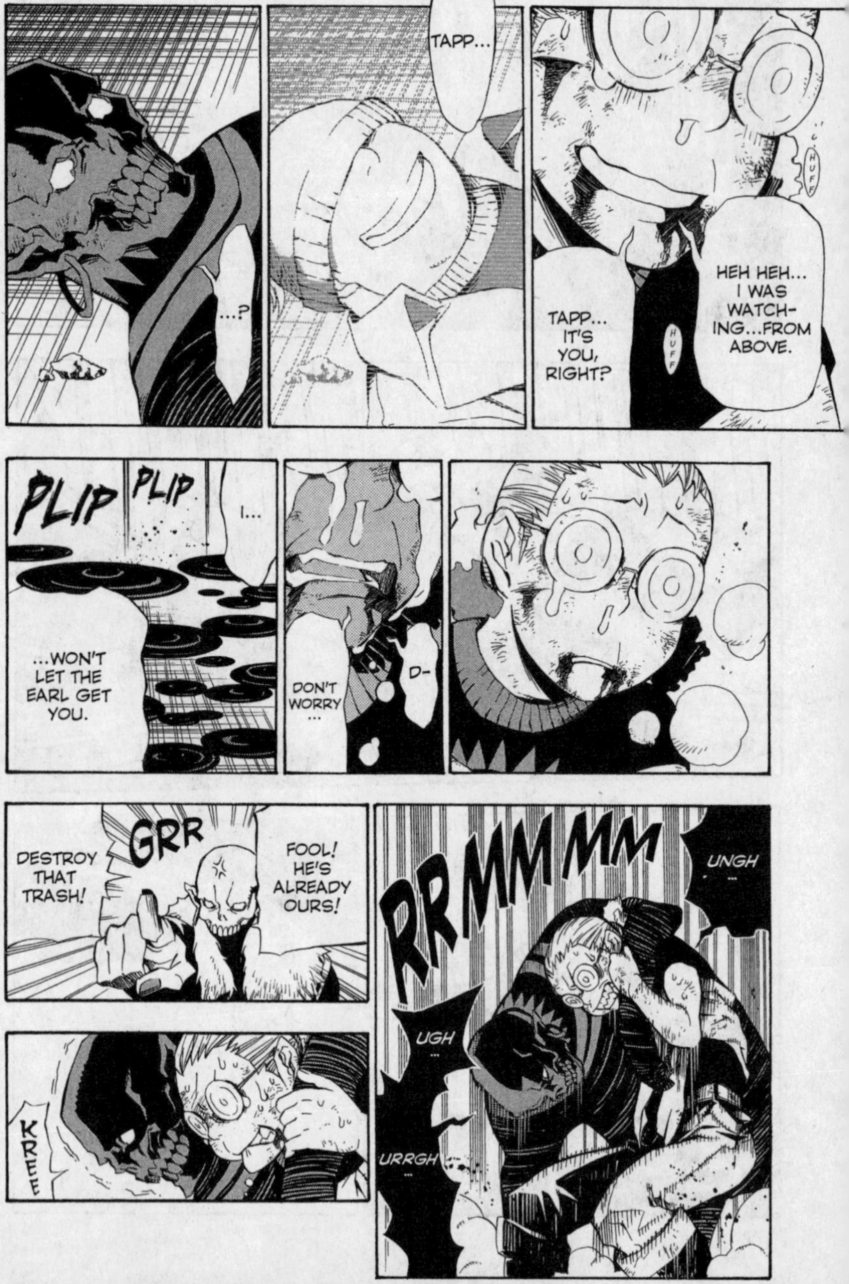
HUFF
HEH HEH... I WAS WATCHING...FROM ABOVE.
HUFF
TAPP... IT'S YOU, RIGHT?
TAPP...
...?
D-
DON'T WORRY ...
I...
PLIP
PLIP
...WON'T LET THE EARL GET YOU.
UNGH ...
RRMMMM
UGH ...
URRGH ...
FOOL! HE'S ALREADY OURS!
GRR
DESTROY THAT TRASH!
KREE

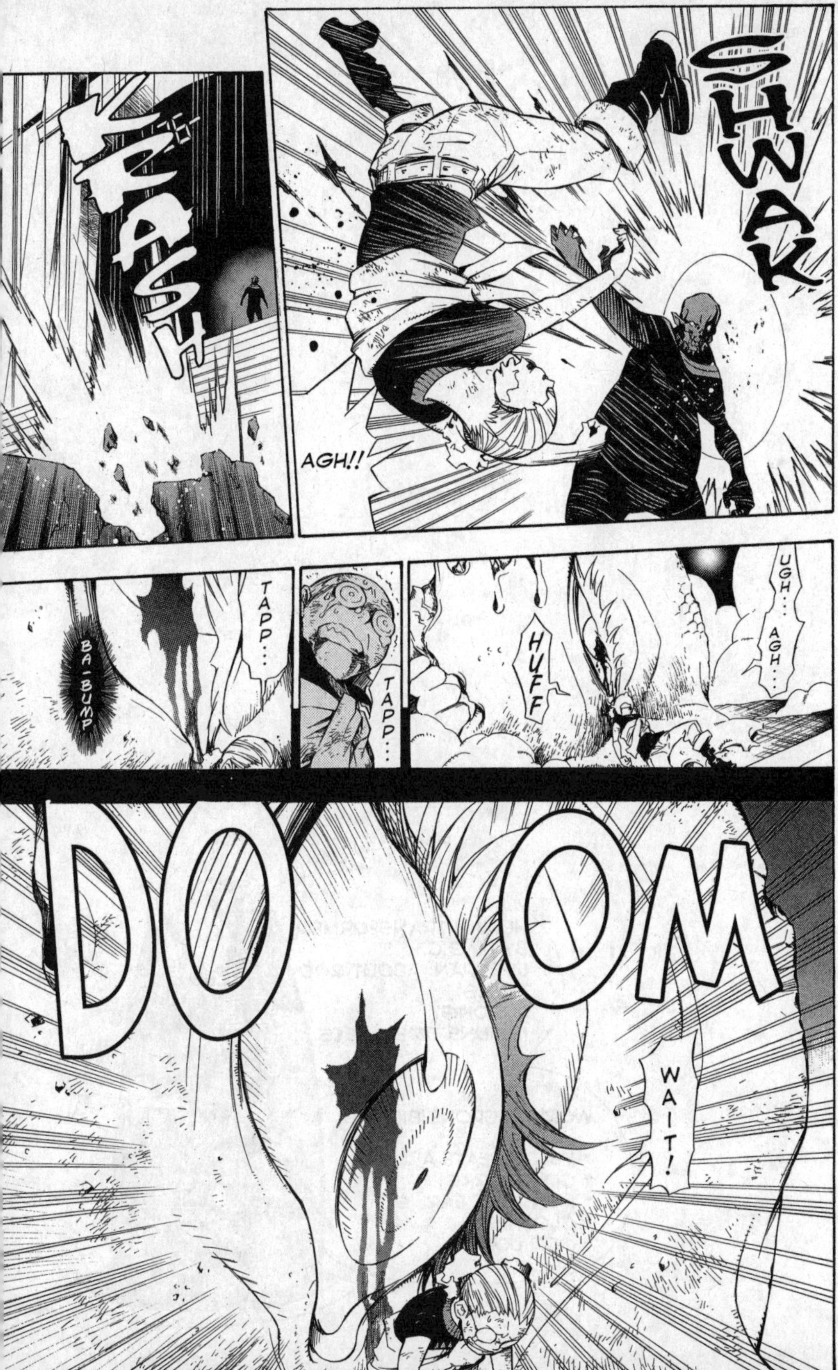
SHWAK
AGH!!
KRASH
UGH... AGH...
HUFF
TAPP...
TAPP...
BA-BUMP
DOOM
WAIT!

SKULL.

HUMAN TRANSFORMED
BY MAGIC.
LIFESPAN: ABOUT 200
YEARS.
STRONG.
IMMUNE TO BULLETS.

WORK RESPONSIBILITIES:

* HELP CREATE AKUMA
* CLEAN ARKS
* MEND THE EARL'S
  CLOTHES
* ODD JOBS

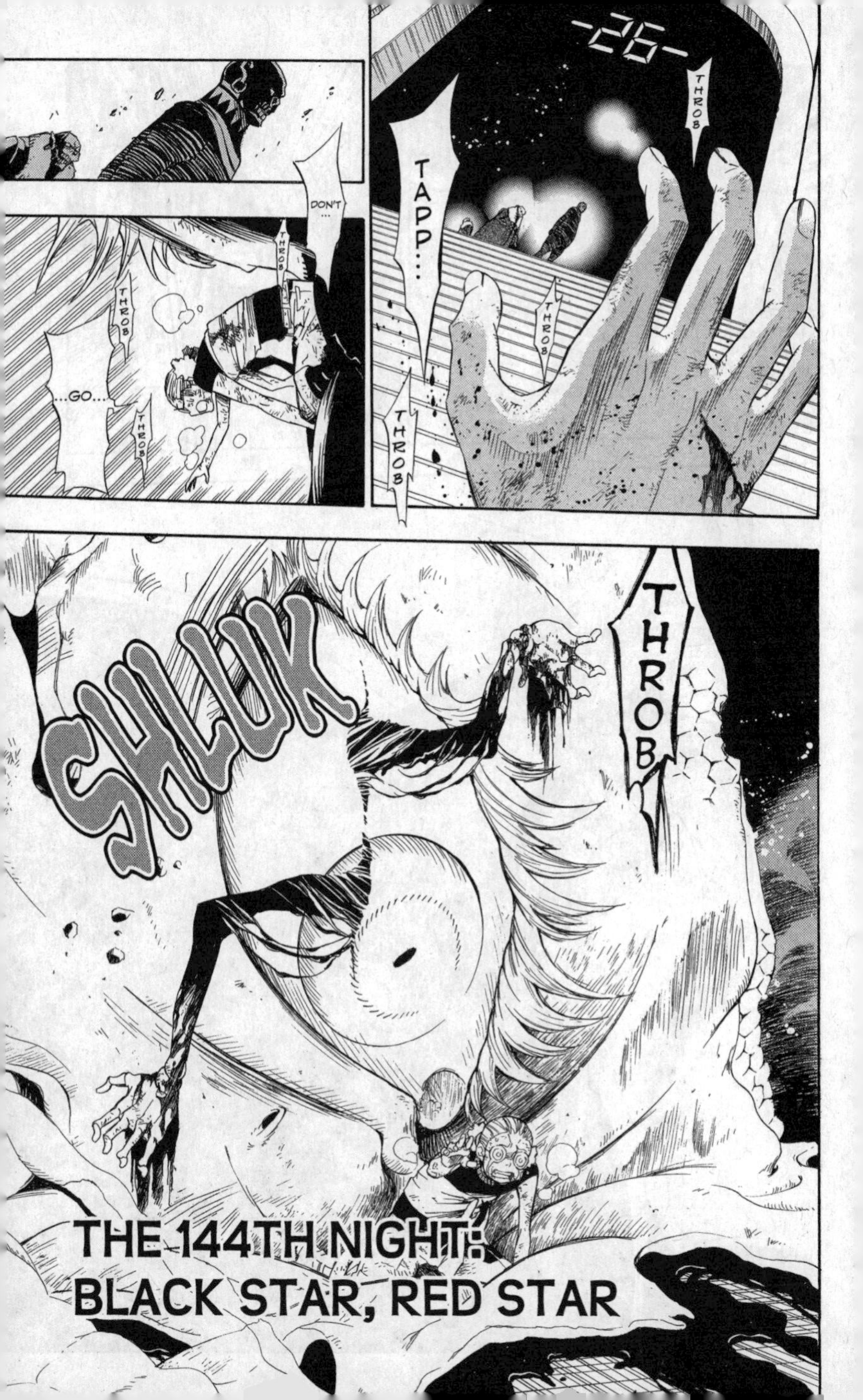
THROB
TAPP...
THROB
THROB
DON'T...
THROB
THROB
...GO...
THROB
THROB
SHLUK

THE 144TH NIGHT: BLACK STAR, RED STAR

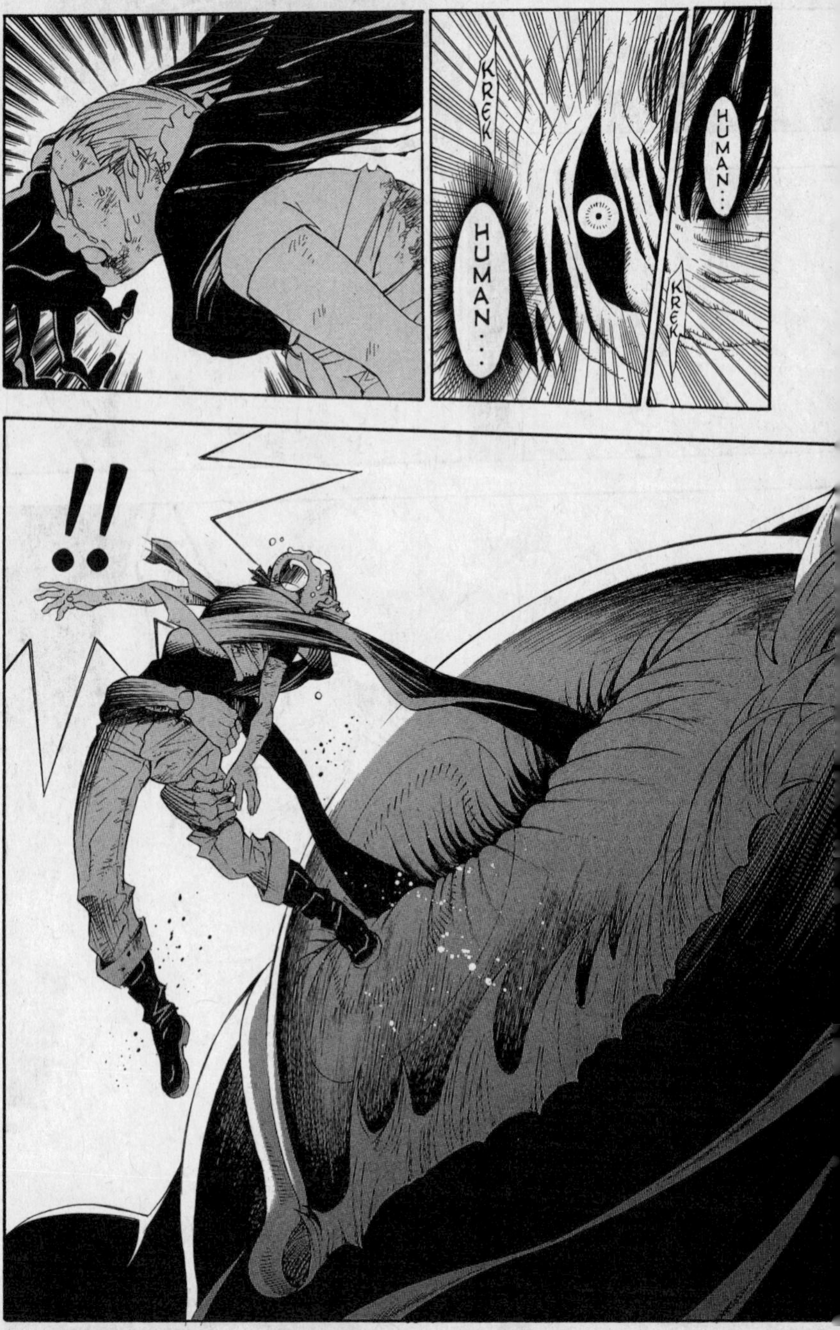
HUMAN...
KREK
KREK
HUMAN...
!!

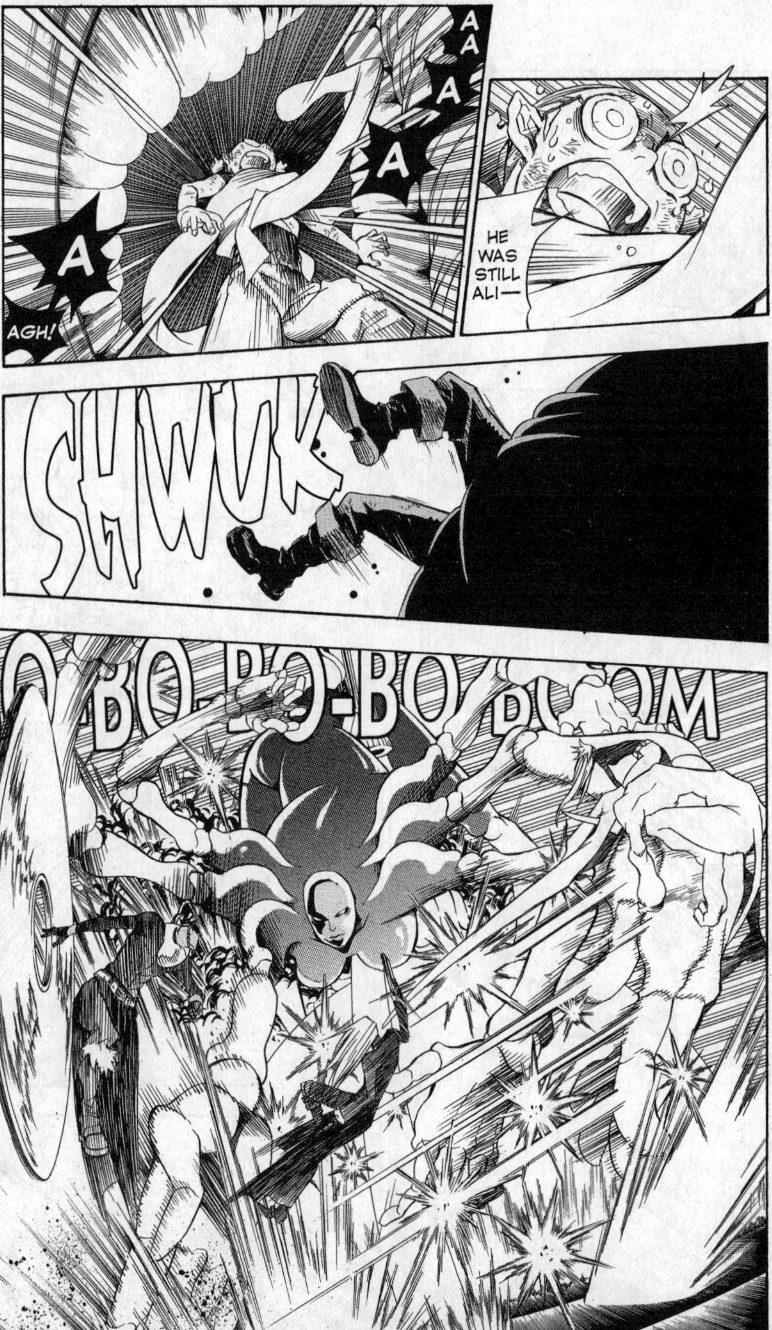
HE WAS STILL ALI—
AAAAA
A
AGH!
SHWUK
BO-BO-BO-BO-BOOM

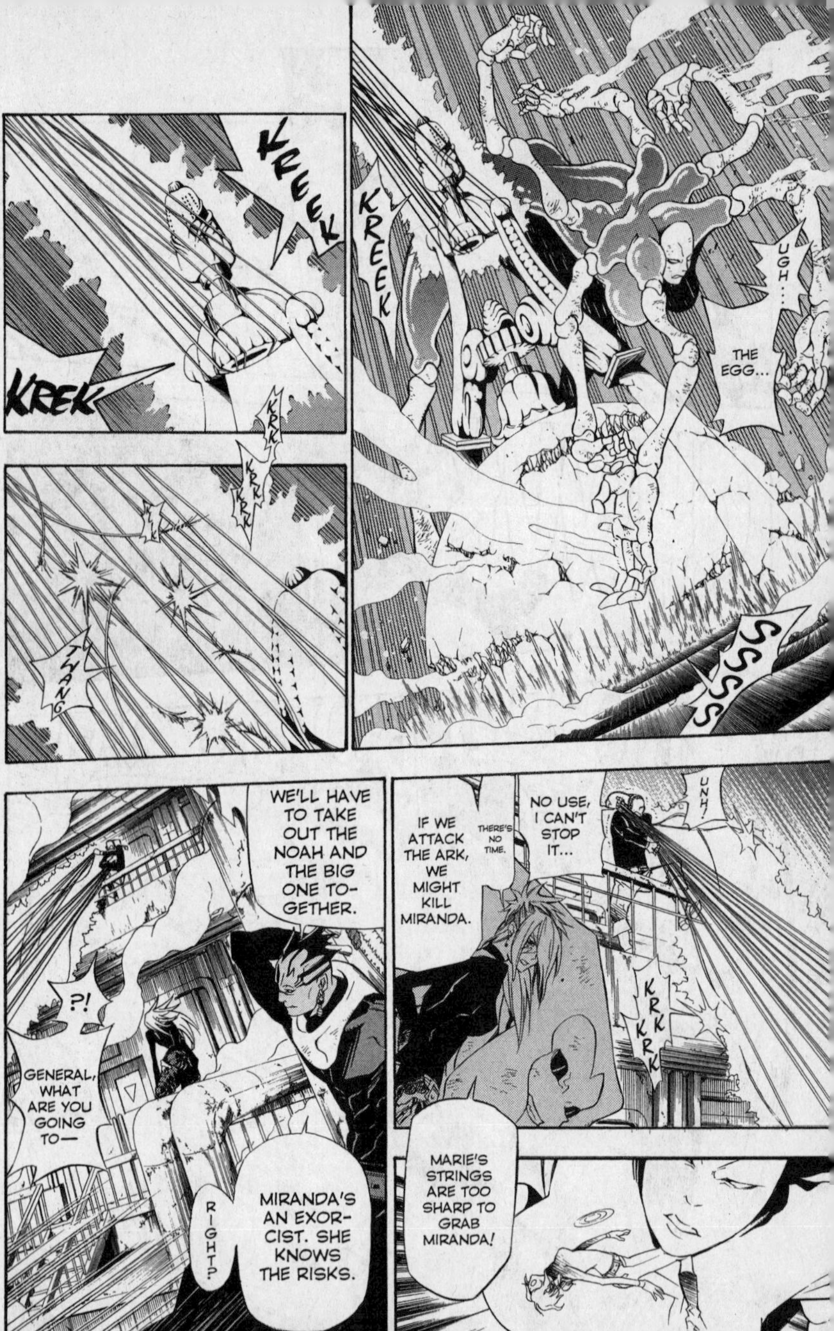
UGH...
THE EGG...
KREEK
SSSSS
KREEEK
KREK
KRK KRK
TWANG
UNH!
NO USE, I CAN'T STOP IT...
THERE'S NO TIME.
IF WE ATTACK THE ARK, WE MIGHT KILL MIRANDA.
KRK KRK
MARIE'S STRINGS ARE TOO SHARP TO GRAB MIRANDA!
WE'LL HAVE TO TAKE OUT THE NOAH AND THE BIG ONE TO-GETHER.
?!
GENERAL, WHAT ARE YOU GOING TO—
MIRANDA'S AN EXOR-CIST. SHE KNOWS THE RISKS.
RIGHT?

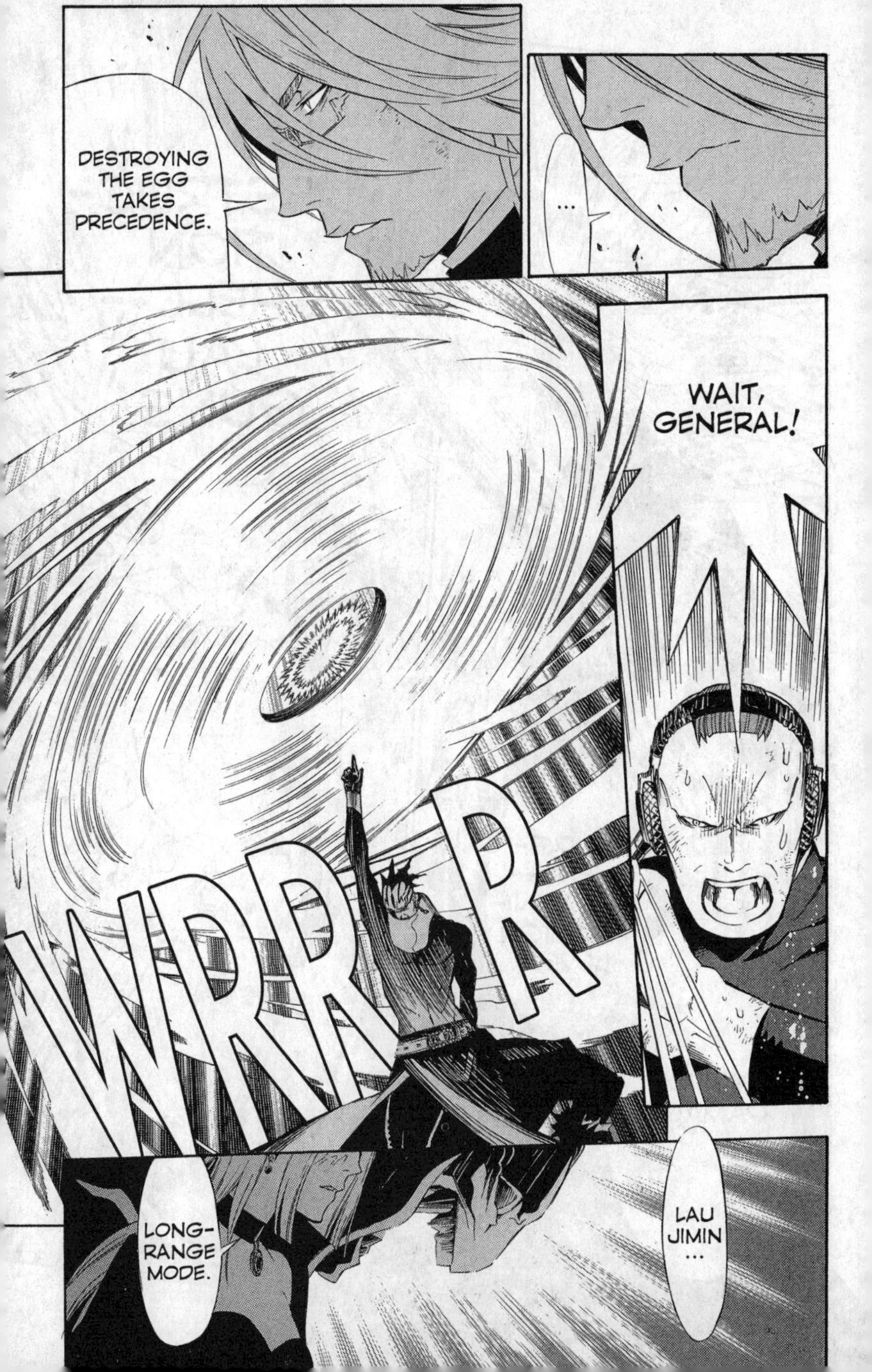
...
DESTROYING THE EGG TAKES PRECEDENCE.
WAIT, GENERAL!
WRRR
LAU JIMIN ...
LONG-RANGE MODE.

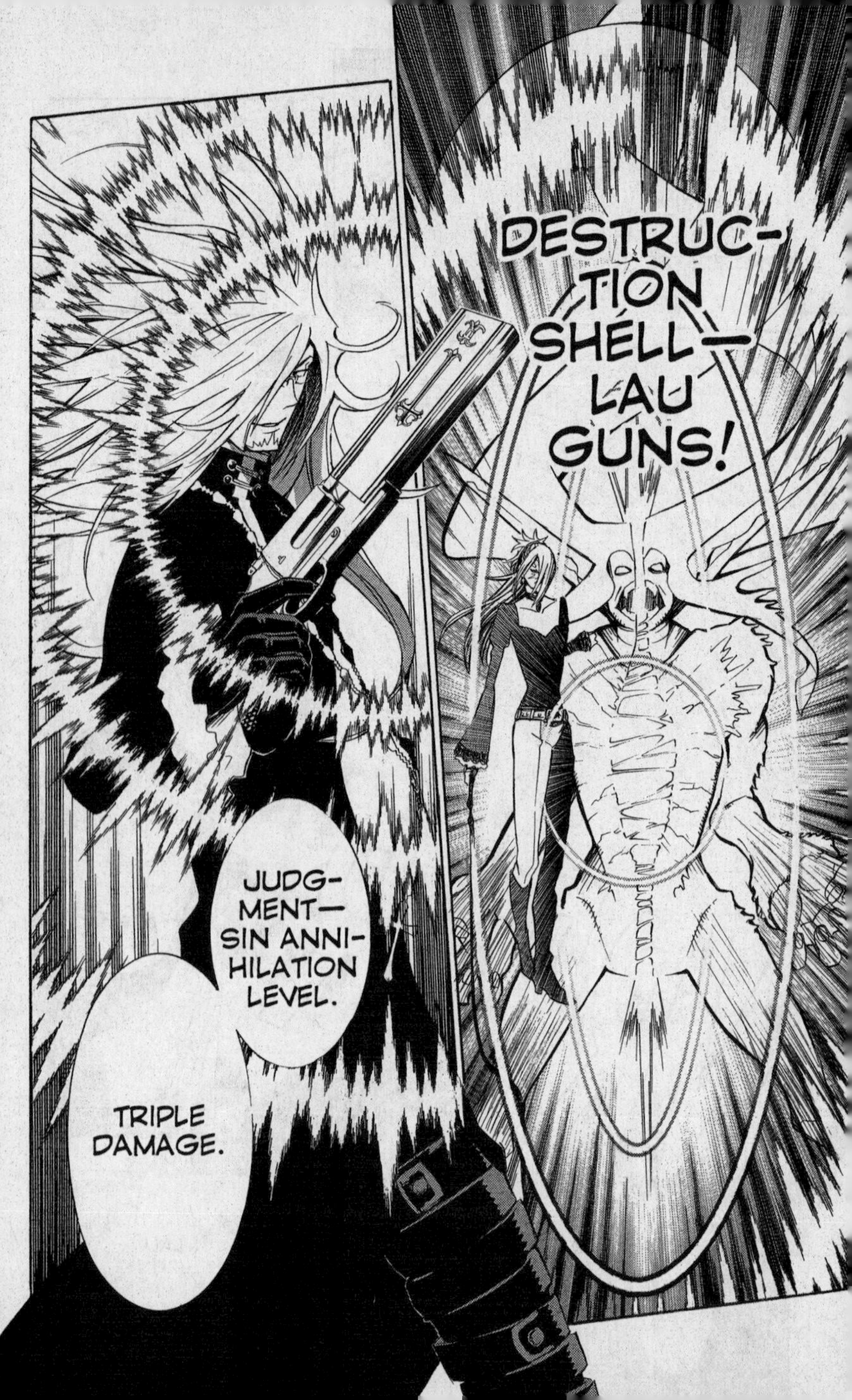
DESTRUCTION SHELL—LAU GUNS!
JUDGMENT—SIN ANNIHILATION LEVEL.
TRIPLE DAMAGE.

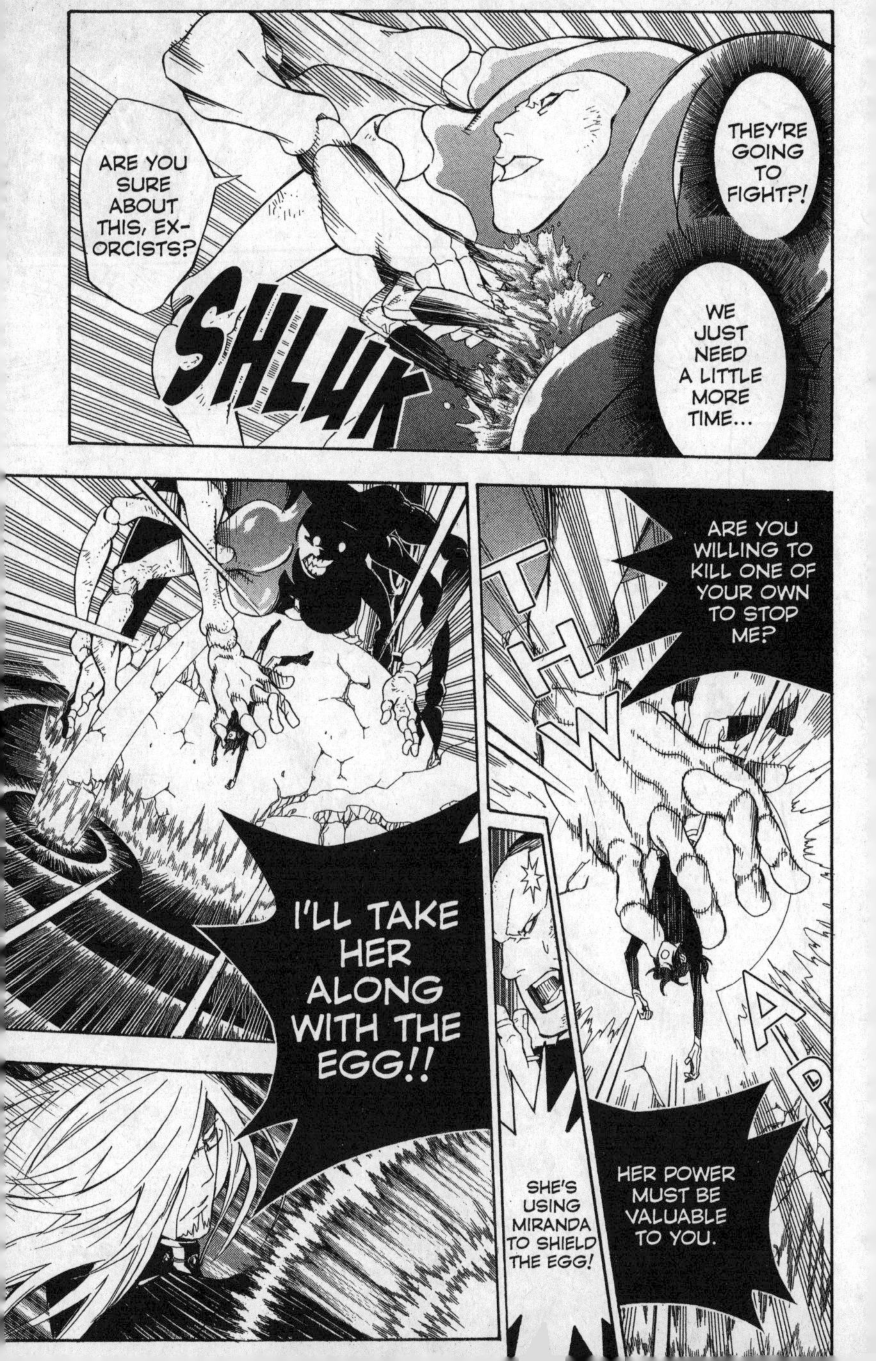
THEY'RE GOING TO FIGHT?!
WE JUST NEED A LITTLE MORE TIME...
ARE YOU SURE ABOUT THIS, EX-ORCISTS?
SHLUK
ARE YOU WILLING TO KILL ONE OF YOUR OWN TO STOP ME?
THWAP
HER POWER MUST BE VALUABLE TO YOU.
SHE'S USING MIRANDA TO SHIELD THE EGG!
I'LL TAKE HER ALONG WITH THE EGG!!

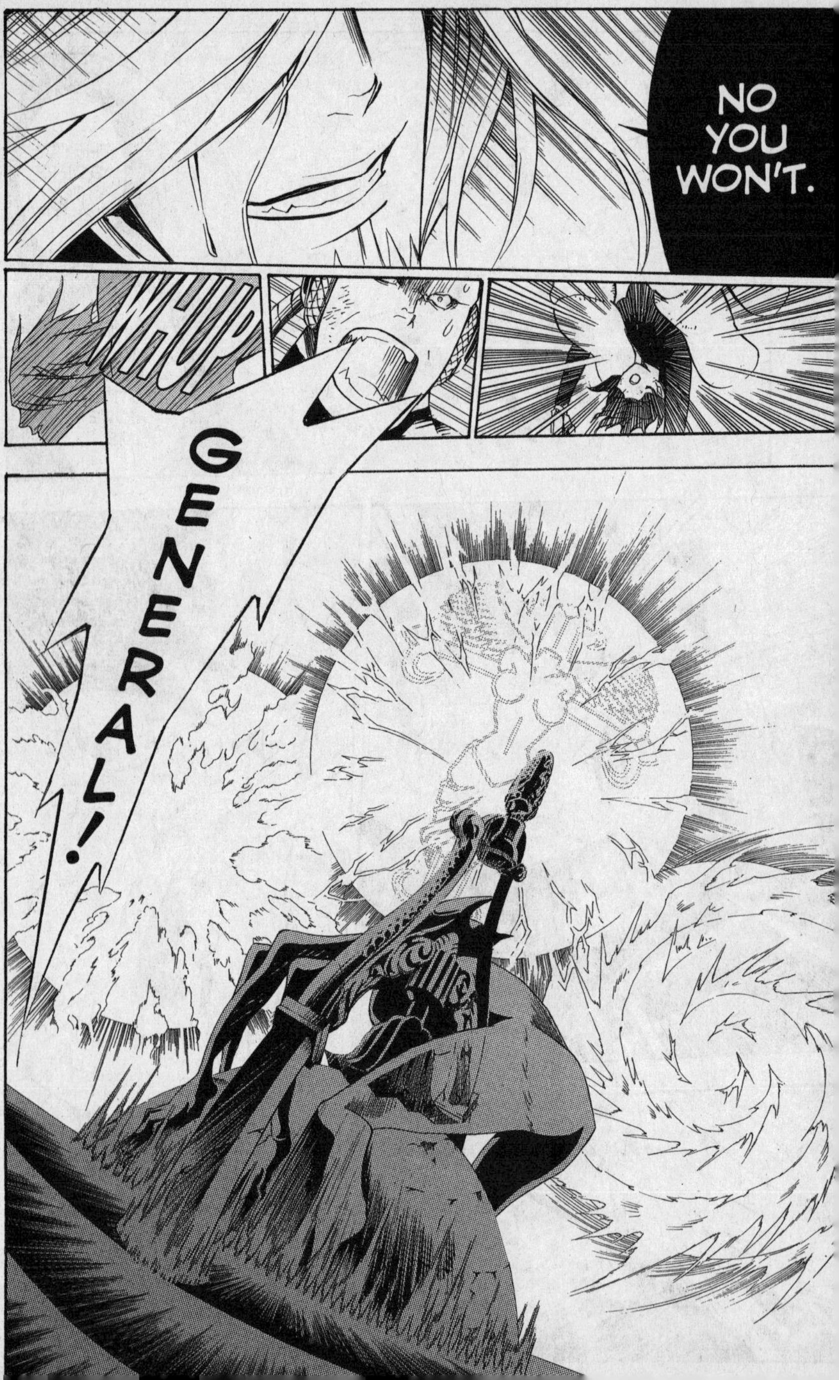
NO YOU WON'T.
GENERAL!
WHUP

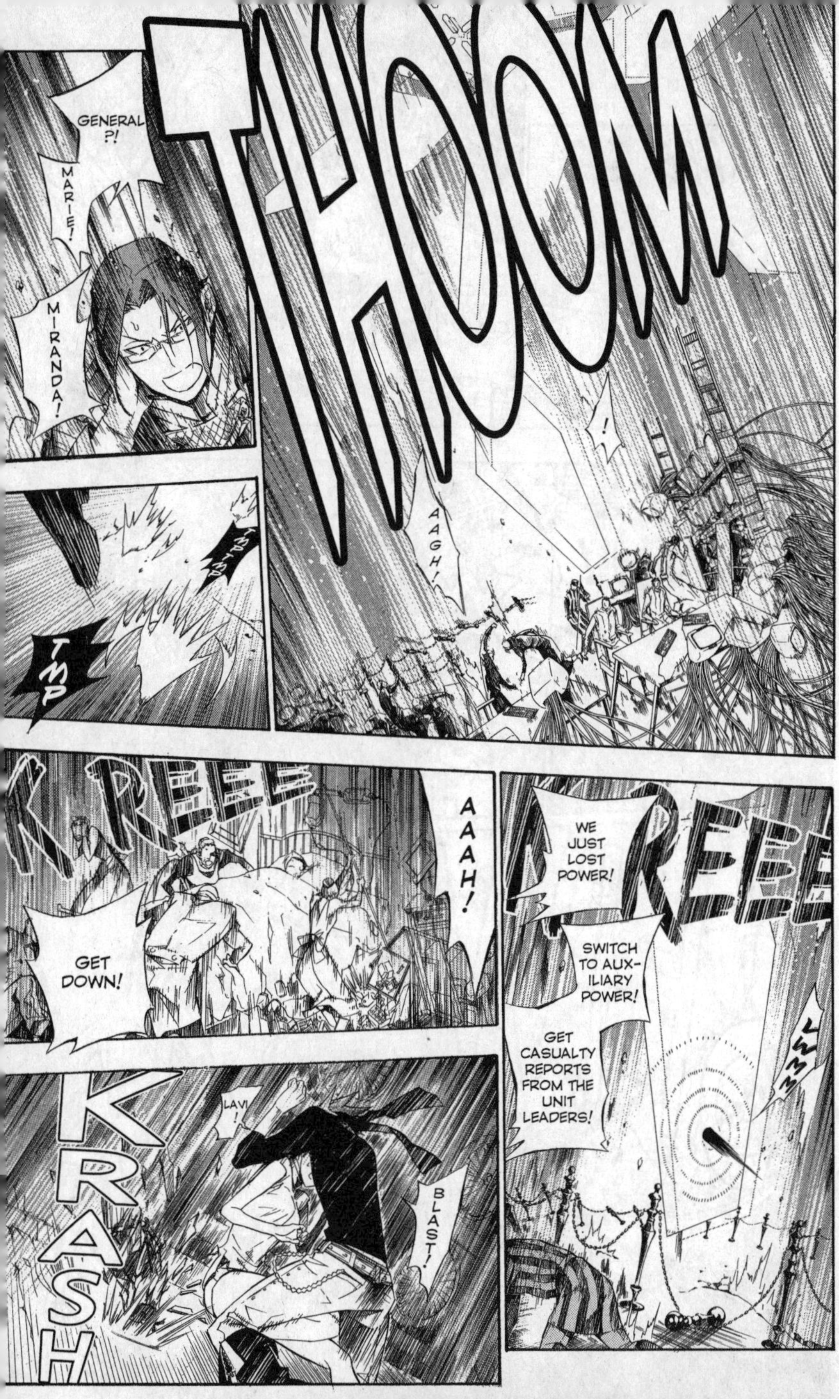
THOOM
!
AAGH!
GENERAL?!
MARIE!
MIRANDA!
TMP
TMP
WE JUST LOST POWER!
REEE
SWITCH TO AUXILIARY POWER!
GET CASUALTY REPORTS FROM THE UNIT LEADERS!
VWMM
KREEE
AAAH!
GET DOWN!
LAVI!
BLAST!
KRASH

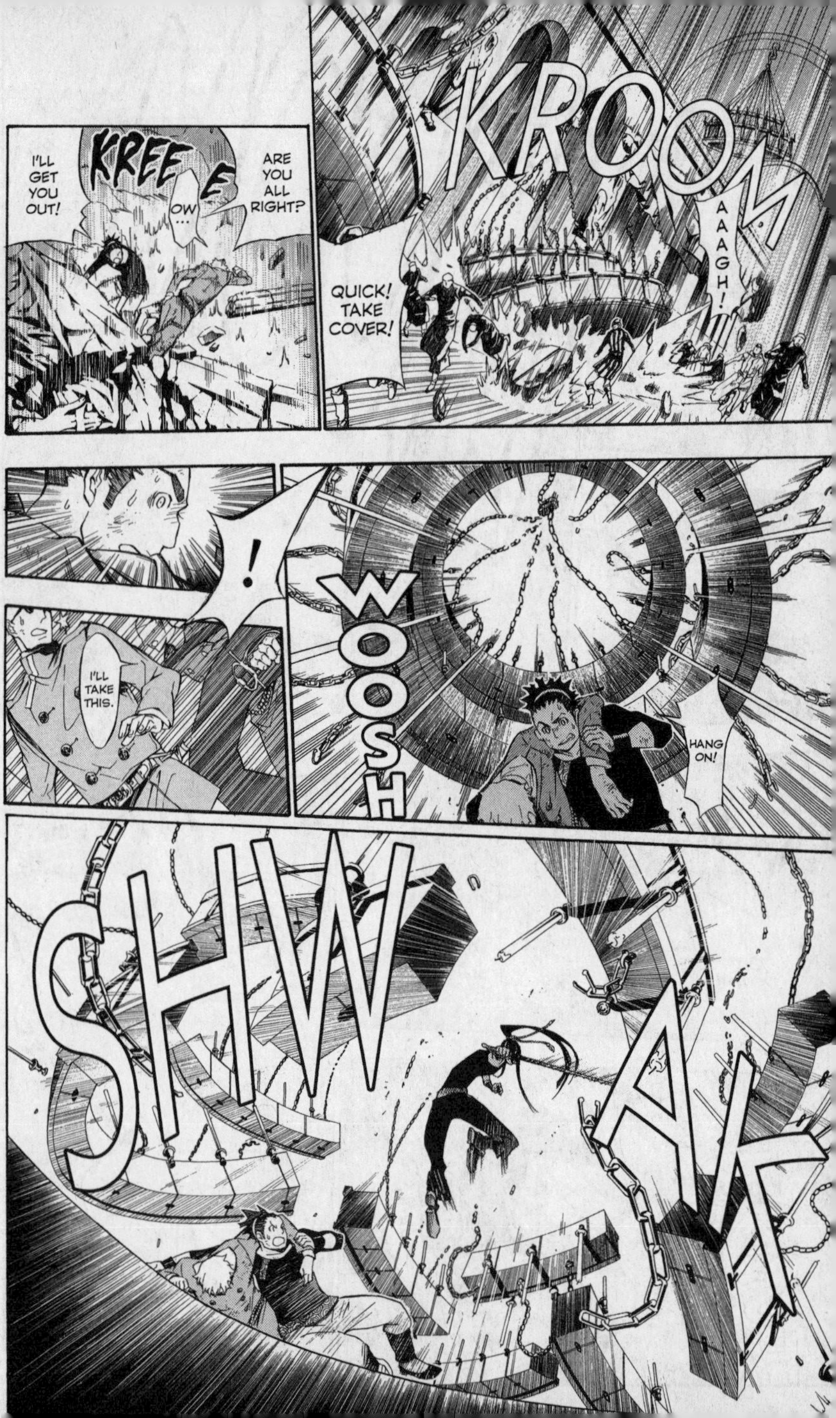
KROOM
AAAGH!
QUICK! TAKE COVER!
KREE E
ARE YOU ALL RIGHT?
OW...
I'LL GET YOU OUT!
HANG ON!
WOOSH
!
I'LL TAKE THIS.
SHWAK

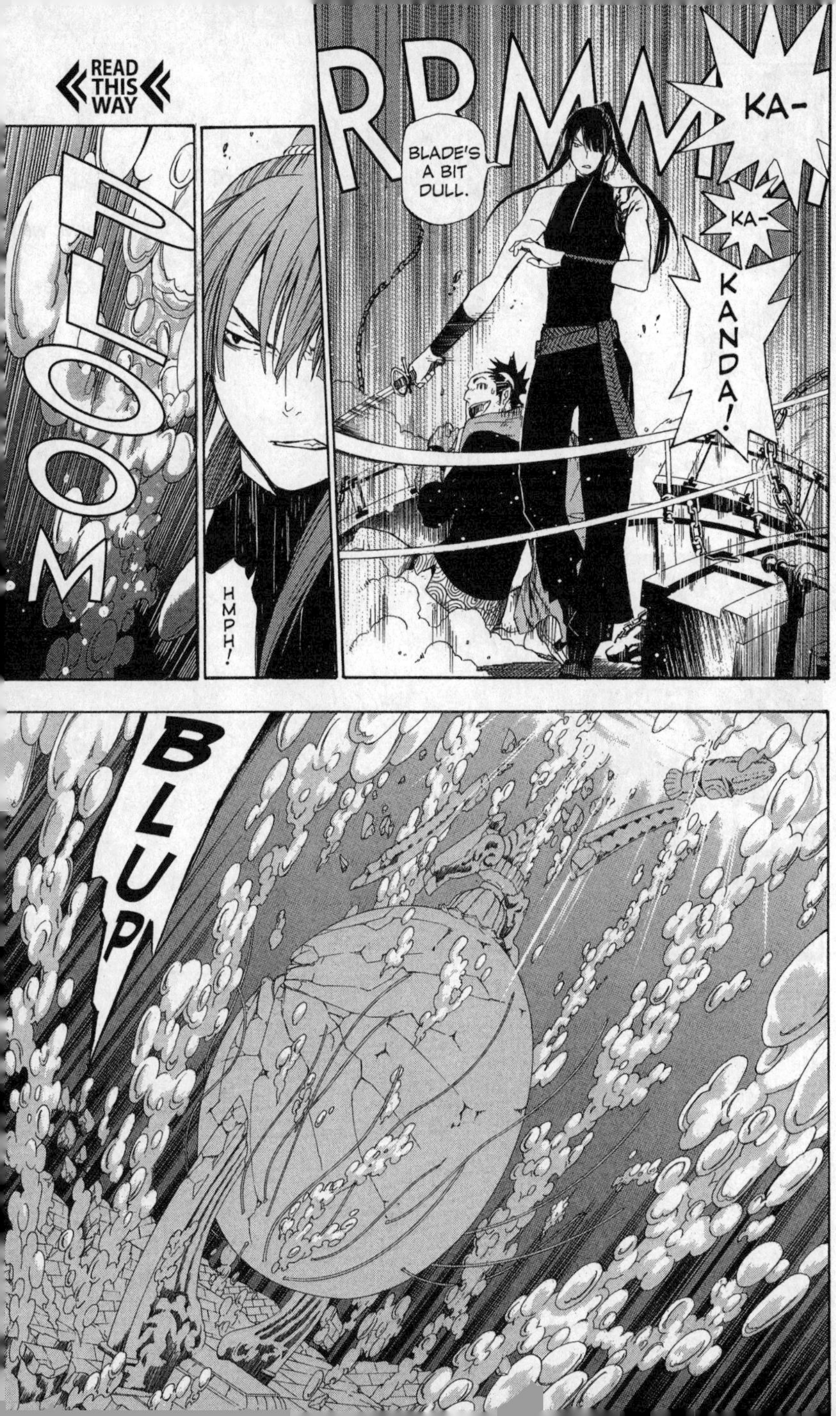
READ THIS WAY
RRMM
KA-
KA-
KANDA!
BLADE'S A BIT DULL.
HMPH!
FLOOOM
BLUP

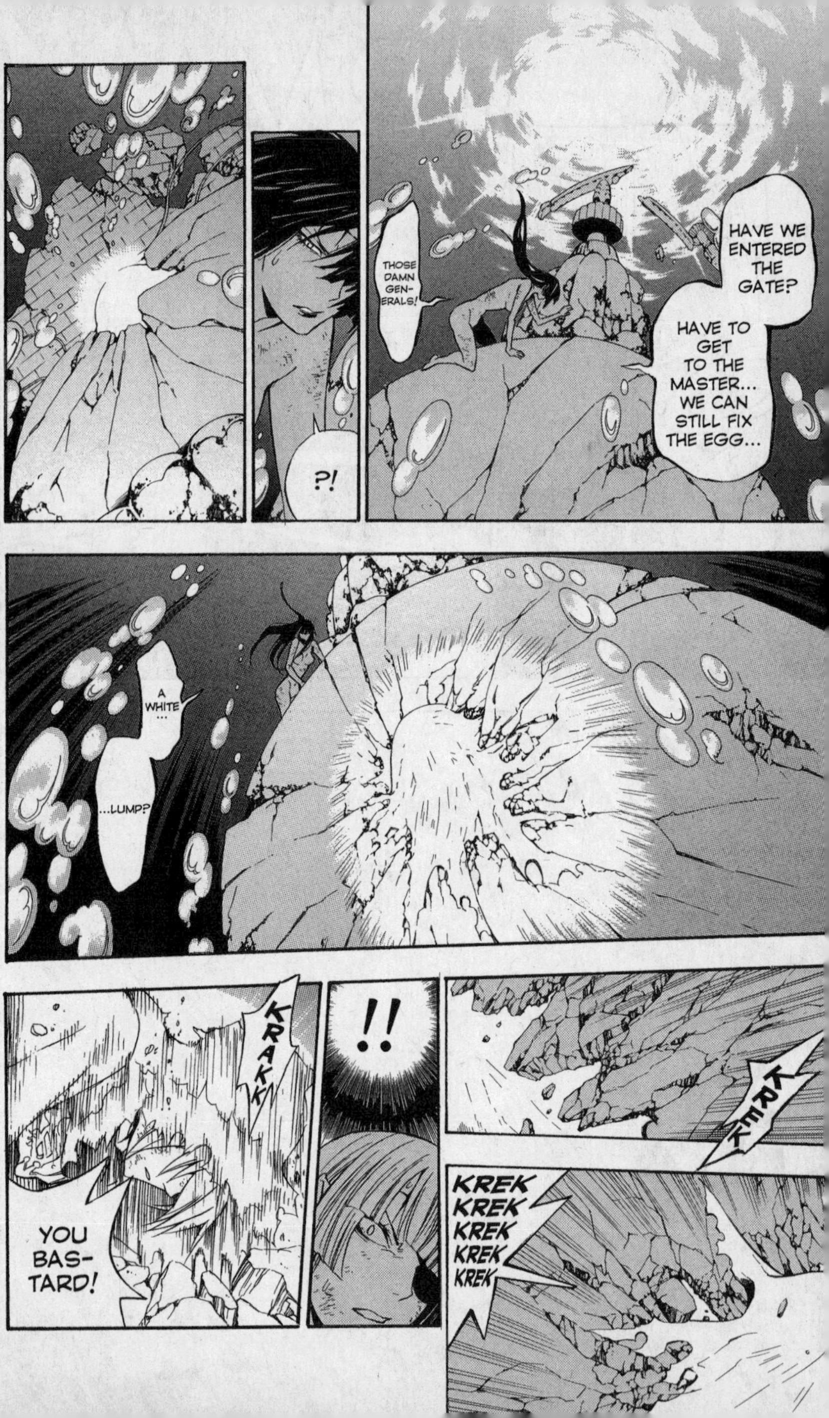
HAVE WE ENTERED THE GATE?
HAVE TO GET TO THE MASTER... WE CAN STILL FIX THE EGG...
THOSE DAMN GEN-ERALS!
?!
A WHITE ...
...LUMP?
KREK
KREK KREK KREK KREK KREK
!!
KRAKK
YOU BAS-TARD!

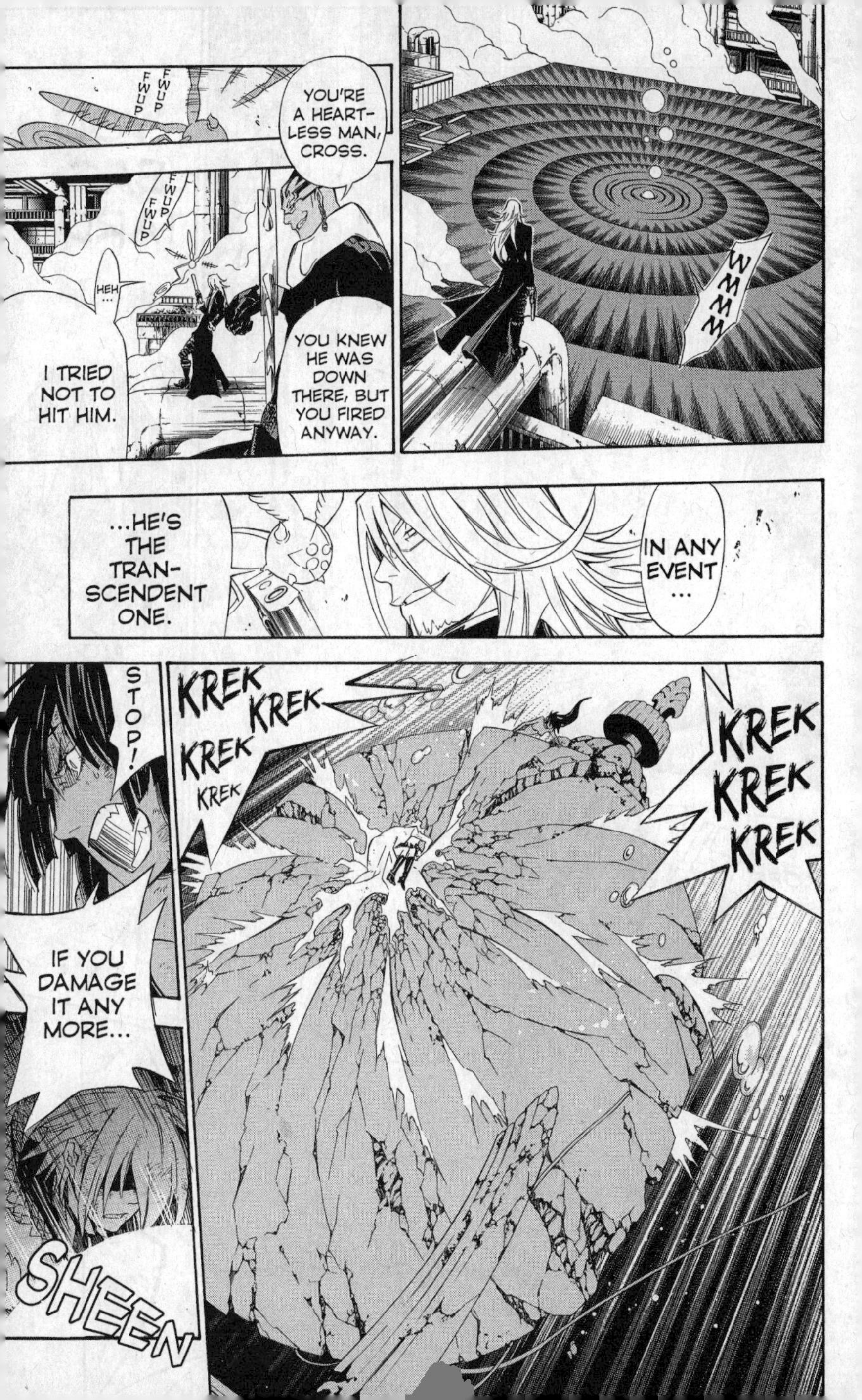
WMMM
FWUP FWUP
YOU'RE A HEART-LESS MAN, CROSS.
FWUP FWUP
YOU KNEW HE WAS DOWN THERE, BUT YOU FIRED ANYWAY.
HEH...
I TRIED NOT TO HIT HIM.
IN ANY EVENT...
...HE'S THE TRAN-SCENDENT ONE.
KREK KREK KREK
KREK KREK KREK KREK
STOP!
IF YOU DAMAGE IT ANY MORE...
SHEEN

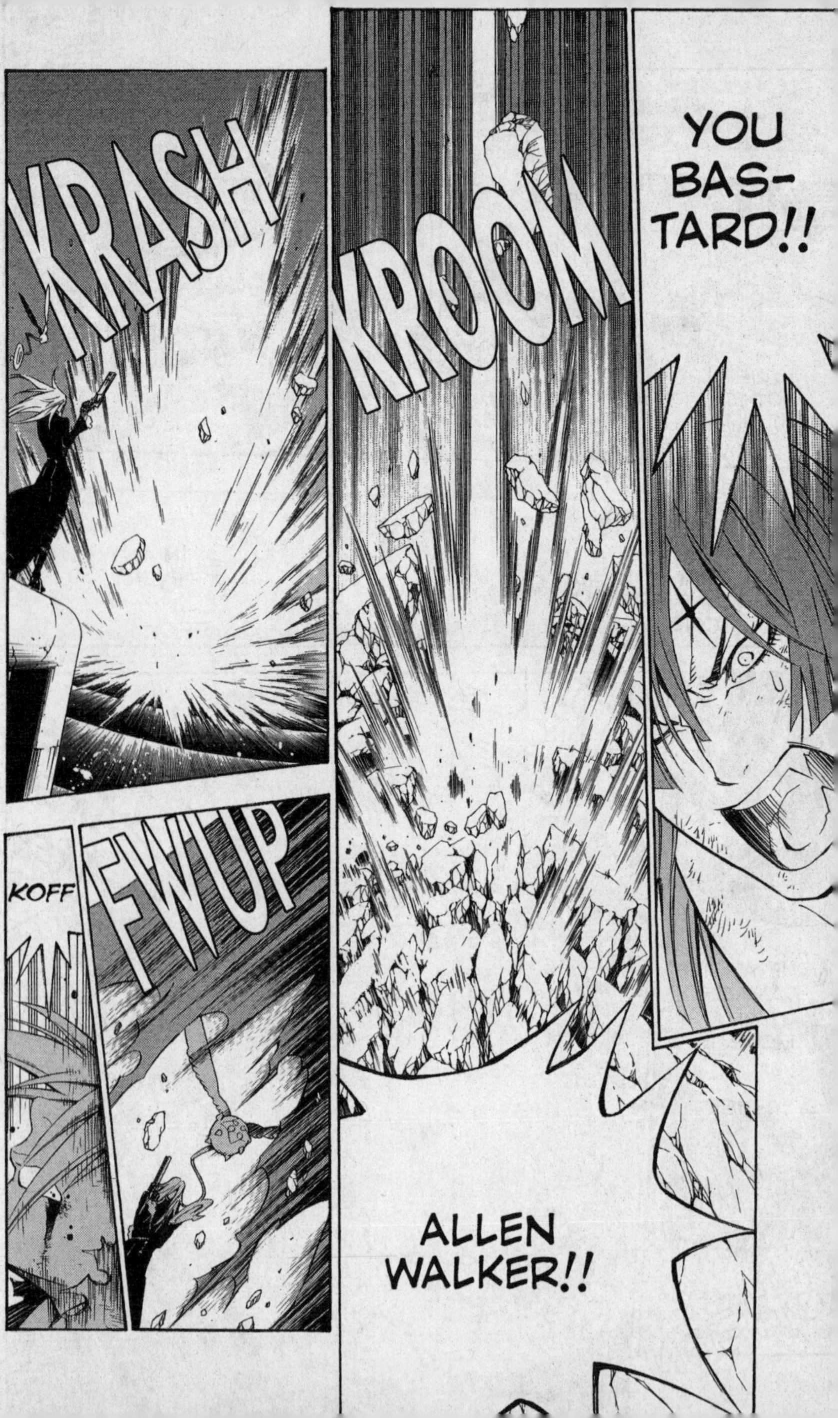
YOU BAS-TARD!!
KROOM
ALLEN WALKER!!
KRASH
FWUP
KOFF

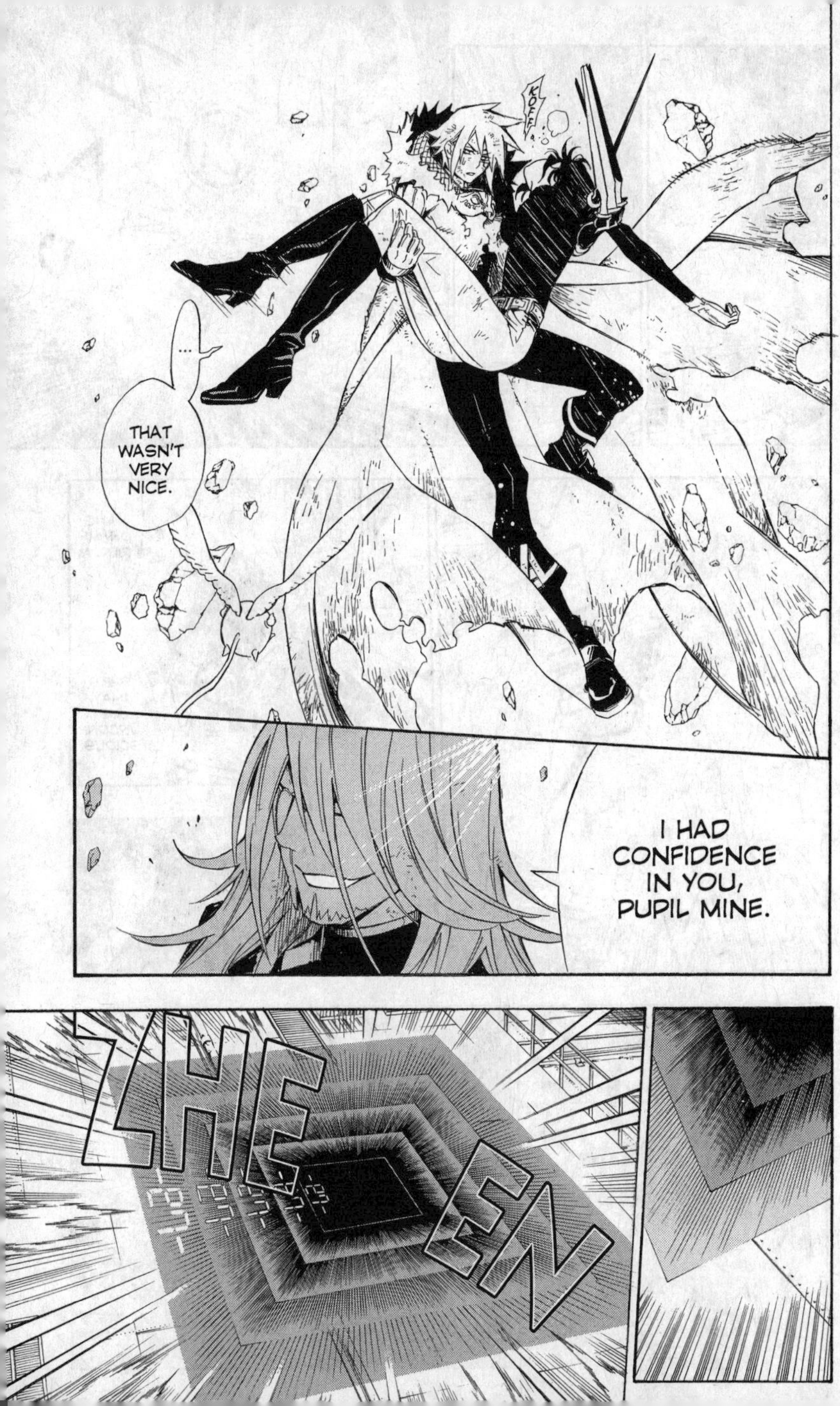
KOFF
...
THAT WASN'T VERY NICE.
I HAD CONFIDENCE IN YOU, PUPIL MINE.
ZHEEEN

ZAP
27
IT CLOSED!
TMP
KREK
SWF
UNH...
HANG ON, MI-RANDA.
SHE'S OKAY, JUST UNCON-SCIOUS.
I'LL GO TO REEV—
EEN
!
HEH...
HEH...
HEH...
HEH...
HEH...
HEH HEH...
HEH...
HEH...

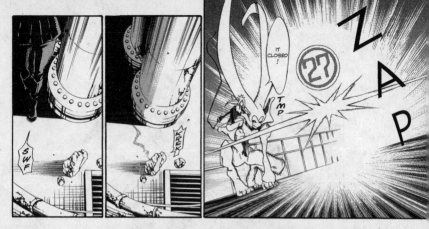

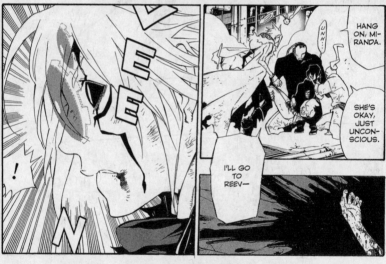

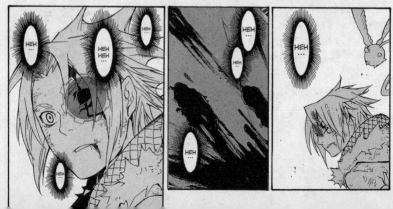

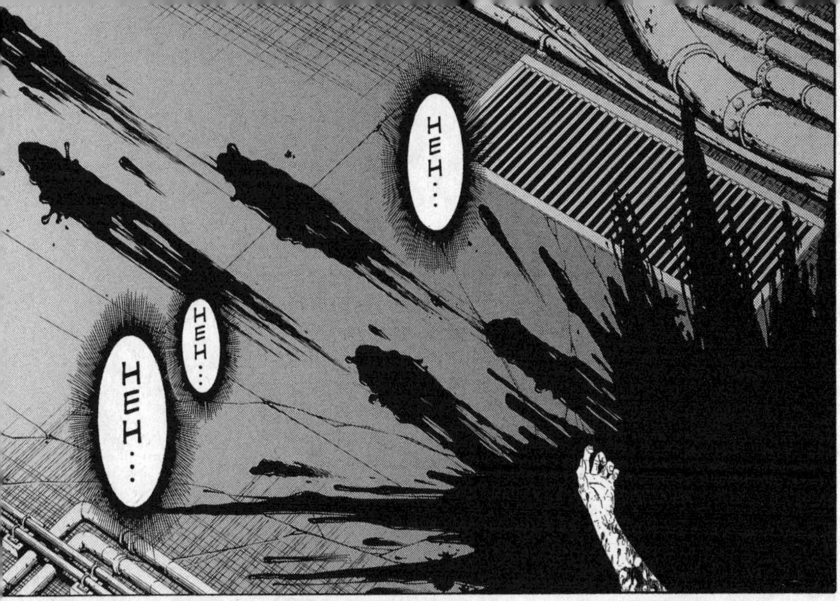
HEH...
HEH...
HEH...

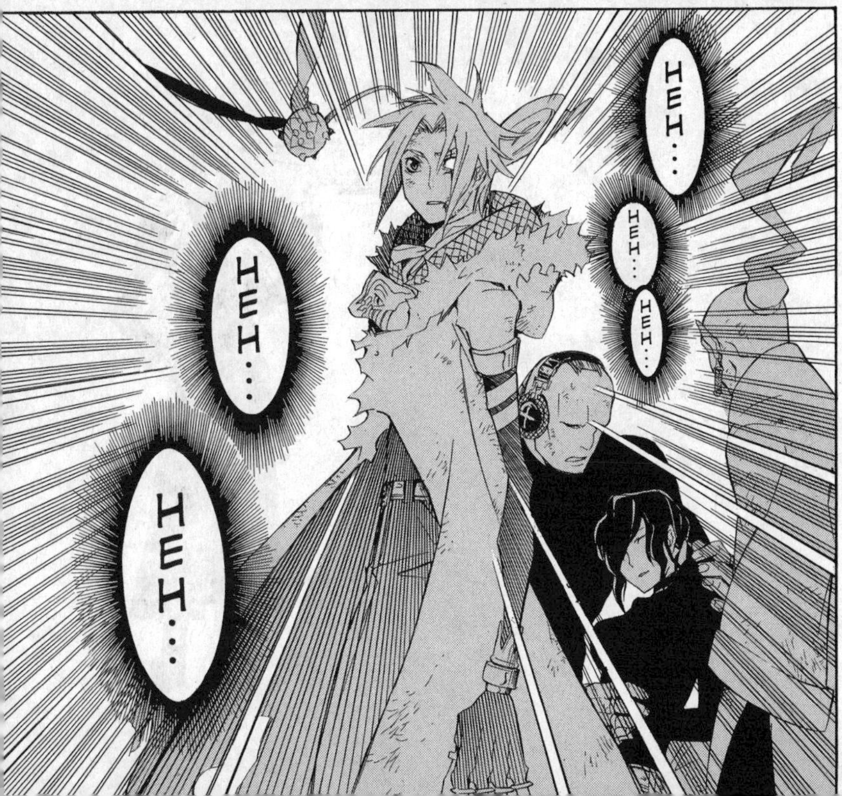
HEH...
HEH...
HEH...
HEH...
HEH...

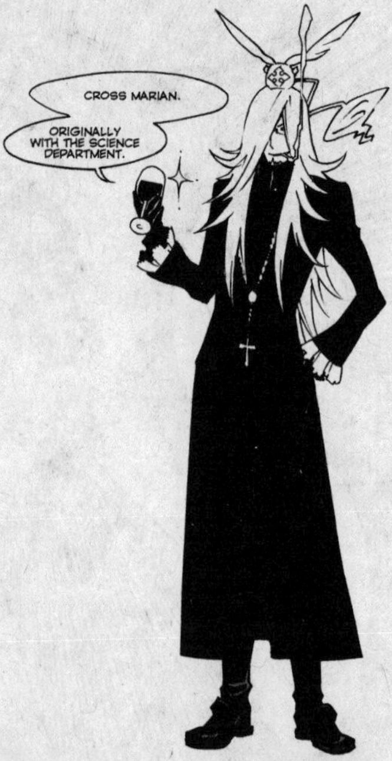
CROSS MARIAN.
ORIGINALLY WITH THE SCIENCE DEPARTMENT.

Darkness 4

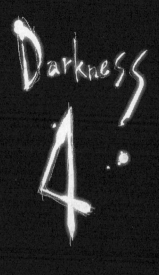

THE 145TH NIGHT: DARKNESS 4

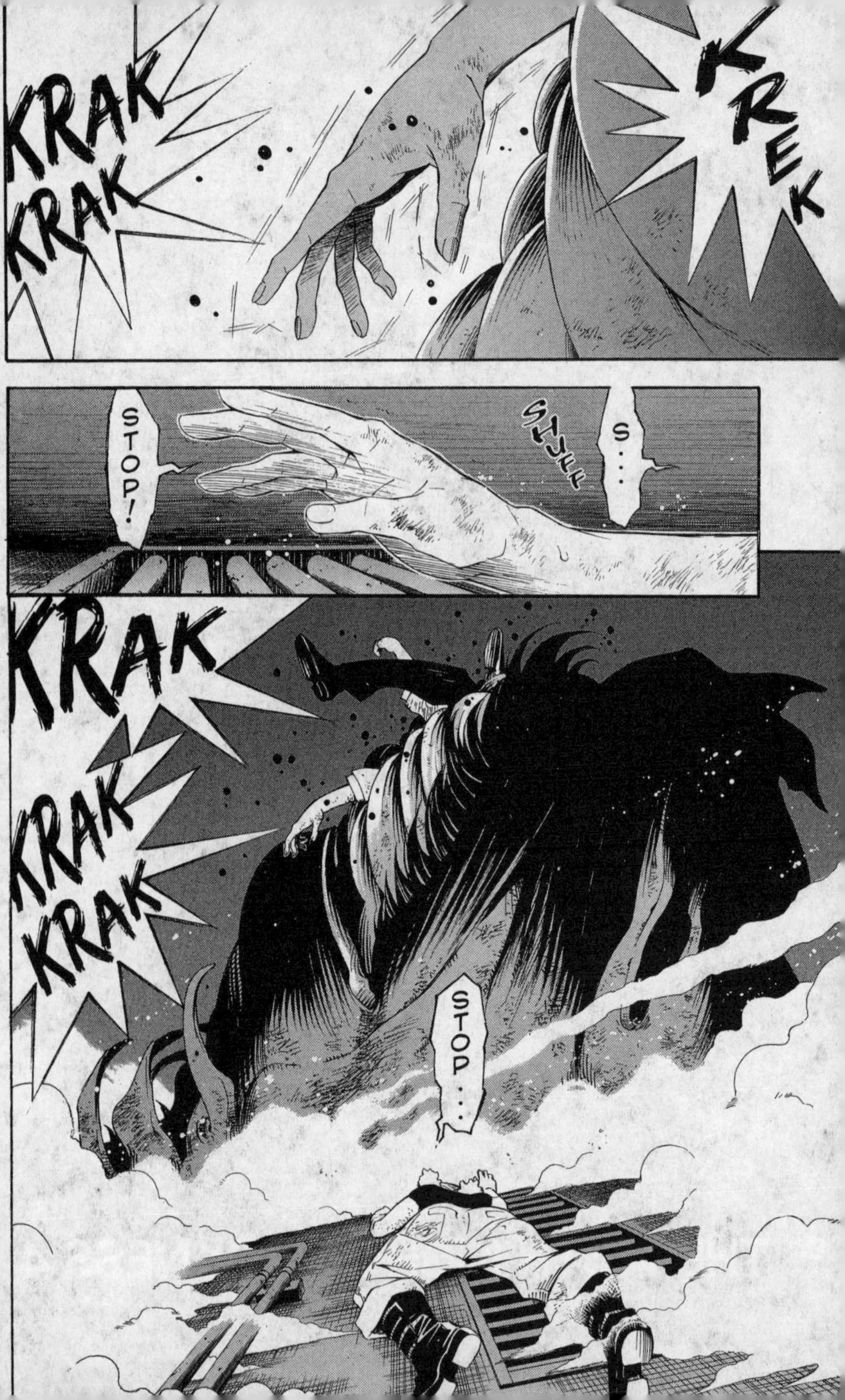
KREK
KRAK KRAK
S...
SHUFF
STOP!
KRAK
KRAK KRAK
STOP...

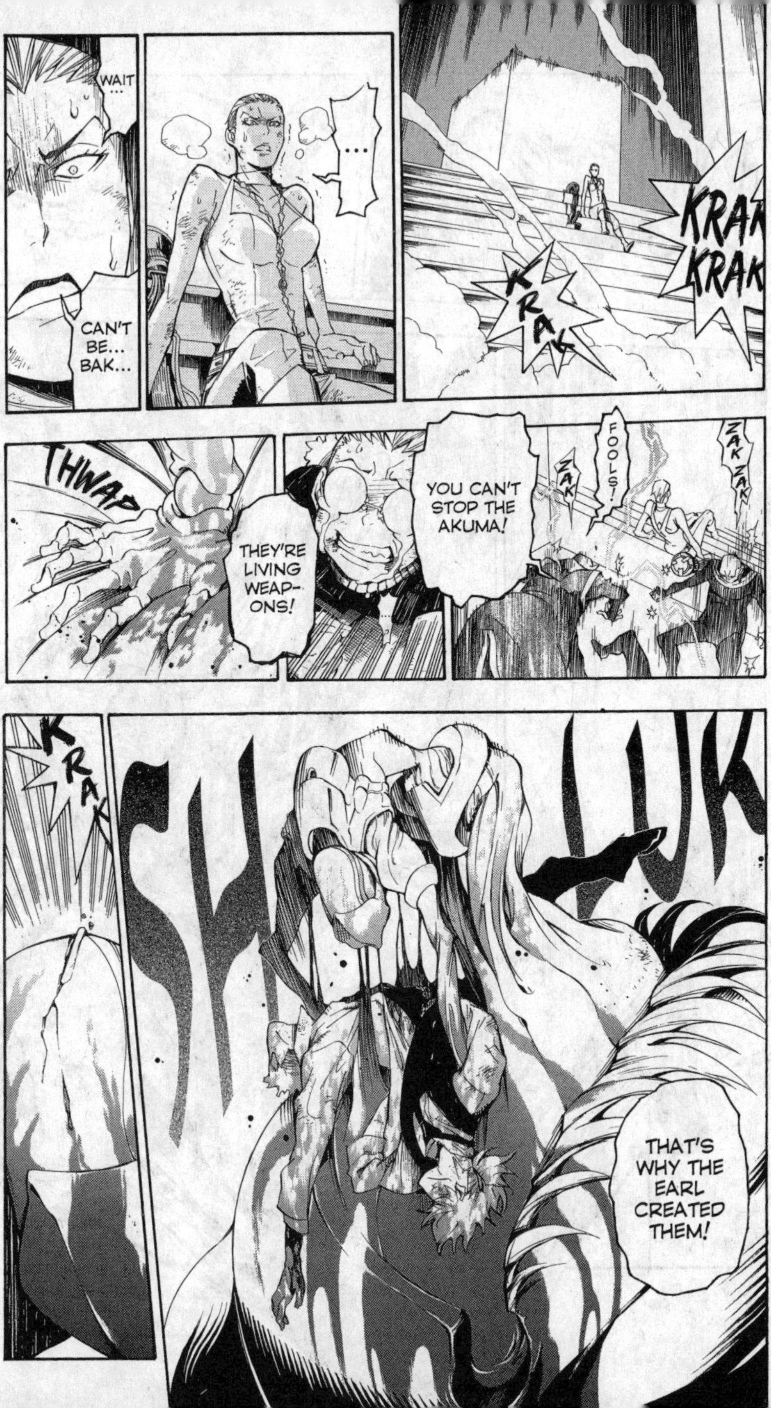
KRAK KRAK
KRAK
...
WAIT...
CAN'T BE... BAK...
FOOLS!
ZAK ZAK
ZAK
YOU CAN'T STOP THE AKUMA!
THEY'RE LIVING WEAPONS!
THWAP
SHLUK
THAT'S WHY THE EARL CREATED THEM!
KRAK

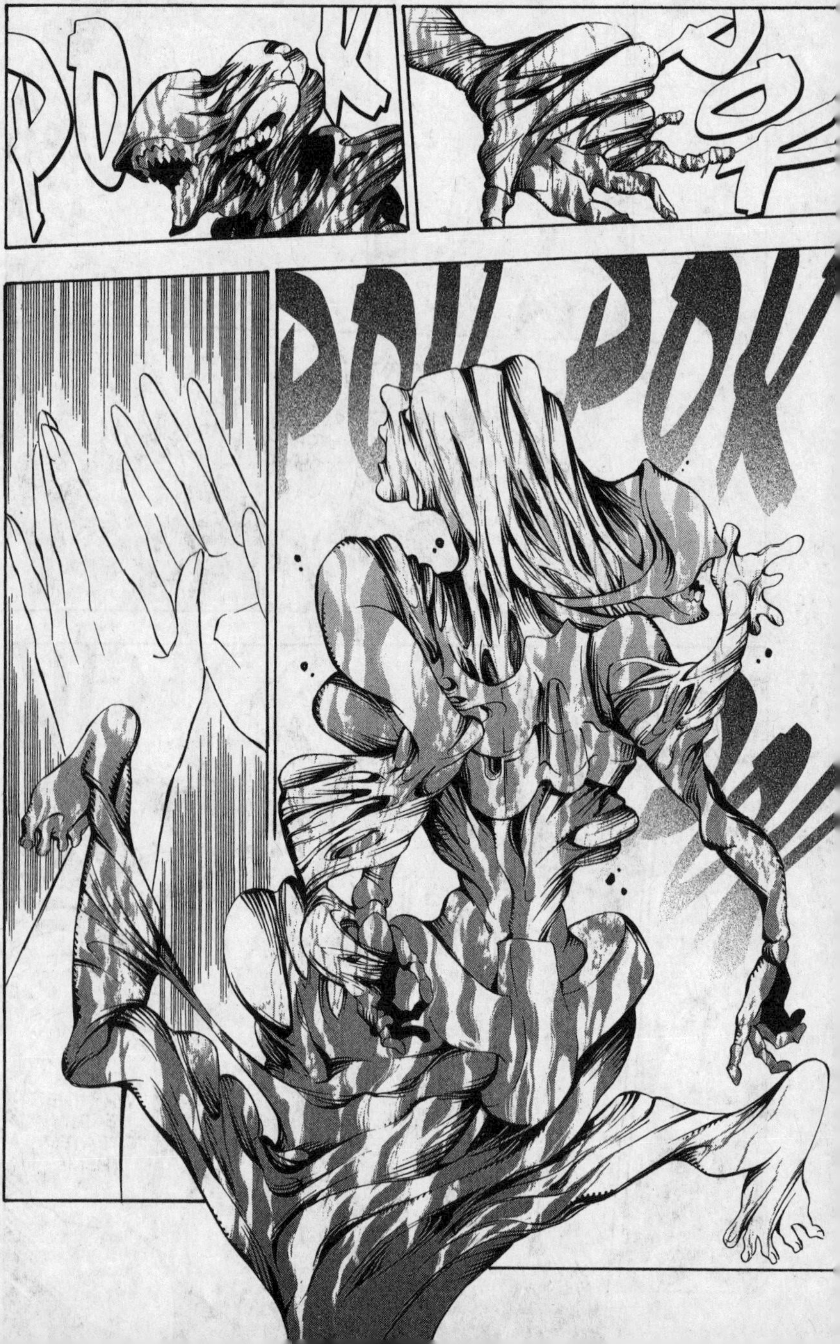
POK
POK
POK POK

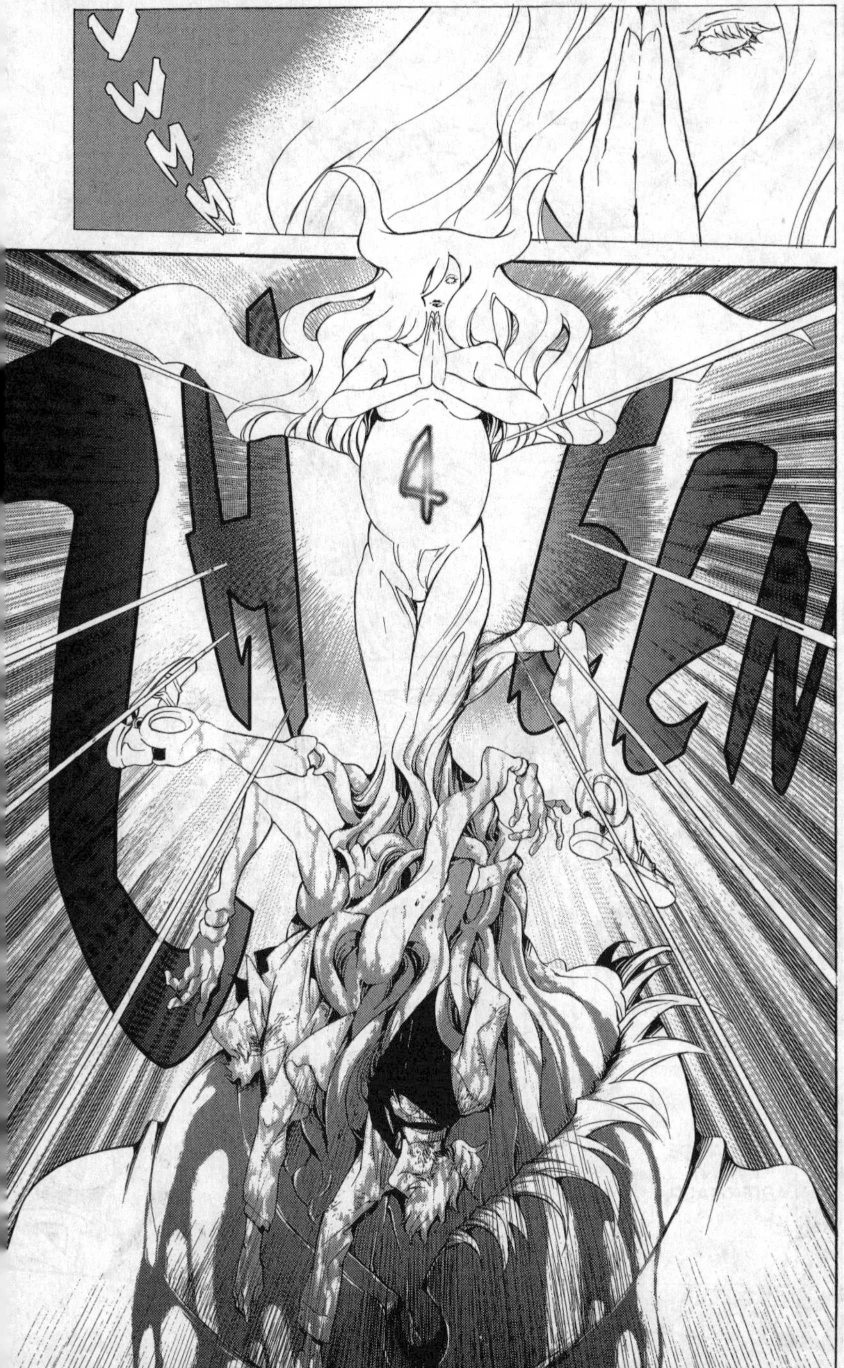
VWMM
CHEN

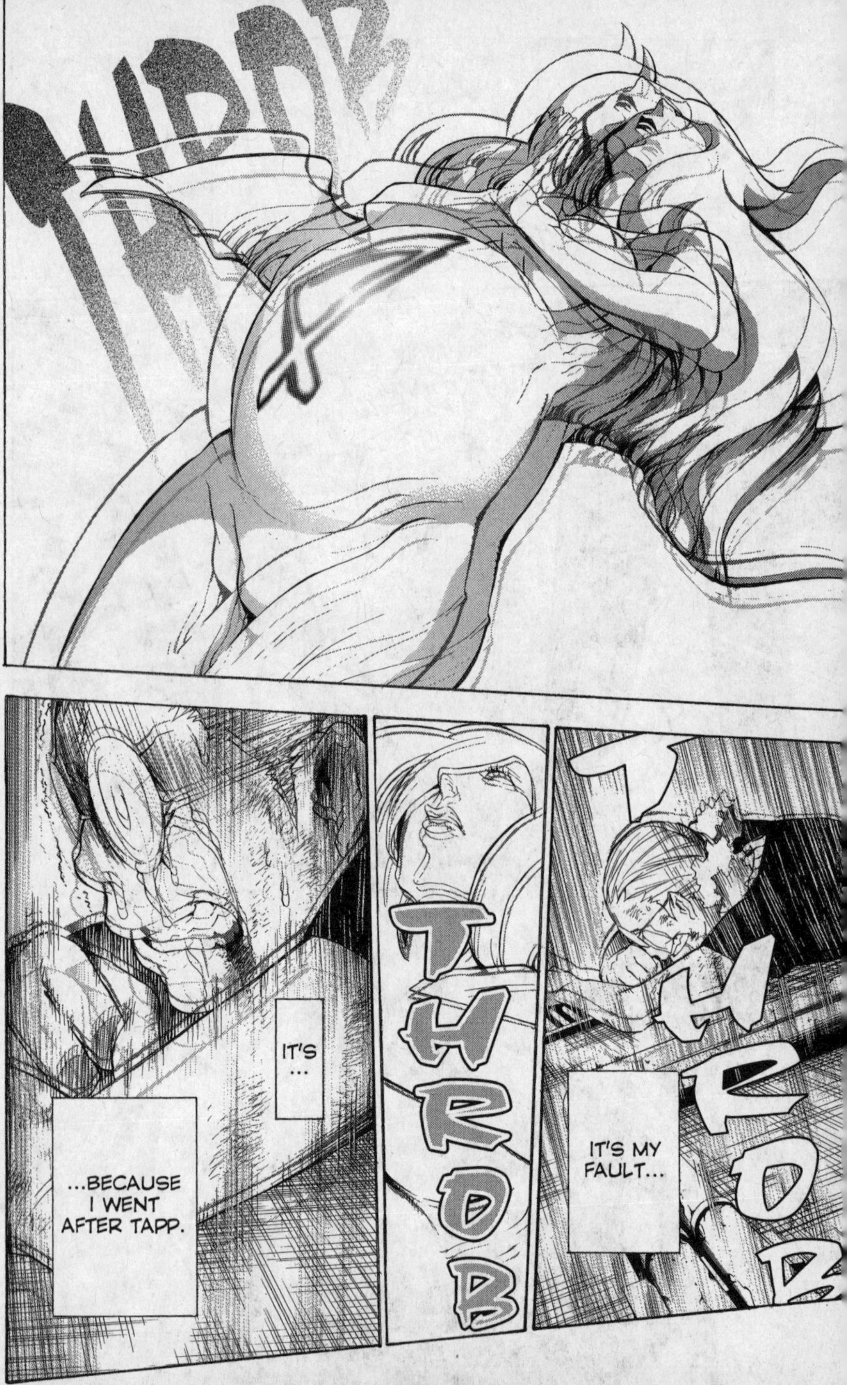
THROB
IT'S MY FAULT...
THROB
IT'S ...
...BECAUSE I WENT AFTER TAPP.

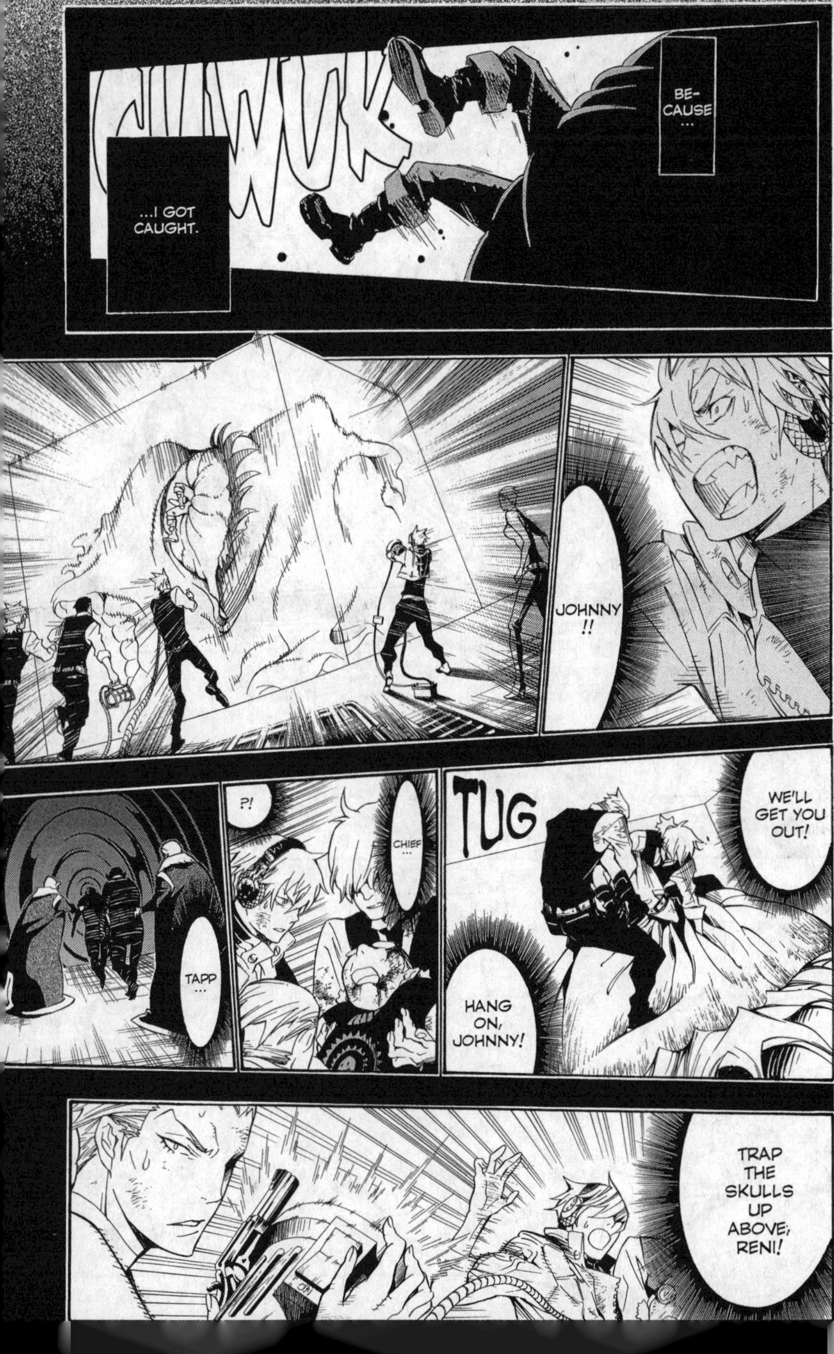
BE-CAUSE...
CHWUK
...I GOT CAUGHT.
JOHNNY!!
WE'LL GET YOU OUT!
TUG
HANG ON, JOHNNY!
CHIEF...
?!
TAPP...
TRAP THE SKULLS UP ABOVE, RENI!

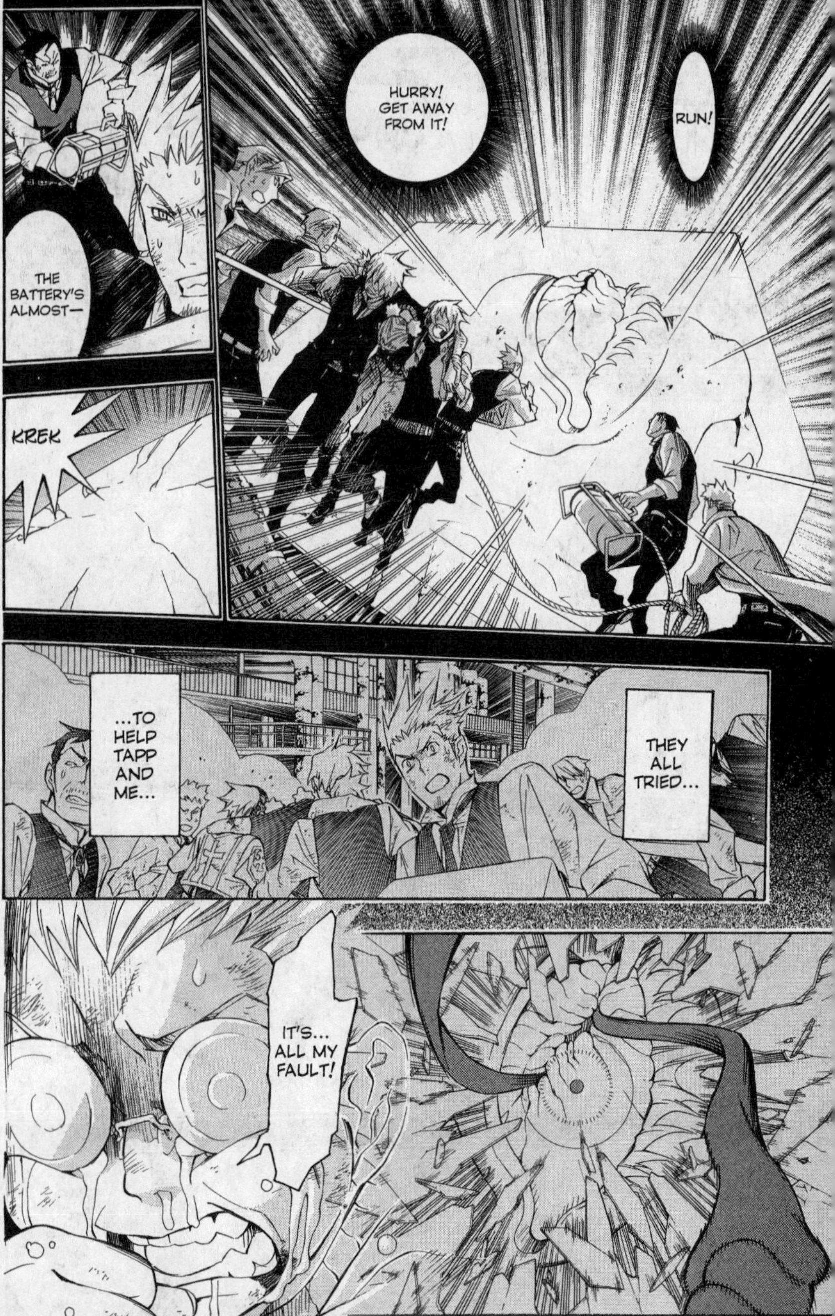
RUN!
HURRY! GET AWAY FROM IT!
THE BATTERY'S ALMOST—
KREK
THEY ALL TRIED...
...TO HELP TAPP AND ME...
IT'S... ALL MY FAULT!

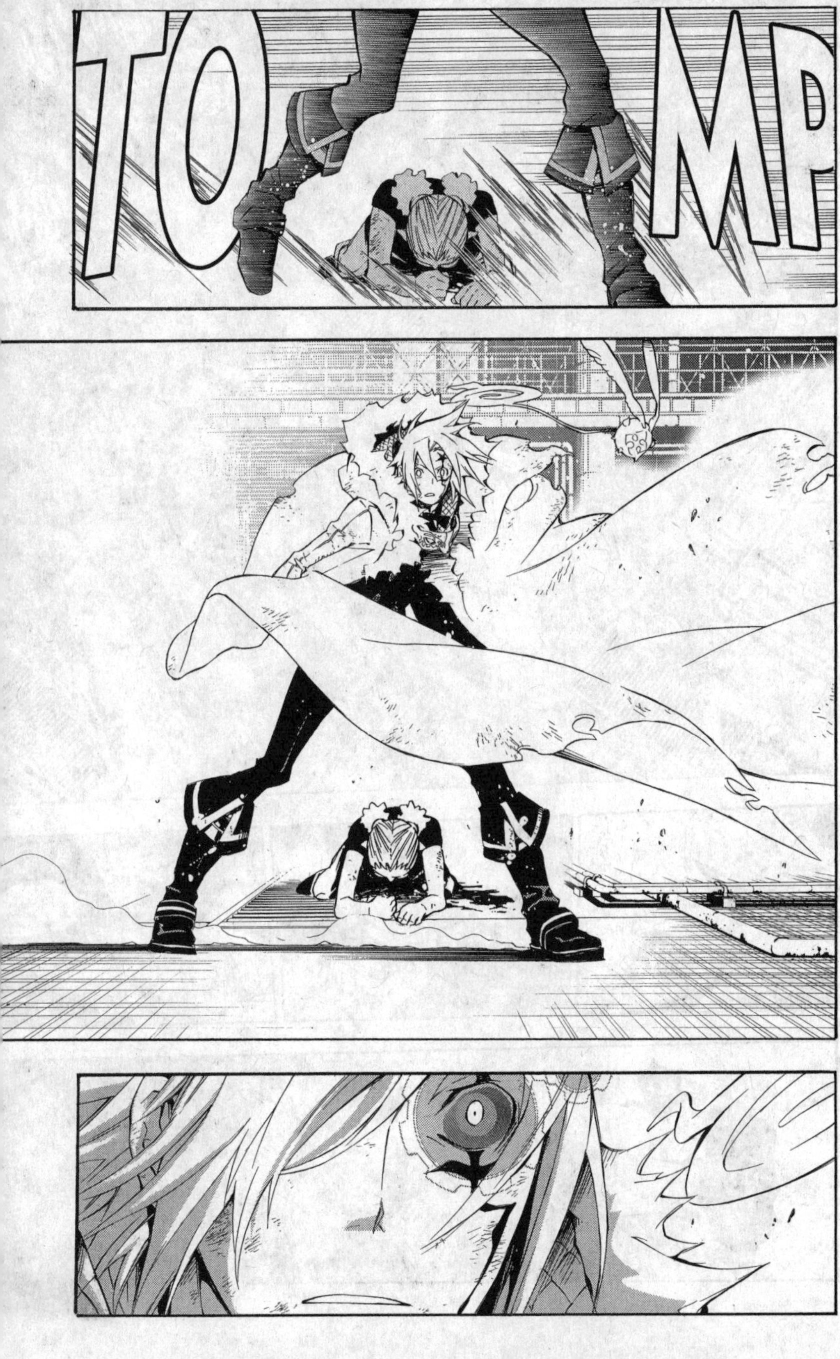
TOMP

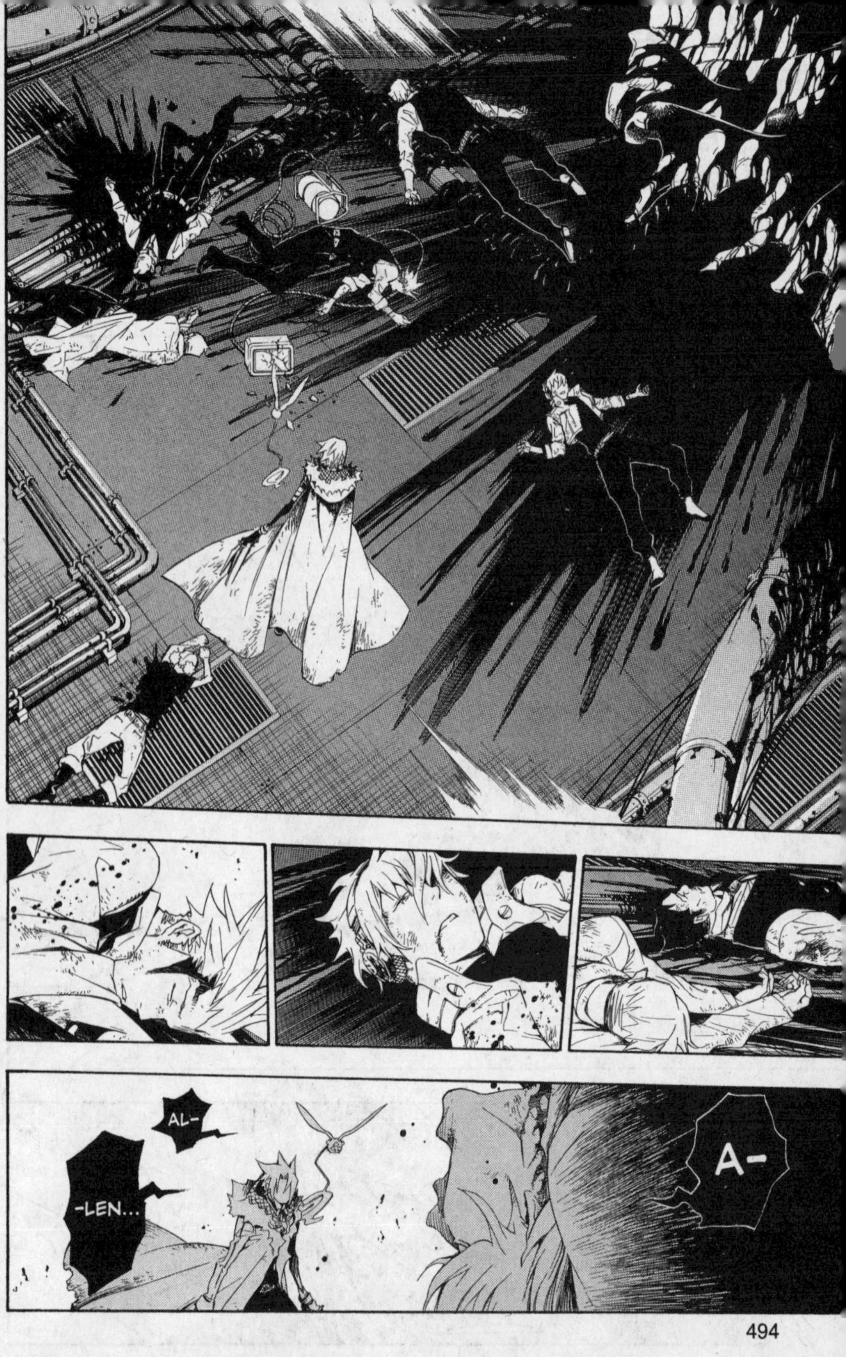
A-
AL-
-LEN...

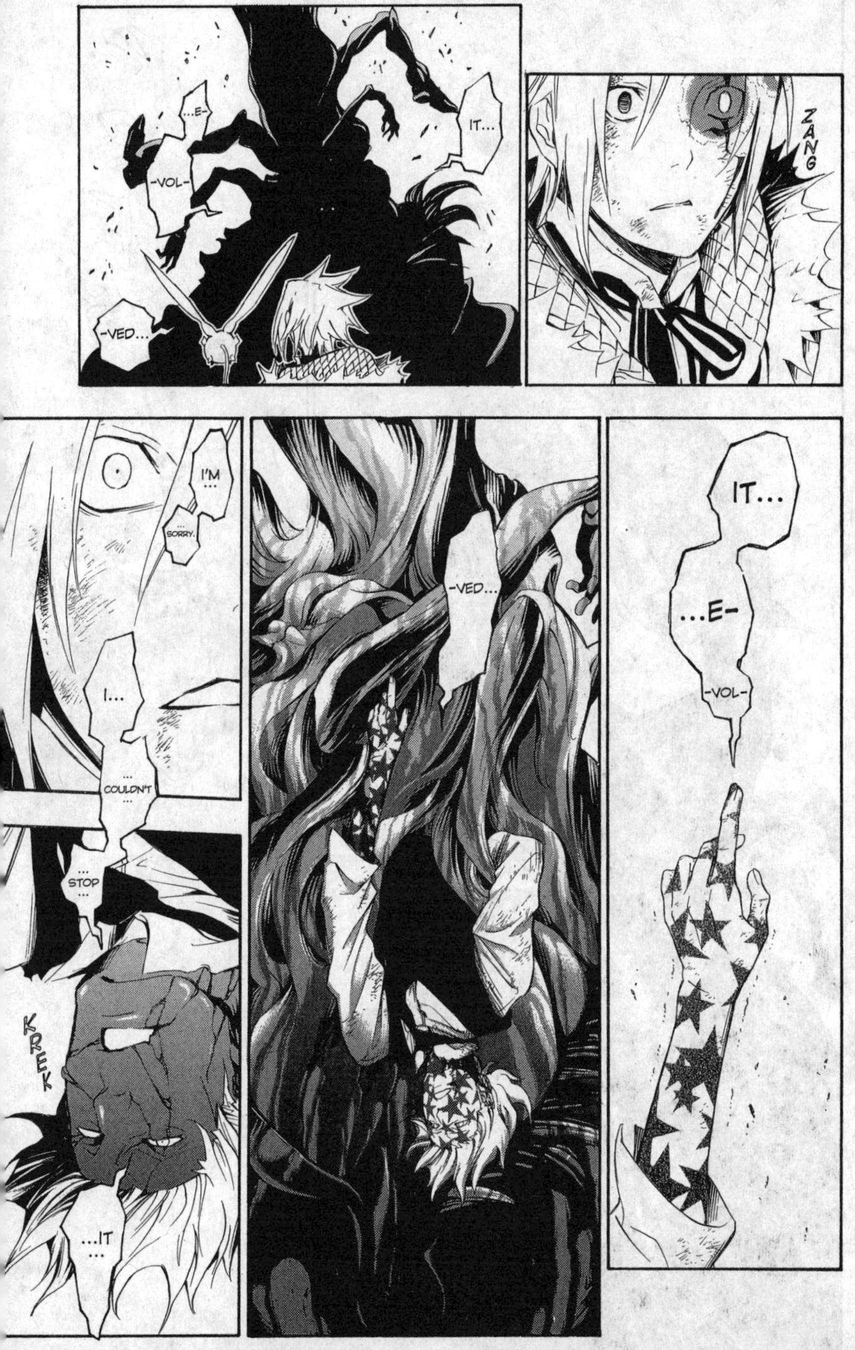
ZANG
IT...
...E-
-VOL-
-VED...
IT...
...E-
-VOL-
-VED...
I'M ...
... SORRY.
I...
... COULDN'T ...
... STOP ...
KREK
...IT ...

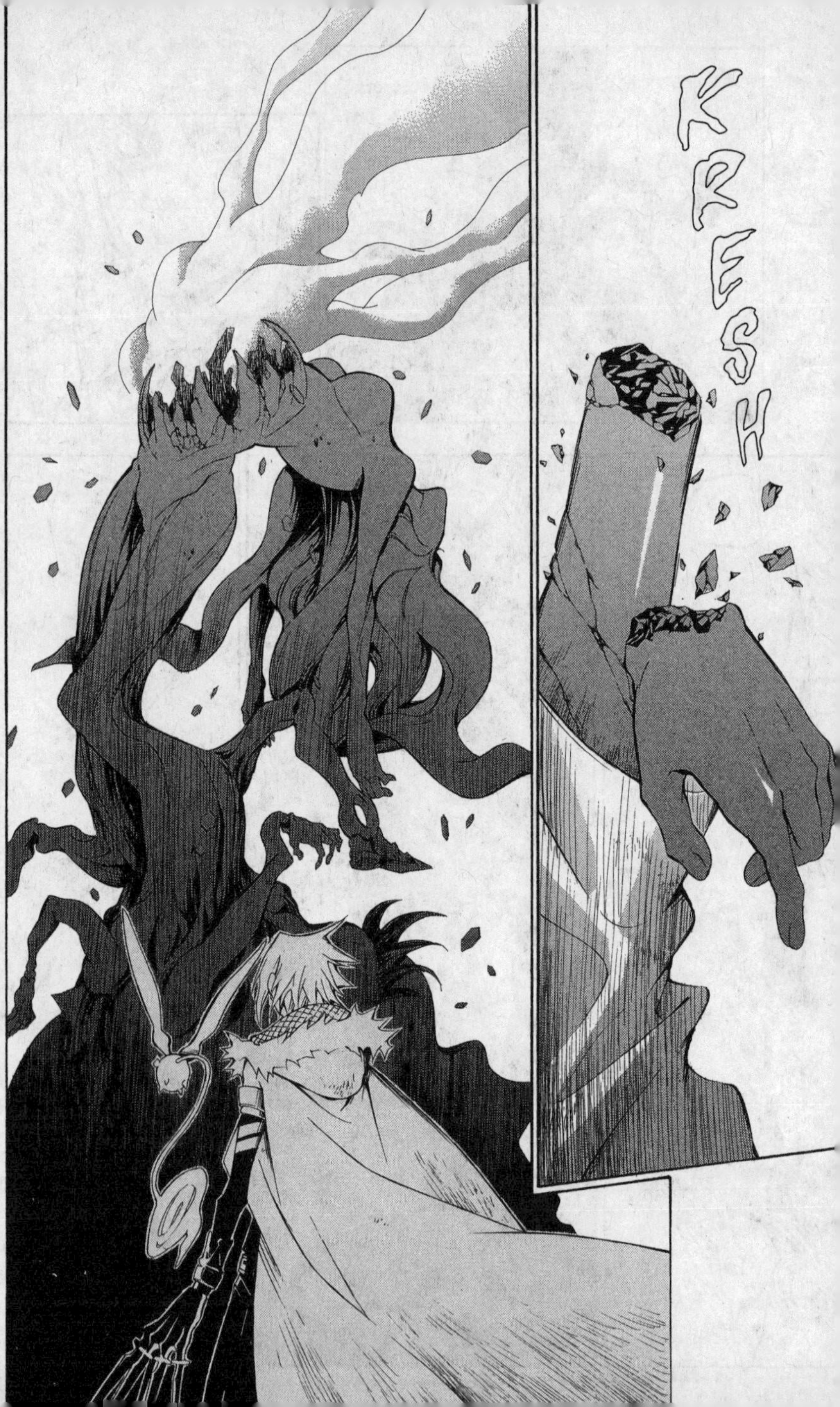
KRESH

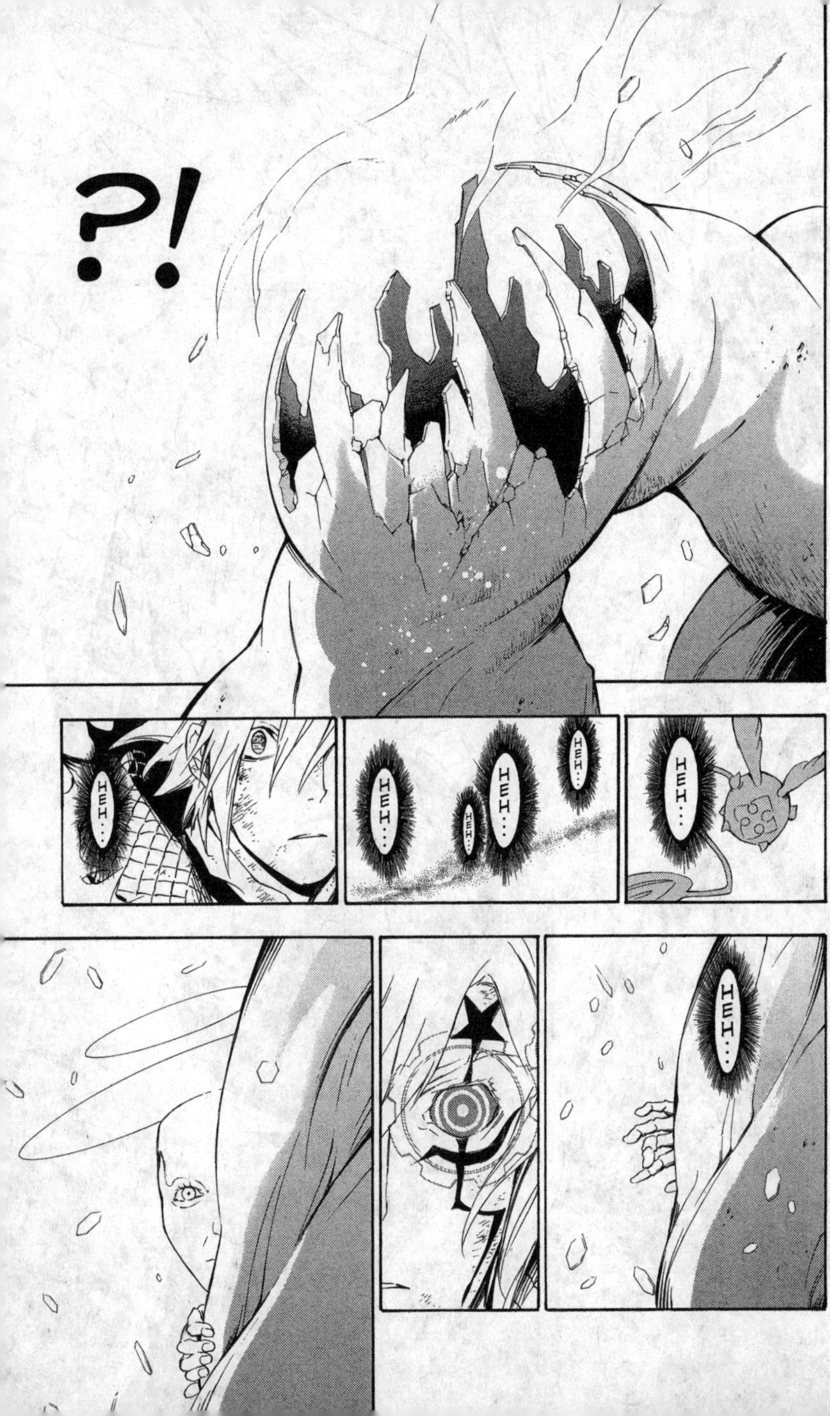
?!
HEH...
HEH...
HEH...
HEH...
HEH...
HEH...
HEH...

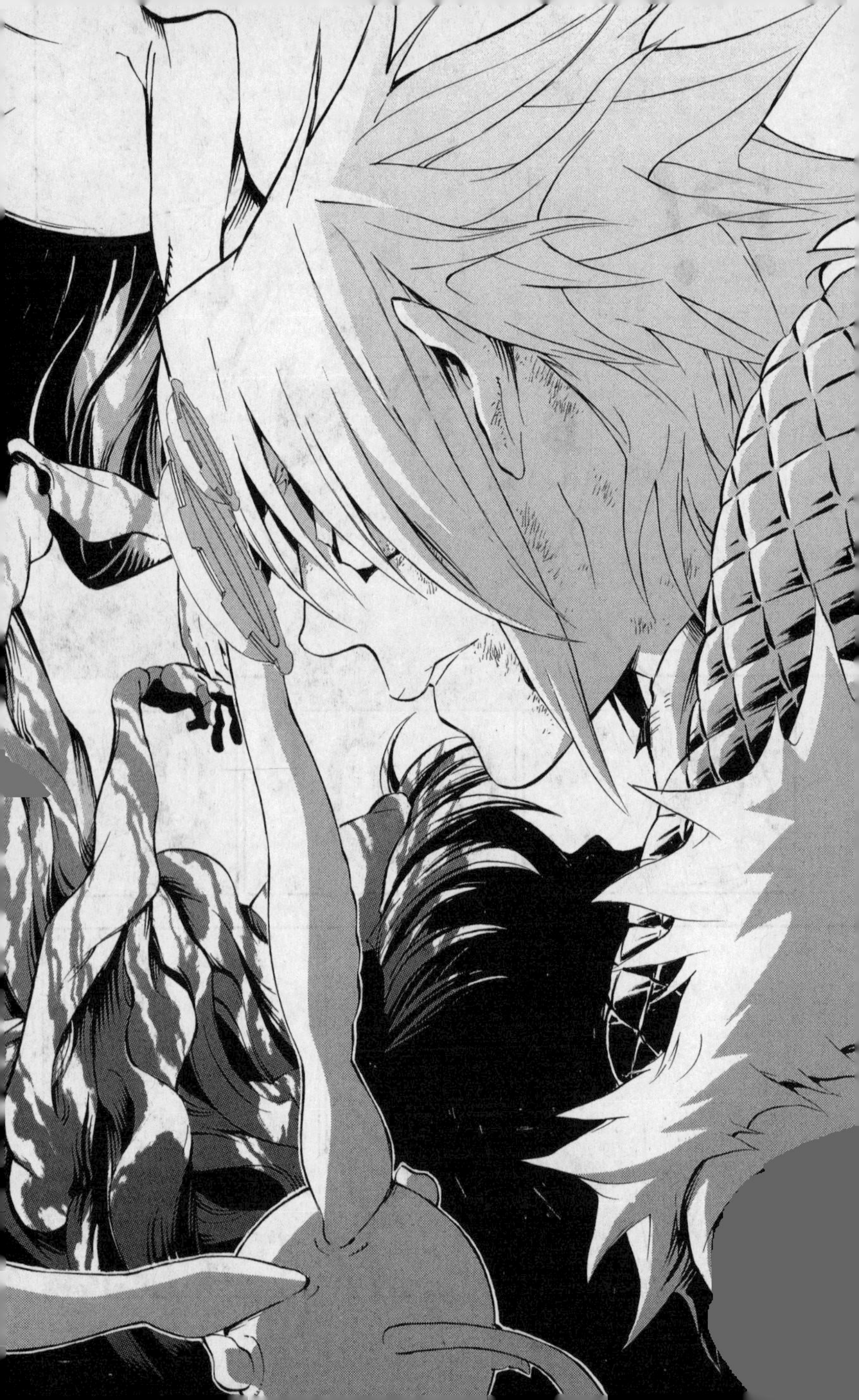

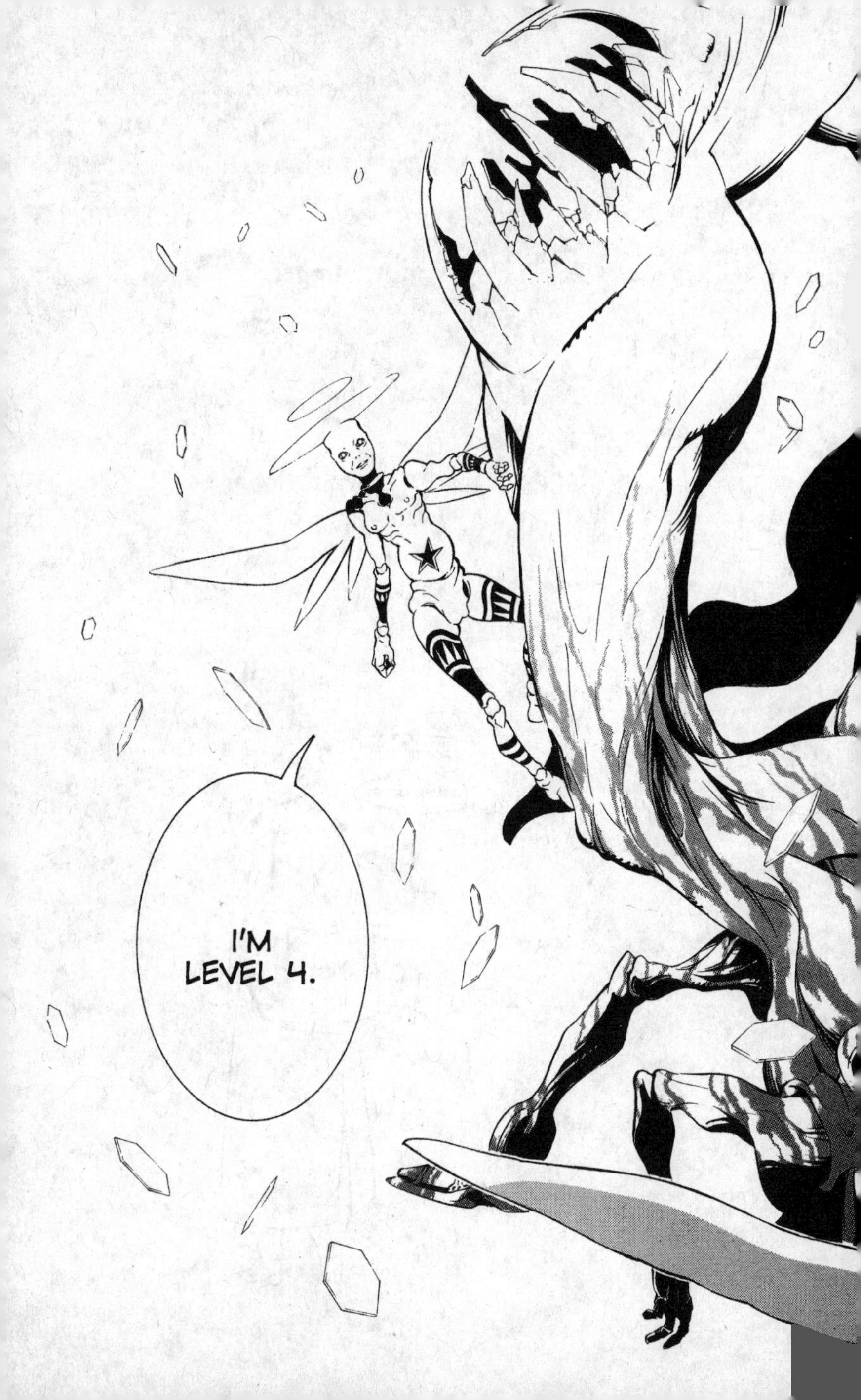
I'M LEVEL 4.

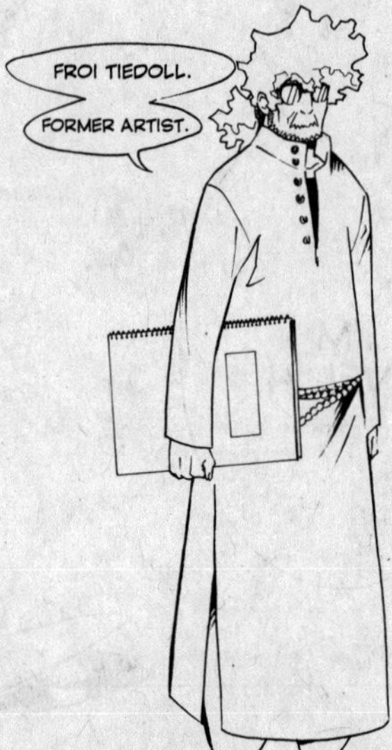
FROI TIEDOLL.
FORMER ARTIST.

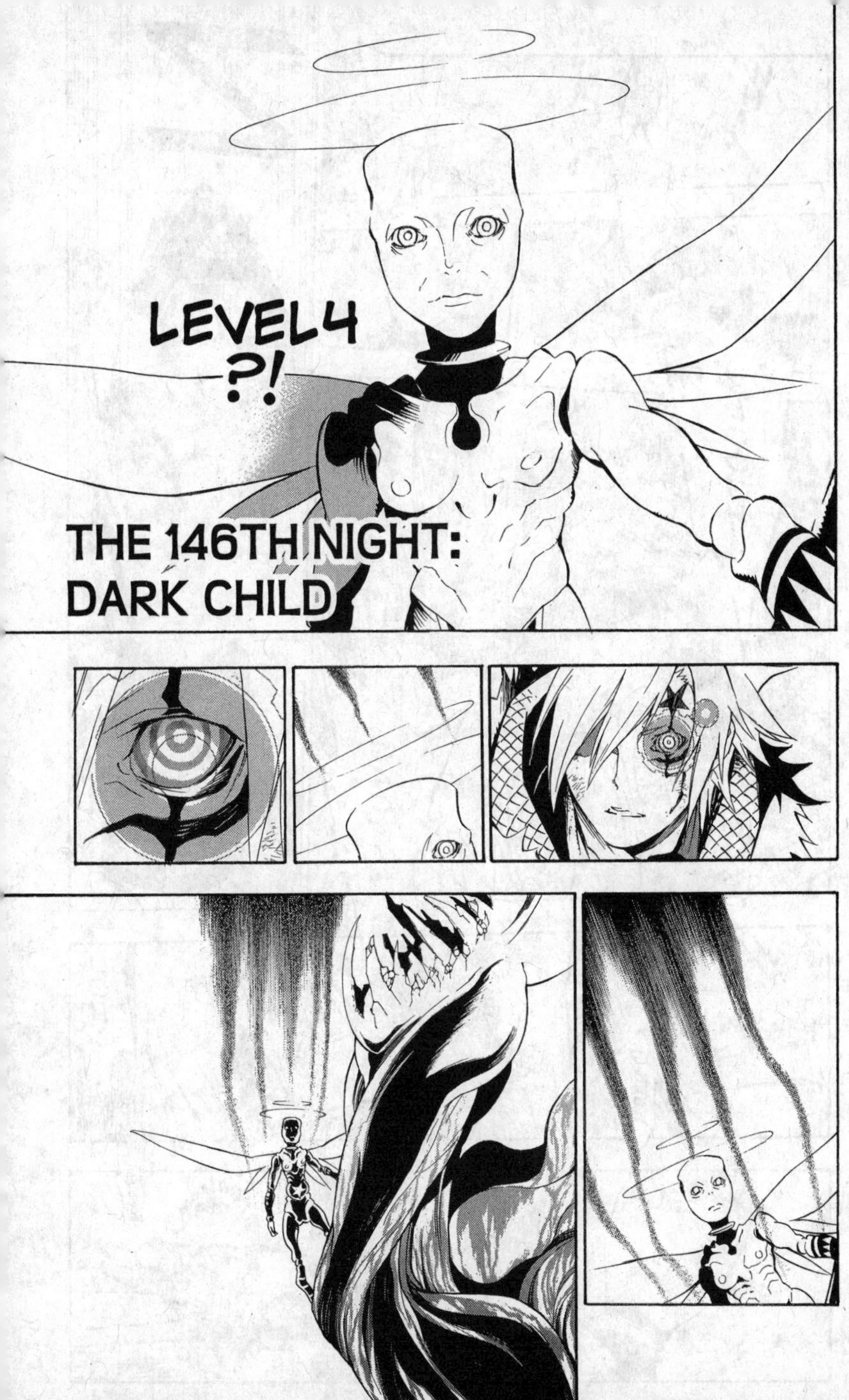
LEVEL 4 ?!
THE 146TH NIGHT: DARK CHILD

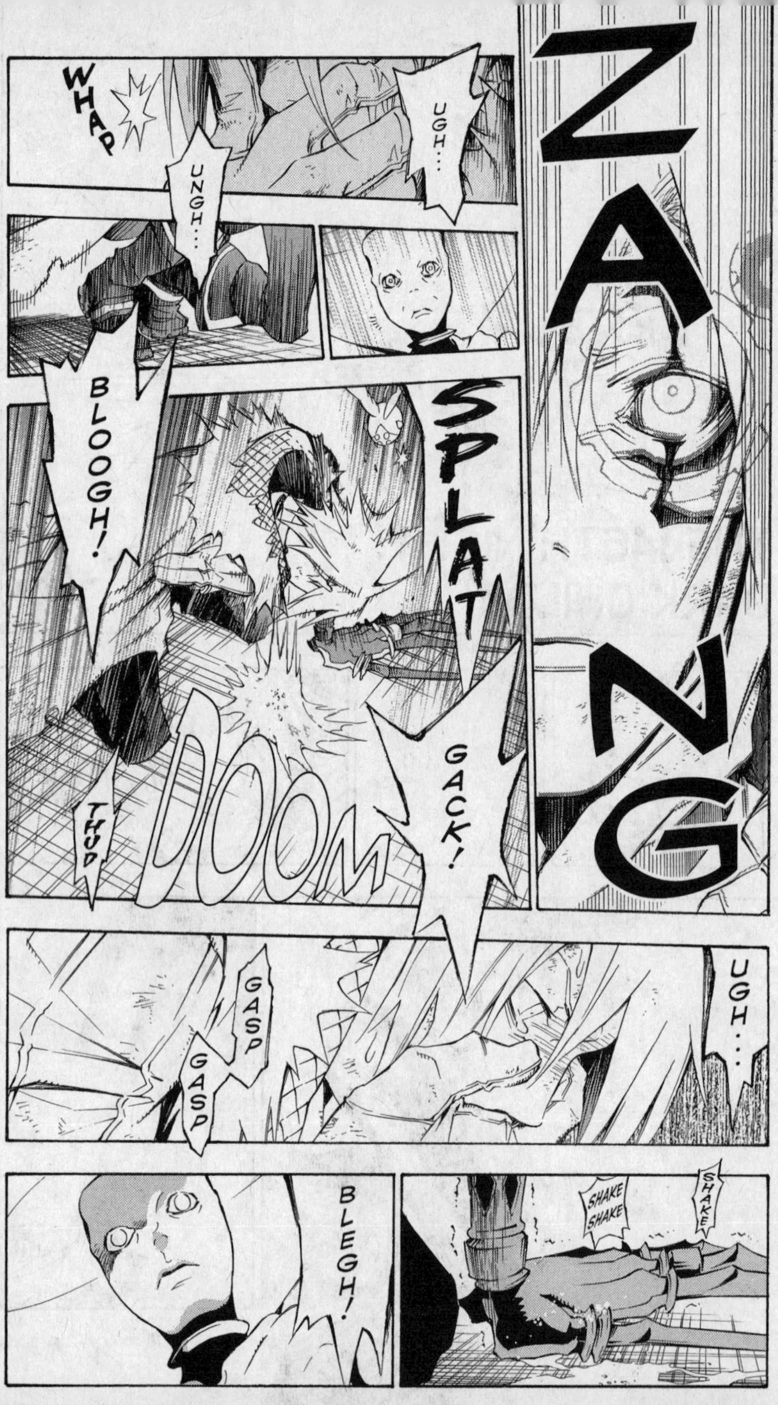
ZANG
UGH...
WHAP
UNGH...
SPLAT
BLOOGH!
GACK!
DOOM
THUD
UGH...
GASP
GASP
SHAKE
SHAKE
SHAKE
BLEGH!

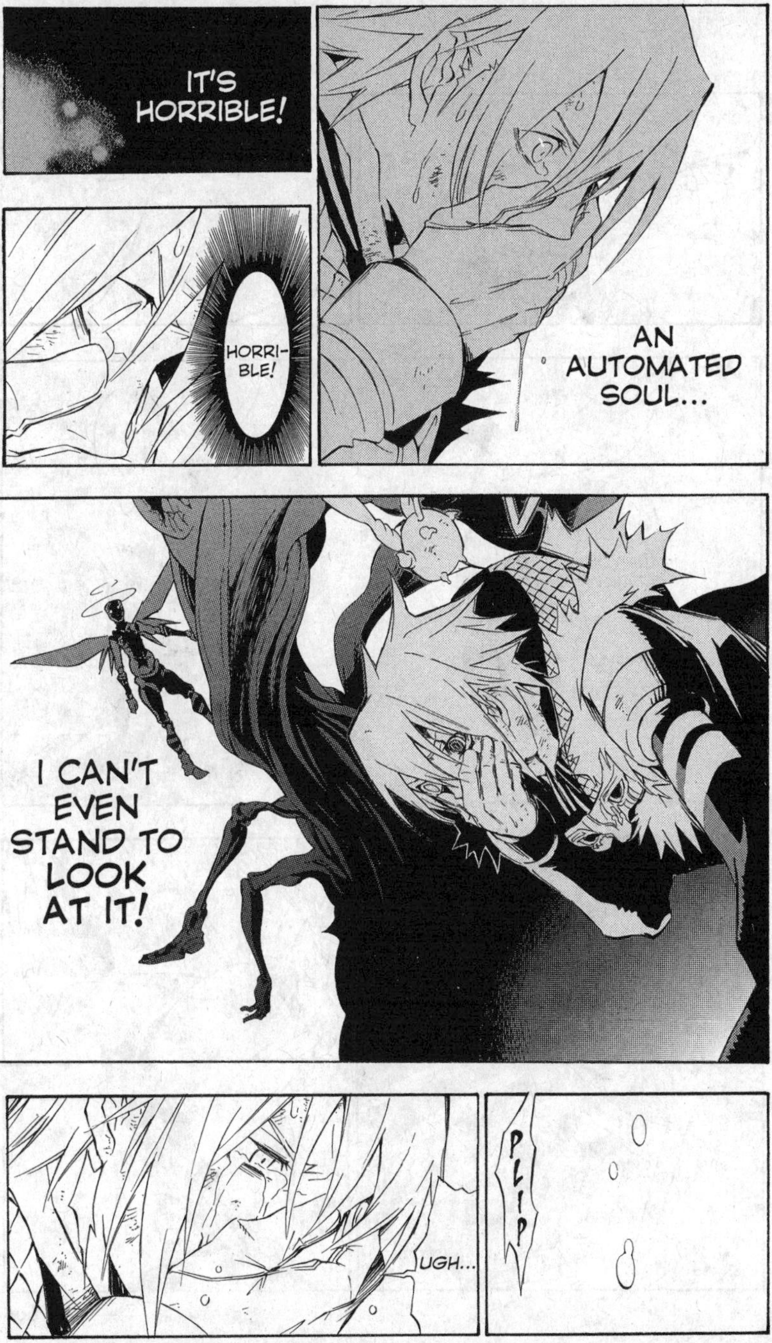
AN AUTOMATED SOUL...
IT'S HORRIBLE!
HORRI-BLE!
I CAN'T EVEN STAND TO LOOK AT IT!
PLIP
UGH...

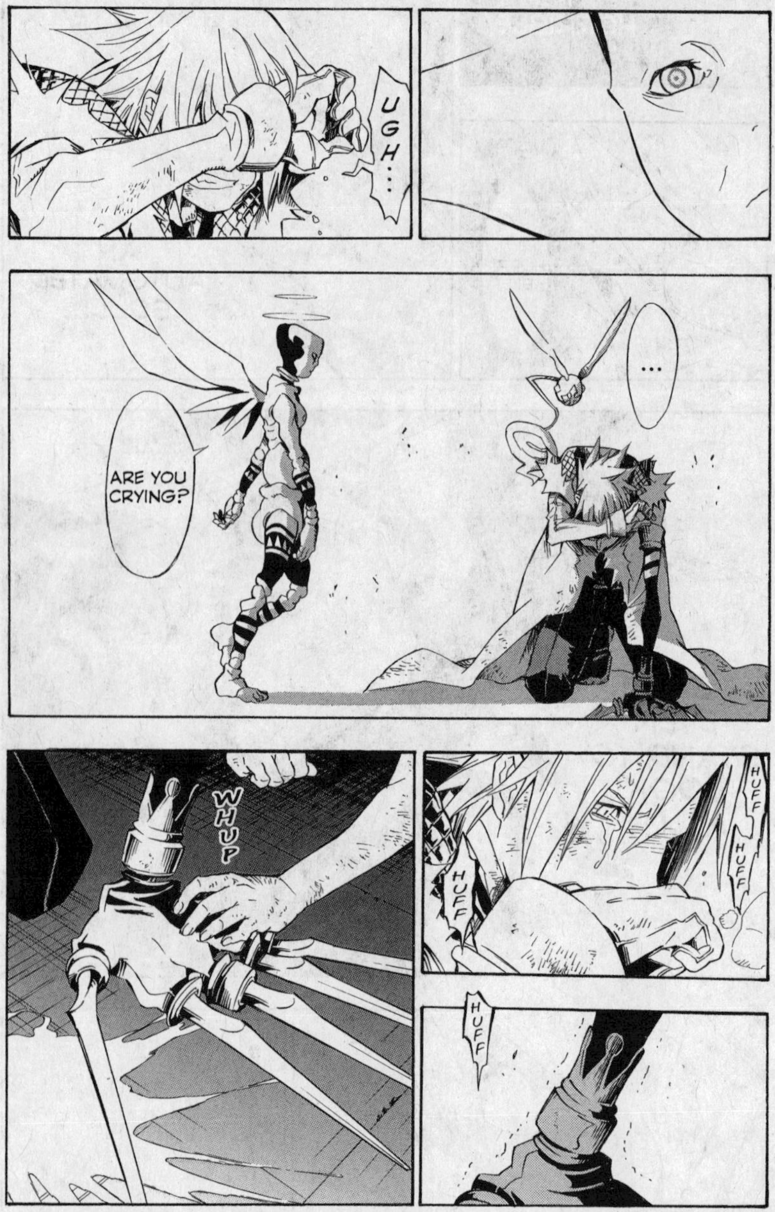
UGH...
...
ARE YOU CRYING?
HUFF
HUFF
HUFF
HUFF
WHUP

READ THIS WAY

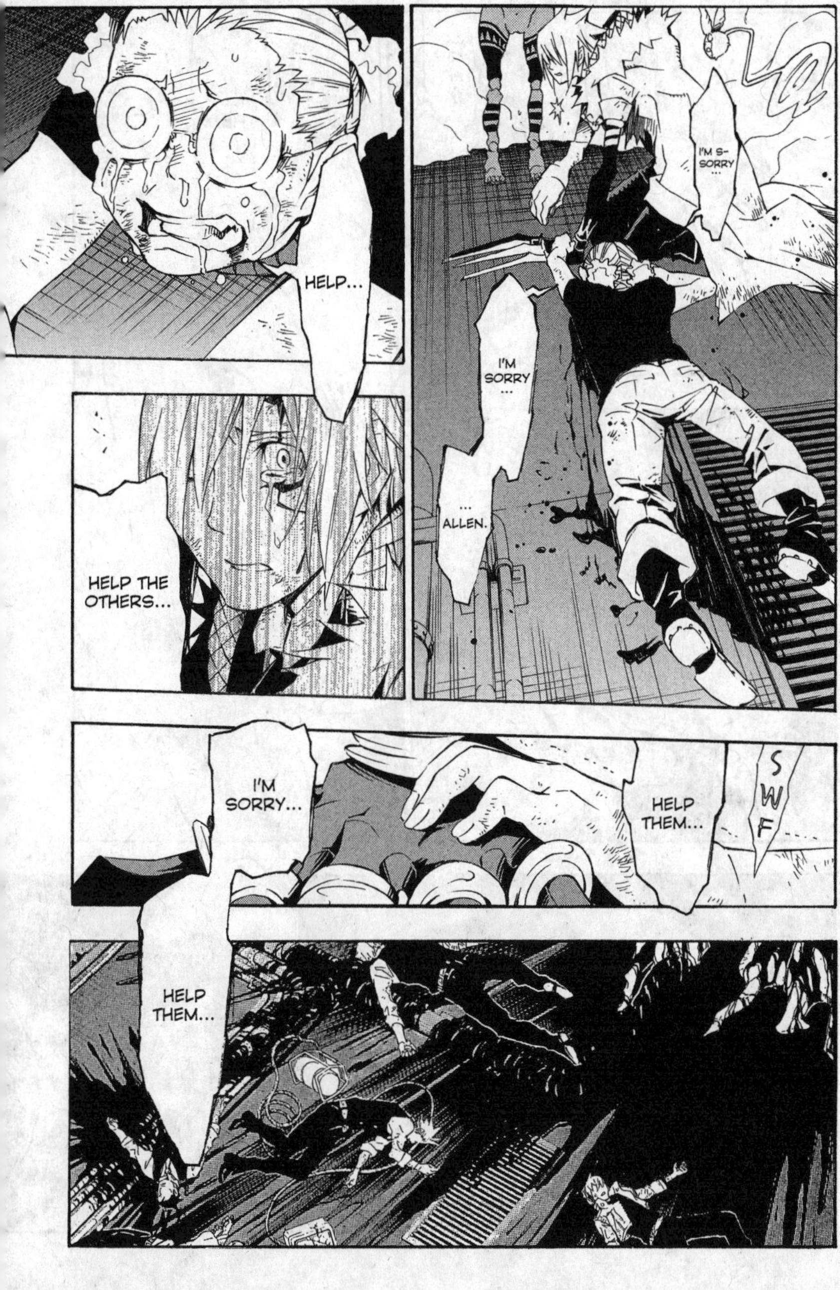

I'M S-SORRY ...
I'M SORRY ...
... ALLEN.
HELP...
HELP THE OTHERS...
SWF
HELP THEM...
I'M SORRY...
HELP THEM...

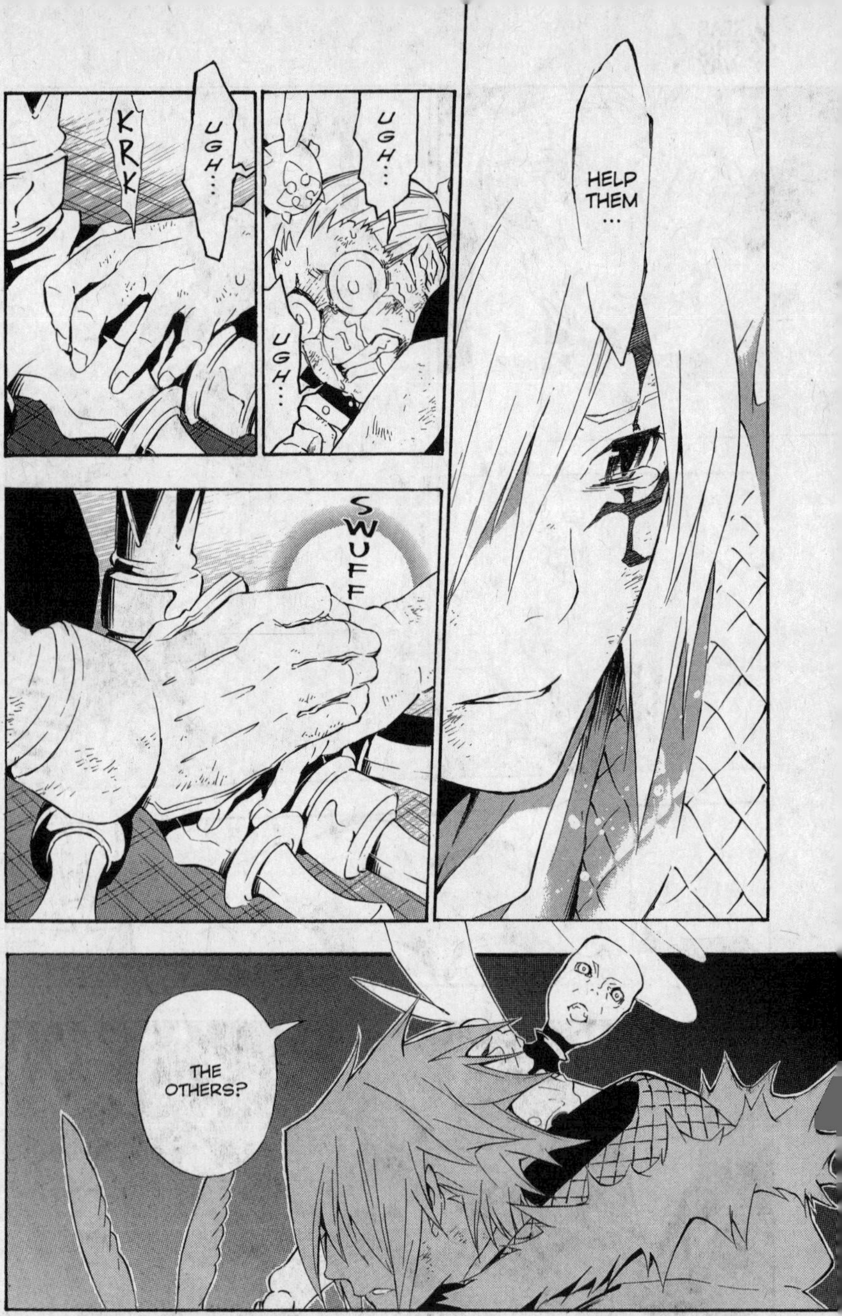
HELP THEM ...
UGH...
UGH...
UGH...
KRK
SWUFF
THE OTHERS?

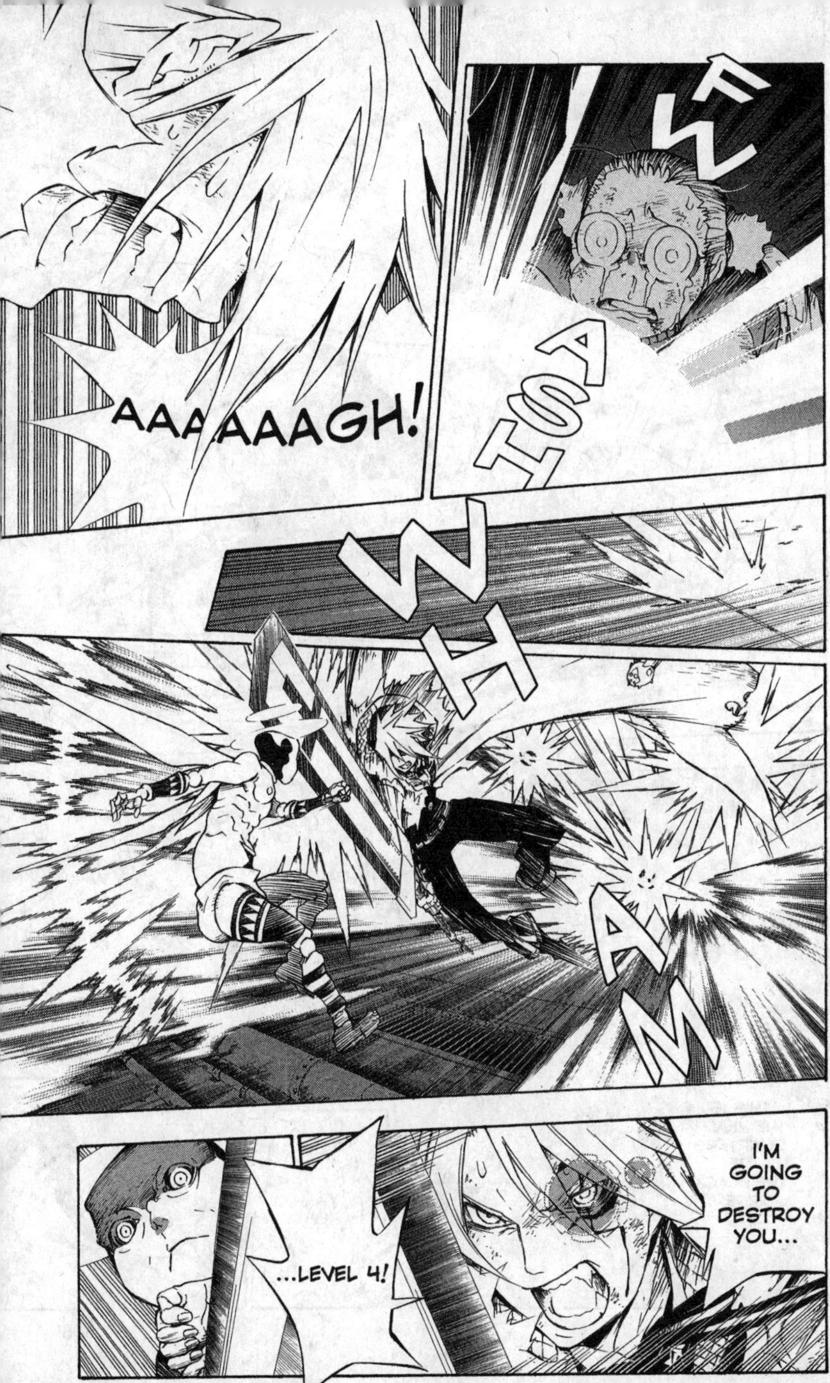
FWASH
AAAAAAAGH!
WHAM
I'M GOING TO DESTROY YOU...
...LEVEL 4!

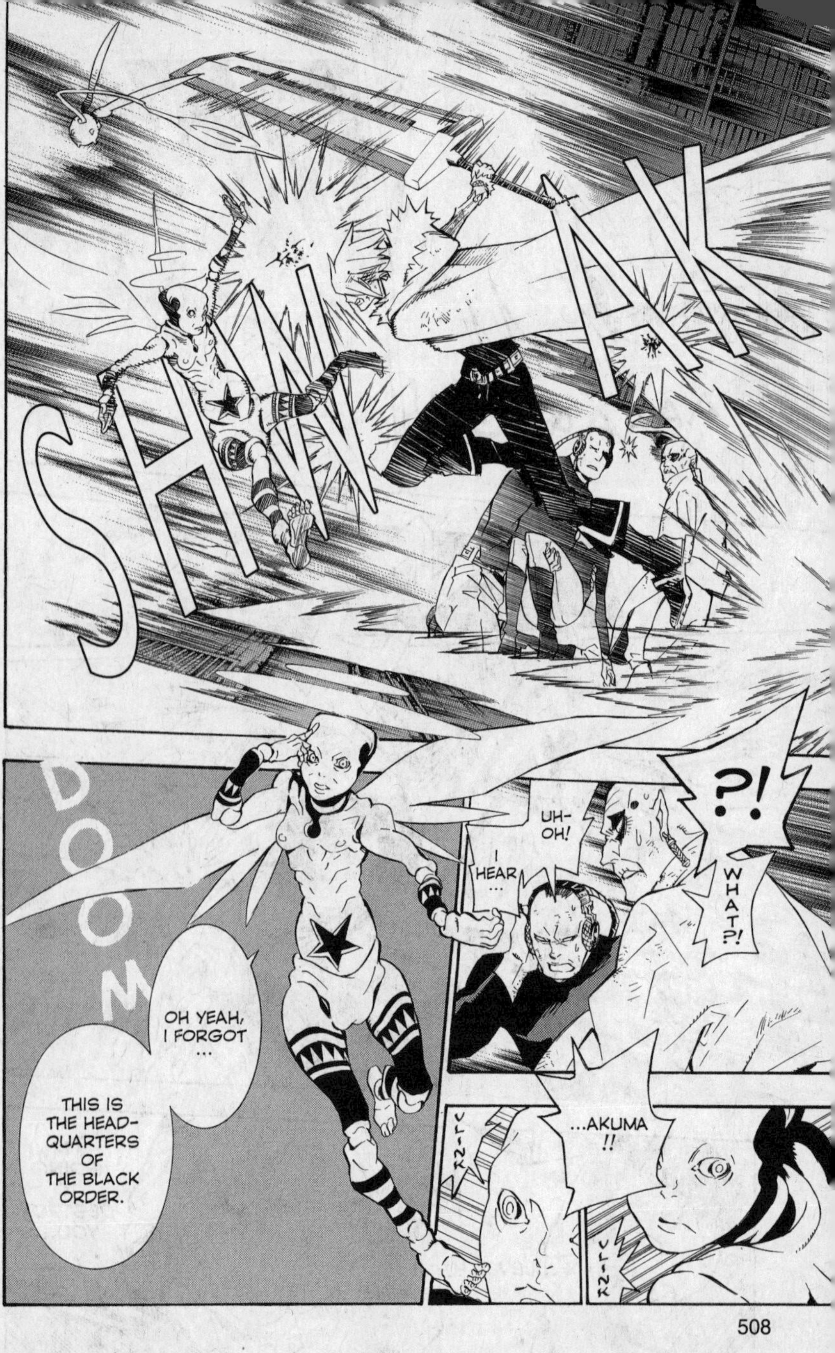
SHWAK
?!
WHAT?!
UH-OH!
I HEAR...
...AKUMA!!
VLINK
VLINK
DOOM
OH YEAH, I FORGOT...
THIS IS THE HEAD-QUARTERS OF THE BLACK ORDER.

READ THIS WAY

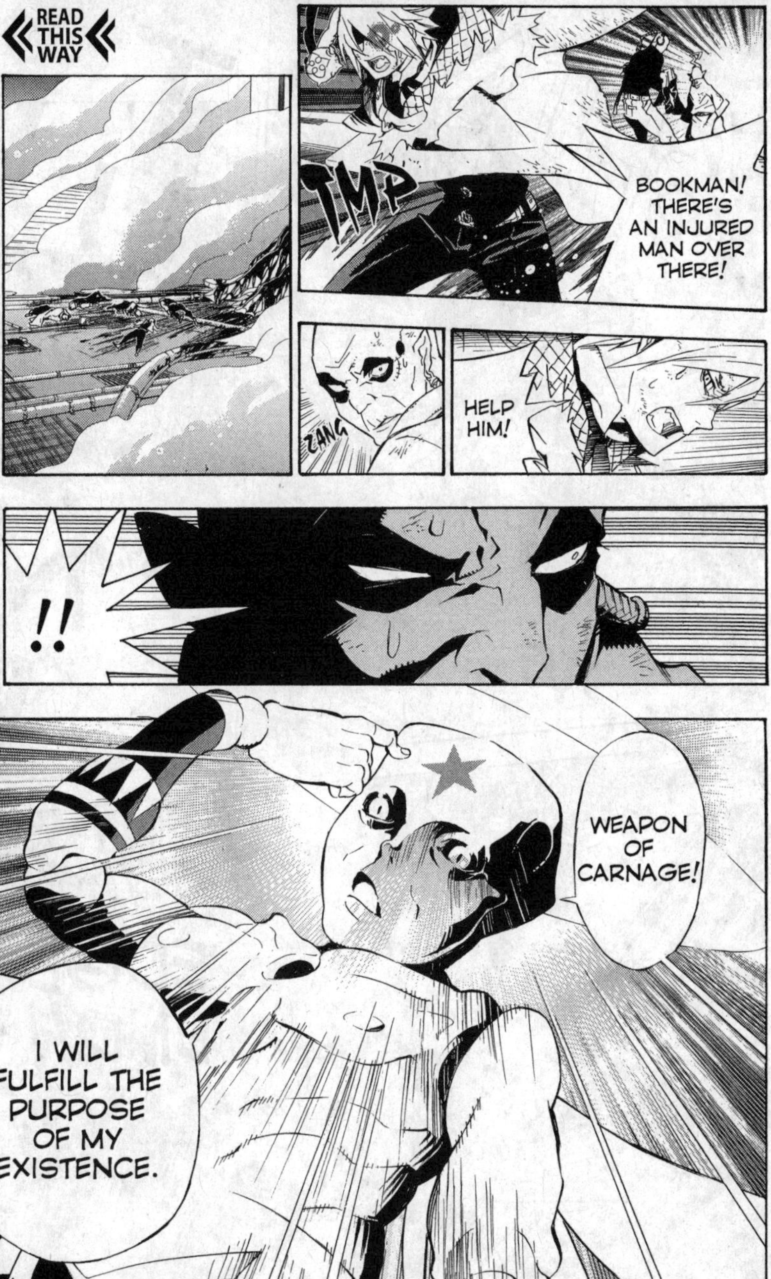
TMP
BOOKMAN! THERE'S AN INJURED MAN OVER THERE!
HELP HIM!
ZANG
!!
WEAPON OF CARNAGE!
I WILL FULFILL THE PURPOSE OF MY EXISTENCE.

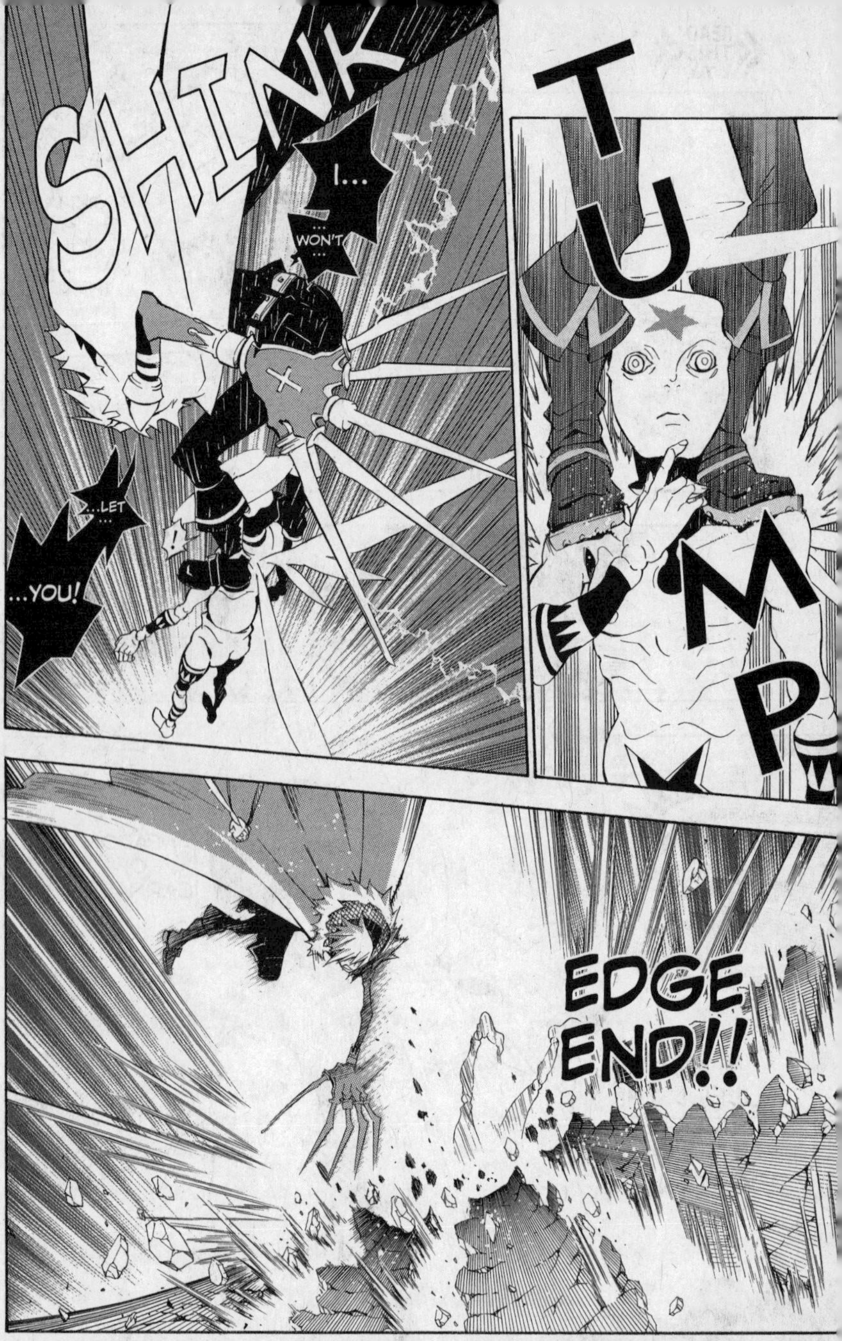
TUMP
SHINK
I...
...WON'T...
!
...LET...
...YOU!
EDGE END!!

?!!

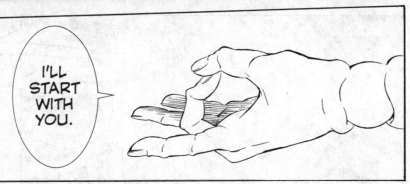

I'LL START WITH YOU.

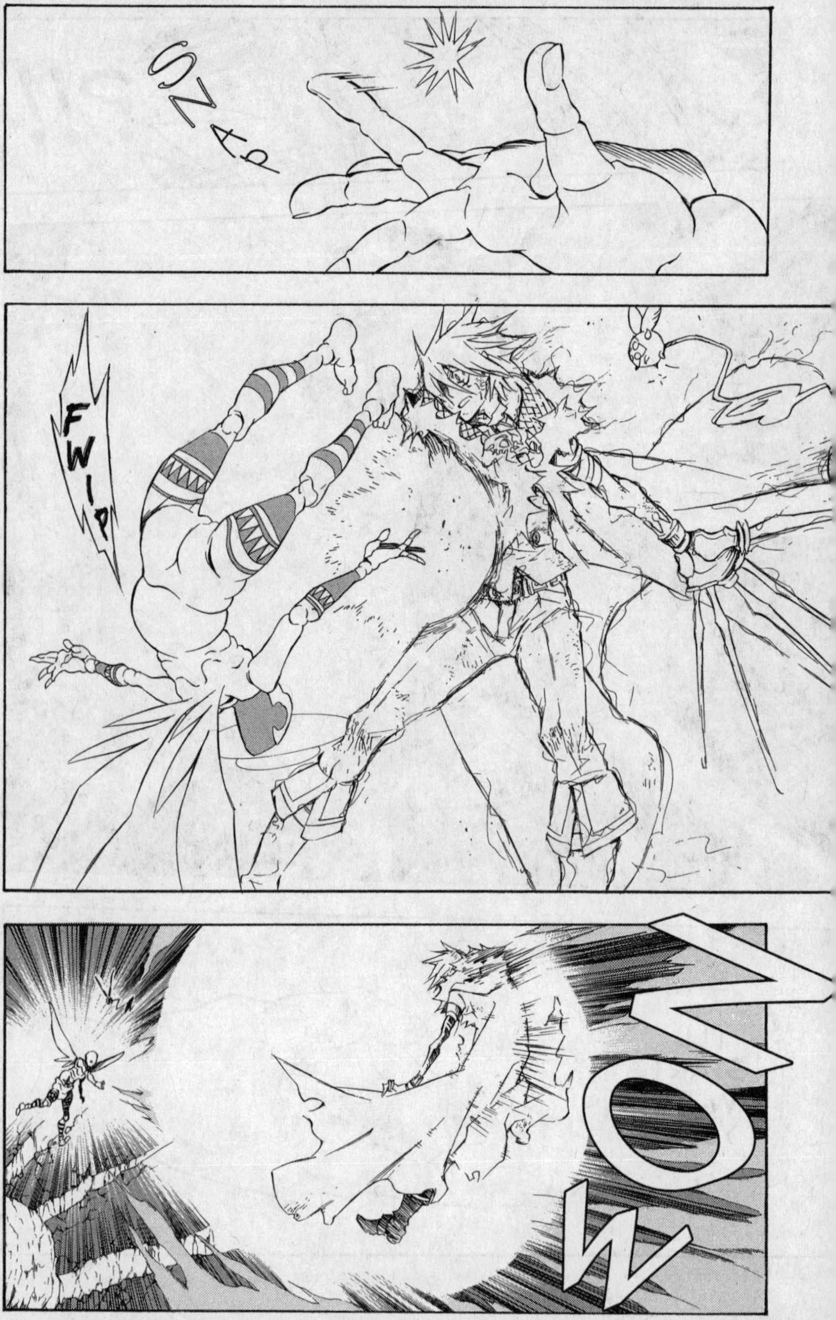
SZAP
FWIP

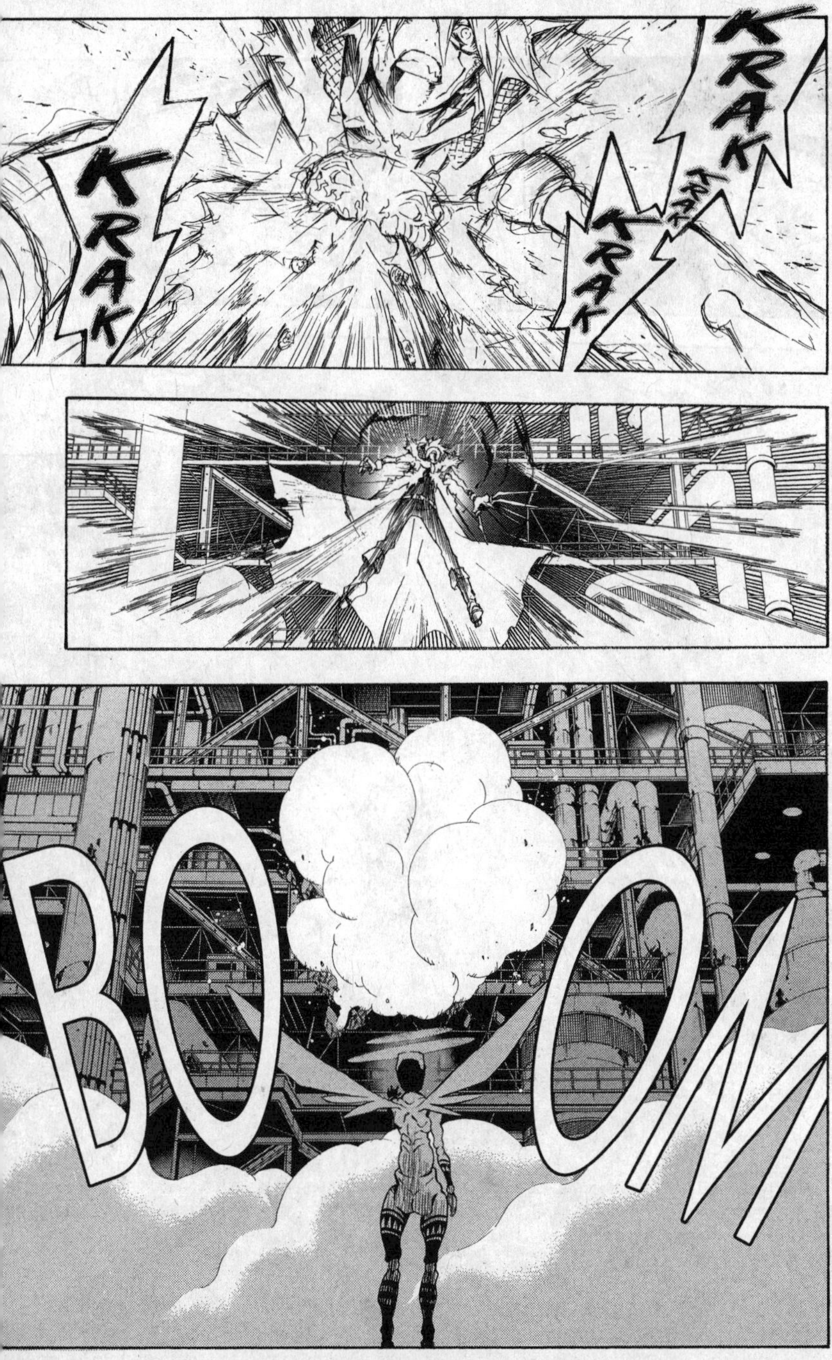
KRAK
KRAK
KRAK
KRAK
BOOM

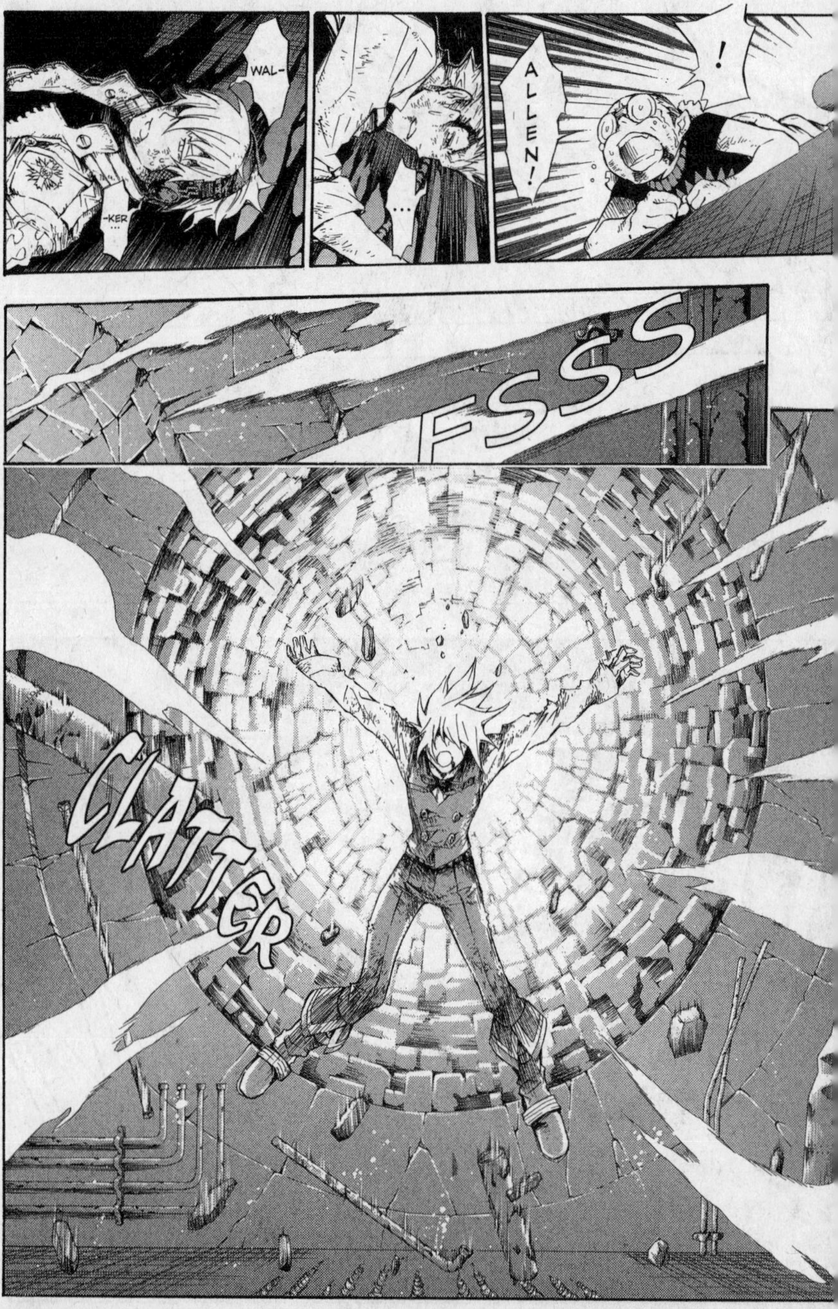
!
ALLEN!
...
WAL-
-KER ...
FSSS
CLATTER

READ THIS WAY

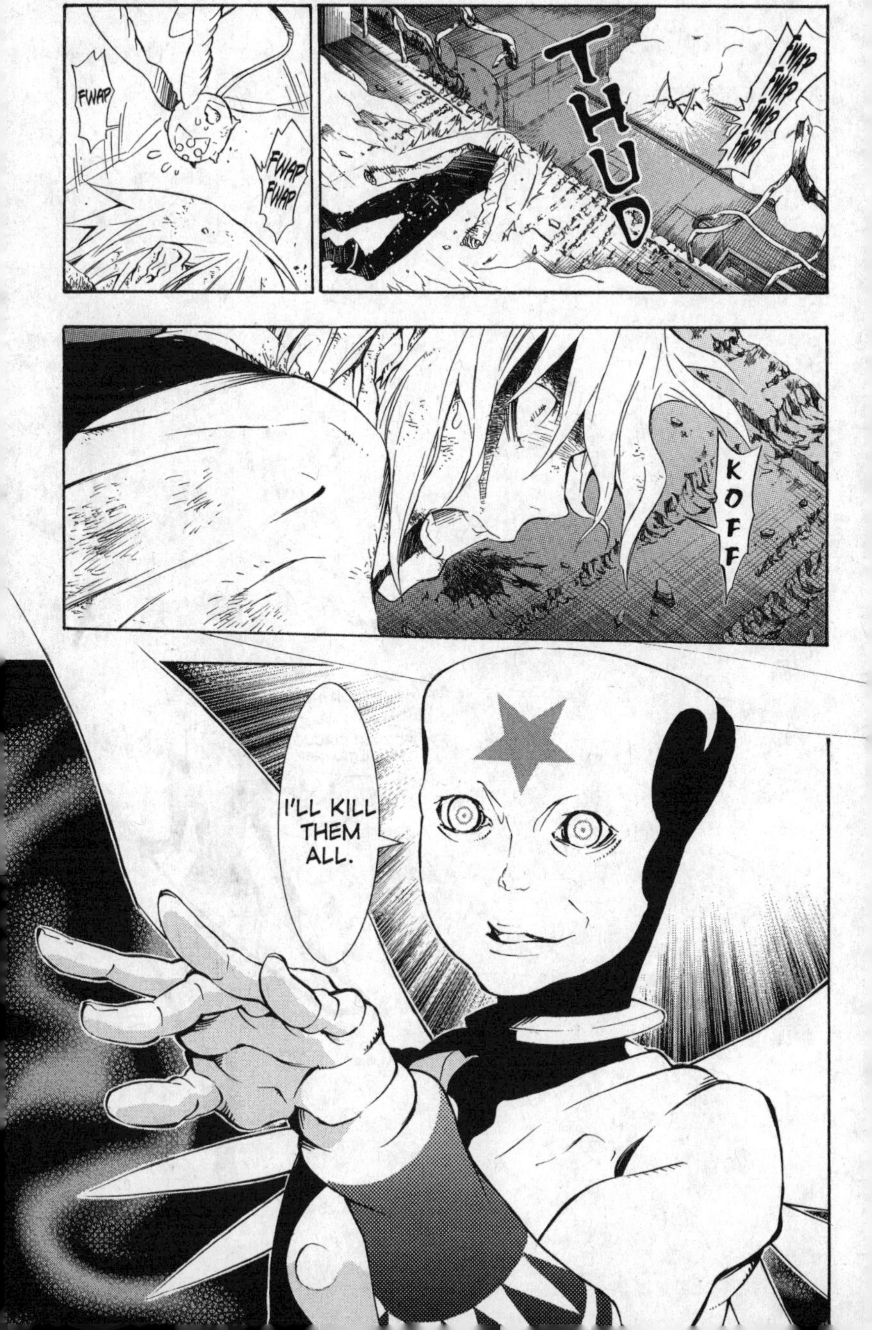
FWIP FWIP FWIP FWIP
THUD
FWAP FWAP
FWAP
KOFF
I'LL KILL THEM ALL.

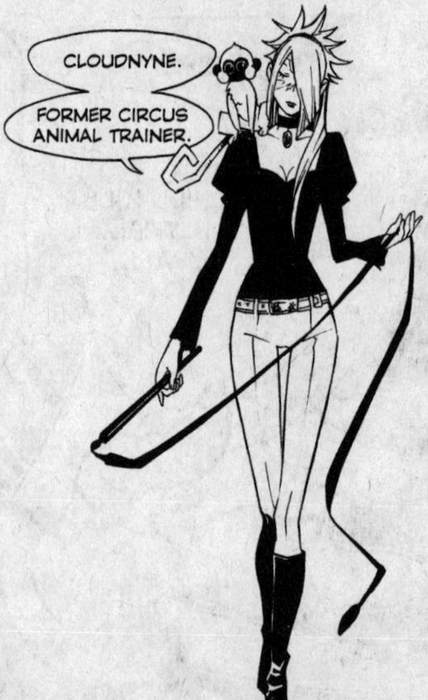
CLOUDNYNE.
FORMER CIRCUS ANIMAL TRAINER.

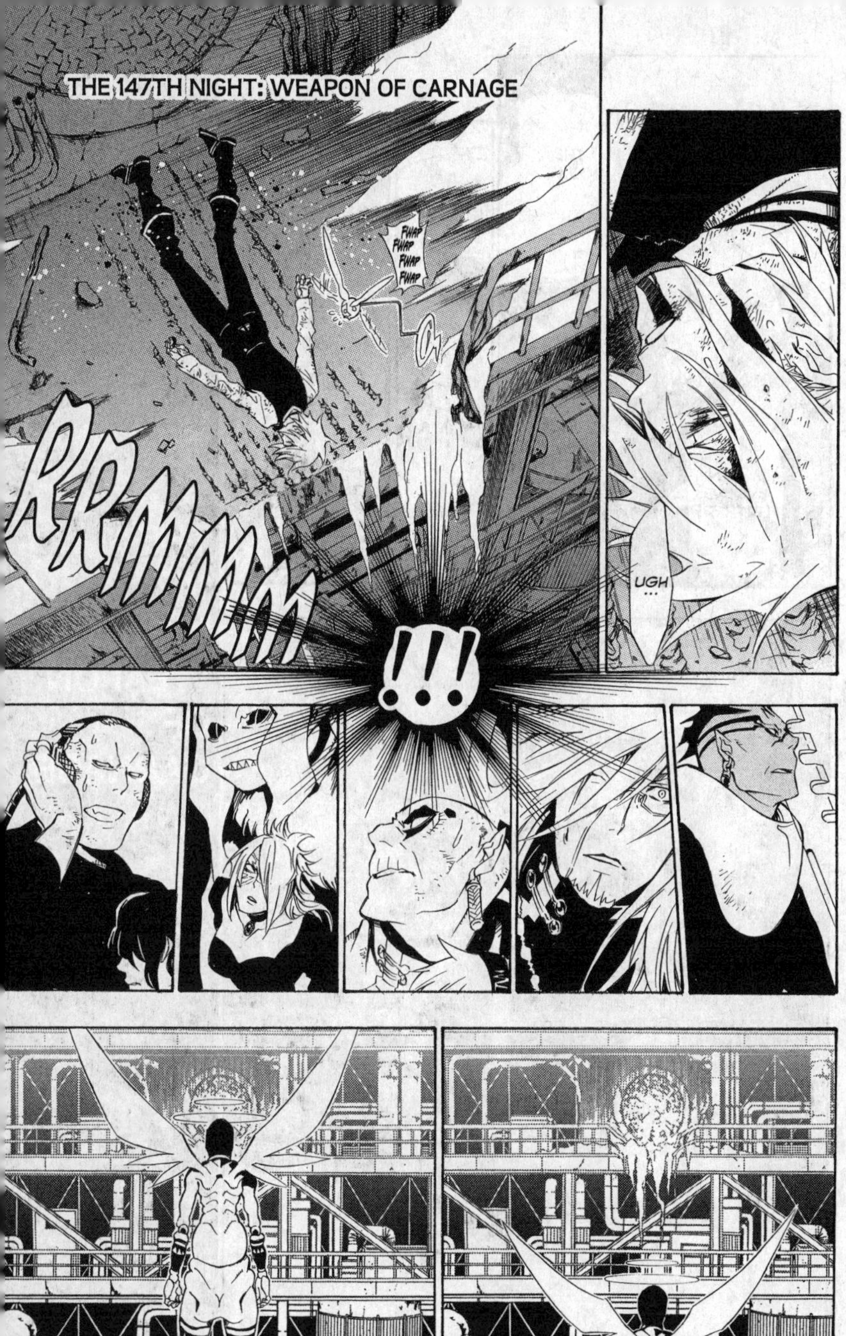
THE 147TH NIGHT: WEAPON OF CARNAGE
UGH...
FWAP FWAP FWAP FWAP
RRMMMM
!!!

THE 147TH NIGHT: WEAPON OF CARNAGE

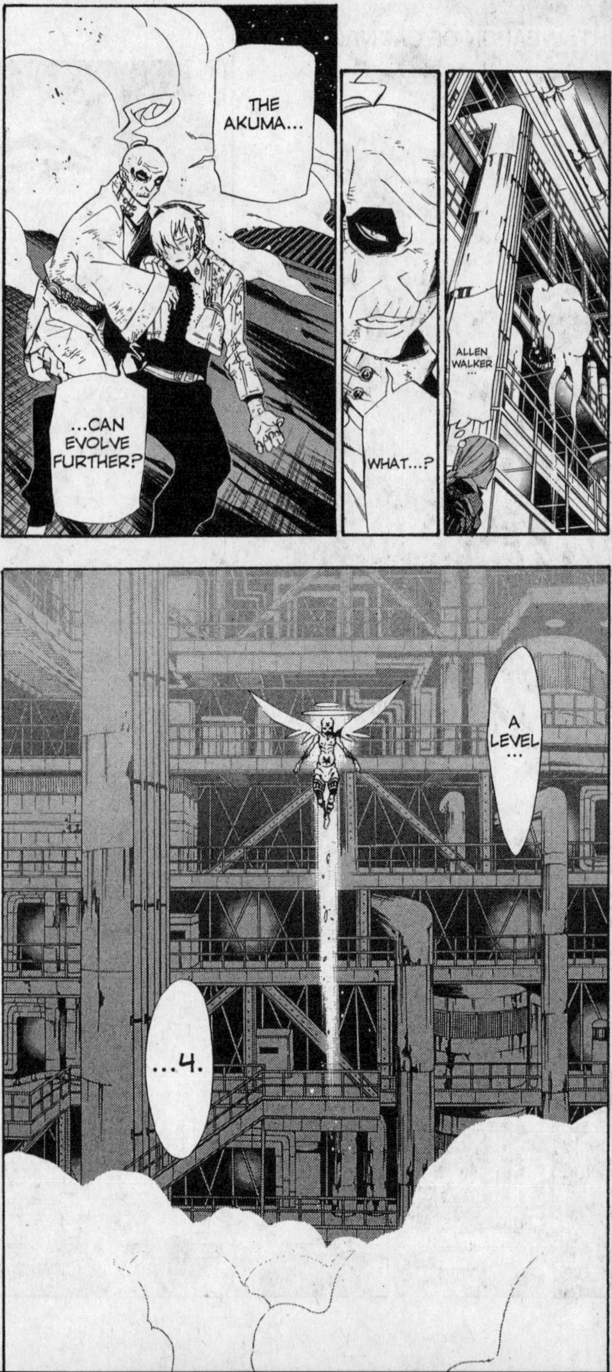
ALLEN WALKER ...
WHAT...?
THE AKUMA...
...CAN EVOLVE FURTHER?
A LEVEL ...
...4.

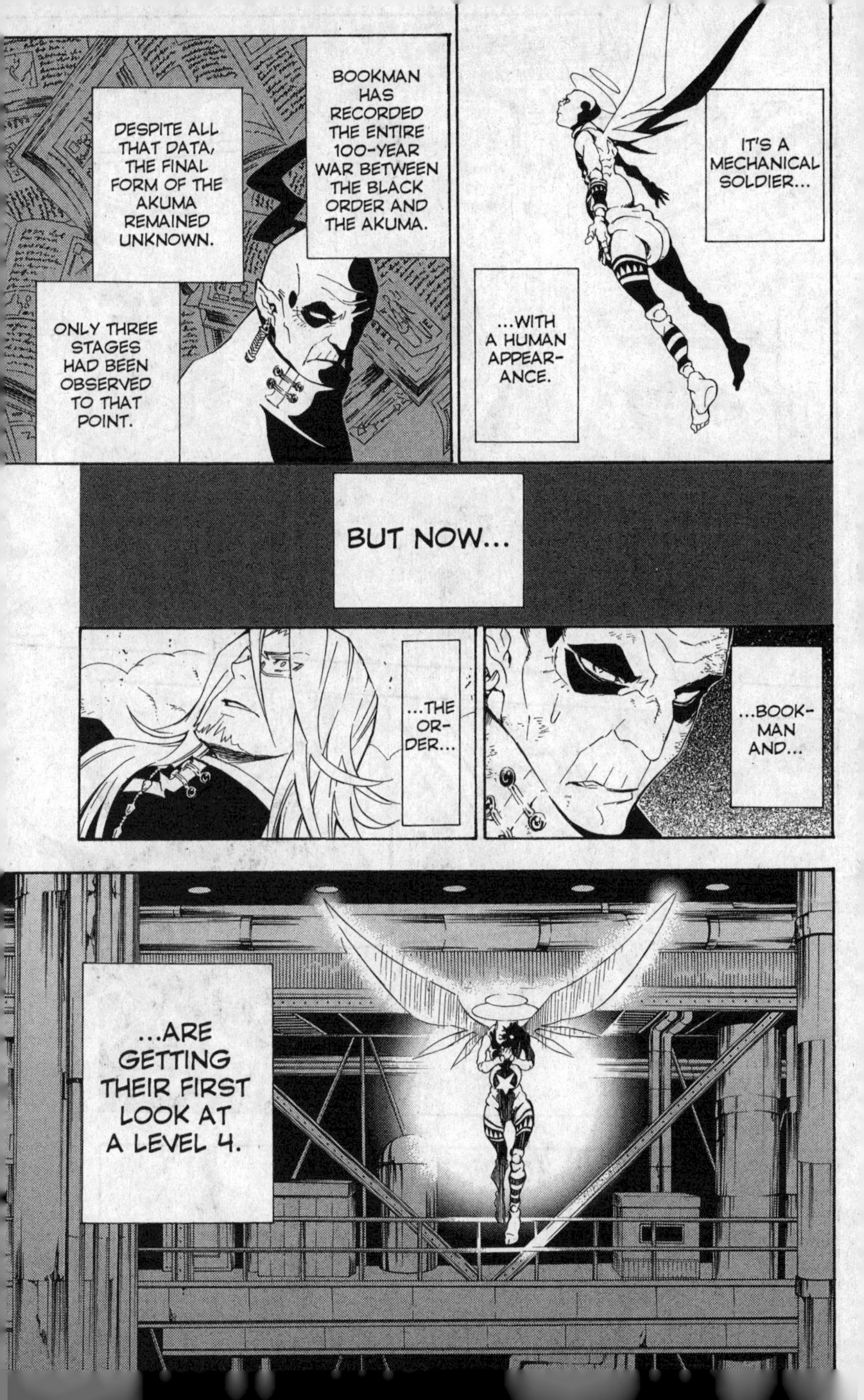
IT'S A MECHANICAL SOLDIER...
...WITH A HUMAN APPEARANCE.
BOOKMAN HAS RECORDED THE ENTIRE 100-YEAR WAR BETWEEN THE BLACK ORDER AND THE AKUMA.
DESPITE ALL THAT DATA, THE FINAL FORM OF THE AKUMA REMAINED UNKNOWN.
ONLY THREE STAGES HAD BEEN OBSERVED TO THAT POINT.
BUT NOW...
...BOOKMAN AND...
...THE ORDER...
...ARE GETTING THEIR FIRST LOOK AT A LEVEL 4.

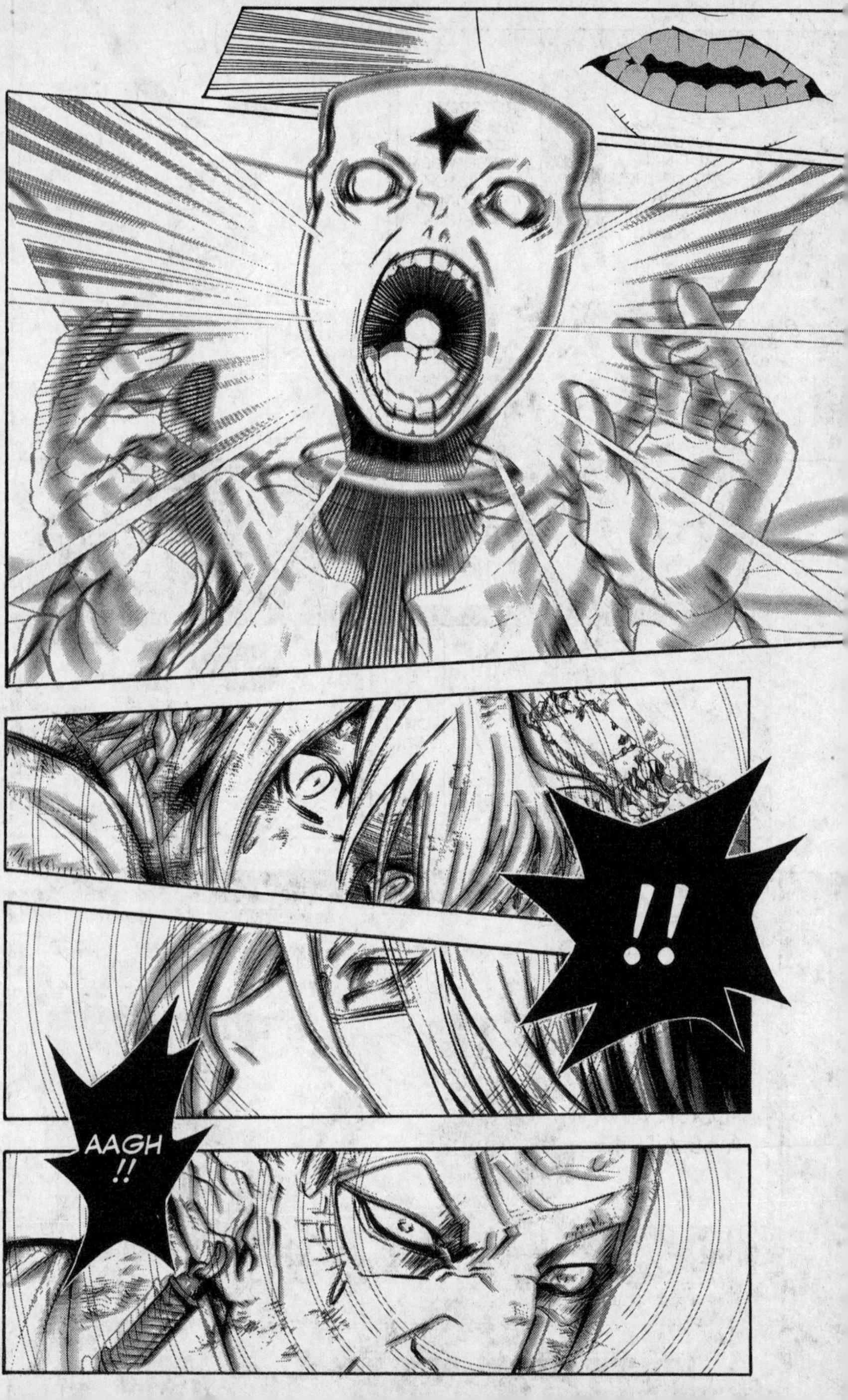
!!
AAGH !!

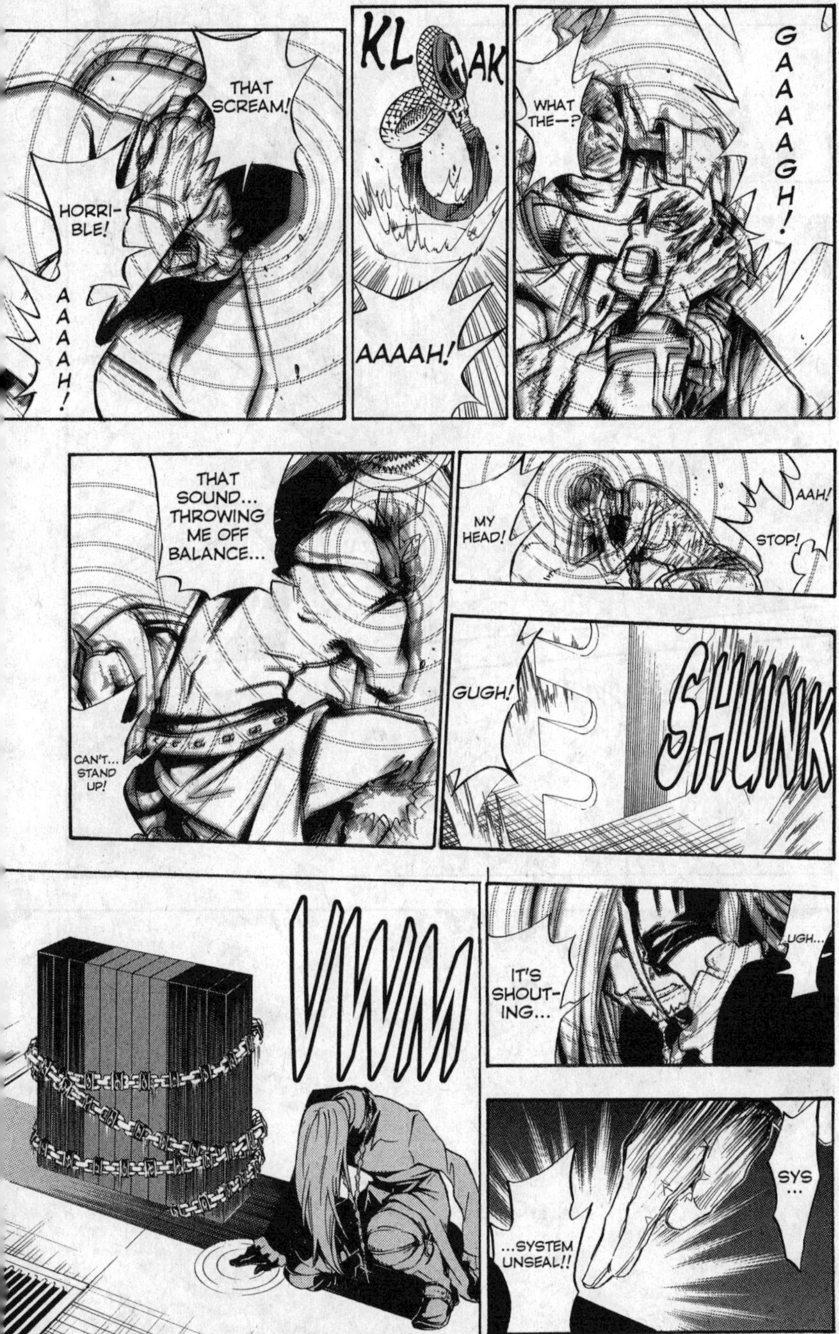
WHAT THE—?
GAAAAGH!
KLAK
AAAAH!
THAT SCREAM!
HORRIBLE!
AAAAH!
AAH!
MY HEAD!
STOP!
SHUNK
GUGH!
THAT SOUND... THROWING ME OFF BALANCE...
CAN'T... STAND UP!
UGH...
IT'S SHOUTING...
SYS...
...SYSTEM UNSEAL!!
VWM

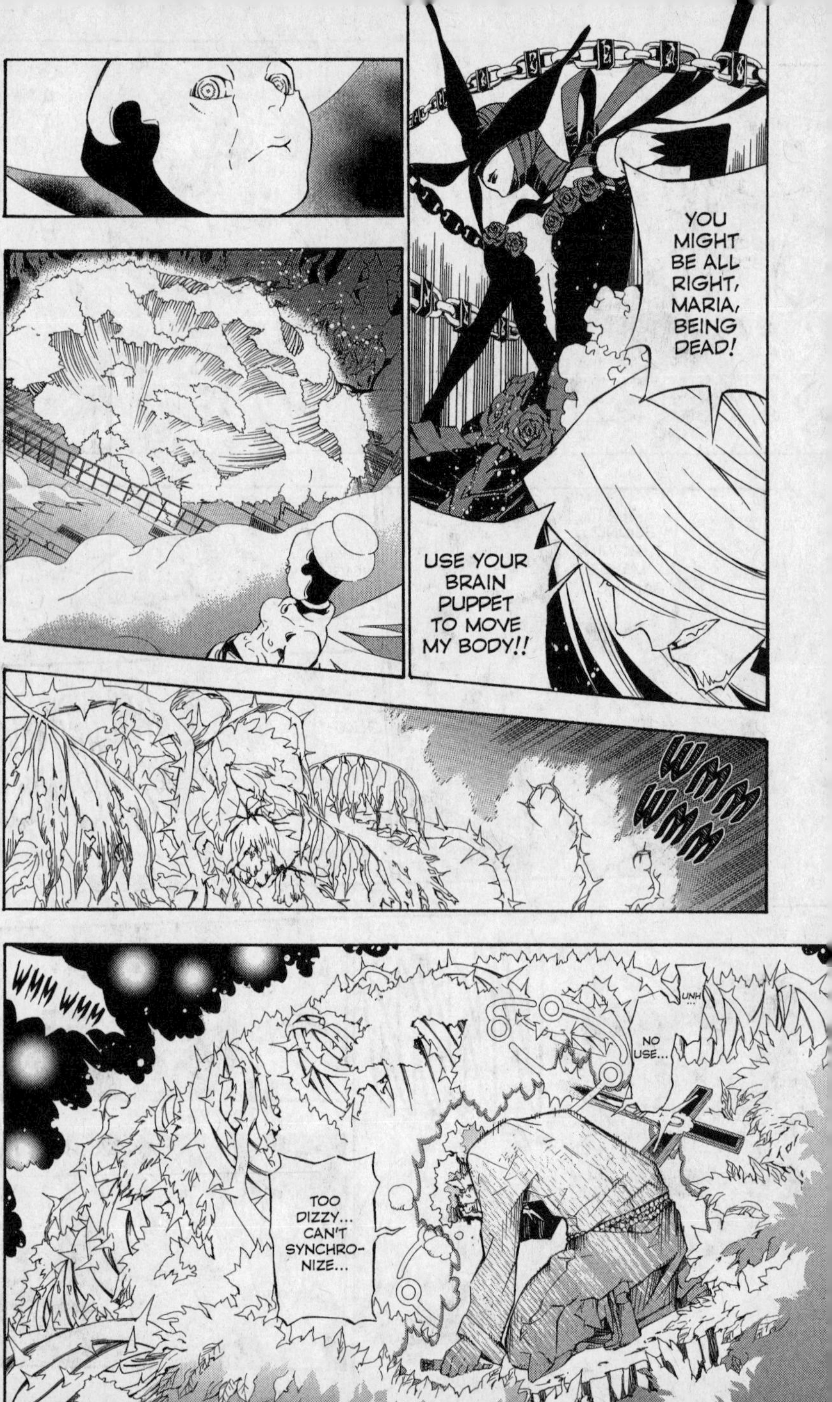
YOU MIGHT BE ALL RIGHT, MARIA, BEING DEAD!
USE YOUR BRAIN PUPPET TO MOVE MY BODY!!
WMM WMM
WMM WMM
UNH...
NO USE...
TOO DIZZY... CAN'T SYNCHRO-NIZE...

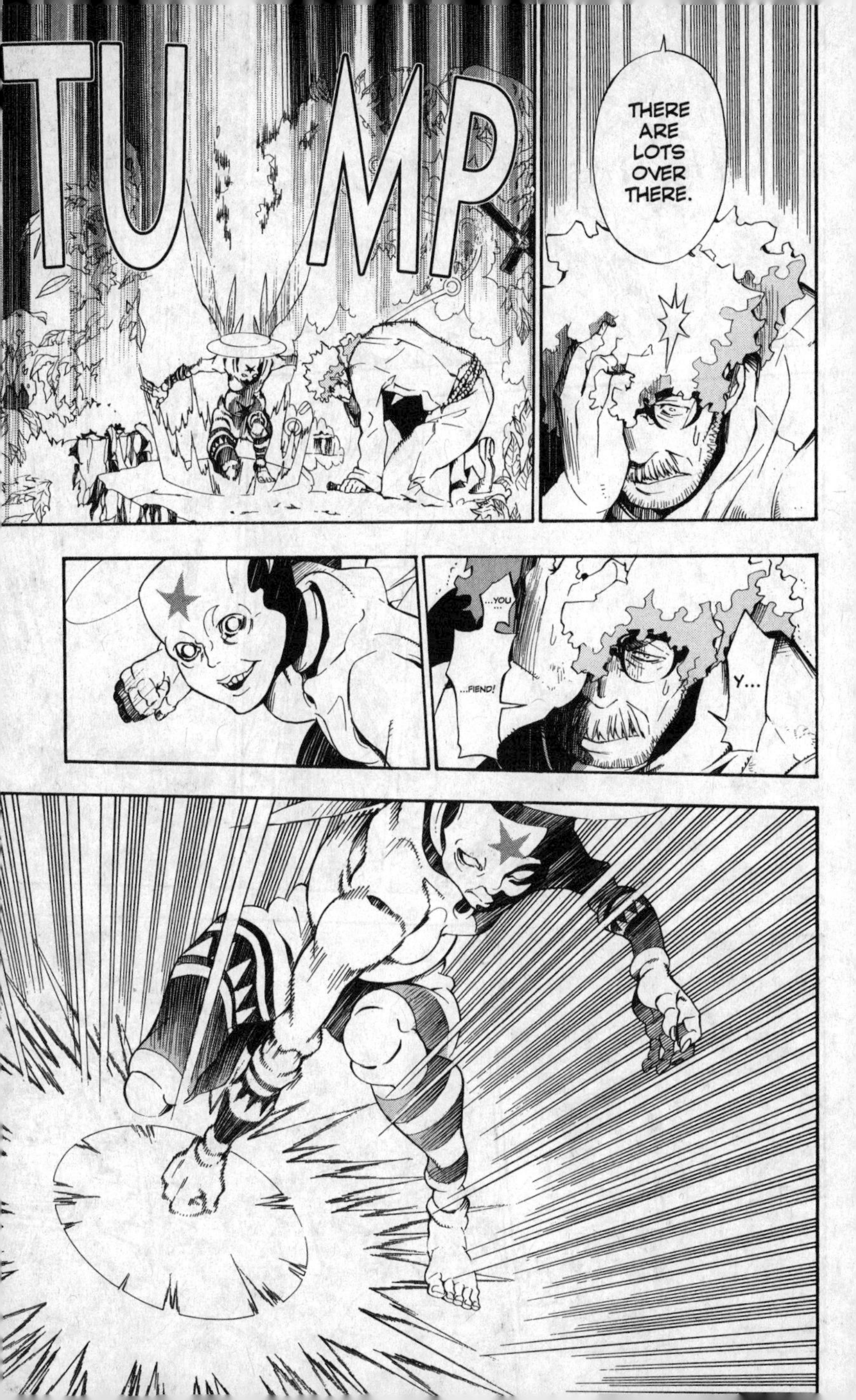
THERE ARE LOTS OVER THERE.
TUMP
Y...
...YOU...
...FIEND!

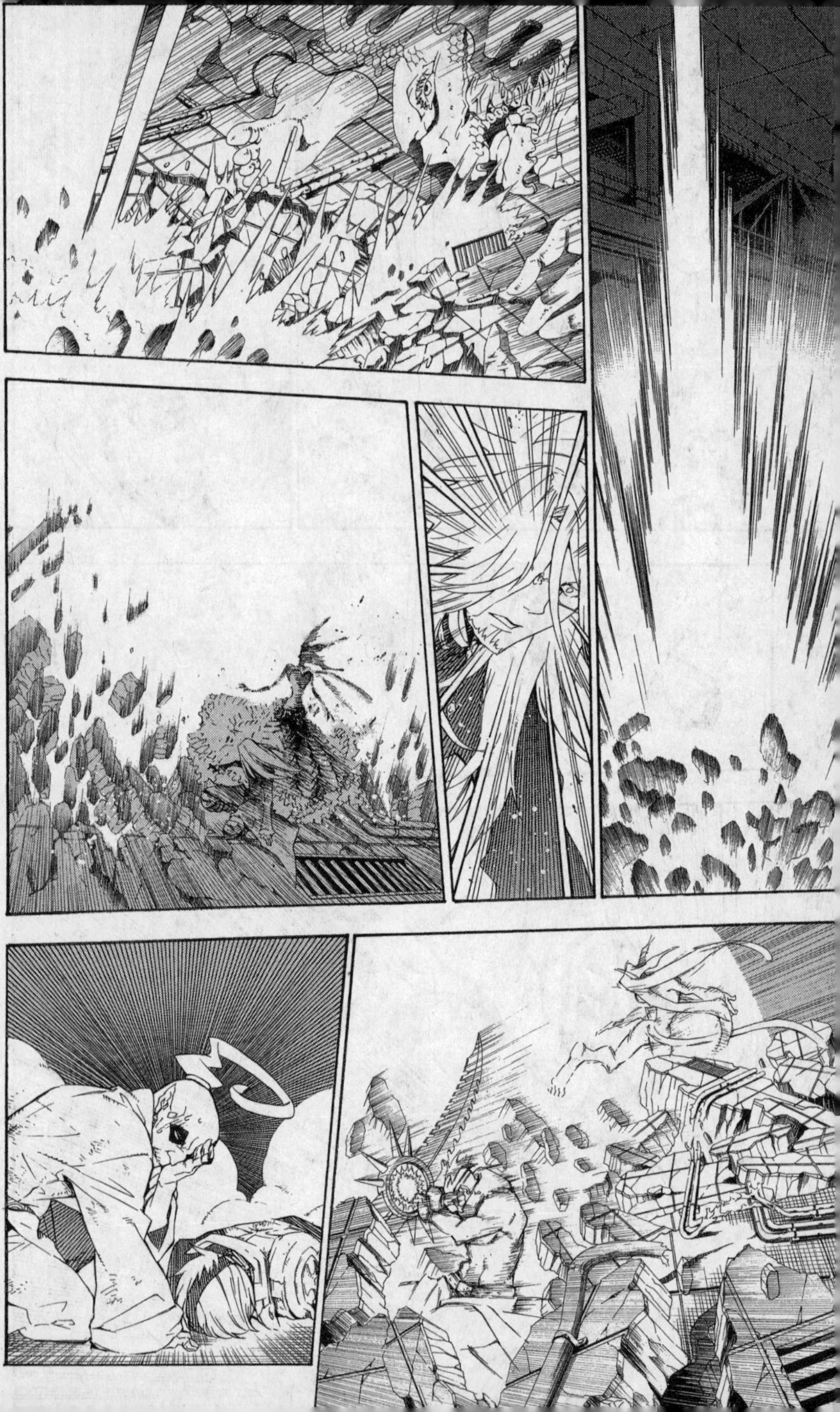

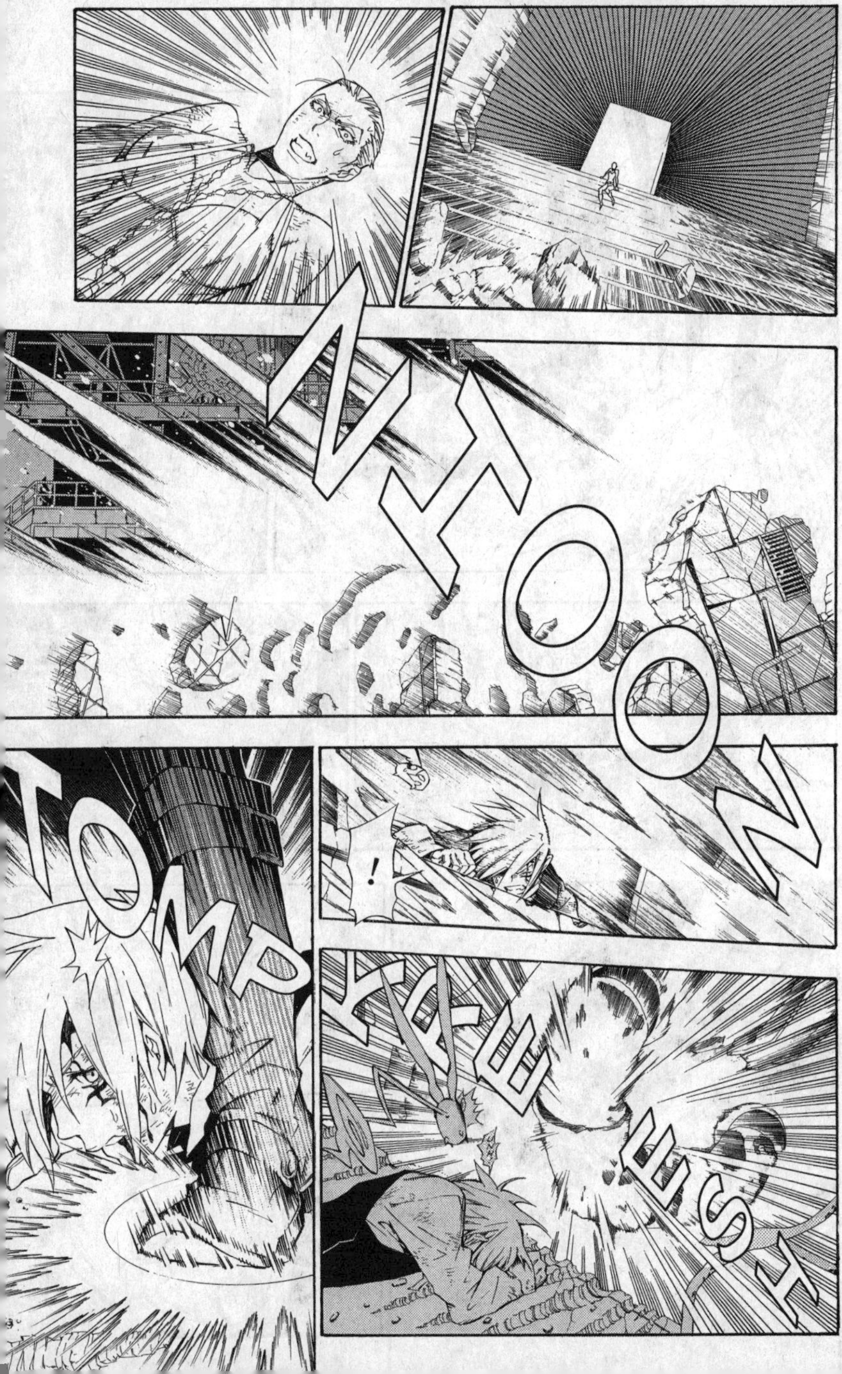
!
TOMP

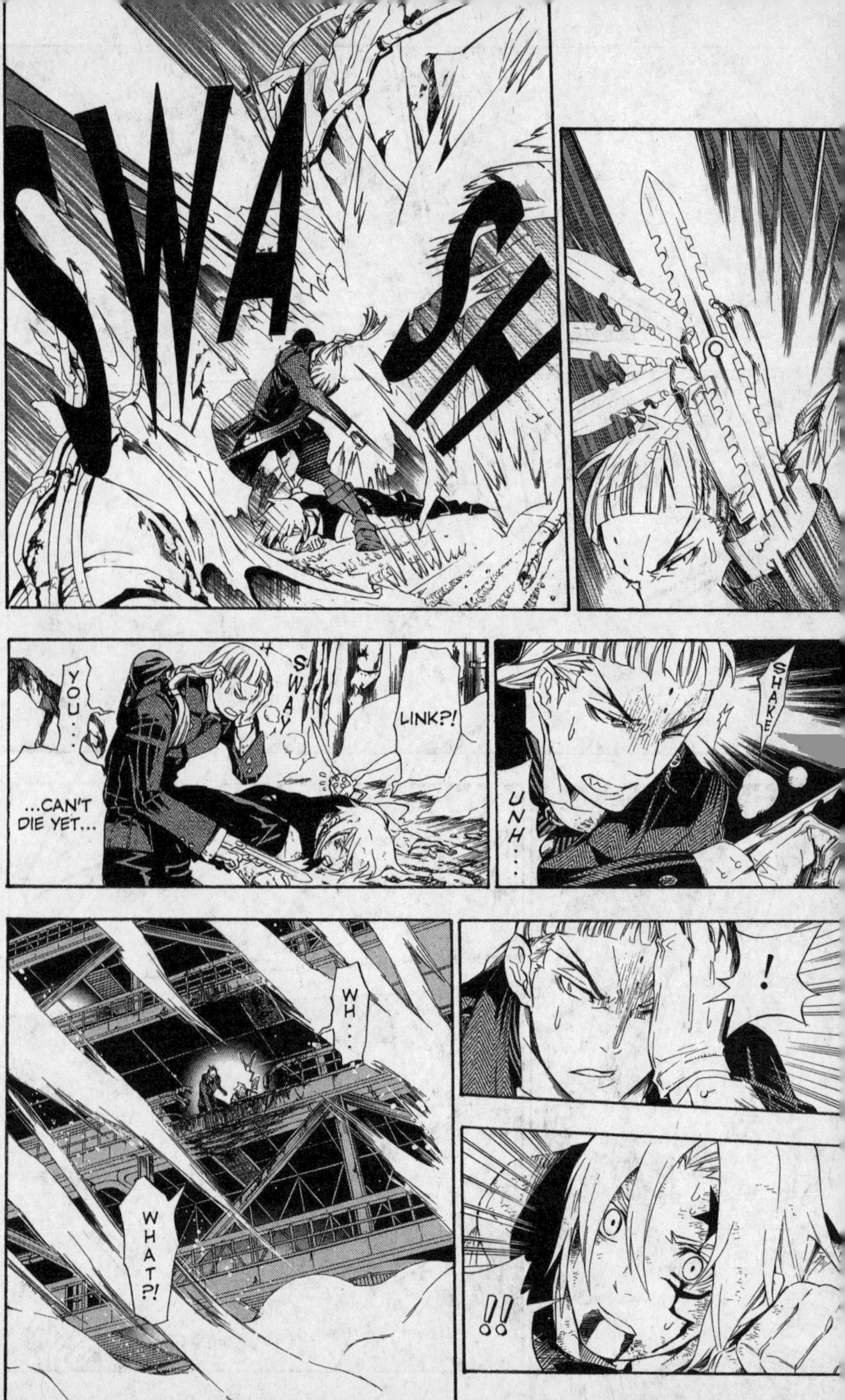
SWASH
SHAKE
UNH...
LINK?!
SWAY
YOU...
...CAN'T DIE YET...
!
!!
WH...
WHAT?!

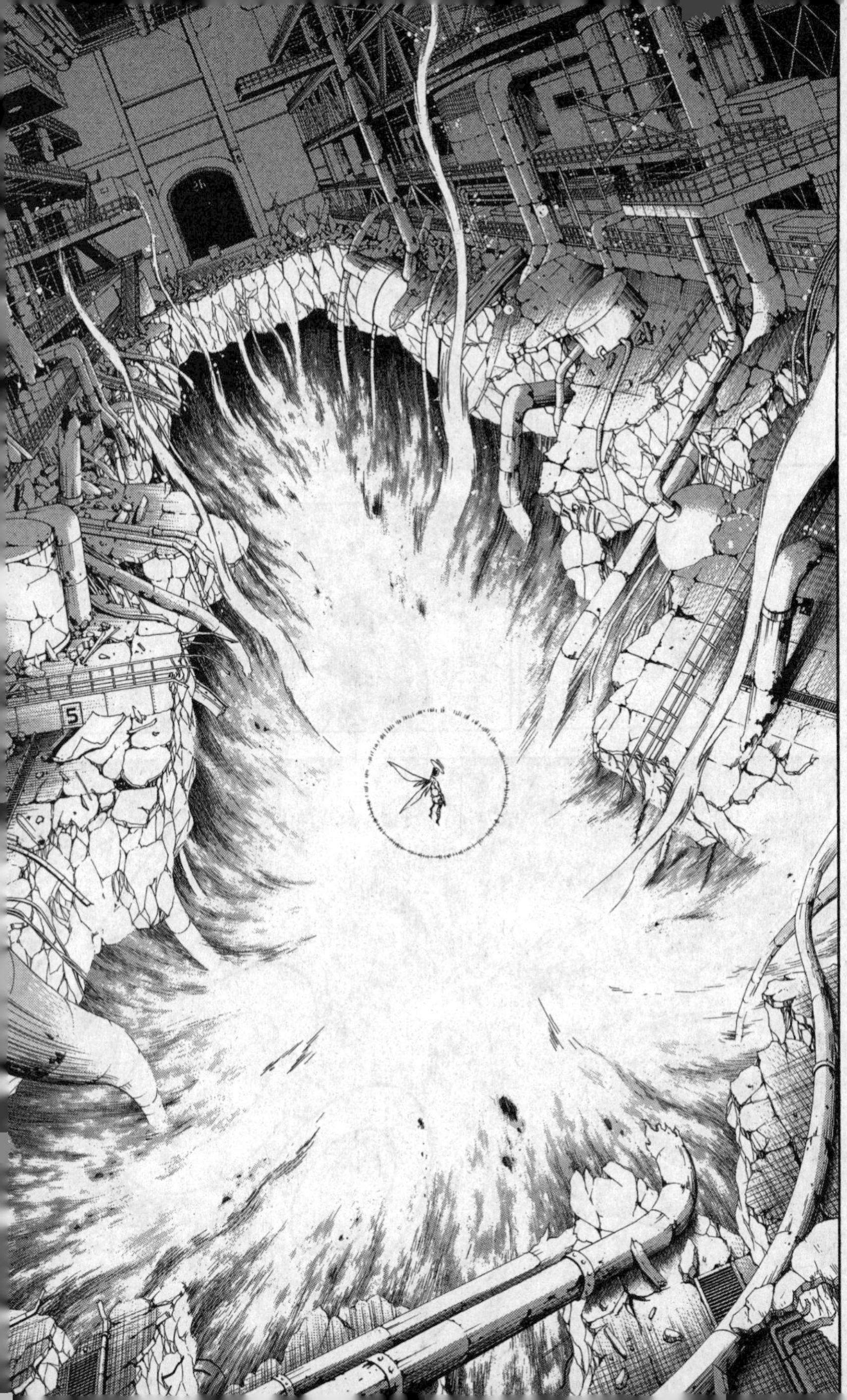
5

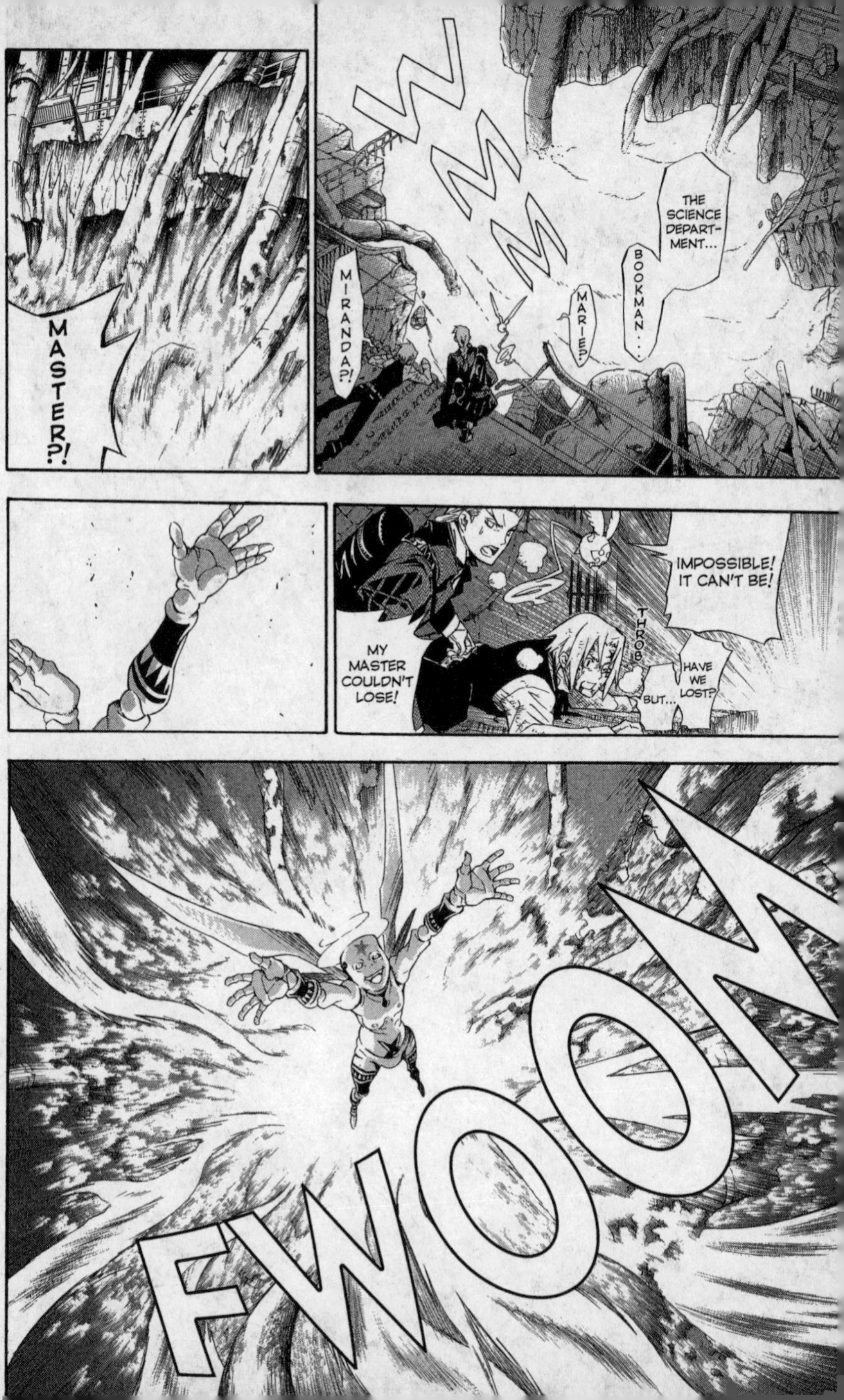
THE SCIENCE DEPART-MENT...
BOOKMAN...
WMMM
MARIE?
MIRANDA?!
MASTER?!
IMPOSSIBLE! IT CAN'T BE!
THROB
HAVE WE LOST?
BUT...
MY MASTER COULDN'T LOSE!
FWOOM

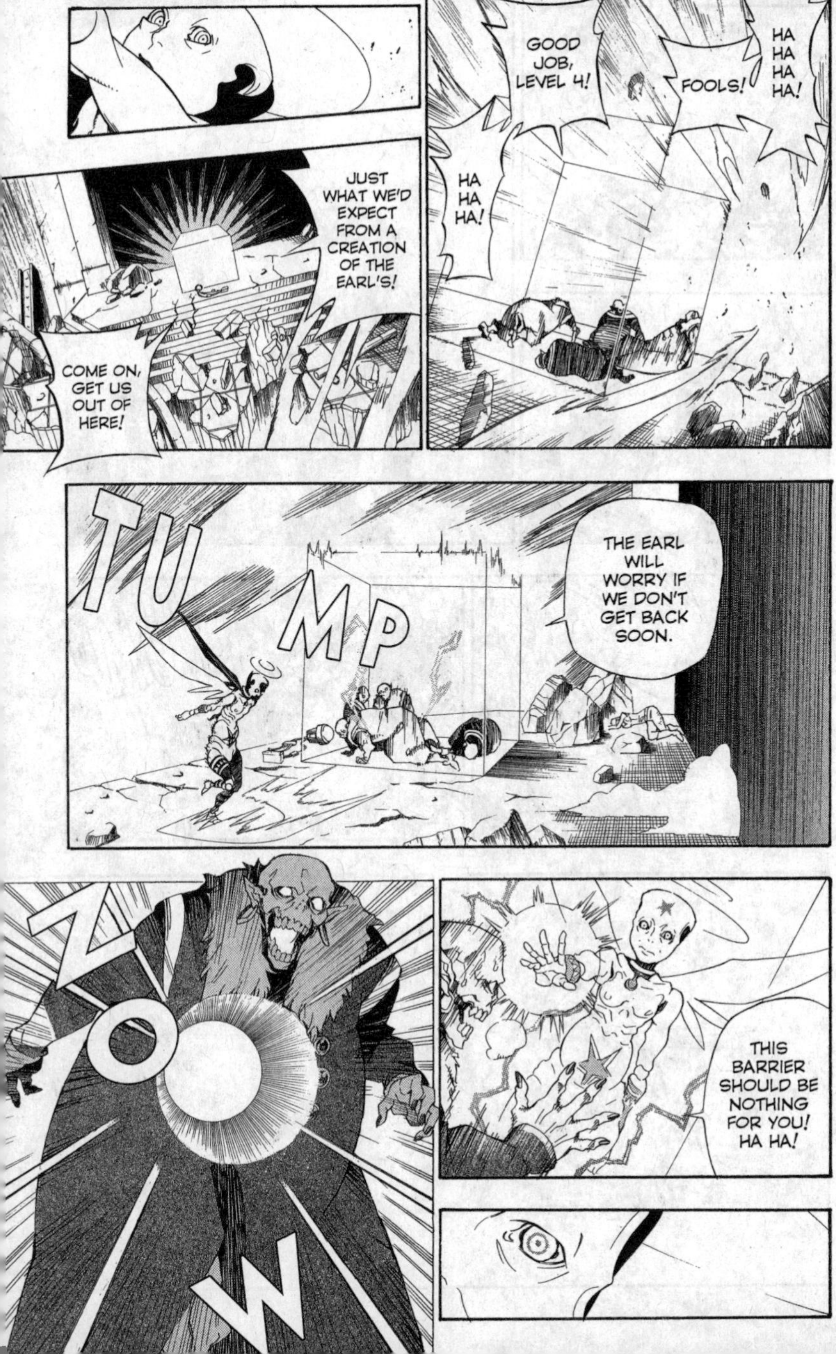
HA HA HA HA!
FOOLS!
GOOD JOB, LEVEL 4!
HA HA HA!
JUST WHAT WE'D EXPECT FROM A CREATION OF THE EARL'S!
COME ON, GET US OUT OF HERE!
THE EARL WILL WORRY IF WE DON'T GET BACK SOON.
TUMP
THIS BARRIER SHOULD BE NOTHING FOR YOU! HA HA!
ZOW

HUH?

...

WHUP

WHA... YOU!

YOU'VE KILLED ME!

DIRTY...

...DOUBLE-CROSSER!

FWUMP

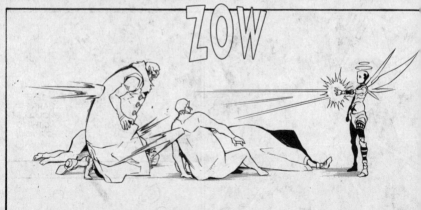

ZOW

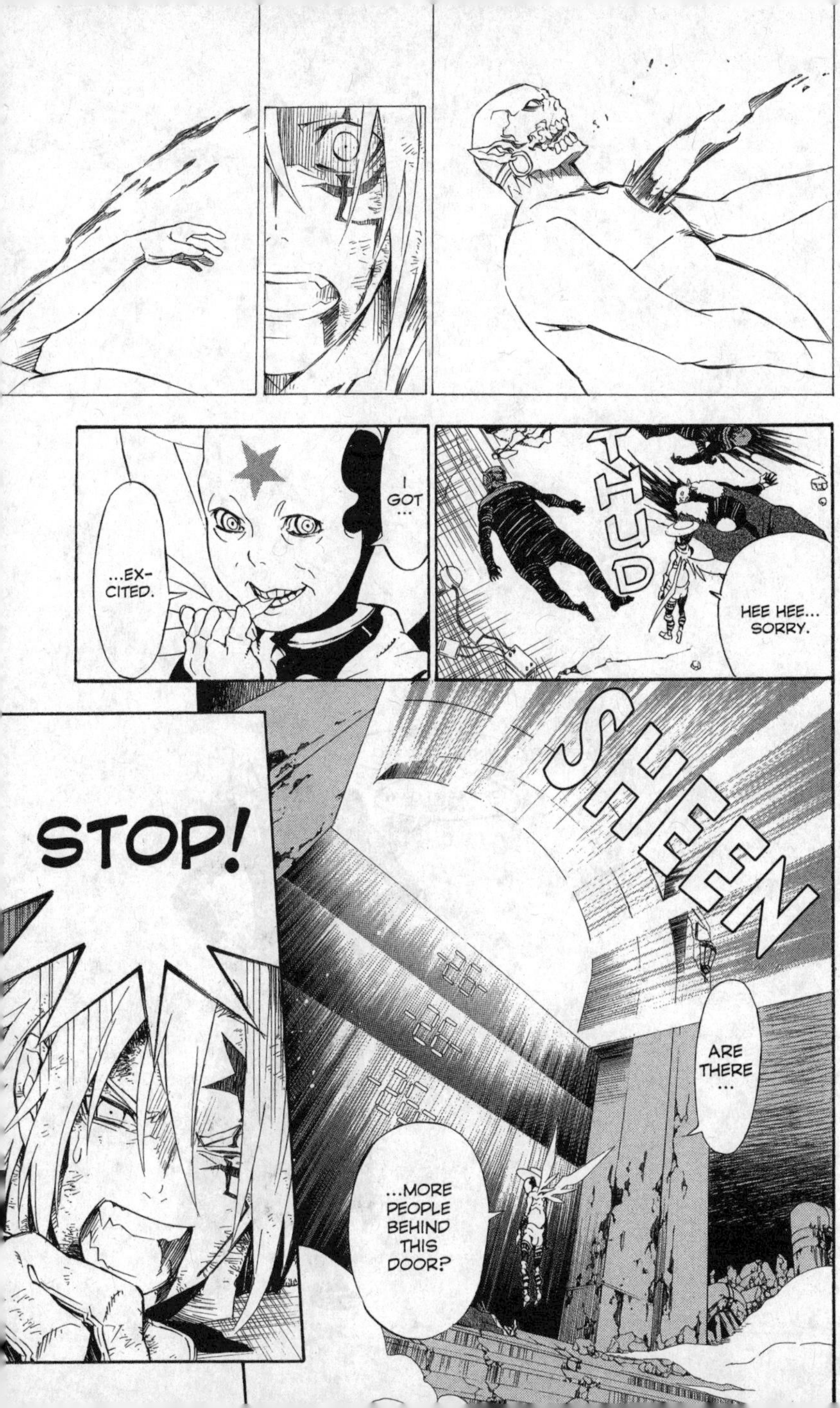
THUD
HEE HEE... SORRY.
I GOT...
...EXCITED.
SHEEN
ARE THERE...
...MORE PEOPLE BEHIND THIS DOOR?
STOP!

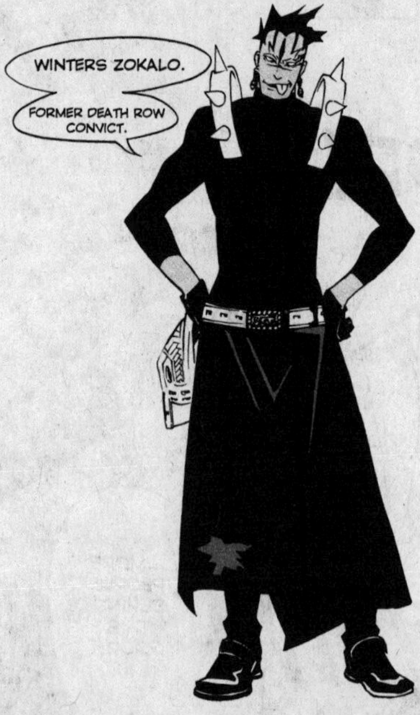
WINTERS ZOKALO.
FORMER DEATH ROW CONVICT.

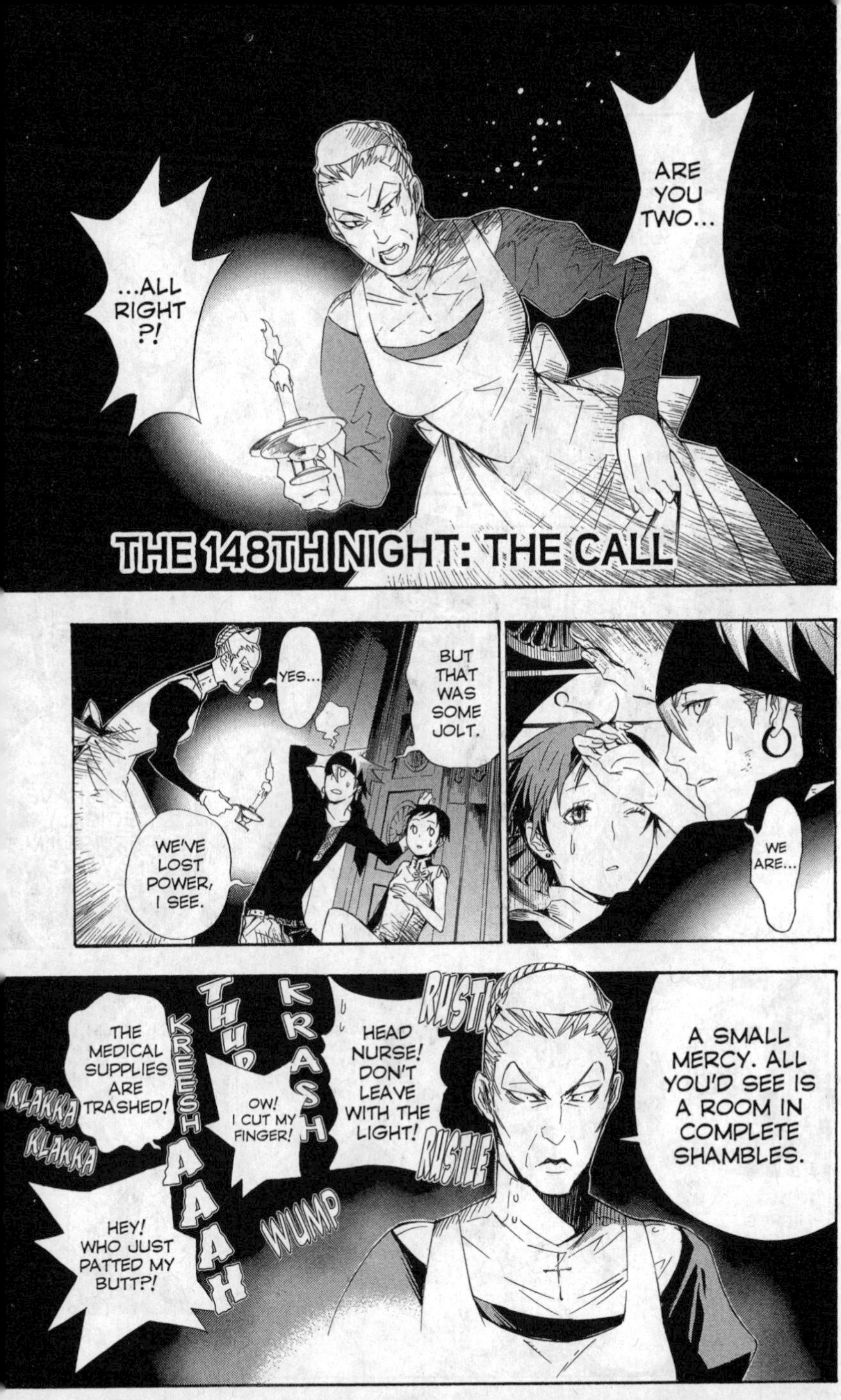
ARE YOU TWO...
...ALL RIGHT?!
THE 148TH NIGHT: THE CALL
WE ARE...
BUT THAT WAS SOME JOLT.
YES...
WE'VE LOST POWER, I SEE.
A SMALL MERCY. ALL YOU'D SEE IS A ROOM IN COMPLETE SHAMBLES.
RUSTLE
KRASH
HEAD NURSE! DON'T LEAVE WITH THE LIGHT!
THUD
OW! I CUT MY FINGER!
KREESH
THE MEDICAL SUPPLIES ARE TRASHED!
KLAKKA KLAKKA
RUSTLE
WUMP
AAAAH
HEY! WHO JUST PATTED MY BUTT?!

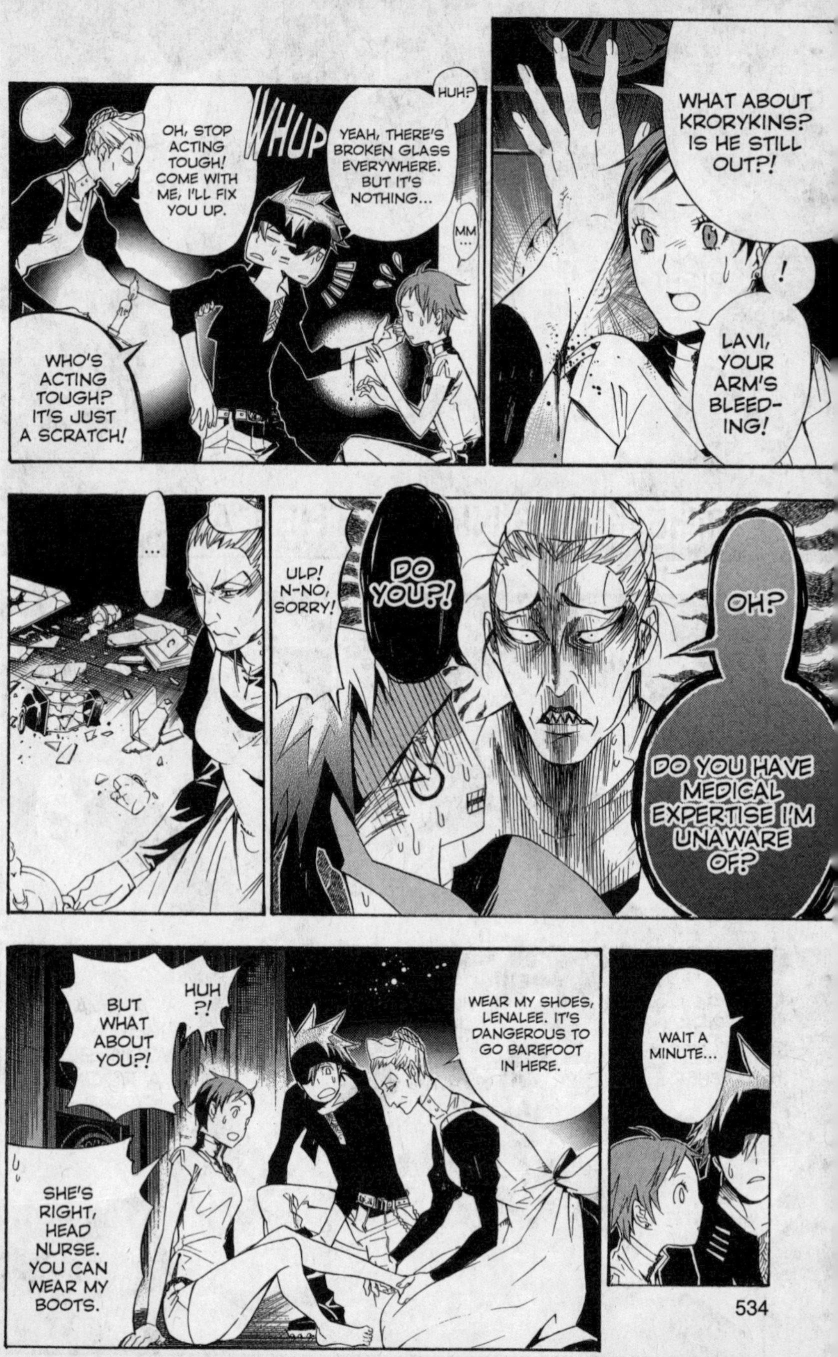
WHAT ABOUT KRORYKINS? IS HE STILL OUT?!
!
LAVI, YOUR ARM'S BLEED-ING!
HUH?
YEAH, THERE'S BROKEN GLASS EVERYWHERE. BUT IT'S NOTHING...
MM...
WHUP
OH, STOP ACTING TOUGH! COME WITH ME, I'LL FIX YOU UP.
WHO'S ACTING TOUGH? IT'S JUST A SCRATCH!
OH?
DO YOU HAVE MEDICAL EXPERTISE I'M UNAWARE OF?
DO YOU?!
ULP! N-NO, SORRY!
...
WAIT A MINUTE...
WEAR MY SHOES, LENALEE. IT'S DANGEROUS TO GO BAREFOOT IN HERE.
HUH?!
BUT WHAT ABOUT YOU?!
SHE'S RIGHT, HEAD NURSE. YOU CAN WEAR MY BOOTS.

READ THIS WAY

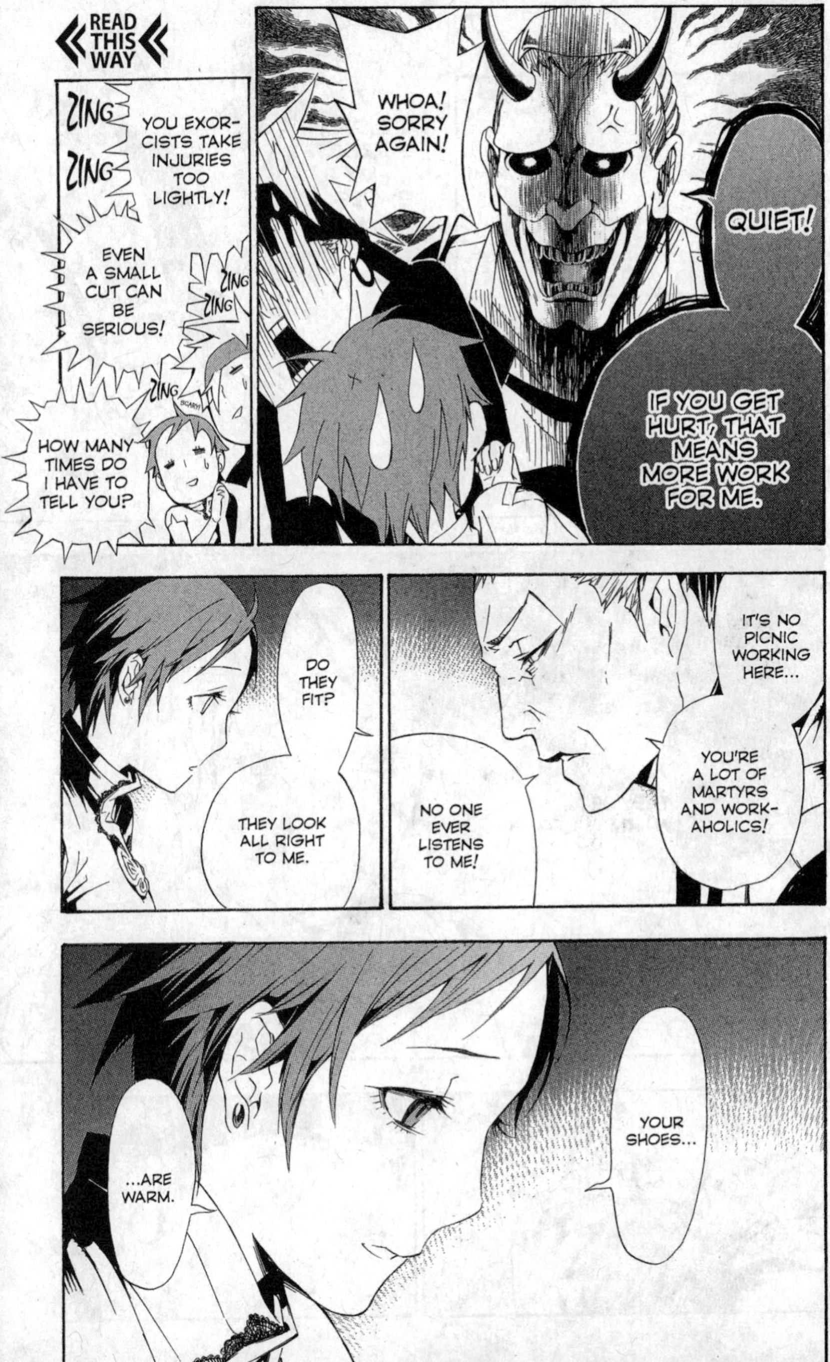
WHOA! SORRY AGAIN!
QUIET!
IF YOU GET HURT, THAT MEANS MORE WORK FOR ME.
ZING
ZING
YOU EXORCISTS TAKE INJURIES TOO LIGHTLY!
ZING
ZING
EVEN A SMALL CUT CAN BE SERIOUS!
ZING
HOW MANY TIMES DO I HAVE TO TELL YOU?
IT'S NO PICNIC WORKING HERE...
YOU'RE A LOT OF MARTYRS AND WORK-AHOLICS!
NO ONE EVER LISTENS TO ME!
DO THEY FIT?
THEY LOOK ALL RIGHT TO ME.
YOUR SHOES...
...ARE WARM.

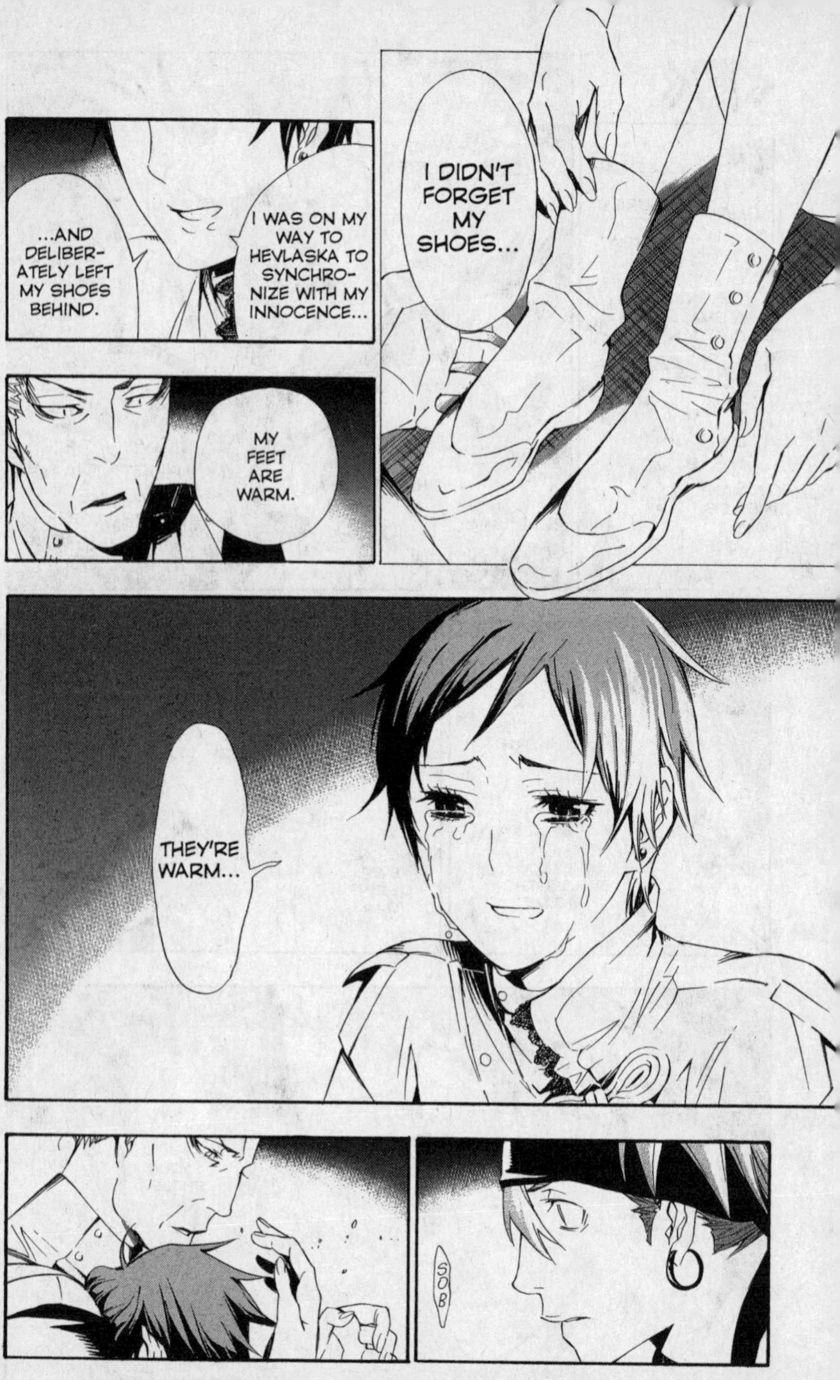
I DIDN'T FORGET MY SHOES...
I WAS ON MY WAY TO HEVLASKA TO SYNCHRONIZE WITH MY INNOCENCE...
...AND DELIBERATELY LEFT MY SHOES BEHIND.
MY FEET ARE WARM.
THEY'RE WARM...
SOB

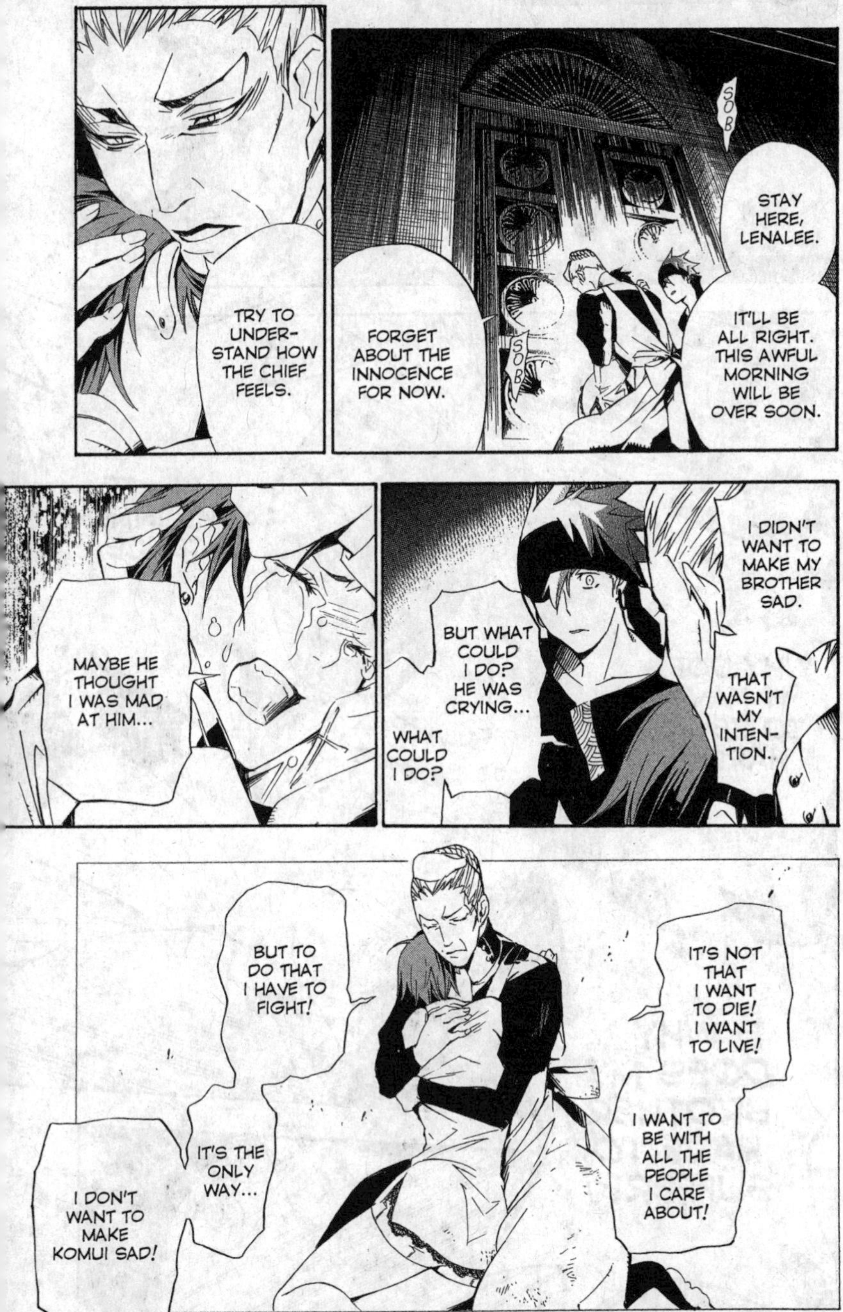
SOB
STAY HERE, LENALEE.
IT'LL BE ALL RIGHT. THIS AWFUL MORNING WILL BE OVER SOON.
SOB
FORGET ABOUT THE INNOCENCE FOR NOW.
TRY TO UNDER-STAND HOW THE CHIEF FEELS.
I DIDN'T WANT TO MAKE MY BROTHER SAD.
THAT WASN'T MY INTEN-TION.
BUT WHAT COULD I DO? HE WAS CRYING...
WHAT COULD I DO?
MAYBE HE THOUGHT I WAS MAD AT HIM...
IT'S NOT THAT I WANT TO DIE! I WANT TO LIVE!
I WANT TO BE WITH ALL THE PEOPLE I CARE ABOUT!
BUT TO DO THAT I HAVE TO FIGHT!
IT'S THE ONLY WAY...
I DON'T WANT TO MAKE KOMUI SAD!

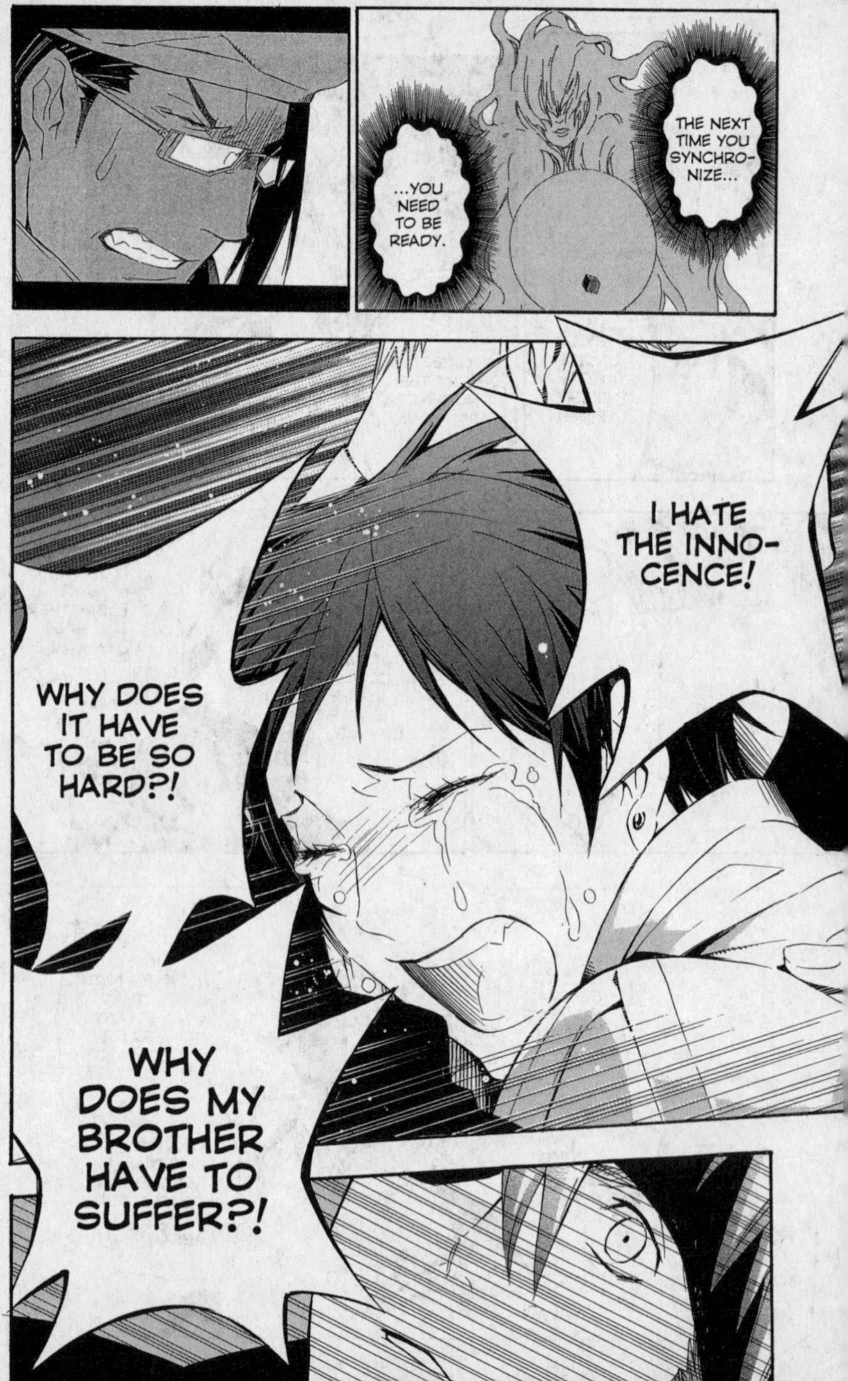
THE NEXT TIME YOU SYNCHRO-NIZE...
...YOU NEED TO BE READY.
I HATE THE INNO-CENCE!
WHY DOES IT HAVE TO BE SO HARD?!
WHY DOES MY BROTHER HAVE TO SUFFER?!

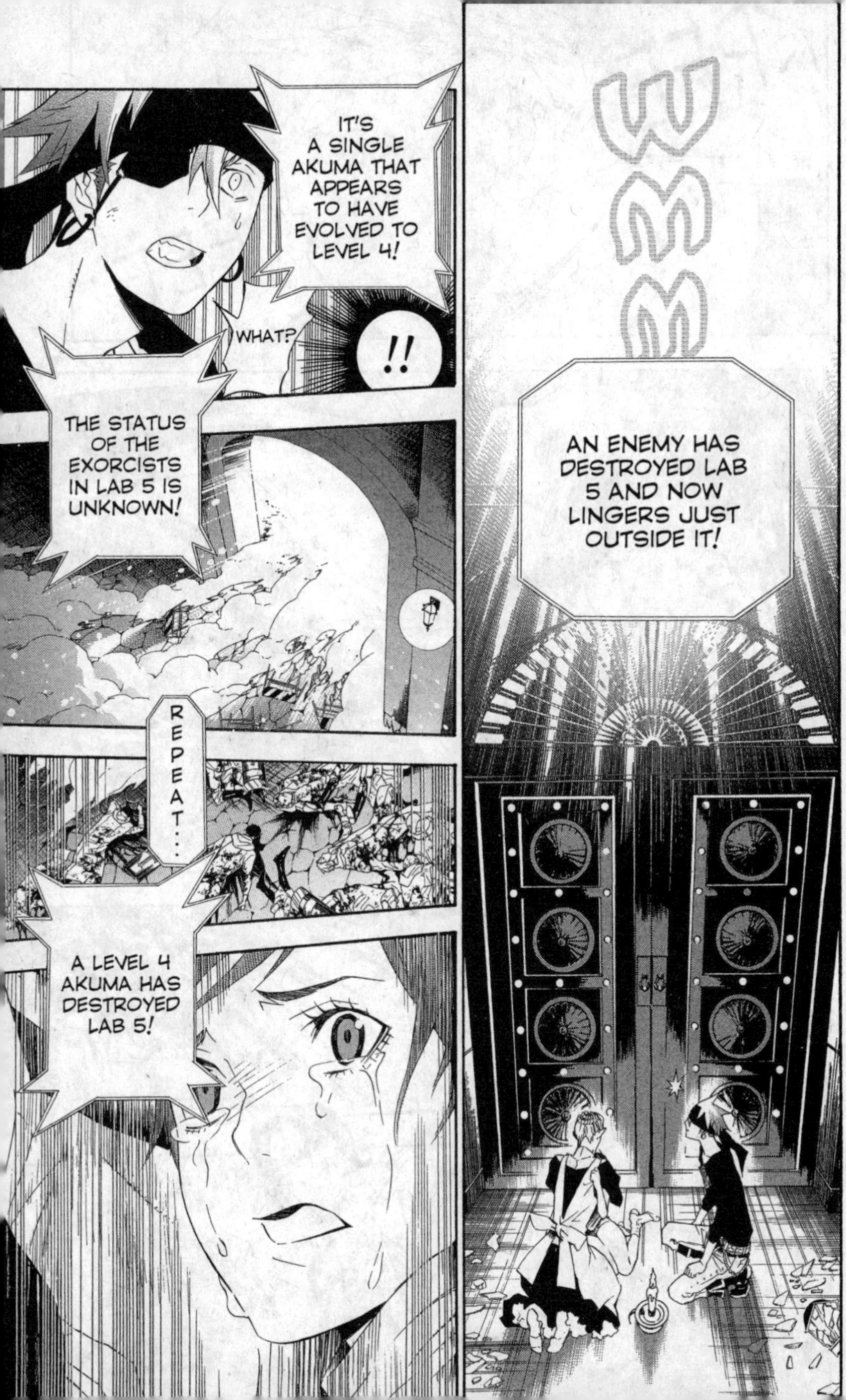

AN ENEMY HAS DESTROYED LAB 5 AND NOW LINGERS JUST OUTSIDE IT!
IT'S A SINGLE AKUMA THAT APPEARS TO HAVE EVOLVED TO LEVEL 4!
!!
WHAT?
THE STATUS OF THE EXORCISTS IN LAB 5 IS UNKNOWN!
REPEAT...
A LEVEL 4 AKUMA HAS DESTROYED LAB 5!

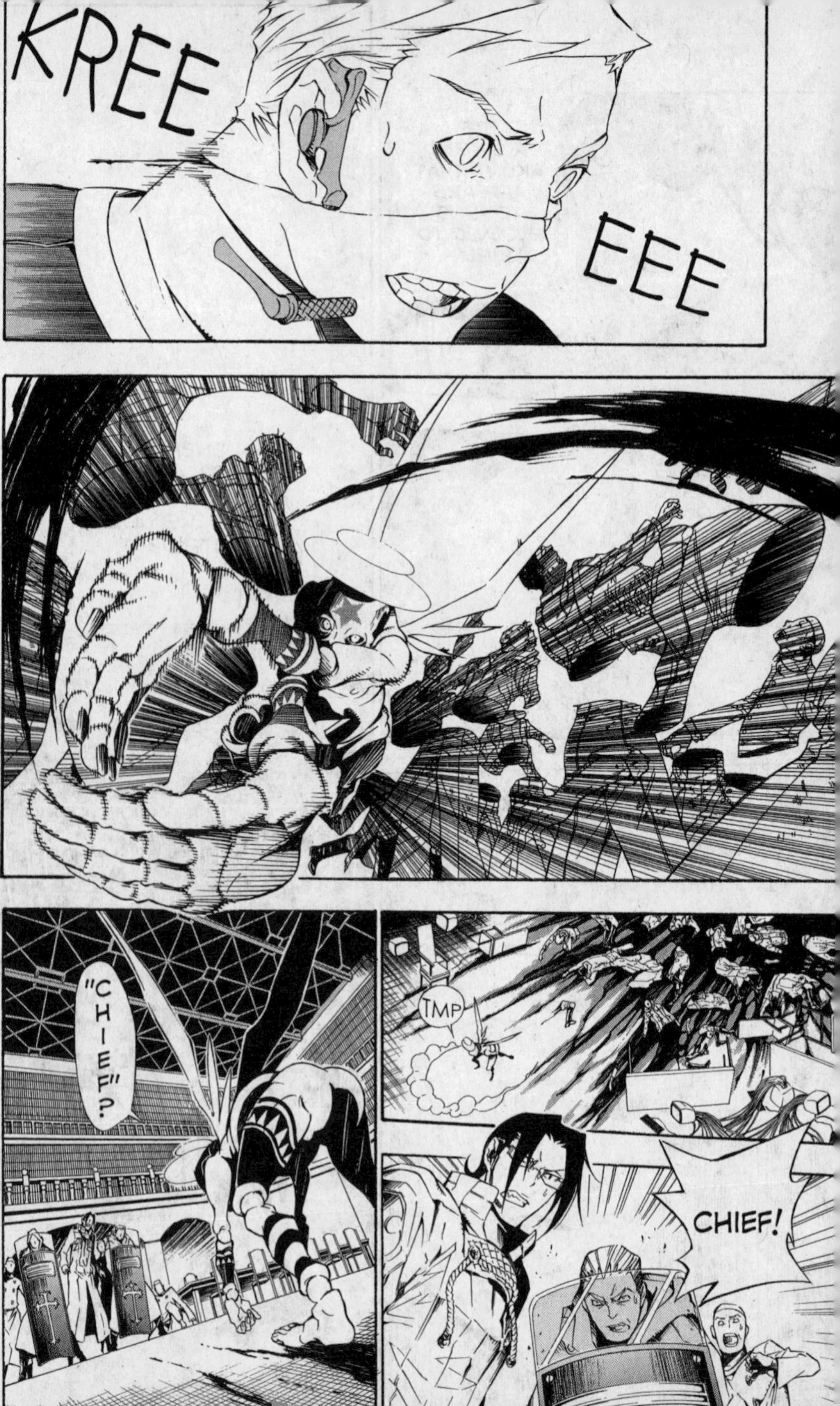
KREE
EEE
TMP
CHIEF!
"CHIEF"?

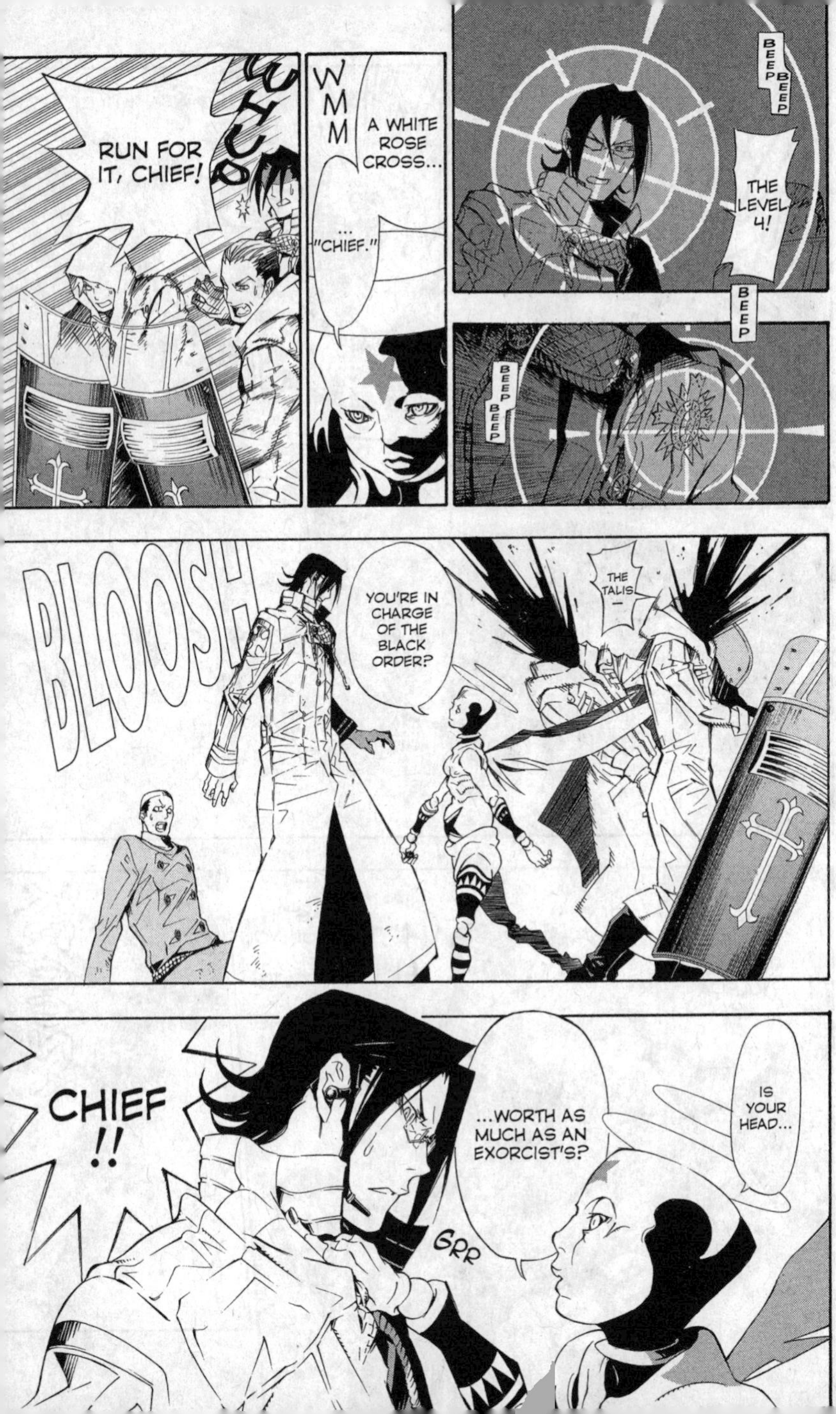
BEEP BEEP BEEP
THE LEVEL 4!
BEEP
BEEP BEEP BEEP
WMM
A WHITE ROSE CROSS...
..."CHIEF."
WHUD
RUN FOR IT, CHIEF!
THE TALIS—
YOU'RE IN CHARGE OF THE BLACK ORDER?
BLOOSH
IS YOUR HEAD...
...WORTH AS MUCH AS AN EXORCIST'S?
GRR
CHIEF !!

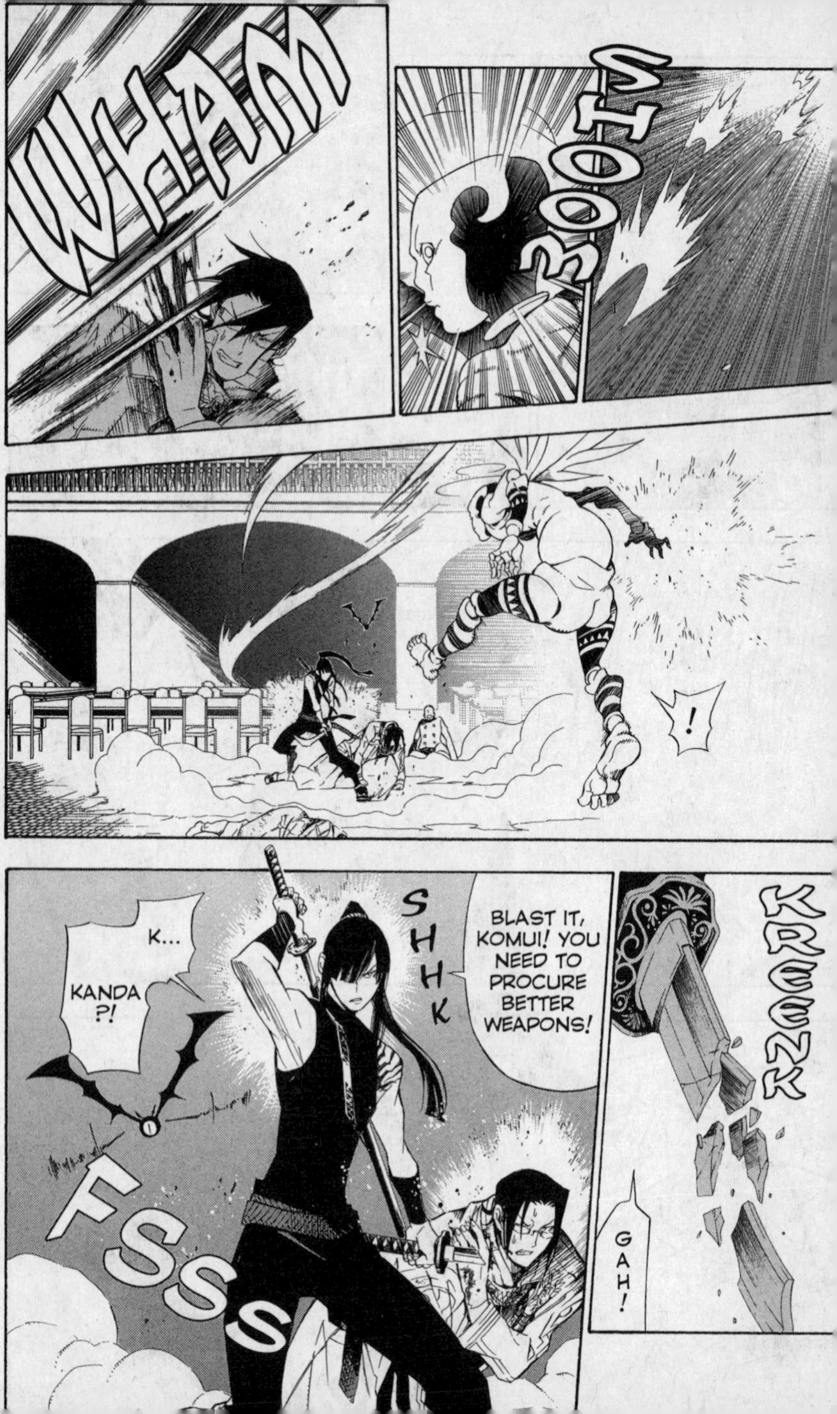
SHOOM
WHAM
!
KRENK
GAH!
BLAST IT, KOMUI! YOU NEED TO PROCURE BETTER WEAPONS!
SHHK
K... KANDA?!
FSSS

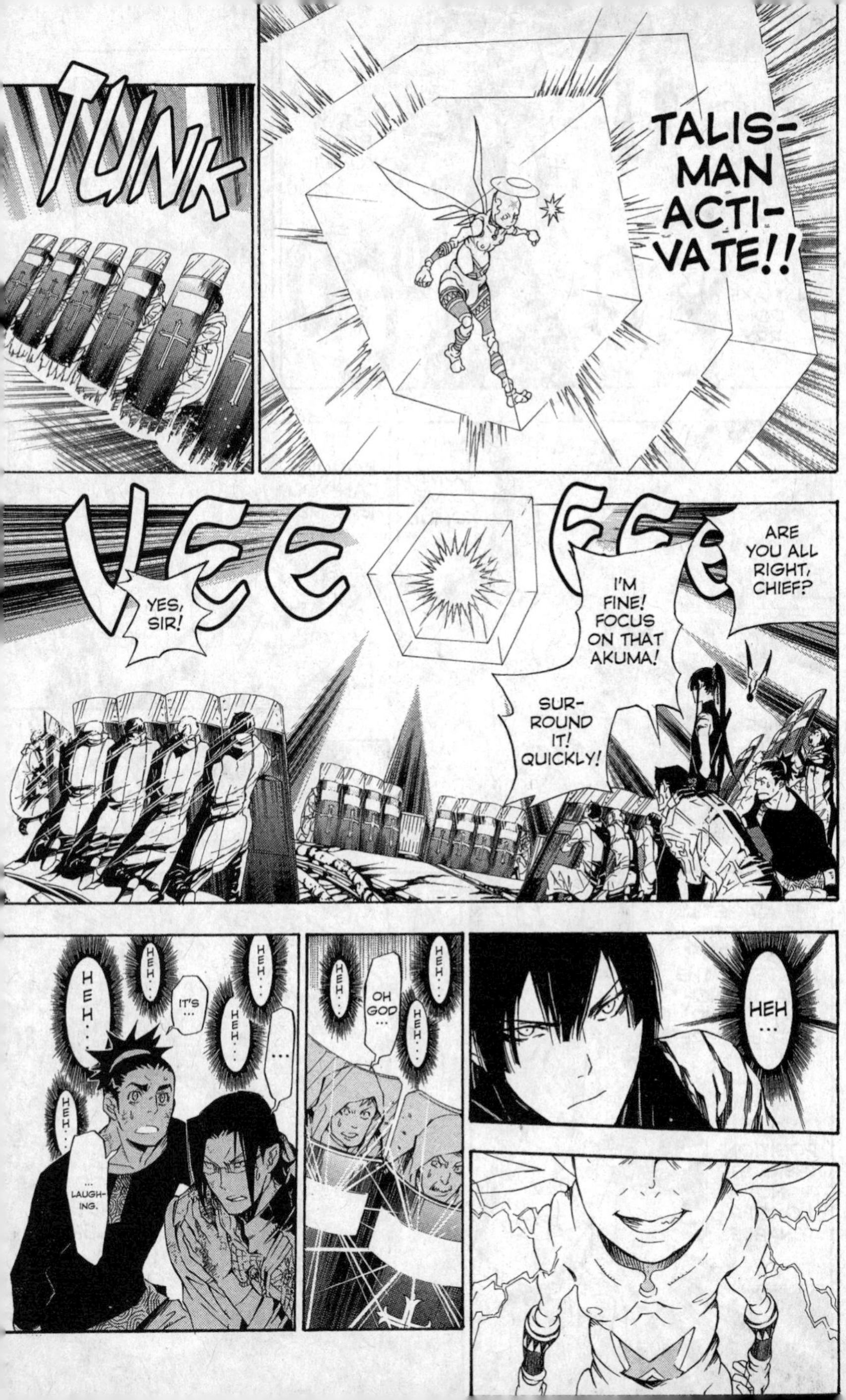
TALIS-MAN ACTI-VATE!!
TUNK
ARE YOU ALL RIGHT, CHIEF?
I'M FINE! FOCUS ON THAT AKUMA!
SUR-ROUND IT! QUICKLY!
YES, SIR!
VEEEEEE
HEH ...
HEH...
OH GOD ...
HEH...
HEH...
HEH...
IT'S ...
HEH...
HEH...
...
HEH...
... LAUGH-ING.

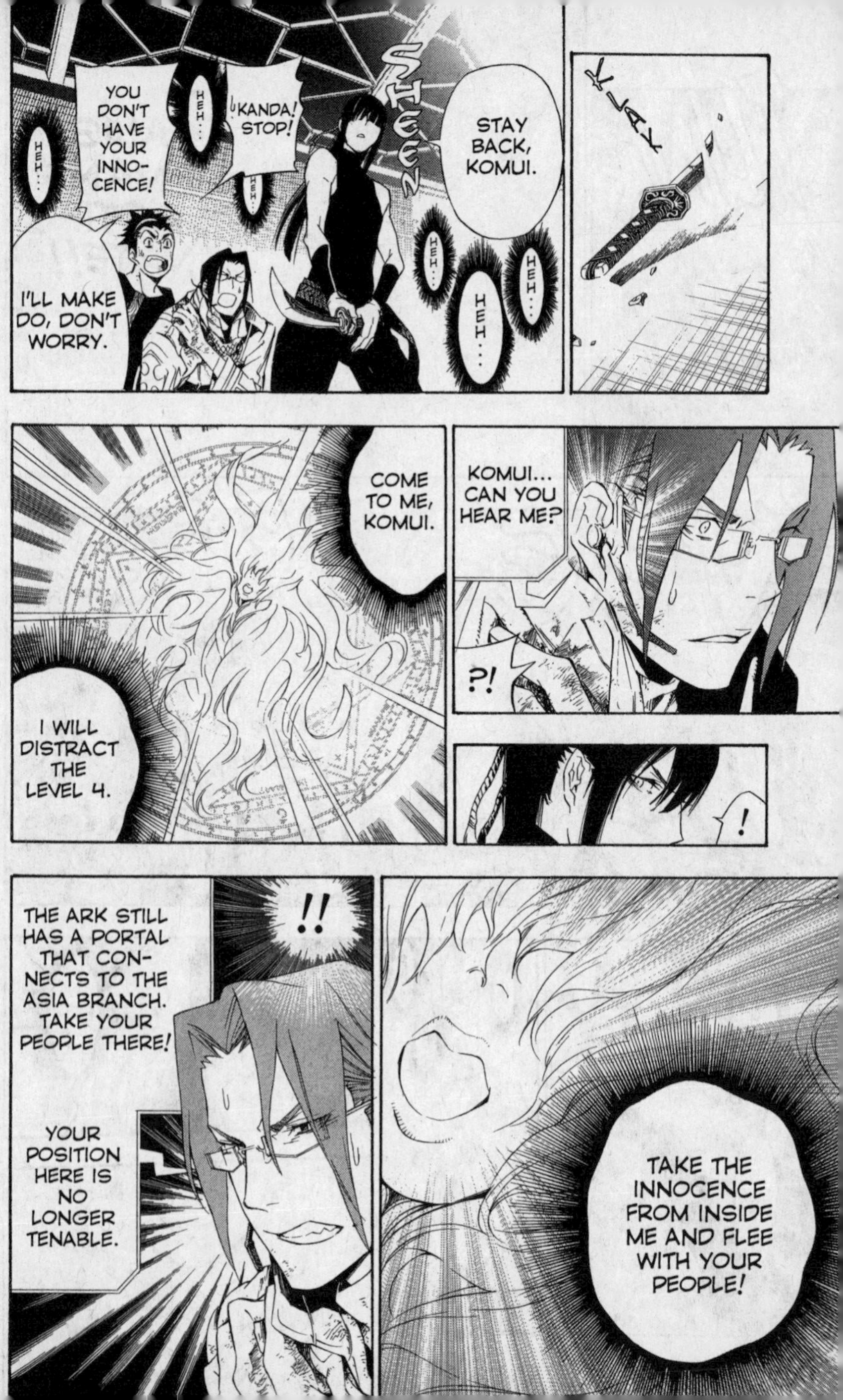
STAY BACK, KOMUI.
SHEEN
HEH...
HEH...
HEH...
KANDA! STOP!
HEH...
HEH...
YOU DON'T HAVE YOUR INNOCENCE!
HEH...
I'LL MAKE DO, DON'T WORRY.
KOMUI... CAN YOU HEAR ME?
?!
!
COME TO ME, KOMUI.
I WILL DISTRACT THE LEVEL 4.
TAKE THE INNOCENCE FROM INSIDE ME AND FLEE WITH YOUR PEOPLE!
!!
THE ARK STILL HAS A PORTAL THAT CONNECTS TO THE ASIA BRANCH. TAKE YOUR PEOPLE THERE!
YOUR POSITION HERE IS NO LONGER TENABLE.

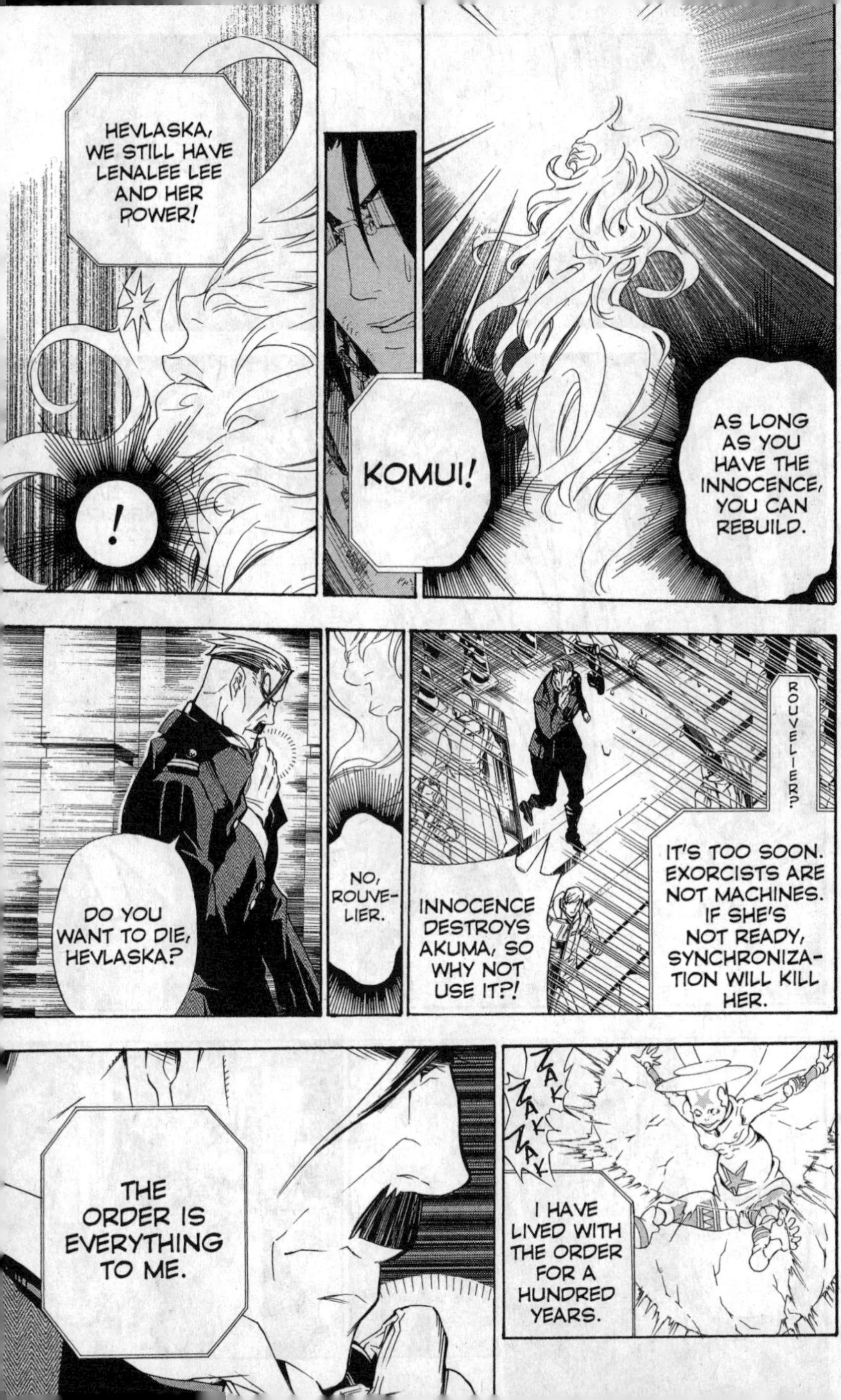
AS LONG AS YOU HAVE THE INNOCENCE, YOU CAN REBUILD.
KOMUI!
HEVLASKA, WE STILL HAVE LENALEE LEE AND HER POWER!
!
ROUVELIER?
IT'S TOO SOON. EXORCISTS ARE NOT MACHINES. IF SHE'S NOT READY, SYNCHRONIZATION WILL KILL HER.
INNOCENCE DESTROYS AKUMA, SO WHY NOT USE IT?!
NO, ROUVELIER.
DO YOU WANT TO DIE, HEVLASKA?
ZAK ZAK ZAK
I HAVE LIVED WITH THE ORDER FOR A HUNDRED YEARS.
THE ORDER IS EVERYTHING TO ME.

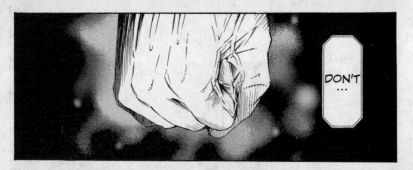

DON'T
...

SPECIAL
INSPEC-
TOR!!

THWAM

LENALEE
LEE...

ROUVE-
LIER...

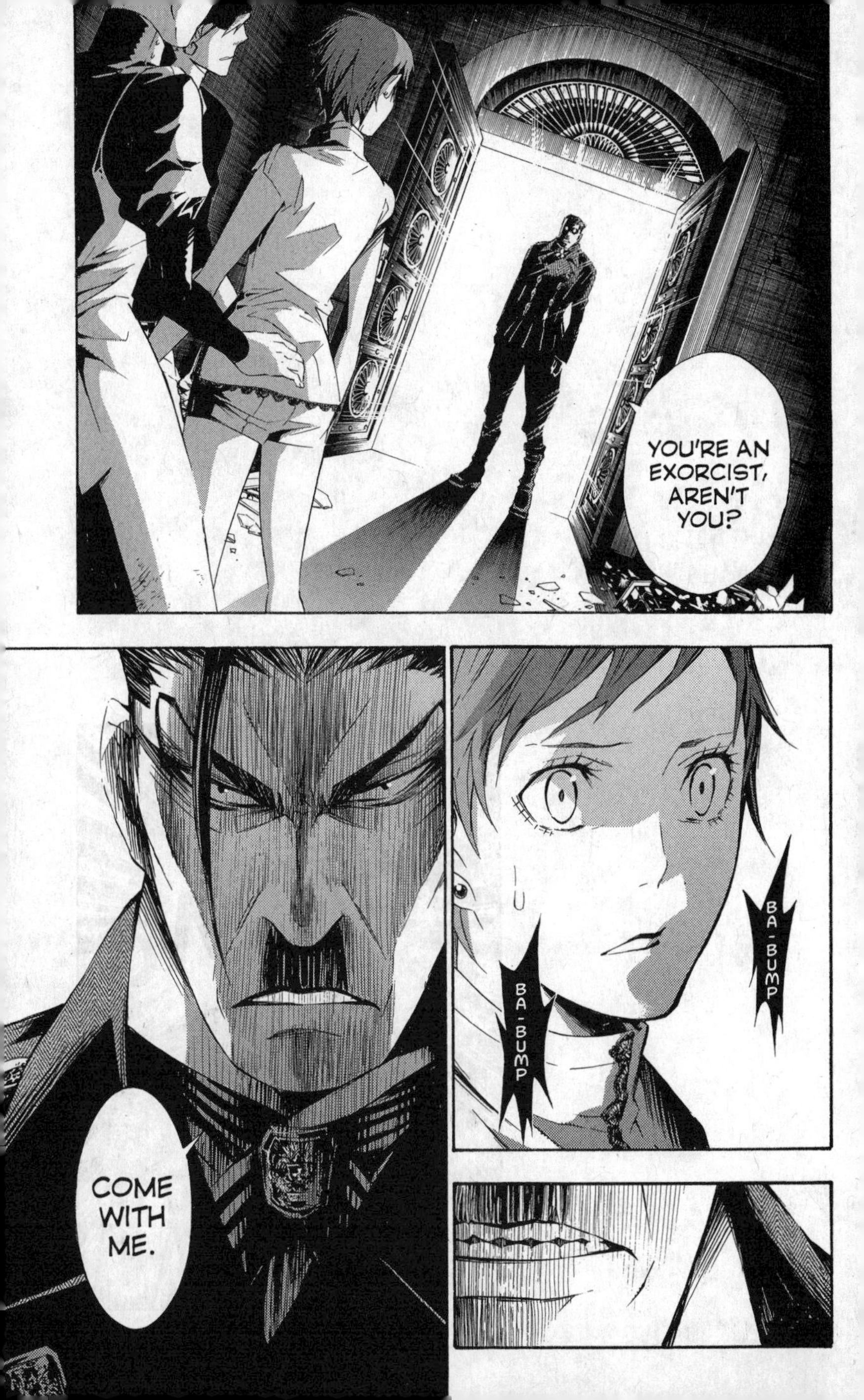
YOU'RE AN EXORCIST, AREN'T YOU?
BA-BUMP
BA-BUMP
COME WITH ME.

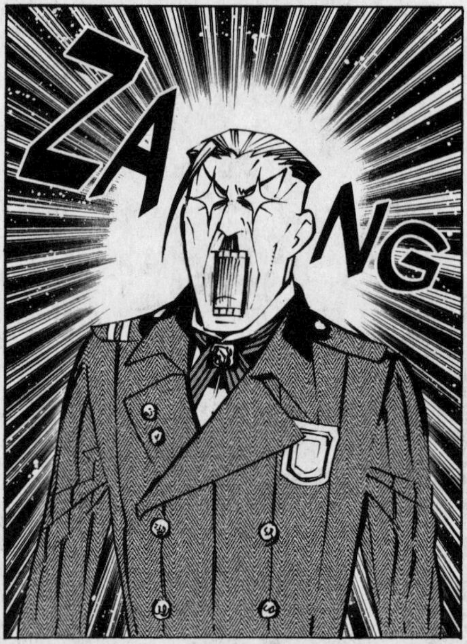
ZANG

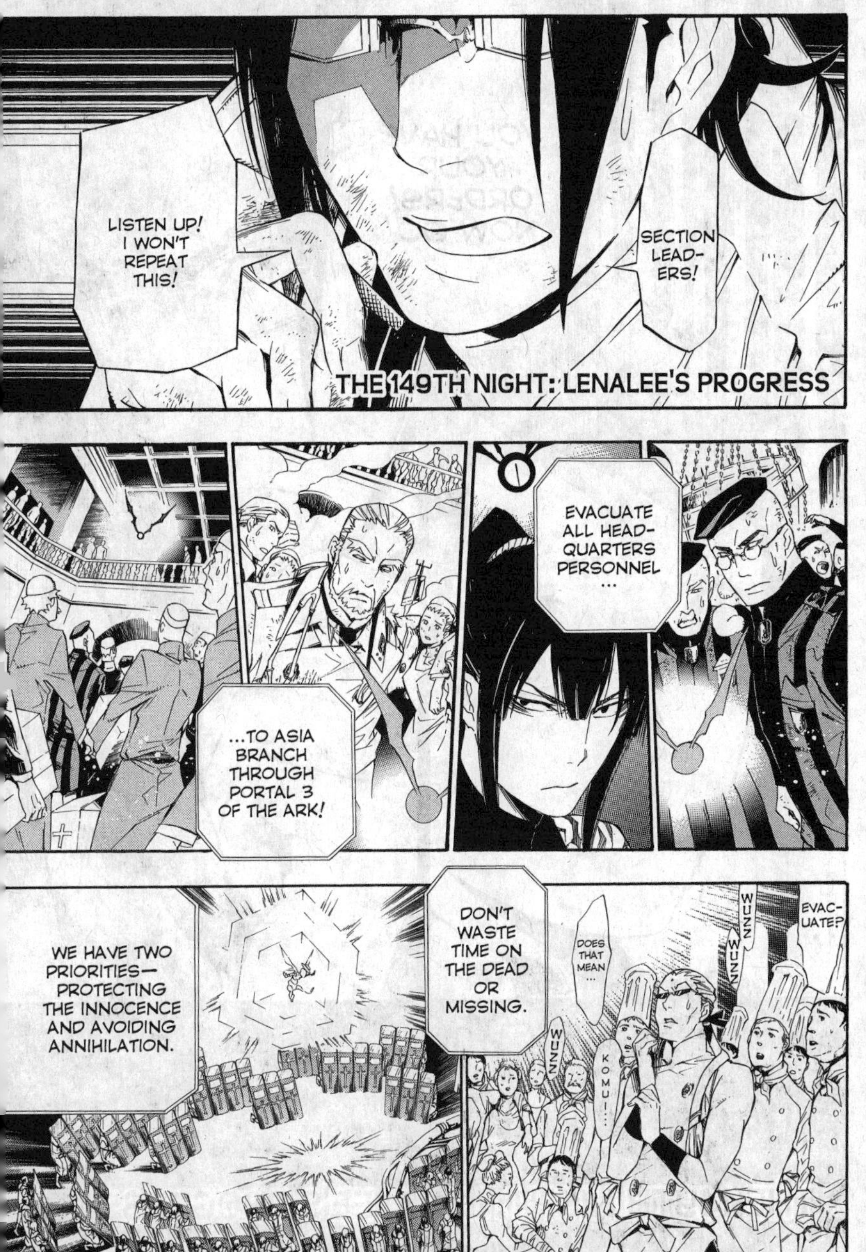
SECTION LEADERS!
LISTEN UP! I WON'T REPEAT THIS!
THE 149TH NIGHT: LENALEE'S PROGRESS
EVACUATE ALL HEADQUARTERS PERSONNEL ...
...TO ASIA BRANCH THROUGH PORTAL 3 OF THE ARK!
EVACUATE?
WUZZ WUZZ
DOES THAT MEAN ...
WUZZ
KOMUI...
DON'T WASTE TIME ON THE DEAD OR MISSING.
WE HAVE TWO PRIORITIES—PROTECTING THE INNOCENCE AND AVOIDING ANNIHILATION.

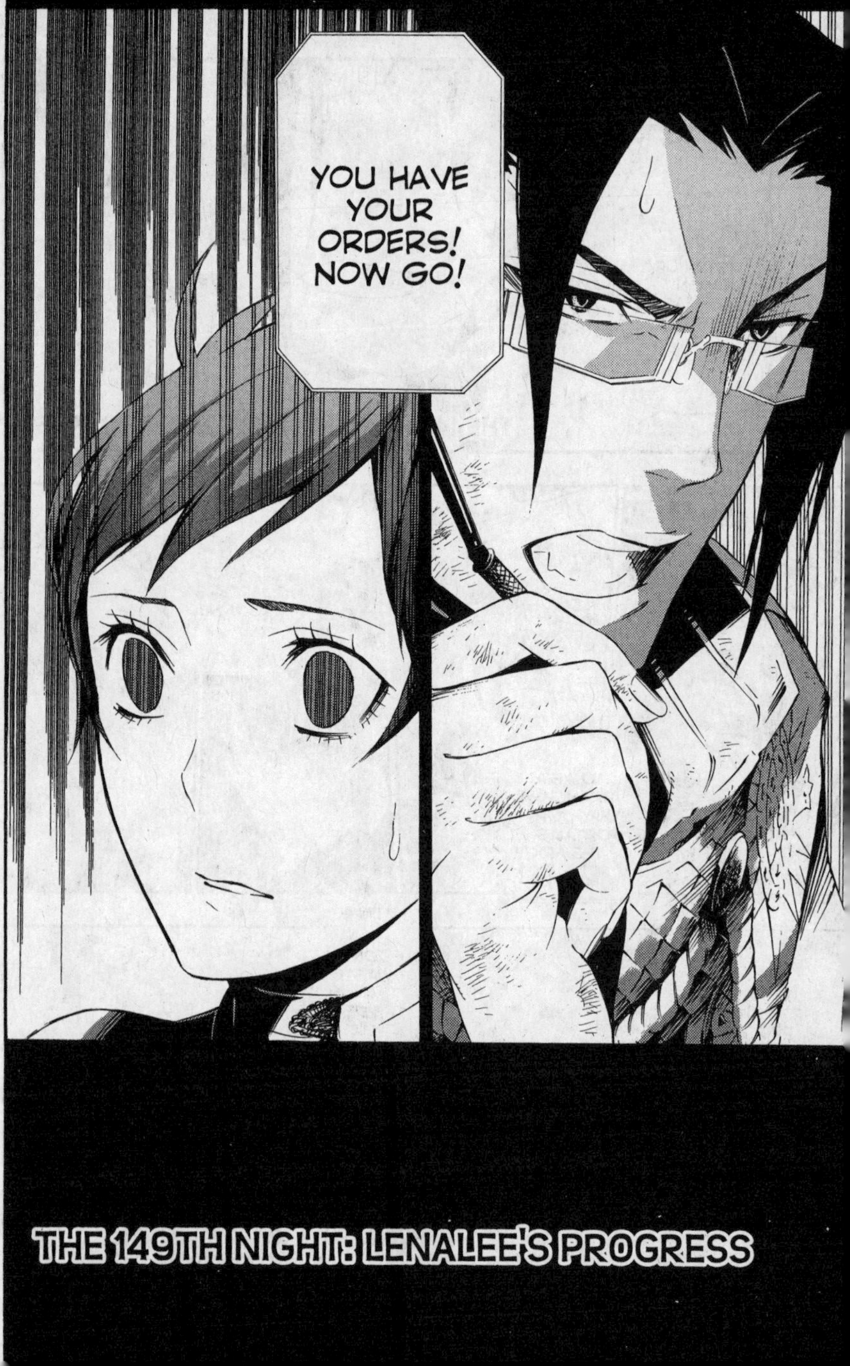
YOU HAVE YOUR ORDERS! NOW GO!

THE 149TH NIGHT: LENALEE'S PROGRESS

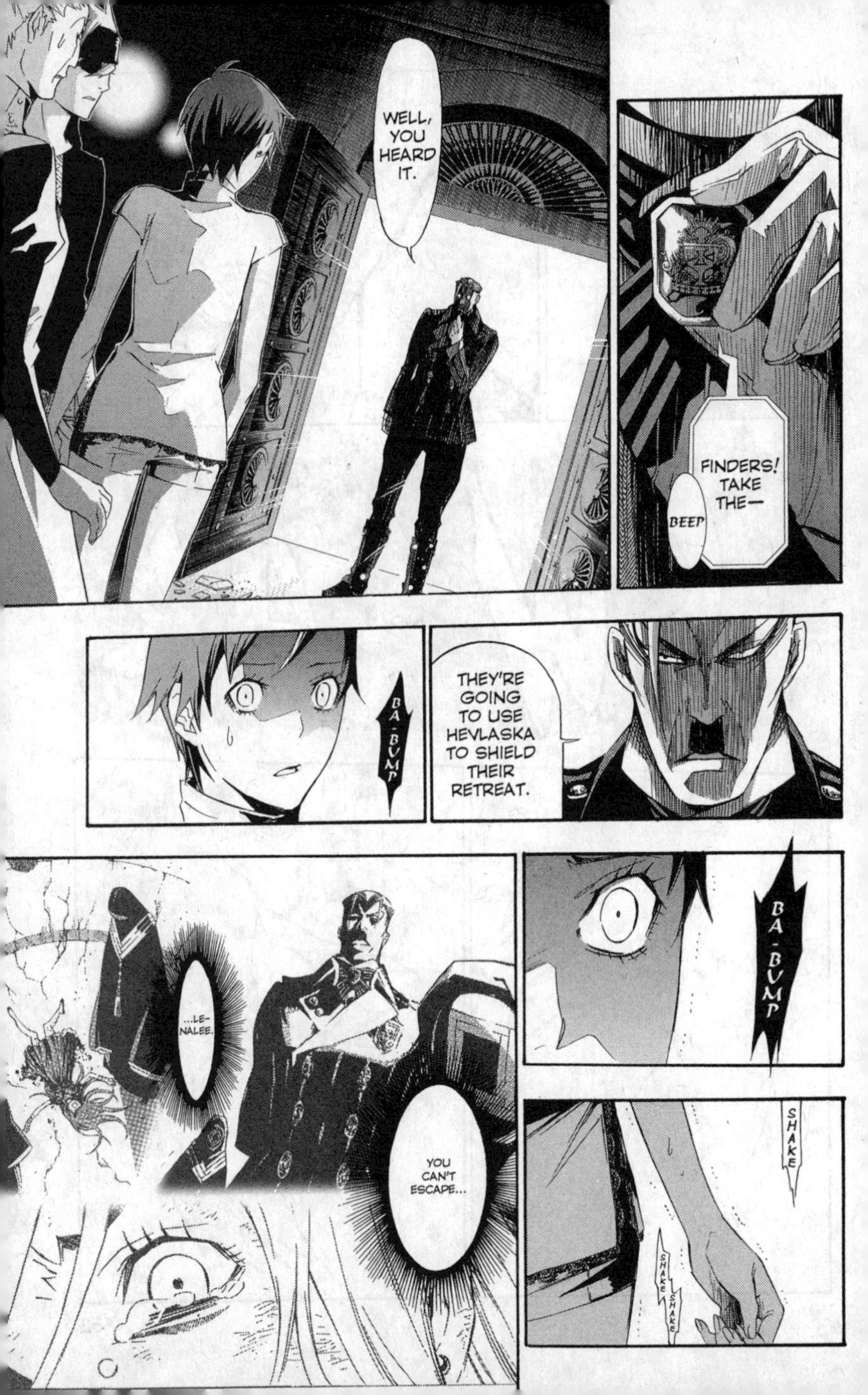
FINDERS! TAKE THE—
BEEP
WELL, YOU HEARD IT.
THEY'RE GOING TO USE HEVLASKA TO SHIELD THEIR RETREAT.
BA-BUMP
BA-BUMP
SHAKE
SHAKE SHAKE
...LE-NALEE.
YOU CAN'T ESCAPE...

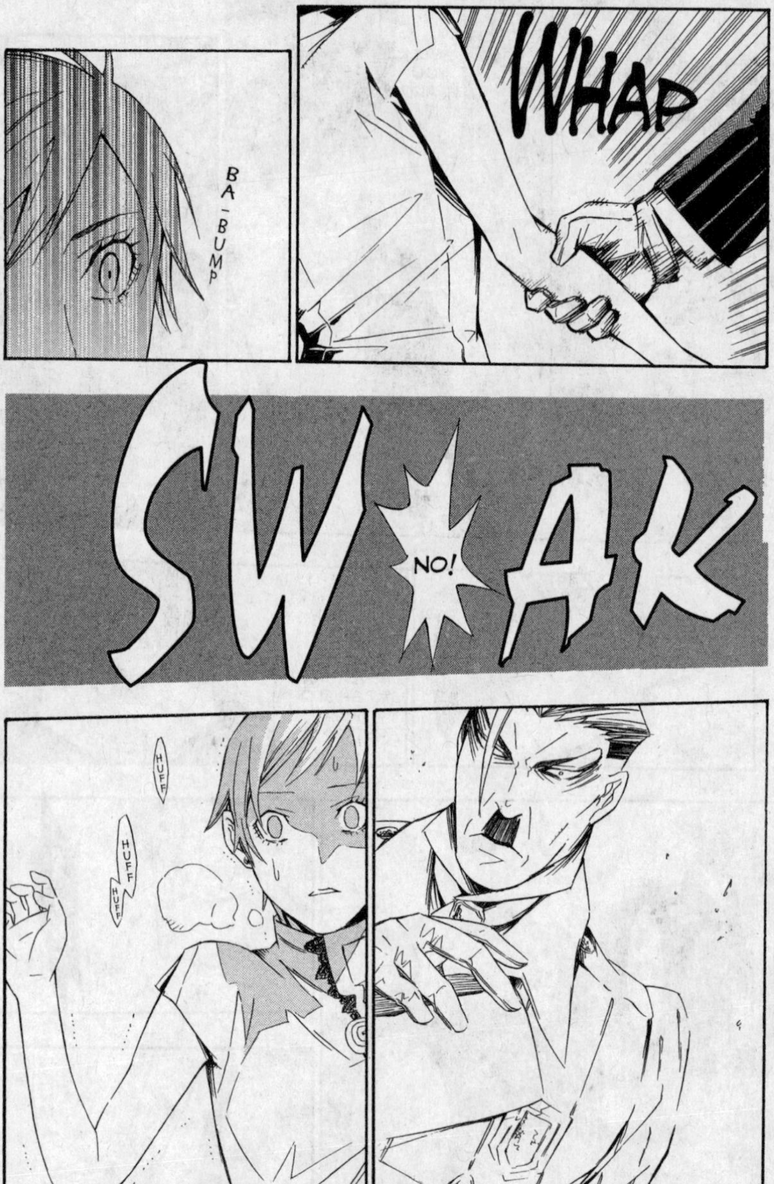
WHAP
BA-BUMP
SWAK
NO!
HUFF
HUFF
HUFF

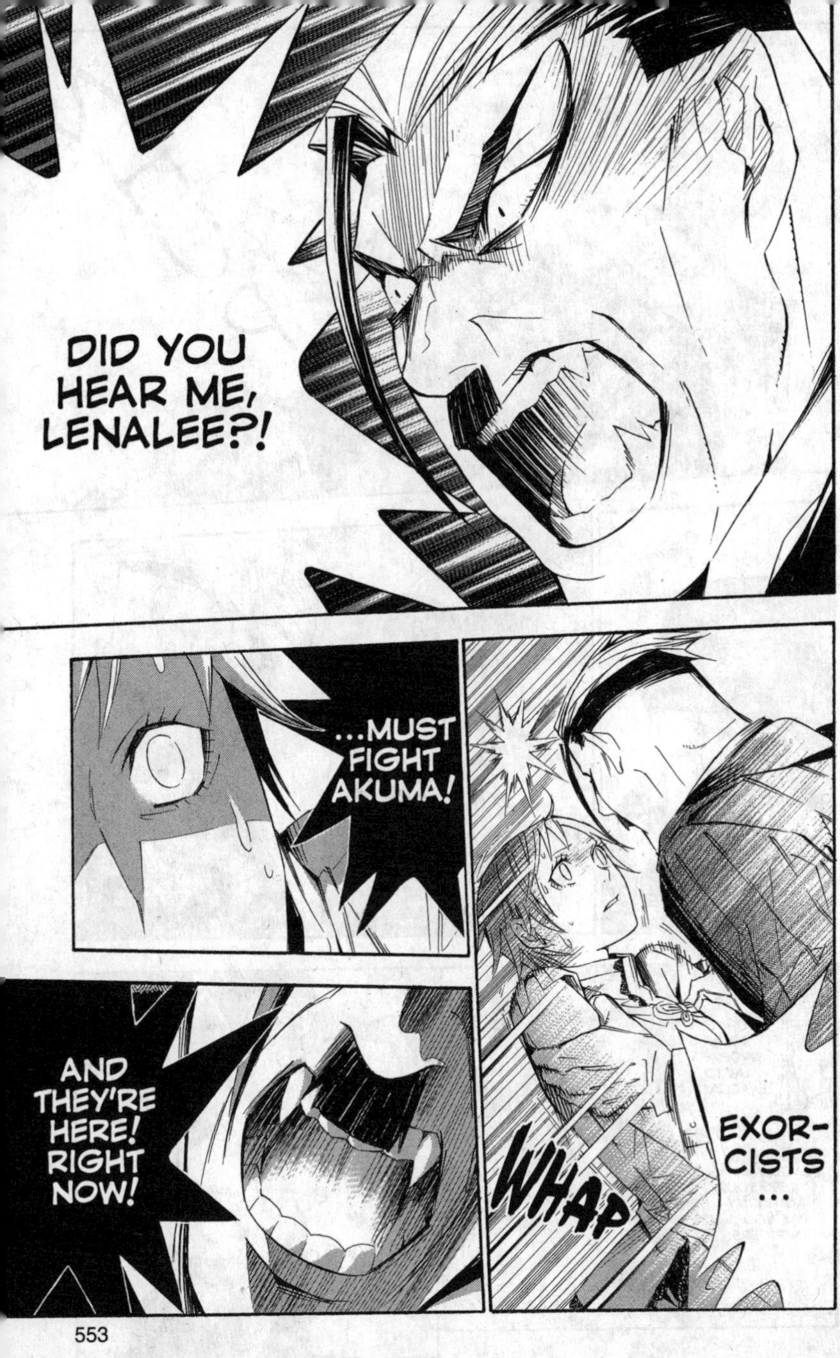
DID YOU HEAR ME, LENALEE?!
EXOR-CISTS ...
WHAP
...MUST FIGHT AKUMA!
AND THEY'RE HERE! RIGHT NOW!

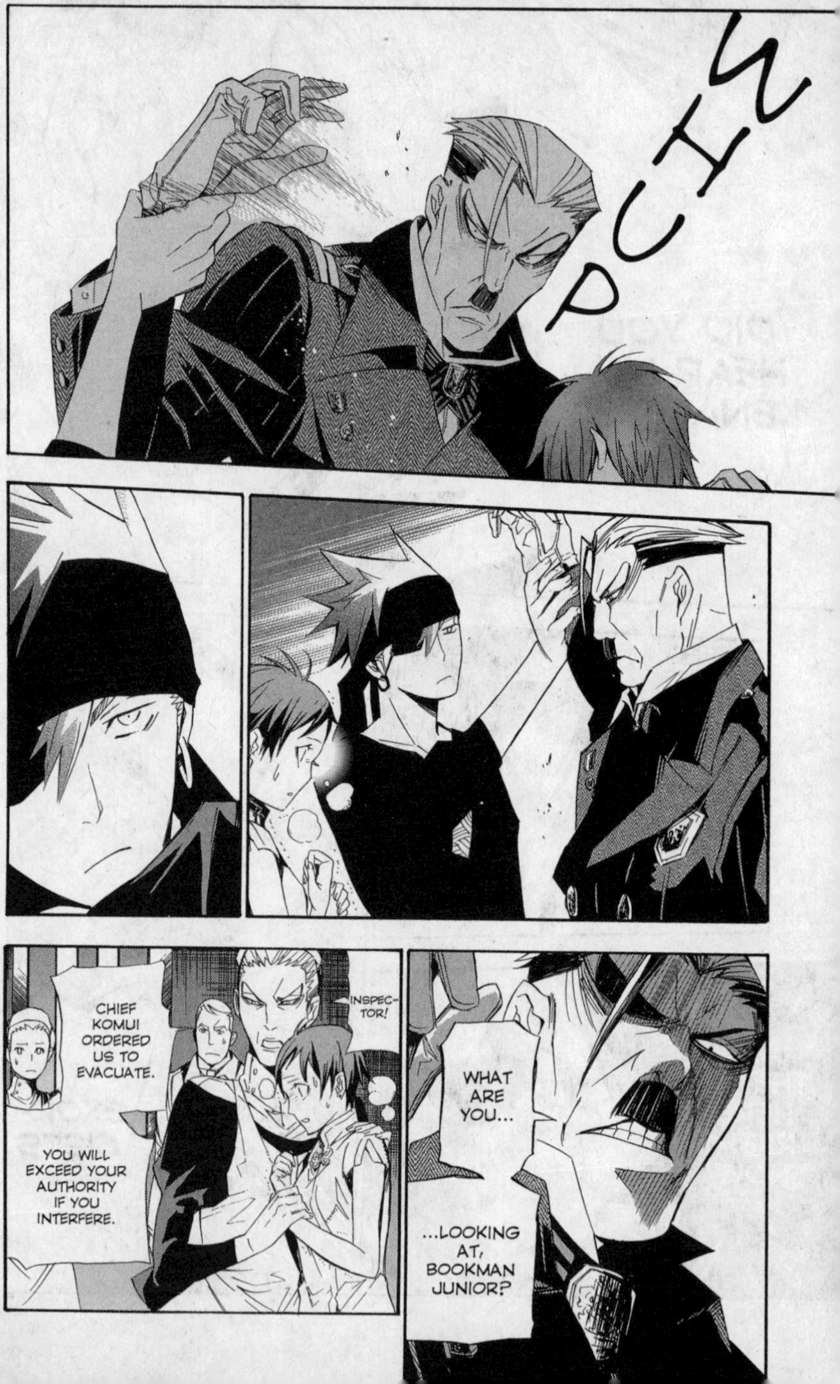
WHUP
WHAT ARE YOU...
...LOOKING AT, BOOKMAN JUNIOR?
INSPECTOR!
CHIEF KOMUI ORDERED US TO EVACUATE.
YOU WILL EXCEED YOUR AUTHORITY IF YOU INTERFERE.

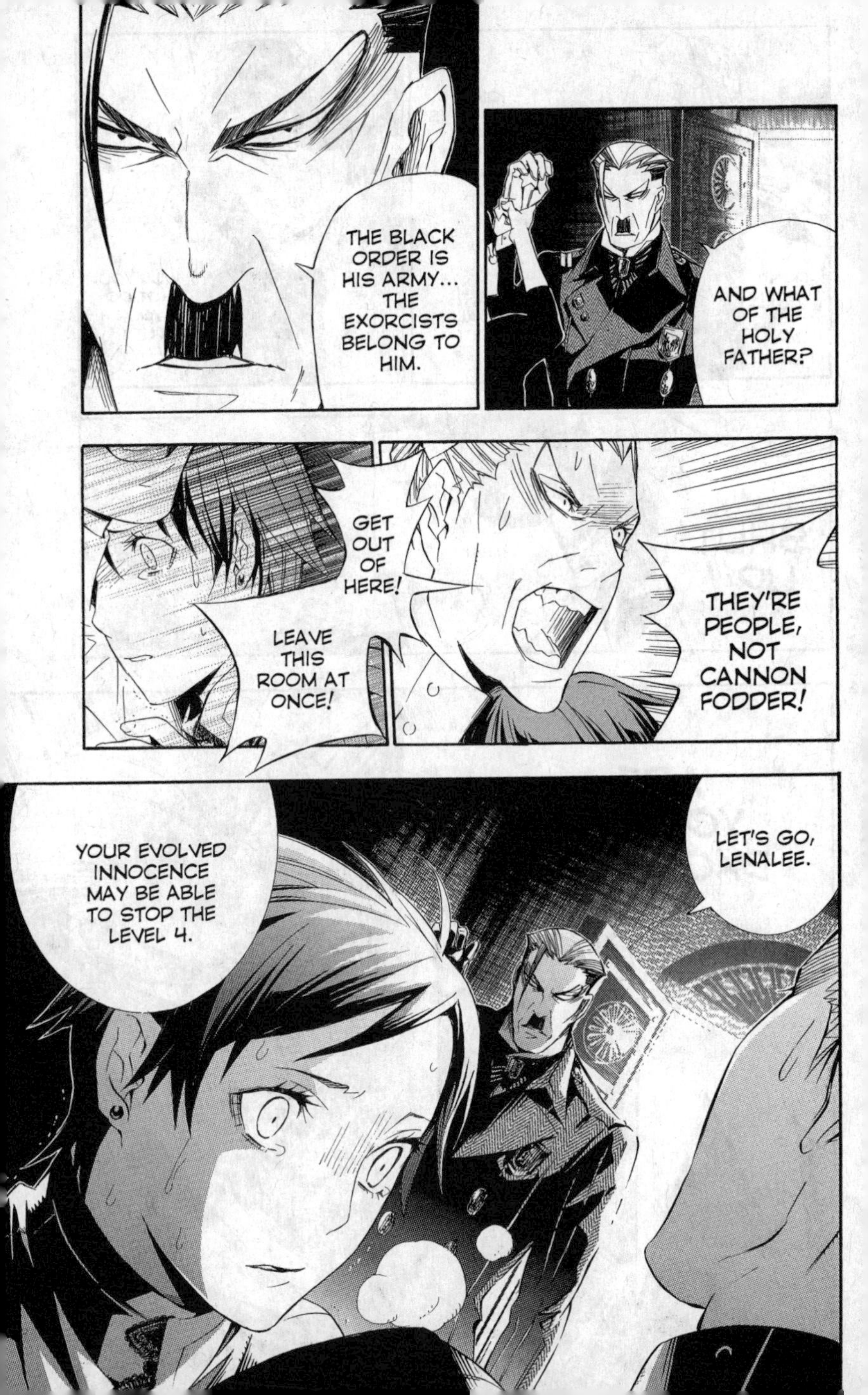
AND WHAT OF THE HOLY FATHER?
THE BLACK ORDER IS HIS ARMY... THE EXORCISTS BELONG TO HIM.
THEY'RE PEOPLE, NOT CANNON FODDER!
GET OUT OF HERE!
LEAVE THIS ROOM AT ONCE!
LET'S GO, LENALEE.
YOUR EVOLVED INNOCENCE MAY BE ABLE TO STOP THE LEVEL 4.

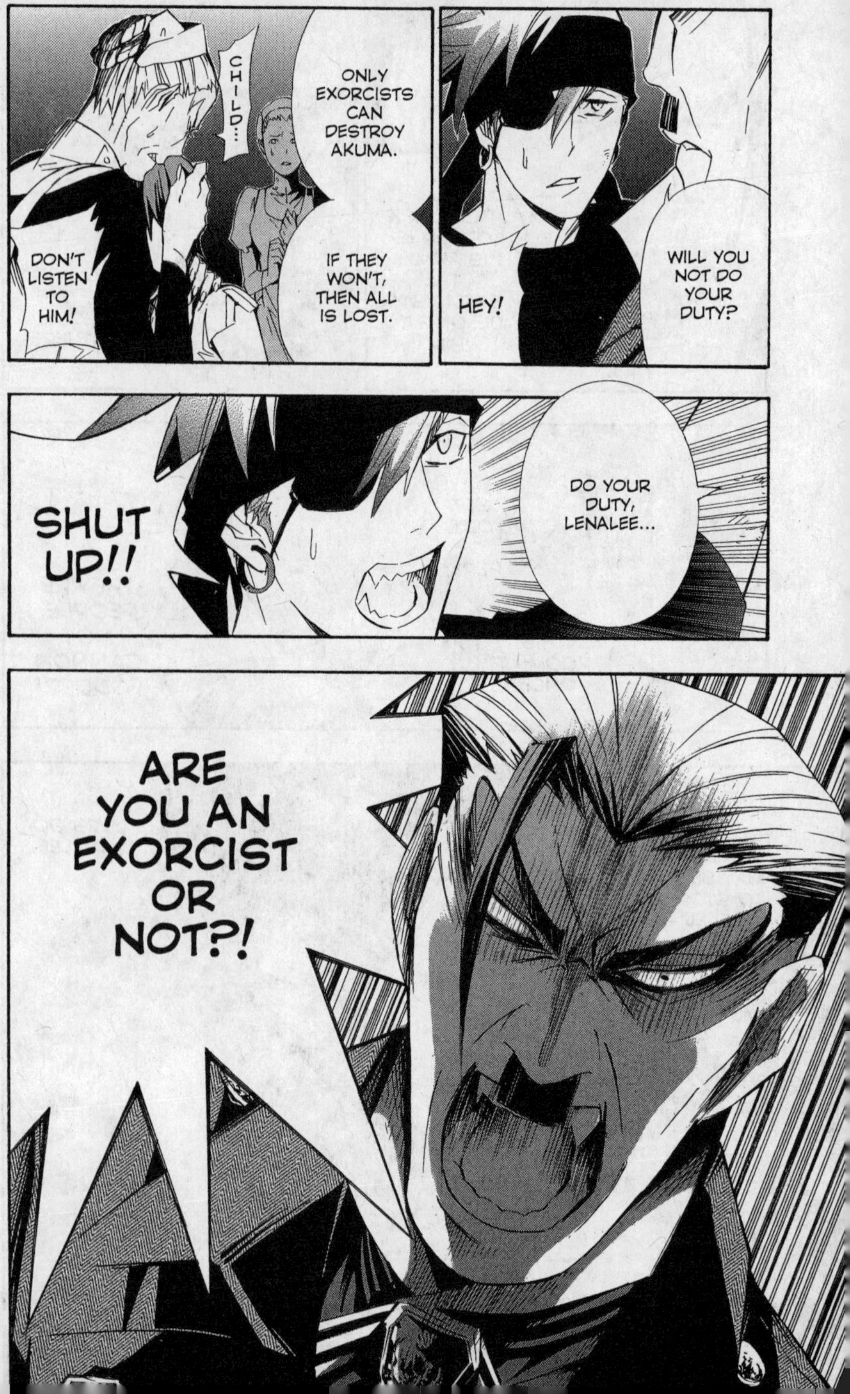
WILL YOU NOT DO YOUR DUTY?
HEY!
ONLY EXORCISTS CAN DESTROY AKUMA.
IF THEY WON'T, THEN ALL IS LOST.
CHILD...
DON'T LISTEN TO HIM!
DO YOUR DUTY, LENALEE...
SHUT UP!!
ARE YOU AN EXORCIST OR NOT?!

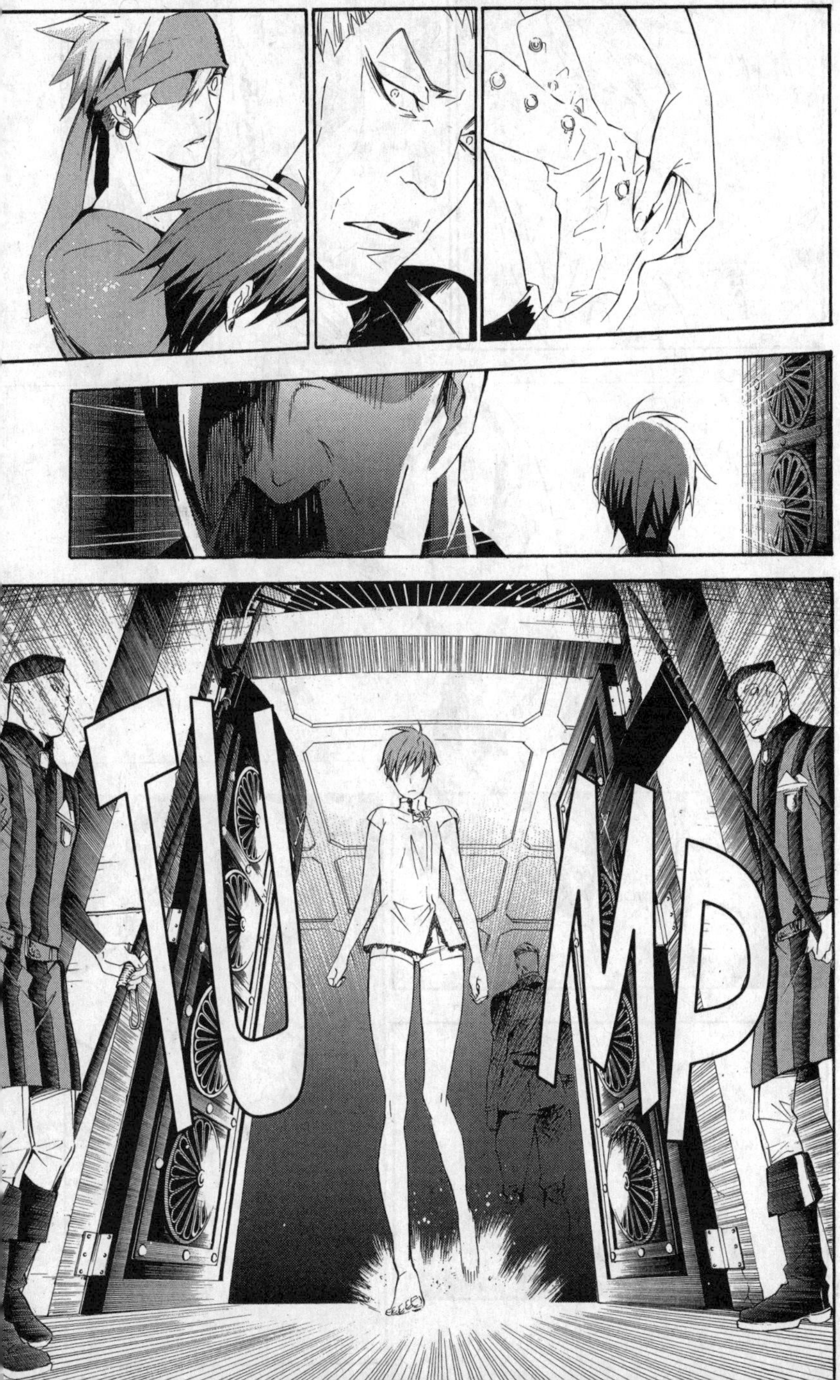
TUMP

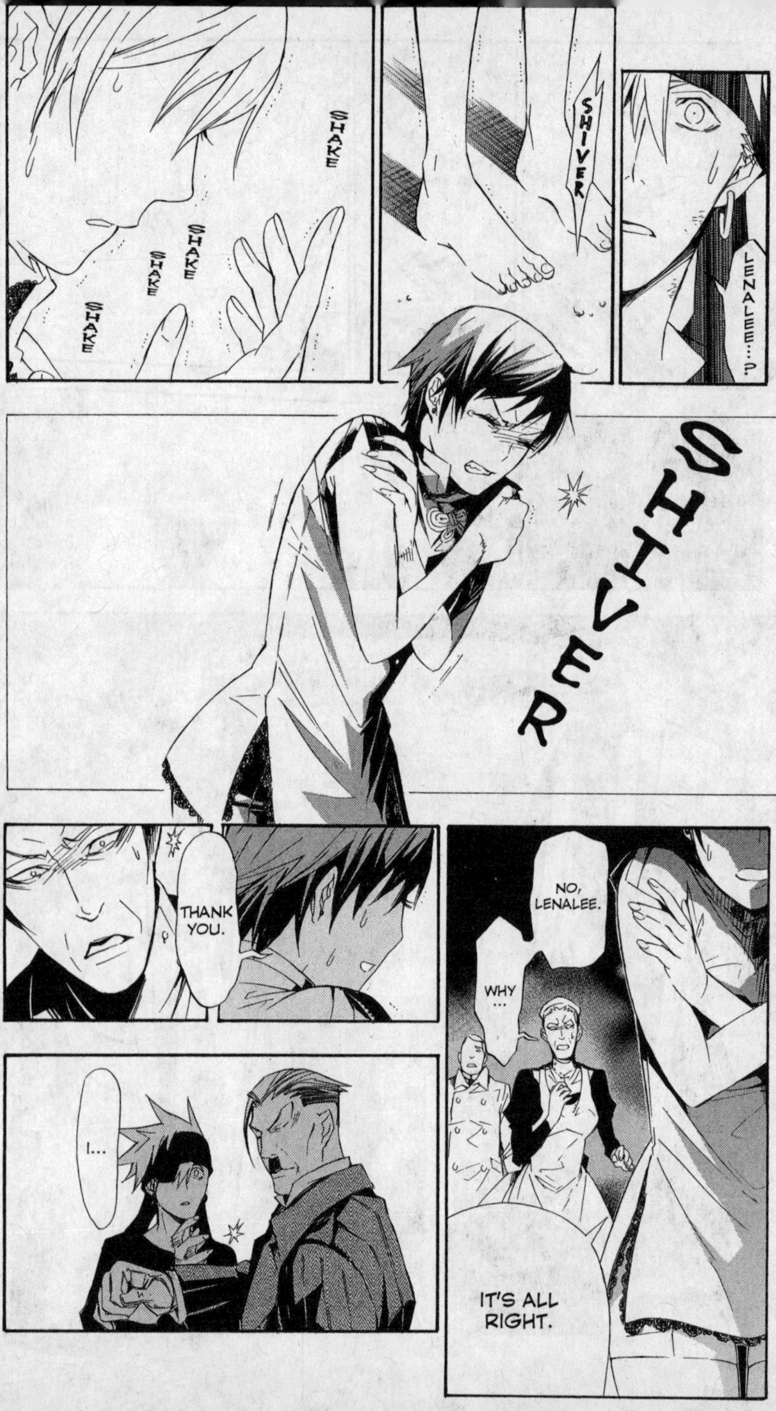
LENALEE...?
SHIVER
SHAKE
SHAKE
SHAKE
SHAKE
SHIVER
NO, LENALEE.
WHY ...
IT'S ALL RIGHT.
THANK YOU.
I...

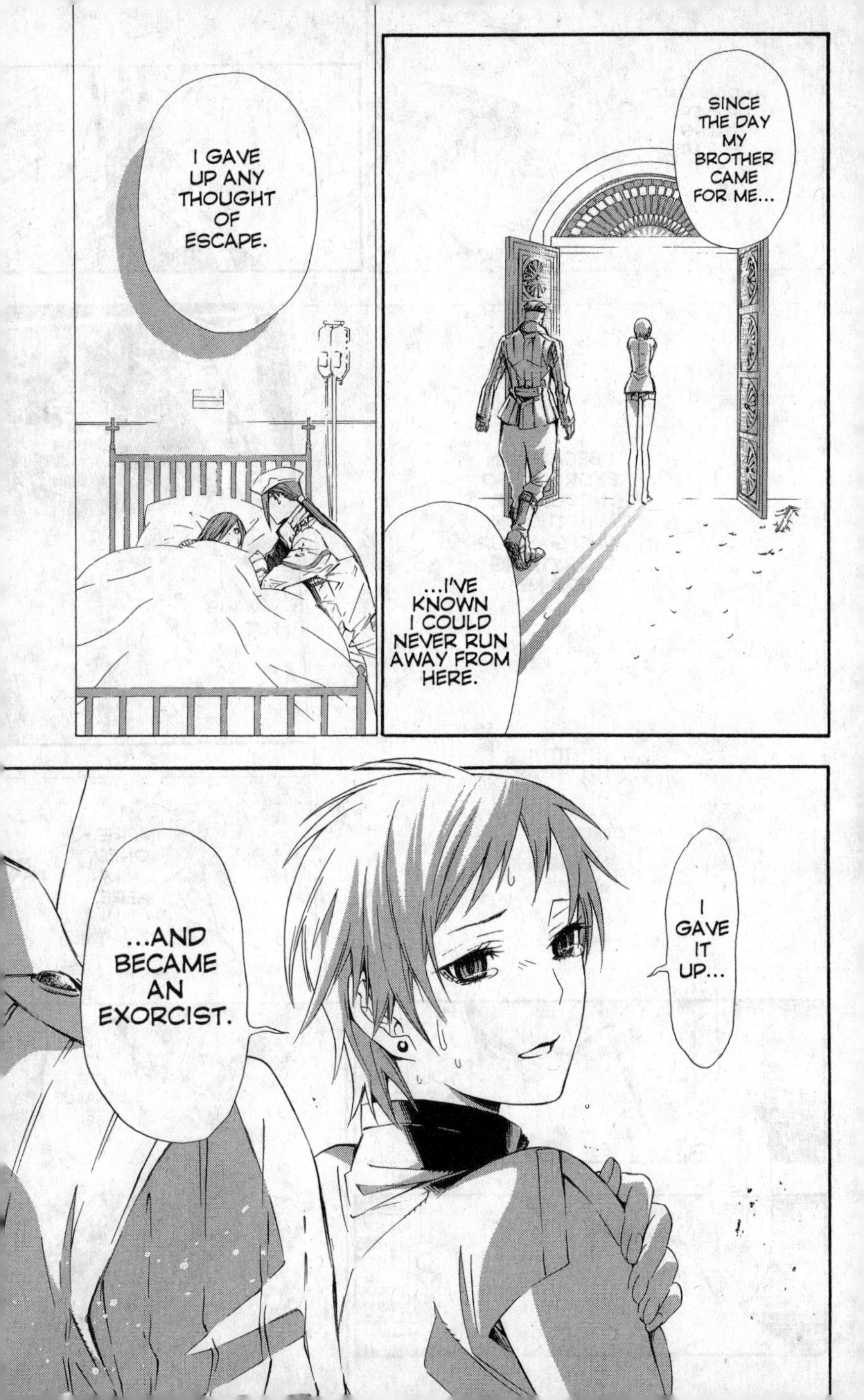
SINCE THE DAY MY BROTHER CAME FOR ME...
...I'VE KNOWN I COULD NEVER RUN AWAY FROM HERE.
I GAVE UP ANY THOUGHT OF ESCAPE.
I GAVE IT UP...
...AND BECAME AN EXORCIST.

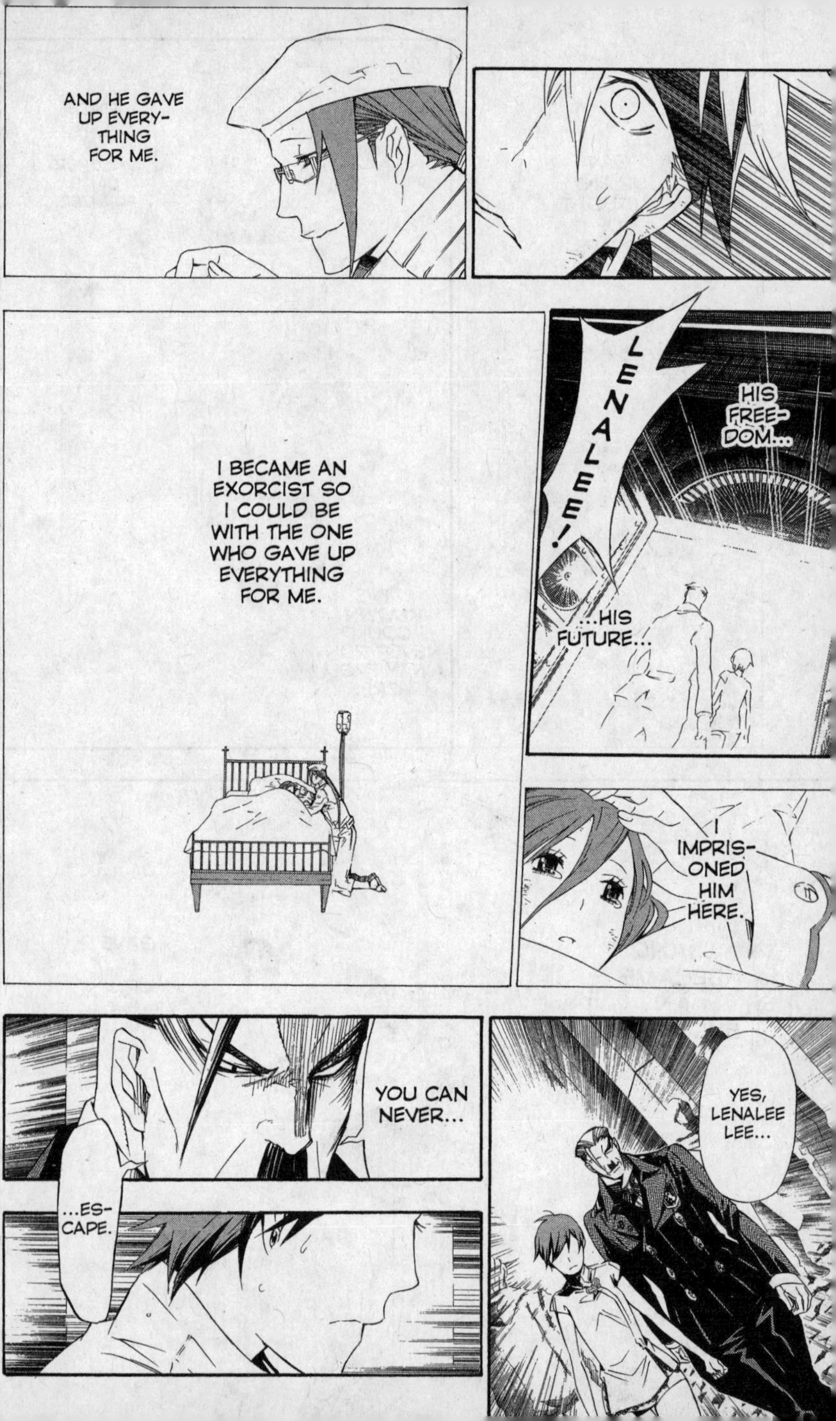
AND HE GAVE UP EVERY-THING FOR ME.
LENALEE!
HIS FREE-DOM...
...HIS FUTURE...
I IMPRIS-ONED HIM HERE.
I BECAME AN EXORCIST SO I COULD BE WITH THE ONE WHO GAVE UP EVERYTHING FOR ME.
YES, LENALEE LEE...
YOU CAN NEVER...
...ES-CAPE.

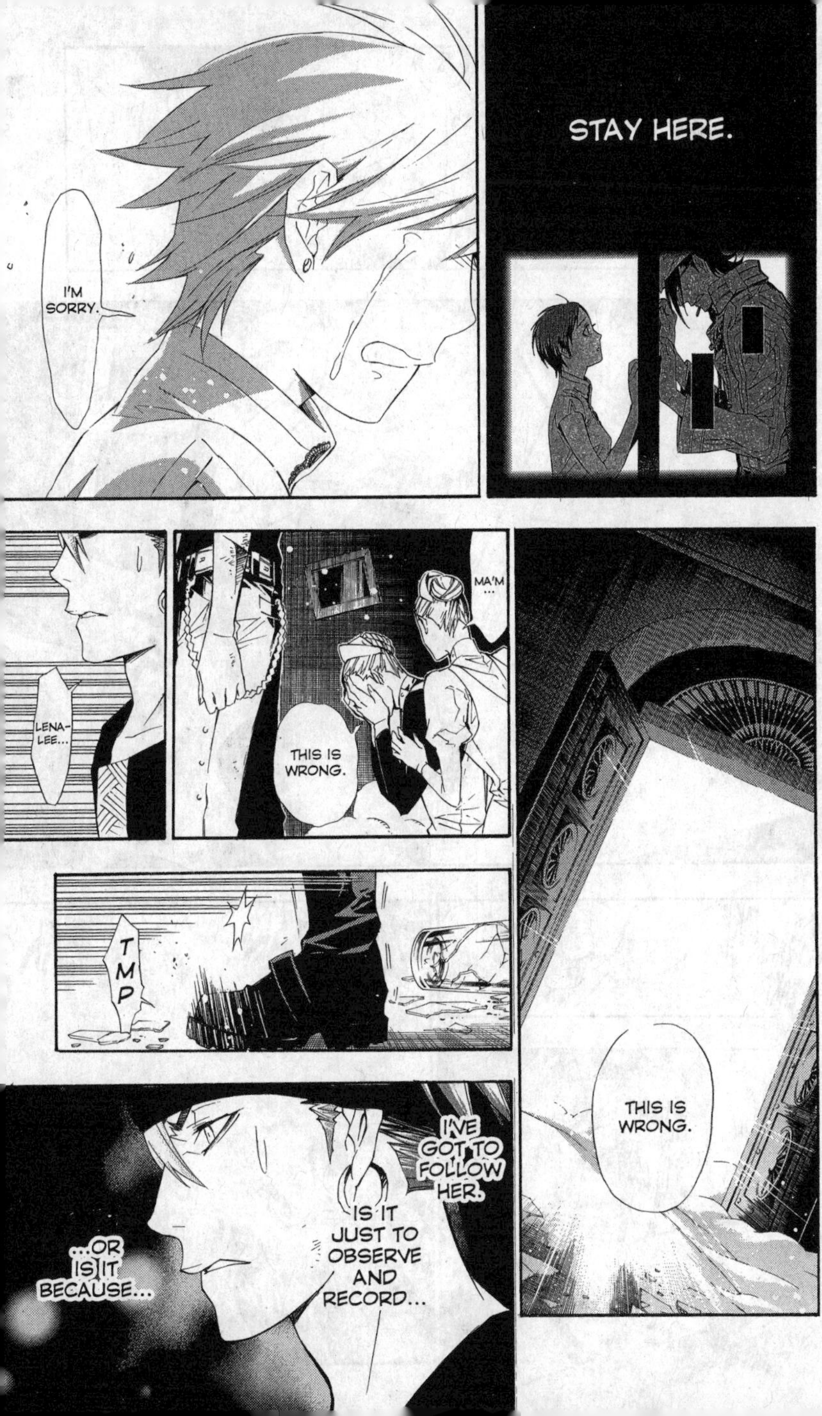
STAY HERE.
I'M SORRY.
THIS IS WRONG.
MA'M ...
THIS IS WRONG.
LENA-LEE...
TMP
I'VE GOT TO FOLLOW HER.
IS IT JUST TO OBSERVE AND RECORD...
...OR IS IT BECAUSE...

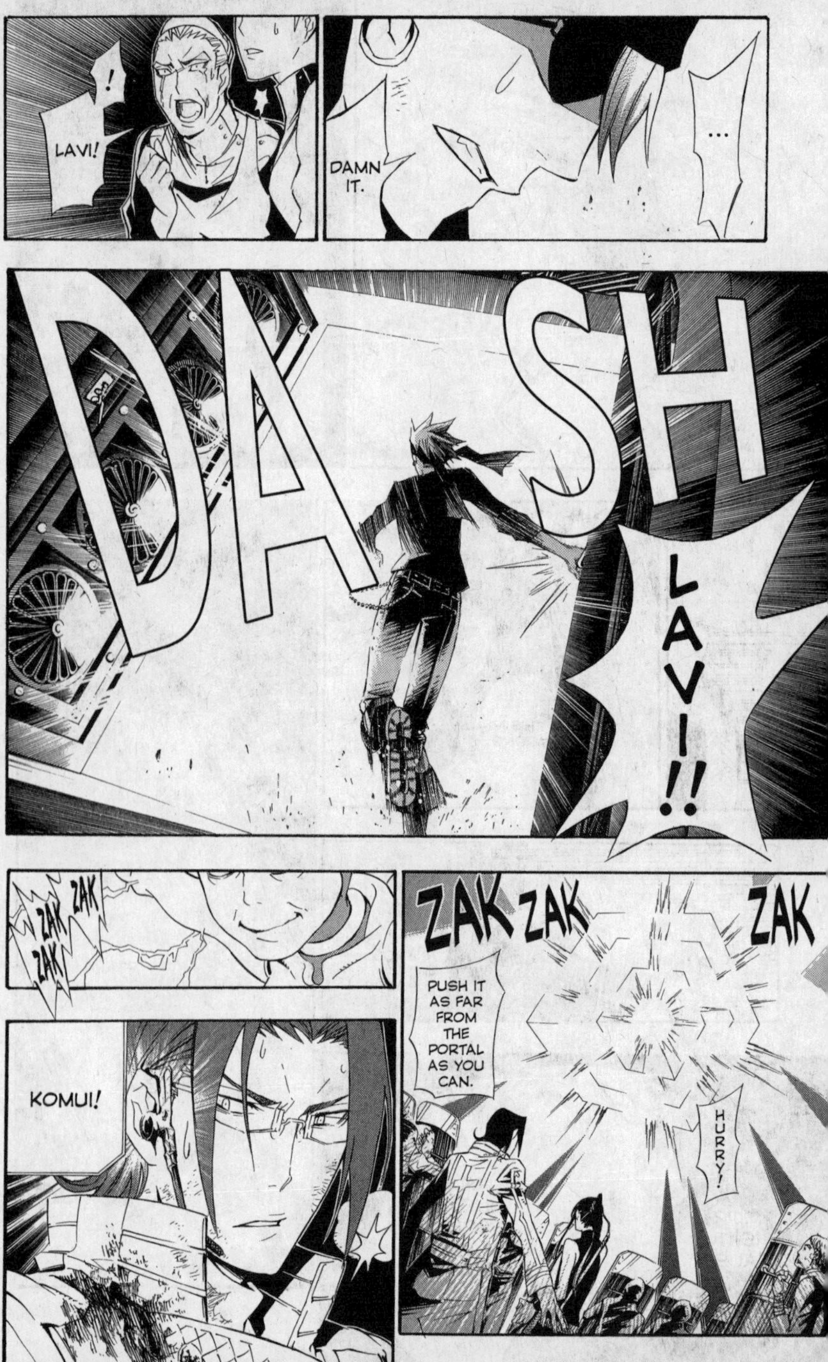
...
DAMN IT.
!
LAVI!
DASH
LAVI!!
ZAK
ZAK
ZAK
PUSH IT AS FAR FROM THE PORTAL AS YOU CAN.
HURRY!
ZAK
ZAK
ZAK
KOMUI!

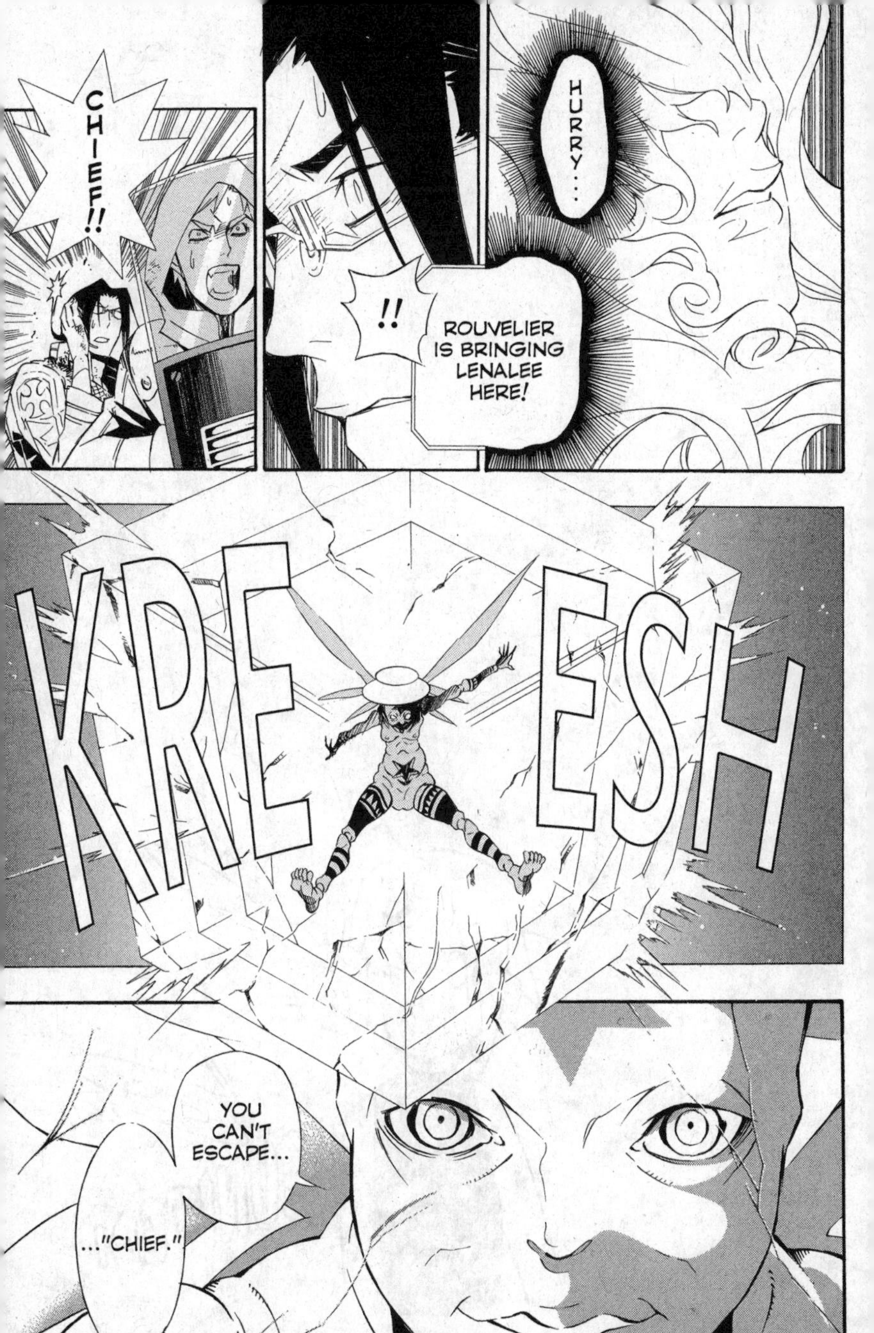
HURRY...
ROUVELIER IS BRINGING LENALEE HERE!
!!
CHIEF!!
KREESH
YOU CAN'T ESCAPE...
..."CHIEF."

VOL.15 BLACK STAR, RED STAR (END)

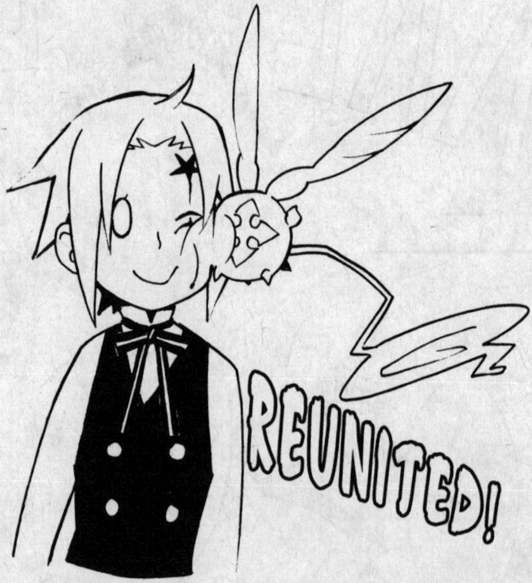
REUNITED!

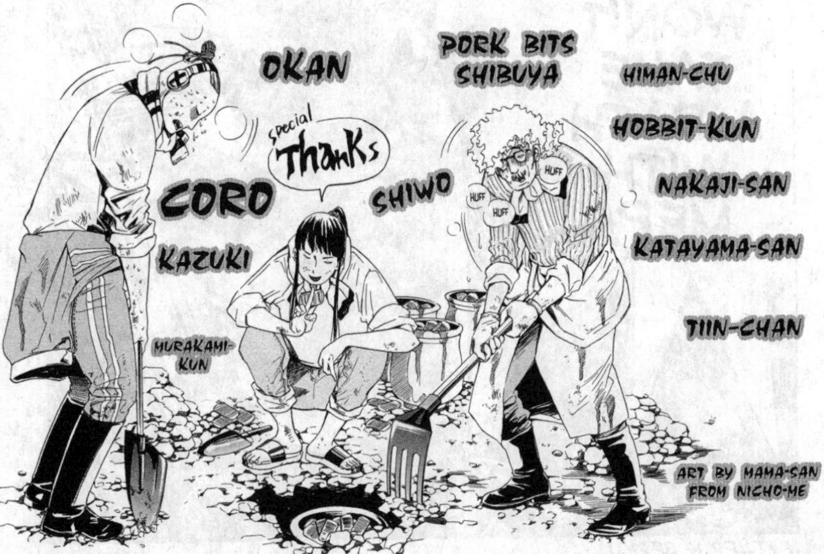
special Thanks
PORK BITS SHIBUYA
OKAN
HIMAN-CHU
HOBBIT-KUN
NAKAJI-SAN
KATAYAMA-SAN
TIIN-CHAN
SHIWO
CORO
KAZUKI
MURAKAMI-KUN
HUFF
HUFF
HUFF
ART BY MAMA-SAN FROM NICHO-ME

THE PEOPLE OF D.GRAY HOUSE: THE LONELY FATHER

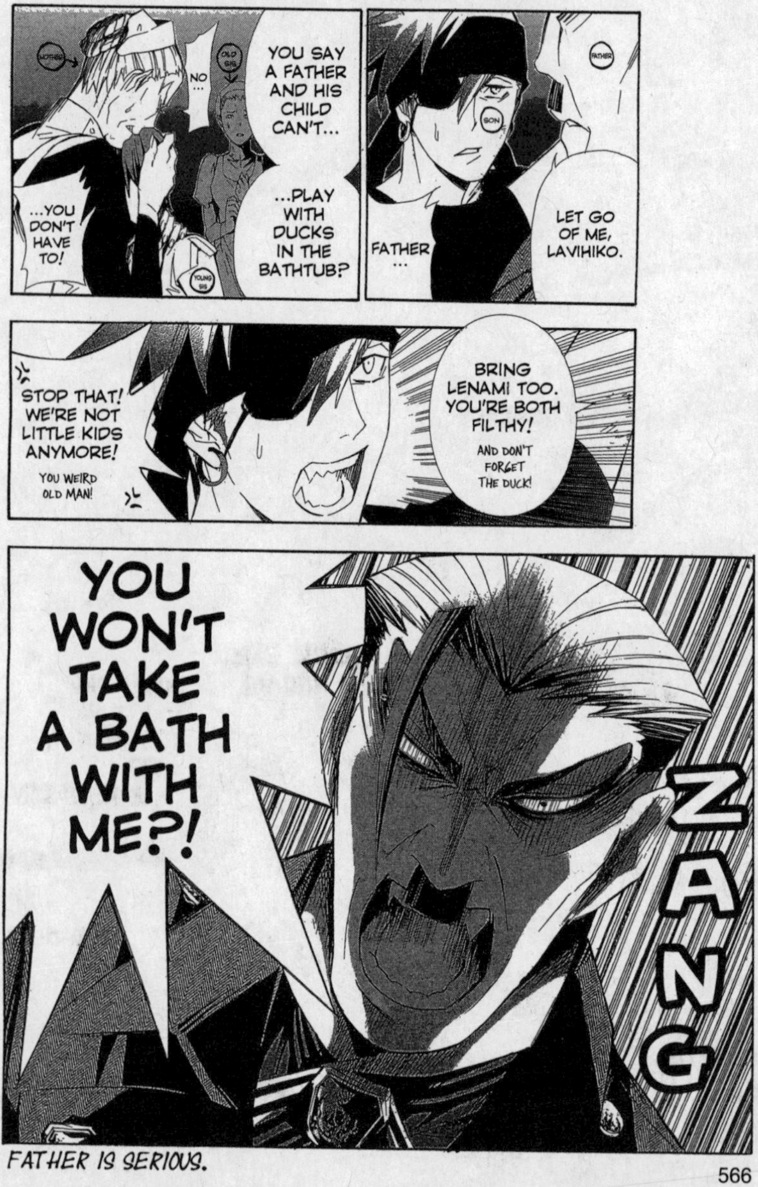
FATHER
SON
LET GO OF ME, LAVIHIKO.
FATHER ...
YOU SAY A FATHER AND HIS CHILD CAN'T...
...PLAY WITH DUCKS IN THE BATHTUB?
OLD SIS
NO ...
MOTHER
...YOU DON'T HAVE TO!
YOUNG SIS
BRING LENAMI TOO. YOU'RE BOTH FILTHY!
AND DON'T FORGET THE DUCK!
STOP THAT! WE'RE NOT LITTLE KIDS ANYMORE!
YOU WEIRD OLD MAN!
YOU WON'T TAKE A BATH WITH ME?!
ZANG

FATHER IS SERIOUS.

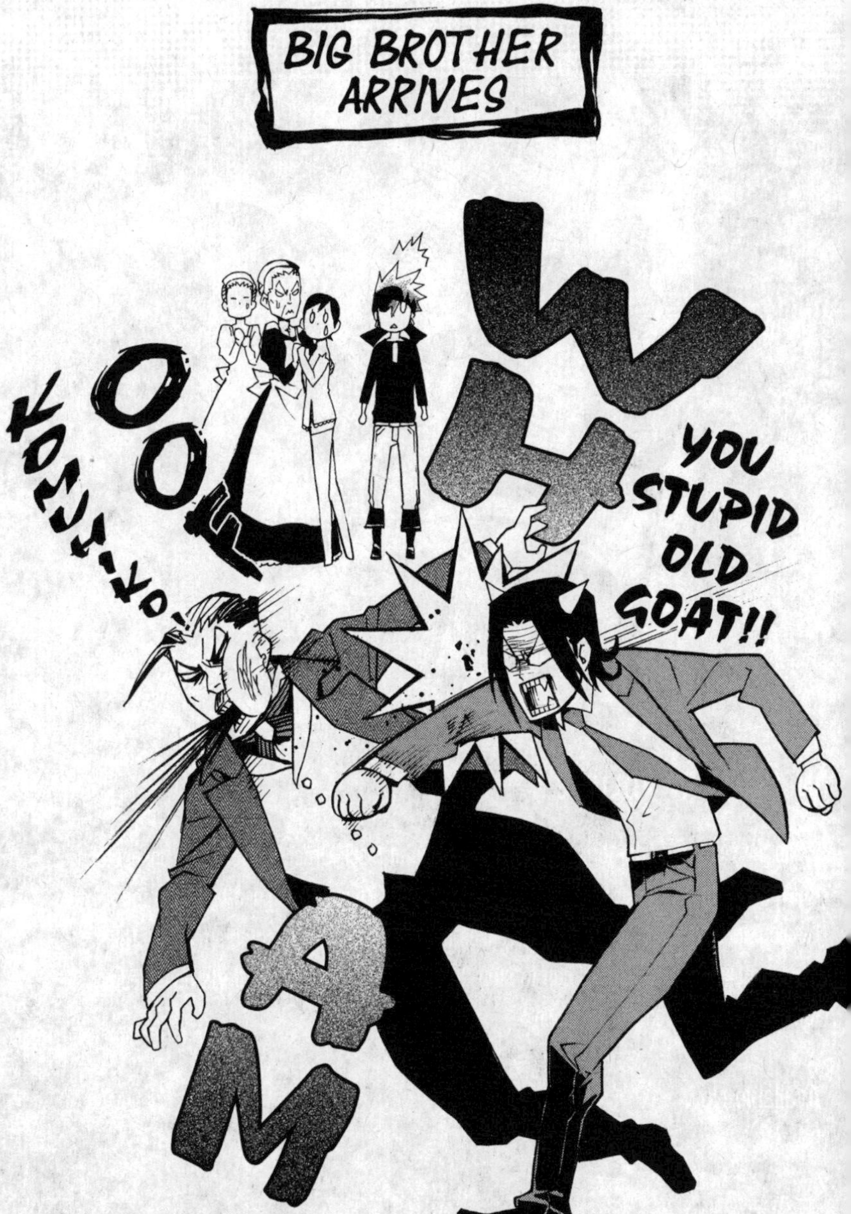
BIG BROTHER ARRIVES
WHAM
YOU STUPID OLD GOAT!!
KOMUI-KO!!
OO

THE PEOPLE OF D.GRAY HOUSE (THE END)

...XT VOLUME...

...4 akuma threatens all who remain at Black Order headqua... ...s Lenalee to a meeting with Hevlaska. Komui, consumed by... ...follow, but that only causes the Level 4 akuma to come a... ...ts do all they can to stop the Level 4, but their best effort... ...even slow it down!

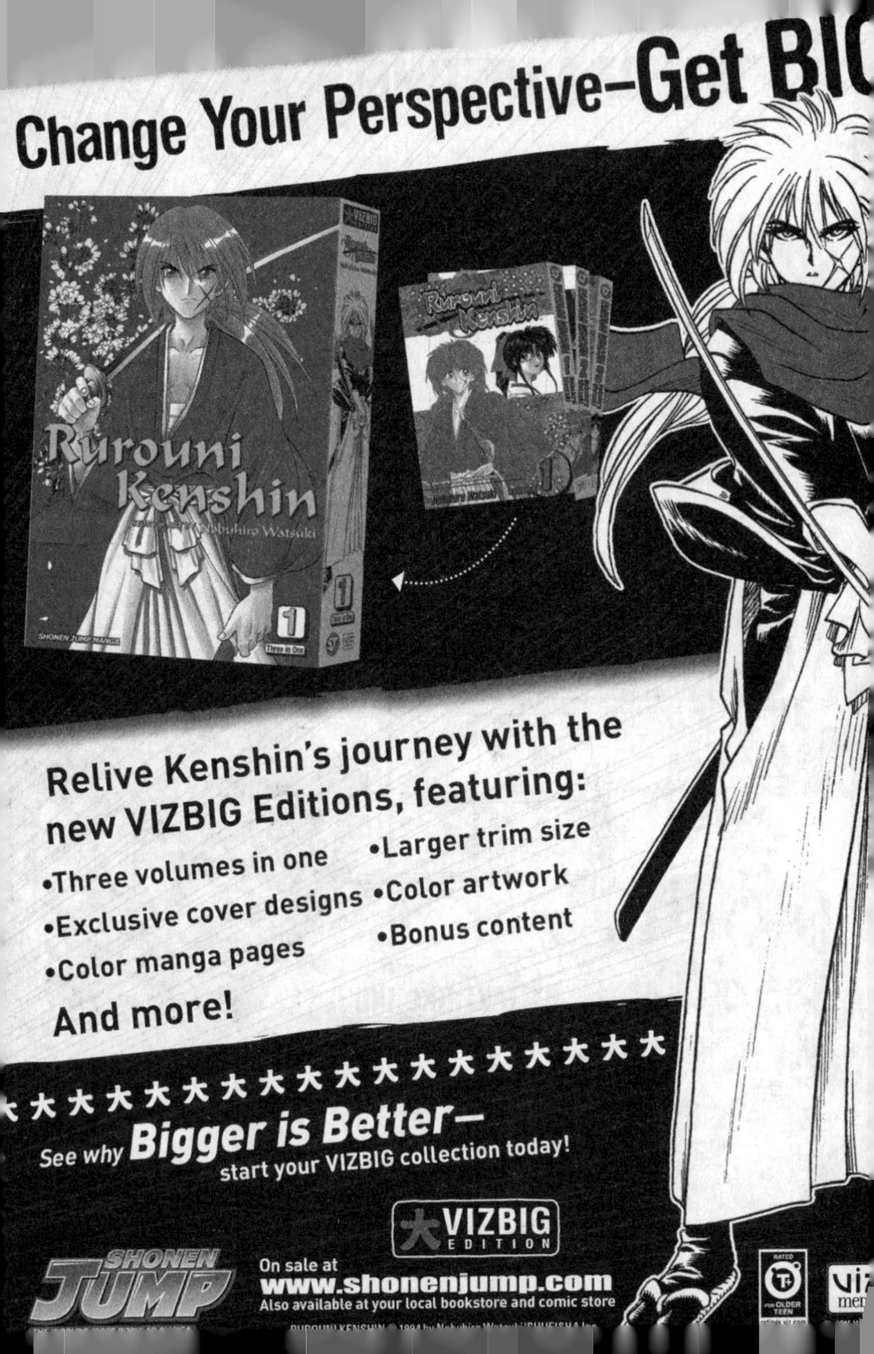
Change Your Perspective—Get BIG
Rurouni Kenshin
Nobuhiro Watsuki
SHONEN JUMP MANGA
Three in One
Relive Kenshin's journey with the new VIZBIG Editions, featuring:
•Three volumes in one
•Larger trim size
•Exclusive cover designs
•Color artwork
•Color manga pages
•Bonus content
And more!
See why Bigger is Better—
start your VIZBIG collection today!
VIZBIG EDITION
SHONEN JUMP
On sale at
www.shonenjump.com
Also available at your local bookstore and comic store
RATED T+ FOR OLDER TEEN

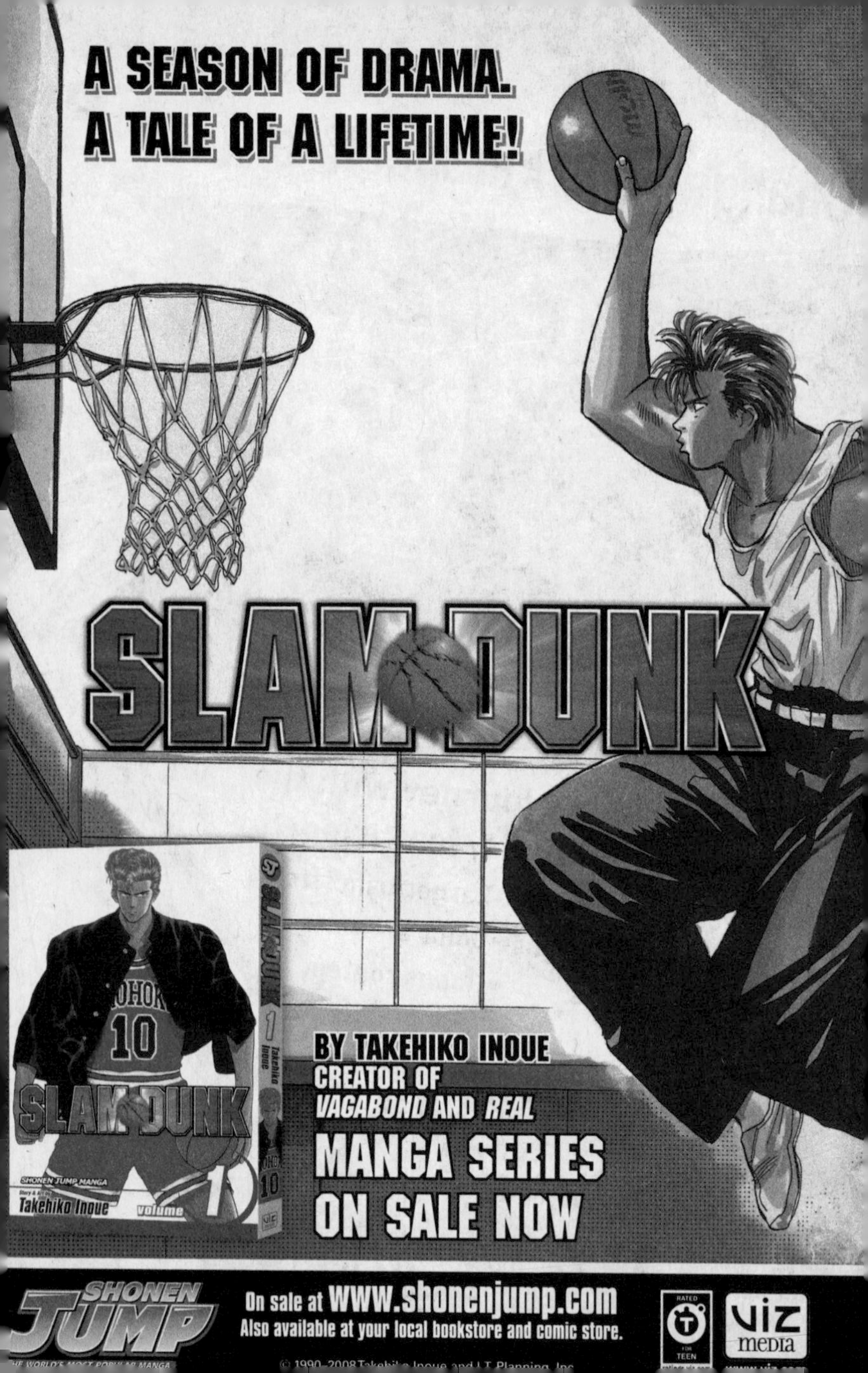
A SEASON OF DRAMA.
A TALE OF A LIFETIME!
SLAM DUNK
SLAM DUNK
SHONEN JUMP MANGA
Story & Art by
Takehiko Inoue
volume 1
BY TAKEHIKO INOUE
CREATOR OF
VAGABOND AND REAL
MANGA SERIES
ON SALE NOW
SHONEN JUMP
On sale at www.shonenjump.com
Also available at your local bookstore and comic store.
RATED T FOR TEEN
VIZ media
© 1990–2008 Takehiko Inoue and I.T. Planning, Inc.

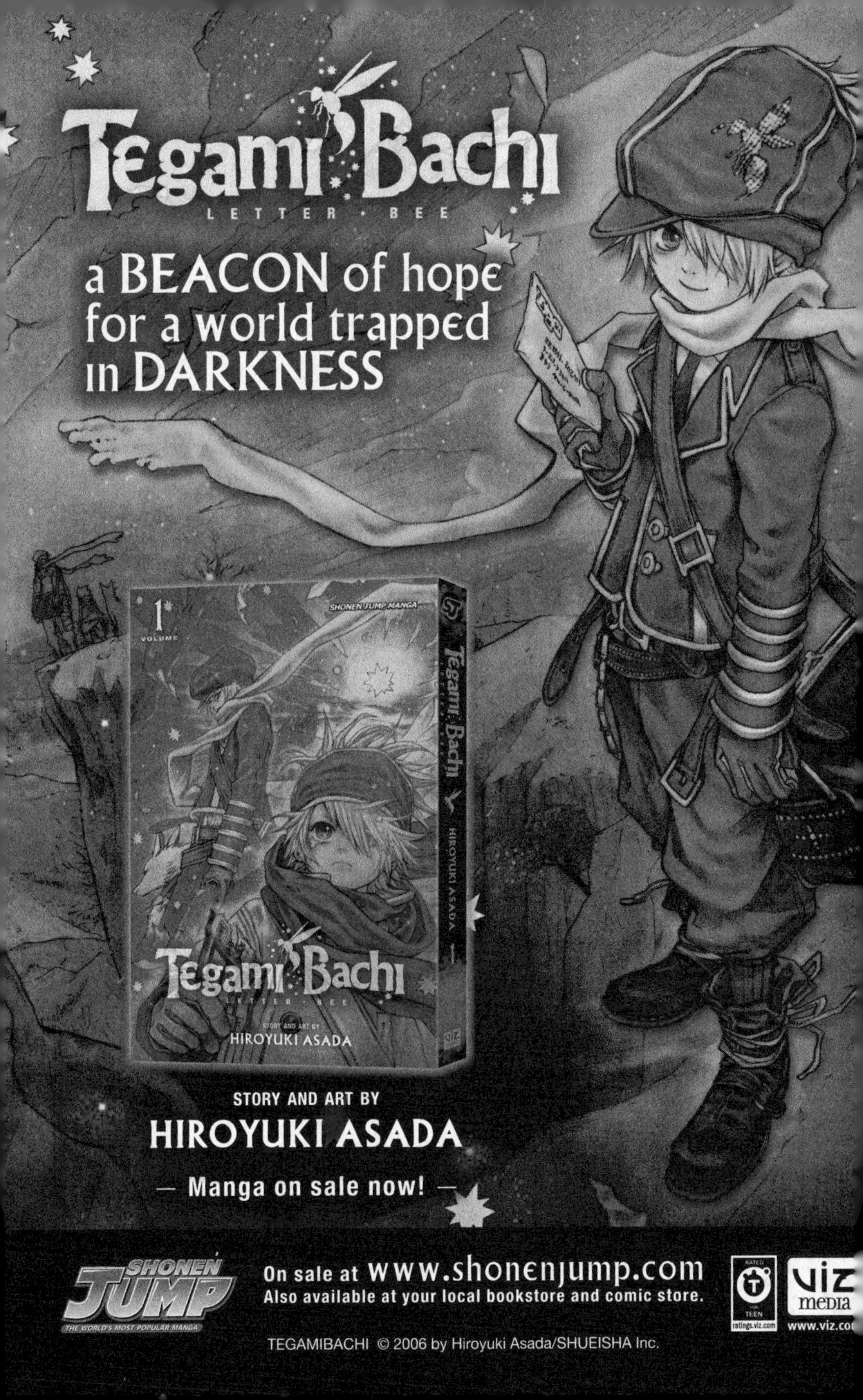
Tegami Bachi
LETTER BEE
a BEACON of hope for a world trapped in DARKNESS
1 VOLUME
SHONEN JUMP MANGA
Tegami Bachi
LETTER BEE
STORY AND ART BY
HIROYUKI ASADA
STORY AND ART BY
HIROYUKI ASADA
— Manga on sale now! —
SHONEN JUMP
THE WORLD'S MOST POPULAR MANGA
On sale at www.shonenjump.com
Also available at your local bookstore and comic store.
RATED T TEEN
ratings.viz.com
VIZ media
www.viz.com
TEGAMIBACHI © 2006 by Hiroyuki Asada/SHUEISHA Inc.

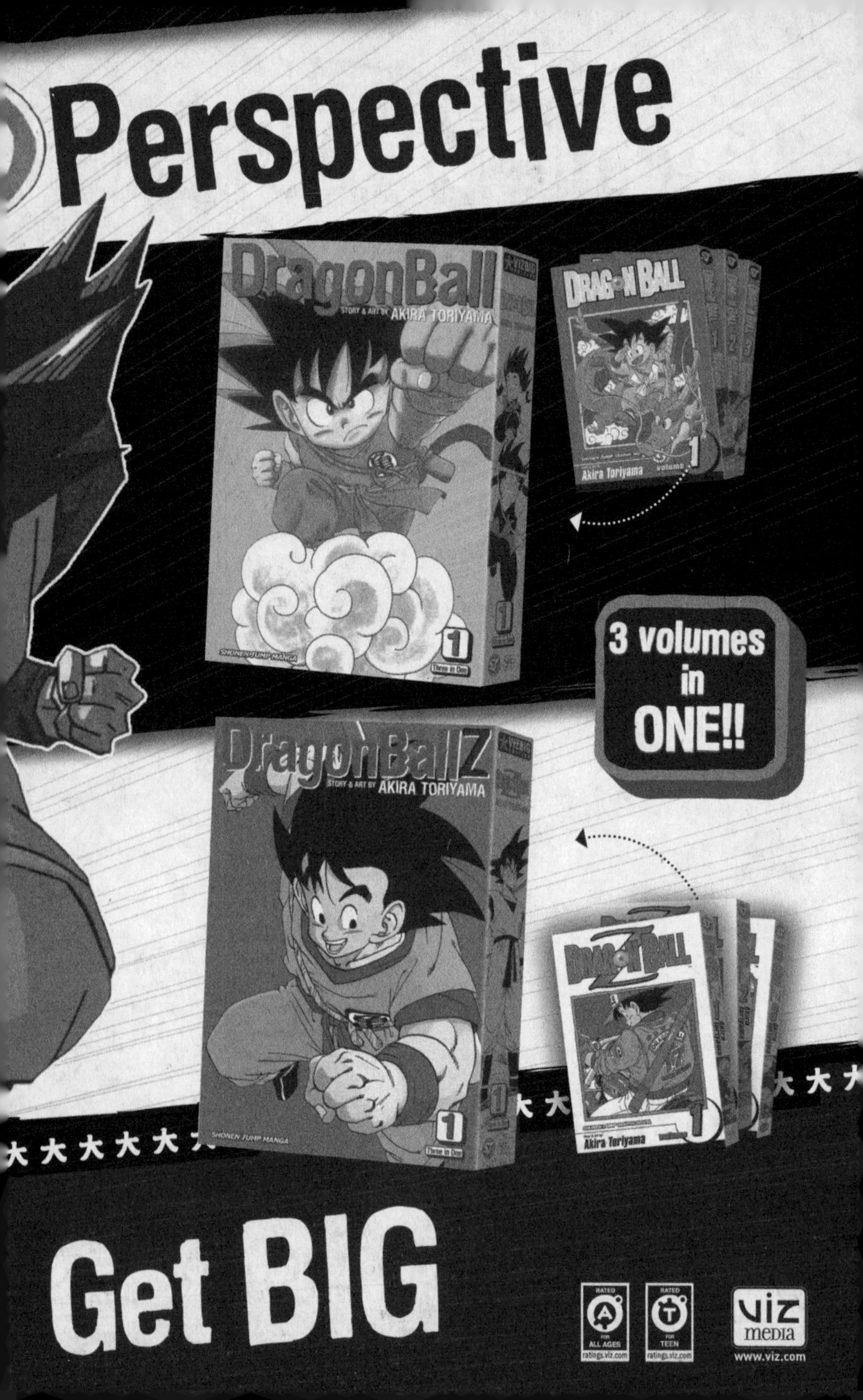
Perspective
DragonBall
STORY & ART BY AKIRA TORIYAMA
SHONEN JUMP MANGA
1
Three in One
DRAGON BALL
Akira Toriyama
volume 1
3 volumes in ONE!!
DragonBall Z
STORY & ART BY AKIRA TORIYAMA
SHONEN JUMP MANGA
1
Three in One
DRAGON BALL Z
Akira Toriyama
Get BIG
RATED A FOR ALL AGES ratings.viz.com
RATED T FOR TEEN ratings.viz.com
viz media
www.viz.com

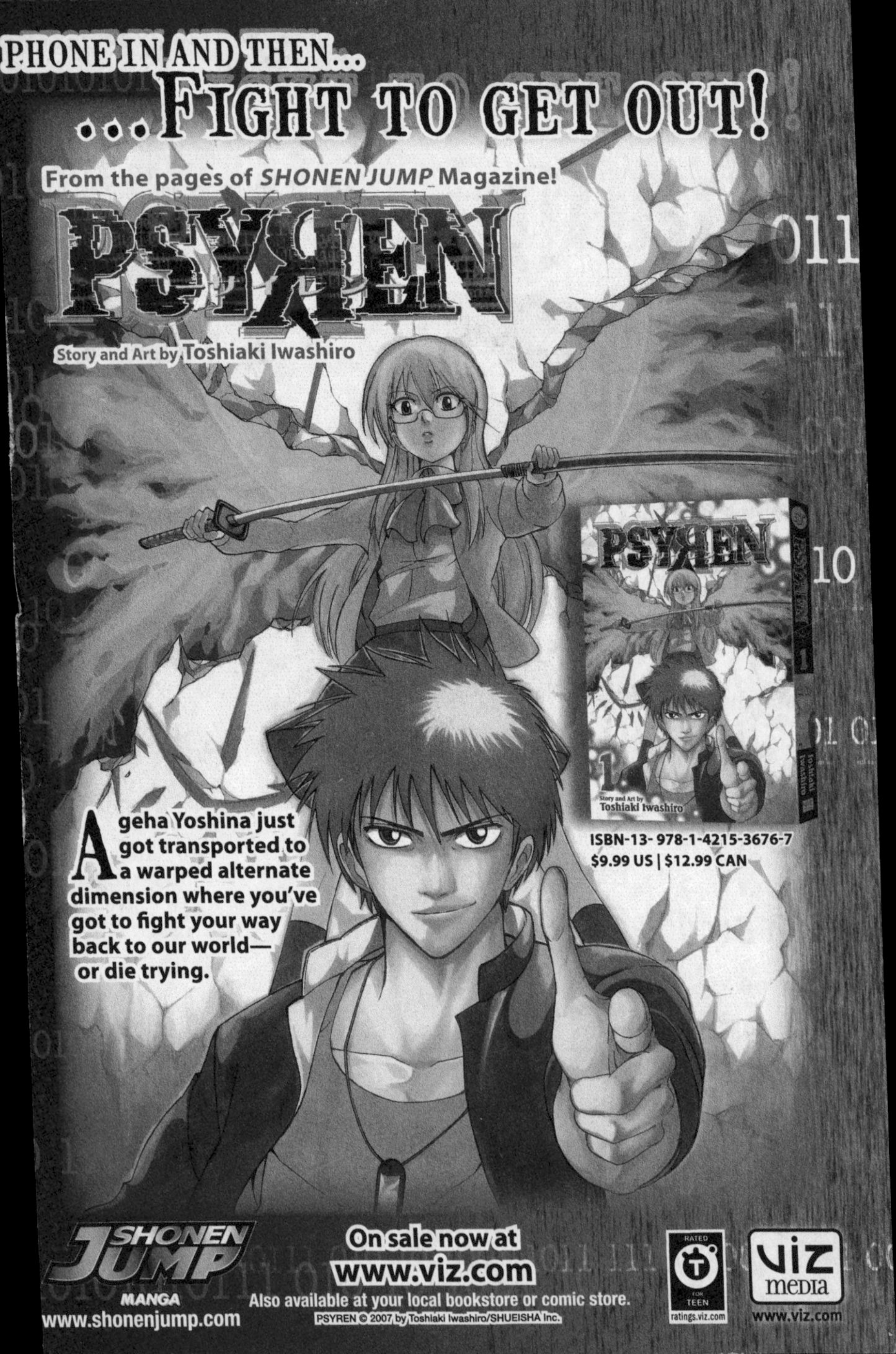
PHONE IN AND THEN...
...FIGHT TO GET OUT!
From the pages of SHONEN JUMP Magazine!
PSYREN
Story and Art by Toshiaki Iwashiro
PSYREN
1
Story and Art by Toshiaki Iwashiro
Toshiaki Iwashiro
ISBN-13- 978-1-4215-3676-7
$9.99 US | $12.99 CAN
Ageha Yoshina just got transported to a warped alternate dimension where you've got to fight your way back to our world—or die trying.
SHONEN JUMP
MANGA
www.shonenjump.com
On sale now at
www.viz.com
Also available at your local bookstore or comic store.
PSYREN © 2007 by Toshiaki Iwashiro/SHUEISHA Inc.
RATED
T
FOR TEEN
ratings.viz.com
VIZ media
www.viz.com

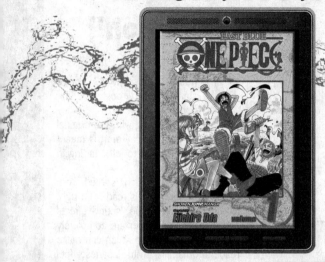

You're Reading in the Wrong Direction!!

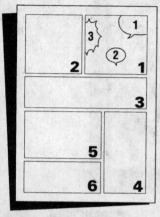

Whoops! Guess what? You're starting at the wrong end of the comic!

It's true! In keeping with the original Japanese format, **D.Gray-man** is meant to be read from right to left, starting in the upper-right corner.

Unlike English, which is read from left to right, Japanese is read from right to left, meaning action, sound effects and word-balloon order are completely reversed... something which can make readers unfamiliar with Japanese feel pretty backwards themselves. For this reason, manga or Japanese comics published in the U.S. in English have sometimes been published "flopped"—that is, printed in exact reverse order, as though seen from the other side of a mirror.

By flopping pages, U.S. publishers can avoid confusing readers, but the compromise is not without its downside. For one thing, a character in a flopped manga series who once wore in the original Japanese version a T-shirt emblazoned with "M A Y" (as in "the merry month of") now wears one which reads "Y A M"! Additionally, many manga creators in Japan are themselves unhappy with the process, as some feel the mirror-imaging of their art skews their original intentions.

We are proud to bring you Katsura Hoshino's **D.Gray-man** in the original unflopped format. For now, though, turn to the other side of the book and let the adventure begin...!

—Editor